THE SPORTS ILLUSTRATED

1992 SPORTS ALMANAC

By the Editors of Sports Illustrated

LITTLE, BROWN AND COMPANY

Boston   Toronto   London

First Edition

ISBN 0-316-80799-0

Library of Congress Cataloging-in-Publication information is available.

Production Services: Editorial Inc. of Rockport, Massachusetts

Design by Penny Darras-Maxwell

Typesetting by Editorial Inc. in Times Roman and Helvetica, with *Sports Illustrated* display type, on the Ventura 3.0 system.

10 9 8 7 6 5 4 3 2 1

COM

Published simultaneously in Canada by
Little, Brown & Company (Canada) Limited

PRINTED IN THE UNITED STATES OF AMERICA

Reference books are judged by two seemingly irreconcilable standards. They must be thorough, yet they must be wieldy. Pliny the Elder, the Roman historian, got it half right. Aiming to gather in one place absolutely everything that was known about the natural world in the first century A.D., Pliny produced a *Natural History* that could scarcely have been more thorough. It ran 37 volumes, qualifying as a handy desktop reference only for those with very large desks.

We hope that the new *1992 Sports Illustrated Sports Almanac* succeeds on both counts. It is our first almanac, and in its single volume you'll find essays summarizing the events of the past year in all major sports; a wide variety of statistics from both 1991 and the more distant past; plus a section of capsule biographies identifying some 500 prominent names in sports.

The *Almanac* will serve a very practical purpose around our office. Most of the writers and editors at *Sports Illustrated* began their careers at the magazine as reporters, a position that sometimes means traveling to events like the World Series to help writers collect material, but usually means fact-checking stories for accuracy. A reporter's career is never very old before he or she is scrambling, at odd hours and in the face of tight deadlines, to verify everything our writers have written before we go to press. What do Kenyon and Hobart Colleges have in common? What, in God's name, is Sphairistike?

We always knew we could find the answers to questions like these in our library. But that source contains more than 6500 volumes. Wouldn't it be nice, we used to think, if most of this information were gathered in one book? Well, now it is.

We know from experience that one of the best sources of information is our readers. So please don't hesitate to send us any suggestions, additions or corrections you might have.

By the way, both Kenyon and Hobart have current streaks of NCAA championships starting in 1980, Kenyon in Division III men's swimming and Hobart in Division III men's lacrosse. Sphairistike is the name Major Walter Clopton Wingfield gave the game he patented in 1874, which we know by the shorter and more easily spelled name of tennis.

John Papanek

CONTENTS

Sports Illustrated

**A SERIES
TO SAVOR**

*It was a magical
year in sports,
and for the
Cinderella Twins,
the World Series
had a storybook
ending.*

ACKNOWLEDGMENTS

As long as this book is, at times it has seemed that the list of people who made it possible is even longer.

It goes without saying that a publication of this nature could never be produced without the support and encouragement of the public relations officials and other executives who work in all the sports we have covered in these pages, and we gratefully acknowledge their contributions separately.

At one time or another everyone on SI's staff got involved with this book, but certain people deserve special mention:

Picture Research: Robert E. Mitchell, Jeffrey Weig.

Art Direction: Steven Hoffman, Barbara Chilenskas, Craig Gartner, Peter Herbert, F. Darrin Perry.

Statistical sections, by chapter: Baseball—James Rodewald, Desmond M. Wallace; Pro Football—Stefanie Krasnow; College Football—John Walters; Pro Basketball—Desmond M. Wallace; College Basketball—Timothy Crothers; Hockey—Paul Fichtenbaum; Tennis—Stefanie Scheer; Golf—Jane Bachman Wulf; Boxing—Steve Hymon, Richard O'Brien; Horse Racing—Stefanie Scheer; Motor Sports—Steve Hymon, Richard O'Brien; Bowling—J. B. Morris; Soccer—Jeff Bradley; NCAA Sports—John Walters; Olympics—Kelli Anderson; Track & Field—Sally Guard, Richard O'Brien; Swimming—Kelli Anderson; Skiing—Sally Guard; Figure Skating—Stefanie Scheer; Miscellaneous Sports—Desmond M. Wallace; Awards—John Walters.

We want to thank our publisher, Little, Brown and Company—another division of our parent company, Time Warner—and in particular Roger Donald and Irv Goodman for getting this project off the ground and for sharing their expertise so generously.

Mark Godich deserves special mention. He was with us for three crucial months this summer before taking over as managing editor at *Golf Shop Operations*, a *Golf Digest* publication, and was invaluable in helping us assemble and organize material for this volume.

As for the actual making of the book, Editorial Inc. of Rockport, Massachusetts, handled all of our production services. Laura Fillmore's staff was tireless. Particular thanks there to production assistant MaryEllen Oliver, composition manager Amanda Sylvester and primary compositor Hagop Hagopian, and most of all to the project manager, Eugene R. Bailey, without whose steady control this book could never have happened.

JOE MARSHALL
Editorial Director/Books

In compiling the *Sports Illustrated 1992 Sports Almanac*, the editors would like to thank the media relations offices of the following organizations for their assistance in providing information and materials relating to their sports: Major League Baseball; the Canadian Football League; the National Football League; the National Collegiate Athletic Association; the National Basketball Association; the National Hockey League; the Association of Tennis Professionals; the World Tennis Association; the U.S. Tennis Association; the U.S. Golf Association; the Ladies Professional Golf Association; the Professional Golfers Association; Thoroughbred Racing Communications, Inc.; the U.S. Trotting Association; the Breeders' Cup; Churchill Downs; the New York Racing Association Inc.; the Maryland Jockey Club; Championship Auto Racing Teams; the National Hot Rod Association; the International Motor Sports Association; the National Association for Stock Car Auto Racing; the Professional Bowlers Association; the Ladies Professional Bowlers Tour; the Major Soccer League: the *Fédération Internationale De Football Association*; the U.S. Soccer Association; the U.S. Olympic Committee; The Athletics Congress; U.S. Swimming; U.S. Diving; U.S. Skiing; U.S. Skating; the U.S. Chess Federation; U.S. Curling; the Iditarod Trail Committee; the International Game Fish Association; the U.S. Gymnastics Federation; the Lacrosse Foundation; the American Power Boat Association; the Professional Rodeo Cowboys Association; U.S. Rowing; the American Softball Association; the Triathlon Association; the National Archery Association; USA Wrestling; the U.S. Squash Racquets Association; the U.S. Polo Association; and the U.S. Volleyball Association.

The following sources were consulted in gathering information:

Baseball *The Baseball Encyclopedia*, Macmillan Publishing Co., 1990; *Total Baseball*, Warner Books, 1991; *Baseballistics*, St. Martin's Press, 1990; *The Book of Baseball Records*, Seymour Siwoff, publisher, 1991; *The Complete Baseball Record Book*, The Sporting News Publishing Co., 1991; *The Sporting News Baseball Guide*, The Sporting News Publishing Co., 1991; *The Sporting News Baseball Register*, The Sporting News Publishing Co., 1991; *National League Green Book—1991*, The Sporting News Publishing Co., 1991; *The 1991 American League Red Book*, The Sporting News Publishing Co., 1991.

Pro Football *The Official 1990 National Football League Record & Fact Book*, The National Football League, 1990; *The Official National Football League Encyclopedia*, New American Library, 1990; *The Sporting News Football Guide*, The Sporting News Publishing Co., 1991; *The Sporting News Football Register*, The Sporting News Publishing Co., 1991.

College Football *1990 NCAA Football*, The National Collegiate Athletic Association, 1990.

Pro Basketball *The Official NBA Basketball Encyclopedia*, Villard Books, 1989; *The Sporting News Official 1990–91 NBA Guide*, The Sporting News Publishing Co., 1990.

College Basketball *1990 NCAA Basketball*, The National Collegiate Athletic Association, 1990.

Hockey *The National Hockey League Official Guide & Record Book 1990–91*, The National Hockey League, 1990.

Tennis   *1991 Official USTA Tennis Yearbook*, H. O. Zimman, Inc., 1991; *IBM/ATP Tour 1991 Player Guide*, Association of Tennis Professionals, 1991; *WTA Official 1991 Media Guide*, Women's Tennis Association, 1991.

Golf   *PGA Tour Book 1991*, PGA Tour Creative Services, 1991; *LPGA 1991 Player Guide*, LPGA Communications Department, 1991; *Senior PGA Tour Book 1991*, PGA Tour Creative Services, 1991; *USGA Yearbook 1991*, U.S. Golf Association, 1991.

Boxing   *The Ring 1986–87 Record Book and Boxing Encyclopedia*, The Ring Publishing Corp., 1987. (To subscribe to *The Ring* magazine, write to P.O. Box 768, Rockville Centre, New York 11571-9905; or call (516) 678-7464); *Computer Boxing Update*, Ralph Citro, Inc., 1989.

Horse Racing   *The American Racing Manual 1991*, Daily Racing Form, Inc., 1991; *1991 Directory and Record Book*, The Thoroughbred Racing Associations, 1991; *The Trotting and Pacing Guide, 1991*, United States Trotting Association, 1991; *Breeders' Cup 1990 Statistics*, Breeders' Cup Limited, 1990; *N Y R A Media Guide 1991*, The New York Racing Association, 1991; *The 117th Kentucky Derby Media Guide, 1991*, Churchill Downs Public Relations Dept., 1991; *The 117th Preakness Press Guide, 1991*, Maryland Jockey Club, 1991.

Motor Sports   *The Official NASCAR Yearbook and Press Guide 1991*, UMI Publications, Inc., 1991; *1991 Indianapolis 500 Media Fact Book*, Indy 500 Publications, 1991; *IMSA 1990 Yearbook*, International Motor Sports Association, 1990; *1991 Winston Drag Racing Series Media Guide*, Sports Marketing Enterprises, 1991.

Bowling   *1991 Professional Bowlers Association Press, Radio and Television Guide*, Professional Bowlers Association, Inc., 1991; *The Ladies Pro Bowlers Tour 1991 Souvenir Tour Guide*, Ladies Pro Bowlers Tour, 1991.

Soccer   *Major Soccer League Official Guide 1990–91*, Major Soccer League, Inc., 1990; *Rothmans Football Yearbook 1990–91*, Queen Anne Press, 1990; *American Professional Soccer League 1991 Media Guide*, APSL Media Relations Department, 1991; *The European Football Yearbook*, Facer Publications Limited, 1988.

NCAA Sports   *1989–90 National Collegiate Championships*, The National Collegiate Athletic Association, 1989.

Olympics   *The Complete Book of the Olympics*, Penguin Books, 1984; *The Seoul Olympian*, Seoul Olympic Organizing Committee, 1988.

Track and Field   *American Athletics Annual 1991*, The Athletics Congress/USA, 1991.

Swimming   *6th World Swimming Championships Media Guide*, The World Swimming Championships Organizing Committee, 1991.

Skiing   *U.S. Ski Team 1991 Media Guide / USSA Directory*, U.S. Ski Association, 1990; *Ski Racing Annual Competition Guide 1991–92*, Ski Racing International, 1991; *Ski Magazine's Encyclopedia of Skiing*, Harper & Row, 1974; *Caffè Lavazza Ski World Cup Press Kit*, Biorama, 1991.

Scorecard

Sports Illustrated

ASICS   JOHN HANCOCK

16

King Of The Road

SALVADOR GARCIA OF MEXICO WINS THE NEW YORK MARATHON

MANNY MILLAN

A summary of late Fall 1991 events.

AUTO RACING

For the first time since 1986, the points battle for the CART-PPG Cup came down to the final race of the season, the Monterey Grand Prix at Laguna Seca Raceway in Monterey, CA on October 20. Michael Andretti, driving a Chevrolet-powered Lola, won both the race and his first series title by averaging 103.604 over 84 laps of the 2.214-mile circuit to beat Al Unser Jr by 11.99 seconds.

Geoff Brabham of Australia won his record fourth straight IMSA driving title when he finished third at the Camel Grand Prix at Del Mar, CA, on October 13. The late Peter Gregg of the U.S. held the previous record, winning three straight from 1973 to 1975.

Gant won four consecutive NASCAR races and barely missed a fifth straight.

Ayrton Senna of Brazil, 31, clinched his third Formula One driving title in Suzuka, Japan, when he finished second in the Japanese Grand Prix. Senna's closest competitor, Nigel Mansell of Britain, who needed to win the final two races of the year, crashed early in the race.

Harry Gant, 51, driving an Oldsmobile, became the fourth driver since 1972 to win four straight NASCAR races when he won the Goody's 500 in Martinsville, VA, on September 23. That followed wins at the Southern 500 in Darlington, SC, on September 1; the Miller 400 in Richmond, VA, on September 7; and the Peak 500 in Dover, DE, on September 15. Gant's streak ended on September 29 at the Tyson Holly Farms 400, in North Wilkesboro, NC, when his brakes failed on his last pit stop and Dale Earnhardt beat him by 1.5 seconds.

At Pomona, CA, on Nov. 2, the Winston Finals decided the National Hot Rod Association's points champion in both the Top Fuel and the Funny Car classes. Joe Amato took the Top Fuel crown, and John Force won the Funny Car championship.

BASEBALL

Tom Kelly and Bobby Cox, the managers of World Series rivals Minnesota and Atlanta, were named Managers of the Year in the American and National leagues, respectively. Each brought a team from last in its division to first, a feat no major league team had accomplished this century. The Braves had the worst record in baseball in 1990, and this year trailed the Dodgers by 9½ games at the All Star break. Cox had been named Manager of the Year in the American League in 1985 when he led the Toronto Blue Jays to the American League playoffs.

Howard's fourth-down TD catch helped Michigan beat Notre Dame.

PRO BASKETBALL

The names of the first ten members of the 1992 U.S. Olympic basketball team were announced on September 21. They are centers Patrick Ewing and David Robinson; forwards Charles Barkley, Larry Bird, Karl Malone, Chris Mullin and Scottie Pippen; and guards Magic Johnson, Michael Jordan and John Stockton. One more NBA player and a college player will be named to the team sometime next year. The team will play its first games in the zone qualifying tournament in Portland, OR, June 27 to July 5.

BOXING

Michael Watson, a 26-year-old English super middleweight boxer, needed two brain operations after being battered while losing a WBO title fight to Chris Eubank in London, on September 21. Referee Roy Francis stopped the fight 29 seconds into the 12th round. A month after the operations, Watson was still in a coma but was responding to light and touch.

Mark Breland, 28, the 1984 Olympic welterweight boxing champion, retired after getting knocked out by Jorge Vaca in the sixth round of their junior middleweight fight in Sacramento on September 13. Breland, who won the WBA welterweight title twice, fought 34 times as a professional, winning 30, losing three and drawing one.

Heavyweight boxing champion Evander Holyfield's title fight with Mike Tyson, which had been scheduled for November 8, was postponed on October 18 after Tyson suffered a costal condra separation—the separation of a rib from the surrounding cartilage and muscle. The injury, which affects the ribs on Tyson's lower left side, occurred while he was working out in the gym. Don King, Tyson's manager, hoped to re-schedule the fight for January 20, seven days before Tyson is scheduled to stand trial in Indianapolis on charges he raped a Miss Black America contestant in July.

COLLEGE FOOTBALL

By mid-season, two players had separated themselves from the pack as Heisman Trophy favorites. One was Michigan junior Desmond Howard, a 5′9″, 176-pound wide receiver and kick returner from Cleveland. In leading the Wolverines to a 7–1 record, Howard caught 17 TD passes—at least two in each game—and averaged 14.25 points per game. He was also averaging 33.4 yards per kickoff return and 13 yards per punt return.

Michigan's one loss came on September 28, at the hands of Florida State, which was ranked number one in most polls at the end of October. Although Howard caught four passes for 69 yards and two TDs, Florida State nevertheless beat Michigan 51–31. The Seminoles won their first nine games of the season, led by senior quarterback Casey Weldon. The 6'1", 195-pound Weldon completed 129 of 208 passes for 18 TDs, with five interceptions. He is 14–0 as the Seminoles' starting quarterback.

Other undefeated Division I-A teams through November 2 were Miami (FL), which was 7–0, and Washington at 8–0.

San Diego State's freshman running back Marshall Faulk, subbing for an injured teammate, set an NCAA single-game rushing record in his second college game when he ran for 386 yards on 37 carries and scored seven TDs in the Aztecs' 55–34 rout of Pacific. Faulk, a 5'10", 180-pounder from New Orleans, also had 212 yards and five TDs against Hawaii and 114 yards and two TDs against Air Force. When Faulk fractured a rib late in the first half against New Mexico on October 19, he had already gained 153 yards on 14 carries, leaving him 17 yards shy of the 1,000-yard mark for the season.

PRO FOOTBALL

Ten weeks into the NFL season, one team was undefeated and one was winless. Indianapolis (0–9) had not won a game and had fired coach Ron Meyer, while the Washington Redskins had won nine straight, including a 16–13 overtime defeat of Houston on November 3.

In Washington's 42–17 defeat of Cleveland on October 13, Art Monk caught seven passes, giving him 756 in his 12-year career and moving him past Charlie Joiner into second place in career receptions. Monk trails only Steve Largent, who caught 819 passes in his career.

Joe Montana had surgery to repair a torn tendon in his right elbow on October 9, sidelining him for the rest of the season. Without him, the 49ers struggled. After nine games, they were 4–5.

Other milestones:

Miami coach Don Shula got his 300th win as an NFL coach on September 22, when the Dolphins beat the Packers, 16–13, in Miami.

Monk became the NFL's No. 2 career receiver as the Redskins got off to a fast start.

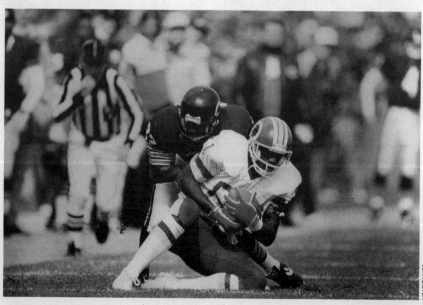

Bo Jackson was declared medically unfit to play by the Los Angeles Raiders team doctor, at least for this season, maybe for life. In his four years Jackson played 38 games, rushing 515 times for 2,782 yards (an average of 73.2 per game) and scoring 16 TDs.

On October 23, the NFL owners voted in Dallas to support the struggling World League of American Football. By a 21–5 vote with two teams passing, they created NFL International, a group that will oversee the WLAF, the American Bowl exhibition games, and worldwide television revenues. Each NFL team promised to contribute $500,000 a year through 1994 to keep the WLAF afloat. Nine of the original 10 WLAF teams will play next season, the one exception being Raleigh-Durham, which folded and will be replaced by Columbus (OH).

GOLF

Seve Ballesteros won his fifth World Match Play title on October 20, beating Zimbabwe's Nick Price 3 and 2 over 36 holes at Wentworth, in Virginia Water, England. The win tied Ballesteros, whose previous triumphs came in 1981, '82, '84 and '85, with Gary Player for most World Match Play titles.

The 1991 PGA Tour concluded November 3, when Craig Stadler won the TOUR Championship on the Pinehurst (NC) Country Club No. 2 Course, defeating Russ Cochran with a birdie on the second playoff hole. This year's leading money winner was Corey Pavin, who took home $979,430. Pavin was followed by Stadler, who raised his earnings to $827,628 with his $360,000 paycheck at Pinehurst. Fred Couples finished third in earnings with $791,749.

The winner of the Vardon Trophy for lowest scoring average was Couples, who averaged 69.59 strokes per round. Couples beat Pavin, who finished with a 69.63 scoring average. Not surprisingly, the longest driver on the 1991 tour was John Daly, whose tee shots averaged 288.9 yards. Second was Greg Norman at 282.3 yards.

RICHARD MACKSON

Zmeskal's all-around gold was the first ever for an American.

GYMNASTICS

At the world championships, which were held in Indianapolis from September 6 to 15, Kim Zmeskal, a 15-year-old from Houston, became the first U.S. woman ever to win the all-around gold medal at a world championship. Zmeskal's teammates, Betty Okino of Elmhurst, IL, and Shannon Miller of Edmond, OK, finished fourth and sixth, respectively, helping the U.S. women's team to a second place finish, behind the Soviet Union but ahead of Romania. Never before had the U.S. won a team medal. In individual events, Miller won the silver medal in the uneven bars, Zmeskal the bronze in the floor exercise and Okino the bronze in the beam.

The U.S. men did not win any medals, but did finish fifth in the team competition. Scott Keswick, a UCLA senior from Las Vegas, finished fourth in the high bar, sixth in the still rings and 10th in the all-around.

HARNESS RACING

Now in its seventh year, harness racing's Breeders Crown series, an event for the sport's best two- and three-year-olds, produced some notable milestones at Pompano Park in Pompano Beach, FL, on Oct. 25. John Campbell drove three winners on the day, with his first win pushing him over the $100 million mark in career earnings. Campbell is the first driver in harness racing history to top that mark. One of Campbell's winners, Miss Easy, set a world record for three-year-old fillies on a ⅝ mile track of 1:52²⁄₅ in the Three-Year-Old Filly Pace.

Giant Victory, the Hambletonian champion, all but sealed Trotter of the Year honors with a 1½ length win in the 3-year-old Colt Trot.

Race	Winner	Driver	Purse ($)
Two-Year-Old Filly Trot	Armbro Keepsake	John Campbell	150,000
Three-Year-Old Filly Trot	Twelve Speed	Ron Waples	155,027
Three-Year-Old Colt Trot	Giant Victory	Ron Pierce	182,703
Three-Year-Old Filly Pace	Miss Easy	John Campbell	150,000
Two-Year-Old Filly Pace	Hazleton Kay	John Campbell	158,000
Two-Year-Old Colt Pace	Digger Almahurst	Doug Brown	188,500
Three-Year-Old-Colt Pace	Three Wizzards	Bill Gale	178,703

ICE HOCKEY

The National Hockey League, its future clouded by uncertainty, decided to open its 75th season with a celebration of its past. Opening Day belonged to the six original NHL franchises. Boston beat the New York Rangers 5–3 and Detroit tied Chicago in overtime. Marking the anniversary in a more unusual fashion, the Toronto Maple Leafs, arrayed in dark suits and fedoras, traveled five hours by train to Montreal, where the Canadiens edged the Leafs 4–3. It was a nice touch, but could not divert attention from a host of problems now facing the league:

Its collective bargaining agreement expired on September 15, and there has been little progress in negotiations.

The league's two conditional franchises for next season both got off to rocky starts. The Tampa Bay Lightning failed to meet a

Lindros spurned the NHL, then helped the host team win the Canada Cup.

June deadline for a $22.5 million payment on its $50 million expansion fee. The Ottawa Senators made their payment, but their plans to construct an arena are threatened by a zoning dispute. As a result, they are having trouble attracting investors.

The league came within hours of starting the season without any U.S. TV contract. The NHL was forced to settle, on opening day, for a "one-year extension" to its three-year, $51 million contract with SportsChannel America, which expired at the end of the 1990-91 season. The deal, which calls for the televising of up to three regular-season games per week plus the entire postseason, was worth $5.5 million, a mere one third of what SCA payed the league for each of the past three years.

Teen star Eric Lindros, the No. 1 pick in the 1991 draft and a potentially great drawing card for the league, turned down the Quebec Nordiques' offer of a contract rumored to be worth $3 million and opted to play junior hockey instead for the Oshawa Generals of the Ontario Hockey League.

The Edmonton Oilers traded away some of their biggest stars. First, on September 19, Edmonton sent two of its Stanley Cup linchpins, goaltender Grant Fuhr and forward Glenn Anderson, along with forward Craig Berube, to Toronto for forwards Vincent Damphousse and Scott Thornton, defenseman Luke Richardson, goaltender Peter Ing, and future considerations. On October 4, Edmonton traded 30-year-old center Mark Messier to the New York Rangers, who promptly made him their captain. In exchange, the Rangers sent Bernie Nicholls and two young players, Steven Rice and Louis Debrusk, to Edmonton. The New York Islanders also traded away two marquis players in separate deals on October 25, sending Pat LaFontaine to the Buffalo Sabres and captain Brent Sutter to the Chicago Blackhawks.

On the ice, Pittsburgh defenseman Paul Coffey had two assists in the Penguins' 8–5 win over the Islanders on October 17 to break Denis Potvin's NHL scoring record for defensemen.

Canada beat the U.S. in two straight games to win the best-of-three Canada Cup final. To reach the final, the U.S. beat Finland 7–3 in the semifinals.

MARATHON

The 22nd New York City Marathon was run on November 3rd. The first finisher in an impressive women's field was Liz McColgan of Scotland, who was running her first marathon. McColgan, who had won the 10,000 meters at the World Championships nine weeks earlier, finished in 2:27:23, 55 seconds ahead of the Soviet Union's Olga Markova. The men's winner was Salvador Garcia of Mexico, who ran 2:09:28.

OLYMPICS

Robert Helmick resigned as president of the United States Olympic Committee (USOC) on September 18, two weeks after *USA Today* revealed that Helmick had accepted over $127,000 from Olympic-related clients. The 54-year-old Des Moines lawyer had been USOC president since March of 1985. William Hybl, a 49-year-old corporate executive from Colorado Springs, was picked to serve the 13 remaining months of Helmick's term.

KEVIN HORAN

Under scrutiny for his business dealings, Helmick resigned as USOC president.

THOROUGHBRED RACING

At the eighth running of the Breeders' Cup, which was held on November 2 at Churchill Downs in Louisville, KY, Arazi, a two-year-old with Pat Valenzuela up, made a dramatic bid for Horse of the Year honors by blazing to a 4¾ lengths win over Bertrando in the $1,000,000 Juvenile. Arazi, who is trained by François Boutin in France, covered the 1¹⁄₁₆ miles in 1:44³⁄₅.

Other results:

Race	Distance	Winner	Jockey	Trainer	Purse ($)
Sprint	6 furlongs	Sheikh Albadou	Pat Eddery	Alex Scott	$1,000,000
Juvenile Fillies	1¹⁄₁₆ miles	Pleasant Stage	Eddie Delahoussaye	Christopher Speckert	$1,000,000
Distaff	1⅛ miles	Dance Smartly	Pat Day	Jim Day	$1,000,000
Mile	1 mile	Opening Verse	Pat Valenzuela	Richard Lundy	$1,000,000
Turf	1½ miles	Miss Alleged	Eric Legrix	Pascal Bary	$2,000,000
Classic	1¼ miles	Black Tie Affair	Jerry Bailey	Ernie Poulos	$3,000,000

TRACK AND FIELD

Gail Devers-Robert capped an astonishing recovery when she set an American record in the 100-meter hurdles, clocking 12.48 at a meet in Berlin on September 10. Devers-Roberts had been suffering from Graves Disease for almost three years and had only started full training in May.

MANNY MILLAN

Devers-Roberts made a record-setting comeback from Graves Disease.

TRIATHLON

Mark Allen, 33, of Cardiff, CA, won his third straight Ironman Triathlon, pulling away from Greg Welch of Australia just short of the midway point in the marathon and finishing in 8:09:15. Welch was second in 8:24:34.

Among the women, Paula Newby-Fraser, a 29-year-old Zimbabwean who now lives in Encinitas, CA, took the lead for good early in the cycle portion of the race and finished in 9:07:52.

WRESTLING

The world championships were held from October 3 and 7, in Varna, Bulgaria. John Smith of Stillwater, OK, winner of the 1990 Sullivan Award, won his fifth straight world title. In the final of the 136.5-pound class, Smith beat Giovanni Schillaci of Italy 8–1.

Two other U.S. wrestlers won their first world titles. At 114.5 pounds, Zeke Jones of Bloomsburg, PA, beat Valentin Jordanov of Bulgaria 8–3, while Kevin Jackson of Ames, IA, won the 180.5-pound class by outpointing Josef Lohyna of Czechoslovakia 2–0 at 40 seconds of overtime after a scoreless five-minute regulation. Other gold medalists:

105.5 Vugar Orudzhez, Soviet Union
125.5 Sergei Smal, Soviet Union
149.5 Arsen Fadzaev, Soviet Union
163 Amir Khadem, Iran
198 Maharbek Khadartsev, Soviet Union
220 Leri Khabelov, Soviet Union
286 Andreas Schroder, Germany

The Year in Sport

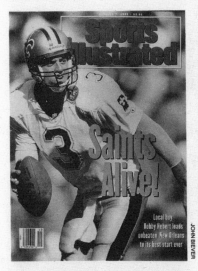

Saints Alive!

Local boy Bobby Hebert leads unbeaten New Orleans to its best start ever

JOHN BIEVER

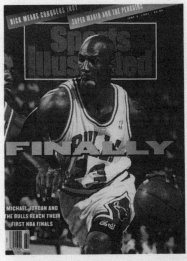

RICK MEARS CONQUERS INDY · SUPER MARIO AND THE PENGUINS

FINALLY

MICHAEL JORDAN AND THE BULLS REACH THEIR FIRST NBA FINALS

MANNY MILLAN

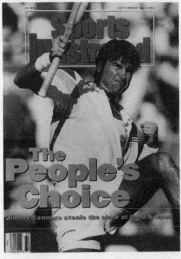

The People's Choice

Jimmy Connors steals the show at the U.S. Open

CARYN LEVY

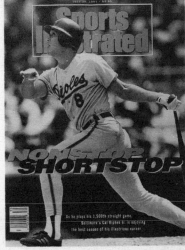

NONSTOP SHORTSTOP

As he plays his 1,500th straight game, Baltimore's Cal Ripken Jr. is enjoying the best season of his illustrious career

RONALD C. MODRA

The Lessons We Learned

The year in sport taught us not to trust in dynasties or the comportment of our heroes | by RON FIMRITE

THE YEAR 1991 BROUGHT US FULL THROTTLE into what one hundred years ago the French called, in their world-weary wisdom, "le fin de siècle." And as the 20th century, the only one most of us have ever known, cranks down, assessments should be made, judgments rendered, and verities confirmed in sports as in all else. Has this past year taught us anything at all? It is safe to say that some lessons have been hammered home.

We have learned, for example, that the old adage, "If it ain't broke, don't fix it," is as obsolete as communism. The San Francisco 49ers were 14–2 in the regular season and missed out on a third straight Super Bowl appearance in '91 by two measly points, a 15–13 loss to the New York Giants in the NFC Championship Game. And yet, their front office couldn't resist tinkering with this well-oiled mechanism, allowing future Hall of Famers Roger Craig and Ronnie Lott to be grabbed by the Los Angeles Raiders. Then, as if to further complicate matters, Joe

Montana went down with a torn tendon in his throwing arm in training camp and that perennial bridesmaid, Steve Young, at long last became the quarterback.

The 49ers were suddenly a different team. And their conquerors, the Super Bowl champion Giants, didn't exactly leave well enough alone either after their nail-biting, 20–19 win over the Buffalo Bills in the all-New York State XXV. First, coach Bill Parcells quit, determining, for the moment at least, that he would rather be a rookie broadcaster than the field boss of a defending NFL champion. And then his successor, Ray Handley, demoted ace quarterback Phil Simms and replaced him with Simms's understudy, Jeff Hostetler. Sure, Hostetler did yeoman work in the big one, after replacing the injured Simms late in the regular season. But it was Simms, after all, who got the Giants there in the first place. So, broke or not, fix it.

Some truths, of course, remain self-evident, one being that for job security, man-

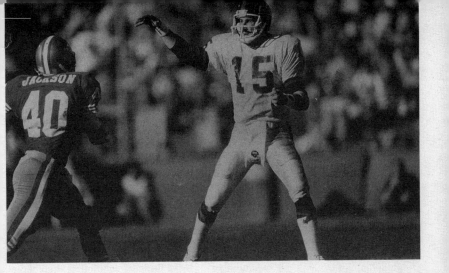

aging a baseball team is the equivalent of
marrying Elizabeth Taylor. Even so, this
was a vintage year for the managerial deep
six. All told, 13 field generals went over the
side, three of them—Don Zimmer (Chicago
Cubs), John Wathan (Kansas City Royals),
and Frank Robinson (Baltimore Orioles)—
in the space of three days in the not so merry
month of May, and four more in four days
in October.

It is, however, a baseball tradition for the
old guard to resurface, so Buck Rodgers,
dumped by the Montreal Expos in May, was
summoned in August to replace the deposed
Doug Rader with the California Angels. The
African-American managerial rotation also
remained constant. On May 22, Hal McRae
became major league baseball's third active
black manager when he supplanted Wathan
in Kansas City. The next day, he became the
second (behind Cito Gaston of the Toronto
Blue Jays) when Robinson was fired and
succeeded by Johnny Oates.

We probably considered it merely an ab-
erration when a record nine no-hitters were
thrown in 1990, but by now we fin-de-
sièclers know that this once extraordinary
feat is as ubiquitous as artificial turf. Eight
more of these erstwhile gems were tossed in
'91: one of them by a committee of four
Baltimore pitchers; two, by Montreal's
Mark Gardner and Dennis Martinez, within

48 hours of each other; and, predictably, yet
another, his seventh, by Commander White-
wash himself, Nolan Ryan of the Texas
Rangers.

The Expos duo's no-no's deserve special
mention. Gardner's went the requisite nine
innings, but he lost the no-hitter and the
game to the Los Angeles Dodgers, 1–0, in
the 10th on the night of July 26. Then, on the
afternoon of the 28th, Martinez avenged this
agonizing defeat with a dead-solid perfect
game against these same powerless Dodgers. There were so many no-hitters, in fact,
that baseball decided not to count those that
went less than nine innings or in which the
pitcher gave up a hit in an extra inning, as
Gardner did.

Ah, but just when we might have deluded
ourselves into thinking of this as a pitcher's
year, there occurred some tremendous offensive explosions. On July 23, a major
league record was tied when four hitters—
the Pittsburgh Pirates' Gary Redus, the
Royals' Todd Benzinger, the Orioles'
Randy Milligan, and the Seattle Mariners'
Ken Griffey Jr.—all hit grand slam home
runs. A week later, Carlos Quintana of the

Martinez led this year's no-hit brigade with a perfect game against the Dodgers.

Boston Red Sox tied another record by driving in six runs in one inning, the third, in an 11–6 Boston win over Texas. And three days after that, Texas pitcher Mike Jeffcoat became the first American League pitcher to drive in a run—with his first big league hit, a double—since the grievous introduction of the designated hitter in 1973. At 32, Jeffcoat could well finish his career with a 1.000 batting average.

Speaking of offensive, a dubious record of sorts may have been achieved when both Rob Dibble of the Cincinnati Reds and Cleveland's Albert Belle conked spectators with balls hurled into the seats. Dibble's toss was the more remarkable, since he found his mark, a woman in centerfield, a good 400 feet from the pitcher's mound. It was an accidental strike, he protested, very much like his errant heave that popped Chicago base runner Doug Dascenzo in the legs later in the season. The oft-suspended Dibble announced after this latest misdemeanor that he would seek counseling. He might well

pass his old manager Pete Rose, fresh out of the pokey, on the way to the couch.

We have long known that baseball statistics have a way of piling up like underclothes in the laundry basket, and 1991 was another big year for numbers-mongers. Rickey Henderson, pouting because at $3 million per year he considered himself underpaid by the Oakland Athletics, and hurting from injuries both real and imagined, nevertheless passed Lou Brock as the game's leading base thief when he stole his 939th on the first of May. And Baltimore's Cal Ripken, a *rara avis* who apparently enjoys playing every day, passed 1,500 consecutive games played on his way to Lou Gehrig's long-sacred record of 2,130.

In the fin de siècle, winners rarely repeat. Consider the season-long travails of the World Series champion Reds and the American League pennant-winning Athletics. They were replaced by two teams, Atlanta and Minnesota, which had finished dead last in 1990. Despite that humble background, the Braves and the Twins produced as thrilling a World Series as this century has seen, with Minnesota winning the seventh game 1–0 in 10 innings.

Look as well upon the Runnin' Rebels of college basketball's UNLV. Irony of ironies, the Rebs had their apparently richly deserved NCAA suspension deferred for a year so they might have a chance to repeat as college champions. And they were indeed undefeated until they fell, 79–77, in the Final Four semifinals to Duke, a team they had defeated by 30 points in the 1990 title game. The Blue Devils, who had made it to the Final Four five times in the last six years and nine times all told, beat the Jayhawks of Kansas, 72–65, for their first national championship.

In the women's Final Four, Tennessee's Lady Vols won their third title in the last five years, beating the Virginia Cavaliers, 70–67, before an encouraging crowd of 7,865 in New Orleans' Lakefront Arena. The distaff game seems to be catching on, a new and welcome truth.

Although the first-time champions had their day—among them the National

MANNY MILLAN

Hockey League's Pittsburgh Penguins and the National Basketball Association's Chicago Bulls—there were some notable repeaters. Rick Mears, for one, won his fourth Indy 500, joining the redoubtable A. J. Foyt and Al Unser Sr. as the only quadruple champions in this dangerous competition. But the Bulls' maiden NBA win was particularly gratifying, because it gave their celestial guard, Michael Jordan, a chance to look his contemporary greats, the Los Angeles Lakers' Magic Johnson and Larry Bird of the Boston Celtics, in the eye as a champion in his own right. It took Jordan seven years to reach the finals, but he made it all worth-

Christian Laettner of Duke showed UNLV's Stacey Augmon that repeating wasn't going to be easy in 1991.

while, averaging 31.2 points in the five games against the Lakers, and setting a five-game record with 14 steals, while also averaging 6.6 rebounds per game. "The championship, in the minds of a lot of people, is a sign of, well, greatness," Jordan commented after his team's 108–101 win in Game Five. "I guess they can say that about me now." Come now, sir, they've been saying that all along.

Jordan reached new heights with his first NBA title but risked falling from grace over an Olympic invitation.

Jordan's well-polished image as a swell fellow both on and off the court was inadvertently sullied, however, when he expressed his reluctance to represent his country in the 1992 Olympic Games, the first in which NBA stars will be allowed to play. Jordan explained that he had already been on the '84 Olympic team and that, besides, he would rather spend his free time working on his golf game. Then he began to hear rumblings from his adoring public. When he sensed his patriotism was being questioned, he changed his stance and agreed, if reluctantly, to go to Barcelona.

Slackers, after all, don't sell shoes. That's a new adage of the fin de siècle.

One athlete who won't have to worry about the Olympics, one way or the other, is teenage tennis star Monica Seles, because by refusing to play for her native Yugoslavia in the Federation Cup, she forfeited her right to go. Actually, the 17-year-old Seles spent much of the year among the missing. After winning the first two Grand Slam events, the French and the Australian Opens, she also skipped Wimbledon, pleading shin splints. As partial compensation for these missed paydays, the willowy Seles signed on to model No Excuses sportswear, thereby following in the less than discreet footsteps of Donna Rice and Marla Maples, both of whom made names for themselves off the tennis court. No Excuses spokesman Neil Cole explained that Monica simply "looks great in our jeans." We sometimes forget she is but a child. Another lesson worth learning.

Wimbledon was otherwise distinguished by the model deportment and modest attire of the normally disagreeable popinjay, Andre Agassi. "I have to admit I got caught up in the excitement and classiness of it all," said Agassi of his first appearance at the All England Lawn Tennis and Croquet Club in four years. But a well-turned-out Agassi made it only to the quarterfinals in a tournament that took on a decidedly Teutonic character. Three of the four players in the final matches were German. Michael Stich defeated his countryman Boris Becker for the men's championship, and Steffi Graf knocked off Argentina's Gabriela Sabatini in the women's title match. Both winners were 22, about average in a game dominated at the fin de siècle by cherubs. This was Graf's third Wimbledon title, but the 6′4″ Stich, who toppled Becker in straight sets, emerged from the legions of the unknown, having been ranked 42nd in the world.

At the end of August, these same formidable Germans invaded the U.S. Open at Flushing Meadow, N.Y. But a real graybeard, 39-year-old Jimmy Connors, captivated the crowd with a series of thrilling matches that carried all the way to the semifinals, where he was unceremoniously dispatched in straight sets by French Open winner Jim Courier. Courier in turn was demolished in straight sets in the finals, 6–2, 6–4, 6–0, by Stefan Edberg of Sweden. Those were the only sets that Courier lost in the entire tournament. On the women's side, Seles resurfaced to beat another golden oldie, Martina Navratilova, for the title, also in straight sets, thus completing a shutout of Americans on their own turf.

Actually, it was a big year for foreigners, wherever they were. A Welshman, Ian Woosnam, won our Masters golf tournament, finishing one stroke ahead of a Spaniard, José-Maria Olazabal; and an Australian, Ian Baker-Finch, won the British Open by two strokes over Aussie mate Michael Harwood. The London Monarchs defeated the Barcelona Dragons 21–0 to become the champions of the new World League of American Football. And Raghib (Rocket) Ismail, late of Notre Dame, snubbed our NFL to play for the Toronto Argonauts in the Canadian Football League. The Rocket had a 91-yard would-be game-winning punt return called back against Colorado in the Orange Bowl, but it is unlikely that the dropped flag sent him scurrying in despair for the border. Try instead a four-

year contract, with incentives, worth as much as $26.2 million, the richest in the history of the CFL, as the motive for his defection.

Still, our own sprinters did set the track world ablaze in August by sweeping the 100 meters at the World Track and Field Championships in Tokyo. It was the fastest race in the history of the event, with six of the eight competitors finishing under 10 seconds flat. Carl Lewis won in the world-record time of 9.86, hurrying past his Santa Monica Track Club teammate Leroy Burrell two lanes to his left in the last 10 meters. Burrell, who is legally blind in his right eye, never saw him coming. And yet Burrell surpassed his own previous world record of 9.90 by finishing second in 9.88. Dennis Mitchell, who grew up not far from both Lewis and Burrell in the Delaware Valley, was third in 9.91.

An interested spectator of these speedy doings was Ben Johnson, who had run 9.79 in the 1988 Olympics, a record quickly expunged, along with an earlier 9.83, when he

Seles was roughed up for skipping Wimbledon, but in the other three Grand Slam events she was untouchable.

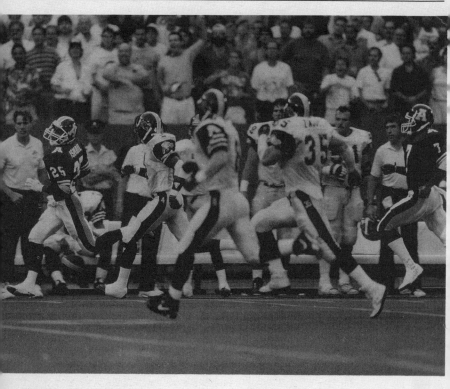

tested positive for steroids. A drug-free Johnson doesn't run nearly so fast, and he made the Canadian team only as a member of the 4 x 100-meter relay team. For the 30-year-old Lewis it was, amazingly enough, the first world record he had ever earned on the track. When Johnson's mark was taken off the books, the 9.92 Lewis ran finishing second in the '88 Games became the official record, but King Carl always dismissed it as a mere technicality. This one he got on his own. "It was the most incredible race of all time," he said afterward, "and the old man pulled it out."

Lewis was not able, though, to break the record he most coveted, Bob Beamon's 23-year-old mark of 29′ 2½″ in the long jump, set at the 1968 Mexico City Olympics. On his fourth attempt in Tokyo, Lewis surpassed Beamon's mark by a quarter of an inch, but the record was ruled invalid by wind meters that measured the breezes at an

Ismail jumped to Canada and picked up right where he left off, going 73 yards with his first kick return.

unacceptably brisk level. As Lewis stood watching, the wind died down and 27-year-old Mike Powell took off on a remarkable 29′ 4½″ leap, finally laying to rest track and field's oldest recognized outdoor record. Powell, heretofore overshadowed by the flamboyant Lewis, could not resist gloating. Turning to Lewis after his triumph, Powell said, "This is not to say, 'In your face,' but in your face."

But Lewis should be mindful of another thought for the fin de siècle: Never count out a golden oldie. Take George Foreman, who at 43 and nearer 300 pounds than 200, survived 12 grueling rounds with heavyweight champion Evander Holyfield before losing the decision. The ponderous former champ had waded through a succession of pushovers before reaching Holyfield, but his gallant showing gave heart to the overweight and overaged everywhere. Holyfield's next opponent was scheduled to be Mike Tyson, who had a much worse year out of the ring than in it. In September Tyson was indicted on a rape charge that stemmed from an accusation made by a contestant at the Miss Black America beauty pageant in Indianapolis. Tyson, who had been invited to attend the pageant, which was part of the Indiana Black Expo, was also hit with two multi-million-dollar civil suits—one by yet another contestant and one by the pageant director, alleging that Tyson fondled a number of women at the pageant. If he is convicted of the rape charge, and three related charges, Tyson could find himself in prison well into the next century.

This century may have seen the last of Sugar Ray Leonard in the ring after the 34-year-old former multi-champion was badly beaten by the much younger Terry Norris in a junior middleweight championship bout. It was Leonard's first venture among the younger set after some years of working the senior circuit with the likes of Tommy Hearns, Roberto Duran, and Marvelous Marvin Hagler.

We also learned in '91 that Bo knows more about Bo than the doctors do. Jackson, in his football mode with the Los Angeles Raiders, had his hip banged up so badly in a playoff game with the Cincinnati Bengals that his baseball employers, the Royals, acting on supposedly competent medical advice, unloaded him. Undeterred, Bo signed on with the Chicago White Sox and by September was back in the major leagues. Who knows, he might even try football again.

The Phillies' Lenny Dykstra had worse luck with his health. Driving home from a bachelor party with teammate Darren Daulton in early May, he crashed his car and suffered multiple injuries that included a broken collarbone. He was on the disabled list for two months before returning to action in July. Then, six weeks after his return, he rebroke the collarbone in yet another crash,

Foreman's strong showing against Holyfield gave heart to the overaged and overweight.

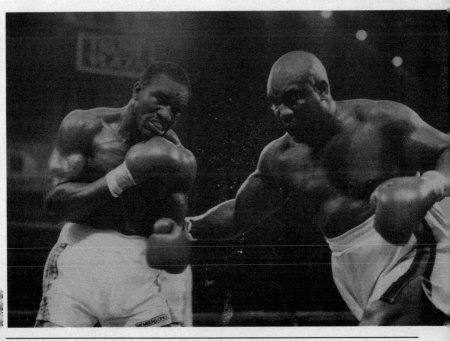

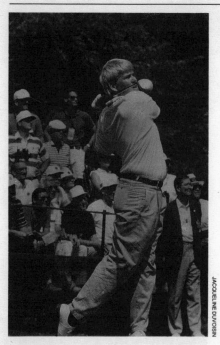

JACQUELINE DUVOISIN

Long drives were the key to success for PGA champion John Daly, who had to make one just to get to Crooked Stick.

finally, ump Joe West grew so agitated by an instant replay calling into question one of his decisions on the Shea Stadium scoreboard that he threatened to forfeit the game to the St. Louis Cardinals if the New York Mets didn't extinguish the offending video screen. The Mets complied. Perhaps a first.

It's always wise to seek out fresh new faces, and the freshest of 1991 must have been young John Daly's. The stocky 25-year-old rookie golf pro from Dardanelle, Ark., hits the ball so hard he considers a 300-yard drive worthy of a mulligan. He got into the PGA Championship at the inappropriately named Crooked Stick course in Carmel, Ind., only as a last-minute replacement for a player, Nick Price, who dropped out. Daly had been a ninth alternate. In order to be on time at the first tee, he drove all night from Memphis and then popped his opening drive 364 yards. Daly shot a 69 in that first round and went on to win the PGA title by three strokes on a course that none other than Jack Nicklaus had once described as the most difficult he had ever played.

Daly's mighty swing is hardly out of the manual. He takes the club so far back that his bulky frame corkscrews into a Stan Musial stance. And then, whipping the club around at an estimated 140 miles an hour—30 miles an hour faster than the average pro—he blasts orbital shots, not all of which find the fairway. Daly, in fact, got so discouraged with his game while playing at the University of Arkansas that he considered pursuing another line of work. His fiancée, Bettye Fulford, persuaded him to stick it out, so he joined the PGA Tour in March. Within six months he had won his first major, a title worth $230,000—$30,000 of which he donated to establish a scholarship fund for the two children of a spectator killed by lightning at the PGA tournament. Big hitter. Bigger heart.

And so we close out another year of this departing century. And as we stand on the threshold of a new one, we naturally wonder who among these fin de siècle heroes will still be around when we ring in the Big 21. I don't know about you, but my money is on big George Foreman.

this one against the unpadded outfield wall at Cincinnati's Riverfront Stadium. He was finished for the season.

This was not a particularly salubrious year for umpires, either. One, Steve Palermo, was shot and wounded trying heroically to stop a robbery in Dallas. Another, Gary Darling, was accused by Reds manager Lou Piniella of harboring a bias against his team. The Major League Umpires Association then sued Piniella for $5 million, claiming defamation of Darling's character. Piniella was last observed filing a motion to dismiss the claim, though he has apologized to Darling. Then, Gene Orza, general counsel of the players union, complained to *The New York Times* that umpires were treated as "a sacrosanct community of monks" and that too many of them were overbearing and vindictive. Ump Bruce Froemming ruled Orza out of line for "shooting off his mouth." And

Nov 8, 1990 — Free agent outfielder Darryl Strawberry leaves the New York Mets after eight seasons, signing a five-year, $20.25 million deal with the Los Angeles Dodgers.

Nov 20 — The American League hands Boston Red Sox pitcher Roger Clemens a five-game suspension and $10,000 fine for his outburst during the fourth game of the American League Championship Series.

Dec 5 — In the biggest trade at the baseball winter meetings, San Diego sends Joe Carter and Roberto Alomar to Toronto for Fred McGriff and Tony Fernandez.

Jan 7, 1991 — Pete Rose is released from Marion (Ill.) Federal Prison Camp after serving a five-month sentence for income tax evasion. Rose reports to a halfway house in Cincinnati.

Feb 4 — A committee rules that permanently ineligible baseball players be left off the Hall of Fame ballot, effectively disqualifying Pete Rose from consideration until he is reinstated.

Feb 8 — Roger Clemens becomes the highest-paid player in baseball history when he signs a four-year, $21.5 million contract with the Boston Red Sox.

Feb 14 — An arbitrator awards Cy Young winner Doug Drabek of the Pittsburgh Pirates a one-year, $3.35 million contract, the richest such award in baseball arbitration history.

Feb 26 — The veterans committee elects Bill Veeck and Tony Lazzeri to the Baseball Hall of Fame. They join Rod Carew, Ferguson Jenkins and Gaylord Perry, who had been elected earlier, as 1991 inductees.

Mar 12 — One day after a two-inning pasting by the Boston Red Sox, Hall of Fame pitcher Jim Palmer ends his comeback bid with the Baltimore Orioles.

Mar 28 — The Los Angeles Dodgers waive popular lefthander Fernando Valenzuela, a mainstay in the team's starting rotation since 1981.

Apr 3 — The Chicago White Sox sign the injured Bo Jackson to an incentive-laced three-year, $8.15 million contract.

Apr 8 — Hours before the first pitch of the season is to be thrown, Major League Baseball averts an umpires' strike by reaching agreement with the Major League Umpires Association on a four-year contract.

Apr 18 — The Chicago White Sox open the new Comiskey Park with a 16–0 loss to the Detroit Tigers before a crowd of 42,191.

Apr 23 — Nick Leyva of the Philadelphia Phillies becomes the first managerial casualty of the 1991 season.

May 1 — Nolan Ryan of the Texas Rangers pitches his record seventh career no-hitter in a 3–0 victory over the Toronto Blue Jays.

May 1 — Rickey Henderson steals the 939th base of his career in a game against the New York Yankees, surpassing Lou Brock as the game's alltime stolen base leader.

May 6 — Lenny Dykstra and Darren Daulton of the Philadelphia Phillies are seriously injured in an early-morning one-car accident after the bachelor party of teammate John Kruk. Dykstra is charged with driving under the influence.

May 8 — Howard Spira is convicted on eight counts of extortion, including five charges that he tried to extort money from deposed Yankees owner George Steinbrenner. But baseball commissioner Fay Vincent says the verdict will have no effect on his ruling that Steinbrenner may have no involvement in running the Yankees.

May 21 — The Chicago Cubs, mired near the bottom of the National League East standings despite three key free agent signings, fire manager Don Zimmer. He is replaced the next day by Jim Essian.

May 22 — The Kansas City Royals, in last place in the American League West after expecting to challenge for the division title, fire manager John Wathan. He is replaced two days later by Hal McRae.

Drabek hit the arbitration jackpot.

DAVID LIAM KYLE

Winfield joined the 400-home run club.

May 23 — The Baltimore Orioles fire Frank Robinson, one of only two black managers in the major leagues. He is replaced by Johnny Oates.

May 23 — Tommy Greene of the Philadelphia Phillies throws a no-hitter in a 2–0 victory over Montreal. Greene strikes out 10 and walks seven.

May 29 — Orel Hershiser of the Los Angeles Dodgers returns to the mound 13 months after being sidelined by a career-threatening arm injury. He gives up four earned runs on nine hits during a four-inning stint against the Houston Astros.

June 3 — The Montreal Expos fire manager Buck Rodgers and replace him with Tom Runnells.

June 10 — The National League expansion committee recommends that Denver and Miami be awarded franchises for the 1993 season. Major league owners give their rubber-stamp approval at a later meeting.

July 6 — Cleveland's John McNamara becomes the sixth managerial casualty of the season. He is replaced by Mike Hargrove.

July 7 — American League umpire Steve Palermo is shot while helping two waitresses who were being robbed outside a Dallas restaurant.

July 9 — Cal Ripken Jr of the Baltimore Orioles hits a three-run home run as the American League wins the All-Star Game for the fourth consecutive year, 4–2.

July 13 — Four Baltimore Orioles pitchers— Bob Milacki, Mike Flanagan, Mark Williamson and Gregg Olson—combine to no-hit the Oakland Athletics, 2–0.

July 23 — Gary Redus (Pirates), Todd Benzinger (Royals), Randy Milligan (Orioles) and Ken Griffey Jr (Mariners) hit grand slams on the same night, tying a major league record.

July 28 — Dennis Martinez of the Montreal Expos pitches a perfect game in a 2–0 victory over the Los Angeles Dodgers. Martinez's gem comes less than 48 hours after teammate Mark Gardner pitches nine innings of no-hit ball, only to lose the no-hitter and the game to the Dodgers in the 10th, 1–0.

July 30 — Carlos Quintana ties a major league record by driving in six runs during the third inning of Boston's 11–6 victory over Texas.

Aug 2 — Texas reliever Mike Jeffcoat becomes the first American League pitcher to drive in a run since the designated hitter rule went into effect in 1973. In his first career at-bat, Jeffcoat doubles during the ninth inning of the Rangers' 15–1 rout of Milwaukee.

Aug 6 — With his 24th save in as many opportunities, Toronto reliever Tom Henke sets a major league record in the Blue Jays' 2–1 victory over the Detroit Tigers.

Aug 11 — Chicago White Sox pitcher Wilson Alvarez, 21, making only his second major league start, throws a no-hitter in a 7–0 victory over the Baltimore Orioles.

Aug 14 — Dave Winfield of the California Angels hits his 400th career home run during a game against the Minnesota Twins, becoming the 23rd player to reach the mark.

Aug 26 — Bret Saberhagen of Kansas City pitches a no-hitter in the Royals' 7–0 victory over the Chicago White Sox.

Aug 26 — The California Angels, having fallen from first to last in the American League West in little more than a month, fire manager Doug Rader and replace him with Buck Rodgers.

Sep 2 — Bo Jackson, trying to rebound from a hip injury that threatened his athletic career, returns to the major leagues and goes 0-for-3 in the Chicago White Sox' 5–1 defeat of Kansas City, the team that released him.

Sep 4 — Major League Baseball announces it will remove the asterisk from Roger Maris's home run record.

Sep 6 — The California Angels name former Cardinal manager Whitey Herzog Senior Vice President and Director of Player Personnel.

Sep 11 — Kent Mercker, Mark Wohlers and Alejandro Pena pitch the first combined no-hitter in National League history in the Atlanta Braves' 1–0 victory over the San Diego Padres.

Sep 15 — Smoky Burgess, former holder of the major league career pinch-hit record, dies at age 64.

Sep 16 — Atlanta outfielder Otis Nixon, a catalyst in the Braves' rise to the top of the National League West, is suspended for 60 days after testing positive for cocaine use.

Sep 22 — The Pittsburgh Pirates clinch the NL East with a 2–1 victory over Philadelphia, becoming the first NL team to repeat as division champs since the Dodgers and Phillies in 1978.

Sep 24 — Deion Sanders of the Atlanta Falcons rejoins the Atlanta Braves for the stretch drive. Sanders, used as a pinch-runner and defensive replacement, continues to practice football during the day and plays in the Falcons' Sep. 29 game against New Orleans.

Sep 29 — The Minnesota Twins become the first team to go from last one season to first the next, clinching the American League West when Chicago loses to Seattle.

Sep 29 — The New York Mets fire manager Bud Harrelson.

Oct 1 — Lee Smith of St. Louis sets a National League record with his 46th save in a game against the Montreal Expos.

Oct 2 — Tom Glavine of Atlanta becomes the major leagues' first 20-game winner as the Braves beat Cincinnati, 6–3. After the Los Angeles Dodgers' 9–4 loss to San Diego, the Braves and Dodgers are tied atop the National League West with three games left.

Oct 2 — Toronto clinches the American League East with a 6–5 win over the California Angels. The Blue Jays become the first team to draw four million in attendance.

Oct 5 — Atlanta becomes the second team this season to go from last one season to first the next, clinching the pennant by beating Houston while the Dodgers are losing to San Francisco.

Oct 6 — David Cone of the New York Mets ties the National League record for strikeouts in a game by fanning 19 Phillies in a 7–0 win.

Oct 7 — Leo Durocher, who won 2,008 games, three pennants and the 1954 World Series as a manager, dies in Palm Springs, CA, at age 86.

Oct 7 — The New York Yankees fire manager Stump Merrill after a 71–91 fifth-place finish.

Oct 8 — Despite a second-place finish, the Boston Red Sox fire manager Joe Morgan and replace him with Butch Hobson, the manager of their class AAA team at Pawtucket, RI.

Oct 8 — The Milwaukee Brewers name Sal Bando to replace Harry Dalton as general manager. Dalton becomes a senior vice president.

Oct 9 — In Sal Bando's first move as Milwaukee's general manager, he fires Tom Trebelhorn, manager of the Brewers for the past five years, despite the fact that Milwaukee had won 40 of its last 59 games this year to finish above .500.

Oct 10 — The New York Mets hire Jeff Torborg, who had managed the Chicago White Sox to two straight second-place finishes, to replace Bud Harrelson as manager.

Oct 10 — Seattle fires Jim Lefebvre as manager even though he led the Mariners to their first winning season in their 15-year history.

Oct 13 — The Minnesota Twins defeat the Toronto Blue Jays 8–5 to win the American League Championship Series four games to one. Kirby Puckett, who hit .429 with two homers and six RBIs, is named the Series MVP.

Oct 17 — Atlanta Braves shut out the Pirates 4–0 in Pittsburgh to win the National League Championship Series four games to three.

Oct 18 — Jim Essian of the Cubs becomes the 13th manager fired this season.

Oct 27 — The Minnesota Twins defeat the Atlanta Braves 1–0 on a 10th-inning, bases-loaded hit over a drawn-in outfield by pinch hitter Gene Larken to win the World Series four games to three. The Twins' Jack Morris pitches the final game shutout and is named Series MVP.

Oct 28 — The Seibu Lions defeat the Hiroshima Toyo Carp 7–1 in the seventh game to win their seventh Japanese championship.

Oct 29 — Bill Plummer is named the 10th manager in the Seattle Mariners' 15-year history.

Oct 29 — Buck Showalter, who was fired as the New York Yankees' third base coach three weeks earlier, is rehired as the team's new manager.

Oct 29 — Bobby Cox, who led the Atlanta Braves from last place in 1990 to the pennant in 1991, is named National League manager of the year.

Oct 30 — The Minnesota Twins' Tom Kelly, who became the first manager to lead a team from last place to a World Series championship, is named manager of the year in the American League.

Oct 30 — The Milwaukee Brewers select Houston Astros coach Phil Garner as their new manager.

Boxing

Hearns beat Hill for his sixth title.

Dec 8, 1990 — Mike Tyson knocks out Alex Stewart in the first round of their heavyweight fight in Atlantic City.

Feb 9, 1991 — Sugar Ray Leonard fails in his comeback bid, losing a 12-round decision to WBC junior middleweight champion Terry Norris.

Mar 18 — Mike Tyson beats Razor Ruddock in a heavyweight bout that, in a controversial decision, is halted in the seventh round by referee Richard Steele.

Apr 19 — Evander Holyfield retains his undisputed heavyweight title with a 12-round decision over George Foreman in Atlantic City.

June 3 — Tommy Hearns, 32, wins his sixth title in 14 years with a decision over Virgil Hill in a WBA light heavyweight fight.

June 28 — Mike Tyson scores a unanimous 12-round decision in a rematch with Razor Ruddock.

Sep 9 — Mike Tyson is indicted on charges of raping a teenage beauty contestant in her Indianapolis hotel room during the Miss Black America pageant in July.

Sep 21 — IBF bantamweight champion Orlando Canizales wins a 12-round decision over Fernie Morales, who requires emergency surgery for a blood clot after the fight.

Oct 18 — Mike Tyson pulls out of his Nov 8 fight against heavyweight champion Evander Holyfield, citing a rib injury.

Oct 19 — Prince Charles Williams retains his IBF light heavyweight title with a second-round TKO of Fred Delgado in Williamson, WV.

College Basketball

Nov 29, 1990 — In an unprecedented move, the NCAA restores the eligibility of defending national basketball champion UNLV for the 1991 NCAA men's basketball tournament. The Runnin' Rebels, on probation from a case dating to 1977, accept alternative penalties that include a ban on postseason play in 1992.

Dec 10 — North Carolina and Kentucky, tied for the all-time lead in college basketball victories at 1,483, square off in Chapel Hill, N.C. The Tar Heels prevail, 84–81.

Jan 5, 1991 — Kevin Bradshaw of U.S. International scores 72 points in a game against Loyola Marymount, breaking the previous record of 69 set by Pete Maravich almost 21 years earlier.

Jan 12 — No. 2 Virginia defeats No. 3 North Carolina State 123–120 in triple overtime in a meeting of women's college basketball powers.

Feb 10 — No. 1 UNLV defeats No. 2 Arkansas 112–105 in a college basketball showdown in Fayetteville, Ark.

Mar 14 — Syracuse becomes the first No. 2 seed to be bounced in the first round of the NCAA men's basketball tournament by falling to Richmond 73–69 in an East Regional game.

No. 1 UNLV pounded No. 2 Arkansas.

College Basketball (*Cont.*)

Mar 23 — Kansas and undefeated UNLV advance to college basketball's Final Four. UNLV defeats Seton Hall 77–65 in the West Regional final, and Kansas stuns Arkansas 93–81 in the Southeast.

Mar 24 — The Final Four field is set: Duke beats St. John's 78–61 in the Midwest, and North Carolina edges Temple 79–77 in the East.

Mar 30 — Duke ends UNLV's bid to repeat as men's national basketball champion with a 79–77 victory at the Final Four in Indianapolis. Kansas reaches the final with a 79–73 victory over North Carolina.

Mar 30 — Virginia ousts Connecticut 61–55, and Tennessee defeats Stanford 68–60 at the women's Final Four in New Orleans.

Mar 31 — Tennessee beats Virginia 70–67 in overtime to capture its third women's NCAA basketball championship in five years.

Apr 1 — On its ninth trip to the Final Four, Duke outlasts Kansas 72–65 to win its first NCAA basketball championship.

Apr 15 — In the wake of a 12–20 season, Digger Phelps resigns under pressure after 20 seasons as Notre Dame basketball coach.

June 7 — The embattled Jerry Tarkanian announces he will coach one more season, then step down as basketball coach at UNLV.

College Football

Nov 3, 1990 — No. 1 Virginia loses at home to Georgia Tech, 41–38.

Nov 17 — No. 1 Notre Dame is knocked off the top spot for the second time, 24–21 by 18th-ranked Penn State.

Dec 1 — BYU quarterback Ty Detmer, who would finish with an NCAA-record 5,188 yards passing in 1990, wins the Heisman Trophy. Hours later, he throws four interceptions in a 59–28 loss to Hawaii.

Jan 1, 1991 — Colorado defeats Notre Dame in the Orange Bowl for a share of college football's national championship, only after Raghib Ismail's 91-yard punt return for a touchdown with 1:05 left is nullified by a clipping penalty. The Associated Press votes Colorado No. 1, but United Press International sides with Georgia Tech, which completes an unbeaten season with a rout of Nebraska in the Florida Citrus Bowl.

May 6 — Roy Lee (Chucky) Mullins, the Mississippi football player who was paralyzed in a 1989 football game and became a symbol of the potential for racial harmony in the state, dies of complications from a blood clot in his lungs at the age of 21.

Aug 28 — Penn State overwhelms codefending national champion Georgia Tech 34–22 in the Kickoff Classic.

Sep 7 — Ty Detmer, with 11,606 yards, becomes the NCAA's career passing leader in BYU's 27–23 loss to UCLA.

Sep 14 — Jeff Ireland kicks a 35-yard field goal with 51 seconds left, lifting Baylor over Colorado, 16–14, and ending college football's longest winning streak at 11 games.

Sep 14 — Freshman Marshall Faulk rushes for an NCAA record 386 yards and scores seven touchdowns in San Diego State's 55–34 victory over Pacific. Faulk, who enters the game only after an injury to a teammate, plays only about three quarters.

Sep 21 — Ty Detmer becomes the NCAA's all-time total offense leader (11,409 yards) in BYU's 33–7 loss to Penn State.

Sep 28 — No. 1 Florida State whips No. 3 Michigan, 51–31. It is the second most points ever allowed by a Wolverines football team.

Oct 12 — Florida upsets undefeated Tennessee 35–18 in front of the largest crowd ever to see a football game in the state of Florida, 85,135. In other upsets, Texas downs undefeated Oklahoma 10–7, and Rice beats undefeated Baylor 20–17.

Florida State's offense ran over Michigan.

Oct 12 — Michael Lerch of Princeton sets NCAA Division I-AA records with 370 receiving yards and 463 all-purpose yards in Princeton's 59–37 win over Brown. The receiving yardage ties the NCAA all-division mark.

Oct 19 — In a battle of unbeaten teams, Washington defeats California 24–17 to get the inside track on a trip to the Rose Bowl.

Oct 19 — Shawn Graves of Wofford College, a 5′8″, 160-pound junior who was born without any chest muscles on the right side of his body, becomes the NCAA's all-time rushing quarterback, surpassing the record of 3,612 yards set by Air Force's Dee Dowis between 1986 and 1989.

Oct 24 — The Big 10 suspends Indiana football coach Bill Mallory for the Hoosiers' Oct 26 conference game against Wisconsin for criticizing officials during Indiana's loss at Michigan.

Golf

Nov 28, 1990 — Charles S. Mechem Jr is named commissioner of the LPGA.

Jan 13, 1991 — Phil Mickelson, 20, birdies the 72nd hole to win the Northern Telecom Open in Tucson, becoming the youngest amateur to win a PGA Tour event and only the second since 1954.

Mar 1 — Paul Azinger, in contention after the second round of the Doral Ryder Open, is disqualified after a television viewer phones in a rules violation that occurred during the first round.

Mar 31 — Amy Alcott coasts to an eight-shot victory at the Nabisco Dinah Shore.

Apr 14 — Welshman Ian Woosnam wins the Masters by one shot over Jose Maria Olazabal. Tom Watson finishes two back.

Apr 21 — Jack Nicklaus wins the PGA Seniors Championship for his fourth Seniors title in six career appearances.

May 5 — Using its controversial system of monitoring television broadcasts, the PGA Tour overrules the contending Tom Kite on a rules interpretation during the final round of the GTE Byron Nelson Classic.

June 4 — The PGA Tour policy board votes to abolish the practice of monitoring telecasts for possible rules violations.

June 13 — Spectator Bill Fadell, 27, is killed by lightning during the first round of the U.S. Open golf tournament. Five others are injured after seeking cover under a tree as a storm blew across the Hazeltine National layout in Chaska, MN.

June 17 — Payne Stewart rallies to defeat Scott Simpson 75–77 in an 18-hole U.S. Open playoff.

June 30 — Meg Mallon birdies the 18th hole to win the LPGA Championship by one shot over Pat Bradley and Ayako Okamoto.

July 14 — Meg Mallon wins her second major in two weeks, shooting a final-round 68 for a two-shot victory over Pat Bradley at the U.S. Women's Open at Colonial Country Club in Fort Worth.

July 21 — Ian Baker-Finch wins the British Open at Royal Birkdale by two shots over fellow Australian Michael Harwood.

July 29 — Jack Nicklaus shoots a 65 to defeat Chi Chi Rodriguez by four shots in an 18-hole playoff for the U.S. Senior Open championship at Oakland Hills Country Club in Birmingham, MI.

Aug 8 — For the second time in as many months, a spectator is killed by lightning at a major golf event. Thomas Weaver, 39, was en route to and some 50 yards from his car when he was struck during the opening round of the PGA.

Aug 11 — Long-hitting John Daly, who got into the field as the ninth alternate, coasts to a three-shot victory in the PGA Championship at Crooked Stick in Carmel, IN.

V. J. LOVERO

Alcott trounced the Dinah Shore field.

Golf (*Cont.*)

Aug 13 — Captain Dave Stockton fills out the US Ryder Cup roster by naming Ray Floyd and Chip Beck to the 12-man team.

Sep 15 — Nancy Scranton, winless in seven LPGA seasons, shoots a final-round 68 to win the du Maurier Classic by three shots.

Sep 22 — Pat Bradley wins the Safeco Classic in a playoff against Rosie Jones, becoming the LPGA's first $4 million woman.

Sep 29 — The United States regains the Ryder Cup with a 14½–13½ victory over Europe on the Ocean Course at Kiawah Island. In the final and deciding match, Bernhard Langer misses a six-foot par putt at the 18th hole that gives Hale Irwin a tie and the half-point the U.S. needs for victory.

Sep 29 — Pat Bradley becomes the 12th player to qualify for the LPGA Hall of Fame by virtue of

her victory at the MBS Classic in Bueno Park, CA, her 30th LPGA career win.

Oct 11 — At the Las Vegas Invitational, Chip Beck shoots a 59, becoming only the second player ever to accomplish the feat on the pro tour. His round consists of 13 birdies and five pars.

Oct 13 — Andrew Magee and D. A. Weibring break the PGA scoring record for 90 holes, finishing the Las Vegas Invitational tied at 31 under par with scores of 329, four strokes better than the previous record. Magee wins the tournament with a par on the second playoff hole.

Oct 27 — Former San Francisco 49er quarterback John Brodie shoots a final round 68 to win his first PGA title at the Security Pacific Senior Classic in Los Angeles.

Hockey

Nov 24, 1990 — Fred Shero, who guided the Philadelphia Flyers to the Stanley Cup championship in 1974 and 1975 and had the fourth-best winning percentage in NHL history, dies of cancer at the age of 65.

Dec 7 — The NHL awards expansion franchises for the 1992–93 season to Ottawa and Tampa.

Jan 19, 1991 — Vincent Damphousse of Toronto scores four goals to lead the Campbell Conference to an 11–5 rout of the Wales Conference at the NHL All-Star Game in Chicago.

Jan 25 — Brett Hull of the St. Louis Blues becomes the fifth player in NHL history to score 50 goals in his team's first 50 games.

Jan 26 — Returning to the lineup from a back injury that sidelined him since the start of the season, Mario Lemieux contributes three assists in Pittsburgh's 6–5 victory at Quebec.

Mar 4 — The New Jersey Devils fire coach John Cunniff and replace him with Tom McVie.

Apr 1 — Winnipeg coach Bob Murdoch is fired after failing to lead the Jets to the NHL playoffs. He is eventually replaced by John Paddock.

May 25 — The Pittsburgh Penguins end the Minnesota North Stars' magical playoff ride with an 8–0 victory in Game 6 of the Stanley Cup finals. It is the Penguins' first Stanley Cup.

May 29 — Rick Ley is fired as coach of the Hartford Whalers, despite compiling a franchise-best winning percentage of .494 in two seasons. He will be replaced by Jimmy Roberts.

May 30 — Mike Milbury steps down as coach of the Boston Bruins to work full time in his role as assistant general manager. He is replaced by Rick Bowness.

June 22 — Quebec makes Eric Lindros the first pick of the NHL entry draft.

June 27 — Edmonton Oilers coach John Muckler moves to the Buffalo Sabres as director of operations. The Oilers name Ted Green to replace him.

Aug 30 — Bob Johnson, coach of the Stanley Cup champion Pittsburgh Penguins, undergoes emergency surgery for the removal of a brain tumor.

Pittsburgh won its first Stanley Cup.

Hockey (*Cont.*)

Sep 3 — An arbitrator awards all-star defenseman Scott Stevens to the New Jersey Devils as compensation for the St. Louis Blues' signing of free agent Brendan Shanahan. Stevens had moved via the NHL's free-agent system the previous summer, jumping from Washington to St. Louis.

Sep 19 — The Edmonton Oilers trade goaltender Grant Fuhr and forwards Glenn Anderson and Craig Berube to Toronto for forwards Vincent Damphousse and Scott Thornton, defenseman Luke Richardson, goaltender Peter Ing and future considerations.

Oct 3 — The NHL opens its 75th anniversary season with games involving only its six original teams: Boston, New York, Detroit, Chicago, Montreal and Toronto.

Oct 4 — The Edmonton Oilers trade center Mark Messier to the New York Rangers for center Bernie Nicholls and a pair of promising forwards, Louie DeBrusk and Steven Rice.

Oct 17 — Paul Coffey of the Pittsburgh Penguins becomes the highest-scoring defenseman in National Hockey League history, surpassing Denis Potvin's mark of 1,053 career points during an 8–5 win over Potvin's former team, the New York Islanders.

Horse Racing

Nov 15, 1990 — Alydar, runner-up to Affirmed in each of the 1978 Triple Crown races, is put down after a freak stall accident.

Nov 16 — Northern Dancer, winner of the 1964 Kentucky Derby and Preakness, is put down at the age of 29 after being stricken with colic.

Apr 8, 1991 — Bill Shoemaker, the winningest jockey in horse racing history, is paralyzed in a one-vehicle accident near Arcadia, Calif.

Apr 25 — Laz Barrera, a four-time winner of the Eclipse Award as the top U.S. trainer and winner of the Triple Crown with Affirmed in 1978, dies of heart failure at the age of 66.

May 4 — Strike the Gold rallies down the stretch to win the Kentucky Derby.

May 18 — Late entry Hansel wins the Preakness. Kentucky Derby winner Strike the Gold is sixth.

June 8 — Hansel wins the Belmont by a head over Strike the Gold.

Aug 3 — Favored Giant Victory wins the 66th running of the Hambletonian.

Oct 17 — Angel Cordero Jr rides Don't Cross the Law to victory at Belmont Park for his 7,000th win since beginning his career on the American mainland in 1962.

Oct 25 — John Campbell drives winners in three of eight Breeders Crown races at Pompano Beach, FL, to become the first harness driver to top $100,000 million in career winnings. One of his winning horses, Miss Easy, sets a world record for three-year-old fillies on a ⅝ mile track of 1:52⅖.

Hansel (in lead) took the Preakness.

Nov 18, 1990 — Dale Earnhardt finishes third in the Atlanta Journal 500, which is good enough to earn him his fourth Winston Cup title. At the same race, Mike Rich, crewman for Bill Elliott, is killed in a pit-road accident.

Nov 25 — Billy Vukovich III, 27, 1988 Indianapolis 500 Rookie of the Year, is killed in a sprint car accident at Mesa Marin Speedway in California.

Dec 23 — Wendell Scott, 69, who broke the color barrier in stock car racing during the 1950s, dies of cancer in Danville, VA.

3, 1991 — A team of five drivers—John Winter, Frank Jelinski, Henri Pescarolo, Hurley Haywood and Bob Wollek—win the 24 Hours of Daytona, averaging 106.633 mph in a Porsche 962C.

Feb 17 — Ernie Irvan holds off Dale Earnhardt and Davey Allison and wins his first Daytona 500.

Mar 17 — John Andretti, nephew of Mario, cousin of Michael and Jeff, wins the first Indy Car race ever held in Australia, at Surfer's Paradise in Queensland.

May 11 — A. J. Foyt, 56, still in severe pain from a late-season crash in 1990, qualifies for the Indianapolis 500, at 222.443 mph. He will start his 34th straight Indy in the middle of the front row.

May 19 — Willy T. Ribbs becomes the first black driver to qualify for the Indy 500.

May 26 — Rick Mears joins A. J. Foyt and Al Unser Sr as the only four-time winners of the Indianapolis 500.

June 2 — Micheal, John, and Mario Andretti finish 1-2-3 in an Indy Car race at West Allis, WI.

June 23 — Volker Weidler, Johnny Herbert, and Bertrand Gachot team up in a Mazda 787B to win the 24 Hours of LeMans, averaging 127.589 mph.

Aug 11 — J. D. McDuffie is killed in a crash early in the Winston Cup race at Watkins Glen, NY.

Sep 22 — Harry Gant becomes only the fourth driver since 1972 to win four consecutive NASCAR races with his victory in the Goody's 500 at Martinsville, VA.

Irvan celebrated his first Daytona win.

GEORGE TIEDEMANN

Sep 29 — Harry Gant fails in his bid to win a fifth consecutive NASCAR event when he experiences brake problems late in the Holly Farms 400. Dale Earnhardt overtakes Gant with nine laps left. Gant, who led much of the race, settles for second.

Oct 13 — With a third-place finish in the Camel Grand Prix at the Del Mar (CA) Fairgrounds, Geoff Brabham becomes the first driver to win the IMSA Camel GT Prototype championship in four consecutive years.

Oct 20 — Michael Andretti wins his first CART points title as he finishes first at the final race of the season held at Laguna Seca Raceway in Monterey, CA.

Oct 20 — Brazil's Ayrton Senna clinches his third Formula One world championship with a second place finish at the Japanese Grand Prix.

Nov 30, 1990 — Larry Bird of the Boston Celtics becomes the 15th player in NBA history to reach 20,000 career points during a game against the Washington Bullets.

Dec 3 — The New York Knicks release coach Stu Jackson 15 games into the NBA season. He is replaced by John MacLeod.

Dec 20 — The Indiana Pacers fire coach Bob Versace, replacing him with assistant Bob Hill.

Dec 30 — Scott Skiles of the Orlando Magic hands out 30 assists in a 155–116 victory over the Denver Nuggets, breaking an NBA record that stood for 13 years.

Feb 10, 1991 — MVP Charles Barkley scores 17 points and grabs 22 rebounds as the East defeats the West 116–114 in the NBA All-Star Game in Charlotte.

Apr 15 — Magic Johnson of the Los Angeles Lakers becomes the NBA's all-time assist leader during the second quarter of a game against the Dallas Mavericks. Johnson passes Oscar Robertson, who had 9,887 assists.

PETER READ MILLER

Ewing (33) remained a Knick.

May 20 — Michael Jordan of the Chicago Bulls is named MVP of the NBA.

May 27 — The Chicago Bulls complete a four-game sweep of the two-time defending NBA champion Detroit Pistons with a 115–94 victory.

May 31 — The New York Knicks name Pat Riley their new head coach, replacing John MacLeod, who had left to take the head job at Notre Dame.

June 12 — The Chicago Bulls defeat the Los Angeles Lakers 108–101 for their first NBA championship. Michael Jordan is named series MVP.

June 17 — Kevin Loughery is named coach of the Miami Heat, but in an unusual twist, the Atlanta Hawks say they won't release Loughery from his contract as an assistant until after the June 26 draft. Loughery replaces Ron Rothstein.

June 19 — The Minnesota Timberwolves name Jimmy Rodgers to replace the fired Bill Musselman.

June 26 — The Charlotte Hornets make Larry Johnson of UNLV the No. 1 pick in the NBA draft.

July 23 — The Charlotte Hornets move coach Gene Littles to the front office and replace him on the bench with director of player personnel Allan Bristow.

July 29 — Patrick Ewing loses his bid to become a free agent when an arbitrator rules he is bound to the New York Knicks for four more seasons. Ewing, citing a clause in his contract that calls for him to be among the NBA's four highest-paid players, had sought to become a restricted free agent.

Sep 4 — The Detroit Pistons waive 35-year-old guard Vinnie Johnson, who made the winning shot in Game 5 of the 1990 NBA Finals to give the Pistons their second consecutive title.

Oct 16 — Roy Tarpley of the Dallas Mavericks is banned from the NBA for life after violating terms of his drug after-care program a third time.

Oct 30 — The Charlotte Hornets sign the No. 1 pick in the NBA draft, UNLV forward Larry Johnson, to a six-year contract worth a reported average of $3.3 million a year.

Pro Football

Nov 5, 1990 — Cleveland Browns coach Bud Carson is fired.

Nov 7 — One day after Arizona voters reject a proposed Martin Luther King Jr holiday, NFL commissioner Paul Tagliabue recommends that Tempe be denied the 1993 Super Bowl.

Nov 11 — Derrick Thomas of the Kansas City Chiefs gets an NFL-record seven sacks against Seattle, but Seahawks quarterback Dave Krieg eludes Thomas's grasp on the final play to throw a game-winning touchdown.

Nov 25 — One week before they are scheduled to square off, the NFL's last remaining unbeatens go down. The San Francisco 49ers lose to the Los Angeles Rams, and the New York Giants fall in Philadelphia.

Nov 25 — Winnipeg wins the CFL's Grey Cup with a 50–11 thrashing of Edmonton.

Nov 27 — NFL commissioner Paul Tagliabue fines the New England Patriots and three players a total of $72,500 for their roles in a locker-room harassment incident involving *Boston Herald* sportswriter Lisa Olson.

Dec 3 — Tampa Bay Buccaneers coach Ray Perkins is fired.

Dec 9 — With 26 yards on 15 carries, the Giants' Ottis Anderson becomes the eighth player in NFL history to rush for 10,000 yards.

Dec 19 — Bo Jackson, who had played in baseball's All-Star Game in July, becomes the first professional athlete named an all-star in two sports with his selection for the NFL's Pro Bowl.

Dec 31 — George Allen, the legendary NFL coach who had come out of retirement to lead Long Beach State to a 6–5 record in 1990, dies of a coronary spasm at the age of 72.

Jan 5, 1991 — The Washington Redskins defeat the Philadelphia Eagles 20–6 in an NFC wild-card game. In the AFC, Miami rallies to beat Kansas City 17–16.

Jan 6 — Cincinnati beats Houston 41–14, and Chicago whips New Orleans 16–6 in other NFL first-round games.

Jan 7 — The New England Patriots name Dick MacPherson of Syracuse as head coach. The announcement comes just weeks after Miami athletic director Sam Jankovich takes over as Patriots general manager.

Jan 8 — The Philadelphia Eagles fire controversial coach Buddy Ryan, who was 43–35–1 in regular-season play but 0–3 in the postseason.

Jan 12 — Buffalo beats Miami 44–34 in an AFC divisional playoff. In the NFC, San Francisco defeats Washington 28–10.

Jan 13 — The Los Angeles Raiders beat Cincinnati 20–10 in the other AFC divisional playoff, but Raiders running back Bo Jackson suffers a career-threatening hip injury. In the NFC, the New York Giants rout Chicago 31–3.

Jan 20 — The Bills whip the Raiders 51–3, and the Giants bounce the two-time defending Super Bowl champion 49ers 15–13, setting up an all–New York State Super Bowl.

Jan 24 — Notre Dame's Raghib (Rocket) Ismail, the most versatile player in college football, announces he will forego his senior season and declare for the NFL draft.

Jan 27 — The Giants beat the Bills 20–19 in Super Bowl XXV as Scott Norwood's 47-yard field goal sails wide right in the closing seconds.

Jan 28 — Harold (Red) Grange, who starred as a running back at the University of Illinois and then for the Chicago Bears, dies of complications from pneumonia at the age of 87.

A hip injury threatened Jackson's career.

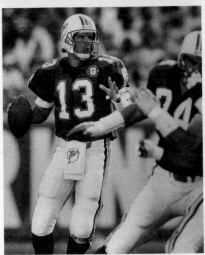

JOHN BIEVER

Marino became the NFL's best paid.

Feb 3 — Jim Kelly leads the AFC to a 23–21 victory over the NFC in the Pro Bowl in Honolulu.

Feb 5 — Bill Belichick, defensive coordinator of the New York Giants, takes over as Cleveland's head coach.

Feb 20 — Robert Tisch buys 50% of the New York Giants from Tim Mara.

Mar 23 — The World League of American Football makes its debut as the London Monarchs go on the road to defeat the Frankfurt Galaxy 24–11.

Mar 25 — Plan B free agent Ronnie Lott, the defensive force in San Francisco's four Super Bowl championships, signs a two-year, $1.8 million contract with the Los Angeles Raiders.

Apr 21 — Raghib Ismail spurns the NFL and signs the richest contract in football history with the CFL's Toronto Argonauts, a four-year deal worth $18.2 million guaranteed, with the potential for an additional payout of $8 million.

Apr 21 — The Dallas Cowboys, having traded up for the No. 1 pick in the NFL draft, select Miami defensive tackle Russell Maryland.

May 15 — Bill Parcells, coach of the two-time Super Bowl champion New York Giants, resigns. He is replaced by assistant coach Ray Handley.

June 9 — London defeats Barcelona 21–0 at Wembley Stadium in London to capture the first World League of American Football championship.

July 18 — Raghib Ismail gains 213 all-purpose yards in his Canadian Football League debut, a 41–18 Toronto victory over Hamilton.

July 27 — Running back Earl Campbell, guard John Hannah, lineman Stan Jones, kicker Jan Stenerud and former Dallas Cowboys president Tex Schramm are inducted into the Pro Football Hall of Fame.

Aug 5 — Pro football legend Paul Brown, who founded the Cleveland Browns and the Cincinnati Bengals, dies of complications from pneumonia at the age of 82.

Aug 20 — The Miami Dolphins announce the signing of quarterback Dan Marino to a five-year contract worth a reported $25 million, making Marino the highest-paid player in the NFL.

Sep 1 — On the opening day of the NFL season, the Philadelphia Eagles lose quarterback Randall Cunningham for the year with two torn ligaments in his left knee.

Sep 8 — Jim Kelly throws for 363 yards and six touchdowns as Buffalo routs Pittsburgh 52–34.

Sep 19 — In the wake of criticism from coaches, players and fans, the NFL announces it will soften its stance on end zone celebrations.

Sep 22 — Don Shula gets his 300th career NFL victory in Miami's 16–13 win over Green Bay.

Oct 1 — The Indianapolis Colts, who scored only 40 points while losing their first five games, fire coach Ron Meyer. He is replaced by defensive coordinator Rick Venturi.

Oct 8 — Bo Jackson flunks his football physical with the Los Angeles Raiders.

Oct 9 — The 49ers' Joe Montana undergoes surgery on his right elbow, sidelining him for the remainder of the season.

Oct 13 — Art Monk of the Washington Redskins takes over second place on the all-time receiving list with his 751st reception, moving past Charlie Joiner during a seven-catch, 104-yard, one-touchdown performance against Cleveland.

Oct 23 — NFL owners vote to keep the World League of American Football alive, at least through 1994, by creating NFL International, an umbrella organization that will also supervise foreign exhibition games and licensing and marketing operations overseas. The Raleigh-Durham franchise is replaced by Columbus (Ohio).

Oct 27 — Morten Andersen of New Orleans kicks a 60-yard field goal, tying the second-longest in NFL history, but the Saints lose to Chicago 20–17, leaving the Washington Redskins as the only undefeated team in the NFL.

Nov 18, 1990 — Monica Seles and Gabriela Sabatini, respective winners of the French and U.S. Opens, make history at the Virginia Slims Championships by playing the first five-set women's match in 89 years. Seles wins.

Dec 1 — Making good use of a controversial homecourt advantage—a slow red-clay surface laid down in St. Petersburg, FL—the United States wins the Davis Cup for the first time since 1982 by defeating Australia.

Dec 13 — Alice Marble, the top female tennis player in the United States from 1936 to 1940 and a four-time U.S. Open champion, dies at age 77.

Dec 16 — Pete Sampras wins the first Grand Slam Cup in Munich with a 6–3, 6–4, 6–2 victory over Brad Gilbert. The $2 million first prize is the richest in tennis history.

Jan 26, 1991 — Monica Seles beats Jana Novotna 5–7, 6–3, 6–1 to become the youngest women's singles winner in the history of the Australian championships.

Jan 27 — Boris Becker beats Ivan Lendl 1–6, 6–4, 6–4, 6–4 to win the Australian Open men's crown.

Mar 3 — John McEnroe beats brother Patrick 3–6, 6–2, 6–4 in the finals of an ATP event in Chicago.

June 8 — Monica Seles wins the French Open women's singles title with a 6–3, 6–4 victory over Arantxa Sanchez Vicario.

DAVID WALBERG

Courier won his first Grand Slam event.

June 9 — Jim Courier rallies to defeat Andre Agassi in the French Open men's final 3–6, 6–4, 2–6, 6–1, 6–4.

July 6 — Steffi Graf rediscovers her game and defeats Gabriela Sabatini 6–4, 3–6, 8–6 in the Wimbledon women's singles final.

July 7 — In an all-German final, Michael Stich defeats Boris Becker 6–4, 7–6, 6–4 for the Wimbledon men's singles title.

July 22 — The Women's Tennis Association fines Monica Seles $20,000 for her participation in the nonsanctioned Pathmark Classic in Mahwah, N.J. The announcement comes one day after Seles, the world's top-ranked women's player, loses in the finals of the Pathmark to Jennifer Capriati 6–3, 7–5.

July 28 — The doubles team of Conchita Martinez and Arantxa Sanchez Vicario of Spain defeats Gigi Fernandez and Zina Garrison, giving Spain a 2–1 victory over the United States in the finals of the Federation Cup.

Aug 4 — Monica Seles loses the No. 1 ranking in women's tennis after a three-set loss to Jennifer Capriati in the finals of the Mazda Classic. Steffi Graf returns to the top spot, although a shoulder injury would force her to yield the ranking to Seles after only one week.

Sep 2 — Jimmy Connors celebrates his 39th birthday with a five-set victory over Aaron Krickstein in the fourth round of the U. S. Open. Connors, who trailed 5–2 in the fifth set, wins the four-hour, 41-minute match 3–6, 7–6 (10–8), 1–6, 6–3, 7–6 (7–4).

Sep 7 — Monica Seles wins her third Grand Slam title of 1991 with a 7–6 (7–1), 6–1 victory over Martina Navratilova in the U.S. Open women's final.

Sep 8 — Stefan Edberg defeats Jim Courier 6–2, 6–4, 6–0 in the most lopsided U.S. Open men's final since 1986.

Sep 22 — The United States advances to the Davis Cup final against France as Andre Agassi defeats Germany's Carl-Uwe Steeb 6–2, 6–2, 6–3 in the fifth and deciding match.

Track and Field

Jan 11, 1991 — Ben Johnson, running for the first time since testing positive for steroid use at the 1988 Summer Olympics, finishes second in the 50-yard dash at a meet in Hamilton, Ontario.

Feb 13 — Leroy Burrell wins the 60-meter dash in a world-record time of 6.40 at an indoor meet in Madrid. When officials question Burrell's start, he offers to run again, and wins in a world-record 6.48.

June 14 — Leroy Burrell wins the 100-meter dash in a world-record 9.90 seconds at the U.S. Championships in New York.

Aug 5 — Sergei Bubka of the Soviet Union becomes the first to clear 20 feet outdoors in the pole vault (20′ 0″) at a meet in Malmö, Sweden.

Aug 7 — The U.S. 4x100-meter relay team of Mike Marsh, Leroy Burrell, Dennis Mitchell and Carl Lewis turns in a world-record time of 37.67 at a meet in Zurich.

Aug 25 — Carl Lewis wins the 100-meter dash in a world-record 9.86 seconds at the World Track and Field Championships in Tokyo. An unprecedented six athletes finish the race in less than 10 seconds.

Aug 30 — Mike Powell leaps 29′ 4½″ at the World Track and Field Championships in Tokyo, breaking the longest-standing record in track and field: Bob Beamon's 29′ 2½″, set at the 1968 Olympics.

Sep 1 — Carl Lewis anchors the U.S. 4x100-meter relay team to a world-record time of 37.50 at the World Track and Field Championships in Tokyo. Other relay members: Andre Cason, Leroy Burrell and Dennis Mitchell.

Burrell briefly held a 100-meter record.

Nov 27, 1990 — Tamara McKinney, winner of 18 World Cup races and one overall title in her 13 years with the U.S. ski team, retires at the age of 28.

Dec 4 — Jay Bias, 20, brother of former Maryland basketball star Len Bias, is shot and killed after an argument outside a shopping mall in Hyattsville, MD. Len Bias died of a cocaine overdose two days after the Boston Celtics made him the second pick in the 1986 NBA draft.

Jan 8, 1991 — At its annual convention in Nashville, the NCAA votes to eliminate athletic dormitories over the course of the next five years.

Jan 16 — A pall is cast over the sports world as war breaks out in the Persian Gulf. Officials at North Carolina and North Carolina State react by postponing their Atlantic Coast Conference basketball game only 30 minutes before tip-off.

Feb 15 — Chuck Daly of the Detroit Pistons is named coach of the US Olympic basketball team for 1992, the first year NBA players will be allowed to compete.

Feb 16 — Tonya Harding becomes the first U.S. woman skater to successfully land a triple Axel in competition en route to winning the U.S. Figure Skating Championships. Todd Eldredge wins his second consecutive men's title.

Mar 16 — Kristi Yamaguchi leads the U.S. women to a sweep of the World Figure Skating Championships in Munich.

June 13 — *The National*, America's first and only sports daily newspaper, publishes its final edition, less than 17 months after start-up.

July 7 — The United States wins its first major soccer title, beating Honduras 4–3 on penalty kicks after a scoreless game for the championship of the North and Central American and Caribbean Region Gold Cup before 39,873 at the Los Angeles Coliseum.

July 11 — Herschel Walker qualifies for a spot on the 1992 U.S. Olympic and World Cup bobsled teams.

July 28 — Miguel Induráin of Spain coasts to a three-minute, 36-second victory in the Tour de France. Two-time defending champion Greg LeMond finishes seventh, more than 13 minutes back.

Aug 18 — On the final day of the Pan American Games, host Cuba accumulates 17 gold medals to the U.S.'s six and claims the gold medal championship of the 16-day competition 140–130. Overall, the U.S. enjoys a 352–265 medal edge.

Sep 14 — Kim Zmeskal, a 15-year-old from Houston, becomes the first U.S. woman ever to win the all-around gold medal at a world gymnastics championship. The U.S. women's team finishes second behind the Soviet Union, the U.S men's team fifth.

Sep 18 — Robert Helmick resigns as United States Olympic Committee president amid questions about whether he had used his office for personal gain.

Sep 21 — Ten NBA players are named to the 1992 U.S. Olympic basketball team. They are: Charles Barkley, Larry Bird, Patrick Ewing, Magic Johnson, Michael Jordan, Karl Malone, Chris Mullin, Scottie Pippen, David Robinson and John Stockton.

Sep 27 — William Hybl replaces Robert Helmick as USOC president.

Oct 19 — Mark Allen of Cardiff, CA, wins his third straight Ironman Triathlon in a time of 8:18:32. Paula Newby-Fraser of Zimbabwe takes the women's title for the fourth time in the last six years, finishing 26th overall with a time of 9:07:52.

Oct 19 — North Korea upsets the U.S. National soccer team 2–1 in Washington, D.C.

Oct 24 — Midfielder Hugo Perez is named U.S. Soccer male athlete of the year. The female athlete of the year award goes to Michelle Akers-Stahl for the second straight year.

Harding nailed a triple axel.

Baseball

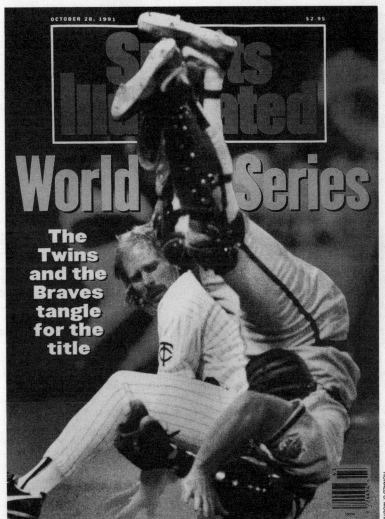

OCTOBER 28, 1991 $2.95

Sports Illustrated

World   Series

The
Twins
and the
Braves
tangle
for the
title

RONALD C. MODRA

The Grandest Finale

An upside-down baseball season ended with the best World Series ever | by TIM KURKJIAN

THE ONLY WAY THE WILD, WACKY, WONDER-ful 1991 baseball season could possibly end was with a World Series to remember. It was more than that. It was unforgettable, unbelievable and unnerving. "Was this the best World Series ever?" asked Twins outfielder Randy Bush. "It had to be, right? What could top it?"

Good question. Four of the seven games were decided on the final swing of the bat; no World Series had ever had more than two games end that way. The last hack of the 1991 Series belonged to Twins pinch-hitter Gene Larkin, whose deep fly ball over the drawn-in outfield scored Dan Gladden with the winning run in the 10th inning, giving the Twins a riveting 1–0 victory over the Atlanta Braves in Game 7.

"It was a beautiful game," said Twins pitcher Jack Morris. "It was a beautiful series."

It was a matchup of two Cinderellas—the first two teams in major league history to go from last place one year to first the next. Neither team was supposed to finish above fourth place in its respective division in 1991, but they dazzled and dizzied the nation with four one-run games and three extra-inning games. Morris, the Series MVP (in three starts, he allowed only three runs in 23 innings), won Game 7 with a complete-game, six-hitter for his second win of the Series. In the eighth, Morris escaped a second-and-third, none-out jam. The Braves, meanwhile, dodged major trouble in the eighth and ninth before Alejandro Pena loaded the bases with one out in the 10th, setting up Larkin's game-winner.

"This has got to go down in World Series history along with Bobby Thomson's homer in Game 7," said Braves pitcher John Smoltz, whose memory lapse can be forgiven.

Getting to Game 7 of the World Series was a fantastic journey. The Twins won the first two games, 5–2 and 3–2 at the Metrodome. The Braves won the next three

MICHAEL ZAGARIS

Atlanta's Lonnie Smith steamrolled the Twins' Brian Harper, but was still out at the plate in Game 4.

at Atlanta-Fulton County Stadium, sending the series back to Minnesota with Atlanta in front three games to two. Remarkably, a number of supposed experts were certain this series was over, what with Atlanta's impressive Steve Avery, the MVP of the NLCS with 16⅔ scoreless innings pitched, facing erratic Scott Erickson in Game 6. Erickson gave his team six effective—but shaky—innings to keep the score tied after seven. And this night belonged to Twins center fielder Kirby Puckett, who put on one of the greatest one-man displays in Series history. He had tripled home a run in the first, then scored for a 2–0 lead. He made a brilliant leaping catch at the fence in left center in the third, killing what could have been a huge rally. He hit a 390-ft. sacrifice fly in fifth for a 3–2 lead. In the 11th, he faced Charlie Leibrandt, who was pitching in relief for the first time in two years, and Puckett launched a 2–1 pitch over the left-center field fence, forcing a Game 7. "I felt like I went 15 rounds with Evander Holyfield," said Puckett. Asked if he was tired, he said, "I'll get my rest when I'm dead." There was no rest for the managers. "This is a storybook," said Twins manager Tom Kelly. "Who has the script? Who is writing this thing? Can you imagine this? It's unbelievable. Six great chapters. Only one to go."

And fittingly, the last chapter was a classic.

The Twins got to the Series by wiping out the Toronto Blue Jays in five games in the ALCS, winning three straight at Toronto's SkyDome to wrap it up. Atlanta had a much tougher time outlasting the Pirates. Things looked bleak for the Braves when they lost, 1–0, in Atlanta in Game 5 to fall behind, 3–2, in the series. But the Braves won the two final games in Pittsburgh, 1–0 and 4–0. In Game 6, Avery pitched his second 1–0 gem of the series, allowing only three hits in eight innings. Said Pirates pitching coach Ray Miller, "Koufax and Gibson couldn't have pitched better."

Game 7 of the NLCS was almost anticlimatic. The Braves scored three times off John Smiley in the first inning (knocking him out of the game), then watched Smoltz pitch a six-hitter to bring the World Series to Atlanta for the first time.

The Braves had gotten to the playoffs by outlasting the Dodgers. Atlanta finished the season with eight wins in nine games to wrap up the division title on the next to last day of the season. It was that old Dodger nemesis, the San Francisco Giants, who eliminated LA on the final weekend. Watch for the same thing to happen in 2002—the Giants have knocked the Dodgers out of the race in 1951, '62, '71, '82 and '91. This season was especially painful to Tommy Lasorda's club, considering the financial investment made in the offseason to win the West. "It's very frustrating," said rightfielder Darryl Strawberry, who signed a five-year, $20-million deal with LA in November 1990. "Especially when you don't feel the best team won." The Pirates, meanwhile, won the NL East by 14 games to become the first team to win that division in back-to-back years since the 1977–78 Phillies.

The Twins weren't supposed to win the AL West, but Kelly considered his team a contender in spring training. "We've go some pitching," he said. "In the past I'd have three starters, but one was always Free Toliver." The Twins started out 2–9, bu won their first 15 games in June to become serious contenders. It was obvious the Twins were destined for something special when they beat the three-time defending American League champion A's, 8–6, on August 3 despite six Oakland homers. That dropped the A's four games out of first; Oakland finished in fourth, 11 games out.

The Blue Jays won the AL East by seven games, but it wasn't easy. They led by eight games on July 15, but by September 21, their lead had wilted to one-half game over the

Does Anybody Here Want This Job?

CITO GASTON LOOKED AWFUL. He felt worse. As the 1991 American League Championship Series opened, the manager of the Toronto Blue Jays was suffering from a herniated disk in his back *and* a nasty case of food poisoning from some mystic pizza. "I haven't felt good for a long time," Gaston told a press gathering at the Metrodome. "My back has been like this for four months; it hurts all day, every day. I don't know if going in the hospital for 10 days did any good: I walked in; I came out in a wheelchair."

It was that kind of year for managers. From opening day through mid-October, 13 skippers were squashed—a record for one season. The list started with Philadelphia's Nick Leyva, and included the Cubs' Don Zimmer, Kansas City's John Wathan, Baltimore's Frank Robinson, Montreal's Buck Rodgers, California's Doug Rader, Cleveland's

John McNamara, the Mets' Bud Harrelson, the Yankees' Stump Merrill, Boston's Joe Morgan, Milwaukee's Tom Trebelhorn, Seattle's Jim Lefebvre and the Cubs' Jim Essian.

But even for those managers who kept their jobs, '91 was a traumatic year. In June, Dodgers manager Tommy Lasorda's son died. In July, Pirates manager Jim Leyland had what he thought was a heart attack on the team plane, forcing it to make an emergency landing. Said Leyland afterwards of his severe chest pains, "I thought I was going to die." So did Chicago skipper Jeff Torborg when an engine of the White Sox plane caught fire in September, also requiring an emergency landing. "Never been more scared in my life," said Torborg.

The Twins' Tom Kelly spent much of the summer suffering from a painful case of shingles. The Giants' Roger Craig had angioplasty to clear coronary blockage. Braves manager Bobby Cox limped to the mound all year on wounded knees, but that he could handle. Worse was the night he was almost strangled by a maniacal shower attachment in Philadelphia.

Red Sox—who had trailed by 11½ on August 7. Columnists across the continent again started calling them the Toronto Blow Jays, but the team won seven of its next 10 to secure the title.

The pennant races capped one of the most memorable, mystifying and mercurial major league seasons in history. The entire AL West played .500 or better, including the Mariners, who broke the .500 barrier for the first time in their 15-year existence. Meanwhile, four teams with legitimate pennant aspirations in spring training—the Reds, Cubs, Mets, and Giants—finished under .500.

But the '91 season was more about comebacks than crashes. Besides the Twins and Braves, there were the Cardinals, who let third baseman Terry Pendleton, outfielder Vince Coleman and reliever Ken Dayley leave via free agency, but won 14 more games than they did in 1990. The Cardinals hit a grand total of only 68 home runs, but blended youth with defense with speed with closer Lee Smith to finish in second place in a division that had them reserved for last.

There were the Tigers, who finished in a second-place tie in the AL East—a division that supposedly only had two contenders. The Tigers defied accepted beliefs on what it takes to win, proving you don't have to have good pitching (they had a team ERA of 4.51) and that it's okay to strike out with regularity (they set a league record with 1,185). If, that is, you have a Cecil Fielder

"It was like a Hitchcock movie," Cox said.

There were other horror shows, many of them the work of some frightful bullpens: Teams lost 121 games that they had led with three outs to go. After a grueling 7–5 loss in Houston on July 30, Cardinals manager Joe Torre said, "I'm going back to the hotel to watch *The Silence of the Lambs*—just to relax."

The Reds' Lou Piniella *never* relaxed. Not only did his team self-destruct, but he got sued by the umpires union. And no manager had a worse season than Harrelson. It go so bad that, in August, he refused to go to the mound at Shea Stadium to make a pitching change because he feared being booed by the home fans. When he was fired in September, his underachieving team was 74–80. He said he was surprised by his dismissal.

Meanwhile, across town, Merrill was pounded in the press for benching Yankee first baseman Don Mattingly in August because Mattingly refused to get his hair cut. (Actually, Merrill was just carrying out the orders of general manager Gene Michael.)

They get fired when things go wrong,

yet get little credit when things go right. A lot went right this year for Cox, but during the final weekend of the regular season at Atlanta-Fulton County Stadium, when the Braves won their division title, Cox, in uniform, was approached by a TV anchorwoman. She put the microphone forward and said, "I'm Brenda Wood with Channel 5, and you are...?" It was that kind of year.

Morgan got a pink slip despite guiding Boston to a second-place finish.

Strawberry cost the Dodgers big bucks but couldn't deliver a pennant.

cord for most games caught (88) by a teenager. California's Dave Winfield hit his 400th homer. And eight no-hitters were thrown, including 44-year-old Nolan Ryan's seventh.

It was as much a season for the goofy as it was for the great. Seattle catcher Dave Valle fell asleep on the team bus, no one woke him, and he missed the team's flight to Texas. This is the same man who, for most of the summer, was batting in the .150's, prompting a Seattle bar to link the price of drinks every Tuesday night to Valle's batting average. Giants outfielder Willie McGee's glove was stolen, so he and Mets outfielder Vince Coleman shared Coleman's glove for a game.

It was the year the players fought back. Oakland's Jose Canseco jawed with a fan in New York after the fan made comments about Canseco's much-publicized rendezvous with Madonna. Cleveland outfielder Albert Belle intentionally hit a fan with a thrown ball at Cleveland Stadium after the fan had mockingly invited Belle, a recovering alcoholic, to a keg party.

It was a season in which Reds reliever Rob Dibble fought, period. He was suspended for intentionally throwing a pitch at Houston's Eric Yelding. He was suspended again for throwing a ball over 400 feet into the center field stands and hitting a schoolteacher in the arm. He was fined for intentionally throwing at a baserunner, Chicago's Doug Dascenzo.

It was a year of individual comebacks. Bo Jackson, whom doctors said might never play again because of a hip injury, returned to the major leagues in September, and hit three homers. Texas pitcher Jose Guzman went 13–7 after missing two years with a right shoulder injury; Milwaukee's Bill Wegman went 15–7 after two years of arm injuries, and Yankees reliever Steve Howe, long plagued by drug problems, went 3–1 with a 1.68 ERA, pitching in the major leagues for the first time since 1987.

But when it was all over, 1991 would be remembered best as the year that two Cinderella teams put on the greatest World Series show ever.

to take up the slack. Detroit's first baseman (44 HRs, 133 RBIs) became the first player to lead or tie for the major league lead in homers and RBIs in consecutive years since Jimmie Foxx (1932–33).

Fielder wasn't alone in individual accomplishment. Baltimore's Cal Ripken was the game's best player in '91, hitting .323 with 34 home runs, 114 RBIs, 210 hits, 46 doubles and only 46 strikeouts. Oakland's Rickey Henderson broke Lou Brock's record (938) for stolen bases in a career (finishing the season with 994). St. Louis's Smith set the National League single-season record for saves (47) in a season. Boston's Jeff Reardon set a record by saving at least 20 games for a 10th consecutive year. Toronto's Joe Carter became the first player ever to drive in 100 runs in three consecutive years for three different teams. Texas's Pudge Rodriguez, 19 years old, set the re-

Final Standings

National League

EASTERN DIVISION

Team	Won	Lost	Pct	GB	Home	Away
Pittsburgh	98	64	.605	—	52-32	46-32
St. Louis	84	78	.519	14	52-32	32-46
Philadelphia	78	84	.481	20	47-36	31-48
Chicago	77	83	.481	20	46-37	31-46
New York	77	84	.478	20½	40-42	37-42
Montreal	71	90	.441	26½	33-35	38-55

WESTERN DIVISION

Team	Won	Lost	Pct	GB	Home	Away
Atlanta	94	68	.580	—	48-33	46-35
Los Angeles	93	69	.574	1	54-27	39-42
San Diego	84	78	.519	10	42-39	42-39
San Francisco	75	87	.463	19	43-38	32-49
Cincinnati	74	88	.457	20	39-42	35-46
Houston	65	97	.401	29	37-44	28-53

American League

EASTERN DIVISION

Team	Won	Lost	Pct	GB	Home	Away
Toronto	91	71	.562	—	46-35	45-36
Boston	84	78	.519	7	43-38	41-40
Detroit	84	78	.519	7	49-32	35-46
Milwaukee	83	79	.512	8	43-37	40-42
New York	71	91	.438	20	39-42	32-49
Baltimore	67	95	.414	24	33-48	34-47
Cleveland	57	105	.352	34	30-52	27-53

WESTERN DIVISION

Team	Won	Lost	Pct	GB	Home	Away
Minnesota	95	67	.586	—	51-30	44-37
Chicago	87	75	.537	8	46-35	41-40
Texas	85	77	.525	10	46-35	39-42
Oakland	84	78	.519	11	47-34	37-44
Seattle	83	79	.512	12	45-36	38-43
Kansas City	82	80	.506	13	40-41	42-39
California	81	81	.500	14	40-41	41-40

1991 Playoffs

National League Championship Series

Oct 9 .... Pittsburgh 5 vs. Atlanta 1
Oct 10 .... Atlanta 1 at Pittsburgh 0
Oct 12 .... Atlanta 10 vs. Pittsburgh 3
Oct 13 .... Pittsburgh 3 at Atlanta 2 (10 innings)
Oct 14 .... Pittsburgh 1 at Atlanta 0
Oct 16 .... Atlanta 1 at Pittsburgh 0
Oct 17 .... Atlanta 4 at Pittsburgh 0
(Atlanta wins series 4-3)

American League Championship Series

Oct 8 .... Minnesota 5 vs. Toronto 4
Oct 9 .... Toronto 5 at Minnesota 2
Oct 11 .... Minnesota 3 at Toronto 2 (10 innings)
Oct 12 .... Minnesota 9 at Toronto 3
Oct 13 .... Minnesota 8 at Toronto 5
(Minnesota wins series 4-1)

World Series

Oct 19 .... Minnesota 5 vs. Atlanta 2
Oct 20 .... Minnesota 3 vs. Atlanta 2
Oct 22 .... Atlanta 5 vs. Minnesota 4 (12 innings)
Oct 23 .... Atlanta 3 vs. Minnesota 2
Oct 24 .... Atlanta 14 vs. Minnesota 5
Oct 26 .... Minnesota 4 vs. Atlanta 3 (11 innings)
Oct 27 .... Minnesota 1 vs. Atlanta 0 (10 innings)
(Minnesota wins series 4-3)

Going Down Swinging — Late in the 1991 season Chicago Cubs outfielder Andre Dawson paid a $1,000 fine for disputing a strike call by umpire Joe West. On the memo line of his check Dawson wrote, "Donation for the blind."

Composite Box Scores

National League Championship Series

ATLANTA

BATTING	AB	R	H	HR	RBI	Avg
Hunter	18	2	6	1	4	.333
Olson	24	3	8	1	4	.333
Treadway	3	0	1	0	0	.333
Bream	10	1	3	1	3	.300
Gant	27	4	7	1	3	.259
Glavine	4	0	1	0	0	.250
Gregg	4	0	1	0	0	.250
L. Smith	24	3	6	0	0	.250
Belliard	19	0	4	0	1	.211
Justice	25	4	5	1	2	.200
Lemke	20	1	4	0	1	.200
Smoltz	5	0	1	0	0	.200
Pendleton	30	1	5	0	1	.167
Avery	7	0	1	0	0	.143
4 others	9	0	0	0	0	.000
Totals	229	19	53	5	19	.231

PITCHING	G	IP	H	BB	SO	ERA
Avery (2-0)	2	16.1	9	4	17	0.00
Pena	4	4.1	1	0	4	0.00
Wohlers	3	1.2	3	1	1	0.00
Clancy	1	.1	0	0	0	0.00
Leibrandt	1	6.2	8	3	6	1.35
Smoltz (2-0)	2	15.1	14	3	15	1.76
Stanton	3	3.2	4	3	3	2.45
Glavine (0-2)	2	14.0	12	6	11	3.21
Mercker (0-1)	1	.2	0	2	0	13.50
Totals	7	63.0	51	22	57	1.57

PITTSBURGH

BATTING	AB	R	H	HR	RBI	Avg
Varsho	2	0	1	0	0	.500
Bell	29	2	12	1	1	.414
LaValliere	6	0	2	0	1	.333
Bonilla	23	2	7	0	1	.304
Buechele	23	2	7	0	1	.304
Slaught	17	0	4	0	1	.235
Merced	9	1	2	1	1	.222
Drabek	5	0	1	0	1	.200
Lind	25	0	4	0	3	.160
Van Slyke	25	3	4	1	2	.160
Redus	19	1	3	0	0	.158
Bonds	27	1	4	0	0	.148
7 others	18	0	0	0	0	.000
Totals	228	12	51	3	11	.224

PITCHING	G	IP	H	BB	SO	ERA
Belinda (1-0)	3	5.0	0	3	4	0.00
Mason	3	4.1	3	1	2	0.00
Patterson	1	2.0	1	0	3	0.00
Drabek (1-1)	2	15.0	10	5	10	0.60
Z. Smith (1-1)	2	14.2	15	3	10	0.61
Walk	3	9.2	5	3	5	1.93
Tomlin	1	6.0	6	2	1	3.00
Kipper	1	2.0	2	0	1	4.50
Landrum	1	1.0	2	2	2	9.00
Smiley (0-2)	2	2.2	8	1	3	23.63
Rodriguez	1	1.0	1	2	1	27.00
Totals	7	63.0	53	22	42	2.57

American League Championship Series

TORONTO

BATTING	AB	R	H	HR	RBI	Avg
Alomar	19	3	9	0	4	.474
White	22	5	8	0	0	.364
Borders	19	0	5	0	2	.263
Carter	19	3	5	1	4	.263
Wilson	8	1	2	0	0	.250
Gruber	21	1	5	0	4	.238
Olerud	19	1	4	0	3	.211
Lee	16	3	2	0	0	.125
Mulliniks	8	1	1	0	0	.125
Maldonado	20	1	2	0	1	.100
3 others	2	0	0	0	0	.000
Totals	173	19	43	1	18	.249

PITCHING	G	IP	H	BB	SO	ERA
Acker	1	.2	1	0	1	0.00
Henke	2	2.2	0	1	5	0.00
Wells	4	7.2	6	2	9	2.35
Key	1	6.0	5	1	1	3.00
Guzman (1-0)	1	5.2	4	4	2	3.18
Timlin (0-1)	4	5.2	5	2	5	3.18
Ward (0-1)	2	4.1	4	1	6	6.23
Candiotti (0-1)	2	7.2	17	2	5	8.22
MacDonald	1	1.0	1	1	0	9.00
Stottlemyre (0-1)	1	3.2	7	1	3	9.82
Totals	5	45.0	50	15	37	4.60

MINNESOTA

BATTING	AB	R	H	HR	RBI	Avg
Puckett	21	4	9	2	6	.429
Knoblauch	20	5	7	0	3	.350
Mack	18	4	6	0	3	.333
Pagliarulo	15	3	5	1	3	.333
Davis	17	3	5	0	2	.294
Harper	18	1	5	0	1	.278
Gladden	23	4	6	0	3	.261
Gagne	17	2	4	0	1	.235
Hrbek	21	0	3	0	3	.143
6 others	11	1	0	0	0	.000
Totals	181	27	50	3	25	.276

PITCHING	G	IP	H	BB	SO	ERA
West (1-0)	2	5.2	1	4	4	0.00
Willis	3	5.1	2	0	3	0.00
Aguilera	3	3.1	1	0	3	0.00
Guthrie (1-0)	2	2.2	0	0	0	0.00
Bedrosian	2	1.1	3	2	2	0.00
Morris (2-0)	2	13.1	17	1	7	4.05
Erickson	2	4.0	3	5	2	4.50
Tapani (0-1)	2	10.1	16	3	9	7.84
Totals	5	46.0	43	15	30	3.33

World Series Composite Box Score

Atlanta

BATTING SUMMARY

	AB	R	H	HR	RBI	Avg
Lemke	24	4	10	0	4	.417
Belliard	16	0	6	0	4	.375
Pendleton	30	6	11	2	3	.367
Gant	30	3	8	0	4	.267
Justice	27	5	7	2	6	.259
Treadway	4	1	1	0	0	.250
Smith	26	5	6	3	3	.231
Olson	27	3	6	0	1	.222
Hunter	21	2	4	1	3	.190
Blauser	6	0	1	0	0	.167
Bream	24	0	3	0	0	.125
Cabrera	1	0	0	0	0	.000
Mitchell	2	0	0	0	0	.000
Gregg	3	0	0	0	0	.000
4 pitchers	8	0	0	0	0	.000
Totals	249	29	63	8	29	.253

PITCHING SUMMARY

	G	IP	H	BB	SO	ERA
Stanton (1-0)	5	7.1	5	2	7	0.00
Wohlers	3	1.2	2	2	1	0.00
Mercker	2	1.0	0	0	1	0.00
Smoltz	2	14.1	13	1	11	1.26
Glavine (1-1)	2	13.1	8	7	8	2.70
Pena (0-1)	3	5.1	6	3	7	3.38
Avery	2	13.0	10	1	8	3.46
Clancy (1-0)	3	4.1	3	4	2	4.15
St. Claire	1	1.0	1	0	0	9.00
Leibrandt (0-2)	2	4.0	8	1	3	11.25
Totals	7	65.1	56	21	48	2.89

Minnesota

BATTING SUMMARY

	AB	R	H	HR	RBI	Avg
Larkin	4	0	2	0	1	.500
Newman	2	0	1	0	1	.500
Harper	21	2	8	0	1	.381
Leius	14	2	5	1	2	.357
Knoblauch	26	3	8	0	2	.308
Pagliarulo	11	1	3	1	2	.273
Puckett	24	4	6	2	4	.250
Bush	4	0	1	0	0	.250
Gladden	30	5	7	0	0	.233
Davis	18	4	4	2	4	.222
Ortiz	5	0	1	0	1	.200
Gagne	24	1	4	1	3	.167
Mack	23	0	3	0	1	.130
Hrbek	26	2	3	1	2	.115
Brown	2	0	0	0	0	.000
Sorrento	2	0	0	0	0	.000
4 pitchers	5	0	0	0	0	.000
Totals	241	24	56	8	24	.232

PITCHING SUMMARY

	G	IP	H	BB	SO	ERA
Morris (2-0)	3	23.0	18	9	15	1.17
Aguilera (1-1)	4	5.0	6	1	3	1.80
Guthrie (0-1)	4	4.0	3	4	3	2.25
Leach	2	2.1	2	0	2	3.86
Tapani (1-1)	2	12.0	13	2	7	4.50
Erickson	2	10.2	10	4	5	5.06
Willis	4	7.0	6	2	2	5.14
Bedrosian	3	3.1	3	0	2	5.40
West	2	0	2	4	0	—
Totals	7	67.1	63	26	39	3.74

Game 1: Minnesota 5, Atlanta 2; at Minnesota, attendance 55,108
Recap: Twins shortstop Greg Gagne's three-run homer in the fifth provided the margin of victory. The Braves could muster only six scattered hits off Jack Morris, Mark Guthrie, and Rick Aguilera.

Game 2: Minnesota 3, Atlanta 2; at Minnesota, attendance 55,145
Recap: Rookie third baseman Scott Leius homered to left for the winning run in the eighth. The game had been tied after Chili Davis smashed a two-run shot in the first and Atlanta scratched back with runs on sacrifice flies in the second and in the fifth. Reliever Rick Aguilera struck out the side in the ninth to preserve the victory.

Game 3: Atlanta 5, Minnesota 4 (12 innings); at Atlanta, attendance 50,878
Recap: Back home in Atlanta, the Braves took a 4-1 lead in Game 3. Minnesota rallied though, and tied the score in the eighth on a two-run homer by Chili Davis. But in the 12th, Dave Justice singled, stole second, and scored the winning run just beating the tag by Twins catcher Brian Harper, on a Mark Lemke base hit to left.

Game 4: Atlanta 3, Minnesota 2; at Atlanta, attendance 50,878
Recap: Mark Lemke again provided the key hit for the Braves. With the score tied at two in the bottom of the ninth, Lemke tripled to the left centerfield wall off of lefthander Mark Guthrie. After a change of pitchers, he scored on a Tommy Gregg sacrifice fly.

Game 5: Atlanta 14, Minnesota 5; at Atlanta, attendance 50,878
Recap: The Braves exploded in the fourth, seventh, and eighth for a combined 13 runs as Atlanta took a 3-2 lead in the Series. The onslaught began with a two-run Dave Justice homer in the fourth which forced five Minnesota pitchers into the game. Lonnie Smith hit his third round-tripper of the Series and Brian Hunter his first.

Game 6: Minnesota 4, Atlanta 3 (11 innings); at Minnesota, attendance 55,155
Recap: Kirby Puckett ended an 11-inning thriller with a game-winning home run. Atlanta had tied the game in the seventh on a fielder's choice. Minnesota relievers pitched five innings of shutout baseball.

Game 7: Minnesota 1, Atlanta 0 (10 innings); at Minnesota, attendance 55,118
Recap: MVP Jack Morris pitched all 10 innings of this World Series classic. In the 10th, scrappy Dan Gladden stretched a single to left center into a double and eventually scored the only run of the game on a Gene Larkin single. The Braves had a golden opportunity to win the Series in the eighth. With none out, Lonnie Smith, on first after singling, lost sight of the ball on a Terry Pendleton double and paused at second just long enough to prevent him from coming all the way around to score. Instead, he stopped at third and was stranded.

National League Batting

BATTING AVERAGE

Pendleton, Atl	.319
Morris, Cin	.318
Gwynn, SD	.317
McGee, SF	.312
Jose, StL	.305
Larkin, Cin	.302
Bonilla, Pitt	.302
Clark, SF	.301
Sabo, Cin	.301
Calderon, Mont	.300

HOME RUNS

Johnson, NY	38
Williams, SF	34
Gant, Atl	32
Dawson, Chi	31
McGriff, SD	31
Clark, SF	29
O'Neill, Cin	28
Strawberry, LA	28
Mitchell, SF	27
2 tied	26

RUNS BATTED IN

Johnson, NY	117
Bonds, Pitt	116
Clark, SF	116
McGriff, SD	106
Gant, Atl	105
Dawson, Chi	104
Bonilla, Pitt	100
Sandberg, Chi	100
Strawberry, LA	99
Williams, SF	98

HITS

Pendleton, Atl	187
Butler, LA	182
Sabo, Cin	175
Bonilla, Pitt	174
Jose, StL	173
Clark, SF	170
Finley, Hou	170
Sandberg, Chi	170

RUNS SCORED

Butler, LA	112
Johnson, NY	108
Sandberg, Chi	104
Bonilla, Pitt	102
Gant, Atl	101
Bell, Pitt	96
O. Smith, StL	96
Bonds, Pitt	95

DOUBLES

Bonilla, Pitt	44
Jose, StL	40
O'Neill, Cin	36
Zeile, StL	36
Gant, Atl	35
Sabo, Cin	35
Johnson, NY	34
Pendleton, Atl	34

TRIPLES

Lankford, StL	15
Gwynn, SD	11
Finley, Hou	10
Gonzalez, Hou	9
Grissom, Mont	9

TOTAL BASES

Clark, SF	303
Pendleton, Atl	303
Johnson, NY	302
Sabo, Cin	294
Williams, SF	294

SLUGGING PERCENTAGE

Clark, SF	.536
Johnson, NY	.535
Pendleton, Atl	.517
Bonds, Pitt	.514
Larkin, Cin	.506

ON-BASE PERCENTAGE

Bonds, Pitt	.410
Butler, LA	.401
McGriff, SD	.396
Bonilla, Pitt	.391
Bagwell, Hou	.387
O. Smith, StL	.380

STOLEN BASES

Grissom, Mont	76
Nixon, Atl	72
DeShields, Mont	56
Lankford, StL	44
Bonds, Pitt	43
Butler, LA	38

BASES ON BALLS

Butler, LA	108
Bonds, Pitt	107
McGriff, SD	105
DeShields, Mont	95
Bonilla, Pitt	90
Sandberg, Chi	87

National League Pitching

EARNED RUN AVERAGE

De. Martinez, Mont	2.39
Rijo, Cin	2.51
Glavine, Atl	2.55
Belcher, LA	2.62
Harnisch, Hou	2.70
DeLeon, StL	2.71
Morgan, LA	2.78

WINS

Smiley, Pitt	20-8
Glavine, Atl	20-11
Avery, Atl	18-8
Martinez, LA	17-13
Smith, Pitt	16-10
Mulholland, Phil	16-13
6 tied	15

STRIKEOUTS

Cone, NY	241
Maddux, Chi	198
Glavine, Atl	192
Harnisch, Hou	172
Rijo, Cin	172
Benes, SD	167
Belcher, LA	156

SAVES

L. Smith, StL	47
Dibble, Cin	31
Franco, NY	30
Williams, Phil	30
Righetti, SF	24
Lefferts, SD	23

GAMES PITCHED

Jones, Mont	77
Assenmacher, Chi	75
Stanton, Atl	74
Agosto, StL	72
Burke, Mont-NY	72

INNINGS PITCHED

Maddux, Chi	263.0
Glavine, Atl	246.2
Morgan, LA	236.1
Drabek, Pitt	234.2
Cone, NY	232.2

COMPLETE GAMES

Glavine, Atl	9
De. Martinez, Mont	9
Mulholland, Phil	8
Maddux, Chi	7
Martinez, LA	6
Smith, Pitt	6

SHUTOUTS

De. Martinez, Mont	5
Martinez, LA	4
Black, SF	3
Mulholland, Phil	3
Smith, Pitt	3

American League Batting

BATTING AVERAGE

Franco, Tex .... .341
Boggs, Bos .... .332
Randolph, Mil .... .327
Griffey Jr, Sea .... .327
Molitor, Mil .... .325
C. Ripken, Balt .... .323
Palmeiro, Tex .... .322
Puckett, Minn .... .319
Thomas, Chi .... .318
Tartabull, KC .... .316

HITS

Molitor, Mil 216
C. Ripken, Balt 210
Palmeiro, Tex 203
Sierra, Tex 203
Franco, Tex 201
Sax, NY 198
Puckett, Minn 195
Alomar, Tor 188

TRIPLES

Johnson, Chi 13
Molitor, Mil 13
Alomar, Tor 11
Devereaux, Balt 10
White, Tor 10

ON-BASE PERCENTAGE

Thomas, Chi .... .453
Randolph, Mil .... .424
Boggs, Bos .... .421
Franco, Tex .... .408
E. Martinez, Sea .... .405
R. Henderson, Oak .... .400

HOME RUNS

Canseco, Oak 44
Fielder, Det 44
C. Ripken, Balt 34
Carter, Tor 33
Thomas, Chi 32
Tartabull, KC 31
Tettleton, Det 31
Davis, Minn 29
3 tied 28

RUNS SCORED

Molitor, Mil 133
Canseco, Oak 115
Palmeiro, Tex 115
Sierra, Tex 110
White, Tor 110
Franco, Tex 108
R. Henderson, Oak 105
Thomas, Chi 104

TOTAL BASES

C. Ripken, Balt 368
Palmeiro, Tex 336
Sierra, Tex 332
Molitor, Mil 325
Carter, Tor 321

STOLEN BASES

R. Henderson, Oak 58
Alomar, Tor 53
Raines, Chi 51
Polonia, Cal 48
Cuyler, Det 41
Franco, Tex 36

RUNS BATTED IN

Fielder, Det 133
Canseco, Oak 122
Sierra, Tex 116
C. Ripken, Balt 114
Thomas, Chi 109
Carter, Tor 108
Gonzalez, Tex 102
Griffey Jr, Sea 100
Tartabull, KC 100
Ventura, Chi 100

DOUBLES

Palmeiro, Tex 49
C. Ripken, Balt 46
Sierra, Tex 44
Boggs, Bos 42
Carter, Tor 42
Griffey Jr, Sea 42
Reed, Bos 42
Alomar, Tor 41

SLUGGING PERCENTAGE

Tartabull, KC .... .593
C. Ripken, Balt .... .566
Canseco, Oak .... .556
Thomas, Chi .... .553
Palmeiro, Tex .... .532

BASES ON BALLS

Thomas, Chi 138
Tettleton, Det 101
R. Henderson, Oak 98
Clark, Bos 96
Davis, Minn 95
McGwire, Oak 93

American League Pitching

EARNED RUN AVERAGE

Clemens, Bos 2.62
Candiotti, Clev-Tor 2.65
Wegman, Mil 2.84
J. Abbott, Cal 2.89
Ryan, Tex 2.91
Moore, Oak.......................... 2.96
Tapani, Minn........................ 2.99

SAVES

Harvey, Cal 46
Eckersley, Oak 43
Aguilera, Minn 42
Reardon, Bos 40
Montgomery, KC 33
Henke, Tor 32

WINS

Erickson, Minn 20-8
Gullickson, Det................. 20-9
Langston, Cal.................... 19-8
Finley, Cal 18-9
Clemens, Bos.................... 18-10
J. Abbott, Cal 18-11
Morris, Minn 18-12

GAMES PITCHED

D. Ward, Tor 81
Jackson, Sea 72
Olson, Balt 72
Swift, Sea 71
Eichhorn, Cal 70
Jeffcoat, Tex 70

STRIKEOUTS

Clemens, Bos 241
Johnson, Sea 228
Ryan, Tex 203
McDowell, Chi....................... 191
Langston, Cal....................... 183
Finley, Cal............................ 171
Swindell, Clev 169

INNINGS PITCHED

Clemens, Bos 271.1
McDowell, Chi.................. 253.2
Morris, Minn 246.2
Langston, Cal.................. 246.1
Tapani, Minn.................... 244.0
J. Abbott, Cal 243.0

COMPLETE GAMES

McDowell, Chi....................... 15
Clemens, Bos 13
Morris, Minn 10
Navarro, Mil 10
Terrell, Det 8

SHUTOUTS

Clemens, Bos 4
Appier, KC 3
Erickson, Minn 3
Holman, Sea.............................3
McDowell, Chi...........................3

1991 Team Statistics

National League

TEAM BATTING	BA	AB	R	H	TB	2B	3B	HR	RBI	SB	BB	SO
Atlanta Braves	.258	5456	749	1407	2145	255	30	141	704	165	563	906
Chicago Cubs	.253	5522	695	1395	2156	232	26	159	654	123	442	879
Cincinnati Reds	.258	5501	689	1419	2215	250	27	164	654	124	488	1006
Houston Astros	.244	5504	605	1345	1908	240	43	79	570	125	502	1027
Los Angeles Dodgers	.253	5408	665	1366	1939	191	29	108	605	126	583	957
Montreal Expos	.246	5412	579	1329	1934	236	42	95	536	221	484	1056
New York Mets	.244	5359	640	1305	1954	250	24	117	605	153	578	789
Philadelphia Phillies	.241	5521	629	1332	1979	248	33	111	590	92	490	1026
Pittsburgh Pirates	.263	5449	768	1433	2170	259	50	126	725	124	620	901
St. Louis Cardinals	.255	5362	651	1366	1915	239	53	68	599	202	532	857
San Diego Padres	.244	5408	636	1321	1960	204	36	121	591	101	501	1069
San Francisco Giants	.246	5463	649	1345	2079	215	48	141	605	95	471	973

TEAM PITCHING	ERA	W	L	Sho	CG	SV	Inn	H	R	ER	BB	SO
Atlanta Braves	3.49	94	68	7	18	48	1452.2	1304	644	563	481	969
Chicago Cubs	4.03	77	83	4	12	40	1456.2	1415	734	653	542	927
Cincinnati Reds	3.83	74	88	11	7	43	1440.0	1372	691	613	560	997
Houston Astros	4.00	65	97	13	7	36	1453.0	1347	717	646	651	1033
Los Angeles Dodgers	3.06	93	69	14	15	40	1458.0	1312	565	496	500	1028
Montreal Expos	3.64	71	90	14	12	39	1440.1	1304	655	583	584	909
New York Mets	3.56	77	84	11	12	39	1437.1	1403	646	568	410	1028
Philadelphia Phillies	3.86	78	84	11	16	35	1463.0	1346	680	628	670	988
Pittsburgh Pirates	3.44	98	64	11	18	51	1456.2	1411	632	557	401	919
St. Louis Cardinals	3.69	84	78	5	9	51	1435.1	1367	648	588	454	822
San Diego Padres	3.57	84	78	11	14	47	1452.2	1385	646	577	457	921
San Francisco Giants	4.03	75	87	10	10	45	1442.0	1397	697	646	544	905

American League

TEAM BATTING	BA	AB	R	H	TB	2B	3B	HR	RBI	SB	BB	SO
Baltimore Orioles	.254	5604	686	1421	2245	256	29	170	660	50	528	974
Boston Red Sox	.269	5530	731	1486	2219	305	25	126	691	59	593	820
California Angels	.255	5470	653	1396	2044	245	29	115	607	94	448	928
Chicago White Sox	.262	5594	758	1464	2185	226	39	139	722	134	610	896
Cleveland Indians	.254	5470	576	1390	1915	236	26	79	546	84	449	888
Detroit Tigers	.247	5547	817	1372	2310	259	26	209	778	109	699	1185
Kansas City Royals	.264	5584	727	1475	2198	290	41	117	689	119	523	969
Milwaukee Brewers	.271	5611	799	1523	2224	247	53	116	750	106	556	802
Minnesota Twins	.280	5556	776	1557	2331	270	42	140	733	107	526	747
New York Yankees	.256	5541	674	1418	2146	249	19	147	630	109	473	861
Oakland Athletics	.248	5410	760	1342	2103	246	19	159	716	151	642	981
Seattle Mariners	.255	5494	702	1400	2104	268	29	126	665	97	588	811
Texas Rangers	.270	5703	829	1539	2420	288	31	177	774	102	596	1039
Toronto Blue Jays	.257	5489	684	1412	2196	295	45	133	649	148	499	1043

TEAM PITCHING	ERA	W	L	Sho	CG	SV	Inn	H	R	ER	BB	SO
Baltimore Orioles	4.59	67	95	8	8	42	1457.2	1534	796	743	504	868
Boston Red Sox	4.01	84	78	13	15	45	1439.2	1405	712	642	530	999
California Angels	3.69	81	81	10	18	50	1441.2	1351	649	591	543	990
Chicago White Sox	3.79	87	75	8	28	40	1478.0	1302	681	622	601	923
Cleveland Indians	4.23	57	105	8	22	33	1441.1	1551	759	678	441	862
Detroit Tigers	4.51	84	78	8	18	38	1450.1	1570	794	726	593	739
Kansas City Royals	3.92	82	80	12	17	41	1466.0	1473	722	639	529	1004
Milwaukee Brewers	4.14	83	79	11	23	41	1463.2	1498	744	674	527	859
Minnesota Twins	3.69	95	67	12	21	53	1449.1	1402	652	595	488	876
New York Yankees	4.42	71	91	11	3	37	1444.0	1510	777	709	506	936
Oakland Athletics	4.57	84	78	10	14	49	1444.1	1425	776	734	655	892
Seattle Mariners	3.79	83	79	13	10	48	1464.1	1387	674	616	628	1003
Texas Rangers	4.47	85	77	10	9	41	1479.0	1486	814	734	662	1022
Toronto Blue Jays	3.50	91	71	16	10	60	1462.2	1301	622	569	523	971

National League Team-by-Team Statistical Leaders

Atlanta Braves

BATTING	BA	G	AB	R	H	TB	2B	3B	HR	RBI	SB	BB	SO
Belliard, Rafael	.249	149	353	36	88	101	9	2	0	27	3	22	63
Blauser, Jeff	.259	129	352	49	91	144	14	3	11	54	5	54	59
Bream, Sid	.253	91	265	32	67	112	12	0	11	45	0	25	31
Gant, Ron	.251	154	561	101	141	278	35	3	32	105	34	71	104
Heath, Mike	.209	49	139	4	29	37	3	1	1	12	0	7	26
Hunter, Brian	.251	97	271	32	68	122	16	1	12	50	0	17	48
Justice, David	.275	109	396	67	109	199	25	1	21	87	8	65	81
Lemke, Mark	.234	136	269	36	63	84	11	2	2	23	1	29	27
Nixon, Otis	.297	124	401	81	119	131	10	1	0	26	72	47	40
Olson, Greg	.241	133	411	46	99	142	25	0	6	44	1	44	48
Pendleton, Terry	.319	153	586	94	187	303	34	8	22	86	10	43	70
Sanders, Deion	.191	54	110	16	21	38	1	2	4	13	11	12	23
Smith, Lonnie	.275	122	353	58	97	139	19	1	7	44	9	50	64
Treadway, Jeff	.320	106	306	41	98	128	17	2	3	32	2	23	19

PITCHING	ERA	W	L	G	GS	CG	SV	INN	H	R	ER	BB	SO
Avery, Steve	3.38	18	8	35	35	3	0	210.1	189	89	79	65	137
Berenguer, Juan	2.24	0	3	49	0	0	17	64.1	43	18	16	20	53
Clancy, Jim	5.71	3	2	24	0	0	3	34.2	36	23	22	14	17
Freeman, Marvin	3.00	1	0	34	0	0	1	48.0	37	19	16	13	34
Glavine, Tom	2.55	20	11	34	34	9	0	246.2	201	83	70	69	192
Leibrandt, Charlie	3.49	15	13	36	36	1	0	229.2	212	105	89	56	128
Mahler, Rick	5.65	1	1	13	2	0	0	28.2	33	20	18	13	10
Mercker, Kent	2.58	5	3	50	4	0	6	73.1	56	23	21	35	62
Pena, Alejandro	1.40	2	0	15	0	0	11	19.1	11	3	3	3	13
Reynoso, Armando	6.17	2	1	6	5	0	0	23.1	26	18	16	10	10
Smith, Pete J.	5.06	1	3	14	10	0	0	48.0	48	33	27	22	29
Smoltz, John	3.80	14	13	36	36	5	0	229.2	206	101	97	77	148
Stanton, Mike	2.88	5	5	74	0	0	7	78.0	62	27	25	21	54
St. Claire, Randy	4.08	0	0	19	0	0	0	28.2	31	17	13	9	30

Chicago Cubs

BATTING	BA	G	AB	R	H	TB	2B	3B	HR	RBI	SB	BB	SO
Bell, George A.	.285	149	558	63	159	261	27	0	25	86	2	32	62
Berryhill, Damon	.189	62	159	13	30	52	7	0	5	14	1	11	41
Dascenzo, Doug	.255	118	239	40	61	75	11	0	1	18	14	24	26
Dawson, Andre	.272	149	563	69	153	275	21	4	31	104	4	22	80
Dunston, Shawon	.260	142	492	59	128	200	22	7	12	50	21	23	64
Grace, Mark	.273	160	619	87	169	231	28	5	8	58	3	70	53
Landrum, Ced.	.233	56	86	28	20	24	2	1	0	6	27	10	18
Salazar, Luis	.258	103	333	34	86	144	14	1	14	38	0	15	45
Sandberg, Ryne	.291	158	585	104	170	284	32	2	26	100	22	87	89
Smith, Dwight	.228	90	167	16	38	58	7	2	3	21	2	11	32
Villanueva, Hector	.276	71	192	23	53	104	10	1	13	32	0	21	30
Vizcaino, Jose	.262	93	145	7	38	43	5	0	0	10	2	5	18
Walker, Chico	.257	124	374	51	96	126	10	1	6	34	13	33	57
Walton, Jerome	.219	123	270	42	59	89	13	1	5	17	7	19	55
Wilkins, Rick	.222	86	203	21	45	72	9	0	6	22	3	19	56

PITCHING	ERA	W	L	G	GS	CG	SV	INN	H	R	ER	BB	SO
Assenmacher, Paul	3.24	7	8	75	0	0	15	102.2	85	41	37	31	117
Bielecki, Mike	4.50	13	11	39	25	0	0	172.0	169	91	86	54	72
Boskie, Shawn	5.23	4	9	28	20	0	0	129.0	150	78	75	52	62
Castillo, Frank	4.35	6	7	18	18	4	0	111.2	107	56	54	33	73
Harkey, Mike	5.30	0	2	4	4	0	0	18.2	21	11	11	6	15
Jackson, Danny	6.75	1	5	17	14	0	0	70.2	89	59	53	48	31
Lancaster, Les	3.52	9	7	64	11	1	3	156.0	150	68	61	49	102
Maddux, Greg	3.35	15	11	37	37	7	0	263.0	232	113	98	66	198
McElroy, Chuck	1.95	6	2	71	0	0	3	101.1	73	33	22	57	92
Scanlan, Bob	3.89	7	8	40	13	0	1	111.0	114	60	48	40	44
Slocumb, Heath	3.45	2	1	52	0	0	1	62.2	53	29	24	30	34
Smith, Dave S.	6.00	0	6	35	0	0	17	33.0	39	22	22	19	16
Sutcliffe, Rick	4.10	6	5	19	18	0	0	96.2	96	52	44	45	52
Wilson, Steve	4.38	0	0	8	0	0	0	12.1	13	7	6	5	9

National League Team-by-Team Statistical Leaders

Cincinnati Reds

BATTING	BA	G	AB	R	H	TB	2B	3B	HR	RBI	SB	BB	SO
Benzinger, Todd	.187	51	123	7	23	33	3	2	1	11	2	10	20
Braggs, Glenn	.260	85	250	36	65	108	10	0	11	39	11	23	46
Davis, Eric	.235	89	285	39	67	110	10	0	11	33	14	48	92
Doran, Bill D.	.280	111	361	51	101	135	12	2	6	35	5	46	39
Duncan, Mariano	.258	100	333	46	86	137	7	4	12	40	5	12	57
Hatcher, Billy	.262	138	442	45	116	159	25	3	4	41	11	26	55
Larkin, Barry	.302	123	464	88	140	235	27	4	20	69	24	55	64
Martinez, Carmelo	.232	53	138	12	32	55	5	0	6	19	0	15	37
Morris, Hal	.318	136	478	72	152	229	33	1	14	59	10	46	61
Oliver, Joe	.216	94	269	21	58	102	11	0	11	41	0	18	53
O'Neill, Paul	.256	152	532	71	136	256	36	0	28	91	12	73	107
Quinones, Luis	.222	97	212	15	47	69	4	3	4	20	1	21	31
Reed, Jeff	.267	91	270	20	72	100	15	2	3	31	0	23	38
Sabo, Chris	.301	153	582	91	175	294	35	3	26	88	19	44	79
Winningham, Herm	.225	98	169	17	38	49	6	1	1	4	4	11	40

PITCHING	ERA	W	L	G	GS	CG	SV	INN	H	R	ER	BB	SO
Armstrong, Jack	5.48	7	13	27	24	1	0	139.2	158	90	85	54	93
Browning, Tom	4.18	14	14	36	36	1	0	230.1	241	124	107	56	115
Carman, Don	5.25	0	2	28	0	0	1	36.0	40	23	21	19	15
Charlton, Norm	2.91	3	5	39	11	0	1	108.1	92	37	35	34	77
Dibble, Rob	3.17	3	5	67	0	0	31	82.1	67	32	29	25	124
Gross, Kip	3.47	6	4	29	9	1	0	85.2	93	43	33	40	40
Hammond, Chris	4.06	7	7	20	18	0	0	99.2	92	51	45	48	50
Hill, Milt	3.78	1	1	22	0	0	0	33.1	36	14	14	8	20
Myers, Randy	3.55	6	13	58	12	1	6	132.0	116	61	52	80	108
Power, Ted	3.62	5	3	68	0	0	3	87.0	87	37	35	31	51
Rijo, Jose	2.51	15	6	30	30	3	0	204.1	165	69	57	55	172
Sanford, Mo	3.86	1	2	5	5	0	0	28.0	19	14	12	15	31
Scudder, Scott	4.35	6	9	27	14	0	1	101.1	91	52	49	56	51

Houston Astros

BATTING	BA	G	AB	R	H	TB	2B	3B	HR	RBI	SB	BB	SO
Anthony, Eric	.153	39	118	11	18	27	6	0	1	7	1	12	41
Bagwell, Jeff	.294	156	554	79	163	242	26	4	15	82	7	75	116
Biggio, Craig	.295	149	546	79	161	204	23	4	4	46	19	53	71
Caminiti, Ken	.253	152	574	65	145	220	30	3	13	80	4	46	85
Candaele, Casey	.262	151	461	44	121	167	20	7	4	50	9	40	49
Cedeno, Andujar	.243	67	251	27	61	105	13	2	9	36	4	9	74
Davidson, Mark	.190	85	142	10	27	39	6	0	2	15	0	12	28
Finley, Steve	.285	159	596	84	170	242	28	10	8	54	34	42	65
Gonzalez, Luis	.254	137	473	51	120	205	28	9	13	69	10	40	101
Ramirez, Rafael	.236	101	233	17	55	68	10	0	1	20	3	13	40
Rhodes, Karl	.213	44	136	7	29	37	3	1	1	12	2	14	26
Simms, Mike	.203	49	123	18	25	39	5	0	3	16	1	18	38
Yelding, Eric	.243	78	276	19	67	83	11	1	1	20	11	13	46
Young, Gerald	.218	108	142	26	31	39	3	1	1	11	16	24	17

PITCHING	ERA	W	L	G	GS	CG	SV	INN	H	R	ER	BB	SO
Bowen, Ryan	5.15	6	4	14	13	0	0	71.2	73	43	41	36	49
Capel, Mike	3.03	1	3	25	0	0	3	32.2	33	14	11	15	23
Clancy, Jim	2.78	0	3	30	0	0	5	55.0	37	19	17	20	33
Corsi, Jim	3.71	0	5	47	0	0	0	77.2	76	37	32	23	53
Deshaies, Jim	4.98	5	12	28	28	1	0	161.0	156	90	89	72	98
Gardner, Chris	4.01	1	2	5	4	0	0	24.2	19	12	11	14	12
Harnisch, Pete	2.70	12	9	33	33	4	0	216.2	169	71	65	83	172
Henry, Dwayne	3.19	3	2	52	0	0	2	67.2	51	25	24	39	51
Hernandez, Xavier	4.71	2	7	32	6	0	3	63.0	66	34	33	32	55
Jones, Jimmy	4.39	6	8	26	22	1	0	135.1	143	73	66	51	88
Kile, Darryl	3.69	7	11	37	22	0	0	153.2	144	81	63	84	100
Osuna, Al	3.42	7	6	71	0	0	12	81.2	59	39	31	46	68
Portugal, Mark	4.49	10	12	32	27	1	1	168.1	163	91	84	59	120
Schilling, Curt	3.81	3	5	56	0	0	8	75.2	79	35	32	39	71

Los Angeles Dodgers

BATTING	BA	G	AB	R	H	TB	2B	3B	HR	RBI	SB	BB	SO
Butler, Brett	.296	161	615	112	182	211	13	5	2	38	38	108	79
Carter, Gary	.246	101	248	22	61	93	14	0	6	26	2	22	26
Daniels, Kal	.249	137	461	54	115	183	15	1	17	73	6	63	116
Gonzalez, Jose	.000	42	28	3	0	0	0	0	0	0	0	2	9
Griffin, Alfredo	.243	109	350	27	85	95	6	2	0	27	5	22	49
Gwynn, Chris	.252	94	139	18	35	57	5	1	5	22	1	10	23
Harris, Lenny	.287	145	429	59	123	150	16	1	3	38	12	37	32
Javier, Stan	.205	121	176	21	36	50	5	3	1	11	7	16	36
Murray, Eddie	.260	153	576	69	150	232	23	1	19	96	10	55	74
Offerman, Jose	.195	52	113	10	22	24	2	0	0	3	3	25	32
Samuel, Juan	.271	153	594	74	161	231	22	6	12	58	23	49	133
Scioscia, Mike	.264	119	345	39	91	135	16	2	8	40	4	47	32
Sharperson, Mike	.278	105	216	24	60	81	11	2	2	20	1	25	24
Strawberry, Darryl	.265	139	505	86	134	248	22	4	28	99	10	75	125

PITCHING	ERA	W	L	G	GS	CG	SV	INN	H	R	ER	BB	SO
Belcher, Tim	2.62	10	9	33	33	2	0	209.1	189	76	61	75	156
Candelaria, John	3.74	1	1	59	0	0	2	33.2	31	16	14	11	38
Cook, Dennis	0.51	1	0	20	1	0	0	17.2	12	3	1	7	8
Crews, Tim	3.43	2	3	60	0	0	6	76.0	75	30	29	19	53
Gott, Jim	2.96	4	3	55	0	0	2	76.0	63	28	25	32	73
Gross, Kevin	3.58	10	11	46	10	0	3	115.2	123	55	46	50	95
Hartley, Mike	4.42	2	0	40	0	0	1	57.0	53	29	28	37	44
Hershiser, Orel	3.46	7	2	21	21	0	0	112.0	112	43	43	32	73
Howell, Jay	3.18	6	5	44	0	0	16	51.0	39	19	18	11	40
Martinez, Ramon	3.27	17	13	33	33	6	0	220.1	190	89	80	69	150
McDowell, Roger	2.55	6	3	33	0	0	7	42.1	39	12	12	16	22
Morgan, Mike	2.78	14	10	34	33	5	1	236.1	197	85	73	61	140
Ojeda, Bob	3.18	12	9	31	31	2	0	189.1	181	78	67	70	120
Wetteland, John	0.00	1	0	6	0	0	0	9.0	5	2	0	3	9
Wilson, Steve	0.00	0	0	11	0	0	2	8.1	1	0	0	4	5

Montreal Expos

BATTING	BA	G	AB	R	H	TB	2B	3B	HR	RBI	SB	BB	SO
Barberie, Bret	.353	57	136	16	48	70	12	2	2	18	0	20	22
Calderon, Ivan	.300	134	470	69	141	226	22	3	19	75	31	53	64
DeShields, Delino	.238	151	563	83	134	187	15	4	10	51	56	95	151
Fitzgerald, Mike R.	.202	71	198	17	40	61	5	2	4	28	4	22	35
Foley, Tom	.208	86	168	12	35	48	11	1	0	15	2	14	30
Galarraga, Andres	.219	107	375	34	82	126	13	2	9	33	5	23	86
Grissom, Marquis	.267	148	558	73	149	208	23	9	6	39	76	34	89
Hassey, Ron	.227	52	119	5	27	38	8	0	1	14	1	13	16
Martinez, Dave	.295	124	396	47	117	166	18	5	7	42	16	20	54
Owen, Spike	.255	139	424	39	108	155	22	8	3	26	2	42	61
Reyes, Gilberto	.217	83	207	11	45	54	9	0	0	13	2	19	51
Santovenia, Nelson	.250	41	96	7	24	35	5	0	2	14	0	2	18
Walker, Larry	.290	137	487	59	141	223	30	2	16	64	14	42	102
Wallach, Tim	.225	151	577	60	130	193	22	1	13	73	2	50	100

PITCHING	ERA	W	L	G	GS	CG	SV	INN	H	R	ER	BB	SO
Barnes, Brian	4.22	5	8	28	27	1	0	160.0	135	82	75	84	117
Boyd, Oil Can	3.52	6	8	19	19	1	0	120.1	115	49	47	40	82
Burke, Tim	4.11	3	4	37	0	0	5	46.0	41	24	21	14	25
Fassero, Jeff	2.44	2	5	51	0	0	8	55.1	39	17	15	17	42
Frey, Steve	4.99	0	1	31	0	0	1	39.2	43	31	22	23	21
Gardner, Mark	3.85	9	11	27	27	0	0	168.1	139	78	72	75	107
Haney, Chris	4.04	3	7	16	16	0	0	84.2	94	49	38	43	51
Jones, Barry	3.35	4	9	77	0	0	13	88.2	76	35	33	33	46
Mahler, Rick	3.62	1	3	10	6	0	0	37.1	37	17	15	15	17
Martinez, Dennis	2.39	14	11	31	31	9	0	222.0	187	70	59	62	123
Nabholz, Chris	3.63	8	7	24	24	1	0	153.2	134	66	62	57	99
Piatt, Doug	2.60	0	0	21	0	0	0	34.2	29	11	10	17	29
Rojas, Mel	3.75	3	3	37	0	0	6	48.0	42	21	20	13	37
Ruskin, Scott	4.24	4	4	64	0	0	6	63.2	57	31	30	30	46
Sampen, Bill	4.00	9	5	43	8	0	0	92.1	96	49	41	46	52

National League Team-by-Team Statistical Leaders

New York Mets

BATTING	BA	G	AB	R	H	TB	2B	3B	HR	RBI	SB	BB	SO
Boston, Daryl	.275	137	255	40	70	106	16	4	4	21	15	30	42
Brooks, Hubie	.238	103	357	48	85	146	11	1	16	50	3	44	62
Carreon, Mark	.260	106	254	18	66	84	6	0	4	21	2	12	26
Cerone, Rick	.273	90	227	18	62	81	13	0	2	16	1	30	24
Coleman, Vince	.255	72	278	45	71	91	7	5	1	17	37	39	47
Elster, Kevin	.241	115	348	33	84	122	16	2	6	36	2	40	53
Herr, Tommy	.194	70	155	17	30	40	7	0	1	14	7	32	21
Jefferies, Gregg	.272	136	486	59	132	182	19	2	9	62	26	47	38
Johnson, Howard	.259	156	564	108	146	302	34	4	38	117	30	78	120
Magadan, Dave	.258	124	418	58	108	143	23	0	4	51	1	83	50
McReynolds, Kevin	.259	143	522	65	135	217	32	1	16	74	6	49	46
Miller, Keith A.	.280	98	275	41	77	113	22	1	4	23	14	23	44
O'Brien, Charlie	.185	69	168	16	31	43	6	0	2	14	0	17	25
Sasser, Mackey	.272	96	228	18	62	95	14	2	5	35	0	9	19
Templeton, Garry	.228	80	219	20	50	67	9	1	2	20	3	9	29

PITCHING	ERA	W	L	G	GS	CG	SV	INN	H	R	ER	BB	SO
Burke, Tim	2.75	3	3	35	0	0	1	55.2	55	22	17	12	34
Cone, Dave	3.29	14	14	34	34	5	0	232.2	204	95	85	73	241
Darling, Ron	3.87	5	6	17	17	0	0	102.1	96	50	44	28	58
Fernandez, Sid	2.86	1	3	8	8	0	0	44.0	36	18	14	9	31
Franco, John	2.93	5	9	52	0	0	30	55.1	61	27	18	18	45
Gooden, Dwight	3.60	13	7	27	27	3	0	190.0	185	80	76	56	150
Innis, Jeff	2.66	0	2	69	0	0	0	84.2	66	30	25	23	47
Pena, Alejandro	2.71	6	1	44	0	0	4	63.0	63	20	19	19	49
Schourek, Pete	4.27	5	4	35	8	1	2	86.1	82	49	41	43	67
Simons, Doug	5.19	2	3	42	1	0	1	60.2	55	40	35	19	38
Viola, Frank	3.97	13	15	35	35	3	0	231.1	259	112	102	54	132
Whitehurst, Wally	4.19	7	12	36	20	0	1	133.1	142	67	62	25	87
Young, Anthony	3.10	2	5	10	8	0	0	49.1	48	20	17	12	20

Philadelphia Phillies

BATTING	BA	G	AB	R	H	TB	2B	3B	HR	RBI	SB	BB	SO
Backman, Wally	.243	94	185	20	45	57	12	0	0	15	3	30	30
Chamberlain, Wes	.240	101	383	51	92	153	16	3	13	50	9	31	73
Daulton, Darren	.196	89	285	36	56	104	12	0	12	42	5	41	66
Dykstra, Len	.297	63	246	48	73	105	13	5	3	12	24	37	20
Fletcher, Darrin	.228	46	136	5	31	42	8	0	1	12	0	5	15
Hayes, Charlie	.230	142	460	34	106	167	23	1	12	53	3	16	75
Hayes, Von	.225	77	284	43	64	81	15	1	0	21	9	31	42
Hollins, David	.298	56	151	18	45	77	10	2	6	21	1	17	26
Jordan, Ricky	.272	101	301	38	82	136	21	3	9	49	0	14	49
Kruk, John	.294	152	538	84	158	260	27	6	21	92	7	67	100
Lake, Steve	.228	58	158	12	36	45	4	1	1	11	0	2	26
Morandini, Mickey	.249	98	325	38	81	103	11	4	1	20	13	29	45
Murphy, Dale	.252	153	544	66	137	226	33	1	18	81	1	48	93
Ready, Randy	.249	76	205	32	51	66	10	1	1	20	2	47	25
Thon, Dickie	.252	146	539	44	136	189	18	4	9	44	11	25	84

PITCHING	ERA	W	L	G	GS	CG	SV	INN	H	R	ER	BB	SO
Akerfelds, Darrel	5.26	2	1	30	0	0	0	49.2	49	30	29	27	31
Ashby, Andy	6.00	1	5	8	8	0	0	42.0	41	28	28	19	26
Boever, Joe	3.84	3	5	68	0	0	0	98.1	90	45	42	54	89
Combs, Pat	4.90	2	6	14	13	1	0	64.1	64	41	35	43	41
Cox, Danny	4.57	4	6	23	17	0	0	102.1	98	57	52	39	46
DeJesus, Jose	3.42	10	9	31	29	3	1	181.2	147	74	69	128	118
Greene, Tommy	3.38	13	7	36	27	3	0	207.2	177	85	78	66	154
Grimsley, Jason	4.87	1	7	12	12	0	0	61.0	54	34	33	41	42
Hartley, Mike	3.76	2	1	18	0	0	1	26.1	21	11	11	10	19
McDowell, Roger	3.20	3	6	38	0	0	3	59.0	61	28	21	32	28
Mulholland, Terry	3.61	16	13	34	34	8	0	232.0	231	100	93	49	142
Ritchie, Wally	2.50	1	2	39	0	0	0	50.1	44	17	14	17	26
Ruffin, Bruce	3.78	4	7	31	15	1	0	119.0	125	52	50	38	85
Searcy, Steve	4.15	2	1	18	0	0	0	30.1	29	16	14	14	21
Williams, Mitch	2.34	12	5	69	0	0	30	88.1	56	24	23	62	84

National League Team-by-Team Statistical Leaders

Pittsburgh Pirates

BATTING	BA	G	AB	R	H	TB	2B	3B	HR	RBI	SB	BB	SO
Bell, Jay	.270	157	608	96	164	260	32	8	16	67	10	52	99
Bonds, Barry	.292	153	510	95	149	262	28	5	25	116	43	107	73
Bonilla, Bobby	.302	157	577	102	174	284	44	6	18	100	2	90	67
Buechele, Steve	.246	31	114	16	28	47	5	1	4	19	0	10	28
King, Jeff	.239	33	109	16	26	41	1	1	4	18	3	14	15
LaValliere, Mike	.289	108	336	25	97	121	11	2	3	41	2	33	27
Lind, Jose	.265	150	502	53	133	170	16	6	3	54	7	30	56
McClendon, Lloyd	.288	85	163	24	47	75	7	0	7	24	2	18	23
Merced, Orlando	.275	120	411	83	113	164	17	2	10	50	8	64	81
Redus, Gary	.246	98	252	45	62	99	12	2	7	24	17	28	39
Slaught, Don	.295	77	220	19	65	87	17	1	1	29	1	21	32
Van Slyke, Andy	.265	138	491	87	130	219	24	7	17	83	10	71	85
Varsho, Gary	.273	99	187	23	51	78	11	2	4	23	9	19	34
Webster, Mitch	.175	36	97	9	17	31	3	4	1	9	0	9	31
Wehner, John	.340	37	106	15	36	43	7	0	0	7	3	7	17
Wilkerson, Curt	.188	85	191	20	36	53	9	1	2	18	2	15	40

PITCHING	ERA	W	L	G	GS	CG	SV	INN	H	R	ER	BB	SO
Belinda, Stan	3.45	7	5	60	0	0	16	78.1	50	30	30	35	71
Drabek, Doug	3.07	15	14	35	35	5	0	234.2	245	92	80	62	142
Heaton, Neal	4.33	3	3	42	1	0	0	68.2	72	37	33	21	34
Kipper, Bob	4.65	2	2	52	0	0	4	60.0	66	34	31	22	38
Landrum, Bill	3.18	4	4	61	0	0	17	76.1	76	32	27	19	45
Mason, Roger	3.03	3	2	24	0	0	3	29.2	21	11	10	6	21
Palacios, Vincente	3.75	6	3	36	7	1	3	81.2	69	34	34	38	64
Patterson, Bob	4.11	4	3	54	1	0	2	65.2	67	32	30	15	57
Smiley, John	3.08	20	8	33	32	2	0	207.2	194	78	71	44	129
Smith, Zane	3.20	16	10	35	35	6	0	228.0	234	95	81	29	120
Tomlin, Randy	2.98	8	7	31	27	4	0	175.0	170	75	58	54	104
Walk, Bob	3.60	9	2	25	20	0	0	115.0	104	53	46	35	67

St. Louis Cardinals

BATTING	BA	G	AB	R	H	TB	2B	3B	HR	RBI	SB	BB	SO
Gedman, Rich	.106	46	94	7	10	20	1	0	3	8	0	4	15
Gilkey, Bernard	.216	81	268	28	58	84	7	2	5	20	14	39	33
Guerrero, Pedro	.272	115	427	41	116	154	12	1	8	70	4	37	46
Hudler, Rex	.227	101	207	21	47	64	10	2	1	15	12	10	29
Jose, Felix	.305	154	568	69	173	249	40	6	8	77	20	50	113
Lankford, Ray	.251	151	566	83	142	222	23	15	9	69	44	41	114
Oquendo, Jose	.240	127	366	37	88	110	11	4	1	26	1	67	48
Pagnozzi, Tom	.264	140	459	38	121	161	24	5	2	57	9	36	63
Pena, Geronimo	.243	104	185	38	45	74	8	3	5	17	15	18	45
Perry, Gerald	.240	109	242	29	58	92	8	4	6	36	15	22	34
Smith, Ozzie	.285	150	550	96	157	202	30	3	3	50	35	83	36
Thompson, Milt	.307	115	326	55	100	144	16	5	6	34	16	32	53
Wilson, Craig	.171	60	82	5	14	16	2	0	0	13	0	6	10
Zeile, Todd	.280	155	565	76	158	233	36	3	11	81	17	62	94

PITCHING	ERA	W	L	G	GS	CG	SV	INN	H	R	ER	BB	SO
Agosto, Juan	4.81	5	3	72	0	0	2	86.0	92	52	46	39	34
Carpenter, Cris	4.23	10	4	59	0	0	0	66.0	53	31	31	20	47
Clark, Mark	4.03	1	1	7	2	0	0	22.1	17	10	10	11	13
Cormier, Rheal	4.12	4	5	11	10	2	0	67.2	74	35	31	8	38
DeLeon, Jose	2.71	5	9	28	28	1	0	162.2	144	57	49	61	118
Fraser, Willie	4.93	3	3	35	0	0	0	49.1	44	28	27	21	25
Hill, Ken	3.57	11	10	30	30	0	0	181.1	147	76	72	67	121
McClure, Bob	3.13	1	1	32	0	0	0	23.0	24	8	8	8	15
Moyer, Jamie	5.74	0	5	8	7	0	0	31.1	38	21	20	16	20
Olivares, Omar	3.71	11	7	28	24	0	1	167.1	148	72	69	61	91
Smith, Bryn	3.85	12	9	31	31	3	0	198.2	188	95	85	45	94
Smith, Lee	2.34	6	3	67	0	0	47	73.0	70	19	19	13	67
Terry, Scott	2.80	4	4	65	0	0	1	80.1	76	31	25	32	52
Tewksbury, Bob	3.25	11	12	30	30	3	0	191.0	206	86	69	38	75

National League Team-by-Team Statistical Leaders

San Diego Padres

BATTING	BA	G	AB	R	H	TB	2B	3B	HR	RBI	SB	BB	SO
Abner, Shawn	.165	53	115	15	19	28	4	1	1	5	0	7	25
Clark, Jerald	.228	118	369	26	84	130	16	0	10	47	2	31	90
Coolbaugh, Scott	.217	60	180	12	39	55	8	1	2	15	0	19	45
Faries, Paul	.177	57	130	13	23	28	3	1	0	7	3	14	21
Fernandez, Tony	.272	145	558	81	152	201	27	5	4	38	23	55	74
Gwynn, Tony	.317	134	530	69	168	229	27	11	4	62	8	34	19
Howard, Thomas	.249	106	281	30	70	100	12	3	4	22	10	24	57
Howell, Jack	.206	58	160	24	33	56	3	1	6	16	0	18	33
Jackson, Darrin	.262	122	359	51	94	171	12	1	21	49	5	27	66
McGriff, Fred	.278	153	528	84	147	261	19	1	31	106	4	105	135
Roberts, Bip	.281	117	424	66	119	147	13	3	3	32	26	37	71
Santiago, Benito	.267	152	580	60	155	234	22	3	17	87	8	23	114
Teufel, Tim	.228	97	307	39	70	119	16	0	11	42	8	49	69

PITCHING	ERA	W	L	G	GS	CG	SV	INN	H	R	ER	BB	SO
Andersen, Larry E.	2.30	3	4	38	0	0	13	47.0	39	13	12	13	40
Benes, Andy	3.03	15	11	33	33	4	0	223.0	194	76	75	59	167
Bones, Ricky	4.83	4	6	11	11	0	0	54.0	57	33	29	18	31
Costello, John	3.09	1	0	27	0	0	0	35.0	37	15	12	17	24
Gardner, Wes	7.08	0	1	14	0	0	1	20.1	27	16	16	12	9
Harris, Greg W.	2.23	9	5	20	20	3	0	133.0	116	42	33	27	95
Hurst, Bruce	3.29	15	8	31	31	4	0	221.2	201	89	81	59	141
Lefferts, Craig	3.91	1	6	54	0	0	23	69.0	74	35	30	14	48
Maddux, Mike	2.46	7	2	64	1	0	5	98.2	78	30	27	27	57
Melendez, Jose	3.27	8	5	31	9	0	3	93.2	77	35	34	24	60
Nolte, Eric	11.05	3	2	6	6	0	0	22.0	37	27	27	10	15
Peterson, Adam	4.45	3	4	13	11	0	0	54.2	50	33	27	28	37
Rasmussen, Dennis	3.74	6	13	24	24	1	0	146.2	155	74	61	49	75
Rodriguez, Rich	3.26	3	1	64	1	0	0	80.0	66	31	29	44	40
Whitson, Ed	5.03	4	6	13	12	2	0	78.2	93	47	44	17	40

San Francisco Giants

BATTING	BA	G	AB	R	H	TB	2B	3B	HR	RBI	SB	BB	SO
Anderson, Dave C.	.248	100	226	24	56	71	5	2	2	13	2	12	35
Bass, Kevin	.233	124	361	43	84	132	10	4	10	40	7	36	56
Clark, Will	.301	148	565	84	170	303	32	7	29	116	4	51	91
Decker, Steve	.206	79	233	11	48	72	7	1	5	24	0	16	44
Felder, Mike	.264	132	348	51	92	114	10	6	0	18	21	30	31
Kennedy, Terry	.234	69	171	12	40	58	7	1	3	13	0	11	31
Leonard, Mark	.240	63	129	14	31	46	7	1	2	14	0	12	25
Lewis, Darren	.248	72	222	41	55	69	5	3	1	15	13	36	30
Litton, Greg	.181	59	127	13	23	35	7	1	1	15	0	11	25
Manwaring, Kirt	.225	67	178	16	40	49	9	0	0	19	1	9	22
McGee, Willie	.312	131	497	67	155	203	30	3	4	43	17	34	74
Mitchell, Kevin	.256	113	371	52	95	191	13	1	27	69	2	43	57
Thompson, Robby	.262	144	492	74	129	220	24	5	19	48	14	63	95
Uribe, Jose	.221	90	231	23	51	70	8	4	1	12	3	20	33
Williams, Matt D.	.268	157	589	72	158	294	24	5	34	98	5	33	128

PITCHING	ERA	W	L	G	GS	CG	SV	INN	H	R	ER	BB	SO
Beck, Rod	3.78	1	1	31	0	0	1	52.1	53	22	22	13	38
Black, Bud	3.99	12	16	34	34	3	0	214.1	201	104	95	71	104
Brantley, Jeff	2.45	5	2	67	0	0	15	95.1	78	27	26	52	81
Burkett, John	4.18	12	11	36	34	3	0	206.2	223	103	96	60	131
Downs, Kelly	4.19	10	4	45	11	0	0	111.2	99	59	52	53	62
Hickerson, Bryan	3.60	2	2	17	6	0	0	50.0	53	20	20	17	43
LaCoss, Mike	7.23	1	5	18	5	0	0	47.1	61	39	38	24	30
McClellan, Paul	4.56	3	6	13	12	1	0	71.0	68	41	36	25	44
Oliveras, Francisco	3.86	6	6	55	1	0	3	79.1	69	36	34	22	48
Remlinger, Mike	4.37	2	1	8	6	1	0	35.0	36	17	17	20	19
Righetti, Dave	3.39	2	7	61	0	0	24	71.2	64	29	27	28	51
Robinson, Don	4.38	5	9	34	16	0	1	121.1	123	64	59	50	78
Wilson, Trevor	3.56	13	11	44	29	2	0	202.0	173	87	80	77	139

American League Team-by-Team Statistical Leaders

Baltimore Orioles

BATTING	BA	G	AB	R	H	TB	2B	3B	HR	RBI	SB	BB	SO
Anderson, Brady	.230	113	256	40	59	83	12	3	2	27	12	38	44
Bell, Juan	.172	100	209	26	36	52	9	2	1	15	0	8	51
Davis, Glenn	.227	49	176	29	40	81	9	1	10	28	4	16	29
Devereaux, Mike	.260	149	608	82	158	262	27	10	19	59	16	47	115
Evans, Dwight	.270	101	270	35	73	102	9	1	6	38	2	54	54
Gomez, Leo	.233	118	391	40	91	160	17	2	16	45	1	40	82
Hoiles, Chris	.243	107	341	36	83	131	15	0	11	31	0	29	61
Horn, Sam	.233	121	317	45	74	159	16	0	23	61	0	41	99
Hulett, Tim	.204	79	206	29	42	72	9	0	7	18	0	13	49
Martinez, Chito	.269	67	216	32	58	111	12	1	13	33	1	11	51
Melvin, Bob	.250	79	228	11	57	70	10	0	1	23	0	11	46
Milligan, Randy	.263	141	483	57	127	196	17	2	16	70	0	84	108
Orsulak, Joe	.278	143	486	57	135	174	22	1	5	43	6	28	45
Ripken, Cal	.323	162	650	99	210	368	46	5	34	114	6	53	46
Ripken, Billy	.216	104	287	24	62	75	11	1	0	14	0	15	31
Segui, David	.278	86	212	15	59	72	7	0	2	22	1	12	19
Worthington, Craig	.225	31	102	11	23	38	3	0	4	12	0	12	14

PITCHING	ERA	W	L	G	GS	CG	SV	INN	H	R	ER	BB	SO
Ballard, Jeff	5.60	6	12	26	22	0	0	123.2	153	91	77	28	37
Flanagan, Mike	2.38	2	7	64	1	0	3	98.1	84	27	26	25	55
Frohwirth, Todd	1.87	7	3	51	0	0	3	96.1	64	24	20	29	77
Johnson, Dave W.	7.07	4	8	22	14	0	0	84.0	127	68	66	24	38
Kilgus, Paul	5.08	0	2	38	0	0	1	62.0	60	38	35	24	32
McDonald, Ben	4.84	6	8	21	21	1	0	126.1	126	71	68	43	85
Mesa, Jose	5.97	6	11	23	23	2	0	123.2	151	86	82	62	64
Milacki, Bob	4.01	10	9	31	26	3	0	184.0	175	86	82	53	108
Mussina, Mike	2.87	4	5	12	12	2	0	87.2	77	31	28	21	52
Olson, Gregg	3.18	4	6	72	0	0	31	73.2	74	28	26	29	72
Poole, Jim Ri.	2.00	3	2	24	0	0	0	36.0	19	10	8	9	34
Rhodes, Arthur	8.00	0	3	8	8	0	0	36.0	47	35	32	23	23
Robinson, Jeff M.	5.18	4	9	21	19	0	0	104.1	119	62	60	51	65
Smith, Roy	5.60	5	4	17	14	0	0	80.1	99	52	50	24	25
Williamson, Mark	4.48	5	5	65	0	0	4	80.1	87	42	40	35	53

Boston Red Sox

BATTING	BA	G	AB	R	H	TB	2B	3B	HR	RBI	SB	BB	SO
Boggs, Wade	.332	144	546	93	181	251	42	2	8	51	1	89	32
Brumley, A. Mike	.212	63	118	16	25	30	5	0	0	5	2	10	22
Brunansky, Tom	.229	142	459	54	105	179	24	1	16	70	1	49	72
Burks, Ellis	.251	130	474	56	119	200	33	3	14	56	6	39	81
Clark, Jack	.249	140	481	75	120	224	18	1	28	87	0	96	133
Greenwell, Mike	.300	147	544	76	163	228	26	6	9	83	15	43	35
Lyons, Steve	.241	87	212	15	51	75	10	1	4	17	10	11	35
Marzano, John	.263	49	114	10	30	38	8	0	0	9	0	1	16
Pena, Tony	.231	141	464	45	107	149	23	2	5	48	8	37	53
Plantier, Phil	.331	53	148	27	49	91	7	1	11	35	1	23	38
Quintana, Carlos	.295	149	478	69	141	197	21	1	11	71	1	61	66
Reed, Jody	.283	153	618	87	175	236	42	2	5	60	6	60	53
Rivera, Luis	.258	129	414	64	107	159	22	3	8	40	4	35	86
Vaughn, Mo	.260	74	219	21	57	81	12	0	4	32	2	26	43

PITCHING	ERA	W	L	G	GS	CG	SV	INN	H	R	ER	BB	SO
Bolton, Tom	5.24	8	9	25	19	0	0	110.0	136	72	64	51	64
Clemens, Roger	2.62	18	10	35	35	13	0	271.1	219	93	79	65	241
Darwin, Danny	5.16	3	6	12	12	0	0	68.0	71	39	39	15	42
Fossas, Tony	3.47	3	2	64	0	0	1	57.0	49	27	22	28	29
Gardiner, Mike	4.85	9	10	22	22	0	0	130.0	140	79	70	47	91
Gray, Jeff	2.34	2	3	50	0	0	1	61.2	39	17	16	10	41
Harris, Greg A.	3.85	11	12	53	21	1	2	173.0	157	79	74	69	127
Hesketh, Joe	3.29	12	4	39	17	0	0	153.1	142	59	56	53	104
Kiecker, Dana	7.36	2	3	18	5	0	0	40.1	56	34	33	23	21
Lamp, Dennis	4.70	6	3	51	0	0	0	92.0	100	54	48	31	57
Morton, Kevin	4.59	6	5	16	15	1	0	86.1	93	49	44	40	45
Reardon, Jeff	3.03	1	4	57	0	0	40	59.1	54	21	20	16	44
Young, Matt	5.18	3	7	19	16	0	0	88.2	92	55	51	53	69

American League Team-by-Team Statistical Leaders

California Angels

BATTING	BA	G	AB	R	H	TB	2B	3B	HR	RBI	SB	BB	SO
Abner, Shawn	.228	41	101	12	23	37	6	1	2	9	1	4	18
Felix, Junior	.283	66	230	32	65	85	10	2	2	26	7	11	55
Gaetti, Gary	.246	152	586	58	144	222	22	1	18	66	5	33	104
Gallagher, Dave	.293	90	270	32	79	99	17	0	1	30	2	24	43
Hill, Donnie	.239	77	209	36	50	63	8	1	1	20	1	30	21
Joyner, Wally	.301	143	551	79	166	269	34	3	21	96	2	52	66
Parker, Dave	.232	119	466	45	108	167	22	2	11	56	3	29	91
Parrish, Lance	.216	119	402	38	87	156	12	0	19	51	0	35	117
Polonia, Luis	.296	150	604	92	179	229	28	8	2	50	48	52	74
Schofield, Dick C.	.225	134	427	44	96	111	9	3	0	31	8	50	69
Sojo, Luis	.258	113	364	38	94	119	14	1	3	20	4	14	26
Tingley, Ron	.200	45	115	11	23	33	7	0	1	13	1	8	34
Venable, Max	.246	82	187	24	46	67	8	2	3	21	2	11	30
Winfield, Dave	.262	150	568	75	149	268	27	4	28	86	7	56	109

PITCHING	ERA	W	L	G	GS	CG	SV	INN	H	R	ER	BB	SO
Abbott, Jim	2.89	18	11	34	34	5	0	243.0	222	85	78	73	158
Bailes, Scott	4.18	1	2	42	0	0	0	51.2	41	26	24	22	41
Bannister, Floyd	3.96	0	0	16	0	0	0	25.0	25	12	11	10	16
Beasley, Chris	3.38	0	1	22	0	0	0	26.2	26	14	10	10	14
Eichhorn, Mark	1.98	3	3	70	0	0	1	81.2	63	21	18	13	49
Fetters, Mike	4.84	2	5	19	4	0	0	44.2	53	29	24	28	24
Finley, Chuck	3.80	18	9	34	34	4	0	227.1	205	102	96	101	171
Grahe, Joe	4.81	3	7	18	10	1	0	73.0	84	43	39	33	40
Harvey, Bryan	1.60	2	4	67	0	0	46	78.2	51	20	14	17	101
Langston, Mark	3.00	19	8	34	34	7	0	246.1	190	89	82	96	183
Lewis, Scott	6.27	3	5	16	11	0	0	60.1	81	43	42	21	37
McCaskill, Kirk	4.26	10	19	30	30	1	0	177.2	193	93	84	66	71
Robinson, Jeff D.	5.37	0	3	39	0	0	3	57.0	56	34	34	29	57

Chicago White Sox

BATTING	BA	G	AB	R	H	TB	2B	3B	HR	RBI	SB	BB	SO
Cora, Joey	.241	100	228	37	55	63	2	3	0	18	11	20	21
Fisk, Carlton	.241	134	460	42	111	190	25	0	18	74	1	32	86
Fletcher, Scott	.206	90	248	14	51	66	10	1	1	28	0	17	26
Grebeck, Craig	.281	107	224	37	63	103	16	3	6	31	1	38	40
Guillen, Ozzie	.273	154	524	52	143	178	20	3	3	49	21	11	38
Huff, Mike	.268	51	97	14	26	35	4	1	1	15	3	12	18
Jackson, Bo	.225	23	71	8	16	29	4	0	3	14	0	12	25
Johnson, Lance	.274	159	588	72	161	201	14	13	0	49	26	26	58
Karkovice, Ron	.246	75	167	25	41	69	13	0	5	22	0	15	42
Merullo, Matt	.229	80	140	8	32	48	1	0	5	21	0	9	18
Newson, Warren	.295	71	132	20	39	56	5	0	4	25	2	28	34
Pasqua, Dan	.259	134	417	71	108	194	22	5	18	66	0	62	86
Raines, Tim	.268	155	609	102	163	210	20	6	5	50	51	83	68
Snyder, Cory	.188	50	117	10	22	35	4	0	3	11	0	6	41
Sosa, Sammy	.203	116	316	39	64	106	10	1	10	33	13	14	98
Thomas, Frank E.	.318	158	559	104	178	309	31	2	32	109	1	138	112
Ventura, Robin	.284	157	606	92	172	268	25	1	23	100	2	80	67

PITCHING	ERA	W	L	G	GS	CG	SV	INN	H	R	ER	BB	SO
Alvarez, Wilson	3.51	3	2	10	9	2	0	56.1	47	26	22	29	32
Drahman, Brian	3.23	3	2	28	0	0	0	30.2	21	12	11	13	18
Fernandez, Alex	4.51	9	13	34	32	2	0	191.2	186	100	96	88	145
Garcia, Ramon	5.40	4	4	16	15	0	0	78.1	79	50	47	31	45
Hibbard, Greg	4.31	11	11	32	29	5	0	194.0	196	107	93	57	71
Hough, Charlie	4.02	9	10	31	29	4	0	199.1	167	98	89	94	107
McDowell, Jack	3.41	17	10	35	35	15	0	253.2	212	97	96	82	191
Pall, Donn	2.41	7	2	51	0	0	0	71.0	59	22	19	20	40
Patterson, Ken	2.83	3	0	43	0	0	1	63.2	48	22	20	35	32
Perez, Melido	3.12	8	7	49	8	0	1	135.2	111	49	47	52	128
Radinsky, Scott	2.02	5	5	67	0	0	8	71.1	53	18	16	23	49
Thigpen, Bobby	3.49	7	5	67	0	0	30	69.2	63	32	27	38	47

Cleveland Indians

BATTING	BA	G	AB	R	H	TB	2B	3B	HR	RBI	SB	BB	SO
Aldrete, Mike	.262	85	183	22	48	59	6	1	1	19	1	36	37
Alomar, Sandy Jr.	.217	51	184	10	40	49	9	0	0	7	0	8	24
Baerga, Carlos	.288	158	593	80	171	236	28	2	11	69	3	48	74
Belle, Albert	.282	123	461	60	130	249	31	2	28	95	3	25	99
Browne, Jerry	.228	107	290	28	66	78	5	2	1	29	2	27	29
Cole, Alex	.295	122	387	58	114	137	17	3	0	21	27	58	47
Fermin, Felix	.262	129	424	30	111	128	13	2	0	31	5	26	27
Huff, Mike	.240	51	146	28	35	49	6	1	2	10	11	25	30
Macoby, Brook	.234	66	231	14	54	77	9	1	4	24	0	16	32
James, Chris	.238	115	437	31	104	139	16	2	5	41	3	18	61
Lewis, Mark	.264	84	314	29	83	100	15	1	0	30	2	15	45
Martinez, Carlos	.284	72	257	22	73	102	14	0	5	30	3	10	43
Skinner, Joel	.243	99	284	23	69	86	14	0	1	24	0	14	67
Whiten, Mark	.256	70	258	34	66	109	14	4	7	26	4	19	50

PITCHING	ERA	W	L	G	GS	CG	SV	INN	H	R	ER	BB	SO
Blair, Willie	6.75	2	3	11	5	0	0	36.0	58	27	27	10	13
Candiotti, Tom	2.24	7	6	15	15	3	0	108.1	88	35	27	28	86
Hillegas, Shawn	4.34	3	4	51	3	0	7	83.0	67	42	40	46	66
Jones, Doug	5.54	4	8	36	4	0	7	63.1	87	42	39	17	48
King, Eric	4.60	6	11	25	24	2	0	150.2	166	83	77	44	59
Nagy, Charles	4.13	10	15	33	33	6	0	211.1	228	103	97	66	109
Nichols, Rod	3.54	2	11	31	16	3	1	137.1	145	63	54	30	76
Olin, Steven	3.36	3	6	48	0	0	17	56.1	61	26	21	23	38
Orosco, Jesse	3.74	2	0	47	0	0	0	45.2	52	20	19	15	36
Otto, Dave	4.23	2	8	18	14	1	0	100.0	108	52	47	27	47
Shaw, Jeff	3.36	0	5	29	1	0	1	72.1	72	34	27	27	31
Swindell, Greg	3.48	9	16	33	33	7	0	238.0	241	112	92	31	169
York, Mike	6.75	1	4	14	4	0	0	34.2	45	29	26	19	19

Detroit Tigers

BATTING	BA	G	AB	R	H	TB	2B	3B	HR	RBI	SB	BB	SO
Allanson, Andy	.232	60	151	10	35	48	10	0	1	16	0	7	31
Barnes, Skeeter	.289	75	159	28	46	78	13	2	5	17	10	9	24
Bergman, Dave	.237	86	194	23	46	79	10	1	7	29	1	35	40
Cuyler, Milton	.257	154	475	77	122	160	15	7	3	33	41	52	92
Deer, Rob	.179	134	448	64	80	173	14	2	25	64	1	89	175
Fielder, Cecil	.261	162	624	102	163	320	25	0	44	133	0	78	151
Fryman, Travis	.259	149	557	65	144	249	36	3	21	91	12	40	149
Incaviglia, Pete	.214	97	337	38	72	119	12	1	11	38	1	36	92
Livingstone, Scott	.291	44	127	19	37	48	5	0	2	11	2	10	25
Moseby, Lloyd	.262	74	260	37	68	103	15	1	6	35	8	21	43
Phillips, Tony	.284	146	564	87	160	247	28	4	17	72	10	79	95
Shelby, John	.154	53	143	19	22	41	8	1	3	8	0	8	23
Tettleton, Mickey	.263	154	501	85	132	246	17	2	31	89	3	101	131
Trammell, Alan	.248	101	375	57	93	140	20	0	9	55	11	37	39
Whitaker, Lou	.279	138	470	94	131	230	26	2	23	78	4	90	45

PITCHING	ERA	W	L	G	GS	CG	SV	INN	H	R	ER	BB	SO
Aldred, Scott	5.18	2	4	11	11	1	0	57.1	58	37	33	30	35
Cerutti, John	4.57	3	6	38	8	1	2	88.2	94	49	45	37	29
Gakeler, Dan	5.74	1	4	31	7	0	2	73.2	73	52	47	39	43
Gibson, Paul	4.59	5	7	68	0	0	8	96.0	112	51	49	48	52
Gleaton, Jerry Don	4.06	3	2	47	0	0	1	75.1	74	37	34	39	47
Gullickson, Bill	3.90	20	9	35	35	4	0	226.1	256	109	98	44	91
Henneman, Mike	2.88	10	2	60	0	0	21	84.1	81	29	27	34	61
Leiter, Mark	4.21	9	7	38	15	1	1	134.2	125	66	63	50	103
Meacham, Rusty	5.20	2	1	10	4	0	0	27.2	35	17	16	11	14
Petry, Dan	4.94	2	3	17	6	0	0	54.2	66	35	30	19	18
Ritz, Kevin	11.74	0	3	11	5	0	0	15.1	17	22	20	22	9
Searcy, Steve	8.41	1	2	16	5	0	0	40.2	52	40	38	30	32
Tanana, Frank	3.77	13	12	33	33	3	0	217.1	217	98	91	78	107
Terrell, Walt	4.24	12	14	35	33	8	0	218.2	257	115	103	79	80

American League Team-by-Team Statistical Leaders

Kansas City Royals

BATTING	BA	G	AB	R	H	TB	2B	3B	HR	RBI	SB	BB	S
Benzinger, Todd	.294	78	293	29	86	113	15	3	2	40	2	17	4
Brett, George	.255	131	505	77	129	203	40	2	10	61	2	58	7
Cromartie, Warren	.313	69	131	13	41	55	7	2	1	20	1	15	1
Eisenreich, Jim	.301	135	375	47	113	147	22	3	2	47	5	20	3
Gibson, Kirk	.236	132	462	81	109	186	17	6	16	55	18	69	10
Howard, Dave	.216	94	236	20	51	61	7	0	1	17	3	16	4
Macfarlane, Mike	.277	84	267	34	74	135	18	2	13	41	1	17	5
Martinez, Carmelo	.207	44	121	17	25	43	6	0	4	17	0	27	2
Mayne, Brent	.251	85	231	22	58	75	8	0	3	31	2	23	4
McRae, Brian	.261	152	629	86	164	234	28	9	8	64	20	24	9
Pecota, Bill	.286	125	398	53	114	159	23	2	6	45	16	41	4
Seitzer, Kevin	.265	85	234	28	62	82	11	3	1	25	4	29	2
Shumpert, Terry	.217	144	369	45	80	119	16	4	5	34	17	30	7
Stillwell, Kurt	.265	122	385	44	102	139	17	1	6	51	3	33	5
Tartabull, Danny	.316	132	484	78	153	287	35	3	31	100	6	65	12
Thurman, Gary	.277	80	184	24	51	66	9	0	2	13	15	11	4

PITCHING	ERA	W	L	G	GS	CG	SV	INN	H	R	ER	BB	SO
Appier, Kevin	3.42	13	10	34	31	6	0	207.2	205	97	79	61	15
Aquino, Luis	3.44	8	4	38	18	1	3	157.0	152	67	60	47	8
Boddicker, Mike	4.08	12	12	30	29	1	0	180.2	188	89	82	59	7
Crawford, Steve	5.98	3	2	33	0	0	1	46.2	60	31	31	18	3
Davis, Storm	4.96	3	9	51	9	1	2	114.1	140	69	63	46	5
Davis, Mark W.	4.45	6	3	29	5	0	1	62.2	55	36	31	39	4
Gordon, Tom	3.87	9	14	45	14	1	1	158.0	129	76	68	87	16
Gubicza, Mark	5.68	9	12	26	26	0	0	133.0	168	90	84	42	8
Johnston, Joel	0.40	1	0	13	0	0	0	22.1	9	1	1	9	2
Magnante, Mike	2.45	0	1	38	0	0	0	55.0	55	19	15	23	4
Montgomery, Jeff	2.90	4	4	67	0	0	33	90.0	83	32	29	28	7
Saberhagen, Bret	3.07	13	8	28	28	7	0	196.1	165	76	67	45	13

Milwaukee Brewers

BATTING	BA	G	AB	R	H	TB	2B	3B	HR	RBI	SB	BB	S
Bichette, Dante	.238	134	445	53	106	175	18	3	15	59	14	22	10
Dempsey, Rick	.231	61	147	15	34	51	5	0	4	21	0	23	20
Ganter, Jim	.283	140	526	63	149	190	27	4	2	47	4	27	3
Hamilton, Darryl	.311	122	405	64	126	156	15	6	1	57	16	33	3
Maldonado, Candy	.207	34	111	11	23	44	6	0	5	20	1	13	2
Molitor, Paul	.325	158	665	133	216	325	32	13	17	75	19	77	6
Randolph, Willie	.327	124	431	60	141	161	14	3	0	54	4	75	3
Sheffield, Gary	.194	50	175	25	34	56	12	2	2	22	5	19	1
Spiers, Bill	.283	133	414	71	117	166	13	6	8	54	14	34	5
Stubbs, Franklin	.213	103	362	48	77	130	16	2	11	38	13	35	7
Surhoff, B.J.	.289	143	505	57	146	188	19	4	5	68	5	26	3
Sveum, Dale	.241	90	266	33	64	97	19	1	4	43	2	32	7
Vaughn, Greg	.244	145	542	81	132	247	24	5	27	98	2	62	125
Yount, Robin	.260	130	503	66	131	189	20	4	10	77	6	54	7

PITCHING	ERA	W	L	G	GS	CG	SV	INN	H	R	ER	BB	SO
August, Don	5.47	9	8	28	23	1	0	138.1	166	87	84	47	62
Bosio, Chris	3.25	14	10	32	32	5	0	204.2	187	80	74	58	117
Brown, Kevin D.	5.51	2	4	15	10	0	0	63.2	66	39	39	34	36
Crim, Chuck	4.63	8	5	66	0	0	3	91.1	115	52	47	25	39
Henry, Doug	1.00	2	1	32	0	0	15	36.0	16	4	4	14	28
Higuera, Ted	4.46	3	2	7	6	0	0	36.1	37	18	18	10	3
Holmes, Darren	4.72	1	4	40	0	0	3	76.1	90	43	40	27	5
Hunter, Jim	7.26	0	5	8	6	0	0	31.0	45	26	25	17	14
Knudson, Mark	7.97	1	3	12	7	0	0	35.0	54	33	31	15	23
Lee, Mark O.	3.86	2	5	62	0	0	1	67.2	72	33	29	31	43
Machado, Julio	3.45	3	3	54	0	0	3	88.2	65	36	34	55	
Navarro, Jaime	3.92	15	12	34	34	10	0	234.0	237	117	102	73	114
Nunez, Edwin	6.04	2	1	23	0	0	8	25.1	28	20	17	13	24
Plesac, Dan	4.29	2	7	45	10	0	8	92.1	92	49	44	39	61
Wegman, Bill	2.84	15	7	28	28	7	0	193.1	176	76	61	40	89

American League Team-by-Team Statistical Leaders

Minnesota Twins

BATTING	BA	G	AB	R	H	TB	2B	3B	HR	RBI	SB	BB	SO
Bush, Randy	.303	93	165	21	50	80	10	1	6	23	0	24	25
Davis, Chili	.277	153	534	84	148	271	34	1	29	93	5	95	117
Gagne, Greg	.265	139	408	52	108	161	23	3	8	42	11	26	72
Gladden, Dan	.247	126	461	65	114	164	14	9	6	52	15	36	60
Harper, Brian	.311	123	441	54	137	197	28	1	10	69	1	14	22
Hrbek, Kent	.284	132	462	72	131	213	20	1	20	89	4	67	48
Knoblauch, Chuck	.281	151	565	78	159	198	24	6	1	50	25	59	40
Larkin, Gene	.286	98	255	34	73	95	14	1	2	19	2	30	21
Leius, Scott	.286	109	199	35	57	83	7	2	5	20	5	30	35
Mack, Shane	.310	143	442	79	137	234	27	8	18	74	13	34	79
Munoz, Pedro	.283	51	138	15	39	69	7	1	7	26	3	9	31
Newman, Al	.191	118	246	25	47	52	5	0	0	19	4	23	21
Ortiz, Junior	.209	61	134	9	28	35	5	1	0	11	0	15	12
Pagliarulo, Mike	.279	121	365	38	102	140	20	0	6	36	1	21	55
Puckett, Kirby	.319	152	611	92	195	281	29	6	15	89	11	31	78

PITCHING	ERA	W	L	G	GS	CG	SV	INN	H	R	ER	BB	SO
Abbott, Paul	4.75	3	1	15	3	0	0	47.1	38	27	25	36	43
Aguilera, Rick	2.35	4	5	63	0	0	42	69.0	44	20	18	30	61
Anderson, Allan	4.96	5	11	29	22	2	0	134.1	148	82	74	42	51
Bedrosian, Steve	4.42	5	3	56	0	0	6	77.1	70	42	38	35	44
Edens, Tom	4.09	2	2	8	6	0	0	33.0	34	15	15	10	19
Erickson, Scott	3.18	20	8	32	32	5	0	204.0	189	80	72	71	108
Guthrie, Mark	4.32	7	5	41	12	0	2	98.0	116	52	47	41	72
Leach, Terry	3.61	1	2	50	0	0	0	67.1	82	28	27	14	32
Morris, Jack	3.43	18	12	35	35	10	0	246.2	226	107	94	92	163
Neagle, Denny	4.05	0	1	7	3	0	0	20.0	28	9	9	7	14
Tapani, Kevin	2.99	16	9	34	34	4	0	244.0	225	84	81	40	135
West, David	4.54	4	4	15	12	0	0	71.1	66	37	36	28	52
Willis, Carl	2.63	8	3	40	0	0	2	89.0	76	31	26	19	53

New York Yankees

BATTING	BA	G	AB	R	H	TB	2B	3B	HR	RBI	SB	BB	SO
Barfield, Jesse	.225	84	284	37	64	127	12	0	17	48	1	36	80
Espinoza, Alvaro	.256	148	480	51	123	165	23	2	5	33	4	16	57
Geren, Bob	.219	64	128	7	28	37	3	0	2	12	0	9	31
Hall, Mel	.285	141	492	67	140	224	23	2	19	80	0	26	40
Kelly, Pat	.242	96	298	35	72	101	12	4	3	23	12	15	52
Kelly, Roberto	.267	126	486	68	130	216	22	2	20	69	32	45	77
Maas, Kevin	.220	148	500	69	110	195	14	1	23	63	5	83	128
Mattingly, Don	.288	152	587	64	169	231	35	0	9	68	2	46	42
Meulens, Hensley	.222	96	288	37	64	92	8	1	6	29	3	18	97
Nokes, Matt	.268	135	456	52	122	214	20	0	24	77	3	25	49
Sax, Steve	.304	158	652	85	198	270	38	2	10	56	31	41	38
Sheridan, Pat	.204	62	113	13	23	38	3	0	4	7	1	13	30
Velarde, Randy	.245	80	184	19	45	61	11	1	1	15	3	18	43
Williams, Bernie	.238	85	320	43	76	112	19	4	3	34	10	48	57

PITCHING	ERA	W	L	G	GS	CG	SV	INN	H	R	ER	BB	SO
Cadaret, Greg	3.62	8	6	68	5	0	3	121.2	110	52	49	59	105
Cary, Chuck	5.91	1	6	10	9	0	0	53.1	61	35	35	32	34
Eiland, Dave	5.33	2	5	18	13	0	0	72.2	87	51	43	23	18
Farr, Steve	2.19	5	5	60	0	0	23	70.0	57	19	17	20	60
Guetterman, Lee	3.68	3	4	64	0	0	6	88.0	91	42	36	25	35
Habyan, John	2.30	4	2	66	0	0	2	90.0	73	28	23	20	70
Howe, Steve	1.68	3	1	37	0	0	3	48.1	39	12	9	7	34
Johnson, Jeff	5.95	6	11	23	23	0	0	127.0	156	89	84	33	62
Kamieniecki, Scott	3.90	4	4	9	9	0	0	55.1	54	24	24	22	34
Leary, Tim	6.49	4	10	28	18	1	0	120.2	150	89	87	57	83
Mills, Alan	4.41	1	1	6	2	0	0	16.1	16	9	8	8	11
Monteleone, Rich	3.64	3	1	26	0	0	0	47.0	42	27	19	19	34
Perez, Pascual	3.18	2	4	14	14	0	0	73.2	68	26	26	24	41
Plunk, Eric	4.76	2	5	43	8	0	0	111.2	128	69	59	62	103
Sanderson, Scott	3.81	16	10	34	34	2	0	208.0	200	95	88	29	130
Taylor, Wade	6.27	7	12	23	22	0	0	116.1	144	85	81	53	72

Oakland Athletics

BATTING	BA	G	AB	R	H	TB	2B	3B	HR	RBI	SB	BB	S
Baines, Harold	.295	141	488	76	144	231	25	1	20	90	0	72	6
Blankenship, Lance	.249	90	185	33	46	63	8	0	3	21	12	23	4
Bordick, Mike	.238	90	235	21	56	63	5	1	0	21	3	14	3
Canseco, Jose	.266	154	572	115	152	318	32	1	44	122	26	78	15
Gallego, Mike	.247	159	482	67	119	178	15	4	12	49	6	67	8
Henderson, Dave	.276	150	572	86	158	266	33	0	25	85	6	58	11
Henderson, Rickey	.268	134	470	105	126	199	17	1	18	57	58	98	7
Jacoby, Brook	.213	56	188	14	40	52	12	0	0	20	2	11	2
Law, Vance	.209	74	134	11	28	37	7	1	0	9	0	18	2
McGwire, Mark	.201	154	483	62	97	185	22	0	22	75	2	93	11
Quirk, Jamie	.261	76	203	16	53	60	4	0	1	17	0	16	2
Riles, Ernest	.214	108	281	30	60	91	8	4	5	32	3	31	4
Steinbach, Terry	.274	129	456	50	125	176	31	1	6	67	2	22	7
Weiss, Walter	.226	40	133	15	30	38	6	1	0	13	6	12	1
Wilson, Willie	.238	113	294	38	70	92	14	4	0	28	20	18	4

PITCHING	ERA	W	L	G	GS	CG	SV	INN	H	R	ER	BB	S
Chitren, Steve	4.33	1	4	56	0	0	4	60.1	59	31	29	32	4
Darling, Ron	4.08	3	7	12	12	0	0	75.0	64	34	34	38	6
Dressendorfer, Kirk	5.45	3	3	7	7	0	0	34.2	33	28	21	21	1
Eckersley, Dennis	2.96	5	4	67	0	0	43	76.0	60	26	25	9	8
Hawkins, Andy	4.79	4	4	15	14	1	0	77.0	68	41	41	36	4
Honeycutt, Rick	3.58	2	4	43	0	0	0	37.2	37	16	15	20	2
Klink, Joe	4.35	10	3	62	0	0	2	62.0	60	30	30	21	3
Moore, Mike	2.96	17	8	33	33	3	0	210.0	176	75	69	105	15
Nelson, Gene	6.84	1	5	44	0	0	0	48.2	60	38	37	23	2
Show, Eric	5.92	1	2	23	5	0	0	51.2	62	36	34	17	2
Slusarski, Joe	5.27	5	7	20	19	1	0	109.1	121	69	64	52	6
Stewart, Dave	5.18	11	11	35	35	2	0	226.0	245	135	130	105	14
Welch, Bob	4.58	12	13	35	35	7	0	220.0	220	124	112	91	10
Young, Curt	5.00	4	2	41	1	0	0	68.1	74	38	38	34	2

Seattle Mariners

BATTING	BA	G	AB	R	H	TB	2B	3B	HR	RBI	SB	BB	S
Bradley, Scott	.203	83	172	10	35	42	7	0	0	11	0	19	1
Briley, Greg	.260	139	381	39	99	128	17	3	2	26	23	27	5
Buhner, Jay	.244	137	406	64	99	202	14	4	27	77	0	53	11
Cochrane, Dave	.247	65	178	16	44	63	13	0	2	22	0	9	3
Cotto, Henry	.305	66	177	35	54	82	6	2	6	23	16	10	2
Davis, Alvin	.221	145	462	39	102	155	15	1	12	69	0	56	7
Griffey, Ken Sr.	.282	30	85	10	24	34	7	0	1	9	0	13	1
Griffey, Ken Jr.	.327	154	548	76	179	289	42	1	22	100	18	71	8
Jones, Tracy	.251	79	175	30	44	63	8	1	3	24	2	18	2
Martinez, Edgar	.307	150	544	98	167	246	35	1	14	52	0	84	7
Martinez, Tino	.205	36	112	11	23	37	2	0	4	9	0	11	2
O'Brien, Pete M.	.248	152	560	58	139	225	29	3	17	88	0	44	6
Powell, Alonzo	.216	57	111	16	24	41	6	1	3	12	0	11	2
Reynolds, Harold	.254	161	631	95	160	215	34	6	3	57	28	72	6
Schaefer, Jeff	.250	84	164	19	41	53	7	1	1	11	3	5	2
Valle, Dave	.194	132	324	38	63	97	8	1	8	32	0	34	4
Vizquel, Omar	.230	142	426	42	98	125	16	4	1	41	7	45	3

PITCHING	ERA	W	L	G	GS	CG	SV	INN	H	R	ER	BB	SO
Bankhead, Scott	4.90	3	6	17	9	0	0	60.2	73	35	33	21	2
Delucia, Rich	5.09	12	13	32	31	0	0	182.0	176	107	103	78	9
Hanson, Erik	3.81	8	8	27	27	2	0	174.2	182	82	74	56	14
Holman, Brian	3.69	13	14	30	30	5	0	195.1	199	86	80	77	10
Jackson, Mike R.	3.25	7	7	72	0	0	14	88.2	64	35	32	34	7
Johnson, Randy D.	3.98	13	10	33	33	2	0	201.1	151	96	89	152	22
Jones, Calvin	2.53	2	2	27	0	0	2	46.1	33	14	13	29	4
Krueger, Bill	3.60	11	8	35	25	1	0	175.0	194	82	70	60	9
Murphy, Rob	3.00	0	1	57	0	0	4	48.0	47	17	16	19	3
Swan, Russ	3.43	6	2	63	0	0	2	78.2	81	35	30	28	3
Swift, Bill C.	1.99	1	2	71	0	0	17	90.1	74	22	20	26	4

American League Team-by-Team Statistical Leaders

Texas Rangers

BATTING	BA	G	AB	R	H	TB	2B	3B	HR	RBI	SB	BB	SO
Buechele, Steve	.267	121	416	58	111	186	17	2	18	66	0	39	69
Diaz, Mario	.264	96	182	24	48	58	7	0	1	22	0	15	18
Downing, Brian	.278	123	407	76	113	185	17	2	17	49	1	58	70
Franco, Julio	.341	146	589	108	201	279	27	3	15	78	36	65	78
Gonzalez, Juan	.264	142	545	78	144	261	34	1	27	102	4	42	118
Huson, Jeff	.213	119	268	36	57	77	8	3	2	26	8	39	32
Palmeiro, Rafael	.322	159	631	115	203	336	49	3	26	88	4	68	72
Palmer, Dean	.187	81	268	38	50	108	9	2	15	37	0	32	98
Petralli, Geno	.271	87	199	21	54	70	8	1	2	20	2	21	25
Pettis, Gary	.216	137	282	37	61	78	7	5	0	19	29	54	91
Reimer, Kevin	.269	136	394	46	106	188	22	0	20	69	0	33	93
Rodriguez, Ivan	.264	88	280	24	74	99	16	0	3	27	0	5	42
Sierra, Ruben	.307	161	661	110	203	332	44	5	25	116	16	56	91
Stanley, Mike	.249	95	181	25	45	69	13	1	3	25	0	34	44

PITCHING	ERA	W	L	G	GS	CG	SV	INN	H	R	ER	BB	SO
Alexander, Gerald	5.24	5	3	30	9	0	0	89.1	93	56	52	48	50
Barfield, John	4.54	4	4	28	9	0	1	83.1	96	51	42	22	27
Bohanon, Brian	4.84	4	3	11	11	1	0	61.1	66	35	33	23	34
Boyd, Oil Can	6.68	2	7	12	12	0	0	62.0	81	47	46	17	33
Brown, J. Kevin	4.40	9	12	33	33	0	0	210.2	233	116	103	90	96
Gossage, Goose	3.57	4	2	44	0	0	1	40.1	33	16	16	16	28
Guzman, Jose	3.08	13	7	25	25	5	0	169.2	152	67	58	84	125
Jeffcoat, Mike	4.63	5	3	70	0	0	1	79.2	104	46	41	25	43
Mathews, Terry	3.61	4	0	34	2	0	1	57.1	54	24	23	18	51
Rogers, Kenny	5.42	10	10	63	9	0	5	109.2	121	80	66	61	73
Rosenthal, Wayne	5.25	1	4	36	0	0	1	70.1	72	43	41	36	61
Russell, Jeff	3.29	6	4	68	0	0	30	79.1	71	36	29	26	52
Ryan, Nolan	2.91	12	6	27	27	2	0	173.0	102	58	56	72	203
Witt, Bobby	6.09	3	7	17	16	1	0	88.2	84	66	60	74	82

Toronto Blue Jays

BATTING	BA	G	AB	R	H	TB	2B	3B	HR	RBI	SB	BB	SO
Alomar, Roberto	.295	161	637	88	188	278	41	11	9	69	53	57	86
Borders, Pat	.244	105	291	22	71	103	17	0	5	36	0	11	45
Carter, Joe	.273	162	638	89	174	321	42	3	33	108	20	49	112
Gonzales, Rene	.195	71	118	16	23	29	3	0	1	6	0	12	22
Gruber, Kelly	.252	113	429	58	108	190	18	2	20	65	12	31	70
Lee, Manny	.234	138	445	41	104	128	18	3	0	29	7	24	107
Maldonado, Candy	.277	52	177	26	49	79	9	0	7	28	3	23	53
Mulliniks, Rance	.250	97	240	27	60	80	12	1	2	24	0	44	44
Myers, Greg	.262	107	309	25	81	127	22	0	8	36	0	21	45
Olerud, John	.256	139	454	64	116	199	30	1	17	68	0	68	84
Sprague, Ed Jr.	.275	61	160	17	44	63	7	0	4	20	0	19	43
Tabler, Pat	.216	82	185	20	40	50	5	1	1	21	0	29	21
White, Devon	.282	156	642	110	181	292	40	10	17	60	33	55	135
Whiten, Mark	.221	46	149	12	33	49	4	3	2	19	0	11	35
Wilson, Mookie	.241	86	241	26	58	84	12	4	2	28	11	8	35

PITCHING	ERA	W	L	G	GS	CG	SV	INN	H	R	ER	BB	SO
Acker, Jim	5.20	3	5	54	4	0	1	88.1	77	53	51	36	44
Boucher, Denis	4.58	0	3	7	7	0	0	35.1	39	20	18	16	16
Candiotti, Tom	2.98	6	7	19	19	3	0	129.2	114	47	43	45	81
Fraser, Willie	6.15	0	2	13	1	0	0	26.1	33	20	18	11	12
Guzman, Juan	2.99	10	3	23	23	1	0	138.2	98	53	46	66	123
Henke, Tom	2.32	0	2	49	0	0	32	50.1	33	13	13	11	53
Key, Jimmy	3.05	16	12	33	33	2	0	209.1	207	84	71	44	125
MacDonald, Bob	2.85	3	3	45	0	0	0	53.2	51	19	17	25	24
Stieb, Dave	3.17	4	3	9	9	1	0	59.2	52	22	21	23	29
Stottlemyre, Todd	3.78	15	8	34	34	0	0	219.0	194	97	92	75	116
Timlin, Mike	3.16	11	6	63	3	0	3	108.1	94	43	38	50	85
Ward, Duane	2.77	7	6	81	0	0	23	107.1	80	36	33	33	132
Wells, Dave	3.72	15	10	40	28	2	1	198.1	188	88	82	49	106

FOR THE RECORD • Year by Year

The World Series

Results

1903 ....Boston (A) 5, Pittsburgh (N) 3	1948 ....Cleveland (A) 4, Boston (N) 2
1904 ....No series	1949 ....New York (A) 4, Brooklyn (N) 1
1905 ....New York (N) 4, Philadelphia (A) 1	1950 ....New York (A) 4, Philadelphia (N) 0
1906 ....Chicago (A) 4, Chicago (N) 2	1951 ....New York (A) 4, New York (N) 2
1907 ....Chicago (N) 4, Detroit (A) 0; 1 tie	1952 ....New York (A) 4, Brooklyn (N) 3
1908 ....Chicago (N) 4, Detroit (A) 1	1953 ....New York (A) 4, Brooklyn (N) 2
1909 ....Pittsburgh (N) 4, Detroit (A) 3	1954 ....New York (N) 4, Cleveland (A) 0
1910 ....Philadelphia (A) 4, Chicago (N) 1	1955 ....Brooklyn (N) 4, New York (A) 3
1911 ....Philadelphia (A) 4, New York (N) 2	1956 ....New York (A) 4, Brooklyn (N) 3
1912 ....Boston (A) 4, New York (N) 3; 1 tie	1957 ....Milwaukee (N) 4, New York (A) 3
1913 ....Philadelphia (A) 4, New York (N) 1	1958 ....New York (A) 4, Milwaukee (N) 3
1914 ....Boston (N) 4, Philadelphia (A) 0	1959 ....Los Angeles (N) 4, Chicago (A) 2
1915 ....Boston (A) 4, Philadelphia (A) 1	1960 ....Pittsburgh (N) 4, New York (A) 3
1916 ....Boston (A) 4, Brooklyn (N) 1	1961 ....New York (A) 4, Cincinnati (N) 1
1917 ....Chicago (A) 4, New York (N) 2	1962 ....New York (A) 4, San Francisco (N) 3
1918 ....Boston (A) 4, Chicago (N) 2	1963 ....Los Angeles (N) 4, New York (A) 0
1919 ....Cincinnati (N) 5, Chicago (A) 3	1964 ....St Louis (N) 4, New York (A) 3
1920 ....Cleveland (A) 5, Brooklyn (N) 2	1965 ....Los Angeles (N) 4, Minnesota (A) 3
1921 ....New York (N) 5, New York (A) 3	1966 ....Baltimore (A) 4, Los Angeles (N) 0
1922 ....New York (N) 4, New York (A) 0; 1 tie	1967 ....St Louis (N) 4, Boston (A) 3
1923 ....New York (A) 4, New York (N) 2	1968 ....Detroit (A) 4, St Louis (N) 3
1924 ....Washington (A) 4, New York (N) 3	1969 ....New York (N) 4, Baltimore (A) 1
1925 ....Pittsburgh (N) 4, Washington (A) 3	1970 ....Baltimore (A) 4, Cincinnati (N) 1
1926 ....St Louis (N) 4, New York (A) 3	1971 ....Pittsburgh (N) 4, Baltimore (A) 3
1927 ....New York (A) 4, Pittsburgh (N) 0	1972 ....Oakland (A) 4, Cincinnati (N) 3
1928 ....New York (A) 4, St Louis (N) 0	1973 ....Oakland (A) 4, New York (N) 3
1929 ....Philadelphia (A) 4, Chicago (N) 1	1974 ....Oakland (A) 4, Los Angeles (N) 1
1930 ....Philadelphia (A) 4, St Louis (N) 2	1975 ....Cincinnati (N) 4, Boston (A) 3
1931 ....St Louis (N) 4, Philadelphia (A) 3	1976 ....Cincinnati (N) 4, New York (A) 0
1932 ....New York (A) 4, Chicago (N) 0	1977 ....New York (A) 4, Los Angeles (N) 2
1933 ....New York (N) 4, Washington (A) 1	1978 ....New York (A) 4, Los Angeles (N) 2
1934 ....St Louis (N) 4, Detroit (A) 3	1979 ....Pittsburgh (N) 4, Baltimore (A) 3
1935 ....Detroit (A) 4, Chicago (N) 2	1980 ....Philadelphia (N) 4, Kansas City (A) 2
1936 ....New York (A) 4, New York (N) 2	1981 ....Los Angeles (N) 4, New York (A) 2
1937 ....New York (A) 4, New York (N) 1	1982 ....St Louis (N) 4, Milwaukee (A) 3
1938 ....New York (A) 4, Chicago (N) 0	1983 ....Baltimore (A) 4, Philadelphia (N) 1
1939 ....New York (A) 4, Cincinnati (N) 0	1984 ....Detroit (A) 4, San Diego (N) 1
1940 ....Cincinnati (N) 4, Detroit (A) 3	1985 ....Kansas City (A) 4, St Louis (N) 3
1941 ....New York (A) 4, Brooklyn (N) 1	1986 ....New York (N) 4, Boston (A) 3
1942 ....St Louis (N) 4, New York (A) 1	1987 ....Minnesota (A) 4, St Louis (N) 3
1943 ....New York (A) 4, St Louis (N) 1	1988 ....Los Angeles (N) 4, Oakland (A) 1
1944 ....St Louis (N) 4, St Louis (A) 2	1989 ....Oakland (A) 4, San Francisco (N) 0
1945 ....Detroit (A) 4, Chicago (N) 3	1990 ....Cincinnati (N) 4, Oakland (A) 0
1946 ....St Louis (N) 4, Boston (A) 3	1991 ....Minnesota (A) 4, Atlanta (N) 3
1947 ....New York (A) 4, Brooklyn (N) 3	

A Matter of Perspective

Oakland A's star Jose Canseco was declared a superman in 1989 when he became the first 40–40 man in baseball history—the first player to hit 40 home runs and steal 40 bases in the same season. Less well known is the fact that baseball also has a 40–.400 man—a player who hit 40 home runs and batted .400 in the same year. He is Rogers Hornsby, who in 1922 socked 42 round trippers and hit .401 for the St. Louis Cardinals. Hornsby's 152 RBIs helped him win the Triple Crown that year, and he also led the National League in runs, hits, doubles, total bases, on-base percentage, and slugging percentage. Stolen bases, you ask? Only 17, no match for a superman like Canseco.

The World Series (*Cont.*)

Most Valuable Players

1955	Johnny Podres, Bklyn
1956	Don Larsen, NY (A)
1957	Lew Burdette, Mil
1958	Bob Turley, NY (A)
1959	Larry Sherry, LA
1960	Bobby Richardson, NY (A)
1961	Whitey Ford, NY (A)
1962	Ralph Terry, NY (A)
1963	Sandy Koufax, LA
1964	Bob Gibson, StL
1965	Sandy Koufax, LA
1966	Frank Robinson, Balt
1967	Bob Gibson, StL
1968	Mickey Lolich, Det
1969	Donn Clendenon, NY (N)
1970	Brooks Robinson, Balt
1971	Roberto Clemente, Pitt
1972	Gene Tenace, Oak
1973	Reggie Jackson, Oak
1974	Rollie Fingers, Oak
1975	Pete Rose, Cin
1976	Johnny Bench, Cin
1977	Reggie Jackson, NY (A)
1978	Bucky Dent, NY (A)
1979	Willie Stargell, Pitt
1980	Mike Schmidt, Phil
1981	Ron Cey, LA
	Pedro Guerrero, LA
	Steve Yeager, LA
1982	Darrell Porter, StL
1983	Rick Dempsey, Balt
1984	Alan Trammell, Det
1985	Bret Saberhagen, KC
1986	Ray Knight, NY (N)
1987	Frank Viola, Minn
1988	Orel Hershiser, LA
1989	Dave Stewart, Oak
1990	Jose Rijo, Cin
1991	Jack Morris, Minn

Career Batting Leaders

GAMES

Yogi Berra	75
Mickey Mantle	65
Elston Howard	54
Hank Bauer	53
Gil McDougald	53
Phil Rizzuto	52
Joe DiMaggio	51
Frankie Frisch	50
Pee Wee Reese	44
Roger Maris	41
Babe Ruth	41

AT BATS

Yogi Berra	259
Mickey Mantle	230
Joe DiMaggio	199
Frankie Frisch	197
Gil McDougald	190
Hank Bauer	188
Phil Rizzuto	183
Elston Howard	171
Pee Wee Reese	169
Roger Maris	152

HITS

Yogi Berra	71
Mickey Mantle	59
Frankie Frisch	58
Joe DiMaggio	54
Pee Wee Reese	46
Hank Bauer	46
Phil Rizzuto	45
Gil McDougald	45
Lou Gehrig	43
Eddie Collins	42
Babe Ruth	42
Elston Howard	42

BATTING AVERAGE

Pepper Martin	.418
Lou Brock	.391
Thurman Munson	.373
George Brett	.373
Hank Aaron	.364
Frank Baker	.363
Roberto Clemente	.362
Lou Gehrig	.361
Reggie Jackson	.357
Carl Yastrzemski	.352

HOME RUNS

Mickey Mantle	18
Babe Ruth	15
Yogi Berra	12
Duke Snider	11
Reggie Jackson	10
Lou Gehrig	10
Frank Robinson	8
Bill Skowron	8
Joe DiMaggio	8
Goose Goslin	7
Hank Bauer	7
Gil McDougald	7

RUNS BATTED IN

Mickey Mantle	40
Yogi Berra	39
Lou Gehrig	35
Babe Ruth	33
Joe DiMaggio	30
Bill Skowron	29
Duke Snider	26
Reggie Jackson	24
Bill Dickey	24
Hank Bauer	24
Gil McDougald	24

RUNS

Mickey Mantle	42
Yogi Berra	41
Babe Ruth	37
Lou Gehrig	30
Joe DiMaggio	27
Roger Maris	26
Elston Howard	25
Gil McDougald	23
Jackie Robinson	22
Gene Woodling	21
Reggie Jackson	21
Duke Snider	21
Phil Rizzuto	21
Hank Bauer	21

STOLEN BASES

Lou Brock	14
Eddie Collins	14
Frank Chance	10
Davey Lopes	10
Phil Rizzuto	10
Honus Wagner	9
Frankie Frisch	9
Johnny Evers	8
Pepper Martin	7
Joe Morgan	7

TOTAL BASES

Mickey Mantle	123
Yogi Berra	117
Babe Ruth	96
Lou Gehrig	87
Joe DiMaggio	84
Duke Snider	79
Hank Bauer	75
Reggie Jackson	74
Frankie Frisch	74
Gil McDougald	72

Career Batting Leaders (*Cont.*)

SLUGGING AVERAGE

Reggie Jackson	.755
Babe Ruth	.744
Lou Gehrig	.731
Al Simmons	.658
Lou Brock	.655
Pepper Martin	.636
Hank Greenberg	.624
Charlie Keller	.611
Jimmie Foxx	.609
Hank Aaron	.600

STRIKEOUTS

Mickey Mantle	54
Elston Howard	37
Duke Snider	33
Babe Ruth	30
Gil McDougald	29
Bill Skowron	26
Hank Bauer	25
Reggie Jackson	24
Bob Meusel	24
Frank Robinson	23
George Kelly	23
Tony Kubek	23
Joe DiMaggio	23

Career Pitching Leaders

GAMES

Whitey Ford	22
Rollie Fingers	16
Allie Reynolds	15
Bob Turley	15
Clay Carroll	14
Clem Labine	13
Waite Hoyt	12
Catfish Hunter	12
Art Nehf	12
Paul Derringer	11
Carl Erskine	11
Rube Marquard	11
Christy Mathewson	11
Vic Raschi	11

INNINGS PITCHED

Whitey Ford	146
Christy Mathewson	102
Red Ruffing	86
Chief Bender	85
Waite Hoyt	84
Bob Gibson	81
Art Nehf	79
Allie Reynolds	77
Jim Palmer	65
Catfish Hunter	63

WINS

Whitey Ford	10
Bob Gibson	7
Red Ruffing	7
Allie Reynolds	7
Lefty Gomez	6
Chief Bender	6
Waite Hoyt	6
Jack Coombs	5
Three Finger Brown	5
Herb Pennock	5
Christy Mathewson	5
Vic Raschi	5
Catfish Hunter	5

LOSSES

Whitey Ford	8
Eddie Plank	5
Schoolboy Rowe	5
Joe Bush	5
Rube Marquard	5
Christy Mathewson	5

SAVES

Rollie Fingers	6
Allie Reynolds	4
Johnny Murphy	4
Roy Face	3
Herb Pennock	3
Kent Tekulve	3
Firpo Marberry	3
Will McEnaney	3
Todd Worrell	3
Tug McGraw	3

EARNED RUN AVERAGE

Jack Billingham	.36
Harry Brecheen	.83
Babe Ruth	.87
Sherry Smith	.89
Sandy Koufax	.95
Hippo Vaughn	1.00
Monte Pearson	1.01
Christy Mathewson	1.15
Babe Adams	1.29
Eddie Plank	1.32

SHUTOUTS

Christy Mathewson	4
Three Finger Brown	3
Whitey Ford	3
Bill Hallahan	2
Lew Burdette	2
Bill Dinneen	2
Sandy Koufax	2
Allie Reynolds	2
Art Nehf	2
Bob Gibson	2

COMPLETE GAMES

Christy Mathewson	1
Chief Bender	
Bob Gibson	
Red Ruffing	
Whitey Ford	
George Mullin	
Eddie Plank	
Art Nehf	
Waite Hoyt	

STRIKEOUTS

Whitey Ford	9
Bob Gibson	9
Allie Reynolds	6
Sandy Koufax	6
Red Ruffing	6
Chief Bender	5
George Earnshaw	5
Waite Hoyt	4
Christy Mathewson	4
Bob Turley	4

BASES ON BALLS

Whitey Ford	3
Allie Reynolds	3
Art Nehf	3
Jim Palmer	3
Bob Turley	2
Paul Derringer	2
Red Ruffing	2
Don Gullett	2
Burleigh Grimes	2
Vic Raschi	2

National League Results

1969	New York (E) 3, Atlanta (W) 0
1970	Cincinnati (W) 3, Pittsburgh (E) 0
1971	Pittsburgh (E) 3, San Francisco (W) 1
1972	Cincinnati (W) 3, Pittsburgh (E) 2
1973	New York (E) 3, Cincinnati (W) 2
1974	Los Angeles (W) 3, Pittsburgh (E) 1
1975	Cincinnati (W) 3, Pittsburgh (E) 0
1976	Cincinnati (W) 3, Philadelphia (E) 0
1977	Los Angeles (W) 3, Philadelphia (E) 1
1978	Los Angeles (W) 3, Philadelphia (E) 1
1979	Pittsburgh (E) 3, Cincinnati (W) 0
1980	Philadelphia (E) 3, Houston (W) 2
1981	Los Angeles (W) 3, Montreal (E) 2
1982	St Louis (E) 3, Atlanta (W) 0
1983	Philadelphia (E) 3, Los Angeles (W) 1
1984	San Diego (W) 3, Chicago (E) 2
1985	St Louis (E) 4, Los Angeles (W) 2
1986	New York (E) 4, Houston (W) 2
1987	St Louis (E) 4, San Francisco (W) 3
1988	Los Angeles (W) 4, New York (E) 3
1989	San Francisco (W) 4, Chicago (E) 1
1990	Cincinnati (W) 4, Pittsburgh (E) 2
1991	Atlanta (W) 4, Pittsburgh (E) 3

American League Results

1969	Baltimore (E) 3, Minnesota (W) 0
1970	Baltimore (E) 3, Minnesota (W) 0
1971	Baltimore (E) 3, Oakland (W) 0
1972	Oakland (W) 3, Detroit (E) 2
1973	Oakland (W) 3, Baltimore (E) 2
1974	Oakland (W) 3, Baltimore (E) 1
1975	Boston (E) 3, Oakland (W) 0
1976	New York (E) 3, Kansas City (W) 2
1977	New York (E) 3, Kansas City (W) 2
1978	New York (E) 3, Kansas City (W) 1
1979	Baltimore (E) 3, California (W) 1
1980	Kansas City (W) 3, New York (E) 0
1981	New York (E) 3, Oakland (W) 0
1982	Milwaukee (E) 3, California (W) 2
1983	Baltimore (E) 3, Chicago (W) 1
1984	Detroit (E) 3, Kansas City (W) 0
1985	Kansas City (W) 4, Toronto (E) 3
1986	Boston (E) 4, California (W) 3
1987	Minnesota (W) 4, Detroit (E) 1
1988	Oakland (W) 4, Boston (E) 0
1989	Oakland (W) 4, Toronto (E) 1
1990	Oakland (W) 4, Boston (E) 0
1991	Minnesota (W) 4, Toronto (E) 1

NLCS Most Valuable Player

1977	Dusty Baker, LA
1978	Steve Garvey, LA
1979	Willie Stargell, Pitt
1980	Manny Trillo, Phil
1981	Burt Hooton, LA
1982	Darrell Porter, StL
1983	Gary Matthews, Phil
1984	Steve Garvey, SD
1985	Ozzie Smith, StL
1986	Mike Scott, Hou
1987	Jeffrey Leonard, SF
1988	Orel Hershiser, LA
1989	Will Clark, SF
1990	Randy Myers, Cin Ron Dibble, Cin
1991	Steve Avery, Atl

ALCS Most Valuable Players

1980	Frank White, KC
1981	Graig Nettles, NY
1982	Fred Lynn, Calif
1983	Mike Boddicker, Balt
1984	Kirk Gibson, Det
1985	George Brett, KC
1986	Marty Barrett, Bos
1987	Gary Gaetti, Minn
1988	Dennis Eckersley, Oak
1989	Rickey Henderson, Oak
1990	Dave Stewart, Oak
1991	Kirby Puckett, Minn

The All-Star Game

Results

Date	Winner	Score	Site
7-6-33	American	4-2	Comiskey Park, Chi
7-10-34	American	9-7	Polo Grounds, NY
7-8-35	American	4-1	Municipal Stadium, Clev
7-7-36	National	4-3	Braves Field, Bos
7-7-37	American	8-3	Griffith Stadium, Wash
7-6-38	National	4-1	Crosley Field, Cin
7-11-39	American	3-1	Yankee Stadium, NY
7-10-40	National	4-0	Sportsman's Park, StL
7-8-41	American	7-5	Briggs Stadium, Det
7-6-42	American	3-1	Polo Grounds, NY
7-13-43	American	5-3	Shibe Park, Phil
7-11-44	National	7-1	Forbes Field, Pitt
1945	No game due to wartime travel restrictions		
7-9-46	American	12-0	Fenway Park, Bos
7-8-47	American	2-1	Wrigley Field, Chi
7-13-48	American	5-2	Sportsman's Park, StL
7-12-49	American	11-7	Ebbets Field, Bklyn
7-11-50	National	4-3	Comiskey Park, Chi

Results (*Cont.*)

Date	Winner	Score	Site
7-10-51	National	8-3	Briggs Stadium, Det
7-8-52	National	3-2	Shibe Park, Phil
7-14-53	National	5-1	Crosley Field, Cin
7-13-54	American	11-9	Municipal Stadium, Clev
7-12-55	National	6-5	County Stadium, Mil
7-10-56	National	7-3	Griffith Stadium, Wash
7-9-57	American	6-5	Busch Stadium, StL
7-8-58	American	4-3	Memorial Stadium, Balt
7-7-59	National	5-4	Forbes Field, Pitt
8-3-59	American	5-3	Memorial Coliseum, LA
7-11-60	National	5-3	Municipal Stadium, KC
7-13-60	National	6-0	Yankee Stadium, NY
7-11-61	National	5-4	Candlestick Park, SF
7-31-61	Tie*	1-1	Fenway Park, Bos
7-10-62	National	3-1	D.C. Stadium, Wash
7-30-62	American	9-4	Wrigley Field, Chi
7-9-63	National	5-3	Municipal Stadium, Clev
7-7-64	National	7-4	Shea Stadium, NY
7-13-65	National	6-5	Metropolitan Stadium, Minn
7-12-66	National	2-1	Busch Stadium, StL
7-11-67	National	2-1	Anaheim Stadium, Anaheim
7-9-68	National	1-0	Astrodome, Hou
7-23-69	National	9-3	R.F.K. Memorial Stadium, Wash
7-14-70	National	5-4	Riverfront Stadium, Cin
7-13-71	American	6-4	Tiger Stadium, Det
7-25-72	National	4-3	Atlanta Stadium, Atl
7-24-73	National	7-1	Royals Stadium, KC
7-23-74	National	7-2	Three Rivers Stadium, Pitt
7-15-75	National	6-3	County Stadium, Mil
7-13-76	National	7-1	Veterans Stadium, Phil
7-19-77	National	7-5	Yankee Stadium, NY
7-11-78	National	7-3	San Diego Stadium, SD
7-17-79	National	7-6	Kingdome, Sea
7-8-80	National	4-2	Dodger Stadium, LA
8-9-81	National	5-4	Municipal Stadium, Clev
7-13-82	National	4-1	Olympic Stadium, Mon
7-6-83	American	13-3	Comiskey Park, Chi
7-10-84	National	3-1	Candlestick Park, SF
7-16-85	National	6-1	Metrodome, Minn
7-15-86	American	3-2	Astrodome, Hou
7-14-87	National	2-0	Oakland Coliseum, Oak
7-12-88	American	2-1	Riverfront Stadium, Cin
7-11-89	American	5-3	Anaheim Stadium, Anaheim
7-10-90	American	2-0	Wrigley Field, Chi
7-9-91	American	4-2	SkyDome, Toronto

*Game called because of rain after 9 innings.

Most Valuable Players

1962	Maury Wills, LA	NL		1976	George Foster, Cin	NL
	Leon Wagner, LA	AL		1977	Don Sutton, LA	NL
1963	Willie Mays, SF	NL		1978	Steve Garvey, LA	NL
1964	Johnny Callison, Phil	NL		1979	Dave Parker, Pitt	NL
1965	Juan Marichal, SF	NL		1980	Ken Griffey, Cin	NL
1966	Brooks Robinson, Balt	AL		1981	Gary Carter, Mont	NL
1967	Tony Perez, Cin	NL		1982	Dave Concepcion, Cin	NL
1968	Willie Mays, SF	NL		1983	Fred Lynn, Calif	AL
1969	Willie McCovey, SF	NL		1984	Gary Carter, Mont	NL
1970	Carl Yastrzemski, Bos	AL		1985	LaMarr Hoyt, SD	NL
1971	Frank Robinson, Balt	AL		1986	Roger Clemens, Bos	AL
1972	Joe Morgan, Cin	NL		1987	Tim Raines, Mont	NL
1973	Bobby Bonds, SF	NL		1988	Terry Steinbach, Oak	AL
1974	Steve Garvey, LA	NL		1989	Bo Jackson, KC	AL
1975	Bill Madlock, Chi	NL		1990	Julio Franco, Tex	AL
	Jon Matlack, NY	NL		1991	Cal Ripken Jr, Balt	AL

Most Valuable Players

NATIONAL LEAGUE

Year	Name and Team	Position	Noteworthy
1911	Wildfire Schulte, Chi	Outfield	21 HR†, 121 RBI†, .300
1912	*Larry Doyle, NY	Second base	10 HR, 90 RBI, .330
1913	Jake Daubert, Bklyn	First base	52 RBI, .350†
1914	*Johnny Evers, Bos	Second base	F.A. .976†, .279
1915-23	No selection		
1924	Dazzy Vance, Bklyn	Pitcher	28†-6, 2.16 ERA†, 262 K†
1925	Rogers Hornsby, StL	Second base, Manager	39 HR†, 143 RBI†, .403†
1926	*Bob O'Farrell, StL	Catcher	7 HR, 68 RBI, .293
1927	*Paul Waner, Pitt	Outfield	237 hits†, 131 RBI†, .380†
1928	*Jim Bottomley, StL	First base	31 HR†, 136 RBI†, .325
1929	*Rogers Hornsby, Chi	Second base	39 HR, 149 RBI, 156 runs†, .380
1930	No selection		
1931	*Frankie Frisch, StL	Second base	4 HR, 82 RBI, 28 SB†, .311
1932	Chuck Klein, Phil	Outfield	38 HR†, 137 RBI, 226 hits†, .348
1933	*Carl Hubbell, NY	Pitcher	23†-12, 1.66 ERA†, 10 SO†
1934	*Dizzy Dean, StL	Pitcher	30†-7, 2.66 ERA, 195 K†
1935	*Gabby Hartnett, Chi	Catcher	13 HR, 91 RBI, .344
1936	*Carl Hubbell, NY	Pitcher	26†-6, 2.31 ERA†
1937	Joe Medwick, StL	Outfield	31 HR‡, 154 RBI†, 111 runs†, .374†
1938	Ernie Lombardi, Cin	Catcher	19 HR, 95 RBI, .342†
1939	*Bucky Walters, Cin	Pitcher	27†-11, 2.29 ERA†, 137 K‡
1940	*Frank McCormick, Cin	First base	19 HR, 127 RBI, 191 hits‡, .309
1941	*Dolph Camilli, Bklyn	First base	34 HR†, 120 RBI†, .285
1942	*Mort Cooper, StL	Pitcher	22†-7, 1.78 ERA†, 10 SO†
1943	*Stan Musial, StL	Outfield	13 HR, 81 RBI, 220 hits†, .357†
1944	*Marty Marion, StL	Shortstop	F.A. .972†, 63 RBI
1945	*Phil Cavarretta, Chi	First base	6 HR, 97 RBI, .355†
1946	*Stan Musial, StL	First base, Outfield	103 RBI, 124 runs†, 228 hits†, .365†
1947	Bob Elliott, Bos	Third base	22 HR, 113 RBI, .317
1948	Stan Musial, StL	Outfield	39 HR, 131 RBI†, .376†
1949	*Jackie Robinson, Bklyn	Second base	16 HR, 124 RBI, 37 SB†, .342†
1950	*Jim Konstanty, Phil	Pitcher	16-7, 22 saves†, 2.66 ERA
1951	Roy Campanella, Bklyn	Catcher	33 HR, 108 RBI, .325
1952	Hank Sauer, Chi	Outfield	37 HR‡, 121 RBI†, .270
1953	*Roy Campanella, Bklyn	Catcher	41 HR, 142 RBI†, .312
1954	*Willie Mays, NY	Outfield	41 HR, 110 RBI, 13 3B†, .345†
1955	*Roy Campanella, Bklyn	Catcher	32 HR, 107 RBI, .318
1956	*Don Newcombe, Bklyn	Pitcher	27†-7, 3.06 ERA
1957	*Hank Aaron, Mil	Outfield	44 HR†, 132 RBI†, .322
1958	Ernie Banks, Chi	Shortstop	47 HR†, 129 RBI†, .313
1959	Ernie Banks, Chi	Shortstop	45 HR, 143 RBI†, .304
1960	*Dick Groat, Pitt	Shortstop	2 HR, 50 RBI, .325†
1961	*Frank Robinson, Cin	Outfield	37 HR, 124 RBI, .323
1962	Maury Wills, LA	Shortstop	104 SB†, 208 hits, .299, GG
1963	*Sandy Koufax, LA	Pitcher	25‡-5, 1.88 ERA†, 306 K†
1964	*Ken Boyer, StL	Third Base	24 HR, 119 RBI†, .295
1965	Willie Mays, SF	Outfield	52 HR†, 112 RBI, .317, GG
1966	Roberto Clemente, Pitt	Outfield	29 HR, 119 RBI, 202 hits, .317, GG
1967	*Orlando Cepeda, StL	First base	25 HR, 111 RBI†, .325
1968	*Bob Gibson, StL	Pitcher	22-9, 1.12 ERA†, 268 K†, 13 SO†, GG
1969	Willie McCovey, SF	First base	45 HR†, 126 RBI†, .320
1970	*Johnny Bench, Cin	Catcher	45 HR†, 148 RBI†, .293, GG
1971	Joe Torre, StL	Third base	24 HR, 137 RBI†, .363†
1972	*Johnny Bench, Cin	Catcher	40 HR†, 125 RBI†, .270, GG
1973	Pete Rose, Cin	Outfield	5 HR, 64 RBI, .338†, 230 hits†
1974	*Steve Garvey, LA	First base	21 HR, 111 RBI, 200 hits, .312, GG
1975	*Joe Morgan, Cin	Second base	17 HR, 94 RBI, 67 SB, .327, GG
1976	*Joe Morgan, Cin	Second base	27 HR, 111 RBI, 60 SB, .320, GG
1977	George Foster, Cin	Outfield	52 HR†, 149 RBI†, .320
1978	Dave Parker, Pitt	Outfield	30 HR, 117 RBI, .334†, GG
1979	Keith Hernandez, StL	First base	11 HR, 105 RBI, 210 hits, .344†, GG
	*Willie Stargell, Pitt	First base	32 HR, 82 RBI, .281
1980	*Mike Schmidt, Phil	Third base	48 HR†, 121 RBI†, .286, GG

Most Valuable Players (*Cont.*)

NATIONAL LEAGUE (*Cont.*)

Year	Name and Team	Position	Noteworthy
1981	Mike Schmidt, Phil	Third base	31 HR†, 91 RBI†, 78 runs†, .316, GG
1982	*Dale Murphy, Atl	Outfield	36 HR, 109 RBI‡, .281, GG
1983	Dale Murphy, Atl	Outfield	36 HR, 121 RBI‡, .302, GG
1984	*Ryne Sandberg, Chi	Second base	19 HR, 84 RBI, 114 runs†, .314, GG
1985	*Willie McGee, StL	Outfield	10 HR, 82 RBI, 18 3B†, .353†, GG
1986	Mike Schmidt, Phil	Third base	37 HR†, 119 RBI†, .290, GG
1987	Andre Dawson, Chi	Outfield	49 HR†, 137 RBI†, .287, GG
1988	*Kirk Gibson, LA	Outfield	25 HR, 76 RBI, 106 runs, .290
1989	*Kevin Mitchell, SF	Outfield	47 HR†, 125 RBI†, .291
1990	*Barry Bonds, Pitt	Outfield	33 HR, 114 RBI, .301

AMERICAN LEAGUE

Year	Name and Team	Position	Noteworthy
1911	Ty Cobb, Det	Outfield	8 HR, 144 RBI, 24 3B†, .420†
1912	*Tris Speaker, Bos	Outfield	10 HR‡, 98 RBI, 53 2B†, .383
1913	Walter Johnson, Wash	Pitcher	36†-7, 1.09 ERA†, 11 SO†, 243 K†
1914	*Eddie Collins, Phil	Second base	2 HR, 85 RBI, 122 runs†, .344
1915-21	No selection		
1922	George Sisler, StL	First base	8 HR, 105 RBI, 246 hits†, .420†
1923	*Babe Ruth, NY	Outfield	41 HR†, 131 RBI†, .393
1924	*Walter Johnson, Wash	Pitcher	23†-7, 2.72 ERA†, 158 K†
1925	*Roger Peckinpaugh, Wash	Shortstop	4 HR, 64 RBI, .294
1926	George Burns, Clev	First base	114 RBI, 216 hits‡, 64 2B†, .358
1927	*Lou Gehrig, NY	First base	47 HR, 175 RBI†, 52 2B†, .373
1928	Mickey Cochrane, Phil	Catcher	10 HR, 57 RBI, .293
1929	No selection		
1930	No selection		
1931	*Lefty Grove, Phil	Pitcher	31†-4, 2.06 ERA†, 175 K†
1932	Jimmie Foxx, Phil	First base	58 HR†, 169 RBI†, 151 runs†, .364
1933	Jimmie Foxx, Phil	First base	48 HR†, 163 RBI†, .356†
1934	*Mickey Cochrane, Det	Catcher	2 HR, 76 RBI, .320
1935	*Hank Greenberg, Det	First base	36 HR‡, 170 RBI†, 203 hits, .328
1936	*Lou Gehrig, NY	First base	49 HR†, 152 RBI, 167 runs†, .354
1937	Charlie Gehringer, Det	Second base	14 HR, 96 RBI, 133 runs, .371†
1938	Jimmie Foxx, Bos	First base	50 HR, 175 RBI†, .349†
1939	*Joe DiMaggio, NY	Outfield	30 HR, 126 RBI, .381†
1940	*Hank Greenberg, Det	Outfield	41 HR†, 150 RBI†, 50 2B†, .340
1941	*Joe DiMaggio, NY	Outfield	30 HR, 125 RBI, .357
1942	*Joe Gordon, NY	Second base	18 HR, 103 RBI, .322
1943	*Spud Chandler, NY	Pitcher	20†-4, 1.64 ERA†, 5 SO‡
1944	Hal Newhouser, Det	Pitcher	29†-9, 2.22 ERA†, 187 K†
1945	*Hal Newhouser, Det	Pitcher	25†-9, 1.81 ERA†, 8 SO†, 212 K†
1946	*Ted Williams, Bos	Outfield	38 HR, 123 RBI, 142 runs†, .342
1947	*Joe DiMaggio, NY	Outfield	20 HR, 97 RBI, .315
1948	*Lou Boudreau, Clev	Shortstop	18 HR, 106 RBI, .355
1949	Ted Williams, Bos	Outfield	43 HR†, 159 RBI†, 150 runs†, .343
1950	*Phil Rizzuto, NY	Shortstop	125 runs, 200 hits, .324
1951	*Yogi Berra, NY	Catcher	27 HR, 88 RBI, .294
1952	Bobby Shantz, Phil	Pitcher	24†-7, 2.48 ERA
1953	Al Rosen, Clev	Third base	43 HR†, 145 RBI†, 115 runs†, .336
1954	Yogi Berra, NY	Catcher	22 HR, 125 RBI, .307
1955	Yogi Berra, NY	Catcher	27 HR, 108 RBI, .272
1956	*Mickey Mantle, NY	Outfield	52 HR†, 130 RBI†, 132 runs†, .353†
1957	*Mickey Mantle, NY	Outfield	34 HR, 94 RBI, 121 runs†, .365
1958	Jackie Jensen, Bos	Outfield	35 HR, 122 RBI†, .286
1959	*Nellie Fox, Chi	Second base	2 HR, 70 RBI, .306, GG
1960	*Roger Maris, NY	Outfield	39 HR, 112 RBI†, .283, GG
1961	*Roger Maris, NY	Outfield	61 HR†, 142 RBI†, .269
1962	*Mickey Mantle, NY	Outfield	30 HR, 89 RBI, .321, GG
1963	*Elston Howard, NY	Catcher	28 HR, 85 RBI, .287, GG
1964	Brooks Robinson, Balt	Third base	28 HR, 118 RBI†, .317, GG
1965	*Zoilo Versalles, Minn	Shortstop	126 runs†, 45 2B‡, 12 3B‡, GG

Most Valuable Players (*Cont.*)

AMERICAN LEAGUE (*Cont.*)

Year	Name and Team	Position	Noteworthy
1966	*Frank Robinson, Balt	Outfield	49 HR†, 122 RBI†, 122 runs†, .316†
1967	*Carl Yastrzemski, Bos	Outfield	44 HR‡, 121 RBI†, 112 runs†, .326†, GG
1968	*Denny McLain, Det	Pitcher	31†-6, 1.96 ERA, 280 K
1969	*Harmon Killebrew, Minn	Third base, First base	49 HR†, 140 RBI†, .276
1970	*Boog Powell, Balt	First base	35 HR, 114 RBI, .297
1971	*Vida Blue, Oak	Pitcher	24-8, 1.82 ERA†, 8 SO†, 301 K
1972	Dick Allen, Chi	First base	37 HR†, 113 RBI†, .308
1973	*Reggie Jackson, Oak	Outfield	32 HR†, 117 RBI†, 99 runs†, .293
1974	Jeff Burroughs, Tex	Outfield	25 HR, 118 RBI†, .301
1975	*Fred Lynn, Bos	Outfield	21 HR, 105 RBI, 103 runs†, .331, GG
1976	*Thurman Munson, NY	Catcher	17 HR, 105 RBI, .302
1977	Rod Carew, Minn	First base	100 RBI, 128 runs†, 239 hits†, .388†
1978	Jim Rice, Bos	Outfield, designated hitter	46 HR†, 139 RBI†, 213 hits†, .315
1979	*Don Baylor, Calif	Outfield, designated hitter	36 HR, 139 RBI†, 120 runs†, .296
1980	*George Brett, KC	Third base	24 HR, 118 RBI, .390†
1981	*Rollie Fingers, Mil	Pitcher	6-3, 28 saves†, 1.04 ERA
1982	*Robin Yount, Mil	Shortstop	29 HR, 114 RBI, 210 hits†, .331, GG
1983	*Cal Ripken, Balt	Shortstop	27 HR, 102 RBI, 121 runs†, 211 hits†, .318
1984	*Willie Hernandez, Det	Pitcher	9-3, 32 saves, 1.92 ERA
1985	Don Mattingly, NY	First base	35 HR, 145 RBI†, 48 2B†, .324, GG
1986	*Roger Clemens, Bos	Pitcher	24†-4, 2.48 ERA†, 238 K
1987	George Bell, Tor	Outfield	47 HR, 134 RBI†, .308
1988	*Jose Canseco, Oak	Outfield	42 HR†, 124 RBI†, 40 SB, .307
1989	Robin Yount, Mil	Outfield	21 HR, 103 RBI, 101 runs, .318
1990	*Rickey Henderson, Oak	Outfield	28 HR, 119 runs†, 65 SB†, .325

*Played for pennant or, after 1968, division winner.

†Led league.

‡Tied for league lead.

Notes: 2B=doubles; 3B=triples; F.A.=fielding average; GG=won Gold Glove, award begun in 1957; K=strikeouts; SO=shutouts; SB=stolen bases.

Rookie of the Year

NATIONAL LEAGUE		AMERICAN LEAGUE	
1947*	Jackie Robinson, Bklyn (1B)	1949	Roy Sievers, StL (OF)
1948*	Alvin Dark, Bos (SS)	1950	Walt Dropo, Bos (1B)
1949	Don Newcombe, Bklyn (P)	1951	Gil McDougald, NY (3B)
1950	Sam Jethroe, Bos (OF)	1952	Harry Byrd, Phil (P)
1951	Willie Mays, NY (OF)	1953	Harvey Kuenn, Det (SS)
1952	Joe Black, Bklyn (P)	1954	Bob Grim, NY (P)
1953	Junior Gilliam, Bklyn (2B)	1955	Herb Score, Clev (P)
1954	Wally Moon, StL (OF)	1956	Luis Aparicio, Chi (SS)
1955	Bill Virdon, StL (OF)	1957	Tony Kubek, NY (OF, SS)
1956	Frank Robinson, Cin (OF)	1958	Albie Pearson, Wash (OF)
1957	Jack Sanford, Phil (P)	1959	Bob Allison, Wash (OF)
1958	Orlando Cepeda, SF (1B)	1960	Ron Hansen, Balt (SS)
1959	Willie McCovey, SF (1B)	1961	Don Schwall, Bos (P)
1960	Frank Howard, LA (OF)	1962	Tom Tresh, NY (SS)
1961	Billy Williams, Chi (OF)	1963	Gary Peters, Chi (P)
1962	Ken Hubbs, Chi (2B)	1964	Tony Oliva, Minn (OF)
1963	Pete Rose, Cin (2B)	1965	Curt Blefary, Balt (OF)
1964	Dick Allen, Phil (3B)	1966	Tommie Agee, Chi (OF)
1965	Jim Lefebvre, LA (2B)	1967	Rod Carew, Minn (2B)
1966	Tommy Helms, Cin (2B)	1968	Stan Bahnsen, NY (P)
1967	Tom Seaver, NY (P)	1969	Lou Piniella, KC (OF)
1968	Johnny Bench, Cin (C)	1970	Thurman Munson, NY (C)
1969	Ted Sizemore, LA (2B)	1971	Chris Chambliss, Clev (1B)
1970	Carl Morton, Mont (P)	1972	Carlton Fisk, Bos (C)
1971	Earl Williams, Atl (C)	1973	Al Bumbry, Balt (OF)

Rookie of the Year (*Cont.*)

NATIONAL LEAGUE

Year	Player
1972	Jon Matlack, NY (P)
1973	Gary Matthews, SF (OF)
1974	Bake McBride, StL (OF)
1975	John Montefusco, SF (P)
1976	Pat Zachry, Cin (P)
	Butch Metzger, SD (P)
1977	Andre Dawson, Mont (OF)
1978	Bob Horner, Atl (3B)
1979	Rick Sutcliffe, LA (P)
1980	Steve Howe, LA (P)
1981	Fernando Valenzuela, LA (P)
1982	Steve Sax, LA (2B)
1983	Darryl Strawberry, NY (OF)
1984	Dwight Gooden, NY (P)
1985	Vince Coleman, StL (OF)
1986	Todd Worrell, StL (P)
1987	Benito Santiago, SD (C)
1988	Chris Sabo, Cin (3B)
1989	Jerome Walton, Chi (OF)
1990	Dave Justice, Atl (OF)

AMERICAN LEAGUE

Year	Player
1974	Mike Hargrove, Tex (1B)
1975	Fred Lynn, Bos (OF)
1976	Mark Fidrych, Det (P)
1977	Eddie Murray, Balt (DH)
1978	Lou Whitaker, Det (2B)
1979	Alfredo Griffin, Tor (SS)
	John Castino, Minn (3B)
1980	Joe Charboneau, Clev (OF)
1981	Dave Righetti, NY (P)
1982	Cal Ripken, Balt (SS)
1983	Ron Kittle, Chi (OF)
1984	Alvin Davis, Sea (1B)
1985	Ozzie Guillen, Chi (SS)
1986	Jose Canseco, Oak (OF)
1987	Mark McGwire, Oak (1B)
1988	Walt Weiss, Oak (SS)
1989	Gregg Olson, Balt (P)
1990	Sandy Alomar Jr, Clev (C)

*Just one selection for both leagues.

Cy Young Award

Year	Player	W-L	Sv	ERA		Year	Player	W-L	Sv	ERA
1956	*Don Newcombe, Bklyn (NL)	27-7	0	3.06		1962	Don Drysdale, LA (NL)	25-9	1	2.83
1957	Warren Spahn, Mil (NL)	21-11	3	2.69		1963	*Sandy Koufax, LA (NL)	25-5	0	1.88
1958	Bob Turley, NY (AL)	21-7	1	2.97		1964	Dean Chance, LA (AL)	20-9	4	1.65
1959	Early Wynn, Chi (AL)	22-10	0	3.17		1965	Sandy Koufax, LA (NL)	26-8	2	2.04
1960	Vernon Law, Pitt (NL)	20-9	0	3.08		1966	Sandy Koufax, LA (NL)	27-9	0	1.73
1961	Whitey Ford, NY (AL)	25-4	0	3.21						

NATIONAL LEAGUE

Year	Player	W-L	Sv	ERA
1967	Mike McCormick, SF	22-10	0	2.85
1968	*Bob Gibson, StL	22-9	0	1.12
1969	Tom Seaver, NY	25-7	0	2.21
1970	Bob Gibson, StL	23-7	0	3.12
1971	Ferguson Jenkins, Chi	24-13	0	2.77
1972	Steve Carlton, Phil	27-10	0	1.97
1973	Tom Seaver, NY	19-10	0	2.08
1974	Mike Marshall, LA	15-12	21	2.42
1975	Tom Seaver, NY	22-9	0	2.38
1976	Randy Jones, SD	22-14	0	2.74
1977	Steve Carlton, Phil	23-10	0	2.64
1978	Gaylord Perry, SD	21-6	0	2.72
1979	Bruce Sutter, Chi	6-6	37	2.23
1980	Steve Carlton, Phil	24-9	0	2.34
1981	F. Valenzuela, LA	13-7	0	2.48
1982	Steve Carlton, Phil	23-11	0	3.10
1983	John Denny, Phil	19-6	0	2.37
1984	†Rick Sutcliffe, Chi	16-1	0	2.69
1985	Dwight Gooden, NY	24-4	0	1.53
1986	Mike Scott, Hou	18-10	0	2.22
1987	Steve Bedrosian, Phil	5-3	40	2.83
1988	Orel Hershiser, LA	23-8	1	2.26
1989	Mark Davis, SD	4-3	44	1.85
1990	Doug Drabek, Pitt	22-6	0	2.76

AMERICAN LEAGUE

Year	Player	W-L	Sv	ERA
1967	Jim Lonborg, Bos	22-9	0	3.16
1968	*Denny McLain, Det	31-6	0	1.96
1969	Denny McLain, Det	24-9	0	2.80
	Mike Cuellar, Balt	23-11	0	2.38
1970	Jim Perry, Minn	24-12	0	3.03
1971	*Vida Blue, Oak	24-8	0	1.82
1972	Gaylord Perry, Clev	24-16	1	1.92
1973	Jim Palmer, Balt	22-9	1	2.40
1974	Catfish Hunter, Oak	25-12	0	2.49
1975	Jim Palmer, Balt	23-11	1	2.09
1976	Jim Palmer, Balt	22-13	0	2.51
1977	Sparky Lyle, NY	13-5	26	2.17
1978	Ron Guidry, NY	25-3	0	1.74
1979	Mike Flanagan, Balt	23-9	0	3.08
1980	Steve Stone, Balt	25-7	0	3.23
1981	*Rollie Fingers, Mil	6-3	28	1.04
1982	Pete Vuckovich, Mil	18-6	0	3.34
1983	LaMarr Hoyt, Chi	24-10	0	3.66
1984	*Willie Hernandez, Det	9-3	32	1.92
1985	Bret Saberhagen, KC	20-6	0	2.87
1986	*Roger Clemens, Bos	24-4	0	2.48
1987	Roger Clemens, Bos	20-9	0	2.97
1988	Frank Viola, Minn	24-7	0	2.64
1989	Bret Saberhagen, KC	23-6	0	2.16
1990	Bob Welch, Oak	27-6	0	2.95

*Pitchers who won the MVP and Cy Young awards in the same season.

†NL games only. Sutcliffe pitched 15 games with Cleveland before being traded to the Cubs.

Career Individual Batting

GAMES

Pete Rose	3562
Carl Yastrzemski	3308
Hank Aaron	3298
Ty Cobb	3034
Stan Musial	3026
Willie Mays	2992
Rusty Staub	2951
Brooks Robinson	2896
Al Kaline	2834
Eddie Collins	2826
Reggie Jackson	2820
Frank Robinson	2808
Tris Speaker	2789
Honus Wagner	2789
Tony Perez	2777
Mel Ott	2734
Graig Nettles	2700
Darrell Evans	2687
Rabbit Maranville	2670
Joe Morgan	2649

AT BATS

Pete Rose	14053
Hank Aaron	12364
Carl Yastrzemski	11988
Ty Cobb	11429
Stan Musial	10972
Willie Mays	10881
Brooks Robinson	10654
Honus Wagner	10441
Lou Brock	10332
Luis Aparicio	10230
Tris Speaker	10208
Al Kaline	10116
Rabbit Maranville	10078
Frank Robinson	10006
Robin Yount	9997
Eddie Collins	9949
Reggie Jackson	9864
Tony Perez	9778
Rusty Staub	9720
Vada Pinson	9645

HOME RUNS

Hank Aaron	755
Babe Ruth	714
Willie Mays	660
Frank Robinson	586
Harmon Killebrew	573
Reggie Jackson	563
Mike Schmidt	548
Mickey Mantle	536
Jimmie Foxx	534
Ted Williams	521
Willie McCovey	521
Eddie Mathews	512
Ernie Banks	512
Mel Ott	511
Lou Gehrig	493
Willie Stargell	475
Stan Musial	475
Carl Yastrzemski	452
Dave Kingman	442
Billy Williams	426

HITS

Pete Rose	4256
Ty Cobb	4191
Hank Aaron	3771
Stan Musial	3630
Tris Speaker	3515
Carl Yastrzemski	3419
Honus Wagner	3418
Eddie Collins	3311
Willie Mays	3283
Nap Lajoie	3244
Paul Waner	3152
Rod Carew	3053
Lou Brock	3023
Al Kaline	3007
Roberto Clemente	3000
Cap Anson	3000
Sam Rice	2987
Sam Crawford	2964
Willie Keeler	2947
Frank Robinson	2943

BATTING AVERAGE

Ty Cobb	.367
Rogers Hornsby	.358
Joe Jackson	.356
Ed Delahanty	.346
Wade Boggs	.345
Ted Williams	.344
Tris Speaker	.344
Billy Hamilton	.344
Willie Keeler	.343
Dan Brouthers	.342
Babe Ruth	.342
Harry Heilmann	.342
Pete Browning	.341
Bill Terry	.341
George Sisler	.340
Lou Gehrig	.340
Jesse Burkett	.339
Nap Lajoie	.338
Riggs Stephenson	.336
Al Simmons	.334

RUNS

Ty Cobb	2245
Babe Ruth	2174
Hank Aaron	2174
Pete Rose	2165
Willie Mays	2062
Stan Musial	1949
Lou Gehrig	1888
Tris Speaker	1881
Mel Ott	1859
Frank Robinson	1829
Eddie Collins	1818
Carl Yastrzemski	1816
Ted Williams	1798
Charlie Gehringer	1774
Jimmie Foxx	1751
Honus Wagner	1735
Willie Keeler	1727
Cap Anson	1719
Jesse Burkett	1718
Billy Hamilton	1692

DOUBLES

Tris Speaker	792
Pete Rose	746
Stan Musial	725
Ty Cobb	724
Nap Lajoie	658
Carl Yastrzemski	646
Honus Wagner	643
Hank Aaron	624
Paul Waner	603
George Brett	599
Charlie Gehringer	574
Harry Heilmann	542
Rogers Hornsby	541
Joe Medwick	540
Al Simmons	539
Lou Gehrig	535
Al Oliver	529
Cap Anson	528
Frank Robinson	528
Ted Williams	525

TRIPLES

Sam Crawford	312
Ty Cobb	297
Honus Wagner	252
Jake Beckley	243
Roger Connor	233
Tris Speaker	223
Fred Clarke	220
Dan Brouthers	205
Joe Kelley	194
Paul Waner	190
Bid McPhee	188
Eddie Collins	187
Sam Rice	184
Ed Delahanty	183
Jesse Burkett	183
Edd Roush	182
Ed Konetchy	181
Buck Ewing	178
Rabbit Maranville	177
Stan Musial	177

BASES ON BALLS

Babe Ruth	2056
Ted Williams	2019
Joe Morgan	1865
Carl Yastrzemski	1845
Mickey Mantle	1734
Mel Ott	1708
Eddie Yost	1614
Darrell Evans	1605
Stan Musial	1599
Pete Rose	1566
Harmon Killebrew	1559
Lou Gehrig	1508
Mike Schmidt	1507
Eddie Collins	1503
Willie Mays	1463
Jimmie Foxx	1452
Eddie Mathews	1444
Frank Robinson	1420
Hank Aaron	1402
Dwight Evans	1391

Career Individual Batting (*Cont.*)

RUNS BATTED IN		STOLEN BASES		TOTAL BASES	
Hank Aaron	2297	Rickey Henderson	994	Hank Aaron	6856
Babe Ruth	2211	Lou Brock	938	Stan Musial	6134
Lou Gehrig	1990	Billy Hamilton	915	Willie Mays	6066
Ty Cobb	1961	Ty Cobb	892	Ty Cobb	5863
Stan Musial	1951	Eddie Collins	743	Babe Ruth	5793
Jimmie Foxx	1921	Arlie Latham	739	Pete Rose	5752
Willie Mays	1903	Max Carey	738	Carl Yastrzemski	5539
Mel Ott	1861	Honus Wagner	703	Frank Robinson	5373
Carl Yastrzemski	1844	Joe Morgan	689	Tris Speaker	5104
Ted Williams	1839	Tim Raines	685	Lou Gehrig	5059
Al Simmons	1827	Tom Brown	657	Mel Ott	5041
Frank Robinson	1812	Bert Campaneris	649	Jimmie Foxx	4956
Honus Wagner	1732	Willie Wilson	632	Ted Williams	4884
Cap Anson	1715	George Davis	616	Honus Wagner	4868
Reggie Jackson	1702	Dummy Hoy	594	Al Kaline	4852
Tony Perez	1652	Maury Wills	586	Reggie Jackson	4834
Ernie Banks	1636	Vince Coleman	586	Rogers Hornsby	4712
Goose Goslin	1609	Davey Lopes	557	Ernie Banks	4706
Dave Winfield	1602	Cesar Cedeno	550	Al Simmons	4685

SLUGGING AVERAGE		PINCH HITS		STRIKEOUTS	
Babe Ruth	.690	Manny Mota	150	Reggie Jackson	2597
Ted Williams	.634	Smoky Burgess	145	Willie Stargell	1936
Lou Gehrig	.632	Greg Gross	143	Mike Schmidt	1883
Jimmie Foxx	.609	Jose Morales	123	Tony Perez	1867
Hank Greenberg	.605	Jerry Lynch	116	Dave Kingman	1816
Joe DiMaggio	.579	Red Lucas	114	Bobby Bonds	1757
Rogers Hornsby	.577	Steve Braun	113	Lou Brock	1730
Johnny Mize	.562	Terry Crowley	108	Dale Murphy	1720
Stan Musial	.559	Gates Brown	107	Mickey Mantle	1710
Willie Mays	.557	Denny Walling	107	Harmon Killebrew	1699
Mickey Mantle	.557	Mike Lum	103	Dwight Evans	1697
Hank Aaron	.555	Rusty Staub	100	Lee May	1570
Ralph Kiner	.548	Vic Davalillo	95	Dick Allen	1556
Hack Wilson	.545	Larry Biittner	95	Willie McCovey	1550
Chuck Klein	.543	Jerry Hairston	94	Frank Robinson	1532
Duke Snider	.540	Jim Dwyer	94	Willie Mays	1526
Frank Robinson	.537	Dave Philley	93	Rick Monday	1513
Al Simmons	.535	Joel Youngblood	93	Greg Luzinski	1495
Dick Allen	.534	Jay Johnstone	92	Eddie Mathews	1487

Career Individual Pitching

GAMES		INNINGS PITCHED		WINS	
Hoyt Wilhelm	1070	Cy Young	7356	Cy Young	511
Kent Tekulve	1050	Pud Galvin	5941	Walter Johnson	416
Lindy McDaniel	987	Walter Johnson	5923	Christy Mathewson	373
Rollie Fingers	944	Phil Niekro	5403	Grover Alexander	373
Gene Garber	931	Gaylord Perry	5351	Warren Spahn	363
Cy Young	906	Don Sutton	5280	Kid Nichols	361
Sparky Lyle	899	Warren Spahn	5244	Pud Galvin	361
Jim Kaat	898	Steve Carlton	5217	Tim Keefe	342
Goose Gossage	897	Grover Alexander	5189	Steve Carlton	329
Don McMahon	874	Nolan Ryan	5163	Eddie Plank	327
Phil Niekro	864	Kid Nichols	5084	John Clarkson	326
Roy Face	848	Tim Keefe	5061	Don Sutton	324
Tug McGraw	824	Bert Blyleven	4837	Phil Niekro	318
Walter Johnson	801	Mickey Welch	4802	Gaylord Perry	314
Gaylord Perry	777	Tom Seaver	4783	Nolan Ryan	314
Charlie Hough	776	Christy Mathewson	4782	Old Hoss Radbourn	311
Don Sutton	774	Tommy John	4708	Tom Seaver	311
Nolan Ryan	767	Robin Roberts	4689	Mickey Welch	308
Darold Knowles	765	Early Wynn	4564	Lefty Grove	300
Tommy John	760	Tony Mullane	4540	Early Wynn	300

Career Individual Pitching (*Cont.*)

LOSSES

Cy Young	.315
Pud Galvin	.308
Walter Johnson	.279
Nolan Ryan	.278
Phil Niekro	.274
Gaylord Perry	.265
Jack Powell	.256
Don Sutton	.256
Eppa Rixey	.251
Robin Roberts	.245
Warren Spahn	.245
Early Wynn	.244
Steve Carlton	.244
Bert Blyleven	.238
Jim Kaat	.237
Gus Weyhing	.235
Tommy John	.231
Ted Lyons	.230
Bob Friend	.230
Ferguson Jenkins	.226

SAVES

Rollie Fingers	.341
Jeff Reardon	.327
Lee Smith	.312
Goose Gossage	.308
Bruce Sutter	.300
Dave Righetti	.248
Dan Quisenberry	.244
Sparky Lyle	.238
Hoyt Wilhelm	.227
Gene Garber	.218
Dave Smith	.216
John Franco	.211
Roy Face	.193
Dennis Eckersley	.188
Mike Marshall	.188
Tom Henke	.186
Kent Tekulve	.184
Steve Bedrosian	.184
Tug McGraw	.180
Ron Perranoski	.179

SHUTOUTS

Walter Johnson	110
Grover Alexander	90
Christy Mathewson	80
Cy Young	76
Eddie Plank	69
Warren Spahn	63
Nolan Ryan	61
Tom Seaver	61
Bert Blyleven	60
Don Sutton	58
Ed Walsh	57
Three Finger Brown	57
Pud Galvin	57
Bob Gibson	56
Steve Carlton	55
Jim Palmer	53
Gaylord Perry	53
Juan Marichal	52
Rube Waddell	50
Vic Willis	50

WINNING PERCENTAGE

Dwight Gooden	.714
Bob Caruthers	.692
Dave Foutz	.690
Whitey Ford	.690
Roger Clemens	.687
Lefty Grove	.680
Vic Raschi	.667
Christy Mathewson	.665
Larry Corcoran	.663
Sam Leever	.658
Sal Maglie	.657
Sandy Koufax	.655
Johnny Allen	.654
Ron Guidry	.651
Lefty Gomez	.649
Three Finger Brown	.649
John Clarkson	.648
Dizzy Dean	.644
Grover Alexander	.642
Deacon Phillippe	.639

EARNED RUN AVERAGE

Ed Walsh	1.82
Addie Joss	1.88
Three Finger Brown	2.06
Monte Ward	2.10
Christy Mathewson	2.13
Rube Waddell	2.16
Walter Johnson	2.17
Orval Overall	2.24
Tommy Bond	2.25
Will White	2.28
Ed Reulbach	2.28
Jim Scott	2.32
Eddie Plank	2.34
Larry Corcoran	2.36
Eddie Cicotte	2.37
George McQuillan	2.38
Ed Killian	2.38
Doc White	2.38
Nap Rucker	2.42
Jeff Tesreau	2.43

COMPLETE GAMES

Cy Young	750
Pud Galvin	639
Tim Keefe	557
Kid Nichols	532
Walter Johnson	531
Mickey Welch	525
Old Hoss Radbourn	489
John Clarkson	485
Tony Mullane	469
Jim McCormick	466
Gus Weyhing	448
Grover Alexander	438
Christy Mathewson	435
Jack Powell	422
Eddie Plank	412
Will White	394
Amos Rusie	392
Vic Willis	388
Warren Spahn	382
Jim Whitney	377

STRIKEOUTS

Nolan Ryan	5511
Steve Carlton	4136
Tom Seaver	3640
Bert Blyleven	3631
Don Sutton	3574
Gaylord Perry	3534
Walter Johnson	3508
Phil Niekro	3342
Ferguson Jenkins	3192
Bob Gibson	3117
Jim Bunning	2855
Mickey Lolich	2832
Cy Young	2796
Warren Spahn	2583
Bob Feller	2581
Jerry Koosman	2556
Frank Tanana	2537
Tim Keefe	2527
Christy Mathewson	2502
Don Drysdale	2486

BASES ON BALLS

Nolan Ryan	2686
Steve Carlton	1833
Phil Niekro	1809
Early Wynn	1775
Bob Feller	1764
Bobo Newsom	1732
Amos Rusie	1704
Gus Weyhing	1566
Red Ruffing	1541
Charlie Hough	1476
Bump Hadley	1442
Warren Spahn	1434
Earl Whitehill	1431
Tony Mullane	1409
Sad Sam Jones	1396
Tom Seaver	1390
Gaylord Perry	1379
Mike Torrez	1371
Walter Johnson	1355
Don Sutton	1343

Individual Batting (Single Season)

HITS

George Sisler, 1920 257
Bill Terry, 1930 254
Lefty O'Doul, 1929..................254
Al Simmons, 1925 253
Rogers Hornsby, 1922 250
Chuck Klein, 1930 250
Ty Cobb, 1911 248
George Sisler, 1922 246
Willie Keeler, 1897 243
Babe Herman, 1930 241
Heinie Manush, 1928 241

BATTING AVERAGE

Hugh Duffy, 1894 438
Tip O'Neill, 1887....................435
Willie Keeler, 1897 432
Ross Barnes, 1876................429
Rogers Hornsby, 1924 424
Jesse Burkett, 1895..............423
Nap Lajoie, 1901 422
George Sisler, 1922 420
Ty Cobb, 1911 420
Tuck Turner, 1894................416

DOUBLES

Earl Webb, 1931......................67
George Burns, 1926 64
Joe Medwick, 1936..................64
Hank Greenberg, 1934 63
Paul Waner, 1932....................62
Charlie Gehringer, 1936 60
Tris Speaker, 1923 59
Chuck Klein, 1930 59
Billy Herman, 1936..................57
Billy Herman, 1935 57

TOTAL BASES

Babe Ruth, 1921 457
Rogers Hornsby, 1922 450
Lou Gehrig, 1927....................447
Chuck Klein, 1930 445
Jimmie Foxx, 1932 438
Stan Musial, 1948..................429
Hack Wilson, 1930 423
Chuck Klein, 1932 420
Lou Gehrig, 1930....................419
Joe DiMaggio, 1937 418

TRIPLES

Owen Wilson, 1912................ 36
Heinie Reitz, 1894.................. 31
Dave Orr, 1886........................ 31
Perry Werden, 1893................ 29
Harry Davis, 1897.................. 28
Sam Thompson, 1894............ 27
George Davis, 1893................ 27
Jimmy Williams, 1899 27
George Treadway, 1894 26
Long John Reilly, 1890 26
Joe Jackson, 1912 26
Sam Crawford, 1914 26
Kiki Cuyler, 1925 26

HOME RUNS

Roger Maris, 1961 61
Babe Ruth, 1927 60
Babe Ruth, 1921 59
Hank Greenberg, 1938 58
Jimmie Foxx, 1932.................. 58
Hack Wilson, 1930 56
Babe Ruth, 1920.................... 54
Mickey Mantle, 1961 54
Babe Ruth, 1928.................... 54
Ralph Kiner, 1949 54

RUNS BATTED IN

Hack Wilson, 1930 190
Lou Gehrig, 1931 184
Hank Greenberg, 1937 183
Jimmie Foxx, 1938................ 175
Lou Gehrig, 1927 175
Lou Gehrig, 1930 174
Babe Ruth, 1921 171
Hank Greenberg, 1935 170
Chuck Klein, 1930 170
Jimmie Foxx, 1932................ 169

STRIKEOUTS

Bobby Bonds, 1970................ 189
Bobby Bonds, 1969................ 187
Rob Deer, 1987...................... 186
Pete Incaviglia, 1986.............. 185
Cecil Fielder, 1990 182
Mike Schmidt, 1975 180
Rob Deer, 1986...................... 179
Jose Canseco, 1986 175
Dave Nicholson, 1963............ 175
Gorman Thomas, 1979.......... 175
Rob Deer, 1991...................... 175

RUNS

Billy Hamilton, 1894.............. 196
Babe Ruth, 1921.................... 177
Tom Brown, 1891 177
Joe Kelley, 1894.................... 167
Tip O'Neill, 1887.................... 167
Lou Gehrig, 1936.................. 167
Billy Hamilton, 1895.............. 166
Willie Keeler, 1894................ 165
Babe Ruth, 1928.................... 163
Lou Gehrig, 1931.................. 163
Arlie Latham, 1887................ 163

STOLEN BASES

Rickey Henderson, 1982 130
Lou Brock, 1974.................... 118
Vince Coleman, 1985 110
Vince Coleman, 1987 109
Rickey Henderson, 1983 108
Vince Coleman, 1986 107
Maury Wills, 1962.................. 104
Rickey Henderson, 1980 100
Ron LeFlore, 1980.................. 97
Ty Cobb, 1915 96
Omar Moreno, 1980................ 96

BASES ON BALLS

Babe Ruth, 1923.................... 170
Ted Williams, 1947 162
Ted Williams, 1949 162
Ted Williams, 1946 156
Eddie Yost, 1956 151
Eddie Joost, 1949.................. 149
Babe Ruth, 1920.................... 148
Jimmy Wynn, 1969................ 148
Eddie Stanky, 1945................ 148
Jimmy Sheckard, 1911 147

SLUGGING AVERAGE

Babe Ruth, 1920....................847
Babe Ruth, 1921....................846
Babe Ruth, 1927....................772
Lou Gehrig, 1927....................765
Babe Ruth, 1923....................764
Rogers Hornsby, 1925............756
Jimmie Foxx, 1932.................749
Babe Ruth, 1924....................739
Babe Ruth, 1926....................737
Ted Williams, 1941 735

Making Contact

Who was the greatest contact hitter in baseball? A lot of people cite Ty Cobb or, among power hitters, Ted Williams, but the honor has to go to Joe Sewell, the Hall of Fame shortstop and .312 lifetime hitter who played for the Cleveland Indians from 1920–30 and for the New York Yankees from 1931–33. Sewell struck out just 114 times in 7,132 at bats—a phenomenal ratio of one whiff for every 62.5 trips to the plate. In 1925 Sewell came to the plate 608 times and had just four strikeouts. Cobb ranks second among high average hitters with a strikeout for every 32 at bats. Among sluggers with 500 or more home runs, Williams leads the way with a strikeout once every 10.8 at bats. Reggie Jackson, by contrast, whiffed once for every 3.7 trips to the plate.

Individual Pitching (Single Season)

GAMES

Mike Marshall, 1974 106
Kent Tekulve, 1979 94
Mike Marshall, 1973 92
Kent Tekulve, 1978 91
Wayne Granger, 1969 90
Mike Marshall, 1979 90
Kent Tekulve, 1987 90
Mark Eichhorn, 1987 89
Wilbur Wood, 1968 88
Rob Murphy, 1987 87

GAMES STARTED

Amos Rusie, 1893 52
Jack Chesbro, 1904 51
Frank Killen, 1896 50
Amos Rusie, 1894 50
Pink Hawley, 1895 50
Ted Breitenstein, 1894 50
Ted Breitenstein, 1895 50
Ed Walsh, 1908 49
Wilbur Wood, 1972 49
Joe McGinnity, 1903 48
Jouett Meekin, 1894 48
Frank Killen, 1893 48
Wilbur Wood, 1973 48

INNINGS PITCHED

Amos Rusie, 1893 482
Ed Walsh, 1908 464
Jack Chesbro, 1904 455
Ted Breitenstein, 1894 447
Pink Hawley, 1895 444
Amos Rusie, 1894 444
Joe McGinnity, 1903 434
Frank Killen, 1896 432
Ted Breitenstein, 1895 430
Kid Nichols, 1893 425

WINS

Jack Chesbro, 1904 41
Ed Walsh, 1908 40
Christy Mathewson, 1908 37
Walter Johnson, 1913 36
Jouett Meekin, 1894 36
Amos Rusie, 1894 36
Joe McGinnity, 1904 35
Cy Young, 1895 35
Smoky Joe Wood, 1912 34
Frank Killen, 1893 34

LOSSES

Red Donahue, 1897 33
Jim Hughey, 1899 30
Ted Breitenstein, 1895 30
Vic Willis, 1905 29
Bill Hart, 1896 29
Jack Taylor, 1898 29
Still Bill Hill, 1896 28
Duke Esper, 1893 28
Paul Derringer, 1933 27
Bill Hart, 1897 27
George Bell, 1910 27
Willie Sudhoff, 1898 27
Dummy Taylor, 1901 27
Pink Hawley, 1894 27

WINNING PERCENTAGE

Roy Face, 1959 .... .947
Johnny Allen, 1937 .... .938
Ron Guidry, 1978 .... .893
Freddie Fitzsimmons, 1940 ... .889
Lefty Grove, 1931 .... .886
Bob Stanley, 1978 .... .882
Preacher Roe, 1951 .... .880
Tom Seaver, 1981 .... .875
Smoky Joe Wood, 1912 .... .872
David Cone, 1988 .... .870

SAVES

Bobby Thigpen, 1990 57
Dennis Eckersley, 1990 48
Lee Smith, 1991 47
Bryan Harvey, 1991 46
Dave Righetti, 1986 46
Bruce Sutter, 1984 45
Dan Quisenberry, 1983 45
Dennis Eckersley, 1988 45
Dan Quisenberry, 1984 44
Mark Davis, 1989 44
Doug Jones, 1990 43
Jeff Reardon, 1988 42

EARNED RUN AVERAGE

Dutch Leonard, 1914 .... 1.01
Three Finger Brown, 1906 ... 1.04
Walter Johnson, 1913 .... 1.09
Bob Gibson, 1968 .... 1.12
Christy Mathewson, 1909 ..... 1.14
Jack Pfiester, 1907 .... 1.15
Addie Joss, 1908 .... 1.16
Carl Lundgren, 1907 .... 1.17
Grover Alexander, 1915 .... 1.22
Cy Young, 1908 .... 1.26

SHUTOUTS

Grover Alexander, 1916 16
Bob Gibson, 1968 13
Jack Coombs, 1910 13
Grover Alexander, 1915 12
Christy Mathewson, 1908 12
Dean Chance, 1964 11
Walter Johnson, 1913 11
Sandy Koufax, 1963 11
Ed Walsh, 1908 11

COMPLETE GAMES

Amos Rusie, 1893 50
Jack Chesbro, 1904 48
Ted Breitenstein, 1894 46
Ted Breitenstein, 1895 46
Vic Willis, 1902 45
Amos Rusie, 1894 45
Kid Nichols, 1893 44
Cy Young, 1894 44
Joe McGinnity, 1903 44
Pink Hawley, 1895 44
Frank Killen, 1896 44

STRIKEOUTS

Nolan Ryan, 1973 383
Sandy Koufax, 1965 382
Nolan Ryan, 1974 367
Rube Waddell, 1904 349
Bob Feller, 1946 348
Nolan Ryan, 1977 341
Nolan Ryan, 1972 329
Nolan Ryan, 1976 327
Sam McDowell, 1965 325
Sandy Koufax, 1966 317

BASES ON BALLS

Amos Rusie, 1893 218
Cy Seymour, 1898 213
Bob Feller, 1938 208
Nolan Ryan, 1977 204
Nolan Ryan, 1974 202
Amos Rusie, 1894 200
Bob Feller, 1941 194
Bobo Newsom, 1938 192
Ted Breitenstein, 1894 191
Tony Mullane, 1893 189

Manager of the Year

NATIONAL LEAGUE

1983 .... Tommy Lasorda, LA
1984 .... Jim Frey, Chi
1985 .... Whitey Herzog, StL
1986 .... Hal Lanier, Hou
1987 .... Buck Rodgers, Mont
1988 .... Tommy Lasorda, LA
1989 .... Don Zimmer, Chi
1990 .... Jim Leyland, Pitt

AMERICAN LEAGUE

1983 .... Tony La Russa, Chi
1984 .... Sparky Anderson, Det
1985 .... Bobby Cox, Tor
1986 .... John McNamara, Bos
1987 .... Sparky Anderson, Det
1988 .... Tony La Russa, Oak
1989 .... Frank Robison, Balt
1990 .... Jeff Torborg, Chi

Baseball Hall of Fame

PLAYER

Name	Position	Career Dates	Year Selected
Hank Aaron	OF	1954-76	1982
Grover Alexander	P	1911-30	1938
Cap Anson	1B	1876-97	1939
Luis Aparicio	SS	1956-73	1984
Luke Appling	SS	1930-50	1964
Earl Averill	OF	1929-41	1975
Frank Baker	3B	1908-22	1955
Dave Bancroft	SS	1915-30	1971
Ernie Banks	SS-1B	1953-71	1977
Jake Beckley	1B	1888-1907	1971
Cool Papa Bell*	OF		1974
Johnny Bench	C	1967-83	1989
Chief Bender	P	1903-25	1953
Yogi Berra	C	1946-65	1972
Jim Bottomley	1B	1922-37	1974
Lou Boudreau	SS	1938-52	1970
Roger Bresnahan	C	1897-1915	1945
Lou Brock	OF	1961-79	1985
Dan Brouthers	1B	1879-1904	1945
Three Finger Brown	P	1903-16	1949
Jesse Burkett	OF	1890-1905	1946
Roy Campanella	C	1948-57	1969
Rod Carew	1B-2B	1967-85	1991
Max Carey	OF	1910-29	1961
Frank Chance	1B	1898-1914	1946
Oscar Charleston*	OF		1976
Jack Chesbro	P	1899-1909	1946
Fred Clarke	OF	1894-1915	1945
John Clarkson	P	1882-94	1963
Roberto Clemente	OF	1955-72	1973
Ty Cobb	OF	1905-28	1936
Mickey Cochrane	C	1925-37	1947
Eddie Collins	2B	1906-30	1939
Jimmy Collins	3B	1895-1908	1945
Earle Combs	OF	1924-35	1970
Roger Connor	1B	1880-97	1976
Stan Coveleski	P	1912-28	1969
Sam Crawford	OF	1899-1917	1957
Joe Cronin	SS	1926-45	1956
Candy Cummings	P	1872-77	1939
Kiki Cuyler	OF	1921-38	1968
Ray Dandridge*	3B		1987
Dizzy Dean	P	1930-47	1953
Ed Delahanty	OF	1888-1903	1945
Bill Dickey	C	1928-46	1954
Martin Dihigo*	P-OF		1977
Joe DiMaggio	OF	1936-51	1955
Bobby Doerr	2B	1937-51	1986
Don Drysdale	P	1956-69	1984
Hugh Duffy	OF	1888-1906	1945
Johnny Evers	2B	1902-29	1939
Buck Ewing	C	1880-97	1946
Red Faber	P	1914-33	1964
Bob Feller	P	1936-56	1962
Rick Ferrell	C	1929-47	1984
Elmer Flick	OF	1898-1910	1963
Whitey Ford	P	1950-67	1974
Jimmie Foxx	1B	1925-45	1951
Frankie Frisch	2B	1919-37	1947
Pud Galvin	P	1879-92	1965
Lou Gehrig	1B	1923-39	1939
Charlie Gehringer	2B	1924-42	1949
Bob Gibson	P	1959-75	1981
Josh Gibson*	C		1972
Lefty Gomez	P	1930-43	1972
Goose Goslin	OF	1921-38	1968
Hank Greenberg	1B	1930-47	1956
Burleigh Grimes	P	1916-34	1964
Lefty Grove	P	1925-41	1947
Chick Hafey	OF	1924-37	1971
Jesse Haines	P	1918-37	1970
Billy Hamilton	OF	1888-1901	1961
Gabby Hartnett	C	1922-41	1955
Harry Heilmann	OF	1914-32	1952
Billy Herman	2B	1931-47	1975
Harry Hooper	OF	1909-25	1971
Rogers Hornsby	2B	1915-37	1942
Waite Hoyt	P	1918-38	1969
Carl Hubbell	P	1928-43	1947
Catfish Hunter	P	1965-79	1987
Monte Irvin*	OF	1949-56	1973
Travis Jackson	SS	1922-36	1982
Ferguson Jenkins	P	1965-83	1991
Hugh Jennings	SS	1891-1918	1945
Judy Johnson*	3B		1975
Walter Johnson	P	1907-27	1936
Addie Joss	P	1902-10	1978
Al Kaline	OF	1953-74	1980
Tim Keefe	P	1880-93	1964
Willie Keeler	OF	1892-1910	1939
George Kell	3B	1943-57	1983
Joe Kelley	OF	1891-1908	1971
George Kelly	1B	1915-32	1973
King Kelly	C	1878-93	1945
Harmon Killebrew	1B-3B	1954-75	1984
Ralph Kiner	OF	1946-55	1975
Chuck Klein	OF	1928-44	1980
Sandy Koufax	P	1955-66	1972
Nap Lajoie	2B	1896-1916	1937
Tony Lazzeri	2B	1926-39	1991
Bob Lemon	P	1941-58	1976
Buck Leonard*	1B		1977
Fred Lindstrom	3B	1924-36	1976
Pop Lloyd*	SS-1B		1977
Ernie Lombardi	C	1931-47	1986
Ted Lyons	P	1923-46	1955
Mickey Mantle	OF	1951-68	1974
Heinie Manush	OF	1923-39	1964
Rabbit Maranville	SS-2B	1912-35	1954
Juan Marichal	P	1960-75	1983
Rube Marquard	P	1908-25	1971
Eddie Mathews	3B	1952-68	1978
Christy Mathewson	P	1900-16	1936
Willie Mays	OF	1951-73	1979
Tommy McCarthy	OF	1884-96	1946
Willie McCovey	1B	1959-80	1986
Joe McGinnity	P	1899-1908	1946
Joe Medwick	OF	1932-48	1968
Johnny Mize	1B	1936-53	1981
Joe Morgan	2B	1963-84	1990
Stan Musial	OF-1B	1941-63	1969
Kid Nichols	P	1890-1906	1949
Jim O'Rourke	OF	1876-1904	1945
Mel Ott	OF	1926-47	1951
Satchel Paige*	P	1948-65	1971
Jim Palmer	P	1965-84	1990
Herb Pennock	P	1912-34	1948
Gaylord Perry	P	1962-83	1991

PLAYER (*Cont.*)

	Position	Career Dates	Year Selected		Position	Career Dates	Year Selected
Eddie Plank	P	1901-17	1946	Bill Terry	1B	1923-36	1954
Hoss Radbourn	P	1880-91	1939	Sam Thompson	OF	1885-1906	1974
Pee Wee Reese	SS	1940-58	1984	Joe Tinker	SS	1902-16	1946
Sam Rice	OF	1915-35	1963	Pie Traynor	3B	1920-37	1948
Eppa Rixey	P	1912-33	1963	Dazzy Vance	P	1915-35	1955
Robin Roberts	P	1948-66	1976	Arky Vaughan	SS	1932-48	1985
Brooks Robinson	3B	1955-77	1983	Rube Waddell	P	1897-1910	1946
Frank Robinson	OF	1956-76	1982	Honus Wagner	SS	1897-1917	1936
Jackie Robinson	2B	1947-56	1962	Bobby Wallace	SS	1894-1918	1953
Edd Roush	OF	1913-31	1962	Ed Walsh	P	1904-17	1946
Red Ruffing	P	1924-47	1967	Lloyd Waner	OF	1927-45	1967
Amos Rusie	P	1889-1901	1977	Paul Waner	OF	1926-45	1952
Babe Ruth	OF	1914-35	1936	Monte Ward	2B-P	1878-94	1964
Ray Schalk	C	1912-29	1955	Mickey Welch	P	1880-92	1973
Red Schoendienst	2B	1945-63	1989	Zach Wheat	OF	1909-27	1959
Joe Sewell	SS	1920-33	1977	Hoyt Wilhelm	P	1952-72	1985
Al Simmons	OF	1924-44	1953	Billy Williams	OF	1959-76	1987
George Sisler	1B	1915-30	1939	Ted Williams	OF	1939-60	1966
Enos Slaughter	OF	1938-59	1985	Hack Wilson	OF	1923-34	1979
Duke Snider	OF	1947-64	1980	Early Wynn	P	1939-63	1972
Warren Spahn	P	1942-65	1973	Carl Yastrzemski	OF	1961-83	1989
Al Spalding	P	1871-78	1939	Cy Young	P	1890-1911	1937
Tris Speaker	OF	1907-28	1937	Ross Youngs	OF	1917-26	1972
Willie Stargell	OF-1B	1962-82	1988				

Note: Career dates indicate first and last appearances in the majors.

*Elected on the basis of his career in the Negro leagues.

UMPIRES

	Year Selected
Al Barlick	1989
Jocko Conlan	1974
Tom Connolly	1953
Billy Evans	1973
Cal Hubbard	1976
Bill Klem	1953

MERITORIOUS SERVICE

	Year Selected
Ed Barrow (manager-executive)	1953
Morgan Bulkeley (executive)	1937
Alexander Cartwright (executive)	1938
Henry Chadwick (writer-executive)	1938
Happy Chandler (commissioner)	1982
Charles Comiskey (manager-executive)	1939
Rube Foster (player-manager-executive)	1981
Ford Frick (commissioner-executive)	1970
Warren Giles (executive)	1979
Will Harridge (executive)	1972
Ban Johnson (executive)	1937
Kenesaw M. Landis (commissioner)	1944
Larry MacPhail (executive)	1978
Branch Rickey (manager-executive)	1967
Al Spalding (player-executive)	1939
Bill Veeck (owner)	1991
George Weiss (executive)	1971
George Wright (player-manager)	1937
Harry Wright (player-manager-executive)	1953
Tom Yawkey (executive)	1980

MANAGER

	Years Managed	Year Selected
Walt Alston	1954-76	1983
Clark Griffith	1901-20	1946
Bucky Harris	1924-56	1975
Miller Huggins	1913-29	1964
Al Lopez	1951-69	1977
Connie Mack	1894-1950	1937
Joe McCarthy	1926-50	1957
John McGraw	1899-1932	1937
Bill McKechnie	1915-46	1962
Wilbert Robinson	1902-31	1945
Casey Stengel	1934-65	1966

30 Home Runs and 30 Stolen Bases

Year	Player and Team	HR	SB
1922	Ken Williams, StL	39	37
1956	Willie Mays, NY (N)	36	40
1957	Willie Mays, NY (N)	35	38
1963	Hank Aaron, Mil	44	31
1969	Bobby Bonds, SF	32	45
1970	Tommy Harper, Mil	31	38
1973	Bobby Bonds, SF	39	43
1975	Bobby Bonds, NY (A)	32	30
1977	Bobby Bonds, Calif	37	41
1978	Bobby Bonds, Chi (A)-Tex	31	43
1983	Dale Murphy, Atl	36	30
1987	Joe Carter, Clev	32	31
1987	Eric Davis, Cin	37	50
1987	Howard Johnson, NY (N)	36	32
1987	Darryl Strawberry, NY (N)	39	36
1988	Jose Canseco, Oak	42	40
1989	Howard Johnson, NY (N)	36	41
1990	Barry Bonds, Pitt	33	52
1990	Ron Gant, Atl	32	33
1991	Ron Gant, Atl	32	34
1991	Howard Johnson, NY (N)	38	30

No-Hit Games, 9 Innings or More

NATIONAL LEAGUE

Date	Pitcher and Game
1876 ..... July 15	George Bradley, StL vs Hart 2-0
1880 ..... June 12	John Richmond, Wor vs Clev 1-0 (perfect game)
June 17	Monte Ward, Prov vs Buff 5-0 (perfect game)
Aug 19	Larry Corcoran, Chi vs Bos 6-0
Aug 20	Pud Galvin, Buff at Wor 1-0
1882 ..... Sep 20	Larry Corcoran, Chi vs Wor 5-0
Sep 22	Tim Lovett, Bklyn vs NY 4-0
1883 ..... July 25	Hoss Radbourn, Prov at Clev 8-0
Sep 13	Hugh Daily, Clev at Phil 1-0
1884 ..... June 27	Larry Corcoran, Chi vs Prov 6-0
Aug 4	Pud Galvin, Buff at Det 18-0
1885 ..... July 27	John Clarkson, Chi at Prov 4-0
Aug 29	Charles Ferguson, Phil vs Prov 1-0
1891 ..... July 31	Amos Rusie, NY vs Bklyn 6-0
June 22	Tom Lovett, Bklyn vs NY 4-0
1892 ..... Aug 6	Jack Stivetts, Bos vs Bklyn 11-0
Aug 22	Alex Sanders, Lou vs Balt 6-2
Oct 15	Bumpus Jones, Cin vs Pitt 7-1 (first major league game)
1893 ..... Aug 16	Bill Hawke, Balt vs Wash 5-0
1897 ..... Sep 18	Cy Young, Clev vs Cin 6-0
1898 ..... Apr 22	Ted Breitenstein, Cin vs Pitt 11-0
Apr 22	Jim Hughes, Balt vs Bos 8-0
July 8	Frank Donahue, Phil vs Bos 5-0
Aug 21	Walter Thornton, Chi vs Bklyn 2-0
1899 ..... May 25	Deacon Phillippe, Lou vs NY 7-0
Aug 7	Vic Willis, Bos vs Wash 7-1
1900 ..... July 12	Noodles Hahn, Cin vs Phil 4-0
1901 ..... July 15	Christy Mathewson, NY at StL 5-0
1903 ..... Sep 18	Chick Fraser, Phil at Chi 10-0
1904 ..... June 11	Bob Wicker, Chi at NY 1-0 (hit in 10th; won in 12th)
1905 ..... June 13	Christy Mathewson, NY at Chi 1-0
1906 ..... May 1	John Lush, Phil at Bklyn 6-0
July 20	Mal Eason, Bklyn at StL 2-0
Aug 1	Harry McIntire, Bklyn vs Pitt 0-1 (hit in 11th; lost in 13th)
1907 ..... May 8	Frank Pfeffer, Bos vs Cin 6-0
Sep 20	Nick Maddox, Pitt vs Bklyn 2-1
1908 ..... July 4	George Wiltse, NY vs Phil 1-0 (10 innings)
Sep 5	Nap Rucker, Bklyn vs Bos 6-0
1909 ..... Apr 15	Leon Ames, NY vs Bklyn 0-3 (hit in 10th; lost in 13th)
1912 ..... Sep 6	Jeff Tesreau, NY at Phil 3-0
1914 ..... Sep 9	George Davis, Bos vs Phil 7-0
1915 ..... Apr 15	Rube Marquard, NY vs Bklyn 2-0
Aug 31	Jimmy Lavender, Chi at NY 2-0
1916 ..... June 16	Tom Hughes, Bos vs Pitt 2-0
1917 ..... May 2	Jim Vaughn, Chi vs Cin 0-1 (hit in 10th; lost in 10th)
May 2	Fred Toney, Cin at Chi 1-0 (10 innings)
1919 ..... May 11	Hod Eller, Cin vs StL 6-0
1922 ..... May 7	Jesse Barnes, NY vs Phil 6-0
1924 ..... July 17	Jesse Haines, StL vs Bos 5-0
1925 ..... Sep 13	Dazzy Vance, Bklyn vs Phil 10-1
1929 ..... May 8	Carl Hubbell, NY vs Pitt 11-0
1934 ..... Sep 21	Paul Dean, StL vs Bklyn 3-0

Date	Pitcher and Game
1938 ..... June 11	Johnny Vander Meer, Cin vs Bos 3-0
June 15	Johnny Vander Meer, Cin at Bklyn 6-0
1940 ..... Apr 30	Tex Carleton, Bklyn at Cin, 3-0
1941 ..... Aug 30	Lon Warneke, StL at Cin 2-0
1944 ..... Apr 27	Jim Tobin, Bos vs Bklyn 2-0
May 15	Clyde Shoun, Cin vs Bos 1-0
1946 ..... Apr 23	Ed Head, Bklyn vs Bos 5-0
1947 ..... June 18	Ewell Blackwell, Cin vs Bos 6-0
1948 ..... Sep 9	Rex Barney, Bklyn at NY 2-0
1950 ..... Aug 11	Vern Bickford, Bos vs Bklyn 7-0
1951 ..... May 6	Cliff Chambers, Pitt at Bos 3-0
1952 ..... June 19	Carl Erskine, Bklyn vs Chi 5-0
1954 ..... June 12	Jim Wilson, Mil vs Phil 2-0
1955 ..... May 12	Sam Jones, Chi vs Pitt 4-0
1956 ..... May 12	Carl Erskine, Bklyn vs NY 3-0
Sep 25	Sal Maglie, Bklyn vs Phil 5-0
1959 ..... May 26	Harvey Haddix, Pitt at Mil 0-1 (hit in 13th; lost in 13th)
1960 ..... May 15	Don Cardwell, Chi vs StL 4-0
Aug 18	Lew Burdette, Mil vs Phil 1-0
Sep 16	Warren Spahn, Mil vs Phil 4-0
1961 ..... Apr 28	Warren Spahn, Mil vs SF 1-0
1962 ..... June 30	Sandy Koufax, LA vs NY 5-0
1963 ..... May 11	Sandy Koufax, LA vs SF 8-0
May 17	Don Nottebart, Hou vs Phil 4-1
June 15	Juan Marichal, SF vs Hou 1-0
1964 ..... Apr 23	Ken Johnson, Hou vs Cin 0-1
June 4	Sandy Koufax, LA at Phil 3-0
June 21	Jim Bunning, Phil at NY 6-0 (perfect game)
1965 ..... June 14	Jim Maloney, Cin vs NY 0-1 (hit in 11th; lost in 11th)
Aug 19	Jim Maloney, Cin at Chi 1-0 (10 innings)
Sep 9	Sandy Koufax, LA vs Chi 1-0 (perfect game)
1967 ..... June 18	Don Wilson, Hou vs Atl 2-0
1968 ..... July 29	George Culver, Cin at Phil 6-1
Sep 17	Gaylord Perry, SF vs StL 1-0
Sep 18	Ray Washburn, StL at SF 2-0
1969 ..... Apr 17	Bill Stoneman, Mont at Phil 7-0
Apr 30	Jim Maloney, Cin vs Hou 10-0
May 1	Don Wilson, Hou at Cin 4-0
Aug 19	Ken Holtzman, Chi vs Atl 3-0
Sep 20	Bob Moose, Pitt at NY 4-0
1970 ..... June 12	Dock Ellis, Pitt at SD 2-0
July 20	Bill Singer, LA vs Phil 5-0
1971 ..... June 3	Ken Holtzman, Chi at Cin 1-0
June 23	Rick Wise, Phil at Cin 4-0
Aug 14	Bob Gibson, StL at Pitt 11-0
1972 ..... Apr 16	Burt Hooton, Chi vs Phil 4-0
Sep 2	Milt Pappas, Chi vs SD 8-0
Oct 2	Bill Stoneman, Mont vs NY 7-0
1973 ..... Aug 5	Phil Niekro, Atl vs SD 9-0
1975 ..... Aug 24	Ed Halicki, SF vs NY 6-0
1976 ..... July 9	Larry Dierker, Hou vs Mont 6-0
Aug 9	John Candelaria, Pitt vs LA 2-0
Sep 29	John Montefusco, SF at Atl 9-0

Note: Includes the games struck from the record book on September 4, 1991, when baseball's committee on statistical accuracy voted to define no-hitters as games of 9 innings or more that end with a team getting no hits.

No-Hit Games, 9 Innings or More (*Cont.*)

NATIONAL LEAGUE (*Cont.*)

Date		Pitcher and Game	Date		Pitcher and Game
1978	Apr 16	Bob Forsch, StL vs Phil 5-0	1990	June 29	Fernando Valenzuela, LA vs StL 6-0
	June 16	Tom Seaver, Cin vs StL 4-0		Aug 15	Terry Mulholland, Phil vs SF 6-0
1979	Apr 7	Ken Forsch, Hou vs Atl 6-0	1991	May 23	Tommy Greene, Phil at Mont 2-0
1980	June 27	Jerry Reuss, LA at SF 8-0		July 26	Mark Gardner, Mont at LA 0-1 (hit in 10th, lost in 10th)
1981	May 10	Charlie Lea, Mont vs SF 4-0			
	Sep 26	Nolan Ryan, Hou vs LA 5-0		July 28	Dennis Martinez, Mont at LA 2-0 (perfect game)
1983	Sep 26	Bob Forsch, StL vs Mont 3-0			
1986	Sep 25	Mike Scott, Hou vs SF 2-0		Sept 11	Kent Mercker (6), Mark Wohlers (2), and Alejandro Pena (1), Atl at SD 1-0
1988	Sep 16	Tom Browning, Cin vs LA 1-0 (perfect game)			

AMERICAN LEAGUE

Date		Pitcher and Game	Date		Pitcher and Game
1901	May 9	Earl Moore, Clev vs Chi 2-4 (hit in 10th; lost in 10th)	1945	Sep 9	Dick Fowler, Phil vs StL 1-0
			1946	Apr 30	Bob Feller, Clev at NY 1-0
1902	Sep 20	Jimmy Callahan, Chi vs Det 3-0	1947	July 10	Don Black, Clev vs Phil 3-0
1904	May 5	Cy Young, Bos vs Phil 3-0 (perfect game)		Sep 3	Bill McCahan, Phil vs Wash 3-0
			1948	June 30	Bob Lemon, Clev at Det 2-0
	Aug 17	Jesse Tannehill, Bos at Chi 6-0	1951	July 1	Bob Feller, Clev vs Det 2-1
1905	July 22	Weldon Henley, Phil at StL 6-0		July 12	Allie Reynolds, NY at Clev 1-0
	Sep 6	Frank Smith, Chi at Det 15-0		Sep 28	Allie Reynolds, NY vs Bos 8-0
	Sep 27	Bill Dinneen, Bos vs Chi 2-0	1952	May 15	Virgil Trucks, Det vs Wash 1-0
1908	June 30	Cy Young, Bos at NY 8-0		Aug 25	Virgil Trucks, Det at NY 1-0
	Sep 18	Bob Rhoades, Clev vs Bos 2-1	1953	May 6	Bobo Holloman, StL vs Phil 6-0 (first major league start)
	Sep 20	Frank Smith, Chi vs Phil 1-0			
	Oct 2	Addie Joss, Clev vs Chi 1-0 (perfect game)	1956	July 14	Mel Parnell, Bos vs Chi 4-0
				Oct 8	Don Larsen, NY (A) vs Bklyn (N) 2-0 (World Series)
1910	Apr 20	Addie Joss, Clev at Chi 1-0			
	May 12	Chief Bender, Phil vs Clev 4-0	1957	Aug 20	Bob Keegan, Chi vs Wash 6-0
	Aug 30	Tom Hughes, NY vs Clev 0-5 (hit in 10th; lost in 11th)	1958	July 20	Jim Bunning, Det at Bos 3-0
				Sep 20	Hoyt Wilhelm, Balt vs NY 1-0
1911	July 29	Joe Wood, Bos vs StL 5-0	1962	May 5	Bo Belinsky, LA vs Balt 2-0
	Aug 27	Ed Walsh, Chi vs Bos 5-0		June 26	Earl Wilson, Bos vs LA 2-0
1912	July 4	George Mullin, Det vs StL 7-0		Aug 1	Bill Monbouquette, Bos at Chi 1-0
	Aug 30	Earl Hamilton, StL at Det 5-1		Aug 26	Jack Kralick, Minn vs KC 1-0
1914	May 14	Jim Scott, Chi at Wash 0-1 (hit in 10th; lost in 10th)	1965	Sep 16	Dave Morehead, Bos vs Clev 2-0
			1966	June 10	Sonny Siebert, Clev vs Wash 2-0
	May 31	Joe Benz, Chi vs Clev 6-1	1967	Apr 30	Steve Barber (8⅔) and Stu Miller (⅓), Balt vs Det 1-2
1916	June 21	George Foster, Bos vs NY 2-0			
	Aug 26	Joe Bush, Phil vs Clev 5-0		Aug 25	Dean Chance, Minn at Clev 2-1
	Aug 30	Dutch Leonard, Bos vs StL 4-0		Sep 10	Joel Horlen, Chi vs Det 6-0
1917	Apr 14	Ed Cicotte, Chi at StL 11-0	1968	Apr 27	Tom Phoebus, Balt vs Bos 6-0
	Apr 24	George Mogridge, NY at Bos 2-1		May 8	Catfish Hunter, Oak vs Minn 4-0 (perfect game)
	May 5	Ernie Koob, StL vs Chi 1-0			
	May 6	Bob Groom, StL vs Chi 3-0	1969	Aug 13	Jim Palmer, Balt vs Oak 8-0
	June 23	Ernie Shore, Bos vs Wash 4-0 (perfect game)	1970	July 3	Clyde Wright, Calif vs Oak 4-0
				Sep 21	Vida Blue, Oak vs Minn 6-0
1918	June 3	Dutch Leonard, Bos at Det 5-0	1973	Apr 27	Steve Busby, KC at Det 3-0
1919	Sep 10	Ray Caldwell, Clev at NY 3-0		May 15	Nolan Ryan, Calif at KC 3-0
1920	July 1	Walter Johnson, Wash at Bos 1-0		July 15	Nolan Ryan, Calif at Det 6-0
1922	Apr 30	Charlie Robertson, Chi at Det 2-0 (perfect game)		July 30	Jim Bibby, Tex at Oak 6-0
			1974	June 19	Steve Busby, KC at Mil 2-0
1923	Sep 4	Sam Jones, NY at Phil 2-0		July 19	Dick Bosman, Clev vs Oak 4-0
	Sep 7	Howard Ehmke, Bos at Phil 4-0		Sep 28	Nolan Ryan, Calif vs Minn 4-0
1926	Aug 21	Ted Lyons, Chi at Bos 6-0	1975	June 1	Nolan Ryan, Calif vs Balt 1-0
1931	Apr 29	Wes Ferrell, Clev vs StL 9-0		Sep 28	Vida Blue (5), Glenn Abbott and Paul Lindblad (1), Rollie Fingers (2), Oak vs Calif 5-0
	Aug 8	Bob Burke, Wash vs Bos 5-0			
1934	Sep 18	Bobo Newsom, StL vs Bos 1-2 (hit in 10th; lost in 10th)	1976	July 28	John Odom (5) and Francisco Barrios (4), Chi at Oak 2-1
1935	Aug 31	Vern Kennedy, Chi vs Clev 5-0			
1937	June 1	Bill Dietrich, Chi vs StL 8-0	1977	May 14	Jim Colborn, KC vs Tex 6-0
1938	Aug 27	Monte Pearson, NY vs Clev 13-0		May 30	Dennis Eckersley, Clev vs Calif 1-0
1940	Apr 16	Bob Feller, Chi at Clev 1-0 (opening day)		Sep 22	Bert Blyleven, Tex at Calif 6-0

No-Hit Games, 9 Innings or More (*Cont.*)

AMERICAN LEAGUE (*Cont.*)

Date	Pitcher and Game	Date	Pitcher and Game
1981 ......May 15	Len Barker, Clev vs Tor 3-0 (perfect game)	1990 ......June 11	Nolan Ryan, Tex at Oak 5-0
1983 ......July 4	Dave Righetti, NY vs Bos 4-0	June 29	Dave Stewart, Oak at Tor 5-0
Sep 29	Mike Warren, Oak vs Chi 3-0	July 1	Andy Hawkins, NY at Chi 0-4 (pitched 8 innings of 9-inning game)
1984 ......Apr 7	Jack Morris, Det at Chi 4-0	Sep 2	Dave Stieb, Tor at Clev 3-0
Sep 30	Mike Witt, Calif at Tex 1-0 (perfect game)	1991 ......May 1	Nolan Ryan, Tex vs Tor 3-0
1986 ......Sep 19	Joe Cowley, Chi at Calif 7-1	July 13	Bob Milacki (6), Mike Flanagan (1), Mark Williamson (1), and Gregg Olson (1), Balt at Oak 2-0
1987 ......Apr 15	Juan Nieves, Mil at Balt 7-0	Aug 11	Wilson Alvarez, Chi at Balt 7-0
1990 ......Apr 11	Mark Langston (7), Mike Witt (2), Calif vs Sea 1-0	Aug 26	Bret Saberhagen, KC vs Chi 7-0
June 2	Randy Johnson, Sea vs Det 2-0		

Longest Hitting Streak

NATIONAL LEAGUE

Player and Team	Year	G
Willie Keeler, Balt	1897	44
Pete Rose, Cin	1978	44
Bill Dahlen, Chi	1894	42
Tommy Holmes, Bos	1945	37
Billy Hamilton, Phil	1894	36
Fred Clarke, Lou	1895	35
Benito Santiago, SD	1987	34
George Davis, NY	1893	33
Rogers Hornsby, StL	1922	32
Ed Delahanty, Phil	1899	31
Willie Davis, LA	1969	31
Rico Carty, Atl	1970	31
Elmer Smith, Cin	1898	30
Stan Musial, StL	1950	30

AMERICAN LEAGUE

Player and Team	Year	G
Joe DiMaggio, NY	1941	56
George Sisler, StL	1922	41
Ty Cobb, Det	1911	40
Paul Molitor, Mil	1987	39
Ty Cobb, Det	1917	35
George Sisler, StL	1925	34
John Stone, Det	1930	34
George McQuinn, StL	1938	34
Dom DiMaggio, Bos	1949	34
Heinie Manush, Wash	1933	33
Sam Rice, Wash	1924	31
Ken Landreaux, Minn	1980	31
Tris Speaker, Bos	1912	30
Goose Goslin, Det	1934	30
Ron LeFlore, Det	1976	30
George Brett, KC	1980	30

Triple Crown Hitters

NATIONAL LEAGUE

Player and Team	Year	HR	RBI	BA
Paul Hines, Prov	1878	4	50	.358
Hugh Duffy, Bos	1894	18	145	.438
Heinie Zimmerman,* Chi	1912	14	103	.372
Rogers Hornsby, StL	1922	42	152	.401
	1925	39	143	.403
Chuck Klein, Phil	1933	28	120	.368
Joe Medwick, StL	1937	31	154	.374

*Zimmerman ranked first in RBIs as calculated by Ernie Lanigan, but only third as calculated by Information Concepts Inc.

AMERICAN LEAGUE

Player and Team	Year	HR	RBI	BA
Nap Lajoie, Phil	1901	14	125	.422
Ty Cobb, Det	1909	9	115	.377
Jimmie Foxx, Phil	1933	48	163	.356
Lou Gehrig, NY	1934	49	165	.363
Ted Williams, Bos	1942	36	137	.356
	1947	32	114	.343
Mickey Mantle, NY	1956	52	130	.353
Frank Robinson, Balt	1966	49	122	.316
Carl Yastrzemski, Bos	1967	44	121	.326

Using His Head

A nonpitcher who bats righthanded and throws lefthanded has always been a baseball oddity. The Athletics' Rickey Henderson and the Mets' Mark Carreon are the only two active players in the club, which includes President Bush and Eddie Gaedel, the 3'7" midget who pinch hit for Bill Veeck's St. Louis Browns in 1951. "My father [former major leaguer Camilo Carreon] saw my lefthanded swing at an early age and changed me," says Carreon. As for being in such a select group, he says, "Well, I'm using both sides of my brain, which is good, I think."

Triple Crown Pitchers

NATIONAL LEAGUE					
Player and Team	Year	W	L	SO	ERA
Tommy Bond, Bos...........1877	1877	40	17	170	2.11
Hoss Radbourn, Prov 1884	1884	60	12	441	1.38
Tim Keefe, NY 1888	1888	35	12	333	1.74
John Clarkson, Bos 1889	1889	49	19	284	2.73
Amos Rusie, NY 1894	1894	36	13	195	2.78
Christy Mathewson, NY 1905	1905	31	8	206	1.27
	1908	37	11	259	1.43
Grover Alexander, Phil 1915	1915	31	10	241	1.22
	1916	33	12	167	1.55
	1917	30	13	201	1.86
Hippo Vaughn, Chi 1918	1918	22	10	148	1.74
Grover Alexander, Chi......1920	1920	27	14	173	1.91
Dazzy Vance, Bklyn 1924	1924	28	6	262	2.16
Bucky Walters, Cin 1939	1939	27	11	137	2.29
Sandy Koufax, LA............1963	1963	25	5	306	1.88
	1965	26	8	382	2.04
	1966	27	9	317	1.73
Steve Carlton, Phil...........1972	1972	27	10	310	1.97
Dwight Gooden, NY.........1985	1985	24	4	268	1.53

AMERICAN LEAGUE					
Player and Team	Year	W	L	SO	ERA
Cy Young, Bos 1901	1901	33	10	158	1.62
Rube Waddell, Phil.........1905	1905	26	11	287	1.48
Walter Johnson, Wash ...1913	1913	36	7	303	1.09
	1918	23	13	162	1.27
	1924	23	7	158	2.72
Lefty Grove, Phil.............1930	1930	28	5	209	2.54
	1931	31	4	175	2.06
Lefty Gomez, NY............1934	1934	26	5	158	2.33
	1937	21	11	194	2.33
Hal Newhouser, Det.......1945	1945	25	9	212	1.81

Joe DiMaggio's 1941 Hitting Streak

Game No.	Date	Team and Pitcher	AB	R	H
1	5-15	Chicago, Smith	4	0	1
2	5-16	Chicago, Lee	4	2	2
3	5-17	Chicago, Rigney	3	1	1
4	5-18	St Louis, Harris, Niggeling	3	3	3
5	5-19	St Louis, Galehouse	3	0	1
6	5-20	St Louis, Auker	5	1	1
7	5-21	Detroit, Rowe, Benton	5	0	2
8	5-22	Detroit, McKain	4	0	1
9	5-23	Boston, Newsome	5	0	1
10	5-24	Boston, Johnson	4	2	1
11	5-25	Boston, Grove	4	0	1
12	5-27	Washington, Chase, Anderson, Carrasquel	5	3	4
13	5-28	Washington, Hudson	4	1	1
14	5-29	Washington, Sundra	3	1	1
15	5-30	Boston, Johnson	2	1	1
16	5-30	Boston, Harris	3	0	1
17	6-1	Cleveland, Milnar	4	1	1
18	6-1	Cleveland, Harder	4	0	1
19	6-2	Cleveland, Feller	4	2	2
20	6-3	Detroit, Trout	4	1	1
21	6-5	Detroit, Newhouser	5	1	1
22	6-7	St Louis, Muncrief, Allen, Caster	5	2	3
23	6-8	St Louis, Auker	4	3	2
24	6-8	St Louis, Caster, Kramer	4	1	2
25	6-10	Chicago, Rigney	5	1	1
26	6-12	Chicago, Lee	4	1	2
27	6-14	Cleveland, Feller	2	0	1
28	6-15	Cleveland, Bagby	3	1	1
29	6-16	Cleveland, Milnar	5	0	1
30	6-17	Chicago, Rigney	4	1	1
31	6-18	Chicago, Lee	3	0	1
32	6-19	Chicago, Smith, Ross	3	2	3
33	6-20	Detroit, Newsom, McKain	5	3	4
34	6-21	Detroit, Trout	4	0	1
35	6-22	Detroit, Newhouser, Newsom	5	1	2
36	6-24	St Louis, Muncrief	4	1	1
37	6-25	St Louis, Galehouse	4	1	1
38	6-26	St Louis, Auker	4	0	1
39	6-27	Philadelphia, Dean	3	1	2
40	6-28	Philadelphia, Babich, Harris	5	1	2
41	6-29	Washington, Leonard	4	1	1
42	6-29	Washington, Anderson	5	1	1
43	7-1	Boston, Harris, Ryba	4	0	2
44	7-1	Boston, Wilson	3	1	1
45	7-2	Boston, Newsome	5	1	1
46	7-5	Philadelphia, Marchildon	4	2	1
47	7-6	Philadelphia, Babich, Hadley	5	2	4
48	7-6	Philadelphia, Knott	4	0	2
49	7-10	St Louis, Niggeling	2	0	1
50	7-11	St Louis, Harris, Kramer	5	1	4
51	7-12	St Louis, Auker, Muncrief	5	1	2
52	7-13	Chicago, Lyons, Hallett	4	2	3
53	7-13	Chicago, Lee	4	0	1
54	7-14	Chicago, Rigney	3	0	1
55	7-15	Chicago, Smith	4	1	2
56	7-16	Cleveland, Milnar, Krakauskas	4	3	3
		Totals	223	56	91

Consecutive Games Played,
500 or More Games

Lou Gehrig	2130	Frank McCormick	652
Cal Ripken Jr	1573*	Sandy Alomar	648
Everett Scott	1307	Eddie Brown	618
Steve Garvey	1207	Roy McMillan	585
Billy Williams	1117	George Pinckney	577
Joe Sewell	1103	Steve Brodie	574
Stan Musial	895	Aaron Ward	565
Eddie Yost	829	Candy LaChance	540
Gus Suhr	822	Buck Freeman	535
Nellie Fox	798	Fred Luderus	533
Pete Rose	745	Clyde Milan	511
Dale Murphy	740	Charlie Gehringer	511
Richie Ashburn	730	Vada Pinson	508
Ernie Banks	717	Tony Cuccinello	504
Earl Averill	673	Charlie Gehringer	504
Pete Rose	678	Omar Moreno	503

*Streak in progress at the end of the 1991 season.

Unassisted Triple Plays

Player and Team	Date	Pos	Opp	Opp Batter
Neal Ball, Clev	7-19-09	SS	Bos	Amby McConnell
Bill Wambsganss, Clev	10-10-20	2B	Bklyn	Clarence Mitchell
George Burns, Bos	9-14-23	1B	Clev	Frank Brower
Ernie Padgett, Bos	10-6-23	SS	Phil	Walter Holke
Glenn Wright, Pitt	5-7-25	SS	StL	Jim Bottomley
Jimmy Cooney, Chi	5-30-27	SS	Pitt	Paul Waner
Johnny Neun, Det	5-31-27	1B	Clev	Homer Summa
Ron Hansen, Wash	7-30-68	SS	Clev	Joe Azcue

National League

Pennant Winners

Year	Team	Manager	W	L	Pct	GA
1900	Brooklyn	Ned Hanlon	82	54	.603	4½
1901	Pittsburgh	Fred Clarke	90	49	.647	7½
1902	Pittsburgh	Fred Clarke	103	36	.741	27½
1903	Pittsburgh	Fred Clarke	91	49	.650	6½
1904	New York	John McGraw	106	47	.693	13
1905	New York	John McGraw	105	48	.686	9
1906	Chicago	Frank Chance	116	36	.763	20
1907	Chicago	Frank Chance	107	45	.704	17
1908	Chicago	Frank Chance	99	55	.643	1
1909	Pittsburgh	Fred Clarke	110	42	.724	6½
1910	Chicago	Frank Chance	104	50	.675	13
1911	New York	John McGraw	99	54	.647	7½
1912	New York	John McGraw	103	48	.682	10
1913	New York	John McGraw	101	51	.664	12½
1914	Boston	George Stallings	94	59	.614	10½
1915	Philadelphia	Pat Moran	90	62	.592	7
1916	Brooklyn	Wilbert Robinson	94	60	.610	2½
1917	New York	John McGraw	98	56	.636	10
1918	Chicago	Fred Mitchell	84	45	.651	10½
1919	Cincinnati	Pat Moran	96	44	.686	9
1920	Brooklyn	Wilbert Robinson	93	61	.604	7
1921	New York	John McGraw	94	59	.614	4
1922	New York	John McGraw	93	61	.604	7
1923	New York	John McGraw	95	58	.621	4½
1924	New York	John McGraw	93	60	.608	1½
1925	Pittsburgh	Bill McKechnie	95	58	.621	8½
1926	St Louis	Rogers Hornsby	89	65	.578	2
1927	Pittsburgh	Donie Bush	94	60	.610	1½
1928	St Louis	Bill McKechnie	95	59	.617	2

Pennant Winners (*Cont.*)

Year	Team	Manager	W	L	Pct	GA
1929	Chicago	Joe McCarthy	98	54	.645	10½
1930	St Louis	Gabby Street	92	62	.597	2
1931	St Louis	Gabby Street	101	53	.656	13
1932	Chicago	Charlie Grimm	90	64	.584	4
1933	New York	Bill Terry	91	61	.599	5
1934	St Louis	Frankie Frisch	95	58	.621	2
1935	Chicago	Charlie Grimm	100	54	.649	4
1936	New York	Bill Terry	92	62	.597	5
1937	New York	Bill Terry	95	57	.625	3
1938	Chicago	Gabby Hartnett	89	63	.586	2
1939	Cincinnati	Bill McKechnie	97	57	.630	4½
1940	Cincinnati	Bill McKechnie	100	53	.654	12
1941	Brooklyn	Leo Durocher	100	54	.649	2½
1942	St Louis	Billy Southworth	106	48	.688	2
1943	St Louis	Billy Southworth	105	49	.682	18
1944	St Louis	Billy Southworth	105	49	.682	14½
1945	Chicago	Charlie Grimm	98	56	.636	3
1946	St Louis*	Eddie Dyer	98	58	.628	2
1947	Brooklyn	Burt Shotton	94	60	.610	5
1948	Boston	Billy Southworth	91	62	.595	6½
1949	Brooklyn	Burt Shotton	97	57	.630	1
1950	Philadelphia	Eddie Sawyer	91	63	.591	2
1951	New York†	Leo Durocher	98	59	.624	1
1952	Brooklyn	Chuck Dressen	96	57	.627	4½
1953	Brooklyn	Chuck Dressen	105	49	.682	13
1954	New York	Leo Durocher	97	57	.630	5
1955	Brooklyn	Walt Alston	98	55	.641	13½
1956	Brooklyn	Walt Alston	93	61	.604	1
1957	Milwaukee	Fred Haney	95	59	.617	8
1958	Milwaukee	Fred Haney	92	62	.597	8
1959	Los Angeles‡	Walt Alston	88	68	.564	2
1960	Pittsburgh	Danny Murtaugh	95	59	.617	7
1961	Cincinnati	Fred Hutchinson	93	61	.604	4
1962	San Francisco#	Al Dark	103	62	.624	1
1963	Los Angeles	Walt Alston	99	63	.611	6
1964	St Louis	Johnny Keane	93	69	.574	1
1965	Los Angeles	Walt Alston	97	65	.599	2
1966	Los Angeles	Walt Alston	95	67	.586	1½
1967	St Louis	Red Schoendienst	101	60	.627	10½
1968	St Louis	Red Schoendienst	97	65	.599	9
1969	New York (E)	Gil Hodges	100	62	.617	8
1970	Cincinnati (W)	Sparky Anderson	102	60	.630	14½
1971	Pittsburgh (E)	Danny Murtaugh	97	65	.599	7
1972	Cincinnati (W)	Sparky Anderson	95	59	.617	10½
1973	New York (E)	Yogi Berra	82	79	.509	1½
1974	Los Angeles (W)	Walt Alston	102	60	.630	4
1975	Cincinnati (W)	Sparky Anderson	108	54	.667	20
1976	Cincinnati (W)	Sparky Anderson	102	60	.630	10
1977	Los Angeles (W)	Tommy Lasorda	98	64	.605	10
1978	Los Angeles (W)	Tommy Lasorda	95	67	.586	2½
1979	Pittsburgh (E)	Chuck Tanner	98	64	.605	2
1980	Philadelphia (E)	Dallas Green	91	71	.562	1
1981	Los Angeles (W)	Tommy Lasorda	63	47	.573	**
1982	St Louis (E)	Whitey Herzog	92	70	.568	3
1983	Philadelphia (E)	Pat Corrales, Paul Owens	90	72	.556	6
1984	San Diego (W)	Dick Williams	92	70	.568	12
1985	St Louis (E)	Whitey Herzog	101	61	.623	3
1986	New York (E)	Dave Johnson	108	54	.667	21½
1987	St Louis (E)	Whitey Herzog	95	67	.586	3
1988	Los Angeles (W)	Tommy Lasorda	94	67	.584	7
1989	San Francisco (W)	Roger Craig	92	70	.568	3
1990	Cincinnati (W)	Lou Piniella	91	71	.562	5
1991	Atlanta (W)	Bobby Cox	94	68	.580	1

*Defeated Brooklyn, two games to none, in playoff for pennant. †Defeated Brooklyn, two games to one, in playoff for pennant. ‡Defeated Milwaukee, two games to none, in playoff for pennant. #Defeated Los Angeles, two games to one, in playoff for pennant. **First half 36-21; second half 27-26.

Leading Batsmen

Year	Player and Team	BA	Year	Player and Team	BA
1900	Honus Wagner, Pitt	.381	1946	Stan Musial, StL	.365
1901	Jesse Burkett, StL	.382	1947	Harry Walker, StL-Phil	.363
1902	Ginger Beaumont, Pitt	.357	1948	Stan Musial, StL	.376
1903	Honus Wagner, Pitt	.355	1949	Jackie Robinson, Bklyn	.342
1904	Honus Wagner, Pitt	.349	1950	Stan Musial, StL	.346
1905	Cy Seymour, Cin	.377	1951	Stan Musial, StL	.355
1906	Honus Wagner, Pitt	.339	1952	Stan Musial, StL	.336
1907	Honus Wagner, Pitt	.350	1953	Carl Furillo, Bklyn	.344
1908	Honus Wagner, Pitt	.354	1954	Willie Mays, NY	.345
1909	Honus Wagner, Pitt	.339	1955	Richie Ashburn, Phil	.338
1910	Sherry Magee, Phil	.331	1956	Hank Aaron, Mil	.328
1911	Honus Wagner, Pitt	.334	1957	Stan Musial, StL	.351
1912	Heinie Zimmerman, Chi	.372	1958	Richie Ashburn, Phil	.350
1913	Jake Daubert, Bklyn	.350	1959	Hank Aaron, Mil	.355
1914	Jake Daubert, Bklyn	.329	1960	Dick Groat, Pitt	.325
1915	Larry Doyle, NY	.320	1961	Roberto Clemente, Pitt	.351
1916	Hal Chase, Cin	.339	1962	Tommy Davis, LA	.346
1917	Edd Roush, Cin	.341	1963	Tommy Davis, LA	.326
1918	Zach Wheat, Bklyn	.335	1964	Roberto Clemente, Pitt	.339
1919	Edd Roush, Cin	.321	1965	Roberto Clemente, Pitt	.329
1920	Rogers Hornsby, StL	.370	1966	Matty Alou, Pitt	.342
1921	Rogers Hornsby, StL	.397	1967	Roberto Clemente, Pitt	.357
1922	Rogers Hornsby, StL	.401	1968	Pete Rose, Cin	.335
1923	Rogers Hornsby, StL	.384	1969	Pete Rose, Cin	.348
1924	Rogers Hornsby, StL	.424	1970	Rico Carty, Atl	.366
1925	Rogers Hornsby, StL	.403	1971	Joe Torre, StL	.363
1926	Bubbles Hargrave, Cin	.353	1972	Billy Williams, Chi	.333
1927	Paul Waner, Pitt	.380	1973	Pete Rose, Cin	.338
1928	Rogers Hornsby, Bos	.387	1974	Ralph Garr, Atl	.353
1929	Lefty O'Doul, Phil	.398	1975	Bill Madlock, Chi	.354
1930	Bill Terry, NY	.401	1976	Bill Madlock, Chi	.339
1931	Chick Hafey, StL	.349	1977	Dave Parker, Pitt	.338
1932	Lefty O'Doul, Bklyn	.368	1978	Dave Parker, Pitt	.334
1933	Chuck Klein, Phil	.368	1979	Keith Hernandez, StL	.344
1934	Paul Waner, Pitt	.362	1980	Bill Buckner, Chi	.324
1935	Arky Vaughan, Pitt	.385	1981	Bill Madlock, Pitt	.341
1936	Paul Waner, Pitt	.373	1982	Al Oliver, Mont	.331
1937	Joe Medwick, StL	.374	1983	Bill Madlock, Pitt	.323
1938	Ernie Lombardi, Cin	.342	1984	Tony Gwynn, SD	.351
1939	Johnny Mize, StL	.349	1985	Willie McGee, StL	.353
1940	Debs Garms, Pitt	.355	1986	Tim Raines, Mont	.334
1941	Pete Reiser, Bklyn	.343	1987	Tony Gwynn, SD	.370
1942	Ernie Lombardi, Bos	.330	1988	Tony Gwynn, SD	.313
1943	Stan Musial, StL	.357	1989	Tony Gwynn, SD	.336
1944	Dixie Walker, Bklyn	.357	1990	Willie McGee, StL	.335
1945	Phil Cavarretta, Chi	.355	1991	Terry Pendleton, Atl	.319

Leaders in Runs Scored

Year	Player and Team	Runs	Year	Player and Team	Runs
1900	Roy Thomas, Phil	131	1914	George Burns, NY	100
1901	Jesse Burkett, StL	139	1915	Gavvy Cravath, Phil	89
1902	Honus Wagner, Pitt	105	1916	George Burns, NY	105
1903	Ginger Beaumont, Pitt	137	1917	George Burns, NY	103
1904	George Browne, NY	99	1918	Heinie Groh, Cin	88
1905	Mike Donlin, NY	124	1919	George Burns, NY	86
1906	Honus Wagner, Pitt	103	1920	George Burns, NY	115
	Frank Chance, Chi	103	1921	Rogers Hornsby, StL	131
1907	Spike Shannon, NY	104	1922	Rogers Hornsby, StL	141
1908	Fred Tenney, NY	101	1923	Ross Youngs, NY	121
1909	Tommy Leach, Pitt	126	1924	Frankie Frisch, NY	121
1910	Sherry Magee, Phil	110		Rogers Hornsby, StL	121
1911	Jimmy Sheckard, Chi	121	1925	Kiki Cuyler, Pitt	144
1912	Bob Bescher, Cin	120	1926	Kiki Cuyler, Pitt	113
1913	Tommy Leach, Chi	99	1927	Lloyd Waner, Pitt	133
	Max Carey, Pitt	99		Rogers Hornsby, NY	133

Leaders in Runs Scored (*Cont.*)

Year	Player and Team	Runs	Year	Player and Team	Runs
1928	Paul Waner, Pitt	142	1961	Willie Mays, SF	129
1929	Rogers Hornsby, Chi	156	1962	Frank Robinson, Cin	134
1930	Chuck Klein, Phil	158	1963	Hank Aaron, Mil	121
1931	Bill Terry, NY	121	1964	Dick Allen, Phil	125
	Chuck Klein, Phil	121	1965	Tommy Harper, Cin	126
1932	Chuck Klein, Phil	152	1966	Felipe Alou, Atl	122
1933	Pepper Martin, StL	122	1967	Hank Aaron, Atl	113
1934	Paul Waner, Pitt	122		Lou Brock, StL	113
1935	Augie Galan, Chi	133	1968	Glenn Beckert, Chi	98
1936	Arky Vaughan, Pitt	122	1969	Bobby Bonds, SF	120
1937	Joe Medwick, StL	111		Pete Rose, Cin	120
1938	Mel Ott, NY	116	1970	Billy Williams, Chi	137
1939	Billy Werber, Cin	115	1971	Lou Brock, StL	126
1940	Arky Vaughan, Pitt	113	1972	Joe Morgan, Cin	122
1941	Pete Reiser, Bklyn	117	1973	Bobby Bonds, SF	131
1942	Mel Ott, NY	118	1974	Pete Rose, Cin	110
1943	Arky Vaughan, Bklyn	112	1975	Pete Rose, Cin	112
1944	Bill Nicholson, Chi	116	1976	Pete Rose, Cin	130
1945	Eddie Stanky, Bklyn	128	1977	George Foster, Cin	124
1946	Stan Musial, StL	124	1978	Ivan DeJesus, Chi	104
1947	Johnny Mize, NY	137	1979	Keith Hernandez, StL	116
1948	Stan Musial, StL	135	1980	Keith Hernandez, StL	111
1949	Pee Wee Reese, Bklyn	132	1981	Mike Schmidt, Phil	78
1950	Earl Torgeson, Bos	120	1982	Lonnie Smith, StL	120
1951	Stan Musial, StL	124	1983	Tim Raines, Mont	133
	Ralph Kiner, Pitt	124	1984	Ryne Sandberg, Chi	114
1952	Stan Musial, StL	105	1985	Dale Murphy, Atl	118
	Solly Hemus, StL	105	1986	Von Hayes, Phil	107
1953	Duke Snider, Bklyn	132		Tony Gwynn, SD	107
1954	Stan Musial, StL	120	1987	Tim Raines, Mont	123
	Duke Snider, Bklyn	120	1988	Brett Butler, SF	109
1955	Duke Snider, Bklyn	126	1989	Howard Johnson, NY	104
1956	Frank Robinson, Cin	122		Will Clark, SF	104
1957	Hank Aaron, Mil	118		Ryne Sandberg, Chi	104
1958	Willie Mays, SF	121	1990	Ryne Sandberg, Chi	116
1959	Vada Pinson, Cin	131	1991	Brett Butler, LA	112
1960	Bill Bruton, Mil	112			

Leaders in Hits

Year	Player and Team	Hits	Year	Player and Team	Hits
1900	Willie Keeler, Bklyn	208	1924	Rogers Hornsby, StL	227
1901	Jesse Burkett, StL	228	1925	Jim Bottomley, StL	227
1902	Ginger Beaumont, Pitt	194	1926	Eddie Brown, Bos	201
1903	Ginger Beaumont, Pitt	209	1927	Paul Waner, Pitt	237
1904	Ginger Beaumont, Pitt	185	1928	Freddy Lindstrom, NY	231
1905	Cy Seymour, Cin	219	1929	Lefty O'Doul, Phil	254
1906	Harry Steinfeldt, Chi	176	1930	Bill Terry, NY	254
1907	Ginger Beaumont, Bos	187	1931	Lloyd Waner, Pitt	214
1908	Honus Wagner, Pitt	201	1932	Chuck Klein, Phil	226
1909	Larry Doyle, NY	172	1933	Chuck Klein, Phil	223
1910	Honus Wagner, Pitt	178	1934	Paul Waner, Pitt	217
	Bobby Byrne, Pitt	178	1935	Billy Herman, Chi	227
1911	Doc Miller, Bos	192	1936	Joe Medwick, StL	223
1912	Heinie Zimmerman, Chi	207	1937	Joe Medwick, StL	237
1913	Gavvy Cravath, Phil	179	1938	Frank McCormick, Cin	209
1914	Sherry Magee, Phil	171	1939	Frank McCormick, Cin	209
1915	Larry Doyle, NY	189	1940	Stan Hack, Chi	191
1916	Hal Chase, Cin	184		Frank McCormick, Cin	191
1917	Heinie Groh, Cin	182	1941	Stan Hack, Chi	186
1918	Charlie Hollocher, Chi	161	1942	Enos Slaughter, StL	188
1919	Ivy Olson, Bklyn	164	1943	Stan Musial, StL	220
1920	Rogers Hornsby, StL	218	1944	Stan Musial, StL	197
1921	Rogers Hornsby, StL	235		Phil Cavarretta, Chi	197
1922	Rogers Hornsby, StL	250	1945	Tommy Holmes, Bos	224
1923	Frankie Frisch, NY	223	1946	Stan Musial, StL	228

Leaders in Hits (*Cont.*)

Year	Player and Team	Hits	Year	Player and Team	Hits
1947	Tommy Holmes, Bos	191	1970	Pete Rose, Cin	205
1948	Stan Musial, StL	230		Billy Williams, Chi	205
1949	Stan Musial, StL	207	1971	Joe Torre, StL	230
1950	Duke Snider, Bklyn	199	1972	Pete Rose, Cin	198
1951	Richie Ashburn, Phil	221	1973	Pete Rose, Cin	230
1952	Stan Musial, StL	194	1974	Ralph Garr, Atl	214
1953	Richie Ashburn, Phil	205	1975	Dave Cash, Phil	213
1954	Don Mueller, NY	212	1976	Pete Rose, Cin	215
1955	Ted Kluszewski, Cin	192	1977	Dave Parker, Pitt	215
1956	Hank Aaron, Mil	200	1978	Steve Garvey, LA	202
1957	Red Schoendienst, NY-Mil	200	1979	Garry Templeton, StL	211
1958	Richie Ashburn, Phil	215	1980	Steve Garvey, LA	200
1959	Hank Aaron, Mil	223	1981	Pete Rose, Phil	140
1960	Willie Mays, SF	190	1982	Al Oliver, Mont	204
1961	Vada Pinson, Cin	208	1983	Jose Cruz, Hou	189
1962	Tommy Davis, LA	230		Andre Dawson, Mont	189
1963	Vada Pinson, Cin	204	1984	Tony Gwynn, SD	213
1964	Roberto Clemente, Pitt	211	1985	Willie McGee, StL	216
	Curt Flood, StL	211	1986	Tony Gwynn, SD	211
1965	Pete Rose, Cin	209	1987	Tony Gwynn, SD	218
1966	Felipe Alou, Atl	218	1988	Andres Galarraga, Mont	184
1967	Roberto Clemente, Pitt	209	1989	Tony Gwynn, SD	203
1968	Felipe Alou, Atl	210	1990	Brett Butler, SF	192
	Pete Rose, Cin	210		Lenny Dykstra, Phil	192
1969	Matty Alou, Pitt	231	1991	Terry Pendleton, Atl	187

Home Run Leaders

Year	Player and Team	HR	Year	Player and Team	HR
1900	Herman Long, Bos	12	1930	Hack Wilson, Chi	56
1901	Sam Crawford, Cin	16	1931	Chuck Klein, Phil	31
1902	Tommy Leach, Pitt	6	1932	Chuck Klein, Phil	38
1903	Jimmy Sheckard, Bklyn	9		Mel Ott, NY	38
1904	Harry Lumley, Bklyn	9	1933	Chuck Klein, Phil	28
1905	Fred Odwell, Cin	9	1934	Ripper Collins, StL	35
1906	Tim Jordan, Bklyn	12		Mel Ott, NY	35
1907	Dave Brain, Bos	10	1935	Wally Berger, Bos	34
1908	Tim Jordan, Bklyn	12	1936	Mel Ott, NY	33
1909	Red Murray, NY	7	1937	Mel Ott, NY	31
1910	Fred Beck, Bos	10		Joe Medwick, StL	31
	Wildfire Schulte, Chi	10	1938	Mel Ott, NY	36
1911	Wildfire Schulte, Chi	21	1939	Johnny Mize, StL	28
1912	Heinie Zimmerman, Chi	14	1940	Johnny Mize, StL	43
1913	Gavvy Cravath, Phil	19	1941	Dolph Camilli, Bklyn	34
1914	Gavvy Cravath, Phil	19	1942	Mel Ott, NY	30
1915	Gavvy Cravath, Phil	24	1943	Bill Nicholson, Chi	29
1916	Dave Robertson, NY	12	1944	Bill Nicholson, Chi	33
1917	Dave Robertson, NY	12	1945	Tommy Holmes, Bos	28
	Gavvy Cravath, Phil	12	1946	Ralph Kiner, Pitt	23
1918	Gavvy Cravath, Phil	8	1947	Ralph Kiner, Pitt	51
1919	Gavvy Cravath, Phil	12		Johnny Mize, NY	51
1920	Cy Williams, Phil	15	1948	Ralph Kiner, Pitt	40
	Cy Williams, Chi	12		Johnny Mize, NY	40
1921	George Kelly, NY	23	1949	Ralph Kiner, Pitt	54
1922	Rogers Hornsby, StL	42	1950	Ralph Kiner, Pitt	47
1923	Cy Williams, Phil	41	1951	Ralph Kiner, Pitt	42
1924	Jack Fournier, Bklyn	27	1952	Ralph Kiner, Pitt	37
1925	Rogers Hornsby, StL	39		Hank Sauer, Chi	37
1926	Hack Wilson, Chi	21	1953	Eddie Mathews, Mil	47
1927	Hack Wilson, Chi	30	1954	Ted Kluszewski, Cin	49
	Cy Williams, Phil	30	1955	Willie Mays, NY	51
1928	Hack Wilson, Chi	31	1956	Duke Snider, Bklyn	43
	Jim Bottomley, StL	31	1957	Hank Aaron, Mil	44
1929	Chuck Klein, Phil	43	1958	Ernie Banks, Chi	47

Home Run Leaders (*Cont.*)

Year	Player and Team	HR	Year	Player and Team	HR
1959	Eddie Mathews, Mil	46	1976	Mike Schmidt, Phil	38
1960	Ernie Banks, Chi	41	1977	George Foster, Cin	52
1961	Orlando Cepeda, SF	46	1978	George Foster, Cin	40
1962	Willie Mays, SF	49	1979	Dave Kingman, Chi	48
1963	Hank Aaron, Mil	44	1980	Mike Schmidt, Phil	48
	Willie McCovey, SF	44	1981	Mike Schmidt, Phil	31
1964	Willie Mays, SF	47	1982	Dave Kingman, NY	37
1965	Willie Mays, SF	52	1983	Mike Schmidt, Phil	40
1966	Hank Aaron, Atl	44	1984	Dale Murphy, Atl	36
1967	Hank Aaron, Atl	39		Mike Schmidt, Phil	36
1968	Willie McCovey, SF	36	1985	Dale Murphy, Atl	37
1969	Willie McCovey, SF	45	1986	Mike Schmidt, Phil	37
1970	Johnny Bench, Cin	45	1987	Andre Dawson, Chi	49
1971	Willie Stargell, Pitt	48	1988	Darryl Strawberry, NY	39
1972	Johnny Bench, Cin	40	1989	Kevin Mitchell, SF	47
1973	Willie Stargell, Pitt	44	1990	Ryne Sandberg, Chi	40
1974	Mike Schmidt, Phil	36	1991	Howard Johnson, NY	38
1975	Mike Schmidt, Phil	38			

Runs Batted In Leaders

Year	Player and Team	RBI	Year	Player and Team	RBI
1900	Elmer Flick, Phil	110	1941	Dolph Camilli, Bklyn	120
1901	Honus Wagner, Pitt	126	1942	Johnny Mize, NY	110
1902	Honus Wagner, Pitt	91	1943	Bill Nicholson, Chi	128
1903	Sam Mertes, NY	104	1944	Bill Nicholson, Chi	122
1904	Bill Dahlen, NY	80	1945	Dixie Walker, Bklyn	124
1905	Cy Seymour, Cin	121	1946	Enos Slaughter, StL	130
1906	Jim Nealon, Pitt	83	1947	Johnny Mize, NY	138
	Harry Steinfeldt, Chi	83	1948	Stan Musial, StL	131
1907	Sherry Magee, Phil	85	1949	Ralph Kiner, Pitt	127
1908	Honus Wagner, Pitt	109	1950	Del Ennis, Phil	126
1909	Honus Wagner, Pitt	100	1951	Monte Irvin, NY	121
1910	Sherry Magee, Phil	123	1952	Hank Sauer, Chi	121
1911	Wildfire Schulte, Chi	121	1953	Roy Campanella, Bklyn	142
1912	Heinie Zimmerman, Chi	103	1954	Ted Kluszewski, Cin	141
1913	Gavvy Cravath, Phil	128	1955	Duke Snider, Bklyn	136
1914	Sherry Magee, Phil	103	1956	Stan Musial, StL	109
1915	Gavvy Cravath, Phil	115	1957	Hank Aaron, Mil	132
1916	Heinie Zimmerman, Chi-NY	83	1958	Ernie Banks, Chi	129
1917	Heinie Zimmerman, NY	102	1959	Ernie Banks, Chi	143
1918	Sherry Magee, Phil	76	1960	Hank Aaron, Mil	126
1919	Hi Myers, Bklyn	73	1961	Orlando Cepeda, SF	142
1920	George Kelly, NY	94	1962	Tommy Davis, LA	153
	Rogers Hornsby, StL	94	1963	Hank Aaron, Mil	130
1921	Rogers Hornsby, StL	126	1964	Ken Boyer, StL	119
1922	Rogers Hornsby, StL	152	1965	Deron Johnson, Cin	130
1923	Irish Meusel, NY	125	1966	Hank Aaron, Atl	127
1924	George Kelly, NY	136	1967	Orlando Cepeda, StL	111
1925	Rogers Hornsby, StL	143	1968	Willie McCovey, SF	105
1926	Jim Bottomley, StL	120	1969	Willie McCovey, SF	126
1927	Paul Waner, Pitt	131	1970	Johnny Bench, Cin	148
1928	Jim Bottomley, StL	136	1971	Joe Torre, StL	137
1929	Hack Wilson, Chi	159	1972	Johnny Bench, Cin	125
1930	Hack Wilson, Chi	190	1973	Willie Stargell, Pitt	119
1931	Chuck Klein, Phil	121	1974	Johnny Bench, Cin	129
1932	Don Hurst, Phil	143	1975	Greg Luzinski, Phil	120
1933	Chuck Klein, Phil	120	1976	George Foster, Cin	121
1934	Mel Ott, NY	135	1977	George Foster, Cin	149
1935	Wally Berger, Bos	130	1978	George Foster, Cin	120
1936	Joe Medwick, StL	138	1979	Dave Winfield, SD	118
1937	Joe Medwick, StL	154	1980	Mike Schmidt, Phil	121
1938	Joe Medwick, StL	122	1981	Mike Schmidt, Phil	91
1939	Frank McCormick, Cin	128	1982	Dale Murphy, Atl	109
1940	Johnny Mize, StL	137		Al Oliver, Mont	109

Runs Batted In Leaders (*Cont.*)

Year	Player and Team	RBI	Year	Player and Team	RBI
1983	Dale Murphy, Atl	121	1987	Andre Dawson, Chi	137
1984	Gary Carter, Mont	106	1988	Will Clark, SF	109
	Mike Schmidt, Phil	106	1989	Kevin Mitchell, SF	125
1985	Dave Parker, Cin	125	1990	Matt Williams, SF	122
1986	Mike Schmidt, Phil	119	1991	Howard Johnson, NY	117

Leading Base Stealers

Year	Player and Team	SB	Year	Player and Team	SB
1900	George Van Haltren, NY	45	1954	Bill Bruton, Mil	34
	Patsy Donovan, StL	45	1955	Bill Bruton, Mil	35
1901	Honus Wagner, Pitt	48	1956	Willie Mays, NY	40
1902	Honus Wagner, Pitt	43	1957	Willie Mays, NY	38
1903	Jimmy Sheckard, Bklyn	67	1958	Willie Mays, SF	31
	Frank Chance, Chi	67	1959	Willie Mays, SF	27
1904	Honus Wagner, Pitt	53	1960	Maury Wills, LA	50
1905	Billy Maloney, Chi	59	1961	Maury Wills, LA	35
	Art Devlin, NY	59	1962	Maury Wills, LA	104
1906	Frank Chance, Chi	57	1963	Maury Wills, LA	40
1907	Honus Wagner, Pitt	61	1964	Maury Wills, LA	53
1908	Honus Wagner, Pitt	53	1965	Maury Wills, LA	94
1909	Bob Bescher, Cin	54	1966	Lou Brock, StL	74
1910	Bob Bescher, Cin	70	1967	Lou Brock, StL	52
1911	Bob Bescher, Cin	80	1968	Lou Brock, StL	62
1912	Bob Bescher, Cin	67	1969	Lou Brock, StL	53
1913	Max Carey, Pitt	61	1970	Bobby Tolan, Cin	57
1914	George Burns, NY	62	1971	Lou Brock, StL	64
1915	Max Carey, Pitt	36	1972	Lou Brock, StL	63
1916	Max Carey, Pitt	63	1973	Lou Brock, StL	70
1917	Max Carey, Pitt	46	1974	Lou Brock, StL	118
1918	Max Carey, Pitt	58	1975	Davey Lopes, LA	77
1919	George Burns, NY	40	1976	Davey Lopes, LA	63
1920	Max Carey, Pitt	52	1977	Frank Taveras, Pitt	70
1921	Frankie Frisch, NY	49	1978	Omar Moreno, Pitt	71
1922	Max Carey, Pitt	51	1979	Omar Moreno, Pitt	77
1923	Max Carey, Pitt	51	1980	Ron LeFlore, Mont	97
1924	Max Carey, Pitt	49	1981	Tim Raines, Mont	71
1925	Max Carey, Pitt	46	1982	Tim Raines, Mont	78
1926	Kiki Cuyler, Pitt	35	1983	Tim Raines, Mont	90
1927	Frankie Frisch, StL	48	1984	Tim Raines, Mont	75
1928	Kiki Cuyler, Chi	37	1985	Vince Coleman, StL	110
1929	Kiki Cuyler, Chi	43	1986	Vince Coleman, StL	107
1930	Kiki Cuyler, Chi	37	1987	Vince Coleman, StL	109
1931	Frankie Frisch, StL	28	1988	Vince Coleman, StL	81
1932	Chuck Klein, Phil	20	1989	Vince Coleman, StL	65
1933	Pepper Martin, StL	26	1990	Vince Coleman, StL	77
1934	Pepper Martin, StL	23	1991	Marquis Grissom, Mont	76
1935	Augie Galan, Chi	22			
1936	Pepper Martin, StL	23			
1937	Augie Galan, Chi	23			
1938	Stan Hack, Chi	16			
1939	Stan Hack, Chi	17			
	Lee Handley, Pitt	17			
1940	Lonny Frey, Cin	22			
1941	Danny Murtaugh, Phil	18			
1942	Pete Reiser, Bklyn	20			
1943	Arky Vaughan, Bklyn	20			
1944	Johnny Barrett, Pitt	28			
1945	Red Schoendienst, StL	26			
1946	Pete Reiser, Bklyn	34			
1947	Jackie Robinson, Bklyn	29			
1948	Richie Ashburn, Phil	32			
1949	Jackie Robinson, Bklyn	37			
1950	Sam Jethroe, Bos	35			
1951	Sam Jethroe, Bos	35			
1952	Pee Wee Reese, Bklyn	30			
1953	Bill Bruton, Mil	26			

THEY SAID IT

Dave Winfield, Angels outfielder, on hitting in front of Dave Parker (a newcomer to California this season) in the batting order: "You're going to hear pitchers saying, 'Nobody told me there'd be Daves like these.'"

Leading Pitchers—Winning Percentage

Year	Pitcher and Team	W	L	Pct	Year	Pitcher and Team	W	L	Pct
1900	Jesse Tannehill, Pitt	20	6	.769	1947	Larry Jansen, NY	21	5	.808
1901	Jack Chesbro, Pitt	21	10	.677	1948	Harry Brecheen, StL	20	7	.741
1902	Jack Chesbro, Pitt	28	6	.824	1949	Preacher Roe, Bklyn	15	6	.714
1903	Sam Leever, Pitt	25	7	.781	1950	Sal Maglie, NY	18	4	.818
1904	Joe McGinnity, NY	35	8	.814	1951	Preacher Roe, Bklyn	22	3	.880
1905	Sam Leever, Pitt	20	5	.800	1952	Hoyt Wilhelm, NY	15	3	.833
1906	Ed Reulbach, Chi	19	4	.826	1953	Carl Erskine, Bklyn	20	6	.769
1907	Ed Reulbach, Chi	17	4	.810	1954	Johnny Antonelli, NY	21	7	.750
1908	Ed Reulbach, Chi	24	7	.774	1955	Don Newcombe, Bklyn	20	5	.800
1909	Christy Mathewson, NY	25	6	.806	1956	Don Newcombe, Bklyn	27	7	.794
	Howie Camnitz, Pitt	25	6	.806	1957	Bob Buhl, Mil	18	7	.720
1910	King Cole, Chi	20	4	.833	1958	Warren Spahn, Mil	22	11	.667
1911	Rube Marquard, NY	24	7	.774		Lew Burdette, Mil	20	10	.667
1912	Claude Hendrix, Pitt	24	9	.727	1959	Roy Face, Pitt	18	1	.947
1913	Bert Humphries, Chi	16	4	.800	1960	Ernie Broglio, StL	21	9	.700
1914	Bill James, Bos	26	7	.788	1961	Johnny Podres, LA	18	5	.783
1915	Grover Alexander, Phil	31	10	.756	1962	Bob Purkey, Cin	23	5	.821
1916	Tom Hughes, Bos	16	3	.842	1963	Ron Perranoski, LA	16	3	.842
1917	Ferdie Schupp, NY	21	7	.750	1964	Sandy Koufax, LA	19	5	.792
1918	Claude Hendrix, Chi	19	7	.731	1965	Sandy Koufax, LA	26	8	.765
1919	Dutch Ruether, Cin	19	6	.760	1966	Juan Marichal, SF	25	6	.806
1920	Burleigh Grimes, Bklyn	23	11	.676	1967	Dick Hughes, StL	16	6	.727
1921	Bill Doak, StL	15	6	.714	1968	Steve Blass, Pitt	18	6	.750
1922	Pete Donohue, Cin	18	9	.667	1969	Tom Seaver, NY	25	7	.781
1923	Dolf Luque, Cin	27	8	.771	1970	Bob Gibson, StL	23	7	.767
1924	Emil Yde, Pitt	16	3	.842	1971	Don Gullett, Cin	16	6	.727
1925	Bill Sherdel, StL	15	6	.714	1972	Gary Nolan, Cin	15	5	.750
1926	Ray Kremer, Pitt	20	6	.769	1973	Tommy John, LA	16	7	.696
1927	Larry Benton, Bos-NY	17	7	.708	1974	Andy Messersmith, LA	20	6	.769
1928	Larry Benton, NY	25	9	.735	1975	Don Gullett, Cin	15	4	.789
1929	Charlie Root, Chi	19	6	.760	1976	Steve Carlton, Phil	20	7	.741
1930	Freddie Fitzsimmons, NY	19	7	.731	1977	John Candelaria, Pitt	20	5	.800
1931	Paul Derringer, StL	18	8	.692	1978	Gaylord Perry, SD	21	6	.778
1932	Lon Warneke, Chi	22	6	.786	1979	Tom Seaver, Cin	16	6	.727
1933	Ben Cantwell, Bos	20	10	.667	1980	Jim Bibby, Pitt	19	6	.760
1934	Dizzy Dean, StL	30	7	.811	1981*	Tom Seaver, Cin	14	2	.875
1935	Bill Lee, Chi	20	6	.769	1982	Phil Niekro, Atl	17	4	.810
1936	Carl Hubbell, NY	26	6	.813	1983	John Denny, Phil	19	6	.760
1937	Carl Hubbell, NY	22	8	.733	1984	Rick Sutcliffe, Chi	16	1	.941
1938	Bill Lee, Chi	22	9	.710	1985	Orel Hershiser, LA	19	3	.864
1939	Paul Derringer, Cin	25	7	.781	1986	Bob Ojeda, NY	18	5	.783
1940	Freddie Fitzsimmons, Bklyn	16	2	.889	1987	Dwight Gooden, NY	15	7	.682
1941	Elmer Riddle, Cin	19	4	.826	1988	David Cone, NY	20	3	.870
1942	Larry French, Bklyn	15	4	.789	1989	Mike Bielecki, Chi	18	7	.720
1943	Mort Cooper, StL	21	8	.724	1990	Doug Drabeck, Pitt	22	6	.786
1944	Ted Wilks, StL	17	4	.810	1991	John Smiley, Pitt	20	8	.714
1945	Harry Brecheen, StL	15	4	.789		Jose Rijo, Cin	15	6	.714
1946	Murray Dickson, StL	15	6	.714					

*1981 percentages based on 10 or more victories.   Note: Based on 15 or more victories.

Orel Hershiser's 59-Inning Consecutive Scoreless Streak, 1988

Date	Opponent/Site	Inn	H	R	ER	BB	SO	Score
Aug. 30	at Montreal	4	1	0	0	2	4	4-2
Sep. 5	at Atlanta	9	4	0	0	1	8	3-0
Sep. 10	Cincinnati	9	7	0	0	3	8	5-0
Sep. 14	Atlanta	9	6	0	0	2	8	1-0
Sep. 19	at Houston	9	4	0	0	0	5	1-0
Sep. 23	at San Francisco	9	5	0	0	2	2	3-0
Sep. 28	at San Diego	10	4	0	0	1	3	1-2
Totals		59	31	0	0	11	38	

Leading Pitchers—Earned-Run Average

Year	Pitcher and Team	ERA	Year	Pitcher and Team	ERA
1900	Rube Waddell, Pitt	2.37	1946	Howie Pollet, StL	2.10
1901	Jesse Tannehill, Pitt	2.18	1947	Warren Spahn, Bos	2.33
1902	Jack Taylor, Chi	1.33	1948	Harry Brecheen, StL	2.24
1903	Sam Leever, Pitt	2.06	1949	Dave Koslo, NY	2.50
1904	Joe McGinnity, NY	1.61	1950	Jim Hearn, StL-NY	2.49
1905	Christy Mathewson, NY	1.27	1951	Chet Nichols, Bos	2.88
1906	Three Finger Brown, Chi	1.04	1952	Hoyt Wilhelm, NY	2.43
1907	Jack Pfiester, Chi	1.15	1953	Warren Spahn, Mil	2.10
1908	Christy Mathewson, NY	1.43	1954	Johnny Antonelli, NY	2.29
1909	Christy Mathewson, NY	1.14	1955	Bob Friend, Pitt	2.84
1910	George McQuillan, Phil	1.60	1956	Lew Burdette, Mil	2.71
1911	Christy Mathewson, NY	1.99	1957	Johnny Podres, Bklyn	2.66
1912	Jeff Tesreau, NY	1.96	1958	Stu Miller, SF	2.47
1913	Christy Mathewson, NY	2.06	1959	Sam Jones, SF	2.82
1914	Bill Doak, StL	1.72	1960	Mike McCormick, SF	2.70
1915	Grover Alexander, Phil	1.22	1961	Warren Spahn, Mil	3.01
1916	Grover Alexander, Phil	1.55	1962	Sandy Koufax, LA	2.54
1917	Grover Alexander, Phil	1.83	1963	Sandy Koufax, LA	1.88
1918	Hippo Vaughn, Chi	1.74	1964	Sandy Koufax, LA	1.74
1919	Grover Alexander, Chi	1.72	1965	Sandy Koufax, LA	2.04
1920	Grover Alexander, Chi	1.91	1966	Sandy Koufax, LA	1.73
1921	Bill Doak, StL	2.58	1967	Phil Niekro, Atl	1.87
1922	Rosy Ryan, NY	3.00	1968	Bob Gibson, StL	1.12
1923	Dolf Luque, Cin	1.93	1969	Juan Marichal, SF	2.10
1924	Dazzy Vance, Bklyn	2.16	1970	Tom Seaver, NY	2.81
1925	Dolf Luque, Cin	2.63	1971	Tom Seaver, NY	1.76
1926	Ray Kremer, Pitt	2.61	1972	Steve Carlton, Phil	1.98
1927	Ray Kremer, Pitt	2.47	1973	Tom Seaver, NY	2.08
1928	Dazzy Vance, Bklyn	2.09	1974	Buzz Capra, Atl	2.28
1929	Bill Walker, NY	3.08	1975	Randy Jones, SD	2.24
1930	Dazzy Vance, Bklyn	2.61	1976	John Denny, StL	2.52
1931	Bill Walker, NY	2.26	1977	John Candelaria, Pitt	2.34
1932	Lon Warneke, Chi	2.37	1978	Craig Swan, NY	2.43
1933	Carl Hubbell, NY	1.66	1979	J.R. Richard, Hou	2.71
1934	Carl Hubbell, NY	2.30	1980	Don Sutton, LA	2.21
1935	Cy Blanton, Pitt	2.59	1981	Nolan Ryan, Hou	1.69
1936	Carl Hubbell, NY	2.31	1982	Steve Rogers, Mont	2.40
1937	Jim Turner, Bos	2.38	1983	Atlee Hammaker, SF	2.25
1938	Bill Lee, Chi	2.66	1984	Alejandro Pena, LA	2.48
1939	Bucky Walters, Cin	2.29	1985	Dwight Gooden, NY	1.53
1940	Bucky Walters, Cin	2.48	1986	Mike Scott, Hou	2.22
1941	Elmer Riddle, Cin	2.24	1987	Nolan Ryan, Hou	2.76
1942	Mort Cooper, StL	1.77	1988	Joe Magrane, StL	2.18
1943	Howie Pollet, StL	1.75	1989	Scott Garrelts, SF	2.28
1944	Ed Heusser, Cin	2.38	1990	Danny Darwin, Hou	2.21
1945	Hank Borowy, Chi	2.14	1991	Dennis Martinez, Mont	2.39

Note: Based on 10 complete games through 1950, then 154 innings until National League expanded in 1962, when it became 162 innings. In strike-shortened 1981, one inning per game required.

Leading Pitchers—Strikeouts

Year	Pitcher and Team	SO	Year	Pitcher and Team	SO
1900	Rube Waddell, Pitt	133	1912	Grover Alexander, Phil	195
1901	Noodles Hahn, Cin	233	1913	Tom Seaton, Phil	168
1902	Vic Willis, Bos	226	1914	Grover Alexander, Phil	214
1903	Christy Mathewson, NY	267	1915	Grover Alexander, Phil	241
1904	Christy Mathewson, NY	212	1916	Grover Alexander, Phil	167
1905	Christy Mathewson, NY	206	1917	Grover Alexander, Phil	200
1906	Fred Beebe, Chi-StL	171	1918	Hippo Vaughn, Chi	148
1907	Christy Mathewson, NY	178	1919	Hippo Vaughn, Chi	141
1908	Christy Mathewson, NY	259	1920	Grover Alexander, Chi	173
1909	Orval Overall, Chi	205	1921	Burleigh Grimes, Bklyn	136
1910	Christy Mathewson, NY	190	1922	Dazzy Vance, Bklyn	134
1911	Rube Marquard, NY	237	1923	Dazzy Vance, Bklyn	197

Leading Pitchers—Strikeouts (*Cont.*)

Year	Player and Team	SO	Year	Player and Team	SO
1924	Dazzy Vance, Bklyn	262	1957	Jack Sanford, Phil	188
1925	Dazzy Vance, Bklyn	221	1958	Sam Jones, StL	225
1926	Dazzy Vance, Bklyn	140	1959	Don Drysdale, LA	242
1927	Dazzy Vance, Bklyn	184	1960	Don Drysdale, LA	246
1928	Dazzy Vance, Bklyn	200	1961	Sandy Koufax, LA	269
1929	Pat Malone, Chi	166	1962	Don Drysdale, LA	232
1930	Bill Hallahan, StL	177	1963	Sandy Koufax, LA	306
1931	Bill Hallahan, StL	159	1964	Bob Veale, Pitt	250
1932	Dizzy Dean, StL	191	1965	Sandy Koufax, LA	382
1933	Dizzy Dean, StL	199	1966	Sandy Koufax, LA	317
1934	Dizzy Dean, StL	195	1967	Jim Bunning, Phil	253
1935	Dizzy Dean, StL	182	1968	Bob Gibson, StL	268
1936	Van Lingle Mungo, Bklyn	238	1969	Ferguson Jenkins, Chi	273
1937	Carl Hubbell, NY	159	1970	Tom Seaver, NY	283
1938	Clay Bryant, Chi	135	1971	Tom Seaver, NY	289
1939	Claude Passeau, Phil-Chi	137	1972	Steve Carlton, Phil	310
	Bucky Walters, Cin	137	1973	Tom Seaver, NY	251
1940	Kirby Higbe, Phil	137	1974	Steve Carlton, Phil	240
1941	Johnny Vander Meer, Cin	202	1975	Tom Seaver, NY	243
1942	Johnny Vander Meer, Cin	186	1976	Tom Seaver, NY	235
1943	Johnny Vander Meer, Cin	174	1977	Phil Niekro, Atl	262
1944	Bill Voiselle, NY	161	1978	J.R. Richard, Hou	303
1945	Preacher Roe, Pitt	148	1979	J.R. Richard, Hou	313
1946	Johnny Schmitz, Chi	135	1980	Steve Carlton, Phil	286
1947	Ewell Blackwell, Cin	193	1981	Fernando Valenzuela, LA	180
1948	Harry Brecheen, StL	149	1982	Steve Carlton, Phil	286
1949	Warren Spahn, Bos	151	1983	Steve Carlton, Phil	275
1950	Warren Spahn, Bos	191	1984	Dwight Gooden, NY	276
1951	Warren Spahn, Bos	164	1985	Dwight Gooden, NY	268
	Don Newcombe, Bklyn	164	1986	Mike Scott, Hou	306
1952	Warren Spahn, Bos	183	1987	Nolan Ryan, Hou	270
1953	Robin Roberts, Phil	198	1988	Nolan Ryan, Hou	228
1954	Robin Roberts, Phil	185	1989	Jose DeLeon, StL	201
1955	Sam Jones, Chi	198	1990	David Cone, NY	233
1956	Sam Jones, Chi	176	1991	David Cone, NY	241

American League

Pennant Winners

Year	Team	Manager	W	L	Pct	GA*
1901	Chicago	Clark Griffith	83	53	.610	4
1902	Philadelphia	Connie Mack	83	53	.610	5
1903	Boston	Jimmy Collins	91	47	.659	14½
1904	Boston	Jimmy Collins	95	59	.617	1½
1905	Philadelphia	Connie Mack	92	56	.622	2
1906	Chicago	Fielder Jones	93	58	.616	3
1907	Detroit	Hughie Jennings	92	58	.613	1½
1908	Detroit	Hughie Jennings	90	63	.588	½
1909	Detroit	Hughie Jennings	98	54	.645	3½
1910	Philadelphia	Connie Mack	102	48	.680	14½
1911	Philadelphia	Connie Mack	101	50	.669	13½
1912	Boston	Jake Stahl	105	47	.691	14
1913	Philadelphia	Connie Mack	96	57	.627	6½
1914	Philadelphia	Connie Mack	99	53	.651	8½
1915	Boston	Bill Carrigan	101	50	.669	2½
1916	Boston	Bill Carrigan	91	63	.591	2
1917	Chicago	Pants Rowland	100	54	.649	9
1918	Boston	Ed Barrow	75	51	.595	2½
1919	Chicago	Kid Gleason	88	52	.629	3½
1920	Cleveland	Tris Speaker	98	56	.636	2
1921	New York	Miller Huggins	98	55	.641	4½
1922	New York	Miller Huggins	94	60	.610	1
1923	New York	Miller Huggins	98	54	.645	16

Pennant Winners (*Cont.*)

Year	Team	Manager	W	L	Pct	GA*
1924	Washington	Bucky Harris	92	62	.597	2
1925	Washington	Bucky Harris	96	55	.636	8½
1926	New York	Miller Huggins	91	63	.591	3
1927	New York	Miller Huggins	110	44	.714	19
1928	New York	Miller Huggins	101	53	.656	2½
1929	Philadelphia	Connie Mack	104	46	.693	18
1930	Philadelphia	Connie Mack	102	52	.662	8
1931	Philadelphia	Connie Mack	107	45	.704	13½
1932	New York	Joe McCarthy	107	47	.695	13
1933	Washington	Joe Cronin	99	53	.651	7
1934	Detroit	Mickey Cochrane	101	53	.656	7
1935	Detroit	Mickey Cochrane	93	58	.616	3
1936	New York	Joe McCarthy	102	51	.667	19½
1937	New York	Joe McCarthy	102	52	.662	13
1938	New York	Joe McCarthy	99	53	.651	9½
1939	New York	Joe McCarthy	106	45	.702	17
1940	Detroit	Del Baker	90	64	.584	1
1941	New York	Joe McCarthy	101	53	.656	17
1942	New York	Joe McCarthy	103	51	.669	9
1943	New York	Joe McCarthy	98	56	.636	13½
1944	St Louis	Luke Sewell	89	65	.578	1
1945	Detroit	Steve O'Neill	88	65	.575	1½
1946	Boston	Joe Cronin	104	50	.675	12
1947	New York	Bucky Harris	97	57	.630	12
1948	Cleveland†	Lou Boudreau	97	58	.626	1
1949	New York	Casey Stengel	97	57	.630	1
1950	New York	Casey Stengel	98	56	.636	3
1951	New York	Casey Stengel	98	56	.636	5
1952	New York	Casey Stengel	95	59	.617	2
1953	New York	Casey Stengel	99	52	.656	8½
1954	Cleveland	Al Lopez	111	43	.721	8
1955	New York	Casey Stengel	96	58	.623	3
1956	New York	Casey Stengel	97	57	.630	9
1957	New York	Casey Stengel	98	56	.636	8
1958	New York	Casey Stengel	92	62	.597	10
1959	Chicago	Al Lopez	94	60	.610	5
1960	New York	Casey Stengel	97	57	.630	8
1961	New York	Ralph Houk	109	53	.673	8
1962	New York	Ralph Houk	96	66	.593	5
1963	New York	Ralph Houk	104	57	.646	10½
1964	New York	Yogi Berra	99	63	.611	1
1965	Minnesota	Sam Mele	102	60	.630	7
1966	Baltimore	Hank Bauer	97	63	.606	9
1967	Boston	Dick Williams	92	70	.568	1
1968	Detroit	Mayo Smith	103	59	.636	12
1969	Baltimore (E)‡	Earl Weaver	109	53	.673	19
1970	Baltimore (E)‡	Earl Weaver	108	54	.667	15
1971	Baltimore (E)‡	Earl Weaver	101	57	.639	12
1972	Oakland (W)‡	Dick Williams	93	62	.600	5½
1973	Oakland (W)‡	Dick Williams	94	68	.580	6
1974	Oakland (W)‡	Al Dark	90	72	.556	5
1975	Boston (E)‡	Darrell Johnson	95	65	.594	4½
1976	New York (E)‡	Billy Martin	97	62	.610	10½
1977	New York (E)‡	Billy Martin	100	62	.617	2½
1978	New York (E)†‡	Billy Martin, Bob Lemon	100	63	.613	1
1979	Baltimore (E)‡	Earl Weaver	102	57	.642	8
1980	Kansas City (W)‡	Jim Frey	97	65	.599	14
1981	New York (E)‡	Gene Michael, Bob Lemon	59	48	.551	#
1982	Milwaukee (E)‡	Buck Rodgers, Harvey Kuenn	95	67	.586	1

There's Gold in Them Thar Cards

This is for all of you whose mother threw out your baseball cards. Early in 1991 Los Angeles Kings hockey great Wayne Gretzky and team owner Bruce McNall purchased a c.1910 Honus Wagner baseball card at a Sotheby's auction for $451,000.

Pennant Winners (*Cont.*)

Year	Team	Manager	W	L	Pct	GA*
1983	Baltimore (E)‡	Joe Altobelli	98	64	.605	6
1984	Detroit (E)‡	Sparky Anderson	104	58	.642	15
1985	Kansas City (W)‡	Dick Howser	91	71	.562	1
1986	Boston (E)‡	John McNamara	95	66	.590	5½
1987	Minnesota (W)‡	Tom Kelly	85	77	.525	2
1988	Oakland (W)‡	Tony La Russa	104	58	.642	13
1989	Oakland (W)‡	Tony La Russa	99	63	.611	7
1990	Oakland (W)‡	Tony La Russa	103	59	.636	9
1991	Minnesota (W)	Tom Kelly	95	67	.586	8

*Games ahead of second-place club. †Defeated Boston in one-game playoff. ‡Won championship series. #First half 34-22; second 25-26.

Leading Batsmen

Year	Player and Team	BA	Year	Player and Team	BA
1901	Nap Lajoie, Phil	.422	1947	Ted Williams, Bos	.343
1902	Ed Delahanty, Wash	.376	1948	Ted Williams, Bos	.369
1903	Nap Lajoie, Clev	.355	1949	George Kell, Det	.343
1904	Nap Lajoie, Clev	.381	1950	Billy Goodman, Bos	.354
1905	Elmer Flick, Clev	.306	1951	Ferris Fain, Phil	.344
1906	George Stone, StL	.358	1952	Ferris Fain, Phil	.327
1907	Ty Cobb, Det	.350	1953	Mickey Vernon, Wash	.337
1908	Ty Cobb, Det	.324	1954	Bobby Avila, Clev	.341
1909	Ty Cobb, Det	.377	1955	Al Kaline, Det	.340
1910	Nap Lajoie, Clev*	.383	1956	Mickey Mantle, NY	.353
1911	Ty Cobb, Det	.420	1957	Ted Williams, Bos	.388
1912	Ty Cobb, Det	.410	1958	Ted Williams, Bos	.328
1913	Ty Cobb, Det	.390	1959	Harvey Kuenn, Det	.353
1914	Ty Cobb, Det	.368	1960	Pete Runnels, Bos	.320
1915	Ty Cobb, Det	.369	1961	Norm Cash, Det	.361
1916	Tris Speaker, Clev	.386	1962	Pete Runnels, Bos	.326
1917	Ty Cobb, Det	.383	1963	Carl Yastrzemski, Bos	.321
1918	Ty Cobb, Det	.382	1964	Tony Oliva, Minn	.323
1919	Ty Cobb, Det	.384	1965	Tony Oliva, Minn	.321
1920	George Sisler, StL	.407	1966	Frank Robinson, Balt	.316
1921	Harry Heilmann, Det	.394	1967	Carl Yastrzemski, Bos	.326
1922	George Sisler, StL	.420	1968	Carl Yastrzemski, Bos	.301
1923	Harry Heilmann, Det	.403	1969	Rod Carew, Minn	.332
1924	Babe Ruth, NY	.378	1970	Alex Johnson, Calif	.329
1925	Harry Heilmann, Det	.393	1971	Tony Oliva, Minn	.337
1926	Heinie Manush, Det	.378	1972	Rod Carew, Minn	.318
1927	Harry Heilmann, Det	.398	1973	Rod Carew, Minn	.350
1928	Goose Goslin, Wash	.379	1974	Rod Carew, Minn	.364
1929	Lew Fonseca, Clev	.369	1975	Rod Carew, Minn	.359
1930	Al Simmons, Phil	.381	1976	George Brett, KC	.333
1931	Al Simmons, Phil	.390	1977	Rod Carew, Minn	.388
1932	Dale Alexander, Det-Bos	.367	1978	Rod Carew, Minn	.333
1933	Jimmie Foxx, Phil	.356	1979	Fred Lynn, Bos	.333
1934	Lou Gehrig, NY	.363	1980	George Brett, KC	.390
1935	Buddy Myer, Wash	.349	1981	Carney Lansford, Bos	.336
1936	Luke Appling, Chi	.388	1982	Willie Wilson, KC	.332
1937	Charlie Gehringer, Det	.371	1983	Wade Boggs, Bos	.361
1938	Jimmie Foxx, Bos	.349	1984	Don Mattingly, NY	.343
1939	Joe DiMaggio, NY	.381	1985	Wade Boggs, Bos	.368
1940	Joe DiMaggio, NY	.352	1986	Wade Boggs, Bos	.357
1941	Ted Williams, Bos	.406	1987	Wade Boggs, Bos	.363
1942	Ted Williams, Bos	.356	1988	Wade Boggs, Bos	.366
1943	Luke Appling, Chi	.328	1989	Kirby Puckett, Minn	.339
1944	Lou Boudreau, Clev	.327	1990	George Brett, KC	.329
1945	Snuffy Stirnweiss, NY	.309	1991	Julio Franco, Tex	.341
1946	Mickey Vernon, Wash	.353			

*League president Ban Johnson declared Ty Cobb batting champion with a .385 average, beating Lajoie's .384. However, subsequent research has led to the revision of Lajoie's average to .383 and Cobb's to .382.

Leaders in Runs Scored

Year	Player and Team	Runs	Year	Player and Team	Runs
1901	Nap Lajoie, Phil	145	1948	Tommy Henrich, NY	138
1902	Dave Fultz, Phil	110	1949	Ted Williams, Bos	150
1903	Patsy Dougherty, Bos	108	1950	Dom DiMaggio, Bos	131
1904	Patsy Dougherty, Bos-NY	113	1951	Dom DiMaggio, Bos	113
1905	Harry Davis, Phil	92	1952	Larry Doby, Clev	104
1906	Elmer Flick, Clev	98	1953	Al Rosen, Clev	115
1907	Sam Crawford, Det	102	1954	Mickey Mantle, NY	129
1908	Matty McIntyre, Det	105	1955	Al Smith, Clev	123
1909	Ty Cobb, Det	116	1956	Mickey Mantle, NY	132
1910	Ty Cobb, Det	106	1957	Mickey Mantle, NY	121
1911	Ty Cobb, Det	147	1958	Mickey Mantle, NY	127
1912	Eddie Collins, Phil	137	1959	Eddie Yost, Det	115
1913	Eddie Collins, Phil	125	1960	Mickey Mantle, NY	119
1914	Eddie Collins, Phil	122	1961	Mickey Mantle, NY	132
1915	Ty Cobb, Det	144		Roger Maris, NY	132
1916	Ty Cobb, Det	113	1962	Albie Pearson, LA	115
1917	Donie Bush, Det	112	1963	Bob Allison, Minn	99
1918	Ray Chapman, Clev	84	1964	Tony Oliva, Minn	109
1919	Babe Ruth, Bos	103	1965	Zoilo Versalles, Minn	126
1920	Babe Ruth, NY	158	1966	Frank Robinson, Balt	122
1921	Babe Ruth, NY	177	1967	Carl Yastrzemski, Bos	112
1922	George Sisler, StL	134	1968	Dick McAuliffe, Det	95
1923	Babe Ruth, NY	151	1969	Reggie Jackson, Oak	123
1924	Babe Ruth, NY	143	1970	Carl Yastrzemski, Bos	125
1925	Johnny Mostil, Chi	135	1971	Don Buford, Balt	99
1926	Babe Ruth, NY	139	1972	Bobby Murcer, NY	102
1927	Babe Ruth, NY	158	1973	Reggie Jackson, Oak	99
1928	Babe Ruth, NY	163	1974	Carl Yastrzemski, Bos	93
1929	Charlie Gehringer, Det	131	1975	Fred Lynn, Bos	103
1930	Al Simmons, Phil	152	1976	Roy White, NY	104
1931	Lou Gehrig, NY	163	1977	Rod Carew, Minn	128
1932	Jimmie Foxx, Phil	151	1978	Ron LeFlore, Det	126
1933	Lou Gehrig, NY	138	1979	Don Baylor, Calif	120
1934	Charlie Gehringer, Det	134	1980	Willie Wilson, KC	133
1935	Lou Gehrig, NY	125	1981	Rickey Henderson, Oak	89
1936	Lou Gehrig, NY	167	1982	Paul Molitor, Mil	136
1937	Joe DiMaggio, NY	151	1983	Cal Ripken, Balt	121
1938	Hank Greenberg, Det	144	1984	Dwight Evans, Bos	121
1939	Red Rolfe, NY	139	1985	Rickey Henderson, NY	146
1940	Ted Williams, Bos	134	1986	Rickey Henderson, NY	130
1941	Ted Williams, Bos	135	1987	Paul Molitor, Mil	114
1942	Ted Williams, Bos	141	1988	Wade Boggs, Bos	128
1943	George Case, Wash	102	1989	Rickey Henderson, NY-Oak	113
1944	Snuffy Stirnweiss, NY	125		Wade Boggs, Bos	113
1945	Snuffy Stirnweiss, NY	107	1990	Rickey Henderson, Oak	119
1946	Ted Williams, Bos	142	1991	Paul Molitor, Mil	133
1947	Ted Williams, Bos	125			

Leaders in Hits

Year	Player and Team	Hits	Year	Player and Team	Hits
1901	Nap Lajoie, Phil	229	1915	Ty Cobb, Det	208
1902	Piano Legs Hickman, Bos-Clev	194	1916	Tris Speaker, Clev	211
1903	Patsy Dougherty, Bos	195	1917	Ty Cobb, Det	225
1904	Nap Lajoie, Clev	211	1918	George Burns, Phil	178
1905	George Stone, StL	187	1919	Ty Cobb, Det	191
1906	Nap Lajoie, Clev	214		Bobby Veach, Det	191
1907	Ty Cobb, Det	212	1920	George Sisler, StL	257
1908	Ty Cobb, Det	188	1921	Harry Heilmann, Det	237
1909	Ty Cobb, Det	216	1922	George Sisler, StL	246
1910	Nap Lajoie, Clev	227	1923	Charlie Jamieson, Clev	222
1911	Ty Cobb, Det	248	1924	Sam Rice, Wash	216
1912	Ty Cobb, Det	227	1925	Al Simmons, Phil	253
1913	Joe Jackson, Clev	197	1926	George Burns, Clev	216
1914	Tris Speaker, Bos	193		Sam Rice, Wash	216

Leaders in Hits (*Cont.*)

Year	Player and Team	Hits	Year	Player and Team	Hits
1927	Earle Combs, NY	231	1958	Nellie Fox, Chi	187
1928	Heinie Manush, StL	241	1959	Harvey Kuenn, Det	198
1929	Dale Alexander, Det	215	1960	Minnie Minoso, Chi	184
	Charlie Gehringer, Det	215	1961	Norm Cash, Det	193
1930	Johnny Hodapp, Clev	225	1962	Bobby Richardson, NY	209
1931	Lou Gehrig, NY	211	1963	Carl Yastrzemski, Bos	183
1932	Al Simmons, Phil	216	1964	Tony Oliva, Minn	217
1933	Heinie Manush, Wash	221	1965	Tony Oliva, Minn	185
1934	Charlie Gehringer, Det	214	1966	Tony Oliva, Minn	191
1935	Joe Vosmik, Clev	216	1967	Carl Yastrzemski, Bos	189
1936	Earl Averill, Clev	232	1968	Bert Campaneris, Oak	177
1937	Beau Bell, StL	218	1969	Tony Oliva, Minn	197
1938	Joe Vosmik, Bos	201	1970	Tony Oliva, Minn	204
1939	Red Rolfe, NY	213	1971	Cesar Tovar, Minn	204
1940	Rip Radcliff, StL	200	1972	Joe Rudi, Oak	181
	Barney McCosky, Det	200	1973	Rod Carew, Minn	203
	Doc Cramer, Bos	200	1974	Rod Carew, Minn	218
1941	Cecil Travis, Wash	218	1975	George Brett, KC	195
1942	Johnny Pesky, Bos	205	1976	George Brett, KC	215
1943	Dick Wakefield, Det	200	1977	Rod Carew, Minn	239
1944	Snuffy Stirnweiss, NY	205	1978	Jim Rice, Bos	213
1945	Snuffy Stirnweiss, NY	195	1979	George Brett, KC	212
1946	Johnny Pesky, Bos	208	1980	Willie Wilson, KC	230
1947	Johnny Pesky, Bos	207	1981	Rickey Henderson, Oak	135
1948	Bob Dillinger, StL	207	1982	Robin Yount, Mil	210
1949	Dale Mitchell, Clev	203	1983	Cal Ripken, Balt	211
1950	George Kell, Det	218	1984	Don Mattingly, NY	207
1951	George Kell, Det	191	1985	Wade Boggs, Bos	240
1952	Nellie Fox, Chi	192	1986	Don Mattingly, NY	238
1953	Harvey Kuenn, Det	209	1987	Kirby Puckett, Minn	207
1954	Nellie Fox, Chi	201		Kevin Seitzer, KC	207
	Harvey Kuenn, Det	201	1988	Kirby Puckett, Minn	234
1955	Al Kaline, Det	200	1989	Kirby Puckett, Minn	215
1956	Harvey Kuenn, Det	196	1990	Rafael Palmeiro, Tex	191
1957	Nellie Fox, Chi	196	1991	Paul Molitor, Mil	216

Home Run Leaders

Year	Player and Team	HR	Year	Player and Team	HR
1901	Nap Lajoie, Phil	13	1926	Babe Ruth, NY	47
1902	Socks Seybold, Phil	16	1927	Babe Ruth, NY	60
1903	Buck Freeman, Bos	13	1928	Babe Ruth, NY	54
1904	Harry Davis, Phil	10	1929	Babe Ruth, NY	46
1905	Harry Davis, Phil	8	1930	Babe Ruth, NY	49
1906	Harry Davis, Phil	12	1931	Babe Ruth, NY	46
1907	Harry Davis, Phil	8		Lou Gehrig, NY	46
1908	Sam Crawford, Det	7	1932	Jimmie Foxx, Phil	58
1909	Ty Cobb, Det	9	1933	Jimmie Foxx, Phil	48
1910	Jake Stahl, Bos	10	1934	Lou Gehrig, NY	49
1911	Frank Baker, Phil	9	1935	Jimmie Foxx, Phil	36
1912	Frank Baker, Phil	10		Hank Greenberg, Det	36
	Tris Speaker, Bos	10	1936	Lou Gehrig, NY	49
1913	Frank Baker, Phil	13	1937	Joe DiMaggio, NY	46
1914	Frank Baker, Phil	9	1938	Hank Greenberg, Det	58
1915	Braggo Roth, Chi-Clev	7	1939	Jimmie Foxx, Bos	35
1916	Wally Pipp, NY	12	1940	Hank Greenberg, Det	41
1917	Wally Pipp, NY	9	1941	Ted Williams, Bos	37
1918	Babe Ruth, Bos	11	1942	Ted Williams, Bos	36
	Tilly Walker, Phil	11	1943	Rudy York, Det	34
1919	Babe Ruth, Bos	29	1944	Nick Etten, NY	22
1920	Babe Ruth, NY	54	1945	Vern Stephens, StL	24
1921	Babe Ruth, NY	59	1946	Hank Greenberg, Det	44
1922	Ken Williams, StL	39	1947	Ted Williams, Bos	32
1923	Babe Ruth, NY	41	1948	Joe DiMaggio, NY	39
1924	Babe Ruth, NY	46	1949	Ted Williams, Bos	43
1925	Bob Meusel, NY	33	1950	Al Rosen, Clev	37

Home Run Leaders (*Cont.*)

Year	Player and Team	HR	Year	Player and Team	H
1951	Gus Zernial, Chi-Phil	33	1974	Dick Allen, Chi	3.
1952	Larry Doby, Clev	32	1975	Reggie Jackson, Oak	3
1953	Al Rosen, Clev	43		George Scott, Mil	3
1954	Larry Doby, Clev	32	1976	Graig Nettles, NY	3
1955	Mickey Mantle, NY	37	1977	Jim Rice, Bos	3
1956	Mickey Mantle, NY	52	1978	Jim Rice, Bos	4
1957	Roy Sievers, Wash	42	1979	Gorman Thomas, Mil	4
1958	Mickey Mantle, NY	42	1980	Reggie Jackson, NY	4
1959	Rocky Colavito, Clev	42		Ben Oglivie, Mil	4
	Harmon Killebrew, Wash	42	1981	Tony Armas, Oak	2
1960	Mickey Mantle, NY	40	1981	Dwight Evans, Bos	2
1961	Roger Maris, NY	61		Bobby Grich, Calif	2
1962	Harmon Killebrew, Minn	48		Eddie Murray, Balt	2
1963	Harmon Killebrew, Minn	45	1982	Reggie Jackson, Calif	3
1964	Harmon Killebrew, Minn	49		Gorman Thomas, Mil	3
1965	Tony Conigliaro, Bos	32	1983	Jim Rice, Bos	3
1966	Frank Robinson, Balt	49	1984	Tony Armas, Bos	4
1967	Harmon Killebrew, Minn	44	1985	Darrell Evans, Det	4
	Carl Yastrzemski, Bos	44	1986	Jesse Barfield, Tor	4
1968	Frank Howard, Wash	44	1987	Mark McGwire, Oak	4
1969	Harmon Killebrew, Minn	49	1988	Jose Canseco, Oak	4
1970	Frank Howard, Wash	44	1989	Fred McGriff, Tor	3
1971	Bill Melton, Chi	33	1990	Cecil Fielder, Det	5
1972	Dick Allen, Chi	37	1991	Jose Canseco, Oak	4
1973	Reggie Jackson, Oak	32		Cecil Fielder, Det	4

Runs Batted In Leaders

Year	Player and Team	RBI	Year	Player and Team	RB
1907	Ty Cobb, Det	116	1941	Joe DiMaggio, NY	12
1908	Ty Cobb, Det	108	1942	Ted Williams, Bos	13
1909	Ty Cobb, Det	107	1943	Rudy York, Det	118
1910	Sam Crawford, Det	120	1944	Vern Stephens, StL	10
1911	Ty Cobb, Det	144	1945	Nick Etten, NY	11
1912	Frank Baker, Phil	133	1946	Hank Greenberg, Det	12
1913	Frank Baker, Phil	126	1947	Ted Williams, Bos	11
1914	Sam Crawford, Det	104	1948	Joe DiMaggio, NY	15
1915	Sam Crawford, Det	112	1949	Ted Williams, Bos	15
	Bobby Veach, Det	112		Vern Stephens, Bos	159
1916	Del Pratt, StL	103	1950	Walt Dropo, Bos	144
1917	Bobby Veach, Det	103		Vern Stephens, Bos	144
1918	Bobby Veach, Det	78	1951	Gus Zernial, Chi-Phil	129
1919	Babe Ruth, Bos	114	1952	Al Rosen, Clev	105
1920	Babe Ruth, NY	137	1953	Al Rosen, Clev	145
1921	Babe Ruth, NY	171	1954	Larry Doby, Clev	126
1922	Ken Williams, StL	155	1955	Ray Boone, Det	116
1923	Babe Ruth, NY	131		Jackie Jensen, Bos	116
1924	Goose Goslin, Wash	129	1956	Mickey Mantle, NY	130
1925	Bob Meusel, NY	138	1957	Roy Sievers, Wash	114
1926	Babe Ruth, NY	145	1958	Jackie Jensen, Bos	122
1927	Lou Gehrig, NY	175	1959	Jackie Jensen, Bos	112
1928	Babe Ruth, NY	142	1960	Roger Maris, NY	112
	Lou Gehrig, NY	142	1961	Roger Maris, NY	142
1929	Al Simmons, Phil	157	1962	Harmon Killebrew, Minn	126
1930	Lou Gehrig, NY	174	1963	Dick Stuart, Bos	118
1931	Lou Gehrig, NY	184	1964	Brooks Robinson, Balt	118
1932	Jimmie Foxx, Phil	169	1965	Rocky Colavito, Clev	108
1933	Jimmie Foxx, Phil	163	1966	Frank Robinson, Balt	122
1934	Lou Gehrig, NY	165	1967	Carl Yastrzemski, Bos	121
1935	Hank Greenberg, Det	170	1968	Ken Harrelson, Bos	109
1936	Hal Trosky, Clev	162	1969	Harmon Killebrew, Minn	140
1937	Hank Greenberg, Det	183	1970	Frank Howard, Wash	126
1938	Jimmie Foxx, Bos	175	1971	Harmon Killebrew, Minn	119
1939	Ted Williams, Bos	145	1972	Dick Allen, Chi	113
1940	Hank Greenberg, Det	150	1973	Reggie Jackson, Oak	117

Runs Batted In Leaders (*Cont.*)

Year	Player and Team	RBI	Year	Player and Team	RBI
974	Jeff Burroughs, Tex	118	1984	Tony Armas, Bos	123
975	George Scott, Mil	109	1985	Don Mattingly, NY	145
976	Lee May, Balt	109	1986	Joe Carter, Clev	121
977	Larry Hisle, Minn	119	1987	George Bell, Tor	134
978	Jim Rice, Bos	139	1988	Jose Canseco, Oak	124
979	Don Baylor, Calif	139	1989	Ruben Sierra, Tex	119
980	Cecil Cooper, Mil	122	1990	Cecil Fielder, Det	132
981	Eddie Murray, Balt	78	1991	Cecil Fielder, Det	133
982	Hal McRae, KC	133			
983	Cecil Cooper, Mil	126			
	Jim Rice, Bos	126			

Note: Runs batted in not compiled before 1907; officially adopted in 1920.

Leading Base Stealers

Year	Player and Team	SB	Year	Player and Team	SB
1901	Frank Isbell, Chi	48	1945	Snuffy Stirnweiss, NY	33
1902	Topsy Hartsel, Phil	54	1946	George Case, Clev	28
1903	Harry Bay, Clev	46	1947	Bob Dillinger, StL	34
1904	Elmer Flick, Clev	42	1948	Bob Dillinger, StL	28
	Harry Bay, Clev	42	1949	Bob Dillinger, StL	20
1905	Danny Hoffman, Phil	46	1950	Dom DiMaggio, Bos	15
1906	Elmer Flick, Clev	39	1951	Minnie Minoso, Clev-Chi	31
	John Anderson, Wash	39	1952	Minnie Minoso, Chi	22
1907	Ty Cobb, Det	49	1953	Minnie Minoso, Chi	25
1908	Patsy Dougherty, Chi	47	1954	Jackie Jensen, Bos	22
1909	Ty Cobb, Det	76	1955	Jim Rivera, Chi	25
1910	Eddie Collins, Phil	81	1956	Luis Aparicio, Chi	21
1911	Ty Cobb, Det	83	1957	Luis Aparicio, Chi	28
1912	Clyde Milan, Wash	88	1958	Luis Aparicio, Chi	29
1913	Clyde Milan, Wash	75	1959	Luis Aparicio, Chi	56
1914	Fritz Maisel, NY	74	1960	Luis Aparicio, Chi	51
1915	Ty Cobb, Det	96	1961	Luis Aparicio, Chi	53
1916	Ty Cobb, Det	68	1962	Luis Aparicio, Chi	31
1917	Ty Cobb, Det	55	1963	Luis Aparicio, Balt	40
1918	George Sisler, StL	45	1964	Luis Aparicio, Balt	57
1919	Eddie Collins, Chi	33	1965	Bert Campaneris, KC	51
1920	Sam Rice, Wash	63	1966	Bert Campaneris, KC	52
1921	George Sisler, StL	35	1967	Bert Campaneris, KC	55
1922	George Sisler, StL	51	1968	Bert Campaneris, Oak	62
1923	Eddie Collins, Chi	49	1969	Tommy Harper, Sea	73
1924	Eddie Collins, Chi	42	1970	Bert Campaneris, Oak	42
1925	John Mostil, Chi	43	1971	Amos Otis, KC	52
1926	John Mostil, Chi	35	1972	Bert Campaneris, Oak	52
1927	George Sisler, StL	27	1973	Tommy Harper, Bos	54
1928	Buddy Myer, Bos	30	1974	Bill North, Oak	54
1929	Charlie Gehringer, Det	27	1975	Mickey Rivers, Calif	70
1930	Marty McManus, Det	23	1976	Bill North, Oak	75
1931	Ben Chapman, NY	61	1977	Freddie Patek, KC	53
1932	Ben Chapman, NY	38	1978	Ron LeFlore, Det	68
1933	Ben Chapman, NY	27	1979	Willie Wilson, KC	83
1934	Bill Werber, Bos	40	1980	Rickey Henderson, Oak	100
1935	Bill Werber, Bos	29	1981	Rickey Henderson, Oak	56
1936	Lyn Lary, StL	37	1982	Rickey Henderson, Oak	130
1937	Bill Werber, Phil	35	1983	Rickey Henderson, Oak	108
	Ben Chapman, Wash-Bos	35	1984	Rickey Henderson, Oak	66
1938	Frank Crosetti, NY	27	1985	Rickey Henderson, NY	80
1939	George Case, Wash	51	1986	Rickey Henderson, NY	87
1940	George Case, Wash	35	1987	Harold Reynolds, Sea	60
1941	George Case, Wash	33	1988	Rickey Henderson, NY	93
1942	George Case, Wash	44	1989	Rickey Henderson, NY-Oak	77
1943	George Case, Wash	61	1990	Rickey Henderson, Oak	65
1944	Snuffy Stirnweiss, NY	55	1991	Rickey Henderson, Oak	58

Leading Pitchers—Winning Percentage

Year	Pitcher and Team	W	L	Pct	Year	Pitcher and Team	W	L	Pct
1901	Clark Griffith, Chi	24	7	.774	1948	Jack Kramer, Bos	18	5	.783
1902	Bill Bernhard, Phil-Clev	18	5	.783	1949	Ellis Kinder, Bos	23	6	.793
1903	Earl Moore, Clev	22	7	.759	1950	Vic Raschi, NY	21	8	.724
1904	Jack Chesbro, NY	41	12	.774	1951	Bob Feller, Clev	22	8	.733
1905	Jess Tannehill, Bos	22	9	.710	1952	Bobby Shantz, Phil	24	7	.774
1906	Eddie Plank, Phil	19	6	.760	1953	Ed Lopat, NY	16	4	.800
1907	Wild Bill Donovan, Det	25	4	.862	1954	Sandy Consuegra, Chi	16	3	.842
1908	Ed Walsh, Chi	40	15	.727	1955	Tommy Byrne, NY	16	5	.762
1909	George Mullin, Det	29	8	.784	1956	Whitey Ford, NY	19	6	.760
1910	Chief Bender, Phil	23	5	.821	1957	Dick Donovan, Chi	16	6	.727
1911	Chief Bender, Phil	17	5	.773		Tom Sturdivant, NY	16	6	.727
1912	Smoky Joe Wood, Bos	34	5	.872	1958	Bob Turley, NY	21	7	.750
1913	Walter Johnson, Wash	36	7	.837	1959	Bob Shaw, Chi	18	6	.750
1914	Chief Bender, Phil	17	3	.850	1960	Jim Perry, Clev	18	10	.643
1915	Smoky Joe Wood, Bos	15	5	.750	1961	Whitey Ford, NY	25	4	.862
1916	Eddie Cicotte, Chi	15	7	.682	1962	Ray Herbert, Chi	20	9	.690
1917	Reb Russell, Chi	15	5	.750	1963	Whitey Ford, NY	24	7	.774
1918	Sad Sam Jones, Bos	16	5	.762	1964	Wally Bunker, Balt	19	5	.792
1919	Eddie Cicotte, Chi	29	7	.806	1965	Mudcat Grant, Minn	21	7	.750
1920	Jim Bagby, Clev	31	12	.721	1966	Sonny Siebert, Clev	16	8	.667
1921	Carl Mays, NY	27	9	.750	1967	Joel Horlen, Chi	19	7	.731
1922	Joe Bush, NY	26	7	.788	1968	Denny McLain, Det	31	6	.838
1923	Herb Pennock, NY	19	6	.760	1969	Jim Palmer, Balt	16	4	.800
1924	Walter Johnson, Wash	23	7	.767	1970	Mike Cuellar, Balt	24	8	.750
1925	Stan Coveleski, Wash	20	5	.800	1971	Dave McNally, Balt	21	5	.808
1926	George Uhle, Clev	27	11	.711	1972	Catfish Hunter, Oak	21	7	.750
1927	Waite Hoyt, NY	22	7	.759	1973	Catfish Hunter, Oak	21	5	.808
1928	General Crowder, StL	21	5	.808	1974	Mike Cuellar, Balt	22	10	.688
1929	Lefty Grove, Phil	20	6	.769	1975	Mike Torrez, Balt	20	9	.690
1930	Lefty Grove, Phil	28	5	.848	1976	Bill Campbell, Minn	17	5	.773
1931	Lefty Grove, Phil	31	4	.886	1977	Paul Splittorff, KC	16	6	.727
1932	Johnny Allen, NY	17	4	.810	1978	Ron Guidry, NY	25	3	.893
1933	Lefty Grove, Phil	24	8	.750	1979	Mike Caldwell, Mil	16	6	.727
1934	Lefty Gomez, NY	26	5	.839	1980	Steve Stone, Balt	25	7	.781
1935	Eldon Auker, Det	18	7	.720	1981*	Pete Vuckovich, Mil	14	4	.778
1936	Monte Pearson, NY	19	7	.731	1982	Pete Vuckovich, Mil	18	6	.750
1937	Johnny Allen, Clev	15	1	.938		Jim Palmer, Balt	15	5	.750
1938	Red Ruffing, NY	21	7	.750	1983	Richard Dotson, Chi	22	7	.759
1939	Lefty Grove, Bos	15	4	.789	1984	Doyle Alexander, Tor	17	6	.739
1940	Schoolboy Rowe, Det	16	3	.842	1985	Ron Guidry, NY	22	6	.786
1941	Lefty Gomez, NY	15	5	.750	1986	Roger Clemens, Bos	24	4	.857
1942	Ernie Bonham, NY	21	5	.808	1987	Roger Clemens, Bos	20	9	.690
1943	Spud Chandler, NY	20	4	.833	1988	Frank Viola, Minn	24	7	.774
1944	Tex Hughson, Bos	18	5	.783	1989	Bret Saberhagen, KC	23	6	.793
1945	Hal Newhouser, Det	25	9	.735	1990	Bob Welch, Oak	27	6	.818
1946	Boo Ferriss, Bos	25	6	.806	1991	Scott Erickson, Minn	20	8	.714
1947	Allie Reynolds, NY	19	8	.704					

Note: Based on 15 or more victories.

*1981 percentages based on 10 or more victories.

Leading Pitchers—Earned-Run Average

Year	Pitcher and Team	ERA	Year	Pitcher and Team	ERA
1913	Walter Johnson, Wash	1.14	1924	Walter Johnson, Wash	2.72
1914	Dutch Leonard, Bos	1.01	1925	Stan Coveleski, Wash	2.84
1915	Smoky Joe Wood, Bos	1.49	1926	Lefty Grove, Phil	2.51
1916	Babe Ruth, Bos	1.75	1927	Wilcy Moore,* NY	2.28
1917	Eddie Cicotte, Chi	1.53	1928	Garland Braxton, Wash	2.52
1918	Walter Johnson, Wash	1.27	1929	Lefty Grove, Phil	2.81
1919	Walter Johnson, Wash	1.49	1930	Lefty Grove, Phil	2.54
1920	Bob Shawkey, NY	2.46	1931	Lefty Grove, Phil	2.06
1921	Red Faber, Chi	2.47	1932	Lefty Grove, Phil	2.84
1922	Red Faber, Chi	2.80	1933	Monte Pearson, Clev	2.33
1923	Stan Coveleski, Clev	2.76	1934	Lefty Gomez, NY	2.33

Leading Pitchers—Earned-Run Average (*Cont.*)

Year	Pitcher and Team	ERA	Year	Pitcher and Team	ERA
1935	Lefty Grove, Bos	2.70	1964	Dean Chance, LA	1.65
1936	Lefty Grove, Bos	2.81	1965	Sam McDowell, Clev	2.18
1937	Lefty Gomez, NY	2.33	1966	Gary Peters, Chi	1.98
1938	Lefty Grove, Bos	3.07	1967	Joe Horlen, Chi	2.06
1939	Lefty Grove, Bos	2.54	1968	Luis Tiant, Clev	1.60
1940	Bob Feller, †Clev	2.62	1969	Dick Bosman, Wash	2.19
1941	Thornton Lee, Chi	2.37	1970	Diego Segui, Oak	2.56
1942	Ted Lyons, Chi	2.10	1971	Vida Blue, Oak	1.82
1943	Spud Chandler, NY	1.64	1972	Luis Tiant, Bos	1.91
1944	Dizzy Trout, Det	2.12	1973	Jim Palmer, Balt	2.40
1945	Hal Newhouser, Det	1.81	1974	Catfish Hunter, Oak	2.49
1946	Hal Newhouser, Det	1.94	1975	Jim Palmer, Balt	2.09
1947	Spud Chandler, NY	2.46	1976	Mark Fidrych, Det	2.34
1948	Gene Bearden, Clev	2.43	1977	Frank Tanana, Calif	2.54
1949	Mel Parnell, Bos	2.78	1978	Ron Guidry, NY	1.74
1950	Early Wynn, Clev	3.20	1979	Ron Guidry, NY	2.78
1951	Saul Rogovin, Det-Chi	2.78	1980	Rudy May, NY	2.47
1952	Allie Reynolds, NY	2.07	1981	Steve McCatty, Oak	2.32
1953	Ed Lopat, NY	2.43	1982	Rick Sutcliffe, Clev	2.96
1954	Mike Garcia, Clev	2.64	1983	Rick Honeycutt, Tex	2.42
1955	Billy Pierce, Chi	1.97	1984	Mike Boddicker, Balt	2.79
1956	Whitey Ford, NY	2.47	1985	Dave Stieb, Tor	2.48
1957	Bobby Shantz, NY	2.45	1986	Roger Clemens, Bos	2.48
1958	Whitey Ford, NY	2.01	1987	Jimmy Key, Tor	2.76
1959	Hoyt Wilhelm, Balt	2.19	1988	Allan Anderson, Minn	2.45
1960	Frank Baumann, Chi	2.68	1989	Bret Saberhagen, KC	2.16
1961	Dick Donovan, Wash	2.40	1990	Roger Clemens, Bos	1.93
1962	Hank Aguirre, Det	2.21	1991	Roger Clemens, Bos	2.62
1963	Gary Peters, Chi	2.33			

Note: Based on 10 complete games through 1950, then, 154 innings until the American League expanded in 1961, when it became 162 innings. In strike-shortened 1981, one inning per game required. Earned runs not tabulated in American League prior to 1913.

*Wilcy Moore pitched only six complete games—he started 12—in 1927, but was recognized as leader because of 213 innings pitched.

†Ernie Bonham, New York, had 1.91 ERA and 10 complete games in 1940, but appeared in only 12 games and 99 innings, and Bob Feller was recognized as leader.

Leading Pitchers—Strikeouts

Year	Pitcher and Team	SO	Year	Pitcher and Team	SO
1901	Cy Young, Bos	159	1926	Lefty Grove, Phil	194
1902	Rube Waddell, Phil	210	1927	Lefty Grove, Phil	174
1903	Rube Waddell, Phil	301	1928	Lefty Grove, Phil	183
1904	Rube Waddell, Phil	349	1929	Lefty Grove, Phil	170
1905	Rube Waddell, Phil	286	1930	Lefty Grove, Phil	209
1906	Rube Waddell, Phil	203	1931	Lefty Grove, Phil	175
1907	Rube Waddell, Phil	226	1932	Red Ruffing, NY	190
1908	Ed Walsh, Chi	269	1933	Lefty Gomez, NY	163
1909	Frank Smith, Chi	177	1934	Lefty Gomez, NY	158
1910	Walter Johnson, Wash	313	1935	Tommy Bridges, Det	163
1911	Ed Walsh, Chi	255	1936	Tommy Bridges, Det	175
1912	Walter Johnson, Wash	303	1937	Lefty Gomez, NY	194
1913	Walter Johnson, Wash	243	1938	Bob Feller, Clev	240
1914	Walter Johnson, Wash	225	1939	Bob Feller, Clev	246
1915	Walter Johnson, Wash	203	1940	Bob Feller, Clev	261
1916	Walter Johnson, Wash	228	1941	Bob Feller, Clev	260
1917	Walter Johnson, Wash	188	1942	Bobo Newsom, Wash	113
1918	Walter Johnson, Wash	162		Tex Hughson, Bos	113
1919	Walter Johnson, Wash	147	1943	Allie Reynolds, Clev	151
1920	Stan Coveleski, Clev	133	1944	Hal Newhouser, Det	187
1921	Walter Johnson, Wash	143	1945	Hal Newhouser, Det	212
1922	Urban Shocker, StL	149	1946	Bob Feller, Clev	348
1923	Walter Johnson, Wash	130	1947	Bob Feller, Clev	196
1924	Walter Johnson, Wash	158	1948	Bob Feller, Clev	164
1925	Lefty Grove, Phil	116	1949	Virgil Trucks, Det	153

Leading Pitchers—Strikeouts (*Cont.*)

Year	Pitcher and Team	SO	Year	Pitcher and Team	SO
1950	Bob Lemon, Clev	170	1971	Mickey Lolich, Det	30▮
1951	Vic Raschi, NY	164	1972	Nolan Ryan, Calif	32▮
1952	Allie Reynolds, NY	160	1973	Nolan Ryan, Calif	38▮
1953	Billy Pierce, Chi	186	1974	Nolan Ryan, Calif	36▮
1954	Bob Turley, Balt	185	1975	Frank Tanana, Calif	26▮
1955	Herb Score, Clev	245	1976	Nolan Ryan, Calif	32▮
1956	Herb Score, Clev	263	1977	Nolan Ryan, Calif	34▮
1957	Early Wynn, Clev	184	1978	Nolan Ryan, Calif	26▮
1958	Early Wynn, Chi	179	1979	Nolan Ryan, Calif	22▮
1959	Jim Bunning, Det	201	1980	Len Barker, Clev	18▮
1960	Jim Bunning, Det	201	1981	Len Barker, Clev	12▮
1961	Camilo Pascual, Minn	221	1982	Floyd Bannister, Sea	20▮
1962	Camilo Pascual, Minn	206	1983	Jack Morris, Det	23▮
1963	Camilo Pascual, Minn	202	1984	Mark Langston, Sea	20▮
1964	Al Downing, NY	217	1985	Bert Blyleven, Clev-Minn	206
1965	Sam McDowell, Clev	325	1986	Mark Langston, Sea	24▮
1966	Sam McDowell, Clev	225	1987	Mark Langston, Sea	26▮
1967	Jim Lonborg, Bos	246	1988	Roger Clemens, Bos	29▮
1968	Sam McDowell, Clev	283	1989	Nolan Ryan, Tex	30▮
1969	Sam McDowell, Clev	279	1990	Nolan Ryan, Tex	23▮
1970	Sam McDowell, Clev	304	1991	Roger Clemens, Bos	24▮

The Commissioners of Baseball

Kenesaw Mountain Landis	Elected November 12, 1920. Served until his death on November 25, 1944.
Happy Chandler	Elected April 24, 1945. Served until July 15, 1951.
Ford Frick	Elected September 20, 1951. Served until November 16, 1965.
William Eckert	Elected November 17, 1965. Served until December 20, 1968.
Bowie Kuhn	Elected February 8, 1969. Served until September 30, 1984.
Peter Ueberroth	Elected March 3, 1984. Took office October 1, 1984. Served through March 31, 1989.
A. Bartlett Giamatti	Elected September 8, 1988. Took office April 1, 1989. Served until his death on September 1, 1989.
Francis Vincent Jr	Appointed Acting Commissioner September 2, 1989. Elected Commissioner September 13, 1989.

An Unbreakable Record

Fans like to argue about which records are least likely to be broken, but surely Johnny Vander Meer's mark of two straight no hitters has to head the list. Pitching three straight no hitters is scarcely imaginable. Vander Meer didn't do badly in history's only attempt at a third straight no-hit game. After no-hitting the Bees (a.k.a. the Braves) in Boston and the Dodgers in Brooklyn in June 1938, he held the Bees hitless in Cincinnati's Crosley Field for three innings in his next start and went on to win a four-hitter. Vander Meer's 21 consecutive hitless innings is a National League mark, but not a major league record. In 1904 Cy Young, then with the Boston Red Sox, pitched 24 straight hitless innings, including the first perfect game off the standard mount.

Pro Football

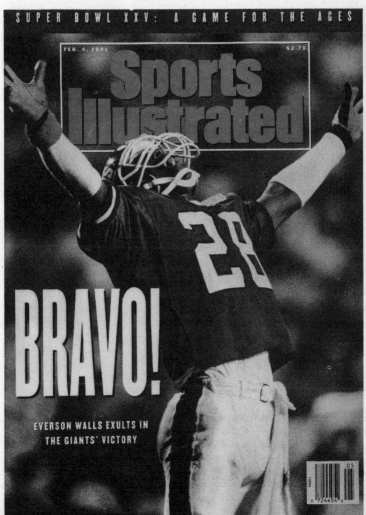

SUPER BOWL XXV: A GAME FOR THE AGES

FEB. 4, 1991 $2.75

Sports Illustrated

BRAVO!

EVERSON WALLS EXULTS IN
THE GIANTS' VICTORY

AL TIELEMANS

Two That Got Away

Rocket Ismail opted for big money in Canada and Bill Parcells quit while he was on top | by PETER KING

T IS NOT UNUSUAL THESE DAYS FOR THE biggest sports headlines to be made off the field. Sometimes what goes on in the off-season eclipses what occurred when the games were played. And so it was in the seven months between Scott Norwood's dramatic missed field goal attempt that enabled the New York Giants to escape with a 20–19 victory against the Buffalo Bills in Super Bowl XXV and the kickoff of the 1991 National Football League season. The big news was made by two guys from New Jersey and a new league that was a big hit in Europe.

Raghib (Rocket) Ismail, who grew up on the mean streets of Newark and went on to become an All-America wide receiver and return specialist at Notre Dame, shunned the chance to be the No. 1 pick in the NFL draft on April 21 and instead signed the richest contract in football history—a four-year deal worth at least $18 million—with the Toronto Argonauts of the Canadian Football League.

Less than a month later, Giants coach Bill Parcells cleaned out his office and for the last time drove the short distance from Giants Stadium to his home in the north Jersey suburbs, where he was born and raised. Parcells retired on May 15 at the tender coaching age of 49, with an 85-52-1 record in eight seasons at the helm of the Giants. "I have given everything I have," said Parcells, whose 1986 club also won the Super Bowl, "and I just don't think I could give quite the same anymore." But he didn't rule out the possibility of returning to coaching one day, and associates suspected that Parcells needed only a one- or two-year break before he would be tempted to return as a coach or general manager.

Parcells eschewed the sophisticated and fancy-Dan offensive game plans of the Bill Walshes and Don Shulas and instead approached the game as a brutal science, which football purists believe it is. "Power football wins," Parcells said over and over down the stretch of the 1990 regular season, when the Giants steamrolled to a 13–3 record.

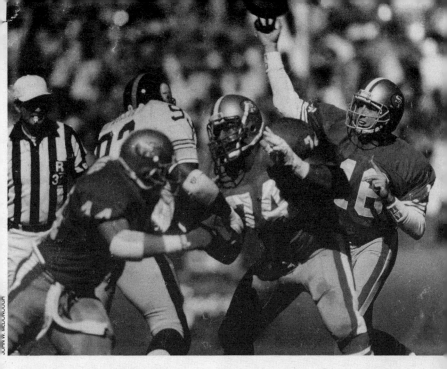

Within hours of Parcells's decision to retire, the Giants promoted assistant coach Ray Handley into the head job. A computer and math whiz, Handley had planned to leave the Giants after the Super Bowl and enter law school. But Parcells had talked his running backs coach into staying with the team and named him offensive coordinator in February. Whereas Parcells was gruff, moody and manipulative with his players, Handley was soft-spoken and reserved. The new coach also offered up a change in philosophy: Handley said he would open up the offense.

The promise of wide-open offenses was the marketing pitch of the new World League of American Football, the latest attempt to tantalize pro football fans in the spring. Unlike the ill-fated United States Football League, however, the WLAF was not in competition with the NFL and actually was funded in part by 26 of the 28 NFL owners. The new 10-team league had franchises in London, Barcelona, Frankfurt and Montreal, plus six American cities, most of which were con-

Montana had what for him was a subpar year, but it was good enough to win league MVP honors.

sidered to be potential pro football hotbeds.

The teams were hastily assembled through a draft of free agents, made up primarily of former college standouts who had failed to make the NFL grade, and the inaugural season began March 23. Ten weeks later, the franchises with the three best records were London (9–1), Barcelona (8–2) and Frankfurt (7–3), and London had attracted the most fans—an average of 40,481. No U.S.-based team fared better than 5–5, and the bottom five teams in attendance were all in American cities.

Fittingly, the London Monarchs and Barcelona Dragons advanced to the first World Bowl, which was played in front of 61,108 fans at London's Wembley Stadium. London quarterback Stan Gelbaugh, the WLAF's offensive most valuable player, completed 18 of 25 passes for 191 yards and two touchdowns, and defensive back Dan

Crossman intercepted three passes to lead the Monarchs to a 21–0 victory. The caliber of play during the season was shaky most of the time and the TV ratings for games shown on ABC and USA Cable Network slumped as the season wore on, but the European fans, happy to have their own American football teams to root for, were more forgiving than their American counterparts and embraced the league enthusiastically.

Still, the sudden change at the controls of the Super Bowl champion and the hearty welcome that American football received on the continent did not create nearly the uproar that was to unfold after Ismail's announcement in January that he was forfeiting his final year of eligibility at Notre Dame to enter the NFL draft. With pro scouts rating the pool of available talent an average crop at best, Ismail rocketed to the top of most draft experts' checklists the day he made public his decision to turn pro early.

There was no questioning Ismail's value as a breakaway threat who could arouse interest in any NFL city, but club personnel directors were taken aback by the demands of Rocket's team of agents and attorneys. Braced by an early offer of $6 million for two years from Argonauts owner Bruce McNall, Ismail's advisers sought the richest rookie contract in NFL history for their client. But Ismail had built his reputation on

Less Bang for the Buck

JUST BEFORE NEW NFL commissioner Paul Tagliabue presided over his first league meetings, in March 1990, he negotiated the biggest TV contract in the history of professional sports. He and the chairman of the NFL's television committee, Cleveland Browns majority owner Art Modell, struck a deal with the three major networks and cable outlets ESPN and TNT. Over four years, NFL clubs would split $3.64 billion. That's billion. With a *B.*

The TV contract took effect with the 1990 season, with each club collecting an initial installment of $26.1 million. In the final year of the deal, 1993, each team will get a check for $39 million. "Paul Tagliabue has come of age very, very quickly as a sports commissioner," Modell said after the 28 NFL owners unanimously approved terms of the new contract.

The days of the megajumps in TV revenue for sports leagues were supposed to be history. In the final year of the NFL's previous TV contract, each team had made $17.02 million, and most owners thought they would be fortunate to average $24 million or $25 million a year during the life of the new deal.

But when cable-TV mogul Ted Turner, owner of the TBS superstation, decided he wanted a piece of the NFL action for his TNT cable network, he waved a blank check in front of Tagliabue and Modell and challenged them to make room for a second cable outlet, in addition to ESPN, on the schedule of televised games. So the NFL was able to up the bidding for cable dates, and then it piggybacked these increases into its negotiations with the big three of CBS, NBC and ABC. The final result: Each team would average $32.5 million per season in TV revenue from 1990 to 1993.

But money wasn't the only thing that came out of the TV negotiations. As a means of generating more TV revenue—and, he thought, more late-season interest among NFL fans—Tagliabue added one wild-card berth from each of the two conferences to the playoff system. That meant that six of the 14 teams in the AFC and six of the 14 teams in the NFC would now qualify for the playoffs.

That was good news for teams that

kick returns, not even as a wide receiver, so it was inconceivable to the NFL brass that he should be paid money beyond that previously reserved for franchise quarterbacks. Ismail had touched the ball an average of only 8.3 times per game in three college seasons, and he had missed all or part of six games with nicks or bruises in his sophomore and junior seasons. There were doubts about the durability of the 5'10", 175-pounder.

Since New England held the first pick, the Patriots were free to negotiate with Ismail in the time leading up to the draft. His advisers wanted $14.5 million over five years. So the woebegone Patriots played hot potato with the first pick, trying to trade it to Atlanta, Denver and Dallas, and finally striking a deal with the Cowboys 48 hours before the draft. New England received a first-round pick (No. 11 overall), a second-round pick and three players.

Everyone in the league thought, Troy Aikman to Rocket Ismail, a match made for Madison Avenue. But the Cowboys thought different. "We never were going to pick him when we made the trade," Dallas owner Jerry Jones revealed later. The Cowboys had traded up to get University of Miami defensive tackle Russell Maryland, a decision that was cinched after the Cowboys got a look at the new demands from Ismail's advisers:

had fared as well as 10–6 and yet been squeezed out of the postseason by the league's tiebreaker system. But it was not-so-good news for the three division champions in each conference. Under the old system, all six division winners received byes into the second round of the playoffs. But under the new format, the division champ with the worst record in each conference now had to play the wild-card team with the worst record in the first round.

In 1990, the Chicago Bears (11–5) of the NFC Central and the Cincinnati Bengals (9–7) of the AFC Central were the division winners who had to play in the wild-card round. Though the Bears didn't whine about it—"I'd personally rather have a smaller number of teams make the playoffs, but a lot of people felt the TV deal was very important," Chicago president Mike McCaskey said—the league took some heat from fans, coaches and the media for expanding the playoffs.

As one club executive put it, "Our prob-lem right now as a league is we're running everything as a business. We need to get back to running it as a football business. Every decision we make is based on money, not the sport."

In negotiating a new TV contract, the new commissioner got a big deal by offering a bigger playoff format.

JOHN BIEVER

$16.8 million for five years, plus performance incentives. And Maryland did come cheap by comparison, signing a five-year, $6.8 million contract within hours of being the first player selected.

Twice rebuffed, Ismail cast his lot with McNall, the owner of the NHL's Los Angeles Kings who collects athletes the way he collects rare coins. He was going to try to save the struggling CFL with Ismail the same way he had kept hockey alive in Southern California by acquiring Wayne Gretzky for the Kings. McNall landed pro football's newest marquee performer and Ismail got the richest contract in football history—a four-year deal worth $18.2 million guaranteed ($14 million in income, plus a $4.2 million marketing package), with the potential to earn as much as $4 million in attendance incentives and up to $4 million in other business ventures over the same period.

Who could blame Ismail for defecting to Canada? Or Parcells for going out on top? They were just two unexpected developments that came on the heels of a strange 1990 NFL season.

That campaign began with the anticipation of the San Francisco 49ers' becoming the first NFL champions in three straight years since the Green Bay Packers (1965, '66, '67) of a generation before. Led by quarterback Joe Montana and wide receiver Jerry Rice, who had starred in Super Bowl victories against the Cincinnati Bengals and Denver Broncos in the two preceding seasons, the 49ers were favored to succeed in their bid to "threepeat," with their strongest opposition expected to come from their NFC West rival Los Angeles Rams and their dynamic young quarterback, Jim Everett.

If either team faltered, the Philadelphia Eagles or Kansas City Chiefs had the potential to step up and become a champion, and the resurgent Broncos were talking confidently of rebounding from their third Super Bowl slaughter in four seasons. But talk of possible Super Bowl XXV matchups did not include the Giants, a team that was getting very old very quickly, or the Bills, who had been distracted the year before by extensive bickering among themselves, or the L.A. Raiders, who were unsettled at quarterback and whose offensive weapon—Bo Jackson—wasn't a full-time player.

So what happened when they played the games?

Well, the 49ers had a very nice year, going 14–2 during the regular season and then beating the Washington Redskins in the divisional playoffs. But in the NFC Championship Game at Candlestick Park, the aging Giants beat San Francisco 15–13 on Matt Bahr's 42-yard field goal as time ran out. What happened to the Rams? Oh, they beat the 49ers once during the regular season, but they won only four other games and finished 5–11, doomed by a new defensive scheme that yielded 26 points a game.

After a 2–4 start, the Eagles won eight of 10 to make the playoffs. But they lost in the first round for the third year in a row, and three days later they lost coach Buddy Ryan as well—fired for failing to take the Eagles any further in five years.

Denver's confidence, as it turned out, was

shaky from the start—coach Dan Reeves missed three weeks of training camp with a heart condition—and the Broncos plummeted to 5–11. As for the Chiefs, they continued to improve (11–5) under coach Marty Schottenheimer, but they were not consistent enough to go the distance, and lost in a playoff.

***

By midseason, the only race in the NFC was for the three wild-card playoff spots. New York and San Francisco both started 10–0, but a *Monday Night Football* matchup of unbeatens in early December was ruined when the Eagles beat the Giants and the Rams defeated the 49ers the week before the showdown.

Despite going 3–3 to finish the season, the Giants still won the NFC East by three games. The Bears (11–5) won the NFC Central by five games over the rest of the division—Tampa Bay, Detroit, Green Bay and Minnesota all went 6–10. The 49ers clinched the NFC West by Thanksgiving, or so it seemed, winning the division by six games over New Orleans (8–8). The Eagles (10–6), Redskins (10–6) and Saints won the wild cards.

In contrast, the AFC had three great divisional races. In the East, Buffalo and Miami ran neck and neck all season, with the Bills needing a win (24–14) over the Dolphins in Week 15 to clinch the title. In the Central, Cincinnati, Houston and Pittsburgh all finished atop the division with 9–7 records, leaving their fate in the hands of the NFL tiebreaker system. Cincinnati was declared the champion because the Bengals were 3–1 in head-to-head meetings with Houston and Pittsburgh. The Oilers were awarded a wild-card spot for having the best conference record (8–4) of the other 9–7 teams in the AFC, the Steelers and the Seattle Seahawks. In the West, Kansas City mashed the Raiders twice during the regular season, wearing them down with 240-pound back Barry Word and his 262-pound sidekick, Christian Okoye. But the Raiders, getting a career year from quarterback Jay Schroeder and bonus mileage out of veteran running back Marcus Allen, won their last five games to finish 12–4 and edge the Chiefs by a game. Kansas City joined Miami and Houston as wild cards.

Bills quarterback Jim Kelly won the NFL passing title with a rating of 101.2, but, more important, he won new respect in Buffalo as well as from the rest of the league. A year earlier, Kelly had been the target of some teammates' accusations of selfishness, but early on in 1990 he established himself as such an effective team leader that offensive coordinator Ted Marchibroda turned the responsibility of calling plays over to him in December. Not since Steeler quarterback Terry Bradshaw called his own plays in 1981 had an NFL quarterback fully run the offense on the field.

Still, Montana won his second straight league MVP award, though his year was hardly vintage. (He threw a career-high 16 interceptions.) If ever there was a season when a receiver deserved to be voted MVP, it was 1990. Montana's favorite target, the graceful and powerful Rice, led the NFL

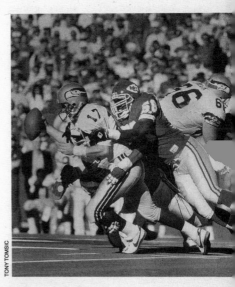

The Chiefs' Derrick Thomas sacked the Seahawks seven times to set a single-game league record.

TONY TOMSIC

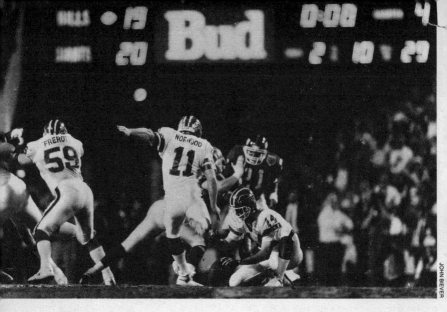

JOHN BIEVER

with 100 receptions and 1,502 receiving yards—18 receptions and 208 yards more than his closest competition.

On defense, two newcomers stood out. Bears rookie cornerback Mark Carrier led the NFL with 10 interceptions and earned a start in the Pro Bowl. Derrick Thomas, the Chiefs' second-year linebacker, had a league-record seven sacks in a game against Seattle and finished the season with a league-high 20 sacks.

***

The Super Bowl pitted the quick-thinking Bills, with their no-huddle offense and Kelly's play-calling wizardry, against the prehistoric Giants. "All that matters," Parcells kept reminding his players, "is who's left standing at the end." Led by the most improbable of heroes—backup quarterback Jeff Hostetler, who had replaced the injured Phil Simms with two games to play in the regular season—the Giants rallied from a 12–3 deficit in the second quarter on

Norwood was so pumped up that he pushed the potential Super Bowl winning field goal wide to the right.

a warm, humid day in Tampa to take a 20–19 lead late in the game. And New York, despite its age, plodding nature and the heat, was the dominant team, holding the ball for 40½ minutes to Buffalo's 19½.

"The no-huddle was supposed to wear us down," Giants linebacker Pepper Johnson said. "People were saying it'd be hot and humid and that we'd be dragging. But they were the ones sucking air at the end. Our offense beat them."

And then came Norwood's 47-yard field goal attempt. "I was so pumped up for the kick," Norwood said, "that my plant leg went about three or four inches ahead of where it should have been, and I ended up pushing the kick right." Too far to the right. By about four feet.

Typical of the 1990 season.

FOR THE RECORD • 1990 – 1991

1990 NFL Final Standings

American Football Conference

EASTERN DIVISION

	W	L	T	Pct	Pts	OP
*Buffalo	13	3	0	.813	428	263
†Miami	12	4	0	.750	336	242
Indianapolis	7	9	0	.438	281	353
NY Jets	6	10	0	.375	295	345
New England	1	15	0	.063	181	446

CENTRAL DIVISION

	W	L	T	Pct	Pts	OP
*Cincinnati	9	7	0	.563	360	352
†Houston	9	7	0	.563	405	307
Pittsburgh	9	7	0	.563	292	240
Cleveland	3	13	0	.188	228	462

WESTERN DIVISION

	W	L	T	Pct	Pts	OP
*LA Raiders	12	4	0	.750	337	268
†Kansas City	11	5	0	.688	369	257
Seattle	9	7	0	.563	306	286
San Diego	6	10	0	.375	315	281
Denver	5	11	0	.313	331	374

National Football Conference

EASTERN DIVISION

	W	L	T	Pct	Pts	OP
*NY Giants	13	3	0	.813	335	211
†Philadelphia	10	6	0	.625	396	299
†Washington	10	6	0	.625	381	301
Dallas	7	9	0	.438	244	308
Phoenix	5	11	0	.313	268	396

CENTRAL DIVISION

	W	L	T	Pct	Pts	OP
*Chicago	11	5	0	.688	348	280
Tampa Bay	6	10	0	.375	264	367
Detroit	6	10	0	.375	373	413
Green Bay	6	10	0	.375	271	347
Minnesota	6	10	0	.375	351	326

WESTERN DIVISION

	W	L	T	Pct	Pts	OP
*San Francisco	14	2	0	.875	353	239
†New Orleans	8	8	0	.500	274	275
LA Rams	5	11	0	.313	345	412
Atlanta	5	11	0	.313	348	365

* Division Champion. † Wild Card team.

1991 NFL Playoffs

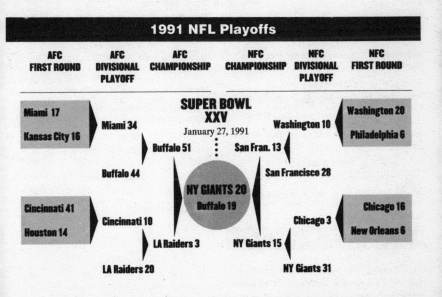

AFC FIRST ROUND — **AFC DIVISIONAL PLAYOFF** — **AFC CHAMPIONSHIP** — **NFC CHAMPIONSHIP** — **NFC DIVISIONAL PLAYOFF** — **NFC FIRST ROUND**

SUPER BOWL XXV
January 27, 1991

NY GIANTS 20
Buffalo 19

Miami 17 / Kansas City 16 → Miami 34
Buffalo 51
Buffalo 44
Cincinnati 41 / Houston 14 → Cincinnati 10
LA Raiders 3
LA Raiders 20

Washington 20 / Philadelphia 6 → Washington 10
San Fran. 13
San Francisco 28
Chicago 16 / New Orleans 6 → Chicago 3
NY Giants 15
NY Giants 31

NFL Playoff Boxscores

AFC Wild Card Games

Kansas City	3	7	6	0 —16	Houston	0	0	7	7 — 14
Miami	0	3	0	14 —17	Cincinnati	10	10	14	7 — 41

FIRST QUARTER

Kansas City: FG Lowery 27, 9:56. Drive: 28 yards, 9 plays.

SECOND QUARTER

Miami: FG Stoyanovich 58, :05. Drive: 40 yards, 9 plays.
Kansas City: S. Paige 26 pass from DeBerg (Lowery kick), 13:06. Drive: 61 yards, 4 plays.

THIRD QUARTER

Kansas City: FG Lowery 25, 10:14. Drive: 63 yards, 11 plays.
Kansas City: FG Lowery 38, 12:05. Drive: 8 yards, 4 plays.

FOURTH QUARTER

Miami: T. Paige 1 pass from Marino (Stoyanovich kick), 2:42. Drive: 66 yards, 10 plays.
Miami: Clayton 12 pass from Marino (Stoyanovich kick), 11:32. Drive: 85 yards, 11 plays.

A: 67,276; T: 2:59.

FIRST QUARTER

Cincinnati: Woods 1 run (Breech kick), 6:24. Drive: 70 yards, 11 plays.
Cincinnati: FG Breech 27, 13:50. Drive: 51 yards, 11 plays.

SECOND QUARTER

Cincinnati: Green 2 pass from Esiason (Breech kick), 5:42. Drive: 16 yards, 4 plays.
Cincinnati: FG Breech 30, 14:17. Drive: 75 yards, 16 plays.

THIRD QUARTER

Cincinnati: Ball 3 run (Breech kick), 3:26. Drive: 33 yards, 5 plays.
Cincinnati: Esiason 10 run (Breech kick), 3:51. Drive: 10 yards, 1 play.
Houston: Givins 16 pass from Carlson (Garcia kick), 9:45. Drive: 80 yards, 10 plays.

FOURTH QUARTER

Cincinnati: Kattus 9 pass from Esiason (Breech kick), :51. Drive: 75 yards, 9 plays.
Houston: Givins 5 pass from Carlson (Garcia kick), 8:01. Drive: 75 yards, 6 plays.

A: 60,012; T: 3:05.

NFC Wild Card Games

Washington	0	10	10	0 —20	New Orleans	0	3	0	3 — 6
Philadelphia	3	3	0	0 — 6	Chicago	3	7	3	3 —16

FIRST QUARTER

Philadelphia: FG Ruzek 37, 8:29. Drive: 55 yards, 7 plays.

SECOND QUARTER

Philadelphia: FG Ruzek 28, 4:42. Drive: 15 yards, 7 plays.
Washington: Monk 16 pass from Rypien (Lohmiller kick), 9:06. Drive: 68 yards, 5 plays.
Washington: FG Lohmiller 20, 14:56. Drive: 47 yards, 7 plays.

THIRD QUARTER

Washington: FG Lohmiller 19, 12:31. Drive: 29 yards, 7 plays.
Washington: Clark 3 pass from Rypien (Lohmiller kick), 14:57. Drive: 55 yards, 5 plays.

A: 65,287; T: 2:55.

FIRST QUARTER

Chicago: FG Butler 19, 4:54. Drive: 32 yards, 6 plays.

SECOND QUARTER

Chicago: Thornton 18 pass from Tomczak (Butler kick), 1:51. Drive: 62 yards, 6 plays.
New Orleans: FG Andersen 47, 13:22. Drive: 18 yards, 6 plays.

THIRD QUARTER

Chicago: FG Butler 22, 8:31. Drive: 60 yards, 16 plays.

FOURTH QUARTER

New Orleans: FG Andersen 38, 9:06. Drive: 59 yards, 14 plays.
Chicago: FG Butler 21, 12:13. Drive: 76 yards, 9 plays.

A: 60,676; T: 3:14.

THEY SAID IT

Mike Baab, Cleveland Browns center, on his team's defensive backfield: "Our defensive backs were like a river. There was a lot more activity at the mouth than at the source."

NFL Playoff Boxscores (*Cont.*)

AFC Divisional Games

Cincinnati	0	3	0	7 — 10
LA Raiders	0	7	3	10 — 20

Miami	3	14	3	14 — 34
Buffalo	13	14	3	14 — 44

SECOND QUARTER

Cincinnati: FG Breech 27, 2:53. Drive: 87 yards, 9 plays.
LA Raiders: Fernandez 13 pass from Schroeder (Jaeger kick), 7:31. Drive: 80 yards, 8 plays.

THIRD QUARTER

LA Raiders: FG Jaeger 49, 9:19. Drive: 45 yards, 8 plays.

FOURTH QUARTER

Cincinnati: Jennings 8 pass from Esiason (Breech kick), 3:11. Drive: 71 yards, 13 plays.
LA Raiders: Horton 41 pass from Schroeder (Jaeger kick), 6:08. Drive: 80 yards, 7 plays.
LA Raiders: FG Jaeger 25, 14:41. Drive: 62 yards, 10 plays.

A: 92,045; T: 2:35.

FIRST QUARTER

Buffalo: Reed 40 pass from Kelly (Norwood kick), 1:54. Drive: 76 yards, 5 plays.
Miami: FG Stoyanovich 49, 8:00. Drive: 40 yards, 10 plays.
Buffalo: FG Norwood 24, 10:11. Drive: 57 yards, 6 plays.
Buffalo: FG Norwood 22, 14:09. Drive: 33 yards, 9 plays.

SECOND QUARTER

Buffalo: Thomas 5 run (Norwood kick), 2:56. Drive: 67 yards, 5 plays.
Miami: Duper 64 pass from Marino (Stoyanovich kick), 5:06. Drive: 80 yards, 4 plays.
Buffalo: Lofton 13 pass from Kelly (Norwood kick), 9:49. Drive: 68 yards, 11 plays.
Miami: Marino 2 run (Stoyanovich kick), 14:39. Drive: 47 yards, 7 plays.

THIRD QUARTER

Miami: FG Stoyanovich 22, 4:57. Drive: 62 yards, 8 plays.
Buffalo: FG Norwood 28, 13:22. Drive: 37 yards, 9 plays.

FOURTH QUARTER

Miami: Foster 2 pass from Marino (Stoyanovich kick), :55. Drive: 43 yards, 6 plays.
Buffalo: Thomas 5 run (Norwood kick), 4:32. Drive: 63 yards, 10 plays.
Buffalo: Reed 26 pass from Kelly (Norwood kick), 5:08. Drive: 29 yards, 2 plays.
Miami: Martin 8 pass from Marino (Stoyanovich kick), 13:45. Drive: 91 yards, 15 plays.

A: 77,087; T: 3:23.

THEY SAID IT

Lindy Infante, Green Bay Packers coach, looking on the bright side of finishing the 1990 season 6–10: "I won't have to run around the country and collect a whole bunch of Coach of the Year trophies."

NFC Divisional Games

Washington	10	0	0	0 — 10
San Francisco	7	14	0	7 — 28

Chicago	0	3	0	0 — 3
NY Giants	10	7	7	7 — 31

FIRST QUARTER

Washington: Monk 31 pass from Rypien (Lohmiller kick), 5:48. Drive: 74 yards, 8 plays.
San Francisco: Rathman 1 run (Cofer kick), 10:06. Drive: 74 yards, 8 plays.
Washington: FG Lohmiller 44, 14:24. Drive:43 yards, 9 plays.

SECOND QUARTER

San Francisco: Rice 10 pass from Montana (Cofer kick), 3:52. Drive: 80 yards, 10 plays.
San Francisco: Sherrard 8 pass from Montana (Cofer kick), 8:29. Drive: 89 yards, 5 plays.

FOURTH QUARTER

San Francisco: M. Carter 61 interception return (Cofer kick), 14:03.

A: 65,292; T: 2:57.

FIRST QUARTER

NY Giants: FG Bahr 46, 5:40. Drive: 5 yards, 4 plays.
NY Giants: Baker 21 pass from Hostetler (Bahr kick), 13:56. Drive: 75 yards, 9 plays.

SECOND QUARTER

Chicago: FG Butler 33, 8:43. Drive: 20 yards, 5 plays.
NY Giants: Cross 5 pass from Hostetler (Bahr kick), 14:27. Drive: 80 yards, 11 plays.

THIRD QUARTER

NY Giants: Hostetler 3 run (Bahr kick), 4:19. Drive: 49 yards, 11 plays.

FOURTH QUARTER

NY Giants: Carthon 1 run (Bahr kick), 14:53. Drive: 51 yards, 16 plays.

A: 77,025; T: 2:52.

AFC Championship

LA Raiders	3	0	0	0 — 3
Buffalo	21	20	0	10 — 51

FIRST QUARTER

Buffalo: Lofton 13 pass from Kelly (Norwood kick), 3:30. Drive: 75 yards, 9 plays.
LA Raiders: FG Jaeger 41, 5:49. Drive: 57 yards, 6 plays.
Buffalo: Thomas 12 run (Norwood kick), 6:59. Drive: 66 yards, 4 plays.
Buffalo: Talley 27 interception return (Norwood kick), 11:51.

SECOND QUARTER

Buffalo: Davis 1 run (kick blocked), 5:58. Drive: 57 yards, 13 plays.
Buffalo: Davis 3 run (Norwood kick), 11:42. Drive: 80 yards, 7 plays.
Buffalo: Lofton 8 pass from Kelly (Norwood kick), 13:54. Drive: 61 yards, 6 plays.

FOURTH QUARTER

Buffalo: Davis 1 run (Norwood kick), :02. Drive: 78 yards, 9 plays.
Buffalo: FG Norwood 39, 2:46. Drive: 6 yards, 4 plays.

A: 80,324; T: 3:17.

NFC Championship

NY Giants	3	3	3	6 — 15
San Francisco	3	3	7	0 — 13

FIRST QUARTER

San Francisco: FG Cofer 47, 5:07. Drive: 44 yards, 10 plays.
NY Giants: FG Bahr 28, 12:19. Drive: 69 yards, 15 plays.

SECOND QUARTER

NY Giants: FG Bahr 42, 14:00. Drive: 56 yards, 14 plays.
San Francisco: FG Cofer 35, 14:57. Drive: 48 yards, 7 plays.

THIRD QUARTER

San Francisco: Taylor 61 pass from Montana (Cofer kick), 4:32. Drive: 61 yards, 1 play.
NY Giants: FG Bahr 46, 10:35. Drive: 49 yards, 10 plays.

FOURTH QUARTER

NY Giants: FG Bahr 38, 9:13. Drive: 41 yards, 8 plays.
NY Giants: FG Bahr 42, 15:00. Drive: 33 yards, 7 plays.

A: 65,750; T: 3:07.

Super Bowl Boxscore

Buffalo	3	9	0	7 — 19
NY Giants	3	7	7	3 — 20

FIRST QUARTER

NY Giants: FG Bahr 28, 7:14. Drive: 58 yards, 11 plays. Key plays: Meggett 10 run; Hostetler 16 pass to Ingram on 3rd and 7. NY Giants 3, Buffalo 0.
Buffalo: FG Norwood 23, 9:09. Drive: 66 yards, 6 plays. Key play: Kelly 61 pass to Lofton. Buffalo 3, NY Giants 3.

SECOND QUARTER

Buffalo: D. Smith 1 run (Norwood kick), 2:30. Drive: 80 yards, 12 plays. Key plays: Kelly 20 pass to Reed; Kelly 13 pass to Thomas. Buffalo 10, NY Giants 3.
Buffalo: Safety, Hostetler tackled in end zone, 6:33. Buffalo 12, NY Giants 3.
NY Giants: Baker 14 pass from Hostetler (Bahr kick), 14:35. Drive: 87 yards, 10 plays. Key plays: Hostetler 22 pass to Ingram; Hostetler 7 pass to Cross on 3rd and 6. Buffalo 12, NY Giants 10.

THIRD QUARTER

NY Giants: Anderson 1 run (Bahr kick), 9:29. Drive: 75 yards, 14 plays. Key plays: Hostetler 11 pass to Meggett on 3rd and 8; Anderson 24 run on 3rd and 1. NY Giants 17, Buffalo 12.

FOURTH QUARTER

Buffalo: Thomas 31 run (Norwood kick), :08. Drive: 63 yards, 4 plays. Key play: Kelly 19 pass to K. Davis. Buffalo 19, NY Giants 17.
NY Giants: FG Bahr 21, 7:40. Drive: 74 yards, 14 plays. Key plays: Hostetler 16 pass to Bavaro on 3rd and 7; Meggett 6 run on 3rd and 5. NY Giants 20, Buffalo 19.
Missed field goal attempt: Buffalo, Norwood 47.

A: 73,813. T: 3:19.

The Smell Is Bearable

Lucky men in Chicago can now slap on a little Mike Ditka—the cologne, that is. The stuff, which has a light, spicy, sandalwood scent, isn't cheap. It costs $24 for a four-ounce bottle and is only available in the Chicago area. "You can be tough in the ways you have to be tough," says Ditka, who selected the scent from among five submitted to him by the manufacturer, "but not in the way you smell."

Team Statistics

	Buffalo	NY Giants
FIRST DOWNS	18	24
Rushing	8	10
Passing	9	13
Penalty	1	1
THIRD DOWN EFF	1-8	9-16
FOURTH DOWN EFF	0-0	0-1
TOTAL NET YARDS	371	386
Total plays	56	73
Avg gain	6.6	5.3
NET YARDS RUSHING	166	172
Rushes	25	39
Avg per rush	6.6	4.4
NET YARDS PASSING	205	214
Completed-Att.	18-30	20-32
Yards per pass	6.6	6.3
Sacked-yards lost	1-7	2-8
Had intercepted	0	0
PUNTS-Avg.	6-39	4-44
TOTAL RETURN YARDS	114	85
Punt returns	0-0	2-37
Kickoff returns	6-114	3-48
Interceptions	0-0	0-0
PENALTIES-Yds	6-35	5-31
FUMBLES-Lost	1-0	0-0
TIME OF POSSESSION	19:27	40:33

Passing

BUFFALO

	Comp	Att	Yds	Int	TD
Kelly	18	30	212	0	0

NY GIANTS

	Comp	Att	Yds	Int	TD
Hostetler	20	32	222	0	1

Rushing

BUFFALO

	No.	Yds	Lg	TD
Thomas	15	135	31	1
Kelly	6	23	9	0
K. Davis	2	4	3	0
Mueller	1	3	3	0
D. Smith	1	1	1	1

NY GIANTS

	No.	Yds	Lg	TD
Anderson	21	102	24	1
Meggett	9	48	17	0
Carthon	3	12	5	0
Hostetler	6	10	5	0

Receiving

BUFFALO

	No.	Yds	Lg	TD
Reed	8	62	20	0
Thomas	5	55	15	0
K. Davis	2	23	19	0
McKeller	2	11	6	0
Lofton	1	61	61	0

NY GIANTS

	No.	Yds	Lg	TD
Ingram	5	74	22	0
Bavaro	5	50	19	0
Cross	4	39	13	0
Baker	2	31	17	1
Meggett	2	18	11	0
Anderson	1	7	7	0
Carthon	1	3	3	0

Defense

BUFFALO

	Tck	Ast	Fum	Int	Sack
L. Smith	8	0	0	0	0
Conlan	8	0	0	0	0
Wright	6	1	0	0	1
Odomes	5	0	0	0	0
Seals	5	0	0	0	0
Kelso	4	2	0	0	0
Bennett	4	1	0	0	0
Bentley	3	1	0	0	0
B. Smith	3	0	0	0	1
K. Jackson	2	1	0	0	0
Bailey	2	1	0	0	0
Talley	2	2	0	0	0
Lodich	2	0	0	0	0
Baldinger	2	0	0	0	0
Tasker	2	0	0	0	0
J. Williams	1	0	0	0	0
Drane	1	0	0	0	0
Tuten	1	0	0	0	0
Gardner	1	0	0	0	0
Mueller	1	0	0	0	0

NY GIANTS

	Tck	Ast	Fum	Int	Sack
Collins	6	0	0	0	0
Reasons	6	0	0	0	0
Howard	6	1	0	0	0
Thompson	4	0	0	0	0
G. Jackson	4	0	0	0	0
Banks	3	1	0	0	0
Johnson	3	0	0	0	0
Walls	2	1	0	0	0
Guyton	2	0	0	0	0
Taylor	2	0	0	0	0
Marshall	2	0	0	0	1
Bahr	2	0	0	0	0
Rouson	2	0	0	0	0
Washington	1	0	0	0	0
Tillman	1	0	0	0	0
Brown	1	0	0	0	0
P. Williams	0	1	0	0	0

1990 All-NFL Team

OFFENSE

Jerry Rice, San Francisco (AP, PFWA)	Wide Receiver
Andre Rison, Atlanta (AP, PFWA)	Wide Receiver
Keith Jackson, Philadelphia (AP, PFWA)	Tight End
Jim Lachey, Washington (AP, PFWA)	Tackle
Anthony Munoz, Cincinnati (AP, PFWA)	Tackle
Bruce Matthews, Houston (AP, PFWA)	Guard
Randall McDaniel, Minnesota (AP)	Guard
Steve Wisniewski, Los Angeles Raiders (PFWA)	Guard
Kent Hull, Buffalo (AP, PFWA)	Center
Joe Montana, San Francisco (AP)	Quarterback
Randall Cunningham, Philadelphia (PFWA)	Quarterback
Barry Sanders, Detroit (AP, PFWA)	Running Back
Thurman Thomas, Buffalo (AP, PFWA)	Running Back

DEFENSE

Bruce Smith, Buffalo (AP, PFWA)	Defensive End
Reggie White, Philadelphia (AP, PFWA)	Defensive End
Michael Dean Perry, Cleveland (AP, PFWA)	Defensive Tackle
Jerome Brown, Philadelphia (AP)	Defensive Tackle
Ray Childress, Houston (PFWA)	Defensive Tackle
Charles Haley, San Francisco (AP, PFWA)	Outside Linebacker
Derrick Thomas, Kansas City (AP, PFWA)	Outside Linebacker
Pepper Johnson, New York Giants (AP, PFWA)	Inside Linebacker
John Offerdahl, Miami (AP, PFWA)	Inside Linebacker
Albert Lewis, Kansas City (AP, PFWA)	Cornerback
Rod Woodson, Pittsburgh (AP, PFWA)	Cornerback
Joey Browner, Minnesota (AP, PFWA)	Safety
Ronnie Lott, San Francisco (AP, PFWA)	Safety

SPECIALISTS

Nick Lowery, Kansas City (AP, PFWA)	Kicker
Sean Landeta, New York Giants (AP, PFWA)	Punter
Mel Gray, Detroit (AP, PFWA)	Kick Returner
Dave Meggett, New York Giants (PFWA)	Punt Returner

Selected by the Associated Press and the Professional Football Writers of America.

1990 AFC Team-by-Team Results

BUFFALO BILLS (13-3)

26	INDIANAPOLIS	10
7	at Miami	30
30	at New York Jets	7
29	DENVER	28
38	LA RAIDERS	24
	OPEN DATE	
30	NY JETS	27
27	at New England	10
42	at Cleveland	0
45	PHOENIX	14
14	NEW ENGLAND	0
24	at Houston	27
30	PHILADELPHIA	23
31	at Indianapolis	7
17	at New York Giants	13
24	MIAMI	14
14	at Washington	29
428		**263**

CINCINNATI BENGALS (9-7)

25	NY JETS	20
21	at San Diego	16
41	NEW ENGLAND	7
16	at Seattle	31
34	at LA Rams (OT)	31
17	at Houston	48
34	at Cleveland	13
17	at Atlanta	38
7	NEW ORLEANS	21
	OPEN DATE	
27	PITTSBURGH	3
20	INDIANAPOLIS	34
16	at Pittsburgh	12
17	SAN FRANCISCO (OT)	20
7	at LA Raiders	24
40	HOUSTON	20
21	CLEVELAND	14
360		**352**

CLEVELAND BROWNS (3-13)

13	Pittsburgh	3
21	at NY Jets	24
14	SAN DIEGO	24
0	at Kansas City	34
30	at Denver	29
20	at New Orleans	25
13	CINCINNATI	34
17	at San Francisco	20
0	BUFFALO	42
	OPEN DATE	
23	HOUSTON	35
13	MIAMI	30
23	LA RAMS	38
14	at Houston	58
13	ATLANTA	10
0	at Pittsburgh	35
14	at Cincinnati	21
228		**462**

DENVER BRONCOS (5-11)

9	at LA Raiders	14
24	KANSAS CITY	23
34	SEATTLE (OT)	31
28	at Buffalo	29
29	CLEVELAND	30
29	PITTSBURGH	34
27	at Indianapolis	17
	OPEN DATE	
22	at Minnesota	27
7	at San Diego	19
13	CHICAGO (OT)	16
27	at Detroit	40
20	LA RAIDERS	23
20	at Kansas City	31
20	SAN DIEGO	10
12	at Seattle	17
22	GREEN BAY	13
331		374

HOUSTON OILERS (9-7)

27	at Atlanta	47
9	at Pittsburgh	20
24	INDIANAPOLIS	10
17	at San Diego	7
21	SAN FRANCISCO	24
48	CINCINNATI	17
23	NEW ORLEANS	10
12	NY JETS	17
13	at LA Rams	17
	OPEN DATE	
35	at Cleveland	23
27	BUFFALO	24
10	at Seattle (OT)	13
58	CLEVELAND	14
27	at Kansas City	10
20	at Cincinnati	40
34	PITTSBURGH	14
405		307

INDIANAPOLIS COLTS (7-9)

10	at Buffalo	26
14	NEW ENGLAND	16
10	at Houston	24
24	at Philadelphia	23
23	KANSAS CITY	19
	OPEN DATE	
17	DENVER	27
7	MIAMI	27
7	NEW YORK GIANTS	24
13	at New England	10
17	NEW YORK JETS	14
34	at Cincinnati	20
17	at Phoenix	20
7	BUFFALO	31
29	at New York Jets	21
35	WASHINGTON	28
17	at Miami	23
281		353

KANSAS CITY CHIEFS (11-5)

24	MINNESOTA	21
23	at Denver	24
17	at Green Bay	3
34	CLEVELAND	0
19	at Indianapolis	23
43	DETROIT	24
7	at Seattle	19
	OPEN DATE	
9	LA RAIDERS	7
16	SEATTLE	17
27	SAN DIEGO	10
27	at LA Raiders	24
37	at New England	7
31	DENVER	20
10	HOUSTON	27
24	at San Diego	21
21	at Chicago	10
369		257

LOS ANGELES RAIDERS (12-4)

14	DENVER	9
17	at Seattle	13
20	PITTSBURGH	3
24	CHICAGO	10
24	at Buffalo	38
24	SEATTLE	17
24	at San Diego	9
	OPEN DATE	
7	at Kansas City	9
16	GREEN BAY	29
13	at Miami	10
24	KANSAS CITY	27
23	at Denver	20
38	at Detroit	31
24	CINCINNATI	7
28	at Minnesota	24
17	SAN DIEGO	12
337		268

MIAMI DOLPHINS (12-4)

27	at New England	24
30	BUFFALO	7
3	at NY Giants	20
28	at Pittsburgh	6
20	NY JETS	16
	OPEN DATE	
17	NEW ENGLAND	10
27	at Indianapolis	7
23	PHOENIX	3
17	at NY Jets	3
10	LA RAIDERS	13
30	at Cleveland	13
20	at Washington	42
23	PHILADELPHIA (OT)	20
24	SEATTLE	17
14	at Buffalo	24
23	INDIANAPOLIS	17
336		242

NEW ENGLAND PATRIOTS (1-15)

24	MIAMI	27
16	at Indianapolis	14
7	at Cincinnati	41
13	NY JETS	37
20	SEATTLE	33
	OPEN DATE	
10	at Miami	17
10	BUFFALO	27
20	at Philadelphia	48
10	INDIANAPOLIS	13
0	at Buffalo	14
14	at Phoenix	34
7	KANSAS CITY	37
3	at Pittsburgh	24
10	WASHINGTON	25
7	at NY Jets	42
10	NY GIANTS	13
181		446

NEW YORK JETS (6-10)

20	at Cincinnati	25
24	CLEVELAND	21
7	BUFFALO	30
37	at New England	13
16	at Miami	20
3	SAN DIEGO	39
27	at Buffalo	30
17	at Houston	12
24	DALLAS	9
3	MIAMI	17
14	at Indianapolis	17
7	PITTSBURGH	24
17	at San Diego	38
	OPEN DATE	
21	INDIANAPOLIS	29
42	NEW ENGLAND	7
16	at Tampa Bay	14
295		345

PITTSBURGH STEELERS (9-7)

3	at Cleveland	13
20	HOUSTON	9
3	at LA Raiders	20
6	MIAMI	28
36	SAN DIEGO	14
34	at Denver	17
7	at San Francisco	27
41	LA RAMS	10
21	ATLANTA	9
	OPEN DATE	
3	at Cincinnati	27
24	at NY Jets	7
12	CINCINNATI	16
24	NEW ENGLAND	3
9	at New Orleans	6
35	CLEVELAND	0
14	at Houston	34
292		240

SAN DIEGO CHARGERS (6-10)

14	at Dallas	17
16	CINCINNATI	21
24	at Cleveland	14
7	HOUSTON	17
14	at Pittsburgh	36
39	at NY Jets	3
9	LA RAIDERS	24
41	TAMPA BAY	10
31	at Seattle	14
19	DENVER	7
10	at Kansas City	27
10	SEATTLE (OT)	13
38	NY JETS	17
	OPEN DATE	
10	at Denver	20
21	KANSAS CITY	24
12	at LA Raiders	17
315		**281**

SEATTLE SEAHAWKS (9-7)

0	at Chicago	17
13	LA RAIDERS	17
31	at Denver (OT)	34
31	CINCINNATI	16
33	at New England	20
17	at LA Raiders	24
19	KANSAS CITY	7
	OPEN DATE	
14	SAN DIEGO	31
17	at Kansas City	16
21	MINNESOTA	24
13	at San Diego (OT)	10
13	HOUSTON (OT)	10
20	at Green Bay	14
17	at Miami	24
17	DENVER	12
30	DETROIT	10
306		**286**

ATLANTA FALCONS (5-11)

47	HOUSTON	27
14	at Detroit	21
13	at San Francisco	19
	OPEN DATE	
28	NEW ORLEANS	27
35	SAN FRANCISCO	45
24	at LA Rams	44
38	CINCINNATI	17
9	at Pittsburgh	21
24	at Chicago	30
23	PHILADELPHIA	24
7	at New Orleans	10
17	at Tampa Bay	23
13	PHOENIX	24
10	at Cleveland	13
20	LA RAMS	13
26	DALLAS	7
348		**365**

CHICAGO BEARS (11-5)

17	SEATTLE	0
31	at Green Bay	13
19	MINNESOTA	16
10	at LA Raiders	24
27	GREEN BAY	13
38	LA RAMS	9
	OPEN DATE	
31	at Phoenix	21
26	at Tampa Bay	6
30	ATLANTA	24
16	at Denver (OT)	13
13	at Minnesota	41
23	DETROIT (OT)	17
9	at Washington	10
21	at Detroit	38
27	TAMPA BAY	14
10	KANSAS CITY	21
348		**280**

DALLAS COWBOYS (7-9)

17	SAN DIEGO	14
7	NY GIANTS	28
15	at Washington	19
17	at NY Giants	31
14	TAMPA BAY	10
3	at Phoenix	20
17	at Tampa Bay	13
20	PHILADELPHIA	21
9	at NY Jets	24
6	SAN FRANCISCO	24
24	at LA Rams	21
27	WASHINGTON	17
17	NEW ORLEANS	13
	OPEN DATE	
41	PHOENIX	10
3	at Philadelphia	17
7	at Atlanta	26
244		**308**

DETROIT LIONS (6-10)

21	TAMPA BAY	38
21	ATLANTA	14
20	at Tampa Bay	23
21	GREEN BAY	24
34	at Minnesota	27
24	at Kansas City	43
	OPEN DATE	
27	at New Orleans	10
38	WASHINGTON (OT)	41
7	MINNESOTA	17
0	at NY Giants	20
40	DENVER	27
17	at Chicago (OT)	23
31	LA RAIDERS	38
38	CHICAGO	21
24	at Green Bay	17
10	at Seattle	30
373		**413**

GREEN BAY PACKERS (6-10)

36	LA RAMS	24
13	CHICAGO	31
3	KANSAS CITY	17
24	at Detroit	21
13	at Chicago	27
14	at Tampa Bay	26
	OPEN DATE	
24	MINNESOTA	10
20	SAN FRANCISCO	24
29	at LA Raiders	16
24	at Phoenix	21
20	TAMPA BAY	10
7	at Minnesota	23
14	SEATTLE	20
0	at Philadelphia	31
17	DETROIT	24
13	at Denver	22
271		**347**

LOS ANGELES RAMS (5-11)

24	at Green Bay	36
35	at Tampa Bay	14
21	PHILADELPHIA	27
	OPEN DATE	
31	CINCINNATI (OT)	34
9	at Chicago	38
44	ATLANTA	24
10	at Pittsburgh	41
17	HOUSTON	13
7	NY GIANTS	31
21	DALLAS	24
28	at San Francisco	26
38	at Cleveland	23
20	NEW ORLEANS	24
10	SAN FRANCISCO	26
13	at Atlanta	20
17	at New Orleans	20
345		**412**

MINNESOTA VIKINGS (6-10)

21	at Kansas City	24
32	NEW ORLEANS	3
16	at Chicago	19
20	TAMPA BAY (OT)	23
27	DETROIT	34
24	at Philadelphia	32
	OPEN DATE	
10	at Green Bay	24
27	DENVER	22
17	at Detroit	7
24	at Seattle	21
41	CHICAGO	13
23	GREEN BAY	7
15	at NY Giants	23
13	at Tampa Bay	26
24	LA RAIDERS	28
17	SAN FRANCISCO	20
351		**326**

NEW ORLEANS SAINTS (8-8)

12	SAN FRANCISCO	13
3	at Minnesota	32
28	PHOENIX	7
	OPEN DATE	
27	at Atlanta	28
25	CLEVELAND	20
10	at Houston	23
10	DETROIT	27
21	at Cincinnati	7
35	TAMPA BAY	7
17	at Washington	31
10	ATLANTA	7
13	at Dallas	17
24	at LA Rams	20
6	PITTSBURGH	9
13	at San Francisco	10
20	LA RAMS	17
274		**275**

NEW YORK GIANTS (13-3)

27	PHILADELPHIA	20
28	at Dallas	7
20	MIAMI	3
31	DALLAS	17
	OPEN DATE	
24	at Washington	20
20	PHOENIX	19
21	WASHINGTON	10
24	at Indianapolis	7
31	at LA Rams	7
20	DETROIT	0
13	at Philadelphia	31
3	at San Francisco	7
23	MINNESOTA	15
13	BUFFALO	17
24	at Phoenix	21
13	at New England	10
335		**211**

PHILADELPHIA EAGLES (10-6)

20	at NY Giants	27
21	PHOENIX	23
27	at LA Rams	21
23	INDIANAPOLIS	24
	OPEN DATE	
32	MINNESOTA	24
7	at Washington	13
21	at Dallas	20
48	NEW ENGLAND	20
28	WASHINGTON	14
24	at Atlanta	23
31	NY GIANTS	13
23	at Buffalo	30
20	at Miami (OT)	23
31	GREEN BAY	0
17	DALLAS	3
23	at Phoenix	21
396		**299**

PHOENIX CARDINALS (5-11)

0	at Washington	31
23	at Philadelphia	21
7	at New Orleans	28
10	WASHINGTON	38
	OPEN DATE	
20	DALLAS	3
19	at NY Giants	20
21	CHICAGO	31
3	at Miami	23
14	at Buffalo	45
21	GREEN BAY	24
34	NEW ENGLAND	14
20	INDIANAPOLIS	17
24	at Atlanta	13
10	at Dallas	41
21	NY GIANTS	24
21	PHILADELPHIA	23
268		**396**

SAN FRANCISCO 49ERS (14-2)

13	at New Orleans	12
26	WASHINGTON	13
19	ATLANTA	13
	OPEN DATE	
24	at Houston	21
45	at Atlanta	35
27	PITTSBURGH	7
20	CLEVELAND	17
24	at Green Bay	20
24	at Dallas	6
31	TAMPA BAY	7
17	LA RAMS	28
7	NY GIANTS	3
20	at Cincinnati (OT)	17
26	at LA Rams	10
10	NEW ORLEANS	13
20	at Minnesota	17
353		**239**

TAMPA BAY BUCCANEERS (6-10)

38	at Detroit	21
14	LA RAMS	35
23	DETROIT	20
23	at Minnesota (OT)	20
10	at Dallas	14
26	GREEN BAY	14
13	DALLAS	17
10	at San Diego	41
6	CHICAGO	26
7	at New Orleans	35
7	at San Francisco	31
10	at Green Bay	20
23	ATLANTA	17
	OPEN DATE	
26	MINNESOTA	13
14	at Chicago	27
14	NY JETS	16
264		**367**

WASHINGTON REDSKINS (10-6)

31	PHOENIX	0
13	at San Francisco	26
19	DALLAS	15
38	at Phoenix	10
	OPEN DATE	
20	NY GIANTS	24
13	PHILADELPHIA	7
10	at NY Giants	21
41	at Detroit (OT)	38
14	at Philadelphia	28
31	NEW ORLEANS	17
17	at Dallas	27
42	MIAMI	20
10	CHICAGO	9
25	at New England	10
28	at Indianapolis	35
29	BUFFALO	14
381		**301**

American Football Conference
Scoring

TOUCHDOWNS	TD	Rush	Rec	Ret	Pts	KICKING	PAT	FG	Lg	Pts
Fenner, Sea	15	14	1	0	90	Lowery, KC	37/38	34/37	48	139
Allen, LA Raiders	13	12	1	0	78	Norwood, Buff	50/52	20/29	48	110
Thomas, Buff	13	11	2	0	78	Treadwell, Den	34/36	25/34	49	109
White, Hou	12	8	4	0	72	Johnson, Sea	33/34	23/32	51	102
Hoge, Pitt	10	7	3	0	60	Leahy, NY Jets	32/32	23/26	47	101
Brooks, Cin	9	5	4	0	54	Stoyanovich, Mia	37/37	21/25	53	100
Brown, Cin	9	0	9	0	54	Anderson, Pitt	32/32	20/25	48	92
Givins, Hou	9	0	9	0	54	Breech, Cin	41/44	17/21	46	92
Smith, Mia	9	8	1	0	54	Jaeger, LA Raiders	40/42	15/20	50	85
						Carney, SD	27/28	19/21	43	84

Note: 3 tied with 48 points.

Passing

	Att	Comp	Pct Comp	Yds	Avg Gain	TD	Pct TD	Int	Pct Int	Lg	Rating Pts
Kelly, Buff	346	219	63.3	2829	8.18	24	6.9	9	2.6	71	101.2
Moon, Hou	584	362	62.0	4689	8.03	33	5.7	13	2.2	t87	96.8
DeBerg, KC	444	258	58.1	3444	7.76	23	5.2	4	0.9	t90	96.3
Schroeder, LA Raiders	334	182	54.5	2849	8.53	19	5.7	9	2.7	t68	90.8
Marino, Mia	531	306	57.6	3563	6.71	21	4.0	11	2.1	t69	82.6
Brister, Pitt	387	223	57.6	2725	7.04	20	5.2	14	3.6	90	81.6
Elway, Den	502	294	58.6	3526	7.02	15	3.0	14	2.8	66	78.5
O'Brien, NY Jets	411	226	55.0	2855	6.95	13	3.2	10	2.4	t69	77.3
Esiason, Cin	402	224	55.7	3031	7.54	24	6.0	22	5.5	53	77.0
George, Ind	334	181	54.2	2152	6.44	16	4.8	13	3.9	75	73.8

Pass Receiving

RECEPTIONS	No.	Yds	Avg	Lg	TD	YARDS	Yds	No.	Avg	Lg	TD
Jeffires, Hou	74	1048	14.2	t87	8	Jeffires, Hou	1048	74	14.2	t87	8
Hill, Hou	74	1019	13.8	57	5	Paige, KC	1021	65	15.7	t86	5
Williams, Sea (RB)	73	699	9.6	60	0	Hill, Hou	1019	74	13.8	57	5
Givins, Hou	72	979	13.6	t80	9	Gault, LA Raiders	985	50	19.7	t68	3
Reed, Buff	71	945	13.3	t56	8	Givins, Hou	979	72	13.6	t80	9
Bentley, Ind (RB)	71	664	9.4	73	2	Reed, Buff	945	71	13.3	t56	8
Duncan, Hou	66	785	11.9	t37	1	A. Miller, SD	933	63	14.8	t31	7
Paige, KC	65	1021	15.7	t86	5	Jackson, Den	926	57	16.2	66	4
A. Miller, SD	63	933	14.8	t31	7	Hester, Ind	924	54	17.1	t64	6
Brooks, Ind	62	823	13.3	75	5	Fryar, NE	856	54	15.9	56	4

Rushing

	Att	Yds	Avg	Lg	TD
Thomas, Buff	271	1297	4.8	t80	11
Butts, SD	265	1225	4.6	52	8
Humphrey, Den	288	1202	4.2	t37	7
Word, KC	204	1015	5.0	t53	4
Brooks, Cin	195	1004	5.1	t56	5
Fenner, Sea	215	859	4.0	36	14
Smith, Mia	226	831	3.7	33	8
Stephens, NE	212	808	3.8	26	2
Okoye, KC	245	805	3.3	32	7
Hoge, Pitt	203	772	3.8	t41	7

Total Yards from Scrimmage

	Total	Rush	Rec
Thomas, Buff	1829	1297	532
Williams, Sea	1413	714	699
Humphrey, Den	1354	1202	152
Butts, SD	1342	1225	117
Brooks, Cin	1273	1004	269
Bentley, Ind	1220	556	664
Hoge, Pitt	1114	772	342
White, Hou	1070	702	368
Mack, Clev	1062	702	360
Jeffires, Hou	1048	0	1048

Interceptions

	No.	Yds	Lg	TD
R. Johnson, Hou	8	100	35	1
Byrd, SD	7	63	24	0
Ross, KC	5	97	40	0
McMillan, NY Jets	5	92	25	0
Oliver, Mia	5	87	35	0
Williams, Mia	5	82	t42	1
Woodson, Pitt	5	67	34	0

Sacks

D. Thomas, KC	20.0
B. Smith, Buff	19.0
O'Neal, SD	13.5
Byrd, NY Jets	13.0
Green, Sea	12.5
S. Jones, Hou	12.5
Townsend, LA Raiders	12.5

American Football Conference (*Cont.*)

Punting

	No.	Yds	Avg	Net Avg	TB	In 20	Lg	Blk	Ret	Ret Yds
Horan, Den	58	2575	44.4	38.9	6	14	67	1	22	159
Stark, Ind	71	3084	43.4	37.4	3	24	61	1	42	334
Johnson, Cin	64	2705	42.3	34.3	8	12	70	0	36	352
Roby, Mia	72	3022	42.0	35.6	3	20	62	0	40	397
Hansen, NE	90	3752	41.7	33.6	8	18	69	2	50	503

Punt Returns

	No.	Yds	Avg	Lg	TD
Verdin, Ind	31	396	12.8	36	0
Woodson, Pitt	38	398	10.5	t52	1
Warren, Sea	28	269	9.6	39	0
T. Brown, LA Raiders	34	295	8.7	39	0
Price, Cin	29	251	8.7	t66	1

Kickoff Returns

	No.	Yds	Avg	Lg	TD
Clark, Den	20	505	25.3	75	0
Elder, SD	24	571	23.8	90	0
Woodson, Pitt	35	764	21.8	49	0
Warren, Sea	23	478	20.8	71	0
Martin, NE	25	515	20.6	38	0

National Football Conference

Scoring

TOUCHDOWNS	TD	Rush	Rec	Ret	Pts
B. Sanders, Det	16	13	3	0	96
Gary, LA Rams	15	14	1	0	90
Anderson, Chi	13	10	3	0	78
Rice, SF	13	0	13	0	78
Anderson, NY Giants	11	11	0	0	66
E. Smith, Dall	11	11	0	0	66
Rison, Atl	10	0	10	0	60
Walker, Minn	9	5	4	0	54
Williams, Phil	9	0	9	0	54

Note: 4 tied with 48 points.

KICKING	PAT	FG	Lg	Pts
Lohmiller, Wash	41/41	30/40	56	131
Butler, Chi	36/37	26/37	52	114
Cofer, SF	39/39	24/36	56	111
Ruzek, Phil	45/48	21/29	53	108
Davis, Atl	40/40	22/33	53	106
Jacke, GB	28/29	23/30	53	97
Christie, TB	27/27	23/27	54	96
Andersen, NO	29/29	21/27	52	92
Lansford, LA Rams	42/43	15/24	46	87
Del Greco, Phoe	31/31	17/27	50	82

Passing

	Att	Comp	Pct Comp	Yds	Avg Gain	TD	Pct TD	Int	Pct Int	Lg	Rating Pts
Simms, NY Giants	311	184	59.2	2284	7.34	15	4.8	4	1.3	t80	92.7
Cunningham, Phil	465	271	58.3	3466	7.45	30	6.5	13	2.8	t95	91.6
Montana, SF	520	321	61.7	3944	7.58	26	5.0	16	3.1	t78	89.0
Harbaugh, Chi	312	180	57.7	2178	6.98	10	3.2	6	1.9	t80	81.9
Peete, Det	271	142	52.4	1974	7.28	13	4.8	8	3.0	t68	79.8
Everett, LA Rams	554	307	55.4	3989	7.20	23	4.2	17	3.1	t55	79.3
Miller, Atl	388	222	57.2	2735	7.05	17	4.4	14	3.6	t75	78.7
Rypien, Wash	304	166	54.6	2070	6.81	16	5.3	11	3.6	t53	78.4
Testaverde, TB	365	203	55.6	2818	7.72	17	4.7	18	4.9	t89	75.6
Majkowski, GB	264	150	56.8	1925	7.29	10	3.8	12	4.5	t76	73.5

Pass Receiving

RECEPTIONS	No.	Yds	Avg	Lg	TD
Rice, SF	100	1502	15.0	t64	13
Rison, Atl	82	1208	14.7	t75	10
Byars, Phil (RB)	81	819	10.1	54	3
Ellard, LA Rams	76	1294	17.0	t50	4
Clark, Wash	75	1112	14.8	t53	8
A. Carter, Minn	70	1008	14.4	t56	8
Monk, Wash	68	770	11.3	44	5
Sharpe, GB	67	1105	16.5	t76	6
Martin, Dall	64	732	11.4	45	0
Johnson, Det	64	727	11.4	t44	6

YARDS	Yds	No.	Avg	Lg	TD
Rice, SF	1502	100	15.0	t64	13
Ellard, LA Rams	1294	76	17.0	t50	4
Rison, Atl	1208	82	14.7	t75	10
Clark, Wash	1112	75	14.8	t53	8
Sharpe, GB	1105	67	16.5	t76	6
Anderson, LA Rams	1097	51	21.5	t55	4
A. Carter, Minn	1008	70	14.4	t56	8
Clark, Det	914	52	17.6	57	8
E. Martin, NO	912	63	14.5	58	5
Byars, Phil (RB)	819	81	10.1	54	3

National Football Conference (*Cont.*)

Rushing

	Att	Yds	Avg	Lg	TD
B. Sanders, Det	255	1304	5.1	t45	13
Byner, Wash	297	1219	4.1	22	6
Anderson, Chi	260	1078	4.1	52	10
Cunningham, Phil	118	942	8.0	t52	5
E. Smith, Dall	241	937	3.9	t48	11
Johnson, Phoe	234	926	4.0	41	5
Gary, LA Rams	204	808	4.0	48	14
Anderson, NY Giants	225	784	3.5	28	11
Walker, Minn	184	770	4.2	t58	5
Rozier, Hou-Atl	163	717	4.4	67	3

Total Yards from Scrimmage

	Total	Rush	Rec
B. Sanders, Det	1784	1304	480
Anderson, Chi	1562	1078	484
Rice, SF	1502	0	1502
Byner, Wash	1498	1219	279
Ellard, LA Rams	1315	21	1294
Rison, Atl	1208	0	1208
Johnson, Phoe	1167	926	241
E. Smith, Dall	1165	937	228
Sharpe, GB	1119	14	1105
Muster, Chi	1116	664	452

Interceptions

	No.	Yds	Lg	TD
Carrier, Chi	10	39	14	0
Haddix, TB	7	231	t65	3
Browner, Minn	7	103	31	1
Waymer, SF	7	64	24	0
Mayhew, Wash	7	20	15	0
Walls, NY Giants	6	80	40	1
Stinson, Chi	6	66	30	0

Sacks

Haley, SF	16.0
White, Phil	14.0
Greene, LA Rams	13.0
Dent, Chi	12.0
Doleman, Minn	11.0
Swilling, NO	11.0

Punting

	No.	Yds	Avg	Net Avg	TB	In 20	Lg	Blk	Ret	Ret Yds
Landeta, NY Giants	75	3306	44.1	37.3	11	24	67	0	41	291
Saxon, Dall	79	3413	43.2	35.6	8	20	62	0	43	438
Camarillo, Phoe	67	2865	42.8	37.4	5	16	63	0	41	258
Barnhardt, NO	70	2990	42.7	36.2	6	20	65	1	43	302
Newsome, Minn	78	3299	42.3	33.2	8	19	61	1	44	513

Punt Returns

	No.	Yds	Avg	Lg	TD
Bailey, Chi	36	399	11.1	t95	1
Meggett, NY Giants	43	467	10.9	t68	1
Gray, Det	34	361	10.6	39	0
Query, GB	32	308	9.6	25	0
Sanders, Atl	29	250	8.6	t79	1

Kickoff Returns

	No.	Yds	Avg	Lg	TD
Meggett, NY Giants	21	492	23.4	58	0
Gray, Det	41	939	22.9	65	0
Wilson, GB	35	798	22.8	36	0
Green, LA Rams	25	560	22.4	t99	1
Walker, Minn	44	966	22.0	64	0

Fancy-Free Football

NFL might as well stand for No Fun League. At their annual meetings last spring in Hawaii, NFL owners directed games officials to strictly enforce rules barring touchdown celebrations. Spikes are O.K. High Fives are O.K. But from now on not much else is.

Even the Ickey Shuffle is no longer safe. Paul Tagliabue can now fine the Bengals if running back Ickey Woods does his trademark, post-TD hip-hop, even if he does it near his own bench.

"We have the best athletes in the world, and they're paid to be athletes, not dancers," said Saints president Jim Finks. "Where does it stop? Somebody's going to out-Ickey Ickey."

Of course, the owners' decision wasn't met with open arms.

"They want us to open the oven and have every cookie look the same," said Atlanta coach Jerry Glanville. "These are football players. They're human. They've got emotions. Let 'em dance."

Cincinnati coach Sam Wyche has thought up one way around the new directive. Let's go to the videotape, he says. "We are certainly a league in love with the instant replay," Wyche said. "So now when Ickey scores, he'll just point to our big video screen in the end zone. Then we'll replay one of his classic shuffles. Let the memory of the shuffle live on."

Unless, of course, the league outlaws pointing at scoreboards.

1990 NFL Team Leaders

AFC Total Offense

	Total Yds	Yds Rush	Yds Pass	Time of Poss	Avg Pts/Game
Houston	6222	1417	4805	31:35	25.3
Buffalo	5276	2080	3196	28:39	26.8
Kansas City	5215	1948	3267	31:30	23.1
Denver	5213	1872	3341	30:50	20.7
Cincinnati	5063	2120	2943	29:21	22.5
Miami	5047	1535	3512	30:09	21.0
San Diego	4940	2257	2683	30:19	19.7
NY Jets	4886	2127	2759	30:05	18.4
LA Raiders	4716	2028	2688	29:28	21.1
Seattle	4583	1749	2834	30:47	19.1
Pittsburgh	4525	1880	2645	30:06	18.3
Cleveland	4367	1220	3147	27:12	14.3
New England	4163	1398	2765	28:21	11.3
Indianapolis	4155	1282	2873	26:27	17.6

AFC Total Defense

	Opp Total Yds	Opp Yds Rush	Opp Yds Pass	Avg PA/Game
Pittsburgh	4115	1615	2500	15.0
LA Raiders	4413	1716	2697	16.8
San Diego	4425	1515	2910	17.6
Miami	4547	1831	2716	15.1
Buffalo	4607	1808	2799	16.4
Seattle	4609	1605	3004	17.9
Houston	4635	1575	3060	19.2
Kansas City	4881	1640	3241	16.1
Cleveland	5190	2105	3085	28.9
Denver	5345	1963	3382	23.4
NY Jets	5455	2018	3437	21.6
Cincinnati	5605	2085	3520	22.0
Indianapolis	5614	2212	3402	22.1
New England	5697	2676	3021	27.9

NFC Total Offense

	Total Yds	Yds Rush	Yds Pass	Time of Poss	Avg Pts/Game
San Francisco	5895	1718	4177	32:49	22.1
Philadelphia	5700	2556	3144	33:19	24.8
Washington	5562	2083	3479	32:19	23.8
LA Rams	5430	1612	3818	29:59	21.6
Atlanta	5055	1594	3461	31:05	21.8
Minnesota	5034	1867	3167	29:34	21.9
Chicago	4980	2436	2544	33:06	21.8
Detroit	4977	1927	3050	25:33	23.3
NY Giants	4805	2049	2756	32:15	20.9
Phoenix	4745	1912	2833	28:38	16.6
Green Bay	4675	1369	3306	29:34	16.9
New Orleans	4476	1850	2626	29:59	17.1
Tampa Bay	4475	1626	2849	28:11	16.5
Dallas	4081	1500	2581	28:44	15.3

NFC Total Defense

	Opp Total Yds	Opp Yds Rush	Opp Yds Pass	Avg PA/Game
NY Giants	4206	1459	2747	13.2
San Francisco	4273	1258	3015	14.9
Chicago	4492	1572	2920	17.5
Dallas	4615	1976	2639	19.3
Philadelphia	4660	1169	3491	18.7
Minnesota	4717	2074	2643	20.4
Washington	4730	1587	3143	18.8
New Orleans	4878	1559	3319	17.2
Phoenix	5216	2318	2898	24.8
Atlanta	5270	1357	3913	22.8
LA Rams	5411	1649	3762	25.8
Green Bay	5442	2059	3383	21.7
Tampa Bay	5479	2223	3256	22.9
Detroit	5734	2388	3346	25.8

Takeaways/Giveaways

AFC

	Takeaways Int	Fum	Total	Giveaways Int	Fum	Total	Net Diff
Kansas City	20	25	45	5	14	19	26
Buffalo	18	17	35	11	10	21	14
Pittsburgh	24	18	42	15	17	32	10
NY Jets	18	11	29	11	13	24	5
Miami	19	8	27	12	15	27	0
LA Raiders	13	9	22	10	14	24	–2
San Diego	19	11	30	19	13	32	–2
Houston	21	12	33	15	21	36	–3
Cincinnati	15	16	31	23	12	35	–4
New England	14	18	32	20	16	36	–4
Seattle	12	18	30	20	16	36	–6
Denver	10	15	25	18	14	32	–7
Indianapolis	9	15	24	21	10	31	–7
Cleveland	13	9	22	23	5	46	–24

NFC

	Takeaways Int	Fum	Total	Giveaways Int	Fum	Total	Net Diff
NY Giants	23	11	34	5	9	14	20
Chicago	31	14	45	12	14	26	19
Washington	21	12	33	22	6	28	5
Philadelphia	19	11	30	13	15	28	2
San Francisco	17	14	31	16	14	30	1
LA Rams	12	19	31	17	14	31	0
Detroit	17	18	35	20	16	36	–1
Tampa Bay	25	17	42	24	19	43	–1
Dallas	11	19	30	24	9	33	–3
Atlanta	17	18	35	18	21	39	–4
Minnesota	22	11	33	24	13	37	–4
Phoenix	16	11	27	18	14	32	–5
New Orleans	8	19	27	23	16	39	–12
Green Bay	16	14	30	21	22	43	–13

THEY SAID IT

Pat Leahy, veteran New York Jets place-kicker, taking issue with the adage that the legs are the first thing to go on an athlete: "It's the hair."

League Rankings

	Offense			Defense				Offense			Defense		
	Total	Rush	Pass	Total	Rush	Pass		Total	Rush	Pass	Total	Rush	Pass
Atlanta	10	21	6	19	3	28	Miami	11	22	4	7	16	5
Buffalo	6	7	10	8	15	7	Minnesota	12	15	11	13	21	3
Chicago	13	2	28	6	7	10	New England	26	25	20	27	28	13
Cincinnati	9	5	15	25	22	26	New Orleans	23	16	26	15	6	19
Cleveland	25	28	12	17	23	15	NY Giants	17	8	22	2	4	6
Dallas	28	23	27	10	18	2	NY Jets	16	4	21	23	19	24
Denver	8	14	7	20	17	21	Philadelphia	3	1	13	12	1	25
Detroit	14	11	14	28	27	20	Phoenix	18	12	19	18	26	8
Green Bay	20	26	8	22	20	22	Pittsburgh	22	13	25	1	11	1
Houston	1	24	1	11	8	14	San Diego	15	3	24	5	5	9
Indianapolis	27	27	16	26	24	23	San Francisco	2	18	2	3	2	12
Kansas City	7	10	9	16	12	17	Seattle	21	17	18	9	10	11
LA Raiders	19	9	23	4	14	4	Tampa Bay	24	19	17	24	25	18
LA Rams	5	20	3	21	13	27	Washington	4	6	5	14	9	16

1990 AFC Team-by-Team Statistical Leaders

Buffalo Bills

	TD						
SCORING	Rush	Rec	Ret	PAT	FG	S	Pts
Norwood	0	0	0	50/52	20/29	0	110
Thomas	11	2	0	0/0	0/0	0	78
Reed	0	8	0	0/0	0/0	0	48
K. Davis	4	1	0	0/0	0/0	0	30
McKeller	0	5	0	0/0	0/0	0	30

RUSHING	No.	Yds	Avg	Lg	TD
Thomas	271	1297	4.8	t80	11
K. Davis	64	302	4.7	47	4
Mueller	59	207	3.5	20	2
D. Smith	20	82	4.1	13	2
Kelly	22	63	2.9	15	0

PASSING	Att	Comp	Pct Comp	Yds	Avg Gain	TD	Int	Rating Pts
Kelly	346	219	63.3	2829	8.18	24	9	101.2
Reich	63	36	57.1	469	7.44	2	0	91.3

RECEIVING	No.	Yds	Avg	Lg	TD
Reed	71	945	13.3	t56	8
Thomas	49	532	10.9	63	2
Lofton	35	712	20.3	71	4
McKeller	34	464	13.6	43	5
D. Smith	21	225	10.7	39	0

INTERCEPTIONS: Jackson, 3

PUNTING	No.	Yds	Avg	Net Avg	TB	In 20	Lg	Blk
Tuten	53	2107	39.8	34.2	4	12	55	0

SACKS: B. Smith, 19.0

Cincinnati Bengals

	TD						
SCORING	Rush	Rec	Ret	PAT	FG	S	Pts
Breech	0	0	0	41/44	17/25	0	92
Brooks	5	4	0	0/0	0/0	0	54
Brown	0	9	0	0/0	0/0	0	54
Woods	6	0	0	0/0	0/0	0	36
Holman	0	5	0	0/0	0/0	0	30

RUSHING	No.	Yds	Avg	Lg	TD
Brooks	195	1004	5.1	t56	5
Green	83	353	4.3	39	1
Woods	64	268	4.2	32	6
Taylor	51	216	4.2	24	2
Esiason	50	157	3.1	21	0

PASSING	Att	Comp	Pct Comp	Yds	Avg Gain	TD	Int	Rating Pts
Esiason	402	224	55.7	3031	7.54	24	22	77.0
Wilhelm	19	12	63.2	117	6.16	0	0	80.4

RECEIVING	No.	Yds	Avg	Lg	TD
Brown	44	706	16.0	t50	9
McGee	43	737	17.1	52	1
Holman	40	596	14.9	53	5
Brooks	26	269	10.3	35	4
Woods	20	162	8.1	22	0

INTERCEPTIONS: Bussey, 4

PUNTING	No.	Yds	Avg	Net Avg	TB	In 20	Lg	Blk
Johnson	64	2705	42.3	34.3	8	12	70	0

SACKS: Francis, 8.0

Big Deals

I'll trade you a whole team for your draft pick. In effect, that's what the Los Angeles Rams said to the Dallas Texans in June of 1952 when they traded 11 players for the draft selection rights to University of California linebacker Les Richter. The Rams were also involved in the second largest swap for a single player. In 1959 they dealt seven veterans, a draft choice, and a player to be named later to the Chicago Cardinals for running back Ollie Matson.

Cleveland Browns

SCORING	Rush	Rec	Ret	PAT	FG	S	Pts
Bauric	0	0	0	24/27	14/20	0	66
Mack	5	2	0	0/0	0/0	0	42
Metcalf	1	1	2	0/0	0/0	0	24
Slaughter	0	4	0	0/0	0/0	0	24
Hoard	3	0	0	0/0	0/0	0	18

RUSHING	No.	Yds	Avg	Lg	TD
Mack	158	702	4.4	26	5
Metcalf	80	248	3.1	17	1
Hoard	58	149	2.6	42	3
Gainer	30	81	2.7	9	1
Slaughter	5	29	5.8	17	0

PASSING	Att	Comp	Pct Comp	Yds	Avg Gain	TD	Int	Rating Pts
Kosar	423	230	54.4	2562	6.06	10	15	65.7
Pagel	148	69	46.6	819	5.53	3	8	48.2

RECEIVING	No.	Yds	Avg	Lg	TD
Slaughter	59	847	14.4	50	4
Metcalf	57	452	7.9	35	1
Langhorne	45	585	13.0	39	2
Brennan	45	568	12.6	28	2
Mack	42	360	8.6	30	2

INTERCEPTIONS: Wright, 3

PUNTING	No.	Yds	Avg	Net Avg	TB	In 20	Lg	Blk
Wagner	74	2879	38.9	30.9	2	13	65	4

SACKS: Perry, 11.5

Denver Broncos

SCORING	Rush	Rec	Ret	PAT	FG	S	Pts
Treadwell	0	0	0	34/36	25/34	0	109
Humphrey	7	0	0	0/0	0/0	0	42
Jackson	1	4	0	0/0	0/0	0	30
Bratton	3	1	0	0/0	0/0	0	24
Young	0	4	0	0/0	0/0	0	24

RUSHING	No.	Yds	Avg	Lg	TD
Humphrey	288	1202	4.2	t37	7
Elway	50	258	5.2	21	3
Winder	42	120	2.9	19	2
Bratton	27	82	3.0	10	3
Ezor	23	81	3.5	15	0

PASSING	Att	Comp	Pct Comp	Yds	Avg Gain	TD	Int	Rating Pts
Elway	502	294	58.6	3526	7.02	15	14	78.5
Kubiak	22	11	50.0	145	6.59	0	4	31.6

RECEIVING	No.	Yds	Avg	Lg	TD
Jackson	57	926	16.2	66	4
Johnson	54	747	13.8	49	3
Kay	29	282	9.7	22	0
Bratton	29	276	9.5	63	1
Young	28	385	13.8	42	4

INTERCEPTIONS: Henderson, Montgomery, Atwater, 2

PUNTING	No.	Yds	Avg	Net Avg	TB	In 20	Lg	Blk
Horan	58	2575	44.4	38.9	6	14	67	1

SACKS: Fletcher, 11.0

Houston Oilers

SCORING	Rush	Rec	Ret	PAT	FG	S	Pts
White	8	4	0	0/0	0/0	0	72
Garcia	0	0	0	26/28	14/20	0	68
Givins	0	9	0	0/0	0/0	0	54
Jeffires	0	8	0	0/0	0/0	0	48
Zendejas	0	0	0	20/21	7/12	0	41

RUSHING	No.	Yds	Avg	Lg	TD
White	168	702	4.2	22	8
Pinkett	66	268	4.1	19	0
Moon	55	215	3.9	17	2
V. Jones	14	75	5.4	14	0

PASSING	Att	Comp	Pct Comp	Yds	Avg Gain	TD	Int	Rating Pts
Moon	584	362	62.0	4689	8.03	33	13	96.8
Carlson	55	37	67.3	383	6.96	4	2	96.3

RECEIVING	No.	Yds	Avg	Lg	TD
Jeffires	74	1048	14.2	t87	8
Hill	74	1019	13.8	57	5
Givins	72	979	13.6	t80	9
Duncan	66	785	11.9	t37	1
White	39	368	9.4	29	4

INTERCEPTIONS: R. Johnson, 8

PUNTING	No.	Yds	Avg	Net Avg	TB	In 20	Lg	Blk
Gr. Montgomery	34	1530	45.0	36.6	5	7	60	0

SACKS: S. Jones, 12.5

Indianapolis Colts

SCORING	Rush	Rec	Ret	PAT	FG	S	Pts
Biasucci	0	0	0	32/33	17/24	0	83
Bentley	4	2	0	0/0	0/0	0	36
Hester	0	6	0	0/0	0/0	0	36
Brooks	0	5	0	0/0	0/0	0	30
Morgan	0	5	0	0/0	0/0	0	30

RUSHING	No.	Yds	Avg	Lg	TD
Dickerson	166	677	4.1	43	4
Bentley	137	556	4.1	t26	4
Trudeau	10	28	2.8	9	0
Clark	7	10	1.4	11	0
Hester	4	9	2.3	10	0

PASSING	Att	Comp	Pct Comp	Yds	Avg Gain	TD	Int	Rating Pts
George	334	181	54.2	2152	6.44	16	13	73.8
Trudeau	144	84	58.3	1078	7.49	6	6	78.4

RECEIVING	No.	Yds	Avg	Lg	TD
Bentley	71	664	9.4	73	2
Brooks	62	823	13.3	75	5
Hester	54	924	17.1	t64	6
Morgan	23	364	15.8	t42	5
Dickerson	18	92	5.1	17	0

INTERCEPTIONS: Prior, 3

PUNTING	No.	Yds	Avg	Net Avg	TB	In 20	Lg	Blk
Stark	71	3084	43.4	37.4	3	24	61	1

SACKS: Clancy, 7.5

Kansas City Chiefs

SCORING	TD Rush	Rec	Ret	PAT	FG	S	Pts
Lowery	0	0	0	37/38	34/37	0	139
Okoye	7	0	0	0/0	0/0	0	42
B. Jones	0	5	0	0/0	0/0	0	30
Paige	0	5	0	0/0	0/0	0	30
R. Thomas	0	4	0	0/0	0/0	0	24

RUSHING	No.	Yds	Avg	Lg	TD
Word	204	1015	5.0	t53	4
Okoye	245	805	3.3	32	7
McNair	14	61	4.4	13	0
B. Jones	10	47	4.7	14	0

PASSING	Att	Comp	Pct Comp	Yds	Avg Gain	TD	Int	Rating Pts
DeBerg	444	258	58.1	3444	7.76	23	4	96.3
Pelluer	5	2	40.0	14	2.80	0	1	8.3

RECEIVING	No.	Yds	Avg	Lg	TD
Paige	65	1021	15.7	t86	5
R. Thomas	41	545	13.3	t47	4
Harry	41	519	12.7	60	2
McNair	40	507	12.7	65	2
B. Jones	19	137	7.2	19	5

INTERCEPTIONS: Ross, 5

PUNTING	No.	Yds	Avg	Net Avg	TB	In 20	Lg	Blk
Barker	64	2479	38.7	33.4	1	16	56	0

SACKS: D. Thomas, 20.0

Los Angeles Raiders

SCORING	TD Rush	Rec	Ret	PAT	FG	S	Pt
Jaeger	0	0	0	40/42	15/20	0	8
Allen	12	1	0	0/0	0/0	0	7
Fernandez	0	5	0	0/0	0/0	0	3
Jackson	5	0	0	0/0	0/0	0	3
Smith	2	3	0	0/0	0/0	0	3

RUSHING	No.	Yds	Avg	Lg	TD
Jackson	125	698	5.6	88	5
Allen	179	682	3.8	28	12
Smith	81	327	4.0	17	2
Bell	47	164	3.5	21	1

PASSING	Att	Comp	Pct Comp	Yds	Avg Gain	TD	Int	Ratin Pts
Schroeder	334	182	54.5	2849	8.53	19	9	90.

RECEIVING	No.	Yds	Avg	Lg	TD
Fernandez	52	839	16.1	t66	5
Gault	50	985	19.7	t68	3
Horton	33	404	12.2	36	3
T. Brown	18	265	14.7	51	3
Allen	15	189	12.6	30	1

INTERCEPTIONS: Anderson, McDaniel, and Harden, 3

PUNTING	No.	Yds	Avg	Net Avg	TB	In 20	Lg	Blk
Gossett	60	2315	38.6	33.6	4	19	57	2

SACKS: Townsend, 12.5

Miami Dolphins

SCORING	TD Rush	Rec	Ret	PAT	FG	S	Pts
Stoyanovich	0	0	0	37/37	21/25	0	100
Smith	8	1	0	0/0	0/0	0	54
Paige	2	4	0	0/0	0/0	0	36
Duper	0	5	0	0/0	0/0	0	30
Clayton	0	3	0	0/0	0/0	0	18

RUSHING	No.	Yds	Avg	Lg	TD
Smith	226	831	3.7	33	8
Logan	79	317	4.0	17	2
Stradford	37	138	3.7	15	1
Paige	32	95	3.0	11	2
Higgs	10	67	6.7	27	0

PASSING	Att	Comp	Pct Comp	Yds	Avg Gain	TD	Int	Rating Pts
Marino	531	306	57.6	3563	6.71	21	11	82.6
Secules	7	3	42.9	17	2.43	0	1	10.7

RECEIVING	No.	Yds	Avg	Lg	TD
Duper	52	810	15.6	t60	5
Jensen	44	365	8.3	18	1
Paige	35	247	7.1	t17	4
Clayton	32	406	12.7	43	3
Edmunds	31	446	14.4	35	1

INTERCEPTIONS: Oliver, 5

PUNTING	No.	Yds	Avg	Net Avg	TB	In 20	Lg	Blk
Roby	72	3022	42.0	35.6	3	20	62	0

SACKS: Cross, 11.5

New England Patriots

SCORING	TD Rush	Rec	Ret	PAT	FG	S	Pts
Staurovsky	0	0	0	19/19	16/22	0	67
Cook	0	5	0	0/0	0/0	0	30
Fryar	0	4	0	0/0	0/0	0	24
Stephens	2	1	0	0/0	0/0	0	18
Dykes	0	2	0	0/0	0/0	0	12

RUSHING	No.	Yds	Avg	Lg	TD
Stephens	212	808	3.8	26	2
Allen	63	237	3.8	29	1
Adams	28	111	4.0	13	0
Perryman	32	97	3.0	13	1
Hodson	12	79	6.6	23	0

PASSING	Att	Comp	Pct Comp	Yds	Avg Gain	TD	Int	Rating Pts
Wilson	265	139	52.5	1625	6.13	6	11	61.6
Hodson	156	85	54.5	968	6.21	4	5	68.5

RECEIVING	No.	Yds	Avg	Lg	TD
Fryar	54	856	15.9	56	4
Cook	51	455	8.9	t35	5
Dykes	34	549	16.1	t35	2
Stephens	28	196	7.0	43	1
McMurtry	22	240	10.9	26	0

INTERCEPTIONS: Lippett, Hurst, and Marion, 4

PUNTING	No.	Yds	Avg	Net Avg	TB	In 20	Lg	Blk
Hansen	90	3752	41.7	33.6	8	18	69	2

SACKS: B. Williams, 6.0

New York Jets

SCORING	Rush	Rec	TD Ret	PAT	FG	S	Pts
Leahy	0	0	0	32/32	23/26	0	101
Baxter	6	0	0	0/0	0/0	0	36
F. McNeil	6	0	0	0/0	0/0	0	36
Moore	0	6	0	0/0	0/0	0	36
Toon	0	6	0	0/0	0/0	0	36

RUSHING	No.	Yds	Avg	Lg	TD
Thomas	123	620	5.0	41	1
Baxter	124	539	4.3	t28	6
F. McNeil	99	458	4.6	29	6
Hector	91	377	4.1	22	2
O'Brien	21	72	3.4	15	0

PASSING	Att	Comp	Pct Comp	Yds	Avg Gain	TD	Int	Rating Pts
O'Brien	411	226	55.0	2855	6.95	13	10	77.3
Eason	28	13	46.4	155	5.54	0	1	49.0

RECEIVING	No.	Yds	Avg	Lg	TD
Toon	57	757	13.3	t46	6
Moore	44	692	15.7	t69	6
Boyer	40	334	8.4	25	1
Thomas	20	204	10.2	55	1
Mathis	19	245	12.9	23	0

INTERCEPTIONS: McMillan, 5

PUNTING	No.	Yds	Avg	Net Avg	TB	In 20	Lg	Blk
Prokop	59	2363	40.1	34.7	3	18	58	0

SACKS: Byrd, 13.0

Pittsburgh Steelers

SCORING	Rush	Rec	TD Ret	PAT	FG	S	Pts
Anderson	0	0	0	32/32	20/25	0	92
Hoge	7	3	0	0/0	0/0	0	60
Green	0	7	0	0/0	0/0	0	42
W. Williams	3	1	0	0/0	0/0	0	24

RUSHING	No.	Yds	Avg	Lg	TD
Hoge	203	772	3.8	t41	7
Worley	109	418	3.8	38	0
W. Williams	68	389	5.7	t70	3
Foster	36	203	5.6	38	1
Brister	25	64	2.6	11	0

PASSING	Att	Comp	Pct Comp	Yds	Avg Gain	TD	Int	Rating Pts
Brister	387	223	57.6	2725	7.04	20	14	81.6
Strom	21	14	66.7	162	7.71	0	1	69.9

RECEIVING	No.	Yds	Avg	Lg	TD
Lipps	50	682	13.6	37	3
Hoge	40	342	8.6	27	3
Green	34	387	11.4	46	7
Mularkey	32	365	11.4	28	3
Hill	25	391	15.6	66	0

INTERCEPTIONS: Woodson, 5

PUNTING	No.	Yds	Avg	Net Avg	TB	In 20	Lg	Blk
Stryzinski	65	2454	37.8	34.1	5	18	51	1

SACKS: G. Williams, 6.0

San Diego Chargers

SCORING	Rush	Rec	TD Ret	PAT	FG	S	Pts
Carney	0	0	0	27/28	19/21	0	84
Butts	8	0	0	0/0	0/0	0	48
A. Miller	0	7	0	0/0	0/0	0	42
Bernstine	4	0	0	0/0	0/0	0	24

RUSHING	No.	Yds	Avg	Lg	TD
Butts	265	1225	4.6	52	8
Bernstine	124	589	4.8	t40	4
Harmon	66	363	5.5	41	0
Lewis	4	25	6.3	t10	1
Tolliver	14	22	1.6	14	0

PASSING	Att	Comp	Pct Comp	Yds	Avg Gain	TD	Int	Rating Pts
Tolliver	410	216	52.7	2574	6.28	16	16	68.9
Vlasic	40	19	47.5	168	4.20	1	2	46.7

RECEIVING	No.	Yds	Avg	Lg	TD
A. Miller	63	933	14.8	t31	7
Harmon	46	511	11.1	t36	2
McEwen	29	325	11.2	32	3
Walker	23	240	10.4	23	1
Butts	16	117	7.3	26	0

INTERCEPTIONS: Byrd, 7

PUNTING	No.	Yds	Avg	Net Avg	TB	In 20	Lg	Blk
Kidd	61	2442	40.0	36.6	2	14	59	1

SACKS: O'Neal, 13.5

Seattle Seahawks

SCORING	Rush	Rec	TD Ret	PAT	FG	S	Pts
Johnson	0	0	0	33/34	23/32	0	102
Fenner	14	1	0	0/0	0/0	0	90
Chadwick	0	4	0	0/0	0/0	0	24
Kane	0	4	0	0/0	0/0	0	24

RUSHING	No.	Yds	Avg	Lg	TD
Fenner	215	859	4.0	36	14
Williams	187	714	3.8	25	3
Krieg	32	115	3.6	25	0
Jones	5	20	4.0	5	0
Blades	3	19	6.3	12	0

PASSING	Att	Comp	Pct Comp	Yds	Avg Gain	TD	Int	Rating Pts
Krieg	448	265	59.2	3194	7.13	15	20	73.6

RECEIVING	No.	Yds	Avg	Lg	TD
Williams	73	699	9.6	60	0
Kane	52	776	14.9	t63	4
Blades	49	525	10.7	24	3
Chadwick	27	478	17.7	t54	4
Skansi	22	257	11.7	t25	2

INTERCEPTIONS: Robinson and Harper, 3

PUNTING	No.	Yds	Avg	Net Avg	TB	In 20	Lg	Blk
Donnelly	67	2722	40.6	34.4	8	18	54	0

SACKS: Green, 12.5

Atlanta Falcons

SCORING	Rush	TD Rec	Ret	PAT	FG	S	Pts
Davis	0	0	0	40/40	22/33	0	106
Rison	0	10	0	0/0	0/0	0	60
Broussard	4	0	0	0/0	0/0	0	24
Dixon	0	4	0	0/0	0/0	0	24
Johnson	3	1	0	0/0	0/0	0	24

RUSHING	No.	Yds	Avg	Lg	TD
Rozier, Hou-Atl	163	717	4.4	67	3
Broussard	126	454	3.6	t50	4
Jones	49	185	3.8	22	0
Johnson	30	106	3.5	12	3
Miller	26	99	3.8	18	1

PASSING	Att	Comp	Pct Comp	Yds	Avg Gain	TD	Int	Rating Pts
Miller	388	222	57.2	2735	7.05	17	14	78.7
Campbell	76	36	47.4	527	6.93	3	4	61.7

RECEIVING	No.	Yds	Avg	Lg	TD
Rison	82	1208	14.7	t75	10
Dixon	38	399	10.5	34	4
Collins	34	503	14.8	61	2
Haynes	31	445	14.4	60	0
Broussard	24	160	6.7	18	0

INTERCEPTIONS: Sanders, Case, Dimry, Jordan, and Butler, 3

PUNTING	No.	Yds	Avg	Net Avg	TB	In 20	Lg	Blk
Fulhage	70	2913	41.6	36.0	4	15	59	0

SACKS: Green, 6.0

Chicago Bears

SCORING	Rush	TD Rec	Ret	PAT	FG	S	Pts
Butler	0	0	0	36/37	26/37	0	114
Anderson	10	3	0	0/0	0/0	0	78
Muster	6	0	0	0/0	0/0	0	36
Harbaugh	4	0	0	0/0	0/0	0	24
Davis	0	3	0	0/0	0/0	0	18
Morris	0	3	0	0/0	0/0	0	18

RUSHING	No.	Yds	Avg	Lg	TD
Anderson	260	1078	4.1	52	10
Muster	141	664	4.7	28	6
Harbaugh	51	321	6.3	17	4
Green	27	126	4.7	14	0
Bailey	26	86	3.3	9	0

PASSING	Att	Comp	Pct Comp	Yds	Avg Gain	TD	Int	Rating Pts
Harbaugh	312	180	57.7	2178	6.98	10	6	81.9
Tomczak	104	39	37.5	521	5.01	3	5	43.8

RECEIVING	No.	Yds	Avg	Lg	TD
Muster	47	452	9.6	48	0
Anderson	42	484	11.5	t50	3
Davis	39	572	14.7	51	3
Morris	31	437	14.1	t67	3
Gentry	23	320	13.9	t80	2

INTERCEPTIONS: Carrier, 10

PUNTING	No.	Yds	Avg	Net Avg	TB	In 20	Lg	Blk
Buford	76	3073	40.4	33.5	7	22	59	2

SACKS: Dent, 12.0

Dallas Cowboys

SCORING	Rush	TD Rec	Ret	PAT	FG	S	Pts
Willis	0	0	0	18/25	26/26	0	80
E. Smith	11	0	0	0/0	0/0	0	66
Irvin	0	5	0	0/0	0/0	0	30
Novacek	0	4	0	0/0	0/0	0	24
Johnston	1	1	0	0/0	0/0	0	12

RUSHING	No.	Yds	Avg	Lg	TD
E. Smith	241	937	3.9	t48	11
Agee	53	213	4.0	28	0
Aikman	40	172	4.3	20	1
Highsmith	19	48	2.5	7	0
Dixon	11	43	3.9	18	0

PASSING	Att	Comp	Pct Comp	Yds	Avg Gain	TD	Int	Rating Pts
Aikman	399	226	56.6	2579	6.46	11	18	66.6

RECEIVING	No.	Yds	Avg	Lg	TD
Martin	64	732	11.4	45	0
Novacek	59	657	11.1	41	4
Agee	30	272	9.1	30	1
E. Smith	24	228	9.5	57	0
Irvin	20	413	20.7	t61	5

INTERCEPTIONS: Holt and Washington, 3

PUNTING	No.	Yds	Avg	Net Avg	TB	In 20	Lg	Blk
Saxon	79	3413	43.2	35.6	8	20	62	0

SACKS: Jones and Stubbs, 7.5

Detroit Lions

SCORING	Rush	TD Rec	Ret	PAT	FG	S	Pts
B. Sanders	13	3	0	0/0	0/0	0	96
Murray	0	0	0	34/34	13/19	0	73
Clark	0	8	0	0/0	0/0	0	48
Johnson	0	6	0	0/0	0/0	0	36
Peete	6	0	0	0/0	0/0	0	36

RUSHING	No.	Yds	Avg	Lg	TD
B. Sanders	255	1304	5.1	t45	13
Peete	48	365	7.6	37	6
Gagliano	46	145	3.2	22	0
Ware	7	64	9.1	30	0

PASSING	Att	Comp	Pct Comp	Yds	Avg Gain	TD	Int	Rating Pts
Peete	271	142	52.4	1974	7.28	13	8	79.8
Gagliano	159	87	54.7	1190	7.48	10	10	73.6

RECEIVING	No.	Yds	Avg	Lg	TD
Johnson	64	727	11.4	t44	6
Clark	53	932	17.6	57	4
B. Sanders	35	462	13.2	t47	3
Matthews	30	349	11.6	52	1
Greer	20	332	16.6	t68	3

INTERCEPTIONS: W. White, 5

PUNTING	No.	Yds	Avg	Net Avg	TB	In 20	Lg	Blk
Arnold	63	2560	40.6	35.3	5	10	59	0

SACKS: Cofer, 10.0

Green Bay Packers

SCORING	Rush	Rec	Ret	PAT	FG	S	Pts
Jacke	0	0	0	28/29	23/30	0	97
Sharpe	0	6	0	0/0	0/0	0	36
West	0	5	0	0/0	0/0	0	30
Query	0	2	1	0/0	0/0	0	18

RUSHING	No.	Yds	Avg	Lg	TD
Haddix	98	311	3.2	13	0
Thompson	76	264	3.5	37	1
Majkowski	29	186	6.4	24	1
Woodside	46	182	4.0	21	1
Fullwood	44	124	2.8	16	1

PASSING	Att	Comp	Pct Comp	Yds	Avg Gain	TD	Int	Rating Pts
Majkowski	264	150	56.8	1925	7.29	10	12	73.5
Dilweg	192	101	52.6	1267	6.60	8	7	72.1

RECEIVING	No.	Yds	Avg	Lg	TD
Sharpe	67	1105	16.5	t76	6
Kemp	44	527	12.0	29	2
Query	34	458	13.5	t47	2
Weathers	33	390	11.8	29	1
Fontenot	31	293	9.5	59	1

INTERCEPTIONS: Butler, Holmes, and Murphy, 3

PUNTING	No.	Yds	Avg	Net Avg	In TB	20	Lg	Blk
Bracken	64	2431	38.0	32.7	2	17	59	1

SACKS: T. Harris, 7.0

Minnesota Vikings

SCORING	Rush	Rec	Ret	PAT	FG	S	Pts
Reveiz, SD-Mn	0	0	0	26/27	13/19	0	65
Igwebuike	0	0	0	19/19	14/16	0	61
Walker	5	4	0	0/0	0/0	0	54
A. Carter	0	8	0	0/0	0/0	0	48
H. Jones	0	7	0	0/0	0/0	0	42

RUSHING	No.	Yds	Avg	Lg	TD
Walker	184	770	4.2	t58	5
Fenney	87	376	4.3	27	2
Gannon	52	268	5.2	27	1
Anderson	59	207	3.5	14	2

PASSING	Att	Comp	Pct Comp	Yds	Avg Gain	TD	Int	Rating Pts
Gannon	349	182	52.1	2278	6.53	16	16	65.9
Wilson	146	82	56.2	1155	7.91	9	8	79.6

RECEIVING	No.	Yds	Avg	Lg	TD
A. Carter	70	1008	14.4	t56	8
H. Jones	51	810	15.9	t75	7
Jordan	45	636	14.1	38	3
Walker	35	315	9.0	32	4
C. Carter	27	413	15.3	t78	3

INTERCEPTIONS: Browner, 7

PUNTING	No.	Yds	Avg	Net Avg	In TB	20	Lg	Blk
Newsome	78	3299	42.3	33.2	8	19	61	1

SACKS: Doleman, 11.0

Los Angeles Rams

SCORING	Rush	Rec	Ret	PAT	FG	S	Pts
Gary	14	1	0	0/0	0/0	0	90
Lansford	0	0	0	42/43	15/24	0	87
McGee	1	4	0	0/0	0/0	0	30
Ellard	0	4	0	0/0	0/0	0	24
Anderson	0	4	0	0/0	0/0	0	24
Delpino	0	4	0	0/0	0/0	0	24

RUSHING	No.	Yds	Avg	Lg	TD
Gary	204	808	4.0	48	14
Green	68	261	3.8	31	0
McGee	44	234	5.3	19	1
Warner	49	139	2.8	9	1
Dupree	19	72	3.8	13	0

PASSING	Att	Comp	Pct Comp	Yds	Avg Gain	TD	Int	Rating Pts
Everett	554	307	55.4	3989	7.20	23	17	79.3

RECEIVING	No.	Yds	Avg	Lg	TD
Ellard	76	1294	17.0	t50	4
Anderson	51	1097	21.5	t55	4
Holohan	49	475	9.7	28	2
McGee	47	388	8.3	25	4

INTERCEPTIONS: Humphery and Newsome, 4

PUNTING	No.	Yds	Avg	Net Avg	In TB	20	Lg	Blk
English	68	2663	39.2	31.9	2	8	58	0

SACKS: Greene, 13.0

New Orleans Saints

SCORING	Rush	Rec	Ret	PAT	FG	S	Pts
Andersen	0	0	0	29/29	21/27	0	92
Mayes	7	0	0	0/0	0/0	0	42
E. Martin	0	5	0	0/0	0/0	0	30
Heyward	4	0	0	0/0	0/0	0	24
Turner	0	4	0	0/0	0/0	0	24

RUSHING	No.	Yds	Avg	Lg	TD
Heyward	129	599	4.6	t47	4
Mayes	138	510	3.7	18	7
Fenerty	73	355	4.9	t60	2
Hilliard	90	284	3.2	17	0
Fourcade	15	77	5.1	12	1

PASSING	Att	Comp	Pct Comp	Yds	Avg Gain	TD	Int	Rating Pts
Walsh, Dall-NO	336	179	53.3	2010	5.98	12	13	67.2
Fourcade	116	50	43.1	785	6.77	3	8	46.1

RECEIVING	No.	Yds	Avg	Lg	TD
E. Martin	63	912	14.5	58	5
Perriman	36	382	10.6	29	2
Turner	21	396	18.9	t68	4
Fenerty	18	209	11.6	28	0

INTERCEPTIONS: Maxie, Cook, Atkins, and Thompson, 2

PUNTING	No.	Yds	Avg	Net Avg	In TB	20	Lg	Blk
Barnhardt	70	2990	42.7	36.2	6	20	65	1

SACKS: Swilling, 11.0

New York Giants

SCORING	TD Rush	Rec	Ret	PAT	FG	S	Pts
Bahr	0	0	0	29/30	17/23	0	80
Anderson	11	0	0	0/0	0/0	0	66
Bavaro	0	5	0	0/0	0/0	0	30
Ingram	0	5	0	0/0	0/0	0	30

RUSHING	No.	Yds	Avg	Lg	TD
Anderson	225	784	3.5	28	11
Hampton	109	455	4.2	41	2
Tillman	84	231	2.8	17	1
Hostetler	39	190	4.9	30	2
Meggett	22	164	7.5	51	0

PASSING	Att	Comp	Pct Comp	Yds	Avg Gain	TD	Int	Rating Pts
Simms	311	184	59.2	2284	7.34	15	4	92.7
Hostetler	87	47	54.0	614	7.06	3	1	83.2

RECEIVING	No.	Yds	Avg	Lg	TD
Meggett	39	410	10.5	38	1
Bavaro	33	393	11.9	61	5
Hampton	32	274	8.6	t27	2
Baker	26	541	20.8	t80	4
Ingram	26	499	19.2	t57	5

INTERCEPTIONS: Walls, 6

PUNTING	No.	Yds	Avg	Net Avg	TB	In 20	Lg	Blk
Landeta	75	3306	44.1	37.3	11	24	67	0

SACKS: Taylor, 10.5

Phoenix Cardinals

SCORING	TD Rush	Rec	Ret	PAT	FG	S	Pts
Del Greco	0	0	0	31/31	17/27	0	82
Johnson	5	0	0	0/0	0/0	0	30
Green	0	4	0	0/0	0/0	0	24
Jones	0	4	0	0/0	0/0	0	24
Proehl	0	4	0	0/0	0/0	0	24
Thompson	4	0	0	0/0	0/0	0	24

RUSHING	No.	Yds	Avg	Lg	TD
Johnson	234	926	4.0	41	5
Rosenbach	86	470	5.5	25	3
Thompson	106	390	3.7	40	4
Flagler	13	85	6.5	t29	1

PASSING	Att	Comp	Pct Comp	Yds	Avg Gain	TD	Int	Rating Pts
Rosenbach	437	237	54.2	3098	7.09	16	17	72.8

RECEIVING	No.	Yds	Avg	Lg	TD
Proehl	56	802	14.3	t45	4
Green	53	797	15.0	54	4
Jones	43	724	16.8	t68	4
Johnson	25	241	9.6	35	0
J. Smith	18	225	12.5	t45	2

INTERCEPTIONS: McDonald, 4

PUNTING	No.	Yds	Avg	Net Avg	TB	In 20	Lg	Blk
Camarillo	67	2865	42.8	37.4	5	16	63	0

SACKS: Harvey, 10.0

Philadelphia Eagles

SCORING	TD Rush	Rec	Ret	PAT	FG	S	Pts
Ruzek	0	0	0	45/48	21/29	0	108
Williams	0	9	0	0/0	0/0	0	54
Barnett	0	8	0	0/0	0/0	0	48
K. Jackson	0	6	0	0/0	0/0	0	36
Cunningham	5	0	0	0/0	0/0	0	30

RUSHING	No.	Yds	Avg	Lg	TD
Cunningham	118	942	8.0	t52	5
Sherman	164	685	4.2	36	1
Toney	132	452	3.4	20	1
Sanders	56	208	3.7	39	1

PASSING	Att	Comp	Pct Comp	Yds	Avg Gain	TD	Int	Rating Pts
Cunningham	465	271	58.3	3466	7.45	30	13	91.6
McMahon	9	6	66.7	63	7.00	0	0	86.8

RECEIVING	No.	Yds	Avg	Lg	TD
Byars	81	819	10.1	54	3
K. Jackson	50	670	13.4	t37	6
Williams	37	602	16.3	t45	9
Barnett	36	721	20.0	t95	8
Sherman	23	167	7.3	26	3

INTERCEPTIONS: Hopkins, 5

PUNTING	No.	Yds	Avg	Net Avg	TB	In 20	Lg	Blk
Feagles	72	3026	42.0	35.5	3	20	60	2

SACKS: White, 15.0

San Francisco 49ers

SCORING	TD Rush	Rec	Ret	PAT	FG	S	Pts
Cofer	0	0	0	39/39	24/36	0	111
Rice	0	13	0	0/0	0/0	0	78
Rathman	7	0	0	0/0	0/0	0	42
Taylor	0	7	0	0/0	0/0	0	42
Jones	0	5	0	0/0	0/0	0	30

RUSHING	No.	Yds	Avg	Lg	TD
D. Carter	114	460	4.0	t74	1
Craig	141	439	3.1	26	1
Rathman	101	318	3.1	22	7
Sydney	35	166	4.7	19	2
Montana	40	162	4.1	20	1

PASSING	Att	Comp	Pct Comp	Yds	Avg Gain	TD	Int	Rating Pts
Montana	520	321	61.7	3944	7.58	26	16	89.0
Young	62	38	61.3	427	6.89	2	0	92.6

RECEIVING	No.	Yds	Avg	Lg	TD
Rice	100	1502	15.0	t64	13
Jones	56	747	13.3	t67	5
Taylor	49	748	15.3	t78	7
Rathman	48	327	6.8	28	0

INTERCEPTIONS: Waymer, 7

PUNTING	No.	Yds	Avg	Net Avg	TB	In 20	Lg	Blk
Helton	69	2537	36.8	30.9	8	15	56	1

SACKS: Haley, 16.0

Tampa Bay Buccaneers

SCORING	TD Rush	Rec	Ret	PAT	FG	S	Pts
Christie	0	0	0	27/27	23/27	0	96
G. Anderson	3	2	0	0/0	0/0	0	30
Hill	0	5	0	0/0	0/0	0	30
Carrier	0	4	0	0/0	0/0	0	24

RUSHING	No.	Yds	Avg	Lg	TD
G. Anderson	166	646	3.9	22	3
Cobb	151	480	3.2	17	2
Testaverde	38	280	7.4	t48	1
Harvey	27	113	4.2	14	0

PASSING	Att	Comp	Pct Comp	Yds	Avg Gain	TD	Int	Rating Pts
Testaverde	365	203	55.6	2818	7.72	17	18	75.6
Chandler	83	42	50.6	464	5.59	1	6	41.4

RECEIVING	No.	Yds	Avg	Lg	TD
Carrier	49	813	16.6	t68	4
Hill	42	641	15.3	t48	5
Cobb	39	299	7.7	17	0
G. Anderson	38	464	12.2	74	2
Hall	31	464	15.0	t54	2

INTERCEPTIONS: Haddix, 7

PUNTING	No.	Yds	Avg	Net Avg	TB	In 20	Lg	Blk
Royals	72	2902	40.3	34.0	5	8	62	0

SACKS: Thomas, 7.5

Washington Redskins

SCORING	TD Rush	Rec	Ret	PAT	FG	S	Pts
Lohmiller	0	0	0	41/41	30/40	0	131
Clark	0	8	0	0/0	0/0	0	48
Byner	6	1	0	0/0	0/0	0	42
Riggs	6	0	0	0/0	0/0	0	36

RUSHING	No.	Yds	Avg	Lg	TD
Byner	297	1219	4.1	22	6
Riggs	123	475	3.9	20	6
Humphries	23	106	4.6	17	2
Dupard	19	85	4.5	11	0

PASSING	Att	Comp	Pct Comp	Yds	Avg Gain	TD	Int	Rating Pts
Rypien	304	166	54.6	2070	6.81	16	11	78.4
Humphries	156	91	58.3	1015	6.51	3	10	57.5

RECEIVING	No.	Yds	Avg	Lg	TD
Clark	75	1112	14.8	t53	8
Monk	68	770	11.3	44	5
Sanders	56	727	13.0	38	3
Byner	31	279	9.0	19	1
Bryant	26	248	9.5	37	1

INTERCEPTIONS: Mayhew, 7

PUNTING	No.	Yds	Avg	Net Avg	TB	In 20	Lg	Blk
Mojsiejenko	43	1687	39.2	34.2	0	17	53	1

SACKS: Stokes, 7.5

Coach of Coaches

In 1984, as a rookie beat man covering the Cincinnati Bengals at their Wilmington, Ohio, training camp, I grew weary of standing on the sidelines for practice every day, hour after tedious hour. One hot morning, I was standing next to the man in the straw hat who ran the team, and I blurted out, "Boy, football practice can sure be boring. How can you take watching this, day after day?"

Rookie mistake. Paul Brown's sharp and wounded look told me that. "Boring?" he shot back. "This is ... this is our lifeblood. This is how we build our business." Shaking his head, he left my side, presumably to watch the rest of the practice with someone who appreciated the sport.

Brown may have appreciated the game more than any other man who ever lived. When he died on August 5 at the age of 82 from complications of pneumonia, football lost a great friend.

He started building champions at Massillon (Ohio) High in 1932, and from there, he went on to coach at Ohio State. In 1946 he formed the professional team in Cleveland that bears his name, and he coached the Browns to seven championships, four in the All-America Conference and three in the NFL. He lost control of the Browns to Art Modell in 1961, but in 1968 he started all over again, creating the Cincinnati Bengals, which he coached until 1975.

Brown brought myriad innovations to football. He invented the playbook, for instance. He was the first coach to signal plays from the sidelines, and in the mid-'50s he went so far as to put a radio transmitter in the helmet of Browns quarterback George Ratterman. He pioneered college scouting, training camps and game films.

Among his Browns were offensive guard Chuck Noll and defensive back Don Shula, and among his Bengals was the current Cincinnati coach, Sam Wyche. Weeb Ewbank, Bud Grant and Bill Walsh all coached under Brown. Students of Brown, in fact, have won 11 of the 25 Super Bowls.

In recent years, Brown was often the NFL's lone voice of dissent against the forces of expansion, television and commercialism. He despised instant replay, for one, but his arguments ("It just adds another layer of error," he said) fell on deaf ears.

The Bengals listened to him, though. Until his recent illness, he was spending six or seven hours a day with the team, offering suggestions and going over the films with Wyche and the coaches. Wyche never bristled at Brown's input. "Working under Paul Brown is like living next to a library," Wyche once said. "I'd be a fool if I didn't check books out."

The players were generally fond of Brown too, and they thought of him as a member of the team. Before an exhibition game in Detroit three days before Brown's death, quarterback Boomer Esiason wrote PB between the stripes of his helmet, hoping Brown, at home, would see the tribute. "I do it for anybody who's hurt and can't be in the huddle with me," Esiason said.

The huddle. Brown probably invented that, too.

—PETER KING

1991 NFL Draft

First- and Second-round picks of the 56th annual NFL Draft held April 21–22 in New York City.

First Round

Team	Selection	Position
1. ...... Dallas*	Russell Maryland, Miami	DT
2. ...... Cleveland	Eric Turner, UCLA	S
3. ...... Atlanta	Bruce Pickens, Nebraska	CB
4. ...... Denver	Mike Croel, Nebraska	LB
5. ...... LA Rams	Todd Lyght, Notre Dame	CB
6. ...... Phoenix	Eric Swann, Bay State Titans	DE
7. ...... Tampa Bay	Charles McRae, Tennessee	OT
8. ...... Philadelphia†	Antone Davis, Tennessee	OT
9. ...... San Diego	Stanley Richard, Texas	CB
10. .... Detroit	Herman Moore, Virginia	WR
11. .... New England‡	Pat Harlow, USC	OT
12. .... Dallas	Alvin Harper, Tennessee	WR
13. .... Atlanta#	Mike Pritchard, Colorado	WR
14. .... New England**	Leonard Russell, Arizona State	RB
15. .... Pittsburgh	Huey Richardson, Florida	LB
16. .... Seattle	Dan McGwire, San Diego State	QB
17. .... Washington††	Bobby Wilson, Michigan State	DT
18. .... Cincinnati	Alfred Williams, Colorado	LB
19. .... Green Bay‡‡	Vincent Clark, Ohio State	CB
20. .... Dallas##	Kelvin Pritchett, Mississippi***	DT
21. .... Kansas City	Harvey Williams, Louisiana State	RB
22. .... Chicago	Stan Thomas, Texas	OT
23. .... Miami	Randal Hill, Miami	WR
24. .... LA Raiders	Todd Marinovich, USC	QB
25. .... San Francisco	Ted Washington, Louisville	DT
26. .... Buffalo	Henry Jones, Illinois	S
27. .... NY Giants	Jarrod Bunch, Michigan	RB

Note: NY Jets (8th) forfeited their 1991 1st-round selection by picking Syracuse wide receiver Rob Moore in the 1990 supplemental draft.

*From New England. †From Green Bay. ‡From Minnesota through Dallas. #From Indianapolis. **From New Orleans through Dallas. ††From Houston through New England and Dallas. ‡‡From Philadelphia. ##From Washington.

***Dallas traded the rights to Pritchett to Detroit for Lions' own 2nd- and 3rd-round 1990 picks plus the 1990 4th-round choice Detroit had received from Miami.

Second Round

Team	Selection	Position
28. .... Houston*	Mike Dumas, Indiana	DB
29. .... Cleveland	Ed King, Auburn	OG
30. .... Denver	Reggie Johnson, Florida State	TE
31. .... LA Rams	Roman Phifer, UCLA	LB
32. .... Phoenix	Mike Jones, N Carolina State	DE
33. .... Atlanta	Brett Favre, Southern Miss	QB
34. .... NY Jets	Browning Nagle, Louisville	QB
35. .... Green Bay	Esera Tuaolo, Oregon State	DT
36. .... San Diego	George Thornton, Alabama	DT
37. .... Dallas†	Dixon Edwards, Michigan State	LB
38. .... Houston‡	Darryl Lewis, Arizona	DB
39. .... San Diego#	Eric Bieniemy, Colorado	RB
40. .... Indianapolis	Shane Curry, Miami	DE
41. .... New England**	Jerome Henderson, Clemson	DB
42. .... New Orleans	Wesley Carroll, Miami	WR
43. .... LA Raiders††	Nick Bell, Iowa	RB
44. .... Houston	John Flannery, Syracuse	C
45. .... San Francisco‡‡	Ricky Watters, Notre Dame	RB
46. .... Pittsburgh	Jeff Graham, Ohio State	WR
47. .... San Diego##	Eric Moten, Michigan State	OG
48. .... Philadelphia	Jesse Campbell, N Carolina St	DB
49. .... Chicago	Chris Zorich, Notre Dame	DT
50. .... Kansas City	Joe Valerio, Pennsylvania	OT
51. .... Seattle***	Doug Thomas, Clemson	WR
52. .... Cincinnati†††	Lamar Rogers, Auburn	DT
53. .... San Francisco	John Johnson, Clemson	LB
54. .... Buffalo	Phil Hansen, N Dakota State	DE
55. .... NY Giants	Kanavis McGhee, Colorado	LB

*From New England. †From Detroit. ‡From Minnesota through Dallas. #From Tampa Bay. **From Dallas. ††From Seattle. ‡‡From Cincinnati. ##From Washington. ***From LA Raiders. †††From Miami through San Francisco.

1991 World League of American Football

Final Standings

EUROPEAN DIVISION

	W	L	T	Pct	Pts/Tm	Pts/Opp
London	9	1	0	.900	310	121
Barcelona	8	2	0	.800	206	126
Frankfurt	7	3	0	.700	155	139

NORTH AMERICAN/EAST DIVISION

	W	L	T	Pct	Pts/Tm	Pts/Opp
NY/NJ	5	5	0	.500	257	155
Orlando	5	5	0	.500	242	286
Montreal	4	6	0	.400	145	244
Raleigh-Durham	0	10	0	.000	123	300

NORTH AMERICAN/WEST DIVISION

	W	L	T	Pct	Pts/Tm	Pts/Opp
Birmingham	5	5	0	.500	140	140
San Antonio	4	6	0	.400	176	196
Sacramento	3	7	0	.300	179	226

Playoff Results

SEMIFINALS

London 42, NY/NJ 26
Barcelona 10, Birmingham 3

1991 World Bowl

June 9, 1991 at Wembley Stadium, London

Barcelona	0	0	0	0 — 0
London	7	14	0	0 —21

FIRST QUARTER

London: Horton 59 pass from Gelbaugh
(P. Alexander kick), 15:00.

SECOND QUARTER

London: Crossman 20 interception return
(P. Alexander kick), 2:42.
London: Garrett 14 pass from Gelbaugh
(P. Alexander kick), 14:17.

A: 61,108.

THEY SAID IT

Dave McGinnis, Chicago Bears linebacker coach, on how to stop the Detroit Lions offense: "The key to Detroit's run-'n-shoot is when Barry Sanders runs, you shoot him."

WLAF Individual Leaders

PASSING

	Att	Comp	Pct Comp	Yds	Avg Gain	TD	Pct TD	Int	Pct Int	Lg	Rating Pts
Gelbaugh, London	303	189	62.4	2655	8.76	17	5.6	12	4.0	t96	92.8
Erney, Barcelona	158	79	50.0	1186	7.51	8	5.1	2	1.3	t81	86.6
Graham, NY/NJ	272	157	57.7	2407	8.85	8	2.9	8	2.9	t64	84.6
Bell, Orlando	325	181	55.7	2214	6.81	17	5.2	14	4.3	t75	76.4
Elkins, Sacramento	312	153	49.0	2068	6.63	13	4.2	13	4.2	t60	67.1

RECEIVING

RECEPTIONS	No.	Yds	Avg	Lg	TD
Garrett, London (RB)	71	620	8.7	47	1
B. Williams, Orlando	59	811	13.7	t42	11
Parker, Sacramento	52	801	15.4	41	8
Horton, London	43	931	21.7	t96	8
Turner, NY/NJ	41	629	15.3	52	1

YARDS	Yds	No.	Avg	Lg	TD
Horton, London	931	43	21.7	t96	8
B. Williams, Orlando	811	59	13.7	t42	11
Parker, Sacramento	801	52	15.4	41	8
Taylor, Barcelona	745	35	21.3	t81	6
Gilbreath, NY/NJ	643	40	16.1	46	1

RUSHING

	Att	Yds	Avg	Lg	TD
Wilkerson, NY/NJ	117	717	6.1	74	7
Baker, Frankfurt	199	648	3.3	26	5
Blake, San Antonio	120	554	4.6	26	5
Harris, Mont-Birm	135	540	4.0	t41	3
Johnson, Montreal	110	423	3.8	t20	1

Other Statistical Leaders

Points (TDs)	Williams, Orlando	66
	Wilkerson, NY/NJ	66
Points (Kicking)	Alexander, London	60
Yards from Scrimmage	Baker, Frankfurt	1071
Interceptions	Parker, NY/NJ	11
Sacks	Lockett, London	13.5
Punting Avg.	Mohr, Montreal	34.0
Punt Return Avg.	Tucker, Orlando	20.7
Kickoff Return Avg.	Painter, Orlando	24.9

1990 Canadian Football League

EASTERN DIVISION

	W	L	T	Pts	Pct	PF	PA	vs Div
Winnipeg	12	6	0	24	.667	472	398	7-3
Toronto	10	8	0	20	.556	689	538	6-4
Ottawa	7	11	0	14	.389	540	602	3-7
Hamilton	6	12	0	12	.333	476	628	4-6

WESTERN DIVISION

	W	L	T	Pts	Pct	PF	PA	vs Div
Calgary	11	6	1	23	.639	588	566	5-4-1
Edmonton	10	8	0	20	.556	612	510	6-4
Saskatchewan	9	9	0	18	.500	557	592	4-6
B.C.	6	11	1	13	.361	520	620	4-5-1

Regular Season Statistical Leaders

Points (TDs)	Smith, Toronto	120
Points (Kicking)	Ridgway, Saskatchewan	233
Yards (Rushing)	Mimbs, Winnipeg	1341
Yards (Passing)	Austin, Saskatchewan	4604
Yards (Receiving)	Smith, Toronto	1826
Yards from Scrimmage	Mimbs, Winnipeg	1879
Passer Rating	Ham, Edmonton	79.9
Receptions	Ellis, Edmonton	106
Sacks	Hill, Edmonton	17

1990 Playoff Results

DIVISION SEMIFINALS

Eastern: TORONTO 34, Ottawa 25
Western: EDMONTON 43, Saskatchewan 27

FINALS

Eastern: WINNIPEG 20, Toronto 17
Western: EDMONTON 43, Calgary 23

1990 Grey Cup Championship

Nov. 25, 1990, at BC Place Stadium, Vancouver

Edmonton Eskimos	0	4	0	7 —11
Winnipeg Blue Bombers	10	0	28	12 —50

A: 46,968.

THEY SAID IT

Ralph Campbell, one of the Hogettes, the unofficial male Redskin cheerleaders who dress up as women, on his group's wardrobe: "Our designer is Calvin Swine."

Making a List

The Pro Football Hall of Fame inducted four players—running back Earl Campbell, guard John Hannah, defensive lineman Stan Jones and kicker Jan Stenerud—and one club executive, former Dallas Cowboy president Tex Schramm, in ceremonies in July in Canton, Ohio. Here is a list of 10 others who SI's Dr. Z, Paul Zimmerman, believes should also be in the Hall:

- **Al Davis,** 1963–present, Oakland and Los Angeles Raiders. Coach, scout, commissioner, owner ... he's done it all. Bad marks in conduct have kept him out, but it's a joke that he hasn't made it.
- **Cliff Harris,** Defensive back, 1970–79, Dallas Cowboys. Among free safeties there are killer types and rover types, and Harris was the best killer type I ever saw.
- **Richie Jackson,** Defensive end, 1966–72, Oakland Raiders, Denver Broncos and Cleveland Browns. My two favorite defensive ends are Deacon Jones and "Tombstone" Jackson. Unfortunately, the latter's career was cut short by a knee injury.
- **Jimmy Johnson,** Defensive back, 1961–76, San Francisco 49ers. The two greatest corners ever are Johnson and Night Train Lane (inducted in 1974). Case closed.
- **Alex Karras,** Defensive tackle, 1958–70, Detroit Lions. He's so identifiable as an actor that people forget how great a player he was, and for how long.

- **John Mackey,** Tight end, 1963–72, Baltimore Colts and San Diego Chargers. Politics (he fought the NFL's antitrust exemption) was his undoing. His numbers aren't that impressive, but he provided great leadership.
- **Dick Plasman,** End, 1937–47, Chicago Bears and Chicago Cardinals. Films of the '30s and '40s reveal him to have been an offensive and defensive terror. Plasman, by the way, was the last man to play without a helmet.
- **Mel Renfro,** Defensive back, 1964–77, Dallas Cowboys. What, another Dallas safety? You bet, and you could make a case for Charlie Waters, too.
- **John Riggins,** Fullback, 1971–85, New York Jets and Washington Redskins. The "Big Diesel" was putting thousand-yard seasons together well into his '30s.
- **Mac Speedie,** End, 1946–52, Cleveland Browns. "McSpeedie" should have made the Hall ahead of his fellow receiver, Dante Lavelli, who was inducted in 1975.

FOR THE RECORD • Year by Year

The Super Bowl

Results

Date	Winner (Share)	Loser (Share)	Score	Site (Attendance)
I 1-15-67	Green Bay ($15,000)	Kansas City ($7,500)	35-10	Los Angeles (61,946)
II 1-14-68	Green Bay ($15,000)	Oakland ($7,500)	33-14	Miami (75,546)
III 1-12-69	NY Jets ($15,000)	Baltimore ($7,500)	16-7	Miami (75,389)
IV 1-11-70	Kansas City ($15,000)	Minnesota ($7,500)	23-7	New Orleans (80,562)
V 1-17-71	Baltimore ($15,000)	Dallas ($7,500)	16-13	Miami (79,204)
VI 1-16-72	Dallas ($15,000)	Miami ($7,500)	24-3	New Orleans (81,023)
VII 1-14-73	Miami ($15,000)	Washington ($7,500)	14-7	Los Angeles (90,182)
VIII 1-13-74	Miami ($15,000)	Minnesota ($7,500)	24-7	Houston (71,882)
IX 1-12-75	Pittsburgh ($15,000)	Minnesota ($7,500)	16-6	New Orleans (80,997)
X 1-18-76	Pittsburgh ($15,000)	Dallas ($7,500)	21-17	Miami (80,187)
XI 1-9-77	Oakland ($15,000)	Minnesota ($7,500)	32-14	Pasadena (103,438)
XII 1-15-78	Dallas ($18,000)	Denver ($9,000)	27-10	New Orleans (75,583)
XIII 1-21-79	Pittsburgh ($18,000)	Dallas ($9,000)	35-31	Miami (79,484)
XIV 1-20-80	Pittsburgh ($18,000)	Los Angeles ($9,000)	31-19	Pasadena (103,985)
XV 1-25-81	Oakland ($18,000)	Philadelphia ($9,000)	27-10	New Orleans (76,135)
XVI 1-24-82	San Francisco ($18,000)	Cincinnati ($9,000)	26-21	Pontiac (81,270)
XVII 1-30-83	Washington ($36,000)	Miami ($18,000)	27-17	Pasadena (103,667)
XVIII 1-22-84	LA Raiders ($36,000)	Washington ($18,000)	38-9	Tampa (72,920)
XIX 1-20-85	San Francisco ($36,000)	Miami ($18,000)	38-16	Stanford (84,059)
XX 1-26-86	Chicago ($36,000)	New England ($18,000)	46-10	New Orleans (73,818)
XXI 1-25-87	NY Giants ($36,000)	Denver ($18,000)	39-20	Pasadena (101,063)
XXII 1-31-88	Washington ($36,000)	Denver ($18,000)	42-10	San Diego (73,302)
XXIII 1-22-89	San Francisco ($36,000)	Cincinnati ($18,000)	20-16	Miami (75,129)
XXIV 1-28-90	San Francisco ($36,000)	Denver ($18,000)	55-10	New Orleans (72,919)
XXV 1-27-91	NY Giants ($36,000)	Buffalo ($18,000)	20-19	Tampa (73,813)

Most Valuable Players

	Position
I .... Bart Starr, GB	QB
II .... Bart Starr, GB	QB
III .... Joe Namath, NY Jets	QB
IV .... Len Dawson, KC	QB
V .... Chuck Howley, Dall	LB
VI .... Roger Staubach, Dall	QB
VII .... Jake Scott, Mia	S
VIII .... Larry Csonka, Mia	RB
IX .... Franco Harris, Pitt	RB
X .... Lynn Swann, Pitt	WR
XI .... Fred Biletnikoff, Oak	WR
XII .... Randy White, Dall	DT
	Harvey Martin, Dall	DE
XIII .... Terry Bradshaw, Pitt	QB
XIV .... Terry Bradshaw, Pitt	QB
XV .... Jim Plunkett, Oak	QB
XVI .... Joe Montana, SF	QB
XVII .... John Riggins, Wash	RB
XVIII .... Marcus Allen, LA Raiders	RB
XIX .... Joe Montana, SF	QB
XX .... Richard Dent, Chi	DE
XXI .... Phil Simms, NY Giants	QB
XXII .... Doug Williams, Wash	QB
XXIII .... Jerry Rice, SF	WR
XXIV .... Joe Montana, SF	QB
XXV .... Ottis Anderson, NY Giants	RB

Composite Standings

	W	L	Pct	Pts	Opp Pts
Pittsburgh Steelers 4		0	1.000	103	73
San Francisco 49ers 4		0	1.000	139	63
Green Bay Packers 2		0	1.000	68	24
NY Giants 2		0	1.000	59	39
Chicago Bears................1		0	1.000	46	10
NY Jets..........................1		0	1.000	16	7
Oakland/LA Raiders 3		1	.750	111	66
Washington Redskins....2		2	.500	85	79
Baltimore Colts 1		1	.500	23	29
Kansas City Chiefs........1		1	.500	33	42
Dallas Cowboys.............2		3	.400	112	85
Miami Dolphins..............2		3	.400	74	103
Buffalo Bills....................0		1	.000	19	20
LA Rams........................0		1	.000	19	31
New England Patriots......0		1	.000	10	46
Philadelphia Eagles........0		1	.000	10	27
Cincinnati Bengals.........0		2	.000	37	46
Denver Broncos.............0		4	.000	50	163
Minnesota Vikings 0		4	.000	34	95

THEY SAID IT

Eugene Lockhart, a linebacker traded in the offseason by the Dallas Cowboys to the New England Patriots, while cleaning out his locker: "It's a cold business—a cold, cold business. And it's even colder in New England."

Career Leaders
Passing

	GP	Att	Comp	Pct Comp	Yds	Avg Gain	TD	Pct TD	Int	Pct Int	Lg	Rating Pts
Joe Montana, SF	4	122	83	68.0	1142	9.36	11	9.0	0	0.0	44	127.8
Jim Plunkett, Raiders	2	46	29	63.0	433	9.41	4	8.7	0	0.0	t80	122.8
Terry Bradshaw, Pitt	4	84	49	58.3	932	11.10	9	10.7	4	4.8	t75	112.8
Bart Starr, GB	2	47	29	61.7	452	9.62	3	6.4	1	2.1	t62	106.0
Roger Staubach, Dall	4	98	61	62.2	734	7.49	8	8.2	4	4.1	t45	95.4
Len Dawson, KC	2	44	28	63.6	353	8.02	2	4.5	2	4.5	t46	84.8
Bob Griese, Mia	3	41	26	63.4	295	7.20	1	2.4	2	4.9	t28	72.7
Dan Marino, Mia	1	50	29	58.0	318	6.36	1	2.0	2	4.0	30	66.9
Joe Theismann, Wash	2	58	31	53.4	386	6.66	2	3.4	4	6.9	60	57.1
John Elway, Den	3	101	46	45.5	669	6.62	2	1.9	6	5.9	t56	49.5
Fran Tarkenton, Minn	3	89	46	51.7	489	5.49	1	1.1	6	6.7	30	43.7

Note: Minimum 40 attempts.

Rushing

	GP	Yds	Att	Avg	Lg	TD
Franco Harris, Pitt	4	354	101	3.5	25	4
Larry Csonka, Mia	3	297	57	5.2	49	2
John Riggins, Wash	2	230	64	3.6	t43	2
Timmy Smith, Wash	1	204	22	9.3	t58	2
Roger Craig, SF	3	198	52	3.8	18	2
Marcus Allen, LA Raiders	1	191	20	9.6	t74	2
Tony Dorsett, Dall	2	162	31	5.2	29	1
Mark van Eeghen, Oak	2	148	36	4.1	11	0
Rocky Bleier, Pitt	4	144	44	3.3	18	0
Walt Garrison, Dall	2	139	26	5.3	19	0

Receiving

	GP	No.	Yds	Avg	Lg	TD
Roger Craig, SF	3	20	212	10.6	40	2
Jerry Rice, SF	2	18	363	20.2	44	4
Lynn Swann, Pitt	4	16	364	22.8	t64	3
Chuck Foreman, Minn	3	15	139	9.3	26	0
Cliff Branch, Raiders	3	14	181	12.9	50	3
Preston Pearson, Balt-Pitt-Dall	5	12	105	8.8	14	0
John Stallworth, Pitt	4	11	268	24.4	t75	3
Dan Ross, Cin	1	11	104	9.5	16	2
Otis Taylor, KC	2	10	138	13.8	t46	1
Dwight Clark, SF	2	10	122	12.2	33	0

Single-Game Leaders
Scoring

POINTS

	Pts
Roger Craig: XIX, San Francisco vs Miami (1 R, 2 P)	18
Jerry Rice: XXIV, San Francisco vs Denver (3 P)	18
Don Chandler: II, Green Bay vs Oakland (3 PAT, 4 FG)	15

TOUCHDOWNS

	No.
Joe Montana: XXIV, San Francisco vs Denver	5
Terry Bradshaw: XIII, Pittsburgh vs Dallas	4
Doug Williams: XXII, Washington vs Denver	4
Roger Staubach: XIII, Dallas vs Pittsburgh	3
Jim Plunkett: XV, Oakland vs Philadelphia	3
Joe Montana: XIX, San Francisco vs Miami	3
Phil Simms: XXI, NY Giants vs Denver	3

Rushing Yards

	Yds
Timmy Smith: XXII, Washington vs Denver	204
Marcus Allen: XVIII, LA Raiders vs Washington	191
John Riggins: XVII, Washington vs Miami	166
Franco Harris: IX, Pittsburgh vs Minnesota	158
Larry Csonka: VIII, Miami vs Minnesota	145
Clarence Davis: XI, Oakland vs Minnesota	137
Thurman Thomas: XXV, Buffalo vs NY Giants	135
Matt Snell: III, NY Jets vs Baltimore	121

Receiving Yards

	Yds
Jerry Rice: XXIII, San Francisco vs Cincinnati	215
Ricky Sanders: XXII, Washington vs Denver	193
Lynn Swann: X, Pittsburgh vs Dallas	161
Jerry Rice: XXIV, San Francisco vs Denver	148
Max McGee: I, Green Bay vs Kansas City	138
George Sauer: III, NY Jets vs Baltimore	133
Willie Gault: XX, Chicago vs New England	129

Receptions

	No.
Dan Ross: XVI, Cincinnati vs San Francisco	11
Jerry Rice: XXIII, San Francisco vs Cincinnati	11
Tony Nathan: XIX, Miami vs San Francisco	10
Ricky Sanders: XXII, Washington vs Denver	9
George Sauer: III, NY Jets vs Baltimore	8
Roger Craig: XXIII, San Francisco vs Cincinnati	8
Andre Reed: XXV, Buffalo vs NY Giants	8

Passing Yards

	Yds
Joe Montana: XXIII, San Francisco vs Cincinnati	357
Doug Williams: XXII, Washington vs Denver	340
Joe Montana: XIX, San Francisco vs Miami	331
Terry Bradshaw: XIII, Pittsburgh vs Dallas	318
Dan Marino: XIX, Miami vs San Francisco	318
Terry Bradshaw: XIV, Pittsburgh vs LA Rams	309
John Elway: XXI, Denver vs NY Giants	304
Ken Anderson: XVI, Cincinnati vs San Francisco	300

1933
NFL championship — Chicago Bears 23, NY Giants 21

1934
NFL championship — NY Giants 30, Chicago Bears 13

1935
NFL championship — Detroit 26, NY Giants 7

1936
NFL championship — Green Bay 21, Boston 6

1937
NFL championship — Washington 28, Chicago Bears 21

1938
NFL championship — NY Giants 23, Green Bay 17

1939
NFL championship — Green Bay 27, NY Giants 0

1940
NFL championship — Chicago Bears 73, Washington 0

1941
W. div playoff — Chicago Bears 33, Green Bay 14
NFL championship — Chicago Bears 37, NY Giants 9

1942
NFL championship — Washington 14, Chicago Bears 6

1943
E. div playoff — Washington 28, NY Giants 0
NFL championship — Chicago Bears 41, Washington 21

1944
NFL championship — Green Bay 14, NY Giants 7

1945
NFL championship — Cleveland 15, Washington 14

1946
NFL championship — Chicago Bears 24, NY Giants 14

1947
E. div playoff — Philadelphia 21, Pittsburgh 0
NFL championship — Chicago Cardinals 28, Philadelphia 21

1948
NFL championship — Philadelphia 7, Chicago Cardinals 0

1949
NFL championship — Philadelphia 14, Los Angeles 0

1950
Am. Conf. playoff — Cleveland 8, NY Giants 3
Nat. Conf. playoff — Los Angeles 24, Chicago Bears 14
NFL championship — Cleveland 30, Los Angeles 28

1951
NFL championship — Los Angeles 24, Cleveland 17

1952
Nat. Conf. playoff — Detroit 31, Los Angeles 21
NFL championship — Detroit 17, Cleveland 7

1953
NFL championship — Detroit 17, Cleveland 16

1954
NFL championship — Cleveland 56, Detroit 10

1955
NFL championship — Cleveland 38, Los Angeles 14

1956
NFL championship — NY Giants 47, Chicago Bears 7

1957
W. Conf playoff — Detroit 31, San Francisco 27
NFL championship — Detroit 59, Cleveland 14

1958
E. Conf playoff — NY Giants 10, Cleveland 0
NFL championship — Baltimore 23, NY Giants 17

1959
NFL championship — Baltimore 31, NY Giants 16

1960
NFL championship — Philadelphia 17, Green Bay 13
AFL championship — Houston 24, LA Chargers 16

1961
NFL championship — Green Bay 37, NY Giants 0
AFL championship — Houston 10, San Diego 3

1962
NFL championship — Green Bay 16, NY Giants 7
AFL championship — Dallas Texans 20, Houston 17

1963
NFL championship — Chicago 14, NY Giants 0
AFL E. div playoff — Boston 26, Buffalo 8
AFL championship — San Diego 51, Boston 10

1964
NFL championship — Cleveland 27, Baltimore 0
AFL championship — Buffalo 20, San Diego 7

1965
NFL W. Conf playoff — Green Bay 13, Baltimore 10
NFL championship — Green Bay 23, Cleveland 12
AFL championship — Buffalo 23, San Diego 0

1966
NFL championship — Green Bay 34, Dallas 27
AFL championship — Kansas City 31, Buffalo 7

1967
NFL E. Conf championship — Dallas 52, Cleveland 14
NFL W. Conf championship — Green Bay 28, Los Angeles 7
NFL championship — Green Bay 21, Dallas 17
AFL championship — Oakland 40, Houston 7

1968

NFL E. Conf championship	Cleveland 31, Dallas 20
NFL W. Conf championship	Baltimore 24, Minnesota 14
NFL championship	Baltimore 34, Cleveland 0
AFL W. div playoff	Oakland 41, Kansas City 6
AFL championship	NY Jets 27, Oakland 23

1969

NFL E. Conf championship	Cleveland 38, Dallas 14
NFL W. Conf championship	Minnesota 23, Los Angeles 20
NFL championship	Minnesota 27, Cleveland 7
AFL div playoffs	Kansas City 13, NY Jets 6
	Oakland 56, Houston 7
AFL championship	Kansas City 17, Oakland 7

1970

AFC div playoffs	Baltimore 17, Cincinnati 0
	Oakland 21, Miami 14
AFC championship	Baltimore 27, Oakland 17
NFC div playoffs	Dallas 5, Detroit 0
	San Francisco 17, Minnesota 14
NFC championship	Dallas 17, San Francisco 10

1971

AFC div playoffs	Miami 27, Kansas City 24
	Baltimore 20, Cleveland 3
AFC championship	Miami 21, Baltimore 0
NFC div playoffs	Dallas 20, Minnesota 12
	San Francisco 24, Washington 20
NFC championship	Dallas 14, San Francisco 3

1972

AFC div playoffs	Pittsburgh 13, Oakland 7
	Miami 20, Cleveland 14
AFC championship	Miami 21, Pittsburgh 17
NFC div playoffs	Dallas 30, San Francisco 28
	Washington 16, Green Bay 3
NFC championship	Washington 26, Dallas 3

1973

AFC div playoffs	Oakland 33, Pittsburgh 14
	Miami 34, Cincinnati 16
AFC championship	Miami 27, Oakland 10
NFC div playoffs	Minnesota 27, Washington 20
	Dallas 27, Los Angeles 16
NFC championship	Minnesota 27, Dallas 10

1974

AFC div playoffs	Oakland 28, Miami 26
	Pittsburgh 32, Buffalo 14
AFC championship	Pittsburgh 24, Oakland 13
NFC div playoffs	Minnesota 30, St Louis 14
	Los Angeles 19, Washington 10
NFC championship	Minnesota 14, Los Angeles 10

1975

AFC div playoffs	Pittsburgh 28, Baltimore 10
	Oakland 31, Cincinnati 28
AFC championship	Pittsburgh 16, Oakland 10
NFC div playoffs	Los Angeles 35, St Louis 23
	Dallas 17, Minnesota 14
NFC championship	Dallas 37, Los Angeles 7

1976

AFC div playoffs	Oakland 24, New England 21
	Pittsburgh 40, Baltimore 14
AFC championship	Oakland 24, Pittsburgh 7
NFC div playoffs	Minnesota 35, Washington 20
	Los Angeles 14, Dallas 12
NFC championship	Minnesota 24, Los Angeles 13

1977

AFC div playoffs	Denver 34, Pittsburgh 21
	Oakland 37, Baltimore 31
AFC championship	Denver 20, Oakland 17
NFC div playoffs	Dallas 37, Chicago 7
	Minnesota 14, Los Angeles 7
NFC championship	Dallas 23, Minnesota 6

1978

AFC 1st-round playoff	Houston 17, Miami 9
AFC div playoffs	Houston 31, New England 14
	Pittsburgh 33, Denver 10
AFC championship	Pittsburgh 34, Houston 5
NFC 1st-round playoff	Atlanta 14, Philadelphia 13
NFC div playoffs	Dallas 27, Atlanta 20
	Los Angeles 34, Minnesota 10
NFC championship	Dallas 28, Los Angeles 0

1979

AFC 1st-round playoff	Houston 13, Denver 7
AFC div playoffs	Houston 17, San Diego 14
	Pittsburgh 34, Miami 14
AFC championship	Pittsburgh 27, Houston 13
NFC 1st-round playoff	Philadelphia 27, Chicago 17
NFC div playoffs	Tampa Bay 24, Philadelphia 17
	Los Angeles 21, Dallas 19
NFC championship	Los Angeles 9, Tampa Bay 0

1980

AFC 1st-round playoff	Oakland 27, Houston 7
AFC div playoffs	San Diego 20, Buffalo 14
	Oakland 14, Cleveland 12
AFC championship	Oakland 34, San Diego 27
NFC 1st-round playoff	Dallas 34, Los Angeles 13
NFC div playoffs	Philadelphia 31, Minnesota 16
	Dallas 30, Atlanta 27
NFC championship	Philadelphia 20, Dallas 7

Offensive Line

One day last spring someone somehow changed the recording used at the Minnesota Vikings' offices. Instead of the regular message, callers heard this: "Thank you for calling the most rotten, stinking team in the history of man. That's right, you have reached the Minnesota Vikings."

1981

AFC 1st-round playoff	Buffalo 31, NY Jets 27
AFC div playoffs	San Diego 41, Miami 38
	Cincinnati 28, Buffalo 21
AFC championship	Cincinnati 27, San Diego 7
NFC 1st-round playoff	NY Giants 27, Philadelphia 21
NFC div playoffs	Dallas 38, Tampa Bay 0
	San Francisco 38, NY Giants 24
NFC championship	San Francisco 28, Dallas 27

1982

AFC 1st-round playoffs	Miami 28, New England 13
	LA Raiders 27, Cleveland 10
	NY Jets 44, Cincinnati 17
	San Diego 31, Pittsburgh 28
AFC 2nd-round playoffs	NY Jets 17, LA Raiders 14
	Miami 34, San Diego 13
AFC championship	Miami 14, NY Jets 0
NFC 1st-round playoffs	Washington 31, Detroit 7
	Green Bay 41, St Louis 16
	Minnesota 30, Atlanta 24
	Dallas 30, Tampa Bay 17
NFC 2nd-round playoffs	Washington 21, Minnesota 7
	Dallas 37, Green Bay 26
NFC championship	Washington 31, Dallas 17

1983

AFC 1st-round playoff	Seattle 31, Denver 7
AFC div playoffs	Seattle 27, Miami 20
	LA Raiders 38, Pittsburgh 10
AFC championship	LA Raiders 30, Seattle 14
NFC 1st-round playoff	LA Rams 24, Dallas 17
NFC div playoffs	San Francisco 24, Detroit 23
	Washington 51, LA Rams 7
NFC championship	Washington 24, San Francisco 21

1984

AFC 1st-round playoff	Seattle 13, LA Raiders 7
AFC div playoffs	Miami 31, Seattle 10
	Pittsburgh 24, Denver 17
AFC championship	Miami 45, Pittsburgh 28
NFC 1st-round playoff	NY Giants 16, LA Rams 13
NFC div playoffs	San Francisco 21, NY Giants 10
	Chicago 23, Washington 19
NFC championship	San Francisco 23, Chicago 0

1985

AFC 1st-round playoff	New England 26, NY Jets 14
AFC div playoffs	Miami 24, Cleveland 21
	New England 27, LA Raiders 20
AFC championship	New England 31, Miami 14
NFC 1st-round playoff	NY Giants 17, San Francisco 3
NFC div playoffs	LA Rams 20, Dallas 0
	Chicago 21, NY Giants 0
NFC championship	Chicago 24, LA Rams 0

1986

AFC 1st-round playoff	NY Jets 35, Kansas City 15
AFC div playoffs	Cleveland 23, NY Jets 20
	Denver 22, New England 17
AFC championship	Denver 23, Cleveland 20
NFC 1st-round playoff	Washington 19, LA Rams 7
NFC div playoffs	Washington 27, Chicago 13
	NY Giants 49, San Francisco 3
NFC championship	NY Giants 17, Washington 0

1987

AFC 1st-round playoff	Houston 23, Seattle 20
AFC div playoffs	Cleveland 38, Indianapolis 21
	Denver 34, Houston 10
AFC championship	Denver 38, Cleveland 33
NFC 1st-round playoff	Minnesota 44, New Orleans 10
NFC div playoffs	Minnesota 36, San Francisco 24
	Washington 21, Chicago 17
NFC championship	Washington 17, Minnesota 10

1988

AFC 1st-round playoff	Houston 24, Cleveland 23
AFC div playoffs	Cincinnati 21, Seattle 13
	Buffalo 17, Houston 10
AFC championship	Cincinnati 21, Buffalo 10
NFC 1st-round playoff	Minnesota 28, LA Rams 17
NFC div playoffs	Chicago 20, Philadelphia 12
	San Francisco 34, Minnesota 9
NFC championship	San Francisco 28, Chicago 3

1989

AFC 1st-round playoff	Pittsburgh 26, Houston 23
AFC div playoffs	Cleveland 34, Buffalo 30
	Denver 24, Pittsburgh 23
AFC championship	Denver 37, Cleveland 21
NFC 1st-round playoff	LA Rams 21, Philadelphia 7
NFC div playoffs	LA Rams 19, NY Giants 13
	San Francisco 41, Minnesota 13
NFC championship	San Francisco 30, LA Rams 3

1990

AFC 1st-round playoffs	Miami 17, Kansas City 16
	Cincinnati 41, Houston 14
AFC div playoffs	Buffalo 44, Miami 34
	LA Raiders 20, Cincinnati 10
AFC championship	Buffalo 51, LA Raiders 3
NFC 1st-round playoffs	Chicago 16, New Orleans 6
	Washington 20, Philadelphia 6
NFC div playoffs	NY Giants 31, Chicago 3
	San Francisco 28, Washington 10
NFC championship	NY Giants 15, San Francisco 13

All-Time NFL Individual Statistical Leaders

Career Leaders

Scoring

	Yrs	TD	FG	PAT	Pts
George Blanda	26	9	335	943	2002
Jan Stenerud	19	0	373	580	1699
Jim Turner	16	1	304	521	1439
Mark Moseley	16	0	300	482	1382
Jim Bakken	17	0	282	534	1380
Fred Cox	15	0	282	519	1365
Pat Leahy	17	0	278	528	1362
Lou Groza	17	1	234	641	1349
Chris Bahr	14	0	241	490	1213
Nick Lowery	12	0	259	375	1152
Gino Cappelletti	11	42	176	350	1130
Ray Wersching	15	0	222	456	1122
Don Cockroft	13	0	216	432	1080
Garo Yepremian	14	0	210	444	1074
Jim Breech	12	0	201	459	1062
Bruce Gossett	11	0	219	374	1031
Eddie Murray	11	0	225	341	1016
Sam Baker	15	2	179	428	977
Matt Bahr	12	0	199	378	975
Rafael Septien	10	0	180	420	960

Cappelletti's total includes four two-point conversions.

Rushing

	Yrs	Att	Yds	Avg	Lg	TD
Walter Payton	13	3,838	16,726	4.4	76	110
Tony Dorsett	12	2,936	12,739	4.3	99	77
Jim Brown	9	2,359	12,312	5.2	80	106
Franco Harris	13	2,949	12,120	4.1	75	91
Eric Dickerson	8	2,616	11,903	4.6	85	86
John Riggins	14	2,916	11,352	3.9	66	104
O. J. Simpson	11	2,404	11,236	4.7	94	61
Ottis Anderson	12	2,499	10,101	4.0	76	80
Earl Campbell	8	2,187	9,407	4.3	81	74
Jim Taylor	10	1,941	8,597	4.4	84	83
Joe Perry	14	1,737	8,378	4.8	78	53
Larry Csonka	11	1,891	8,081	4.3	54	64
Marcus Allen	9	1,960	7,957	4.1	61	75
Gerald Riggs	9	1,911	7,940	4.2	58	58
Freeman McNeil	10	1,704	7,604	4.5	69	36
Mike Pruitt	11	1,844	7,378	4.0	77	51
James Brooks	10	1,515	7,347	4.9	65	47
Leroy Kelly	10	1,727	7,274	4.2	70	74
George Rogers	7	1,692	7,176	4.2	79	54
Roger Craig	8	1,686	7,064	4.2	71	50

Touchdowns

	Yrs	Rush	Pass Rec	Ret	Total TD
Jim Brown	9	106	20	0	126
Walter Payton	13	110	15	0	125
John Riggins	14	104	12	0	116
Lenny Moore	12	63	48	2	113
Don Hutson	11	3	99	3	105
Steve Largent	14	1	100	0	101
Franco Harris	13	91	9	0	100
Marcus Allen	9	75	17	1	93
Jim Taylor	10	83	10	0	93
Tony Dorsett	12	77	13	1	91

	Yrs	Rush	Pass Rec	Ret	Total TD
Bobby Mitchell	11	18	65	8	91
Eric Dickerson	8	86	4	0	90
Leroy Kelly	10	74	13	3	90
Charley Taylor	13	11	79	0	90
Don Maynard	15	0	88	0	88
Lance Alworth	11	2	85	0	87
Paul Warfield	13	1	85	0	86
Ottis Anderson	12	80	5	0	85
Tommy McDonald	12	0	84	1	85
Jerry Rice	6	4	79	0	83

Boo-Boo by the Bay

San Francisco 49ers owner Eddie DeBartolo announced last spring that he was changing the team's tastefully understated helmet logo, an interlocking block SF, to a garish 49ers emblem that resembles something one might expect to see on a children's toy or a professional wrestler's frock. This supposedly bold move into the '90s was greeted by predictable hoots of derision all over the Bay Area. Talk-show shots were besieged by angry protests. A *San Francisco Examiner* poll, which attracted the biggest reader response since the 49er quarterback controversy of 1988 (Joe Montana versus Steve Young) resulted in 7,392 votes against the new insignia and only 583 for it. Similar polls conducted by *The Sacramento Bee* and the *San Jose Mercury News* elicited overwhelmingly anti-logo sentiments.

Poor Eddie. For all the great teams he has financed from his home in Youngstown, Ohio, he still couldn't read the soul of San Francisco. He didn't understand that these are a people who sharply oppose any break with tradition—the 49ers have had the same helmet logo since 1962—and who retain some feelings for aesthetics in a barbaric age.

You'd have thought Eddie learned his lesson 14 years ago when he bought the team and hired as his front-office honcho the infamous Joe Thomas, a philistine who said tradition be damned. Thomas actually removed the office photos of such 49er legends as Frankie Albert, Joe Perry, Leo Nomellini, Hugh McElhenny and Y.A. Tittle. Thomas was nearly run out of town on a rail, and his successor, Bill Walsh, wisely restored historical perspective to the operation. Eddie just didn't get the message.

But this time he apparently did. Just a couple of days after the news conference at which the new logo was unveiled, DeBartolo announced the 49ers would retain their original logo.

Career Leaders (*Cont.*)
Combined Yards Gained

	Yrs	Total	Rush	Rec	Int Ret	Punt Ret	Kickoff Ret	Fum Ret
Walter Payton	13	21,803	16,726	4,538	0	0	539	0
Tony Dorsett	12	16,326	12,739	3,554	0	0	0	33
Jim Brown	9	15,459	12,312	2,499	0	0	648	0
Franco Harris	13	14,622	12,120	2,287	0	0	233	−18
O.J. Simpson	11	14,368	11,236	2,142	0	0	990	0
Bobby Mitchell	11	14,078	2,735	7,954	0	699	2,690	0
James Brooks	10	13,709	7,347	3,274	0	565	2,523	0
Eric Dickerson	8	13,643	11,903	1,725	0	0	0	15
John Riggins	14	13,435	11,352	2,090	0	0	0	−7
Steve Largent	14	13,396	83	13,089	0	68	156	0
Greg Pruitt	12	13,262	5,672	3,069	0	2,007	2,514	0
Ottis Anderson	12	13,151	10,101	3,021	0	0	0	29
Ollie Matson	14	12,884	5,173	3,285	51	595	3,746	34
Tim Brown	10	12,684	3,862	3,399	0	639	4,781	3
Lenny Moore	12	12,451	5,174	6,039	0	56	1,180	2
Don Maynard	15	12,379	70	11,834	0	132	343	0
Charlie Joiner	18	12,367	22	12,146	0	0	194	5
Leroy Kelly	10	12,330	7,274	2,281	0	990	1,784	1
James Lofton	13	12,236	246	11,963	0	0	0	27
Floyd Little	9	12,173	6,323	2,418	0	893	2,523	16

Passing

	Yrs	Att	Comp	Pct Comp	Yds	Avg Gain	TD	Pct TD	Int	Pct Int	Rating Pts
Joe Montana	12	4,579	2,914	63.6	34,998	7.64	242	5.3	123	2.7	93.4
Dan Marino	8	4,181	2,480	59.3	31,416	7.51	241	5.8	136	3.3	88.5
Jim Kelly	5	2,088	1,251	59.9	15,730	7.53	105	5.0	72	3.4	85.8
Boomer Esiason	7	2,687	1,520	56.6	21,381	7.96	150	5.6	98	3.6	85.8
Roger Staubach	11	2,958	1,685	57.0	22,700	7.67	153	5.2	109	3.7	83.4
Neil Lomax	8	3,153	1,817	57.6	22,771	7.22	136	4.3	90	2.9	82.7
Sonny Jurgensen	18	4,262	2,433	57.1	32,224	7.56	255	6.0	189	4.4	82.6
Len Dawson	19	3,741	2,136	57.1	28,711	7.67	239	6.4	183	4.9	82.6
Dave Krieg	11	3,291	1,909	58.0	24,052	7.31	184	5.6	136	4.1	82.3
Ken O'Brien	7	2,878	1,697	59.0	20,444	7.10	109	3.8	78	2.7	82.2
Jim Everett	5	2,038	1,154	56.6	15,345	7.53	101	5.0	73	3.6	82.2
Ken Anderson	16	4,475	2,654	59.3	32,838	7.34	197	4.4	160	3.6	81.9
Danny White	13	2,950	1,761	59.7	21,959	7.44	155	5.3	132	4.5	81.7
Bart Starr	16	3,149	1,808	57.4	24,718	7.85	152	4.8	138	4.4	80.5
Fran Tarkenton	18	6,467	3,686	57.0	47,003	7.27	342	5.3	266	4.1	80.4
Bernie Kosar	6	2,363	1,364	57.7	16,450	6.96	85	3.6	62	2.6	80.3
Dan Fouts	15	5,604	3,297	58.8	43,040	7.68	254	4.5	242	4.3	80.2
Warren Moon	7	3,025	1,701	56.2	22,989	7.60	134	4.4	112	3.7	79.9
Tony Eason	8	1,564	911	58.2	11,142	7.12	61	3.9	51	3.3	79.7
Jim McMahon	9	1,840	1,056	57.4	13,398	7.28	77	4.2	66	3.6	79.3

1,500 or more attempts. The passing ratings are based on performance standards established for completion percentage, interception percentage, touchdown percentage, and average gain. Passers are allocated points according to how their marks compare with those standards.

Receiving

	Yrs	No.	Yds	Avg	Lg	TD		Yrs	No.	Yds	Avg	Lg	TD
Steve Largent	14	819	13,089	16.0	74	100	Harold Jackson	16	579	10,372	17.9	79	76
Charlie Joiner	18	750	12,146	16.2	87	65	Lionel Taylor	10	567	7,195	12.7	80	45
Art Monk	11	730	9,935	13.6	79	52	Wes Chandler	11	559	8,966	16.0	85	56
Ozzie Newsome	13	662	7,980	12.1	74	47	Stanley Morgan	14	557	10,716	19.2	76	72
Charley Taylor	13	649	9,110	14.0	88	79	J.T. Smith	13	544	6,974	12.8	77	35
James Lofton	13	642	11,963	18.6	80	61	Lance Alworth	11	542	10,266	18.9	85	85
Don Maynard	15	633	11,834	18.7	87	88	Kellen Winslow	9	541	6,741	12.5	67	45
Raymond Berry	13	631	9,275	14.7	70	68	John Stallworth	14	537	8,723	16.2	74	63
Harold Carmichael	14	590	8,985	15.2	85	79	Roy Green	12	522	8,496	16.3	83	66
Fred Biletnikoff	14	589	8,974	15.2	82	76	Bobby Mitchell	11	521	7,954	15.3	99	65

Career Leaders (*Cont.*)

Interceptions

	Yrs	No.	Yds	Avg	Lg	TD
Paul Krause	16	81	1185	14.6	81	3
Emlen Tunnell	14	79	1282	16.2	55	4
Dick "Night Train" Lane	14	68	1207	17.8	80	5
Ken Riley	15	65	596	9.2	66	5
Dick LeBeau	13	62	762	12.3	70	3
Dave Brown	16	62	698	11.3	90	5

Punting

	Yrs	No.	Yds	Avg	Lg	Blk
Sammy Baugh	16	338	15,245	45.1	85	9
Tommy Davis	11	511	22,833	44.7	82	2
Yale Lary	11	503	22,279	44.3	74	4
Rohn Stark	9	664	29,267	44.1	72	6
Horace Gillom	7	385	16,872	43.8	80	5

Punt Returns

	Yrs	No.	Yds	Avg	Lg	TD
George McAfee	8	112	1431	12.8	74	2
Jack Christiansen	8	85	1084	12.8	89	8
Claude Gibson	5	110	1381	12.6	85	3
Clarence Verdin	5	76	931	12.3	73	2
Bill Dudley	9	124	1515	12.2	96	3

Kickoff Returns

	Yrs	No.	Yds	Avg	Lg	TD
Gale Sayers	7	91	2781	30.6	103	6
Lynn Chandnois	7	92	2720	29.6	93	3
Abe Woodson	9	193	5538	28.7	105	5
Claude "Buddy" Young	6	90	2514	27.9	104	2
Travis Williams	5	102	2801	27.5	105	5

Single-Season Leaders

Scoring

POINTS

	Year	TD	PAT	FG	Pts
Paul Hornung, GB	1960	15	41	15	176
Mark Moseley, Wash	1983	0	62	33	161
Gino Cappelletti, Bos	1964	7	38	25	155
Gino Cappelletti, Bos	1961	8	48	17	147
Paul Hornung, GB	1961	10	41	15	146
Jim Turner, NY Jets	1968	0	43	34	145
John Riggins, Wash	1983	24	0	0	144
Kevin Butler, Chi	1985	0	51	31	144
Tony Franklin, NE	1986	0	44	32	140
Gary Anderson, Pitt	1985	0	40	33	139

Note: Cappelletti's 1964 total includes a two-point conversion.

TOUCHDOWNS

	Year	Rush	Rec	Ret	Total
John Riggins, Wash	1983	24	0	0	24
O. J. Simpson, Buff	1975	16	7	0	23
Jerry Rice, SF	1987	1	22	0	23
Gale Sayers, Chi	1966	14	6	2	22

FIELD GOALS

	Year	Att	No.
Ali Haji-Sheikh, NY Giants	1983	42	35
Jim Turner, NY Jets	1968	46	34
Chester Marcol, GB	1972	48	33
Mark Moseley, Wash	1983	47	33

Rushing

YARDS GAINED

	Year	Att	Yds	Avg
Eric Dickerson, LA Rams	1984	379	2105	5.6
O. J. Simpson, Buff	1973	332	2003	6.0
Earl Campbell, Hou	1980	373	1934	5.2
Jim Brown, Clev	1963	291	1883	6.4
Walter Payton, Chi	1977	339	1852	5.5
Eric Dickerson, LA Rams	1986	404	1821	4.5
O. J. Simpson, Buff	1975	329	1817	5.5
Eric Dickerson, LA Rams	1983	390	1808	4.6
Marcus Allen, LA Raiders	1985	390	1759	4.6
Gerald Riggs, Atl	1985	397	1719	4.3

AVERAGE GAIN

	Year	Avg
Beattie Feathers, Chi	1934	9.94
Randall Cunningham, Phil	1990	7.98
Bobby Douglass, Chi	1972	6.87
Dan Towler, LA Rams	1951	6.78

TOUCHDOWNS

	Year	No.
John Riggins, Wash	1983	24
Joe Morris, NY Giants	1985	21
Jim Taylor, GB	1962	19
Earl Campbell, Hou	1979	19
Chuck Muncie, SD	1981	19

Heap Big Score

The most points ever scored by a team in an NFL game occurred, curiously enough, in a championship. In the 1940 title game the Chicago Bears triumphed 73–0 over the Washington Redskins, a team they had lost to earlier that year by the score of—students of numerology, take note—7–3. The Redskins set the regular season scoring record in 1966 when they trounced the New York Giants 72–41. The only other team to score 70 points in a game is the Los Angeles Rams, who beat the Baltimore Colts 70–27 in 1950.

Single-Season Leaders (*Cont.*)
Passing

YARDS GAINED

	Year	Att	Comp	Pct	Yds
Dan Marino, Mia	1984	564	362	64.2	5084
Dan Fouts, SD	1981	609	360	59.1	4802
Dan Marino, Mia	1986	623	378	60.7	4746
Dan Fouts, SD	1980	589	348	59.1	4715
Warren Moon, Hou	1990	584	362	62.0	4689
Neil Lomax, StL	1984	560	345	61.6	4614
Lynn Dickey, GB	1983	484	289	59.7	4458
Dan Marino, Mia	1988	606	354	58.4	4434
Bill Kenney, KC	1983	603	346	57.4	4348
Don Majkowski, GB	1989	599	353	58.9	4318
Jim Everett, LA Rams	1989	518	304	58.7	4310

PASS RATING

	Year	Rat.
Joe Montana, SF	1989	112.4
Milt Plum, Clev	1960	110.4
Sammy Baugh, Wash	1945	109.9
Dan Marino, Mia	1984	108.9

TOUCHDOWNS

	Year	No.
Dan Marino, Mia	1984	48
Dan Marino, Mia	1986	44
George Blanda, Hou	1961	36
Y. A. Tittle, NY Giants	1963	36

Receiving

RECEPTIONS

	Year	No.	Yds
Art Monk, Wash	1984	106	1372
Charley Hennigan, Hou	1964	101	1546
Lionel Taylor, Den	1961	100	1176
Jerry Rice, SF	1990	100	1502
Todd Christensen, LA Raiders	1986	95	1153
Johnny Morris, Chi	1964	93	1200
Al Toon, NY Jets	1988	93	1067
Lionel Taylor, Den	1960	92	1235
Todd Christensen, LA Raiders	1983	92	1247
Roger Craig, SF	1985	92	1016
Art Monk, Wash	1985	91	1226
J. T. Smith, StL	1967	91	1117

YARDS GAINED

	Year	Yds
Charley Hennigan, Hou	1961	1746
Lance Alworth, SD	1965	1602
Jerry Rice, SF	1986	1570
Roy Green, StL	1984	1555

TOUCHDOWNS

	Year	No.
Jerry Rice, SF	1987	22
Mark Clayton, Mia	1984	18
Don Hutson, GB	1942	17
Elroy "Crazylegs" Hirsch, LA Rams	1951	17
Bill Groman, Hou	1961	17
Jerry Rice, SF	1989	17

All-Purpose Yards

	Year	Run	Rec	Ret	Total
Lionel James, SD	1985	516	1027	992	2535
Terry Metcalf, StL	1975	816	378	1268	2462
Mack Herron, NE	1974	824	474	1146	2444
Gale Sayers, Chi	1966	1231	447	762	2440
Timmy Brown, Phil	1963	841	487	1100	2428
Tim Brown, LA Raiders	1988	50	725	1542	2317
Marcus Allen, LA Raiders	1985	1759	555	–6	2308
Timmy Brown, Phil	1962	545	849	912	2306
Gale Sayers, Chi	1965	867	507	898	2272
Eric Dickerson, LA Rams	1984	2105	139	15	2259
O. J. Simpson, Buff	1975	1817	426	0	2243

Punting

	Year	No.	Yds	Avg
Sammy Baugh, Wash	1940	35	1799	51.4
Yale Lary, Det	1963	35	1713	48.9
Sammy Baugh, Wash	1941	30	1462	48.7
Yale Lary, Det	1961	52	2516	48.4
Sammy Baugh, Wash	1942	37	1783	48.2

Sacks

	Year	No.
Mark Gastineau, NY Jets	1984	22
Reggie White, Phil	1987	21
Chris Doleman, Minn	1989	21
Lawrence Taylor, NY Giants	1986	20.5

Interceptions

	Year	No.
Dick "Night Train" Lane, LA Rams	1952	14
Dan Sandifer, Wash	1948	13
Spec Sanders, NY Yanks	1950	13
Lester Hayes, Oak	1980	13

Kickoff Returns

	Year	Avg
Travis Williams, GB	1967	41.1
Gale Sayers, Chi	1967	37.7
Ollie Matson, Chi Cardinals	1958	35.5
Jim Duncan, Balt	1970	35.4
Lynn Chandnois, Pitt	1952	35.2

Punt Returns

	Year	Avg
Herb Rich, Balt	1950	23.0
Jack Christiansen, Det	1952	21.5
Dick Christy, NY Titans	1961	21.3
Bob Hayes, Dall	1968	20.8

Single-Game Leaders
Scoring

POINTS

	Date	Pts
Ernie Nevers, Cards vs Bears	11-28-29	40
Dub Jones, Clev vs Chi Bears	11-25-51	36
Gale Sayers, Chi Bears vs SF	12-12-65	36
Paul Hornung, GB vs Balt	10-8-61	33

On Thanksgiving Day, 1929, Nevers scored all the Cardinals' points on six rushing TDs and four PATs. The Cards defeated Red Grange and the Bears, 40-6. Jones and Sayers each rushed for six touchdowns in their teams victories. Hornung scored four touchdowns and kicked 6 PATs and a field goal in a 45-7 win over the Colts.

FIELD GOALS

	Date	No.
Jim Bakken, StL vs Pitt	9-24-67	7
Rich Karlis, Minn vs LA Rams	11-5-89	7
Eight players tied with 6 FGs each.		

Bakken was 7 for 9, Karlis 7 for 7.

TOUCHDOWNS

	Date	No
Ernie Nevers, Cards vs Bears	11-28-29	6
Dub Jones, Clev vs Chi Bears	11-25-51	6
Gale Sayers, Chi vs SF	12-12-65	6
Bob Shaw, Chi Cards vs Balt	10-2-50	5
Jim Brown, Clev vs Balt	11-1-59	5
Abner Haynes, Dall Texans vs Oak	11-26-61	5
Billy Cannon, Hous vs NY Titans	12-10-61	5
Cookie Gilchrist, Buff vs NY Jets	12-8-63	5
Paul Hornung, GB vs Balt	12-12-65	5
Kellen Winslow, SD vs Oak	11-22-81	5
Jerry Rice, SF vs Atl	10-14-90	5

Rushing

YARDS GAINED

	Date	Yds
Walter Payton, Chi vs Minn	11-20-77	275
O. J. Simpson, Buff vs Det	11-25-76	273
O. J. Simpson, Buff vs NE	9-16-73	250
Willie Ellison, LA Rams vs NO	12-5-71	247
Cookie Gilchrist, Buff vs NY Jets	12-8-63	243

TOUCHDOWNS

	Date	No.
Ernie Nevers, Cards vs Bears	11-28-29	6
Jim Brown, Clev vs Balt	11-1-59	5
Cookie Gilchrist, Buff vs NY Jets	12-8-63	5

CARRIES

	Date	No.
Jamie Morris, Wash vs Cin	12-17-88	45
Butch Woolfolk, NY Giants vs Phil	11-20-83	43
James Wilder, TB vs GB	9-30-84	43
James Wilder, TB vs Pitt	10-30-83	42
Franco Harris, Pitt vs Cin	10-17-76	41
Gerald Riggs, Atl vs LA Rams	11-17-85	41

Passing

YARDS GAINED

	Date	Yds
Norm Van Brocklin, LA vs NY Yanks	9-28-51	554
Warren Moon, Hou vs KC	12-16-90	527
Dan Marino, Mia vs NY Jets	10-23-88	521
Phil Simms, NY Giants vs Cin	10-13-85	513
Vince Ferragamo, LA Rams vs Chi	12-26-82	509
Y. A. Tittle, NY Giants vs Wash	10-28-62	505

COMPLETIONS

	Date	No.
Richard Todd, NY Jets vs SF	9-21-80	42
Ken Anderson, Cin vs SD	12-20-82	40
Phil Simms, NY Giants vs Cin	10-13-85	40
Dan Marino, Mia vs Buff	11-16-86	39
Tommy Kramer, Minn vs Clev	12-14-80	38
Tommy Kramer, Minn vs GB	11-29-81	38
Joe Ferguson, Buff vs Mia	10-9-83	38

TOUCHDOWNS

	Date	No.
Sid Luckman, Chi Bears vs NY Giants	11-14-43	7
Adrian Burk, Phil vs Wash	10-17-54	7
George Blanda, Hou vs NY Titans	11-19-61	7
Y. A. Tittle, NY Giants vs Wash	10-28-62	7
Joe Kapp, Minn vs Balt	9-28-69	7

THEY SAID IT

Eric Dickerson, Indianapolis Colts running back, on his apparently fading ability: "If I've lost a step, it's a step a lot of other guys never had."

Single-Game Leaders (*Cont.*)
Receiving

YARDS GAINED

	Date	Yds
Flipper Anderson, LA Rams vs NO	11-26-89	336
Stephone Paige, KC vs SD	12-22-85	309
Jim Benton, Clev vs Det	11-22-45	303
Cloyce Box, Det vs Balt	12-3-50	302
John Taylor, SF vs LA Rams	12-11-89	286

RECEPTIONS

	Date	No.
Tom Fears, LA Rams vs GB	12-3-50	18
Clark Gaines, NY Jets vs SF	9-21-80	17
Sonny Randle, StL vs NY Giants	11-4-62	16
Rickey Young, Minn vs NE	12-16-79	15
William Andrews, Atl vs Pitt	11-15-81	15

TOUCHDOWNS

	Date	No.
Bob Shaw, Chi Cards vs Balt	10-2-50	5
Kellen Winslow, SD vs Oak	11-22-81	5
Jerry Rice, SF vs Atl	10-14-90	5

All-Purpose Yards

	Date	Yds
Billy Cannon, Hou vs NY Titans	12-10-61	373
Lionel James, SD vs LA Raiders	11-10-85	345
Timmy Brown, Phil vs StL	12-16-62	341
Gale Sayers, Chi vs Minn	12-18-66	339
Gale Sayers, Chi vs SF	12-12-65	336

Pro Bowl All-Time Results

Date	Result	Date	Result
1-15-39	NY Giants 13, Pro All-Stars 10	1-21-68	AFL East 25, West 24
1-14-40	Green Bay 16, NFL All-Stars 7	1-21-68	NFL West 38, East 20
12-29-40	Chi Bears 28, NFL All-Stars 14	1-19-69	AFL West 38, East 25
1-4-42	Chi Bears 35, NFL All-Stars 24	1-19-69	NFL West 10, East 7
12-27-42	NFL All-Stars 17, Washington 14	1-17-70	AFL West 26, East 3
1-14-51	American Conf 28, National Conf 27	1-18-70	NFL West 16, East 13
1-12-52	National Conf 30, American Conf 13	1-24-71	NFC 27, AFC 6
1-10-53	National Conf 27, American Conf 7	1-23-72	AFC 26, NFC 13
1-17-54	East 20, West 9	1-21-73	AFC 33, NFC 28
1-16-55	West 26, East 19	1-20-74	AFC 15, NFC 13
1-15-56	East 31, West 30	1-20-75	NFC 17, AFC 10
1-13-57	West 19, East 10	1-26-76	NFC 23, AFC 20
1-12-58	West 26, East 7	1-17-77	AFC 24, NFC 14
1-11-59	East 28, West 21	1-23-78	NFC 14, AFC 13
1-17-60	West 38, East 21	1-29-79	NFC 13, AFC 7
1-15-61	West 35, East 31	1-27-80	NFC 37, AFC 27
1-7-62	AFL West 47, East 27	2-1-81	NFC 21, AFC 7
1-14-62	NFL West 31, East 30	1-31-82	AFC 16, NFC 13
1-13-63	AFL West 21, East 14	2-6-83	NFC 20, AFC 19
1-13-63	NFL East 30, West 20	1-29-84	NFC 45, AFC 3
1-12-64	NFL West 31, East 17	1-27-85	AFC 22, NFC 14
1-19-64	AFL West 27, East 24	2-2-86	NFC 28, AFC 24
1-10-65	NFL West 34, East 14	2-1-87	AFC 10, NFC 6
1-16-65	AFL West 38, East 14	2-7-88	AFC 15, NFC 6
1-15-66	AFL All-Stars 30, Buffalo 19	1-29-89	NFC 34, AFC 3
1-15-66	NFL East 36, West 7	2-4-90	NFC 27, AFC 21
1-21-67	AFL East 30, West 23	2-3-91	AFC 23, NFC 21
1-22-67	NFL East 20, West 10		

Date	Results (Attendance)
8-31-34	Chi Bears 0, All-Stars 0 (79,432)
8-29-35	Chi Bears 5, All-Stars 0 (77,450)
9-3-36	All-Stars 7, Detroit 7 (76,000)
9-1-37	All-Stars 6, Green Bay 0 (84,560)
8-31-38	All-Stars 28, Washington 16 (74,250)
8-30-39	NY Giants 9, All-Stars 0 (81,456)
8-29-40	Green Bay 45, All-Stars 28 (84,567)
8-28-41	Chi Bears 37, All-Stars 13 (98,203)
8-28-42	Chi Bears 21, All-Stars 0 (101,100)
8-25-43	All-Stars 27, Washington 7 (48,471)
8-30-44	Chi Bears 24, All-Stars 21 (48,769)
8-30-45	Green Bay 19, All-Stars 7 (92,753)
8-23-46	All-Stars 16, Los Angeles 0 (97,380)
8-22-47	All-Stars 16, Chi Bears 0 (105,840)
8-20-48	Chi Cardinals 28, All-Stars 0 (101,220)
8-12-49	Philadelphia 38, All-Stars 0 (93,780)
8-11-50	All-Stars 17, Philadelphia 7 (88,885)
8-17-51	Cleveland 33, All-Stars 0 (92,180)
8-15-52	Los Angeles 10, All-Stars 7 (88,316)
8-14-53	Detroit 24, All-Stars 10 (93,818)
8-13-54	Detroit 31, All-Stars 6 (93,470)
8-12-55	All-Stars 30, Cleveland 27 (75,000)

Date	Results (Attendance)
8-10-56	Cleveland 26, All-Stars 0 (75,000)
8-9-57	NY Giants 22, All-Stars 12 (75,000)
8-15-58	All-Stars 35, Detroit 19 (70,000)
8-14-59	Baltimore 29, All-Stars 0 (70,000)
8-12-60	Baltimore 32, All-Stars 7 (70,000)
8-4-61	Philadelphia 28, All-Stars 14 (66,000)
8-3-62	Green Bay 42, All-Stars 20 (65,000)
8-2-63	All-Stars 20, Green Bay 17 (65,000)
8-7-64	Chicago 28, All-Stars 17 (65,000)
8-6-65	Cleveland 24, All-Stars 16 (68,000)
8-5-66	Green Bay 38, All-Stars 0 (72,000)
8-4-67	Green Bay 27, All-Stars 0 (70,934)
8-2-68	Green Bay 34, All-Stars 17 (69,917)
8-1-69	NY Jets 26, All-Stars 24 (74,208)
7-31-70	Kansas City 24, All-Stars 3 (69,940)
7-30-71	Baltimore 24, All-Stars 17 (52,289)
7-28-72	Dallas 20, All-Stars 7 (54,162)
7-27-73	Miami 14, All-Stars 3 (54,103)
1974	No game
8-1-75	Pittsburgh 21, All-Stars 14 (54,103)
7-23-76	Pittsburgh 24, All-Stars 0 (52,895)

All-Time Winningest NFL Coaches

Most Career Wins, Start of 1991 Season

Coach	Yrs	Teams	Regular Season W	L	T	Pct	Career W	L	T	Pct
George Halas	40	Bears	319	148	31	.672	325	151	31	.672
Don Shula	28	Colts, Dolphins	281	123	6	.693	298	137	6	.683
Tom Landry	29	Cowboys	250	162	6	.605	270	178	6	.601
Curly Lambeau	33	Packers, Cardinals, Redskins	226	132	22	.623	229	134	22	.623
Chuck Noll	22	Steelers	186	139	1	.572	202	147	1	.579
Chuck Knox	18	Rams, Bills, Seahawks	164	105	1	.609	171	116	1	.596
Paul Brown	21	Browns, Bengals	166	100	6	.621	170	108	6	.609
Bud Grant	18	Vikings	158	96	5	.620	168	108	5	.607
Steve Owen	23	Giants	151	100	17	.595	153	108	17	.582
Hank Stram	17	Chiefs, Saints	131	97	10	.571	136	100	10	.573
Weeb Ewbank	20	Colts, Jets	130	129	7	.502	134	130	7	.507
Sid Gillman	18	Rams, Chargers, Oilers	122	99	7	.550	123	104	7	.541
George Allen	12	Rams, Redskins	116	47	5	.705	118	54	5	.681
Don Coryell	14	Cardinals, Chargers	111	83	1	.572	114	89	1	.561
Joe Gibbs	10	Redskins	101	51	0	.664	113	55	0	.673
John Madden	10	Raiders	103	32	7	.750	112	39	7	.731
Buddy Parker	15	Cardinals, Lions, Steelers	104	75	9	.577	107	76	9	.581
Vince Lombardi	10	Packers, Redskins	96	34	6	.728	105	35	6	.740
Bill Walsh	10	49ers	92	59	1	.609	102	63	1	.617
Lou Saban	16	Patriots, Bills, Broncos	95	99	7	.490	97	100	7	.493

Top Winning Percentages

	W	L	T	Pct
Vince Lombardi	105	35	6	.740
John Madden	112	39	7	.731
Don Shula	298	137	6	.683
George Allen	118	54	5	.681
Joe Gibbs	113	55	0	.673
George Halas	325	151	31	.672
Curly Lambeau	229	134	22	.623
Bill Walsh	102	63	1	.617
Paul Brown	170	108	6	.609
Bud Grant	168	108	5	.607

THEY SAID IT

Terry Bradshaw, former Pittsburgh Steelers quarterback, now a CBS announcer: "If a receiver's open, throw it to him. If he's not, throw it to him anyway. Let the guy show his athletic ability."

All-Time Number-One Draft Choices

Year	Team	Selection	Position
1936	Philadelphia	Jay Berwanger, Chicago	HB
1937	Philadelphia	Sam Francis, Nebraska	FB
1938	Cleveland	Corbett Davis, Indiana	FB
1939	Chicago Cardinals	Ki Aldrich, Texas Christian	C
1940	Chicago Cardinals	George Cafego, Tennessee	HB
1941	Chicago Bears	Tom Harmon, Michigan	HB
1942	Pittsburgh	Bill Dudley, Virginia	HB
1943	Detroit	Frank Sinkwich, Georgia	HB
1944	Boston	Angelo Bertelli, Notre Dame	QB
1945	Chicago Cardinals	Charley Trippi, Georgia	HB
1946	Boston	Frank Dancewicz, Notre Dame	QB
1947	Chicago Bears	Bob Fenimore, Oklahoma A&M	HB
1948	Washington	Harry Gilmer, Alabama	QB
1949	Philadelphia	Chuck Bednarik, Pennsylvania	C
1950	Detroit	Leon Hart, Notre Dame	E
1951	New York Giants	Kyle Rote, Southern Methodist	HB
1952	Los Angeles	Bill Wade, Vanderbilt	QB
1953	San Francisco	Harry Babcock, Georgia	E
1954	Cleveland	Bobby Garrett, Stanford	QB
1955	Baltimore	George Shaw, Oregon	QB
1956	Pittsburgh	Gary Glick, Colorado A&M	DB
1957	Green Bay	Paul Hornung, Notre Dame	HB
1958	Chicago Cardinals	King Hill, Rice	QB
1959	Green Bay	Randy Duncan, Iowa	QB
1960	Los Angeles	Billy Cannon, Louisiana State	RB
1961	Minnesota	Tommy Mason, Tulane	RB
	Buffalo (AFL)	Ken Rice, Auburn	G
1962	Washington	Ernie Davis, Syracuse	RB
	Oakland (AFL)	Roman Gabriel, North Carolina State	QB
1963	Los Angeles	Terry Baker, Oregon State	QB
	Kansas City (AFL)	Buck Buchanan, Grambling	DT
1964	San Francisco	Dave Parks, Texas Tech	E
	Boston (AFL)	Jack Concannon, Boston College	QB
1965	New York Giants	Tucker Frederickson, Auburn	RB
	Houston (AFL)	Lawrence Elkins, Baylor	E
1966	Atlanta	Tommy Nobis, Texas	LB
	Miami (AFL)	Jim Grabowski, Illinois	RB
1967	Baltimore	Bubba Smith, Michigan State	DT
1968	Minnesota	Ron Yary, Southern California	T
1969	Buffalo (AFL)	O. J. Simpson, Southern California	RB
1970	Pittsburgh	Terry Bradshaw, Louisiana Tech	QB
1971	New England	Jim Plunkett, Stanford	QB
1972	Buffalo	Walt Patulski, Notre Dame	DE
1973	Houston	John Matuszak, Tampa	DE
1974	Dallas	Ed Jones, Tennessee State	DE
1975	Atlanta	Steve Bartkowski, California	QB
1976	Tampa Bay	Lee Roy Selmon, Oklahoma	DE
1977	Tampa Bay	Ricky Bell, Southern California	RB
1978	Houston	Earl Campbell, Texas	RB
1979	Buffalo	Tom Cousineau, Ohio State	LB
1980	Detroit	Billy Sims, Oklahoma	RB
1981	New Orleans	George Rogers, South Carolina	RB
1982	New England	Kenneth Sims, Texas	DT
1983	Baltimore	John Elway, Stanford	QB
1984	New England	Irving Fryar, Nebraska	WR
1985	Buffalo	Bruce Smith, Virginia Tech	DE
1986	Tampa Bay	Bo Jackson, Auburn	RB
1987	Tampa Bay	Vinny Testaverde, Miami	QB
1988	Atlanta	Aundray Bruce, Auburn	LB
1989	Dallas	Troy Aikman, UCLA	QB
1990	Indianapolis	Jeff George, Illinois	QB
1991	Dallas	Russell Maryland, Miami	DT

From 1947 through 1958, the first selection in the draft was a bonus pick, awarded to the winner of a random draw. That club, in turn, forfeited its last-round draft choice. The winner of the bonus choice was eliminated from future draws. The system was abolished after 1958, by which time all clubs had received a bonus choice.

Members of the Pro Football Hall of Fame

Herb Adderley
Lance Alworth
Doug Atkins
Morris "Red" Badgro
Cliff Battles
Sammy Baugh
Chuck Bednarik
Bert Bell
Bobby Bell
Raymond Berry
Charles W. Bidwill, Sr.
Fred Biletnikoff
George Blanda
Mel Blount
Terry Bradshaw
Jim Brown
Paul Brown
Roosevelt Brown
Willie Brown
Buck Buchanan
Dick Butkus
Earl Campbell
Tony Canadeo
Joe Carr
Guy Chamberlin
Jack Christiansen
Earl "Dutch" Clark
George Connor
Jimmy Conzelman
Larry Csonka
Willie Davis
Len Dawson
Mike Ditka
Art Donovan
John "Paddy" Driscoll
Bill Dudley
Glen "Turk" Edwards
Weeb Ewbank
Tom Fears
Ray Flaherty

Len Ford
Dan Fortmann
Frank Gatski
Bill George
Frank Gifford
Sid Gillman
Otto Graham
Harold "Red" Grange
Joe Greene
Forrest Gregg
Bob Griese
Lou Groza
Joe Guyon
George Halas
Jack Ham
John Hannah
Franco Harris
Ed Healey
Mel Hein
Ted Hendricks
Wilbur "Pete" Henry
Arnie Herber
Bill Hewitt
Clarke Hinkle
Elroy "Crazylegs" Hirsch
Paul Hornung
Ken Houston
Cal Hubbard
Sam Huff
Lamar Hunt
Don Hutson
John Henry Johnson
David "Deacon" Jones
Stan Jones
Sonny Jurgensen
Walt Kiesling
Frank "Bruiser" Kinard
Earl "Curly" Lambeau
Jack Lambert
Tom Landry

Dick "Night Train" Lane
Jim Langer
Willie Lanier
Yale Lary
Dante Lavelli
Bobby Layne
Alphonse "Tuffy" Leemans
Bob Lilly
Vince Lombardi
Sid Luckman
Roy "Link" Lyman
Tim Mara
Gino Marchetti
George Preston Marshall
Ollie Matson
Don Maynard
George McAfee
Mike McCormack
Hugh McElhenny
Johnny "Blood" McNally
Mike Michalske
Wayne Millner
Bobby Mitchell
Ron Mix
Lenny Moore
Marion Motley
George Musso
Bronko Nagurski
Joe Namath
Earle "Greasy" Neale
Ernie Nevers
Ray Nitschke
Leo Nomellini
Merlin Olsen
Jim Otto
Steve Owen
Alan Page
Clarence "Ace" Parker
Jim Parker
Joe Perry

Pete Pihos
Hugh "Shorty" Ray
Dan Reeves
Jim Ringo
Andy Robustelli
Art Rooney
Pete Rozelle
Bob St. Clair
Gale Sayers
Joe Schmidt
Tex Schramm
Art Shell
O. J. Simpson
Bart Starr
Roger Staubach
Ernie Stautner
Jan Stenerud
Ken Strong
Joe Stydahar
Fran Tarkenton
Charley Taylor
Jim Taylor
Jim Thorpe
Y. A. Tittle
George Trafton
Charley Trippi
Emlen Tunnell
Clyde "Bulldog" Turner
Johnny Unitas
Gene Upshaw
Norm Van Brocklin
Steve Van Buren
Doak Walker
Paul Warfield
Bob Waterfield
Arnie Weinmeister
Bill Willis
Larry Wilson
Alex Wojciechowicz
Willie Wood

Don Shula

Miami Dolphins coach Don Shula's overall career total of 298 victories ranks fifth among all-time coaches in the history of professional and major college football (Division I). Only George Halas (Bears; 325 wins), Paul "Bear" Bryant (Maryland, Kentucky, Texas A&M, Alabama; 323), Amos Alonzo Stagg (Springfield, Chicago, Pacific; 314), and Glenn "Pop" Warner (Georgia, Cornell, Carlisle, Pittsburgh, Stanford, Temple; 313) have more victories than Shula, a former defensive back who began his coaching career as an assistant with the Detroit Lions in 1960. Shula was named head coach of the Baltimore Colts in 1963 and moved to the Dolphins in 1970.

Shula is the winningest active coach among NFL and Division I coaches. Penn State's Joe Paterno (229 victories), Florida State's Bobby Bowden (205), the Pittsburgh Steelers' Chuck Noll (202), and Iowa's Hayden Fry (179) round out the Top 5. Only Shula and Hall of Fame coaches Halas and Tom Landry have coached more than 400 regular-season NFL games. Shula has individually amassed more victories in his 28-year NFL career than have 14 of the current 28 NFL teams.

The Canadian Football League Grey Cup

Year	Results	Site	Attendance
1909	U of Toronto 26, Parkdale 6	Toronto	3,807
1910	U of Toronto 16, Hamilton Tigers 7	Hamilton	12,000
1911	U of Toronto 14, Toronto 7	Toronto	13,687
1912	Hamilton Alerts 11, Toronto 4	Hamilton	5,337
1913	Hamilton Tigers 44, Parkdale 2	Hamilton	2,100
1914	Toronto 14, U of Toronto 2	Toronto	10,500
1915	Hamilton Tigers 13, Toronto RAA 7	Toronto	2,808
1916-19	No game		
1920	U of Toronto 16, Toronto 3	Toronto	10,088
1921	Toronto 23, Edmonton 0	Toronto	9,558
1922	Queen's U 13, Edmonton 1	Kingston	4,700
1923	Queen's U 54, Regina 0	Toronto	8,629
1924	Queen's U 11, Balmy Beach 3	Toronto	5,978
1925	Ottawa Senators 24, Winnipeg 1	Ottawa	6,900
1926	Ottawa Senators 10, Toronto U 7	Toronto	8,276
1927	Balmy Beach 9, Hamilton Tigers 6	Toronto	13,676
1928	Hamilton Tigers 30, Regina 0	Hamilton	4,767
1929	Hamilton Tigers 14, Regina 3	Hamilton	1,906
1930	Balmy Beach 11, Regina 6	Toronto	3,914
1931	Montreal AAA 22, Regina 0	Montreal	5,112
1932	Hamilton Tigers 25, Regina 6	Hamilton	4,806
1933	Toronto 4, Sarnia 3	Sarnia	2,751
1934	Sarnia 20, Regina 12	Toronto	8,900
1935	Winnipeg 18, Hamilton Tigers 12	Hamilton	6,405
1936	Sarnia 26, Ottawa RR 20	Toronto	5,883
1937	Toronto 4, Winnipeg 3	Toronto	11,522
1938	Toronto 30, Winnipeg 7	Toronto	18,778
1939	Winnipeg 8, Ottawa 7	Ottawa	11,738
1940	Ottawa 12, Balmy Beach 5	Ottawa	1,700
1940	Ottawa 8, Balmy Beach 2	Toronto	4,998
1941	Winnipeg 18, Ottawa 16	Toronto	19,065
1942	Toronto RCAF 8, Winnipeg RCAF 5	Toronto	12,455
1943	Hamilton F Wild 23, Winnipeg RCAF 14	Toronto	16,423
1944	Montreal St H-D Navy 7, Hamilton F Wild 6	Hamilton	3,871
1945	Toronto 35, Winnipeg 0	Toronto	18,660
1946	Toronto 28, Winnipeg 6	Toronto	18,960
1947	Toronto 10, Winnipeg 9	Toronto	18,885
1948	Calgary 12, Ottawa 7	Toronto	20,013
1949	Montreal Als 28, Calgary 15	Toronto	20,087
1950	Toronto 13, Winnipeg 0	Toronto	27,101
1951	Ottawa 21, Saskatchewan 14	Toronto	27,341
1952	Toronto 21, Edmonton 11	Toronto	27,391
1953	Hamilton Ticats 12, Winnipeg 6	Toronto	27,313
1954	Edmonton 26, Montreal 25	Toronto	27,321
1955	Edmonton 34, Montreal 19	Vancouver	39,417
1956	Edmonton 50, Montreal 27	Toronto	27,425
1957	Hamilton 32, Winnipeg 7	Toronto	27,051
1958	Winnipeg 35, Hamilton 28	Vancouver	36,567
1959	Winnipeg 21, Hamilton 7	Toronto	33,133
1960	Ottawa 16, Edmonton 6	Vancouver	38,102
1961	Winnipeg 21, Hamilton 14	Toronto	32,651
1962	Winnipeg 28, Hamilton 27	Toronto	32,655
1963	Hamilton 21, British Columbia 10	Vancouver	36,545
1964	British Columbia 34, Hamilton 24	Toronto	32,655
1965	Hamilton 22, Winnipeg 16	Toronto	32,655
1966	Saskatchewan 29, Ottawa 14	Vancouver	36,553
1967	Hamilton 24, Saskatchewan 1	Ottawa	31,358
1968	Ottawa 24, Calgary 21	Toronto	32,655
1969	Ottawa 29, Saskatchewan 11	Montreal	33,172
1970	Montreal 23, Calgary 10	Toronto	32,669
1971	Calgary 14, Toronto 11	Vancouver	34,484
1972	Hamilton 13, Saskatchewan 10	Hamilton	33,993
1973	Ottawa 22, Edmonton 18	Toronto	36,653
1974	Montreal 20, Edmonton 7	Vancouver	34,450

The Canadian Football League Grey Cup (Cont.)

Year	Results	Site	Attendance
1975	Edmonton 9, Montreal 8	Calgary	32,454
1976	Ottawa 23, Saskatchewan 20	Toronto	53,467
1977	Montreal 41, Edmonton 6	Montreal	68,318
1978	Edmonton 20, Montreal 13	Toronto	54,695
1979	Edmonton 17, Montreal 9	Montreal	65,113
1980	Edmonton 48, Hamilton 10	Toronto	54,661
1981	Edmonton 26, Ottawa 23	Montreal	52,478
1982	Edmonton 32, Toronto 16	Toronto	54,741
1983	Toronto 18, British Columbia 17	Vancouver	59,345
1984	Winnipeg 47, Hamilton 17	Edmonton	60,081
1985	British Columbia 37, Hamilton 24	Montreal	56,723
1986	Hamilton 39, Edmonton 15	Vancouver	59,621
1987	Edmonton 38, Toronto 36	Vancouver	59,478
1988	Winnipeg 22, British Columbia 21	Ottawa	50,604
1989	Saskatchewan 43, Hamilton 40	Toronto	54,088
1990	Winnipeg 50, Edmonton 11	Vancouver	46,968

In 1909, Earl Grey, the Governor-General of Canada, donated a trophy for the Rugby Football Championship of Canada. The trophy, which subsequently became known as the Grey Cup, was originally open only to teams registered with the Canada Rugby Union. Since 1954, it has been awarded to the winner of the Canadian Football League's championship game.

AMERICAN FOOTBALL LEAGUE I

Year	Champion	Record
1926	Philadelphia Quakers	7-2

AMERICAN FOOTBALL LEAGUE II

Year	Champion	Record
1936	Boston Shamrocks	8-3
1937	LA Bulldogs	8-0

AMERICAN FOOTBALL LEAGUE III

Year	Champion	Record
1940	Columbus Bullies	8-1-1
1941	Columbus Bullies	5-1-2

ALL-AMERICAN FOOTBALL CONFERENCE

Year	Championship Game
1946	Cleveland 14, NY Yankees 9
1947	Cleveland 14, NY Yankees 3
1948	Cleveland 49, Buffalo 7
1949	Cleveland 21, San Francisco 7

WORLD FOOTBALL LEAGUE

Year	World Bowl Championship
1974	Birmingham 22, Florida 21
1975	Disbanded midseason

UNITED STATES FOOTBALL LEAGUE

Year	Championship Game
1983	Michigan 24, Philadelphia 22, Denver
1984	Philadelphia 23, Arizona 3, Tampa
1985	Baltimore 28, Oakland 24, East Rutherford, NJ

Rocketing Economy

The moment in February he announced he was leaving school a year early to enter the NFL draft, Raghib (Rocket) Ismail became the prospective No. 1 pick in an otherwise starless pool of college talent.

"There's nobody like him in football today," said Bills general manager Bill Polian. "He becomes a weapon no matter how he's used." Well, Ismail's army of agents—Team Rocket—took the words of Polian and other NFL executives to the bargaining table. Buoyed by a substantial offer from the Toronto Argonauts of the Canadian Football League, Team Rocket proceeded to price Ismail out of the NFL in the days leading up to the April 21 draft. They asked New England for $14.5 million over five years, and upped the ante to $16.8 million over five years when the Dallas Cowboys acquired the top pick from the Patriots two days before the draft.

In the end, no NFL team wanted Rocket at the price he was asking, and Toronto's offer became so good that there was no need to negotiate seriously with New England or Dallas. So 11 hours before the NFL draft began, Rocket launched his pro career with the Argos, signing the richest contract in football history: a four-year deal worth a guaranteed $18.2 million with incentives that could push the total to more than $26 million.

Just how good was Toronto owner Bruce McNall's offer? Well, one NFL source told Sports Illustrated that on the eve of the draft, Team Rocket faxed the Cowboys a contract ultimatum, asking for an average of $3.36 million a year guaranteed and calling it "non-negotiable." Team Rocket also asked for incentives that stunned the Cowboys. Among the 22 potential bonuses were $750,000 if the Cowboys reached the Super Bowl, and a dizzying demand of $250,000 if Ismail scored 10 touchdowns in a season, $500,000 if he scored 15 and $750,000 if he scored 20.

And now you know why the Rocket flew north.

College Football

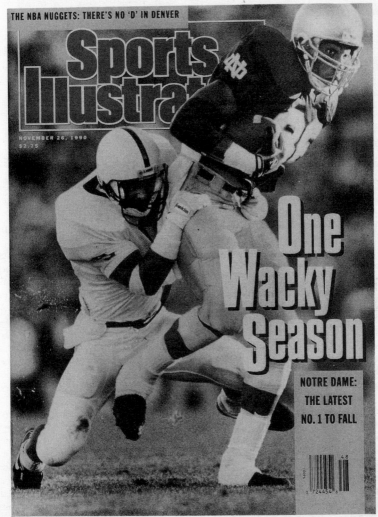

THE NBA NUGGETS: THERE'S NO 'D' IN DENVER

Sports Illustrated

NOVEMBER 26, 1990
$2.75

One Wacky Season

NOTRE DAME:
THE LATEST
NO. 1 TO FALL

HEINZ KLUETMEIER

A Split Decision

Colorado and Georgia Tech shared national title honors in a season of upsets | by AUSTIN MURPHY

ET 1990 BE REMEMBERED AS THE YEAR IN which the college football bowl selection process became so chaotic—and, ultimately, so unsatisfactory in determining a national champion—that the antiquated system finally succumbed to a much needed overhaul. Throughout the '90 season an eloquent case for a major revamping was made by the bowl representatives themselves.

This was not altogether intentional.

Unable to abide by the NCAA's simple rule—bowl bids will not be extended until the Saturday after the third Thursday of November—the bowls jumped the gun, cutting deals that yielded a batch of dull-as-dishwater matchups. Disgusted, the NCAA threatened to do away with the traditional selection system. In early January 1991, taking action to save their own skins, all 19 members of the Football Bowl Association adopted a plan to police themselves. To wit, any bowl found to have tendered an invitation in advance of the deadline would be fined $250,000.

Impressive, but it did not go far enough to satisfy many of the sport's most important schools, who came up with a plan of their own. To increase the likelihood of a national championship game—a New Year's Day matchup of the Nos. 1 and 2 teams—an alliance was struck among some decidedly odd bedfellows. After the '92 regular season, the highest-ranked team from among the newly constituted Big East (which will include powerhouse Miami among its eight football-playing schools), the ACC and Notre Dame will play the highest ranked team from among the Big Eight (in the Orange Bowl), the Southwest Conference (Cotton Bowl) or the Southeastern Conference (Sugar Bowl). However, if the Nos. 1 and 2 teams are both from the alliance of Notre Dame, the Big East and the ACC, then the Fiesta Bowl will provide a site for the championship game.

If this sounds complicated, it is nothing

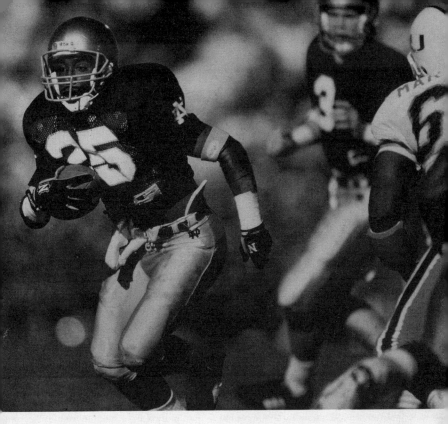

The Rocket almost danced off with a national championship, then danced off to the CFL.

compared to the chaos that surrounded the New Year's Day games following the '90 season. In the waning moments of the Orange Bowl, Colorado clung to a 10–9 lead over Notre Dame. If the Buffaloes could hang on they would clinch at least a share of the national championship. With 65 seconds left, the Buffaloes had a fourth-and-36 on their own 47-yard line, and Notre Dame's Raghib (Rocket) Ismail was back to receive the punt.

"I was sure they'd kick it out of bounds," recalled Ismail.

Ah, but this was the climax of the 1990 season, a campaign of such profound disarray that it could only end on an illogical note, which Colorado punter Tom Rouen provided by booming a beautiful 44-yard spiral

into Ismail's waiting arms. The replays would show six Buffaloes getting at least a hand on Ismail as he streaked 91 yards into the end zone for an apparent touchdown. It was not to be. The play was nullified by a clipping penalty. Football historians can call the play Ismail's 91-Yard Trot for Naught.

As it turned out, the clip was as painful to Georgia Tech as it was to the Irish. By dismantling Nebraska in the Citrus Bowl, 45–21, the Rambling Wreck had preserved its status as Division I-A's only undefeated team (Tech finished 11-0-1, the lone blight on its record a mystifying 13–13 tie with North Carolina). Had Notre Dame beaten Colorado, Georgia Tech would have won the national championship outright. Instead, the clip gave the Buffaloes the game, an 11-1-1 record and a half share of the title: The coaches' panel at UPI (which in 1991 moved to *USA Today*) crowned Tech No. 1 by a single point; Colorado got the nod from

In a Heisman showdown Miami's Erickson completed 28 of 52 passes for 299 yards but was outdone by. . . .

the media, who vote in the AP poll, despite a controversial 33–31 victory over Missouri, courtesy of game officials who allowed the Buffaloes a touchdown on a fifth down.

For the first time since 1978, when Alabama and Southern Cal shared the championship, a season ended on a split decision. It was an appropriate finale for a season during which 17 teams received first-place AP poll votes.

The confusion began long before the players reported for August two-a-days. In February 1990, Notre Dame announced that it would defect from the College Football Association, a consortium of 64 Division I-A programs. Notre Dame, the CFA's top TV drawing card, cut its own lucrative deal with NBC. In June 1990 the CFA learned that it would lose another prestigious school in 1993 when Penn State will become the

11th member of the Big Ten, which is not part of the CFA. Over the next few months Arkansas bolted the Southwest Conference for the fatter attendance and TV revenue of the SEC, South Carolina surrendered its independence and also joined the SEC, and Florida State hitched up with the ACC. Finally, Rutgers, Temple, Virginia Tech and West Virginia announced that they would join Pitt, Boston College, Syracuse and Miami in a football Big East that would be every bit as formidable as that league's basketball configuration. The word *superconference* had entered the lexicon of college athletics.

Yet, as conferences grew, there was also growing pressure on big-time programs to cut costs. At the NCAA convention in January 1990, scholarships were reduced from 100 to 95, which would eventually provide the added benefit of spreading the talent out. As it happened, parity arrived ahead of schedule.

On Sept. 8 defending national champion

Miami was visiting Brigham Young for a game billed as a duel of quarterbacking Heisman hopefuls, the Hurricanes' Craig Erickson versus BYU's Ty Detmer. While Erickson completed a respectable 28 of 52 passes for 299 yards, Detmer was an incandescent 38 of 54 for 406 yards and three touchdowns as the Cougars upset the favored top-ranked Hurricanes 28–21.

The timing of the win proved serendipitous for Detmer. The Miami game was one of only two that BYU would play on network television during the '90 season, and it gave Detmer's Heisman candidacy an immeasurable boost. His primary competition for the prize would come from Ismail, who enjoyed considerably more national TV exposure. In the end the sheer heft of Detmer's numbers overwhelmed the Heisman electors. Detmer outpointed Ismail by a surprisingly wide margin, 1,482 to 1,177.

By season's end Detmer had set 42 NCAA records (and tied five more), and he

BYU's Detmer, who connected on 38 of 54 passes for 406 yards and three TDs in the Cougars' 28–21 upset win.

still had a season of eligibility remaining. Detmer's decision to use that eligibility and return for his senior year set him apart from 29 other underclassmen, such as Ismail, who, due largely to the NFL's annual threat to impose a wage scale on rookies, chose to make themselves eligible for the draft.

Miami's loss to BYU thrust Notre Dame into the top spot. In addition to preparing his team for its opener with Michigan, Irish head coach Lou Holtz was busy issuing denials. He insisted that he had not turned a blind eye to anabolic steroid use on the squad, as charged by former Notre Dame lineman Steve Huffman in an August 1990 issue of *Sports Illustrated*. Holtz denied allegations that during his 1984–85 tenure as coach at Minnesota he had given an academic adviser $500 to pass along to a player.

Seemingly oblivious to these off-field tempests, the Irish led charmed lives for the first fortnight of their season. Thanks to a Joe Montana–like comeback engineered by sophomore quarterback Rick Mirer in his first collegiate start, Notre Dame erased a 24–14 deficit to beat Michigan 28–24. A week later Michigan State had the Irish on

the ropes in East Lansing. With the Spartans ahead late in the game, Mirer threw a dreadful pass that hit Michigan State cornerback Todd Murray squarely on the numbers, then bounced into the hands of the Irish's Adrian Jarrell at the State two-yard line. Notre Dame scored the winning touchdown moments later. In ensuing interviews, Holtz intimated that perhaps the Almighty was looking out for Notre Dame.

Then the Irish sailed into the safe harbor of their schedule—successive home games against Purdue, Stanford and Air Force—which, of course, in nonsensical '90, meant they were ripe for a fall. Few people, however, expected it to come at the hands of Stanford, which had never won in South Bend. Fewer still expected an upset when the Irish took a 24–7 lead with 6:30 to play in the first half.

Plucky Stanford never panicked. Coach Dennis Green refused to throw a long bomb to end the first half because he did not want to appear desperate. Calmly, gradually, the Cardinal got back in the game. It turned two of Notre Dame's three fumbled punt returns into touchdowns and hung on for dear life to win 36–31.

Having enjoyed, thanks to Stanford, a week as the nation's No. 1 team, Michigan became the country's best two-loss team when it dropped a heartbreaker to Michigan State, 28–27. When the Wolverines pulled to within one point of the Spartans with six seconds left to play, first-year Michigan coach Gary Moeller decided to go for the two-point conversion. The attempt failed (replays later showed blatant pass interference by State), but Moeller and his team got high marks for going down the way a top team should.

The Michigan loss vaulted Virginia, then 6–0, into the No. 1 spot in the polls for the first time in the school's 103-year football history. It also set up the Game of the Year: the Nov. 3 meeting between Virginia and Georgia Tech, those unbeaten powerhouses from, of all places, the ACC, where football is widely regarded as an elaborate excuse to tailgate. Scott Sisson's 37-yard field goal with seven seconds remaining gave Tech a 41–38 win and lanced the bubble of Virginia's dream season.

The Cavaliers would go on to lose two more games, to Maryland and Virginia Tech, as well as the services of quarterback

Terry Kirby's running helped Virginia vault to No. 1 for the first time ever.

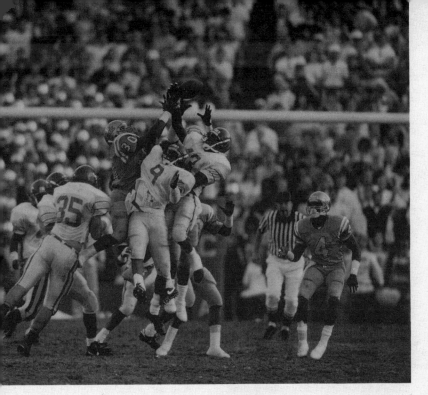

The battle for No. 1 was a free-for-all, just like the fight for this pass in USC's 45–42 win over UCLA.

Shawn Moore, who suffered a dislocated thumb in his right (throwing) hand against the Terrapins. Virginia's nosedive demonstrated (1) Moore's importance to the team and (2) that the bowl selection process had become a travesty.

Almost three weeks before the date on which bowl invitations could be officially extended, only one of the seven major New Year's Day games lacked an informal agreement. After its loss to Georgia Tech, Virginia agreed to play in the Sugar Bowl, a commitment that effectively stripped that game of any national significance. And having lined up Notre Dame to take on the Big Eight champ, Orange Bowl functionaries winced as the Irish took leave of the national championship picture, losing 24–21 in South Bend to Penn State.

The Fiesta Bowl, played in Tempe, Ariz., had a different sort of problem. Its cachet had evaporated after Arizonans voted not to enact a state holiday honoring Dr. Martin Luther King. Players from Virginia, Notre Dame and Penn State let it be known that they did not care to play in Arizona on New Year's Day. The Fiesta finally came up with willing participants in Louisville and Alabama. The Cardinals, in their sixth season under Howard Schnellenberger, were desperate to play in a major bowl; having finished the regular season with four losses, the Crimson Tide counted itself lucky to be playing anywhere on Jan. 1. In its first bowl appearance since 1977, the Cardinals routed Alabama 34–7. The loss was the Tide's second worst defeat in 43 bowl appearances.

The Sugar Bowl, stuck with Virginia against SEC champion Tennessee, could only watch in frustration as the team it should have lassoed, Miami, traveled to the Cotton Bowl, where the Hurricanes eviscerated Texas 46–3. The 10–1 Longhorns had

Miami's Russell Maryland won the Outland Trophy and was picked No. 1 in the NFL draft by the Dallas Cowboys.

held faint hopes for a national championship. Miami quickly snatched it away. The only suspense in the game was whether the Hurricanes would go over 200 yards in penalties. They did, finishing with 202, including two 15-yarders for "excessive celebration." Said Hurricanes wide receiver Randal (Thrill) Hill, "This week we got the message from coach [Dennis Erickson] to do 'whatever it takes' to win." So much for Miami's attempts to overhaul its renegade image.

On bowl day the upstart ACC fared well against the more established conferences: Clemson trashed the Big Ten's Illinois 30–0, and Georgia Tech dominated virtually every aspect of play in creaming the Nebraska Cornhuskers in the Citrus. Curiously, though they were the nation's lone undefeated team, the Yellow Jackets had entered the Citrus

two-point underdogs to 19th-ranked Nebraska. The odds-makers could not bring themselves to take Tech seriously.

In head coach Bobby Ross's first two seasons at Tech, 1987 and '88, the Yellow Jackets at one point lost 13 straight ACC games. After getting off to a dispiriting 0–3 start in '89, Tech turned the corner, winning seven of its last eight. On Oct. 28, 1989, Tech lost to Duke 30–19. They did not lose a game the rest of that season and marched through the '90 campaign with only the tie against North Carolina staining an otherwise perfect record.

Having humbled Nebraska, Tech players and coaches huddled in their Orlando hotel rooms to watch Notre Dame and Colorado in the Orange Bowl. When the officials brought back Ismail's electrifying gallop and the Buffaloes hung on to win, the national championship race was over—split between a team from a roundball conference and a team that had used a five-down series to secure one of its 11 wins. All in all, a perfect ending to an imperfect season.

Final Polls

Associated Press

		Record	Pts	Head Coach	SI Preseason Top 20
1	Colorado (39)	11-1-1	1475	Bill McCartney	7
2	Georgia Tech (20)	11-0-1	1441	Bobby Ross	
3	Miami (FL) (1)	10-2-0	1388	Dennis Erickson	1
4	Florida St	10-2-0	1303	Bobby Bowden	3
5	Washington	10-2-0	1246	Don James	18
6	Notre Dame	9-3-0	1179	Lou Holtz	2
7	Michigan	9-3-0	1025	Gary Moeller	5
8	Tennessee	9-2-2	993	Johnny Majors	6
9	Clemson	10-2-0	950	Ken Hatfield	16
10	Houston	10-1-0	940	John Jenkins	
11	Penn St	9-3-0	907	Joe Paterno	14
12	Texas	10-2-0	887	David McWilliams	
13	Florida	9-2-0	863	Steve Spurrier	
14	Louisville	10-1-1	775	Howard Schnellenberger	
15	Texas A&M	9-3-1	627	R. C. Slocum	
16	Michigan St	8-3-1	610	George Perles	17
17	Oklahoma	8-3-0	452	Gary Gibbs	
18	Iowa	8-4-0	370½	Hayden Fry	
19	Auburn	8-3-1	288	Pat Dye	4
20	Southern Cal	8-4-1	266	Larry Smith	8
21	Mississippi	9-3-0	253	Billy Brewer	
22	Brigham Young	10-3-0	246	LaVell Edwards	15
23	Virginia	8-4-0	188	George Welsh	19
24	Nebraska	9-3-0	185	Tom Osborne	9
25	Illinois	8-4-0	146½	John Mackovic	12

Note: As voted by panel of 60 sportswriters and broadcasters following bowl games (1st-place votes in parentheses).

United Press International

		Pts	Prev Rank			Pts	Prev Rank
1	Georgia Tech (30)	847	2	14	Michigan St	120	20
2	Colorado (27)	846	1	15	Virginia	65	23
3	Miami (FL) (2)	763	4	16	Iowa	57	15
4	Florida St	677	5	17	Brigham Young	41	9
5	Washington	664	7		Nebraska	41	13
6	Notre Dame	548	6	19	Auburn	39	
7	Tennessee	449	10	20	San Jose St	16	25
8	Michigan	426	12	21	Syracuse	12	
9	Clemson	420	11	22	Southern Cal	9	18
10	Penn St	301	8	23	Mississippi	7	14
11	Texas	268	3	24	Illinois	6	17
12	Louisville	245	16	25	Virginia Tech	5	
13	Texas A&M	204	19				

Note: As voted by panel of 50 Division I-A head coaches; 15 points for 1st, 14 for 2nd, etc.; 1st-place votes in parentheses. Teams on probation (ineligible for poll): Florida, Houston, Oklahoma, Oklahoma St, S Carolina.

Bowls and Playoffs

NCAA Division I-A Bowl Results

Date	Bowl	Result	Payout/Team ($)	Attendance
12-8-90	California	San Jose St 48, Central Michigan 24	275,000	25,431
12-15-90	Independence	Louisiana Tech 34, Maryland 34	600,000	48,325
12-25-90	Aloha	Syracuse 28, Arizona 0	600,000	14,185
12-27-90	Liberty	Air Force 23, Ohio St 11	1 million	13,144
12-28-90	All American	N Carolina St 31, Southern Miss 27	600,000	44,000
12-28-90	Blockbuster	Florida St 24, Penn St 17	1.6 million	74,021
12-29-90	Peach	Auburn 27, Indiana 23	900,000	38,912

NCAA Division I-A Bowl Results (*Cont.*)

Date	Bowl	Result	Payout/Team ($)	Attendance
12-29-90	Freedom	Colorado St 32, Oregon 31	600,000	41,450
12-29-90	Holiday	Texas A&M 65, Brigham Young 14	1.2 million	61,441
12-31-90	Hancock	Michigan St 17, Southern Cal 16	880,000	50,562
12-31-90	Copper	California 17, Wyoming 15	600,000	36,340
1-1-91	Gator	Michigan 35, Mississippi 3	1.2 million	68,927
1-1-91	Hall of Fame	Clemson 30, Illinois 0	1 million	63,154
1-1-91	Citrus	Georgia Tech 45, Nebraska 21	1.35 million	72,328
1-1-91	Cotton	Miami (FL) 46, Texas 3	3 million	73,521
1-1-91	Fiesta	Louisville 34, Alabama 7	2.5 million	69,098
1-1-91	Rose	Washington 46, Iowa 34	6 million	101,273
1-1-91	Orange	Colorado 10, Notre Dame 9	4.2 million	77,062
1-1-91	Sugar	Tennessee 23, Virginia 22	3.25 million	75,132

NCAA Division I-AA Championship Boxscore

Nevada	3	3	0	7 —13
Georgia Southern	7	7	6	16 —36

First Quarter
GS: Joe Ross 14 run (Mike Dowis kick), 11:34.
NV: FG Kevin McKelvie 37, 5:05.

Second Quarter
GS: Raymond Gross 8 run (Dowis kick), 2:38.
NV: FG McKelvie 44, 0:03.

Third Quarter
GS: Darryl Hopkins 3 run (kick failed).

Fourth Quarter
GS: Hopkins 18 run (Dowis kick), 14:52.

NV: Ross Ortega 3 pass from Chris Vargas (McKelvie kick), 6:22.
GS: FG Dowis 41, 1:06.
GS: Alex Mash 15 interception return (kick failed), 0:44.

	NV	Georgia Southern
First downs	21	20
Rushing yardage	56	323
Passing yardage	265	69
Return yardage	0	97
Passes (att-comp-int)	53-27-2	5-2-0
Punts (no.-avg)	6-38.8	2-37.0
Fumbles (no.-lost)	1-1	5-4
Penalties (no.-yards)	10-77	8-66

Small College Championship Summaries

NCAA DIVISION II

First round: Mississippi Col 70, Wofford 19; Jacksonville St 38, N Alabama 14; Indiana (PA) 48, Winston-Salem 0; Edinboro 38, Virginia Union 14; N Dakota St 17, Northern Colorado 7; Cal Poly-SLO 14, Cal St-Northridge 7; Pittsburg St 59, NE Missouri St 3; E Texas St 20, Grand Valley St 14.
Quarterfinals: Pittsburg St 60, E Texas St 28; Indiana (PA) 14, Edinboro 7; Mississippi Col 14, Jacksonville St 7; N Dakota St 47, Cal Poly-SLO 0.
Semifinals: Indiana (PA) 27, Mississippi Col 8; N Dakota St 39, Pittsburg St 29.
Championship: 12-8-90 Florence, AL

Indiana (PA)	3	8	0	0 —11
N Dakota St	7	7	30	7 —51

NCAA DIVISION III

First round: Hofstra 35, Cortland St 9; Trenton St 24, Ithaca 14; Washington & Jefferson 10, Ferrum 7; Lycoming 17, Carnegie Mellon 7; Dayton 24, Augustana (IL) 14; Allegheny 26, Mount Union 15; St Thomas (MN) 24, WI-Whitewater 23; Central (IA) 24, Redlands 7.
Quarterfinals: Hofstra 38, Trenton St 3; Lycoming 24, Washington & Jefferson 0; Allegheny 31, Dayton 23; Central (IA) 33, St Thomas (MN) 32.
Semifinals: Lycoming 20, Hofstra 10; Allegheny 24, Central (IA) 7.
Championship: 12-8-90 Bradenton, FL

Allegheny	0	0	7	7	7 —21
Lycoming	7	7	0	0	0 —14

NAIA DIVISION I PLAYOFFS

Quarterfinals: Carson-Newman 35, Southwest St 6; Central Arkansas 26, Northeastern St 14; Central St (OH) 48, Fort Hays St 10; Mesa St 37, Western New Mexico 30 (OT).
Semifinals: Central St (OH) 41, Carson-Newman 14; Mesa St 10, Central Arkansas 9.
Championship: 12-8-90 Grand Junction, CO

Central St (OH)	14	0	10	14 —38
Mesa St	0	7	0	9 —16

NAIA DIVISION II PLAYOFFS

First round: Westminster 47, Georgetown (KY) 13; Peru St 24, WI-La Crosse 3; Pacific Lutheran 37, Concordia 3; Baker 55, Bethany 7; Dickinson St 28, Chadron St 3; Central Washington 43, Greenville 13; William Jewell 26, Austin 23 (OT); Tarleton St 24, St Mary of the Plains 14.
Quarterfinals: Baker 56, William Jewell 29; Peru St 38, Dickinson St 34; Central Washington 24, Pacific Lutheran 6; Westminster 19, Tarleton St 17.
Semifinals: Westminster 24, Central Washington 17; Peru St 27, Baker 3.
Championship: 12-15-90 Omaha, NE

Peru St	0	7	0	10 —17
Westminster	0	0	7	0 — 7

Awards

Heisman Memorial Trophy

Player/School	Class	Pos	1st	2nd	3rd	Total
Ty Detmer, Brigham Young	Jr	QB	316	208	118	1482
Raghib Ismail, Notre Dame	Jr	FL	237	174	118	1177
Eric Bieniemy, Colorado	Sr	RB	114	153	150	798
Shawn Moore, Virginia	Sr	QB	46	96	135	465
David Klingler, Houston	Jr	QB	7	27	50	125
Herman Moore, Virginia	Jr	WR	6	14	22	68
Greg Lewis, Washington	Sr	RB	4	5	19	41
Craig Erickson, Miami (FL)	Sr	QB	0	6	19	31
Darren Lewis, Texas A&M	Sr	RB	0	9	13	31
Mike Mayweather, Army	Sr	RB	3	4	3	20

Note: Former Heisman winners and the media vote, with ballots allowing for 3 names (3 points for 1st, 2 for 2nd, 1 for 3rd).

Offensive Players of the Year

Maxwell Award (Player)............................Ty Detmer, Brigham Young, QB
Walter Camp Player of the Year (Back)....Raghib Ismail, Notre Dame, FL
Davey O'Brien Award (QB)........................Ty Detmer, Brigham Young
Doak Walker Award (RB).........................Greg Lewis, Washington

Other Awards

Rockne Award (Lineman) ....Chris Zorich, Notre Dame, NT
Vince Lombardi/Rotary Award (Lineman) ..Chris Zorich, Notre Dame, NT
Outland Trophy (Interior lineman)............Russell Maryland, Miami (FL), DT
Butkus Award (Linebacker).......................Alfred Williams, Colorado, LB
Jim Thorpe Award (Defensive back).........Darryl Lewis, Arizona, CB
Sporting News Player of the Year............Raghib Ismail, Notre Dame, FL
Walter Payton Award (Div I-AA Player) ....Walter Dean, Grambling, RB
Harlon Hill Trophy (Div II Player) ....Chris Simdorn, N Dakota St, QB

Coaches' Awards

Bobby Dodd Award...................................Bobby Ross, Georgia Tech
Walter Camp Award..................................Bobby Ross, Georgia Tech
Bear Bryant FWAA Award ....Bobby Ross, Georgia Tech
Eddie Robinson Award (Div I-AA)............Gene McDowell, Central Florida

AFCA Coaches of the Year

NCAA I-A ....Bobby Ross, Georgia Tech
NCAA I-AA..Tim Stowers, Georgia Southern
NCAA II and NAIA I ....Rocky Hager, N Dakota St
NCAA III and NAIA II ....Ken O'Keefe, Allegheny

Consensus All-America Football Team

OFFENSE

*Raghib Ismail, Notre Dame, Jr............Wide receiver
Herman Moore, Virginia, Jr..................Wide receiver
*Chris Smith, Brigham Young, Sr ....Tight end
*Antone Davis, Tennessee, Sr ....OL
*Joe Garten, Colorado, Sr.....................OL
*Ed King, Auburn, Jr...............................OL
Stacy Long, Clemson, Sr........................OL
John Flannery, Syracuse, Sr...................Center
Ty Detmer, Brigham Young, Jr..............Quarterback
*Eric Bieniemy, Colorado, Sr.................Running back
Darren Lewis, Texas A&M, Sr...............Running back
*Philip Doyle, Alabama, Sr ....PK

*Unanimous selection.

DEFENSE

*Russell Maryland, Miami (FL), Sr.......DL
*Chris Zorich, Notre Dame, Sr.............DL
Moe Gardner, Illinois, Sr......................DL
David Rocker, Auburn, Sr....................DL
*Alfred Williams, Colorado, Sr.............Linebacker
*Michael Stonebreaker,
Notre Dame, Sr ....Linebacker
Maurice Crum, Miami (FL), Sr.............Linebacker
*Tripp Welborne, Michigan, Sr ....Defensive back
*Darryl Lewis, Arizona, Sr ....Defensive back
*Ken Swilling, Georgia Tech, Jr...........Defensive back
Todd Lyght, Notre Dame, Sr ....Defensive back
Brian Greenfield, Pittsburgh, Sr...........Punter

Note: Made up of the selections from 5 different teams: Associated Press, United Press International, Football Writers Association, American Football Coaches Association and Walter Camp Foundation.

Division I-A

ATLANTIC COAST CONFERENCE

	Conference			Full Season				
	W	L	T	W	L	T	Pts	OP
Georgia Tech	6	0	1	10	0	1	334	165
Clemson	5	2	0	9	2	0	303	109
Virginia	5	2	0	8	3	0	442	204
Maryland	4	3	0	6	5	0	203	250
N Carolina	3	3	1	6	4	1	227	186
N Carolina St	3	4	0	6	5	0	267	162
Duke	1	6	0	4	7	0	240	295
Wake Forest	0	7	0	3	8	0	247	351

BIG EIGHT CONFERENCE

	Conference			Full Season				
	W	L	T	W	L	T	Pts	OP
Colorado	7	0	0	10	1	1	389	220
Nebraska	5	2	0	9	2	0	413	147
Oklahoma	5	2	0	8	3	0	401	174
Iowa St	2	4	1	4	6	1	270	307
Kansas	2	4	1	3	7	1	213	365
Kansas St	2	5	0	5	6	0	255	293
Missouri	2	5	0	4	7	0	278	360
Oklahoma St	2	5	0	4	7	0	233	309

BIG TEN CONFERENCE

	Conference			Full Season				
	W	L	T	W	L	T	Pts	OP
Iowa	6	2	0	8	3	0	393	242
Illinois	6	2	0	8	3	0	293	216
Michigan	6	2	0	8	3	0	354	195
Michigan St	6	2	0	7	3	1	295	207
Ohio St	5	2	1	7	3	1	338	197
Minnesota	5	3	0	6	5	0	224	281
Indiana	3	4	1	6	4	1	306	211
Northwestern	1	7	0	2	9	0	210	370
Purdue	1	7	0	2	9	0	177	337
Wisconsin	0	8	0	1	10	0	133	285

BIG WEST CONFERENCE

	Conference			Full Season				
	W	L	T	W	L	T	Pts	OP
San Jose St	7	0	0	8	2	1	387	204
Fresno St	5	1	1	8	2	1	346	230
Utah St	5	1	1	5	5	1	287	310
Long Beach St	4	3	0	6	5	0	249	331
NV-Las Vegas	3	4	0	4	7	0	239	324
Pacific	2	5	0	4	7	0	353	411
New Mexico St	1	6	0	1	10	0	200	422
Cal St-Fullerton	0	7	0	1	11	0	223	485

MID-AMERICAN CONFERENCE

	Conference			Full Season				
	W	L	T	W	L	T	Pts	OP
Toledo	7	1	0	9	2	0	284	178
Central Michigan	7	1	0	8	2	1	259	98
Ball St	5	3	0	7	4	0	204	121
Western Michigan	5	3	0	7	4	0	249	235
Miami (OH)	4	3	1	5	5	1	200	225
Bowling Green	2	4	2	3	5	2	138	163
Eastern Michigan	2	6	0	2	9	0	179	301
Kent St	2	6	0	2	9	0	177	328
Ohio	0	7	0	1	9	1	162	342

Division I-A (*Cont.*)

PACIFIC-10 CONFERENCE

	Conference			Full Season				
	W	L	T	W	L	T	Pts	OP
Washington	7	1	0	9	2	0	394	150
Southern Cal	5	2	1	8	3	1	332	257
Oregon	4	3	0	8	3	0	310	189
California	4	3	1	6	4	1	308	326
Arizona	5	4	0	7	4	0	267	283
Stanford	4	4	0	5	6	0	263	284
UCLA	4	4	0	5	6	0	305	332
Arizona St	2	5	0	4	7	0	272	294
Washington St	2	6	0	3	8	0	286	381
Oregon St	1	6	0	1	10	0	152	371

SOUTHEASTERN CONFERENCE

	Conference			Full Season				
	W	L	T	W	L	T	Pts	OP
Florida*	6	1	0	9	2	0	387	171
Tennessee	5	1	1	8	2	2	442	198
Mississippi	5	2	0	9	2	0	257	191
Alabama	5	2	0	7	4	0	253	127
Auburn	4	2	1	7	3	1	256	193
Kentucky	3	4	0	4	7	0	228	316
Louisiana St	2	5	0	5	6	0	183	238
Georgia	2	5	0	4	7	0	185	293
Mississippi St	1	6	0	5	6	0	207	236
Vanderbilt	1	6	0	1	10	0	227	457

*Florida not eligible for conference title.

SOUTHWEST ATHLETIC CONFERENCE

	Conference			Full Season				
	W	L	T	W	L	T	Pts	OP
Texas	8	0	0	10	1	0	355	181
Houston*	7	1	0	10	1	0	511	303
Texas A&M	5	2	1	8	3	1	400	218
Baylor	5	2	1	6	4	1	225	202
Rice	3	5	0	5	6	0	256	258
Texas Christian	3	5	0	5	6	0	292	353
Texas Tech	3	5	0	4	7	0	322	356
Arkansas	1	7	0	3	8	0	263	360
Southern Meth	0	8	0	1	10	0	197	426

*Houston not eligible for conference title.

WESTERN ATHLETIC CONFERENCE

	Conference			Full Season				
	W	L	T	W	L	T	Pts	OP
Brigham Young	7	1	0	10	2	0	510	285
Colorado St	6	1	0	8	4	0	340	271
San Diego St	5	2	0	6	5	0	459	386
Wyoming	5	3	0	9	3	0	312	280
Hawaii	4	4	0	7	5	0	374	257
Air Force	3	4	0	6	5	0	239	272
Utah	2	6	0	4	7	0	214	342
New Mexico	1	6	0	2	10	0	279	400
UTEP	1	7	0	3	8	0	191	342

Division I-A (*Cont.*)

INDEPENDENTS

	Full Season					
	W	L	T	Pct	Pts	OP
Louisville	9	1	1	.864	311	142
Florida St	9	2	0	.818	435	189
Miami (FL)	9	2	0	.818	401	181
Notre Dame	9	2	0	.818	350	249
Penn St	9	2	0	.818	280	155
Louisiana Tech	8	3	0	.727	331	185
Southern Miss	8	3	0	.727	193	141
Temple	7	4	0	.636	261	269
Syracuse	6	4	2	.583	313	213
Army	6	5	0	.545	295	264
Northern Illinois	6	5	0	.545	333	260
S Carolina	6	5	0	.545	282	237
Virginia Tech	6	5	0	.545	245	227
E Carolina	5	6	0	.455	254	267
Navy	5	6	0	.455	209	294
Southwestern Louisiana	5	6	0	.455	197	242
Memphis St	4	6	1	.409	212	233
Boston Col	4	7	0	.364	190	288
Tulane	4	7	0	.364	237	253
W Virginia	4	7	0	.364	217	238
Akron	3	7	1	.318	233	263
Pittsburgh	3	7	1	.318	240	293
Rutgers	3	8	0	.273	173	302
Tulsa	3	8	0	.273	183	281
Cincinnati	1	10	0	.091	172	460

Division I-AA

BIG SKY CONFERENCE

	Conference			Full Season				
	W	L	T	W	L	T	Pts	OP
Nevada	7	1	0	10	1	0	356	184
Boise St	6	2	0	8	3	0	290	183
Idaho	6	2	0	8	3	0	409	279
Montana	4	4	0	7	4	0	372	275
Eastern Washington	3	5	0	5	6	0	300	360
Northern Arizona	3	5	0	5	6	0	290	417
Weber St	3	5	0	5	6	0	309	307
Montana St	3	5	0	4	7	0	268	304
Idaho St	1	7	0	3	8	0	265	359

GATEWAY COLLEGIATE ATHLETIC CONFERENCE

	Conference			Full Season				
	W	L	T	W	L	T	Pts	OP
Northern Iowa	5	1	0	8	3	0	331	189
SW Missouri St	5	1	0	9	2	0	378	178
Eastern Illinois	3	3	0	5	6	0	180	219
Illinois St	3	3	0	5	6	0	198	189
Western Illinois	3	3	0	3	8	0	194	314
Indiana St	1	5	0	4	7	0	263	289
Southern Illinois	1	5	0	2	9	0	174	313

THEY SAID IT

The late Bear Bryant in 1973 on the role of athletics on campus: "It's kind of hard to rally around a math class."

Division I-AA (*Cont.*)

IVY GROUP

	Conference			Full Season				
	W	L	T	W	L	T	Pts	OP
Dartmouth	6	1	0	7	2	1	211	121
Cornell	6	1	0	7	3	0	263	212
Yale	5	2	0	6	4	0	233	223
Harvard	3	4	0	5	5	0	199	206
Pennsylvania	3	4	0	3	7	0	155	197
Princeton	2	5	0	3	7	0	168	224
Brown	2	5	0	2	8	0	160	299
Columbia	1	6	0	1	9	0	115	292

MID-EASTERN ATHLETIC CONFERENCE

	Conference			Full Season				
	W	L	T	W	L	T	Pts	OP
Florida A&M	6	0	0	7	4	0	349	289
N Carolina A&T	5	1	0	9	2	0	311	175
Delaware St	4	2	0	7	3	0	330	257
Howard	3	3	0	6	5	0	261	205
S Carolina St	2	4	0	4	6	0	191	176
Bethune-Cookman	1	5	0	4	7	0	211	312
Morgan St	0	6	0	1	10	0	81	412

OHIO VALLEY CONFERENCE

	Conference			Full Season				
	W	L	T	W	L	T	Pts	OP
Eastern Kentucky	5	1	0	10	1	0	352	155
Middle Tennessee St	5	1	0	10	1	0	384	101
Tennessee St	3	2	0	7	4	0	268	261
Morehead St	3	2	0	5	6	0	268	223
Tennessee Tech	3	3	0	6	5	0	242	256
Murray St	1	5	0	2	9	0	95	429
Austin Peay	0	6	0	0	11	0	108	339

PATRIOT LEAGUE

	Conference			Full Season				
	W	L	T	W	L	T	Pts	OP
Holy Cross	5	0	0	9	1	1	339	106
Bucknell	3	2	0	7	4	0	337	278
Colgate	3	2	0	7	4	0	296	248
Lehigh	3	2	0	7	4	0	329	211
Lafayette	1	4	0	4	7	0	223	318
Fordham	0	5	0	1	9	0	127	342

Note: Formerly Colonial League.

SOUTHERN CONFERENCE

	Conference			Full Season				
	W	L	T	W	L	T	Pts	OP
Furman	6	1	0	8	3	0	345	178
Appalachian St	5	2	0	6	5	0	171	266
TN-Chattanooga	4	2	0	6	5	0	227	243
Citadel	4	3	0	7	4	0	266	192
Marshall	4	3	0	6	5	0	310	162
Western Carolina	2	5	0	3	8	0	169	362
Virginia Military	1	5	0	4	7	0	251	346
East Tennessee St	1	6	0	2	9	0	240	330

Division I-AA (*Cont.*)

SOUTHLAND CONFERENCE

	Conference			Full Season				
	W	L	T	W	L	T	Pts	OP
NE Louisiana	5	1	0	7	4	0	194	191
McNeese St	4	2	0	5	6	0	183	265
SW Texas St	3	3	0	6	5	0	268	220
NW Louisiana	3	3	0	5	6	0	203	203
Sam Houston St	3	3	0	4	7	0	163	187
N Texas	2	4	0	6	5	0	223	211
SF Austin St	1	5	0	2	9	0	190	252

SOUTHWESTERN ATHLETIC CONFERENCE

	Conference			Full Season				
	W	L	T	W	L	T	Pts	OP
Jackson St	5	1	0	8	3	0	418	234
Alabama St	4	2	0	8	2	1	384	177
Grambling	3	3	0	8	3	0	364	227
Mississippi Valley	3	3	0	5	6	0	237	327
Southern	2	4	0	4	7	0	231	277
Texas Southern	2	4	0	4	7	0	223	363
Alcorn St	2	4	0	2	7	0	128	268

YANKEE CONFERENCE

	Conference			Full Season				
	W	L	T	W	L	T	Pts	OP
Massachusetts	7	1	0	8	1	1	224	137
New Hampshire	5	3	0	7	3	1	301	186
Connecticut	5	3	0	6	5	0	308	281
Delaware	5	3	0	6	5	0	216	233
Villanova	5	3	0	6	5	0	204	161
Boston U	4	4	0	5	6	0	246	273
Rhode Island	2	6	0	5	6	0	245	193
Maine	2	6	0	3	8	0	200	281
Richmond	1	7	0	1	10	0	133	312

INDEPENDENTS

	Full Season					
	W	L	T	Pct	Pts	OP
Youngstown St	11	0	0	1.000	323	126
William & Mary	9	2	0	.818	391	270
Central Florida	8	3	0	.727	365	181
Georgia Southern	8	3	0	.727	297	225
Liberty	7	4	0	.636	296	236
Samford	6	4	1	.591	268	233
James Madison	5	6	0	.455	228	191
Nicholls St	4	7	0	.364	272	287
Arkansas St	3	7	1	.318	200	313
Western Kentucky	2	8	0	.200	159	234
Towson St	2	9	0	.182	163	336
Northeastern	1	10	0	.091	144	342

THEY SAID IT

LaVell Edwards, BYU football coach, on whether he prefers speed or quickness in his receivers: "I'd like to have them both, but if they had both, they'd be at Southern California."

1990 NCAA Individual Leaders

Division I-A

SCORING

	Class	GP	TD	XP	FG	Pts	Pts/Game
Stacey Robinson, Northern Illinois	Sr	11	19	6	0	120	10.91
Aaron Craver, Fresno St	Sr	10	18	0	0	108	10.80
Roman Anderson, Houston	Jr	11	0	58	19	115	10.45
Amp Lee, Florida St.	So	11	18	0	0	108	9.82
Andy Trakas, San Diego St	So	11	0	53	18	107	9.73
Darren Lewis, Texas A&M	Sr	12	19	0	0	114	9.50
Eric Bieniemy, Colorado	Sr	11	17	0	0	102	9.27
Carlos Huerta, Miami (FL)	Jr	11	0	50	17	101	9.18
Michale Pollak, Texas	Sr	11	0	39	20	99	9.00
Greg Burke, Tennessee	Sr	12	0	50	19	107	8.92

FIELD GOALS

	Class	GP	FGA	FG	Pct	FG/Game
Philip Doyle, Alabama	Sr	11	29	24	82.8	2.18
Clint Gwaltney, N Carolina	Jr	11	27	21	77.8	1.91
Michale Pollak, Texas	Sr	11	26	20	76.9	1.82
Chris Gardocki, Clemson	Jr	11	24	19	79.2	1.73
John Kasay, Georgia	Sr	11	24	19	79.2	1.73
Roman Anderson, Houston	Jr	11	25	19	76.0	1.73
Bob Wright, Temple	Sr	11	25	19	76.0	1.73
Jeff Shudak, Iowa St	Sr	11	27	19	70.4	1.73
Andy Trakas, San Diego St	So	11	26	18	69.2	1.64
Rusty Hanna, Toledo	So	11	29	18	62.1	1.64

TOTAL OFFENSE

			Rushing		Passing		Total Offense			
	Class	GP	Car	Net	Att	Yds	Yds	Yds/Play	TDR*	Yds/Game
David Klingler, Houston	Jr	11	61	81	643	5140	5221	7.42	55	474.64
Ty Detmer, Brigham Young	Jr	12	73	−166	562	5188	5022	7.91	45	418.50
Troy Kopp, Pacific	So	9	57	−35	428	3311	3276	6.75	32	364.00
Dan McGwire, San Diego St	Sr	11	35	−169	449	3833	3664	7.57	28	333.09
Craig Erickson, Miami (FL)	Sr	11	46	26	393	3363	3389	7.72	25	308.09
Shane Matthews, Florida	So	11	72	−27	378	2952	2925	6.50	27	265.91
Ralph Martini, San Jose St	Sr	11	51	−5	362	2928	2923	7.08	25	265.73
Tommy Maddox, UCLA	Fr	10	90	148	327	2682	2830	6.79	19	257.27
Shawn Moore, Virginia	Sr	10	94	306	241	2262	2568	7.67	29	256.80
Mark Barsotti, Fresno St	Jr	11	61	248	346	2534	2782	6.84	14	252.91

*Touchdowns responsible for.

RUSHING

	Class	GP	Car	Yds	Avg	TD	Yds/Game
Gerald Hudson, Oklahoma St	Sr	11	279	1642	5.9	10	149.27
Eric Bieniemy, Colorado	Sr	11	288	1628	5.7	17	148.00
Darren Lewis, Texas A&M	Sr	12	291	1691	5.8	18	140.92
Greg Lewis, Washington	Sr	10	229	1279	5.6	8	127.90
Tico Duckett, Michigan St	So	11	249	1376	5.5	10	125.09
Roger Grant, Utah St	Jr	11	266	1370	5.2	8	124.55
Mike Mayweather, Army	Sr	11	274	1338	4.9	10	121.64
Trevor Cobb, Rice	So	11	283	1325	4.7	10	120.45
Sheldon Canley, San Jose St	Sr	11	296	1248	4.2	12	113.45
Stacey Robinson, Northern Illinois	Sr	11	193	1238	6.4	19	112.55

Acknowledging the Crowd

Back in 1986 when LSU field goal kicker Ronnie Lewis was jeered by the crowd during the Tigers' loss to Miami of Ohio in Baton Rouge, Lewis responded with an obscene gesture—actually he delivered it with both hands—as he ran off the field. Later, then-LSU coach Bill Arnsparger denied Lewis had done it, but a photograph in the Baton Rouge State-Times clearly showed Lewis signing off with vigor. One observer, trying to be helpful, suggested that Lewis might be signalling, "We're No. 11."

Division I-A (*Cont.*)

PASSING EFFICIENCY

	Class	GP	Att	Comp	Pct Comp	Yds	Yds/Att	TD	Int	Rating Pts
Shawn Moore, Virginia	Sr	10	241	144	59.75	2262	9.39	21	8	160.7
Ty Detmer, Brigham Young	Jr	12	562	361	64.23	5188	9.23	41	28	155.9
Casey Weldon, Florida St	Jr	11	182	112	61.54	1600	8.79	12	4	152.7
Dan McGwire, San Diego St	Sr	11	449	270	60.13	3833	8.54	27	7	148.6
David Klingler, Houston	Jr	11	643	374	58.16	5140	7.99	54	20	146.8
Craig Erickson, Miami (FL)	Sr	11	393	225	57.25	3363	8.56	22	7	144.0
Shane Matthews, Florida	So	11	378	229	60.58	2952	7.81	23	12	139.9
Garrett Gabriel, Hawaii	Sr	12	320	165	51.56	2752	8.60	25	16	139.6
Troy Kopp, Pacific	So	9	428	243	56.78	3311	7.74	31	14	139.1
Rick Mirer, Notre Dame	So	11	200	110	55.00	1824	9.12	8	6	138.8

Note: Minimum 15 attempts per game.

RECEPTIONS PER GAME

	Class	GP	No.	Yds	TD	R/Game
Manny Hazard, Houston	Sr	10	78	946	9	7.80
Bobby Slaughter, Louisiana Tech	Sr	11	78	994	5	7.09
Eric Morgan, New Mexico	Sr	12	80	1043	6	6.67
Andy Boyce, Brigham Young	Sr	12	79	1241	13	6.58
Patrick Rowe, San Diego St	Jr	11	71	1392	8	6.45
Frank Wycheck, Maryland	Fr	9	58	509	1	6.44
Dennis Arey, San Diego St	Sr	11	68	1118	10	6.18
Keenan McCardell, NV-Las Vegas	Sr	11	68	1046	8	6.18

RECEIVING YARDS PER GAME

	Class	GP	No.	Yds	TD	Yds/Game
Patrick Rowe, San Diego St	Jr	11	71	1392	8	126.55
Aaron Turner, Pacific	So	11	66	1264	11	114.91
Herman Moore, Virginia	Jr	11	54	1190	13	108.18
Andy Boyce, Brigham Young	Sr	12	79	1241	13	103.42
Dennis Arey, San Diego St	Sr	11	68	1118	10	101.64

ALL-PURPOSE RUNNERS

	Class	GP	Rush	Rec	PR	KOR	Yds	Yds/Game
Glyn Milburn, Stanford	So	11	729	632	267	594	2222	202.00
Sheldon Canley, San Jose St	Sr	11	1248	386	5	574	2213	201.18
Chuck Weatherspoon, Houston	Sr	11	1097	560	196	185	2038	185.27
Eric Bieniemy, Colorado	Sr	11	1628	159	0	31	1818	165.27
Jeff Sydner, Hawaii	So	12	390	820	483	265	1958	163.17

INTERCEPTIONS

	Class	GP	No.	Yds	TD	Int/Game
Jerry Parks, Houston	Jr	11	8	124	1	.73
Will White, Florida	So	10	7	116	0	.70
Darryl Lewis, Arizona	Sr	11	7	192	2	.64
Shawn Vincent, Akron	Sr	11	7	191	0	.64
Ron Carpenter, Miami (OH)	Jr	11	7	164	1	.64
Darren Perry, Penn St	Sr	11	7	125	1	.64
Mike Welch, Baylor	Sr	11	7	80	0	.64
Ozzie Jackson, Akron	Sr	11	7	50	0	.64

PUNTING

	Class	No.	Avg
Cris Shale, Bowling Green	Sr	66	46.77
Brian Greenfield, Pittsburgh	Sr	50	45.60
Jason Hanson, Washington St	Jr	59	45.41
Chris Gardocki, Clemson	Jr	53	44.34
Greg Hertzog, W Virginia	Sr	62	43.50

Note: Minimum of 3.6 per game.

PUNT RETURNS

	Class	No.	Yds	TD	Avg
Dave McCloughan, Colorado	Sr	32	524	2	16.38
Beno Bryant, Washington	So	36	560	3	15.56
Jeff Graham, Ohio St	Sr	22	327	2	14.86
Tony James, Mississippi St	So	23	341	2	14.83
Tripp Welborne, Michigan	Sr	31	455	0	14.68

Note: Minimum 1.2 per game.

Division I-A (*Cont.*)

KICKOFF RETURNS

	Class	No.	Yds	TD	Avg
Dale Carter, Tennessee	Jr	17	507	1	29.82
Desmond Howard, Michigan	Jr	16	472	1	29.50
Tyrone Hughes, Nebraska	So	18	523	1	29.06
Ray Washington, New Mexico St	Jr	22	638	1	29.00
Randy Jones, Duke	Sr	24	678	2	28.25

Note: Minimum of 1.2 per game.

Division I-A Single-Game Highs

RUSHING AND PASSING

Rushing and passing plays: 94*—Matt Vogler, Texas Christian, Nov 3 (vs Houston).

Rushing and passing yards: 732†—David Klingler, Houston, Dec 2 (vs Arizona St).

Rushing plays: 47—Jason Davis, Louisiana Tech, Sep 29 (vs Southwestern Louisiana).

Net rushing yards: 312—Mark Brus, Tulsa, Oct 27 (vs New Mexico St).

Passes attempted: 79‡—Matt Vogler, Texas Christian, Nov 3 (vs Houston).

Passes completed: 48#—David Klingler, Houston, Oct 20 (vs Southern Meth).

Passing yards: 716**—David Klingler, Houston, Dec 2 (vs Arizona St).

*NCAA I-A record. Old record: 79—Dave Telford, Fresno St, 1987, and Donny Harrison, Ohio, 1983.

†NCAA I-A record. Old record: 696—Matt Vogler, Texas Christian, 1990.

‡NCAA I-A record. Old record: 76—David Klingler, Houston, 1990.

#NCAA I-A record. Old record: 45—Sandy Schwab, Northwestern, 1982.

**NCAA I-A record. Old record: 690—Matt Vogler, Texas Christian, 1990.

RECEIVING AND RETURNS

Passes caught: 18—Richard Woodley, Texas Christian, Nov 10 (vs Texas Tech).

Receiving yards: 265—Aaron Turner, Pacific, Oct 20 (vs New Mexico St).

Punt return yards: 151—Paul Agema, Western Michigan, Oct 6 (vs Akron).

Kickoff return yards: 237—Dwayne Owens, Oregon St, Nov 10 (vs Southern Cal).

Division I-AA

SCORING

	Class	GP	TD	XP	FG	Pts	Pts/Game
Barry Bourassa, New Hampshire	So	9	16	0	0	96	10.67
Erick Torain, Lehigh	Sr	11	19	2	0	116	10.55
Brian Mitchell, Northern Iowa	Jr	11	0	31	26	109	9.91
Brady Jones, Samford	Sr	11	18	0	0	108	9.82
Walter Dean, Grambling	Sr	11	17	0	0	102	9.27

FIELD GOALS

	Class	GP	FGA	FG	Pct	FG/Game
Brian Mitchell, Northern Iowa	Jr	11	27	26	96.3	2.36
Kevin McKelvie, Nevada	Sr	11	24	21	87.5	1.91
Darren Goodman, Idaho St	Jr	11	28	20	71.4	1.82
Eric Roberts, McNeese St	Jr	11	25	19	76.0	1.73
Matt Crews, Middle Tennessee St	Jr	11	24	17	70.8	1.55
Mark Klein, Sam Houston St	Jr	11	26	17	65.4	1.55

Division I-AA (*Cont.*)

TOTAL OFFENSE

	Class	GP	Rushing				Passing		Total Offense			
			Car	Gain	Loss	Net	Att	Yds	Yds	Yds/Play	TDR*	Yds/Game
Jamie Martin, Weber St	So	11	80	282	269	13	428	3700	3713	7.31	25	337.55
Dave Goodwin, Colgate	Sr	11	60	183	256	–73	453	3352	3279	6.39	23	298.09
Glenn Kempa, Lehigh	Jr	10	28	35	94	–59	402	2990	2931	6.82	19	293.10
Grady Bennett, Montana	Sr	11	84	415	213	202	401	3005	3207	6.61	28	291.55
Stan Greene, Boston U	Sr	11	108	367	334	33	459	3135	3168	5.59	21	288.00

*Touchdowns responsible for.

RUSHING

	Class	GP	Car	Yds	Avg	TD	Yds/Game
Walter Dean, Grambling	Sr	11	221	1401	6.3	15	127.36
Devon Pearce, Idaho	Jr	11	267	1393	5.2	15	126.64
Derrick Franklin, Indiana St	Jr	11	284	1301	4.6	6	118.27
Reggie Rivers, SW Texas St	Sr	10	215	1145	5.3	5	114.50
Joe Campbell, Middle Tennessee St	Jr	10	151	1136	7.5	13	113.60

PASSING EFFICIENCY

	Class	GP	Att	Comp	Yds	Pct Comp	Yds/Att	TD	Int	Rating Pts
Connell Maynor, N Carolina A&T	Jr	11	191	123	1699	64.4	8.90	16	10	156.3
Jay Johnson, Northern Iowa	So	11	275	150	2768	54.6	10.07	15	7	152.0
Matt Degennaro, Connecticut	Sr	10	257	160	1977	62.3	7.69	21	8	147.6
Ricky Jones, Alabama St	Jr	11	249	126	2213	50.6	8.89	21	10	145.1
Tom Ciaccio, Holy Cross	Jr	11	324	196	2611	60.5	8.06	24	14	144.0

Note: Minimum 15 attempts per game.

RECEPTIONS PER GAME

	Class	GP	No.	Yds	TD	R/Game
Kasey Dunn, Idaho	Jr	11	88	1164	7	8.00
Mike Trevathan, Montana	Sr	10	71	1006	7	7.10
Mark Didio, Connecticut	Jr	11	78	1153	10	7.09
Rodd Torbert, Brown	Jr	10	67	908	6	6.70
Gary Comstock, Columbia	Sr	10	67	811	3	6.70

RECEIVING YARDS PER GAME

	Class	GP	No.	Yds	TD	Yds/Game
Kasey Dunn, Idaho	Jr	11	88	1164	7	105.82
David Jones, Delaware St	Sr	10	53	1049	8	104.90
Mark Didio, Connecticut	Jr	11	78	1153	10	104.82
Horace Hamm, Lehigh	Jr	11	61	1148	5	104.36
George Delaney, Colgate	Jr	11	67	1146	7	104.18

ALL-PURPOSE RUNNERS

	Class	GP	Rush	Rec	PR	KOR	Yds	Yds/Game
Barry Bourassa, New Hampshire	So	9	957	276	133	368	1734	192.67
John McNiff, Cornell	Jr	10	998	163	0	455	1616	161.60
Reggie Rivers, SW Texas St	Sr	10	1145	89	0	374	1608	160.80
Treamelle Taylor, Nevada	Sr	11	0	893	388	446	1727	157.00
Jamie Jones, Eastern Illinois	Jr	11	1055	270	0	282	1607	146.09
Cisco Richard, NE Louisiana	Sr	11	548	617	179	263	1607	146.09

INTERCEPTIONS

	Class	GP	No.	Yds	TD	Int/Game
Aeneas Williams, Southern	Sr	11	11	173	1	1.00
Claude Pettaway, Maine	Sr	11	11	161	1	1.00
Cedric Walker, SF Austin St	Fr	11	10	11	0	.91
Ricky Hill, S Carolina St	Jr	10	9	166	0	.90
Robert Turner, Jackson St	Fr	11	9	212	4	.82
William Carroll, Florida A&M	So	11	9	134	0	.82

Division I-AA (*Cont.*)

PUNTING

	Class	No.	Avg
Colin Godfrey, Tennessee St	So	57	45.86
Paul Alsbury, SW Texas St	Sr	39	44.85
Pumpy Tudors, TN-Chattanooga	Jr	63	44.60
Duffy Daugherty, Idaho St	Sr	57	42.35
Chad McCarty, NE Louisiana	So	71	41.49

Note: Minimum 3.6 per game.

Division II

SCORING

	Class	GP	TD	XP	FG	Pts	Pts/Game
Ernest Priester, Edinboro	Sr	8	16	0	0	96	12.0
Eric Lynch, Grand Valley St	Jr	11	21	2	0	128	11.6
Shawn Graves, Wofford	So	9	17	2	0	104	11.6
Chris Simdorn, N Dakota St	Sr	9	17	0	0	102	11.3
Andrew Hill, Indiana (PA)	Jr	10	18	4	0	112	11.2

FIELD GOALS

	Class	GP	FGA	FG	Pct	FG/Game
Jack McTyre, Valdosta St	Sr	10	23	17	73.9	1.70
Mike Estrella, St Mary's (CA)	Fr	10	22	16	72.7	1.60
Jay Masek, Chadron St	Sr	10	23	15	65.2	1.50
Bryan Seward, Ashland	Fr	11	22	16	72.7	1.45
Dennis Brown, Abilene Christian	Jr	10	17	14	82.4	1.40

TOTAL OFFENSE

	Class	GP	Yds	Yds/Game
Andy Breault, Kutztown	Jr	11	3173	288.5
Jay McLucas, New Haven	Sr	10	2856	285.6
Sam Mannery, California (PA)	Sr	10	2819	281.9
Maurice Heard, Tuskegee	Jr	11	2885	262.3
Bill Bair, Mansfield	So	10	2608	260.8

RUSHING

	Class	GP	Car	Yds	TD	Yds/Game
David Jones, Chadron St	Sr	10	225	1570	14	157.0
Shawn Graves, Wofford	So	9	151	1324	17	147.1
Derrick Price, West Chester	Sr	10	291	1457	7	145.7
Jeremy Monroe, Michigan Tech	Fr	10	185	1395	15	139.5
Jeff Cameron, Hillsdale	Sr	11	299	1462	18	132.9

PASSING EFFICIENCY

	Class	GP	Att	Comp	Yds	Pct Comp	TD	Int	Rating Pts
Tony Aliucci, Indiana (PA)	Jr	10	181	111	1801	61.3	21	10	172.0
Mitch Nicholson, Winston-Salem	Jr	11	171	85	1651	49.7	22	5	167.2
Jack Hull, Grand Valley St	Jr	11	241	134	2152	55.6	19	5	152.4
Maurice Heard, Tuskegee	Jr	11	359	182	2974	50.7	34	14	143.6
Don Bailey, Portland St	Sr	11	204	137	1629	67.1	10	9	141.4

Note: Minimum 15 attempts per game.

RECEPTIONS PER GAME

	Class	GP	No.	Yds	TD	C/Game
Mark Steinmeyer, Kutztown	Jr	11	86	940	5	7.8
Ken Duimstra, Cal St-Chico	Sr	10	78	884	8	7.8
Pierre Fils, New Haven	Sr	9	63	1121	11	7.0
Anthony Thomas, Alabama A&M	So	11	74	869	8	6.7
Kelvin Jeffrey, Newberry	Jr	11	73	772	2	6.6

Division II (*Cont.*)

RECEIVING YARDS PER GAME

	Class	GP	No.	Yds	TD	Yds/Game
Ernest Priester, Edinboro	Sr	8	45	1060	14	132.5
Pierre Fils, New Haven	Sr	9	63	1121	11	124.6
Anthony Cooley, N Carolina Central	Sr	10	45	1058	7	105.8
Keith Miller, W Texas St	Jr	11	61	1130	9	102.7
Millard Hamilton, Clark Atlanta	Sr	10	50	997	12	99.7

INTERCEPTIONS

	Class	GP	No.	Yds	Int/Game
Eric Turner, E Texas St	Jr	11	10	105	.91
Anthony Devine, Millersville	So	10	9	143	.90
Bryan Schroeder, Winona St	Sr	11	9	49	.82
Jimmy Hooker, E Texas St	Jr	10	8	3	.80
David Cook, Saginaw Valley	Sr	10	8	73	.80

PUNTING

	Class	No.	Avg
Mark Bounds, W Texas St	Jr	69	46.3
Doug O'Neil, Cal Poly-SLO	So	57	45.8
Eric Fadness, Fort Lewis	So	53	43.2
Eric Weetman, Cal St-Chico	Sr	60	42.9
Joe Harkreader, S Dakota	Sr	52	42.1

Note: Minimum 3.6 per game.

1990 NCAA Division I-A Team Leaders

Offense

SCORING

	GP	Pts	Avg
Houston	11	511	46.5
Brigham Young	12	510	42.5
San Diego St	11	459	41.7
Virginia	11	442	40.2
Florida St	11	435	39.5
Nebraska	11	413	37.5
Tennessee	12	442	36.8
Miami (FL)	11	401	36.5
Oklahoma	11	401	36.5
Washington	11	394	35.8

RUSHING

	GP	Car	Yds	Avg	TD	Yds/Game
Northern Illinois	11	619	3791	6.1	36	344.6
Nebraska	11	641	3740	5.8	36	340.0
Army	11	746	3647	4.9	30	331.5
Texas A&M	12	661	3829	5.8	37	319.1
Oklahoma	11	637	3182	5.0	41	289.3
Colorado	12	629	3254	5.2	33	271.2
Air Force	11	653	2942	4.5	28	267.5
Virginia	11	520	2831	5.4	31	257.4
Clemson	11	623	2808	4.5	24	255.3
Michigan St	11	590	2793	4.7	34	253.9

TOTAL OFFENSE

	GP	Plays	Yds	Avg	TD*	Yds/Game
Houston	11	905	6455	7.1	63	586.82
Brigham Young	12	968	6788	7.0	64	565.67
San Diego St	11	927	5798	6.3	57	527.09
Virginia	11	804	5516	6.9	55	501.45
Miami (FL)	11	842	5312	6.3	49	482.91
Texas A&M	12	875	5653	6.5	50	471.08
San Jose St	11	872	5116	5.9	51	465.09
Pacific	11	835	5080	6.1	47	461.82
Fresno St	11	868	5026	5.8	45	456.91
Florida	11	855	4978	5.8	44	452.55

*Defensive and special teams TDs not included.

THEY SAID IT

Hugh Campbell, then football coach at Whitworth College in Spokane, Wash., after his team defeated Whitman 70–30: "It wasn't as easy as you think. It's hard to stay awake that long."

PASSING

	GP	Att	Comp	Yds	Pct Comp	Yds/Att	TD	Int	Yds/Game
Houston	11	659	386	5213	58.6	7.9	54	20	473.9
Brigham Young	12	580	373	5379	64.3	9.3	41	29	448.3
San Diego St	11	485	287	4086	59.2	8.4	29	8	371.5
Pacific	11	535	303	4051	56.6	7.6	40	16	368.3
Miami (FL)	11	434	246	3573	56.7	8.2	22	8	324.8
Missouri	11	404	246	3248	60.9	8.0	18	19	295.3
Texas Christian	11	511	258	3237	50.5	6.3	24	20	294.3
San Jose St	11	393	219	3208	55.7	8.2	27	15	291.6
Florida	11	415	246	3197	59.3	7.7	25	16	290.6
New Mexico	12	510	237	3221	46.5	6.3	18	23	268.4

Single-Game Highs

Points scored: 84—Houston, Nov 17 (vs Eastern Washington).
Net rushing yards: 733—Northern Illinois, Oct 6 (vs Fresno St).
Passing yards: 716—Houston, Dec 2 (vs Arizona St).
Total yards: 827—Houston, Nov 3 (vs Texas Christian).
Fewest total yards allowed: 17—N Carolina St, Sep 1 (vs Western Carolina).
Passes attempted: 81*—Houston, Oct 20 (vs Southern Meth).
Passes completed: 53—Houston, Oct 20 (vs Southern Meth).

*NCAA I-A record. Old record: 79—Texas Christian, 1990.

Defense

SCORING

	GP	Pts	Avg
Central Michigan	11	98	8.9
Clemson	11	109	9.9
Ball St	11	121	11.0
Alabama	11	127	11.5
Southern Mississippi	11	141	12.8
Louisville	11	142	12.9
Nebraska	11	147	13.4
Washington	11	150	13.6
Penn St	11	155	14.1
N Carolina St	11	162	14.7

RUSHING

	GP	Car	Yds	Avg	TD	Yds/Game
Washington	11	392	735	1.9	10	66.8
Clemson	11	369	789	2.1	5	71.7
Miami (FL)	11	387	877	2.3	7	79.7
San Jose St	11	410	916	2.2	9	83.3
Florida	11	386	941	2.4	8	85.5
Alabama	11	402	1007	2.5	6	91.5
Penn St	11	401	1040	2.6	8	94.5
Iowa	11	392	1095	2.8	14	99.5
Central Michigan	11	392	1097	2.8	2	99.7
Ball St	11	461	1120	2.4	8	101.8

TOTAL DEFENSE

	GP	Plays	Yds	Avg	Yds/Game
Clemson	11	678	2386	3.5	216.9
Ball St	11	708	2449	3.5	222.6
Alabama	11	711	2523	3.5	229.4
Central Michigan	11	681	2559	3.8	232.6
Florida	11	708	2834	4.0	257.6
Louisville	11	737	2855	3.9	259.5
Nebraska	11	724	2898	4.0	263.5
Auburn	11	738	3002	4.1	272.9
Miami (OH)	11	765	3036	4.0	276.0
N Carolina St	11	772	3054	4.0	277.6

TURNOVER MARGIN

		Turnovers Gained			Turnovers Lost			Margin/
	GP	Fum	Int	Total	Fum	Int	Total	Game
Washington	11	17	20	37	6	8	14	2.09
Tennessee	12	19	24	43	3	17	20	1.92
Florida St	11	15	21	36	6	10	16	1.82
Oklahoma	11	18	19	37	14	8	22	1.36
Kansas St	11	16	19	35	8	12	20	1.36
Georgia Tech	11	16	24	40	13	13	26	1.27
Penn St	11	8	23	31	8	9	17	1.27

PASSING EFFICIENCY

	GP	Att	Comp	Yds	Pct Comp	Yds/Att	TD	Pct TD	Int	Pct Int	Rating Pts
Alabama	11	309	141	1516	45.6	4.91	5	1.62	15	4.85	82.47
Central Michigan	11	289	129	1462	44.6	5.06	6	2.08	15	5.19	83.60
Ball St	11	247	116	1329	47.0	5.38	4	1.62	17	6.88	83.74
Miami (OH)	11	244	106	1327	43.4	5.44	8	3.28	15	6.15	87.65
Texas	11	314	129	1780	41.1	5.67	7	2.23	13	4.14	87.78
Clemson	11	309	149	1597	48.2	5.17	5	1.62	14	4.53	87.91
Tennessee	12	336	163	1737	48.5	5.17	12	3.57	24	7.14	89.44
Louisville	11	279	141	1641	50.5	5.88	4	1.43	19	6.81	91.06
Fresno St	11	346	144	2109	41.6	6.10	5	1.45	11	3.18	91.23
Penn St	11	361	178	2023	49.3	5.60	9	2.49	23	6.37	91.86

National Champions

Year	Champion	Record	Bowl Game	Head Coach
1883	Yale	8-0-0	No bowl	Ray Tompkins (Captain)
1884	Yale	9-0-0	No bowl	Eugene L. Richards (Captain)
1885	Princeton	9-0-0	No bowl	Charles DeCamp (Captain)
1886	Yale	9-0-1	No bowl	Robert N. Corwin (Captain)
1887	Yale	9-0-0	No bowl	Harry W. Beecher (Captain)
1888	Yale	13-0-0	No bowl	Walter Camp
1889	Princeton	10-0-0	No bowl	Edgar Poe (Captain)
1890	Harvard	11-0-0	No bowl	George A. Stewart
				George C. Adams
1891	Yale	13-0-0	No bowl	Walter Camp
1892	Yale	13-0-0	No bowl	Walter Camp
1893	Princeton	11-0-0	No bowl	Tom Trenchard (Captain)
1894	Yale	16-0-0	No bowl	William C. Rhodes
1895	Pennsylvania	14-0-0	No bowl	George Woodruff
1896	Princeton	10-0-1	No bowl	Garrett Cochran
1897	Pennsylvania	15-0-0	No bowl	George Woodruff
1898	Harvard	11-0-0	No bowl	W. Cameron Forbes
1899	Harvard	10-0-1	No bowl	Benjamin H. Dibblee
1900	Yale	12-0-0	No bowl	Malcolm McBride
1901	Michigan	11-0-0	Won Rose	Fielding Yost
1902	Michigan	11-0-0	No bowl	Fielding Yost
1903	Princeton	11-0-0	No bowl	Art Hillebrand
1904	Pennsylvania	12-0-0	No bowl	Carl Williams
1905	Chicago	11-0-0	No bowl	Amos Alonzo Stagg
1906	Princeton	9-0-1	No bowl	Bill Roper
1907	Yale	9-0-1	No bowl	Bill Knox
1908	Pennsylvania	11-0-1	No bowl	Sol Metzger
1909	Yale	10-0-0	No bowl	Howard Jones
1910	Harvard	8-0-1	No bowl	Percy Houghton
1911	Princeton	8-0-2	No bowl	Bill Roper
1912	Harvard	9-0-0	No bowl	Percy Houghton
1913	Harvard	9-0-0	No bowl	Percy Houghton
1914	Army	9-0-0	No bowl	Charley Daly
1915	Cornell	9-0-0	No bowl	Al Sharpe
1916	Pittsburgh	8-0-0	No bowl	Pop Warner
1917	Georgia Tech	9-0-0	No bowl	John Heisman
1918	Pittsburgh	4-1-0	No bowl	Pop Warner
1919	Harvard	9-0-1	Won Rose	Bob Fisher
1920	California	9-0-0	Won Rose	Andy Smith
1921	Cornell	8-0-0	No bowl	Gil Dobie
1922	Cornell	8-0-0	No bowl	Gil Dobie
1923	Illinois	8-0-0	No bowl	Bob Zuppke
1924	Notre Dame	10-0-0	Won Rose	Knute Rockne
1925	Alabama (H)	10-0-0	Won Rose	Wallace Wade
	Dartmouth (D)	8-0-0	No bowl	Jesse Hawley
1926	Alabama (H)	9-0-1	Tied Rose	Wallace Wade
	Stanford (D)(H)	10-0-1	Tied Rose	Pop Warner
1927	Illinois	7-0-1	No bowl	Bob Zuppke
1928	Georgia Tech (H)	10-0-0	Won Rose	Bill Alexander
	Southern Cal (D)	9-0-1	No bowl	Howard Jones
1929	Notre Dame	9-0-0	No bowl	Knute Rockne
1930	Notre Dame	10-0-0	No bowl	Knute Rockne
1931	Southern Cal	10-1-0	Won Rose	Howard Jones
1932	Southern Cal (H)	10-0-0	Won Rose	Howard Jones
	Michigan (D)	8-0-0	No bowl	Harry Kipke
1933	Michigan	7-0-1	No bowl	Harry Kipke
1934	Minnesota	8-0-0	No bowl	Bernie Bierman
1935	Minnesota (H)	8-0-0	No bowl	Bernie Bierman
	Southern Meth (D)	12-1-0	Lost Rose	Matty Bell
1936	Minnesota	7-1-0	No bowl	Bernie Bierman
1937	Pittsburgh	9-0-1	No bowl	Jack Sutherland

Year	Champion	Record	Bowl Game	Head Coach
1938	Texas Christian (AP)	11-0-0	Won Sugar	Dutch Meyer
	Notre Dame (D)	8-1-0	No bowl	Elmer Layden
1939	Southern Cal (D)	8-0-2	Won Rose	Howard Jones
	Texas A&M (AP)	11-0-0	Won Sugar	Homer Norton
1940	Minnesota	8-0-0	No bowl	Bernie Bierman
1941	Minnesota	8-0-0	No bowl	Bernie Bierman
1942	Ohio St	9-1-0	No bowl	Paul Brown
1943	Notre Dame	9-1-0	No bowl	Frank Leahy
1944	Army	9-0-0	No bowl	Red Blaik
1945	Army	9-0-0	No bowl	Red Blaik
1946	Notre Dame	8-0-1	No bowl	Frank Leahy
1947	Notre Dame	9-0-0	No bowl	Frank Leahy
	Michigan*	10-0-0	Won Rose	Fritz Crisler
1948	Michigan	9-0-0	No bowl	Bennie Oosterbaan
1949	Notre Dame	10-0-0	No bowl	Frank Leahy
1950	Oklahoma	10-1-0	Lost Sugar	Bud Wilkinson
1951	Tennessee	10-1-0	Lost Sugar	Bob Neyland
1952	Michigan St	9-0-0	No bowl	Biggie Munn
1953	Maryland	10-1-0	Lost Orange	Jim Tatum
1954	Ohio St	10-0-0	Won Rose	Woody Hayes
	UCLA (UP)	9-0-0	No bowl	Red Sanders
1955	Oklahoma	11-0-0	Won Orange	Bud Wilkinson
1956	Oklahoma	10-0-0	No bowl	Bud Wilkinson
1957	Auburn	10-0-0	No bowl	Shug Jordan
	Ohio St (UP)	9-1-0	Won Rose	Woody Hayes
1958	Louisiana St	11-0-0	Won Sugar	Paul Dietzel
1959	Syracuse	11-0-0	Won Cotton	Ben Schwartzwalder
1960	Minnesota	8-2-0	Lost Rose	Murray Warmath
1961	Alabama	11-0-0	Won Sugar	Bear Bryant
1962	Southern Cal	11-0-0	Won Rose	John McKay
1963	Texas	11-0-0	Won Cotton	Darrell Royal
1964	Alabama	10-1-0	Lost Orange	Bear Bryant
1965	Alabama	9-1-1	Won Orange	Bear Bryant
	Michigan St (UPI)	10-1-0	Lost Rose	Duffy Daugherty
1966	Notre Dame	9-0-1	No bowl	Ara Parseghian
1967	Southern Cal	10-1-0	Won Rose	John McKay
1968	Ohio St	10-0-0	Won Rose	Woody Hayes
1969	Texas	11-0-0	Won Cotton	Darrell Royal
1970	Nebraska	11-0-1	Won Orange	Bob Devaney
	Texas (UPI)	10-1-0	Lost Cotton	Darrell Royal
1971	Nebraska	13-0-0	Won Orange	Bob Devaney
1972	Southern Cal	12-0-0	Won Rose	John McKay
1973	Notre Dame	11-0-0	Won Sugar	Ara Parseghian
	Alabama (UPI)	11-1-0	Lost Sugar	Bear Bryant
1974	Oklahoma	11-0-0	No bowl	Barry Switzer
	Southern Cal (UPI)	10-1-1	Won Rose	John McKay
1975	Oklahoma	11-1-0	Won Orange	Barry Switzer
1976	Pittsburgh	12-0-0	Won Sugar	Johnny Majors
1977	Notre Dame	11-1-0	Won Cotton	Dan Devine
1978	Alabama	11-1-0	Won Sugar	Bear Bryant
	Southern Cal (UPI)	12-1-0	Won Rose	John Robinson
1979	Alabama	12-0-0	Won Sugar	Bear Bryant
1980	Georgia	12-0-0	Won Sugar	Vince Dooley
1981	Clemson	12-0-0	Won Orange	Danny Ford
1982	Penn St	11-1-0	Won Sugar	Joe Paterno
1983	Miami (FL)	11-1-0	Won Orange	Howard Schnellenberger
1984	Brigham Young	13-0-0	Won Holiday	LaVell Edwards
1985	Oklahoma	11-1-0	Won Orange	Barry Switzer
1986	Penn St	12-0-0	Won Fiesta	Joe Paterno
1987	Miami (FL)	12-0-0	Won Orange	Jimmy Johnson
1988	Notre Dame	12-0-0	Won Fiesta	Lou Holtz
1989	Miami (FL)	11-1-0	Won Sugar	Dennis Erickson
1990	Colorado	11-1-1	Won Orange	Bill McCartney
	Georgia Tech (UPI)	11-0-1	Won Citrus	Bobby Ross

*The AP, which had voted Notre Dame No. 1, took a second vote, giving the national title to Michigan after its 49-0 win over Southern Cal in the Rose Bowl.

Note: Selectors: Helms Athletic Foundation (H) 1883-1935, The Dickinson System (D) 1924-40, The Associated Press (AP) 1936-90, and United Press International (UP) 1958-90.

Results of Major Bowl Games

Rose Bowl

1-1-2	Michigan 49, Stanford 0
1-1-16	Washington St 14, Brown 0
1-1-17	Oregon 14, Pennsylvania 0
1-1-18	Mare Island 19, Camp Lewis 7
1-1-19	Great Lakes 17, Mare Island 0
1-1-20	Harvard 7, Oregon 6
1-1-21	California 28, Ohio St 0
1-2-22	Washington & Jefferson 0, California 0
1-1-23	Southern Cal 14, Penn St 3
1-1-24	Navy 14, Washington 14
1-1-25	Notre Dame 27, Stanford 10
1-1-26	Alabama 20, Washington 19
1-1-27	Alabama 7, Stanford 7
1-2-28	Stanford 7, Pittsburgh 6
1-1-29	Georgia Tech 8, California 7
1-1-30	Southern Cal 47, Pittsburgh 14
1-1-31	Alabama 24, Washington St 0
1-1-32	Southern Cal 21, Tulane 12
1-2-33	Southern Cal 35, Pittsburgh 0
1-1-34	Columbia 7, Stanford 0
1-1-35	Alabama 29, Stanford 13
1-1-36	Stanford 7, Southern Meth 0
1-1-37	Pittsburgh 21, Washington 0
1-1-38	California 13, Alabama 0
1-2-39	Southern Cal 7, Duke 3
1-1-40	Southern Cal 14, Tennessee 0
1-1-41	Stanford 21, Nebraska 13
1-1-42	Oregon St 20, Duke 16
1-1-43	Georgia 9, UCLA 0
1-1-44	Southern Cal 29, Washington 0
1-1-45	Southern Cal 25, Tennessee 0
1-1-46	Alabama 34, Southern Cal 14
1-1-47	Illinois 45, UCLA 14
1-1-48	Michigan 49, Southern Cal 0
1-1-49	Northwestern 20, California 14
1-2-50	Ohio St 17, California 14
1-1-51	Michigan 14, California 6
1-1-52	Illinois 40, Stanford 7
1-1-53	Southern Cal 7, Wisconsin 0
1-1-54	Michigan St 28, UCLA 20
1-1-55	Ohio St 20, Southern Cal 7
1-2-56	Michigan St 17, UCLA 14
1-1-57	Iowa 35, Oregon St 19
1-1-58	Ohio St 10, Oregon 7
1-1-59	Iowa 38, California 12
1-1-60	Washington 44, Wisconsin 8
1-2-61	Washington 17, Minnesota 7
1-1-62	Minnesota 21, UCLA 3
1-1-63	Southern Cal 42, Wisconsin 37
1-1-64	Illinois 17, Washington 7
1-1-65	Michigan 34, Oregon St 7
1-1-66	UCLA 14, Michigan St 12
1-2-67	Purdue 14, Southern Cal 13
1-1-68	Southern Cal 14, Indiana 3
1-1-69	Ohio St 27, Southern Cal 16
1-1-70	Southern Cal 10, Michigan 3
1-1-71	Stanford 27, Ohio St 17
1-1-72	Stanford 13, Michigan 12
1-1-73	Southern Cal 42, Ohio St 17
1-1-74	Ohio St 42, Southern Cal 21
1-1-75	Southern Cal 18, Ohio St 17
1-1-76	UCLA 23, Ohio St 10
1-1-77	Southern Cal 14, Michigan 6
1-2-78	Washington 27, Michigan 20
1-1-79	Southern Cal 17, Michigan 10
1-1-80	Southern Cal 17, Ohio St 16

1-1-81	Michigan 23, Washington 6
1-1-82	Washington 28, Iowa 0
1-1-83	UCLA 24, Michigan 14
1-2-84	UCLA 45, Illinois 9
1-1-85	Southern Cal 20, Ohio St 17
1-1-86	UCLA 45, Iowa 28
1-1-87	Arizona St 22, Michigan 15
1-1-88	Michigan St 20, Southern Cal 17
1-2-89	Michigan 22, Southern Cal 14
1-1-90	Southern Cal 17, Michigan 10
1-1-91	Washington 46, Iowa 34

City: Pasadena.

Stadium: Rose Bowl.

Capacity: 104,091.

Automatic Berths: Pacific-10 champ vs Big 8 champ (since 1947).

Playing Sites: Tournament Park (1902, 1916-22), Rose Bowl (1923-41, since 1943), Duke Stadium, Durham, NC (1942).

Orange Bowl

1-1-35	Bucknell 26, Miami (FL) 0
1-1-36	Catholic 20, Mississippi 19
1-1-37	Duquesne 13, Mississippi St 12
1-1-38	Auburn 6, Michigan St 0
1-2-39	Tennessee 17, Oklahoma 0
1-1-40	Georgia Tech 21, Missouri 7
1-1-41	Mississippi St 14, Georgetown 7
1-1-42	Georgia 40, Texas Christian 26
1-1-43	Alabama 37, Boston College 21
1-1-44	Louisiana St 19, Texas A&M 14
1-1-45	Tulsa 26, Georgia Tech 12
1-1-46	Miami (FL) 13, Holy Cross 6
1-1-47	Rice 8, Tennessee 0
1-1-48	Georgia Tech 20, Kansas 14
1-1-49	Texas 41, Georgia 28
1-2-50	Santa Clara 21, Kentucky 13
1-1-51	Clemson 15, Miami (FL) 14
1-1-52	Georgia Tech 17, Baylor 14
1-1-53	Alabama 61, Syracuse 6
1-1-54	Oklahoma 7, Maryland 0
1-1-55	Duke 34, Nebraska 7
1-2-56	Oklahoma 20, Maryland 6
1-1-57	Colorado 27, Clemson 21
1-1-58	Oklahoma 48, Duke 21
1-1-59	Oklahoma 21, Syracuse 6
1-1-60	Georgia 14, Missouri 0
1-2-61	Missouri 21, Navy 14
1-1-62	Louisiana St 25, Colorado 7
1-1-63	Alabama 17, Oklahoma 0
1-1-64	Nebraska 13, Auburn 7
1-1-65	Texas 21, Alabama 17
1-1-66	Alabama 39, Nebraska 28
1-2-67	Florida 27, Georgia Tech 12
1-1-68	Oklahoma 26, Tennessee 24
1-1-69	Penn St 15, Kansas 14
1-1-70	Penn St 10, Missouri 3
1-1-71	Nebraska 17, Louisiana St 12
1-1-72	Nebraska 38, Alabama 6
1-1-73	Nebraska 40, Notre Dame 6
1-1-74	Penn St 16, Louisiana St 9
1-1-75	Notre Dame 13, Alabama 11
1-1-76	Oklahoma 14, Michigan 6
1-1-77	Ohio St 27, Colorado 10
1-2-78	Arkansas 31, Oklahoma 6

Results of Major Bowl Games (*Cont.*)

Orange Bowl (*Cont.*)

1-1-79 ....Oklahoma 31, Nebraska 24
1-1-80 ....Oklahoma 24, Florida St 7
1-1-81 ....Oklahoma 18, Florida St 17
1-1-82 ....Clemson 22, Nebraska 15
1-1-83 ....Nebraska 21, Louisiana St 20
1-2-84 ....Miami (FL) 31, Nebraska 30
1-1-85 ....Washington 28, Oklahoma 17
1-1-86 ....Oklahoma 25, Penn St 10
1-1-87 ....Oklahoma 42, Arkansas 8
1-1-88 ....Miami (FL) 20, Oklahoma 14
1-2-89 ....Miami (FL) 23, Nebraska 3
1-1-90 ....Notre Dame 21, Colorado 6
1-1-91 ....Colorado 10, Notre Dame 9

City: Miami.

Stadium: Orange Bowl.

Capacity: 75,500.

Automatic Berths: Big 8 champ (1954-64, since 1976).

Sugar Bowl

1-1-35 ....Tulane 20, Temple 14
1-1-36 ....Texas Christian 3, Louisiana St 2
1-1-37 ....Santa Clara 21, Louisiana St 14
1-1-38 ....Santa Clara 6, Louisiana St 0
1-2-39 ....Texas Christian 15, Carnegie Tech 7
1-1-40 ....Texas A&M 14, Tulane 13
1-1-41 ....Boston Col 19, Tennessee 13
1-1-42 ....Fordham 2, Missouri 0
1-1-43 ....Tennessee 14, Tulsa 7
1-1-44 ....Georgia Tech 20, Tulsa 18
1-1-45 ....Duke 29, Alabama 26
1-1-46 ....Oklahoma St 33, St Mary's (CA) 13
1-1-47 ....Georgia 20, N Carolina 10
1-1-48 ....Texas 27, Alabama 7
1-1-49 ....Oklahoma 14, N Carolina 6
1-2-50 ....Oklahoma 35, Louisiana St 0
1-1-51 ....Kentucky 13, Oklahoma 7
1-1-52 ....Maryland 28, Tennessee 13
1-1-53 ....Georgia Tech 24, Mississippi 7
1-1-54 ....Georgia Tech 42, W Virginia 19
1-1-55 ....Navy 21, Mississippi 0
1-2-56 ....Georgia Tech 7, Pittsburgh 0
1-1-57 ....Baylor 13, Tennessee 7
1-1-58 ....Mississippi 39, Texas 7
1-1-59 ....Louisiana St 7, Clemson 0
1-1-60 ....Mississippi 21, Louisiana St 0
1-2-61 ....Mississippi 14, Rice 6
1-1-62 ....Alabama 10, Arkansas 3
1-1-63 ....Mississippi 17, Arkansas 13
1-1-64 ....Alabama 12, Mississippi 7
1-1-65 ....Louisiana St 13, Syracuse 10
1-1-66 ....Missouri 20, Florida 18
1-2-67 ....Alabama 34, Nebraska 7
1-1-68 ....Louisiana St 20, Wyoming 13
1-1-69 ....Arkansas 16, Georgia 2
1-1-70 ....Mississippi 27, Arkansas 22
1-1-71 ....Tennessee 34, Air Force 13
1-1-72 ....Oklahoma 40, Auburn 22
12-31-72 ....Oklahoma 14, Penn St 0
12-31-73 ....Notre Dame 24, Alabama 23
12-31-74 ....Nebraska 13, Florida 10
12-31-75 ....Alabama 13, Penn St 6
1-1-77 ....Pittsburgh 27, Georgia 3
1-2-78 ....Alabama 35, Ohio St 6
1-1-79 ....Alabama 14, Penn St 7

Sugar Bowl (*Cont.*)

1-1-80 ....Alabama 24, Arkansas 9
1-1-81 ....Georgia 17, Notre Dame 10
1-1-82 ....Pittsburgh 24, Georgia 20
1-1-83 ....Penn St 27, Georgia 23
1-2-84 ....Auburn 9, Michigan 7
1-1-85 ....Nebraska 28, Louisiana St 10
1-1-86 ....Tennessee 35, Miami (FL) 7
1-1-87 ....Nebraska 30, Louisiana St 15
1-1-88 ....Syracuse 16, Auburn 16
1-2-89 ....Florida St 13, Auburn 7
1-1-90 ....Miami (FL) 33, Alabama 25
1-1-91 ....Tennessee 23, Virginia 22

City: New Orleans.

Stadium: Louisiana Superdome.

Capacity: 69,548.

Automatic Berths: Southeastern champ (since 1977).

Playing Sites: Tulane Stadium (1935-74), Superdome (since 1974).

Cotton Bowl

1-1-37 ....Texas Christian 16, Marquette 6
1-1-38 ....Rice 28, Colorado 14
1-2-39 ....St. Mary's (CA) 20, Texas Tech 13
1-1-40 ....Clemson 6, Boston Col 3
1-1-41 ....Texas A&M 13, Fordham 12
1-1-42 ....Alabama 29, Texas A&M 21
1-1-43 ....Texas 14, Georgia Tech 7
1-1-44 ....Texas 7, Randolph Field 7
1-1-45 ....Oklahoma St 34, Texas Christian 0
1-1-46 ....Texas 40, Missouri 27
1-1-47 ....Arkansas 0, Louisiana St 0
1-1-48 ....Southern Meth 13, Penn St 13
1-1-49 ....Southern Meth 21, Oregon 13
1-2-50 ....Rice 27, N Carolina 13
1-1-51 ....Tennessee 20, Texas 14
1-1-52 ....Kentucky 20, Texas Christian 7
1-1-53 ....Texas 16, Tennessee 0
1-1-54 ....Rice 28, Alabama 6
1-1-55 ....Georgia Tech 14, Arkansas 6
1-2-56 ....Mississippi 14, Texas Christian 13
1-1-57 ....Texas Christian 28, Syracuse 27
1-1-58 ....Navy 20, Rice 7
1-1-59 ....Texas Christian 0, Air Force 0
1-1-60 ....Syracuse 23, Texas 14
1-2-61 ....Duke 7, Arkansas 6
1-1-62 ....Texas 12, Mississippi 7
1-1-63 ....Louisiana St 13, Texas 0
1-1-64 ....Texas 28, Navy 6
1-1-65 ....Arkansas 10, Nebraska 7
1-1-66 ....Louisiana St 14, Arkansas 7
12-31-66 ....Georgia 24, Southern Meth 9
1-1-68 ....Texas A&M 20, Alabama 16
1-1-69 ....Texas 36, Tennessee 13
1-1-70 ....Texas 21, Notre Dame 17
1-1-71 ....Notre Dame 24, Texas 11
1-1-72 ....Penn St 30, Texas 6
1-1-73 ....Texas 17, Alabama 13
1-1-74 ....Nebraska 19, Texas 3
1-1-75 ....Penn St 41, Baylor 20
1-1-76 ....Arkansas 31, Georgia 10
1-1-77 ....Houston 30, Maryland 21
1-2-78 ....Notre Dame 38, Texas 10
1-1-79 ....Notre Dame 35, Houston 34
1-1-80 ....Houston 17, Nebraska 14

Cotton Bowl (*Cont.*)

1-1-81 ....Alabama 30, Baylor 2
1-1-82 ....Texas 14, Alabama 12
1-1-83 ....Southern Meth 7, Pittsburgh 3
1-2-84 ....Georgia 10, Texas 9
1-1-85 ....Boston Col 45, Houston 28
1-1-86 ....Texas A&M 36, Auburn 16
1-1-87 ....Ohio St 28, Texas A&M 12
1-1-88 ....Texas A&M 35, Notre Dame 10
1-2-89 ....UCLA 17, Arkansas 3
1-1-90 ....Tennessee 31, Arkansas 27
1-1-91 ....Miami (FL) 46, Texas 3

City: Dallas.

Stadium: Cotton Bowl.

Capacity: 72,032.

Automatic Berths: Southwest champ (since 1942).

Playing Sites: Fair Park Stadium (1937), Cotton Bowl (since 1938).

John Hancock Bowl

1-1-36 ....Hardin-Simmons 14, New Mexico St 14
1-1-37 ....Hardin-Simmons 34, UTEP 6
1-1-38 ....W Virginia 7, Texas Tech 6
1-2-39 ....Utah 26, New Mexico 0
1-1-40 ....Catholic 0, Arizona St 0
1-1-41 ....Case Reserve 26, Arizona St 13
1-1-42 ....Tulsa 6, Texas Tech 0
1-1-43 ....2nd Air Force 13, Hardin-Simmons 7
1-1-44 ....Southwestern (TX) 7, New Mexico 0
1-1-45 ....Southwestern (TX) 35, U Mexico 0
1-1-46 ....New Mexico 34, Denver 24
1-1-47 ....Cincinnati 18, Virginia Tech 6
1-1-48 ....Miami (OH) 13, Texas Tech 12
1-1-49 ....W Virginia 21, UTEP 12
1-2-50 ....UTEP 33, Georgetown 20
1-1-51 ....West Texas St 14, Cincinnati 13
1-1-52 ....Texas Tech 25, Pacific 14
1-1-53 ....Pacific 26, Southern Miss 7
1-1-54 ....UTEP 37, Southern Miss 14
1-1-55 ....UTEP 47, Florida St 20
1-2-56 ....Wyoming 21, Texas Tech 14
1-1-57 ....George Washington 13, UTEP 0
1-1-58 ....Louisville 34, Drake 20
12-31-58 ....Wyoming 14, Hardin-Simmons 6
12-31-59 ....New Mexico St 28, N Texas 8
12-31-60 ....New Mexico St 20, Utah St 13
12-30-61 ....Villanova 17, Wichita St 9
12-31-62 ....W Texas St 15, Ohio 14
12-31-63 ....Oregon 21, Southern Meth 14
12-26-64 ....Georgia 7, Texas Tech 0
12-31-65 ....UTEP 13, Texas Christian 12
12-24-66 ....Wyoming 28, Florida St 20
12-30-67 ....UTEP 14, Mississippi 7
12-28-68 ....Auburn 34, Arizona 10
12-20-69 ....Nebraska 45, Georgia 6
12-19-70 ....Georgia Tech 17, Texas Tech 9
12-18-71 ....Louisiana St 33, Iowa St 15
12-30-72 ....N Carolina 32, Texas Tech 28
12-29-73 ....Missouri 34, Auburn 17
12-28-74 ....Mississippi St 26, N Carolina 24
12-26-75 ....Pittsburgh 33, Kansas 19
1-2-77 ....Texas A&M 37, Florida 14
12-31-77 ....Stanford 24, Louisiana St 14
12-23-78 ....Texas 42, Maryland 0
12-22-79 ....Washington 14, Texas 7

John Hancock Bowl (*Cont.*)

12-27-80 ....Nebraska 31, Mississippi St 17
12-26-81 ....Oklahoma 40, Houston 14
12-25-82 ....N Carolina 26, Texas 10
12-24-83 ....Alabama 28, Southern Meth 7
12-22-84 ....Maryland 28, Tennessee 27
12-28-85 ....Georgia 13, Arizona 13
12-25-86 ....Alabama 28, Washington 6
12-25-87 ....Oklahoma St 35, W Virginia 33
12-24-88 ....Alabama 29, Army 28
12-30-89 ....Pittsburgh 31, Texas A&M 28
12-31-90 ....Michigan St 17, Southern Cal 16

City: El Paso.

Stadium: Sun Bowl.

Capacity: 52,000.

Automatic Berths: None.

Name Changes: Sun Bowl (1936-86), John Hancock Sun Bowl (1987-88), John Hancock Bowl (since 1989).

Playing Sites: Kidd Field (1936-62), Sun Bowl (since 1963).

Gator Bowl

1-1-46 ....Wake Forest 26, S Carolina 14
1-1-47 ....Oklahoma 34, N Carolina St 13
1-1-48 ....Maryland 20, Georgia 20
1-1-49 ....Clemson 24, Missouri 23
1-2-50 ....Maryland 20, Missouri 7
1-1-51 ....Wyoming 20, Washington & Lee 7
1-1-52 ....Miami (FL) 14, Clemson 0
1-1-53 ....Florida 14, Tulsa 13
1-1-54 ....Texas Tech 35, Auburn 13
12-31-54 ....Auburn 33, Baylor 13
12-31-55 ....Vanderbilt 25, Auburn 13
12-29-56 ....Georgia Tech 21, Pittsburgh 14
12-28-57 ....Tennessee 3, Texas A&M 0
12-27-58 ....Mississippi 7, Florida 3
1-2-60 ....Arkansas 14, Georgia Tech 7
12-31-60 ....Florida 13, Baylor 12
12-30-61 ....Penn St 30, Georgia 15
12-29-62 ....Florida 17, Penn St 7
12-28-63 ....N Carolina 35, Air Force 0
1-2-65 ....Florida St 36, Oklahoma 19
12-31-65 ....Georgia Tech 31, Texas Tech 21
12-31-66 ....Tennessee 18, Syracuse 12
12-30-67 ....Penn St 17, Florida St 17
12-28-68 ....Missouri 35, Alabama 10
12-27-69 ....Florida 14, Tennessee 13
1-2-71 ....Auburn 35, Mississippi 28
12-31-71 ....Georgia 7, N Carolina 3
12-30-72 ....Auburn 24, Colorado 3
12-29-73 ....Texas Tech 28, Tennessee 19
12-30-74 ....Auburn 27, Texas 3
12-29-75 ....Maryland 13, Florida 0
12-27-76 ....Notre Dame 20, Penn St 9
12-30-77 ....Pittsburgh 34, Clemson 3
12-29-78 ....Clemson 17, Ohio St 15
12-28-79 ....N Carolina 17, Michigan 15
12-29-80 ....Pittsburgh 37, S Carolina 9
12-28-81 ....N Carolina 31, Arkansas 27
12-30-82 ....Florida St 31, W Virginia 12
12-30-83 ....Florida 14, Iowa 6
12-28-84 ....Oklahoma St 21, S Carolina 14
12-30-85 ....Florida St 34, Oklahoma St 23
12-27-86 ....Clemson 27, Stanford 21
12-31-87 ....Louisiana St 30, S Carolina 13
1-1-89 ....Georgia 34, Michigan St 27

Gator Bowl (*Cont.*)

12-30-89 ....Clemson 27, W Virginia 7
1-1-91 ....Michigan 35, Mississippi 3

City: Jacksonville, FL.

Stadium: Gator Bowl.

Capacity: 82,000. Automatic Berths: None.

Florida Citrus Bowl

1-1-47 ....Catawba 31, Maryville (TN) 6
1-1-48 ....Catawba 7, Marshall 0
1-1-49 ....Murray St 21, Sul Ross St 21
1-2-50 ....St Vincent 7, Emory & Henry 6
1-1-51 ....Morris Harvey 35, Emory & Henry 14
1-1-52 ....Stetson 35, Arkansas St 20
1-1-53 ....E Texas St 33, Tennessee Tech 0
1-1-54 ....E Texas St 7, Arkansas St 7
1-1-55 ....NE-Omaha 7, Eastern Kentucky 6
1-2-56 ....Juniata 6, Missouri Valley 6
1-1-57 ....W Texas St 20, Southern Miss 13
1-1-58 ....E Texas St 10, Southern Miss 9
12-27-58 ....E Texas St 26, Missouri Valley 7
1-1-60 ....Middle Tennessee St 21,
                        Presbyterian 12
12-30-60 ....Citadel 27, Tennessee Tech 0
12-29-61 ....Lamar 21, Middle Tennessee St 14
12-22-62 ....Houston 49, Miami (OH) 21
12-28-63 ....Western Kentucky 27, Coast Guard 0
12-12-64 ....E Carolina 14, Massachusetts 13
12-11-65 ....E Carolina 31, Maine 0
12-10-66 ....Morgan St 14, West Chester 6
12-16-67 ....TN-Martin 25, West Chester 8
12-27-68 ....Richmond 49, Ohio 42
12-26-69 ....Toledo 56, Davidson 33
12-28-70 ....Toledo 40, William & Mary 12
12-28-71 ....Toledo 28, Richmond 3
12-29-72 ....Tampa 21, Kent 18
12-22-73 ....Miami (OH) 16, Florida 7
12-21-74 ....Miami (OH) 21, Georgia 10
12-20-75 ....Miami (OH) 20, S Carolina 7
12-18-76 ....Oklahoma St 49, Brigham Young 21
12-23-77 ....Florida St 40, Texas Tech 17
12-23-78 ....N Carolina St 30, Pittsburgh 17
12-22-79 ....Louisiana St 34, Wake Forest 10
12-20-80 ....Florida 35, Maryland 20
12-19-81 ....Missouri 19, Southern Miss 17
12-18-82 ....Auburn 33, Boston Col 26
12-17-83 ....Tennessee 30, Maryland 23
12-22-84 ....Georgia 17, Florida St 17
12-28-85 ....Ohio St 10, Brigham Young 7
1-1-87 ....Auburn 16, Southern Cal 7
1-1-88 ....Clemson 35, Penn St 10
1-2-89 ....Clemson 13, Oklahoma 6
1-1-90 ....Illinois 31, Virginia 21
1-1-91 ....Georgia Tech 45, Nebraska 21

City: Orlando, FL.

Stadium: Florida Citrus Bowl-Orlando.

Capacity: 52,300. Automatic Berths: None.

Name Change: Tangerine Bowl (1947-82), Florida Citrus Bowl (since 1983).

Playing Sites: Tangerine Bowl (1947-72, 1974-82), Florida Field, Gainesville (1973), Orlando Stadium (1983-85), Florida Citrus Bowl-Orlando (since 1986). Tangerine Bowl, Orlando Stadium, and Florida Citrus Bowl-Orlando are identical site.

Liberty Bowl

12-19-59 ....Penn St 7, Alabama 0
12-17-60 ....Penn St 41, Oregon 12
12-16-61 ....Syracuse 15, Miami (FL) 14
12-15-62 ....Oregon St 6, Villanova 0
12-21-63 ....Mississippi St 16, N Carolina St 12
12-19-64 ....Utah 32, W Virginia 6
12-18-65 ....Mississippi 13, Auburn 7
12-10-66 ....Miami (FL) 14, Virginia Tech 7
12-16-67 ....N Carolina St 14, Georgia 7
12-14-68 ....Mississippi 34, Virginia Tech 17
12-13-69 ....Colorado 47, Alabama 33
12-12-70 ....Tulane 17, Colorado 3
12-20-71 ....Tennessee 14, Arkansas 13
12-18-72 ....Georgia Tech 31, Iowa St 30
12-17-73 ....N Carolina St 31, Kansas 18
12-16-74 ....Tennessee 7, Maryland 3
12-22-75 ....Southern Cal 20, Texas A&M 0
12-20-76 ....Alabama 36, UCLA 6
12-19-77 ....Nebraska 21, N Carolina 17
12-23-78 ....Missouri 20, Louisiana St 15
12-22-79 ....Penn St 9, Tulane 6
12-27-80 ....Purdue 28, Missouri 25
12-30-81 ....Ohio St 31, Navy 28
12-29-82 ....Alabama 21, Illinois 15
12-29-83 ....Notre Dame 19, Boston Col 18
12-27-84 ....Auburn 21, Arkansas 15
12-27-85 ....Baylor 21, Louisiana St 7
12-29-86 ....Tennessee 21, Minnesota 14
12-29-87 ....Georgia 20, Arkansas 17
12-28-88 ....Indiana 34, S Carolina 10
12-28-89 ....Mississippi 42, Air Force 29
12-27-90 ....Air Force 23, Ohio St 11

City: Memphis.

Stadium: Liberty Bowl Memorial Stadium.

Capacity: 63,000.

Automatic Berths: winner of Commander-in-Chief's Trophy (Air Force, Army, Navy).

Playing Sites: Philadelphia (Municipal Stadium, 1959-63), Atlantic City (Convention Center, 1964), Memphis (since 1965).

Peach Bowl

12-30-68 ....Louisiana St 31, Florida St 27
12-30-69 ....W Virginia 14, S Carolina 3
12-30-70 ....Arizona St 48, N Carolina 26
12-30-71 ....Mississippi 41, Georgia Tech 18
12-29-72 ....N Carolina St 49, W Virginia 13
12-28-73 ....Georgia 17, Maryland 16
12-28-74 ....Vanderbilt 6, Texas Tech 6
12-31-75 ....W Virginia 13, N Carolina St 10
12-31-76 ....Kentucky 21, N Carolina 0
12-31-77 ....N Carolina St 24, Iowa St 14
12-25-78 ....Purdue 41, Georgia Tech 21
12-31-79 ....Baylor 24, Clemson 18
1-2-81 ....Miami (FL) 20, Virginia Tech 10
12-31-81 ....W Virginia 26, Florida 6
12-31-82 ....Iowa 28, Tennessee 22

Peach Bowl (*Cont.*)

12-30-83 .... Florida St 28, N Carolina 3
12-31-84 .... Virginia 27, Purdue 24
12-31-85 .... Army 31, Illinois 29
12-31-86 .... Virginia Tech 25, N Carolina St 24
1-2-88 .... Tennessee 27, Indiana 22
12-31-88 .... N Carolina St 28, Iowa 23
12-30-89 .... Syracuse 19, Georgia 18
12-29-90 .... Auburn 27, Indiana 23

City: Atlanta.
Stadium: Atlanta Fulton County Stadium.
Capacity: 59,800.
Automatic Berths: None.
Playing Sites: Grant Field (1968-70), Atlanta Stadium (since 1971).

Fiesta Bowl

12-27-71 .... Arizona St 45, Florida St 38
12-23-72 .... Arizona St 49, Missouri 35
12-21-73 .... Arizona St 28, Pittsburgh 7
12-28-74 .... Oklahoma St 16, Brigham Young 6
12-26-75 .... Arizona St 17, Nebraska 14
12-25-76 .... Oklahoma 41, Wyoming 7
12-25-77 .... Penn St 42, Arizona St 30
12-25-78 .... Arkansas 10, UCLA 10
12-25-79 .... Pittsburgh 16, Arizona 10
12-26-80 .... Penn St 31, Ohio St 19
1-1-82 .... Penn St 26, Southern Cal 10
1-1-83 .... Arizona St 32, Oklahoma 21
1-2-84 .... Ohio St 28, Pittsburgh 23
1-1-85 .... UCLA 39, Miami (FL) 37
1-1-86 .... Michigan 27, Nebraska 23
1-2-87 .... Penn St 14, Miami (FL) 10
1-1-88 .... Florida St 31, Nebraska 28
1-2-89 .... Notre Dame 34, W Virginia 21
1-1-90 .... Florida St 41, Nebraska 17
1-1-91 .... Louisville 34, Alabama 7

City: Tempe, AZ.
Stadium: Sun Devil Stadium.
Capacity: 74,000.
Automatic Berths: None.

Independence Bowl

12-13-76 .... McNeese St 20, Tulsa 16
12-17-77 .... Louisiana Tech 24, Louisville 14
12-16-78 .... E Carolina 35, Louisiana Tech 13
12-15-79 .... Syracuse 31, McNeese St 7
12-13-80 .... Southern Miss 16, McNeese St 14
12-12-81 .... Texas A&M 33, Oklahoma St 16
12-11-82 .... Wisconsin 14, Kansas St 3
12-10-83 .... Air Force 9, Mississippi 3
12-15-84 .... Air Force 23, Virginia Tech 7
12-21-85 .... Minnesota 20, Clemson 13
12-20-86 .... Mississippi 20, Texas Tech 17
12-19-87 .... Washington 24, Tulane 12
12-23-88 .... Southern Miss 38, UTEP 18
12-16-89 .... Oregon 27, Tulsa 24
12-15-90 .... Louisiana Tech 34, Maryland 34

City: Shreveport, LA.
Stadium: Independence Stadium.
Capacity: 50,560.
Automatic Berths: None.

All-American Bowl

12-22-77 .... Maryland 17, Minnesota 7
12-20-78 .... Texas A&M 28, Iowa St 12
12-29-79 .... Missouri 24, S Carolina 14
12-27-80 .... Arkansas 34, Tulane 15
12-31-81 .... Mississippi St 10, Kansas 0
12-31-82 .... Air Force 36, Vanderbilt 28
12-22-83 .... W Virginia 20, Kentucky 16
12-29-84 .... Kentucky 20, Wisconsin 19
12-31-85 .... Georgia Tech 17, Michigan St 14
12-31-86 .... Florida St 27, Indiana 13
12-22-87 .... Virginia 22, Brigham Young 16
12-29-88 .... Florida 14, Illinois 10
12-28-89 .... Texas Tech 49, Duke 21
12-28-90 .... N Carolina St 31, Southern Mississippi 27

City: Birmingham, AL.
Stadium: Legion Field.
Capacity: 75,808.
Automatic Berths: None.
Name Change: Hall of Fame Classic (1977-84), All-American Bowl (since 1985).

Holiday Bowl

12-22-78 .... Navy 23, Brigham Young 16
12-21-79 .... Indiana 38, Brigham Young 37
12-19-80 .... Brigham Young 46, Southern Meth 45
12-18-81 .... Brigham Young 38, Washington St 36
12-17-82 .... Ohio St 47, Brigham Young 17
12-23-83 .... Brigham Young 21, Missouri 17
12-21-84 .... Brigham Young 24, Michigan 17
12-22-85 .... Arkansas 18, Arizona St 17
12-30-86 .... Iowa 39, San Diego St 38
12-30-87 .... Iowa 20, Wyoming 19
12-30-88 .... Oklahoma St 62, Wyoming 14
12-29-89 .... Penn St 50, Brigham Young 39
12-29-90 .... Texas A&M 65, Brigham Young 14

City: San Diego.
Stadium: Jack Murphy Stadium.
Capacity: 60,750.
Automatic Berths: Western Athletic champ (except 1985).

California Bowl

12-19-81 .... Toledo 27, San Jose St 25
12-18-82 .... Fresno St 29, Bowling Green 28
12-17-83 .... Northern Illinois 20, Cal St-Fullerton 13
12-15-84 .... NV-Las Vegas 30, Toledo 13*
12-14-85 .... Fresno St 51, Bowling Green 7
12-13-86 .... San Jose St 37, Miami (OH) 7
12-12-87 .... Eastern Michigan 30, San Jose St 27
12-10-88 .... Fresno St 35, Western Michigan 30
12-9-89 .... Fresno St 27, Ball St 6
12-8-90 .... San Jose St 48, Central Michigan 24

* Toledo won later by forfeit.
City: Fresno, CA.
Stadium: Bulldog Stadium.
Capacity: 30,000.
Automatic Berths: Mid-American and Big West champs.

Aloha Bowl

12-25-82 ....Washington 21, Maryland 20
12-26-83 ....Penn St 13, Washington 10
12-29-84 ....Southern Meth 27, Notre Dame 20
12-28-85 ....Alabama 24, Southern Cal 3
12-27-86 ....Arizona 30, N Carolina 21
12-25-87 ....UCLA 20, Florida 16
12-25-88 ....Washington St 24, Houston 22
12-25-89 ....Michigan St 33, Hawaii 13
12-25-90 ....Syracuse 28, Arizona 0

City: Honolulu.

Stadium: Aloha Stadium.

Capacity: 50,000.

Automatic Berths: None.

Freedom Bowl

12-16-84 ....Iowa 55, Texas 17
12-30-85 ....Washington 20, Colorado 17
12-30-86 ....UCLA 31, Brigham Young 10
12-30-87 ....Arizona St 33, Air Force 28
12-29-88 ....Brigham Young 20, Colorado 17
12-30-89 ....Washington 34, Florida 7
12-29-90 ....Colorado St 32, Oregon 31

City: Anaheim.

Stadium: Anaheim Stadium.

Capacity: 70,500.

Automatic Berths: None.

Hall of Fame Bowl

12-23-86 ....Boston Col 27, Georgia 24
1-2-88 ....Michigan 28, Alabama 24
1-2-89 ....Syracuse 23, Louisiana St 10
1-1-90 ....Auburn 31, Ohio St 14
1-1-91 ....Clemson 30, Illinois 0

City: Tampa.

Stadium: Tampa Stadium.

Capacity: 74,315.

Automatic Berths: None.

Copper Bowl

12-31-89 ....Arizona 17, N Carolina St 10
12-31-90 ....California 17, Wyoming 15

City: Tucson.

Stadium: Arizona Stadium.

Capacity: 57,000.

Automatic Berths: None.

Blockbuster Bowl

12-28-90 ....Florida St 24, Penn St 17

City: Miami.

Stadium: Joe Robbie.

Capacity: 75,000.

Automatic Berths: None.

Bluebonnet Bowl (Discontinued)

12-19-59 ....Clemson 23, Texas Christian 7
12-17-60 ....Texas 3, Alabama 3
12-16-61 ....Kansas 33, Rice 7
12-22-62 ....Missouri 14, Georgia Tech 10
12-21-63 ....Baylor 14, LSU 7
12-19-64 ....Tulsa 14, Mississippi 7
12-18-65 ....Tennessee 27, Tulsa 6
12-17-66 ....Texas 19, Mississippi 0
12-23-67 ....Colorado 31, Miami (FL) 21
12-31-68 ....Southern Meth 28, Oklahoma 27
12-31-69 ....Houston 36, Auburn 7
12-31-70 ....Alabama 24, Oklahoma 24
12-31-71 ....Colorado 29, Houston 17
12-30-72 ....Tennessee 24, LSU 17
12-29-73 ....Houston 47, Tulane 7
12-23-74 ....N Carolina St 31, Houston 31
12-27-75 ....Texas 38, Colorado 21
12-31-76 ....Nebraska 27, Texas Tech 24
12-31-77 ....Southern Cal 47, Texas A&M 28
12-31-78 ....Stanford 25, Georgia 22
12-31-79 ....Purdue 27, Tennessee 22
12-31-80 ....N Carolina 16, Texas 7
12-31-81 ....Michigan 33, UCLA 14
12-31-82 ....Arkansas 28, Florida 24
12-31-83 ....Oklahoma St 24, Baylor 14
12-31-84 ....W Virginia 31, Texas Christian 14
12-31-85 ....Air Force 24, Texas 16
12-31-86 ....Baylor 21, Colorado 9
12-31-87 ....Texas 32, Pittsburgh 27

City: Houston.

Name change: Astro-Bluebonnet Bowl (1968-76).

Playing sites: Rice Stadium (1959-67, 1985-86), Astrodome (1968-84, 1987).

These Records Are Made to Be Broken

Forgive those weary statisticians at the NCAA if they wrote in the name David Klingler in pencil following the 1990 season. Klingler, the quarterback at Houston, still had one year of eligibility remaining after erasing 15 of former teammate and Heisman Trophy winner Andre Ware's NCAA records. Among the 33 records Klingler set or tied in 1990 are:

Single Season:
    Most yards gained, total offense (5221)
    Most yards gained per game, total offense (474.6)
    Most passes completed (374)
    Most passes completed per game (34)
    Most touchdowns scored passing (54)

Single Game:
    Most yards passing (716)
    Most touchdowns passing (11)

The 6–3, 210-lb junior led Houston to a 10–1 record but could garner no better than a fifth-place finish in the Heisman voting. Two QBs, Virginia's Shawn Moore and BYU's Ty Detmer, finished ahead of Klingler. Detmer, the Heisman winner, broke or tied eleven NCAA records, one-third as many as his Cougar counterpart.

NCAA Divisional Championships

Division I-AA

Year	Winner	Runner-Up	Score
1978	Florida A&M	Massachusetts	35-28
1979	Eastern Kentucky	Lehigh	30-7
1980	Boise St	Eastern Kentucky	3I-29
1981	Idaho St	Eastern Kentucky	34-23
1982	Eastern Kentucky	Delaware	17-14
1983	Southern Illinois	Western Carolina	43-7
1984	Montana St	Louisiana Tech	19-6
1985	Georgia Southern	Furman	44-42
1986	Georgia Southern	Arkansas St	48-21
1987	NE Louisiana	Marshall	43-42
1988	Furman	Georgia Southern	17-12
1989	Georgia Southern	SF Austin St	37-34
1990	Georgia Southern	NV-Reno	36-13

Division II

Year	Winner	Runner-Up	Score
1973	Louisiana Tech	Western Kentucky	34-0
1974	Central Michigan	Delaware	54-14
1975	Northern Michigan	Western Kentucky	16-14
1976	Montana St	Akron	24-13
1977	Lehigh	Jacksonville St	33-0
1978	Eastern Illinois	Delaware	10-9
1979	Delaware	Youngstown St	38-21
1980	Cal Poly SLO	Eastern Illinois	21-13
1981	SW Texas St	N Dakota St	42-13
1982	SW Texas St	UC-Davis	34-9
1983	N Dakota St	Central St (OH)	41-21
1984	Troy St	N Dakota St	18-17
1985	N Dakota St	N Alabama	35-7
1986	N Dakota St	S Dakota	27-7
1987	Troy St	Portland St	31-17
1988	N Dakota St	Portland St	35-21
1989	Mississippi Col	Jacksonville St	3-0
1990	N Dakota St	Indiana (PA)	51-11

Division III

Year	Winner	Runner-Up	Score
1973	Wittenberg	Juniata	41-0
1974	Central (IA)	Ithaca	10-8
1975	Wittenberg	Ithaca	28-0
1976	St John's (MN)	Towson St	31-28
1977	Widener	Wabash	39-36
1978	Baldwin-Wallace	Wittenberg	24-10
1979	Ithaca	Wittenberg	14-10
1980	Dayton	Ithaca	63-0
1981	Widener	Dayton	17-10
1982	W Georgia	Augustana (IL)	14-0
1983	Augustana (IL)	Union (NY)	21-17
1984	Augustana (IL)	Central (IA)	21-12
1985	Augustana (IL)	Ithaca	20-7
1986	Augustana (IL)	Salisbury St	31-3
1987	Wagner	Dayton	19-3
1988	Ithaca	Central (IA)	39-24
1989	Dayton	Union (NY)	17-7
1990	Allegheny	Lycoming	21-14 (OT)

NAIA Divisional Championships

Division I

Year	Winner	Runner-Up	Score
1956	St Joseph's (IN)		0-0
	Montana State		
1957	Kansas St-Pittsburg	Hillsdale (MI)	27-26
1958	Northeastern Oklahoma	Northern Arizona	19-13
1959	Texas A&I	Lenoir-Rhyne (NC)	20-7
1960	Lenoir-Rhyne	Humboldt St (CA)	15-14
1961	Kansas St-Pittsburg	Linfield (OR)	12-7
1962	Central St (OK)	Lenoir-Rhyne (NC)	28-13
1963	St John's (MN)	Prairie View (TX)	33-27
1964	Concordia-Moorhead		7-7
	Sam Houston		
1965	St John's (MN)	Linfield (OR)	33-0
1966	Waynesburg (PA)	WI-Whitewater	42-21
1967	Fairmont St (WV)	Eastern Washington	28-21
1968	Troy St (MI)	Texas A&I	43-35
1969	Texas A&I	Concordia-Moorhead	32-7
1970	Texas A&I	Wofford (SC)	48-7
1971	Livingston (AL)	Arkansas Tech	14-12
1972	E Texas St	Carson-Newman	21-18
1973	Abilene Christian	Elon (NC)	42-14
1974	Texas A&I	Henderson St (AR)	34-23
1975	Texas A&I	Salem (WV)	37-0
1976	Texas A&I	Central Arkansas	26-0
1977	Abilene Christian	Southwestern Oklahoma	24-7
1978	Angelo St	Elon (NC)	34-14
1979	Texas A&I	Central St (OK)	20-14
1980	Elon (NC)	Northeastern Oklahoma	17-10
1981	Elon (NC)	Pittsburg St	3-0
1982	Central St (OK)	Mesa (CO)	14-11
1983	Carson-Newman (TN)	Mesa (CO)	36-28
1984	Carson-Newman (TN)		19-19
	Central Arkansas		
1985	Central Arkansas		10-10
	Hillsdale (MI)		
1986	Carson-Newman (TN)	Cameron (OK)	17-0
1987	Cameron (OK)	Carson-Newman (TN)	30-2
1988	Carson-Newman (TN)	Adams St (CO)	56-21
1989	Carson-Newman (TN)	Emporia St (KS)	34-20
1990	Central St (OH)	Mesa St (CO)	38-16

Division II

Year	Winner	Runner-Up	Score
1970	Westminster (PA)	Anderson (IN)	21-16
1971	California Lutheran	Westminster (PA)	30-14
1972	Missouri Southern	Northwestern (IA)	21-14
1973	Northwestern (IA)	Glenville St (WV)	10-3
1974	Texas Lutheran	Missouri Valley	42-0
1975	Texas Lutheran	California Lutheran	34-8
1976	Westminster (PA)	Redlands (CA)	20-13
1977	Westminster (PA)	California Lutheran	17-9
1978	Concordia-Moorhead	Findlay (OH)	7-0
1979	Findlay (OH)	Northwestern (IA)	51-6
1980	Pacific Lutheran	Wilmington	38-10
1981	Austin Col		24-24
	Concordia-Moorhead		
1982	Linfield (OR)	William Jewell (MO)	33-15
1983	Northwestern (IA)	Pacific Lutheran	25-21
1984	Linfield (OR)	Northwestern (IA)	33-22
1985	WI-La Crosse	Pacific Lutheran	24-7
1986	Linfield (OR)	Baker (KS)	17-0
1987	Pacific Lutheran	Wisconsin-Stevens Point*	16-16
1988	Westminster (PA)	WI-La Crosse	21-14
1989	Westminster (PA)	WI-La Crosse	51-30
1990	Peru St (NEB)	Westminster (PA)	17-7

*Forfeited 1987 season due to use of an ineligible player.

Awards

Heisman Memorial Trophy

Awarded to the best college football player by the Downtown Athletic Club of New York City. The trophy is named after John W. Heisman, who coached Georgia Tech to the national championship in 1917 and later served as DAC athletic director.

Year	Player, College, Position	Year	Player, College, Position
1935	Jay Berwanger, Chicago, HB	1963	*Roger Staubach, Navy, QB
1936	Larry Kelley, Yale, E	1964	John Huarte, Notre Dame, QB
1937	Clint Frank, Yale, HB	1965	Mike Garrett, Southern Cal, HB
1938	†Davey O'Brien, Texas Christian, QB	1966	Steve Spurrier, Florida, QB
1939	Nile Kinnick, Iowa, HB	1967	Gary Beban, UCLA, QB
1940	Tom Harmon, Michigan, HB	1968	O. J. Simpson, Southern Cal, HB
1941	†Bruce Smith, Minnesota, HB	1969	Steve Owens, Oklahoma, HB
1942	Frank Sinkwich, Georgia, HB	1970	Jim Plunkett, Stanford, QB
1943	Angelo Bertelli, Notre Dame, QB	1971	Pat Sullivan, Auburn, QB
1944	Les Horvath, Ohio St, QB	1972	Johnny Rodgers, Nebraska, FL
1945	*†Doc Blanchard, Army, FB	1973	John Cappelletti, Penn St, HB
1946	Glenn Davis, Army, HB	1974	*Archie Griffin, Ohio St, HB
1947	†John Lujack, Notre Dame, QB	1975	Archie Griffin, Ohio St, HB
1948	*Doak Walker, Southern Meth, HB	1976	†Tony Dorsett, Pittsburgh, HB
1949	†Leon Hart, Notre Dame, E	1977	Earl Campbell, Texas, HB
1950	*Vic Janowicz, Ohio St, HB	1978	*Billy Sims, Oklahoma, HB
1951	Dick Kazmaier, Princeton, HB	1979	Charles White, Southern Cal, HB
1952	Billy Vessels, Oklahoma, HB	1980	George Rogers, S Carolina, HB
1953	John Lattner, Notre Dame, HB	1981	Marcus Allen, Southern Cal, HB
1954	Alan Ameche, Wisconsin, FB	1982	*Herschel Walker, Georgia, HB
1955	Howard Cassady, Ohio St, HB	1983	Mike Rozier, Nebraska, HB
1956	Paul Hornung, Notre Dame, QB	1984	Doug Flutie, Boston Col, QB
1957	John Crow, Texas A&M, HB	1985	Bo Jackson, Auburn, HB
1958	Pete Dawkins, Army, HB	1986	Vinny Testaverde, Miami (FL), QB
1959	Billy Cannon, Louisiana St, HB	1987	Tim Brown, Notre Dame, WR
1960	Joe Bellino, Navy, HB	1988	*Barry Sanders, Oklahoma St, RB
1961	Ernie Davis, Syracuse, HB	1989	*Andre Ware, Houston, QB
1962	Terry Baker, Oregon St, QB	1990	Ty Detmer, Brigham Young, QB

*Juniors (all others seniors).

†Winners who played for national championship teams the same year.

Note: Former Heisman winners and national media vote, with ballots allowing for three names (3 points for first, 2 for second, and 1 for third).

Jim Thorpe Award

Given to the best defensive back of the year, the award is presented by the Jim Thorpe Athletic Club of Oklahoma City.

Year	Player, College	Year	Player, College
1986	Thomas Everett, Baylor	1988	Deion Sanders, Florida St
1987	Bennie Blades, Miami (FL)	1989	Mark Carrier, Southern Cal
	Rickey Dixon, Oklahoma	1990	Darryl Lewis, Arizona

Outland Trophy

Given to the outstanding interior lineman, who is selected by the Football Writers Association of America.

Year	Player, College, Position	Year	Player, College, Position
1946	George Connor, Notre Dame, T	1961	Merlin Olsen, Utah St, T
1947	Joe Steffy, Army, G	1962	Bobby Bell, Minnesota, T
1948	Bill Fischer, Notre Dame, G	1963	Scott Appleton, Texas, T
1949	Ed Bagdon, Michigan St, G	1964	Steve DeLong, Tennessee, T
1950	Bob Gain, Kentucky, T	1965	Tommy Nobis, Texas, G
1951	Jim Weatherall, Oklahoma, T	1966	Loyd Phillips, Arkansas, T
1952	Dick Modzelewski, Maryland, T	1967	Ron Yary, Southern Cal, T
1953	J. D. Roberts, Oklahoma, G	1968	Bill Stanfill, Georgia, T
1954	Bill Brooks, Arkansas, G	1969	Mike Reid, Penn St, DT
1955	Calvin Jones, Iowa, G	1970	Jim Stillwagon, Ohio St, MG
1956	Jim Parker, Ohio St, G	1971	Larry Jacobson, Nebraska, DT
1957	Alex Karras, Iowa, T	1972	Rich Glover, Nebraska, MG
1958	Zeke Smith, Auburn, G	1973	John Hicks, Ohio St, OT
1959	Mike McGee, Duke, T	1974	Randy White, Maryland, DE
1960	Tom Brown, Minnesota, G	1975	Lee Roy Selmon, Oklahoma, DT

Outland Trophy (Cont.)

Year	Player, College, Position	Year	Player, College, Position
1976	*Ross Browner, Notre Dame, DE	1984	Bruce Smith, Virginia Tech, DT
1977	Brad Shearer, Texas, DT	1985	Mike Ruth, Boston Col, NG
1978	Greg Roberts, Oklahoma, G	1986	Jason Buck, Brigham Young, DT
1979	Jim Ritcher, N Carolina St, C	1987	Chad Hennings, Air Force, DT
1980	Mark May, Pittsburgh, OT	1988	Tracy Rocker, Auburn, DT
1981	*Dave Rimington, Nebraska, C	1989	Mohammed Elewonibi, Brigham Young, G
1982	Dave Rimington, Nebraska, C	1990	Russell Maryland, Miami (FL), DT
1983	Dean Steinkuhler, Nebraska, G		

*Juniors (all others seniors).

Vince Lombardi/Rotary Award

Given to the outstanding college lineman of the year, the award is sponsored by the Rotary Club of Houston.

Year	Player, College, Position	Year	Player, College, Position
1970	Jim Stillwagon, Ohio St, MG	1981	Kenneth Sims, Texas, DT
1971	Walt Patulski, Notre Dame, DE	1982	Dave Rimington, Nebraska, C
1972	Rich Glover, Nebraska, MG	1983	Dean Steinkuhler, Nebraska, G
1973	John Hicks, Ohio St, OT	1984	Tony Degrate, Texas, DT
1974	Randy White, Maryland, DT	1985	Tony Casillas, Oklahoma, NG
1975	Lee Roy Selmon, Oklahoma, DT	1986	Cornelius Bennett, Alabama, LB
1976	Wilson Whitley, Houston, DT	1987	Chris Spielman, Ohio St, LB
1977	Ross Browner, Notre Dame, DE	1988	Tracy Rocker, Auburn, DT
1978	Bruce Clark, Penn St, DT	1989	Percy Snow, Michigan St, LB
1979	Brad Budde, Southern Cal, G	1990	Chris Zorich, Notre Dame, NG
1980	Hugh Green, Pittsburgh, DE		

Butkus Award

Given to the top collegiate linebacker, the award was established by the Downtown Athletic Club of Orlando and named for college hall of famer Dick Butkus of Illinois.

Year	Player, College	Year	Player, College
1985	Brian Bosworth, Oklahoma	1988	Derrick Thomas, Alabama
1986	Brian Bosworth, Oklahoma	1989	Percy Snow, Michigan St
1987	Paul McGowan, Florida St	1990	Alfred Williams, Colorado

Davey O'Brien National Quarterback Award

Given to the No. 1 quarterback in the nation by the Davey O'Brien Educational and Charitable Trust of Fort Worth. Named for Texas Christian hall of fame quarterback Davey O'Brien (1936-38).

Year	Player, College	Year	Player, College
1981	Jim McMahon, Brigham Young	1986	Vinny Testaverde, Miami (FL)
1982	Todd Blackledge, Penn St	1987	Don McPherson, Syracuse
1983	Steve Young, Brigham Young	1988	Troy Aikman, UCLA
1984	Doug Flutie, Boston Col	1989	Andre Ware, Houston
1985	Chuck Long, Iowa	1990	Ty Detmer, Brigham Young

Note: Originally known as the Davey O'Brien Memorial Trophy, honoring the outstanding football player in the Southwest as follows: 1977—Earl Campbell, Texas, RB; 1978—Billy Sims, Oklahoma, RB; 1979—Mike Singletary, Baylor, LB; 1980—Mike Singletary, Baylor, LB.

Maxwell Award

Given to the nation's outstanding college football player by the Maxwell Football Club of Philadelphia.

Year	Player, College, Position	Year	Player, College, Position
1937	Clint Frank, Yale, HB	1948	Chuck Bednarik, Pennsylvania, C
1938	Davey O'Brien, Texas Christian, QB	1949	Leon Hart, Notre Dame, E
1939	Nile Kinnick, Iowa, HB	1950	Reds Bagnell, Pennsylvania, HB
1940	Tom Harmon, Michigan, HB	1951	Dick Kazmaier, Princeton, HB
1941	Bill Dudley, Virginia, HB	1952	John Lattner, Notre Dame, HB
1942	Paul Governali, Columbia, QB	1953	John Lattner, Notre Dame, HB
1943	Bob Odell, Pennsylvania, HB	1954	Ron Beagle, Navy, E
1944	Glenn Davis, Army, HB	1955	Howard Cassady, Ohio St, HB
1945	Doc Blanchard, Army, FB	1956	Tommy McDonald, Oklahoma, HB
1946	Charley Trippi, Georgia, HB	1957	Bob Reifsnyder, Navy, T
1947	Doak Walker, Southern Meth, HB	1958	Pete Dawkins, Army, HB

Maxwell Award (*Cont.*)

Year	Player, College, Position
1959	Rich Lucas, Penn St, QB
1960	Joe Bellino, Navy, HB
1961	Bob Ferguson, Ohio St, FB
1962	Terry Baker, Oregon St, QB
1963	Roger Staubach, Navy, QB
1964	Glenn Ressler, Penn St, C
1965	Tommy Nobis, Texas, LB
1966	Jim Lynch, Notre Dame, LB
1967	Gary Beban, UCLA, QB
1968	O. J. Simpson, Southern Cal, RB
1969	Mike Reid, Penn St, DT
1970	Jim Plunkett, Stanford, QB
1971	Ed Marinaro, Cornell, RB
1972	Brad Van Pelt, Michigan St, DB
1973	John Cappelletti, Penn St, RB
1974	Steve Joachim, Temple, QB

Year	Player, College, Position
1975	Archie Griffin, Ohio St, RB
1976	Tony Dorsett, Pittsburgh, RB
1977	Ross Browner, Notre Dame, DE
1978	Chuck Fusina, Penn St, QB
1979	Charles White, Southern Cal, RB
1980	Hugh Green, Pittsburgh, DE
1981	Marcus Allen, Southern Cal, RB
1982	Herschel Walker, Georgia, RB
1983	Mike Rozier, Nebraska, RB
1984	Doug Flutie, Boston Col, QB
1985	Chuck Long, Iowa, QB
1986	Vinny Testaverde, Miami (FL), QB
1987	Don McPherson, Syracuse, QB
1988	Barry Sanders, Oklahoma St, RB
1989	Anthony Thompson, Indiana, RB
1990	Ty Detmer, Brigham Young, QB

Walter Payton Player of the Year Award

Given to the top Division I-AA football player, the award is sponsored by Sports Network and voted on by Division I-AA sports information directors.

Year	Player, College, Position
1987	Kenny Gamble, Colgate, RB
1988	Dave Meggett, Towson St, RB
1989	John Friesz, Idaho, QB
1990	Walter Dean, Grambling, RB

The Harlon Hill Trophy

Given to the outstanding NCAA Division II college football player, the award is sponsored by the National Harlon Hill Awards Committee, Florence, AL.

Year	Player, College, Position
1986	Jeff Bentrim, N Dakota St, QB
1987	Johnny Bailey, Texas A&I, RB
1988	Johnny Bailey, Texas A&I, RB
1989	Johnny Bailey, Texas A&I, RB
1990	Chris Simdorn, N Dakota St, QB

NCAA Division I-A Individual Records

Career

SCORING

Most Points Scored: 394—Anthony Thompson, Indiana, 1986-89

Most Points Scored per Game: 11.9—Bob Gaiters, New Mexico St, 1959-60

Most Touchdowns Scored: 65—Anthony Thompson, Indiana, 1986-89

Most Touchdowns Scored per Game: 1.93—Ed Marinaro, Cornell, 1969-71

Most Touchdowns Scored, Rushing: 64—Anthony Thompson, Indiana, 1986-89

Most Touchdowns Scored, Passing: 84—Jim McMahon, Brigham Young, 1977-78, 80-81

Most Touchdowns Scored, Receiving: 38—Clarkston Hines, Duke, 1986-89

Most Touchdowns Scored, Interception Returns: 5—Ken Thomas, San Jose St, 1979-82; Jackie Walker, Tennessee, 1969-71

Most Touchdowns Scored, Punt Returns: 7—Johnny Rodgers, Nebraska, 1970-72; Jack Mitchell, Oklahoma, 1946-48

Most Touchdowns Scored, Kickoff Returns: 6—Anthony Davis, Southern Cal, 1972-74

PASSING

Highest Passing Efficiency Rating: 156.9—Jim McMahon, Brigham Young, 1977-78, 80-81 (1060 attempts, 653 completions, 34 interceptions, 9536 yards, 84 TD passes)

Most Passes Attempted: 1484—Todd Santos, San Diego St, 1984-87

Most Passes Attempted per Game: 39.6—Mike Perez, San Jose St, 1986-87

Most Passes Completed: 910—Todd Santos, San Diego St, 1984-87

Most Passes Completed per Game: 25.9—Doug Gaynor, Long Beach St, 1984-85

Highest Completion Percentage: 65.2—Steve Young, Brigham Young, 1981-83

Most Yards Gained: 11,425—Todd Santos, San Diego St, 1984-87

Most Yards Gained per Game: 309.7—Mike Perez, San Jose St, 1986-87

TOTAL OFFENSE

Most Plays: 1722—Todd Santos, San Diego St, 1984-87

Most Plays per Game: 48.5—Doug Gaynor, Long Beach St, 1984-85

Most Yards Gained: 11,317—Doug Flutie, Boston Col, 1981-84 (10,579 passing, 738 rushing)

Most Yards Gained per Game: 309.1—Mike Perez, San Jose St, 1986-87

Most 300+ Yard Games: 18—Steve Young, Brigham Young, 1981-83

RUSHING

Most Rushes: 1215—Steve Bartalo, Colorado St, 1983-86 (4813 yds)

Most Rushes per Game: 34.0—Ed Marinaro, Cornell, 1969-71

Most Yards Gained: 6082—Tony Dorsett, Pittsburgh, 1973-76

Most Yards Gained per Game: 174.6—Ed Marinaro, Cornell, 1969-71

Most 100+ Yard Games: 33—Tony Dorsett, Pittsburgh, 1973-76; Archie Griffin, Ohio St, 1972-75

Most 200+ Yard Games: 11—Marcus Allen, Southern Cal, 1978-81

SPECIAL TEAMS

Highest Punt Return Average: 23.6—Jack Mitchell, Oklahoma, 1946-48

Highest Kickoff Return Average: 36.2—Forrest Hall, San Francisco, 1946-47

Highest Average Yards per Punt: 45.6—Reggie Roby, Iowa, 1979-82

RECEIVING

Most Passes Caught: 263—Terance Mathis, New Mexico, 1985-87, 89

Most Passes Caught per Game: 10.0—Howard Twilley, Tulsa, 1963-65

Most Yards Gained: 4254—Terance Mathis, New Mexico, 1985-87, 89

Most Yards Gained per Game: 128.6—Howard Twilley, Tulsa, 1963-65

Highest Average Gain per Reception: 25.7—Wesley Walker, California, 1973-75

ALL-PURPOSE RUNNING

Most Plays: 1347—Steve Bartalo, Colorado St, 1983-86 (1215 rushes, 132 receptions)

Most Yards Gained: 7172—Napoleon McCallum, Navy, 1981-85 (4179 rushing, 796 receiving, 858 punt returns, 1339 kickoff returns)

Most Yards Gained per Game: 193.7—Howard Stevens, Louisville, 1971-72

Highest Average Gain per Play: 17.4—Anthony Carter, Michigan, 1979-82.

INTERCEPTIONS

Most Passes Intercepted: 29—Al Brosky, Illinois, 1950-52

Most Passes Intercepted per Game: 1.07—Al Brosky, Illinois, 1950-52

Most Yards on Interception Returns: 470—John Provost, Holy Cross, 1972-74

Highest Average Gain per Interception: 26.5—Tom Pridemore, W Virginia, 1975-77

Single Season

SCORING

Most Points Scored: 234—Barry Sanders, Oklahoma St, 1988

Most Points Scored per Game: 21.27—Barry Sanders, Oklahoma St, 1988

Most Touchdowns Scored: 39—Barry Sanders, Oklahoma St, 1988

Most Touchdowns Scored, Rushing: 37—Barry Sanders, Oklahoma St, 1988

Most Touchdowns Scored, Passing: 54—David Klingler, Houston, 1990

Most Touchdowns Scored, Receiving: 22—Emmanuel Hazard, Houston, 1989

Most Touchdowns Scored, Interception Returns: 3—by many players

Most Touchdowns Scored, Punt Returns: 4—James Henry, Southern Miss, 1987; Golden Richards, Brigham Young, 1971; Cliff Branch, Colorado, 1971

Most Touchdowns Scored, Kickoff Returns: Terance Mathis, New Mexico, 1989; Willie Gault, Tennessee, 1980; Anthony Davis, Southern Cal, 1974; Stan Brown, Purdue, 1970; Forrest Hall, San Francisco, 1946

PASSING

Highest Passing Efficiency Rating: 176.9—Jim McMahon, Brigham Young, 1980 (445 attempts, 284 completions, 18 interceptions, 4571 yards, 47 TD passes)

Most Passes Attempted: 643—David Klingler, Houston, 1990

Most Passes Attempted per Game: 58.4—David Klingler, Houston, 1990

Most Passes Completed: 374—David Klingler, Houston, 1990

Most Passes Completed per Game: 34.0—David Klingler, Houston, 1990

Highest Completion Percentage: 71.3—Steve Young, Brigham Young, 1983

Most Yards Gained: 5188—Ty Detmer, Brigham Young, 1990

Most Yards Gained per Game: 471.6—Ty Detmer, Brigham Young, 1990

THEY SAID IT

LaVell Edwards, BYU football coach, noting in 1976 that his squad that year included 20 Mormon missionaries: "If we don't win our first few games, we might start looking for some hell raisers."

TOTAL OFFENSE

Most Plays: 704—David Klingler, Houston, 1990
Most Yards Gained: 5221—David Klingler, Houston, 1990
Most Yards Gained per Game: 474.6—David Klingler, Houston, 1990
Most 300+ Yard Games: 11—Jim McMahon, Brigham Young, 1980

RUSHING

Most Rushes: 403—Marcus Allen, Southern Cal, 1981
Most Rushes per Game: 39.6—Ed Marinaro, Cornell, 1971
Most Yards Gained: 2628—Barry Sanders, Oklahoma St, 1988
Most Yards Gained per Game: 238.9—Barry Sanders, Oklahoma St, 1988
Most 100+ Yard Games: 11—by 9 players, most recently Barry Sanders, Oklahoma St, 1988

THEY SAID IT

Ray Jenkins, then Montana State football coach, assessing his team's prospects in 1959: "We definitely will be improved this year. Last year we lost 10 games. This year we only scheduled nine."

RECEIVING

Most Passes Caught: 142—Emmanuel Hazard, Houston, 1989
Most Passes Caught per Game: 13.4—Howard Twilley, Tulsa, 1965
Most Yards Gained: 1779—Howard Twilley, Tulsa, 1965
Most Yards Gained per Game: 177.9—Howard Twilley, Tulsa, 1965
Highest Average Gain per Reception: 27.9—Elmo Wright, Houston, 1968

ALL-PURPOSE RUNNING

Most Plays: 432—Marcus Allen, Southern Cal, 1981
Most Yards Gained: 3250—Barry Sanders, Oklahoma St, 1988
Most Yards Gained per Game: 295.5—Barry Sanders, Oklahoma St, 1988
Highest Average Gain per Play: 18.2—Jim Sandusky, San Diego St, 1983

INTERCEPTIONS

Most Passes Intercepted: 14—Al Worley, Washington, 1968
Most Yards on Interception Returns: 302—Charles Phillips, Southern Cal, 1974
Highest Average Gain per Interception: 50.6—Norm Thompson, Utah, 1969

SPECIAL TEAMS

Highest Punt Return Average: 25.9—Bill Blackstock, Tennessee, 1951
Highest Kickoff Return Average: 38.2—Forrest Hall, San Francisco, 1946
Highest Average Yards per Punt: 49.8—Reggie Roby, Iowa, 1981

Single Game

SCORING

Most Points Scored: 48—Howard Griffith, Illinois, 1990 (vs Southern Illinois)
Most Field Goals: 7—Dale Klein, Nebraska, 1985 (vs Missouri)
Most Extra Points (Kick): 13—Terry Leiweke, Houston, 1968 (vs Tulsa)
Most Extra Points (2-Pts): 6—Jim Pilot, New Mexico St, 1961 (vs Hardin-Simmons)

TOTAL OFFENSE

Most Yards Gained: 732—David Klingler, Houston, 1990 (vs Arizona St)

RUSHING

Most Yards Gained: 377—Anthony Thompson, Indiana, 1989 (vs Wisconsin)
Most Touchdowns Rushed: 8—Howard Griffith, Illinois, 1990 (vs Southern Illinois)

PASSING

Most Passes Completed: 48—David Klingler, Houston, 1990 (vs Southern Methodist)
Most Yards Gained: 716—David Klingler, Houston, 1990 (vs Arizona St)
Most Touchdowns Passed: 11—David Klingler, Houston, 1990 [vs Eastern Washington (I-AA)]

RECEIVING

Most Passes Caught: 22—Jay Miller, Brigham Young, 1973 (vs New Mexico)
Most Yards Gained: 349—Chuck Hughes, UTEP, 1965 (vs N Texas St)
Most Touchdown Catches: 6—Tim Delaney, San Diego St, 1969 (vs New Mexico St)

THEY SAID IT

George Perles, Michigan State football coach and renowned malapropist, on women in the locker room: "I think we probably expose our players to the media as well as anybody."

Career

Scoring

POINTS (KICKERS)

	Years	Pts
Derek Schmidt, Florida St	1984-87	393
Luis Zendejas, Arizona St	1981-84	368
Jeff Jaeger, Washington	1983-86	358
Roman Anderson, Houston*	1988-	354
John Lee, UCLA	1982-85	353
Max Zendejas, Arizona	1982-85	353
Kevin Butler, Georgia	1981-84	353

POINTS (NON-KICKERS)

	Years	Pts
Anthony Thompson, Indiana	1986-89	394
Tony Dorsett, Pittsburgh	1973-76	356
Glenn Davis, Army	1943-46	354
Art Luppino, Arizona	1953-56	337
Steve Owens, Oklahoma	1967-69	336

POINTS PER GAME (NON-KICKERS)

	Years	Pts/Game
Bob Gaiters, New Mexico St	1959-60	11.9
Ed Marinaro, Cornell	1969-71	11.8
Bill Burnett, Arkansas	1968-70	11.3
Steve Owens, Oklahoma	1967-69	11.2
Eddie Talboom, Wyoming	1948-50	10.8

Total Offense

YARDS GAINED

	Years	Yds
Doug Flutie, Boston Col	1981-84	11,317
Ty Detmer, Brigham Young	1988-90*	10,664
Todd Santos, San Diego St	1984-87	10,513
Kevin Sweeney, Fresno St	1982-86	10,252
Brian McClure, Bowling Green	1982-85	9,774

YARDS PER GAME

	Years	Yds/Game
Mike Perez, San Jose St	1986-87	309.1
Doug Gaynor, Long Beach St	1984-85	305.0
Tony Eason, Illinois	1981-82	299.5
Steve Young, Brigham Young	1981-83	284.4
Doug Flutie, Boston Col	1981-84	269.5

Rushing

YARDS GAINED

	Years	Yds
Tony Dorsett, Pittsburgh	1973-76	6082
Charles White, Southern Cal	1976-79	5598
Herschel Walker, Georgia	1980-82	5259
Archie Griffin, Ohio St	1972-75	5177
Anthony Thompson, Indiana	1986-89	4965

YARDS PER GAME

	Years	Yds/Game
Ed Marinaro, Cornell	1969-71	174.6
O. J. Simpson, Southern Cal	1967-68	164.4
Herschel Walker, Georgia	1980-82	159.4
Tony Dorsett, Pittsburgh	1973-76	141.4
Mike Rozier, Nebraska	1981-83	136.6

TOUCHDOWNS RUSHING

	Years	TD
Anthony Thompson, Indiana	1986-89	64
Steve Owens, Oklahoma	1967-69	56
Tony Dorsett, Pittsburgh	1973-76	55
Ed Marinaro, Cornell	1969-71	50
Mike Rozier, Nebraska	1981-83	49

* Still Active.

Passing

PASSING EFFICIENCY

	Years	Rating
Jim McMahon, Brigham Young	1977-78,80-81	156.9
Steve Young, Brigham Young	1982,84-86	149.8
Robbie Bosco, Brigham Young	1981-83	149.4
Chuck Long, Iowa	1981-85	148.9
Andre Ware, Houston	1987-89	143.3

Note: Minimum 500 completions.

YARDS GAINED

	Years	Yds
Todd Santos, San Diego St	1984-87	11,425
Ty Detmer, Brigham Young	1988-90*	11,000
Kevin Sweeney, Fresno St	1982-86	10,623
Doug Flutie, Boston Col	1981-84	10,579
Brian McClure, Bowling Green	1982-85	10,280
Ben Bennett, Duke	1980-83	9,614

Note: Minimum 500 completions.

COMPLETIONS

	Years	Comp
Todd Santos, San Diego St	1984-87	910
Brian McClure, Bowling Green	1982-85	900
Ben Bennett, Duke	1980-83	820
John Elway, Stanford	1979-82	774
Jack Trudeau, Illinois	1981,83-85	736

Note: Minimum 500 completions.

TOUCHDOWNS PASSING

	Years	TD
Ty Detmer, Brigham Young	1988-90*	86
Jim McMahon, Brigham Young	1977-78,80-81	84
Joe Adams, Tennessee St	1977-80	81
John Elway, Stanford	1979-82	77
Andre Ware, Houston	1987-89	75

Receiving

CATCHES

	Years	No.
Terance Mathis, New Mexico	1985-87,89	263
Mark Templeton, Long Beach St	1983-86	262
Howard Twilley, Tulsa	1963-65	261
David Williams, Illinois	1983-85	245
Marc Zeno, Tulane	1984-87	236

CATCHES PER GAME

	Years	No./Game
Emmanuel Hazard, Houston	1989-90	12.9
Howard Twilley, Tulsa	1963-65	10.0
Jason Phillips, Houston	1987-88	9.4
Neal Sweeney, Tulsa	1965-66	7.4
David Williams, Illinois	1983-85	7.4

YARDS GAINED

	Years	Yds
Terance Mathis, New Mexico	1985-87,89	4254
Marc Zeno, Tulane	1984-87	3725
Ron Sellers, Florida St	1966-68	3598
Elmo Wright, Houston	1968-70	3347
Howard Twilley, Tulsa	1963-65	3343

TOUCHDOWN CATCHES

	Years	TD
Clarkston Hines, Duke	1986-89	38
Terance Mathis, New Mexico	1985-87,89	36
Elmo Wright, Houston	1968-70	34
Howard Twilley, Tulsa	1963-65	32
Emmanuel Hazard, Houston	1989-90	31

Career (*Cont.*)

All-Purpose Running

YARDS GAINED	Years	Yds
Napoleon McCallum, Navy	1981-85	7172
Darrin Nelson, Stanford	1977-78,80-81	6885
Terance Mathis, New Mexico	1985-87,89	6691
Tony Dorsett, Pittsburgh	1973-76	6615
Paul Palmer, Temple	1983-86	6609

YARDS PER GAME	Years	Yds/Game
Sheldon Canley, San Jose St.	1988-90*	205.8
Howard Stevens, Louisville	1971-72	193.7
O. J. Simpson, Southern Cal	1967-68	192.9
Ed Marinaro, Cornell	1969-71	183.0
Herschel Walker, Georgia	1980-82	174.2

Big Crowds in Michigan

The University of Michigan has hosted the 10 largest regular-season college-football crowds in the 42 seasons that official national attendance records have been maintained.

Crowd	Date	Results
106,255	11-17-79	Michigan 15, Ohio St 18
106,208	10-08-88	Michigan 17, Michigan St 3
106,141	10-11-86	Michigan 27, Michigan St 6
106,115	11-19-83	Michigan 24, Ohio St 21
106,113	10-09-82	Michigan 31, Michigan St 17
106,111	11-19-77	Michigan 14, Ohio St 6
106-104	10-22-88	Michigan 31, Indiana 6
106,102	11-23-85	Michigan 27, Ohio St 17
106,098	9-12-87	Michigan 7, Notre Dame 26
106,043	11-21-81	Michigan 9, Ohio St 14

Interceptions

PLAYER/SCHOOL	Years	Int
Al Brosky, Illinois	1950-52	2*
John Provost, Holy Cross	1972-74	2
Martin Bayless, Bowling Green	1980-83	2
Tom Curtis, Michigan	1967-69	2*
Tony Thurman, Boston Col	1981-84	2*

Punting Average

PLAYER/SCHOOL	Years	Avg
Reggie Roby, Iowa	1979-82	45.*
Greg Montgomery, Michigan St	1985-87	45.
Tom Tupa, Ohio St	1984-87	45.2
Barry Helton, Colorado	1984-87	44.9
Ray Guy, Southern Miss	1970-72	44.7

Note: At least 150 punts kicked.

Punt Return Average

PLAYER/SCHOOL	Years	Avg
Jack Mitchell, Oklahoma	1946-48	23.6
Gene Gibson, Cincinnati	1949-50	20.5
Eddie Macon, Pacific	1949-51	18.9
Jackie Robinson, UCLA	1939-40	18.8
Mike Fuller, Auburn	1972-74	17.7
Bobby Dillon, Texas	1949-51	17.7

Note: At least 1.2 punt returns per game.

Kickoff Return Average

PLAYER/SCHOOL	Years	Avg
Forrest Hall, San Francisco	1946-47	36.2
Anthony Davis, Southern Cal	1972-74	35.1
Overton Curtis, Utah St	1957-58	31.0
Altie Taylor, Utah St	1966-68	29.3
Stan Brown, Purdue	1968-70	28.8

*Denotes player is still active.

Note: At least 1.2 kickoff returns per game.

Single Season

Scoring

POINTS	Year	Pts
Barry Sanders, Oklahoma St.	1988	234
Mike Rozier, Nebraska	1983	174
Lydell Mitchell, Penn St	1971	174
Art Luppino, Arizona	1954	166
Bobby Reynolds, Nebraska	1950	157

FIELD GOALS	Year	FG
John Lee, UCLA	1984	29
Paul Woodside, W Virginia	1982	28
Luis Zendejas, Arizona St	1983	28
Fuad Reveiz, Tennessee	1982	27

Note: Three tied with 25 each.

All-Purpose Running

YARDS GAINED	Year	Yds
Barry Sanders, Oklahoma St.	1988	3250
Mike Pringle, Fullerton St	1989	2690
Paul Palmer, Temple	1986	2633
Marcus Allen, Southern Cal	1981	2559
Sheldon Canley, San Jose St.	1989	2513

YARDS PER GAME	Years	Yds/Game
Barry Sanders, Oklahoma St.	1988	295.5
Byron "Whizzer" White, Colorado	1937	246.3
Mike Pringle, Fullerton St	1989	244.6
Paul Palmer, Temple	1986	239.4
Marcus Allen, Southern Cal	1981	232.6

Total Offense

YARDS GAINED

	Year	Yds
David Klingler, Houston	1990	5221
Ty Detmer, Brigham Young	1990	5022
Andre Ware, Houston	1989	4661
Jim McMahon, Brigham Young	1980	4627
Ty Detmer, Brigham Young	1989	4433

YARDS PER GAME

	Year	Yds/Game
David Klingler, Houston	1990	474.6
Andre Ware, Houston	1989	423.7
Ty Detmer, Brigham Young	1990	418.5
Steve Young, Brigham Young	1983	395.1
Scott Mitchell, Utah	1988	390.8

Rushing

YARDS GAINED

	Year	Yds
Barry Sanders, Oklahoma St.	1988	2628
Marcus Allen, Southern Cal.	1981	2342
Mike Rozier, Nebraska	1983	2148
Tony Dorsett, Pittsburgh	1976	1948
Lorenzo White, Michigan St	1985	1908

YARDS PER GAME

	Year	Yds/Game
Barry Sanders, Oklahoma St.	1988	238.9
Marcus Allen, Southern Cal.	1981	212.9
Ed Marinaro, Cornell	1971	209.0
Charles White, Southern Cal.	1979	180.3
Mike Rozier, Nebraska	1983	179.0

TOUCHDOWNS RUSHING

	Year	TD
Barry Sanders, Oklahoma St.	1988	37
Mike Rozier, Nebraska	1983	29
Ed Marinaro, Cornell	1971	24
Anthony Thompson, Indiana	1988	24
Anthony Thompson, Indiana	1989	24

Passing

PASSING EFFICIENCY

	Year	Rating
Jim McMahon, Brigham Young	1980	176.9
Ty Detmer, Brigham Young	1989	175.6
Jerry Rhome, Tulsa	1964	172.6
Steve Young, Brigham Young	1983	168.5
Vinny Testaverde, Miami (FL)	1986	165.8
Brian Dowling, Yale	1968	165.8

YARDS GAINED

	Year	Yds
Ty Detmer, Brigham Young	1990	5188
David Klingler, Houston	1990	5140
Andre Ware, Houston	1989	4699
Jim McMahon, Brigham Young	1980	4571
Ty Detmer, Brigham Young	1989	4560

COMPLETIONS

	Year	Att	Comp
David Klingler, Houston	1990	643	374
Andre Ware, Houston	1989	578	365
Ty Detmer, Brigham Young	1990	562	361
Robbie Bosco, Brigham Young	1985	511	338
Scott Mitchell, Utah	1988	533	323

Note: Minimum 15 attempts per game.

TOUCHDOWNS PASSING

	Year	TD
David Klingler, Houston	1990	54
Jim McMahon, Brigham Young	1980	47
Andre Ware, Houston	1989	46
Ty Detmer, Brigham Young	1990	41
Dennis Shaw, San Diego St.	1969	39

Receiving

CATCHES

	Year	GP	No.
Emmanuel Hazard, Houston	1989	11	142
Howard Twilley, Tulsa	1965	10	134
Jason Phillips, Houston	1988	11	108
James Dixon, Houston	1988	11	102
David Williams, Illinois	1984	11	101

CATCHES PER GAME

	Year	No.	No./Game
Howard Twilley, Tulsa	1965	134	13.4
Emmanuel Hazard, Houston	1989	142	12.9
Jason Phillips, Houston	1988	108	9.8
Jerry Hendren, Idaho	1969	95	9.5
Howard Twilley, Tulsa	1964	95	9.5

YARDS GAINED

	Year	Yds
Howard Twilley, Tulsa	1965	1779
Emmanuel Hazard, Houston	1989	1689
Chuck Hughes, UTEP*	1965	1519
Henry Ellard, Fresno St	1982	1510
Ron Sellers, Florida St	1968	1496

*UTEP was Texas Western in 1965.

TOUCHDOWN CATCHES

	Year	TD
Emmanuel Hazard, Houston	1989	22
Tom Reynolds, San Diego St.	1969	18
Dennis Smith, Utah	1989	18
Clarkston Hines, Duke	1989	17
Howard Twilley, Tulsa	1965	16
Dan Bitson, Tulsa	1989	16

Single Game

Scoring

POINTS

	Opponent	Year	Pts
Howard Griffith, Illinois	Southern Illinois	1990	48
Jim Brown, Syracuse	Colgate	1956	43
Showboat Boykin, Mississippi	Mississippi St	1951	42
Fred Wendt, UTEP*	New Mexico St	1948	42
Dick Bass, Pacific	San Diego St	1958	38

*UTEP was Texas Mines in 1948.

FIELD GOALS

	Opponent	Year	FG
Dale Klein, Nebraska	Missouri	1985	7
Mike Prindle, Western Michigan	Marshall	1984	7

Note: Klein's distances were 32-22-43-44-29-43-43.
Prindle's distances were 32-44-42-23-48-41-27.

Single Game (*Cont.*)

Total Offense

YARDS GAINED	Opponent	Year	Yds
David Klingler, Houston...	Arizona St	1990	732
Matt Vogler, Texas Christian	Houston	1990	696
David Klingler, Houston...	Texas Christian	1990	625
Scott Mitchell, Utah	Air Force	1988	625
Tony Kopp, Pacific	New Mexico St	1990	601

Passing

YARDS GAINED	Opponent	Year	Yds
David Klingler, Houston............	Arizona St	1990	716
Matt Vogler, Texas Christian	Houston	1990	690
Scott Mitchell, Utah	Air Force	1988	631
Jeremy Leach, New Mexico	Utah	1989	622
Dave Wilson, Illinois	Ohio St	1980	621

COMPLETIONS	Opponent	Year	Comp
David Klingler, Houston.............	Southern Methodist	1990	48
Sandy Schwab, Northwestern...	Michigan	1982	45
Chuck Hartlieb, Iowa	Indiana	1988	44
Jim McMahon, Brigham Young...	Colorado St	1981	44
Gary Schofield, Wake Forest	Maryland	1981	43

TOUCHDOWNS PASSING	Opponent	Year	TD
David Klingler, Houston.............	E. Wash	1990	11

Note: Klingler's TD passes were 5-48-29-7-3-7-40-10-7-8-51.

Rushing

YARDS GAINED	Opponent	Year	Yd
Anthony Thompson, Indiana................	Wisconsin	1989	37
Rueben Mayes, Washington St	Oregon	1984	35
Mike Pringle, California St-Fullerton........	New Mexico St	1989	35
Eddie Lee Ivery, Georgia Tech.....................	Air Force	1978	35
Eric Allen, Michigan St	Purdue	1971	35

TOUCHDOWNS RUSHING	Opponent	Year	
Howard Griffith, Illinois	Southern Illinois	1990	

Note: Griffith's TD runs were 5-51-7-41-5-18-5-3.

Receiving

CATCHES	Opponent	Year	N
Jay Miller, Brigham Young ...	New Mexico	1973	2
Rick Eber, Tulsa...................	Idaho St	1967	2
Howard Twilley, Tulsa	Colorado St	1965	1
Ron Fair, Arizona St.............	Washington St	1989	1
Emmanuel Hazard, Houston	Texas Christian	1989	1
Emmanuel Hazard, Houston	Texas	1989	1

YARDS GAINED	Opponent	Year	Yd
Chuck Hughes, UTEP*............	N Texas St	1965	34
Rick Eber, Tulsa.......................	Idaho St	1967	32
Harry Wood, Tulsa	Idaho St	1967	31
Jeff Evans, New Mexico St.......	Southern Illinois	1978	31
Tom Reynolds, San Diego St...	Utah St	1971	29

*UTEP was Texas Western in 1965.

TOUCHDOWN CATCHES	Opponent	Year	TD
Tim Delaney, San Diego St...	New Mexico St	1969	6

Note: Delaney's TD catches were 2-22-34-31-30-9.

Longest Plays (since 1941)

RUSHING	Opponent	Year	Yds
Gale Sayers, Kansas................	Nebraska	1963	99
Max Anderson, Arizona St........	Wyoming	1967	99
Ralph Thompson, W Texas St...............................	Wichita St	1970	99
Kelsey Finch, Tennessee	Florida	1977	99

PASSING	Opponent	Year	Yds
Fred Owens to Jack Ford, Portland	St Mary's (CA)	1947	99
Bo Burris to Warren McVea, Houston..................	Washington St	1966	99
Colin Clapton to Eddie Jenkins, Holy Cross.............	Boston U	1970	99
Terry Peel to Robert Ford, Houston...............................	Syracuse	1970	99
Terry Peel to Robert Ford, Houston...............................	San Diego St	1972	99
Cris Collinsworth to Derrick Gaffney, Florida..................	Rice	1977	99
Scott Ankrom to James Maness, Texas Christian.....	Rice	1984	99

FIELD GOALS	Opponent	Year	Yds
Steve Little, Arkansas................	Texas	1977	6
Russell Erxleben, Texas............	Rice	1977	6
Joe Williams, Wichita St	Southern Illinois	1978	6
Tony Franklin, Texas A&M	Baylor	1976	6
Russell Erxleben, Texas............	Oklahoma	1977	64
Tony Franklin, Texas A&M	Baylor	1976	64

PUNTS	Opponent	Year	Yd
Pat Brady, Nevada*................	Loyola (CA)	1950	99
George O'Brien, Wisconsin....	Iowa	1952	96

*Note: Nevada was Nevada-Reno in 1950.

DIVISION I-A WINNINGEST TEAMS

All-Time Winning Percentage

	Yrs	W	L	T	Pct	GP	Bowl Record
Notre Dame	102	692	206	40	.759	938	10-6-0
Michigan	111	712	236	33	.742	982	10-12-0
Alabama	95	658	235	43	.728	934	23-17-3
Oklahoma	96	636	230	50	.722	916	18-10-1
Texas	98	671	257	31	.716	959	16-16-2
Southern Cal	98	613	236	51	.710	900	22-12-0
Ohio St	101	633	257	51	.700	941	11-12-0
Penn St	104	646	282	41	.688	969	16-9-2
Nebraska	101	644	284	39	.687	967	14-15-0
Tennessee	94	609	268	52	.684	929	17-14-0
Central Michigan	90	464	242	32	.650	738	3-1-0
Louisiana St	97	561	304	46	.641	911	11-16-1
Army	101	572	310	50	.641	932	2-1-0
Miami (OH)	102	530	293	40	.637	863	5-2-0
Arizona St	78	426	240	24	.635	690	9-5-1
Washington	101	534	303	49	.631	886	11-7-1
Georgia	97	565	322	53	.630	940	13-13-3
Auburn	98	537	324	45	.618	906	12-9-2
Michigan St	94	507	308	43	.617	858	5-5-0
Florida St	44	282	172	16	.617	470	11-7-2
Minnesota	107	547	334	43	.616	924	2-3-0
Arkansas	97	536	343	38	.605	917	9-14-3
UCLA	72	414	268	37	.602	719	9-7-1
Pittsburgh	101	554	361	42	.601	957	8-10-0

Note: Includes bowl games.

All-Time Victories

Michigan	712	Army	572	W Virginia	535
Notre Dame	692	Georgia	565	Washington	534
Texas	671	Louisiana St	561	Colorado	532
Alabama	658	Syracuse	556	Miami (OH)	530
Penn St	646	Pittsburgh	554	N Carolina St	522
Nebraska	644	Minnesota	547	Texas A&M	516
Oklahoma	636	Navy	541	Rutgers	513
Ohio St	633	Auburn	537	Michigan St	507
Southern Cal	613	Arkansas	536	California	506
Tennessee	609	Georgia Tech	536	Clemson	503

Note: Includes bowl games.

NUMBER ONE VS NUMBER TWO

The number 1 and number 2 teams, according to the Associated Press Poll, have met 25 times, including 8 bowl games, since the poll's inception in 1936. The number 1 teams have a 16-7-2 record in these matchups. Notre Dame (3-3-2) has played in 8 of the games.

Date	Results	Stadium
10-9-43	No. 1 Notre Dame 35, No. 2 Michigan 12	Michigan (Ann Arbor)
11-20-43	No. 1 Notre Dame 14, No. 2 Iowa Pre-Flight 13	Notre Dame (South Bend)
12-2-44	No. 1 Army 23, No. 2 Navy 7	Municipal (Baltimore)
11-10-45	No. 1 Army 48, No. 2 Notre Dame 0	Yankee (New York)
12-1-45	No. 1 Army 32, No. 2 Navy 13	Municipal (Philadelphia)
11-9-46	No. 1 Army 0, No. 2 Notre Dame 0	Yankee (New York)
1-1-63	No. 1 Southern Cal 42, No. 2 Wisconsin 37 (Rose Bowl)	Rose Bowl (Pasadena)
10-12-63	No. 2 Texas 28, No. 1 Oklahoma 7	Cotton Bowl (Dallas)
1-1-64	No. 1 Texas 28, No. 2 Navy 6 (Cotton Bowl)	Cotton Bowl (Dallas)
11-19-66	No. 1 Notre Dame 10, No. 2 Michigan St 10	Spartan (East Lansing)
9-28-68	No. 1 Purdue 37, No. 2 Notre Dame 22	Notre Dame (South Bend)
1-1-69	No. 1 Ohio St 27, No. 2 Southern Cal 16 (Rose Bowl)	Rose Bowl (Pasadena)
12-6-69	No. 1 Texas 15, No. 2 Arkansas 14	Razorback (Fayetteville)
11-25-71	No. 1 Nebraska 35, No. 2 Oklahoma 31	Owen Field (Norman)
1-1-72	No. 1 Nebraska 38, No. 2 Alabama 6 (Orange Bowl)	Orange Bowl (Miami)

NUMBER ONE VS NUMBER TWO (*Cont.*)

Date	Results	Stadium
1-1-79	No. 2 Alabama 14, No. 1 Penn St 7 (Sugar Bowl)	Sugar Bowl (New Orleans)
9-26-81	No. 1 Southern Cal 28, No. 2 Oklahoma 24	Coliseum (Los Angeles)
1-1-83	No. 2 Penn St 27, No. 1 Georgia 23 (Sugar Bowl)	Sugar Bowl (New Orleans)
10-19-85	No. 1 Iowa 12, No. 2 Michigan 10	Kinnick (Iowa City)
9-27-86	No. 2 Miami (FL) 28, No. 1 Oklahoma 16	Orange Bowl (Miami)
1-2-87	No. 2 Penn St 14, No. 1 Miami (FL) 10 (Fiesta Bowl)	Fiesta Bowl (Tempe)
11-21-87	No. 2 Oklahoma 17, No. 1 Nebraska 7	Memorial (Lincoln)
1-1-88	No. 2 Miami (FL) 20, No. 1 Oklahoma 14 (Orange Bowl)	Orange Bowl (Miami)
11-26-88	No. 1 Notre Dame 27, No. 2 Southern Cal 10	Coliseum (Los Angeles)
9-16-89	No. 1 Notre Dame 24, No. 2 Michigan 19	Michigan (Ann Arbor)

Longest Winning Streaks

Wins	Team	Yrs	Ended by	Score
47	Oklahoma	1953-57	Notre Dame	7-0
39	Washington	1908-14	Oregon St	0-0
37	Yale	1890-93	Princeton	6-0
37	Yale	1887-89	Princeton	10-0
35	Toledo	1969-71	Tampa	21-0
34	Pennsylvania	1894-96	Lafayette	6-4
31	Oklahoma	1948-50	Kentucky	13-7
31	Pittsburgh	1914-18	Cleveland Naval Reserve	10-9
31	Pennsylvania	1896-98	Harvard	10-0
30	Texas	1968-70	Notre Dame	24-11
29	Michigan	1901-03	Minnesota	6-6
28	Alabama	1978-80	Mississippi St	6-3
28	Oklahoma	1973-75	Kansas	23-3
28	Michigan St	1950-53	Purdue	6-0
27	Nebraska	1901-04	Colorado	6-0

Longest Unbeaten Streaks

No.	W	T	Team	Yrs	Ended by	Score
63	59	4	Washington	1907-17	California	27-0
56	55	1	Michigan	1901-05	Chicago	2-0
50	46	4	California	1920-25	Olympic Club	15-0
48	47	1	Oklahoma	1953-57	Notre Dame	7-0
48	47	1	Yale	1885-89	Princeton	10-0
47	42	5	Yale	1879-85	Princeton	6-5
44	42	2	Yale	1894-96	Princeton	24-6
42	39	3	Yale	1904-08	Harvard	4-0
39	37	2	Notre Dame	1946-50	Purdue	28-14
37	36	1	Oklahoma	1972-75	Kansas	23-3
35	34	1	Minnesota	1903-05	Wisconsin	16-12
34	33	1	Nebraska	1912-16	Kansas	7-3
34	32	2	Princeton	1884-87	Harvard	12-0
34	29	5	Princeton	1877-82	Harvard	1-0
33	30	3	Tennessee	1926-30	Alabama	18-6
33	31	2	Georgia Tech	1914-18	Pittsburgh	32-0
33	30	3	Harvard	1911-15	Cornell	10-0
32	31	1	Nebraska	1969-71	UCLA	20-17
32	30	2	Army	1944-47	Columbia	21-20
32	31	1	Harvard	1898-1900	Yale	28-0
31	30	1	Penn St	1967-70	Colorado	41-13
31	30	1	San Diego St	1967-70	Long Beach St	27-11
31	29	2	Georgia Tech	1950-53	Notre Dame	27-14
30	25	5	Penn St	1919-22	Navy	14-0
30	28	2	Pennsylvania	1903-06	Swarthmore	4-0
28	26	2	Southern Cal	1978-80	Washington	20-10
28	26	2	Army	1947-50	Navy	14-2
28	24	4	Minnesota	1933-36	Northwestern	6-0
28	26	2	Tennessee	1930-33	Duke	10-2
27	26	1	Southern Cal	1931-33	Stanford	13-7
27	24	3	Notre Dame	1910-14	Yale	28-0

Note: Includes bowl games.

Longest Losing Streaks

L		Seasons	Ended Against	Score
44	Columbia	1983-88	Princeton	16-14
34	Northwestern	1979-82	Northern Illinois	31-6
28	Virginia	1958-61	William & Mary	21-6
28	Kansas St	1945-48	Arkansas St	37-6
27	Eastern Michigan	1980-82	Kent St	9-7

Longest Series

GP	Opponents (Series Leader Listed First)	Record	First Game	GP	Opponents (Series Leader Listed First)	Record	First Game
100	Minnesota-Wisconsin	55-37-8	1890	93	Stanford-California	45-37-11	1892
99	Missouri-Kansas	47-43-9	1891	91	Auburn-Georgia Tech	47-39-4	1892
97	Nebraska-Kansas	73-21-3	1892	91	Navy-Army	43-41-7	1890
97	Texas Christian-Baylor	46-44-7	1899	90	Penn St-Pittsburgh	45-41-4	1893
97	Texas-Texas A&M	64-28-5	1894	88	Louisiana St-Tulane*	59-22-7	1893
95	N Carolina-Virginia	53-38-4	1892	88	Clemson-S Carolina	52-32-4	1896
95	Miami (OH)-Cincinnati	51-38-6	1888	88	Kansas-Kansas St	60-23-5	1902
94	Auburn-Georgia	45-42-7	1892	88	Oklahoma-Kansas	59-23-6	1903
94	Oregon-Oregon St	46-38-10	1894	88	Utah-Utah St	57-27-4	1892
93	Purdue-Indiana	57-30-6	1891				

*Disputed series record. Tulane claims 23-58-7 record.

NCAA Coaches' Records

ALL-TIME WINNINGEST DIVISION I-A COACHES

By Percentage

Coach (Alma mater)	Colleges Coached	Yrs	W	L	T	Pct
Knute Rockne (Notre Dame '14)†	Notre Dame 1918-30	13	105	12	5	.881
Frank W. Leahy (Notre Dame '31)†	Boston Col 1939-40; Notre Dame 1941-43, 1946-53	13	107	13	9	.864
George W. Woodruff (Yale '89)†	Pennsylvania 1892-01; Illinois 1903; Carlisle 1905	12	142	25	2	.846
Barry Switzer (Arkansas '60)	Oklahoma 1973-88	16	157	29	4	.837
Percy D. Haughton (Harvard '99)†	Cornell 1899-1900; Harvard 1908-16; Columbia 1923-24	13	96	17	6	.832
Bob Neyland (Army '16)†	Tennessee 1926-34, 1936-40, 1946-52	21	173	31	12	.829
Fielding "Hurry Up" Yost (Lafayette '97)†	Ohio Wesleyan 1897; Nebraska 1898; Kansas 1899; Stanford 1900; Michigan 1901-23, 1925-26	29	196	36	12	.828
Bud Wilkinson (Minnesota '37)†	Oklahoma 1947-63	17	145	29	4	.826
Jock Sutherland (Pittsburgh '18)†	Lafayette 1919-23; Pittsburgh 1924-38	20	144	28	14	.812
Bob Devaney (Alma, MI '39)†	Wyoming 1957-61; Nebraska 1962-72	16	136	30	7	.806
Tom Osborne (Hastings '59)*	Nebraska 1973-present	18	177	41	2	.805
Frank W. Thomas (Notre Dame '23)†	Chattanooga 1925-28; Alabama 1931-42, 1944-46	19	141	33	9	.795
Henry L. Williams (Yale '91)†	Army 1891; Minnesota 1900-21	23	141	34	12	.786
Joe Paterno (Brown '50)*	Penn St 1966-present	25	229	60	3	.784
Gil Dobie (Minnesota '02)†	N Dakota St 1906-07; Washington 1908-16; Navy 1917-19; Cornell 1920-35; Boston Col 1936-38	33	180	45	15	.781
Paul W. "Bear" Bryant (Alabama '36)†	Maryland 1945; Kentucky 1946-53; Texas A&M 1954-57; Alabama 1958-82	38	323	85	17	.780

*Active coach. †Hall of Fame member.

Note: Minimum 10 years as head coach at Division I institutions; record at 4-year colleges only; bowl games included; ties computed as half won, half lost.

Top Winners by Victories

	Yrs	W	L	T	Pct		Yrs	W	L	T	Pct
Paul "Bear" Bryant	38	323	85	17	.780	Warren Woodson	31	203	95	14	.673
Amos Alonzo Stagg	57	314	199	35	.605	Vince Dooley	25	201	77	10	.715
Glenn "Pop" Warner	44	313	106	32	.729	Eddie Anderson	39	201	128	15	.606
Woody Hayes	33	238	72	10	.759	Dana Bible	33	198	72	23	.715
Bo Schembechler	27	234	65	8	.775	Dan McGugin	30	197	55	19	.762
Joe Paterno	25	229	60	3	.789	Fielding Yost	29	196	36	12	.828
Jess Neely	40	207	176	19	.539	Howard Jones	29	194	64	21	.733
Bobby Bowden	25	205	74	3	.734	John Vaught	25	190	61	12	.745

Most Bowl Victories

	W	L	T		W	L	T
Paul "Bear" Bryant	15	12	2	Vince Dooley	8	10	2
*Joe Paterno	13	7	1	*Don James	9	4	0
John Vaught	10	8	0	*Johnny Majors	9	6	0
*Bobby Bowden	10	3	1	*Terry Donahue	7	2	1
Bobby Dodd	9	4	0	Bob Devaney	7	3	0
Barry Switzer	8	5	0	Dan Devine	7	3	0
Darrell Royal	8	7	1	*Lou Holtz	7	6	2
*Tom Osborne	8	10	0	Charlie McClendon	7	6	0

*Active coach.

WINNINGEST ACTIVE COACHES

By Percentage

						Bowls		
Coach, College	Years	W	L	T	Pct*	W	L	T
Tom Osborne, Nebraska	18	177	41	2	.809	8	10	0
Joe Paterno, Penn St	25	229	60	3	.789	13	7	1
LaVell Edwards, Brigham Young	19	175	59	1	.747	5	10	6
Bobby Bowden, Florida St	25	205	74	3	.732	10	3	1
Pat Dye, Auburn	17	143	51	4	.732	7	2	1
Herb Deromedi, Central Michigan	13	94	41	6	.688	0	1	0
Terry Donahue, UCLA	15	116	51	8	.686	7	2	1
Don James, Washington	20	155	75	3	.672	9	4	0
Lou Holtz, Notre Dame	21	162	79	5	.669	7	6	2
Earle Bruce, Colorado St	19	146	75	2	.659	7	5	0

*Ties computed as half win, half loss. Playoff games included.

Note: Minimum 5 years as Division I-A head coach; record at 4-year colleges only.

It's Never Over 'Til It's Over

Consider this next fall when the score is 32–0 at halftime, Paducah Tech is being made to look like carrion against Big Ol' State U., and you, sitting in a seat half a zip code away, realize it's been at least two touchdowns since you've felt any sensation in your toes: If you leave, you might miss out on the greatest comeback in college football history. How could you face your family and friends?

The fans remaining at Miami's Orange Bowl on November 10, 1984, were discomfited not so much by the weather as by ennui. It was a balmy south Florida afternoon and the 8–2 Hurricanes had raced out to a 31–0 halftime lead behind Bernie Kosar. In the locker room, Maryland coach Bobby Ross, disgusted with the effort of his 5–3 Terrapins, threatened to hold a practice that night.

Ross's practices must be hell. His Terps, duly inspired, scored 42 second-half points and stopped a last-minute two-point conversion attempt by Miami to defeat the defending national champs, 42–40. It still ranks as the greatest comeback in Division 1-A history.

Six weeks later, in a repeat performance at the Sun Bowl, Maryland found itself behind by 21 points to Tennessee at the half. Yawn. True to their mascot, the slow and steady tortoise, the Terps outlasted the Vols 28–27.

By Victories

Coach, Winning Percentage	Won	Coach, Winning Percentage	Won
Joe Paterno, Penn St .789	229	Grant Teaff, Baylor .521	155
Bobby Bowden, Florida St .732	205	Don James, Washington .672	155
Hayden Fry, Iowa .561	179	Bill Dooley, Wake Forest .565	150
Tom Osborne, Nebraska .809	177	Earle Bruce, Colorado St .659	146
LaVell Edwards, Brigham Young .747	175	Pat Dye, Auburn .732	143
Lou Holtz, Notre Dame .669	162	Jim Wacker, Texas Christian .610	137
Jim Sweeney, Fresno St .563	159	Bill Mallory, Indiana .593	136
Johnny Majors, Tennessee .610	158		

WINNINGEST ACTIVE DIVISION I-AA COACHES

By Percentage

Coach, College	Yrs	W	L	T	Pct*
Mark Duffner, Holy Cross	5	49	5	1	.891
Jimmy Satterfield, Furman	5	48	15	2	.754
Eddie Robinson, Grambling	48	366	128	15	.734
Roy Kidd, Eastern Kentucky	27	218	79	8	.728
W. C. Gorden, Jackson St	15	114	43	5	.719
Tubby Raymond, Delaware	25	202	83	2	.707
Chris Ault, Nevada	15	126	52	1	.707
William Collick, Delaware St	6	43	20	0	.683
Carmen Cozza, Yale	26	156	82	5	.652
Andy Talley, Villanova	11	65	37	2	.635

*Ties computed as half win, half loss. Playoff games included.

Note: Minimum 5 years as a Division I-A and/or Division I-AA head coach; record at 4-year colleges only.

By Victories

Eddie Robinson, Grambling	366	Phil Albert, Towson St	116
Roy Kidd, Eastern Kentucky	218	W. C. Gorden, Jackson St	114
Tubby Raymond, Delaware	202	Willie Jeffries, S Carolina St	110
Carmen Cozza, Yale	156	Joe Restic, Harvard	107
Chris Ault, NV-Reno	126	Don Read, Montana	107
Bill Bowes, New Hampshire	122	James Donnelly, Middle Tennessee St	100

WINNINGEST ACTIVE DIVISION II COACHES

By Percentage

Coach, College	Yrs	W	L	T	Pct*
Ken Sparks, Carson-Newman	11	104	30	1	.774
Bob Cortese, Fort Hays St	11	92	26	3	.772
Tom Beck, Grand Valley St	19	137	52	1	.724
Dick Lowry, Hillsdale	17	131	51	2	.717
Gene Carpenter, Millersville	22	148	61	4	.704
Willard Bailey, Norfolk St	20	148	62	5	.700
Pokey Allen, Portland St	5	43	19	2	.688
Jim Malosky, MN-Duluth	33	212	95	11	.684
Bill Burgess, Jacksonville St	6	45	20	3	.684
Tom Hollman, Edinboro	7	46	21	2	.681

*Ties computed as half win, half loss. Playoff games included.

Note: Minimum 5 years as a college head coach; record at 4-year colleges only.

By Victories

Jim Malosky, MN-Duluth .684	212	Tom Beck, Grand Valley St .724	137
Fred Martinelli, Ashland .625	191	Dick Lowry, Hillsdale .717	131
Gene Carpenter, Millersville .704	148	Bud Elliott, NW Missouri St .525	123
Willard Bailey, Norfolk St .700	148	Douglas Porter, Fort Valley St .594	121
Ron Harms, Texas A&I .628	140	Claire Boroff, Kearney St .642	118

WINNINGEST ACTIVE DIVISION III COACHES

By Percentage

Coach, College	Yrs	W	L	T	Pct*
Bob Reade, Augustana (IL)	12	117	15	1	.883
Lou Desloges, Plymouth St	5	45	7	1	.858
Mike Kelly, Dayton	10	96	20	1	.825
Al Bagnoli, Union (NY)	9	75	18	0	.806
Ron Schipper, Central (IA)	30	234	59	3	.796
Bill Manlove, Widener	22	179	46	1	.794
Rick Giancola, Montclair St	8	66	18	2	.779
Larry Kehres, Mount Union	5	40	11	2	.774
Walt Hameline, Wagner	10	81	23	2	.774
Jim Luckhardt, Washington & Jefferson	9	67	20	2	.764

*Ties computed as half win, half loss. Playoff games included.

Note: Minimum 5 years as a college head coach; record at 4-year colleges only.

By Victories (Minimum of 100)

John Gagliardi, St John's (MN) .741	275	Roger Harring, WI-LaCrosse .750	174
Ron Schipper, Central (IA) .796	234	Jim Ostendarp, Amherst .664	168
Keith Piper, Denison .591	193	Jim Christopherson, Concordia-Moorhead .718	159
Jim Butterfield, Ithaca .736	179	Frank Girardi, Lycoming .724	132
Bill Manlove, Widener .794	179	Joe McDaniel, Centre .581	130

NAIA Coaches' Records

WINNINGEST ACTIVE NAIA COACHES

By Percentage

DIVISION I

Coach, College	Yrs	W	L	T	Pct*
Ken Sparks, Carson-Newman	11	104	30	1	.774
Billy Joe, Central St (OH)	17	139	47	3	.743
Bob Cortese, Fort Hays St	11	86	31	3	.729
Dennis Miller, Northern St (SD)	6	38	16	0	.704
Jim Malosky, MN-Duluth	33	205	104	9	.659

DIVISION II

Coach, College	Yrs	W	L	T	Pct
Mike Dunbar, Central Washington	5	45	8	1	.842
Ted Kessinger, Bethany	15	123	28	0	.808
Ad Rutschman, Linfield (OR)	23	173	45	3	.790
Frosty Westering, Pacific Lutheran	24	193	67	5	.743
Larry Korver, Northwestern (IA)	24	185	63	5	.741

*Ties computed as half win, half loss. Playoff games included.

Note: Minimum five years as a collegiate head coach and includes record against four-year institutions only.

Victories

DIVISION I		DIVISION II	
Jim Malosky, MN-Duluth	205	Frosty Westering, Pacific Lutheran	193
Buddy Benson, Ouachita Baptist	145	Larry Korver, Northwestern (IA)	186
Billy Joe, Central St (OH)	139	Ad Rutschman, Linfield	175
Ross Fortier, Moorhead St	138	Bill MacArthur, Western Oregon	164
Ken Sparks, Carson-Newman	104	Bob Petrino, Carroll (MT)	124

Pro Basketball

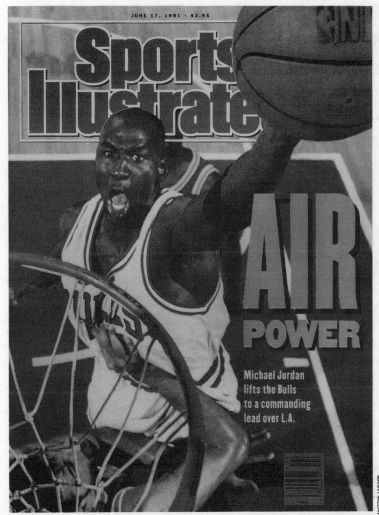

JUNE 17, 1991 · $2.95

Sports
Illustrated

AIR
POWER

Michael Jordan
lifts the Bulls
to a commanding
lead over L.A.

MANNY MILLAN

Michael Was Simply Magic

Michael Jordan, who had everything but an NBA title,
led Chicago to a win over L.A. | by JACK McCALLUM

FOR ALL THAT MAGIC JOHNSON AND LARRY Bird did to elevate the status of the NBA in the decade of the '80s, it should be noted that they also made life extremely difficult for many of their contemporaries. Point guards who came after Magic were invariably asked, Why can't you show his leadership, his on-the-court intelligence, his unselfishness? Similarly, forwards who came after Bird were asked, Why can't you demonstrate his versatility, his work ethic, his ability to get so much out of such seemingly modest natural gifts? And for those few All-Star athletes who avoided such questions, the championship successes of the dynamic duo were invariably thrown in their faces. Magic won a title as a 20-year-old rookie, and it took Bird only one year longer to get his first ring. The assumption was that if you were a *true* Hall of Fame player, your team would win a championship. Magic and Bird made it look....

"Easy," said Michael Jordan, completing the sentence. "The fact that Magic and Bird did it so quickly and so often left the impression that it was easy. Well, I can tell you this—it's not easy."

This, then, was the dilemma for the gravity-defying superstar as he entered the 1990–91 season, his seventh with the Chicago Bulls: Nothing short of a championship would enhance his reputation. He had already proven beyond a doubt that he was the greatest individual player of his generation and perhaps of all time. But the failure of the Bulls to win a championship had somehow become an indictment of his talent. If Jordan, the league's leading scorer with a 31.5 average and the MVP, could somehow make himself less, went the presumption, his teammates would be able to make themselves more.

The Bulls started the season slowly, experiencing trouble with the triangle offense developed by assistant coach Tex Winter and staunchly implemented by head coach Phil Jackson. Jordan referred to it, somewhat

Rodman and Thomas (behind) played dirty with the Bulls, but Jordan and Co. made it a clean sweep.

contemptuously, as "that triangle stuff." Meanwhile, over in the Western Conference, the Los Angeles Lakers were having trouble adapting to the program of their new coach, Mike Dunleavy. When Dunleavy's power-oriented, post-up game that turned the Lakers from Showtime into Slowtime was not instantly successful, rumors surfaced that some of the Lakers were upset with him. But Jackson and Dunleavy stayed the course without panicking and paddled

skillfully through the potential troubled waters of dissension. And in June, theirs were the only two teams still standing. How did it happen? Here is an assessment of the '90–91 season.

***

Frustrated, perhaps, by two years of Piston dominance, several Western Conference teams decided before or during the '90–91 season that changes were needed. It was admirable thinking. But it brought mixed results.

Dallas, for example, redid its roster in a big way, adding guard Fat Lever—he missed most of the season with a knee injury—and forwards Alex English from Denver and Rodney McCray from Sacramento. But the new Mavs couldn't overcome the serious knee injury suffered by their star-crossed franchise player, center Roy Tarpley. They looked good on paper but finished far out of the playoff picture.

The already talented Phoenix Suns seemed to have pulled off a coup when they snatched high-scoring forward Xavier McDaniel from Seattle early in the season. But the added offensive option only seemed to complicate matters, particularly for multi-talented point guard Kevin Johnson, who didn't particularly want or need another option. The Suns had begun the season with a

Bird got off the deck against the Pacers and led the Celtics to a dramatic playoff win over Indiana.

two-game split against the Jazz in, of all places, Tokyo, in what were the first regular-season games ever played outside the continental United States. And they ended it with a four-game playoff set against the Jazz. Only this one didn't end in a split. Utah took the series, and Phoenix, like Dallas, was left to ponder whether or not change had been the correct course of action.

Utah made one major move, acquiring veteran sharpshooter Jeff Malone from Washington, specifically to get further in the playoffs than they had the last two seasons, both of which ended with first-round losses. And Malone did help them get by Phoenix. But the Jazz were then eliminated by Portland, and, in the end, all that the addition of Malone proved was that Utah is now a three-man team instead of a two-man team. At least one more major piece will be needed

before point guard John Stockton (who led the NBA in assists for the fourth straight year) and the Malone boys, Karl and Jeff, can get to the Finals.

Ironically, another team that had change thrust upon it prospered as much as any. When Houston's All-Star center Hakeem Olajuwon was forced to the sidelines with an eye injury on Jan. 3, most observers felt that the Rockets were certain to misfire. But they played well during Olajuwon's 25-game absence and, in the process, locked up coach-of-the-year honors for the formerly lightly regarded Don Chaney.

San Antonio faced a similar unwanted change after point guard Rod Strickland broke a bone in his right hand in a nightclub fight on Feb. 2. He missed 20 games. The Spurs most certainly would have collapsed had a similar fate befallen center David Robinson. One of the enduring debates of the '90s will be the relative merits of the NBA's three premier centers, Robinson, Olajuwon, and the Knicks' Patrick Ewing, and right now it would seem that the younger, quicker and more versatile Robinson has the edge. His individual brilliance, and the return of Strickland, enabled the Spurs to win a dogfight with Utah and Houston and capture the Midwest Division.

Even in the talent-rich Pacific Division, which some observers considered the best in recent NBA history, the Trail Blazers were clearly the cream of the crop. They had speed and quickness, size and strength, All-Star starters and a deep bench, and one other key ingredient—they had been to the Finals one year earlier. The Blazers won their first 11 games, 19 of their first 20, and in January made their roster even stronger by picking up veteran swingman Walter Davis from Denver. That move sent shock waves all the way to Chicago, where an angry Jordan blasted general manager Jerry Krause for not landing Davis, an ex-North Carolina Tar Heel like himself. When the regular season ended, Portland had the NBA's best record (63–19).

***

In the Eastern Conference, the Celtics drew much of the regular-season attention

although they were nowhere near as dominating as the Blazers. Rookie coach Chris Ford had pledged in the preseason that his Celtics would get out and run, and unlike his predecessor, Jimmy Rodgers, he actually insisted that they do so during the season. The result was that opponents were presented with the dual problem of stopping the consistent half-court games of veterans Bird, Robert Parish, and Kevin McHale and also halting the up-tempo styles of shooting guard Reggie Lewis, CBA discovery Kevin Gamble, and the speedy point-guard tandem of Brian Shaw and rookie Dee Brown. Who knows how far the Celts would have gone had Bird's longtime nemesis, a bad back, not

Magic steadied the Lakers after their slow start and kept them on the move into the NBA Finals.

PETER READ MILLER

Brown, the Celtics' high-flying rookie, won the league's Slam Dunk Contest.

brought him down in the second half of the season?

Boston's competition in the Atlantic Division, such as it was, came from Philadelphia, which performed reasonably well without point guard Johnny Dawkins, who went down with a serious knee injury early in the season. The Sixers were easily the funniest team in the league, with an insult-a-minute frontcourt tandem of Charles Barkley, Rick Mahorn, and 7'7" Manute Bol. The

league office found little to chuckle about on the evening of March 26, however, when, during a game against the Nets at Brendan Byrne Arena, Barkley spit at an abusive fan, missed, and hit a young girl. Barkley was subsequently fined $10,000 and suspended for one game.

The Knicks made most of their noise off the court, too. Ewing's huge salary-cap-eating contract, the pouting of point guard Mark Jackson and the lame-duck status of general manager Al Bianchi drew more attention than their mediocre play. Now the Knicks will try to begin a new era (once again) under ex-Laker coach Pat Riley, who came aboard in June with a five-year, $6 million contract.

Even the once proud Central Division, which as recently as three years ago was considered, top to bottom, perhaps the toughest division in the history of the NBA, offered only two legitimate contenders, Detroit and Chicago. The once-promising Cleveland Cavaliers, unlike the Sixers, fell apart completely when their quarterback, Mark Price, went down with a knee injury early in the season. If Price comes back, the Cavs have a chance to rebound in 1991–92; if he doesn't, then general manager Wayne Embry and coach Lenny Wilkens will have to make some changes.

To continue the trend of the disappearing point guard, the Pistons, too, played for 10 weeks without their leader, Isiah Thomas, who had wrist surgery on Jan. 29. True, Detroit's performance was uneven enough to enable the Bulls to win the division title with scarcely a struggle. And when Isiah did return, he didn't seem to be 100%. But going into the playoffs, the healthy and increasingly confident Bulls were sure of one thing—the road to the Finals would go through Detroit.

***

In the playoffs, Golden State was easily the most entertaining team in the early going in the West, eliminating favored San Antonio before losing to the Lakers in five games. But playoff upsets were nothing new for the Warriors. Coach Don Nelson did what he always does: He put a dizzying number of lineup combinations on the floor, handed the ball to his scorers (Chris Mullin, Mitch Richmond and Tim Hardaway), told everybody else to get out of the way, then sat back and let the competition stew and sweat under the playoff pressure. San Antonio collapsed, the Lakers buckled but didn't bow.

In fact, L.A.'s Slowtime offense seemed to gather, well, not speed, but certainly momentum in the postseason, as the Lakers' primary new acquisition, Sam Perkins from Dallas, was able for the first time to truly show his versatility on a national stage. Portland, from afar, seemed to feel the Lakers' hot breath. The Trail Blazers strug-gled in their first two series against the lowly SuperSonics and the more formidable Jazz, and by the time they lined up to face the Lakers, their advantages in depth and overall athletic ability seemed to be negated by the Lakers' experience and composure. When the Trail Blazers showed one major weakness—Kevin Duckworth's poor shooting from the center position—the Lakers pounced on it and won the Western final. That put Magic in the Finals for the ninth time since joining the league in 1979–80.

Chuck Person's long-range shooting and short-range woofing almost produced a first-round upset for Indiana in the East playoffs before the Celtics prevailed in a scintillating five-game series. But the Pacers

Coleman, the top pick in the '90 draft, lived up to his billing when he was named rookie of the year.

AL TIELEMANS

The debate will continue, but for now Robinson tops the list of the NBA's best centers.

seriously depleted Boston's strength, and the Celtics lost three straight (Games 4, 5, and 6) and their second-round series to the Pistons. Detroit's defense and the overall ability of players like Dennis Rodman were too much for the Celts.

The Bulls, meanwhile, picked their way almost disdainfully through the playoff weeds in their side of the bracket. The Knicks were swept. The Sixers were gone in five. And now it was payback time with the Pistons coming to Chicago. The Bulls' defense was by this time a finely tuned machine, and the Pistons were unable to solve it. They tried pushing the Bulls around, but that didn't work, either. Seconds before Chicago completed a four-game sweep at the Palace of Auburn Hills, the Pistons walked off the court, deliberately ignoring the Bulls and refusing to shake their hands, one of the most classless exits in the history of pro sports. "But not really surprising," said Jordan, who had made his displeasure with the Detroit players very public during the series.

***

From the basketball-playing nations of Europe, where both players are national heroes, to Madison Avenue, where both players are megabuck phenomena, the Michael-Magic Finals were a dream come true.

Better yet, the first three games of the championship series, which ended with Chicago leading 2–1, seemed to promise an exciting six- or seven-game outcome. But it was not to be. The sound defensive strategy that the Bulls employed in Game 2 proved to be the difference. They used their size to surround the Lakers' post-up players, their quickness to harass shooting guard Byron Scott, and their youth and suddenly superior depth to wear down Magic. Games 4 and 5 were no contest, with the Bulls winning by 97–82 and 108–101. When it was over, Jordan and his fellow starters, Scottie Pippen, John Paxson, Horace Grant, and Bill Cartwright, were all heading, as has become the tradition for American champions, to Disney World. And in the not-too-distant future Jordan will be taking another, more important trip—to the Hall of Fame.

FOR THE RECORD • 1990 – 1991

NBA Final Standings

Eastern Conference

ATLANTIC DIVISION					CENTRAL DIVISION				
Team	W	L	Pct	GB	Team	W	L	Pct	GB
Boston	56	26	.683		Chicago	61	21	.744	
Philadelphia	44	38	.537	12	Detroit	50	32	.610	11
New York	39	43	.476	17	Milwaukee	48	34	.585	13
Washington	30	52	.366	26	Atlanta	43	39	.524	18
New Jersey	26	56	.317	30	Indiana	41	41	.500	20
Miami	24	58	.293	32	Cleveland	33	49	.402	28
					Charlotte	26	56	.317	35

Western Conference

MIDWEST DIVISION					PACIFIC DIVISION				
Team	W	L	Pct	GB	Team	W	L	Pct	GB
San Antonio	55	27	.671		Portland	63	19	.768	
Utah	54	28	.659	1	LA Lakers	58	24	.707	5
Houston	52	30	.634	3	Phoenix	55	27	.671	8
Orlando	31	51	.378	24	Golden State	44	38	.537	19
Minnesota	29	53	.354	26	Seattle	41	41	.500	22
Dallas	28	54	.341	27	LA Clippers	31	51	.378	32
Denver	20	62	.244	35	Sacramento	25	57	.305	38

1991 NBA Playoffs

CHICAGO BULLS 1991 PLAYOFF STATISTICS

Player	GP	Field Goals		3-Pt FG		Free Throws		Rebounds						
		FGM	Pct	FGM	FGA	FTM	Pct	Off	Total	A	Stl	TO	BS	Avg	Hi
Jordan	17	197	52.4	10	26	125	84.5	18	108	142	40	43	23	31.1	46
Pippen	17	152	50.4	4	17	80	79.2	37	151	99	42	55	19	21.6	32
Grant	17	91	58.3	0	0	44	73.3	56	138	38	15	20	6	13.3	22
Cartwright	17	70	51.9	0	0	22	68.8	25	80	32	9	21	7	9.5	16
Paxson	17	62	53.0	2	14	14	100.0	2	23	53	11	6	0	8.2	20
Armstrong	17	35	50.0	3	5	20	80.0	5	27	43	19	13	1	5.5	18
Hodges	17	33	42.3	11	28	3	75.0	0	4	10	11	11	0	4.7	16
Perdue	17	29	54.7	0	0	12	54.5	32	65	4	2	14	8	4.1	16
Levingston	17	21	51.2	0	0	3	50.0	22	41	7	10	2	7	2.6	10
King	11	8	29.6	0	1	7	63.6	9	22	2	1	9	1	2.1	4
Williams	12	6	46.2	0	1	11	55.0	4	20	3	1	4	3	1.9	5
Hopson	5	2	33.3	0	0	4	44.4	2	4	1	0	1	1	1.6	3
Bulls	17	696	51.4	30	92	345	76.3	212	683	434	161	212	76	103.9	126
Opponents	17	574	45.0	50	152	370	80.3	198	611	327	115	270	65	92.2	107

LA LAKERS 1991 PLAYOFF STATISTICS

Player	GP	Field Goals		3-Pt FG		Free Throws		Rebounds						
		FGM	Pct	FGM	FGA	FTM	Pct	Off	Total	A	Stl	TO	BS	Avg	Hi
Johnson	19	118	44.0	21	71	157	88.2	23	154	240	23	77	0	21.8	44
Worthy	18	161	46.5	4	24	53	73.6	25	73	70	19	40	2	21.1	36
Perkins	19	121	54.8	11	30	83	76.1	41	157	33	15	37	27	17.7	27
Divac	19	97	56.4	1	6	57	80.3	49	127	21	27	41	41	13.3	27
Scott	18	95	51.1	20	38	27	79.4	13	57	29	23	17	4	13.2	27
Teagle	18	47	37.6	0	0	25	78.1	8	28	11	8	16	4	6.6	17
Green	19	41	42.3	4	8	38	70.4	46	102	9	12	19	3	6.5	16
Campbell	14	25	65.8	0	0	7	46.7	8	29	3	6	6	8	4.1	21
Smith	7	6	46.2	0	0	2	66.7	3	3	2	1	6	0	2.0	12
Drew	18	14	42.4	3	11	4	66.7	0	8	21	0	9	0	1.9	8
Thomas	3	1	100.0	0	0	0	—	0	0	0	0	0	0	0.7	2
Thompson	8	2	28.6	0	0	0	—	3	9	0	0	1	3	0.5	2
Lakers	19	728	48.3	64	188	453	78.9	219	747	439	134	279	92	103.8	126
Opponents	19	785	48.7	56	176	327	77.7	239	762	472	158	258	88	102.8	125

NBA Awards

ALL-NBA TEAMS

FIRST TEAM

G Michael Jordan, Chicago
G Magic Johnson, LA Lakers
C David Robinson, San Antonio
F Karl Malone, Utah
F Charles Barkley, Philadelphia

SECOND TEAM

Kevin Johnson, Phoenix
Clyde Drexler, Portland
Patrick Ewing, New York
Dominique Wilkins, Atlanta
Chris Mullin, Golden State

THIRD TEAM

John Stockton, Utah
Joe Dumars, Detroit
Hakeem Olajuwon, Houston
James Worthy, LA Lakers
Bernard King, Washington

Master Lock NBA All-Defensive Teams

FIRST TEAM

G Michael Jordan, Chicago
G Alvin Robertson, Milwaukee
C David Robinson, San Antonio
F Dennis Rodman, Detroit
F Buck Williams, Portland

SECOND TEAM

Joe Dumars, Detroit
John Stockton, Utah
Hakeem Olajuwon, Houston
Scottie Pippen, Chicago
Dan Majerle, Phoenix

All-Rookie Teams
(Chosen Without Regard to Position)

FIRST TEAM	SECOND TEAM
Kendall Gill, Charlotte	Chris Jackson, Denver
Dennis Scott, Orlando	Gary Payton, Seattle
Dee Brown, Boston	Felton Spencer, Minnesota
Lionel Simmons, Sacramento	Travis Mays, Sacramento
Derrick Coleman, New Jersey	Willie Burton, Miami

NBA Individual Leaders

Scoring

	GP	Pts	Avg
Michael Jordan, Chi.	82	2580	31.5
Karl Malone, Utah	82	2382	29.0
Bernard King, Wash	64	1817	28.4
Charles Barkley, Phil	67	1849	27.6
Patrick Ewing, NY	81	2154	26.6
Michael Adams, Den	66	1752	26.5
Dominique Wilkins, Atl	81	2101	25.9
Chris Mullin, GS	82	2107	25.7
David Robinson, SA	82	2101	25.6
Mitch Richmond, GS	77	1840	23.9

Rebounds

	GP	Reb	Avg
David Robinson, SA	82	1063	13.0
Dennis Rodman, Det	82	1026	12.5
Charles Oakley, NY	76	920	12.1
Karl Malone, Utah	82	967	11.8
Patrick Ewing, NY	81	905	11.2
Brad Daugherty, Clev	76	830	10.9
Robert Parish, Bos	81	856	10.6
Benoit Benjamin, LA Clippers/Sea	70	723	10.3
Otis Thorpe, Hou	82	846	10.3
Derrick Coleman, NJ	74	759	10.3

Assists

	GP	Assists	Avg
John Stockton, Utah	82	1164	14.2
Magic Johnson, LA Lakers	79	989	12.5
Michael Adams, Den	66	693	10.5
Kevin Johnson, Phoe	77	781	10.1
Tim Hardaway, GS	82	793	9.7
Isiah Thomas, Det	48	446	9.3
Pooh Richardson, Minn	82	734	9.0
Gary Grant, LA Clippers	68	587	8.6
Sherman Douglas, Mia	73	624	8.5
Scott Skiles, Orl	79	660	8.4

Field-Goal Percentage

	FGA	FGM	Pct
Buck Williams, Port	595	358	60.2
Robert Parish, Bos	811	485	59.8
Kevin Gamble, Bos	933	548	58.7
Charles Barkley, Phil	1167	665	57.0
Vlade Divac, LA Lakers	637	360	56.5
Olden Polynice, Sea/LA Clippers	564	316	56.0
Otis Thorpe, Hou	988	549	55.6
Kevin McHale, Bos	912	504	55.3
David Robinson, SA	1366	754	55.2
John Paxson, Chi	578	317	54.8

Free-Throw Percentage

	FTA	FTM	Pct
Reggie Miller, Ind	600	551	91.8
Jeff Malone, Utah	252	231	91.7
Ricky Pierce, Mil/Sea	471	430	91.3
Kelly Tripucka, Char	167	152	91.0
Magic Johnson, LA Lakers	573	519	90.6
Scott Skiles, Orl	377	340	90.2
Kiki Vandeweghe, NY	288	259	89.9
Jeff Hornacek, Phoe	224	201	89.7
Eddie Johnson, Phoe/Sea	257	229	89.1
Larry Bird, Bos	183	163	89.1

Three-Point Field-Goal Percentage

	FGA	FGM	Pct
Jim Les, Sac	154	71	46.1
Trent Tucker, NY	153	64	41.8
Jeff Hornacek, Phoe	146	61	41.8
Terry Porter, Port	313	130	41.5
Scott Skiles, Orl	228	93	40.8
Danny Ainge, Port	251	102	40.6
Hersey Hawkins, Phil	270	108	40.0
Larry Bird, Bos	198	77	38.9
Glen Rice, Mia	184	71	38.6
Tim Hardaway, GS	252	97	38.5

Steals

	GP	Steals	Avg
Alvin Robertson, Mil	81	246	3.04
John Stockton, Utah	82	234	2.85
Michael Jordan, Chi.	82	223	2.72
Tim Hardaway, GS	82	214	2.61
Scottie Pippen, Chi	82	193	2.35
Mookie Blaylock, NJ	72	169	2.35
Michael Adams, Den	66	147	2.23
Hersey Hawkins, Phil	80	178	2.23
Kevin Johnson, Phoe	77	163	2.12
Chris Mullin, GS	82	173	2.11

Blocked Shots

	GP	BS	Avg
Hakeem Olajuwon, Hou	56	221	3.95
David Robinson, SA	82	320	3.90
Patrick Ewing, NY	81	258	3.19
Manute Bol, Phil	82	247	3.01
Chris Dudley, NJ	61	153	2.51
Larry Nance, Clev	80	200	2.50
Mark Eaton, Utah	80	188	2.35
Kevin McHale, Bos	68	146	2.15
Benoit Benjamin, LA Clippers/Sea	70	145	2.07
Pervis Ellison, Wash	76	157	2.07

NBA Team Statistics

Offense

Team	Field Goals		3-Pt Field Goals		Free Throws		Rebounds		A	Stl	Scoring
	FGM	Pct	3FGM	Pct	FTM	Pct	Off	Total			Avg
Denver	3901	44.0	300	28.3	1726	76.3	1520	4050	2005	856	119.9
Golden State	3566	48.5	270	33.7	2162	78.3	1113	3419	1954	803	116.6
Portland	3577	48.5	341	37.7	1912	75.3	1202	3763	2254	724	114.7
Phoenix	3573	49.6	138	31.9	2064	77.0	1132	3730	2209	687	114.0
Indiana	3450	49.3	249	33.2	2010	81.1	1018	3394	2181	658	111.7
Boston	3695	51.2	109	31.5	1646	82.4	1088	3785	2160	672	111.5
Chicago	3632	51.0	155	36.6	1605	76.0	1148	3490	2212	822	110.0
Atlanta	3349	46.4	271	32.4	2034	80.0	1235	3655	1864	729	109.8
San Antonio	3409	48.8	81	27.3	1883	76.6	1131	3788	2140	670	107.1
Houston	3403	46.7	316	32.0	1631	74.1	1275	3783	1906	796	106.7
Seattle	3500	49.2	136	31.9	1608	75.0	1222	3395	2042	861	106.6
Milwaukee	3337	48.0	257	34.1	1796	80.1	1079	3241	2075	894	106.4
LA Lakers	3343	48.4	226	30.4	1805	79.8	1078	3518	2091	642	106.3
Orlando	3298	45.5	270	35.8	1818	74.3	1233	3662	1809	602	105.9
Philadelphia	3289	47.5	195	31.6	1868	79.0	984	3480	1824	678	105.4
Utah	3214	49.2	148	32.3	1951	78.9	867	3341	2217	652	104.0
LA Clippers	3391	46.4	113	26.0	1596	70.2	1246	3746	2119	725	103.5
New York	3308	48.5	185	33.2	1654	77.0	1053	3489	2172	638	103.1
New Jersey	3311	44.4	161	27.5	1658	73.9	1400	3748	1782	748	102.9
Charlotte	3286	46.7	131	31.4	1725	77.9	1027	3227	2019	759	102.8
Miami	3280	45.9	140	30.2	1649	71.5	1232	3534	1904	757	101.8
Cleveland	3259	47.5	160	33.4	1665	76.5	1011	3340	2240	643	101.7
Washington	3390	46.6	55	19.4	1478	72.9	1173	3563	2081	588	101.4
Detroit	3194	46.5	131	29.8	1686	76.3	1206	3658	1825	487	100.1
Dallas	3245	47.1	193	32.2	1512	76.1	984	3344	1821	581	99.9
Minnesota	3265	44.9	108	28.3	1531	73.5	1275	3388	1885	712	99.6
Sacramento	3086	45.3	216	37.4	1540	73.2	1027	3245	1991	631	96.7

Defense (Opponent's Statistics)

Team	Field Goals		3-Pt Field Goals		Free Throws		Rebounds		Stl	Scoring	
	FGM	Pct	3FGM	Pct	FTM	Pct	Off	Total		Avg	Diff
Detroit	3053	45.3	157	31.2	1674	77.0	1002	3276	581	96.8	+3.3
LA Lakers	3354	46.2	178	31.1	1278	75.2	1131	3318	668	99.6	+6.7
Utah	3217	45.9	205	30.7	1615	77.3	1101	3379	686	100.7	+3.3
Chicago	3267	47.5	190	30.4	1554	77.0	1062	3224	633	101.0	+9.1
San Antonio	3265	44.8	218	31.0	1664	76.1	1122	3392	801	102.6	+4.5
Houston	3337	45.6	183	29.5	1609	77.1	1242	3673	711	103.2	+3.5
New York	3410	47.6	183	33.6	1471	77.3	1119	3455	724	103.3	−0.2
Sacramento	3142	47.0	155	31.6	2045	76.1	1164	3707	699	103.5	−6.8
Minnesota	3320	49.0	171	33.9	1680	75.7	1094	3473	512	103.5	−3.9
Milwaukee	3290	48.6	189	32.9	1755	75.9	1108	3423	704	104.0	+2.5
Cleveland	3459	48.6	163	32.3	1464	76.4	1097	3495	710	104.2	−2.5
Dallas	3346	48.2	178	30.5	1700	74.0	1116	3605	650	104.5	−4.6
Seattle	3285	48.8	207	32.7	1866	75.9	1107	3256	729	105.4	+1.2
Philadelphia	3536	47.6	196	29.7	1388	77.4	1156	3675	691	105.6	−0.2
Boston	3419	45.2	191	31.3	1639	78.6	1192	3396	738	105.7	+5.8
Portland	3320	45.6	236	32.3	1819	77.7	1079	3433	630	106.0	+8.7
Washington	3396	46.6	166	29.9	1763	77.1	1232	3705	728	106.4	−5.0
LA Clippers	3337	46.7	199	33.6	1901	75.2	1115	3609	773	107.0	−3.5
New Jersey	3374	46.8	136	30.8	1927	77.3	1287	3814	831	107.5	−4.5
Phoenix	3462	46.2	182	31.2	1705	76.0	1195	3493	682	107.5	+6.5
Miami	3335	47.8	173	33.7	1997	76.7	1176	3540	853	107.8	−6.0
Charlotte	3408	49.3	158	31.6	1884	77.2	1151	3665	675	108.0	−5.2
Atlanta	3568	49.4	217	34.9	1587	76.7	1080	3579	688	109.0	+0.8
Orlando	3454	47.8	223	33.1	1879	76.7	1095	3595	706	109.9	−4.0
Indiana	3577	49.0	186	30.5	1851	74.3	1202	3515	729	112.1	−0.4
Golden State	3544	48.2	221	32.2	2121	75.8	1292	3772	726	115.0	+1.6
Denver	4076	51.2	194	38.6	2377	77.5	1242	4309	757	130.8	−10.7

Atlanta Hawks

Player	GP	Min	Field Goals		3-Pt FG		Free Throws		Rebounds		A	Stl	TO	BS	Avg
			FGM	Pct	FGA	FGM	FTM	Pct	Off	Total					
Wilkins	81	3,078	770	47.0	249	85	476	82.9	261	732	265	123	201	65	25.9
Rivers	79	2,586	444	43.5	262	88	221	84.4	47	253	340	148	125	47	15.2
Battle	79	1,863	397	46.1	49	14	270	85.4	34	159	217	45	113	6	13.6
Webb	75	2,197	359	44.7	168	54	231	86.8	41	174	417	118	146	6	13.4
Willis	80	2,373	444	50.4	10	4	159	66.8	259	704	99	60	153	40	13.1
Malone	82	1,912	280	46.8	7	0	309	83.1	271	667	68	30	137	74	10.6
Ferrell	78	1,165	174	48.9	3	2	125	80.1	97	179	55	33	78	27	6.1
Robinson	47	674	108	44.6	11	2	47	58.8	20	71	132	32	76	8	5.6
Moncrief	72	1,096	117	48.8	64	21	82	78.1	31	128	104	50	66	9	4.7
McCormick	56	689	93	49.7	3	0	66	73.3	56	165	32	11	45	14	4.5
Koncak	77	1,931	140	43.6	8	1	32	59.3	101	375	124	74	50	76	4.1
Wilson	25	162	21	30.0	2	0	13	50.0	16	40	11	5	17	1	2.2
Wright	4	20	2	66.7	0	0	1	100.0	1	6	0	0	2	0	1.3
Leonard	4	9	0	—	0	0	2	50.0	0	2	0	0	0	1	0.5
Hawks	82	19,755	3,349	46.4	836	271	2,034	80.0	1,235	3,655	1,864	729	1,231	374	109.8
Opponents	82	19,755	3,568	49.4	621	217	1,587	76.7	1,080	3,579	2,320	688	1,291	361	109.0

Boston Celtics

Player	GP	Min	Field Goals		3-Pt FG		Free Throws		Rebounds		A	Stl	TO	BS	Avg
			FGM	Pct	FGA	FGM	FTM	Pct	Off	Total					
Bird	60	2,277	462	45.4	198	77	163	89.1	53	509	431	108	187	58	19.4
Lewis	79	2,878	598	49.1	13	1	281	82.6	119	410	201	98	147	85	18.7
McHale	68	2,067	504	55.3	37	15	228	82.9	145	480	126	25	140	146	18.4
Gamble	82	2,706	548	58.7	7	0	185	81.5	85	267	256	100	148	34	15.6
Parish	81	2,441	485	59.8	1	0	237	76.7	271	856	66	66	153	103	14.9
Shaw	79	2,772	442	46.9	27	3	204	81.9	104	370	602	105	223	34	13.8
Brown	82	1,945	284	46.4	34	7	137	87.3	41	182	344	83	137	14	8.7
Pinckney	70	1,165	131	53.9	1	0	104	89.7	155	341	45	61	45	43	5.2
M. Smith	47	389	95	47.5	24	6	22	81.5	21	56	43	6	37	2	4.6
Kleine	72	850	102	46.8	2	0	54	78.3	71	244	21	15	53	14	3.6
D. Smith	2	16	1	25.0	1	0	3	75.0	0	0	5	1	1	1	2.5
Wynder	6	39	3	25.0	1	0	6	75.0	1	3	8	1	4	0	2.0
Vrankovic	31	166	24	46.2	0	0	10	55.6	15	51	4	1	24	29	1.9
Popson	19	64	13	40.6	0	0	9	90.0	7	14	2	1	6	2	1.8
C. Smith	5	30	3	42.9	0	0	3	60.0	0	2	6	1	3	0	1.8
Celtics	82	19,805	3,695	51.2	346	109	1,646	82.4	1,088	3,785	2,160	672	1,320	565	111.5
Opponents	82	19,805	3,419	45.2	611	191	1,639	78.6	1,192	3,396	2,052	738	1,127	381	105.7

Charlotte Hornets

Player	GP	Min	Field Goals		3-Pt FG		Free Throws		Rebounds		A	Stl	TO	BS	Avg
			FGM	Pct	FGA	FGM	FTM	Pct	Off	Total					
Gilliam	25	949	195	51.3	0	0	104	81.3	86	234	27	34	64	21	19.8
Newman	81	2,477	478	47.0	84	30	385	80.9	94	254	188	100	189	17	16.9
Chapman	70	2,100	410	44.5	148	48	234	83.0	45	191	250	73	131	16	15.7
Reid	80	2,467	360	46.6	2	0	182	70.3	154	502	89	87	153	47	11.3
Gill	82	1,944	376	45.0	14	2	152	83.5	105	263	303	104	163	39	11.0
Curry	76	1,515	337	47.1	86	32	96	84.2	47	199	166	75	80	25	10.6
Gminski	50	1,405	248	47.3	6	1	75	78.9	115	381	60	24	54	22	11.4
Gattison	72	1,552	243	53.2	2	0	164	66.1	136	379	44	48	102	67	9.0
Tripucka	77	1,289	187	45.4	45	15	152	91.0	46	176	159	33	92	13	7.0
Bogues	81	2,299	241	46.0	12	0	86	79.6	58	216	669	137	120	3	7.0
Leckner	40	744	92	46.5	0	0	46	54.8	55	208	21	10	44	11	5.8
Sanders	3	43	6	42.9	0	0	1	50.0	3	9	1	1	1	1	4.3
Keys	44	473	59	40.7	14	3	19	57.6	40	100	18	22	35	15	3.2
Haffner	7	50	8	38.1	2	0	1	50.0	2	4	9	3	4	1	2.4
Hoppen	19	112	18	56.3	1	0	8	80.0	14	30	3	2	12	1	2.3
Cureton	9	159	8	33.3	1	0	1	33.3	6	36	3	0	6	3	1.9
Scheffler	39	227	20	51.3	0	0	19	90.5	21	45	9	6	4	2	1.5
Hornets	82	19,805	3,286	46.7	417	131	1,725	77.9	1,027	3,227	2,019	759	1,290	304	102.8
Opponents	82	19,805	3,408	49.3	500	158	1,884	77.2	1,151	3,665	2,144	675	1,406	480	108.0

Chicago Bulls

Player	GP	Min	Field Goals		3-Pt FG		Free Throws		Rebounds		A	Stl	TO	BS	Avg
			FGM	Pct	FGA	FGM	FTM	Pct	Off	Total					
Jordan	82	3,034	990	53.9	93	29	571	85.1	118	492	453	223	202	83	31.5
Pippen	82	3,014	600	52.0	68	21	240	70.6	163	595	511	193	232	93	17.8
Grant	78	2,641	401	54.7	6	1	197	71.1	266	659	178	95	92	69	12.8
Cartwright	79	2,273	318	49.0	0	0	124	69.7	167	486	126	32	113	15	9.6
Armstrong	82	1,731	304	48.1	30	15	97	87.4	25	149	301	70	107	4	8.8
Paxson	82	1,971	317	54.8	96	42	34	82.9	15	91	297	62	69	3	8.7
King	76	1,198	156	46.7	2	0	107	70.4	72	208	65	24	91	42	5.5
Hodges	73	843	146	42.4	115	44	26	96.3	10	42	97	34	35	2	5.0
Hopson	61	728	104	42.6	5	1	55	66.3	49	109	65	25	59	14	4.3
Perdue	74	972	116	49.4	3	0	75	67.0	122	336	47	23	75	57	4.1
Levingston	78	1,013	127	45.0	4	1	59	64.8	99	225	56	29	50	43	4.0
Williams	51	337	53	51.0	2	1	20	71.4	42	98	16	12	23	13	2.5
Bulls	82	19,755	3,632	51.0	424	155	1,605	76.0	1,148	3,490	2,212	822	1,184	438	110.0
Opponents	82	19,755	3,267	47.5	626	190	1,554	77.0	1,062	3,224	2,016	633	1,402	348	101.0

Cleveland Cavaliers

Player	GP	Min	Field Goals		3-Pt FG		Free Throws		Rebounds		A	Stl	TO	BS	Avg
			FGM	Pct	FGA	FGM	FTM	Pct	Off	Total					
Daugherty	76	2,946	605	52.4	3	0	435	75.1	177	830	253	74	211	46	21.6
Nance	80	2,927	635	52.4	8	2	265	80.3	201	686	237	66	131	200	19.2
Price	16	571	97	49.7	53	18	59	95.2	8	45	166	42	56	2	16.9
Williams	43	1,293	199	46.3	1	0	107	65.2	111	290	100	36	63	69	11.7
Ehlo	82	2,766	344	44.5	149	49	95	67.9	142	388	376	121	160	34	10.1
Valentine	65	1,841	230	46.4	25	6	143	83.1	37	172	351	98	126	12	9.4
Ferry	81	1,661	275	42.8	77	23	124	81.6	99	286	142	43	120	25	8.6
Brown	74	1,485	263	52.4	4	0	101	70.1	78	213	80	26	94	24	8.5
James	37	505	112	44.1	60	24	52	72.2	26	79	32	15	37	5	8.1
Paddio	70	1,181	212	41.9	24	6	74	79.6	38	118	90	20	71	6	7.2
Morton	66	1,207	120	43.8	12	4	113	81.3	41	103	243	61	107	18	5.4
Kerr	57	905	99	44.4	62	28	45	84.9	5	37	131	29	40	4	4.8
Woodson	4	46	5	21.7	1	0	1	100.0	1	2	5	0	5	1	2.8
Bennett	27	334	40	37.4	0	0	35	74.5	30	64	28	8	20	2	4.3
Chievous	18	110	17	37.0	0	0	9	56.3	11	18	2	3	6	1	2.4
Babic	12	52	6	31.6	0	0	7	58.3	6	9	4	1	5	1	1.6
Cavaliers	82	19,830	3,259	47.5	479	160	1,665	76.5	1,011	3,340	2,240	643	1,281	450	101.7
Opponents	82	19,830	3,459	48.6	505	163	1,464	76.4	1,097	3,495	2,150	710	1,226	394	104.2

Dallas Mavericks

Player	GP	Min	Field Goals		3-Pt FG		Free Throws		Rebounds		A	Stl	TO	BS	Avg
			FGM	Pct	FGA	FGM	FTM	Pct	Off	Total					
Tarpley	5	171	43	54.4	1	0	16	88.9	16	55	12	6	13	9	20.4
Blackman	80	2,965	634	48.2	114	40	282	86.5	63	256	301	69	159	19	19.9
Harper	77	2,879	572	46.7	246	89	286	73.1	59	233	548	147	177	14	19.7
Williams	60	1,832	332	50.7	4	0	83	63.8	86	357	95	30	113	88	12.5
McCray	74	2,561	336	49.5	39	13	159	80.3	153	560	259	70	129	51	11.4
Donaldson	82	2,800	327	53.2	0	0	165	72.1	201	727	69	34	146	93	10.0
English	79	1,748	322	43.9	1	0	119	85.0	108	254	105	40	101	25	9.7
White	79	1,901	265	39.8	37	6	159	70.7	173	504	63	81	131	44	8.8
Lever	4	86	9	39.1	3	0	11	78.6	3	15	12	6	10	3	7.3
Upshaw	48	514	104	45.0	29	7	55	85.9	20	55	86	28	39	5	5.6
Davis	80	1,426	159	42.6	85	22	91	77.1	13	118	230	45	77	17	5.4
Alford	34	236	59	50.4	23	7	26	83.9	10	24	22	8	16	1	4.4
Wright	3	8	2	66.7	1	0	2	100.0	1	2	0	1	0	0	2.0
Grandholm	26	168	30	51.7	17	9	10	47.6	20	50	8	2	11	8	3.0
Shasky	57	510	51	44.0	0	0	48	60.8	58	134	11	14	27	20	2.6
Mavericks	82	19,805	3,245	47.1	600	193	1,512	76.1	984	3,344	1,821	581	1,186	397	99.9
Opponents	82	19,805	3,346	48.2	583	178	1,700	74.0	1,116	3,605	2,025	650	1,147	400	104.5

Denver Nuggets

Player	GP	Min	Field Goals		3-Pt FG		Free Throws		Rebounds		A	Stl	TO	BS	Avg
			FGM	Pct	FGA	FGM	FTM	Pct	Off	Total					
Adams	66	2,346	560	39.4	564	167	465	87.9	58	256	693	147	240	6	26.5
Woolridge	53	1,823	490	49.8	4	0	350	79.7	141	361	119	69	152	23	25.1
Davis	39	1,044	316	47.4	33	10	86	91.5	52	123	84	62	63	3	18.7
Jackson	67	1,505	417	41.3	100	24	84	85.7	34	121	206	55	110	4	14.1
Lichti	29	860	166	43.9	47	14	59	85.5	49	112	72	46	33	8	14.0
Williams	51	1,542	323	44.4	131	43	131	84.0	116	247	87	93	76	30	16.1
Rasmussen	70	2,325	405	45.8	5	2	63	67.7	170	678	70	52	81	132	12.5
Farmer	25	443	99	45.8	22	5	46	73.0	27	63	38	13	37	2	10.0
Gaines	10	226	28	40.0	21	5	22	84.6	4	14	91	10	23	2	8.3
Mills	17	279	56	46.7	2	0	16	72.7	31	88	16	16	18	9	7.5
Lane	62	1,383	202	43.8	4	1	58	41.1	280	578	123	51	105	14	7.5
Wolf	74	1,593	234	45.1	15	2	69	83.1	136	400	107	60	95	31	7.3
Liberty	76	1,171	216	42.1	57	17	58	63.0	117	221	64	48	71	19	6.7
Battle	40	682	95	48.5	22	3	50	78.1	62	123	47	41	36	12	6.1
Legler	10	148	25	34.7	12	3	5	83.3	8	18	12	2	4	0	5.8
Cook	58	1,121	118	41.7	3	0	71	55.0	134	326	26	35	50	72	5.3
Anderson	41	659	85	44.0	0	0	44	50.6	67	237	12	25	61	36	5.2
Johnson	21	217	29	42.6	4	0	21	65.6	9	21	77	14	27	2	3.8
Mason	3	21	2	50.0	0	0	6	75.0	3	5	0	1	0	0	3.3
Dunn	17	217	21	44.7	4	1	9	90.0	20	42	24	12	7	1	3.1
Nuggets	82	19,730	3,901	44.0	1,059	300	1,726	76.3	1,520	4,050	2,005	856	1,332	406	119.9
Opponents	82	19,730	4,076	51.2	502	194	2,377	77.5	1,242	4,309	2,492	757	1,527	525	130.8

Detroit Pistons

Player	GP	Min	Field Goals		3-Pt FG		Free Throws		Rebounds		A	Stl	TO	BS	Avg
			FGM	Pct	FGA	FGM	FTM	Pct	Off	Total					
Dumars	80	3,046	622	48.1	45	14	371	89.0	62	187	443	89	189	7	20.4
Thomas	48	1,657	289	43.5	65	19	179	78.2	35	160	446	75	185	10	16.2
Aguirre	78	2,006	420	46.2	78	24	240	75.7	134	374	139	47	128	20	14.2
Edwards	72	1,903	383	48.4	2	1	215	72.9	91	277	65	12	126	30	13.6
Johnson	82	2,390	406	43.4	34	11	135	64.6	110	280	271	75	118	15	11.7
Laimbeer	82	2,668	372	47.8	125	37	123	83.7	173	737	157	38	98	56	11.0
Rodman	82	2,747	276	49.3	30	6	111	63.1	361	1,026	85	65	94	55	8.2
Salley	74	1,649	179	47.5	1	0	186	72.7	137	327	70	52	91	112	7.4
Henderson	23	392	50	42.7	21	7	16	76.2	8	37	62	12	28	2	5.3
Bedford	60	562	106	43.8	13	5	55	70.5	55	131	32	2	32	36	4.5
Long	25	256	35	41.2	6	2	24	96.0	9	32	18	9	14	2	3.8
Hastings	27	113	16	57.1	4	3	13	100.0	14	28	7	0	7	0	1.8
Blanks	38	214	26	42.6	16	2	10	71.4	4	20	26	9	18	2	1.7
Pistons	82	19,805	3,194	46.5	440	131	1,686	76.3	1,206	3,658	1,825	487	1,181	367	100.1
Opponents	82	19,805	3,053	45.3	504	157	1,674	77.0	1,002	3,276	1,736	581	1,127	289	96.8

Golden State Warriors

Player	GP	Min	Field Goals		3-Pt FG		Free Throws		Rebounds		A	Stl	TO	BS	Avg
			FGM	Pct	FGA	FGM	FTM	Pct	Off	Total					
Mullin	82	3,315	777	53.6	133	40	513	88.4	141	443	329	173	245	63	25.7
Richmond	77	3,027	703	49.4	115	40	394	84.7	147	452	238	126	230	34	23.9
Hardaway	82	3,215	739	47.6	252	97	306	80.3	87	332	793	214	270	12	22.9
Marciulionis	50	987	183	50.1	6	1	178	72.4	51	118	85	62	75	4	10.9
Higgins	82	2,024	259	46.3	220	73	185	81.9	109	354	113	52	65	37	9.5
Tolbert	62	1,371	183	42.3	21	7	127	73.8	87	275	76	35	80	38	8.1
Elie	30	624	77	50.7	8	3	74	85.1	46	109	44	19	27	10	7.7
Lister	77	1,552	188	47.8	1	0	115	56.9	121	483	93	20	106	90	6.4
Hill	74	1,192	147	49.2	0	0	96	63.2	157	383	19	33	72	30	5.3
Askew	7	85	12	48.0	0	0	9	81.8	7	11	13	2	6	0	4.7
Petersen	62	834	114	48.3	4	1	50	65.8	69	200	27	13	48	41	4.5
Pritchard	62	773	88	38.4	31	5	62	80.5	16	65	81	30	59	8	3.9
Robinson	24	170	24	40.7	0	0	8	53.3	15	23	11	9	16	1	2.3
Johnson	24	228	34	54.0	0	0	22	59.5	18	57	17	4	25	4	3.8
Warriors	82	19,805	3,566	48.5	801	270	2,162	78.3	1,113	3,419	1,954	803	1,359	378	116.6
Opponents	82	19,805	3,544	48.2	686	221	2,121	75.8	1,292	3,772	2,164	726	1,534	437	115.0

Houston Rockets

Player	GP	Min	FGM	Pct	FGA	FGM	FTM	Pct	Off	Total	A	Stl	TO	BS	Avg
Olajuwon	56	2,062	487	50.8	4	0	213	76.9	219	770	131	121	174	221	21.2
K. Smith	78	2,699	522	52.0	135	49	287	84.4	36	163	554	106	237	11	17.7
Thorpe	82	3,039	549	55.6	7	3	334	69.6	287	846	197	73	217	20	17.5
Maxwell	82	2,870	504	40.4	510	172	217	73.3	41	238	303	127	171	15	17.0
Johnson	73	2,279	416	47.7	15	2	157	72.7	108	330	142	81	122	47	13.6
Floyd	82	1,850	386	41.1	176	48	185	75.2	52	159	317	95	140	17	12.3
Wood	82	1,421	148	42.4	90	28	108	81.2	107	246	94	58	89	16	5.3
Woodson	11	125	21	38.9	6	1	10	83.3	2	11	10	5	7	4	4.8
Winchester	64	607	98	40.0	20	8	35	77.8	34	67	25	16	30	13	3.7
L. Smith	81	1,923	128	48.7	0	0	12	24.0	302	709	88	83	93	22	3.3
Jamerson	37	202	43	38.1	19	5	22	81.5	9	30	27	6	20	1	3.1
Feitl	52	372	52	37.1	3	0	33	75.0	29	100	8	3	25	12	2.6
Bullard	18	63	14	45.2	3	0	11	64.7	6	14	2	3	3	0	2.2
Caldwell	42	343	35	42.2	1	0	7	41.2	43	100	8	19	30	10	1.8
Rockets	**82**	**19,855**	**3,403**	**46.7**	**989**	**316**	**1,631**	**74.1**	**1,275**	**3,783**	**1,906**	**796**	**1,402**	**409**	**106.7**
Opponents	**82**	**19,855**	**3,337**	**45.6**	**621**	**183**	**1,609**	**77.1**	**1,242**	**3,673**	**1,965**	**711**	**1,415**	**357**	**103.2**

Indiana Pacers

Player	GP	Min	FGM	Pct	FGA	FGM	FTM	Pct	Off	Total	A	Stl	TO	BS	Avg
Miller	82	2,972	596	51.2	322	112	551	91.8	81	281	331	109	163	13	22.6
Person	80	2,566	620	50.4	203	69	165	72.1	121	417	238	56	184	17	18.4
Schrempf	82	2,632	432	52.0	40	15	441	81.8	178	660	301	58	175	22	16.1
Fleming	69	1,929	356	53.1	18	4	161	72.9	83	214	369	76	137	13	12.7
M. Williams	73	1,706	261	49.9	7	1	290	87.9	49	176	348	150	150	17	11.1
Smits	76	1,690	342	48.5	0	0	144	76.2	116	357	84	24	86	111	10.9
Thompson	82	1,946	276	48.8	5	1	72	69.2	154	563	147	63	168	63	7.6
Sanders	80	1,357	206	41.7	20	4	47	82.5	73	185	106	37	65	26	5.8
McCloud	74	1,070	131	37.3	124	43	38	77.6	35	118	150	40	91	11	4.6
Dreiling	73	1,031	98	50.5	2	0	63	60.0	66	255	51	24	57	29	3.5
Dinkins	2	5	1	100.0	0	0	0	—	0	1	0	0	0	0	1.0
K. Williams	75	527	93	52.0	3	0	34	68.0	56	131	31	11	41	31	2.9
Wittman	41	355	35	44.3	5	0	4	66.7	6	33	25	10	10	4	1.8
Oldham	4	19	3	50.0	0	0	0	—	0	3	0	0	0	0	1.5
Pacers	**82**	**19,805**	**3,450**	**49.3**	**749**	**249**	**2,010**	**81.1**	**1,018**	**3,394**	**2,181**	**658**	**1,355**	**357**	**111.7**
Opponents	**82**	**19,805**	**3,577**	**49.0**	**609**	**186**	**1,851**	**74.3**	**1,202**	**3,515**	**2,063**	**729**	**1,260**	**353**	**112.1**

Los Angeles Clippers

Player	GP	Min	FGM	Pct	FGA	FGM	FTM	Pct	Off	Total	A	Stl	TO	BS	Avg
Smith	74	2,703	548	46.9	7	0	384	79.3	216	608	134	81	165	145	20.0
Harper	39	1,383	285	39.1	148	48	145	66.8	58	188	209	66	129	35	19.6
Norman	70	2,309	520	50.1	32	6	173	62.9	177	497	159	63	139	63	17.4
Manning	73	2,197	470	51.9	3	0	219	71.6	169	426	196	117	188	62	15.9
Benjamin	39	1,337	229	49.2	0	0	123	72.8	95	469	74	26	138	91	14.9
Polynice	31	1,132	151	57.9	1	0	79	57.2	106	283	26	17	35	13	12.3
Grant	68	2,105	265	45.1	39	9	51	68.9	69	209	587	103	210	12	8.7
Garland	69	1,702	221	42.6	26	4	118	75.2	46	198	317	97	116	10	8.2
Martin	74	1,334	214	42.2	88	27	68	68.0	53	131	65	37	49	31	7.1
Kimble	62	1,004	159	38.0	65	19	92	77.3	42	119	76	30	77	8	6.9
Vaught	73	1,178	175	48.7	2	0	49	66.2	124	349	40	20	49	23	5.5
Garrick	67	949	100	42.4	22	0	60	75.9	40	127	223	62	66	2	3.9
Bannister	47	339	43	53.1	1	0	25	38.5	34	96	9	5	25	7	2.4
Smrek	10	70	3	18.8	0	0	4	50.0	4	19	3	1	1	3	1.0
Butler	9	37	5	26.3	0	0	4	66.7	8	16	1	0	4	0	1.6
Ball	7	26	3	37.5	0	0	2	100.0	5	11	0	0	2	1	1.1
Clippers	**82**	**19,805**	**3,391**	**46.4**	**434**	**113**	**1,596**	**70.2**	**1,246**	**3,746**	**2,119**	**725**	**1,438**	**507**	**103.5**
Opponents	**82**	**19,805**	**3,337**	**46.7**	**593**	**199**	**1,901**	**75.2**	**1,115**	**3,609**	**1,982**	**773**	**1,316**	**491**	**107.0**

NBA Team-by-Team Statistical Leaders (*Cont.*)

Los Angeles Lakers

Player	GP	Min	Field Goals		3-Pt FG		Free Throws		Rebounds		A	Stl	TO	BS	Avg
			FGM	Pct	FGA	FGM	FTM	Pct	Off	Total					
Worthy	78	3,008	716	49.2	90	26	212	79.7	107	356	275	104	127	35	21.4
Johnson	79	2,933	466	47.7	250	80	519	90.6	105	551	989	102	314	17	19.4
Scott	82	2,630	501	47.7	219	71	118	79.7	54	246	177	95	85	21	14.5
Perkins	73	2,504	368	49.5	64	18	229	82.1	167	538	108	64	103	78	13.5
Divac	82	2,310	360	56.5	14	5	196	70.3	205	666	92	106	146	127	11.2
Teagle	82	1,498	335	44.3	9	0	145	81.9	82	181	82	31	83	8	9.9
Green	82	2,164	258	47.6	55	11	223	73.8	201	516	71	59	99	23	9.1
Thompson	72	1,077	113	49.6	2	0	62	70.5	74	228	21	23	47	23	4.0
Smith	64	695	97	44.1	7	0	40	70.2	24	71	135	28	69	12	3.7
Drew	48	496	54	43.2	33	14	17	77.3	5	34	118	15	49	1	2.9
Campbell	52	380	56	45.5	0	0	32	65.3	40	96	10	11	16	38	2.8
Thomas	26	108	17	34.0	0	0	12	57.1	14	31	10	4	13	1	1.8
Brown	7	27	2	66.7	1	1	0	—	0	4	3	0	4	0	0.7
Lakers	82	19,830	3,343	48.4	744	226	1,805	79.8	1,078	3,518	2,091	642	1,203	384	106.3
Opponents	82	19,830	3,354	46.2	573	178	1,278	75.2	1,131	3,318	1,998	668	1,175	334	99.6

Miami Heat

Player	GP	Min	Field Goals		3-Pt FG		Free Throws		Rebounds		A	Stl	TO	BS	Avg
			FGM	Pct	FGA	FGM	FTM	Pct	Off	Total					
Douglas	73	2,562	532	50.4	31	4	284	68.6	78	209	624	121	270	5	18.5
Rice	77	2,646	550	46.1	184	71	171	81.8	85	381	189	101	166	26	17.4
Seikaly	64	2,171	395	48.1	6	2	258	61.9	207	709	95	51	205	86	16.4
Edwards	79	2,000	380	41.0	84	24	171	80.3	80	205	240	130	163	46	12.1
Burton	76	1,928	341	44.1	30	4	229	78.2	111	262	107	72	144	24	12.0
Long	80	2,514	276	49.2	6	1	181	78.7	225	568	176	119	156	43	9.2
Thompson	73	1,481	205	49.9	4	0	89	71.8	120	312	111	32	117	48	6.8
Kessler	78	1,259	199	42.5	4	0	88	67.2	115	336	31	17	108	26	6.2
Davis	55	996	115	48.7	2	1	69	55.6	107	266	39	18	36	28	5.5
Coles	82	1,355	162	41.2	34	6	71	74.7	56	153	232	65	98	12	4.9
Wagner	13	116	24	42.1	17	6	9	81.8	0	7	15	2	12	3	4.8
Sundvold	24	225	43	40.2	35	15	11	100.0	3	9	24	7	16	0	4.7
Askins	39	266	34	42.0	25	6	12	48.0	30	68	19	16	11	13	2.2
Ogg	31	261	24	43.6	2	0	6	60.0	15	49	2	6	8	27	1.7
Heat	82	19,780	3,280	45.9	464	140	1,649	71.5	1,232	3,534	1,904	757	1,551	387	101.8
Opponents	82	19,780	3,335	47.8	514	173	1,997	76.7	1,176	3,540	2,006	853	1,467	502	107.8

Milwaukee Bucks

Player	GP	Min	Field Goals		3-Pt FG		Free Throws		Rebounds		A	Stl	TO	BS	Avg
			FGM	Pct	FGA	FGM	FTM	Pct	Off	Total					
Pierce	46	1,327	359	49.9	93	37	282	90.7	37	117	96	38	93	11	22.5
Ellis	21	624	159	48.6	68	30	58	70.7	38	81	31	16	32	5	19.3
Humphries	80	2,726	482	50.2	161	60	191	79.9	57	220	538	129	151	7	15.2
Robertson	81	2,598	438	48.5	63	23	199	75.7	191	459	444	246	212	16	13.6
Brickowski	75	1,912	372	52.7	2	0	198	79.8	129	426	131	86	160	43	12.6
Roberts	82	2,114	357	53.3	25	4	170	81.3	107	281	135	63	135	29	10.8
Schayes	82	2,228	298	49.9	5	0	274	83.5	174	535	98	55	106	61	10.6
Sikma	77	1,940	295	42.7	135	46	166	84.3	108	441	143	65	130	64	10.4
Grayer	82	1,422	210	43.3	3	0	101	68.7	111	246	123	48	86	9	6.4
Dantley	10	126	19	38.0	3	1	18	69.2	8	13	9	5	6	0	5.7
Lohaus	81	1,219	179	43.1	119	33	37	68.5	59	217	75	50	60	74	5.3
Conner	39	519	38	39.6	3	0	39	75.0	10	55	107	48	31	1	2.9
Henson	68	690	79	41.8	54	18	38	90.5	14	51	131	32	43	0	3.1
Anderson	26	247	27	37.0	1	0	16	57.1	26	75	3	8	22	9	2.7
Stephens	3	6	2	66.7	0	0	2	100.0	0	0	2	0	0	0	2.0
Kornet	32	157	23	37.1	18	5	7	53.8	10	24	9	5	11	1	1.8
Bucks	82	19,855	3,337	48.0	753	257	1,796	80.1	1,079	3,241	2,075	894	1,321	330	106.4
Opponents	82	19,855	3,290	48.6	574	189	1,755	75.9	1,108	3,423	2,023	704	1,531	461	104.0

Minnesota Timberwolves

| Player | GP | Min | Field Goals | | 3-Pt FG | | Free Throws | | Rebounds | | A | Stl | TO | BS | Avg |
			FGM	Pct	FGA	FGM	FTM	Pct	Off	Total					
Campbell	77	2,893	652	43.4	61	16	358	80.3	161	346	214	121	190	48	21.8
Corbin	82	3,196	587	44.8	10	2	296	79.8	185	589	347	162	209	53	18.0
Richardson	82	3,154	635	47.0	128	42	89	53.9	82	286	734	131	174	13	17.1
Mitchell	82	3,121	445	44.1	9	0	307	77.5	188	520	133	66	104	57	14.6
Spencer	81	2,099	195	51.2	1	0	182	72.2	272	641	25	48	77	121	7.1
Glass	51	606	149	43.8	17	2	52	68.4	54	102	42	28	41	9	6.9
Breuer	73	1,505	197	45.3	0	0	35	44.3	114	345	73	35	69	80	5.9
Brooks	80	980	159	43.0	135	45	61	84.7	28	72	204	53	51	5	5.3
Murphy	52	1,063	90	39.6	17	1	70	66.7	92	255	60	25	32	20	4.8
West	75	824	118	48.0	1	0	58	69.0	56	136	48	35	41	23	3.9
Thornton	12	110	4	30.8	0	0	8	80.0	1	15	1	0	9	3	1.3
Coffey	52	320	28	37.3	1	0	12	54.5	42	79	3	6	5	4	1.3
Godfread	10	20	5	41.7	1	0	3	75.0	0	2	0	1	0	4	1.3
Thomas	3	14	1	25.0	0	0	0	—	0	0	1	1	1	0	0.7
Timberwolves	82	19,905	3,265	44.9	381	108	1,531	73.5	1,275	3,388	1,885	712	1,062	440	99.6
Opponents	82	19,905	3,320	49.0	505	171	1,680	75.7	1,094	3,473	2,142	512	1,238	511	103.5

New Jersey Nets

| Player | GP | Min | Field Goals | | 3-Pt FG | | Free Throws | | Rebounds | | A | Stl | TO | BS | Avg |
			FGM	Pct	FGA	FGM	FTM	Pct	Off	Total					
Theus	81	2,955	583	46.8	144	52	292	85.1	69	229	378	85	252	35	18.6
Coleman	74	2,602	514	46.7	38	13	323	73.1	269	759	163	71	217	99	18.4
Blaylock	72	2,585	432	41.6	91	14	139	79.0	67	249	441	169	207	40	14.1
Morris	79	2,553	409	42.5	179	45	179	73.4	210	521	220	138	167	96	13.2
Bowie	62	1,916	314	43.4	22	4	169	73.2	176	480	147	43	141	90	12.9
Petrovic	43	882	211	50.0	59	22	99	86.1	41	92	66	37	69	1	12.6
Anderson	1	18	4	100.0	0	0	0	—	4	6	1	2	1	0	8.0
Gervin	56	743	164	41.6	28	7	90	78.9	40	110	30	19	45	19	7.6
Dudley	61	1,560	170	40.8	0	0	94	53.4	229	511	37	39	80	153	7.1
Mills	38	540	78	46.4	2	0	31	70.5	51	141	17	19	25	20	4.9
Haley	78	1,178	161	46.9	0	0	112	61.9	140	356	31	20	63	21	5.6
Hinson	9	91	20	51.3	0	0	1	33.3	6	19	4	0	6	3	4.4
Conner	35	489	58	52.3	2	0	29	69.0	11	57	58	37	27	1	4.1
George	56	594	80	41.5	2	0	32	80.0	19	47	104	25	42	5	3.4
Buechler	74	859	94	41.6	4	1	43	65.2	61	141	51	33	26	15	3.1
Lee	48	265	19	26.8	15	3	25	89.3	7	30	34	11	20	2	1.4
Nets	82	19,830	3,311	44.4	586	161	1,658	73.9	1,400	3,748	1,782	748	1,423	600	102.9
Opponents	82	19,830	3,374	46.8	442	136	1,927	77.3	1,287	3,814	1,737	831	1,452	540	107.5

New York Knickerbockers

| Player | GP | Min | Field Goals | | 3-Pt FG | | Free Throws | | Rebounds | | A | Stl | TO | BS | Avg |
			FGM	Pct	FGA	FGM	FTM	Pct	Off	Total					
Ewing	81	3,104	845	51.4	6	0	464	74.5	194	905	244	80	291	258	26.6
Vandeweghe	75	2,420	458	49.4	141	51	259	89.9	78	180	110	42	108	10	16.3
G. Wilkins	68	2,164	380	47.3	43	9	169	82.0	78	207	275	82	161	23	13.8
Oakley	76	2,739	307	51.6	2	0	239	78.4	305	920	204	62	215	17	11.2
Jackson	72	1,595	250	49.2	51	13	117	73.1	62	197	452	60	135	9	8.8
Cheeks	76	2,147	241	49.9	20	5	105	81.4	22	173	435	128	108	10	7.8
Starks	61	1,173	180	43.9	93	27	79	75.2	30	131	204	59	74	17	7.6
Tucker	65	1,194	191	44.0	153	64	17	63.0	33	105	111	44	46	9	7.1
Quinnett	68	1,011	139	45.9	43	15	26	72.2	65	145	53	22	52	13	4.7
Mustaf	62	825	106	46.5	1	0	56	64.4	51	169	36	15	61	14	4.3
Walker	54	771	83	43.5	1	0	64	78.0	63	157	13	18	30	30	4.3
E. Wilkins	68	668	114	44.7	1	0	51	56.7	69	180	15	17	50	7	4.1
Gray	8	37	4	33.3	0	0	3	100.0	2	10	0	0	2	1	1.4
Grant	22	107	10	37.0	3	1	5	83.3	1	10	20	9	10	0	1.2
Knickerbockers	82	19,955	3,308	48.5	558	185	1,654	77.0	1,053	3,489	2,172	638	1,379	418	103.1
Opponents	82	19,955	3,410	47.6	545	183	1,471	77.3	1,119	3,455	1,999	724	1,239	368	103.3

Orlando Magic

Player	GP	Min	FGM	Pct	FGA	FGM	FTM	Pct	Off	Total	A	Stl	TO	BS	Avg
Skiles	79	2,714	462	44.5	228	93	340	90.2	57	270	660	89	252	4	17.2
Scott	82	2,336	503	42.5	334	125	153	75.0	62	235	134	62	127	25	15.7
Catledge	51	1,459	292	46.2	5	0	161	62.4	168	355	58	34	107	9	14.6
Anderson	70	1,971	400	46.7	58	17	173	66.8	92	386	106	74	113	44	14.1
Smith	75	1,885	407	45.1	46	9	221	73.4	176	389	169	85	140	35	13.9
Reynolds	80	1,843	344	43.4	34	10	336	80.2	88	299	203	95	172	56	12.9
Turner	71	1,683	259	48.7	15	6	85	75.9	108	363	97	29	126	10	8.6
Vincent	49	975	152	43.1	19	3	99	82.5	17	107	197	30	91	5	8.3
Ansley	67	877	144	54.8	0	0	91	71.7	122	253	25	27	32	7	5.7
Wright	8	136	15	36.6	0	0	13	61.9	10	37	3	3	9	5	5.4
Kite	82	2,225	166	49.1	0	0	63	51.2	189	588	59	25	102	81	4.8
Acres	68	1,313	109	50.9	3	1	66	65.3	140	359	25	25	42	25	4.2
Wiley	34	350	45	41.7	12	6	17	68.0	4	17	73	24	34	0	3.3
Magic	82	19,780	3,298	45.5	754	270	1,818	74.3	1,233	3,662	1,809	602	1,391	306	105.9
Opponents	82	19,780	3,454	47.8	674	223	1,879	76.7	1,095	3,595	2,118	706	1,215	654	109.9

Philadelphia 76ers

Player	GP	Min	FGM	Pct	FGA	FGM	FTM	Pct	Off	Total	A	Stl	TO	BS	Avg
Barkley	67	2,498	665	57.0	155	44	475	72.2	258	680	284	110	210	33	27.6
Hawkins	80	3,110	590	47.0	270	108	479	87.1	48	310	299	178	213	39	22.1
Gilliam	50	1,695	292	47.0	2	0	164	81.6	134	364	78	35	110	32	15.0
Dawkins	4	124	26	63.4	4	1	10	90.9	0	16	28	3	8	0	15.8
Anderson	82	2,340	512	48.5	43	9	165	83.3	103	367	115	65	100	13	14.6
Green	79	2,248	334	46.3	36	8	117	83.0	33	137	413	57	108	6	10.0
Gminski	30	791	109	38.4	8	1	53	84.1	71	201	33	16	31	34	9.1
Mahorn	80	2,439	261	46.7	9	0	189	78.8	151	621	118	79	127	56	8.9
Turner	70	1,407	168	43.9	33	12	64	73.6	36	152	311	63	95	0	5.9
Oliver	73	800	111	40.8	18	5	52	73.2	12	80	88	34	50	4	3.8
Payne	47	444	68	36.0	18	4	26	89.7	17	66	16	10	21	6	3.5
Williams	52	508	72	44.7	2	1	37	66.1	41	111	16	9	40	6	3.5
Farmer	2	13	2	28.6	1	0	2	100.0	2	5	0	0	1	0	3.0
Hoppen	11	43	6	50.0	1	0	8	66.7	4	9	0	1	1	0	1.8
Elie	3	20	2	28.6	2	1	1	50.0	0	1	1	0	3	0	2.0
Bol	82	1,522	65	39.6	14	1	24	58.5	66	350	20	16	63	247	1.9
Harris	6	41	4	25.0	2	0	2	50.0	0	1	0	1	3	0	1.7
Reid	3	37	2	14.3	0	0	0	—	2	9	4	1	3	3	1.3
76ers	82	20,080	3,289	47.5	618	195	1,868	79.0	984	3,480	1,824	678	1,230	479	105.4
Opponents	82	20,080	3,536	47.6	660	196	1,388	77.4	1,156	3,675	2,220	691	1,177	391	105.6

Phoenix Suns

Player	GP	Min	FGM	Pct	FGA	FGM	FTM	Pct	Off	Total	A	Stl	TO	BS	Avg
K. Johnson	77	2,772	591	51.6	44	9	519	84.3	54	271	781	163	269	11	22.2
Chambers	76	2,475	556	43.7	73	20	379	82.6	104	490	194	65	177	52	19.9
McDaniel	66	2,105	451	50.3	5	0	144	72.7	137	476	149	50	144	42	15.8
Hornacek	80	2,733	544	51.8	146	61	201	89.7	74	321	409	111	130	16	16.9
Majerle	77	2,281	397	48.4	86	30	227	76.2	168	418	216	106	114	40	13.6
E. Johnson	15	312	88	47.3	21	6	21	72.4	16	46	17	9	24	2	13.5
Ceballos	63	730	204	48.7	6	1	110	66.3	77	150	35	22	69	5	8.2
West	82	1,957	247	64.7	0	0	135	65.5	171	564	37	32	86	161	7.7
Battle	16	263	38	44.2	2	0	20	69.0	21	53	15	19	17	6	6.0
Knight	64	792	131	42.5	25	6	71	60.2	20	71	191	20	76	7	5.3
Lang	63	1,152	109	57.7	1	0	93	71.5	113	303	27	17	45	127	4.9
Perry	46	587	75	52.1	5	0	43	61.4	53	126	27	23	32	43	4.2
Lockhart	1	2	1	100.0	0	0	2	100.0	0	0	0	0	0	0	4.0
Rambis	62	900	83	49.7	2	0	60	70.6	77	266	64	25	45	11	3.6
Carroll	11	96	13	36.1	0	0	11	91.7	3	24	11	1	12	8	3.4
Nealy	55	573	45	46.4	16	5	28	73.7	44	151	36	24	19	4	2.2
Suns	82	19,730	3,573	49.6	432	138	2,064	77.0	1,132	3,730	2,209	687	1,302	535	114.0
Opponents	82	19,730	3,462	46.2	584	182	1,705	76.0	1,195	3,493	1,972	682	1,282	463	107.5

Portland Trail Blazers

Player	GP	Min	Field Goals		3-Pt FG		Free Throws		Rebounds		A	Stl	TO	BS	Avg
			FGM	Pct	FGA	FGM	FTM	Pct	Off	Total					
Drexler	82	2,852	645	48.2	191	61	416	79.4	212	546	493	144	232	60	21.5
Porter	81	2,665	486	51.5	313	130	279	82.3	52	282	649	158	189	12	17.0
Duckworth	81	2,511	521	48.1	2	0	240	77.2	177	531	89	33	186	34	15.8
Kersey	73	2,359	424	47.8	13	4	232	70.9	169	481	227	101	149	76	14.8
Davis	32	439	87	44.6	3	1	21	91.3	19	58	41	18	25	0	6.1
Robinson	82	1,940	373	46.3	19	6	205	65.3	123	349	151	78	133	76	11.7
Williams	80	2,582	358	60.2	0	0	217	70.5	227	751	97	47	137	47	11.7
Ainge	80	1,710	337	47.2	251	102	114	82.6	45	205	285	63	100	13	11.1
Bryant	53	781	99	48.8	1	0	74	73.3	65	190	27	15	33	12	5.1
Petrovic	18	133	32	45.1	6	1	15	68.2	10	18	20	6	12	0	4.4
Young	75	897	103	38.0	104	36	41	91.1	22	75	141	50	50	7	3.8
Abdelnaby	43	290	55	47.4	0	0	25	56.8	27	89	12	4	22	12	3.1
Cooper	67	746	57	39.3	1	0	33	78.6	54	188	22	7	22	61	2.2
Trail Blazers	82	19,905	3,577	48.5	904	341	1,912	75.3	1,202	3,763	2,254	724	1,309	410	114.7
Opponents	82	19,905	3,320	45.6	730	236	1,819	77.7	1,079	3,433	2,048	630	1,397	352	106.0

Sacramento Kings

Player	GP	Min	Field Goals		3-Pt FG		Free Throws		Rebounds		A	Stl	TO	BS	Avg
			FGM	Pct	FGA	FGM	FTM	Pct	Off	Total					
Carr	77	2,527	628	51.1	3	0	295	75.8	163	420	191	45	171	101	20.1
Tisdale	33	1,116	262	48.3	1	0	136	80.0	75	253	66	23	82	28	20.0
Simmons	79	2,978	549	42.2	11	3	320	73.6	193	697	315	113	230	85	18.0
Mays	64	2,145	294	40.6	197	72	255	77.0	54	178	253	81	159	11	14.3
Sparrow	80	2,375	371	49.1	78	31	58	69.9	45	186	362	83	126	16	10.4
Bonner	34	750	103	44.8	0	0	44	57.9	59	161	49	39	41	5	7.4
Les	55	1,399	119	44.4	154	71	86	83.5	18	111	299	57	75	4	7.2
Causwell	76	1,719	210	50.8	0	0	105	63.6	141	391	69	49	96	148	6.9
Wood	12	222	25	39.7	38	12	19	90.5	5	19	49	5	12	0	6.8
Hansen	36	811	96	37.5	69	19	18	50.0	33	96	90	20	34	5	6.4
Wennington	77	1,455	181	43.6	5	1	74	78.7	101	340	69	46	51	59	5.7
Frederick	35	475	67	39.9	0	0	43	71.7	36	84	44	22	40	13	5.1
Calloway	64	678	75	39.1	2	0	55	69.6	25	78	61	22	51	7	3.2
Colter	19	251	23	41.1	14	5	7	70.0	5	26	37	11	11	1	3.1
Sampson	25	348	34	36.6	5	1	26	41.1	41	111	17	11	27	17	3.0
Leckner	32	378	39	40.6	0	0	16	59.3	27	87	18	4	25	11	2.9
Higgins	7	61	6	60.0	0	0	4	57.1	4	5	2	0	4	2	2.3
Kings	82	19,705	3,086	45.3	578	216	1,540	73.2	1,027	3,245	1,991	631	1,272	513	96.7
Opponents	82	19,705	3,142	47.0	491	155	2,045	76.1	1,164	3,707	1,912	699	1,312	448	103.5

San Antonio Spurs

Player	GP	Min	Field Goals		3-Pt FG		Free Throws		Rebounds		A	Stl	TO	BS	Avg
			FGM	Pct	FGA	FGM	FTM	Pct	Off	Total					
Robinson	82	3,095	754	55.2	7	1	592	76.2	335	1,063	208	127	270	320	25.6
Cummings	67	2,195	503	48.4	33	7	164	68.3	194	521	157	61	131	30	17.6
Elliott	82	3,044	478	49.0	64	20	325	80.8	142	456	238	69	147	33	15.9
Anderson	75	2,592	453	45.7	35	7	170	79.8	68	351	358	79	167	46	14.4
Strickland	58	2,076	314	48.2	33	11	161	76.3	57	219	463	117	156	11	13.8
Williams	22	354	61	48.0	26	14	35	85.4	17	59	46	20	36	11	7.8
Pressey	70	1,683	201	47.2	57	16	110	82.7	50	176	271	63	130	32	7.5
Green	66	1,099	177	46.1	3	0	89	84.8	98	313	52	32	89	13	6.7
Wingate	25	563	53	38.4	9	1	29	70.7	24	75	46	19	42	5	5.4
Lett	7	99	14	48.3	1	0	6	66.7	1	7	2	8	1	4	4.9
Johnson	47	742	101	48.3	5	1	38	69.1	13	56	153	33	47	2	5.1
Higgins	50	464	97	45.8	19	3	28	84.8	18	63	35	8	49	1	4.5
Greenwood	63	1,018	85	50.3	2	0	69	73.4	61	221	52	29	71	25	3.8
Schintzius	42	398	68	43.9	2	0	22	55.0	28	121	17	2	34	29	3.8
Myers	8	103	10	43.5	1	0	9	81.8	2	13	14	3	14	3	3.6
Massenburg	35	161	27	45.0	0	0	28	62.2	23	58	4	4	13	9	2.3
Spurs	82	19,830	3,409	48.8	297	81	1,883	76.6	1,131	3,788	2,140	670	1,445	571	107.1
Opponents	82	19,830	3,265	44.8	704	218	1,664	76.1	1,122	3,392	1,928	801	1,260	437	102.6

Seattle Supersonics

Player	GP	Min	FGM	Pct	FGA	FGM	FTM	Pct	Off	Total	A	Stl	TO	BS	Avg
McDaniel	15	529	139	47.9	3	0	49	71.0	36	81	38	26	40	4	21.8
Pierce	32	840	202	46.3	23	9	148	92.5	30	74	72	22	54	2	17.5
Johnson	66	1,773	455	48.6	99	33	208	91.2	91	225	94	49	98	7	17.4
McKey	73	2,503	438	51.7	19	4	235	84.5	172	423	169	91	158	56	15.3
Ellis	30	800	181	46.3	89	27	62	73.8	28	92	64	33	49	3	15.0
Kemp	81	2,442	462	50.8	12	2	288	66.1	267	679	144	77	202	123	15.0
Benjamin	31	899	157	50.2	0	0	87	69.0	62	254	45	28	97	54	12.9
Threatt	80	2,066	433	51.9	35	10	137	79.2	25	99	273	113	138	8	12.7
Polynice	48	960	165	54.5	0	0	67	58.8	114	270	16	26	53	19	8.3
Payton	82	2,244	259	45.0	13	1	69	71.1	108	243	528	165	180	15	7.2
Cage	82	2,141	226	50.8	3	0	70	62.5	177	558	89	85	83	58	6.4
Barros	66	750	154	49.5	81	32	78	91.8	17	71	111	23	54	1	6.3
Dailey	30	299	73	47.1	1	0	38	61.3	11	32	16	7	19	1	6.1
McMillan	78	1,434	132	43.3	48	17	57	61.3	71	251	371	104	122	20	4.3
Corzine	28	147	17	44.7	0	0	13	59.1	10	33	4	5	2	5	1.7
Meents	13	53	7	25.0	1	1	2	50.0	3	10	8	7	6	4	1.3
Supersonics	**82**	**19,880**	**3,500**	**49.2**	**427**	**136**	**1,608**	**75.0**	**1,222**	**3,395**	**2,042**	**861**	**1,404**	**380**	**106.6**
Opponents	**82**	**19,880**	**3,285**	**48.8**	**633**	**207**	**1,866**	**75.9**	**1,107**	**3,256**	**1,851**	**729**	**1,485**	**446**	**105.4**

Utah Jazz

Player	GP	Min	FGM	Pct	FGA	FGM	FTM	Pct	Off	Total	A	Stl	TO	BS	Avg
K. Malone	82	3,302	847	52.7	14	4	684	77.0	236	967	270	89	244	79	29.0
J. Malone	69	2,466	525	50.8	6	1	231	91.7	36	206	143	50	108	6	18.6
Stockton	82	3,103	496	50.7	168	58	363	83.6	46	237	1,164	234	298	16	17.2
Bailey	82	2,486	399	45.8	3	0	219	80.8	101	407	124	53	130	91	12.4
Edwards	62	1,611	244	52.6	24	6	82	70.1	51	201	108	57	105	29	9.3
Griffith	75	1,005	174	39.1	138	48	34	75.6	17	90	37	42	48	7	5.7
Eaton	80	2,580	169	57.9	0	0	71	63.4	182	667	51	39	99	188	5.1
M. Brown	82	1,391	129	45.4	0	0	132	74.2	109	337	49	29	82	24	4.8
Rudd	82	874	124	43.5	61	17	59	83.1	14	66	216	36	102	2	4.0
Cummings	4	26	4	66.7	0	0	7	70.0	3	5	0	0	2	0	3.8
Toolson	47	470	50	40.3	32	12	25	75.8	32	67	31	14	24	2	2.9
T. Brown	23	267	28	36.4	11	2	20	87.0	24	39	13	4	12	0	3.4
Palmer	28	85	15	33.3	1	0	10	66.7	6	21	6	3	6	4	1.4
Munk	11	29	3	42.9	0	0	7	58.3	5	14	1	1	5	2	1.2
O'Sullivan	21	85	7	43.8	0	0	7	63.6	5	17	4	1	4	1	1.0
Jazz	**82**	**19,780**	**3,214**	**49.2**	**458**	**148**	**1,951**	**78.9**	**867**	**3,341**	**2,217**	**652**	**1,305**	**451**	**104.0**
Opponents	**82**	**19,780**	**3,217**	**45.9**	**667**	**205**	**1,615**	**77.3**	**1,101**	**3,379**	**1,858**	**686**	**1,254**	**409**	**100.7**

Washington Bullets

Player	GP	Min	FGM	Pct	FGA	FGM	FTM	Pct	Off	Total	A	Stl	TO	BS	Avg
King	64	2,401	713	47.2	37	8	383	79.0	114	319	292	56	255	16	28.4
Grant	77	2,842	609	49.8	15	2	185	74.3	179	557	204	91	125	61	18.2
Eackles	67	1,616	345	45.3	59	14	164	73.9	47	128	136	47	115	10	13.0
Williams	33	941	164	41.7	41	10	73	75.3	42	177	133	39	68	6	12.5
Ellison	76	1,942	326	51.3	6	0	139	65.0	224	585	102	49	146	157	10.4
English	70	1,443	251	43.9	31	3	111	70.7	66	147	177	25	114	15	8.8
Workman	73	2,034	234	45.4	50	12	101	75.9	51	242	353	87	136	7	8.0
Walker	71	2,305	230	43.0	9	0	93	60.4	140	498	459	78	154	33	7.8
Robinson	12	255	38	41.8	1	0	7	58.3	14	28	24	7	11	0	6.9
Alarie	42	587	99	44.0	21	5	41	85.4	41	117	45	15	40	8	5.8
Hammonds	70	1,023	155	46.1	4	0	57	72.2	58	206	43	15	54	7	5.2
Irvin	33	316	60	46.5	5	1	50	82.0	24	45	24	15	16	2	5.2
Foster	54	606	97	46.0	5	0	42	68.9	52	151	37	12	45	22	4.4
Jones	62	1,499	67	54.0	0	0	29	58.0	119	359	48	51	46	124	2.6
Smith	5	45	2	50.0	0	0	3	50.0	2	4	4	1	1	0	1.4
Bullets	**82**	**19,855**	**3,390**	**46.6**	**284**	**55**	**1,478**	**72.9**	**1,173**	**3,563**	**2,081**	**588**	**1,360**	**468**	**101.4**
Opponents	**82**	**19,855**	**3,396**	**46.6**	**555**	**166**	**1,763**	**77.1**	**1,232**	**3,705**	**1,861**	**728**	**1,254**	**492**	**106.4**

1991 NBA Draft

First Round

1. Larry Johnson, Charlotte
2. Kenny Anderson, New Jersey
3. Billy Owens, Sacramento
4. Dikembe Mutombo, Denver
5. Steve Smith, Miami
6. Doug Smith, Dallas
7. Luc Longley, Minnesota
8. Mark Macon, Denver
9. Stacey Augmon, Atlanta
10. Brian Williams, Orlando
11. Terrell Brandon, Cleveland
12. Greg Anthony, New York
13. Dale Davis, Indiana
14. Rich King, Seattle
15. Anthony Avent, Atlanta
16. Chris Gatling, Golden State
17. Victor Alexander, Golden State
18. Kevin Brooks, Milwaukee
19. LaBradford Smith, Washington
20. John Turner, Houston
21. Eric Murdock, Utah
22. LeRon Ellis, LA Clippers
23. Stanley Roberts, Orlando
24. Rick Fox, Boston
25. Shaun Vandiver, Golden State
26. Mark Randall, Chicago
27. Pete Chilcutt, Sacramento

Second Round

28. Kevin Lynch, Charlotte
29. George Ackles, Miami
30. Rodney Monroe, Atlanta
31. Randy Brown, Sacramento
32. Chad Gallagher, Phoenix
33. Donald Hodge, Dallas
34. Myron Brown, Minnesota
35. Mike Iuzzolino, Dallas
36. Chris Corchiani, Orlando
37. Elliot Perry, LA Clippers
38. Joe Wylie, LA Clippers
39. Jimmy Oliver, Cleveland
40. Doug Overton, Detroit
41. Sean Green, Indiana
42. Steve Hood, Sacramento
43. Lamont Strothers, Golden State
44. Alvaro Teheran, Philadelphia
45. Bobby Phills, Milwaukee
46. Richard Dumas, Phoenix
47. Keith Hughes, Houston
48. Isaac Austin, Utah
49. Greg Sutton, San Antonio
50. Joey Wright, Phoenix
51. Zan Tabak, Houston
52. Anthony Jones, LA Lakers
53. Von McDade, New Jersey
54. Marcus Kennedy, Portland

Making a List

With the NBA playoffs in full swing, SI's Jack McCallum asked Red Auerbach, who has won 16 NBA titles with the Celtics, to name the 10 players whom he would most want in the playoffs. Said Auerbach, "Look, I had 12 players when I coached. The hell with 10." So here are Red's 12 (in no particular order, he stresses).

1. Bill Russell. The most influential player of his era, maybe of all time. By innovating the art of shot-blocking, he totally dictated tempo.

2. Kareem Abdul-Jabbar. Perhaps the single most potent offensive weapon ever. A durable player, a clutch player.

3. Larry Bird. Plays all parts of the game better than anyone who ever lived.

4. Magic Johnson. The most potent point guard ever.

5. John Havlicek. The ultimate professional. Superb condition, superb attitude, superb defender, superb versatility.

6. Michael Jordan. He's just everywhere. He could do anything.

7. Bob Cousy. When you're in the running game, you have to have Cousy. Next to Magic, the best ever on the break.

8. Jerry West. A very underrated defensive player. And a pressure performer.

9. Oscar Robertson. Like Bird, he did so much. He could rebound, shoot, play defense, and he was strong-willed.

10. Julius Erving. With one move, he could raise a team and destroy the opponent.

11. Charles Barkley. He does what he has to, whether it's outside, inside, rebounding or scoring. A winner.

12. Karl Malone. The thing that sets him apart from Bob Pettit and Elgin Baylor is that he runs the floor like a big guard.

FOR THE RECORD • Year by Year

NBA Champions

Season	Winner	Series	Loser	Winning Coach
1946-47	Philadelphia	4-1	Chicago	Eddie Gottlieb
1947-48	Baltimore	4-2	Philadelphia	Buddy Jeannette
1948-49	Minneapolis	4-2	Washington	John Kundla
1949-50	Minneapolis	4-2	Syracuse	John Kundla
1950-51	Rochester	4-3	New York	Les Harrison
1951-52	Minneapolis	4-3	New York	John Kundla
1952-53	Minneapolis	4-1	New York	John Kundla
1953-54	Minneapolis	4-3	Syracuse	John Kundla
1954-55	Syracuse	4-3	Ft Wayne	Al Cervi
1955-56	Philadelphia	4-1	Ft Wayne	George Senesky
1956-57	Boston	4-3	St Louis	Red Auerbach
1957-58	St Louis	4-2	Boston	Alex Hannum
1958-59	Boston	4-0	Minneapolis	Red Auerbach
1959-60	Boston	4-3	St Louis	Red Auerbach
1960-61	Boston	4-1	St Louis	Red Auerbach
1961-62	Boston	4-3	LA Lakers	Red Auerbach
1962-63	Boston	4-2	LA Lakers	Red Auerbach
1963-64	Boston	4-1	San Francisco	Red Auerbach
1964-65	Boston	4-1	LA Lakers	Red Auerbach
1965-66	Boston	4-3	LA Lakers	Red Auerbach
1966-67	Philadelphia	4-2	San Francisco	Alex Hannum
1967-68	Boston	4-2	LA Lakers	Bill Russell
1968-69	Boston	4-3	LA Lakers	Bill Russell
1969-70	New York	4-3	LA Lakers	Red Holzman
1970-71	Milwaukee	4-0	Baltimore	Larry Costello
1971-72	LA Lakers	4-1	New York	Bill Sharman
1972-73	New York	4-1	LA Lakers	Red Holzman
1973-74	Boston	4-3	Milwaukee	Tommy Heinsohn
1974-75	Golden State	4-0	Washington	Al Attles
1975-76	Boston	4-2	Phoenix	Tommy Heinsohn
1976-77	Portland	4-2	Philadelphia	Jack Ramsay
1977-78	Washington	4-3	Seattle	Dick Motta
1978-79	Seattle	4-1	Washington	Lenny Wilkens
1979-80	LA Lakers	4-2	Philadelphia	Paul Westhead
1980-81	Boston	4-2	Houston	Bill Fitch
1981-82	LA Lakers	4-2	Philadelphia	Pat Riley
1982-83	Philadelphia	4-0	LA Lakers	Billy Cunningham
1983-84	Boston	4-3	LA Lakers	K.C. Jones
1984-85	LA Lakers	4-2	Boston	Pat Riley
1985-86	Boston	4-2	Houston	K.C. Jones
1986-87	LA Lakers	4-2	Boston	Pat Riley
1987-88	LA Lakers	4-3	Detroit	Pat Riley
1988-89	Detroit	4-0	LA Lakers	Chuck Daly
1989-90	Detroit	4-1	Portland	Chuck Daly
1990-91	Chicago	4-1	LA Lakers	Phil Jackson

NBA Finals Most Valuable Player

Year	Player
1969	Jerry West, LA
1970	Willis Reed, NY
1971	Kareem Abdul-Jabbar, Mil
1972	Wilt Chamberlain, LA
1973	Willis Reed, NY
1974	John Havlicek, Bos
1975	Rick Barry, GS
1976	JoJo White, Bos
1977	Bill Walton, Port
1978	Wes Unseld, Wash
1979	Dennis Johnson, Sea
1980	Magic Johnson, LA
1981	Cedric Maxwell, Bos
1982	Magic Johnson, LA
1983	Moes Malone, Phil
1984	Larry Bird, Bos
1985	Kareem Abdul-Jabbar, LA Lakers
1986	Larry Bird, Bos
1987	Magic Johnson, LA Lakers
1988	James Worthy, LA Lakers
1989	Joe Dumars, Det
1990	Isiah Thomas, Det
1991	Michael Jordan, Chi

NBA Awards

NBA Most Valuable Player: Maurice Podoloff Trophy

1955-56 ....Bob Pettit, StL	1973-74 ....Kareem Abdul-Jabbar, Mil
1956-57 ....Bob Cousy, Bos	1974-75 ....Bob McAdoo, Buff
1957-58 ....Bill Russell, Bos	1975-76 ....Kareem Abdul-Jabbar, LA
1958-59 ....Bob Pettit, StL	1976-77 ....Kareem Abdul-Jabbar, LA
1959-60 ....Wilt Chamberlain, Phil	1977-78 ....Bill Walton, Port
1960-61 ....Bill Russell, Bos	1978-79 ....Moses Malone, Hou
1961-62 ....Bill Russell, Bos	1979-80 ....Kareem Abdul-Jabbar, LA
1962-63 ....Bill Russell, Bos	1980-81 ....Julius Erving, Phil
1963-64 ....Oscar Robertson, Cin	1981-82 ....Moses Malone, Hou
1964-65 ....Bill Russell, Bos	1982-83 ....Moses Malone, Phil
1965-66 ....Wilt Chamberlain, Phil	1983-84 ....Larry Bird, Bos
1966-67 ....Wilt Chamberlain, Phil	1984-85 ....Larry Bird, Bos
1967-68 ....Wilt Chamberlain, Phil	1985-86 ....Larry Bird, Bos
1968-69 ....Wes Unseld, Balt	1986-87 ....Magic Johnson, LA Lakers
1969-70 ....Willis Reed, NY	1987-88 ....Michael Jordan, Chi
1970-71 ....Kareem Abdul-Jabbar, Mil	1988-89 ....Magic Johnson, LA Lakers
1971-72 ....Kareem Abdul-Jabbar, Mil	1989-90 ....Magic Johnson, LA Lakers
1972-73 ....Dave Cowens, Bos	1990-91 ....Michael Jordan, Chi

Coach of the Year: Arnold "Red" Auerbach Trophy

1962-63 ....Harry Gallatin, StL	1977-78 ....Hubie Brown, Atl
1963-64 ....Alex Hannum, SF	1978-79 ....Cotton Fitzsimmons, KC
1964-65 ....Red Auerbach, Bos	1979-80 ....Bill Fitch, Bos
1965-66 ....Dolph Schayes, Phil	1980-81 ....Jack McKinney, Ind
1966-67 ....Johnny Kerr, Chi	1981-82 ....Gene Shue, Wash
1967-68 ....Richie Guerin, StL	1982-83 ....Don Nelson, Mil
1968-69 ....Gene Shue, Balt	1983-84 ....Frank Layden, Utah
1969-70 ....Red Holzman, NY	1984-85 ....Don Nelson, Mil
1970-71 ....Dick Motta, Chi	1985-86 ....Mike Fratello, Atl
1971-72 ....Bill Sharman, LA	1986-87 ....Mike Schuler, Port
1972-73 ....Tom Heinsohn, Bos	1987-88 ....Doug Moe, Den
1973-74 ....Ray Scott, Det	1988-89 ....Cotton Fitzsimmons, Phoe
1974-75 ....Phil Johnson, KC-Oma	1989-90 ....Pat Riley, LA Lakers
1975-76 ....Bill Fitch, Clev	1990-91 ....Don Chaney, Hou
1976-77 ....Tom Nissalke, Hou	

Note: Award named after Auerbach in 1986.

NBA Rookie of the Year: Eddie Gottlieb Trophy

1952-53 ....Don Meineke, FW	1971-72 ....Sidney Wicks, Port
1953-54 ....Ray Felix, Balt	1972-73 ....Bob McAdoo, Buff
1954-55 ....Bob Pettit, Mil	1973-74 ....Ernie DiGregorio, Buff
1955-56 ....Maurice Stokes, Roch	1974-75 ....Keith Wilkes, GS
1956-57 ....Tom Heinsohn, Bos	1975-76 ....Alvan Adams, Phoe
1957-58 ....Woody Sauldsberry, Phil	1976-77 ....Adrian Dantley, Buff
1958-59 ....Elgin Baylor, Minn	1977-78 ....Walter Davis, Phoe
1959-60 ....Wilt Chamberlain, Phil	1978-79 ....Phil Ford, KC
1960-61 ....Oscar Robertson, Cin	1979-80 ....Larry Bird, Bos
1961-62 ....Walt Bellamy, Chi	1980-81 ....Darrell Griffith, Utah
1962-63 ....Terry Dischinger, Chi	1981-82 ....Buck Williams, NJ
1963-64 ....Jerry Lucas, Cin	1982-83 ....Terry Cummings, SD
1964-65 ....Willis Reed, NY	1983-84 ....Ralph Sampson, Hou
1965-66 ....Rick Barry, SF	1984-85 ....Michael Jordan, Chi
1966-67 ....Dave Bing, Det	1985-86 ....Patrick Ewing, NY
1967-68 ....Earl Monroe, Balt	1986-87 ....Chuck Person, Ind
1968-69 ....Wes Unseld, Balt	1987-88 ....Mark Jackson, NY
1969-70 ....Kareem Abdul-Jabbar, Mil	1988-89 ....Mitch Richmond, GS
1970-71 ....Dave Cowens, Bos	1989-90 ....David Robinson, SA
Geoff Petrie, Port	1990-91 ....Derrick Coleman, NJ

Hogging the Titles
Between them, the Celtics and the Lakers have won 27 of the NBA's 45 titles. Boston leads all teams with 16 NBA crowns.

NBA Defensive Player of the Year

Season	Player
1982-83	Sidney Moncrief, Mil
1983-84	Sidney Moncrief, Mil
1984-85	Mark Eaton, Utah
1985-86	Alvin Robertson, SA
1986-87	Michael Cooper, LA Lakers
1987-88	Michael Jordan, Chi
1988-89	Mark Eaton, Utah
1989-90	Dennis Rodman, Det
1990-91	Dennis Rodman, Det

NBA Sixth Man Award

Season	Player
1982-83	Bobby Jones, Phil
1983-84	Kevin McHale, Bos
1984-85	Kevin McHale, Bos
1985-86	Bill Walton, Bos
1986-87	Ricky Pierce, Mil
1987-88	Roy Tarpley, Dall
1988-89	Eddie Johnson, Phoe
1989-90	Ricky Pierce, Mil
1990-91	Detlef Schrempf, Ind

NBA Most Improved Player

Season	Player
1985-86	Alvin Robertson, SA
1986-87	Dale Ellis, Sea
1987-88	Kevin Duckworth, Port
1988-89	Kevin Johnson, Phoe
1989-90	Rony Seikaly, Mia
1990-91	Scott Skiles, Orl

Big Score for a Scorer

When Michael Jordan led the Chicago Bulls to the 1990–91 title, he became only the second player in history to lead the NBA in scoring and play on a championship team in the same year. The other was Kareem Abdul-Jabbar, then Lew Alcindor, who accomplished the feat with the Milwaukee Bucks in 1970–71.

J. Walter Kennedy Citizenship Award

Season	Player
1974-75	Wes Unseld, Wash
1975-76	Slick Watts, Sea
1976-77	Dave Bing, Wash
1977-78	Bob Lanier, Det
1978-79	Calvin Murphy, Hou
1979-80	Austin Carr, Clev
1980-81	Mike Glenn, NY
1981-82	Kent Benson, Det
1982-83	Julius Erving, Phil
1983-84	Frank Layden, Utah
1984-85	Dan Issel, Den
1985-86	Michael Cooper, LA Lakers Rory Sparrow, NY
1986-87	Isiah Thomas, Det
1987-88	Alex English, Den
1988-89	Thurl Bailey, Utah
1989-90	Glenn Rivers, Atl
1990-91	Kevin Johnson, Phoe

NBA Executive of the Year

Season	Executive
1972-73	Joe Axelson, KC-Oma
1973-74	Eddie Donovan, Buff
1974-75	Dick Vertlieb, GS
1975-76	Jerry Colangelo, Phoe
1976-77	Ray Patterson, Hou
1977-78	Angelo Drossos, SA
1978-79	Bob Ferry, Wash
1979-80	Red Auerbach, Bos
1980-81	Jerry Colangelo, Phoe
1981-82	Bob Ferry, Wash
1982-83	Zollie Volchok, Sea
1983-84	Frank Layden, Utah
1984-85	Vince Boryla, Den
1985-86	Stan Kasten, Atl
1986-87	Stan Kasten, Atl
1987-88	Jerry Krause, Chi
1988-89	Jerry Colangelo, Phoe
1989-90	Bob Bass, SA
1990-91	Bucky Buckwalter, Port

Selected by *The Sporting News.*

NBA All-Time Individual Leaders

Scoring

MOST POINTS, LIFETIME

Player	Points
Kareem Abdul-Jabbar	38,387
Wilt Chamberlain	31,419
Elvin Hayes	27,313
Oscar Robertson	26,710
John Havlicek	26,395

MOST POINTS, SEASON

Player	Points	Season
Wilt Chamberlain, Phil	4,029	1961-62
Wilt Chamberlain, SF	3,586	1962-63
Michael Jordan, Chi	3,041	1986-87
Wilt Chamberlain, Phil	3,033	1960-61
Wilt Chamberlain, SF	2,948	1963-64

HIGHEST SCORING AVERAGE, CAREER

Player	Avg	Games
Michael Jordan	32.6	509 games
Wilt Chamberlain	30.1	1,045 games
Elgin Baylor	27.4	846 games
Jerry West	27.0	932 games
Bob Pettit	26.4	792 games

HIGHEST SCORING AVERAGE, SEASON
(Minimum of 70 games)

Player	Avg	Season
Wilt Chamberlain, Phil	50.4	1961-62
Wilt Chamberlain, SF	44.8	1962-63
Wilt Chamberlain, Phil	38.4	1960-61
Wilt Chamberlain, Phil	37.6	1959-60
Michael Jordan, Chi	37.1	1986-87

MOST POINTS, GAME: 100—Wilt Chamberlain, Philadelphia vs New York, at Hershey, PA, 3/2/62

Tops Seldom Are Tops

Only four of the NBA's No. 1 draft picks have gone on to win the league's Rookie of the Year award: Derrick Coleman, David Robinson, Ralph Sampson, and Kareem Abdul-Jabbar.

Field Goal Percentage

Highest Field Goal Percentage, Career: .599—Artis Gilmore
Highest Field Goal Percentage, Season: .727—Wilt Chamberlain, LA Lakers, 1972-73 (426/586)

Free Throw Percentage

HIGHEST FREE THROW PERCENTAGE, CAREER

Rick Barry	.900
Calvin Murphy	.892
Bill Sharman	.883
Larry Bird	.880

HIGHEST FREE THROW PERCENTAGE, SEASON

Calvin Murphy, Hou	.958	1980-81
Rick Barry, Hou	.947	1978-79
Ernie DiGregorio, Buff	.945	1976-77
Ricky Sobers, Chi	.9352	1980-81
Rick Barry, Hou	.9346	1979-80

Three-Point Field Goal Percentage*

Most Three-Point Field Goals, Career: Darrell Griffith—1,506
Highest Three-Point Field Goal Percentage, Career: Mark Price—.418
Most Three-Point Field Goals, Season: Michael Adams, Den—167 1990-91
Highest Three-Point Field Goal Percentage, Season: Jon Sundvold, Mia—.522 1988-89
Most Three-Point Field Goals, Game: 9—Dale Ellis, Seattle vs LA Clippers, 4/20/90; 9—Michael Adams, Denver vs LA Clippers, 4/12/91

*First Year of Shot: 1979-80

Steals

Most Steals, Career: 2,194—Maurice Cheeks
Most Steals, Season: 301—Alvin Robertson, San Antonio, 1985-86
Most Steals, Game: 11—Larry Kenon, San Antonio vs Kansas City, 12/26/76

Rebounds

MOST REBOUNDS, CAREER

Wilt Chamberlain	23,924
Bill Russell	21,620
Kareem Abdul-Jabbar	17,440
Elvin Hayes	16,279
Moses Malone	15,150

MOST REBOUNDS, SEASON

Wilt Chamberlain, Phil	2,149	1960-61
Wilt Chamberlain, Phil	2,052	1961-62
Wilt Chamberlain, Phil	1,957	1966-67
Wilt Chamberlain, Phil	1,952	1967-68
Wilt Chamberlain, SF	1,946	1962-63

MOST REBOUNDS, GAME: 55—Wilt Chamberlain, Philadelphia vs Boston, 11/24/60

Assists

MOST ASSISTS, CAREER

Magic Johnson	9,921
Oscar Robertson	9,887
Isiah Thomas	7,431
Lenny Wilkens	7,211
Bob Cousy	6,955

MOST ASSISTS, SEASON

John Stockton, Utah	1,164	1990-91
John Stockton, Utah	1,134	1989-90
John Stockton, Utah	1,128	1987-88
Isiah Thomas, Det	1,123	1984-85
John Stockton, Utah	1,118	1988-89

MOST ASSISTS, GAME: 30—Scott Skiles, Orlando vs Denver, 12/30/90

Blocked Shots

Most Blocked Shots, Career: 3,189—Kareem Abdul-Jabbar
Most Blocked Shots, Season: 456—Mark Eaton, Utah, 1984-85
Most Blocked Shots, Game: 17—Elmore Smith, LA Lakers vs Portland, 10/28/73

NBA Season Leaders

Scoring

1946-47	Joe Fulks, Phil	1389	1964-65	Wilt Chamberlain, SF-Phil	2534
1947-48	Max Zaslofsky, Chi	1007	1965-66	Wilt Chamberlain, Phil	2649
1948-49	George Mikan, Minn	1698	1966-67	Rick Barry, SF	2775
1949-50	George Mikan, Minn	1865	1967-68	Dave Bing, Det	2142
1950-51	George Mikan, Minn	1932	1968-69	Elvin Hayes, SD	2327
1951-52	Paul Arizin, Phil	1674	1969-70	Jerry West, LA	*31.2
1952-53	Neil Johnston, Phil	1564	1971-71	Kareem Abdul-Jabbar, Mil	34.8
1953-54	Neil Johnston, Phil	1759	1972-73	Nate Archibald, KC-Oma	34.0
1954-55	Neil Johnston, Phil	1631	1973-74	Bob McAdoo, Buff	30.6
1955-56	Bob Pettit, StL	1849	1974-75	Bob McAdoo, Buff	34.5
1956-57	Paul Arizin, Phil	1817	1975-76	Bob McAdoo, Buff	31.1
1957-58	George Yardley, Det	2001	1976-77	Pete Maravich, NO	31.1
1958-59	Bob Pettit, StL	2105	1977-78	George Gervin, SA	27.2
1959-60	Wilt Chamberlain, Phil	2707	1978-79	George Gervin, SA	29.6
1960-61	Wilt Chamberlain, Phil	3033	1979-80	George Gervin, SA	33.1
1961-62	Wilt Chamberlain, Phil	4029	1980-81	Adrian Dantley, Utah	30.7
1962-63	Wilt Chamberlain, SF	3586	1981-82	George Gervin, SA	32.3
1963-64	Wilt Chamberlain, SF	2948	1982-83	Alex English, Den	28.4

Scoring (*Cont.*)

1983-84	Adrian Dantley, Utah	30.6	1987-88	Michael Jordan, Chi	35.0
1984-85	Bernard King, NY	32.9	1988-89	Michael Jordan, Chi	32.5
1985-86	Dominique Wilkins, Atl	30.3	1989-90	Michael Jordan, Chi	33.6
1986-87	Michael Jordan, Chi	37.1	1990-91	Michael Jordan, Chi	31.5

*Based on per game average.

Rebounding

1950-51	Dolph Schayes, Syr	1080	1971-72	Wilt Chamberlain, LA	19.2
1951-52	Larry Foust, FW	880	1972-73	Wilt Chamberlain, LA	18.6
	Mel Hutchins, Mil	880	1973-74	Elvin Hayes, Capital	18.1
1952-53	George Mikan, Minn	1007	1974-75	Wes Unseld, Wash	14.8
1953-54	Harry Gallatin, NY	1098	1975-76	Kareem Abdul-Jabbar, LA	16.9
1954-55	Neil Johnston, Phil	1085	1976-77	Bill Walton, Port	14.4
1955-56	Bob Pettit, StL	1164	1977-78	Len Robinson, NO	15.7
1956-57	Maurice Stokes, Roch	1256	1978-79	Moses Malone, Hou	17.6
1957-58	Bill Russell, Bos	1564	1979-80	Swen Nater, SD	15.0
1958-59	Bill Russell, Bos	1612	1980-81	Moses Malone, Hou	14.8
1959-60	Wilt Chamberlain, Phil	1941	1981-82	Moses Malone, Hou	14.7
1960-61	Wilt Chamberlain, Phil	2149	1982-83	Moses Malone, Phil	15.3
1961-62	Wilt Chamberlain, Phil	2052	1983-84	Moses Malone, Phil	13.4
1962-63	Wilt Chamberlain, SF	1946	1984-85	Moses Malone, Phil	13.1
1963-64	Bill Russell, Bos	1930	1985-86	Bill Laimbeer, Det	13.1
1964-65	Bill Russell, Bos	1878	1986-87	Charles Barkley, Phil	14.6
1965-66	Wilt Chamberlain, Phil	1943	1987-88	Michael Cage, LA Clippers	13.03
1966-67	Wilt Chamberlain, Phil	1957	1988-89	Hakeem Olajuwon, Hou	13.5
1967-68	Wilt Chamberlain, Phil	1952	1989-90	Hakeem Olajuwon, Hou	14.0
1968-69	Wilt Chamberlain, LA	1712	1990-91	David Robinson, SA	13.0
1969-70	Elvin Hayes, SD	*16.9			
1970-71	Wilt Chamberlain, LA	18.2			

*Based on per game average.

Assists

1946-47	Ernie Calverly, Prov	202	1969-70	Len Wilkens, Sea	*9.1
1947-48	Howie Dallmar, Phil	120	1970-71	Norm Van Lier, Cin	10.1
1948-49	Bob Davies, Roch	321	1971-72	Jerry West, LA	9.7
1949-50	Dick McGuire, NY	386	1972-73	Nate Archibald, KC-Oma	11.4
1950-51	Andy Phillip, Phil	414	1973-74	Ernie DiGregorio, Buff	8.2
1951-52	Andy Phillip, Phil	539	1974-75	Kevin Porter, Wash	8.0
1952-53	Bob Cousy, Bos	547	1975-76	Don Watts, Sea	8.1
1953-54	Bob Cousy, Bos	578	1976-77	Don Buse, Ind	8.5
1954-55	Bob Cousy, Bos	557	1977-78	Kevin Porter, NJ-Det	10.2
1955-56	Bob Cousy, Bos	642	1978-79	Kevin Porter, Det	13.4
1956-57	Bob Cousy, Bos	478	1979-80	Micheal Richardson, NY	10.1
1957-58	Bob Cousy, Bos	463	1980-81	Kevin Porter, Wash	9.1
1958-59	Bob Cousy, Bos	557	1981-82	Johnny Moore, SA	9.6
1959-60	Bob Cousy, Bos	715	1982-83	Magic Johnson, LA	10.5
1960-61	Oscar Robertson, Cin	690	1983-84	Magic Johnson, LA	13.1
1961-62	Oscar Robertson, Cin	899	1984-85	Isiah Thomas, Det	13.9
1962-63	Guy Rodgers, SF	825	1985-86	Magic Johnson, LA Lakers	12.6
1963-64	Oscar Robertson, Cin	868	1986-87	Magic Johnson, LA Lakers	12.2
1964-65	Oscar Robertson, Cin	861	1987-88	John Stockton, Utah	13.8
1965-66	Oscar Robertson, Cin	847	1988-89	John Stockton, Utah	13.6
1966-67	Guy Rodgers, Chi	908	1989-90	John Stockton, Utah	14.5
1967-68	Wilt Chamberlain, Phil	702	1990-91	John Stockton, Utah	14.2
1968-69	Oscar Robertson, Cin	772			

*Based on per game average.

A Slow Start

Bill Russell played on 11 NBA championship teams, won the league's MVP award five times, and was a first-team All-Pro on three occasions, but in his first year in pro ball the Rookie of the Year award went to a teammate, Tom Heinsohn.

Field Goal Percentage

1946-47	Bob Feerick, Wash	40.1	1969-70	Johnny Green, Cin	55.9
1947-48	Bob Feerick, Wash	34.0	1970-71	Johnny Green, Cin	58.7
1948-49	Arnie Risen, Roch	42.3	1971-72	Wilt Chamberlain, LA	64.9
1949-50	Alex Groza, Ind	47.8	1972-73	Wilt Chamberlain, LA	72.7
1950-51	Alex Groza, Ind	47.0	1973-74	Bob McAdoo, Buff	54.7
1951-52	Paul Arizin, Phil	44.8	1974-75	Don Nelson, Bos	53.9
1952-53	Neil Johnston, Phil	45.2	1975-76	Wes Unseld, Wash	56.1
1953-54	Ed Macauley, Bos	48.6	1976-77	Kareem Abdul-Jabbar, LA	57.9
1954-55	Larry Foust, FW	48.7	1977-78	Bobby Jones, Den	57.8
1955-56	Neil Johnston, Phil	45.7	1978-79	Cedric Maxwell, Bos	58.4
1956-57	Neil Johnston, Phil	44.7	1979-80	Cedric Maxwell, Bos	60.9
1957-58	Jack Twyman, Cin	45.2	1980-81	Artis Gilmore, Chi	67.0
1958-59	Ken Sears, NY	49.0	1981-82	Artis Gilmore, Chi	65.2
1959-60	Ken Sears, NY	47.7	1982-83	Artis Gilmore, SA	62.6
1960-61	Wilt Chamberlain, Phil	50.9	1983-84	Artis Gilmore, SA	63.1
1961-62	Walt Bellamy, Chi	51.9	1984-85	James Donaldson, LA Clippers	63.7
1962-63	Wilt Chamberlain, SF	52.8	1985-86	Steve Johnson, SA	63.2
1963-64	Jerry Lucas, Cin	52.7	1986-87	Kevin McHale, Bos	60.4
1964-65	Wilt Chamberlain, SF-Phil	51.0	1987-88	Kevin McHale, Bos	60.4
1965-66	Wilt Chamberlain, Phil	54.0	1988-89	Dennis Rodman, Det	59.5
1966-67	Wilt Chamberlain, Phil	68.3	1989-90	Mark West, Phoe	62.5
1967-68	Wilt Chamberlain, Phil	59.5	1990-91	Buck Williams, Port	60.2
1968-69	Wilt Chamberlain, LA	58.3			

Free Throw Percentage

1946-47	Fred Scolari, Wash	81.1	1969-70	Flynn Robinson, Mil	89.8
1947-48	Bob Feerick, Wash	78.8	1970-71	Chet Walker, Chi	85.9
1948-49	Bob Feerick, Wash	85.9	1971-72	Jack Marin, Balt	89.4
1949-50	Max Zaslofsky, Chi	84.3	1972-73	Rick Barry, GS	90.2
1950-51	Joe Fulks, Phil	85.5	1973-74	Ernie DiGregorio, Buff	90.2
1951-52	Bob Wanzer, Roch	90.4	1974-75	Rick Barry, GS	90.4
1952-53	Bill Sharman, Bos	85.0	1975-76	Rick Barry, GS	92.3
1953-54	Bill Sharman, Bos	84.4	1976-77	Ernie DiGregorio, Buff	94.5
1954-55	Bill Sharman, Bos	89.7	1977-78	Rick Barry, GS	92.4
1955-56	Bill Sharman, Bos	86.7	1978-79	Rick Barry, Hou	94.7
1956-57	Bill Sharman, Bos	90.5	1979-80	Rick Barry, Hou	93.5
1957-58	Dolph Schayes, Syr	90.4	1980-81	Calvin Murphy, Hou	95.8
1958-59	Bill Sharman, Bos	93.2	1981-82	Kyle Macy, Phoe	89.9
1959-60	Dolph Schayes, Syr	89.2	1982-83	Calvin Murphy, Hou	92.0
1960-61	Bill Sharman, Bos	92.1	1983-84	Larry Bird, Bos	88.8
1961-62	Dolph Schayes, Syr	89.6	1984-85	Kyle Macy, Phoe	90.7
1962-63	Larry Costello, Syr	88.1	1985-86	Larry Bird, Bos	89.6
1963-64	Oscar Robertson, Cin	85.3	1986-87	Larry Bird, Bos	91.0
1964-65	Larry Costello, Phil	87.7	1987-88	Jack Sikma, Mil	92.2
1965-66	Larry Siegfried, Bos	88.1	1988-89	Magic Johnson, LA Lakers	91.1
1966-67	Adrian Smith, Cin	90.3	1989-90	Larry Bird, Bos	93.0
1967-68	Oscar Robertson, Cin	87.3	1990-91	Reggie Miller, Ind	91.8
1968-69	Larry Siegfried, Bos	86.4			

Three-Point Field Goal Percentage

1979-80	Fred Brown, Sea	44.3
1980-81	Brian Taylor, SD	38.3
1981-82	Campy Russell, NY	43.9
1982-83	Mike Dunleavy, SA	34.5
1983-84	Darrell Griffith, Utah	36.1
1984-85	Byron Scott, LA Lakers	43.3
1985-86	Craig Hodges, Mil	45.1
1986-87	Kiki Vandeweghe, Port	48.1
1987-88	Craig Hodges, Mil-Phoe	49.1
1988-89	Jon Sundvold, Mia	52.2
1989-90	Steve Kerr, Clev	50.7
1990-91	Jim Les, Sac	46.1

Playtime

The bizarre injury-of-the-season award for the 1990–91 campaign goes to Sacramento Kings rookie forward Lionel Simmons. On Feb. 20, days after he was named Player of the Week, Simmons got tendinitis in his right wrist and forearm and missed two games. The cause of the tendinitis was soon revealed: Simmons had been playing too much Nintendo Game Boy. "It's not unusual for Lionel to be focused on something," says Sacramento general manager Jerry Reynolds. "But to hurt himself like *that*?"

NBA Season Leaders (*Cont.*)

Steals

1973-74 .... Larry Steele, Port	2.68
1974-75 .... Rick Barry, GS	2.85
1975-76 .... Don Watts, Sea	3.18
1976-77 .... Don Buse, Ind	3.47
1977-78 .... Ron Lee, Phoe	2.74
1978-79 .... M. L. Carr, Det	2.46
1979-80 .... Micheal Richardson, NY	3.23
1980-81 .... Magic Johnson, LA	3.43
1981-82 .... Magic Johnson, LA	2.67
1982-83 .... Micheal Richardson, GS-NJ	2.84
1983-84 .... Rickey Green, Utah	2.65
1984-85 .... Micheal Richardson, NJ	2.96
1985-86 .... Alvin Robertson, SA	3.67
1986-87 .... Alvin Robertson, SA	3.21
1987-88 .... Michael Jordan, Chi	3.16
1988-89 .... John Stockton, Utah	3.21
1989-90 .... Michael Jordan, Chi	2.77
1990-91 .... Alvin Robertson, Mil	3.04

Blocked Shots

1973-74 .... Elmore Smith, LA	4.85
1974-75 .... Kareem Abdul-Jabbar, Mil	3.26
1975-76 .... Kareem Abdul-Jabbar, LA	4.12
1976-77 .... Bill Walton, Port	3.25
1977-78 .... George Johnson, NJ	3.38
1978-79 .... Kareem Abdul-Jabbar, LA	3.95
1979-80 .... Kareem Abdul-Jabbar, LA	3.41
1980-81 .... George Johnson, SA	3.39
1981-82 .... George Johnson, SA	3.12
1982-83 .... Wayne Rollins, Atl	4.29
1983-84 .... Mark Eaton, Utah	4.28
1984-85 .... Mark Eaton, Utah	5.56
1985-86 .... Manute Bol, Wash	4.96
1986-87 .... Mark Eaton, Utah	4.06
1987-88 .... Mark Eaton, Utah	3.71
1988-89 .... Manute Bol, GS	4.31
1989-90 .... Hakeem Olajuwon, Hou	4.59
1990-91 .... Hakeem Olajuwon, Hou	3.95

NBA All-Star Game Results

Year	Result	Site	Winning Coach	Most Valuable Player
1951	East 111, West 94	Boston	Joe Lapchick	Ed Macauley, Bos
1952	East 108, West 91	Boston	Al Cervi	Paul Arizin, Phil
1953	West 79, East 75	Ft Wayne	John Kundla	George Mikan, Minn
1954	East 98, West 93 (OT)	New York	Joe Lapchick	Bob Cousy, Bos
1955	East 100, West 91	New York	Al Cervi	Bill Sharman, Bos
1956	West 108, East 94	Rochester	Charley Eckman	Bob Pettit, StL
1957	East 109, West 97	Boston	Red Auerbach	Bob Cousy, Bos
1958	East 130, West 118	St Louis	Red Auerbach	Bob Pettit, StL
1959	West 124, East 108	Detroit	Ed Macauley	Bob Pettit, StL
				Elgin Baylor, Minn
1960	East 125, West 115	Philadelphia	Red Auerbach	Wilt Chamberlain, Phil
1961	West 153, East 131	Syracuse	Paul Seymour	Oscar Robertson, Cin
1962	West 150, East 130	St Louis	Fred Schaus	Bob Pettit, StL
1963	East 115, West 108	Los Angeles	Red Auerbach	Bill Russell, Bos
1964	East 111, West 107	Boston	Red Auerbach	Oscar Robertson, Cin
1965	East 124, West 123	St Louis	Red Auerbach	Jerry Lucas, Cin
1966	East 137, West 94	Cincinnati	Red Auerbach	Adrian Smith, Cin
1967	West 135, East 120	San Francisco	Fred Schaus	Rick Barry, SF
1968	East 144, West 124	New York	Alex Hannum	Hal Greer, Phil
1969	East 123, West 112	Baltimore	Gene Shue	Oscar Robertson, Cin
1970	East 142, West 135	Philadelphia	Red Holzman	Willis Reed, NY
1971	West 108, East 107	San Diego	Larry Costello	Lenny Wilkens, Sea
1972	West 112, East 110	Los Angeles	Bill Sharman	Jerry West, LA
1973	East 104, West 84	Chicago	Tom Heinsohn	Dave Cowens, Bos
1974	West 134, East 123	Seattle	Larry Costello	Bob Lanier, Det
1975	East 108, West 102	Phoenix	K. C. Jones	Walt Frazier, NY
1976	East 123, West 109	Philadelphia	Tom Heinsohn	Dave Bing, Wash
1977	West 125, East 124	Milwaukee	Larry Brown	Julius Erving, Phil
1978	East 133, West 125	Atlanta	Billy Cunningham	Randy Smith, Buff
1979	West 134, East 129	Detroit	Lenny Wilkens	David Thompson, Den
1980	East 144, West 135 (OT)	Washington	Billy Cunningham	George Gervin, SA
1981	East 123, West 120	Cleveland	Billy Cunningham	Nate Archibald, Bos
1982	East 120, West 118	New Jersey	Bill Fitch	Larry Bird, Bos
1983	East 132, West 123	Los Angeles	Billy Cunningham	Julius Erving, Phil
1984	East 154, West 145 (OT)	Denver	K. C. Jones	Isiah Thomas, Det
1985	West 140, East 129	Indiana	Pat Riley	Ralph Sampson, Hou
1986	East 139, West 132	Dallas	K. C. Jones	Isiah Thomas, Det
1987	West 154, East 149 (OT)	Seattle	Pat Riley	Tom Chambers, Sea
1988	East 138, West 133	Chicago	Mike Fratello	Michael Jordan, Chi
1989	West 143, East 134	Houston	Pat Riley	Karl Malone, Utah
1990	East 130, West 113	Miami	Chuck Daly	Magic Johnson, LA Lakers
1991	East 116, West 114	Charlotte	Chris Ford	Charles Barkley, Phil

Members of the Basketball Hall of Fame

Contributors

Senda Abbott (1984)
Forest C. "Phog" Allen (1959)
Clair F. Bee (1967)
Walter A. Brown (1965)
John W. Bunn (1964)
Bob Douglas (1971)
Al Duer (1981)
Clifford Fagan (1983)
Harry A. Fisher (1973)
Larry Fleisher (1991)
Edward Gottlieb (1971)
Luther H. Gulick (1959)
Lester Harrison (1979)
Ferenc Hepp (1980)
Edward J. Hickox (1959)

Paul D. "Tony" Hinkle (1965)
Ned Irish (1964)
R. William Jones (1964)
J. Walter Kennedy (1980)
Emil S. Liston (1974)
John B. McLendon (1978)
Bill Mokray (1965)
Ralph Morgan (1959)
Frank Morgenweck (1962)
James Naismith (1959)
Peter F. Newell (1978)
John J. O'Brien (1961)
Larry O'Brien (1991)
Harold G. Olsen (1959)
Maurice Podoloff (1973)

H.V. Porter (1960)
William A. Reid (1963)
Elmer Ripley (1972)
Lynn W. St. John (1962)
Abe Saperstein (1970)
Arthur A. Schabinger (1961)
Amos Alonzo Stagg (1959)
Boris Stankovic (1991)
Edward Steitz (1983)
Chuck Taylor (1968)
Oswald Tower (1959)
Arthur L. Trester (1961)
Clifford Wells (1971)
Lou Wilke (1982)

Players

Nate "Tiny" Archibald (1991)
Paul J. Arizin (1977)
Thomas B. Barlow (1980)
Rick Barry (1986)
Elgin Baylor (1976)
John Beckman (1972)
Dave Bing (1989)
Bennie Borgmann (1961)
Bill Bradley (1982)
Joseph Brennan (1974)
Al Cervi (1984)
Wilt Chamberlain (1978)
Charles "Tarzan" Cooper (1976)
Bob Cousy (1970)
Dave Cowens (1991)
Billy Cunningham (1985)
Bob Davies (1969)
Forrest S. DeBernardi (1961)
Dave DeBusschere (1982)
H. G. "Dutch" Dehnert (1968)
Paul Endacott (1971)
Harold "Bud" Foster (1964)
Walter "Clyde" Frazier (1986)
Max "Marty" Friedman (1971)
Joe Fulks (1977)
Lauren "Laddie" Gale (1976)
Harry "the Horse" Gallatin (1991)
William Gates (1988)

Tom Gola (1975)
Hal Greer (1981)
Robert "Ace" Gruenig (1963)
Clifford O. Hagan (1977)
Victor Hanson (1960)
John Havlicek (1983)
Elvin Hayes (1989)
Tom Heinsohn (1985)
Nat Holman (1964)
Robert J. Houbregs (1986)
Chuck Hyatt (1959)
William C. Johnson (1976)
D. Neil Johnston (1989)
K. C. Jones (1988)
Sam Jones (1983)
Edward "Moose" Krause (1975)
Bob Kurland (1961)
Joe Lapchick (1966)
Clyde Lovellette (1987)
Jerry Lucas (1979)
Angelo "Hank" Luisetti (1959)
C. Edward Macauley (1960)
Branch McCracken (1960)
Jack McCracken (1962)
Bobby McDermott (1987)
Peter P. Maravich (1986)
Slater Martin (1981)
George L. Mikan (1959)

Earl Monroe (1989)
Charles "Stretch" Murphy (1960)
H. O. "Pat" Page (1962)
Bob Pettit (1970)
Andy Phillip (1961)
Jim Pollard (1977)
Frank Ramsey (1981)
Willis Reed (1981)
Oscar Robertson (1979)
John S. Roosma (1961)
Bill Russell (1974)
John "Honey" Russell (1964)
Adolph Schayes (1972)
Ernest J. Schmidt (1973)
John J. Schommer (1959)
Barney Sedran (1962)
Bill Sharman (1975)
Christian Steinmetz (1961)
John A. "Cat" Thompson (1962)
Nate Thurmond (1984)
Jack Twyman (1982)
Wes Unseld (1987)
Robert "Fuzzy" Vandivier (1974)
Edward A. Wachter (1961)
Robert F. Wanzer (1986)
Jerry West (1979)
Lenny Wilkens (1988)
John R. Wooden (1960)

Coaches

Harold Anderson (1984)
Red Auerbach (1968)
Sam Barry (1978)
Ernest A. Blood (1960)
Howard G. Cann (1967)
H. Clifford Carlson (1959)
Ben Carnevale (1969)
Everett Case (1981)
Everett S. Dean (1966)
Edgar A. Diddle (1971)
Bruce Drake (1972)
Clarence Gaines (1981)
Jack Gardner (1983)
Amory T. "Slats" Gill (1967)

Marv Harshman (1984)
Edgar S. Hickey (1978)
Howard A. Hobson (1965)
Red Holzman (1985)
Hank Iba (1968)
Alvin F. "Doggie" Julian (1967)
Frank W. Keaney (1960)
George E. Keogan (1961)
Bob Knight (1991)
Ward L. Lambert (1960)
Harry Litwack (1975)
Kenneth D. Loeffler (1964)
A. C. "Dutch" Lonborg (1972)
Arad A. McCutchan (1980)

Frank McGuire (1976)
Walter E. Meanwell (1959)
Raymond J. Meyer (1978)
Ralph Miller (1987)
Adolph F. Rupp (1968)
Leonard D. Sachs (1961)
Everett F. Shelton (1979)
Dean Smith (1982)
Fred R. Taylor (1985)
Bertha Teague (1984)
Margaret Wade (1984)
Stanley H. Watts (1985)
John R. Wooden (1972)

Note: Year of election in parentheses.

Referees

James E. Enright (1978)
George T. Hepbron (1960)
George Hoyt (1961)
Matthew P. Kennedy (1959)
Lloyd Leith (1982)
Zigmund J. Mihalik (1985)
John P. Nucatola (1977)
Ernest C. Quigley (1961)
J. Dallas Shirley (1979)
David Tobey (1961)
David H. Walsh (1961)

Teams

Buffalo Germans (1961)
First Team (1959)
Original Celtics (1959)
Renaissance (1963)

Note: Year of election in parentheses.

ABA

ABA CHAMPIONS

Year	Champion	Series	Loser	Winning Coach
1968	Pittsburgh Pipers	4-2	New Orleans Bucs	Vince Cazetta
1969	Oakland Oaks	4-1	Indiana Pacers	Alex Hannum
1970	Indiana Pacers	4-2	Los Angeles Stars	Bob Leonard
1971	Utah Stars	4-3	Kentucky Colonels	Bill Sharman
1972	Indiana Pacers	4-2	New York Nets	Bob Leonard
1973	Indiana Pacers	4-3	Kentucky Colonels	Bob Leonard
1974	New York Nets	4-1	Utah Stars	Kevin Loughery
1975	Kentucky Colonels	4-1	Indiana Pacers	Hubie Brown
1976	New York Nets	4-2	Denver Nuggets	Kevin Loughery

POSTSEASON AWARDS

ABA Most Valuable Player

1967-68........Connie Hawkins, Pitt
1968-69........Mel Daniels, Ind
1969-70........Spencer Haywood, Den
1970-71........Mel Daniels, Ind
1971-72........Artis Gilmore, Ken
1972-73........Billy Cunningham, Car
1973-74........Julius Erving, NY
1974-75........Julius Erving, NY
................George McGinnis, Ind
1975-76........Julius Erving, NY

ABA Rookie of the Year

1967-68........Mel Daniels, Minn
1968-69........Warren Armstrong, Oak
1969-70........Spencer Haywood, Den
1970-71........Charlie Scott
................Dan Issel, Ken
1971-72........Artis Gilmore, Ken
1972-73........Brian Taylor, NY
1973-74........Swen Nater, SA
1974-75........Marvin Barnes, SL
1975-76........David Thompson, Den

ABA Coach of the Year

1967-68.........Vince Cazetta, Pitt
1968-69.........Alex Hannum, Oak
1969-70.........Bill Sharman, LA
................Joe Belmont, Den
1970-71.........Al Bianchi, Vir
1971-72.........Tom Nissalke, Dall
1972-73.........Larry Brown, Car
1973-74.........Babe McCarthy, Ken
................Joe Mullaney, Utah
1974-75.........Larry Brown, Den
1975-76.........Larry Brown, Den

A Big Point Spread

Kareem Abdul-Jabbar retired with a career total of 38,387 points, an NBA record that seemed unsurpassable. But don't count out Michael Jordan. At his current pace the Chicago Bulls' superstar would pass Abdul-Jabbar in the 12th game of the 1998–99 season, when Jordan will be 36 years old. Abdul-Jabbar averaged 24.6 points per game over 20 years. In 509 games through the end of the 1990–91 season Air Jordan has soared to 16,599 points for a 32.6 per game average. Now he just needs to keep that pace up for 669 more games.

SEASON LEADERS

Scoring

		GP	Pts	Avg
1968	Connie Hawkins, Pitt	70	1875	26.8
1969	Rick Barry, Oak	35	1190	34.0
1970	Spencer Haywood, Den	84	2519	30.0
1971	Dan Issel, Ken	83	2480	29.4
1972	Charlie Scott, Vir	73	2524	34.6
1973	Julius Erving, Vir	71	2268	31.9
1974	Julius Erving, NY	84	2299	27.4
1975	George McGinnis, Ind	79	2353	29.8
1976	Julius Erving, NY	84	2462	29.3

Rebounds

1967-68	Mel Daniels, Minn	15.6
1968-69	Mel Daniels, Ind	16.5
1969-70	Spencer Haywood, Den	19.5
1970-71	Mel Daniels, Ind	18.0
1971-72	Artis Gilmore, Ken	17.8
1972-73	Artis Gilmore, Ken	17.5
1973-74	Artis Gilmore, Ken	18.3
1974-75	Swen Nater, SA	16.4
1975-76	Artis Gilmore, Ken	15.5

Assists

1967-68	Larry Brown, NO	6.5
1968-69	Larry Brown, Oak	7.1
1969-70	Larry Brown, Wash	7.1
1970-71	Bill Melchionni, NY	8.3
1971-72	Bill Melchionni, NY	8.4
1972-73	Bill Melchionni, NY	7.5
1973-74	Al Smith, Den	8.2
1974-75	Mack Calvin, Den	7.7
1975-76	Don Buse, Ind	8.2

Steals

1973-74	Ted McClain, Car	2.98
1974-75	Brian Taylor, NY	2.80
1975-76	Don Buse, Ind	4.12

Blocked Shots

1973-74	Caldwell Jones, SD	4.00
1974-75	Caldwell Jones, SD	3.24
1975-76	Billy Paultz, SA	3.05

Russell vs. Chamberlain

Who was better, Bill Russell or Wilt Chamberlain? Going by statistics, you would have to give the nod to Chamberlain. In the 142 games they played against each other, Chamberlain averaged almost twice as many points as Russell (28.7 per game to 14.5) and won the battle of the boards (28.7 per game to 23.7). Russell, on the other hand, played on 11 NBA champions, Chamberlain just two.

THEY SAID IT

Chicago Bulls and former North Carolina star Michael Jordan on why he chose geography as his college major: "I knew that I would be going places and I just wanted to know where I was when I got there."

College Basketball

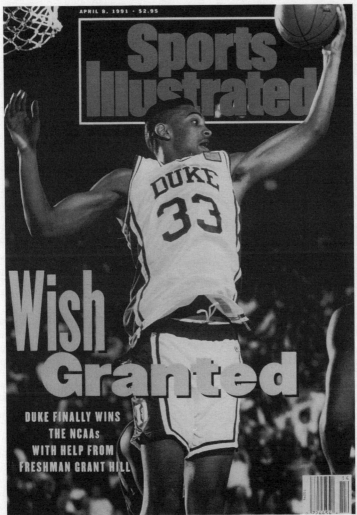

APRIL 8, 1991 · $2.95

Sports Illustrated

Wish Granted

DUKE FINALLY WINS THE NCAAs WITH HELP FROM FRESHMAN GRANT HILL

JOHN W. McDONOUGH

Runnin' Down the Rebs

"Invincible" UNLV was be(Blue)Deviled by Duke, which went on to win its first NCAA crown | by PHIL TAYLOR

E THOUGHT THEY WERE INVIN-cible. Some of us thought they were everything a college basketball team should be; others thought they were everything a college basketball program shouldn't be. But almost everyone agreed on one thing: the famed UNLV Runnin' Rebels were the best team of the 1990–91 season—and maybe the best team ever. The nation marveled at the Rebels. Otherwise rational men suggested that UNLV could compete with NBA expansion teams. *Call off the NCAA tournament! UNLV can't be beat,* one newspaper headline screamed after the Rebels ran their record to 20–0 with a 112–105 humbling of pitiable Arkansas.

It was easy to be drawn into the hype. The Rebels' average margins of victory were often astonishing, especially because coach Jerry Tarkanian didn't often leave his starters on the floor to run up the score when the outcome had long since been decided. Long

Beach State fell twice, by 51 and 47, Nevada-Reno by 50. Michigan State, a Top 20 team, threw everything it had at the Rebels, including the home court advantage—and still lost by 20. Still, we should have known better. But we couldn't help ourselves. We thought they were invincible.

Outwardly, UNLV laughed at that notion. Even as they turned the regular season and most of the NCAA tournament into one long, seemingly effortless victory tour, the only people for whom the Rebels had greater disdain than they did for their opponents were those souls foolish enough to believe that UNLV couldn't lose. "Invincible? There's no such thing as invincible," said UNLV guard Greg Anthony in March.

Whatever else they were, the Rebels were realists. Even with their sneering, their in-your-face finger-pointing and their arrogant on-court demeanor, the Rebels never seemed to be taken in by their own success. Ask them if they thought they would go undefeated and they invariably replied that

superior talent guarantees nothing, that un-defeated does not mean infallible. Then, on a memorable March afternoon in Indianapolis's Hoosier Dome, they proved it.

Or maybe Duke proved it. The Blue Devils had been victims of a 30-point trashing by UNLV in the 1990 championship game. But one year later, they pulled off a stirring 79–77 upset of the Rebels in the NCAA tournament semifinals and went on to win the national championship with a 72–65 victory over Kansas two nights later. It was Duke's first national title in nine trips to the Final Four, including the last four.

The Blue Devils did it by fulfilling every item on the long checklist of how to beat UNLV. They got Anthony, the Rebels' guiding hand, to foul out down the stretch. They used a parade of fresh defenders to keep Larry Johnson, UNLV's All-America forward, in check on offense; and when the Blue Devils had the ball they used center Christian Laettner's mobility and ball handling skills to pull Johnson away from the

With Johnson leading the way, UNLV slammed its way past all 30 of its regular season opponents.

basket, which opened up the middle of the Rebel defense. And finally, they introduced UNLV to a unique concept: a close game in the final minutes, something the Rebels had never dealt with during the regular season.

If it wasn't the perfect game, it was as close as anyone could expect to come against UNLV. With a couple of minutes to play, Duke assistant Mike Brey turned to Tommy Amaker, another Blue Devil assistant. "It would be a shame if we lost this game," Brey said, "because everything is falling into place."

It finally fell completely into place for Duke coach Mike Krzyzewski, who had nothing to show for his four previous trips to the Final Four. After the 1990 loss to UNLV, the joke went like this: the college basketball season is a five-month exercise to determine two things: (1) a national champion and (2) whose turn it is to beat Duke in the Final Four. But 1991 was the year Coach K got to have the last laugh.

"It's never been a monkey on my back," Krzyzewski said, moments after beating Kansas, a surprise entrant in the Final Four.

But while Duke and UNLV both enjoyed the kind of successful years to which they are accustomed, there were plenty of other traditional powers that didn't. It was a season of humility, one in which several of the elite, high-profile programs and coaches found out how the other half lives. Notre Dame, Oklahoma, Louisville and Michigan all had humbling years that ended without their usual NCAA tournament bid.

Notre Dame may have had the most difficult year of all. The Fighting Irish lost their best player, forward LaPhonso Ellis, to academic problems, and several injuries further depleted coach Digger Phelps's roster. Notre Dame struggled to a 12–20 season, during which the university administration answered questions about Phelps's job security with a silence that spoke volumes. Phelps took the hint and announced his resignation April 15, after 20 years as the Notre Dame coach. He was replaced three weeks later with former New York Knicks coach John MacLeod.

Several other well-known coaches also had their rocky moments. Louisville's Denny Crum suffered through a subpar season, but his real problems had to do with the classroom, where his players' academic performances drew increased scrutiny. Only six of the Cardinals's 37 scholarship players who completed their eligibility at the school between 1981 and '90 earned degrees within five years of enrolling at Louisville, and four of Crum's 1990–91 recruits were academically ineligible. Crum didn't help himself when he told Morley Safer of *60 Minutes* that he saw nothing wrong with some of his

New Kids on the Block

EVERY SEASON BRINGS a new crop of freshmen of whom wondrous things are expected, but 1990–91 was noteworthy in that regard. It marked the arrival of one of the most publicized freshmen in years, Indiana guard Damon Bailey, and the most heralded group of newcomers in memory, North Carolina's famed five freshmen— center Eric Montross, forwards Clifford Rozier and Pat Sullivan, and guards Derrick Phelps and Brian Reese. Reality rarely keeps pace with imagination, so it's no surprise that neither Bailey, individually, nor the new Tar Heels, collectively, set the college basketball world afire. Instead, they were erratic, at times showing how good they may eventually become and at other times showing how much they had to learn.

For Bailey, the buildup had started at age 14, when, after watching him play as an eighth-grader, Indiana coach Bob Knight declared in the book *A Season on the Brink* that the kid was "better than any guard we have right now."

Bailey, who lived in Heltonville, Ind., went on to a storybook career at Bedford North Lawrence High, a career so brilliant— the Stars won the state title in Bailey's senior season, before a staggering crowd of 41,046 in the Hoosier Dome as he scored 30 points—that Knight's words looked less like an exaggeration than a prophecy.

At Indiana, Bailey started slowly but he may have come of age in one of the season's best games, the Hoosiers' 97–95 double-overtime loss to second-ranked Ohio State in February in which he made 11 of his 15 shots and led all scorers with 32 points. Bailey finished the season with an 11.4 scoring average.

"I'm sure some people expected me to be some sort of immediate superstar, but I tried not to let that enter my thinking," Bailey said. "I think in a lot of ways the freshman year is the toughest. I've enjoyed

players, in effect, "majoring in basketball."

It may not have been the greatest of seasons for people like Phelps and Crum, but LSU center Shaquille O'Neal had few complaints. O'Neal, a 7'1", 295-pound sophomore, won all the player of the year awards that UNLV's Johnson didn't. His performance overshadowed remarkable years by some of the nation's other top players, including guards Kenny Anderson of Georgia Tech, Steve Smith of Michigan State and Eric Murdock of Providence, and forwards Jimmy Jackson of Ohio State and Billy Owens of Syracuse.

O'Neal proved himself the most dominating big man college basketball has seen since Georgetown's Patrick Ewing terrorized opponents in the early '80s. O'Neal averaged 27.6 points, seventh in the nation, and led the country with 14.7 rebounds per game. He also averaged five blocked shots, third best in the country.

But statistics can only begin to measure the sheer force of O'Neal's presence. His most memorable game may have come in a 92–82 victory over No. 2 Arizona in December, when he had 29 points, 14 rebounds, six blocks and five steals while playing only 28 minutes because of foul trouble and a pulled stomach muscle. He not only carried the Tigers to victory against a superior team, but he also provided one of the season's most enduring images: hanging from the rim and sneering down at the Wildcats after a monster dunk down the stretch—not to mention the Cabbage Patch number he performed near the lane.

"I don't know what he's doing still in college," said forward Todd Merritt of Mississippi State. "He's costing himself an awful lot of money."

And that was before O'Neal decided to forgo what has been estimated to be as much as $30 million over five years by staying in

Indiana's Bailey was certainly no flop, but life as a freshman wasn't a cakewalk either.

MANNY MILLAN

it, but I wouldn't want to go through it again."

North Carolina's five might say the same thing. Recruiting experts called them the best freshman class in history.

But the Carolina class only stayed together one year. After a season in which the freshmen made only sporadic contributions—Montross and Rozier, who averaged 5.8 and 4.9 points per game, respectively, were the group's most prolific scorers—Rozier transferred to Louisville, unhappy with his playing time in Chapel Hill and Dean Smith's age-old system. "I just made a mistake," he said. "Nothing against North Carolina, it just isn't the right place for me."

At about the time Rozier was finalizing his transfer, Michigan was putting the finishing touches on a recruiting class—forwards Chris Webber, Juwan Howard and Jalen Rose and guards Jimmy King and Ray Jackson—that has already been dubbed the best freshman class in the country. They will undoubtedly find that label both a blessing and a curse.

A year after Duke's humiliating loss to UNLV in the final, Hurley showed Hunt the new order of things.

school another year. He would almost certainly have been the No. 1 pick in the June 1991 NBA draft, but he announced in April that he would remain at LSU.

Other star underclassmen couldn't resist the lure of the pros. Anderson, the Yellow Jackets' sophomore prodigy at point guard, left early for the NBA draft, as did Owens, the versatile Syracuse junior.

The women's game didn't have a player as dominant as O'Neal or a team as awesome as UNLV, but like the Rebels, Virginia, led by gifted point guard Dawn Staley, held on to the No. 1 spot most of the season and was the clear favorite to win the title. Alas, the Cavs stumbled just short of the finish line. Tennessee's 70–67 overtime upset of the Cavaliers in the title game at New Orleans gave the Vols their third national championship in five years.

For Tennessee coach Pat Summitt, the championship was the end of an eventful year in which Virginia had a recurring role. Tennessee had lost to Virginia in the East Regional final the previous year. The loss so irked Summitt that the mere mention of Virginia evoked bad memories for her throughout the year.

Flying home from a recruiting trip in September, just before the start of practice for the 1990–91 season, the pregnant Summitt went into labor. As bad luck would have it, Summitt's plane was in Virginia airspace while she was having contractions. Determined not to give birth in Cavalier territory, she insisted on flying on, and Ross Tyler Summitt was safely delivered on the ground in Tennessee.

Little Tyler, as he is known, quickly became a favorite of the Tennessee players, in particular All-America center Daedra Charles, who made a habit of touching the baby for good luck before games throughout the season. The Vols' luck held in the championship game, as they came back from a 60–55 deficit in the last 1:15 of regulation before winning in overtime. Tyler witnessed it all, clad in a tiny shirt with "Cavalier Buster" on the chest.

But in truth, Tyler probably had less to do with Tennessee's success than his mom. Summitt has won more NCAA titles than any other woman coach in NCAA history, and more than any Division I coach other than Wooden, Knight and Kentucky's Adolph Rupp. She has had 37 players earn letters since the 1981–82 season, 27 of whom played on at least one championship team.

One of the few drawbacks to the women's Final Four was that Tennessee and Virginia had to play the championship game less than 24 hours after the completion of Saturday's second semifinal to ensure a national television audience for all three games of the Final Four. Fatigue appeared to take its toll on both teams, although it was overshadowed by the game's dramatic finish. Still, the women would have been better served if they had taken a day's rest between the semis and the final, as the men do.

Perhaps the best thing that could happen to women's basketball is to have a nationally televised championship game as good as the regular-season encounter between two national powers, second-ranked Virginia and No. 3 North Carolina State, which was played in January in Raleigh. Virginia edged the Wolfpack 123–120 in triple overtime in what may have been the best game—men's or women's—of the year.

Virginia recovered from a 20-point deficit in the second half. So, not surprisingly, there were a ton of clutch plays, the last of which came when Tonya Cardoza stole a Wolfpack pass and went the length of the floor to score with 2.5 seconds left in the third overtime and give the Cavs a 122–120 lead. When it was all over, both coaches appropriately used the game as a soapbox to promote women's basketball. "We're worth seeing," said N.C. State coach Kay Yow. "The game, men's and women's, is the same. We just can't play above the rim."

One area in which the women haven't matched the men, thankfully, is in scandals. The season saw its usual share, most notably a pair of related incidents at Texas A&M and Syracuse. The Texas A&M saga eventually cost first-year coach Kermit Davis his job.

Tony Scott, a former Syracuse forward

The most dominating player in college was the 7'1", 295-pound O'Neal, who led the country with 14.7 rebounds a game.

who had transferred to Texas A&M, told the *Syracuse Post-Standard* that Davis had used the services of a New York talent scout, Rob Johnson, to help recruit Scott to Texas A&M, a violation of NCAA rules. Davis denied all the allegations and Scott later recanted his story, but the damage to Davis had been done. He resigned under pressure in March and was replaced by Tony Barone, the fiery former Creighton coach.

The *Post-Standard* uncovered the allegations against Texas A&M as a by-product of its investigation into the Syracuse program, a foray that turned up several other charges of NCAA violations. According to the newspaper, 10 Syracuse players said that together they received hundreds of dollars from Syracuse boosters, and former Syracuse player Rodney Walker said one of his grades on an exam was changed in order to keep him eligible for a game in 1987. Coach Jim Boeheim denied the allegations, and the NCAA is still investigating the charges.

But there were far more pleasant stories to focus on during the season, including the annual emergence of several surprise teams. Nebraska, a perennial contender in the Big Eight—*in football*—and unheralded East Tennessee State had stunningly successful seasons. The Cornhuskers, picked by most to finish no better than in the middle of the pack in their conference, instead ripped off a 26–7 record heading into the NCAA tournament, beating such teams as Michigan State, Kansas, Oklahoma and Missouri. Nebraska, a balanced team without many recognizable players, took its emotional cues from coach Danny Nee, a former helicopter tail gunner in Vietnam who instilled in his players the toughness necessary to do battle in the rugged Big Eight.

"When your coach has told you how he stood in bunkers waist deep in water somewhere in Vietnam, watching the rats swim by and keeping alert for snipers, suddenly going in to play Oklahoma on their home court isn't such an intimidating experience," said Nebraska center Rich King.

East Tennessee State was less of a surprise—the Buccaneers won their Southern Conference, as expected, but the little school

DAMIAN STROHMEYER

Tyler proved a good luck charm for mom and the Tennessee Vols, who won their third NCAA title in five years.

in Johnson City, Tenn., even spent some time in the Top Ten. The Bucs also featured one of the nation's most delightful players, 5'7" playmaker Keith (Mister) Jennings.

Nebraska and East Tennessee both bowed out in the first round of the NCAA tournament, leaving the final mighty mite story of the year to Eastern Michigan. Until the tournament, the Hurons' greatest claim to fame was that they were no longer the Hurons. The school retired the nickname early in the 1990–91 season because it was viewed as an affront to Native Americans.

But the absence of a nickname didn't keep Eastern Michigan from reaching the East Regional semifinals. Largely on the strength of its outstanding point guard, Lorenzo Neely, Eastern Michigan upset Mississippi State and Penn State before North Carolina burst its bubble in the round of 16.

Eastern Michigan's departure left the tournament with no Cinderellas, and with UNLV casting its imposing shadow upon the field, crowning the 1991 national champion seemed little more than a formality. Duke changed all that, of course.

After the Rebels lost, they quickly cleared out of their locker room. The only article of clothing left in the deserted room was a solitary cap sitting on a shelf in one of the UNLV stalls. It was blue, with white letters, and it provided the last word on the 1990–91 season. It said, "Duke."

NCAA Championship Game Boxscore

Kansas 65

KANSAS	Min	FG M-A	FT M-A	Reb O-T	A	PF	TP
Jamison	25	1-10	0-0	2-4	5	4	2
Maddox	19	2-4	0-0	1-3	4	3	4
Randall	33	7-9	3-6	3-10	2	4	18
Brown	31	6-15	0-0	1-4	1	1	16
Jordan	34	4-6	1-2	0-0	3	0	11
Woodberry	18	1-4	0-0	2-4	0	4	2
Scott	15	3-9	0-0	2-2	0	1	6
Tunstall	15	1-5	0-0	1-1	0	3	2
Wagner	3	1-1	0-0	1-1	0	0	2
Johanning	3	1-1	0-0	1-2	1	1	2
Richey	4	0-1	0-0	0-1	0	0	0
Totals	200	27-65	4-8	14-32	16	21	65

Percentages: FG—.415, FT—.500. 3-pt goals: 7-18, .389 (Brown 4-11, Jordan 2-2, Randall 1-1, Richey 0-1, Tunstall 0-1, Jamison 0-2). Team rebounds: 0. Blocked shots: 2 (Maddox, Tunstall). Turnovers: 14 (Jordan 3, Randall 3, Brown 2, Maddox 2, Jamison, Scott, Tunstall, Woodberry). Steals: 10 (Jamison 4, Brown 3, Jordan, Randall, Woodberry).

Duke 72

DUKE	Min	FG M-A	FT M-A	Reb O-T	A	PF	TP
Koubek	17	2-4	0-0	2-4	0	1	5
G. Hill	28	4-6	2-8	0-8	3	1	10
Laettner	32	3-8	12-12	4-10	0	3	18
Hurley	40	3-5	4-4	0-1	9	1	12
T. Hill	23	1-5	0-0	0-4	1	2	3
Davis	24	4-5	0-2	0-2	1	4	8
Palmer	9	0-0	0-0	0-0	0	0	0
Lang	1	0-0	0-0	0-0	0	0	0
McCaffrey	26	6-8	2-2	0-1	0	1	16
Totals	200	23-41	20-28	6-31	14	13	72

Percentages: FG—.561, FT—.714. 3-pt goals: 6-10, .600 (Hurley 2-4, McCaffrey 2-3, T. Hill 1-1, Koubek 1-2). Team rebounds: 1. Blocked shots: 2 (G. Hill 2). Turnovers: 18 (Laettner 4, McCaffrey 4, Hurley 3, G. Hill 2, Koubek 2, Davis, Lang, Palmer). Steals: 6 (G. Hill 2, Hurley 2, Laettner, Koubek).

Halftime: Duke 42, Kansas 34. A: 47,100. Officials: Mickey Crowley, Charles Range, James Burr.

Final AP Top 25

Poll taken before NCAA Tournament. Records entering post-season.

1. UNLV	30-0
2. Arkansas	31-3
3. Indiana	27-4
4. N Carolina	25-5
5. Ohio St	25-3
6. Duke	26-7
7. Syracuse	26-5
8. Arizona	26-6
9. Kentucky	22-6
10. Utah	28-3
11. Nebraska	26-7
12. Kansas	22-7
13. Seton Hall	22-8
14. Oklahoma St	22-7
15. New Mexico St	23-5
16. UCLA	23-8
17. E Tennessee St	26-4
18. Princeton	24-2
19. Alabama	21-9
20. St. John's	20-8
21. Mississippi St	20-8
22. Louisiana St	20-9
23. Texas	22-8
24. DePaul	20-8
25. Southern Miss	21-7

National Invitation Tournament Scores

First round: Providence 98, James Madison 93 (2OT); Cincinnati 82, Ball State 55; Wisconsin 87, Bowling Green 79 (OT); Colorado 71, Michigan 64; Southern Illinois 75, Boise State 74; Stanford 93, Houston 86; Siena 90, Fairleigh Dickinson 85; Fordham 76, S Florida 66; SW Missouri St 57, Coppin St 47; Memphis St 82, AL-Birmingham 76; Arkansas St 78, Rice 71; Oklahoma 111, Tulsa 86; West Virginia 86, Furman 67; Massachusetts 93, La Salle 90; S Carolina 69, George Washington 63; Wyoming 63, Butler 61.

Second round: Providence 85, West Virginia 79; Oklahoma 89, Cincinnati 81 (OT); Stanford 80, Wisconsin 72; Southern Illinois 72, SW Missouri St 69; Arkansas St 58, Memphis St 57; Colorado 83, Wyoming 75; Massachusetts 78, Fordham 74; Siena 63, S Carolina 58.

Third round: Oklahoma 83, Providence 74; Massachusetts 82, Siena 80 (OT); Stanford 78, Southern Illinois 68; Colorado 81, Arkansas St 75.

Semifinals: Stanford 73, Massachusetts 71; Oklahoma 88, Colorado 78.

Championship: Stanford 78, Oklahoma 72.

Consolation game: Colorado 98, Massachusetts 91.

1991 NCAA Basketball Men's Division I Tournament

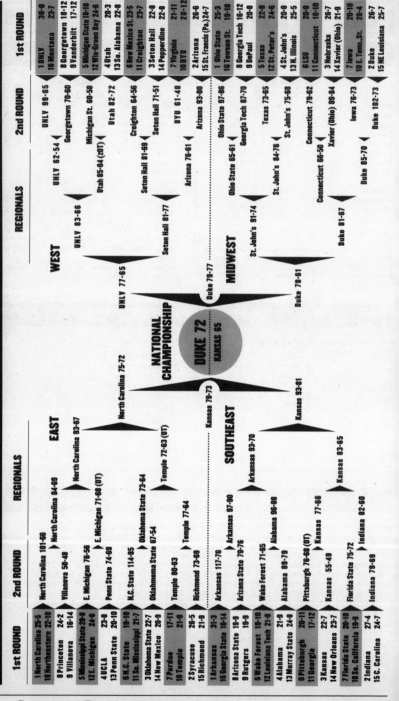

1st ROUND

1 UNLV 30-0
16 Montana 23-7
8 Georgetown 18-12
9 Vanderbilt 17-12
5 Michigan State 18-10
12 Wis-Green Bay 24-6
4 Utah 28-3
13 So. Alabama 22-8
6 New Mexico St. 23-5
11 Creighton 23-7
3 Seton Hall 22-8
14 Pepperdine 22-8
7 Virginia 21-11
10 BYU 20-12
2 Arizona 26-6
15 St. Francis (Pa.) 24-7

1 Ohio State 25-3
16 Towson St. 19-10
8 Georgia Tech 16-12
9 DePaul 20-8
5 Texas 22-8
12 St. Peter's 24-6
4 St. John's 20-8
13 N. Illinois 25-5
6 LSU 20-9
11 Connecticut 18-10
3 Nebraska 26-7
14 Xavier (Ohio) 21-9
7 Iowa 20-10
10 E. Tenn. St. 28-4
2 Duke 26-7
15 NE Louisiana 25-7

2nd ROUND

UNLV 99-65
Georgetown 70-60
Michigan St. 60-58
Utah 82-72
Creighton 64-56
Seton Hall 71-51
BYU 61-48
Arizona 93-80

Ohio State 97-86
Georgia Tech 87-70
Texas 73-65
St. John's 75-68
Connecticut 79-62
Xavier (Ohio) 89-84
Iowa 76-73
Duke 102-73

REGIONALS

WEST

UNLV 62-54
Utah 85-84 (2OT)
Seton Hall 81-69
Arizona 76-61

UNLV 83-66
Seton Hall 81-77

UNLV 77-65

MIDWEST

Ohio State 65-61
St. John's 91-74
Duke 81-67

St. John's 84-76
Duke 85-70

Duke 78-61

NATIONAL CHAMPIONSHIP

DUKE 72
KANSAS 65

Duke 79-77

North Carolina 75-72

Kansas 79-73

EAST

North Carolina 93-67
E. Michigan 71-68 (0T)
Oklahoma State 73-64
Temple 72-63 (0T)

North Carolina 84-69
Temple 77-64

North Carolina 101-66

SOUTHEAST

Arkansas 97-90
Alabama 96-88
Kansas 77-66
Indiana 82-60

Arkansas 93-70
Kansas 83-65

Kansas 93-81

2nd ROUND

North Carolina 101-66
Villanova 50-48
E. Michigan 76-56
Penn State 74-69
N.C. State 114-85
Oklahoma State 67-54
Temple 80-63
Richmond 73-69

Arkansas 117-76
Arizona State 79-76
Wake Forest 71-65
Alabama 89-79
Pittsburgh 76-68 (0T)
Kansas 55-49
Florida State 75-72
Indiana 79-69

1st ROUND

1 North Carolina 25-5
16 Northeastern 22-10
8 Princeton 24-2
9 Villanova 16-14
5 Mississippi State 29-9
12 E. Michigan 23-6
4 UCLA 23-8
13 Penn State 20-10
6 N.C. State 19-10
11 So. Mississippi 21-7
3 Oklahoma State 22-7
14 New Mexico 20-9
7 Purdue 17-11
10 Temple 21-9
2 Syracuse 26-5
15 Richmond 21-9

1 Arkansas 31-3
16 Georgia State 16-14
8 Arizona State 19-9
9 Rutgers 19-9
5 Wake Forest 18-10
12 Louisiana Tech 21-9
4 Alabama 21-9
13 Murray State 24-8
6 Pittsburgh 20-11
11 Georgia 17-12
3 Kansas 22-7
14 New Orleans 23-7
7 Florida State 20-10
10 So. California 19-9
2 Indiana 27-4
15 E. Carolina 24-7

NCAA Men's Division I Conference Standings

American South

	Conference			All Games		
	W	L	Pct	W	L	Pct
New Orleans*	9	3	.750	23	8	.742
Arkansas St	9	3	.750	23	9	.719
La. Tech†	8	4	.667	21	10	.677
SW Louisiana	6	6	.500	21	10	.677
Lamar	4	8	.333	15	13	.536
Cent. Fla.	3	9	.250	10	17	.370
TX-Pan Am	3	9	.250	7	21	.250

Assoc. of Mid-Continent

	Conference			All Games		
	W	L	Pct	W	L	Pct
N. Illinois*	14	2	.875	25	6	.806
WI-Gr. Bay†	13	3	.813	24	7	.774
E. Illinois	10	6	.625	17	12	.586
Cleveland St	8	8	.500	12	16	.429
Northern Iowa	8	8	.500	19	14	.408
Akron	6	10	.375	15	13	.536
Western Illinois	6	10	.375	15	15	.464
IL-Chicago	5	11	.313	15	15	.500
Valparaiso	2	14	.125	5	22	.185

Atlantic Coast

	Conference			All Games		
	W	L	Pct	W	L	Pct
Duke*	11	3	.786	32	7	.821
N Carolina†	10	4	.714	29	6	.829
Wake Forest	8	6	.571	19	11	.633
N Carolina State	8	6	.571	20	11	.645
Georgia Tech	6	8	.429	17	13	.567
Virginia	6	8	.429	21	12	.636
Maryland	5	9	.357	16	12	.571
Clemson	2	12	.167	11	17	.393

Atlantic 10

	Conference			All Games		
	W	L	Pct	W	L	Pct
Rutgers*	14	4	.778	19	10	.655
Temple	13	5	.722	24	10	.706
Penn St††	10	8	.556	21	11	.656
George Wash.	10	8	.556	19	12	.613
Massachusetts	10	8	.556	20	13	.606
Duquesne	10	8	.556	13	15	.464
West Virginia	10	8	.556	17	14	.548
St. Joseph's	7	11	.389	17	17	.433
Rhode Island	6	12	.333	11	17	.393
St. Bonaventure	0	18	.000	5	23	.179

Big East

	Conference			All Games		
	W	L	Pct	W	L	Pct
Syracuse*	12	4	.750	26	6	.813
St John's	10	6	.625	23	9	.719
Connecticut	9	7	.563	20	11	.645
Seton Hall†	9	7	.563	25	9	.735
Pittsburgh	9	7	.563	21	12	.636
Georgetown	8	8	.500	19	13	.594
Providence	7	9	.438	18	12	.600
Villanova	7	9	.438	17	15	.531
Boston Col	1	15	.063	11	19	.366

Big Eight

	Conference			All Games		
	W	L	Pct	W	L	Pct
Oklahoma St*	10	4	.714	24	8	.750
Kansas*	10	4	.714	27	8	.771
Nebraska	9	5	.643	26	8	.765
Missouri†	8	6	.571	20	10	.667
Iowa St	6	8	.429	12	19	.387
Oklahoma	5	9	.357	20	15	.571
Colorado	5	9	.357	19	14	.576
Kansas St	3	11	.214	13	15	.464

Big Sky

	Conference			All Games		
	W	L	Pct	W	L	Pct
Montana*†	13	3	.813	23	8	.742
Nevada	12	4	.750	17	14	.548
Idaho	11	5	.689	19	11	.633
Boise St	10	6	.625	18	11	.621
Idaho St	7	9	.438	11	18	.379
Weber St	7	9	.438	12	16	.429
Montana St	6	10	.375	12	16	.429
Eastern Washington	5	11	.312	11	16	.408
Northern Arizona	1	15	.062	4	23	.148

Big South

	Conference			All Games		
	W	L	Pct	W	L	Pct
Coastal Carolina*†	13	1	.929	24	8	.750
Radford	12	2	.857	22	7	.759
Augusta	9	5	.643	14	16	.467
Davidson	6	8	.429	10	19	.345
Winthrop	5	9	.357	8	20	.286
NC-Asheville	4	10	.285	8	20	.286
Charleston So	4	10	.285	9	19	.321
Campbell	3	11	.214	9	19	.321

Big Ten

	Conference			All Games		
	W	L	Pct	W	L	Pct
Ohio St*	15	3	.833	27	4	.871
Indiana	15	3	.833	29	5	.853
Illinois	11	7	.611	21	10	.677
Michigan St	11	7	.611	19	11	.633
Iowa	9	9	.500	21	11	.656
Purdue	9	9	.500	17	12	.586
Wisconsin	8	10	.444	15	15	.500
Michigan	7	11	.389	14	15	.483
Minnesota	5	13	.278	12	16	.429
Northwestern	0	18	.000	5	23	.179

*Conf. champ; †Conf. tourney winner.

The Price Of Success

CBS paid $143 million for the television rights to the 1991 NCAA basketball tournament, an increase of almost $89 million from the previous year. That's a far cry from 1939, the tournament's first year, when the sponsoring National Association of Basketball Coaches lost about $2,500.

Big West

	Conference			All Games		
	W	L	Pct	W	L	Pct
UNLV*†	18	0	1.000	34	1	.971
New Mex St	15	3	.833	23	6	.793
Pacific U	9	9	.500	14	15	.483
UC Santa Brb	8	10	.444	14	15	.483
Utah St	8	10	.444	11	17	.393
Cal State Fullerton	7	11	.389	14	14	.500
Fresno St	7	11	.389	14	16	.467
Long Beach St	7	11	.389	11	17	.393
UC Irvine	6	12	.333	11	19	.367
San Jose St	5	13	.278	7	20	.259

Colonial Athletic Association

	Conference			All Games		
	W	L	Pct	W	L	Pct
James Madison*	12	2	.857	19	10	.655
Richmond†	10	4	.714	22	10	.688
American U	8	6	.571	15	14	.517
George Mason	8	6	.571	14	16	.467
NC-Wilmington	6	8	.429	11	17	.393
William & Mary	6	8	.429	13	15	.464
E Carolina	4	10	.286	12	16	.429
Navy	2	12	.143	8	21	.259

East Coast

	Conference			All Games		
	W	L	Pct	W	L	Pct
Towson St*†	10	2	.833	19	11	.633
Delaware	8	4	.667	16	13	.552
Drexel	7	5	.583	12	16	.428
Hofstra	7	5	.583	14	14	.500
MD-Baltimore County	4	8	.333	7	22	.241
Rider	4	8	.333	14	16	.467
Central Connecticut	2	10	.167	4	24	.143

Ivy Group

	Conference			All Games		
	W	L	Pct	W	L	Pct
Princeton*	14	0	1.000	24	3	.889
Yale	9	5	.643	15	11	.577
Brown	6	8	.429	11	15	.423
Cornell	6	8	.429	13	13	.500
Harvard	6	8	.429	9	17	.346
Penn	6	8	.429	9	17	.346
Columbia	5	9	.357	7	19	.269
Dartmouth	4	10	.286	9	17	.346

Metro

	Conference			All Games		
	W	L	Pct	W	L	Pct
Southern Miss*	10	4	.714	21	8	.724
Florida St†	9	5	.643	21	11	.656
Cincinnati	8	6	.571	18	12	.600
Tulane	7	7	.500	15	13	.536
Memphis St	7	7	.500	17	15	.531
Virginia Tech	6	8	.429	13	16	.448
S Carolina	5	9	.357	20	13	.606
Louisville	4	10	.286	14	16	.467

Metro Atlantic

	Conference			All Games		
	W	L	Pct	W	L	Pct
Siena*	12	4	.750	25	10	.714
La Salle	12	4	.750	19	10	.655
St Peter's†	11	5	.688	24	7	.774
Iona	11	5	.688	17	13	.567
Manhattan	8	8	.500	13	15	.464
Niagara	6	10	.375	8	20	.286
Loyola, MD	5	11	.313	12	16	.429
Fairfield	4	12	.250	8	20	.286
Canisius	3	13	.188	10	19	.345

Mid-American

	Conference			All Games		
	W	L	Pct	W	L	Pct
Eastern Michigan*†	13	3	.813	26	7	.788
Ball State	10	6	.625	21	10	.677
Miami (OH)	10	6	.625	16	12	.571
Ohio	9	7	.563	16	12	.571
Bowling Green	9	7	.563	17	13	.567
Central Michigan	8	8	.500	14	14	.500
Toledo	7	9	.438	17	16	.515
Kent St	4	12	.250	10	18	.357
Western Michigan	2	14	.125	5	22	.185

Mid-Eastern Athletic

	Conference			All Games		
	W	L	Pct	W	L	Pct
Coppin State*	14	2	.875	19	11	.633
Delaware St	10	6	.625	19	11	.633
N Caro A&T	10	6	.625	17	10	.630
SC State	10	6	.625	13	15	.464
Florida A&M†	9	7	.563	17	14	.548
Howard	7	9	.438	8	20	.286
Morgan State	6	10	.375	7	22	.241
Md.-E Shore	3	13	.188	5	23	.179
Bethune-Cookman	3	13	.188	5	24	.172

*Conf. champ; †Conf. tourney winner.

THEY SAID IT

Rick Pitino, Kentucky basketball coach, when asked about one of his team's defensive alignments: "That's our mother-in-law set—constant nagging and harassment."

Midwestern Collegiate

	Conference			All Games		
	W	L	Pct	W	L	Pct
Xavier, Ohio*†	11	3	.786	22	10	.688
Butler	10	4	.714	18	11	.621
St Louis	8	6	.571	19	14	.576
Dayton	8	6	.571	14	15	.483
Evansville	7	7	.500	14	14	.500
Marquette	7	7	.500	11	18	.379
Loyola (IL)	3	11	.214	10	19	.345
Detroit	2	12	.143	9	19	.321

Missouri Valley

	Conference			All Games		
	W	L	Pct	W	L	Pct
Creighton*†	12	4	.750	24	8	.750
SW Missouri St	11	5	.688	22	12	.647
Tulsa	10	6	.625	18	12	.600
S Illinois	9	7	.563	18	14	.563
Indiana St	9	7	.563	14	14	.500
Wichita St	7	9	.438	14	17	.452
Bradley	6	10	.375	8	20	.286
Drake	4	12	.250	8	21	.276
Illinois St	4	12	.250	5	23	.179

North Atlantic

	Conference			All Games		
	W	L	Pct	W	L	Pct
Northeastern*†	8	2	.800	22	11	.667
Maine	7	3	.700	13	16	.448
Boston U	5	5	.500	11	18	.379
Vermont	5	5	.500	15	13	.536
Hartford	5	5	.500	13	16	.448
New Hampshire	0	10	.000	3	25	.107

Northeast

	Conference			All Games		
	W	L	Pct	W	L	Pct
St. Francis (PA)*†	13	3	.813	24	8	.750
Fairleigh Dickinson	13	3	.813	22	9	.710
Robert Morris	12	4	.750	17	11	.607
Monmouth	10	6	.625	19	10	.655
St. Francis (NY)	8	8	.500	15	14	.517
Mount St Mary's	6	10	.375	8	19	.296
Long Island	4	12	.250	10	18	.357
Marist	4	12	.250	6	22	.214
Wagner	2	14	.125	4	26	.133

Ohio Valley

	Conference			All Games		
	W	L	Pct	W	L	Pct
Murray St*†	10	2	.833	24	9	.727
Eastern Kentucky	9	3	.750	19	10	.655
Tennessee Tech	6	6	.500	12	16	.429
Austin Peay	6	6	.500	15	14	.517
Middle Tennessee	6	6	.500	21	9	.700
Morehead St	4	8	.333	16	13	.552
Tennessee St	1	11	.083	5	23	.179

*Conf. champ; †Conf. tourney winner.

Pacific-10

	Conference			All Games		
	W	L	Pct	W	L	Pct
Arizona*	14	4	.778	28	7	.800
UCLA	11	7	.611	23	9	.719
Arizona St	10	8	.556	20	10	.667
Southern Cal	10	8	.556	19	10	.655
Stanford	8	10	.444	20	13	.606
Washington St	8	10	.444	16	12	.571
Oregon St	8	10	.444	14	14	.500
Oregon	8	10	.444	13	15	.464
California	8	10	.444	13	15	.464
Washington	5	13	.278	14	14	.500

Patriot

	Conference			All Games		
	W	L	Pct	W	L	Pct
Fordham*†	11	1	.917	25	8	.758
Lehigh	10	2	.833	19	10	.655
Holy Cross	8	4	.667	18	12	.600
Bucknell	7	5	.583	18	13	.581
Army	3	9	.250	6	22	.214
Colgate	2	10	.167	5	23	.179
Lafayette	1	11	.083	7	21	.250

Southeastern

	Conference			All Games		
	W	L	Pct	W	L	Pct
Kentucky	14	4	.778	22	6	.786
Mississippi St*	13	5	.722	20	9	.690
Louisiana St*	13	5	.722	20	10	.667
Alabama†	12	6	.667	23	10	.697
Vanderbilt	11	7	.611	17	13	.567
Georgia	9	9	.500	17	13	.567
Florida	7	11	.389	11	17	.393
Auburn	5	13	.278	13	16	.448
Tennessee	3	15	.167	12	22	.353
Mississippi	3	15	.167	9	19	.321

Southern

	Conference			All Games		
	W	L	Pct	W	L	Pct
Furman*	11	3	.786	20	9	.690
E Tenn St†	11	3	.786	28	5	.848
TN-Chatt	11	3	.786	19	10	.655
Appalachian St	7	7	.500	16	14	.533
Marshall	7	7	.500	14	14	.500
VMI	5	9	.357	10	18	.357
W Carolina	3	11	.214	11	17	.393
The Citadel	1	13	.071	6	22	.214

THEY SAID IT

Peter Roby, Harvard basketball coach, on his recruiting philosophy: "If I ask a kid how he did on the boards, and he says, 'Twelve a game,' I know he's not coming to Harvard."

Southland

	Conference			All Games		
	W	L	Pct	W	L	Pct
NE Louisiana*†	13	1	.929	25	8	.758
TX-Arlington	11	3	.786	20	9	.690
North Texas	11	3	.786	17	13	.567
SF Austin	6	8	.429	11	17	.393
Sam Hou St	5	9	.357	7	20	.259
SW Texas St	4	10	.286	10	17	.370
McNeese St	4	10	.286	8	19	.296
N'western St	2	12	.143	6	22	.214

Southwest

	Conference			All Games		
	W	L	Pct	W	L	Pct
Arkansas*†	15	1	.938	34	4	.895
Texas	13	3	.813	23	9	.719
Houston	10	6	.625	18	11	.621
TCU	9	7	.563	18	10	.643
Rice	9	7	.563	16	14	.533
SMU	6	10	.375	12	17	.414
Baylor	4	12	.250	12	15	.444
Texas Tech	4	12	.250	8	23	.258
Texas A&M	2	14	.125	8	21	.276

Southwestern Athletic

	Conference			All Games		
	W	L	Pct	W	L	Pct
Jackson St*†	10	2	.833	17	13	.567
Southern	8	4	.667	19	9	.679
Texas Southern	7	5	.583	13	17	.433
Alabama St	7	5	.583	18	11	.621
Miss Valley St	4	8	.333	9	19	.321
Grambling St	3	9	.250	6	22	.214
Alcorn St	3	9	.250	8	21	.275
Prairie View	0	0	.000	4	21	.160

Sun Belt

	Conference			All Games		
	W	L	Pct	W	L	Pct
S Alabama*†	11	3	.786	22	9	.710
AL-Birmingham	9	5	.643	18	13	.581
South Florida	8	6	.571	19	11	.633
W Kentucky	8	6	.571	14	14	.500
VCU	7	7	.500	14	17	.452
UNC-Charlotte	6	8	.429	14	14	.500
Old Dominion	5	9	.357	14	18	.438
Jacksonville	2	12	.143	6	22	.214

Trans-America

	Conference			All Games		
	W	L	Pct	W	L	Pct
UT-S Antonio*	12	2	.857	21	8	.724
Centenary	10	4	.714	17	12	.586
Ga Southern	9	5	.643	14	13	.519
Stetson	9	5	.643	15	16	.484
Georgia St†	7	7	.500	16	15	.516
Ark-Little Rock	6	8	.429	10	20	.333
Samford	2	12	.143	6	22	.214
Mercer	1	13	.071	2	25	.074

West Coast

	Conference			All Games		
	W	L	Pct	W	L	Pct
Pepperdine*†	13	1	.929	22	9	.710
Loyola Marymount	9	5	.643	16	15	.516
San Diego	8	6	.571	17	12	.586
St Mary's	7	7	.500	13	17	.433
Santa Clara	7	7	.500	16	13	.552
Gonzaga	5	9	.357	14	14	.500
San Francisco	4	10	.286	12	17	.414
Portland	3	11	.214	5	23	.179

Western Athletic

	Conference			All Games		
	W	L	Pct	W	L	Pct
Utah*	15	1	.938	30	4	.882
BYU†	11	5	.688	21	13	.618
New Mexico	10	6	.625	20	10	.667
Wyoming	8	8	.500	20	12	.625
Hawaii	7	9	.467	16	13	.552
UTEP	7	9	.467	16	13	.552
Colorado St	6	10	.375	15	14	.517
San Diego St	6	10	.375	13	16	.448
Air Force	2	14	.125	9	20	.310

Independents

	W	L	Pct
DePaul	20	9	.690
Wright St	19	9	.679
WI-Milwaukee	18	10	.643
Southern Utah	16	12	.571
MO-Kansas City	15	14	.517
Youngstown St	12	16	.429
Brooklyn	11	16	.407
Notre Dame	12	20	.375
Miami (FL)	9	19	.321
SE Louisiana	9	19	.321
Northridge St	8	20	.286
Florida Int'l	6	22	.214
Liberty	5	23	.179
Chicago St	4	24	.143
Nicholls St	3	25	.107
NE Illinois	2	25	.074
U.S. Int'l	2	26	.071

*Conf. champ; †Conf. tourney winner.

THEY SAID IT

Chris Corchiani, North Carolina State basketball player, to ESPN announcer Dick Vitale, after the shiny-pated Vitale suggested Corchiani meet Vitale's then 18-year-old daughter, Terri: "Mr. Vitale, does she have hair?"

SCORING

	Class	GP	FGA	FG	Pct	FGA	FG	FTA	FT	Pct	Reb	Pts	Avg
			Field Goals			3-Pt FG		Free Throws					
Kevin Bradshaw, US Int'l	Sr	28	837	358	42.8	190	60	338	278	82.2	144	1054	37.6
Alphonso Ford, Mississippi Valley	So	28	668	325	48.7	260	86	234	179	76.5	167	915	32.7
Von McDade, WI-Milwaukee	Sr	28	633	274	43.3	242	96	238	186	78.2	152	830	29.6
Steve Rogers, Alabama St	Jr	29	546	273	50.0	147	56	332	250	75.3	206	852	29.4
Terrell Lowery, Loyola Marymount	Jr	31	621	298	48.0	257	103	231	185	80.1	139	884	28.5
Bobby Phills, Southern-BR	Sr	28	641	260	40.6	353	123	211	152	72.0	132	795	28.4
Shaquille O'Neal, Louisiana St	So	28	497	312	62.8	0	0	235	150	63.8	411	774	27.6
John Taft, Marshall	Sr	28	539	256	47.5	197	82	246	170	69.1	193	764	27.3
Rodney Monroe, N Carolina St	Sr	31	641	285	44.5	239	104	183	162	88.5	136	836	27.0
Terrell Brandon, Oregon	Jr	28	556	273	49.1	119	40	187	159	85.0	101	745	26.6
Kenny Anderson, Georgia Tech	So	30	636	278	43.7	185	65	187	155	82.9	171	776	25.9
Eric Murdock, Providence	Sr	32	589	262	44.5	160	56	293	238	81.2	168	818	25.6
Keith Gailes, Loyola (IL)	Sr	26	533	237	44.5	145	50	171	133	77.8	82	657	25.3
Curtis Stuckey, Bradley	Sr	28	568	241	42.4	147	55	217	165	76.0	142	702	25.1
Steve Smith, Michigan St	Sr	30	566	268	47.3	162	66	187	150	80.2	183	752	25.1
Rod Parker, Chicago St	Sr	25	465	221	47.5	95	33	192	146	76.0	63	621	24.8
Tom Davis, Delaware St	Sr	30	518	292	56.4	3	0	266	156	58.6	366	740	24.7
Michael Ervin, Prairie View	Sr	25	532	235	44.2	88	20	183	122	66.7	22	612	24.5
Robert Youngblood, Southern-BR	Sr	28	453	272	60.0	10	3	196	132	67.3	234	679	24.3
Mike Iuzzolino, St Francis (PA)	Sr	32	227	419	54.2	103	195	215	243	88.5	97	772	24.1
Larry Stewart, Coppin St	Sr	30	244	384	63.5	1	1	227	289	78.5	403	716	23.9
Desi Wilson, FDU-Teaneck	Sr	31	266	472	56.4	2	10	204	277	73.6	284	738	23.8
Reggie Isaac, Coppin St	Sr	30	262	571	45.9	83	197	105	144	72.9	100	712	23.7
Terry Boyd, Western Carolina	Jr	28	225	482	46.7	65	172	149	177	84.2	193	664	23.7
Allan Houston, Tennessee	So	34	265	500	48.2	99	231	177	205	86.3	104	806	23.7
Doug Smith, Missouri	Sr	30	275	553	49.7	3	18	156	190	82.1	311	709	23.6
Harold Miner, Southern Cal	So	29	235	519	45.3	59	175	152	190	80.0	159	681	23.5
Victor Alexander, Iowa St	Sr	31	294	446	65.9	0	0	136	201	67.7	280	724	23.4
Marc Brown, Siena	Sr	35	289	602	48.0	83	179	155	194	79.9	139	816	23.3
Billy Owens, Syracuse	Jr	32	282	554	50.9	23	58	157	233	67.4	371	744	23.3

REBOUNDS

	Class	GP	Reb	Avg
Shaquille O'Neal, Louisiana St	So	28	411	14.7
Popeye Jones, Murray St	Jr	33	469	14.2
Larry Stewart, Coppin St	Sr	30	403	13.4
Tim Burroughs, Jacksonville	Jr	27	350	13.0
Warren Kidd, Middle Tennessee St	So	30	370	12.3
Clarence Weatherspoon, Southern Miss	Jr	29	355	12.2
Ervin Johnson, New Orleans	So	30	367	12.2
Tom Davis, Delaware St	Sr	30	366	12.2
Dikembe Mutombo, Georgetown	Sr	32	389	12.2
Dale Davis, Clemson	Sr	28	340	12.1

ASSISTS

	Class	GP	A	Avg
Chris Corchiani, N Carolina St	Sr	31	299	9.6
Danny Tirado, Jacksonville	Jr	28	259	9.3
Terrell Lowery, Loyola Marymount	Jr	31	283	9.1
Keith Jennings, E Tennessee St	Sr	33	301	9.1
Greg Anthony, UNLV	Sr	35	310	8.9
Van Usher, Tennessee Tech	Jr	28	233	8.3
Orlando Smart, San Francisco	Fr	29	237	8.2
Ray Johnson, Sam Houston St	Jr	24	193	8.0
Glover Cody, TX-Arlington	Jr	29	229	7.9
Arnold Bernard, SW Missouri St	Sr	34	257	7.6

3-POINT FIELD GOALS MADE PER GAME

	Class	GP	FG	Avg
Bobby Phills, Southern-BR	Sr	28	123	4.4
Ronnie Schmitz, MO-Kansas City	So	29	116	4.0
Jeff Herdman, UC-Irvine	Sr	30	112	3.7
Doug Day, Radford	So	29	106	3.7
Sean Jackson, Princeton	Jr	27	95	3.5
Kyle Kerlegan, Cal St-Northridge	Jr	28	98	3.5
Andy Kennedy, AL-Birmingham	Sr	31	107	3.5
Von McDade, WI-Milwaukee	Sr	28	96	3.4
Ray Younger, Texas Southern	Sr	29	99	3.4
Scott Draud, Vanderbilt	Sr	30	101	3.4
Rodney Monroe, N Carolina St	Sr	31	104	3.4

3-POINT FIELD GOAL PERCENTAGES

	Class	GP	FGA	FG	Pct
Keith Jennings, E Tennessee St	Sr	33	142	84	59.2
Tony Bennett, WI-Green Bay	Jr	31	150	80	53.3
Mike Iuzzolino, St Francis (PA)	Sr	32	195	103	52.8
Ross Richardson, Loyola Marymount	Fr	25	116	61	52.6
David Mitchell, Samford	So	26	78	41	52.6
Gary Waites, Alabama	Sr	33	101	52	51.5
Todd Leslie, Northwestern	So	28	127	65	51.2
Dave Olson, Eastern Illinois	Jr	29	160	80	50.0
Billy Dreher, California	So	28	112	56	50.0
Lance Vaughn, Boise St	So	29	91	45	49.5

Note: Minimum 1.5 made per game.

STEALS

	Class	GP	S	Avg
Van Usher, Tennessee Tech	Jr	28	104	3.7
Scott Burrell, Connecticut	So	31	112	3.6
Eric Murdock, Providence	Sr	32	111	3.5
Von McDade, WI-Milwaukee	Sr	28	97	3.5
Lynn Smith, St Francis (NY)	Jr	29	100	3.4
Emanual Davis, Delaware St	Sr	25	84	3.4
Ronnie Ellison, TX-San Antonio	Jr	29	97	3.3
Keith Jennings, E Tennessee St	Sr	33	109	3.3
Bobby Phills, Southern-BR	Sr	28	90	3.2
Pat Baldwin, Northwestern	Fr	28	90	3.2

FIELD GOAL PERCENTAGES

	Class	GP	FGA	FG	Pct
Oliver Miller, Arkansas	Jr	38	361	254	70.4
Warren Kidd, Middle Tennessee St	So	30	247	173	70.0
Pete Freeman, Akron	Sr	28	250	175	70.0
Lester James, St Francis (NY)	Jr	29	215	149	69.3
Marcus Kennedy, Eastern Michigan	Sr	33	352	240	68.2
Allen Lightfoot, Montana St	Sr	25	196	130	66.3
Chris Brooks, W Virginia	Sr	31	335	222	66.3
Larry Johnson, UNLV	Sr	35	465	308	66.2
Victor Alexander, Iowa St	Sr	31	446	294	65.9
Luc Longley, New Mexico	Sr	30	349	229	65.6

Note: Minimum 5 made per game.

BLOCKED SHOTS

	Class	GP	BS	Avg
Shawn Bradley, Brigham Young	Fr	34	177	5.2
Cedric Lewis, Maryland	Sr	28	143	5.1
Shaquille O'Neal, Louisiana St	So	28	140	5.0
Dikembe Mutombo, Georgetown	Sr	32	151	4.7
Kevin Roberson, Vermont	Jr	28	104	3.7
Lorenzo Williams, Stetson	Sr	31	113	3.6
Acie Earl, Iowa	So	32	106	3.3
Jim McIlvaine, Marquette	Fr	28	92	3.3
Luc Longley, New Mexico	Sr	30	95	3.2
Damon Lopez, Fordham	Sr	33	100	3.0

FREE-THROW PERCENTAGES

	Class	GP	FTA	FT	Pct
Darin Archbold, Butler	Jr	29	205	187	91.2
William Lewis, Monmouth (NJ)	Jr	28	101	91	90.1
Darwyn Alexander, Oklahoma St	Jr	32	107	96	89.7
Keith Jennings, E Tennessee St	Sr	33	152	136	89.5
Rodney Monroe, N Carolina St	Sr	31	183	162	88.5
Mike Iuzzolino, St Francis (PA)	Sr	32	243	215	88.5
Eddie Bird, Indiana St	Sr	27	94	82	87.2
Davor Marcelic, Southern Utah St	Jr	28	93	81	87.1
Lewis Geter, Ohio	Jr	28	158	137	86.7
Andy Kennedy, AL-Birmingham	Sr	31	193	167	86.5

Note: Minimum 2.5 made per game.

Single-Game Highs

POINTS

72	Kevin Bradshaw, US Intl, Jan 5 (vs Loyola Marymount)
59	Kevin Bradshaw, US Intl, Jan 14 (vs Florida Intl)
56	Brent Price, Oklahoma, Dec 15 (vs Loyola Marymount)
53	Shaquille O'Neal, Louisiana St, Dec 18 (vs Arkansas St)
53	Kevin Bradshaw, US Intl, Jan 24 (vs Cal St-Los Angeles)
53	Kevin Bradshaw, US Intl, Jan 28 (vs Cal St-Northridge)
51	Ronnie Schmitz, MO-Kansas City, Mar 4 (vs US Intl)
50	Von McDade, WI-Milwaukee, Dec 3 (vs Illinois)
50	Kenny Anderson, Georgia Tech, Dec 22 (vs Loyola Marymount)

REBOUNDS

27	Dikembe Mutombo, Georgetown, Mar 8 (vs Connecticut)
23	Popeye Jones, Murray St, Feb 11 (vs Morehead St)
22	Rob Renfroe, Mercer, Dec 3 (vs NC-Asheville)
22	Ervin Johnson, New Orleans, Jan 17 (vs Lamar)
22	Delon Turner, Florida A&M, Feb 7 (vs Morgan)
22	Darrell Harris, Grambling, Feb 9 (vs Prairie View)
22	Billy Owens, Syracuse, Mar 8 (vs Villanova)

ASSISTS

20	Chris Corchiani, N Carolina St, Feb 27 (vs Maryland)
19	Greg Anthony, UNLV, Dec 29 (vs Pacific)
19	Keith Jennings, E Tennessee St, Feb 2 (vs Appalachian St)
18	Terrell Lowery, Loyola Marymount, Dec 29 (vs St Joseph's [PA])

Single-Game Highs (*Cont.*)

3-POINT FIELD GOALS

11 .... Doug Day, Radford, Dec 12 (vs Central Connecticut St)
11 .... Brent Price, Oklahoma, Dec 15 (vs Loyola Marymount)
11 .... Bobby Phills, Southern-BR, Dec 28 (vs Manhattan)
11 .... Terry Brown, Kansas, Jan 5 (vs N Carolina St)

STEALS

11 .... Carl Thomas, Eastern Michigan, Feb 20 (vs Chicago St)
10 .... Delvon Anderson, Montana, Nov 15 (vs Simon Fraser)
10 .... Shawn Griggs, Louisiana St, Feb 23 (vs Tennessee)

BLOCKED SHOTS

14 .... Shawn Bradley, Brigham Young, Dec 7 (vs Eastern Kentucky)
12 .... Cedric Lewis, Maryland, Jan 19 (vs S Florida)
11 .... Dikembe Mutombo, Georgetown, Nov 23 (vs HI-Loa)
10 .... Byron Tucker, George Mason, Nov 23 (vs Miami [FL])
10 .... Kevin Roberson, Vermont, Jan 8 (vs Hartford)
10 .... Damon Lopez, Fordham, Jan 16 (vs Lehigh)
10 .... Shaquille O'Neal, Louisiana St, Jan 26 (vs Florida)
10 .... Derek Stewart, Augusta, Jan 26 (vs Davidson)

NCAA Men's Division I Team Leaders

SCORING OFFENSE

	GP	W	L	Pts	Avg		GP	W	L	Pts	Avg
Southern-BR	28	19	9	2924	104.4	E Tennessee St	33	28	5	3103	94.0
Loyola Marymount	31	16	15	3211	103.6	Southern Utah St	28	16	12	2604	93.0
Arkansas	38	34	4	3783	99.6	Wright St	28	19	9	2594	92.6
UNLV	35	34	1	3420	97.7	UCLA	32	23	9	2954	92.3
Oklahoma	35	20	15	3363	96.1	Alabama St	29	18	11	2656	91.6
TX-Arlington	29	20	9	2743	94.6	Delaware St	30	19	11	2741	91.4

SCORING DEFENSE

	GP	W	L	Pts	Avg		GP	W	L	Pts	Avg
Princeton	27	24	3	1320	48.9	St Peter's	31	24	7	1954	63.0
Northern Illinois	31	25	6	1781	57.5	Monmouth (NJ)	29	19	10	1838	63.4
Yale	26	15	11	1508	58.0	Temple	34	24	10	2177	64.0
WI-Green Bay	31	24	7	1893	61.1	Utah	34	30	4	2184	64.2
Georgetown	32	19	13	1964	61.4	S Carolina	33	20	13	2124	64.4
Colorado St	29	15	14	1783	61.5	Boise St	29	18	11	1873	64.6

SCORING MARGIN

	Off	Def	Mar		Off	Def	Mar
UNLV	97.7	71.0	26.7	Arizona	86.3	71.7	14.6
Arkansas	99.6	80.4	19.2	Kansas	84.2	69.6	14.6
E Tennessee St	94.0	76.8	17.3	Duke	87.7	73.4	14.3
Ohio St	84.6	68.5	16.2	Southern-BR	104.4	90.7	13.8
N Carolina	87.6	71.6	16.0	Princeton	62.4	48.9	13.5
Indiana	84.8	69.2	15.6	Oklahoma St	79.7	66.2	13.5

FIELD GOAL PERCENTAGE

	FGA	FG	Pct		FGA	FG	Pct
UNLV	2441	1305	53.5	Princeton	1112	574	51.6
Indiana	1955	1043	53.4	Appalachian St	1821	939	51.6
New Mexico	1644	868	52.8	Arizona	2121	1091	51.4
Brooklyn	1262	656	52.0	Ohio St	1919	987	51.4
Kansas	2097	1086	51.8	Eastern Michigan	1790	920	51.4
UCLA	2085	1078	51.7	E Tennessee St	2208	1132	51.3

NCAA Men's Division I Team Leaders (*Cont.*)

FIELD GOAL PERCENTAGE DEFENSE

	FGA	FG	Pct		FGA	FG	Pct
Georgetown	1847	680	36.8	UNLV	2235	893	40.0
Northern Illinois	1587	616	38.8	Radford	1826	740	40.5
Connecticut	1753	682	38.9	Seton Hall	1972	801	40.6
New Orleans	1837	725	39.5	Brigham Young	1989	811	40.8
Middle Tennessee St	2007	793	39.5	Toledo	2187	893	40.8
Arizona	2272	903	39.7	Missouri	1900	785	41.3

FREE-THROW PERCENTAGE

	FTA	FT	Pct		FTA	FT	Pct
Butler	922	725	78.6	Indiana St	590	449	76.1
Monmouth (NJ)	547	422	77.1	Penn St	849	644	75.9
Air Force	627	483	77.0	Vanderbilt	641	485	75.7
Northwestern	612	470	76.8	NE Louisiana	704	532	75.6
Wyoming	853	654	76.7	Bucknell	773	584	75.5
N Carolina St	677	516	76.2	Seton Hall	864	651	75.3

3-POINT FIELD GOALS MADE PER GAME

	GP	FG	Avg		GP	FG	Avg
TX-Arlington	29	265	9.1	WI-Milwaukee	28	237	8.5
E Tennessee St	33	301	9.1	Princeton	27	226	8.4
Dayton	29	256	8.8	Loyola Marymount	31	259	8.4
UC-Irvine	30	263	8.8	Western Kentucky	28	233	8.3
Kentucky	28	242	8.6	SW Texas St	27	224	8.3
N Carolina St	31	267	8.6	UNLV	35	282	8.1

3-POINT FIELD GOAL PERCENTAGE

	GP	FGA	FG	Pct		GP	FGA	FG	Pct
WI-Green Bay	31	407	189	46.4	Brown	26	461	198	43.0
Southern Utah St	28	353	158	44.8	Princeton	27	532	226	42.5
St Francis (PA)	32	534	238	44.6	Oklahoma St	32	312	131	42.0
Eastern Illinois	29	457	200	43.8	Holy Cross	30	385	161	41.8
Northern Illinois	31	305	133	43.6	Seton Hall	34	498	208	41.8
Northwestern	28	251	109	43.4	Pittsburgh	33	506	211	41.7

Note: Minimum 3.0 made per game.

NCAA Division I Women's Tournament Scores

First round: SW Missouri St 94, Tennessee Tech 64; Florida St 96, Appalachian St 57; Holy Cross 81, Maryland 74; Vanderbilt 73, S Carolina 64; UNLV 70, Texas Tech 65; Southern Cal 63, Utah 52; Iowa 64, Montana 53; Cal State Fullerton 84, Louisiana Tech 80; James Madison 70, Kentucky 62; Providence 88, Fairfield 87; Toledo 83, Rutgers 65; George Washington 73, Richmond 62; Stephen F. Austin 72, Mississippi 62; Oklahoma St 81, DePaul 80; Northwestern 82, Washington St 62; Lamar 77, Texas 63.
    Second round: Tennessee 55, SW Missouri St 47; Western Kentucky 72, Florida State 69; Auburn 84, Holy Cross 58; Vanderbilt 69, Purdue 63; Georgia 86, UNLV 62; Long Beach St 83, Southern Cal 58; Washington 70, Iowa 53; Stanford 91, Cal State Fullerton 67; James Madison 73, Penn St 71; Clemson 103, Providence 91; Connecticut 81, Toledo 80; N Carolina State 94, George Washington 83; Virginia 74, Stephen F. Austin 72; Oklahoma State 96, Michigan St 94 (3OT); Arkansas 105, Northwestern 68; Lamar 93, Louisiana St 73.
    Regional semifinals: Tennessee 68, Western Kentucky 61; Auburn 58, Vanderbilt 45; Georgia 87, Long Beach St 77; Stanford 73, Washington 47; Clemson 57, James Madison 55; Connecticut 82, N Carolina St 71; Virginia 76, Oklahoma St 61; Lamar 91, Arkansas 75.
    Regional finals: Tennessee 69, Auburn 65; Stanford 75, Georgia 67; Connecticut 60, Clemson 57; Virginia 85, Lamar 70.
    National semifinals: Tennessee 68, Stanford 60; Virginia 61, Connecticut 55.
    National championship: Tennessee 70, Virginia 67 (OT).

Final AP Women's Top 25

The final Associated Press women's poll, as conducted by Mel Greenberg of the *Philadelphia Inquirer*. Poll was taken before the NCAA tournament. Records are entering NCAA tournament play.

1. Penn St. 29-1	14. Stephen F. Austin.....25-4
2. Virginia 27-2	15. Providence 25-5
3. Georgia......................26-3	16. Texas.......................21-8
4. Tennessee................25-5	17. UNLV.......................24-6
5. Purdue......................26-2	18. Long Beach St.........23-7
6. Auburn......................24-5	19. Mississippi...............20-8
7. N Carolina State.......25-5	20. Rutgers....................23-6
8. Louisiana St.............24-6	21. Clemson.................20-10
9. Arkansas 27-3	22. Northwestern...........20-8
10. Western Kentucky 28-2	23. Iowa.........................20-8
11. Stanford...................23-5	24. Lamar......................26-3
12. Washington 23-4	25. Oklahoma St............25-5
13. Connecticut 26-4	

NCAA Women's Division I Scoring Leaders

	Class	GP	TFG	3FG	FT	Pts	Avg
Jan Jensen, Drake	Sr	30	358	6	166	888	29.6
Genia Miller, Cal St-Fullerton	Sr	33	376	0	217	969	29.4
Lisa McMullen, Alabama St.	Jr	28	285	126	119	815	29.1
Tari Phillips, Central Florida	Sr	21	213	13	93	532	25.3
Rehema Stephens, UCLA	Jr	28	273	47	116	709	25.3
Sheila Ethridge, Louisiana Tech	Sr	30	281	75	119	756	25.2
Tarcha Hollis, Grambling	Sr	29	312	1	104	729	25.1
Andrea Congreaves, Mercer	So	27	281	23	77	662	24.5
Lisa Foss, Northern Illinois	Sr	35	340	14	159	853	24.4
Kirsten Brendel, Pennsylvania	Sr	26	230	1	170	631	24.3
Tammy Brown, Campbell	Sr	29	269	0	155	693	23.9
Sarah Behn, Boston Col	So	28	237	33	161	668	23.9
Tracy Lis, Providence	Jr	32	280	46	153	759	23.7
Kieishsha Garnes, San Diego St	Jr	28	271	0	119	661	23.6
Rachel Bouchard, Maine	Sr	26	224	0	162	610	23.5

NCAA Men's Division II Scoring Leaders

	Class	GP	TFG	3FG	FT	Pts	Avg
Gary Mattison, St Augustine's	Sr	26	277	53	159	766	29.5
George Gilmore, Chaminade	Jr	23	205	92	149	651	28.3
Jeff deLaveaga, Cal Lutheran	Jr	26	223	97	181	724	27.8
Tom Murphy, Colorado Christian	Sr	25	270	33	122	695	27.8
Jon Baskin, Mesa St.	Sr	30	325	0	182	832	27.7
Tony Smith, Pfeiffer	Jr	32	290	113	160	853	26.7
Myron Brown, Slippery Rock	Sr	31	253	69	251	826	26.6
Mark Sherrill, Johnson Smith	Jr	30	275	54	170	774	25.8
Isaac Washington, Texas A&I	Sr	28	249	31	172	701	25.0
Ron Rutland, Indianapolis	Sr	28	279	44	94	696	24.9

NCAA Men's Division III Scoring Leaders

	Class	GP	TFG	3FG	FT	Pts	Avg
Andre Foreman, Salisbury St	Jr	29	350	39	175	914	31.5
Terrence Dupree, Polytechnic (NY)	Jr	24	282	6	139	709	29.5
David Hicks, Centre	Sr	25	275	2	180	732	29.3
Chris Jans, Loras	Sr	25	224	133	126	707	28.3
Lamont Strothers, Christopher Newport	Sr	29	279	55	146	759	26.2
James Bradley, Otterbein	Sr	33	325	63	148	861	26.1
Kit Walsh, Sewanee	Sr	25	245	59	99	648	25.9
Dale Turnquist, Bethel (MN)	Sr	28	277	8	151	713	25.5

NCAA Division I Men's Championship Results

NCAA Final Four Results

Year	Winner	Score	Runner-up	Third Place	Fourth Place	Winning Coach
1939	Oregon	46-33	Ohio St	*Oklahoma	*Villanova	Howard Hobson
1940	Indiana	60-42	Kansas	*Duquesne	*Southern Cal	Branch McCracken
1941	Wisconsin	39-34	Washington St	*Pittsburgh	*Arkansas	Harold Foster
1942	Stanford	53-38	Dartmouth	*Colorado	*Kentucky	Everett Dean
1943	Wymong	46-34	Georgetown	*Texas	*DePaul	Everett Shelton
1944	Utah	42-40 (OT)	Dartmouth	*Iowa St	*Ohio St	Vadal Peterson
1945	Oklahoma St	49-45	NYU	*Arkansas	*Ohio St	Hank Iba
1946	Oklahoma St	43-40	N Carolina	Ohio St	California	Hank Iba
1947	Holy Cross	58-47	Oklahoma	Texas	CCNY	Alvin Julian
1948	Kentucky	58-42	Baylor	Holy Cross	Kansas St	Adolph Rupp
1949	Kentucky	46-36	Oklahoma St	Illinois	Oregon St	Adolph Rupp
1950	CCNY	71-68	Bradley	N Carolina St	Baylor	Nat Holman
1951	Kentucky	68-58	Kansas St	Illinois	Oklahoma St	Adolph Rupp
1952	Kansas	80-63	St John's (NY)	Illinois	Santa Clara	Forrest Allen
1953	Indiana	69-68	Kansas	Washington	Louisiana St	Branch McCracken
1954	La Salle	92-76	Bradley	Penn St	Southern Cal	Kenneth Loeffler
1955	San Francisco	77-63	La Salle	Colorado	Iowa	Phil Woolpert
1956	San Francisco	83-71	Iowa	Temple	Southern Meth	Phil Woolpert
1957	N Carolina	54-53†	Kansas	San Francisco	Michigan St	Frank McGuire
1958	Kentucky	84-72	Seattle	Temple	Kansas St	Adolph Rupp
1959	California	71-70	W Virginia	Cincinnati	Louisville	Pete Newell
1960	Ohio St	75-55	California	Cincinnati	NYU	Fred Taylor
1961	Cincinnati	70-65 (OT)	Ohio St	Vacated‡	Utah	Edwin Jucker
1962	Cincinnati	71-59	Ohio St	Wake Forest	UCLA	Edwin Jucker
1963	Loyola (IL)	60-58 (OT)	Cincinnati	Duke	Oregon St	George Ireland
1964	UCLA	98-83	Duke	Michigan	Kansas St	John Wooden
1965	UCLA	91-80	Michigan	Princeton	Wichita St	John Wooden
1966	UTEP	72-65	Kentucky	Duke	Utah	Don Haskins
1967	UCLA	79-64	Dayton	Houston	N Carolina	John Wooden
1968	UCLA	78-55	N Carolina	Ohio St	Houston	John Wooden
1969	UCLA	92-72	Purdue	Drake	N Carolina	John Wooden
1970	UCLA	80-69	Jacksonville	New Mexico St	St Bonaventure	John Wooden
1971	UCLA	68-62	Vacated‡	Vacated‡	Kansas	John Wooden
1972	UCLA	81-76	Florida St	N Carolina	Louisville	John Wooden
1973	UCLA	87-66	Memphis St	Indiana	Providence	John Wooden
1974	N Carolina St	76-64	Marquette	UCLA	Kansas	Norm Sloan
1975	UCLA	92-85	Kentucky	Louisville	Syracuse	John Wooden
1976	Indiana	86-68	Michigan	UCLA	Rutgers	Bob Knight
1977	Marquette	67-59	N Carolina	NV-Las Vegas	NC-Charlotte	Al McGuire
1978	Kentucky	94-88	Duke	Arkansas	Notre Dame	Joe Hall
1979	Michigan St	75-64	Indiana St	DePaul	Penn	Jud Heathcote
1980	Louisville	59-54	Vacated‡	Purdue	Iowa	Denny Crum
1981	Indiana	63-50	N Carolina	Virginia	Louisiana St	Bob Knight
1982	N Carolina	63-62	Georgetown	*Houston	*Louisville	Dean Smith
1983	N Carolina St	54-52	Houston	*Georgia	*Louisville	Jim Valvano
1984	Georgetown	84-75	Houston	*Kentucky	*Virginia	John Thompson
1985	Villanova	66-64	Georgetown	*St John's (NY)	Vacated‡	Rollie Massimino
1986	Louisville	72-69	Duke	*Kansas	*Louisiana St	Denny Crum
1987	Indiana	74-73	Syracuse	*NV-Las Vegas	*Providence	Bob Knight
1988	Kansas	83-79	Oklahoma	*Arizona	*Duke	Larry Brown
1989	Michigan	80-79 (OT)	Seton Hall	*Duke	*Illinois	Steve Fisher
1990	UNLV	103-73	Duke	*Arkansas	*Georgia Tech	Jerry Tarkanian
1991	Duke	72-65	Kansas	*UNLV	*N Carolina	Mike Krzyzewski

*Tied for third place.

†Three overtimes.

‡Student-athletes representing St Joseph's (PA) in 1961, Villanova in 1971 (runner-up), Western Kentucky in 1971 (third), UCLA (1980) and Memphis State (1985) were declared ineligible subsequent to the tournament. Under NCAA rules, the teams' and ineligible student-athletes' records were deleted, and the teams' places in the standings were vacated.

Best NCAA Tournament Single-Game Scoring Performances

Player and Team	Year	Round	FG	3FG	FT	TP
Austin Carr, Notre Dame vs Ohio	1970	1st	25	—	11	61
Bill Bradley, Princeton vs Wichita St	1965	C*	22	—	14	58
Oscar Robertson, Cincinnati vs Arkansas	1958	C	21	—	14	56
Austin Carr, Notre Dame vs Kentucky	1970	2nd	22	—	8	52
Austin Car, Notre Dame vs Texas Christian	1971	1st	20	—	12	52
David Robinson, Navy vs Michigan	1987	1st	22	0	6	50
Elvin Hayes, Houston vs Loyola (IL)	1968	1st	20	—	9	49
Hal Lear, Temple vs Southern Meth	1956	C*	17	—	14	48
Austin Carr, Notre Dame vs Houston	1971	C	17	—	13	47
Dave Corzine, DePaul vs Louisville	1978	2nd	18	—	10	46
Bob Houbregs, Washington vs Seattle	1953	2nd	20	—	5	45
Austin Carr, Notre Dame vs Iowa	1970	C	21	—	3	45
Bo Kimble, Loyola Marymount vs New Mexico St	1990	1st	17	5	6	45

C regional third place; C* third-place game.

NIT Championship Results

Year	Winner	Score	Runner-up	Year	Winner	Score	Runner-up
1938	Temple	60-36	Colorado	1965	St John's (NY)	55-51	Villanova
1939	Long Island U	44-32	Loyola (IL)	1966	BYU	97-84	NYU
1940	Colorado	51-40	Duquesne	1967	Southern Illinois	71-56	Marquette
1941	Long Island U	56-42	Ohio U	1968	Dayton	61-48	Kansas
1942	W Virginia	47-45	Western Kentucky	1969	Temple	89-76	Boston College
1943	St John's (NY)	48-27	Toledo	1970	Marquette	65-53	St John's (NY)
1944	St John's (NY)	47-39	DePaul	1971	N Carolina	84-66	Georgia Tech
1945	DePaul	71-54	Bowling Green	1972	Maryland	100-69	Niagara
1946	Kentucky	46-45	Rhode Island	1973	Virginia Tech	92-91 (OT)	Notre Dame
1947	Utah	49-45	Kentucky	1974	Purdue	97-81	Utah
1948	St Louis	65-52	NYU	1975	Princeton	80-69	Providence
1949	San Francisco	48-47	Loyola (IL)	1976	Kentucky	71-67	NC-Charlotte
1950	CCNY	69-61	Bradley	1977	St Bonaventure	94-91	Houston
1951	BYU	62-43	Dayton	1978	Texas	101-93	N Carolina St
1952	La Salle	75-64	Dayton	1979	Indiana	53-52	Purdue
1953	Seton Hall	58-46	St John's (NY)	1980	Virginia	58-55	Minnesota
1954	Holy Cross	71-62	Duquesne	1981	Tulsa	86-84 (OT)	Syracuse
1955	Duquesne	70-58	Dayton	1982	Bradley	67-58	Purdue
1956	Louisville	93-80	Dayton	1983	Fresno St	69-60	DePaul
1957	Bradley	84-83	Memphis St	1984	Michigan	83-63	Notre Dame
1958	Xavier (OH)	78-74 (OT)	Dayton	1985	UCLA	65-62	Indiana
1959	St John's (NY)	76-71 (OT)	Bradley	1986	Ohio St	73-63	Wyoming
1960	Bradley	88-72	Providence	1987	Southern Miss	84-80	La Salle
1961	Providence	62-59	St Louis	1988	Connecticut	72-67	Ohio St
1962	Dayton	73-67	St John's (NY)	1989	St John's (NY)	73-65	St Louis
1963	Providence	81-66	Canisius	1990	Vanderbilt	74-72	St Louis
1964	Bradley	86-54	New Mexico	1991	Stanford	78-72	Oklahoma

THEY SAID IT

Brian Cunnane, assistant basketball coach at the U.S. Merchant Marine Academy, which went 3-23 this season: "If it's true that losing builds character, then we have more characters than Disney and Warner Brothers combined."

Like Coach, Like Player

In the history of the NCAA basketball tournament, only five individuals have both played and coached in the Final Four: Vic Bubas (North Carolina State '50; Duke '63, '64, '66), Dick Harp (Kansas '40 and '57), Bobby Knight (Ohio State '60–'62; Indiana '73, '76, '81), Bones McKinney (North Carolina '46; Wake Forest '63), and Dean Smith (Kansas '52, '53; North Carolina '67–'69, '72, '77, '81–'82, '91). Knight and Smith are the only two who have won titles as player and coach. Knight was the sixth man on the Buckeyes' 1960 championship team and coached Indiana to titles in 1976 and 1981. Smith played for Kansas' 1952 champions and 30 years later coached Michael Jordan, James Worthy, Sam Perkins, and a bunch of other Tar Heels to an NCAA crown.

ANNUAL SCORING AVERAGE

Year	Player and Team	Ht	Class	GP	FG	3FG	FT	Pts	Avg
1948	Murray Wier, Iowa	5-9	Sr	19	152	—	95	399	21.0
1949	Tony Lavelli, Yale	6-3	Sr	30	228	—	215	671	22.4
1950	Paul Arizin, Villanova	6-3	Sr	29	260	—	215	735	25.3
1951	Bill Mlkvy, Temple	6-4	Sr	25	303	—	125	731	29.2
1952	Clyde Lovellette, Kansas	6-9	Sr	28	315	—	165	795	28.4
1953	Frank Selvy, Furman	6-3	Jr	25	272	—	194	738	29.5
1954	Frank Selvy, Furman	6-3	Sr	29	427	—	355	1209	41.7
1955	Darrell Floyd, Furman	6-1	Jr	25	344	—	209	897	35.9
1956	Darrell Floyd, Furman	6-1	Sr	28	339	—	268	946	33.8
1957	Grady Wallace, S Carolina	6-4	Sr	29	336	—	234	906	31.2
1958	Oscar Robertson, Cincinnati	6-5	So	28	352	—	280	984	35.1
1959	Oscar Robertson, Cincinnati	6-5	Jr	30	331	—	316	978	32.6
1960	Oscar Robertson, Cincinnati	6-5	Sr	30	369	—	273	1011	33.7
1961	Frank Burgess, Gonzaga	6-1	Sr	26	304	—	234	842	32.4
1962	Billy McGill, Utah	6-9	Sr	26	394	—	221	1009	38.8
1963	Nick Werkman, Seton Hall	6-3	Jr	22	221	—	208	650	29.5
1964	Howard Komives, Bowling Green	6-1	Sr	23	292	—	260	844	36.7
1965	Rick Barry, Miama (FL)	6-7	Sr	26	340	—	293	973	37.4
1966	Dave Schellhase, Purdue	6-4	Sr	24	284	—	213	781	32.5
1967	Jim Walker, Providence	6-3	Sr	28	323	—	205	851	30.4
1968	Pete Maravich, Louisiana St	6-5	So	26	432	—	274	1138	43.8
1969	Pete Maravich, Louisiana St	6-5	Jr	26	433	—	282	1148	44.2
1970	Pete Maravich, Louisiana St	6-5	Sr	31	522	—	337	1381	44.5
1971	Johnny Neumann, Mississippi	6-6	So	23	366	—	191	923	40.1
1972	Dwight Lamar, Southwestern Louisiana	6-1	Jr	29	429	—	196	1054	36.3
1973	William Averitt, Pepperdine	6-1	Sr	25	352	—	144	848	33.9
1974	Larry Fogle, Canisius	6-5	So	25	326	—	183	835	33.4
1975	Bob McCurdy, Richmond	6-7	Sr	26	321	—	213	855	32.9
1976	Marshall Rodgers, TX-Pan American	6-2	Sr	25	361	—	197	919	36.8
1977	Freeman Williams, Portland St	6-4	Jr	26	417	—	176	1010	38.8
1978	Freeman Williams, Portland St	6-4	Sr	27	410	—	149	969	35.9
1979	Lawrence Butler, Idaho St	6-3	Sr	27	310	—	192	812	30.1
1980	Tony Murphy, Southern-BR	6-3	Sr	29	377	—	178	932	32.1
1981	Zam Fredrick, S Carolina	6-2	Sr	27	300	—	181	781	28.9
1982	Harry Kelly, Texas Southern	6-7	Jr	29	336	—	190	862	29.7
1983	Harry Kelly, Texas Southern	6-7	Sr	29	333	—	169	835	28.8
1984	Joe Jakubick, Akron	6-5	Sr	27	304	—	206	814	30.1
1985	Xavier McDaniel, Wichita St	6-8	Sr	31	351	—	142	844	27.2
1986	Terrance Bailey, Wagner	6-2	Jr	29	321	—	212	854	29.4
1987	Kevin Houston, Army	5-11	Sr	29	311	63	268	953	32.9
1988	Hersey Hawkins, Bradley	6-3	Sr	31	377	87	284	1125	36.3
1989	Hank Gathers, Loyola Marymount	6-7	Jr	31	419	0	177	1015	32.7
1990	Bo Kimble, Loyola Marymount	6-5	Sr	32	404	92	231	1131	35.3
1991	Kevin Bradshaw, U.S. Int'l	6-6	Sr	28	358	60	278	1054	37.6

Single-Game Records

SCORING HIGHS VS DIVISION I OPPONENT

Pts	Player and Team vs Opponent	Date
72	Kevin Bradshaw, U.S. Int'l vs Loyola Marymount	1-5-91
69	Pete Maravich, Louisiana St vs Alabama	2-7-70
68	Calvin Murphy, Niagara vs Syracuse	12-7-68
66	Jay Handlan, Washington & Lee vs Furman	2-17-51
66	Pete Maravich, Louisiana St vs Tulane	2-10-69
66	Anthony Roberts, Oral Roberts vs N Carolina A&T	2-19-77
65	Anthony Roberts, Oral Roberts vs Oregon	3-9-77
65	Scott Haffner, Evansville vs Dayton	2-18-89
64	Pete Maravich, Louisiana St vs Kentucky	2-21-70
63	Johnny Neumann, Mississippi vs Louisiana St	1-30-71
63	Hersey Hawkins, Bradley vs Detroit	2-22-88

Single-Game Records (*Cont.*)

SCORING HIGHS VS NON-DIVISION I OPPONENT

Pts	Player and Team vs Opponent	Date
100	Frank Selvy, Furman vs Newberry	2-13-54
85	Paul Arizin, Villanova vs Philadelphia NAMC	2-12-49
81	Freeman Williams, Portland St vs Rocky Mountain	2-3-78
73	Bill Mlkvy, Temple vs Wilkes	3-3-51
71	Freeman Williams, Portland St vs Southern Oregon	2-9-77

REBOUNDING HIGHS BEFORE 1973

Reb	Player and Team vs Opponent	Date
51	Bill Chambers, William & Mary vs Virginia	2-14-53
43	Charlie Slack, Marshall vs Morris Harvey	1-12-54
42	Tom Heinsohn, Holy Cross vs Boston College	3-1-55
40	Art Quimby, Connecticut vs Boston U	1-11-55
39	Maurice Stokes, St Francis (PA) vs John Carroll	1-28-55
39	Dave DeBusschere, Detroit vs Central Michigan	1-30-60
39	Keith Swagerty, Pacific vs UC-Santa Barbara	3-5-65

REBOUNDING HIGHS SINCE 1973

Reb	Player and Team vs Opponent	Date
34	David Vaughn, Oral Roberts vs Brandeis	1-8-73
33	Robert Parish, Centenary vs Southern Miss	1-22-73
32	Durand Macklin, Louisiana St vs Tulane	11-26-76
31	Jim Bradley, Northern Illinois vs WI-Milwaukee	2-19-73
31	Calvin Natt, Northeast Louisiana vs Georgia Southern	12-29-76

ASSISTS

A	Player and Team vs Opponent	Date
22	Tony Fairley, Baptist vs Armstrong St	2-9-87
22	Avery Johnson, Southern-BR vs Texas Southern	1-25-88
22	Sherman Douglas, Syracuse vs Providence	1-28-89
21	Mark Wade, NV-Las Vegas vs Navy	12-29-86
21	Kelvin Scarborough, New Mexico vs Hawaii	2-13-87
21	Anthony Manuel, Bradley vs UC-Irvine	12-19-87
21	Avery Johnson, Southern-BR vs Alabama St	1-16-88

STEALS

S	Player and Team vs Opponent	Date
13	Mookie Blaylock, Oklahoma vs Centenary	12-12-87
13	Mookie Blaylock, Oklahoma vs Loyola Marymount	12-17-88
12	Kenny Robertson, Cleveland St vs Wagner	12-3-88
11	Darron Brittman, Chicago St vs McKendree	2-24-86
11	Darron Brittman, Chicago St vs St Xavier	2-8-86
11	Marty Johnson, Towson St vs Bucknell	2-17-88
11	Aldwin Ware, Florida A&M vs Tuskegee	2-24-88
11	Mark Macon, Temple vs Notre Dame	1-29-89
11	Carl Thomas, E Michigan vs Chicago St	2-20-91

BLOCKED SHOTS

BS	Player and Team vs Opponent	Date
14	David Robinson, Navy vs NC-Wilmington	1-4-86
14	Shawn Bradley, Brigham Young vs E Kentucky	12-7-90
12	David Robinson, Navy vs James Madison	1-9-86
12	Derrick Lewis, Maryland vs James Madison	1-28-87
12	Rodney Blake, St Joseph's (PA) vs Cleveland St	12-2-87
12	Walter Palmer, Dartmouth vs Harvard	1-9-88
12	Alan Ogg, AL-Birmingham vs Florida A&M	12-16-88
12	Dikembe Mutombo, Georgetown vs St John's (NY)	1-23-89
12	Shaquille O'Neal, Louisiana St vs Loyola Marymount	2-3-90
12	Cedric Lewis, Maryland vs S Florida	1-19-91

Season Records

POINTS

Player and Team	Year	GP	FG	3FG	FT	Pts
Pete Maravich, Louisiana St.	1970	31	522	—	337	1381
Elvin Hayes, Houston	1968	33	519	—	176	1214
Frank Selvy, Furman	1954	29	427	—	355	1209
Pete Maravich, Louisiana St.	1969	26	433	—	282	1148
Pete Maravich, Lousiana St	1968	26	432	—	274	1138
Bo Kimble, Loyola Marymount	1990	32	404	92	231	1131
Hersey Hawkins, Bradley	1988	31	377	87	284	1125
Austin Carr, Notre Dame	1970	29	444	—	218	1106
Austin Carr, Notre Dame	1971	29	430	—	241	1101
Otis Birdsong, Houston	1977	36	452	—	186	1090

SCORING AVERAGE

Player and Team	Year	GP	FG	FT	Pts	Avg
Pete Maravich, Louisiana St.	1970	31	522	337	1381	44.5
Pete Maravich, Louisiana St.	1969	26	433	282	1148	44.2
Pete Maravich, Louisiana St.	1968	26	432	274	1138	43.8
Frank Selvy, Furman	1954	29	427	355	1209	41.7
Johnny Neumann, Mississippi	1971	23	366	191	923	40.1
Freeman Williams, Portland St.	1977	26	417	176	1010	38.8
Billy McGill, Utah	1962	26	394	221	1009	38.8
Calvin Murphy, Niagara	1968	24	337	242	916	38.2
Austin Carr, Notre Dame	1970	29	444	218	1106	38.1
Austin Carr, Notre Dame	1971	29	430	241	1101	38.0
Kevin Bradshaw, U.S. Int'l	1991	28	358	278	1054	37.6

REBOUNDS

Player and Team	Year	GP	Reb	Player and Team	Year	GP	Reb
Walt Dukes, Seton Hall	1953	33	734	Artis Gilmore, Jacksonville	1970	28	621
Leroy Wright, Pacific	1959	26	652	Tom Gola, La Salle	1955	31	618
Tom Gola, La Salle	1954	30	652	Ed Conlin, Fordham	1953	26	612
Charlie Tyra, Louisville	1956	29	645	Art Quimby, Connecticut	1955	25	611
Paul Silas, Creighton	1964	29	631	Bill Russell, San Francisco	1956	29	609
Elvin Hayes, Houston	1968	33	624	Jim Ware, Oklahoma City	1966	29	607

REBOUND AVERAGE BEFORE 1973

Player and Team	Year	GP	Reb	Avg
Charlie Slack, Marshall	1955	21	538	25.6
Leroy Wright, Pacific	1959	26	652	25.1
Art Quimby, Connecticut	1955	25	611	24.4
Charlie Slack, Marshall	1956	22	520	23.6
Ed Conlin, Fordham	1053	26	612	23.5

REBOUND AVERAGE SINCE 1973

Player and Team	Year	GP	Reb	Avg
Kermit Washington, American	1973	22	439	20.0
Marvin Barnes, Providence	1973	30	571	19.0
Marvin Barnes, Providence	1974	32	597	18.7
Pete Padgett, NV-Reno	1973	26	462	17.8
Jim Bradley, Northern Illinois	1973	24	426	17.8

ASSISTS

Player and Team	Year	GP	A	Player and Team	Year	GP	A
Mark Wade, UNLV	1987	38	406	Sherman Douglas, Syracuse	1989	38	326
Avery Johnson, Southern-BR	1988	30	399	Greg Anthony, UNLV	1991	35	310
Anthony Manuel, Bradley	1988	31	373	Reid Gettys, Houston	1984	37	309
Avery Johnson, Southern-BR	1987	31	333	Carl Golston, Loyola (IL)	1985	33	305
Mark Jackson, St John's (NY)	1986	32	328	Craig Neal, Georgia Tech	1988	32	303

Season Records (*Cont.*)

ASSIST AVERAGE

Player and Team	Year	GP	A	Avg	Player and Team	Year	GP	A	Avg
Avery Johnson, Southern-BR	1988	30	399	13.3	Chris Corchiani, N Carolina St	1991	31	299	9.6
Anthony Manuel, Bradley	1988	31	373	12.0	Tony Fairley, Baptist	1987	28	270	9.6
Avery Johnson, Southern-BR	1987	31	333	10.7	Muggsy Bogues, Wake Forest	1987	29	276	9.5
Mark Wade, NV-Las Vegas	1987	38	406	10.7	Craig Neal, Georgia Tech	1988	32	303	9.5
Glenn Williams, Holy Cross	1989	28	278	9.9	Ron Weingard, Hofstra	1985	24	228	9.5

FIELD-GOAL PERCENTAGE

Player and Team	Year	GP	FG	FGA	Pct
Steve Johnson, Oregon St	1981	28	235	315	74.6
Dwayne Davis, Florida	1989	33	179	248	72.2
Keith Walker, Utica	1985	27	154	216	71.3
Steve Johnson, Oregon St	1980	30	211	297	71.0
Oliver Miller, Arkansas	1991	38	254	361	70.4
Alan Williams, Princeton	1987	25	163	232	70.3
Mark McNamara, California	1982	27	231	329	70.2
Warren Kidd, Middle Tennessee St	1991	30	173	247	70.0
Pete Freeman, Akron	1991	28	175	250	70.0
Joe Senser, West Chester	1977	25	130	186	69.9
Lee Campbell, SW Missouri St	1990	29	192	275	69.8
Stephen Scheffler, Purdue	1990	30	173	248	69.8

Based on qualifiers for annual championships.

FREE-THROW PERCENTAGE

Player and Team	Year	GP	FT	FTA	Pct
Craig Collins, Penn St	1985	27	94	98	95.9
Rod Foster, UCLA	1982	27	95	100	95.0
Carlos Gibson, Marshall	1978	28	84	89	94.4
Jim Barton, Dartmouth	1986	26	65	69	94.2
Jack Moore, Nebraska	1982	27	123	131	93.9
Rob Robbins, New Mexico	1990	34	101	108	93.5
Tommy Boyer, Arkansas	1962	23	125	134	93.3
Damon Goodwin, Dayton	1986	30	95	102	93.1
Brian Magid, George Washington	1980	26	79	85	92.9
Mike Joseph, Bucknell	1990	29	144	155	92.9

Based on qualifiers for annual championships.

THREE-POINT FIELD-GOAL PERCENTAGE

Player and Team	Year	GP	3FG	3FGA	Pct
Glenn Tropf, Holy Cross	1988	29	52	82	63.4
Keith Jennings, E Tennessee St	1991	33	84	142	59.2
Dave Calloway, Monmouth (NJ)	1989	28	48	82	58.5
Steve Kerr, Arizona	1988	38	114	199	57.3
Reginald Jones, Prairie View	1987	28	64	112	57.1
Joel Tribelhorn, Colorado St	1989	33	76	135	56.3
Mike Joseph, Bucknell	1988	28	65	116	56.0
Reginald Jones, Prairie View	1988	27	85	155	54.8
Eric Rhodes, SF Austin St	1987	30	58	106	54.7
Dave Orlandini, Princeton	1988	26	60	110	54.5

Based on qualifiers for annual championships.

STEALS

Player and Team	Year	GP	S
Mookie Blaylock, Oklahoma	1988	39	150
Aldwin Ware, Florida A&M	1988	29	142
Darron Brittman, Chicago St	1986	28	139
Nadav Henefeld, Connecticut	1990	37	138
Mookie Blaylock, Oklahoma	1989	35	131

BLOCKED SHOTS

Player and Team	Year	GP	BS
David Robinson, Navy	1986	35	207
Shawn Bradley, BYU	1991	34	177
Alonzo Mourning, Georgetown	1989	34	169
Dikembe Mutombo, Georgetown	1991	32	151
David Robinson, Navy	1987	32	144

Season Records (*Cont.*)

STEAL AVERAGE

Player and Team	Year	GP	S	Avg
Darron Brittman, Chicago St	1986	28	139	4.96
Aldwin Ware, Florida A&M	1988	29	142	4.90
Ronn McMahon, Eastern Washington	1990	29	130	4.48
Jim Paguaga, St Francis (NY)	1986	28	120	4.29
Marty Johnson, Towson St	1988	30	124	4.13

BLOCKED SHOT AVERAGE

Player and Team	Year	GP	BS	Avg
David Robinson, Navy	1986	35	207	5.91
Shawn Bradley, BYU	1991	34	177	5.21
Cedric Lewis, Maryland	1991	28	143	5.11
Shaquille O'Neal, Louisiana St	1991	28	140	5.00
Alonzo Mourning, Georgetown	1989	34	169	4.97

Career Records

POINTS

Player and Team	Ht	Final Year	GP	FG	3FG*	FT	Pts
Pete Maravich, Louisiana St	6-5	1970	83	1387	—	893	3667
Freeman Williams, Portland St	6-4	1978	106	1369	—	511	3249
Lionel Simmons, La Salle	6-7	1990	131	1244	56	673	3217
Harry Kelly, Texas Southern	6-7	1983	110	1234	—	598	3066
Hersey Hawkins, Bradley	6-3	1988	125	1100	118	690	3008
Oscar Robertson, Cincinnati	6-5	1960	88	1052	—	869	2973
Danny Manning, Kansas	6-10	1988	147	1216	10	509	2951
Alfredrick Hughes, Loyola (IL)	6-5	1985	120	1226	—	462	2914
Elvin Hayes, Houston	6-8	1968	93	1215	—	454	2884
Larry Bird, Indiana St	6-9	1979	94	1154	—	542	2850
Otis Birdsong, Houston	6-4	1977	116	1176	—	480	2832
Kevin Bradshaw, Bethune-Cookman, U.S. Int'l	6-6	1991	111	1027	132	618	2804
Hank Gathers, Southern Cal, Loyola Marymount	6-7	1990	117	1127	0	469	2723
Reggie Lewis, Northeastern	6-7	1987	122	1043	30 (1)	592	2708
Daren Queenan, Lehigh	6-5	1988	118	1024	29	626	2703
Byron Larkin, Xavier (OH)	6-3	1988	121	1022	51	601	2696
David Robinson, Navy	7-1	1987	127	1032	1	604	2669
Wayman Tisdale, Oklahoma	6-9	1985	104	1077	—	507	2661
Michael Brooks, La Salle	6-7	1980	114	1064	—	500	2628
Mark Macon, Temple	6-5	1991	126	980	246	403	2609

*Listed is the number of three-pointers scored since it became the national rule in 1987; the number in the parentheses is number scored prior to 1987—these counted as three points in the game but counted as two-pointers in the national rankings. The three-pointers in the parentheses are not included in total points.

SCORING AVERAGE

Player and Team	Final Year	GP	FG	FT	Pts	Avg
Pete Maravich, Louisiana St	1968	83	1387	893	3667	44.2
Austin Carr, Notre Dame	1971	74	1017	526	2560	34.6
Oscar Robertson, Cincinnati	1960	88	1052	869	2973	33.8
Calvin Murphy, Niagara	1970	77	947	654	2548	33.1
Dwight Lamar, Southwestern Louisiana	1973	57	768	326	1862	32.7
Frank Selvy, Furman	1954	78	922	694	2538	32.5
Rick Mount, Purdue	1970	72	910	503	2323	32.3
Darrell Floyd, Furman	1956	71	868	545	2281	32.1
Nick Werkman, Seton Hall	1964	71	812	649	2273	32.0
Willie Humes, Idaho St	1971	48	565	380	1510	31.5
William Averitt, Pepperdine	1973	49	615	311	1541	31.4
Elgin Baylor, Col Idaho, Seattle	1958	80	956	588	2500	31.3
Elvin Hayes, Houston	1968	93	1215	454	2884	31.0
Freeman Williams, Portland St	1978	106	1369	511	3249	30.7
Larry Bird, Indiana St	1979	94	1154	542	2850	30.3

REBOUNDS

Player and Team	Final Year	GP	Reb
Tom Gola, La Salle	1955	118	2201
Joe Holup, George Washington	1956	104	2030
Charlie Slack, Marshall	1956	88	1916
Ed Conlin, Fordham	1955	102	1884
Dickie Hemric, Wake Forest	1955	104	1802

Career Records (*Cont.*)

REBOUNDS FOR CAREERS BEGINNING IN 1973 OR AFTER

Player and Team	Final Year	GP	Reb
Derrick Coleman, Syracuse	1990	143	1537
Ralph Sampson, Virginia	1983	132	1511
Pete Padgett, NV-Reno	1976	104	1464
Lionel Simmons, La Salle	1990	131	1429
Anthony Bonner, St Louis	1990	133	1424

ASSISTS

Player and Team	Final Year	GP	A
Chris Corchiani, N Carolina St	1991	124	1038
Keith Jennings, E Tennessee St	1991	127	983
Sherman Douglas, Syracuse	1989	138	960
Greg Anthony, Portland, UNLV	1991	138	950
Gary Payton, Oregon St	1990	120	939

FIELD-GOAL PERCENTAGE

Player and Team	Final Year	FG	FGA	Pct
Stephen Scheffler, Purdue	1990	408	596	68.5
Steve Johnson, Oregon St	1981	828	1222	67.8
Murray Brown, Florida St	1980	566	847	66.8
Lee Campbell, SW Missouri St	1990	411	618	66.5
Joe Senser, West Chester	1979	476	719	66.2

Note: Minimum 400 field goals.

FREE-THROW PERCENTAGE

Player and Team	Final Year	FT	FTA	Pct
Greg Starrick, Kentucky, Southern Illinois	1972	341	375	90.9
Jack Moore, Nebraska	1982	446	495	90.1
Steve Henson, Kansas St	1990	361	401	90.0
Steve Alford, Indiana	1987	535	596	89.8
Bob Lloyd, Rutgers	1967	543	605	89.8

Note: Minimum 300 free throws.

THREE-POINT FIELD GOALS MADE

Player and Team	Final Year	GP	3FG
Jeff Fryer, Loyola Marymount	1990	112	363
Dennis Scott, Georgia Tech	1990	99	351
Rodney Monroe, N Carolina St	1991	124	322
Andy Kennedy, Ala-Birmingham	1991	95	318
Dana Barros, Boston Col	1989	91	291

THREE-POINT FIELD-GOAL PERCENTAGE

Player and Team	Final Year	3FG	3FGA	Pct
Keith Jennings, E Tennessee St	1991	223	452	49.3
Kirk Manns, Michigan St	1990	212	446	47.5
Tim Locum, Wisconsin	1991	227	481	47.2
Barry Booker, Vanderbilt	1989	246	535	46.0
Dave Calloway, Monmouth (NJ)	1991	260	567	45.9

Note: Minimum 200 3-point field goals.

STEALS

Player and Team	Final Year	GP	S
Eric Murdock, Providence	1991	117	376
Michael Anderson, Drexel	1988	115	341
Kenny Robertson, New Mexico, Cleveland St	1990	119	341
Keith Jennings, E Tennessee St	1991	127	334
Greg Anthony, Portland, UNLV	1991	138	329

Career Records (*Cont.*)

BLOCKED SHOTS

Player and Team	Final Year	GP	BS
Rodney Blake, St Joseph's (PA)	1988	116	399
Tim Perry, Temple	1988	130	392
Pervis Ellison, Louisville	1989	136	374
Dikembe Mutombo, Georgetown	1991	96	354
David Robinson, Navy	1987	67	351

NCAA Division I Team Leaders

Division I Team All-Time Wins

Team	First Year	Yrs	W	L	T
N Carolina	1911	81	1508	550	0
Kentucky	1903	88	1501	495	1
Kansas	1899	93	1459	677	0
St John's (NY)	1908	84	1444	613	0
Oregon St	1902	90	1387	858	0
Duke	1906	86	1377	693	0
Temple	1895	95	1356	735	0
Notre Dame	1898	86	1335	668	1
Pennsylvania	1902	90	1324	770	0
Syracuse	1901	90	1318	625	0
Washington	1896	89	1291	790	0
Indiana	1901	91	1271	700	0
UCLA	1920	72	1244	561	0
Princeton	1901	91	1242	793	0
Fordham	1903	88	1241	877	0

Note: Years in Division I only.

Division I Team All-Time Winning Percentage

Team	First Year	Yrs	W	L	T	Pct
Kentucky	1903	88	1501	495	1	.752
N Carolina	1911	81	1508	550	0	.733
St Johns (NY)	1908	84	1444	613	0	.702
UCLA	1920	72	1244	561	0	.689
Kansas	1899	93	1459	677	0	.683
Syracuse	1901	90	1318	625	0	.678
Western Kentucky	1915	72	1237	588	0	.678
DePaul	1924	68	1098	533	0	.673
Notre Dame	1898	86	1335	668	1	.667
Duke	1906	86	1377	693	0	.665

Note: Minimum of 25 years in Division I only.

NCAA Division I Men's Winning Streaks

Longest—Full Season

Team	Games	Years	Ended by
UCLA	88	1971-74	Notre Dame (71-70)
San Francisco	60	1955-57	Illinois (62-33)
UCLA	47	1966-68	Houston (71-69)
UNLV	45	1990-91	Duke (79-77)
Texas	44	1913-17	Rice (24-18)
Seton Hall	43	1939-41	LIU-Brooklyn (49-26)
LIU-Brooklyn	43	1935-37	Stanford (45-31)
UCLA	41	1968-69	Southern Cal (46-44)
Marquette	39	1970-71	Ohio St (60-59)
Cincinnati	37	1962-63	Wichita St (65-64)
N Carolina	37	1957-58	W Virginia (75-64)
N Carolina St	36	1974-75	Wake Forest (83-78)
Arkansas	35	1927-29	Texas (26-25)

Longest—Home Court

Team	Games	Years
Kentucky	129	1943-55
St Bonaventure	99	1948-61
UCLA	98	1970-76
Cincinnati	86	1957-64
Marquette	81	1967-73
Arizona	81	1945-51
Lamar	80	1978-84
Long Beach St	75	1968-74
NV-Las Vegas	72	1974-78
Cincinnati	68	1972-78

Longest—Regular Season

Team	Games	Years	Ended by
UCLA	76	1971-74	Notre Dame (71-70)
Indiana	57	1975-77	Toledo (59-57)
Marquette	56	1970-72	Detroit (70-49)
Kentucky	54	1952-55	George Tech (59-58)
San Francisco	51	1955-57	Illinois (62-33)
Pennsylvania	48	1970-72	Temple (57-52)
Ohio St	47	1960-62	Wisconsin (86-67)
Texas	44	1913-17	Rice (24-18)
UCLA	43	1966-68	Houston (71-69)
LIU-Brooklyn	43	1935-37	Stanford (45-31)
Seton Hall	42	1939-41	LIU-Brooklyn (49-26)

NCAA Division I Winningest Men's Coaches

Active Coaches

WINS

Coach and Team	W
Dean Smith, N Carolina	717
Jerry Tarkanian, UNLV	599
Lefty Driesell, James Madison	579
Don Haskins, UTEP	577
Lou Henson, Illinois	576
Norm Stewart, Missouri	571
Bob Knight, Indiana	561
Gene Bartow, AL-Birmingham	553
Glenn Wilkes, Stetson	527
Tom Young, Old Dominion	524

Note: Minimum 5 years as a Division I head coach; includes record at 4-year colleges only.

WINNING PERCENTAGE

Coach and Team	Yrs	W	L	Pct
Jerry Tarkanian, UNLV	23	599	120	.833
Dean Smith, N Carolina	30	717	209	.774
John Chaney, Temple	19	441	130	.772
Jim Boeheim, Syracuse	15	369	114	.764
Pete Gillen, Xavier (OH)	6	141	49	.742
John Thompson, Georgetown	19	442	155	.740
Nolan Richardson, Arkansas	11	260	92	.739
Denny Crum, Louisville	20	477	172	.735
Bob Knight, Indiana	26	561	203	.734
Lou Carnesecca, St John's (NY)	23	507	189	.728

Note: Minimum 5 years as a Division I head coach; includes record at 4-year colleges only.

All-Time Winningest Division I Men's Coaches

WINS

Coach (Team)	W
Adolph Rupp (Kentucky)	875
Hank Iba (NW Missouri St, Colorado, Oklahoma St)	767
Ed Diddle (Western Kentucky)	759
Phog Allen (Baker, Kansas, Haskell, Central Missouri St, Kansas)	746
Ray Meyer (DePaul)	724
Dean Smith (N Carolina)	717
John Wooden (Indiana St, UCLA)	664
Ralph Miller (Wichita St, Iowa, Oregon St)	657
Marv Harshman (Pacific Lutheran, Washington St, Washington)	642
Norm Sloan (Presbyterian, Citadel, N Carolina St, Florida)	627
Cam Henderson (Muskingum, Davis & Elkins, Marshall)	611
Jerry Tarkanian (Long Beach St, UNLV)	599
Amory "Slats" Gill (Oregon St)	599
Abe Lemons (Oklahoma City, Tex-Pan American, Oklahoma City)	597
Guy Lewis (Houston)	592

Note: Minimum 10 head coaching seasons in Division I.

Tops at Two Levels

Five players have been named MVP of the NCAA basketball tournament and of the NBA. They are Bill Russell, Wilt Chamberlain, Lew Alcindor/Kareem Abdul-Jabbar, Bill Walton, and Magic Johnson.

WINNING PERCENTAGE

Coach (Team)	Yrs	W	L	Pct
Jerry Tarkanian (Long Beach St 69-73, UNLV 74-)	23	599	120	.833
Clair Bee (Rider 29-31, LIU-Brooklyn 32-45, 46-51)	21	410	86	.827
Adolph Rupp (Kentucky 31-72)	41	875	190	.822
John Wooden (Indiana St 47-48, UCLA 49-75)	29	664	162	.804
Dean Smith (N Carolina 62-)	30	717	209	.774
George Keogan (St Louis 16, Allegheny 19, Valparaiso 20-21, Notre Dame 24-43)	24	385	117	.767
Jack Ramsay (St Joseph's [PA] 56-66)	11	231	71	.765
Frank Keaney (Rhode Island 21-48)	28	403	124	.765
Jim Boeheim (Syracuse 77-)	15	369	114	.764
Vic Bubas (Duke 60-69)	10	213	67	.761
Charles "Chick" Davies (Duquesne 25-43, 47-48)	21	314	106	.748
Ray Mears (Wittenberg 57-62, Tennessee 63-77)	21	399	135	.747
John Thompson (Georgetown 73-)	19	442	155	.740
Al McGuire (Belmont Abbey 58-64, Marquette 65-77)	20	405	143	.739
Everett Case (N Carolina St 47-64)	18	376	133	.739
Phog Allen (Baker 06-08, Kansas 08-09, Haskell 09, Central Missouri St 13-19, Kansas 20-56)	48	746	264	.739
Nolan Richardson (Tulsa 81-85, Arkansas 86-)	10	260	92	.739
Denny Crum (Louisville 72-)	20	477	172	.735
Bob Knight (Army 66-71, Indiana 72-)	26	561	203	.734
Lou Carnesecca (St John's [NY] 66-70, and 74-)	23	507	189	.728

Note: Minimum 10 head coaching seasons in Division I.

NCAA Division I Women's Championship Results

Year	Winner	Score	Runner-up	Winning Coach
1982	Louisiana Tech	76-62	Cheyney	Sonja Hogg
1983	Southern Cal	69-67	Louisiana Tech	Linda Sharp
1984	Southern Cal	72-61	Tennessee	Linda Sharp
1985	Old Dominion	70-65	Georgia	Marianne Stanley
1986	Texas	97-81	Southern Cal	Jody Conradt
1987	Tennessee	67-44	Louisiana Tech	Pat Summitt
1988	Louisiana Tech	56-54	Auburn	Leon Barmore
1989	Tennessee	76-60	Auburn	Pat Summitt
1990	Stanford	88-81	Auburn	Tara VanDerveer
1991	Tennessee	70-67 (OT)	Virginia	Pat Summitt

NCAA Division I Women's All-Time Individual Leaders

SINGLE-GAME SCORING HIGHS

Pts	Player and Team vs Opponent	Date
60	Cindy Brown, Long Beach St vs San Jose St	1987
58	Kim Perrot, Southwestern Louisiana vs Southeastern Louisiana	1990
58	Lorri Bauman, Drake vs SW Missouri St	1984
55	Patricia Hoskins, Mississippi Valley vs Southern-BR	1989
55	Patricia Hoskins, Mississippi Valley vs Alabama St	1989
54	Wanda Ford, Drake vs SW Missouri St	1986
53	Felisha Edwards, NE Louisiana vs Southern Mississippi	1991
53	Chris Starr, NV-Reno vs Cal St-Sacramento	1983
52	Sheryl Martin, Georgia St vs Stetson	1983
52	Deborah Temple, Delta St vs Tennessee-Martin	1983
52	Lisa Ingram, Northeastern Louisiana vs Louisiana St	1984

SEASON SCORING AVERAGE

Player and Team	Year	GP	FG	3FG	FT	Pts	Avg
Patricia Hoskins, Mississippi Valley	1989	27	345	13	205	908	33.6
Deborah Temple, Delta St	1984	28	373	—	127	873	31.2
Wanda Ford, Drake	1986	30	390	—	139	919	30.6
Anucha Browne, Northwestern	1985	28	341	—	173	855	30.5

SEASON SCORING AVERAGE (*Cont.*)

Player and Team	Year	GP	FG	3FG	FT	Pts	Avg
LeChandra LeDay, Grambling	1988	28	334	36	146	850	30.4
Kim Perrot, Southwestern Louisiana	1990	28	308	95	128	839	30.0
Tina Hutchinson, San Diego St	1984	30	383	—	132	898	29.9
Jan Jensen, Drake	1991	30	358	6	166	888	29.6
Genia Miller, Cal St-Fullerton	1991	33	376	0	217	969	29.4
Barbara Kennedy, Clemson	1982	31	392	—	124	908	29.3
LaTaunya Pollard, Long Beach St	1983	31	376	—	155	907	29.3
Lisa McMullen, Alabama St	1991	28	285	126	119	815	29.1
Tresa Spaulding, BYU	1987	28	347	—	116	810	28.9
Hope Linthicum, Central Connecticut St	1987	23	282	—	101	665	28.9
Pam Hudson, Northwestern Lousiana	1990	29	330	1	168	829	28.6

CAREER POINTS

Player and Team	Year	GP	Pts
Patricia Hoskins, Mississippi Valley	1989	110	3122
Lorri Bauman, Drake	1984	120	3115
Cheryl Miller, Southern Cal	1986	128	3018
Valorie Whiteside, Appalachian St	1988	116	2944
Joyce Walker, Louisiana St	1984	117	2906
Sandra Hodge, New Orleans	1984	107	2860
Karen Pelphrey, Marshall	1986	114	2746
Cindy Brown, Long Beach St	1987	128	2696
Carolyn Thompson, Texas Tech	1984	121	2655
Sue Wicks, Rutgers	1988	125	2655

CAREER SCORING AVERAGE

Player and Team	Yrs	GP	FG	3FG	FT	Pts	Avg
Patricia Hoskins, Mississippi Valley	1985-89	110	1196	24	706	3122	28.4
Sandra Hodge, New Orleans	1981-84	107	1194	—	472	2860	26.7
Lorri Bauman, Drake	1981-84	120	1104	—	907	3115	26.0
Valorie Whiteside, Appalachian St	1984-88	116	1153	0	638	2944	25.4
Joyce Walker, Louisiana St	1981-84	117	1259	—	388	2906	24.8
Tarcha Hollis, Grambling	1988-91	85	904	3	247	2058	24.2
Karen Pelphrey, Marshall	1983-86	114	1175	—	396	2746	24.1
Erma Jones, Bethune-Cookman	1982-84	87	961	—	173	2095	24.1
Cheryl Miller, Southern Cal	1983-86	128	1159	—	700	3018	23.6
Chris Starr, Nevada-Reno	1983-86	101	881	—	594	2356	23.3

NCAA Division II Men's Championship Results

Year	Winner	Score	Runner-up	Third Place	Fourth Place
1957	Wheaton (IL)	89-65	Kentucky Wesleyan	Mount St Mary's (MD)	Cal St-Los Angeles
1958	S Dakota	75-53	St Michael's	Evansville	Wheaton (IL)
1959	Evansville	83-67	SW Missouri St	N Carolina A&T	Cal St-Los Angeles
1960	Evansville	90-69	Chapman	Kentucky Wesleyan	Cornell College
1961	Wittenberg	42-38	SE Missouri St	S Dakota St	Mount St Mary's (MD)
1962	Mount St Mary's (MD)	58-57 (OT)	Cal St-Sacramento	Southern Illinois	Nebraska Wesleyan
1963	S Dakota St	44-42	Wittenberg	Oglethorpe	Southern Illinois
1964	Evansville	72-59	Akron	N Carolina A&T	Northern Iowa
1965	Evansville	85-82 (OT)	Southern Illinois	N Dakota	St Michael's
1966	Kentucky Wesleyan	54-51	Southern Illinois	Akron	N Dakota
1967	Winston-Salem	77-74	SW Missouri St	Kentucky Wesleyan	Illinois St
1968	Kentucky Wesleyan	63-52	Indiana St	Trinity (TX)	Ashland
1969	Kentucky Wesleyan	75-71	SW Missouri St	†Vacated	Ashland
1970	Philadelphia Textile	76-65	Tennessee St	UC-Riverside	Buffalo St
1971	Evansville	97-82	Old Dominion	†Vacated	Kentucky Wesleyan
1972	Roanoke	84-72	Akron	Tennessee St	Eastern Mich
1973	Kentucky Wesleyan	78-76 (OT)	Tennessee St	Assumption	Brockport St
1974	Morgan St	67-52	SW Missouri St	Assumption	New Orleans
1975	Old Dominion	76-74	New Orleans	Assumption	TN-Chattanooga
1976	Puget Sound	83-74	TN-Chattanooga	Eastern Illinois	Old Dominion

NCAA Division II Men's Championship Results (*Cont.*)

Year	Winner	Score	Runner-up	Third Place	Fourth Place
1977	TN-Chattanooga	71-62	Randolph-Macon	N Alabama	Sacred Heart
1978	Cheyney	47-40	WI-Green Bay	Eastern Illinois	Central Florida
1979	N Alabama	64-50	WI-Green Bay	Cheyney	Bridgeport
1980	Virginia Union	80-74	New York Tech	Florida Southern	N Alabama
1981	Florida Southern	73-68	Mount St Mary's (MD)	Cal Poly-SLO	WI-Green Bay
1982	District of Columbia	73-63	Florida Southern	Kentucky Wesleyan	Cal St-Bakersfield
1983	Wright St	92-73	District of Columbia	*Cal St-Bakersfield	*Morningside
1984	Central Missouri St	81-77	St Augustine's	*Kentucky Wesleyan	*N Alabama
1985	Jacksonville St	74-73	S Dakota St	*Kentucky Wesleyan	*Mount St Mary's (MD)
1986	Sacred Heart	93-87	SE Missouri St	*Cheyney	*Florida Southern
1987	Kentucky Wesleyan	92-74	Gannon	*Delta St	*Eastern Montana
1988	Lowell	75-72	AK-Anchorage	Florida Southern	Troy St
1989	N Carolina Central	73-46	SE Missouri St	UC-Riverside	Jacksonville St
1990	Kentucky Wesleyan	93-79	Cal St-Bakersfield	N Dakota	Morehouse
1991	N Alabama	79-72	Bridgeport (CT)	*Cal St-Bakersfield	*Virginia Union

*Indicates tied for third.

†Student-athletes representing American International in 1969 and Southwestern Louisiana in 1971 were declared ineligible subsequent to the tournament. Under NCAA rules, the teams' and ineligible student-athletes' records were deleted, and the teams' places in the final standings were vacated.

NCAA Division II Men's All-Time Individual Leaders

SINGLE-GAME SCORING HIGHS

Pts	Player and Team vs Opponent	Date
113	Bevo Francis, Rio Grande vs Hillsdale	1954
84	Bevo Francis, Rio Grande vs Alliance	1954
82	Bevo Francis, Rio Grande vs Bluffton	1954
80	Paul Crissman, Southern Cal Col vs Pacific Christian	1966
77	William English, Winston-Salem vs Fayetteville St	1968

SEASON SCORING AVERAGE

Player and Team	Year	GP	Pts	Avg
Bevo Francis, Rio Grande	1954	27	1255	46.5
Earl Glass, Mississippi Industrial	1963	19	815	42.9
Earl Monroe, Winston-Salem	1967	32	1329	41.5
John Rinka, Kenyon	1970	23	942	41.0
Willie Shaw, Lane	1964	18	727	40.4

CAREER POINTS

Player and Team	Yrs	Pts
Travis Grant, Kentucky St	1969-72	4045
Bob Hopkins, Grambling	1953-56	3759
Earnest Lee, Clark Atlanta	1984-87	3298
Joe Miller, Alderson-Broaddus	1954-57	3294
Henry Logan, Western Carolina	1965-68	3290

CAREER SCORING AVERAGE

Player and Team	Yrs	GP	Pts	Avg
Travis Grant, Kentucky St	1969-72	121	4045	33.4
John Rinka, Kenyon	1967-70	99	3251	32.8
Florindo Vieira, Quinnipiac	1954-57	69	2263	32.8
Willie Shaw, Lane	1961-64	76	2379	31.3
Mike Davis, Virginia Union	1966-69	89	2758	31.0

NCAA Division III Men's Championship Results

Year	Winner	Score	Runner-up	Third Place	Fourth Place
1975	LeMoyne-Owen	57-54	Glassboro St	Augustana (IL)	Brockport St
1976	Scranton	60-57	Wittenberg	Augustana (IL)	Plattsburgh St
1977	Wittenberg	79-66	Oneonta St	Scranton	Hamline
1978	North Park	69-57	Widener	Albion	Stony Brook
1979	North Park	66-62	Potsdam St	Franklin & Marshall	Centre
1980	North Park	83-76	Upsala	Wittenberg	Longwood
1981	Potsdam St	67-65 (OT)	Augustana (IL)	Ursinus	Otterbein
1982	Wabash	83-62	Potsdam St	Brooklyn	Cal St Stanislaus
1983	Scranton	64-63	Wittenberg	Roanoke	WI-Whitewater
1984	WI-Whitewater	103-86	Clark (MA)	DePauw	Upsala
1985	North Park	72-71	Potsdam St	Nebraska Wesleyan	Widener
1986	Potsdam St	76-73	LeMoyne-Owen	Nebraska Wesleyan	Jersey City St
1987	North Park	106-100	Clark (MA)	Wittenberg	Stockton St
1988	Ohio Wesleyan	92-70	Scranton	Nebraska Wesleyan	Hartwick
1989	WI-Whitewater	94-86	Trenton St	Southern Maine	Centre
1990	Rochester	43-42	DePauw	Washington (MD)	Calvin
1991	Wisconsin Platteville	81-74	Franklin & Marshall	Otterbein	Ramapo (NJ)

Hockey

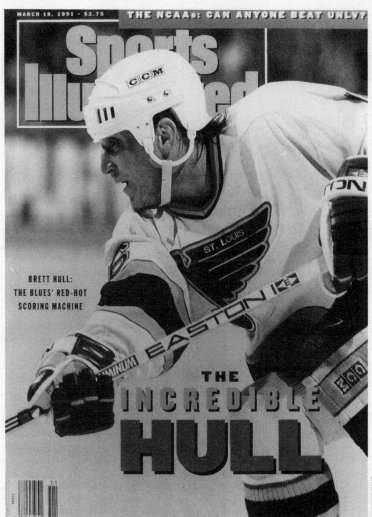

MARCH 18, 1991 · $2.75

THE NCAAs: CAN ANYONE BEAT UNLV?

Sports Illustrated

BRETT HULL:
THE BLUES' RED-HOT
SCORING MACHINE

THE
INCREDIBLE
HULL

The Pens Were Mightier

In a season full of surprises, Pittsburgh won its first Stanley Cup | by JAY GREENBERG

FOR MUCH OF THEIR 24-YEAR HISTORY, THE Pittsburgh Penguins couldn't do anything right. The franchise has had five owners, eight general managers and one bankruptcy and has suffered enough misfortune and incompetence to suggest that only on a hot day in Antarctica would the Penguins ever become champions. But in 1990–91 they did.

Led by Mario Lemieux's magnificent performance, the Penguins beat the Minnesota North Stars four games to two, and won the Stanley Cup. Their 8–0 rout in the sixth game was the largest margin of victory in a Cup-deciding contest. And despite missing Game 3 with back spasms, Lemieux, the graceful and gifted center, scored five goals and seven assists against the North Stars and won the Conn Smythe Trophy as the Most Valuable Player in the playoffs.

At practically every pivotal moment of the finals, Lemieux was the best skater on the ice. It was only the second time in his seven-year career that the Penguins had even made the playoffs, and Lemieux turned the postseason into his personal showcase.

"When somebody that big and that good wants it that badly," said Minnesota center Dave Gagner, "there isn't much you can do." Lemieux, who returned halfway through last season after a career-threatening back infection that followed disk surgery, changed what had been an unpredictable season into one that Pittsburgh would not soon forget.

Wayne Gretzky turned 30, became the first player in NHL history to score 2,000 career points, won a 10th scoring title and even led the Los Angeles Kings to their first Smythe Division title. He also took on a new, middle-aged image: reliable as ever. Still, Gretzky was held in check by Edmonton Oiler superpest Esa Tikkanen as the Kings fell in the second round of the playoffs for the third straight year.

Ray Bourque carried the Boston Bruins to a record 24th consecutive playoff berth, series triumphs over the Hartford Whalers and

Gretzky was as Great as ever in leading the Kings to their first ever division title.

Montreal Canadiens, and won his fourth Norris Trophy as the league's best defenseman. But by the Bruins' series against Pittsburgh, Bourque was tired and simply ordinary.

The smallest player in the league—Theoren Fleury, the Calgary Flames' 5'6", 160-pound forward—became one of its most important with a startling 51-goal season. But in the Flames' first-round loss to the Edmonton Oilers, Fleury was pounded relentlessly and held to two goals.

Chicago Blackhawk rookie goaltender Ed Belfour performed a workload (74 games) and had a goals-against average (2.47) that were representative of a more defensive era. He and flashy second-year center Jeremy Roenick paced Chicago to the league's best regular-season record. But both Blackhawk stars were, at best, average when Chicago was stunned in the first round by Minnesota.

Brett Hull of the St. Louis Blues scored 86 goals and established himself as the game's shooting star, but he and his center, Adam Oates, were largely contained when the Blues, the league's second-best team in the regular season, were upset by the North Stars in the second round.

The Oilers' Mark Messier, the 1989–90 Most Valuable Player, was rendered ineffective by injuries to his thumb and both knees as Minnesota, pulling off its third consecutive upset, eliminated the defending champions in the Campbell Conference finals.

In a year when there was no outstanding team, a larger-than-normal number of fair-to-good ones had a chance to win the Cup. Based on their total collapse after Lemieux left the lineup with his back injury in February of '89, the Penguins appeared to be anything but a Stanley Cup contender entering the '90–91 season. But new coach Bob Johnson, an accomplished master who had built winning programs at the University of Wisconsin and with the Calgary Flames, preached positive thinking and taught defensive responsibility. The Penguins held their own in the first half and went 26-21-3 when Lemieux returned. A strong stretch run helped them come from 15 points behind the New York Rangers to take their first-ever Patrick Division title.

Like their regular-season start, the Penguin playoff run also began on an ominous note. Tom Barrasso suffered a shoulder injury in the first round against the New Jersey Devils, but Pittsburgh rallied behind backup Frank Pietrangelo to win Games 6 and 7. The Penguins then smoked what was supposed to be a tougher, more determined, Washington team in five games. After outplaying Boston in the first two games of the Prince of Wales Conference final—and making just enough mistakes to lose both contests—Pittsburgh outscored the Bruins 20–7 in the next four matches to win the series in six games.

A Shooting Star

THE SAME REASON Brett Hull was never supposed to become a star has helped make him perhaps the most endearing one in hockey. "I've always played with a smile on my face," says the St. Louis Blues right wing, "and it's brought up a lot of questions in people's minds about caring and effort. I've always said, 'What the hell am I doing out here if I'm not having fun?'"

Only the goalies didn't share in Brett Hull's good times in '90–91. Hull, 26, became the fifth player in the game's history to reach 50 goals within the first 50 games of a season. His regular-season total of 86 goals was the third highest in NHL history. In the first year of a four-year, $7.1 million contract that raised him into a salary category previously reserved for Wayne Gretzky and Mario Lemieux, Hull earned every cent.

Just as important, however, for both himself and the game, he kept smiling. With the 30-year-old Gretzky just past his peak, and the sport looking for a new marquee personality, Hull warmly embraced his role as a superstar. Despite the increasing demands on his time and the endless comparisons with Bobby, his Hall of Fame father, Brett's smile continued to come as easily as his goals.

He has the quickest release in the game and one of its harder, heavier shots. His laid-back attitude, cited as the reason he wasn't picked until the sixth round by Calgary (he was traded to the Blues in 1988), has also turned out to be a valuable attribute.

"If I didn't have the kind of personality I have, I'd have been in the loony bin a long time ago," Brett says.

Bobby Hull was the best left wing in the game's history, and Brett understood early on that he would never outskate his father's giant shadow. So instead, the son found shade in it. "I was proud of my dad, but I knew I would never be Bobby Hull," he says. "So I learned to be pleased with myself."

Until two years ago, he was too pleased. The same coaches who were captivated by his genes were turned off by the 20 extra pounds he carried on his 5'11" frame, and disgustedly they reached the same conclusion that so comforted Brett: No, the kid wasn't his old man. But after Hull scored 41 goals in his first full season in St. Louis, Blues coach Brian Sutter informed his lazy young prospect of how much more he could do. The light bulb finally went on in Hull's head. All he was being asked to do was raise his own standards, not meet someone else's. Since then, whenever Hull has found himself getting entangled in others' expectations, he reverts to his own easygoing nature.

"I'm a totally different personality from

The Cup finals turned Pittsburgh's way in Game 4, when the visiting Penguins, in danger of going down 3–1 in the series, survived a furious North Star rally in the final minutes and won 5–3. That victory, secured by an empty-net goal in the final minute, not only proved that the Penguins were resilient, but it was also the first sign that the North Stars' bubble was bursting. With the series tied at two games, Pittsburgh stunned Minnesota with a four-goal first-period burst in Game 5 and won 6–4. In Game 6 Lemieux quickly took control. With the Penguins leading 1–0 and killing off a two-man disadvantage, Lemieux stole the puck, drew a North Star penalty, then scored a shorthanded goal. The rout was on.

Even without a happy ending, the North Stars wrote the best playoff story the NHL has enjoyed in years. There were only 5,730 persons at the Metropolitan Sports Center on Oct. 4, the opening night of the regular sea-

my father," he says about his on-ice personas. The elder Hull roared in on goaltenders with flared nostrils and a stick cocked to deliver one of the hardest slap shots the game has ever known. He was a fiery competitor, driven on every shift, but off the ice he was also admired as one of the game's foremost ambassadors.

There is one area, at least, in which father and son are alike. "One of the best examples I could have had for dealing with being a celebrity was my dad," Brett says. "I don't think anybody would admit to enjoying signing 100 autographs before you can get on a bus or into your car after a game, but I know what's expected of me and I'm going to do it. Reporters ask questions so they can explain to the people who like to come and watch you play what kind of a guy you are. I'm not a phony. And I want the people to know that."

Brett Hull did the impossible—he scored 86 goals and he still remained a nice guy.

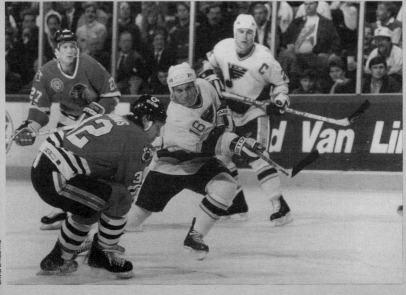

DAVID E. KLUTHO

son. On Nov. 22 the North Stars were 4-14-3. After going 14-6-6 in their final 26 games, they went into the playoffs as a solid threat to pull off a first-round upset, despite netting only 68 points in the regular season. Patient and purposeful like their rookie coach, Bob Gainey, the North Stars refused to be drawn into retaliatory penalties, and Chicago, which took a slew of unnecessary penalties, self-destructed. As the playoffs proceeded, and as the North Stars gained confidence, it was clear that they had more scoring depth than the supposedly superior teams they were defeating.

There were other success stories in hockey last season. Edmonton's Grant Fuhr, who had backstopped the Oilers to four Stanley Cups, admitted to using drugs and was suspended for 60 games. Fuhr came back a new man—"Facing up to things is part of the process of burying them," he said—and as the same fine goalie.

The first wave of Soviet veterans to play in the NHL in 1989–90 were largely disappointing, but in '90–91, Detroit's 21-year-old rookie center, Sergei Fedorov, quickly adjusted to the North American style of play. He looked like a future superstar.

Fedorov was only one of several young stars who emerged. The New York Rangers' Brian Leetch, a brilliant skater and passer with a good sense for when—and when not—to gamble, may be only a year or two away from becoming the best defenseman in the NHL. Oates, a third-line center before Detroit traded him to St. Louis in 1989, developed into one of the game's top threats, scoring 115 points despite missing 19 games with a pulled stomach muscle.

Kid goalies were blooming all over. Belfour needed more than an iron body to carry the low-scoring Blackhawks. He also proved to have an iron will by bouncing back from coach Mike Keenan's frequent quick hooks. Rangers' rookie Mike Richter combined extraordinary quickness with a textbook standup style and was considered among the top handful of NHL goalies. Vancouver's Troy Gamble, who had a 16-16-6 record for a Canucks' team that lost 15 more games than it won, looked like a

DAVID E. KLUTHO

Lemieux showed Jon Casey and the rest of the world he's the best player in hockey.

comer. So did Quebec's Ron Tugnutt, who turned in the goaltending performance of the season in stopping 73 shots in a 3–3 tie in Boston.

The Nordiques, who finished with the NHL's worst record for the third straight season, lacked size, strength and character but not a gifted scorer. Joe Sakic's 109-point season, his second consecutive 100-plus campaign, established the 21-year-old center as one of the game's top players. Now

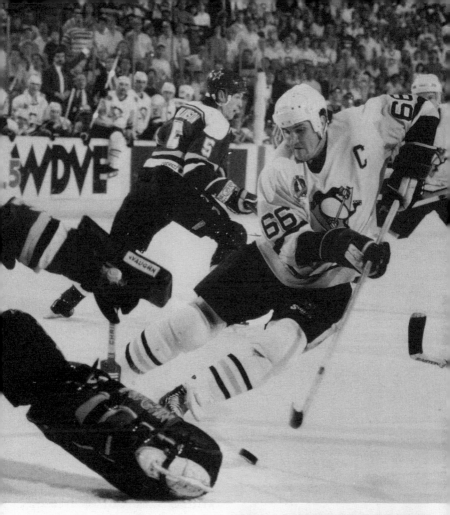

Sakic awaits help. Quebec made Eric Lindros, the most eagerly awaited prospect since Lemieux, the No. 1 pick in the entry draft.

Lindros, 6′4″ and 227 pounds, plays with the raw power of Messier, the NHL's Most Valuable Player in 1989–90. But at 18, Lindros's skills are far more advanced than Messier's were at that same age. Lindros is equally adept at running over defensemen or passing the puck by them and has an excellent touch around the net. He lacks an

The Blackhawks flew to the league's top record behind Belfour and his butterfly style.

PAUL BERESWILL

The 5′6″ Fleury had 51 goals in the regular season but the Oilers got physical with him and held him to two in the playoffs.

exceptionally quick first step, but his long stride and terrific balance make him a strong skater nevertheless. A mean streak, good offensive and defensive sense, and an unselfish attitude complete a package that has been exciting NHL scouts for more than two years.

The NHL, which expanded to San Jose for this season, added two more new franchises for 1992–93 in Tampa Bay and Ottawa. The two franchises agreed to pay the bloated $50 million entrance fee, and despite indications that the NHL had overpriced the franchises, the league remained committed to an expansion from the current 22 teams (24 including Tampa Bay and Ottawa) to 28 by the year 2000. European-born players and a growing number of American prospects will eventually fill in the talent gaps, but the stingy expansion drafts from current NHL clubs will create instantly bad teams. The next few seasons will bring a sharp increase in the number of noncompetitive games.

Nevertheless, an era in which more teams have a chance to win the Stanley Cup has begun. Since 1976, the Montreal Canadiens and the New York Islanders have each won four straight Cups, and Edmonton claimed five in seven years, but the day of the dynasty appears to be over. Last season, for the first time since 1973–74, the NHL crowned a third different champion in three years.

Parity was celebrated most loudly in Pittsburgh, where one image was burned into the memory of Penguin fans: Lemieux extending the Stanley Cup over his head and bringing 24 years of despair to an end.

FOR THE RECORD • 1990 – 1991

NHL Final Team Standings

Clarence Campbell Conference

NORRIS DIVISION

	GP	W	L	T	GF	GA	Pts
Chicago	80	49	23	8	284	211	106
St Louis	80	47	22	11	310	250	105
Detroit	80	34	38	8	273	298	76
Minnesota	80	27	39	14	256	266	68
Toronto	80	23	46	11	241	318	57

SMYTHE DIVISION

	GP	W	L	T	GF	GA	Pts
Los Angeles	80	46	24	10	340	254	102
Calgary	80	46	26	8	344	263	100
Edmonton	80	37	37	6	272	272	80
Vancouver	80	28	43	9	243	315	65
Winnipeg	80	26	43	11	260	288	63

Prince of Wales Conference

ADAMS DIVISION

	GP	W	L	T	GF	GA	Pts
Boston	80	44	24	12	299	264	100
Montreal	80	39	30	11	273	249	89
Buffalo	80	31	30	19	292	278	81
Hartford	80	31	38	11	238	276	73
Quebec	80	16	50	14	236	354	46

PATRICK DIVISION

	GP	W	L	T	GF	GA	Pts
Pittsburgh	80	41	33	6	342	305	88
NY Rangers	80	36	31	13	297	265	85
Washington	80	37	36	7	258	258	81
New Jersey	80	32	33	15	272	264	79
Philadelphia	80	33	37	10	252	267	76
NY Islanders	80	25	45	10	223	290	60

1991 Stanley Cup Playoffs

WALES CONFERENCE

DIVISION SEMIFINALS   DIVISION FINALS   CONFERENCE FINAL

CAMPBELL CONFERENCE

CONFERENCE FINAL   DIVISION FINALS   DIVISION SEMIFINALS

STANLEY CUP

PITTSBURGH (4-2)

Boston
Hartford
→ Boston (4-2)
→ Boston (4-3)
Montreal
Buffalo
→ Montreal (4-2)
→ Pittsburgh (4-2)
Pittsburgh
New Jersey
→ Pittsburgh (4-3)
→ Pittsburgh (4-1)
N.Y. Rangers
Washington
→ Washington (4-2)

Chicago
Minnesota
→ Minnesota (4-2)
→ Minnesota (4-2)
St. Louis
Detroit
→ St. Louis (4-3)
→ Minnesota (4-1)
Los Angeles
Vancouver
→ Los Angeles (4-2)
→ Edmonton (4-2)
Calgary
Edmonton
→ Edmonton (4-3)

So Who Needs a Regular Season?

How meaningful is the NHL's regular season? Consider this: The Chicago Blackhawks finished the year with the most points (106) but got eliminated in the first round of the playoffs. The team that beat the Blackhawks, the Minnesota North Stars, went all the way to the finals despite finishing the regular season with a losing record.

Stanley Cup Playoff Results

(All series best of 7)
DIVISION SEMIFINALS

ADAMS DIVISION

Apr 3	Hartford	5	at Boston	2	Apr 3	Buffalo	5	at Montreal	7
Apr 5	Hartford	3	at Boston	4	Apr 5	Buffalo	4	at Montreal	5
Apr 7	Boston	6	at Hartford	3	Apr 7	Montreal	4	at Buffalo	5
Apr 9	Boston	3	at Hartford	4	Apr 9	Montreal	4	at Buffalo	6
Apr 11	Hartford	1	at Boston	6	Apr 11	Buffalo	3	at Montreal	4*
Apr 13	Boston	3	at Hartford	1	Apr 13	Montreal	5	at Buffalo	1

Boston won series 4-2.   Montreal won series 4-2.

PATRICK DIVISION

Apr 3	New Jersey	3	at Pittsburgh	1	Apr 3	Washington	1	at NY Rangers	2
Apr 5	New Jersey	4	at Pittsburgh	5*	Apr 5	Washington	3	at NY Rangers	0
Apr 7	Pittsburgh	4	at New Jersey	3	Apr 7	NY Rangers	6	at Washington	0
Apr 9	Pittsburgh	1	at New Jersey	4	Apr 9	NY Rangers	4	at Washington	3
Apr 11	New Jersey	4	at Pittsburgh	2	Apr 11	Washington	5	at NY Rangers	4*
Apr 13	Pittsburgh	4	at New Jersey	3	Apr 13	NY Rangers	2	at Washington	4
Apr 15	New Jersey	0	at Pittsburgh	4					

Pittsburgh won series 4-3.   Washington won series 4-2.

NORRIS DIVISION

Apr 4	Minnesota	4	at Chicago	3*	Apr 4	Detroit	6	at St Louis	3
Apr 6	Minnesota	2	at Chicago	5	Apr 6	Detroit	2	at St Louis	4
Apr 8	Chicago	6	at Minnesota	5	Apr 8	St Louis	2	at Detroit	5
Apr 10	Chicago	1	at Minnesota	3	Apr 10	St Louis	3	at Detroit	4
Apr 12	Minnesota	6	at Chicago	0	Apr 12	Detroit	1	at St Louis	6
Apr 14	Chicago	1	at Minnesota	3	Apr 14	St Louis	3	at Detroit	0
					Apr 16	Detroit	2	at St Louis	3

Minnesota won series 4-2.   St Louis won series 4-3.

SMYTHE DIVISION

Apr 4	Vancouver	6	at Los Angeles	5	Apr 4	Edmonton	3	at Calgary	1
Apr 6	Vancouver	2	at Los Angeles	3*	Apr 6	Edmonton	1	at Calgary	3
Apr 8	Los Angeles	1	at Vancouver	2*	Apr 8	Calgary	3	at Edmonton	4
Apr 10	Los Angeles	6	at Vancouver	1	Apr 10	Calgary	2	at Edmonton	5
Apr 12	Vancouver	4	at Los Angeles	7	Apr 12	Edmonton	3	at Calgary	5
Apr 14	Los Angeles	4	at Vancouver	1	Apr 14	Calgary	2	at Edmonton	1*
					Apr 16	Edmonton	5	at Calgary	4*

Los Angeles won series 4-2.   Edmonton won series 4-3.

DIVISION FINALS

ADAMS DIVISION

Apr 17	Montreal	1	at Boston	2
Apr 19	Montreal	4	at Boston	3*
Apr 21	Boston	3	at Montreal	2
Apr 23	Boston	2	at Montreal	6
Apr 25	Montreal	1	at Boston	4
Apr 27	Boston	2	at Montreal	3*
Apr 29	Montreal	1	at Boston	2

Boston won series 4-3.

PATRICK DIVISION

Apr 17	Washington	4	at Pittsburgh	2
Apr 19	Washington	6	at Pittsburgh	7*
Apr 21	Pittsburgh	3	at Washington	1
Apr 23	Pittsburgh	3	at Washington	1
Apr 25	Washington	1	at Pittsburgh	4

Pittsburgh won series 4-1.

NORRIS DIVISION

Apr 18	Minnesota	2	at St Louis	1
Apr 20	Minnesota	2	at St Louis	5
Apr 22	St Louis	1	at Minnesota	5
Apr 24	St Louis	4	at Minnesota	8
Apr 26	Minnesota	2	at St Louis	4
Apr 28	St Louis	2	at Minnesota	3

Minnesota won series 4-2.

SMYTHE DIVISION

Apr 18	Edmonton	3	at Los Angeles	4*
Apr 20	Edmonton	4	at Los Angeles	3†
Apr 22	Los Angeles	3	at Edmonton	4*
Apr 24	Los Angeles	2	at Edmonton	4
Apr 26	Edmonton	2	at Los Angeles	5
Apr 28	Los Angeles	3	at Edmonton	4*

Edmonton won series 4-2.

WALES FINAL

May 1	Pittsburgh	3	at Boston	6
May 3	Pittsburgh	4	at Boston	5*
May 5	Boston	1	at Pittsburgh	4
May 7	Boston	1	at Pittsburgh	4
May 9	Pittsburgh	7	at Boston	2
May 11	Boston	3	at Pittsburgh	5

Pittsburgh won series 4-2.

CAMPBELL FINAL

May 2	Minnesota	3	at Edmonton	1
May 4	Minnesota	2	at Edmonton	7
May 6	Edmonton	3	at Minnesota	7
May 8	Edmonton	1	at Minnesota	5
May 10	Minnesota	3	at Edmonton	2

Minnesota won series 4-1.

STANLEY CUP CHAMPIONSHIP

May 15	Minnesota	5	at Pittsburgh	4
May 17	Minnesota	1	at Pittsburgh	4
May 19	Pittsburgh	1	at Minnesota	3
May 21	Pittsburgh	5	at Minnesota	3
May 23	Minnesota	4	at Pittsburgh	6
May 25	Pittsburgh	8	at Minnesota	0

Pittsburgh won series 4-2.

*Overtime game.   †Double overtime game.

Individual Leaders

SCORING

Player and Team	GP	G	A	Pts	+/–	PM
Mario Lemieux, Pitt	23	16	28	44	14	16
Mark Recchi, Pitt	24	10	24	34	6	33
Kevin Stevens, Pitt	24	17	16	33	14	53
Brian Bellows, Minn	23	10	19	29	6–	30
Dave Gagner, Minn	23	12	15	27	4–	28
Ray Bourque, Bos	19	7	18	25	4–	12
Brian Propp, Minn	23	8	15	23	4–	28
Larry Murphy, Pitt	23	5	18	23	17	44
Neal Broten, Minn	23	9	13	22	2	6
Craig Janney, Bos	18	4	18	22	4–	11
Cam Neely, Bos	19	16	4	20	3–	36
Esa Tikkanen, Edm	18	12	8	20	3	24
Mike Modano, Minn	23	8	12	20	3–	16
Adam Oates, StL	13	7	13	20	7	10
Brett Hull, StL	13	11	8	19	5	4

GOALS

Player and Team	GP	G
Kevin Stevens, Pitt	24	17
Cam Neely, Bos	19	16
Mario Lemieux, Pitt	23	16
Luc Robitaille, LA	12	12
Esa Tikkanen, Edm	18	12
Dave Gagner, Minn	23	12

POWER PLAY GOALS

Player and Team	GP	PP
Cam Neely, Bos	19	9
Brian Propp, Minn	23	8
Kevin Stevens, Pitt	24	7
Brian Bellows, Minn	23	6
Dave Gagner, Minn	23	6
Mario Lemieux, Pitt	23	6

GAME WINNING GOALS

Player and Team	GP	GW
Bobby Smith, Minn	23	5
Cam Neely, Bos	19	4
Ron Francis, Pitt	24	4
Kevin Stevens, Pitt	24	4
Shayne Corson, Mont	13	3
Petr Klima, Edm	18	3
Esa Tikkanen, Edm	18	3
Brian Propp, Minn	23	3

SHORT HAND GOALS

Player and Team	GP	SH
Russ Courtnall, Mont	13	2
Mario Lemieux, Pitt	23	2

ASSISTS

Player and Team	GP	A
Mario Lemieux, Pitt	23	28
Mark Recchi, Pitt	24	24
Brian Bellows, Minn	23	19
Craig Janney, Bos	18	18
Ray Bourque, Bos	19	18
Larry Murphy, Pitt	23	18

PLUS/MINUS

Player and Team	GP	+/–
Joe Mullen, Pitt	22	17
Larry Murphy, Pitt	23	17
Mario Lemieux, Pitt	23	14
Kevin Stevens, Pitt	24	14
Ron Francis, Pitt	24	13
Gordie Roberts, Pitt	24	13
Norm Maciver, Edm	18	10

Goaltending
(Minimum 420 minutes)

GOALS AGAINST AVERAGE

Player and Team	GP	Mins	GA	Avg
Tom Barrasso, Pitt	20	1175	51	2.60
Kelly Hrudey, LA	12	798	37	2.78
Don Beaupre, Wash	11	624	29	2.79
Chris Terreri, NJ	7	428	21	2.94
Mike Vernon, Calg	7	427	21	2.95

SAVE PERCENTAGE

Player and Team	GP	Mins	GA	SA	Pct	W	L
Tom Barrasso, Pitt	20	1175	51	629	.919	12	7
Kelly Hrudey, LA	12	798	37	382	.903	6	6
Chris Terreri, NJ	7	428	21	216	.903	3	4
Don Beaupre, Wash	11	624	29	294	.901	5	5
Patrick Roy, Mont	13	785	40	394	.898	7	5

NHL Awards

Award	Player and Team
Hart Trophy (most valuable player)	Brett Hull, StL
Calder Trophy (rookie of the year)	Ed Belfour, Chi
Vezina Trophy (top goaltender)	Ed Belfour, Chi
Norris Trophy (top defenseman)	Ray Bourque, Bos
Lady Byng Trophy (for gentlemanly play)	Wayne Gretzky, LA
Selke Trophy (top defensive forward)	Dirk Graham, Chi
Adams Award (top coach)	Brian Sutter, StL
Jennings Trophy (best goals against average)	Ed Belfour, Chi
Conn Smythe Trophy (playoff most valuable player)	Mario Lemieux, Pitt

NHL Individual Leaders

Scoring

POINTS

Player and Team	GP	G	A	P	+/−	PM	Player and Team	GP	G	A	P	+/−	PM
Wayne Gretzky, LA	78	41	122	163	30	16	Joe Sakic, Que	80	48	61	109	26−	24
Brett Hull, StL	78	86	45	131	23	22	Steve Yzerman, Det	80	51	57	108	2−	34
Adam Oates, StL	61	25	90	115	15	29	Theo Fleury, Calg	79	51	53	104	48	136
Mark Recchi, Pitt	78	40	73	113	0	48	Al MacInnis, Calg	78	28	75	103	42	90
John Cullen, Pitt-Hart	78	39	71	110	6−	101	Steve Larmer, Chi	80	44	57	101	37	79

GOALS

Player and Team	GP	G
Brett Hull, StL	78	86
Cam Neely, Bos	69	51
Theo Fleury, Calg	79	51
Steve Yzerman, Det	80	51
Mike Gartner, NYR	79	49

GAME WINNING GOALS

Player and Team	GP	GW
Brett Hull, StL	78	11
Jeremy Roenick, Chi	79	10
Mark Recchi, Pitt	78	9
Theo Fleury, Calg	79	9
Steve Larmer, Chi	80	9

ASSISTS

Player and Team	GP	A
Wayne Gretzky, LA	78	122
Adam Oates, StL	61	90
Al MacInnis, Calg	78	75
Ray Bourque, Bos	76	73
Mark Recchi, Pitt	78	73

POWER PLAY GOALS

Player and Team	GP	PP
Brett Hull, StL	78	29
Mike Gartner, NYR	79	22
Joe Nieuwendyk, Calg	79	22
Dave Gagner, Minn	73	20
John MacLean, NJ	78	19

SHORT HAND GOALS

Player and Team	GP	SHG
Dave Reid, Tor	69	8
Theo Fleury, Calg	79	7
Dirk Graham, Chi	80	6
Craig MacTavish, Edm	80	6
Steve Yzerman, Det	80	6

PLUS/MINUS

Player and Team	GP	+/−
Marty McSorley, LA	61	48
Theo Fleury, Calg	79	48
Al MacInnis, Calg	78	42
Jeremy Roenick, Chi	79	38
Steve Larmer, Chi	80	37

Goaltending
(Minimum 25 games)

GOALS AGAINST AVERAGE

Player and Team	GP	Mins	GA	Avg
*Ed Belfour, Chi	74	4127	170	2.47
Don Beaupre, Wash	45	2572	113	2.64
Patrick Roy, Mont	48	2835	128	2.71
Andy Moog, Bos	51	2844	136	2.87
Pete Peeters, Phil	26	1270	61	2.88
Kelly Hrudey, LA	47	2730	132	2.90

* Rookie.

WINS

Player and Team	GP	Mins	W	L	T
*Ed Belfour, Chi	74	4127	43	19	7
Mike Vernon, Calg	54	3121	31	19	3
Tim Cheveldae, Det	65	3615	30	26	5
Vincent Riendeau, StL	44	2671	29	9	6
Tom Barrasso, Pitt	48	2754	27	16	3
Bill Ranford, Edm	60	3415	27	27	3

* Rookie.

SAVE PERCENTAGE

Player and Team	GP	GA	SA	Pct	W	L	T
*Ed Belfour, Chi	74	170	1883	.910	43	19	7
Patrick Roy, Mont	48	128	1362	.906	25	15	6
*Mike Richter, NYR	45	135	1392	.903	21	13	7
Pete Peeters, Phil	26	61	623	.902	9	7	1
Kelly Hrudey, LA	47	132	1321	.900	26	13	6

* Rookie.

SHUTOUTS

Player and Team	GP	Mins	SO	W	L	T
Don Beaupre, Wash	45	2572	5	20	18	3
Andy Moog, Bos	51	2844	4	25	13	9
Bob Essensa, Winn	55	2916	4	19	24	6
*Ed Belfour, Chi	74	4127	4	43	19	7

* Rookie.

Boston Bruins

SCORING

Player	GP	G	A	Pts	+/-	PM
Ray Bourque, D	76	21	73	94	33	75
Craig Janney, C	77	26	66	92	15	8
Cam Neely, R	69	51	40	91	26	98
*Ken Hodge, C	70	30	29	59	11	20
Dave Christian, L	78	32	21	53	8	41
Bob Sweeney, C	80	15	33	48	12	115
Glen Wesley, D	80	11	32	43	0	78
Randy Burridge, L	62	15	13	28	17	40
Petri Skriko, R Van	20	4	4	8	9–	8
Bos	28	5	14	19	4	9
Total	48	9	18	27	5–	17
Garry Galley, D	70	6	21	27	0	84
Jim Wiemer, D	61	4	19	23	3	62
Don Sweeney, D	77	8	13	21	2	67
Dave Poulin, C	31	8	12	20	5	25
*Jeff Lazaro, L	49	5	13	18	7	67
Bob Carpenter, L	29	8	8	16	2	22
Vladimir Ruzicka, C	29	8	8	16	1	19
*Wes Walz, C	56	8	8	16	14–	32
Chris Nilan, R	41	6	9	15	4	277
John Carter, L	50	4	7	11	13–	68
Andy Brickley, L	40	2	9	11	4–	8
Stephane Quintal, D	45	2	6	8	2	89
Allen Pedersen, D	57	2	6	8	15	107
Peter Douris, R	39	5	2	7	12–	9
*Graeme Townshend, L	18	2	5	7	1	12
Nevin Markwart, L	23	3	3	6	0	36
*Ron Hoover, L	15	4	0	4	0	31

GOALTENDING

Player	GP	Mins	Avg	W	L	T	SO
*Matt Delguidice	1	10	.00	0	0	0	0
Andy Moog	51	2844	2.87	25	13	9	4
Rejean Lemelin	33	1829	3.64	17	10	3	1
*Norm Foster	3	184	4.57	2	1	0	0
Team total	80	4872	3.25	44	24	12	5

* Rookie.

Buffalo Sabres

SCORING

Player	GP	G	A	Pts	+/-	PM
Dale Hawerchuk, C	80	31	58	89	2	32
Pierre Turgeon, C	78	32	47	79	14	26
Dave Andreychuk, L	80	36	33	69	11	32
Alexander Mogilny, L	62	30	34	64	14	16
Rick Vaive, R	71	25	27	52	11	74
Christian Ruuttu, C	77	16	34	50	6–	96
Benoit Hogue, C	76	19	28	47	8–	74
Uwe Krupp, D	74	12	32	44	14	66
Grant Ledyard, D	60	8	23	31	13	46
Doug Bodger, D	58	5	23	28	8–	54
Tony Tanti, R Pitt	46	6	12	18	1	44
Buff	10	1	7	8	2	6
Total	56	7	19	26	3	50
Dave Snuggerud, R	80	9	15	24	13–	32
Mikko Makela, L	60	15	7	22	2–	25
Greg Paslawski, R Winn	43	9	10	19	6–	10
Buff	12	2	1	3	0	4
Total	55	11	11	22	6–	14
Mike Ramsey, D	71	6	14	20	14	46
Rob Ray, L	66	8	8	16	11–	348
*Darrin Shannon, L	34	8	6	14	11–	12
Dean Kennedy, D	64	4	8	12	5	119
Mike Hartman, L	60	9	2	11	10–	204
Lou Franceschetti, R Tor	16	1	1	2	2–	30
Buff	35	1	8	9	2	26
Total	51	2	9	11	0	56
*Ken Sutton, D	15	3	6	9	2	13
*Kevin Haller, D	21	1	8	9	9	20

GOALTENDING

Player	GP	Mins	Avg	W	L	T	SO
*Darcy Wakaluk	16	630	3.33	4	5	3	0
Clint Malarchuk	37	2131	3.35	12	14	10	1
Daren Puppa	38	2092	3.38	15	11	6	2
*Dave Littman	1	36	5.00	0	0	0	0
Team total	80	4902	3.40	31	30	19	3

* Rookie.

Calgary Flames

SCORING

Player	GP	G	A	Pts	+/-	PM
Theo Fleury, R	79	51	53	104	48	136
Al MacInnis, D	78	28	75	103	42	90
Joe Nieuwendyk, C	79	45	40	85	19	36
Doug Gilmour, C	78	20	61	81	27	142
Sergei Makarov, R	78	30	49	79	15	44
Gary Suter, D	79	12	58	70	26	102
Gary Roberts, L	80	22	31	53	15	252
*Robert Reichel, C	66	19	22	41	17	22
Joel Otto, C	76	19	20	39	4–	185
Paul Fenton, L Winn	17	4	4	8	4–	18
Tor	30	5	10	15	3–	0
Calg	31	5	7	12	2	10
Total	78	14	21	35	5–	28
*Stephane Matteau, R	78	15	19	34	17	93
Paul Ranheim, L	39	14	16	30	20	4
Carey Wilson, C Hart	45	8	15	23	14–	16
Calg	12	3	3	6	1	2
Total	57	11	18	29	13–	18

Player	GP	G	A	Pts	+/-	PM
Brian MacLellan, L	57	13	14	27	15	55
Frantisek Musil, D Minn	8	0	2	2	0	23
Calg	67	7	14	21	12	160
Total	75	7	16	23	12	183
Jamie Macoun, D	79	7	15	22	29	84
Ric Nattress, D	58	5	13	18	1–	63
Roger Johansson, D	38	4	13	17	9	47
*Tim Sweeney, L	42	7	9	16	1	8
Ronnie Stern, R Vanc	31	2	3	5	14–	171
Calg	13	1	3	4	0	59
Total	44	3	6	9	14–	230

GOALTENDING

Player	GP	Mins	Avg	W	L	T	SO
Rick Wamsley	29	1670	3.05	14	7	5	0
Mike Vernon	54	3121	3.31	31	19	3	1
Steve Guenette	1	60	4.00	1	0	0	0
Team total	80	4859	3.25	46	26	8	1

* Rookie.

Chicago Blackhawks

SCORING

Player	GP	G	A	Pts	+/-	PM
Steve Larmer, R	80	44	57	101	37	79
Jeremy Roenick, C	79	41	53	94	38	80
Michel Goulet, R	74	27	38	65	27	65
Chris Chelios, D	77	12	52	64	23	192
Steve Thomas, L	69	19	35	54	8	129
Adam Creighton, C	72	22	29	51	0	135
Dirk Graham, R	80	24	21	45	12	86
Doug Wilson, D	51	11	29	40	25	32
Troy Murray, C	75	14	23	37	13	74
Tony McKegney, L Que	50	17	16	33	25-	44
Chi	9	0	1	1	2-	4
Total	59	17	17	34	27-	48
Wayne Presley, R	71	15	19	34	11	122
Dave Manson, D	75	14	15	29	20	191
Greg Gilbert, L	72	10	15	25	6	58
Mike Hudson, C	55	7	9	16	5	62
Trent Yawney, D	61	3	13	16	6	77
Paul Gillis, C Que	49	3	8	11	19-	91
Chi	13	0	5	5	1	53
Total	62	3	13	16	18-	144

Player	GP	G	A	Pts	+/-	PM
*Frantisek Kucera, D	40	2	12	14	3	32
Jocelyn Lemieux, R	67	6	7	13	7-	119
Keith Brown, D	45	1	10	11	9	55
Steve Konroyd, D	70	0	11	11	11	40
Bob McGill, D	77	4	5	9	8	153
*Mike Peluso, L	53	6	1	7	3-	320
*Ed Belfour, G	74	0	3	3	0	34
*Stu Grimson, L	35	0	1	1	3-	183

GOALTENDING

Player	GP	Mins	Avg	W	L	T	SO
Jim Waite	1	60	2.00	1	0	0	0
*Dominic Hasek	5	195	2.46	3	0	1	0
*Ed Belfour	74	4127	2.47	43	19	7	4
Jacques Cloutier	10	403	3.57	2	3	0	0
Greg Millen	3	58	4.14	0	1	0	0
Team total	80	4846	2.61	49	23	8	4

* Rookie.

Detroit Red Wings

SCORING

Player	GP	G	A	Pts	+/-	PM
Steve Yzerman, C	80	51	57	108	2-	34
*Sergei Fedorov, C	77	31	48	79	11	66
Kevin Miller, C NYR	63	17	27	44	1	63
Det	11	5	1	6	4-	4
Total	74	22	28	50	3-	67
Shawn Burr, L	80	20	30	50	14	112
Yves Racine, D	62	7	40	47	1	33
Jimmy Carson, C	64	21	25	46	3	28
*Paul Ysebaert, L NJ	11	4	3	7	1	6
Det	51	15	18	33	8-	16
Total	62	19	21	40	7-	22
Dave Barr, R	70	18	22	40	19	55
*Johan Garpenlov, L	71	18	21	39	4-	18
Bob Probert, R	55	16	23	39	3-	315
Doug Crossman, D NYI	16	1	6	7	4-	12
Hart	41	4	19	23	13-	19
Det	17	3	4	7	6-	17
Total	74	8	29	37	23-	48
Brent Fedyk, R	67	16	19	35	21	38
Gerard Gallant, L	45	10	16	26	6	111
Rick Zombo, D	77	4	19	23	2-	57
Steve Chiasson, D	42	3	17	20	0	80
Marc Habscheid, C	46	9	8	17	10-	22
Rick Green, D	65	2	14	16	10	24

GOALTENDING

Player	GP	Mins	Avg	W	L	T	SO
*Scott King	1	45	2.67	0	0	0	0
Glen Hanlon	19	862	3.20	4	6	3	0
Tim Cheveldae	65	3615	3.55	30	26	5	2
Allan Bester	3	178	4.38	0	3	0	0
Alain Chevrier	3	108	6.11	0	2	0	0
*David Gagnon	2	35	10.29	0	1	0	0
Team total	80	4854	3.68	34	38	8	2

* Rookie.

Edmonton Oilers

SCORING

Player	GP	G	A	Pts	+/-	PM
Esa Tikkanen, L	79	27	42	69	22	85
Petr Klima, L	70	40	28	68	24	113
Mark Messier, C	53	12	51	63	15	34
Joe Murphy, R	80	27	35	62	2	35
Craig Simpson, L	75	30	27	57	8-	66
Glenn Anderson, R	74	24	31	55	7-	59
Steve Smith, D	77	13	41	54	14	193
Martin Gelinas, L	73	20	20	40	7-	34
Ken Linseman, C	56	7	29	36	15	94
Craig MacTavish, C	80	17	15	32	1-	76
Anatoli Semenov, L	57	15	16	31	17	26
Charlie Huddy, D	53	5	22	27	4	32
Adam Graves, C	76	7	18	25	21-	127
Chris Joseph, D	49	5	17	22	3	59
Kevin Lowe, D	73	3	13	16	9-	113
Geoff Smith, D	59	1	12	13	13	55
Mark Lamb, C	37	4	8	12	2-	25
Jeff Beukeboom, D	67	3	7	10	6	150
Craig Muni, D	76	1	9	10	10	77
Dave Brown, R	58	3	4	7	7-	160
Norm Maciver, D	21	2	5	7	1	14
Kelly Buchberger, L	64	3	1	4	6-	160
Bill Ranford, G	60	0	4	4	0	6

GOALTENDING

Player	GP	Mins	Avg	W	L	T	SO
Grant Fuhr	13	778	3.01	6	4	3	1
Bill Ranford	60	3415	3.20	27	27	3	0
Kari Takko	11	529	4.20	4	4	0	0
Eldon Reddick	2	120	4.50	0	2	0	0
Team total	80	4850	3.36	37	37	6	1

Hartford Whalers

SCORING

Player	GP	G	A	Pts	+/–	PM
John Cullen, C Hart	13	8	8	16	6–	18
Pitt	65	31	63	94	0	83
Total	78	39	71	110	6–	101
Pat Verbeek, R	80	43	39	82	0	246
Rob Brown, R Pitt	25	6	10	16	0	31
Hart	44	18	24	42	7–	101
Total	69	24	34	58	7–	132
Zarley Zalapski, D Pitt	66	12	36	48	15	59
Hart	11	3	3	6	7–	6
Total	77	15	39	54	8	65
Kevin Dineen, R	61	17	30	47	15–	104
*Bobby Holik, L	78	21	22	43	3–	113
Mark Hunter, R Calg	57	10	15	25	1–	125
Hart	11	4	3	7	3	40
Total	68	14	18	32	2	165
Brad Shaw, D	72	4	28	32	10–	29
Todd Krygier, L	72	13	17	30	1	95
Dean Evason, C	75	6	23	29	6–	170
Paul Cyr, L	70	12	13	25	8–	107
Sylvain Cote, D	73	7	12	19	17–	17
Mike Tomlak, L	64	8	8	16	9–	55
Randy Cunneyworth, L	32	9	5	14	6–	49
Mikael Andersson, L	41	4	7	11	0	8
Adam Burt, D	42	2	7	9	4–	63
*Jim McKenzie, L	41	4	3	7	7–	108
Doug Houda, D Det	22	0	4	4	2–	41
Hart	19	1	2	3	3–	41
Total	41	1	6	7	5–	82
*Terry Yake, C	19	1	4	5	3–	10

GOALTENDING

Player	GP	Mins	Avg	W	L	T	SO
*Daryl Reaugh	20	1010	3.15	7	7	1	1
Peter Sidorkiewicz	52	2953	3.33	21	22	7	1
*Kay Whitmore	18	850	3.67	3	9	3	0
*Ross McKay	1	35	5.14	0	0	0	0
Team total	80	4867	3.40	31	38	11	2

* Rookie.

Minnesota North Stars

SCORING

Player	GP	G	A	Pts	+/–	PM
Dave Gagner, C	73	40	42	82	9	114
Brian Bellows, L	80	35	40	75	13–	43
Brian Propp, L	79	26	47	73	7	58
Neal Broten, C	79	13	56	69	3–	26
Mike Modano, R	79	28	36	64	2	65
Bobby Smith, C	73	15	31	46	9–	60
Ulf Dahlen, R	66	21	18	39	7	6
Mark Tinordi, D	69	5	27	32	1	191
Doug Smail, L Winn	15	1	2	3	6–	10
Minn	57	7	13	20	2–	38
Total	72	8	15	23	8–	48
Brian Glynn, D	66	8	11	19	5–	83
Gaetan Duchesne, L	68	9	9	18	4	18
Perry Berezan, C	52	11	6	17	2–	26
Jim Johnson, D Pitt	24	0	5	5	3–	23
Minn	44	1	9	10	9	100
Total	68	1	14	15	6	123
Curt Giles, D	70	4	10	14	3	48
*Mike Craig, R	39	8	4	12	11–	32

Player	GP	G	A	Pts	+/–	PM
Chris Dahlquist, D Pitt	22	1	2	3	0	30
Minn	42	2	6	8	1–	33
Total	64	3	8	11	1–	63
Neil Wilkinson, D	50	2	9	11	5–	117
Stewart Gavin, L	38	4	4	8	3–	36
Rob Zettler, D	47	1	4	5	10–	109
Shane Churla, R	40	2	2	4	1	284
Shawn Chambers, D	29	1	3	4	2	24
Basil McRae, L	40	1	3	4	8–	224
Jon Casey, G	55	0	2	2	0	22

GOALTENDING

Player	GP	Mins	Avg	W	L	T	SO
Jon Casey	55	3185	2.98	21	20	11	3
Brian Hayward	26	1473	3.14	6	15	3	2
Kari Takko	2	119	6.05	0	2	0	0
Jarmo Myllys	2	78	6.15	0	2	0	0
Team total	80	4876	3.27	27	39	14	5

* Rookie.

Los Angeles Kings

SCORING

Player	GP	G	A	Pts	+/–	PM
Wayne Gretzky, C	78	41	122	163	30	16
Luc Robitaille, L	76	45	46	91	28	68
Tomas Sandstrom, R	68	45	44	89	27	106
Tony Granato, L	68	30	34	64	22	156
Steve Duchesne, D	78	21	41	62	19	66
Todd Elik, C	74	21	37	58	20	58
Dave Taylor, R	73	23	30	53	27	148
*Rob Blake, D	75	12	34	46	3	125
Marty McSorley, D	61	7	32	39	48	221
Bob Kudelski, R	72	23	13	36	9	46
Brian Benning, D	61	7	24	31	12	123
John Tonelli, L	71	14	16	30	3	49
Steve Kasper, C	67	9	19	28	3	33
Larry Robinson, D	62	1	22	23	22	16
Brad Jones, L	53	9	11	20	11	57
Jay Miller, L	66	8	12	20	9	259
Ilkka Sinisalo, R Minn	46	5	12	17	10–	24
LA	7	0	0	0	4	2
Total	53	5	12	17	6–	26
John McIntyre, C Tor	13	0	3	3	0	25
LA	56	8	5	13	6	115
Total	69	8	8	16	6	140
Mike Donnelly, L	53	7	5	12	3	41
Rod Buskas, D	57	3	8	11	14	180
Scott Bjugstad, L	31	2	4	6	5–	12
*Frank Breault, R	17	1	4	5	1–	6
Bob Halkidis, D	34	1	3	4	8	133
Tim Watters, D	45	0	4	4	7	92
Daniel Berthiaume, G	37	0	0	0	0	10
Kelly Hrudey, G	47	0	0	0	0	14

GOALTENDING

Player	GP	Mins	Avg	W	L	T	SO
Kelly Hrudey	47	2730	2.90	26	13	6	3
Daniel Berthiaume	37	2119	3.31	20	11	4	1
Team total	80	4863	3.13	46	24	10	4

*Rookie.

Montreal Canadiens

SCORING

Player	GP	G	A	Pts	+/−	PM
Russ Courtnall, R	79	26	50	76	5	29
Stephane Richer, R	75	31	30	61	0	53
Denis Savard, C	70	28	31	59	1−	52
Stephan Lebeau, C	73	22	31	53	4	24
Shayne Corson, L	71	23	24	47	9	138
Guy Carbonneau, C	78	20	24	44	1−	63
Mike McPhee, L	64	22	21	43	6	56
Mike Keane, R	73	13	23	36	6	50
Brian Skrudland, C	57	15	19	34	12	85
Matt Schneider, D	69	10	20	30	7	63
Petr Svoboda, D	60	4	22	26	5	52
Eric Desjardins, D	62	7	18	25	7	27
*Andrew Cassels, C	54	6	19	25	2	20
Sylvain Lefebvre, D	63	5	18	23	11−	30
*Tom Chorske, L	57	9	11	20	8−	32
J. J. Daigneault, D	51	3	16	19	2−	31
Brent Gilchrist, C	51	6	9	15	3−	10
Donald Dufresne, D	53	2	13	15	5	55
Sylvain Turgeon, L	19	5	6	11	2−	20
Alain Cote, D	28	0	6	6	8	24
Todd Ewen, R	28	3	2	5	4	128
*Benoit Brunet, L	17	1	3	4	1−	0
Patrick Roy, G	48	0	2	2	0	6
*Lyle Odelein, D	52	0	2	2	7	259
*J. C. Bergeron, G	18	0	1	1	0	0
*Andre Racicot, G	21	0	1	1	0	0
Ryan Walter, C	25	0	1	1	3−	12

GOALTENDING

Player	GP	Mins	Avg	W	L	T	SO
Patrick Roy	48	2835	2.71	25	15	6	1
*Andre Racicot	21	975	3.20	7	9	2	1
*Frederic Chabot	3	108	3.33	0	0	1	0
*J. C. Bergeron	18	941	3.76	7	6	2	0
Team total	80	4896	3.07	39	30	11	2

* Rookie.

New Jersey Devils

SCORING

Player	GP	G	A	Pts	+/−	PM
John MacLean, R	78	45	33	78	8	150
Kirk Muller, L	80	19	51	70	1	76
Brendan Shanahan, R	75	29	37	66	4	141
Peter Stastny, C	77	18	42	60	0	53
Claude Lemieux, R	78	30	17	47	8−	105
Patrik Sundstrom, C	71	15	31	46	7	48
Bruce Driver, D	73	9	36	45	11	62
Alexei Kasatonov, D	78	10	31	41	23	76
*Eric Weinrich, D	76	4	34	38	10	48
Doug Brown, R	58	14	16	30	18	4
*Jon Morris, C	53	9	19	28	9	27
*Zdeno Ciger, L	45	8	17	25	3	8
David Maley, L	64	8	14	22	9	151
Laurie Boschman, C	78	11	9	20	1−	79
Ken Daneyko, D	80	4	16	20	10−	249
Viacheslav Fetisov, D	67	3	16	19	5	62
Pat Conacher, L	49	5	11	16	9	27
Lee Norwood, D Det	21	3	7	10	6	50
NJ	28	3	2	5	1−	87
Total	49	6	9	15	5	137
Tommy Albelin, D	47	2	12	14	1	44
*Troy Crowder, R	59	6	3	9	10−	182
Al Stewart, L	41	5	2	7	6−	159
*Myles O'Connor, D	22	3	1	4	3	41
Chris Terreri, G	53	0	3	3	0	2
Sean Burke, G	35	0	0	0	0	18

GOALTENDING

Player	GP	Mins	Avg	W	L	T	SO
Chris Terreri	53	2970	2.91	24	21	7	1
Sean Burke	35	1870	3.59	8	12	8	0
Roland Melanson	1	20	6.00	0	0	0	0
Team total	80	4876	3.25	32	33	15	1

* Rookie.

New York Islanders

SCORING

Player	GP	G	A	Pts	+/−	PM
Pat LaFontaine, C	75	41	44	85	6−	42
David Volek, L	77	22	34	56	10−	57
Brent Sutter, C	75	21	32	53	8−	49
Patrick Flatley, R	56	20	25	45	2−	74
Derek King, L	66	19	26	45	1	44
Randy Wood, L	76	24	18	42	12−	45
Ray Ferraro, C Hart	15	2	5	7	1−	18
NYI	61	19	16	35	11−	52
Total	76	21	21	42	12−	70
Jeff Norton, D	44	3	25	28	13−	16
*Bill Berg, L	78	9	14	23	3−	67
Gary Nylund, D	72	2	21	23	8−	105
Wayne McBean, D	52	5	14	19	21−	47
Joe Reekie, D	66	3	16	19	17	96
Brad Dalgarno, R	41	3	12	15	10−	24
Dave Chyzowski, L	56	5	9	14	19−	61
Hubie McDonough, C	52	6	6	12	14−	10
Brad Lauer, L	44	4	8	12	6−	45
John Tucker, C Buff	18	1	3	4	0	4
NYI	20	3	4	7	1−	4
Total	38	4	7	11	1−	8

Player	GP	G	A	Pts	+/−	PM
Tom Fitzgerald, R	41	5	5	10	9−	42
Craig Ludwig, D	75	1	8	9	24−	77
Ken Baumgartner, L	78	1	6	7	14−	282
Mick Vukota, R	60	2	4	6	13−	238
Richard Pilon, D	60	1	4	5	12−	126
*Greg Parks, C	20	1	2	3	0	4
Dean Chynoweth, D	25	1	1	2	6−	59
Glenn Healy, G	53	0	2	2	0	14
Jeff Hackett, G	30	0	0	0	0	4

GOALTENDING

Player	GP	Mins	Avg	W	L	T	SO
Mark Fitzpatrick	2	120	3.00	1	1	0	0
Glenn Healy	53	2999	3.32	18	24	9	0
Jeff Hackett	30	1508	3.62	5	18	1	0
*Danny Lorenz	2	80	3.75	0	1	0	0
*George Maneluk	4	140	6.43	1	1	0	0
Team total	80	4867	3.58	25	45	10	0

* Rookie.

New York Rangers

SCORING

Player	GP	G	A	Pts	+/–	PM
Brian Leetch, D	80	16	72	88	2	42
Bernie Nicholls, C	71	25	48	73	5	96
Mike Gartner, R	79	49	20	69	9–	53
Darren Turcotte, C	74	26	41	67	5–	37
Brian Mullen, R	79	19	43	62	12	44
James Patrick, D	74	10	49	59	5–	58
John Ogrodnick, L	79	31	23	54	15	10
Ray Sheppard, R	59	24	23	47	8	21
Kelly Kisio, C	51	15	20	35	3	58
Kris King, L	72	11	14	25	1–	156
Jan Erixon, L	53	7	18	25	13	8
Randy Moller, D	61	4	19	23	13	161
Troy Mallette, L	71	12	10	22	8–	252
Mark Janssens, C	67	9	7	16	1–	172
Jody Hull, R	47	5	8	13	2	10
Joe Cirella, D Que	39	2	10	12	28–	59
NYR	19	1	0	1	1	52
Total	58	3	10	13	27–	111
David Shaw, D	77	2	10	12	8	89
Paul Broten, R	28	4	6	10	7	18
Normand Rochefort, D	44	3	7	10	10	35
Joey Kocur, R Det	52	5	4	9	6–	253
NYR	5	0	0	0	1–	36
Total	57	5	4	9	7–	289
Miloslav Horava, D	29	1	6	7	2	12
Mark Hardy, D	70	1	5	6	1–	89
John Vanbiesbrouck, G	40	0	3	3	0	18
*Tie Domi, R	28	1	0	1	5–	185
*Mike Richter, G	45	0	1	1	0	4

GOALTENDING

Player	GP	Mins	Avg	W	L	T	SO
*Mike Richter	45	2596	3.12	21	13	7	0
John Vanbiesbrouck	40	2257	3.35	15	18	6	3
Team total	80	4872	3.26	36	31	13	3

* Rookie.

Philadelphia Flyers

SCORING

Player	GP	G	A	Pts	+/–	PM
Rick Tocchet, R	70	40	31	71	2	150
Per-Erik Eklund, C	73	19	50	69	2–	14
Murray Craven, L	77	19	47	66	2–	53
Ron Sutter, C	80	17	28	45	2	92
Gord Murphy, D	80	11	31	42	7–	58
*Mike Ricci, C	68	21	20	41	8–	64
Scott Mellanby, R	74	20	21	41	8	155
Keith Acton, C	76	14	23	37	9–	131
Terry Carkner, D	79	7	25	32	15–	204
Normand Lacombe, R	74	11	20	31	1–	27
Kjell Samuelsson, D	78	9	19	28	4	82
*Mark Pederson, L Mont	47	8	15	23	3	18
Phil	12	2	1	3	8–	5
Total	59	10	16	26	5–	23
Jiri Latal, D	50	5	21	26	19–	14
Tim Kerr, R	27	10	14	24	8–	8
Derrick Smith, L	72	11	10	21	0	37
*Dale Kushner, L	63	7	11	18	4–	195
Craig Berube, L	74	8	9	17	6–	293
*Murray Baron, D	67	8	8	16	3–	74
*Martin Hostak, C	50	3	10	13	1	22
Mark Howe, D	19	0	10	10	9	8
Tony Horacek, L	34	3	6	9	6	49
Jeff Chychrun, D	36	0	6	6	1	105
Dave Fenyves, D	40	1	4	5	1	28
*Pat Murray, L	16	2	1	3	5–	15
Chris Jensen, R	18	2	1	3	5–	2
*Scott Sandelin, D	15	0	3	3	2–	0

GOALTENDING

Player	GP	Mins	Avg	W	L	T	SO
Pete Peeters	26	1270	2.88	9	7	1	1
Ron Hextall	36	2035	3.13	13	16	5	0
Ken Wregget	30	1484	3.56	10	14	3	0
*Bruce Hoffort	2	39	4.62	1	0	1	0
Team total	80	4853	3.30	33	37	10	1

* Rookie.

Pittsburgh Penguins

SCORING

Player	GP	G	A	Pts	+/–	PM
Mark Recchi, R	78	40	73	113	0	48
Paul Coffey, D	76	24	69	93	18–	128
Ron Francis, C Hart	67	21	55	76	2–	51
Pitt	14	2	9	11	0	21
Total	81	23	64	87	2–	72
Kevin Stevens, L	80	40	46	86	1–	133
*Jaromir Jagr, R	80	27	30	57	4–	42
Mario Lemieux, C	26	19	26	45	8	30
Larry Murphy, D Minn	31	4	11	15	8–	38
Pitt	44	5	23	28	2	30
Total	75	9	34	43	6–	68
Bob Errey, L	79	20	22	42	11	115
Scott Young, R Hart	34	6	9	15	9–	8
Pitt	43	11	16	27	3	33
Total	77	17	25	42	6–	41
Joe Mullen, R	47	17	22	39	9	6
Phil Bourque, L	78	20	14	34	7	106
Bryan Trottier, C	52	9	19	28	5	24
Ulf Samuelsson, D Hart	62	3	18	21	13	174
Pitt	14	1	4	5	4	37
Total	76	4	22	26	17	211
Randy Gilhen, C	72	15	10	25	3	51
Jiri Hrdina, C Calg	14	0	3	3	4–	4
Pitt	37	6	14	20	2–	13
Total	51	6	17	23	6–	17
*Paul Stanton, D	75	5	18	23	11	40
Troy Loney, L	44	7	9	16	10	85

GOALTENDING

Player	GP	Mins	Avg	W	L	T	SO
Tom Barrasso	48	2754	3.59	27	16	3	1
Frank Pietrangelo	25	1311	3.94	10	11	1	0
Wendell Young	18	773	4.04	4	6	2	0
Team total	80	4843	3.78	41	33	6	1

* Rookie.

Quebec Nordiques

SCORING

Player	GP	G	A	Pts	+/–	PM
Joe Sakic, C	80	48	61	109	26–	24
*Mats Sundin, R	80	23	36	59	24–	58
Tony Hrkac, C	70	16	32	48	22–	16
*Stephane Morin, C	48	13	27	40	6	28
Mike Hough, R	63	13	20	33	7–	111
Bryan Fogarty, D	45	9	22	31	11–	24
Guy Lafleur, R	59	12	16	28	10–	2
Steven Finn, D	71	6	13	19	26–	228
Craig Wolanin, D	80	5	13	18	13–	89
Scott Pearson, L Tor	12	0	0	0	5–	20
Que	35	11	4	15	4–	84
Total	47	11	4	15	9–	104
Shawn Anderson, D	31	3	10	13	2	21
*Owen Nolan, R	59	3	10	13	19–	109
Alexei Gusarov, D	36	3	9	12	4–	12
Randy Velischek, D	79	2	10	12	19–	42
*Mike McNeill, C Chi	23	2	2	4	1–	6
Que	14	2	5	7	5	4
Total	37	4	7	11	4	10
Everett Sanipass, L	29	5	5	10	15–	41
Herb Raglan, R StL	32	3	3	6	4	52
Que	15	1	3	4	1	30
Total	47	4	6	10	5	82
Curtis Leschyshyn, D	55	3	7	10	19–	49

GOALTENDING

Player	GP	Mins	Avg	W	L	T	SO
*Stephane Fiset	3	186	3.87	0	2	1	0
Ron Tugnutt	56	3145	4.04	12	29	10	0
*John Tanner	6	228	4.21	1	3	1	0
Jacques Cloutier	15	828	4.42	3	8	2	0
*Scott Gordon	13	484	5.95	0	8	0	0
Team total	80	4883	4.35	16	50	14	0

* Rookie.

St. Louis Blues

SCORING

Player	GP	G	A	Pts	+/–	PM
Brett Hull, R	78	86	45	131	23	22
Adam Oates, C	61	25	90	115	15	29
Dan Quinn, C Van	64	18	31	49	28–	46
StL	14	4	7	11	5–	20
Total	78	22	38	60	33–	66
Jeff Brown, D	67	12	47	59	4	39
Rod Brind'Amour, C	78	17	32	49	2	93
Scott Stevens, D	78	5	44	49	23	150
Dave Lowry, L	79	19	21	40	19	168
Ron Wilson, D	73	10	27	37	1–	54
Paul Cavallini, D	67	10	25	35	19	89
Gino Cavallini, L	78	8	27	35	4	81
Bob Bassen, C	79	16	18	34	17	183
Rich Sutter, R	77	16	11	27	6	122
Garth Butcher, D Van	69	6	12	18	18–	257
StL	13	0	4	4	4	32
Total	82	6	16	22	14–	289
Glen Featherstone, D	68	5	15	20	19	204
Paul MacLean, R	37	6	11	17	2–	24
Mario Marois, D	64	2	14	16	17	81
Steve Tuttle, R	20	3	6	9	2	2
Darin Kimble, R Que	35	2	5	7	5–	114
StL	26	1	1	2	2	128
Total	61	3	6	9	3–	242
Tom Tilley, D	22	2	4	6	5	4
Harold Snepsts, D	54	1	4	5	3	50

GOALTENDING

Player	GP	Mins	Avg	W	L	T	SO
Vincent Riendeau	44	2671	3.01	29	9	6	3
*Pat Jablonski	8	492	3.05	2	3	3	0
*Curtis Joseph	30	1710	3.12	16	10	2	0
Team total	80	4877	3.08	47	22	11	3

* Rookie.

Toronto Maple Leafs

SCORING

Player	GP	G	A	Pts	+/–	PM
Vincent Damphousse, L	79	26	47	73	31–	65
Dave Ellett, D Winn	17	4	7	11	4–	6
Tor	60	8	30	38	4–	69
Total	77	12	37	49	8–	75
Mike Krushelnyski, C LA	15	1	5	6	7	10
Tor	59	17	22	39	6–	48
Total	74	18	27	45	1	58
Brian Bradley, C Van	44	11	20	31	2–	42
Tor	26	0	11	11	7–	20
Total	70	11	31	42	9–	62
Peter Zezel, C Wash	20	7	5	12	13–	10
Tor	32	14	14	28	7–	4
Total	52	21	19	40	20–	14
Michel Petit, D Que	19	4	7	11	15–	47
Tor	54	9	19	28	19–	132
Total	73	13	26	39	34–	179
Wendel Clark, L	63	18	16	34	5–	152
Dave Hannan, C	74	11	23	34	9–	82
Rob Ramage, D	80	10	24	34	2	173
Dan Marois, R	78	21	9	30	16–	112
Gary Leeman, R	52	17	12	29	25–	39
Dave Reid, L	69	15	13	28	10–	18
Lucien Deblois, C Que	14	2	2	4	1	13
Tor	38	10	12	22	4–	30
Total	52	12	14	26	3–	43
Bob Rouse, D Wash	47	5	15	20	7–	65
Tor	13	2	4	6	11–	10
Total	60	7	19	26	18–	75
Mike Foligno, R Buff	31	4	5	9	4	42
Tor	37	8	7	15	3–	65
Total	68	12	12	24	1	107

GOALTENDING

Player	GP	Mins	Avg	W	L	T	SO
*Damian Rhodes	1	60	1.00	1	0	0	0
*Peter Ing	56	3126	3.84	16	29	8	1
Jeff Reese	30	1430	3.86	6	13	3	1
Allan Bester	6	247	4.37	0	4	0	0
Team total	80	4874	3.91	23	46	11	2

* Rookie.

Vancouver Canucks

SCORING

Player	GP	G	A	Pts	+/-	PM
Trevor Linden, R	80	33	36	69	25–	65
Geoff Courtnall, L StL	66	27	30	57	19	56
Van	11	6	2	8	3–	8
Total	77	33	32	65	16	64
Greg Adams, L	55	21	24	45	5–	10
Cliff Ronning, C StL	48	14	18	32	2	10
Van	11	6	6	12	2–	0
Total	59	20	24	44	0	10
Dave Capuano, L	61	13	31	44	1	42
Doug Lidster, D	78	6	32	38	6–	77
Sergio Momesso, L StL	59	10	18	28	12	131
Van	11	6	2	8	1	43
Total	70	16	20	36	13	174
Igor Larionov, C	64	13	21	34	3–	14
Steve Bozek, L	62	15	17	32	6–	22
*Robert Kron, L	76	12	20	32	11–	21
Jyrki Lumme, D	80	5	27	32	15–	59
Tom Kurvers, D Tor	19	0	3	3	12–	8
Van	32	4	23	27	13–	20
Total	51	4	26	30	25–	28
*Garry Valk, R	59	10	11	21	23–	67
*Jay Mazur, R	36	11	7	18	3	14
*Petr Nedved, C	61	10	6	16	21–	20
Stan Smyl, R	45	2	12	14	5–	87
Jim Sandlak, R	59	7	6	13	20–	125

GOALTENDING

Player	GP	Mins	Avg	W	L	T	SO
*Troy Gamble	47	2433	3.45	16	16	6	1
Kirk McLean	41	1969	3.99	10	22	3	0
Bob Mason	6	353	4.93	2	4	0	0
*Steve McKichan	1	20	6.00	0	0	0	0
Steve Weeks	1	59	6.10	0	1	0	0
Team total	80	4856	3.89	28	43	9	1

* Rookie.

Washington Capitals

SCORING

Player	GP	G	A	Pts	+/-	PM
Kevin Hatcher, D	79	24	50	74	10–	69
Mike Ridley, C	79	23	48	71	9	26
Michal Pivonka, C	79	20	49	69	3	34
John Druce, R	80	22	36	58	4	46
Calle Johansson, D	80	11	41	52	2–	23
Kelly Miller, L	80	24	26	50	10	29
Dale Hunter, C	76	16	30	46	22–	234
Dino Ciccarelli, R	54	21	18	39	17–	66
Al Iafrate, D Tor	42	3	15	18	15–	113
Wash	30	6	8	14	1–	124
Total	72	9	23	32	16–	237
Stephen Leach, R	68	11	19	30	9–	99
*Peter Bondra, R	54	12	16	28	0–	47
*Dimitri Khristich, L	40	13	14	27	1–	21
*Mikhail Tatarinov, D	65	8	15	23	4–	82
Nick Kypreos, L	79	9	9	18	4–	196
Dave Tippett, C	61	6	9	15	13–	24
Tim Bergland, C	47	5	9	14	1–	21
Alan May, L	67	4	6	10	0–	264
*Ken Sabourin, D Calg	16	1	3	4	9	36
Wash	28	1	4	5	6	81
Total	44	2	7	9	15	117
Rod Langway, D	56	1	7	8	12	24
Bob Joyce, L	17	3	3	6	3	8
Mike Lalor, D	68	1	5	6	23–	61
Rob Murray, C	17	0	3	3	0	19

GOALTENDING

Player	GP	Mins	Avg	W	L	T	SO
Don Beaupre	45	2572	2.64	20	18	3	5
*Jim Hrivnak	9	432	3.61	4	2	1	0
Mike Liut	35	1834	3.73	13	16	3	0
Team total	80	4850	3.19	37	36	7	5

* Rookie.

Winnipeg Jets

SCORING

Player	GP	G	A	Pts	+/-	PM
Phil Housley, D	78	23	53	76	13–	24
Ed Olczyk, C Tor	18	4	10	14	7–	13
Winn	61	26	31	57	20–	69
Total	79	30	41	71	27–	82
Thomas Steen, C	58	19	48	67	3–	49
Pat Elynuik, R	80	31	34	65	13–	73
Fredrik Olausson, D	71	12	29	41	22–	24
Paul MacDermid, R	69	15	21	36	6–	128
Brent Ashton, L	61	12	24	36	10–	58
Doug Evans, L	70	7	27	34	1–	108
Teppo Numminen, D	80	8	25	33	15–	28
Randy Carlyle, D	52	9	19	28	6	44
Dave McLlwain, R	60	14	11	25	13–	46
*Danton Cole, C	66	13	11	24	14–	24
Moe Mantha, D	57	9	15	24	20–	33
Phil Sykes, L	70	12	10	22	9–	59
Mark Osborne, L Tor	18	3	6	9	6–	4
Winn	37	8	8	16	1–	59
Total	55	11	11	22	11–	63
Scott Arniel, C	75	5	17	22	12–	87

Player	GP	G	A	Pts	+/-	PM
Mark Kumpel, R	53	7	3	10	10–	10
Mike Eagles, C	44	0	9	9	10–	79
Gord Donnelly, D	57	3	4	7	13–	265
Shawn Cronin, D	67	1	5	6	10–	189
*Bryan Marchment, D	28	2	2	4	5–	91
Don Barber, L Minn	7	0	0	0	3–	4
Winn	16	1	2	3	3–	14
Total	23	1	2	3	6–	18
Bob Essensa, G	55	0	3	3	0	6
*Steph Beauregard, G	16	0	1	1	0	2
*Rick Tabaracci, G	24	0	1	1	0	8

GOALTENDING

Player	GP	Mins	Avg	W	L	T	SO
Bob Essensa	55	2916	3.15	19	24	6	4
*Rick Tabaracci	24	1093	3.90	4	9	4	1
*Steph Beauregard	16	836	3.95	3	10	1	0
Team total	80	4860	3.56	26	43	11	5

* Rookie.

NHL All-Star Game

	1	2	2	—	5
Wales	1	2	2	—	5
Campbell	2	5	4	—	11

Wales: Goal: Patrick Roy, Mont; Andy Moog, Bos. Defense: Ray Bourque, Bos; Paul Coffey, Pitt; Garry Galley, Bos; Kevin Hatcher, Wash; Uwe Krupp, Buff; Brian Leetch, NYR. Centers: Joe Sakic, Que; John Cullen, Pitt; Pat LaFontaine, NYI; Brian Skrudland, Mont; Darren Turcotte, NYR. Wingers: Cam Neely, Bos; Rick Tocchet, Phil; John MacLean, NJ; Chris Nilan, Bos; Mark Recchi, Pitt; Kevin Stevens, Pitt; Pat Verbeek, Hart. (Dave Christian, Bos, replaced Nilan, who was injured. Denis Savard, Mont, replaced Skrudland, who was injured. NHL added Guy Lafleur, Que.)

Campbell: Goal: Mike Vernon, Calg; Bill Ranford, Edm. Defense: Chris Chelios, Chi; Al MacInnis, Calg; Phil Housley, Winn; Steve Smith, Edm; Scott Stevens, StL; Gary Suter, Calg. Centers: Wayne Gretzky, LA; Theo Fleury, Calg; Dave Gagner, Minn; Mark Messier, Edm; Jeremy Roenick, Chi; Steve Yzerman, Det. Wingers: Brett Hull, StL; Luc Robitaille, LA; Vincent Damphousse, Tor; Steve Larmer, Chi; Trevor Linden, Van; Tomas Sandstrom, LA. (Adam Oates, StL, replaced Hull, who was injured. NHL added Bobby Smith, Minn.)

First Period: Campbell, Gagner (Roenick, Larmer), 6:17; Wales, LaFontaine (Turcotte) 9:14; Campbell, Damphousse (Oates, S. Smith), 11:36. Penalties—none.

Second Period: Wales, LaFontaine (Hatcher), 1:33; Campbell, Suter, 5:23; Campbell, Gretzky (Sandstrom), 9:10; Campbell, Oates (Yzerman), 9:48; Campbell, Fleury (Messier, Chelios), 14:40; Wales, Tocchet (Verbeek, Sakic), 15:36; Campbell, Roenick (S. Smith, Oates), 17:07. Penalties—none.

Third Period: Wales, MacLean (Cullen, Bourque), (pp) 2:29; Campbell, Chelios (Roenick, Larmer), 5:23; Campbell, Damphousse (Oates, Housley), 8:54; Campbell, Damphousse (Oates, Housley), 11:40; Wales, K. Stevens (Tocchet), (pp) 13:56; Campbell, Damphousse, 17:16. Penalties—Housley, Campbell 0:57, 12:26.

SHOTS ON GOAL

	1	2	3	T
Wales	10	9	22	41
Campbell	15	15	11	41

GOALTENDERS

	Time	SA	GA	ENG	Dec
Wales, Roy	29:48	15	5	0	
Wales, Moog	28:52	13	6	0	L
Campbell, Vernon	28:48	12	2	0	
Campbell, Ranford	28:52	24	3	0	W

PP Conversions: Wales 2/2; Campbell 0/0.

Referee: Terry Gregson.

Linesmen: Dan Schachte, Jerry Pateman.

Attendance: 18,472 (at Chicago Stadium).

Three Stars: 1. Damphousse (Campbell). 2. Oates (Campbell). 3. Roenick (Campbell).

All-Star Game MVP: Damphousse (Campbell).

1991 NHL Draft

First Round

The opening round of the 1991 NHL draft was held in Buffalo on June 22.

	Team	Selection	Position
1	Quebec	Eric Lindros, Oshawa (OHL)	C
2	San Jose	Pat Falloon, Spokane (WHL)	C/R
3	New Jersey	Scott Niedermayer, Kamloops (WHL)	D
4	NY Islanders	Scott Lachance, Boston U	D
5	Winnipeg	Aaron Ward, Michigan	D
6	Philadelphia	Peter Forsberg, MoDo (Sweden)	C
7	Vancouver	Alex Stojanov, Hamilton (OHL)	L
8	Minnesota	Richard Matvichuk, Saskatoon (WHL)	D
9	Hartford	Patrick Poulin, St-Hyacinthe (QMJHL)	L
10	Detroit	Martin Lapointe, Laval (QMJHL)	R
11	New Jersey	Brian Ralston, Detroit (NAJHL)	C
12	Edmonton	Tyler Wright, Swift Current (WHL)	C
13	Buffalo	Phillippe Boucher, Granby (QMJHL)	D
14	Washington	Patrick Peake, Detroit (OHL)	C
15	NY Rangers	Alexei Kovalev, Moscow Dynamo	C
16	Pittsburgh	Markus Naslund, MoDo (Sweden)	R
17	Montreal	Brent Bilodeau, Seattle (WHL)	D
18	Boston	Glenn Murray, Sudbury (OHL)	R
19	Calgary	Niklas Sunblad, AIK (Sweden)	L/R
20	Edmonton	Martin Rucinsky, Litvinov (Czech)	C/L
21	Washington	Trevor Halverson, North Bay (OHL)	L
22	Chicago	Dean McAmmond, Prince Albert (WHL)	C

Notes: NAJHL, North American Junior Hockey League; OHL, Ontario Hockey League; QMJHL, Quebec Major Junior Hockey League; WHL, Western Hockey League.

FOR THE RECORD • Year by Year

The Stanley Cup

Awarded annually to the team that wins the NHL's best-of-seven final-round playoffs. The Stanley Cup is the oldest trophy competed for by professional athletes in North America. It was donated in 1893 by Frederick Arthur, Lord Stanley of Preston.

Results

WINNERS PRIOR TO FORMATION OF NHL IN 1917

1892-93 .... Montreal A.A.A.	1904-05 .... Ottawa Silver Seven
1893-94 .... Montreal A.A.A.	1905-06 .... Ottawa Silver Seven (Feb)
1894-95 .... Montreal Victorias	1905-06 .... Montreal Wanderers (Mar)
1895-96 .... Winnipeg Victorias (Feb)	1906-07 .... Kenora Thistles (Jan)
1895-96 .... Montreal Victorias (Dec)	1906-07 .... Montreal Wanderers (Mar)
1896-97 .... Montreal Victorias	1907-08 .... Montreal Wanderers
1897-98 .... Montreal Victorias	1908-09 .... Ottawa Senators
1898-99 .... Montreal Victorias (Feb)	1909-10 .... Montreal Wanderers
1898-99 .... Montreal Shamrocks (Mar)	1910-11 .... Ottawa Senators
1899-1900 .... Montreal Shamrocks	1911-12 .... Quebec Bulldogs
1900-01 .... Winnipeg Victorias	1912-13 .... Quebec Bulldogs
1901-02 .... Winnipeg Victorias (Jan)	1913-14 .... Toronto Blueshirts
1901-02 .... Montreal A.A.A. (Mar)	1914-15 .... Vancouver Millionaires
1902-03 .... Montreal A.A.A. (Feb)	1915-16 .... Montreal Canadiens
1902-03 .... Ottawa Silver Seven (Mar)	1916-17 .... Seattle Metropolitans
1903-04 .... Ottawa Silver Seven	

NHL WINNERS AND FINALISTS

Season	Champion	Finalist	GP in Final
1917-18	Toronto Arenas	Vancouver Millionaires	5
1918-19	No decision*	No decision*	5
1919-20	Ottawa Senators	Seattle Metropolitans	5
1920-21	Ottawa Senators	Vancouver Millionaires	5
1921-22	Toronto St Pats	Vancouver Millionaires	5
1922-23	Ottawa Senators	Vancouver Millionaires, Edmonton	3, 2
1923-24	Montreal Canadiens	Vancouver Millionaires, Calgary	2, 2
1924-25	Victoria Cougars	Montreal Canadiens	4
1925-26	Montreal Maroons	Victoria Cougars	4
1926-27	Ottawa Senators	Boston Bruins	4
1927-28	New York Rangers	Montreal Maroons	5
1928-29	Boston Bruins	New York Rangers	2
1929-30	Montreal Canadiens	Boston Bruins	2
1930-31	Montreal Canadiens	Chicago Blackhawks	5
1931-32	Toronto Maple Leafs	New York Rangers	3
1932-33	New York Rangers	Toronto Maple Leafs	4
1933-34	Chicago Blackhawks	Detroit Red Wings	4
1934-35	Montreal Maroons	Toronto Maple Leafs	3
1935-36	Detroit Red Wings	Toronto Maple Leafs	4
1936-37	Detroit Red Wings	New York Rangers	5
1937-38	Chicago Blackhawks	Toronto Maple Leafs	4
1938-39	Boston Bruins	Toronto Maple Leafs	5
1939-40	New York Rangers	Toronto Maple Leafs	6
1940-41	Boston Bruins	Detroit Red Wings	4
1941-42	Toronto Maple Leafs	Detroit Red Wings	7
1942-43	Detroit Red Wings	Boston Bruins	4
1943-44	Montreal Canadiens	Chicago Blackhawks	4
1944-45	Toronto Maple Leafs	Detroit Red Wings	7
1945-46	Montreal Canadiens	Boston Bruins	5
1946-47	Toronto Maple Leafs	Montreal Canadiens	6
1947-48	Toronto Maple Leafs	Detroit Red Wings	4
1948-49	Toronto Maple Leafs	Detroit Red Wings	4
1949-50	Detroit Red Wings	New York Rangers	7
1950-51	Toronto Maple Leafs	Montreal Canadiens	5

NHL WINNERS AND FINALISTS (*Cont.*)

Season	Champion	Finalist	GP in Final
1951-52	Detroit Red Wings	Montreal Canadiens	4
1952-53	Montreal Canadiens	Boston Bruins	5
1953-54	Detroit Red Wings	Montreal Canadiens	7
1954-55	Detroit Red Wings	Montreal Canadiens	7
1955-56	Montreal Canadiens	Detroit Red Wings	5
1956-57	Montreal Canadiens	Boston Bruins	5
1957-58	Montreal Canadiens	Boston Bruins	6
1958-59	Montreal Canadiens	Toronto Maple Leafs	5
1959-60	Montreal Canadiens	Toronto Maple Leafs	4
1960-61	Chicago Blackhawks	Detroit Red Wings	6
1961-62	Toronto Maple Leafs	Chicago Blackhawks	6
1962-63	Toronto Maple Leafs	Detroit Red Wings	5
1963-64	Toronto Maple Leafs	Detroit Red Wings	7
1964-65	Montreal Canadiens	Chicago Blackhawks	7
1965-66	Montreal Canadiens	Detroit Red Wings	6
1966-67	Toronto Maple Leafs	Montreal Canadiens	6
1967-68	Montreal Canadiens	St Louis Blues	4
1968-69	Montreal Canadiens	St Louis Blues	4
1969-70	Boston Bruins	St Louis Blues	4
1970-71	Montreal Canadiens	Chicago Blackhawks	7
1971-72	Boston Bruins	New York Rangers	6
1972-73	Montreal Canadiens	Chicago Blackhawks	6
1973-74	Philadelphia Flyers	Boston Bruins	6
1974-75	Philadelphia Flyers	Buffalo Sabres	6
1975-76	Montreal Canadiens	Philadelphia Flyers	4
1976-77	Montreal Canadiens	Boston Bruins	4
1977-78	Montreal Canadiens	Boston Bruins	6
1978-79	Montreal Canadiens	New York Rangers	5
1979-80	New York Islanders	Philadelphia Flyers	6
1980-81	New York Islanders	Minnesota North Stars	5
1981-82	New York Islanders	Vancouver Canucks	4
1982-83	New York Islanders	Edmonton Oilers	4
1983-84	Edmonton Oilers	New York Islanders	5
1984-85	Edmonton Oilers	Philadelphia Flyers	5
1985-86	Montreal Canadiens	Calgary Flames	6
1986-87	Edmonton Oilers	Philadelphia Flyers	7
1987-88	Edmonton Oilers	Boston Bruins	4
1988-89	Calgary Flames	Montreal Canadiens	6
1989-90	Edmonton Oilers	Boston Bruins	5
1990-91	Pittsburgh Penguins	Minnesota North Stars	6

*In the spring of 1919 the Montreal Canadiens traveled to Seattle to meet Seattle, PCHL champions. After 5 games had been played—teams were tied at 2 wins and 1 tie—the series was called off by the local Department of Health because of the influenza epidemic and the death of Canadian defenseman Joe Hall from influenza.

Conn Smythe Trophy

Awarded to the Most Valuable Player of the Stanley Cup playoffs, as selected by the Professional Hockey Writers Association. The trophy is named after the former coach, general manager, president and owner of the Toronto Maple Leafs.

1965	Jean Beliveau, Mont	1979	Bob Gainey, Mont
1966	Roger Crozier, Det	1980	Bryan Trottier, NYI
1967	Dave Keon, Tor	1981	Butch Goring, NYI
1968	Glenn Hall, StL	1982	Mike Bossy, NYI
1969	Serge Savard, Mont	1983	Bill Smith, NYI
1970	Bobby Orr, Bos	1984	Mark Messier, Edm
1971	Ken Dryden, Mont	1985	Wayne Gretzky, Edm
1972	Bobby Orr, Bos	1986	Patrick Roy, Mont
1973	Yvan Cournoyer, Mont	1987	Ron Hextall, Phil
1974	Bernie Parent, Phil	1988	Wayne Gretzky, Edm
1975	Bernie Parent, Phil	1989	Al MacInnis, Calg
1976	Reggie Leach, Phil	1990	Bill Ranford, Edm
1977	Guy Lafleur, Mont	1991	Mario Lemieux, Pitt
1978	Larry Robinson, Mont		

All-Time Stanley Cup Playoff Leaders

Points

	Yrs	GP	G	A	Pts
*Wayne Gretzky, Edm, LA	12	150	93	206	299
*Mark Messier, Edm	12	166	80	135	215
*Jari Kurri, Edm	10	146	92	110	202
*Glenn Anderson, Edm	11	164	81	102	183
*Bryan Trottier, NYI, Pitt	15	198	67	110	177
Jean Beliveau, Mont	17	162	79	97	176
Denis Potvin, NYI	14	185	56	108	164
Mike Bossy, NYI	10	129	85	75	160
Gordie Howe, Det, Hart	20	157	68	92	160
*Bobby Smith, Minn, Mont	12	177	63	92	155
Stan Mikita, Chi	18	155	59	91	150

	Yrs	GP	G	A	Pts
*Brian Propp, Phil, Bos	13	159	64	84	148
*Larry Robinson, Mont, LA	19	225	28	116	144
Jacques Lemaire, Mont	11	145	61	78	139
Phil Esposito, Chi, Bos, NYR	15	130	61	76	137
Guy Lafleur, Mont, NYR	14	128	58	76	134
Bobby Hull, Chi, Hart	14	119	62	67	129
Henri Richard, Mont	18	180	49	80	129
*Paul Coffey, Edm, Pitt	9	117	40	89	129
Yvon Cournoyer, Mont	12	147	64	63	127
Maurice Richard, Mont	15	133	82	44	126
Brad Park, NYR, Bos, Det	17	162	35	90	125

*Active player.

Goals

	Yrs	GP	G
*Wayne Gretzky, Edm, LA	12	150	93
*Jari Kurri, Edm	10	146	92
Mike Bossy, NYI	10	129	85
Maurice Richard, Mont	15	133	82
*Glenn Anderson, Edm	11	164	81
*Mark Messier, Edm	12	166	80
Jean Beliveau, Mont	17	162	79
Gordie Howe, Det, Hart	20	157	68
*Bryan Trottier, NYI, Pitt	15	198	67
Yvan Cournoyer, Mont	12	147	64
*Brian Propp, Phil, Bos, Minn	13	159	64

*Active player.

Assists

	Yrs	GP	A
*Wayne Gretzky, Edm, LA	12	150	206
*Mark Messier, Edm	12	166	135
*Larry Robinson, Mont, LA	19	225	116
*Jari Kurri, Edm	10	146	110
*Bryan Trottier, NYI, Pitt	15	198	110
Denis Potvin, NYI	14	185	108
*Glenn Anderson, Edm	11	164	102
Jean Beliveau, Mont	17	162	97
Gordie Howe, Det, Hart	20	157	92
Stan Mikita, Chi	18	155	91

*Active player.

Goaltending

WINS	W	L	Pct
Billy Smith	88	36	.709
Ken Dryden	80	32	.714
Grant Fuhr	74	32	.698
Jacques Plante	71	37	.657
Turk Broda	58	42	.580
Terry Sawchuk	54	48	.529
Glenn Hall	49	65	.429
Gerry Cheevers	47	35	.573
Gump Worsley	41	25	.621
Bernie Parent	38	33	.535

SHUTOUTS	GP	W	SO
Clint Benedict	48	25	15
Jacques Plante	112	71	15
Turk Broda	101	58	13
Terry Sawchuk	106	54	12
Ken Dryden	112	80	10

GOALS AGAINST AVG	Avg
George Hainsworth	1.93
Turk Broda	1.98
Jacques Plante	2.17
Ken Dryden	2.40
Bernie Parent	2.43

Note: At least 50 games played.

Stanley Cup Coaching Records

Coach	Team	Yrs	Series W	Series L	Games G	Games W	Games L	T	Cups	Pct
Glen Sather	Edm	10	27	21	6	*126	89	37	0	4	.706
Toe Blake	Mont	13	23	18	5	119	82	37	0	8	.689
Hap Day	Tor	9	14	10	4	80	49	31	0	5	.613
Scott Bowman	StL, Mont, Buff	17	37	25	12	186	114	72	0	5	.612
Al Arbour	StL, NYI	14	38	28	10	187	114	73	0	4	.610
Fred Shero	Phil, NYR	8	21	15	6	108	61	47	0	2	.565
Lester Patrick	NYR	12	24	14	10	65	31	26	8	2	.538
Tommy Ivan	Det	7	12	8	4	67	36	31	0	3	.537
Mike Keenan	Phil, Chi	7	17	10	7	99	53	46	0	0	.535
Dick Irvin	Chi, Tor, Mont	24	45	25	20	190	100	88	2	4	.532

*Does not include suspended game, May 24, 1988.

Note: Coaches ranked by winning percentage. Minimum: 65 games.

The 10 Longest Overtime Games

Date	Scorer	OT	Results	Series	Series Winner
3-24-36	Mud Bruneteau	116:30	Det 1 vs Mont M 0	SF	Det
4-3-33	Ken Doraty	104:46	Tor 1 vs Bos 0	SF	Tor
3-23-43	Jack McLean	70:18	Tor 3 vs Det 2	SF	Det
3-28-30	Gus Rivers	68:52	Mont 2 vs NYR 1	SF	Mont
4-18-87	Pat LaFontaine	68:47	NYI 3 vs Wash 2	DSF	NYI
3-27-51	Maurice Richard	61:09	Mont 3 vs Det 2	SF	Mont
3-26-32	Fred Cook	59:32	NYR 4 vs Mont 3	SF	NYR
3-21-39	Mel Hill	59:25	Bos 2 vs NYR 1	SF	Bos
5-15-90	Petr Klima	55:13	Edm 3 vs Bos 2	F	Edm
4-9-31	Cy Wentworth	53:50	Chi 3 vs Mont 2	F	Mont

NHL Awards

Hart Memorial Trophy

Awarded annually "to the player adjudged to be the most valuable to his team." The original trophy was donated by Dr. David A. Hart, father of Cecil Hart, former manager-coach of the Montreal Canadiens. In the decade of the 1980s Wayne Gretzky won the award nine of 10 times.

Winner	Winner
1924 ...... Frank Nighbor, Ott	1958 ...... Gordie Howe, Det
1925 ...... Billy Burch, Ham	1959 ...... Andy Bathgate, NYR
1926 ...... Nels Stewart, Mont M	1960 ...... Gordie Howe, Det
1927 ...... Herb Gardiner, Mont	1961 ...... Bernie Geoffrion, Mont
1928 ...... Howie Morenz, Mont	1962 ...... Jacques Plante, Mont
1929 ...... Roy Worters, NYA	1963 ...... Gordie Howe, Det
1930 ...... Nels Stewart, Mont M	1964 ...... Jean Beliveau, Mont
1931 ...... Howie Morenz, Mont	1965 ...... Bobby Hull, Chi
1932 ...... Howie Morenz, Mont	1966 ...... Bobby Hull, Chi
1933 ...... Eddie Shore, Bos	1967 ...... Stan Mikita, Chi
1934 ...... Aurel Joliat, Mont	1968 ...... Stan Mikita, Chi
1935 ...... Eddie Shore, Bos	1969 ...... Phil Esposito, Bos
1936 ...... Eddie Shore, Bos	1970 ...... Bobby Orr, Bos
1937 ...... Babe Siebert, Mont	1971 ...... Bobby Orr, Bos
1938 ...... Eddie Shore, Bos	1972 ...... Bobby Orr, Bos
1939 ...... Toe Blake, Mont	1973 ...... Bobby Clarke, Phil
1940 ...... Ebbie Goodfellow, Det	1974 ...... Phil Esposito, Bos
1941 ...... Bill Cowley, Bos	1975 ...... Bobby Clarke, Phil
1942 ...... Tom Anderson, Bos	1976 ...... Bobby Clarke, Phil
1943 ...... Bill Cowley, Bos	1977 ...... Guy Lafleur, Mont
1944 ...... Babe Pratt, Tor	1978 ...... Guy Lafleur, Mont
1945 ...... Elmer Lach, Mont	1979 ...... Bryan Trottier, NYI
1946 ...... Max Bentley, Chi	1980 ...... Wayne Gretzky, Edm
1947 ...... Maurice Richard, Mont	1981 ...... Wayne Gretzky, Edm
1948 ...... Buddy O'Connor, NYR	1982 ...... Wayne Gretzky, Edm
1949 ...... Sid Abel, Det	1983 ...... Wayne Gretzky, Edm
1950 ...... Charlie Rayner, NYR	1984 ...... Wayne Gretzky, Edm
1951 ...... Milt Schmidt, Bos	1985 ...... Wayne Gretzky, Edm
1952 ...... Gordie Howe, Det	1986 ...... Wayne Gretzky, Edm
1953 ...... Gordie Howe, Det	1987 ...... Wayne Gretzky, Edm
1954 ...... Al Rollins, Chi	1988 ...... Mario Lemieux, Pitt
1955 ...... Ted Kennedy, Tor	1989 ...... Wayne Gretzky, LA
1956 ...... Jean Beliveau, Mont	1990 ...... Mark Messier, Edm
1957 ...... Gordie Howe, Det	1991 ...... Brett Hull, StL

THEY SAID IT

Tom Watt, Toronto Maple Leaf coach, after another disheartening loss: "If it would have been raining soup, we would have had forks."

Art Ross Trophy

Awarded annually "to the player who leads the league in scoring points at the end of the regular season." The trophy was presented to the NHL in 1947 by Arthur Howie Ross, former manager-coach of the Boston Bruins. The tie-breakers, in order, are as follows: (1) player with most goals, (2) player with fewer games played, (3) player scoring first goal of the season. Bobby Orr is the only defenseman in NHL history to win this trophy, and he won it twice (1970 and 1975).

Winner	Winner	Winner
1918 ....Joe Malone, Mont	1943 .... Doug Bentley, Chi	1968 .... Stan Mikita, Chi
1919 ....Newsy Lalonde, Mont	1944 .... Herb Cain, Bos	1969 .... Phil Esposito, Bos
1920 ....Joe Malone, Que	1945 .... Elmer Lach, Mont	1970 .... Bobby Orr, Bos
1921 ....Newsy Lalonde, Mont	1946 .... Max Bentley, Chi	1971 .... Phil Esposito, Bos
1922 ....Punch Broadbent, Ott	1947 .... *Max Bentley, Chi	1972 .... Phil Esposito, Bos
1923 ....Babe Dye, Tor	1948 .... Elmer Lach, Mont	1973 .... Phil Esposito, Bos
1924 ....Cy Denneny, Ott	1949 .... Roy Conacher, Chi	1974 .... Phil Esposito, Bos
1925 ....Babe Dye, Tor	1950 .... Ted Lindsay, Det	1975 .... Bobby Orr, Bos
1926 ....Nels Stewart, Mont M	1951 .... Gordie Howe, Det	1976 .... Guy Lafleur, Mont
1927 ....Bill Cook, NYR	1952 .... Gordie Howe, Det	1977 .... Guy Lafleur, Mont
1928 ....Howie Morenz, Mont	1953 .... Gordie Howe, Det	1978 .... Guy Lafleur, Mont
1929 ....Ace Bailey, Tor	1954 .... Gordie Howe, Det	1979 .... Bryan Trottier, NYI
1930 ....Cooney Weiland, Bos	1955 .... Bernie Geoffrion, Mont	1980 .... Marcel Dionne, LA
1931 ....Howie Morenz, Mont	1956 .... Jean Beliveau, Mont	1981 .... Wayne Gretzky, Edm
1932 ....Harvey Jackson, Tor	1957 .... Gordie Howe, Det	1982 .... Wayne Gretzky, Edm
1933 ....Bill Cook, NYR	1958 .... Dickie Moore, Mont	1983 .... Wayne Gretzky, Edm
1934 ....Charlie Conacher, Tor	1959 .... Dickie Moore, Mont	1984 .... Wayne Gretzky, Edm
1935 ....Charlie Conacher, Tor	1960 .... Bobby Hull, Chi	1985 .... Wayne Gretzky, Edm
1936 ....Dave Schriner, NYA	1961 .... Bernie Geoffrion, Mont	1986 .... Wayne Gretzky, Edm
1937 ....Dave Schriner, NYA	1962 .... Bobby Hull, Chi	1987 .... Wayne Gretzky, Edm
1938 ....Gordie Drillon, Tor	1963 .... Gordie Howe, Det	1988 .... Mario Lemieux, Pitt
1939 ....Toe Blake, Mont	1964 .... Stan Mikita, Chi	1989 .... Mario Lemieux, Pitt
1940 ....Milt Schmidt, Bos	1965 .... Stan Mikita, Chi	1990 .... Wayne Gretzky, LA
1941 ....Bill Cowley, Bos	1966 .... Bobby Hull, Chi	1991 .... Wayne Gretzky, LA
1942 ....Bryan Hextall, NYR	1967 .... Stan Mikita, Chi	

*Scoring leader prior to inception of Art Ross Trophy in 1947-48.

Lady Byng Memorial Trophy

Awarded annually "to the player adjudged to have exhibited the best type of sportsmanship and gentlemanly conduct combined with a high standard of playing ability." Lady Byng, who first presented the trophy in 1925, was the wife of Canada's Governor-General. She donated a second trophy in 1936 after the first was given permanently to Frank Boucher of the New York Rangers, who won it seven times in eight seasons. Stan Mikita, one of the league's most penalized players during his early years in the NHL, won the trophy twice late in his career (1967 and 1968).

Winner	Winner	Winner
1925 ....Frank Nighbor, Ott	1948 .... Buddy O'Connor, NYR	1970 .... Phil Goyette, StL
1926 ....Frank Nighbor, Ott	1949 .... Bill Quackenbush, Det	1971 .... John Bucyk, Bos
1927 ....Billy Burch, NYA	1950 .... Edgar Laprade, NYR	1972 .... Jean Ratelle, NYR
1928 ....Frank Boucher, NYR	1951 .... Red Kelly, Det	1973 .... Gilbert Perreault, Buff
1929 ....Frank Boucher, NYR	1952 .... Sid Smith, Tor	1974 .... John Bucyk, Bos
1930 ....Frank Boucher, NYR	1953 .... Red Kelly, Det	1975 .... Marcel Dionne, Det
1931 ....Frank Boucher, NYR	1954 .... Red Kelly, Det	1976 .... Jean Ratelle, NYR-Bos
1932 ....Joe Primeau, Tor	1955 .... Sid Smith, Tor	1977 .... Marcel Dionne, LA
1933 ....Frank Boucher, NYR	1956 .... Earl Reibel, Det	1978 .... Butch Goring, LA
1934 ....Frank Boucher, NYR	1957 .... Andy Hebenton, NYR	1979 .... Bob MacMillan, Atl
1935 ....Frank Boucher, NYR	1958 .... Camille Henry, NYR	1980 .... Wayne Gretzky, Edm
1936 ....Doc Romnes, Chi	1959 .... Alex Delvecchio, Det	1981 .... Rick Kehoe, Pitt
1937 ....Marty Barry, Det	1960 .... Don McKenney, Bos	1982 .... Rick Middleton, Bos
1938 ....Gordie Drillon, Tor	1961 .... Red Kelly, Tor	1983 .... Mike Bossy, NYI
1939 ....Clint Smith, NYR	1962 .... Dave Keon, Tor	1984 .... Mike Bossy, NYI
1940 ....Bobby Bauer, Bos	1963 .... Dave Keon, Tor	1985 .... Jari Kurri, Edm
1941 ....Bobby Bauer, Bos	1964 .... Ken Wharram, Chi	1986 .... Mike Bossy, NYI
1942 ....Syl Apps, Tor	1965 .... Bobby Hull, Chi	1987 .... Joe Mullen, Calg
1943 ....Max Bentley, Chi	1966 .... Alex Delvecchio, Det	1988 .... Mats Naslund, Mont
1944 ....Clint Smith, Chi	1967 .... Stan Mikita, Chi	1989 .... Joe Mullen, Calg
1945 ....Billy Mosienko, Chi	1968 .... Stan Mikita, Chi	1990 .... Brett Hull, StL
1946 ....Toe Blake, Mont	1969 .... Alex Delvecchio, Det	1991 .... Wayne Gretzky, LA
1947 ....Bobby Bauer, Bos		

James Norris Memorial Trophy

Awarded annually "to the defense player who demonstrates throughout the season the greatest all-around ability in the position." James Norris was the former owner-president of the Detroit Red Wings. Bobby Orr holds the record for most consecutive times winning the award (eight, 1968-1975).

Winner	Winner	Winner
1954 ....Red Kelly, Det	1967 .... Harry Howell, NYR	1980.....Larry Robinson, Mont
1955 ....Doug Harvey, Mont	1968 .... Bobby Orr, Bos	1981.....Randy Carlyle, Pitt
1956 ....Doug Harvey, Mont	1969 .... Bobby Orr, Bos	1982.....Doug Wilson, Chi
1957 ....Doug Harvey, Mont	1970 .... Bobby Orr, Bos	1983.....Rod Langway, Wash
1958 ....Doug Harvey, Mont	1971 .... Bobby Orr, Bos	1984.....Rod Langway, Wash
1959 ...Tom Johnson, Mont	1972 .... Bobby Orr, Bos	1985.....Paul Coffey, Edm
1960 ....Doug Harvey, Mont	1973 .... Bobby Orr, Bos	1986.....Paul Coffey, Edm
1961 ....Doug Harvey, Mont	1974 .... Bobby Orr, Bos	1987.....Ray Bourque, Bos
1962 ....Doug Harvey, NYR	1975 .... Bobby Orr, Bos	1988.....Ray Bourque, Bos
1963 ....Pierre Pilote, Chi	1976 .... Denis Potvin, NYI	1989.....Chris Chelios, Mont
1964 ....Pierre Pilote, Chi	1977 .... Larry Robinson, Mont	1990.....Ray Bourque, Bos
1965 ....Pierre Pilote, Chi	1978 .... Denis Potvin, NYI	1991.....Ray Bourque, Bos
1966 ....Jacques Laperriere, Mont	1979 .... Denis Potvin, NYI	

Calder Memorial Trophy

Awarded annually "to the player selected as the most proficient in his first year of competition in the National Hockey League." Frank Calder was a former NHL president. Sergei Makarov, who won the award in 1989-1990, was the oldest recipient of the trophy, at 31. Players are no longer eligible for the award if they are 26 or older as of September 15th of the season in question.

Winner	Winner	Winner
1933 ....Carl Voss, Det	1953 .... Gump Worsley, NYR	1973.....Steve Vickers, NYR
1934 ....Russ Blinko, Mont M	1954 .... Camille Henry, NYR	1974.....Denis Potvin, NYI
1935 ....Dave Schriner, NYA	1955 .... Ed Litzenberger, Chi	1975.....Eric Vail, Atl
1936 ....Mike Karakas, Chi	1956 .... Glenn Hall, Det	1976.....Bryan Trottier, NYI
1937 ....Syl Apps, Tor	1957 .... Larry Regan, Bos	1977.....Willi Plett, Atl
1938 ....Cully Dahlstrom, Chi	1958 .... Frank Mahovlich, Tor	1978.....Mike Bossy, NYI
1939 ....Frank Brimsek, Bos	1959 .... Ralph Backstrom, Mont	1979.....Bobby Smith, Minn
1940 ....Kilby MacDonald, NYR	1960 .... Bill Hay, Chi	1980.....Ray Bourque, Bos
1941 ....Johnny Quilty, Mont	1961 .... Dave Keon, Tor	1981.....Peter Stastny, Que
1942 ....Grant Warwick, NYR	1962 .... Bobby Rousseau, Mont	1982.....Dale Hawerchuk, Winn
1943 ....Gaye Stewart, Tor	1963 .... Kent Douglas, Tor	1983.....Steve Larmer, Chi
1944 ....Gus Bodnar, Tor	1964 .... Jacques Laperriere, Mont	1984.....Tom Barrasso, Buff
1945 ....Frank McCool, Tor	1965 .... Roger Crozier, Det	1985.....Mario Lemieux, Pitt
1946 ....Edgar Laprade, NYR	1966 .... Brit Selby, Tor	1986.....Gary Suter, Calg
1947 ....Howie Meeker, Tor	1967 .... Bobby Orr, Bos	1987.....Luc Robitaille, LA
1948 ....Jim McFadden, Det	1968 .... Derek Sanderson, Bos	1988.....Joe Nieuwendyk, Calg
1949 ....Pentti Lund, NYR	1969 .... Danny Grant, Minn	1989.....Brian Leetch, NYR
1950 ....Jack Gelineau, Bos	1970 .... Tony Esposito, Chi	1990.....Sergei Makarov, Calg
1951 ....Terry Sawchuk, Det	1971 .... Gilbert Perreault, Buff	1991.....Ed Belfour, Chi
1952 ....Bernie Geoffrion, Mont	1972 .... Ken Dryden, Mont	

Vezina Trophy

Awarded annually "to the goalkeeper adjudged to be the best at his position." The trophy is named after Georges Vezina, an outstanding goalie for the Montreal Canadiens who collapsed during a game on November 28, 1925, and died a few months later of tuberculosis. The general managers of the 21 NHL teams vote on the award.

Winner	Winner	Winner
1927 ....George Hainsworth, Mont	1939 .... Frank Brimsek, Bos	1951.....Al Rollins, Tor
1928 ....George Hainsworth, Mont	1940 .... Dave Kerr, NYR	1952.....Terry Sawchuk, Det
1929 ....George Hainsworth, Mont	1941 .... Turk Broda, Tor	1953.....Terry Sawchuk, Det
1930 ....Tiny Thompson, Bos	1942 .... Frank Brimsek, Bos	1954.....Harry Lumley, Tor
1931 ....Roy Worters, NYA	1943 .... Johnny Mowers, Det	1955.....Terry Sawchuk, Det
1932 ....Charlie Gardiner, Chi	1944 .... Bill Durnan, Mont	1956.....Jacques Plante, Mont
1933 ....Tiny Thompson, Bos	1945 .... Bill Durnan, Mont	1957.....Jacques Plante, Mont
1934 ....Charlie Gardiner, Chi	1946 .... Bill Durnan, Mont	1958.....Jacques Plante, Mont
1935 ....Lorne Chabot, Chi	1947 .... Bill Durnan, Mont	1959.....Jacques Plante, Mont
1936 ....Tiny Thompson, Bos	1948 .... Turk Broda, Tor	1960.....Jacques Plante, Mont
1937 ....Normie Smith, Det	1949 .... Bill Durnan, Mont	1961.....Johnny Bower, Tor
1938 ....Tiny Thompson, Bos	1950 .... Bill Durnan, Mont	1962.....Jacques Plante, Mont

Vezina Trophy (*Cont.*)

Winner	Winner	Winner
1963 .... Glenn Hall, Chi	1972 .... Tony Esposito, Chi	1981 .... Richard Sevigny, Mont
1964 .... Charlie Hodge, Mont	Gary Smith, Chi	Denis Herron, Mont
1965 .... Terry Sawchuk, Tor	1973 .... Ken Dryden, Mont	Michel Larocque, Mont
Johnny Bower, Tor	1974 .... Bernie Parent, Phil (tie)	1982 .... Bill Smith, NYI
1966 .... Gump Worsley, Mont	Tony Esposito, Chi (tie)	1983 .... Pete Peeters, Bos
Charlie Hodge, Mont	1975 .... Bernie Parent, Phil	1984 .... Tom Barrasso, Buff
1967 .... Glenn Hall, Chi	1976 .... Ken Dryden, Mont	1985 .... Pelle Lindbergh, Phil
Denis Dejordy, Chi	1977 .... Ken Dryden, Mont	1986 .... John Vanbiesbrouck,
1968 .... Gump Worsley, Mont	Michel Larocque, Mont	NYR
Rogie Vachon, Mont	1978 .... Ken Dryden, Mont	1987 .... Ron Hextall, Phil
1969 .... Jacques Plante, StL	Michel Larocque, Mont	1988 .... Grant Fuhr, Edm
Glenn Hall, StL	1979 .... Ken Dryden, Mont	1989 .... Patrick Roy, Mont
1970 .... Tony Esposito, Chi	Michel Larocque, Mont	1990 .... Patrick Roy, Mont
1971 .... Ed Giacomin, NYR	1980 .... Bob Sauve, Buff	1991 .... Ed Belfour, Chi
Gilles Villemure, NYR	Don Edwards, Buff	

Career Records

All-Time Point Leaders

Player	Yrs	GP	G	A	Pts	Pts/game
*1. Wayne Gretzky, Edm, LA	12	925	718	1424	2142	2.316
2. Gordie Howe, Det, Hart	26	1767	801	1049	1850	1.047
3. Marcel Dionne, Det, LA, NYR	18	1348	731	1040	1771	1.314
4. Phil Esposito, Chi, Bos, NYR	18	1282	717	873	1590	1.240
5. Stan Mikita, Chi	22	1394	541	926	1467	1.052
*6. Bryan Trottier, NYI, Pitt	16	1175	509	872	1381	1.175
7. John Bucyk, Det, Bos	23	1540	556	813	1369	.889
8. Guy Lafleur, Mont, NYR, Que	17	1126	560	793	1353	1.201
9. Gilbert Perreault, Buff	17	1191	512	814	1326	1.113
10. Alex Delvecchio, Det	24	1549	456	825	1281	.827
11. Jean Ratelle, NYR, Bos	21	1281	491	776	1267	.989
12. Norm Ullman, Det, Tor	20	1410	490	739	1229	.872
13. Jean Beliveau, Mont	20	1125	507	712	1219	1.084
14. Bobby Clarke, Phil	15	1144	358	852	1210	1.058
15. Bobby Hull, Chi, Winn, Hart	16	1063	610	560	1170	1.101

*Active player.

All-Time Goal-Scoring Leaders

Player	Yrs	GP	G	G/game
1. Gordie Howe, Det, Hart	26	1767	801	.453
2. Marcel Dionne, Det, LA, NYR	18	1348	731	.542
*3. Wayne Gretzky, Edm, LA	12	925	718	.776
4. Phil Esposito, Chi, Bos, NYR	18	1282	717	.559
5. Bobby Hull, Chi, Winn, Hart	16	1063	610	.574
6. Mike Bossy, NYI	10	752	573	.762
7. Guy Lafleur, Mont, NYR, Que	17	1126	560	.497
8. John Bucyk, Det, Bos	23	1540	556	.361
9. Maurice Richard, Mont	18	978	544	.556
10. Stan Mikita, Chi	22	1394	541	.388

*Active player.

All-Time Assist Leaders

Player	Yrs	GP	A	A/game
*1. Wayne Gretzky, Edm, LA	12	925	1424	1.539
2. Gordie Howe, Det, Hart	26	1767	1049	.594
3. Marcel Dionne, Det, LA, NYR	18	1348	1040	.772
4. Stan Mikita, Chi	22	1394	926	.664
5. Phil Esposito, Chi, Bos, NYR	18	1282	873	.681
*6. Bryan Trottier, NYI, Pitt	16	1175	872	.742
7. Bobby Clarke, Phil	15	1144	852	.745
8. Alex Delvecchio, Det	24	1549	825	.533
9. Gilbert Perreault, Buff	17	1191	814	.683
10. John Bucyk, Det, Bos	23	1540	813	.528

*Active player.

Career Records (*Cont.*)

Goaltending Records

ALL-TIME WIN LEADERS

Goaltender	W	L	T	Pct
Terry Sawchuk	435	337	188	.551
Jacques Plante	434	246	137	.615
Tony Esposito	423	307	151	.566
Glenn Hall	407	327	165	.544
Rogie Vachon	355	291	115	.542
Gump Worsley	335	353	150	.489
Harry Lumley	332	324	143	.505
Billy Smith	305	233	105	.556
Turk Broda	302	224	101	.562
Ed Giacomin	289	206	97	.570

ACTIVE GOALTENDING LEADERS

Goaltender	W	L	T	Pct
Andy Moog, Edm, Bos	214	92	45	.673
Grant Fuhr, Edm	226	117	54	.637
Pete Peeters, Phil, Bos, Wash	246	156	51	.610
Rick Wamsley, Mont, StL, Calg	197	121	46	.604
Rejean Lemelin, Atl, Calg, Bos	236	147	63	.599
Kelly Hrudey, NYI, LA	164	128	40	.554
Tom Barrasso, Buff, Pitt	176	145	41	.542
Rollie Melanson, NYI, LA	124	103	33	.540
Clint Malarchuk, Que, Wash, Buff	131	117	42	.524
Don Beaupre, Minn, Wash	174	165	53	.511

Note: Ranked by winning percentage; minimum 250 games played.

ALL-TIME SHUTOUT LEADERS

Goaltender	Team	Yrs	GP	SO
Terry Sawchuk	Det, Bos, Tor, LA, NYR	21	971	103
George Hainsworth	Mont, Tor	11	464	94
Glenn Hall	Det, Chi, StL	18	906	84
Jacques Plante	Mont, NYR, StL, Tor, Bos	18	837	82
Tiny Thompson	Bos, Det	12	553	81
Alex Connell	Ott, Det, NYA, Mont M	12	417	81
Tony Esposito	Mont, Chi	16	886	76
Lorne Chabot	NYR, Tor, Mont, Chi, Mont M, NYA	11	411	73
Harry Lumley	Det, NYR, Chi, Tor, Bos	16	804	71
Roy Worters	Pitt Pir, NYA, *Mont	12	484	66

*Played 1 game for Canadiens in 1929-30, not a shutout.

Coaching Records

Coach	Team	Seasons	W	L	T	Pct*
Scott Bowman	StL, Mont, Buff	1967-87	739	327	210	.661
Toe Blake	Mont	1955-68	500	255	159	.634
Glen Sather	Edm	1979-89	442	241	99	.629
Fred Shero	Phil, NYR	1971-81	390	225	119	.612
Tommy Ivan	Det, Chi	1947-54, 56-58	302	196	112	.587
Emile Francis	NYR, StL	1965-77, 81-83	393	273	112	.577
Al Arbour	StL, NYI	1970-86, 88-91	671	469	218	.574
Billy Reay	Tor, Chi	1957-59, 63-77	542	385	175	.571
Bryan Murray	Wash, Det	1981-91	377	284	94	.561
Dick Irvin	Chi, Tor, Mont	1930-56	690	521	226	.559

*Percentage arrived at by dividing possible points into actual points.

Note: Minimum 600 regular-season games. Ranked by %.

Single-Season Records

Points per Game

Player	Season	GP	Pts	Avg
Wayne Gretzky, Edm	1983-84	74	205	2.77
Wayne Gretzky, Edm	1985-86	80	215	2.69
Wayne Gretzky, Edm	1981-82	80	212	2.65
Mario Lemieux, Pitt	1988-89	76	199	2.62
Wayne Gretzky, Edm	1984-85	80	208	2.60
Wayne Gretzky, Edm	1982-83	80	196	2.45
Wayne Gretzky, Edm	1987-88	64	149	2.33
Wayne Gretzky, Edm	1986-87	79	183	2.32
Mario Lemieux, Pitt	1987-88	77	168	2.18
Wayne Gretzky, LA	1988-89	78	168	2.15

Player	Season	GP	Pts	Avg
Wayne Gretzky, LA	1990-91	78	163	2.08
Mario Lemieux, Pitt	1989-90	59	123	2.08
Wayne Gretzky, Edm	1980-81	80	164	2.05
Bill Cowley, Bos	1943-44	36	71	1.97
Phil Esposito, Bos	1970-71	78	152	1.95
Wayne Gretzky, LA	1989-90	73	142	1.95
Steve Yzerman, Det	1988-89	80	155	1.94
Bernie Nicholls, LA	1988-89	79	150	1.90
Phil Esposito, Bos	1973-74	78	145	1.86
Jari Kurri, Edm	1984-85	73	135	1.85

Goals per Game

Player	Season	GP	G	Avg
Joe Malone, Mont	1917-18	20	44	2.20
Cy Denneny, Ott	1917-18	22	36	1.64
Newsy Lalonde, Mont	1917-18	14	23	1.64
Joe Malone, Que	1919-20	24	39	1.63
Newsy Lalonde, Mont	1919-20	23	36	1.57
Joe Malone, Ham	1920-21	20	30	1.50
Babe Dye, Ham, Tor	1920-21	24	35	1.46
Cy Denneny, Ott	1920-21	24	34	1.42
Reg Noble, Tor	1917-18	20	28	1.40
Newsy Lalonde, Mont	1920-21	24	33	1.38

Note: Minimum 20 goals in one season.

Assists per Game

Player	Season	GP	A	Avg
Wayne Gretzky, Edm	1985-86	80	163	2.04
Wayne Gretzky, Edm	1987-88	64	109	1.70
Wayne Gretzky, Edm	1984-85	80	135	1.69
Wayne Gretzky, Edm	1983-84	74	118	1.59
Wayne Gretzky, Edm	1982-83	80	125	1.56
Wayne Gretzky, LA	1990-91	78	122	1.56
Wayne Gretzky, Edm	1986-87	79	121	1.53
Wayne Gretzky, Edm	1981-82	80	120	1.50
Mario Lemieux, Pitt	1988-89	76	114	1.50
Adam Oates, StL	1990-91	60	90	1.47

Shutout Leaders

	Season	SO	Length of Schedule		Season	SO	Length of Schedule
George Hainsworth, Mont	1928-29	22	44	Bernie Parent, Phil	1973-74	12	78
Alex Connell, Ott	1925-26	15	36	Bernie Parent, Phil	1974-75	12	80
Alex Connell, Ott	1927-28	15	44	Lorne Chabot, NYR	1927-28	11	44
Hal Winkler, Bos	1927-28	15	44	Harry Holmes, Det	1927-28	11	44
Tony Esposito, Chi	1969-70	15	76	Clint Benedict, Mont M	1928-29	11	44
George Hainsworth, Mont	1926-27	14	44	Joe Miller, Pitt Pirates	1928-29	11	44
Clint Benedict, Mont M	1926-27	13	44	Tiny Thompson, Bos	1932-33	11	48
Alex Connell, Ott	1926-27	13	44	Terry Sawchuk, Det	1950-51	11	70
George Hainsworth, Mont	1927-28	13	44	Lorne Chabot, NYR	1926-27	10	44
Roy Worters, NYA	1927-28	13	44	Roy Worters, Pitt Pirates	1927-28	10	44
John Roach, NYR	1928-29	13	44	Clarence Dolson, Det	1928-29	10	44
Roy Worters, NYA	1928-29	13	44	John Roach, Det	1932-33	10	48
Harry Lumley, Tor	1953-54	13	70	Chuck Gardiner, Chi	1933-34	10	48
Tiny Thompson, Bos	1928-29	12	44	Tiny Thompson, Bos	1935-36	10	48
Lorne Chabot, Tor	1928-29	12	44	Frank Brimsek, Bos	1938-39	10	48
Chuck Gardiner, Chi	1930-31	12	44	Bill Durnan, Mont	1948-49	10	60
Terry Sawchuk, Det	1951-52	12	70	Gerry McNeil, Mont	1952-53	10	70
Terry Sawchuk, Det	1953-54	12	70	Harry Lumley, Tor	1952-53	10	70
Terry Sawchuk, Det	1954-55	12	70	Tony Esposito, Chi	1973-74	10	78
Glenn Hall, Det	1955-56	12	70	Ken Dryden, Mont	1976-77	10	80

Single-Game Records

Goals

	Date	G
Joe Malone, Que vs Tor	1-31-20	7
Newsy Lalonde, Mont vs Tor	1-10-20	6
Joe Malone, Que vs Ott	3-10-20	6
Corb Denneny, Tor vs Ham	1-26-21	6
Cy Denneny, Ott vs Ham	3-7-21	6
Syd Howe, Det vs NYR	2-3-44	6
Red Berenson, StL vs Phil	11-7-68	6
Darryl Sittler, Tor vs Bos	2-7-76	6

Assists

	Date	A
Billy Taylor, Det vs Chi	3-16-47	7
Wayne Gretzky, Edm vs Wash	2-15-80	7
Wayne Gretzky, Edm vs Chi	12-11-85	7
Wayne Gretzky, Edm vs Que	2-14-86	7

Note: 19 tied with 6.

Points

	Date	G	A	Pts
Darryl Sittler, Tor vs Bos	2-7-76	6	4	10
Maurice Richard, Mont vs Det	12-28-44	5	3	8
Bert Olmstead, Mont vs Chi	1-9-54	4	4	8
Tom Bladon, Phil vs Clev	12-11-77	4	4	8
Bryan Trottier, NYI vs NYR	12-23-78	5	3	8
Peter Stastny, Que vs Wash	2-22-81	4	4	8
Anton Stastny, Que vs Wash	2-22-81	3	5	8
Wayne Gretzky, Edm vs NJ	11-19-83	3	5	8
Wayne Gretzky, Edm vs Minn	1-4-84	4	4	8
Paul Coffey, Edm vs Det	3-14-86	2	6	8
Mario Lemieux, Pitt vs StL	10-15-88	2	6	8
Bernie Nicholls, LA vs Tor	12-1-88	2	6	8
Mario Lemieux, Pitt vs NJ	12-31-88	5	3	8

On Both Sides of the Law

Paul Stewart is the only current referee who has played in the NHL. Ironically, Stewart, who played most of his 171 games during the 1980s with the Quebec Nordiques, is a former enforcer whose forte was fighting.

NHL All-Star Game

First played in 1947, this game was scheduled before the start of the regular season and used to match the defending Stanley Cup champions against a squad made up of league All-Stars from other teams. In 1966 the games were moved to mid-season, although there was no game that year. The format changed to a conference versus conference showdown in 1969.

Results

Year	Site	Score	Coaches	Attendance
1947	Toronto	All-Stars 4, Toronto 3	Dick Irvin, Hap Day	14,169
1948	Chicago	All-Stars 3, Toronto 1	Tommy Ivan, Hap Day	12,794
1949	Toronto	All-Stars 3, Toronto 1	Tommy Ivan, Hap Day	13,541
1950	Detroit	Detroit 7, All-Stars 1	Tommy Ivan, Lynn Patrick	9,166
1951	Toronto	1st team 2, 2nd team 2	Joe Primeau, Hap Day	11,469
1952	Detroit	1st team 1, 2nd team 1	Tommy Ivan, Dick Irvin	10,680
1953	Montreal	All-Stars 3, Montreal 1	Lynn Patrick, Dick Irvin	14,153
1954	Detroit	All-Stars 2, Detroit 2	King Clancy, Jim Skinner	10,689
1955	Detroit	Detroit 3, All-Stars 1	Jim Skinner, Dick Irvin	10,111
1956	Montreal	All-Stars 1, Montreal 1	Jim Skinner, Toe Blake	13,095
1957	Montreal	All-Stars 5, Montreal 3	Milt Schmidt, Toe Blake	13,003
1958	Montreal	Montreal 6, All-Stars 3	Toe Blake, Milt Schmidt	13,989
1959	Montreal	Montreal 6, All-Stars 1	Toe Blake, Punch Imlach	13,818
1960	Montreal	All-Stars 2, Montreal 1	Punch Imlach, Toe Blake	13,949
1961	Chicago	All-Stars 3, Chicago 1	Sid Abel, Rudy Pilous	14,534
1962	Toronto	Toronto 4, All-Stars 1	Punch Imlach, Rudy Pilous	14,236
1963	Toronto	All-Stars 3, Toronto 3	Sid Abel, Punch Imlach	14,034
1964	Toronto	All-Stars 3, Toronto 2	Sid Abel, Punch Imlach	14,232
1965	Montreal	All-Stars 5, Montreal 2	Billy Reay, Toe Blake	13,529
1967	Montreal	Montreal 3, All-Stars 0	Toe Blake, Sid Abel	14,284
1968	Toronto	Toronto 4, All-Stars 3	Punch Imlach, Toe Blake	15,753
1969	Montreal	East 3, West 3	Toe Blake, Scott Bowman	16,260
1970	St Louis	East 4, West 1	Claude Ruel, Scott Bowman	16,587
1971	Boston	West 2, East 1	Scott Bowman, Harry Sinden	14,790
1972	Minnesota	East 3, West 2	Al MacNeil, Billy Reay	15,423
1973	NY Rangers	East 5, West 4	Tom Johnson, Billy Reay	16,986
1974	Chicago	West 6, East 4	Billy Reay, Scott Bowman	16,426
1975	Montreal	Wales 7, Campbell 1	Bep Guidolin, Fred Shero	16,080
1976	Philadelphia	Wales 7, Campbell 5	Floyd Smith, Fred Shero	16,436
1977	Vancouver	Wales 4, Campbell 3	Scott Bowman, Fred Shero	15,607
1978	Buffalo	Wales 3, Campbell 2 (OT)	Scott Bowman, Fred Shero	16,433
1980	Detroit	Wales 6, Campbell 3	Scott Bowman, Al Arbour	21,002
1981	Los Angeles	Campbell 4, Wales 1	Pat Quinn, Scott Bowman	15,761
1982	Washington	Wales 4, Campbell 2	Al Arbour, Glen Sonmor	18,130
1983	NY Islanders	Campbell 9, Wales 3	Roger Neilson, Al Arbour	15,230
1984	NJ Devils	Wales 7, Campbell 6	Al Arbour, Glen Sather	18,939
1985	Calgary	Wales 6, Campbell 4	Al Arbour, Glen Sather	16,825
1986	Hartford	Wales 4, Campbell 3 (OT)	Mike Keenan, Glen Sather	15,100
1988	St Louis	Wales 6, Campbell 5 (OT)	Mike Keenan, Glen Sather	17,878
1989	Edmonton	Campbell 9, Wales 5	Glen Sather, Terry O'Reilly	17,503
1990	Pittsburgh	Wales 12, Campbell 7	Pat Burns, Terry Crisp	16,236
1991	Chicago	Campbell 11, Wales 5	John Muckler, Mike Milbury	18,472

Note: The Challenge Cup, a series between the NHL All-Stars and the Soviet Union, was played instead of the All-Star Game in 1979. Eight years later, Rendez-Vous '87, a two-game series matching the Soviet Union and the NHL All-Stars, replaced the All-Star Game.

A Rubber Chicken Trick?

Where did the term "hat trick" come from? It first came into usage in cricket around 1875, to refer to the dismissal by the bowler of three batters with three straight balls. The bowler reportedly got a new hat whenever he accomplished this rare feat.

U.S. fans are more used to the term in hockey, in which it came into use in the mid-1950s. In soccer as well as hockey it meant three unanswered goals by one player in a single game. It has also been used in horse racing to refer to a jockey riding a winner in three straight races or in an annual race for three consecutive years. Somewhere along the line (NHL expansion?), the meaning got muddy and hockey goals no longer needed to be unanswered to qualify. Hockey fans have been known to throw hats onto the ice after a hat trick. Then again, they've also thrown shoes and rubber chickens.

Hockey Hall of Fame

Located in Toronto, the Hockey Hall of Fame was officially opened on August 26, 1961. The current president is Ian "Scotty" Morrison, a former NHL referee. There are, at present, 276 members of the Hockey Hall of Fame—192 players, 73 "Builders," and 11 on-ice officials. To be eligible, player and referee/linesman candidates should have been out of the game for three years, but the Hall's Board of Directors can make exceptions.

Players

Sid Abel (1969)
Jack Adams (1959)
Charles "Syl" Apps (1961)
George Armstrong (1975)
Irvine "Ace" Bailey (1975)
Donald H. "Dan" Bain (1945)
Hobey Baker (1945)
Bill Barber (1990)
Marty Barry (1965)
Andy Bathgate (1978)
Jean Beliveau (1972)
Clint Benedict (1965)
Douglas Bentley (1964)
Max Bentley (1966)
Hector "Toe" Blake (1966)
Leo Boivin (1986)
Dickie Boon (1952)
Emile "Butch" Bouchard (1966)
Frank Boucher (1958)
George "Buck" Boucher (1960)
Johnny Bower (1976)
Russell Bowie (1945)
Frank Brimsek (1966)
Harry L. "Punch" Broadbent (1962)
Walter "Turk" Broda (1967)
John Bucyk (1981)
Billy Burch (1974)
Harry Cameron (1962)
Gerry Cheevers (1985)
Francis "King" Clancy (1958)
Aubrey "Dit" Clapper (1947)
Bobby Clarke (1987)
Sprague Cleghorn (1958)
Neil Colville (1967)
Charlie Conacher (1961)
Alex Connell (1958)
Bill Cook (1952)
Arthur Coulter (1974)
Yvan Cournoyer (1982)
Bill Cowley (1968)
Samuel "Rusty" Crawford (1962)
Jack Darragh (1962)
Allan M. "Scotty" Davidson (1950)
Clarence "Hap" Day (1961)
Alex Delvecchio (1977)
Cy Denneny (1959)
Gordie Drillon (1975)
Charles Drinkwater (1950)
Ken Dryden (1983)
Thomas Dunderdale (1974)
Bill Durnan (1964)

Mervyn A. "Red" Dutton (1958)
Cecil "Babe" Dye (1970)
Phil Esposito (1984)
Tony Esposito (1988)
Arthur F. Farrell (1965)
Ferdinand "Fern" Flaman (1990)
Frank Foyston (1958)
Frank Frederickson (1958)
Bill Gadsby (1970)
Chuck Gardiner (1945)
Herb Gardiner (1958)
Jimmy Gardner (1962)
Bernie "Boom Boom" Geoffrion (1972)
Eddie Gerard (1945)
Ed Giacomin (1987)
Rod Gilbert (1982)
Hamilton "Billy" Gilmour (1962)
Frank "Moose" Goheen (1952)
Ebenezer R. "Ebbie" Goodfellow (1963)
Mike Grant (1950)
Wilfred "Shorty" Green (1962)
Si Griffis (1950)
George Hainsworth (1961)
Glenn Hall (1975)
Joe Hall (1961)
Doug Harvey (1973)
George Hay (1958)
William "Riley" Hern (1962)
Bryan Hextall (1969)
Harry "Hap" Holmes (1972)
Tom Hooper (1962)
George "Red" Horner (1965)
Miles "Tim" Horton (1977)
Gordie Howe (1972)
Syd Howe (1965)
Harry Howell (1979)
Bobby Hull (1983)
John "Bouse" Hutton (1962)
Harry M. Hyland (1962)
James "Dick" Irvin (1958)
Harvey "Busher" Jackson (1971)
Ernest "Moose" Johnson (1952)
Ivan "Ching" Johnson (1958)
Tom Johnson (1970)
Aurel Joliat (1947)
Gordon "Duke" Keats (1958)
Leonard "Red" Kelly (1969)
Ted "Teeder" Kennedy (1966)
Dave Keon (1986)

Elmer Lach (1966)
Guy Lafleur (1988)
Edouard "Newsy" Lalonde (1950)
Jacques Laperriere (1987)
Jean "Jack" Laviolette (1962)
Hugh Lehman (1958)
Jacques Lemaire (1984)
Percy LeSueur (1961)
Herbert A. Lewis (1989)
Ted Lindsay (1966)
Harry Lumley (1980)
Frank McGee (1945)
Billy McGimsie (1962)
George McNamara (1958)
Duncan "Mickey" MacKay (1952)
Frank Mahovlich (1981)
Joe Malone (1950)
Sylvio Mantha (1960)
Jack Marshall (1965)
Fred G. "Steamer" Maxwell (1962)
Stan Mikita (1983)
Dicky Moore (1974)
Patrick "Paddy" Moran (1958)
Howie Morenz (1945)
Billy Mosienko (1965)
Frank Nighbor (1947)
Reg Noble (1962)
Herbert "Buddy" O'Connor (1988)
Harry Oliver (1967)
Bert Olmstead (1985)
Bobby Orr (1979)
Bernie Parent (1984)
Brad Park (1988)
Lester Patrick (1947)
Lynn Patrick (1980)
Gilbert Perreault (1990)
Tommy Phillips (1945)
Pierre Pilote (1975)
Didier "Pit" Pitre (1962)
Jacques Plante (1978)
Walter "Babe" Pratt (1966)
Joe Primeau (1963)
Marcel Pronovost (1978)
Harvey Pulford (1945)
Hubert "Bill" Quackenbush (1976)
Frank Rankin (1961)
Jean Ratelle (1985)
Claude "Chuck" Rayner (1973)

Players (*Cont.*)

Kenneth Reardon (1966)
Henri Richard (1979)
Maurice "Rocket" Richard (1961)
George Richardson (1950)
Gordon Roberts (1971)
Art Ross (1945)
Blair Russel (1965)
Ernest Russell (1965)
Jack Ruttan (1962)
Serge Savard (1986)
Terry Sawchuk (1971)
Fred Scanlan (1965)
Milt Schmidt (1961)
Dave "Sweeney" Schriner (1962)
Earl Seibert (1963)
Oliver Seibert (1961)
Eddie Shore (1947)
Albert C. "Babe" Siebert (1964)
Harold "Bullet Joe" Simpson (1962)
Daryl Sittler (1989)
Alfred E. Smith (1962)
Reginald "Hooley" Smith (1972)
Thomas Smith (1973)
Allan Stanley (1981)
Russell "Barney" Stanley (1962)
John "Black Jack" Stewart (1964)
Nels Stewart (1962)
Bruce Stuart (1961)
Hod Stuart (1945)
Frederic "Cyclone" (O.B.E.) Taylor (1947)
Cecil R. "Tiny" Thompson (1959)
Vladislav Tretiak (1989)
Harry J. Trihey (1950)
Norm Ullman (1982)
Georges Vezina (1945)
Jack Walker (1960)
Marty Walsh (1962)
Harry E. Watson (1962)
Ralph "Cooney" Weiland (1971)
Harry Westwick (1962)
Fred Whitcroft (1962)
Gordon "Phat" Wilson (1962)
Lorne "Gump" Worsley (1980)
Roy Worters (1969)

Builders

Charles Adams (1960)
Weston W. Adams (1972)
Thomas "Frank" Ahearn (1962)
John "Bunny" Ahearne (1977)
Montagu Allan (C.V.O.) (1945)
Harold Ballard (1977)
David Bauer (1989)
John Bickell (1978)
George V. Brown (1961)
Walter A. Brown (1962)
Frank Buckland (1975)
Jack Butterfield (1980)
Frank Calder (1947)
Angus D. Campbell (1964)
Clarence Campbell (1966)
Joe Cattarinich (1977)
Joseph "Leo" Dandurand (1963)
Francis Dilio (1964)
George S. Dudley (1958)
James A. Dunn (1968)
Alan Eagleson (1989)
Emile Francis (1982)
Jack Gibson (1976)
Tommy Gorman (1963)
William Hanley (1986)
Charles Hay (1974)
James C. Hendy (1968)
Foster Hewitt (1965)
William Hewitt (1947)
Fred J. Hume (1962)
George "Punch" Imlach (1984)
Tommy Ivan (1974)
William M. Jennings (1975)
Gordon W. Juckes (1979)
John Kilpatrick (1960)
George Leader (1969)
Robert LeBel (1970)
Thomas F. Lockhart (1965)
Paul Loicq (1961)
Frederic McLaughlin (1963)
John Mariucci (1985)
John "Jake" Milford (1984)
Hartland Molson (1973)
Francis Nelson (1947)
Bruce A. Norris (1969)
James Norris, Sr. (1958)
James D. Norris (1962)
William M. Northey (1947)
John O'Brien (1962)
Frank Patrick (1958)
Allan W. Pickard (1958)

Builders (*Cont.*)

Rudy Pilous (1985)
Norman "Bud" Poile (1990)
Samuel Pollock (1978)
Donat Raymond (1958)
John Robertson (1947)
Claude C. Robinson (1947)
Philip D. Ross (1976)
Frank J. Selke (1960)
Harry Sinden (1983)
Frank D. Smith (1962)
Conn Smythe (1958)
Edward M. Snider (1988)
Lord Stanley of Preston (G.C.B.) (1945)
James T. Sutherland (1947)
Anatoli V. Tarasov (1974)
Lloyd Turner (1958)
William Tutt (1978)
Carl Potter Voss (1974)
Fred C. Waghorn (1961)
Arthur Wirtz (1971)
Bill Wirtz (1976)
John A. Ziegler, Jr. (1987)

Referees/Linesmen

John Ashley (1981)
William L. Chadwick (1964)
Chaucer Elliott (1961)
George Hayes (1988)
Robert W. Hewitson (1963)
Fred J. "Mickey" Ion (1961)
Matt Pavelich (1987)
Mike Rodden (1962)
J. Cooper Smeaton (1961)
Roy "Red" Storey (1967)
Frank Udvari (1973)

Note: Year of election to the Hall of Fame is in parentheses after the member's name.

The Goal-a-Game Gang	In 1990-91 the St. Louis Blues' Brett Hull became only the third player in NHL history to score more than 80 goals in a season, netting 86. Wayne Gretzky has done it twice (92 in 1981–82; 87 in 1983–84), and Mario Lemieux once (85 in 1988–89).

Tennis

JULY 15, 1991 · $2.95

Sports Illustrated

I'm Back!

Steffi Graf emerges from 18 months of frustration to win her third Wimbledon title

OPEL

CARYN LEVY

A Season of Unforced Errors

In tennis, events off the court were often as startling as the play on it | by ROBERT SULLIVAN

T WAS A WACKY YEAR ON AND OFF THE COURTS. We had a legend (Bjorn Borg) trying a hapless comeback, as his wife attempted suicide; we had a Madonna wannabe (Monica Seles) as the best woman player in the world; we had a face-off in the stands at the French Open between Steffi Graf's father and an adoring fan; we had a bitter lawsuit between an aging champion (Martina Navratilova) and her former cohabitant; and we had a year in which the biggest winner of all was another legend (Jimmy Connors) who didn't win a darn thing. It was a crazy-sidespin kind of year.

Lewis Carroll would've loved it, and he would have urged us to start at the begin-

ning, a very good place to start. In January at the Australian Open, there were four familiar names in the men's semifinals: Lendl, Edberg, Becker, and McEnroe. But this McEnroe was Patrick, younger brother of John. Patrick went no further, losing to Germany's Boris Becker, who went on to win the event and then capture the No. 1 ranking for the first time in his illustrious career. Becker was so overcome with the moment that prior to the postmatch ceremony, he took a victory jog—in a park near the stadium. Becker and Stefan Edberg of Sweden would play leapfrog with the top spot all year.

In the spring, one man's thoughts turned to flights of lunacy as Borg, who had retired

in 1983 at age 26, announced that he was returning to the tour. While Borg was in Monte Carlo in April for his re-debut, his wife, Loredana Berte, an erstwhile Italian pop-music diva who had stayed behind in Milan, reportedly ingested far too many barbiturates over rumors that Borg was out philandering. She survived, but Borg did not, succumbing 6–2, 6–3 in the first round to Nobody N. Particular (Jordi Arrese for you trivia fans). Borg played with an old-fashioned, small-headed racket and was "coached" by a 79-year-old trainer/guru named Tia Honsai (né Ron Thatcher), whose charge was to cast good vibrations from the stands.

A month after the Borg psychodrama, the French Open was dominated by Seles, but much of the attention was focused on Jim Levee, a very rich, white-haired Floridian who gives gifts—cash, cars, other items of worth—to many of the young, talented women on the tour. The term "Sugar Daddy" seems not to apply in the traditional sense, but it was uttered nonetheless. Anyway, Graf accepted Levee's largesse until Levee switched his primary allegiance to Seles in mid-1990. In the gallery at Stade Roland Garros he shouted loudly for Seles throughout the tournament. At one point, he was heard by, among others, Peter Graf, Steffi's

Stich was unstoppable at Wimbledon, beating the world's top players, Edberg and Becker, in the semis and finals.

father, who at the time was suffering through his daughter's 6–0, 6–2 semifinal thrashing by Arantxa Sanchez Vicario of Spain. Daddy Graf, himself a two-year source of humiliation to Steffi for his alleged sexual indiscretions, proceeded to bop Sugar Daddy Levee on the head.

Americans in Paris were the subtext of the men's division at the French, where an all-Yank final ensued for the first time in 37 years. Andre Agassi, who had led the U.S. to the 1990 Davis Cup title and taken the $600,000 winner's check at the ATP Tour World Championship to round out the previous season, gained his third Grand Slam final in just two years with an impressive semifinal win over Becker. All Agassi could manage, however, was his third Grand Slam runner-up trophy. He fell to 20-year-old Jim Courier, the hottest, hardest-hitting American of '91. Courier, a Florida redhead, whomps the ball from both sides and has a strong serve as well. The French was Courier's first Slam championship, but it won't be his last.

At Wimbledon, Germany's Michael Stich arrived with a vengeance. He beat the world's best players—Edberg and Becker—in the final two rounds with a powerful serve that is among the hardest on the tour and with an all-around game that is well suited for any surface.

Graf won the women's All England title, though the story of the tournament concerned someone who never played a match. Seles mysteriously withdrew a few days before the fortnight, prompting rumors to fly that she (a) had shin splints, (b) was pregnant, or (c) had holed up at Donald Trump's Mar-a-Lago mansion in Palm Beach, Fla. At the same time, Graf bravely battled her own tabloid troubles, which included reheated stuff about Dad and new stuff about Levee, who had threatened at the French Open to "get two bodyguards at Wimbledon and break both of (Dad's) legs."

All this tennis . . . junk . . . kept piling up as the summer progressed. Seles later submitted a doctor's note proving that she was, in fact, suffering from shin splints. Still, she was fined $6,000 by the Women's Tennis Association. Then there was the Texas lawsuit filed against Navratilova by her longtime companion, Judy Nelson. The suit, which was played out in court with tearful testimony from both parties, wasn't settled despite a week's worth of unseemly hearings in September, which only prompted a new round of out-of-court talks.

With all this high-toned news dominating the tennis headlines, it seemed suitable that

An Oldie, Not a Goodie

THE YEAR SHOULD HAVE BELONGED to Stefan Edberg and Monica Seles, tennis's emerging stars. But it was stolen from the kids by a crotchety, foul-mouthed gunslinger who strode forth from his California ranch and picked off enough cowboys to rebolster his reputation as one tough hombre. James Scott Connors, winner of eight Grand Slam titles during the last two decades, was cut down in each tournament he entered during the year, but all of America remains convinced that he won everything in sight.

Connors spent most of 1990 on the sidelines due to injury, and by last February his ranking had nosedived to No. 990. As something of a lark, he accepted a wild-card entry into the French Open. Clay-court rehab is a good idea: You get to hit a lot of balls. *Jheemee,* as the gay Parisians called him, got to hit a lot more than he expected.

Upset victories over Todd Witsken of the U.S. and Ronald Agenor of Haiti set up a compelling confrontation: Connors, at 38, versus Michael Chang, the '89 French champion and a kid half his age. Remarkably, Connors, playing with a gimpy back, was able to even the match at two sets apiece. He looked awfully creaky as he readied himself for the final set, but he did a typically Jimbo thing. He drilled a backhand return for a winner and *then* retired. "Quit while I was ahead," he said later, laughing, sort of.

At Wimbledon, Connors moonlighted in the NBC broadcast booth as he reached the third round before losing to Derrick Rostagno, 7–6, 6–1, 6–4. He then spent most of the summer playing Team Tennis; one month shy of his 39th birthday, he was named the league's male Rookie of the Year.

All of this was mere prelude to the melodrama that unfolded at Flushing Meadow. Connors trailed Patrick McEnroe 6–4, 7–6, 3–0, 40–0 during their first-round match on the tournament's second evening. Facing such a score, a player is wont to hit away, and Connors did, gaining his stride as the vice tightened on the less experienced McEnroe

the tour encamped for its final Slam event in a place called Flushing. The goo continued to seep out during the two weeks (they never dignify the U.S. Open by calling it a "fortnight") in Queens, N.Y. Seles was back, cooing coquettishly at courtside with Kim Basinger-less actor Alec Baldwin; playing braless during all of her matches; and starring in a shameless TV ad for No Excuses jeans, a smarmy bit of video that no 17-year-old should be allowed to see, much less perform in. Wherever she was, Seles was a sight. Bizarrely, she spent the Open metamorphosing from a Madonna wannabe into a Marla Maples wannabe. During her speech after routing Navratilova 7–6, 6–1 in the final for her third Grand Slam title of the year, she even thanked Trump for his support. Only in America could a young, pretty Yugoslav with all the talent in the world pile up so many PR mistakes, zooming toward zero popularity like a heat-seeking missile while soaring toward the top of the rankings. As Seles finished off Navratilova, there was only grudging applause. And as she took her victory cruise around the court, fans thronged to the hundred-dollar-quiche stands, wanting to fortify themselves for the next installment of the soap-opera drama starring Connors (*see sidebar*). Thus, ironically, as Seles was capping a magnificent season, she was being largely ignored. It was as strange a moment as the strange old year had to offer.

and the beery midnight crowd roused itself. At 1:35 in the morning, after nearly 4½ hours, poor McEnroe was done and Connors was on his way toward owning the tournament.

He requested night matches to avoid the heat. He took 40 seconds between points (25 is the rule). And he spoke profanely to an official with impunity. Perhaps the most amazing aspect of the Connors renaissance was that the old goat somehow became lovable without budging as a crass, unsportsmanlike boor. Connors called the chair umpire a "son of a bitch," among other things, during another stirring five-set comeback, this one against Aaron Krickstein. "Get your ass out of the chair," Connors screamed. "You're an abortion."

"Connors has always been an ——," said a former pro. "It's just that now he's everybody's favorite ——."

Yes he was, even after Courier dismissed Connors in the semis, 6–3, 6–3, 6–2. Watching at Flushing, Connors's old friend in gamesmanship, Ilie Nastase, put it well: "What Jimmy has is what we all would kill for—Just one more time."

CARYN LEVY

Connors captivated crowds with the same boorish behavior that used to turn them off.

CARYN LEVY

Thank goodness for Connors, who added some pizzazz, which isn't to say class, to the proceedings. And thank goodness for Edberg, who added some uncommon brilliance.

The match of the tournament was neither of Connors's dynamic five-set comebacks (against Patrick McEnroe in the opening round and against Aaron Krickstein in the fourth round). Nor was it 15-year-old Jennifer Capriati's jump-for-joy triumph over defending champion Gabriela Sabatini in the quarters, nor Seles's three-set thriller over a distraught Capriati in the semis, nor Edberg's near-perfect dissections of Lendl in the semis and Courier in the final. It was none of those, good as they were for their excitement, drama, and competitiveness. The match of the tournament, qualitatively, was a fourth-round straight-set win by Edberg over 19-year-old Michael Chang. The young American and former French Open champion raised himself from a poor summer and issued a fine challenge to the

Seles won the Australian, French and U.S. Opens, but drew more attention for skipping Wimbledon.

superb, sublimely talented Swede. Chang chased down everything, no matter how hard it was hit. He surprised Edberg by sneaking to the net. He served well. He hit passing shots. And yet, all he could manage was to reach one tiebreaker. Edberg played like a taller, stronger Rod Laver. His volleys were precise. His winners off both wings were dazzling. Neither player would be considered a riveting personality, and yet the late-night crowd was thrilled by the pure excellence of the match.

Edberg went on to play precisely the same tennis against Javier Sanchez, Lendl and Courier, none of whom gave him the fight Chang had provided or managed even to take a set. When Edberg closed out Courier with a firm backhand volley down the line, tennis's dissonant year ended on a clear, beautifully struck note.

1991 Grand Slam Champions

Australian Open
Men's Singles

	Winner	Loser	Score
Quarterfinals	Stefan Edberg (1)	Jaime Yzaga	6-2, 6-3, 6-2
	Ivan Lendl (3)	Goran Prpic	6-0, 7-6, 7-6
	Patrick McEnroe	Cristiano Caratti	7-6, 6-3, 4-6, 4-6, 6-2
	Boris Becker (2)	Guy Forget (10)	6-2, 7-6, 6-3
Semifinals	Ivan Lendl	Stefan Edberg	6-4, 5-7, 3-6, 7-6, 6-4
	Boris Becker	Patrick McEnroe	6-7, 6-4, 6-1, 6-4
Final	Boris Becker	Ivan Lendl	1-6, 6-4, 6-4, 6-4

Women's Singles

	Winner	Loser	Score
Quarterfinals	Jana Novotna (10)	Steffi Graf (1)	5-7, 6-4, 8-6
	Arantxa Sanchez Vicario (6)	Gabriela Sabatini (4)	6-1, 6-3
	Mary Joe Fernandez (3)	Katerina Maleeva (5)	6-3, 6-2
	Monica Seles (2)	Anke Huber	6-3, 6-1
Semifinals	Jana Novotna	Arantxa Sanchez Vicario	6-2, 6-4
	Monica Seles	Mary Joe Fernandez	6-3, 0-6, 9-7
Final	Monica Seles	Jana Novotna	5-7, 6-3, 6-1

Doubles

	Winner	Loser	Score
Men's Final	Scott Davis/ David Pate (3)	Patrick McEnroe/ David Wheaton (13)	6-7, 7-6, 6-3, 7-5
Women's Final	Patty Fendick/ Mary Joe Fernandez (4)	Gigi Fernandez/ Jana Novotna (1)	7-6, 6-1
Mixed Final	Jeremy Bates/ Jo Durie	Scott Davis/ Robin White (3)	2-6, 6-4, 6-4

French Open
Men's Singles

	Winner	Loser	Score
Quarterfinals	Jim Courier (9)	Stefan Edberg (1)	6-4, 2-6, 6-3, 6-4
	Michael Stich (12)	Franco Davin	6-4, 6-4, 6-4
	Andre Agassi (4)	Jakob Hlasek	6-3, 6-1, 6-1
	Boris Becker (2)	Michael Chang (10)	6-4, 6-4, 6-2
Semifinals	Jim Courier	Michael Stich	6-2, 6-7, 6-2, 6-4
	Andre Agassi	Boris Becker	7-5, 6-3, 3-6, 6-1
Final	Jim Courier	Andre Agassi	3-6, 6-4, 2-6, 6-1, 6-4

Women's Singles

	Winner	Loser	Score
Quarterfinals	Monica Seles (1)	Conchita Martinez (7)	6-0, 7-5
	Gabriela Sabatini (3)	Jana Novotna (6)	5-7, 7-6, 6-0
	Arantxa Sanchez Vicario (5)	Mary Joe Fernandez (4)	6-3, 6-2
	Steffi Graf (2)	Nathalie Tauziat (13)	6-3, 6-2
Semifinals	Monica Seles	Gabriela Sabatini	6-4, 6-1
	Arantxa Sanchez Vicario	Steffi Graf	6-0, 6-2
Final	Monica Seles	Arantxa Sanchez Vicario	6-3, 6-4

Note: Seedings in parentheses.

French Open (*Cont.*)
Doubles

	Winner	Loser	Score
Men's Final	John Fitzgerald/ Anders Jarryd (9)	Rick Leach/ Jim Pugh (3)	6-0, 7-6
Women's Final	Gigi Fernandez/ Jana Novotna (1)	Larisa Savchenko/ Natalia Zvereva (2)	6-4, 6-0
Mixed Final	Cyril Suk/ Helena Sukova (12)	Paul Haarhuis/ Caroline Vis (14)	3-6, 6-4, 6-1

Wimbledon
Men's Singles

	Winner	Loser	Score
Quarterfinals	Stefan Edberg (1)	Thierry Champion	6-3, 6-2, 7-5
	Michael Stich (6)	Jim Courier (4)	6-3, 7-6, 6-2
	David Wheaton	Andre Agassi (5)	6-2, 0-6, 3-6, 7-6, 6-2
	Boris Becker (2)	Guy Forget (7)	6-7, 7-6, 6-2, 7-6
Semifinals	Michael Stich	Stefan Edberg	4-6, 7-6, 7-6, 7-6
	Boris Becker	David Wheaton	6-4, 7-6, 7-5
Final	Michael Stich	Boris Becker	6-4, 7-6, 6-4

Women's Singles

	Winner	Loser	Score
Quarterfinals	Steffi Graf (1)	Zina Garrison (7)	6-1, 6-3
	Mary Joe Fernandez (5)	Arantxa Sanchez Vicario (4)	6-2, 7-5
	Jennifer Capriati (9)	Martina Navratilova (3)	6-4, 7-5
	Gabriela Sabatini (2)	Laura Gildemeister	6-2, 6-1
Semifinals	Steffi Graf	Mary Joe Fernandez	6-2, 6-4
	Gabriela Sabatini	Jennifer Capriati	6-4, 6-4
Final	Steffi Graf	Gabriela Sabatini	6-4, 3-6, 8-6

Doubles

	Winner	Loser	Score
Men's Final	John Fitzgerald/ Anders Jarryd (2)	Javier Frana/ Leonardo Lavalle	6-3, 6-4, 6-7, 6-1
Women's Final	Larisa Savchenko/ Natalia Zvereva (2)	Gigi Fernandez/ Jana Novotna (1)	6-4, 3-6, 6-4
Mixed Final	John Fitzgerald/ Elizabeth Smylie (2)	Jim Pugh/ Natalia Zvereva (1)	7-6, 6-2

U.S. Open
Men's Singles

	Winner	Loser	Score
Quarterfinals	Jimmy Connors	Paul Haarhuis	4-6, 7-6, 6-4, 6-2
	Jim Courier (4)	Pete Sampras (6)	6-2, 7-6, 7-6
	Ivan Lendl (5)	Michael Stich (3)	6-3, 3-6, 4-6, 7-6, 6-1
	Stefan Edberg (2)	Javier Sanchez	6-3, 6-2, 6-3
Semifinals	Jim Courier	Jimmy Connors	6-3, 6-3, 6-2
	Stefan Edberg	Ivan Lendl	6-3, 6-3, 6-4
Final	Stefan Edberg	Jim Courier	6-2, 6-4, 6-0

Note: Seedings in parentheses.

1991 Grand Slam Champions (*Cont.*)

U.S. Open (*Cont.*)
Women's Singles

	Winner	Loser	Score
Quarterfinals	Steffi Graf (1)	Conchita Martinez (8)	6-1, 6-3
	Martina Navratilova (6)	Arantxa Sanchez Vicario (4)	6-7, 7-6, 6-2
	Jennifer Capriati (7)	Gabriela Sabatini (3)	6-3, 7-6
	Monica Seles (2)	Gigi Fernandez	6-1, 6-2
Semifinals	Martina Navratilova	Steffi Graf	7-6, 6-7, 6-4
	Monica Seles	Jennifer Capriati	6-3, 3-6, 7-6
Final	Monica Seles	Martina Navratilova	7-6, 6-1

Doubles

	Winner	Loser	Score
Men's Final	John Fitzgerald/ Anders Jarryd (1)	Scott Davis/ David Pate (2)	6-3, 3-6, 6-3, 6-3
Women's Final	Pam Shriver/ Natalia Zvereva (6)	Jana Novotna/ Larisa Savchenko	6-4, 4-6, 7-6
Mixed Final	Tom Nijssen/ Manon Bollegraf	Emilio Sanchez/ Arantxa Sanchez Vicario (2)	6-2, 7-6

Note: Seedings in parentheses.

Tournament Results

Men's Tour (Late 1990)

Date	Tournament	Site	Winner	Finalist	Score
Oct 1-Oct 7	Australian Indoor Tennis Championships	Sydney	Boris Becker	Stefan Edberg	7-6, 6-4, 6-4
Oct 8-Oct 14	Seiko Super Tennis	Tokyo	Ivan Lendl	Boris Becker	4-6, 6-3, 7-6
Oct 8-Oct 14	Berlin Open	Berlin	Ronald Agenor	Alexander Volkov	4-6, 6-4, 7-6
Oct 22-Oct 28	Stockholm Open	Stockholm	Boris Becker	Stefan Edberg	6-4, 6-0, 6-3
Oct 29-Nov 4	Open de la Ville de Paris	Paris	Stefan Edberg	Boris Becker	3-3 ret
Nov 12-Nov 18	IBM/ATP Tour World Championship	Frankfurt	Andre Agassi	Stefan Edberg	5-7, 7-6, 7-5, 6-2

Men's Tour (through September 8, 1991)

Date	Tournament	Site	Winner	Finalist	Score
Jan 14-27	Australian Open	Melbourne	Boris Becker	Ivan Lendl	1-6, 6-4, 6-4, 6-4
Feb 11-17	US Pro Indoor Tennis Championships	Philadelphia	Ivan Lendl	Pete Sampras	5-7, 6-4, 3-6, 6-3
Feb 11-17	Donnay Indoor Championship	Brussels	Guy Forget	Andrei Cherkasov	6-3, 7-5, 3-6, 7-6
Feb 18-24	Eurocard Classics	Stuttgart	Stefan Edberg	Jonas Svensson	6-2, 3-6, 7-5, 6-2
Feb 18-24	Volvo Tennis Indoor	Memphis	Ivan Lendl	Michael Stich	7-5, 6-3
Mar 4-10	Newsweek Champions Cup	Indian Wells, CA	Jim Courier	Guy Forget	4-6, 6-3, 4-6, 6-3, 7-6
Mar 15-24	Lipton Intl Players Championships	Key Biscayne	Jim Courier	David Wheaton	4-6, 6-3, 6-4
Apr 8-14	Suntory Japan Open Tennis Championship	Tokyo	Stefan Edberg	Ivan Lendl	6-1, 7-5, 6-0
Apr 8-14	Trofeo Conde de Godo	Barcelona	Emilio Sanchez	Sergi Bruguera	6-4, 7-6, 6-2
Apr 22-28	Volvo Monte Carlo Open	Monte Carlo	Sergi Bruguera	Boris Becker	5-7, 6-4, 7-6, 7-6
May 6-12	Panasonic German Open	Hamburg	Karel Novacek	Magnus Gustafsson	6-3, 6-3, 5-7, 0-6, 6-1
May 13-19	XLVIII Campionati Intl d'Italia	Rome	Emilio Sanchez	Alberto Mancini	6-3, 6-1, 3-0 ret
May 20-26	Peugeot ATP World Team Cup	Dusseldorf	Sweden	Yugoslavia	2-1
May 27-June 9	French Open	Paris	Jim Courier	Andre Agassi	3-6, 6-4, 2-6, 6-1, 6-4
June 24-July 7	Wimbledon Championships	Wimbledon	Michael Stich	Boris Becker	6-4, 7-6, 6-4

Tournament Results (*Cont.*)

Men's Tour (*Cont.*)

Date	Tournament	Site	Winner	Finalist	Score
July 15-21	Mercedes Cup	Stuttgart	Michael Stich	Alberto Mancini	1-6, 7-6, 6-4, 6-2
July 15-21	Sovran Bank Classic	Washington	Andre Agassi	Petr Korda	6-3, 6-4
July 22-28	Player's Ltd Intl Canadian Open Tennis Championships	Montreal	Andrei Chesnokov	Petr Korda	3-6, 6-4, 6-3
July 29-Aug 4	Campionati Intl di Tennis	San Marino	Guillermo Perez-Roldan	Frederic Fontang	6-3, 6-1
Aug 5-11	Thriftway ATP Championship	Cincinnati	Guy Forget	Pete Sampras	2-6, 7-6, 6-4
Aug 12-18	GTE/US Men's Hardcourt Championships	Indianapolis	Pete Sampras	Boris Becker	7-6, 3-6, 6-3
Aug 12-18	Volvo Intl Tennis Tournament	New Haven	Petr Korda	Goran Ivanisevic	6-4, 6-2
Aug 26-Sep 8	US Open	New York	Stefan Edberg	Jim Courier	6-2, 6-4, 6-0

Women's Tour (Late 1990)

Date	Tournament	Site	Winner	Finalist	Score
Sep 10-16	Austrian Open	Kitzbuhel, Austria	Claudia Kohde-Kilsch	Rachel McQuillan	7-6, 6-4
Sep 24-30	Volkswagen Grand Prix	Leipzig	Steffi Graf	Arantxa Sanchez Vicario	6-1, 6-1
Sep 25-30	Nichirei Intl Championships (Tokyo Indoors)	Tokyo	Mary Joe Fernandez	Amy Frazier	3-6, 6-2, 6-3
Oct 8-14	BMW European Indoors	Zurich	Steffi Graf	Gabriela Sabatini	6-3, 6-2
Oct 15-21	Porsche Tennis Grand Prix	Filderstadt, Germany	Mary Joe Fernandez	Barbara Paulus	6-1, 6-3
Oct 22-28	Midland Bank Championships	Brighton, England	Steffi Graf	Helena Sukova	7-5, 6-3
Oct 22-28	Puerto Rico Open	Dorado, P.R.	Jennifer Capriati	Zina Garrison	5-7, 6-4, 6-2
Oct 29-Nov 4	Virginia Slims of California	Oakland	Monica Seles	Martina Navratilova	6-3, 7-6
Nov 5-11	Virginia Slims of New England	Worcester	Steffi Graf	Gabriela Sabatini	7-6, 6-3
Nov 12-18	Virginia Slims Championships	New York	Monica Seles	Gabriela Sabatini	6-4, 5-7, 3-6, 6-4, 6-2

Women's Tour (through September 8, 1991)

Date	Tournament	Site	Winner	Finalist	Score
Dec 31-Jan 6	Danone Open	Brisbane	Helena Sukova	Akiko Kijimuta	6-4, 6-3
Jan 7-13	Holden NSW Open	Sydney	Jana Novotna	Arantxa Sanchez Vicario	6-4, 6-2
Jan 14-27	Australian Open	Melbourne	Monica Seles	Jana Novotna	5-7, 6-3, 6-1
Jan 29-Feb 3	Pan Pacific Open	Tokyo	Gabriela Sabatini	Martina Navratilova	2-6, 6-2, 6-4
Feb 11-17	Virginia Slims of Chicago	Chicago	Martina Navratilova	Zina Garrison	6-1, 6-2
Feb 18-24	Virginia Slims of Oklahoma	Oklahoma City	Jana Novotna	Anne Smith	3-6, 6-3, 6-2
Feb 25-Mar 3	Virginia Slims of Palm Springs	Palm Springs	Martina Navratilova	Monica Seles	6-2, 7-6
Mar 4-10	Virginia Slims of Florida	Boca Raton	Gabriela Sabatini	Steffi Graf	6-4, 7-6
Mar 15-24	Lipton Intl Players Championships	Key Biscayne	Monica Seles	Gabriela Sabatini	6-3, 7-5
Mar 25-31	US Women's Hardcourt Championships	San Antonio	Steffi Graf	Monica Seles	6-4, 6-3
Apr 1-7	Family Circle Magazine Cup	Hilton Head Island, SC	Gabriela Sabatini	Leila Meskhi	6-1, 6-1
Apr 8-14	Bausch & Lomb Championships	Amelia Island, FL	Gabriela Sabatini	Steffi Graf	7-5, 7-6
Apr 15-21	Virginia Slims of Houston	Houston	Monica Seles	Mary Joe Fernandez	6-4, 6-3

Women's Tour (*Cont.*)

Date	Tournament	Site	Winner	Finalist	Score
Apr 22-28	Intl Championships of Spain	Barcelona	Conchita Martinez	Manuela Maleeva-Fragniere	6-4, 6-1
Apr 29-May 5	Citizen Cup	Hamburg	Steffi Graf	Monica Seles	7-5, 6-7, 6-3
May 6-12	Peugeot Italian Open	Rome	Gabriela Sabatini	Monica Seles	6-3, 6-2
May 13-20	Lufthansa Cup German Open	Berlin	Steffi Graf	Monica Seles	6-3, 4-6, 7-6
May 20-26	Geneva European Open	Geneva	Manuela Maleeva-Fragniere	Helen Kelesi	6-3, 3-6, 6-3
May 27-June 9	French Open	Paris	Monica Seles	Arantxa Sanchez Vicario	6-3, 6-4
June 10-16	Dow Classic	Birmingham, England	Martina Navratilova	Natalia Zvereva	6-4, 7-6
June 17-22	Pilkington Glass Championships	Eastbourne, England	Martina Navratilova	Arantxa Sanchez Vicario	6-4, 6-4
June 24-July 7	Wimbledon Championships	Wimbledon	Steffi Graf	Gabriela Sabatini	6-4, 3-6, 8-6
July 15-21	Citroen Austrian Ladies Open	Kitzbuhel, Austria	Conchita Martinez	Judith Wiesner	6-1, 2-6, 6-3
July 29-Aug 4	Mazda Tennis Classic	San Diego, CA	Jennifer Capriati	Monica Seles	4-6, 6-1, 7-6
Aug 5-11	Players Canadian Open	Toronto	Jennifer Capriati	Katerina Maleeva	6-2, 6-3
Aug 12-18	Virginia Slims of L.A.	Los Angeles, CA	Monica Seles	Kimiko Date	6-3, 6-1
Aug 19-25	Virginia Slims of Washington	Washington, D.C.	Arantxa Sanchez Vicario	Katerina Maleeva	6-2, 7-5
Aug 26-Sep 8	US Open	New York	Monica Seles	Martina Navratilova	7-6, 6-1

1990 Singles Leaders

Men

Rank	Player	Tournament Wins	Match Record	Earnings ($)
1	Stefan Edberg	7	70-14	1,995,901
2	Boris Becker	5	71-15	1,587,502
3	Ivan Lendl	5	53-11	1,145,742
4	Andre Agassi	4	45-12	1,741,382
5	Pete Sampras	3	47-17	900,057
6	Andres Gomez	3	37-26	872,613
7	Thomas Muster	3	51-17	605,267
8	Emilio Sanchez	2	50-25	734,286
9	Goran Ivanisevic	1	50-22	720,945
10	Brad Gilbert	3	47-22	555,733
11	Jonas Svensson	1	45-20	441,745
12	Andrei Chesnokov	2	45-21	423,863
13	John McEnroe	1	33-15	372,505
14	Guillermo Perez-Roldan	1	41-21	317,538
15	Michael Chang	1	34-20	416,072
16	Guy Forget	1	40-23	638,358
17	Jakob Hlasek	1	42-24	661,671
18	Jay Berger	1	32-18	349,354
19	Juan Aguilera	2	31-19	311,806
20	Aaron Krickstein	2	38-24	350,183

Note: Compiled by the Association of Tennis Professionals (ATP).

Women

Rank	Player	Tournament Wins	Match Record	Earnings ($)
1	Steffi Graf	10	72-5	1,921,853
2	Monica Seles	9	54-6	1,637,222
3	Martina Navratilova	6	52-7	1,330,794
4	Gabriela Sabatini	2	49-14	975,490
5	Mary Joe Fernandez	2	40-10	518,366
6	Zina Garrison	1	51-20	602,203
7	Katerina Maleeva	1	47-15	418,475
8	Arantxa Sanchez Vicario	2	41-15	517,662
9	Manuela Maleeva-Fragniere	0	42-16	360,215
10	Jana Novotna	1	43-16	645,500
11	Helena Sukova	0	41-17	562,715
12	Natalia Zvereva	2	42-15	462,770
13	Conchita Martinez	3	42-10	248,184
14	Nathalie Tauziat	1	48-21	300,103
15	Jennifer Capriati	1	42-11	283,597
16	Judith Wiesner	0	44-20	251,446
17	Barbara Paulus	1	35-15	184,164
18	Amy Frazier	1	31-14	160,620
19	Leila Meskhi	2	39-17	210,438
20	Rosalyn Fairbank-Nideffer	0	26-20	163,582

Note: Compiled by the Women's Tennis Association (WTA).

1990 Davis Cup

FINALS

United States d. Australia 3-2 at St Petersburg
Andre Agassi (US) d. Richard Fromberg (Aus) 4-6, 6-2, 4-6, 6-2, 6-4
Michael Chang (US) d. Darren Cahill (Aus) 6-2, 7-6, 6-0
Rick Leach and Jim Pugh (US) d. Pat Cash and John Fitzgerald (Aus) 6-4, 6-2, 3-6, 7-6
Darren Cahill (Aus) d. Andre Agassi (US) 6-4, 4-6, ret
Richard Fromberg (Aus) d. Michael Chang (US) 7-5, 2-6, 6-3

1991 Davis Cup

FIRST ROUND

Spain d. Canada 4-1 at Murcia
Argentina d. New Zealand 4-1 at Christchurch
Germany d. Italy 3-2 at Dortmund
Yugoslavia d. Sweden 4-1 at Zagreb
Czechoslovakia d. Austria 4-1 at Prague
Australia d. Belgium 5-0 at Perth
France d. Israel 5-0 at Rennes
United States d. Mexico 3-2 at Mexico City

SECOND ROUND

Yugoslavia d. Czechoslovakia 4-1 at Prague
Germany d. Argentina 5-0 at Berlin
France d. Australia 3-2 at Nimes
United States d. Spain 4-1 at Newport

SEMIFINALS

United States d. Germany 3-2 at Kansas City
Andre Agassi (US) d. Michael Stich (Ger)
Jim Courier (US) d. Carl-Uwe Steeb (Ger)
Michael Stich and Eric Jelen (Ger) d. David Pate
and Scott Davis (US)
Michael Stich (Ger) d. Jim Courier (US)
Andre Agassi (US) d. Carl-Uwe Steeb (Ger)

France d. Yugoslavia 5-0 at Pau, France
Guy Forget (Fra) d. Srdjan Muskatirovic (Yug)
Fabrice Santoro (Fra) d. Slobodan Zivojinovic (Yug)
Guy Forget and Arnaud Boetsch (Fra) d. Slobodan
Zivojinovic and Srdjan Muskatirovic (Yug)
Guy Forget (Fra) d. Slobodan Zivojinovic (Yug)
Fabrice Santoro (Fra) d. Srdjan Muskatirovic (Yug)

FINAL: France vs. United States to be held Nov 29-Dec 1 at Lyon.

1991 Federation Cup

FIRST ROUND

Australia d. Japan 2-1
Poland d. France 2-1
Canada d. Denmark 2-1
China PR d. Brazil 3-0
Finland d. Romania 3-0
Bulgaria d. Hungary 3-0
USSR d. Paraguay 3-0
Indonesia d. Yugoslavia 3-0
Spain d. Belgium 2-1
Germany d. Greece 3-0
Great Britain d. New Zealand 2-0
Switzerland d. Argentina 2-0
Czechoslovakia d. Sweden 2-0
Austria d. Portugal 3-0
Italy d. Israel 2-1
United States d. Netherlands 2-0

SECOND ROUND

Germany d. Canada 2-1
Italy d. Great Britain 2-0
Austria d. Finland 2-1
Indonesia d. Poland 2-1
Switzerland d. China 2-1
Czechoslovakia d. USSR 2-1
Spain d. Australia 3-0
United States d. Bulgaria 3-0

QUARTERFINALS

Czechoslovakia d. Switzerland 2-1
Germany d. Italy 2-1
Spain d. Indonesia 2-0
United States d. Austria 2-1

SEMIFINALS

Spain d. Germany 3-0
Conchita Martinez (Spain) d. Barbara Rittner (Ger)
Arantxa Sanchez Vicario (Spain) d. Anke Huber (Ger)
Conchita Martinez and Arantxa Sanchez Vicario
(Spain) d. Barbara Rittner and Anke Huber (Ger)

United States d. Czechoslovakia 3-0
Jennifer Capriati (US) d. Radka Zrubakova (Czech)
Mary Joe Fernandez (US) d. Jana Novotna (Czech)
Gigi Fernandez and Zina Garrison (US) d. Eva
Sviglerova and Regina Rajchrtova (Czech)

FINALS

Spain d. United States 2-1
Jennifer Capriati (US) d. Conchita Martinez (Spain)
4-6, 7-6, 6-1
Arantxa Sanchez Vicario (Spain) d. Mary Joe
Fernandez (US) 6-3, 6-4
Conchita Martinez and Arantxa Sanchez Vicario
(Spain) d. Gigi Fernandez and Zina Garrison
(US) 3-6, 6-1, 6-1

Note: Held at Nottingham Tennis Center, Nottingham, England, July 21-28.

Grand Slam Tournaments

MEN

Australian Championships

Year	Winner	Finalist	Score
1905	Rodney Heath	A. H. Curtis	4-6, 6-3, 6-4, 6-4
1906	Tony Wilding	H. A. Parker	6-0, 6-4, 6-4
1907	Horace M. Rice	H. A. Parker	6-3, 6-4, 6-4
1908	Fred Alexander	A. W. Dunlop	3-6, 3-6, 6-0, 6-2, 6-3
1909	Tony Wilding	E. F. Parker	6-1, 7-5, 6-2
1910	Rodney Heath	Horace M. Rice	6-4, 6-3, 6-2
1911	Norman Brookes	Horace M. Rice	6-1, 6-2, 6-3
1912	J. Cecil Parke	A. E. Beamish	3-6, 6-3, 1-6, 6-1, 7-5
1913	E. F. Parker	H. A. Parker	2-6, 6-1, 6-2, 6-3
1914	Pat O'Hara Wood	G. L. Patterson	6-4, 6-3, 5-7, 6-1
1915	Francis G. Lowe	Horace M. Rice	4-6, 6-1, 6-1, 6-4
1916-18	No tournament		
1919	A. R. F. Kingscote	E. O. Pockley	6-4, 6-0, 6-3
1920	Pat O'Hara Wood	Ron Thomas	6-3, 4-6, 6-8, 6-1, 6-3
1921	Rhys H. Gemmell	A. Hedeman	7-5, 6-1, 6-4
1922	Pat O'Hara Wood	Gerald Patterson	6-0, 3-6, 3-6, 6-3, 6-2
1923	Pat O'Hara Wood	C. B. St John	6-1, 6-1, 6-3
1924	James Anderson	R. E. Schlesinger	6-3, 6-4, 3-6, 5-7, 6-3
1925	James Anderson	Gerald Patterson	11-9, 2-6, 6-2, 6-3
1926	John Hawkes	J. Willard	6-1, 6-3, 6-1
1927	Gerald Patterson	John Hawkes	3-6, 6-4, 3-6, 18-16, 6-3
1928	Jean Borotra	R. O. Cummings	6-4, 6-1, 4-6, 5-7, 6-3
1929	John C. Gregory	R. E. Schlesinger	6-2, 6-2, 5-7, 7-5
1930	Gar Moon	Harry C. Hopman	6-3, 6-1, 6-3
1931	Jack Crawford	Harry C. Hopman	6-4, 6-2, 2-6, 6-1
1932	Jack Crawford	Harry C. Hopman	4-6, 6-3, 3-6, 6-3, 6-1
1933	Jack Crawford	Keith Gledhill	2-6, 7-5, 6-3, 6-2
1934	Fred Perry	Jack Crawford	6-3, 7-5, 6-1
1935	Jack Crawford	Fred Perry	2-6, 6-4, 6-4, 6-4
1936	Adrian Quist	Jack Crawford	6-2, 6-3, 4-6, 3-6, 9-7
1937	Vivian B. McGrath	John Bromwich	6-3, 1-6, 6-0, 2-6, 6-1
1938	Don Budge	John Bromwich	6-4, 6-2, 6-1
1939	John Bromwich	Adrian Quist	6-4, 6-1, 6-3
1940	Adrian Quist	Jack Crawford	6-3, 6-1, 6-2
1941-45	No tournament		
1946	John Bromwich	Dinny Pails	5-7, 6-3, 7-5, 3-6, 6-2
1947	Dinny Pails	John Bromwich	4-6, 6-4, 3-6, 7-5, 8-6
1948	Adrian Quist	John Bromwich	6-4, 3-6, 6-3, 2-6, 6-3
1949	Frank Sedgman	Ken McGregor	6-3, 6-3, 6-2
1950	Frank Sedgman	Ken McGregor	6-3, 6-4, 4-6, 6-1
1951	Richard Savitt	Ken McGregor	6-3, 2-6, 6-3, 6-1
1952	Ken McGregor	Frank Sedgman	7-5, 12-10, 2-6, 6-2
1953	Ken Rosewall	Mervyn Rose	6-0, 6-3, 6-4
1954	Mervyn Rose	Rex Hartwig	6-2, 0-6, 6-4, 6-2
1955	Ken Rosewall	Lew Hoad	9-7, 6-4, 6-4
1956	Lew Hoad	Ken Rosewall	6-4, 3-6, 6-4, 7-5
1957	Ashley Cooper	Neale Fraser	6-3, 9-11, 6-4, 6-2
1958	Ashley Cooper	Mal Anderson	7-5, 6-3, 6-4
1959	Alex Olmedo	Neale Fraser	6-1, 6-2, 3-6, 6-3
1960	Rod Laver	Neale Fraser	5-7, 3-6, 6-3, 8-6, 8-6
1961	Roy Emerson	Rod Laver	1-6, 6-3, 7-5, 6-4
1962	Rod Laver	Roy Emerson	8-6, 0-6, 6-4, 6-4
1963	Roy Emerson	Ken Fletcher	6-3, 6-3, 6-1
1964	Roy Emerson	Fred Stolle	6-3, 6-4, 6-2
1965	Roy Emerson	Fred Stolle	7-9, 2-6, 6-4, 7-5, 6-1
1966	Roy Emerson	Arthur Ashe	6-4, 6-8, 6-2, 6-3
1967	Roy Emerson	Arthur Ashe	6-4, 6-1, 6-1
1968	Bill Bowrey	Juan Gisbert	7-5, 2-6, 9-7, 6-4

Australian Championships (*Cont.*)

Year	Winner	Finalist	Score
1969*	Rod Laver	Andres Gimeno	6-3, 6-4, 7-5
1970	Arthur Ashe	Dick Crealy	6-4, 9-7, 6-2
1971	Ken Rosewall	Arthur Ashe	6-1, 7-5, 6-3
1972	Ken Rosewall	Mal Anderson	7-6, 6-3, 7-5
1973	John Newcombe	Onny Parun	6-3, 6-7, 7-5, 6-1
1974	Jimmy Connors	Phil Dent	7-6, 6-4, 4-6, 6-3
1975	John Newcombe	Jimmy Connors	7-5, 3-6, 6-4, 7-5
1976	Mark Edmondson	John Newcombe	6-7, 6-3, 7-6, 6-1
1977 (Jan)	Roscoe Tanner	Guillermo Vilas	6-3, 6-3, 6-3
1977 (Dec)	Vitas Gerulaitis	John Lloyd	6-3, 7-6, 5-7, 3-6, 6-2
1978	Guillermo Vilas	John Marks	6-4, 6-4, 3-6, 6-3
1979	Guillermo Vilas	John Sadri	7-6, 6-3, 6-2
1980	Brian Teacher	Kim Warwick	7-5, 7-6, 6-3
1981	Johan Kriek	Steve Denton	6-2, 7-6, 6-7, 6-4
1982	Johan Kriek	Steve Denton	6-3, 6-3, 6-2
1983	Mats Wilander	Ivan Lendl	6-1, 6-4, 6-4
1984	Mats Wilander	Kevin Curren	6-7, 6-4, 7-6, 6-2
1985 (Dec)	Stefan Edberg	Mats Wilander	6-4, 6-3, 6-3
1987 (Jan)	Stefan Edberg	Pat Cash	6-3, 6-4, 3-6, 5-7, 6-3
1988	Mats Wilander	Pat Cash	6-3, 6-7, 3-6, 6-1, 8-6
1989	Ivan Lendl	Miloslav Mecir	6-2, 6-2, 6-2
1990	Ivan Lendl	Stefan Edberg	4-6, 7-6, 5-2 ret
1991	Boris Becker	Ivan Lendl	1-6, 6-4, 6-4, 6-4

*Became Open (amateur and professional) in 1969.

French Championships

Year	Winner	Finalist	Score
1925†	Rene Lacoste	Jean Borotra	7-5, 6-1, 6-4
1926	Henri Cochet	Rene Lacoste	6-2, 6-4, 6-3
1927	Rene Lacoste	Bill Tilden	6-4, 4-6, 5-7, 6-3, 11-9
1928	Henri Cochet	Rene Lacoste	5-7, 6-3, 6-1, 6-3
1929	Rene Lacoste	Jean Borotra	6-3, 2-6, 6-0, 2-6, 8-6
1930	Henri Cochet	Bill Tilden	3-6, 8-6, 6-3, 6-1
1931	Jean Borotra	Claude Boussus	2-6, 6-4, 7-5, 6-4
1932	Henri Cochet	Giorgio de Stefani	6-0, 6-4, 4-6, 6-3
1933	Jack Crawford	Henri Cochet	8-6, 6-1, 6-3
1934	Gottfried von Cramm	Jack Crawford	6-4, 7-9, 3-6, 7-5, 6-3
1935	Fred Perry	Gottfried von Cramm	6-3, 3-6, 6-1, 6-3
1936	Gottfried von Cramm	Fred Perry	6-0, 2-6, 6-2, 2-6, 6-0
1937	Henner Henkel	Henry Austin	6-1, 6-4, 6-3
1938	Don Budge	Roderick Menzel	6-3, 6-2, 6-4
1939	Don McNeill	Bobby Riggs	7-5, 6-0, 6-3
1940	No tournament		
1941‡	Bernard Destremau	n/a	n/a
1942‡	Bernard Destremau	n/a	n/a
1943‡	Yvon Petra	n/a	n/a
1944‡	Yvon Petra	n/a	n/a
1945‡	Yvon Petra	Bernard Destremau	7-5, 6-4, 6-2
1946	Marcel Bernard	Jaroslav Drobny	3-6, 2-6, 6-1, 6-4, 6-3
1947	Joseph Asboth	Eric Sturgess	8-6, 7-5, 6-4
1948	Frank Parker	Jaroslav Drobny	6-4, 7-5, 5-7, 8-6
1949	Frank Parker	Budge Patty	6-3, 1-6, 6-1, 6-4
1950	Budge Patty	Jaroslav Drobny	6-1, 6-2, 3-6, 5-7, 7-5
1951	Jaroslav Drobny	Eric Sturgess	6-3, 6-3, 6-3
1952	Jaroslav Drobny	Frank Sedgman	6-2, 6-0, 3-6, 6-4
1953	Ken Rosewall	Vic Seixas	6-3, 6-4, 1-6, 6-2
1954	Tony Trabert	Arthur Larsen	6-4, 7-5, 6-1
1955	Tony Trabert	Sven Davidson	2-6, 6-1, 6-4, 6-2
1956	Lew Hoad	Sven Davidson	6-4, 8-6, 6-3
1957	Sven Davidson	Herbie Flam	6-3, 6-4, 6-4
1958	Mervyn Rose	Luis Ayala	6-3, 6-4, 6-4
1959	Nicola Pietrangeli	Ian Vermaak	3-6, 6-3, 6-4, 6-1
1960	Nicola Pietrangeli	Luis Ayala	3-6, 6-3, 6-4, 4-6, 6-3

French Championships (*Cont.*)

Year	Winner	Finalist	Score
1961	Manuel Santana	Nicola Pietrangeli	4-6, 6-1, 3-6, 6-0, 6-2
1962	Rod Laver	Roy Emerson	3-6, 2-6, 6-3, 9-7, 6-2
1963	Roy Emerson	Pierre Darmon	3-6, 6-1, 6-4, 6-4
1964	Manuel Santana	Nicola Pietrangeli	6-3, 6-1, 4-6, 7-5
1965	Fred Stolle	Tony Roche	3-6, 6-0, 6-2, 6-3
1966	Tony Roche	Istvan Gulyas	6-1, 6-4, 7-5
1967	Roy Emerson	Tony Roche	6-1, 6-4, 2-6, 6-2
1968*	Ken Rosewall	Rod Laver	6-3, 6-1, 2-6, 6-2
1969	Rod Laver	Ken Rosewall	6-4, 6-3, 6-4
1970	Jan Kodes	Zeljko Franulovic	6-2, 6-4, 6-0
1971	Jan Kodes	Ilie Nastase	8-6, 6-2, 2-6, 7-5
1972	Andres Gimeno	Patrick Proisy	4-6, 6-3, 6-1, 6-1
1973	Ilie Nastase	Nikki Pilic	6-3, 6-3, 6-0
1974	Bjorn Borg	Manuel Orantes	6-7, 6-0, 6-1, 6-1
1975	Bjorn Borg	Guillermo Vilas	6-2, 6-3, 6-4
1976	Adriano Panatta	Harold Solomon	6-1, 6-4, 4-6, 7-6
1977	Guillermo Vilas	Brian Gottfried	6-0, 6-3, 6-0
1978	Bjorn Borg	Guillermo Vilas	6-1, 6-1, 6-3
1979	Bjorn Borg	Victor Pecci	6-3, 6-1, 6-7, 6-4
1980	Bjorn Borg	Vitas Gerulaitis	6-4, 6-1, 6-2
1981	Bjorn Borg	Ivan Lendl	6-1, 4-6, 6-2, 3-6, 6-1
1982	Mats Wilander	Guillermo Vilas	1-6, 7-6, 6-0, 6-4
1983	Yannick Noah	Mats Wilander	6-2, 7-5, 7-6
1984	Ivan Lendl	John McEnroe	3-6, 2-6, 6-4, 7-5, 7-5
1985	Mats Wilander	Ivan Lendl	3-6, 6-4, 6-2, 6-2
1986	Ivan Lendl	Mikael Pernfors	6-3, 6-2, 6-4
1987	Ivan Lendl	Mats Wilander	7-5, 6-2, 3-6, 7-6
1988	Mats Wilander	Henri Leconte	7-5, 6-2, 6-1
1989	Michael Chang	Stefan Edberg	6-1, 3-6, 4-6, 6-4, 6-2
1990	Andres Gomez	Andre Agassi	6-3, 2-6, 6-4, 6-4
1991	Jim Courier	Andre Agassi	3-6, 6-4, 2-6, 6-1, 6-4

*Became Open (amateur and professional) in 1968 but closed to contract professionals in 1972.

†1925 was the first year that entries were accepted from all countries.

‡From 1941 to 1945 the event was called Tournoi de France and was closed to all foreigners.

Wimbledon Championships

Year	Winner	Finalist	Score
1877	Spencer W. Gore	William C. Marshall	6-1, 6-2, 6-4
1878	P. Frank Hadow	Spencer W. Gore	7-5, 6-1, 9-7
1879	John T. Hartley	V. St Leger Gould	6-2, 6-4, 6-2
1880	John T. Hartley	Herbert F. Lawford	6-0, 6-2, 2-6, 6-3
1881	William Renshaw	John T. Hartley	6-0, 6-2, 6-1
1882	William Renshaw	Ernest Renshaw	6-1, 2-6, 4-6, 6-2, 6-2
1883	William Renshaw	Ernest Renshaw	2-6, 6-3, 6-3, 4-6, 6-3
1884	William Renshaw	Herbert F. Lawford	6-0, 6-4, 9-7
1885	William Renshaw	Herbert F. Lawford	7-5, 6-2, 4-6, 7-5
1886	William Renshaw	Herbert F. Lawford	6-0, 5-7, 6-3, 6-4
1887	Herbert F. Lawford	Ernest Renshaw	1-6, 6-3, 3-6, 6-4, 6-4
1888	Ernest Renshaw	Herbert F. Lawford	6-3, 7-5, 6-0
1889	William Renshaw	Ernest Renshaw	6-4, 6-1, 3-6, 6-0
1890	William J. Hamilton	William Renshaw	6-8, 6-2, 3-6, 6-1, 6-1
1891	Wilfred Baddeley	Joshua Pim	6-4, 1-6, 7-5, 6-0
1892	Wilfred Baddeley	Joshua Pim	4-6, 6-3, 6-3, 6-2
1893	Joshua Pim	Wilfred Baddeley	3-6, 6-1, 6-3, 6-2
1894	Joshua Pim	Wilfred Baddeley	10-8, 6-2, 8-6
1895	Wilfred Baddeley	Wilberforce V. Eaves	4-6, 2-6, 8-6, 6-2, 6-3
1896	Harold S. Mahoney	Wilfred Baddeley	6-2, 6-8, 5-7, 8-6, 6-3
1897	Reggie F. Doherty	Harold S. Mahoney	6-4, 6-4, 6-3
1898	Reggie F. Doherty	H. Laurie Doherty	6-3, 6-3, 2-6, 5-7, 6-1
1899	Reggie F. Doherty	Arthur W. Gore	1-6, 4-6, 6-2, 6-3, 6-3
1900	Reggie F. Doherty	Sidney H. Smith	6-8, 6-3, 6-1, 6-2
1901	Arthur W. Gore	Reggie F. Doherty	4-6, 7-5, 6-4, 6-4
1902	H. Laurie Doherty	Arthur W. Gore	6-4, 6-3, 3-6, 6-0

Wimbledon Championships (*Cont.*)

Year	Winner	Finalist	Score
1903	H. Laurie Doherty	Frank L. Riseley	7-5, 6-3, 6-0
1904	H. Laurie Doherty	Frank L. Riseley	6-1, 7-5, 8-6
1905	H. Laurie Doherty	Norman E. Brookes	8-6, 6-2, 6-4
1906	H. Laurie Doherty	Frank L. Riseley	6-4, 4-6, 6-2, 6-3
1907	Norman E. Brookes	Arthur W. Gore	6-4, 6-2, 6-2
1908	Arthur W. Gore	H. Roper Barrett	6-3, 6-2, 4-6, 3-6, 6-4
1909	Arthur W. Gore	M. J. G. Ritchie	6-8, 1-6, 6-2, 6-2, 6-2
1910	Anthony F. Wilding	Arthur W. Gore	6-4, 7-5, 4-6, 6-2
1911	Anthony F. Wilding	H. Roper Barrett	6-4, 4-6, 2-6, 6-2 ret
1912	Anthony F. Wilding	Arthur W. Gore	6-4, 6-4, 4-6, 6-4
1913	Anthony F. Wilding	Maurice E. McLoughlin	8-6, 6-3, 10-8
1914	Norman E. Brookes	Anthony F. Wilding	6-4, 6-4, 7-5
1915-18	No tournament		
1919	Gerald L. Patterson	Norman E. Brookes	6-3, 7-5, 6-2
1920	Bill Tilden	Gerald L. Patterson	2-6, 6-3, 6-2, 6-4
1921	Bill Tilden	Brian I. C. Norton	4-6, 2-6, 6-1, 6-0, 7-5
1922	Gerald L. Patterson	Randolph Lycett	6-3, 6-4, 6-2
1923	Bill Johnston	Francis T. Hunter	6-0, 6-3, 6-1
1924	Jean Borotra	Rene Lacoste	6-1, 3-6, 6-1, 3-6, 6-4
1925	Rene Lacoste	Jean Borotra	6-3, 6-3, 4-6, 8-6
1926	Jean Borotra	Howard Kinsey	8-6, 6-1, 6-3
1927	Henri Cochet	Jean Borotra	4-6, 4-6, 6-3, 6-4, 7-5
1928	Rene Lacoste	Henri Cochet	6-1, 4-6, 6-4, 6-2
1929	Henri Cochet	Jean Borotra	6-4, 6-3, 6-4
1930	Bill Tilden	Wilmer Allison	6-3, 9-7, 6-4
1931	Sidney B. Wood Jr	Francis X. Shields	walkover
1932	Ellsworth Vines	Henry Austin	6-4, 6-2, 6-0
1933	Jack Crawford	Ellsworth Vines	4-6, 11-9, 6-2, 2-6, 6-4
1934	Fred Perry	Jack Crawford	6-3, 6-0, 7-5
1935	Fred Perry	Gottfried von Cramm	6-2, 6-4, 6-4
1936	Fred Perry	Gottfried von Cramm	6-1, 6-1, 6-0
1937	Don Budge	Gottfried von Cramm	6-3, 6-4, 6-2
1938	Don Budge	Henry Austin	6-1, 6-0, 6-3
1939	Bobby Riggs	Elwood Cooke	2-6, 8-6, 3-6, 6-3, 6-2
1940-45	No tournament		
1946	Yvon Petra	Geoff E. Brown	6-2, 6-4, 7-9, 5-7, 6-4
1947	Jack Kramer	Tom P. Brown	6-1, 6-3, 6-2
1948	Bob Falkenburg	John Bromwich	7-5, 0-6, 6-2, 3-6, 7-5
1949	Ted Schroeder	Jaroslav Drobny	3-6, 6-0, 6-3, 4-6, 6-4
1950	Budge Patty	Frank Sedgman	6-1, 8-10, 6-2, 6-3
1951	Dick Savitt	Ken McGregor	6-4, 6-4, 6-4
1952	Frank Sedgman	Jaroslav Drobny	4-6, 6-3, 6-2, 6-3
1953	Vic Seixas	Kurt Nielsen	9-7, 6-3, 6-4
1954	Jaroslav Drobny	Ken Rosewall	13-11, 4-6, 6-2, 9-7
1955	Tony Trabert	Kurt Nielsen	6-3, 7-5, 6-1
1956	Lew Hoad	Ken Rosewall	6-2, 4-6, 7-5, 6-4
1957	Lew Hoad	Ashley Cooper	6-2, 6-1, 6-2
1958	Ashley Cooper	Neale Fraser	3-6, 6-3, 6-4, 13-11
1959	Alex Olmedo	Rod Laver	6-4, 6-3, 6-4
1960	Neale Fraser	Rod Laver	6-4, 3-6, 9-7, 7-5
1961	Rod Laver	Chuck McKinley	6-3, 6-1, 6-4
1962	Rod Laver	Martin Mulligan	6-2, 6-2, 6-1
1963	Chuck McKinley	Fred Stolle	9-7, 6-1, 6-4
1964	Roy Emerson	Fred Stolle	6-4, 12-10, 4-6, 6-3
1965	Roy Emerson	Fred Stolle	6-2, 6-4, 6-4
1966	Manuel Santana	Dennis Ralston	6-4, 11-9, 6-4
1967	John Newcombe	Wilhelm Bungert	6-3, 6-1, 6-1
1968*	Rod Laver	Tony Roche	6-3, 6-4, 6-2
1969	Rod Laver	John Newcombe	6-4, 5-7, 6-4, 6-4
1970	John Newcombe	Ken Rosewall	5-7, 6-3, 6-2, 3-6, 6-1
1971	John Newcombe	Stan Smith	6-3, 5-7, 2-6, 6-4, 6-4
1972	Stan Smith	Ilie Nastase	4-6, 6-3, 6-3, 4-6, 7-5
1973	Jan Kodes	Alex Metreveli	6-1, 9-8, 6-3
1974	Jimmy Connors	Ken Rosewall	6-1, 6-1, 6-4

Wimbledon Championships (*Cont.*)

Year	Winner	Finalist	Score
1975	Arthur Ashe	Jimmy Connors	6-1, 6-1, 5-7, 6-4
1976	Bjorn Borg	Ilie Nastase	6-4, 6-2, 9-7
1977	Bjorn Borg	Jimmy Connors	3-6, 6-2, 6-1, 5-7, 6-4
1978	Bjorn Borg	Jimmy Connors	6-2, 6-2, 6-3
1979	Bjorn Borg	Roscoe Tanner	6-7, 6-1, 3-6, 6-3, 6-4
1980	Bjorn Borg	John McEnroe	1-6, 7-5, 6-3, 6-7, 8-6
1981	John McEnroe	Bjorn Borg	4-6, 7-6, 7-6, 6-4
1982	Jimmy Connors	John McEnroe	3-6, 6-3, 6-7, 7-6, 6-4
1983	John McEnroe	Chris Lewis	6-2, 6-2, 6-2
1984	John McEnroe	Jimmy Connors	6-1, 6-1, 6-2
1985	Boris Becker	Kevin Curren	6-3, 6-7, 7-6, 6-4
1986	Boris Becker	Ivan Lendl	6-4, 6-3, 7-5
1987	Pat Cash	Ivan Lendl	7-6, 6-2, 7-5
1988	Stefan Edberg	Boris Becker	4-6, 7-6, 6-4, 6-2
1989	Boris Becker	Stefan Edberg	6-0, 7-6, 6-4
1990	Stefan Edberg	Boris Becker	6-2, 6-2, 3-6, 3-6, 6-4
1991	Michael Stich	Boris Becker	6-4, 7-6, 6-4

*Became Open (amateur and professional) in 1968 but closed to contract professionals in 1972.

Note: Prior to 1922 the tournament was run on a challenge-round system. The previous year's winner "stood out" of an All Comers event, which produced a challenger to play him for the title.

United States Championships

Year	Winner	Finalist	Score
1881	Richard D. Sears	W. E. Glyn	6-0, 6-3, 6-2
1882	Richard D. Sears	C. M. Clark	6-1, 6-4, 6-0
1883	Richard D. Sears	James Dwight	6-2, 6-0, 9-7
1884	Richard D. Sears	H. A. Taylor	6-0, 1-6, 6-0, 6-2
1885	Richard D. Sears	G. M. Brinley	6-3, 4-6, 6-0, 6-3
1886	Richard D. Sears	R. L. Beeckman	4-6, 6-1, 6-3, 6-4
1887	Richard D. Sears	H. W. Slocum Jr	6-1, 6-3, 6-2
1888‡	H. W. Slocum Jr	H. A. Taylor	6-4, 6-1, 6-0
1889	H. W. Slocum Jr	Q. A. Shaw	6-3, 6-1, 4-6, 6-2
1890	Oliver S. Campbell	H. W. Slocum Jr	6-2, 4-6, 6-3, 6-1
1891	Oliver S. Campbell	Clarence Hobart	2-6, 7-5, 7-9, 6-1, 6-2
1892	Oliver S. Campbell	Frederick H. Hovey	7-5, 3-6, 6-3, 7-5
1893‡	Robert D. Wrenn	Frederick H. Hovey	6-4, 3-6, 6-4, 6-4
1894	Robert D. Wrenn	M. F. Goodbody	6-8, 6-1, 6-4, 6-4
1895	Frederick H. Hovey	Robert D. Wrenn	6-3, 6-2, 6-4
1896	Robert D. Wrenn	Frederick H. Hovey	7-5, 3-6, 6-0, 1-6, 6-1
1897	Robert D. Wrenn	Wilberforce V. Eaves	4-6, 8-6, 6-3, 2-6, 6-2
1898‡	Malcolm D. Whitman	Dwight F. Davis	3-6, 6-2, 6-2, 6-1
1899	Malcolm D. Whitman	J. Parmly Paret	6-1, 6-2, 3-6, 7-5
1900	Malcolm D. Whitman	William A. Larned	6-4, 1-6, 6-2, 6-2
1901‡	William A. Larned	Beals C. Wright	6-2, 6-8, 6-4, 6-4
1902	William A. Larned	Reggie F. Doherty	4-6, 6-2, 6-4, 8-6
1903	H. Laurie Doherty	William A. Larned	6-0, 6-3, 10-8
1904‡	Holcombe Ward	William J. Clothier	10-8, 6-4, 9-7
1905	Beals C. Wright	Holcombe Ward	6-2, 6-1, 11-9
1906	William J. Clothier	Beals C. Wright	6-3, 6-0, 6-4
1907‡	William A. Larned	Robert LeRoy	6-2, 6-2, 6-4
1908	William A. Larned	Beals C. Wright	6-1, 6-2, 8-6
1909	William A. Larned	William J. Clothier	6-1, 6-2, 5-7, 1-6, 6-1
1910	William A. Larned	Thomas C. Bundy	6-1, 5-7, 6-0, 6-8, 6-1
1911	William A. Larned	Maurice E. McLoughlin	6-4, 6-4, 6-2
1912†	Maurice E. McLoughlin	Bill Johnson	3-6, 2-6, 6-2, 6-4, 6-2
1913	Maurice E. McLoughlin	Richard N. Williams	6-4, 5-7, 6-3, 6-1
1914	Richard N. Williams	Maurice E. McLoughlin	6-3, 8-6, 10-8
1915	Bill Johnston	Maurice E. McLoughlin	1-6, 6-0, 7-5, 10-8
1916	Richard N. Williams	Bill Johnston	4-6, 6-4, 0-6, 6-2, 6-4
1917#	R. L. Murray	N. W. Niles	5-7, 8-6, 6-3, 6-3
1918	R. L. Murray	Bill Tilden	6-3, 6-1, 7-5
1919	Bill Johnston	Bill Tilden	6-4, 6-4, 6-3
1920	Bill Tilden	Bill Johnston	6-1, 1-6, 7-5, 5-7, 6-3

United States Championships (*Cont.*)

Year	Winner	Finalist	Score
1921	Bill Tilden	Wallace F. Johnson	6-1, 6-3, 6-1
1922	Bill Tilden	Bill Johnston	4-6, 3-6, 6-2, 6-3, 6-4
1923	Bill Tilden	Bill Johnston	6-4, 6-1, 6-4
1924	Bill Tilden	Bill Johnston	6-1, 9-7, 6-2
1925	Bill Tilden	Bill Johnston	4-6, 11-9, 6-3, 4-6, 6-3
1926	Rene Lacoste	Jean Borotra	6-4, 6-0, 6-4
1927	Rene Lacoste	Bill Tilden	11-9, 6-3, 11-9
1928	Henri Cochet	Francis T. Hunter	4-6, 6-4, 3-6, 7-5, 6-3
1929	Bill Tilden	Francis T. Hunter	3-6, 6-3, 4-6, 6-2, 6-4
1930	John H. Doeg	Francis X. Shields	10-8, 1-6, 6-4, 16-14
1931	Ellsworth Vines	George M. Lott Jr	7-9, 6-3, 9-7, 7-5
1932	Ellsworth Vines	Henri Cochet	6-4, 6-4, 6-4
1933	Fred Perry	Jack Crawford	6-3, 11-13, 4-6, 6-0, 6-1
1934	Fred Perry	Wilmer L. Allison	6-4, 6-3, 1-6, 8-6
1935	Wilmer L. Allison	Sidney B. Wood Jr	6-2, 6-2, 6-3
1936	Fred Perry	Don Budge	2-6, 6-2, 8-6, 1-6, 10-8
1937	Don Budge	Gottfried von Cramm	6-1, 7-9, 6-1, 3-6, 6-1
1938	Don Budge	Gene Mako	6-3, 6-8, 6-2, 6-1
1939	Bobby Riggs	Welby van Horn	6-4, 6-2, 6-4
1940	Don McNeill	Bobby Riggs	4-6, 6-8, 6-3, 6-3, 7-5
1941	Bobby Riggs	Francis Kovacs II	5-7, 6-1, 6-3, 6-3
1942	Ted Schroeder	Frank Parker	8-6, 7-5, 3-6, 4-6, 6-2
1943	Joseph R. Hunt	Jack Kramer	6-3, 6-8, 10-8, 6-0
1944	Frank Parker	William F. Talbert	6-4, 3-6, 6-3, 6-3
1945	Frank Parker	William F. Talbert	14-12, 6-1, 6-2
1946	Jack Kramer	Tom P. Brown	9-7, 6-3, 6-0
1947	Jack Kramer	Frank Parker	4-6, 2-6, 6-1, 6-0, 6-3
1948	Pancho Gonzales	Eric W. Sturgess	6-2, 6-3, 14-12
1949	Pancho Gonzales	Ted Schroeder	16-18, 2-6, 6-1, 6-2, 6-4
1950	Arthur Larsen	Herbie Flam	6-3, 4-6, 5-7, 6-4, 6-3
1951	Frank Sedgman	Vic Seixas	6-4, 6-1, 6-1
1952	Frank Sedgman	Gardnar Mulloy	6-1, 6-2, 6-3
1953	Tony Trabert	Vic Seixas	6-3, 6-2, 6-3
1954	Vic Seixas	Rex Hartwig	3-6, 6-2, 6-4, 6-4
1955	Tony Trabert	Ken Rosewall	9-7, 6-3, 6-3
1956	Ken Rosewall	Lew Hoad	4-6, 6-2, 6-3, 6-3
1957	Mal Anderson	Ashley J. Cooper	10-8, 7-5, 6-4
1958	Ashley J. Cooper	Mal Anderson	6-2, 3-6, 4-6, 10-8, 8-6
1959	Neale Fraser	Alex Olmedo	6-3, 5-7, 6-2, 6-4
1960	Neale Fraser	Rod Laver	6-4, 6-4, 9-7
1961	Roy Emerson	Rod Laver	7-5, 6-3, 6-2
1962	Rod Laver	Roy Emerson	6-2, 6-4, 5-7, 6-4
1963	Rafael Osuna	Frank Froehling III	7-5, 6-4, 6-2
1964	Roy Emerson	Fred Stolle	6-4, 6-2, 6-4
1965	Manuel Santana	Cliff Drysdale	6-2, 7-9, 7-5, 6-1
1966	Fred Stolle	John Newcombe	4-6, 12-10, 6-3, 6-4
1967	John Newcombe	Clark Graebner	6-4, 6-4, 8-6
1968**	Arthur Ashe	Bob Lutz	4-6, 6-3, 8-10, 6-0, 6-4
1968*	Arthur Ashe	Tom Okker	14-12, 5-7, 6-3, 3-6, 6-3
1969**	Stan Smith	Bob Lutz	9-7, 6-3, 6-1
1969*	Rod Laver	Tony Roche	7-9, 6-1, 6-3, 6-2
1970	Ken Rosewall	Tony Roche	2-6, 6-4, 7-6, 6-3
1971	Stan Smith	Jan Kodes	3-6, 6-3, 6-2, 7-6
1972	Ilie Nastase	Arthur Ashe	3-6, 6-3, 6-7, 6-4, 6-3
1973	John Newcombe	Jan Kodes	6-4, 1-6, 4-6, 6-2, 6-3
1974	Jimmy Connors	Ken Rosewall	6-1, 6-0, 6-1
1975	Manuel Orantes	Jimmy Connors	6-4, 6-3, 6-3
1976	Jimmy Connors	Bjorn Borg	6-4, 3-6, 7-6, 6-4
1977	Guillermo Vilas	Jimmy Connors	2-6, 6-3, 7-6, 6-0
1978	Jimmy Connors	Bjorn Borg	6-4, 6-2, 6-2
1979	John McEnroe	Vitas Gerulaitis	7-5, 6-3, 6-3
1980	John McEnroe	Bjorn Borg	7-6, 6-1, 6-7, 5-7, 6-4
1981	John McEnroe	Bjorn Borg	4-6, 6-2, 6-4, 6-3
1982	Jimmy Connors	Ivan Lendl	6-3, 6-2, 4-6, 6-4

United States Championships (*Cont.*)

Year	Winner	Finalist	Score
1983	Jimmy Connors	Ivan Lendl	6-3, 6-7, 7-5, 6-0
1984	John McEnroe	Ivan Lendl	6-3, 6-4, 6-1
1985	Ivan Lendl	John McEnroe	7-6, 6-3, 6-4
1986	Ivan Lendl	Miloslav Mecir	6-4, 6-2, 6-0
1987	Ivan Lendl	Mats Wilander	6-7, 6-0, 7-6, 6-4
1988	Mats Wilander	Ivan Lendl	6-4, 4-6, 6-3, 5-7, 6-4
1989	Boris Becker	Ivan Lendl	7-6, 1-6, 6-3, 7-6
1990	Pete Sampras	Andre Agassi	6-4, 6-3, 6-2
1991	Stefan Edberg	Jim Courier	6-2, 6-4, 6-0

*Became Open (amateur and professional) in 1968.

†Challenge round abolished.

‡No challenge round played.

#National Patriotic Tournament.

**Amateur event held.

WOMEN

Australian Championships

Year	Winner	Finalist	Score
1922	Margaret Molesworth	Esna Boyd	6-3, 10-8
1923	Margaret Molesworth	Esna Boyd	6-1, 7-5
1924	Sylvia Lance	Esna Boyd	6-3, 3-6, 6-4
1925	Daphne Akhurst	Esna Boyd	1-6, 8-6, 6-4
1926	Daphne Akhurst	Esna Boyd	6-1, 6-3
1927	Esna Boyd	Sylvia Harper	5-7, 6-1, 6-2
1928	Daphne Akhurst	Esna Boyd	7-5, 6-2
1929	Daphne Akhurst	Louise Bickerton	6-1, 5-7, 6-2
1930	Daphne Akhurst	Sylvia Harper	10-8, 2-6, 7-5
1931	Coral Buttsworth	Margorie Crawford	1-6, 6-3, 6-4
1932	Coral Buttsworth	Kathrine Le Messurier	9-7, 6-4
1933	Joan Hartigan	Coral Buttsworth	6-4, 6-3
1934	Joan Hartigan	Margaret Molesworth	6-1, 6-4
1935	Dorothy Round	Nancye Wynne Bolton	1-6, 6-1, 6-3
1936	Joan Hartigan	Nancye Wynne Bolton	6-4, 6-4
1937	Nancye Wynne Bolton	Emily Westacott	6-3, 5-7, 6-4
1938	Dorothy Bundy	D. Stevenson	6-3, 6-2
1939	Emily Westacott	Nell Hopman	6-1, 6-2
1940	Nancye Wynne Bolton	Thelma Coyne	5-7, 6-4, 6-0
1941-45	No tournament		
1946	Nancye Wynne Bolton	Joyce Fitch	6-4, 6-4
1947	Nancye Wynne Bolton	Nell Hopman	6-3, 6-2
1948	Nancye Wynne Bolton	Marie Toomey	6-3, 6-1
1949	Doris Hart	Nancye Wynne Bolton	6-3, 6-4
1950	Louise Brough	Doris Hart	6-4, 3-6, 6-4
1951	Nancye Wynne Bolton	Thelma Long	6-1, 7-5
1952	Thelma Long	H. Angwin	6-2, 6-3
1953	Maureen Connolly	Julia Sampson	6-3, 6-2
1954	Thelma Long	J. Staley	6-3, 6-4
1955	Beryl Penrose	Thelma Long	6-4, 6-3
1956	Mary Carter	Thelma Long	3-6, 6-2, 9-7
1957	Shirley Fry	Althea Gibson	6-3, 6-4
1958	Angela Mortimer	Lorraine Coghlan	6-3, 6-4
1959	Mary Carter-Reitano	Renee Schuurman	6-2, 6-3
1960	Margaret Smith	Jan Lehane	7-5, 6-2
1961	Margaret Smith	Jan Lehane	6-1, 6-4
1962	Margaret Smith	Jan Lehane	6-0, 6-2
1963	Margaret Smith	Jan Lehane	6-2, 6-2
1964	Margaret Smith	Lesley Turner	6-3, 6-2
1965	Margaret Smith	Maria Bueno	5-7, 6-4, 5-2 ret
1966	Margaret Smith	Nancy Richey	Default
1967	Nancy Richey	Lesley Turner	6-1, 6-4

Australian Championships (*Cont.*)

Year	Winner	Finalist	Score
1968	Billie Jean King	Margaret Smith	6-1, 6-2
1969*	Margaret Smith Court	Billie Jean King	6-4, 6-1
1970	Margaret Smith Court	Kerry Melville Reid	6-3, 6-1
1971	Margaret Smith Court	Evonne Goolagong	2-6, 7-6, 7-5
1972	Virginia Wade	Evonne Goolagong	6-4, 6-4
1973	Margaret Smith Court	Evonne Goolagong	6-4, 7-5
1974	Evonne Goolagong	Chris Evert	7-6, 4-6, 6-0
1975	Evonne Goolagong	Martina Navratilova	6-3, 6-2
1976	Evonne Goolagong Cawley	Renata Tomanova	6-2, 6-2
1977 (Jan)	Kerry Melville Reid	Dianne Balestrat	7-5, 6-2
1977 (Dec)	Evonne Goolagong Cawley	Helen Gourlay	6-3, 6-0
1978	Chris O'Neil	Betsy Nagelsen	6-3, 7-6
1979	Barbara Jordan	Sharon Walsh	6-3, 6-3
1980	Hana Mandlikova	Wendy Turnbull	6-0, 7-5
1981	Martina Navratilova	Chris Evert Lloyd	6-7, 6-4, 7-5
1982	Chris Evert Lloyd	Martina Navratilova	6-3, 2-6, 6-3
1983	Martina Navratilova	Kathy Jordan	6-2, 7-6
1984	Chris Evert Lloyd	Helena Sukova	6-7, 6-1, 6-3
1985 (Dec)	Martina Navratilova	Chris Evert Lloyd	6-2, 4-6, 6-2
1987 (Jan)	Hana Mandlikova	Martina Navratilova	7-5, 7-6
1988	Steffi Graf	Chris Evert	6-1, 7-6
1989	Steffi Graf	Helena Sukova	6-4, 6-4
1990	Steffi Graf	Mary Joe Fernandez	6-3, 6-4
1991	Monica Seles	Jana Novotna	5-7, 6-3, 6-1

*Became Open (amateur and professional) in 1969.

French Championships

Year	Winner	Finalist	Score
1925†	Suzanne Lenglen	Kathleen McKane	6-1, 6-2
1926	Suzanne Lenglen	Mary K. Browne	6-1, 6-0
1927	Kea Bouman	Irene Peacock	6-2, 6-4
1928	Helen Wills	Eileen Bennett	6-1, 6-2
1929	Helen Wills	Simone Mathieu	6-3, 6-4
1930	Helen Wills Moody	Helen Jacobs	6-2, 6-1
1931	Cilly Aussem	Betty Nuthall	8-6, 6-1
1932	Helen Wills Moody	Simone Mathieu	7-5, 6-1
1933	Margaret Scriven	Simone Mathieu	6-2, 4-6, 6-4
1934	Margaret Scriven	Helen Jacobs	7-5, 4-6, 6-1
1935	Hilde Sperling	Simone Mathieu	6-2, 6-1
1936	Hilde Sperling	Simone Mathieu	6-3, 6-4
1937	Hilde Sperling	Simone Mathieu	6-2, 6-4
1938	Simone Mathieu	Nelly Landry	6-0, 6-3
1939	Simone Mathieu	Jadwiga Jedrzejowska	6-3, 8-6
1940-45	No tournament		
1946	Margaret Osborne	Pauline Betz	1-6, 8-6, 7-5
1947	Patricia Todd	Doris Hart	6-3, 3-6, 6-4
1948	Nelly Landry	Shirley Fry	6-2, 0-6, 6-0
1949	Margaret Osborne duPont	Nelly Adamson	7-5, 6-2
1950	Doris Hart	Patricia Todd	6-4, 4-6, 6-2
1951	Shirley Fry	Doris Hart	6-3, 3-6, 6-3
1952	Doris Hart	Shirley Fry	6-4, 6-4
1953	Maureen Connolly	Doris Hart	6-2, 6-4
1954	Maureen Connolly	Ginette Bucaille	6-4, 6-1
1955	Angela Mortimer	Dorothy Knode	2-6, 7-5, 10-8
1956	Althea Gibson	Angela Mortimer	6-0, 12-10
1957	Shirley Bloomer	Dorothy Knode	6-1, 6-3
1958	Zsuzsi Kormoczi	Shirley Bloomer	6-4, 1-6, 6-2
1959	Christine Truman	Zsuzsi Kormoczi	6-4, 7-5
1960	Darlene Hard	Yola Ramirez	6-3, 6-4
1961	Ann Haydon	Yola Ramirez	6-2, 6-1
1962	Margaret Smith	Lesley Turner	6-3, 3-6, 7-5
1963	Lesley Turner	Ann Haydon Jones	2-6, 6-3, 7-5
1964	Margaret Smith	Maria Bueno	5-7, 6-1, 6-2

French Championships (*Cont.*)

Year	Winner	Finalist	Score
1965	Lesley Turner	Margaret Smith	6-3, 6-4
1966	Ann Jones	Nancy Richey	6-3, 6-1
1967	Francoise Durr	Lesley Turner	4-6, 6-3, 6-4
1968*	Nancy Richey	Ann Jones	5-7, 6-4, 6-1
1969	Margaret Smith Court	Ann Jones	6-1, 4-6, 6-3
1970	Margaret Smith Court	Helga Niessen	6-2, 6-4
1971	Evonne Goolagong	Helen Gourlay	6-3, 7-5
1972	Billie Jean King	Evonne Goolagong	6-3, 6-3
1973	Margaret Smith Court	Chris Evert	6-7, 7-6, 6-4
1974	Chris Evert	Olga Morozova	6-1, 6-2
1975	Chris Evert	Martina Navratilova	2-6, 6-2, 6-1
1976	Sue Barker	Renata Tomanova	6-2, 0-6, 6-2
1977	Mima Jausovec	Florenza Mihai	6-2, 6-7, 6-1
1978	Virginia Ruzici	Mima Jausovec	6-2, 6-2
1979	Chris Evert Lloyd	Wendy Turnbull	6-2, 6-0
1980	Chris Evert Lloyd	Virginia Ruzici	6-0, 6-3
1981	Hana Mandlikova	Sylvia Hanika	6-2, 6-4
1982	Martina Navratilova	Andrea Jaeger	7-6, 6-1
1983	Chris Evert Lloyd	Mima Jausovec	6-1, 6-2
1984	Martina Navratilova	Chris Evert Lloyd	6-3, 6-1
1985	Chris Evert Lloyd	Martina Navratilova	6-3, 6-7, 7-5
1986	Chris Evert Lloyd	Martina Navratilova	2-6, 6-3, 6-3
1987	Steffi Graf	Martina Navratilova	6-4, 4-6, 8-6
1988	Steffi Graf	Natalia Zvereva	6-0, 6-0
1989	Arantxa Sanchez Vicario	Steffi Graf	7-6, 3-6, 7-5
1990	Monica Seles	Steffi Graf	7-6, 6-4
1991	Monica Seles	Arantxa Sanchez Vicario	6-3, 6-4

*Became Open (amateur and professional) in 1968 but closed to contract professionals in 1972.

†1925 was the first year that entries were accepted from all countries.

Wimbledon Championships

Year	Winner	Finalist	Score
1884	Maud Watson	Lilian Watson	6-8, 6-3, 6-3
1885	Maud Watson	Blanche Bingley	6-1, 7-5
1886	Blanche Bingley	Maud Watson	6-3, 6-3
1887	Charlotte Dod	Blanche Bingley	6-2, 6-0
1888	Charlotte Dod	Blanche Bingley Hillyard	6-3, 6-3
1889	Blanche Bingley Hillyard		
1890	Lena Rice		
1891	Charlotte Dod		
1892	Charlotte Dod	Blanche Bingley Hillyard	6-1, 6-1
1893	Charlotte Dod	Blanche Bingley Hillyard	6-8, 6-1, 6-4
1894	Blanche Bingley Hillyard		
1895	Charlotte Cooper		
1896	Charlotte Cooper	Mrs. W. H. Pickering	6-2, 6-3
1897	Blanche Bingley Hillyard	Charlotte Cooper	5-7, 7-5, 6-2
1898	Charlotte Cooper		
1899	Blanche Bingley Hillyard	Charlotte Cooper	6-2, 6-3
1900	Blanche Bingley Hillyard	Charlotte Cooper	4-6, 6-4, 6-4
1901	Charlotte Cooper Sterry	Blanche Bingley Hillyard	6-2, 6-2
1902	Muriel Robb	Charlotte Cooper Sterry	7-5, 6-1
1903	Dorothea Douglass		
1904	Dorothea Douglass	Charlotte Cooper Sterry	6-0, 6-3
1905	May Sutton	Dorothea Douglass	6-3, 6-4
1906	Dorothea Douglass	May Sutton	6-3, 9-7
1907	May Sutton	Dorothea Douglass Lambert Chambers	6-1, 6-4
1908	Charlotte Cooper Sterry		
1909	Dora Boothby		
1910	Dorothea Douglass Lambert Chambers	Dora Boothby	6-2, 6-2
1911	Dorothea Douglass Lambert Chambers	Dora Boothby	6-0, 6-0

Wimbledon Championships (*Cont.*)

Year	Winner	Finalist	Score
1912	Ethel Larcombe		
1913	Dorothea Douglass Lambert Chambers		
1914	Dorothea Douglass Lambert Chambers	Ethel Larcombe	7-5, 6-4
1915-18	No tournament		
1919	Suzanne Lenglen	Dorothea Douglass Lambert Chambers	10-8, 4-6, 9-7
1920	Suzanne Lenglen	Dorothea Douglass Lambert Chambers	6-3, 6-0
1921	Suzanne Lenglen	Elizabeth Ryan	6-2, 6-0
1922	Suzanne Lenglen	Molla Mallory	6-2, 6-0
1923	Suzanne Lenglen	Kathleen McKane	6-2, 6-2
1924	Kathleen McKane	Helen Wills	4-6, 6-4, 6-2
1925	Suzanne Lenglen	Joan Fry	6-2, 6-0
1926	Kathleen McKane Godfree	Lili de Alvarez	6-2, 4-6, 6-3
1927	Helen Wills	Lili de Alvarez	6-2, 6-4
1928	Helen Wills	Lili de Alvarez	6-2, 6-3
1929	Helen Wills	Helen Jacobs	6-1, 6-2
1930	Helen Wills Moody	Elizabeth Ryan	6-2, 6-2
1931	Cilly Aussem	Hilde Kranwinkel	7-5, 7-5
1932	Helen Wills Moody	Helen Jacobs	6-3, 6-1
1933	Helen Wills Moody	Dorothy Round	6-4, 6-8, 6-3
1934	Dorothy Round	Helen Jacobs	6-2, 5-7, 6-3
1935	Helen Wills Moody	Helen Jacobs	6-3, 3-6, 7-5
1936	Helen Jacobs	Hilde Kranwinkel Sperling	6-2, 4-6, 7-5
1937	Dorothy Round	Jadwiga Jedrzejowska	6-2, 2-6, 7-5
1938	Helen Wills Moody	Helen Jacobs	6-4, 6-0
1939	Alice Marble	Kay Stammers	6-2, 6-0
1940-45	No tournament		
1946	Pauline Betz	Louise Brough	6-2, 6-4
1947	Margaret Osborne	Doris Hart	6-2, 6-4
1948	Louise Brough	Doris Hart	6-3, 8-6
1949	Louise Brough	Margaret Osborne duPont	10-8, 1-6, 10-8
1950	Louise Brough	Margaret Osborne duPont	6-1, 3-6, 6-1
1951	Doris Hart	Shirley Fry	6-1, 6-0
1952	Maureen Connolly	Louise Brough	6-4, 6-3
1953	Maureen Connolly	Doris Hart	8-6, 7-5
1954	Maureen Connolly	Louise Brough	6-2, 7-5
1955	Louise Brough	Beverly Fleitz	7-5, 8-6
1956	Shirley Fry	Angela Buxton	6-3, 6-1
1957	Althea Gibson	Darlene Hard	6-3, 6-2
1958	Althea Gibson	Angela Mortimer	8-6, 6-2
1959	Maria Bueno	Darlene Hard	6-4, 6-3
1960	Maria Bueno	Sandra Reynolds	8-6, 6-0
1961	Angela Mortimer	Christine Truman	4-6, 6-4, 7-5
1962	Karen Hantze Susman	Vera Sukova	6-4, 6-4
1963	Margaret Smith	Billie Jean Moffitt	6-3, 6-4
1964	Maria Bueno	Margaret Smith	6-4, 7-9, 6-3
1965	Margaret Smith	Maria Bueno	6-4, 7-5
1966	Billie Jean King	Maria Bueno	6-3, 3-6, 6-1
1967	Billie Jean King	Ann Haydon Jones	6-3, 6-4
1968*	Billie Jean King	Judy Tegart	9-7, 7-5
1969	Ann Haydon Jones	Billie Jean King	3-6, 6-3, 6-2
1970	Margaret Smith Court	Billie Jean King	14-12, 11-9
1971	Evonne Goolagong	Margaret Smith Court	6-4, 6-1
1972	Billie Jean King	Evonne Goolagong	6-3, 6-3
1973	Billie Jean King	Chris Evert	6-0, 7-5
1974	Chris Evert	Olga Morozova	6-0, 6-4
1975	Billie Jean King	Evonne Goolagong Cawley	6-0, 6-1
1976	Chris Evert	Evonne Goolagong Cawley	6-3, 4-6, 8-6
1977	Virginia Wade	Betty Stove	4-6, 6-3, 6-1
1978	Martina Navratilova	Chris Evert	2-6, 6-4, 7-5
1979	Martina Navratilova	Chris Evert Lloyd	6-4, 6-4
1980	Evonne Goolagong Cawley	Chris Evert Lloyd	6-1, 7-6

Wimbledon Championships (*Cont.*)

Year	Winner	Finalist	Score
1981	Chris Evert Lloyd	Hana Mandlikova	6-2, 6-2
1982	Martina Navratilova	Chris Evert Lloyd	6-1, 3-6, 6-2
1983	Martina Navratilova	Andrea Jaeger	6-0, 6-3
1984	Martina Navratilova	Chris Evert Lloyd	7-6, 6-2
1985	Martina Navratilova	Chris Evert Lloyd	4-6, 6-3, 6-2
1986	Martina Navratilova	Hana Mandlikova	7-6, 6-3
1987	Martina Navratilova	Steffi Graf	7-5, 6-3
1988	Steffi Graf	Martina Navratilova	5-7, 6-2, 6-1
1989	Steffi Graf	Martina Navratilova	6-2, 6-7, 6-1
1990	Martina Navratilova	Zina Garrison	6-4, 6-1
1991	Steffi Graf	Gabriela Sabatini	6-4, 3-6, 8-6

*Became Open (amateur and professional) in 1968 but closed to contract professionals in 1972.

Note: Prior to 1922 the tournament was run on a challenge round system. The previous year's winner "stood out" of an All Comers event, which produced a challenger to play her for the title.

United States Championships

Year	Winner	Finalist	Score
1887	Ellen Hansell	Laura Knight	6-1, 6-0
1888	Bertha L. Townsend	Ellen Hansell	6-3, 6-5
1889	Bertha L. Townsend	Louise Voorhes	7-5, 6-2
1890	Ellen C. Roosevelt	Bertha L. Townsend	6-2, 6-2
1891	Mabel Cahill	Ellen C. Roosevelt	6-4, 6-1, 4-6, 6-3
1892	Mabel Cahill	Elisabeth Moore	5-7, 6-3, 6-4, 4-6, 6-2
1893	Aline Terry	Alice Schultze	6-1, 6-3
1894	Helen Hellwig	Aline Terry	7-5, 3-6, 6-0, 3-6, 6-3
1895	Juliette Atkinson	Helen Hellwig	6-4, 6-2, 6-1
1896	Elisabeth Moore	Juliette Atkinson	6-4, 4-6, 6-2, 6-2
1897	Juliette Atkinson	Elisabeth Moore	6-3, 6-3, 4-6, 3-6, 6-3
1898	Juliette Atkinson	Marion Jones	6-3, 5-7, 6-4, 2-6, 7-5
1899	Marion Jones	Maud Banks	6-1, 6-1, 7-5
1900	Myrtle McAteer	Edith Parker	6-2, 6-2, 6-0
1901	Elisabeth Moore	Myrtle McAteer	6-4, 3-6, 7-5, 2-6, 6-2
1902**	Marion Jones	Elisabeth Moore	6-1, 1-0 retired
1903	Elisabeth Moore	Marion Jones	7-5, 8-6
1904	May Sutton	Elisabeth Moore	6-1, 6-2
1905	Elisabeth Moore	Helen Homans	6-4, 5-7, 6-1
1906	Helen Homans	Maud Barger-Wallach	6-4, 6-3
1907	Evelyn Sears	Carrie Neely	6-3, 6-2
1908	Maud Barger-Wallach	Evelyn Sears	6-3, 1-6, 6-3
1909	Hazel Hotchkiss	Maud Barger-Wallach	6-0, 6-1
1910	Hazel Hotchkiss	Louise Hammond	6-4, 6-2
1911	Hazel Hotchkiss	Florence Sutton	8-10, 6-1, 9-7
1912†	Mary K. Browne	Eleanora Sears	6-4, 6-2
1913	Mary K. Browne	Dorothy Green	6-2, 7-5
1914	Mary K. Browne	Marie Wagner	6-2, 1-6, 6-1
1915	Molla Bjurstedt	Hazel Hotchkiss Wightman	4-6, 6-2, 6-0
1916	Molla Bjurstedt	Louise Hammond Raymond	6-0, 6-1
1917‡	Molla Bjurstedt	Marion Vanderhoef	4-6, 6-0, 6-2
1918	Molla Bjurstedt	Eleanor Goss	6-4, 6-3
1919	Hazel Hotchkiss Wightman	Marion Zinderstein	6-1, 6-2
1920	Molla Bjurstedt Mallory	Marion Zinderstein	6-3, 6-1
1921	Molla Bjurstedt Mallory	Mary K. Browne	4-6, 6-4, 6-2
1922	Molla Bjurstedt Mallory	Helen Wills	6-3, 6-1
1923	Helen Wills	Molla Bjurstedt Mallory	6-2, 6-1
1924	Helen Wills	Molla Bjurstedt Mallory	6-1, 6-3
1925	Helen Wills	Kathleen McKane	3-6, 6-0, 6-2
1926	Molla Bjurstedt Mallory	Elizabeth Ryan	4-6, 6-4, 9-7
1927	Helen Wills	Betty Nuthall	6-1, 6-4
1928	Helen Wills	Helen Jacobs	6-2, 6-1
1929	Helen Wills	Phoebe Holcroft Watson	6-4, 6-2
1930	Betty Nuthall	Anna McCune Harper	6-1, 6-4
1931	Helen Wills Moody	Eileen Whitingstall	6-4, 6-1
1932	Helen Jacobs	Carolin Babcock	6-2, 6-2
1933	Helen Jacobs	Helen Wills Moody	8-6, 3-6, 3-0 retired

United States Championships (*Cont.*)

Year	Winner	Finalist	Score
1934	Helen Jacobs	Sarah Palfrey	6-1, 6-4
1935	Helen Jacobs	Sarah Palfrey Fabyan	6-2, 6-4
1936	Alice Marble	Helen Jacobs	4-6, 6-3, 6-2
1937	Anita Lizane	Jadwiga Jedrzejowska	6-4, 6-2
1938	Alice Marble	Nancye Wynne	6-0, 6-3
1939	Alice Marble	Helen Jacobs	6-0, 8-10, 6-4
1940	Alice Marble	Helen Jacobs	6-2, 6-3
1941	Sarah Palfrey Cooke	Pauline Betz	7-5, 6-2
1942	Pauline Betz	Louise Brough	4-6, 6-1, 6-4
1943	Pauline Betz	Louise Brough	6-3, 5-7, 6-3
1944	Pauline Betz	Margaret Osborne	6-3, 8-6
1945	Sarah Palfrey Cooke	Pauline Betz	3-6, 8-6, 6-4
1946	Pauline Betz	Patricia Canning	11-9, 6-3
1947	Louise Brough	Margaret Osborne	8-6, 4-6, 6-1
1948	Margaret Osborne duPont	Louise Brough	4-6, 6-4, 15-13
1949	Margaret Osborne duPont	Doris Hart	6-4, 6-1
1950	Margaret Osborne duPont	Doris Hart	6-4, 6-3
1951	Maureen Connolly	Shirley Fry	6-3, 1-6, 6-4
1952	Maureen Connolly	Doris Hart	6-3, 7-5
1953	Maureen Connolly	Doris Hart	6-2, 6-4
1954	Doris Hart	Louise Brough	6-8, 6-1, 8-6
1955	Doris Hart	Patricia Ward	6-4, 6-2
1956	Shirley Fry	Althea Gibson	6-3, 6-4
1957	Althea Gibson	Louise Brough	6-3, 6-2
1958	Althea Gibson	Darlene Hard	3-6, 6-1, 6-2
1959	Maria Bueno	Christine Truman	6-1, 6-4
1960	Darlene Hard	Maria Bueno	6-4, 10-12, 6-4
1961	Darlene Hard	Ann Haydon	6-3, 6-4
1962	Margaret Smith	Darlene Hard	9-7, 6-4
1963	Maria Bueno	Margaret Smith	7-5, 6-4
1964	Maria Bueno	Carole Graebner	6-1, 6-0
1965	Margaret Smith	Billie Jean Moffitt	8-6, 7-5
1966	Maria Bueno	Nancy Richey	6-3, 6-1
1967	Billie Jean King	Ann Haydon Jones	11-9, 6-4
1968*	Virginia Wade	Billie Jean King	6-4, 6-4
1968#	Margaret Smith Court	Maria Bueno	6-2, 6-2
1969*	Margaret Smith Court	Nancy Richey	6-2, 6-2
1969#	Margaret Smith Court	Virginia Wade	4-6, 6-3, 6-0
1970	Margaret Smith Court	Rosie Casals	6-2, 2-6, 6-1
1971	Billie Jean King	Rosie Casals	6-4, 7-6
1972	Billie Jean King	Kerry Melville	6-3, 7-5
1973	Margaret Smith Court	Evonne Goolagong	7-6, 5-7, 6-2
1974	Billie Jean King	Evonne Goolagong	3-6, 6-3, 7-5
1975	Chris Evert	Evonne Goolagong Cawley	5-7, 6-4, 6-2
1976	Chris Evert	Evonne Goolagong Cawley	6-3, 6-0
1977	Chris Evert	Wendy Turnbull	7-6, 6-2
1978	Chris Evert	Pam Shriver	7-6, 6-4
1979	Tracy Austin	Chris Evert Lloyd	6-4, 6-3
1980	Chris Evert Lloyd	Hana Mandlikova	5-7, 6-1, 6-1
1981	Tracy Austin	Martina Navratilova	1-6, 7-6, 7-6
1982	Chris Evert Lloyd	Hana Mandlikova	6-3, 6-1
1983	Martina Navratilova	Chris Evert Lloyd	6-1, 6-3
1984	Martina Navratilova	Chris Evert Lloyd	4-6, 6-4, 6-4
1985	Hana Mandlikova	Martina Navratilova	7-6, 1-6, 7-6
1986	Martina Navratilova	Helena Sukova	6-3, 6-2
1987	Martina Navratilova	Steffi Graf	7-6, 6-1
1988	Steffi Graf	Gabriela Sabatini	6-3, 3-6, 6-1
1989	Steffi Graf	Martina Navratilova	3-6, 6-4, 6-2
1990	Gabriela Sabatini	Steffi Graf	6-2, 7-6
1991	Monica Seles	Martina Narvatilova	7-6, 6-1

*Became Open (amateur and professional) in 1968.

†Challenge round abolished.

‡National Patriotic Tournament.

#Amateur event held.

**Five-set final abolished.

Singles

Don Budge, 1938
Maureen Connolly, 1953
Rod Laver, 1962, 1969
Margaret Smith Court, 1970
Steffi Graf, 1988

Doubles

Frank Sedgman and Ken McGregor, 1951
Martina Navratilova and Pam Shriver, 1984
Maria Bueno and two partners: Christine Truman (Australian), Darlene Hard (French, Wimbledon and U.S. Championships), 1960

Mixed Doubles

Margaret Smith and Ken Fletcher, 1963
Owen Davidson and two partners: Lesley Turner (Australian), Billie Jean King (French, Wimbledon and U.S. Championships), 1967

The All-Time Champions

Men

Player	Aus. S-D-M	French S-D-M	Wim. S-D-M	U.S. S-D-M	Total
Roy Emerson	6-3-0	2-6-0	2-3-0	2-4-0	28
John Newcombe	2-5-0	0-3-0	3-6-0	2-3-1	25
Frank Sedgman	2-2-2	0-2-2	1-3-2	2-2-2	22
Bill Tilden	*	0-0-1	3-1-0	7-5-4	21
Rod Laver	3-4-0	2-1-1	4-1-2	2-0-0	20
Jean Borotra	1-1-1	2-6-2	2-3-1	0-0-1	20
Fred Stolle	0-3-1	1-2-0	0-2-3	1-3-2	18
Ken Rosewall	4-3-0	2-2-0	0-2-0	2-2-1	18
Neale Fraser	0-3-1	0-3-0	1-2-0	2-3-3	18
Adrian Quist	3-10-0	0-1-0	0-2-0	0-1-0	17
John Bromwich	2-8-1	0-0-0	0-2-2	0-1-1	17
John McEnroe	0-0-0	0-0-1	3-4-0	4-5-0	17
H.L. Doherty	*	*	5-8-0	1-2-0	16
Henri Cochet	*	4-3-2	2-2-0	1-0-1	15
Vic Seixas	0-1-0	0-2-1	1-0-4	1-2-3	15
Jack Crawford	4-4-1	1-1-1	1-1-1	0-0-0	15
Bob Hewitt	0-2-1	0-1-2	0-5-2	0-1-1	15

Women

Player	Aus. S-D-M	French S-D-M	Wim. S-D-M	U.S. S-D-M	Total
Margaret Court	11-8-2	5-4-4	3-2-5	7-7-8	66
Martina Navratilova	3-8-0	2-7-2	9-7-1	4-9-2	54
Billie Jean King	1-0-1	1-1-2	6-10-4	4-5-4	39
Margaret duPont	*	2-3-0	1-5-1	3-13-9	37
Louise Brough	1-1-0	0-3-0	4-5-4	1-12-4	35
Doris Hart	1-1-2	2-5-3	1-4-5	2-4-5	35
Helen Wills Moody	*	4-2-0	8-3-1	7-4-2	30
Elizabeth Ryan	*	0-4-0	0-12-7	0-1-2	26
Suzanne Lenglen	*	6-2-2	6-6-3	0-0-0	25
Pam Shriver	0-7-0	0-4-1	0-5-0	0-5-0	22
Chris Evert	2-0-0	7-2-0	3-1-0	6-0-0	21
Maria Bueno	0-1-0	0-1-1	3-5-0	4-5-0	20
Darlene Hard	*	1-2-2	0-4-3	2-6-0	20
Sarah Palfrey Cooke	*	0-0-1	0-2-0	2-9-4	18
Alice Marble	*	*	1-2-3	4-4-4	18

*Did not compete.

All-American Guy

By appearing in the 1991 Davis Cup, John McEnroe tied Bill Tilden and Stan Smith for most years played in the international event, with 11. McEnroe holds a number of other Davis Cup records: most events (26); most singles matches (49); most singles wins (41); most singles and doubles matches (65); and most total wins (56). In the five Davis Cup finals in which McEnroe has represented his country, the United States has won four.

National Team Competition

Davis Cup

Started in 1900 as the International Lawn Tennis Challenge Trophy by America's Dwight Davis, the runner-up in the 1898 U.S. Championships. A Davis Cup meeting between two countries is known as a tie and is a three-day event consisting of two singles matches, followed by one doubles match and then two more singles matches. The United States boasts the greatest number of wins (29), followed by Australia (20).

Year	Winner	Finalist	Site	Score
1900	United States	Great Britain	Boston	3-0
1901	No tournament			
1902	United States	Great Britain	New York	3-2
1903	Great Britain	United States	Boston	4-1
1904	Great Britain	Belgium	Wimbledon	5-0
1905	Great Britain	United States	Wimbledon	5-0
1906	Great Britain	United States	Wimbledon	5-0
1907	Australasia	Great Britain	Wimbledon	3-2
1908	Australasia	United States	Melbourne	3-2
1909	Australasia	United States	Sydney	5-0
1910	No tournament			
1911	Australasia	United States	Christchurch, NZ	5-0
1912	Great Britain	Australasia	Melbourne	3-2
1913	United States	Great Britain	Wimbledon	3-2
1914	Australasia	United States	New York	3-2
1915-18	No tournament			
1919	Australasia	Great Britain	Sydney	4-1
1920	United States	Australasia	Auckland, NZ	5-0
1921	United States	Japan	New York	5-0
1922	United States	Australasia	New York	4-1
1923	United States	Australasia	New York	4-1
1924	United States	Australia	Philadelphia	5-0
1925	United States	France	Philadelphia	5-0
1926	United States	France	Philadelphia	4-1
1927	France	United States	Philadelphia	3-2
1928	France	United States	Paris	4-1
1929	France	United States	Paris	3-2
1930	France	United States	Paris	4-1
1931	France	Great Britain	Paris	3-2
1932	France	United States	Paris	3-2
1933	Great Britain	France	Paris	3-2
1934	Great Britain	United States	Wimbledon	4-1
1935	Great Britain	United States	Wimbledon	5-0
1936	Great Britain	Australia	Wimbledon	3-2
1937	United States	Great Britain	Wimbledon	4-1
1938	United States	Australia	Philadelphia	3-2
1939	Australia	United States	Philadelphia	3-2
1940-45	No tournament			
1946	United States	Australia	Melbourne	5-0
1947	United States	Australia	New York	4-1
1948	United States	Australia	New York	5-0
1949	United States	Australia	New York	4-1
1950	Australia	United States	New York	4-1
1951	Australia	United States	Sydney	3-2
1952	Australia	United States	Adelaide	4-1
1953	Australia	United States	Melbourne	3-2
1954	United States	Australia	Sydney	3-2
1955	Australia	United States	New York	5-0
1956	Australia	United States	Adelaide	5-0
1957	Australia	United States	Melbourne	3-2
1958	United States	Australia	Brisbane	3-2
1959	Australia	United States	New York	3-2
1960	Australia	Italy	Sydney	4-1
1961	Australia	Italy	Melbourne	5-0
1962	Australia	Mexico	Brisbane	5-0
1963	United States	Australia	Adelaide	3-2
1964	Australia	United States	Cleveland	3-2
1965	Australia	Spain	Sydney	4-1
1966	Australia	India	Melbourne	4-1

Davis Cup (*Cont.*)

Year	Winner	Finalist	Site	Score
1967	Australia	Spain	Brisbane	4-1
1968	United States	Australia	Adelaide	4-1
1969	United States	Romania	Cleveland	5-0
1970	United States	West Germany	Cleveland	5-0
1971	United States	Romania	Charlotte, NC	3-2
1972	United States	Romania	Bucharest	3-2
1973	Australia	United States	Cleveland	5-0
1974	South Africa	India	*	walkover
1975	Sweden	Czechoslovakia	Stockholm	3-2
1976	Italy	Chile	Santiago	4-1
1977	Australia	Italy	Sydney	3-1
1978	United States	Great Britain	Palm Springs	4-1
1979	United States	Italy	San Francisco	5-0
1980	Czechoslovakia	Italy	Prague	4-1
1981	United States	Argentina	Cincinnati	3-1
1982	United States	France	Grenoble	4-1
1983	Australia	Sweden	Melbourne	3-2
1984	Sweden	United States	Gothenburg	4-1
1985	Sweden	West Germany	Munich	3-2
1986	Australia	Sweden	Melbourne	3-2
1987	Sweden	India	Gothenburg	5-0
1988	West Germany	Sweden	Gothenburg	4-1
1989	West Germany	Sweden	Stuttgart	3-2
1990	United States	Australia	St Petersburg	3-2

*India refused to play the final in protest over South Africa's governmental policy of apartheid.

Note: Prior to 1972 the challenge-round system was in effect, with the previous year's winner "standing out" of the competition until the finals. A straight 16-nation tournament has been held since 1981.

Federation Cup

The women's equivalent of the Davis Cup, this competition was started in 1963 by the International Lawn Tennis Federation (now the ITF). Unlike the Davis Cup, though, all entrants gather at one site at one time for a tournament that is concluded within one week. Matches consist of two singles and one doubles. The United States boasts the greatest number of wins (14), followed by Australia (7).

Year	Winner	Finalist	Site	Score
1963	United States	Australia	London	2-1
1964	Australia	United States	Philadelphia	2-1
1965	Australia	United States	Melbourne	2-1
1966	United States	West Germany	Turin	3-0
1967	United States	Great Britain	West Berlin	2-0
1968	Australia	Netherlands	Paris	3-0
1969	United States	Australia	Athens	2-1
1970	Australia	Great Britain	Freiburg	3-0
1971	Australia	Great Britain	Perth	3-0
1972	South Africa	Great Britain	Johannesburg	2-1
1973	Australia	South Africa	Bad Homburg	3-0
1974	Australia	United States	Naples	2-1
1975	Czechoslovakia	Australia	Aix-en-Provence	3-0
1976	United States	Australia	Philadelphia	2-1
1977	United States	Australia	Eastbourne	2-1
1978	United States	Australia	Melbourne	2-1
1979	United States	Australia	Madrid	3-0
1980	United States	Australia	West Berlin	3-0
1981	United States	Great Britain	Nagoya	3-0
1982	United States	West Germany	Santa Clara	3-0
1983	Czechoslovakia	West Germany	Zurich	2-1
1984	Czechoslovakia	Australia	São Paulo	2-1
1985	Czechoslovakia	United States	Tokyo	2-1
1986	United States	Czechoslovakia	Prague	3-0
1987	West Germany	United States	Vancouver	2-1
1988	Czechoslovakia	USSR	Melbourne	2-1
1989	United States	Spain	Tokyo	3-0
1990	United States	USSR	Atlanta	2-1
1991	Spain	United States	Nottingham	2-1

Rankings

ATP Computer Year-End Top 10

1973
Ilie Nastase
John Newcombe
Jimmy Connors
Tom Okker
Stan Smith
Ken Rosewall
Manuel Orantes
Rod Laver
Jan Kodes
Arthur Ashe

1974
Jimmy Connors
John Newcombe
Bjorn Borg
Rod Laver
Guillermo Vilas
Tom Okker
Arthur Ashe
Ken Rosewall
Stan Smith
Ilie Nastase

1975
Jimmy Connors
Guillermo Vilas
Bjorn Borg
Arthur Ashe
Manuel Orantes
Ken Rosewall
Ilie Nastase
John Alexander
Roscoe Tanner
Rod Laver

1976
Jimmy Connors
Bjorn Borg
Ilie Nastase
Manuel Orantes
Raul Ramirez
Guillermo Vilas
Adriano Panatta
Harold Solomon
Eddie Dibbs
Brian Gottfried

1977
Jimmy Connors
Guillermo Vilas
Bjorn Borg
Vitas Gerulaitis
Brian Gottfried
Eddie Dibbs
Manuel Orantes
Raul Ramirez
Ilie Nastase
Dick Stockton

1978
Jimmy Connors
Bjorn Borg
Guillermo Vilas
John McEnroe
Vitas Gerulaitis
Eddie Dibbs
Brian Gottfried
Raul Ramirez
Harold Solomon
Corrado Barazzutti

1979
Bjorn Borg
Jimmy Connors
John McEnroe
Vitas Gerulaitis
Roscoe Tanner
Guillermo Vilas
Arthur Ashe
Harold Solomon
Jose Higueras
Eddie Dibbs

1980
Bjorn Borg
John McEnroe
Jimmy Connors
Gene Mayer
Guillermo Vilas
Ivan Lendl
Harold Solomon
Jose-Luis Clerc
Vitas Gerulaitis
Eliot Teltscher

1981
John McEnroe
Ivan Lendl
Jimmy Connors
Bjorn Borg
Jose-Luis Clerc
Guillermo Vilas
Gene Mayer
Eliot Teltscher
Vitas Gerulaitis
Peter McNamara

1982
John McEnroe
Jimmy Connors
Ivan Lendl
Guillermo Vilas
Vitas Gerulaitis
Jose-Luis Clerc
Mats Wilander
Gene Mayer
Yannick Noah
Peter McNamara

1983
John McEnroe
Ivan Lendl
Jimmy Connors
Mats Wilander
Yannick Noah
Jimmy Arias
Jose Higueras
Jose-Luis Clerc
Kevin Curren
Gene Mayer

1984
John McEnroe
Jimmy Connors
Ivan Lendl
Mats Wilander
Andres Gomez
Anders Jarryd
Henrik Sundstrom
Pat Cash
Eliot Teltscher
Yannick Noah

1985
Ivan Lendl
John McEnroe
Mats Wilander
Jimmy Connors
Stefan Edberg
Boris Becker
Yannick Noah
Anders Jarryd
Miloslav Mecir
Kevin Curren

1986
Ivan Lendl
Boris Becker
Mats Wilander
Yannick Noah
Stefan Edberg
Henri Leconte
Joakim Nystrom
Jimmy Connors
Miloslav Mecir
Andres Gomez

1987
Ivan Lendl
Stefan Edberg
Mats Wilander
Jimmy Connors
Boris Becker
Miloslav Mecir
Pat Cash
Yannick Noah
Tim Mayotte
John McEnroe

Pass the Cream Cheese

More than 3000 match results were reported on the IBM/ATP Tour in 1990, and only twice did a "double bagel"—a 6–0, 6–0 blanking—occur. Guillermo Perez-Roldan defeated Xavier Daufresne in a first-round match at Bologna and Michael Chang shut out Mark Kratzman in another first-round match at London.

ATP Computer Year-End Top 10 (*Cont.*)

1988	1989	1990
Mats Wilander	Ivan Lendl	Stefan Edberg
Ivan Lendl	Boris Becker	Boris Becker
Andre Agassi	Stefan Edberg	Ivan Lendl
Boris Becker	John McEnroe	Andre Agassi
Stefan Edberg	Michael Chang	Pete Sampras
Kent Carlsson	Brad Gilbert	Andres Gomez
Jimmy Connors	Andre Agassi	Thomas Muster
Jakob Hlasek	Aaron Krickstein	Emilio Sanchez
Henri Leconte	Alberto Mancini	Goran Ivanisevic
Tim Mayotte	Jay Berger	Brad Gilbert

WTA Computer Year-End Top 10

1973	1977	1981
Margaret Smith Court	Chris Evert	Chris Evert Lloyd
Billie Jean King	Billie Jean King	Tracy Austin
Evonne Goolagong Cawley	Martina Navratilova	Martina Navratilova
Chris Evert	Virginia Wade	Andrea Jaeger
Rosie Casals	Sue Barker	Hana Mandlikova
Virginia Wade	Rosie Casals	Sylvia Hanika
Kerry Reid	Betty Stove	Pam Shriver
Nancy Gunter	Dianne Balestrat	Wendy Turnbull
Julie Heldman	Wendy Turnbull	Bettina Bunge
Helga Masthoff	Kerry Reid	Barbara Potter

1974	1978	1982
Billie Jean King	Martina Navratilova	Martina Navratilova
Evonne Goolagong Cawley	Chris Evert	Chris Evert Lloyd
Chris Evert	Evonne Goolagong Cawley	Andrea Jaeger
Virginia Wade	Virginia Wade	Tracy Austin
Julie Heldman	Billie Jean King	Wendy Turnbull
Rosie Casals	Tracy Austin	Pam Shriver
Kerry Reid	Wendy Turnbull	Hana Mandlikova
Olga Morozova	Kerry Reid	Barbara Potter
Lesley Hunt	Betty Stove	Bettina Bunge
Francoise Durr	Dianne Balestrat	Sylvia Hanika

1975	1979	1983
Chris Evert	Martina Navratilova	Martina Navratilova
Billie Jean King	Chris Evert Lloyd	Chris Evert Lloyd
Evonne Goolagong Cawley	Tracy Austin	Andrea Jaeger
Martina Navratilova	Evonne Goolagong Cawley	Pam Shriver
Virginia Wade	Billie Jean King	Sylvia Hanika
Margaret Smith Court	Dianne Balestrat	Jo Durie
Olga Morozova	Wendy Turnbull	Bettina Bunge
Nancy Gunter	Virginia Wade	Wendy Turnbull
Francoise Durr	Kerry Reid	Tracy Austin
Rosie Casals	Sue Barker	Zina Garrison

1976	1980	1984
Chris Evert	Chris Evert Lloyd	Martina Navratilova
Evonne Goolagong Cawley	Tracy Austin	Chris Evert Lloyd
Virginia Wade	Martina Navratilova	Hana Mandlikova
Martina Navratilova	Hana Mandlikova	Pam Shriver
Sue Barker	Evonne Goolagong Cawley	Wendy Turnbull
Betty Stove	Billie Jean King	Manuela Maleeva
Dianne Balestrat	Andrea Jaeger	Helena Sukova
Mima Jausovec	Wendy Turnbull	Claudia Kohde-Kilsch
Rosie Casals	Pam Shriver	Zina Garrison
Francoise Durr	Greer Stevens	Kathy Jordan

Young Guns

Monica Seles became the youngest No. 1 in tennis history when she attained that ranking on March 11, 1991, at the age of 17 years, 3 months and 9 days. She was 17 days younger than Tracy Austin, who became No. 1 on April 7, 1980.

WTA Computer Year-End Top 10 (*Cont.*)

1985
Martina Navratilova
Chris Evert Lloyd
Hana Mandlikova
Pam Shriver
Claudia Kohde-Kilsch
Steffi Graf
Manuela Maleeva
Zina Garrison
Helena Sukova
Bonnie Gadusek

1986
Martina Navratilova
Chris Evert Lloyd
Steffi Graf
Hana Mandlikova
Helena Sukova
Pam Shriver
Claudia Kohde-Kilsch
Manuela Maleeva
Kathy Rinaldi
Gabriela Sabatini

1987
Steffi Graf
Martina Navratilova
Chris Evert
Pam Shriver
Hana Mandlikova
Gabriela Sabatini
Helena Sukova
Manuela Maleeva
Zina Garrison
Claudia Kohde-Kilsch

1988
Steffi Graf
Martina Navratilova
Chris Evert
Gabriela Sabatini
Pam Shriver
Manuela Maleeva-Fragniere
Natalia Zvereva
Helena Sukova
Zina Garrison
Barbara Potter

1989
Steffi Graf
Martina Navratilova
Gabriela Sabatini
Zina Garrison
Arantxa Sanchez Vicario
Monica Seles
Conchita Martinez
Helena Sukova
Manuela Maleeva-Fragniere
*Chris Evert

1990
Steffi Graf
Monica Seles
Martina Navratilova
Mary Joe Fernandez
Gabriela Sabatini
Katerina Maleeva
Arantxa Sanchez Vicario
Jennifer Capriati
Manuela Maleeva-Fragniere
Zina Garrison

*When Chris Evert announced her retirement at the 1989 United States Open, she was ranked 4 in the world. That was her last official series tournament.

Prize Money

Top 25 Men's Career Prize Money Leaders

	Earnings ($)
Ivan Lendl	17,511,731
John McEnroe	11,492,690
Stefan Edberg	10,001,536
Boris Becker	9,020,310
Jimmy Connors	8,280,114
Mats Wilander	7,377,193
Guillermo Vilas	4,900,582
Andres Gomez	4,077,165
Andre Agassi	3,833,204
Tomas Smid	3,696,118
Anders Jarryd	3,695,128
Bjorn Borg	3,609,896
Brad Gilbert	3,442,329
Yannick Noah	3,259,485
Emilio Sanchez	3,206,251
Brian Gottfried	2,782,514
Vitas Gerulaitis	2,778,748
Kevin Curren	2,727,295
Wojtek Fibak	2,725,133
Jakob Hlasek	2,704,382
Tim Mayotte	2,652,592
Miloslav Mecir	2,632,538
Guy Forget	2,499,659
Johan Kriek	2,352,329
Henri Leconte	2,295,780

Note: From arrival of Open tennis in 1968 through September 8, 1991.

Top 25 Women's Career Prize Money Leaders

	Earnings ($)
Martina Navratilova	17,254,143
Chris Evert	8,896,195
Steffi Graf	8,080,534
Gabriela Sabatini	4,570,707
Pam Shriver	4,518,808
Helena Sukova	3,744,996
Hana Mandlikova	3,340,959
Monica Seles	3,329,041
Zina Garrison	3,054,504
Wendy Turnbull	2,769,024
Manuela Maleeva-Fragniere	2,151,082
Claudia Kohde-Kilsch	2,129,948
Billie Jean King	1,966,487
Arantxa Sanchez Vicario	1,938,257
Tracy Austin	1,925,415
Jana Novotna	1,907,723
Natalia Zvereva	1,607,835
Kathy Jordan	1,592,111
Lori McNeil	1,549,379
Virginia Wade	1,542,278
Mary Joe Fernandez	1,467,838
Evonne Goolagong Cawley	1,399,431
Andrea Jaeger	1,379,066
Barbara Potter	1,376,580
Rosie Casals	1,364,955

Note: From arrival of Open tennis in 1968 through September 8, 1991.

Open Era Overall Wins

Men's Career Leaders—Tournaments Won

The top tournament-winning men from the institution of Open tennis in 1968 through September 8, 1991.

	W		W
Jimmy Connors	109	John Newcombe	32
Ivan Lendl	91	Manuel Orantes	32
John McEnroe	77	Ken Rosewall	32
Bjorn Borg	65	Stefan Edberg	31
Guillermo Vilas	61	Boris Becker	30
Ilie Nastase	57	Tom Okker	30
Rod Laver	47	Vitas Gerulaitis	27
Stan Smith	39	Jose-Luis Clerc	25
Arthur Ashe	33	Brian Gottfried	25
Mats Wilander	33	Yannick Noah	23

Women's Career Leaders—Matches Won

The top match winners among women since the institution of Open tennis in 1968 through September 8, 1991.

	W	Pct Won		W	Pct Won
Chris Evert	1309	90.3	Virginia Ruzici	490	63.7
Martina Navratilova	1307	88.0	Helena Sukova	470	69.9
Virginia Wade	839	71.6	Dianne Balestrat	468	63.3
Billie Jean King	695	81.8	Margaret Smith Court	464	85.6
Evonne Goolagong Cawley	695	81.5	Zina Garrison	449	71.0
Wendy Turnbull	577	64.4	Sylvia Hanika	423	63.5
Hana Mandlikova	567	74.4	Gabriela Sabatini	410	78.5
Pam Shriver	556	73.7	Claudia Kohde-Kilsch	390	63.5
Rosie Casales	528	63.1	Manuela Maleeva-Fragniere	382	71.4
Steffi Graf	499	88.0	Sue Barker	365	63.7

Making a List

The U.S. Open is the only Grand Slam tournament that has been held on three surfaces—grass, clay, and hard court—and five-time champion Jimmy Connors is the only player to have won it on all three. He also has played more memorable matches at the U.S. Open than anyone else. Here are seven of them, not including his 1991 5-set thrillers.

1974 final—6–1, 6–0, 6–1 win over Ken Rosewall. In the most lopsided final in tournament history, Rosewall fared even worse on the grass at Forest Hills than he had in the Wimbledon final two months earlier, which Connors won 6–1, 6–1, 6–4.

1976 final—6–4, 3–6, 7–6, 6–4 win over Bjorn Borg on clay. Borg won 123 points to Connors' 121, but Jimbo saved four set points in the tiebreaker.

1977 final—2–6, 6–3, 7–6, 6–0 loss to Guillermo Vilas. Connors pushed and shoved photographers as he stormed off the court. Minutes later, he was driving away from the West Side Tennis Club.

1978 round of 16—4–6, 6–4, 6–1, 1–6, 7–5 win over Adriano Panatta on the hard courts at Flushing Meadow. What a point! Serving at 5–6 and deuce in the fifth set, Panatta thought he had ended the rally with a crosscourt volley that bounded 10 feet beyond the sideline. But Connors scrambled after the ball and ripped a one-handed backhand around the net post. The ball landed inches inside the baseline. Panatta double-faulted on the next point to lose the match.

1983 final—6–3, 6–7, 7–5, 6–0 win over Ivan Lendl. Connors won his fifth U.S. Open, surviving a death threat, diarrhea, and 107° heat.

1984 semifinals—6–4, 4–6, 7–5, 4–6, 6–3 loss to McEnroe. The match was the last of the day and ended at 11:13 p.m. Connors nailed 45 winners to McEnroe's 20, but McEnroe won 12 of the first 13 points in the fifth set.

1989 round of 16—6–2, 6–3, 6–1 victory over Stefan Edberg. Edberg was seeded third but Connors demolished him. Along the way, a characteristic curse-fest, directed at umpire Richard Ings, cost Jimbo $2,250 in fines.

International Tennis Hall of Fame

Pauline Betz Addie (1965)
George T. Adee (1964)
Fred B. Alexander (1961)
Wilmer L. Allison (1963)
Manuel Alonso (1977)
Arthur Ashe (1985)
Juliette Atkinson (1974)
Lawrence A. Baker (1975)
Maud Barger-Wallach (1958)
Karl Behr (1969)
Bjorn Borg (1987)
Jean Borotra (1976)
Maureen Connolly Brinker (1968)
John Bromwich (1984)
Norman Everard Brookes (1977)
Mary K. Browne (1957)
Jacques Brugnon (1976)
J. Donald Budge (1964)
Maria E. Bueno (1978)
May Sutton Bundy (1956)
Mabel E. Cahill (1976)
Oliver S. Campbell (1955)
Malcom Chace (1961)
Dorothea Douglass Lambert Chambers (1981)
Louise Brough Clapp (1967)
Clarence Clark (1983)
Joseph S. Clark (1955)
William J. Clothier (1956)
Henri Cochet (1976)
Ashley Cooper (1991)
Margaret Smith Court (1979)
Gottfried von Cramm (1977)
John H. Crawford (1979)
Joseph F. Cullman III (1990)
Allison Danzig (1968)
Sarah Palfrey Danzig (1963)
Dwight F. Davis (1956)
Charlotte Dod (1983)
John H. Doeg (1962)
Laurie Doherty (1980)
Reggie Doherty (1980)
Jaroslav Drobny (1983)
Margaret Osborne duPont (1967)
James Dwight (1955)
Roy Emerson (1982)
Pierre Etchebaster (1978)
Robert Falkenburg (1974)
Neale Fraser (1984)
Charles S. Garland (1969)
Althea Gibson (1971)
Kathleen McKane Godfree (1978)

Richard A. Gonzales (1968)
Evonne Goolagong Cawley (1988)
Bryan M. Grant Jr (1972)
David Gray (1985)
Clarence Griffin (1970)
King Gustaf V of Sweden (1980)
Harold H. Hackett (1961)
Ellen Forde Hansell (1965)
Darlene R. Hard (1973)
Doris J. Hart (1969)
Gladys M. Heldman (1979)
W. E. "Slew" Hester Jr (1981)
Lew Hoad (1980)
Harry Hopman (1978)
Fred Hovey (1974)
Joseph R. Hunt (1966)
Francis T. Hunter (1961)
Shirley Fry Irvin (1970)
Helen Hull Jacobs (1962)
William Johnston (1958)
Ann Haydon Jones (1985)
Perry Jones (1970)
Billie Jean King (1987)
Jan Kodes (1990)
John A. Kramer (1968)
Rene Lacoste (1976)
Al Laney (1979)
William A. Larned (1956)
Arthur D. Larsen (1969)
Rod G. Laver (1981)
Suzanne Lenglen (1978)
Dorothy Round Little (1986)
George M. Lott Jr (1964)
Chuck McKinley (1986)
Maurice McLoughlin (1957)
W. Donald McNeill (1965)
Gene Mako (1973)
Molla Bjurstedt Mallory (1958)
Alice Marble (1964)
Alastair B. Martin (1973)
William McChesney Martin (1982)
Elisabeth H. Moore (1971)
Gardnar Mulloy (1972)
R. Lindley Murray (1958)
Julian S. Myrick (1963)
Ilie Nastase (1991)
John D. Newcombe (1986)
Arthur C. Nielsen Sr (1971)
Betty Nuthall (1977)
Alex Olmedo (1987)
Rafael Osuna (1979)
Mary Ewing Outerbridge (1981)

Frank A. Parker (1966)
Gerald Patterson (1989)
Budge Patty (1977)
Theodore R. Pell (1967)
Fred Perry (1975)
Tom Pettitt (1982)
Nicola Pietrangeli (1986)
Adrian Quist (1984)
Dennis Ralston (1987)
Ernest Renshaw (1983)
Willie Renshaw (1983)
Vincent Richards (1961)
Robert L. Riggs (1967)
Helen Wills Moody Roark (1959)
Anthony D. Roche (1986)
Ellen C. Roosevelt (1975)
Ken Rosewall (1980)
Elizabeth Ryan (1972)
Manuel Santana (1984)
Richard Savitt (1976)
Frederick R. Schroeder (1966)
Eleonora Sears (1968)
Richard D. Sears (1955)
Frank Sedgman (1979)
Pancho Segura (1984)
Vic Seixas Jr (1971)
Francis X. Shields (1964)
Henry W. Slocum Jr (1955)
Stan Smith (1987)
Fred Stolle (1985)
William F. Talbert (1967)
Bill Tilden (1959)
Lance Tingay (1982)
Ted Tinling (1986)
Bertha Townsend Toulmin (1974)
Tony Trabert (1970)
James H. Van Alen (1965)
John Van Ryn (1963)
Guillermo Vilas (1991)
Ellsworth Vines (1962)
Virginia Wade (1989)
Marie Wagner (1969)
Holcombe Ward (1956)
Watson Washburn (1965)
Malcolm D. Whitman (1955)
Hazel Hotchkiss Wightman (1957)
Anthony Wilding (1978)
Richard Norris Williams II (1957)
Sidney B. Wood (1964)
Robert D. Wrenn (1955)
Beals C. Wright (1956)

Note: Years in parentheses are dates of induction.

Golf

AUGUST 19, 1991 · $2.95

Sports Illustrated

THE PREZ AT PLAY

LONG SHOT

BIG HITTER JOHN DALY
IN A BIG PGA UPSET

JACQUELINE DUVOISIN

Monster of the Fairway

In a year of surprises, John Daly's long-driving win at the PGA was the biggest | by JOHN GARRITY

N TINY DARDANELLE, ARK. (POP. 3,621), THEY'LL no doubt remember Aug. 10, 1991, as the day the phones started ringing. They were ringing at the home of the high school football coach, ringing at the full-service gas station, ringing at the corner grocery. Most of all, they were ringing in the pro shop at the nine-hole Bay Ridge Boat and Golf Club.

"You don't know me," went the typical call from a golf writer, "but I'm trying to talk to someone—anyone—who knows John Daly."

"Waaall, I don't *know* him, but I saw him buy a sleeve of golf balls once."

"Perfect! Can I ask you some questions about him?"

Daly, a chunky, hot-tempered 25-year-old PGA Tour rookie, was the fellow who put Dardanelle on the sports map. And he did it by winning the PGA Championship at Crooked Stick Golf Club in Carmel, Ind. Here's a look at what happened in the days leading up to his improbable victory in the final major tournament of the 1991 tour:

Wednesday night. Daly, the ninth alternate, drives all night from Memphis to Indianapolis, not knowing if he will get to play in the PGA.

Thursday morning. Daly, added to the 151-man field when Nick Price withdraws, tees off without benefit of a practice round on a golf course that Jack Nicklaus calls "the toughest I've ever seen."

Friday afternoon. Daly birdies the 445-yard 18th hole with a driver and a seven-iron to take a one-stroke lead at eight under par. Stories begin circulating that he is cutting doglegs with 300-yard-plus drives and hitting greens with skyscraper-high iron shots. Skeptics note that Daly ranks first on the PGA Tour in driving distance and 185th in driving accuracy.

Saturday afternoon. Daly birdies three straight holes on the front side. Galleries desert the dream pairing of Nick Faldo and Ian Woosnam to follow the rookie. CBS, committing all of its ground cameras to

Daly, decides to cover the rest of the field from a blimp. Phones start ringing in Dardanelle.

Saturday night. Daly attends an Indianapolis Colts preseason game at the Hoosier Dome and gets a rousing ovation from the fans.

Sunday afternoon. Daly wins by three shots over Bruce Lietzke and is hailed as the most surprising major-tournament champion since Jack Fleck, who beat Ben Hogan in a playoff to win the 1955 U.S. Open.

So who was John Daly? The former high school placekicker described himself as "sort of a loner" and said he taught himself to play golf as a youngster in Dardanelle, using golf balls he fished out of a pond. Ignoring the advice of teaching pros ("I don't like being told what to do"), the former University of Arkansas golf All-America perfected his power stroke on the South African and Ben Hogan tours before earning his PGA Tour card in 1990. His long-driving secret: a stretch-till-something-tears body coil and a simple thought in midswing: "Kill!"

Said Daly, whose booming game was tailor-made for the 7,289-yard Crooked Stick layout, "I've never hit it this straight before."

Baker-Finch came out of the rough and up from Down Under to win the British Open.

And CBS never had it so good. It was carrying the PGA for the first time in several years—it had been on ABC—and got much higher than expected ratings.

Television also figured in 1991's longest running golf controversy. The trouble started at the Doral Ryder Open in March, when a vigilant home viewer called tournament officials to report that Paul Azinger had dislodged a pebble with his foot while taking a stance in a water hazard. Azinger was subsequently disqualified for signing an incorrect scorecard, touching off a debate over the role of TV and instant replay in rules decisions.

The ensuing decision to place a PGA Tour rules official in the TV trailer to monitor play backfired when veteran Tom Kite hit his ball into a water hazard during the final round of the Byron Nelson Classic in May. Kite dropped and played his ball from where he thought his shot had crossed the boundary of the hazard, only to be overruled by the official in the TV trailer, who ordered Kite to replay the hole from the tee. Embarrassed by another unpopular ruling, the Tour pulled the plug on its experiment.

Undaunted, the video vigilantes struck again at the PGA Championship. As Daly lined up an eagle putt during the third round, several viewers noted that his caddie had let the flagstick touch the putting surface behind the hole—a two-stroke penalty, if called. This time, officials of the PGA of America wisely decided that there was no penalty because the flagstick had not touched precisely where Daly was aiming.

Trend-watchers in '91 saw no letup in the Down Under phenomenon, as two more Australian golfers won significant tournaments. Steve Elkington's victory at The Players Championship and Ian Baker-Finch's British Open win, coming within a year of triumphs by Wayne Grady (PGA), Mike Harwood (British PGA), and Greg Norman (1990 leading money winner), made Crocodile Dundee jokes the in-thing. In the lefthanded compliment department, Arizona State University portsider Phil Mickelson became only the fourth amateur ever to win a Tour event, the Northern Telecom Open in Tucson, and southpaw Russ Cochran earned his first career win, the Western Open. And Billy Andrade, winless in three years on the Tour, got his own trend going with back-to-back wins, the Kemper Open and the Buick Classic, in June.

Elsewhere in Golf . . .

WHEN THE HEAT WAS ON, MEG Mallon came through. She had never won a Ladies Professional Golf Association tournament before her breakthrough win at the Oldsmobile Classic in February, and even then some members of the women's tour said she was "too nice to win." The fifth-year pro buried that canard in late June by winning the LPGA Championship at the Bethesda (Md.) Country Club. In oppressive heat and humidity, she went head-to-head with veterans Pat Bradley and Ayako Okamoto, capping her one-shot victory with a mettle-testing downhill 12-footer for birdie on the 72nd hole. "It's something you dream about," said Mallon, "making a putt on the last green to win a major championship."

Two weeks later, the LPGA's newest star did it again. The field at the U.S. Women's Open, held at Fort Worth's Colonial Country Club, had to contend with 100˚ days and bent-grass greens so stressed that they had to be covered with ice by night and cooled by electric fans by day. Bradley again looked like she would capture her seventh major title, and Amy Alcott, winner of the Dinah Shore in March and one victory away from qualifying for the LPGA Hall of Fame, made a second-round move and by Sunday seemed ready to pounce. But it was Mallon who kept her cool over the final holes, hitting nothing but fairways and greens for a closing 67. Her 283, two shots better than Bradley, was the only subpar score of the week.

Said the 28-year-old Mallon, "No one's more surprised than I am."

On the Senior PGA Tour, an overworked Lee Trevino failed to produce anything approaching his seven-win $1 million-plus 1990 season. The year belonged instead to Jack Nicklaus and Chi Chi Rodriguez—"the big bear and the little mouse from Puerto Rico," as Rodriguez put it. Nicklaus, 51, played in only a handful of senior tournaments, but he won three of the most prestigious events—The Tradition, the PGA Seniors, and the U.S. Senior Open, played at Oakland Hills in Birmingham, Mich. Nicklaus called his 65 in the 18-hole Senior Open playoff with Rodriguez one of the greatest tournament rounds of his career. "You

For drama, no tournament could top the 1991 Masters. Three of the world's greatest players came to the 72nd hole with a chance to win. Spain's Jose Maria Olazabal, who had recovered from a second-round quadruple bogey, drove into a fairway bunker and made bogey. Two-time Masters champ Tom Watson, who had eagled two holes on the final nine to stay in contention, saw his hopes die when he pushed a three-wood into the trees. That left the door open for the little Welshman, Ian Woosnam. Wee Woosie swung from his heels and knocked his final drive completely over and left of the bunker that had caught Olazabal. A wild shot? No, explained Woosnam, because his landing area afforded a clear shot at the green. Woosnam parred the hole to win the Masters, his first major.

The two Opens provided less excitement, but served to validate the reputations of two of the world's better players. Payne Stewart won the U.S. Open at Hazeltine by outlasting former Open champ Scott Simpson in an 18-hole playoff. The decisive shot: Simpson's pull-hook into the water on the par-3 17th hole on Monday. Baker-Finch made easy work of the British Open at Royal Birkdale, firing a final-round, front-nine 29 and cruising to a two-shot win.

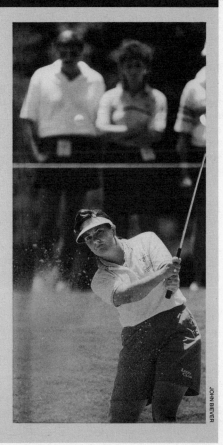

can't catch Jack," said Rodriguez. "Once he puts those paws on you, you're gone."

The one biggie that Nicklaus didn't win was the Senior Players Championship at Dearborn, Mich., which he had won there the year before, and the joke was on Jack because he designed the golf course, the TPC of Michigan. A club pro from Locust Valley, N.Y., Jim Albus, won the tournament.

Other seniors had their moments in '91. Mike Hill, the former beer-truck driver, sparkled for the third straight year, and erstwhile ESPN commentator Jim Colbert made an impressive tour debut, winning the Southwestern Bell Classic outside Kansas City and finishing second several times.

For the most part, though, when the Bear was away, the Mouse did play. Heading into the final six weeks of the Seniors tour, the flamboyant Rodriguez had won four tournaments and was in position to finish atop the Senior Tour money list for the second time.

Mallon's breakthrough year included wins at the LPGA Championship and the U.S. Women's Open.

JOHN BIEVER

JOHN IACONO

And finally, the professional golfers of the United States wrested the Ryder Cup from the professionals of Europe, who had held it since their victory at The Belfry, in Sutton Coldfield, England, in 1985. The scene of the American triumph was an alligator-friendly barrier island in South Carolina and a Pete Dye golf course that was a lot less friendly than the alligators. The Ocean Course at Kiawah Island—a windswept fantasy blending the traditional Scottish links look with marshland, live oak trees and vast sand-and-scrub transition areas—took its toll on both teams, which were tied 8–8 after two days of alternate-shot and better-ball matches.

Paul Azinger, Chip Beck, Corey Pavin, Fred Couples and Lanny Wadkins won their Sunday singles matches, as the Americans took a 14–13 lead with only one match left to be decided. That struggle, pitting three-time U.S. Open champion Hale Irwin against Germany's Bernhard Langer, came down to a six-foot putt on the 18th green. Langer, who had holed a series of character-building putts to square his match with

Woosnam's par on the 72nd hole at the Masters was worth a cheer and a green jacket.

Irwin, needed to make one more to win his match and retain the cup for Europe by virtue of a 14–14 tie. Instead, his ball slid over the right edge of the cup, giving the U.S. team a 14½–13½ win in the biennial event.

A lot of memorable golf was played in '91, but the enduring snapshot will be Daly at Crooked Stick. When he spotted controversial course designer Pete Dye in the crowd after his stunning victory, Daly said, "I *love* your golf course."

Dye beamed. "I have one fan!"

Funny. One fan is all Daly had when he teed off for the first round of the PGA Championship—his fiancée, Bettye Fulford—but he left the golf course three days later in a tight cordon of Indiana State Troopers assigned to protect him from his many new-found admirers. "This is kinda different," he said.

So was John Daly.

FOR THE RECORD • 1990 – 1991

Men's Majors

The Masters
Augusta National GC; Augusta, GA
(par 72; 6,905 yds) April 11-14

Player	Score	Earnings ($)
Ian Woosnam	72-66-67-72—277	243,000
Jose Maria Olazabal	68-71-69-70—278	145,800
Ben Crenshaw	70-73-68-68—279	64,800
Steve Pate	72-73-69-65—279	64,800
Lanny Wadkins	67-71-70-71—279	64,800
Tom Watson	68-68-70-73—279	64,800

U.S. Open
Hazeltine National GC; Chaska, MN
(par 72; 7,149 yds) June 13-17

Player	Score	Earnings ($)
Payne Stewart	67-70-73-72—282	235,000
Scott Simpson	70-68-72-72—282	117,500
Fred Couples	70-70-75-70—285	62,574
Larry Nelson	73-72-72-68—285	62,574
Fuzzy Zoeller	72-73-74-67—286	41,542

Note: Stewart defeated Simpson 75-77 in 18-hole playoff.

British Open
Royal Birkdale; Southport, England
(par 70; 6,940 yds) July 18-21

Player	Score	Earnings ($)
Ian Baker-Finch	71-71-64-66—272	150,000
Mike Harwood	68-70-69-67—274	115,500
Fred Couples	72-69-70-64—275	90,750
Mark O'Meara	71-68-67-69—275	90,750
Bob Tway	75-66-70-66—277	56,375
Eamonn Darcy	73-68-66-70—277	56,375
Jodie Mudd	72-70-72-63—277	56,375

PGA Championship
Crooked Stick GC; Carmel, IN
(par 72; 7,289 yds) August 8-11

Player	Score	Earnings ($)
John Daly	69-67-69-71—276	230,000
Bruce Lietzke	68-69-72-70—279	140,000
Jim Gallagher Jr.	70-72-72-67—281	95,000
Kenny Knox	67-71-70-74—282	75,000
Bob Gilder	73-70-67-73—283	60,000
Steven Richardson	70-72-72-69—283	60,000

Men's Tour Results

Late 1990 PGA Tour Events

Tournament	Final Round	Winner	Score/ Under Par	Earnings ($)
Isuzu Kapalua International	Nov 10	David Peoples	264/–24	150,000
RMCC Invitational	Nov 18	Fred Couples, Raymond Floyd	182/–34	125,000 each
JC Penney Classic	Dec 2	Davis Love III, Beth Daniel	266/–18	100,000 each
Sazale Classic	Dec 9	Fred Couples, Mike Donald	254/–34	90,000 each

1991 PGA Tour Events

Tournament	Final Round	Winner	Score/ Under Par	Earnings ($)
Tournament of Champions	Jan 6	Tom Kite	272/–16	144,000
Northern Telecom Open	Jan 13	Phil Mickelson	272/–16	Amateur
United Hawaiian Open	Jan 20	Lanny Wadkins	270/–18	198,000
Phoenix Open	Jan 27	Nolan Henke	268/–16	180,000
AT&T Pebble Beach Pro-Am	Feb 3	Paul Azinger	274/–14	198,000
Bob Hope Chrysler Classic	Feb 10	Corey Pavin*	331/–29	198,000
Shearson Lehman Brothers Open	Feb 17	Jay Don Blake	268/–20	180,000
Nissan Los Angeles Open	Feb 24	Ted Schulz	272/–12	180,000
Doral Ryder Open	Mar 4	Rocco Mediate*	276/–12	252,000
Honda Classic	Mar 10	Steve Pate	279/–9	180,000
Nestle Invitational	Mar 17	Andrew Magee†	203/–13	180,000
USF&G Classic	Mar 24	Ian Woosnam‡	275/–13	180,000
Players Championship	Mar 31	Steve Elkington	276/–12	288,000
Independent Insurance Agent Open	Apr 7	Rained out; rescheduled Oct 1991		
The Masters	Apr 14	Ian Woosnam	277/–11	243,000
Deposit Guaranty Golf Classic	Apr 14	Larry Silveira*	266/–14	54,000
MCI Heritage Classic	Apr 21	Davis Love III	271/–13	180,000
K Mart Greater Greensboro Open	Apr 28	Mark Brooks#	275/–13	225,000
GTE Byron Nelson Classic	May 5	Nick Price	270/–10	198,000
BellSouth Atlanta Classic	May 12	Corey Pavin*	272/–16	180,000
Memorial Tournament	May 19	Kenny Perry*	273/–15	216,000

1991 PGA Tour Events (*Cont.*)

Tournament	Final Round	Winner	Score/ Under Par	Earnings ($)
Southwestern Bell Colonial	May 26	Tom Purtzer	267/–13	216,000
Kemper Open	June 2	Billy Andrade*	263/–21	180,000
Buick Classic	June 9	Billy Andrade	273/–11	180,000
U.S. Open	June 17	Payne Stewart††	282/–6	235,000
Anheuser-Busch Classic	June 23	Mike Hulbert*	266/–18	180,000
Federal Express St Jude Classic	June 30	Fred Couples	269/–15	180,000
Centel Western Open	July 7	Russ Cochran	275/–13	180,000
New England Classic	July 14	Bruce Fleisher**	268/–16	180,000
British Open	July 21	Ian Baker-Finch	272/–8	150,000
Chattanooga Classic	July 21	Dillard Pruitt	260/–20	126,000
Canon Greater Hartford Open	July 28	Billy Ray Brown*	271/–9	180,000
Buick Open	Aug 4	Brad Faxon*	271/–17	180,000
PGA Championship	Aug 11	John Daly	276/–12	230,000
The International	Aug 18	Jose Maria Olazabal (Stableford scoring)	+10	198,000
NEC World Series of Golf	Aug 25	Tom Purtzer‡	279/–1	216,000
Greater Milwaukee Open	Sep 1	Mark Brooks	270/–18	180,000
Canadian Open	Sep 8	Nick Price	273/–15	180,000
Hardee's Golf Classic	Sep 15	D. A. Weibring	267/–13	180,000
B.C. Open	Sep 22	Fred Couples	269/–15	144,000
Buick Southern Open	Sep 29	David Peoples	276/–12	126,000
H.E.B. Texas Open	Oct 6	Blaine McCallister‡	269/–11	162,000
Las Vegas Invitational	Oct 13	Andrew Magee‡	329/–31	270,000
Walt Disney World-Oldsmobile Classic	Oct 19	Mark O'Meara	267/–21	180,000
TOUR Championship	Nov 3	Craig Stadler‡	279/–5	360,000

*Won on 1st playoff hole.

†Rain shortened to 3 rounds.

‡Won on 2nd playoff hole.

#Won on 3rd playoff hole.

††Won in 18-hole playoff, 75-77.

**Won on 7th playoff hole.

Women's Majors

Nabisco Dinah Shore
Mission Hills CC; Rancho Mirage, CA
(par 72; 6,437 yds) March 28-31

Player	Score	Earnings ($)
Amy Alcott	67-70-68-68—273	90,000
Dottie Mochrie	70-71-71-69—281	55,500
Pat Bradley	70-72-73-67—282	36,000
Patty Sheehan	71-71-70-70—282	36,000
Lori Garbacz	73-71-70-70—284	25,500

U.S. Women's Open
Colonial CC; Fort Worth, TX
(par 71; 6,340 yds) July 11-14

Player	Score	Earnings ($)
Meg Mallon	70-75-71-67—283	110,000
Pat Bradley	69-73-72-71—285	55,000
Amy Alcott	75-68-72-71—286	32,882
Laurel Kean	70-76-71-70—287	23,996
Dottie Mochrie	73-76-68-71—288	17,642
Chris Johnson	76-72-68-72—288	17,642

LPGA Championship
Bethesda CC; Bethesda, MD
(par 71; 6,246 yds) June 27-30

Player	Score	Earnings ($)
Meg Mallon	68-68-71-67—274	150,000
Pat Bradley	68-68-71-68—275	80,000
Ayako Okamoto	70-64-73-68—275	80,000
Beth Daniel	71-70-68-69—278	52,500
Deb Richard	67-70-72-70—279	38,750
Barb Bunkowsky	70-68-70-71—279	38,750

Du Maurier LTD. Classic
Vancouver GC; Coquitlam, British Columbia, Canada (par 71; 7,000 yds) September 12-15

Player	Score	Earnings ($)
Nancy Scranton	72-75-64-68—279	105,000
Debbie Massey	67-70-72-73—282	64,750
Laura Davies	71-71-71-71—284	37,916
Trish Johnson	67-71-73-73—284	37,916
Pamela Wright	72-69-69-74—284	37,916

Women's Tour Results

Late 1990 LPGA Tour Events

Tournament	Final Round	Winner	Score/ Under Par	Earnings ($)
Centel Classic	Oct 7	Beth Daniel	271/–17	150,000
Mazda Japan Classic	Nov 5	Debbie Massey#	133/–11	82,500
JC Penney Classic	Dec 2	Davis Love III, Beth Daniel	266/–18	100,000 each

1991 LPGA Tour Events

Tournament	Final Round	Winner	Score/ Under Par	Earnings ($)
Jamaica Classic	Jan 20	Jane Geddes	207/–6	75,000
Oldsmobile LPGA Classic	Feb 3	Meg Mallon	276/–12	60,000
Phar-Mor at Inverrary	Feb 10	Beth Daniel	209/–7	75,000
Orix Hawaiian Ladies Open	Feb 23	Patty Sheehan	207/–9	52,500
Women's Kemper Open	Mar 2	Deb Richard*	275/–9	75,000
Inamori Classic	Mar 10	Laura Davies	277/–11	60,000
Desert Inn LPGA International	Mar 17	Penny Hammel	211/–5	60,000
Standard Register Ping	Mar 24	Danielle Ammaccapane	283/–9	82,500
Nabisco Dinah Shore	Mar 31	Amy Alcott	273/–15	90,000
Ping/Welch's Championship	Apr 7	Chris Johnson	273/–15	52,500
Sara Lee Classic	May 5	Nancy Lopez	206/–10	63,750
Crestar-Farm Fresh Classic	May 12	Hollis Stacy	282/–6	60,000
Centel Classic	May 19	Pat Bradley	278/–10	165,000
LPGA Corning Classic	May 26	Betsy King	273/–15	60,000
Rochester International	June 2	Rosie Jones	276/–12	60,000
Atlantic City Classic	June 9	Jane Geddes	208/–5	45,000
Lady Keystone Open	June 16	Colleen Walker	207/–9	60,000
McDonald's Championship	June 23	Beth Daniel	273/–11	112,500
Mazda LPGA Championship	June 30	Meg Mallon	274/–10	150,000
Jamie Farr Toledo Classic	July 7	Alice Miller†	205/–8	52,500
U.S. Women's Open	July 14	Meg Mallon	283/–1	110,000
JAL Big Apple Classic	July 21	Betsy King	279/–5	75,000
LPGA Bay State Classic	July 28	Juli Inkster	275/–13	60,000
Phar-Mor in Youngstown	Aug 4	Deb Richard‡	207/–9	75,000
Stratton Mountain Classic	Aug 11	Melissa McNamara	278/–10	67,500
Northgate Classic	Aug 18	Cindy Rarick†	211/–5	60,000
LPGA Chicago Shoot-Out	Aug 25	Martha Nause	275/–13	63,750
Rail Charity Golf Classic	Sep 3	Pat Bradley	197/–19	60,000
Ping-Cellular One Championship	Sep 8	Michelle Estill	208/–8	60,000
Du Maurier Ltd Classic	Sep 15	Nancy Scranton	279/–9	105,000
Safeco Classic	Sep 22	Pat Bradley*	280/–8	60,000
MBS LPGA Classic	Sep 29	Pat Bradley	277/–11	52,500

*Won on 2nd playoff hole.
†Won on 3rd playoff hole.
‡Won on 1st playoff hole.
#Rain shortened to 2 rounds.

Senior Men's Tour Results

Late 1990 Senior Tour Events

Tournament	Final Round	Winner	Score/ Under Par	Earnings ($)
Vantage Championship	Oct 7	Charles Coody	202/–14	202,500
Gatlin Brothers SW Classic	Oct 14	Bruce Crampton	204/–12	45,000
Transamerica Senior Championship	Oct 21	Lee Trevino	205/–11	75,000
Gold Rush at Rancho Murieta	Oct 28	George Archer	204/–12	60,000
Security Pacific Classic	Nov 4	Mike Hill	201/–12	75,000
GTE Kaanapali Classic	Dec 9	Bob Charles	206/–4	67,500
New York Life Champions	Dec 16	Mike Hill#	201/–15	150,000

1991 Senior Tour Events

Tournament	Final Round	Winner	Score/ Under Par	Earnings ($)
Tournament of Champions	Jan 6	Bruce Crampton	279/–9	80,000
Royal Caribbean Classic	Feb 3	Gary Player	200/–13	67,500
GTE Suncoast Classic	Feb 10	Bob Charles	210/–6	67,500
Aetna Challenge	Feb 17	Lee Trevino	205/–11	67,500
GTE West Classic	Mar 3	Chi Chi Rodriguez*	132/–8	67,500
Vantage at the Dominion	Mar 17	Lee Trevino*	137/–7	52,500
Vintage ARCO Invitational	Mar 24	Chi Chi Rodriguez	206/–10	75,000
Fuji Electric Grandslam	Mar 31	Miller Barber	202/–14	77,000
The Tradition at Desert Mountain	Apr 7	Jack Nicklaus	277/–11	120,000
PGA Seniors Championship	Apr 21	Jack Nicklaus	271/–17	85,000
Doug Sanders Kingwood Celebrity Classic	Apr 28	Mike Hill	203/–13	45,000
Las Vegas Senior Classic	May 5	Chi Chi Rodriguez	204/–12	67,500
Murata Reunion Pro-Am	May 12	Chi Chi Rodriguez†	208/–8	60,000
Liberty Mutual Legends of Golf	May 19	Lee Trevino, Mike Hill	252/–36	70,000 each
Bell Atlantic Classic	May 26	Jim Ferree	208/–8	82,500
NYNEX Commemorative	June 2	Charles Coody	193/–17	60,000
Senior Players Championship	June 9	Jim Albus	279/–9	150,000
MONY Syracuse Senior Classic	June 16	Rocky Thompson	199/–17	60,000
PaineWebber Invitational	June 23	Orville Moody	207/–9	67,500
Southwestern Bell Classic	June 30	Jim Colbert	201/–9	67,500
Kroger Senior Classic	July 7	Al Geiberger	203/–10	90,000
Newport Cup	July 14	Larry Ziegler	199/–17	48,750
Ameritech Senior Open	July 21	Mike Hill	200/–16	75,000
U.S. Senior Open	July 28	Jack Nicklaus‡	282/+2	110,000
Northville Long Island Classic	Aug 4	George Archer	204/–12	67,500
Showdown Classic	Aug 11	Dale Douglass	209/–7	52,500
GTE Northwest Classic	Aug 18	Mike Hill	198/–18	60,000
Sunwest Bank/Charley Pride Classic	Aug 25	Lee Trevino	200/–16	52,500
GTE North Classic	Sep 1	George Archer	199/–17	67,500
First of America Classic	Sep 8	Harold Henning#	202/–11	52,500
Digital Seniors Classic	Sep 15	Rocky Thompson	205/–11	60,000
Nationwide Championship	Sep 22	Mike Hill	212/–4	105,000
Bank One Classic	Sep 29	Dewitt Weaver**	207/–9	45,000

*Rain shortened to 2 rounds.

†Won on 4th playoff hole.

‡Won in 18-hole playoff, 65-69.

#Won on 1st playoff hole.

**Won on 2nd playoff hole.

Amateur Results

Tournament	Final Round	Winner	Score	Runner-Up
Junior Amateur	July 27	Tiger Woods	19 holes	Brad Zwetschke
Girls' Junior	Aug 3	Emilee Klein	3 & 2	Kimberly Marshall
Women's Amateur	Aug 10	Amy Fruhwirth	5 & 4	Heidi Voorhees
Men's Amateur	Aug 25	Mitch Voges	7 & 6	Manny Zerman
Senior Amateur	Sep 21	Bill Bosshard	5 & 4	Morris Beecroft
Women's Mid-Amateur	Sep 26	Sarah LeBrun Ingram	6 & 5	Martha Lang

International Results

Tournament	Final Round	Winner	Score
Walker Cup Matches	Sep 6	United States def. Britain/Ireland	14-10
Ryder Cup Matches	Sep 29	United States def. Europe	14½-13½

PGA Tour Final 1991 Money Leaders

Name	Events	Best Finish	Scoring Average	Money ($)
Corey Pavin	25	1 (2)	69.63	979,430
Craig Stadler	21	1	70.06	827,628
Fred Couples	21	1 (2)	69.59	791,749
Tom Purtzer	25	1 (2)	70.36	750,568
Andrew Magee	28	1 (2)	70.55	750,082
Steve Pate	26	1	70.04	727,997
Nick Price	23	1 (2)	70.18	714,389
Davis Love III	28	1	70.38	686,361
Paul Azinger	21	1	70.17	685,603
Russ Cochran	30	1	70.44	684,851

LPGA Tour Final 1990 Money Leaders

Name	Events	Best Finish	Scoring Average	Money ($)
Beth Daniel	23	1 (7)	70.54	863,578
Patty Sheehan	24	1 (5)	70.62	732,618
Betsy King	28	1 (3)	71.32	543,844
Cathy Gerring	29	1 (3)	71.89	487,326
Pat Bradley	28	1 (3)	71.13	480,018
Rosie Jones	24	2 (2)	71.48	353,832
Ayako Okamoto	20	1	71.57	302,885
Nancy Lopez	18	1	71.33	301,262
Danielle Ammaccapane	27	2 (2)	71.92	300,231
Cindy Rarick	29	1	72.18	259,163

Senior Tour Final 1990 Money Leaders

Name	Events	Best Finish	Scoring Average	Money ($)
Lee Trevino	29	1 (7)	68.89	1,190,518
Mike Hill	33	1 (5)	70.06	895,678
Charles Coody	33	1	70.77	762,901
George Archer	33	1 (4)	69.99	749,691
Chi Chi Rodriguez	32	1 (3)	70.11	729,788
Jim Dent	32	1 (4)	70.34	693,214
Bob Charles	28	1 (2)	70.47	548,318
Dale Douglass	32	1	70.91	568,198
Gary Player	23	1	69.96	507,268
Rives McBee	39	1 (2)	71.41	480,329

The Newest "Next Jack Nicklaus"

When 20-year-old Phil Mickelson, an Arizona State junior, won the Northern Telecom Open last January, he became the youngest amateur—and fourth amateur ever—to win a PGA Tour event. In 1954, 23-year-old Gene Littler won the San Diego Open; in 1956, 22-year-old Doug Sanders claimed the Canadian Open; and in 1985, 21-year-old Scott Verplank triumphed in the Western Open. In 1990 Mickelson became the only player other than Jack Nicklaus to win both the NCAA championship and the U.S. Amateur in the same year.

Men's Golf

THE MAJOR TOURNAMENTS
The Masters

Year	Winner	Score	Runner-Up
1934	Horton Smith	284	Craig Wood
1935	*Gene Sarazen (144) (only 36-hole playoff)	282	Craig Wood (149)
1936	Horton Smith	285	Harry Cooper
1937	Byron Nelson	283	Ralph Guldahl
1938	Henry Picard	285	Ralph Guldahl, Harry Cooper
1939	Ralph Guldahl	279	Sam Snead
1940	Jimmy Demaret	280	Lloyd Mangrum
1941	Craig Wood	280	Byron Nelson
1942	*Byron Nelson (69)	280	Ben Hogan (70)
1943-45	No tournament		
1946	Herman Keiser	282	Ben Hogan
1947	Jimmy Demaret	281	Byron Nelson, Frank Stranahan
1948	Claude Harmon	279	Cary Middlecoff
1949	Sam Snead	282	Johnny Bulla, Lloyd Mangrum
1950	Jimmy Demaret	283	Jim Ferrier
1951	Ben Hogan	280	Skee Riegel
1952	Sam Snead	286	Jack Burke, Jr
1953	Ben Hogan	274	Ed Oliver, Jr
1954	*Sam Snead (70)	289	Ben Hogan (71)
1955	Cary Middlecoff	279	Ben Hogan
1956	Jack Burke, Jr	289	Ken Venturi
1957	Doug Ford	282	Sam Snead
1958	Arnold Palmer	284	Doug Ford, Fred Hawkins
1959	Art Wall, Jr	284	Cary Middlecoff
1960	Arnold Palmer	282	Ken Venturi
1961	Gary Player	280	Charles R. Coe, Arnold Palmer
1962	*Arnold Palmer (68)	280	Gary Player (71), Dow Finsterwald (77)
1963	Jack Nicklaus	286	Tony Lema
1964	Arnold Palmer	276	Dave Marr, Jack Nicklaus
1965	Jack Nicklaus	271	Arnold Palmer, Gary Player
1966	*Jack Nicklaus (70)	288	Tommy Jacobs (72), Gay Brewer, Jr (78)
1967	Gay Brewer, Jr	280	Bobby Nichols
1968	Bob Goalby	277	Roberto DeVicenzo
1969	George Archer	281	Billy Casper, George Knudson, Tom Weiskopf
1970	*Billy Casper (69)	279	Gene Littler (74)
1971	Charles Coody	279	Johnny Miller, Jack Nicklaus
1972	Jack Nicklaus	286	Bruce Crampton, Bobby Mitchell, Tom Weiskopf
1973	Tommy Aaron	283	J. C. Snead
1974	Gary Player	278	Tom Weiskopf, Dave Stockton
1975	Jack Nicklaus	276	Johnny Miller, Tom Weiskopf
1976	Ray Floyd	271	Ben Crenshaw
1977	Tom Watson	276	Jack Nicklaus
1978	Gary Player	277	Hubert Green, Rod Funseth, Tom Watson
1979†	*Fuzzy Zoeller (4-3)	280	Ed Sneed (4-4), Tom Watson (4-4)
1980	Seve Ballesteros	275	Gibby Gilbert, Jack Newton
1981	Tom Watson	280	Johnny Miller, Jack Nicklaus
1982	*Craig Stadler (4)	284	Dan Pohl (5)
1983	Seve Ballesteros	280	Ben Crenshaw, Tom Kite
1984	Ben Crenshaw	277	Tom Watson
1985	Bernhard Langer	282	Curtis Strange, Seve Ballesteros, Ray Floyd
1986	Jack Nicklaus	279	Greg Norman, Tom Kite
1987	*Larry Mize (4-3)	285	Seve Ballesteros (5), Greg Norman (4-4)
1988	Sandy Lyle	281	Mark Calcavecchia
1989	*Nick Faldo (5-3)	283	Scott Hoch (5-4)
1990	*Nick Faldo (4-4)	278	Ray Floyd (4-x)
1991	Ian Woosnam	277	Jose Maria Olazabal

*Winner in playoff. Playoff scores are in parentheses. †Playoff cut from 18 holes to sudden death.

Note: Played at Augusta National Golf Club, Augusta, GA.

United States Open Championship

Year	Winner	Score	Runner-Up	Site
1895	Horace Rawlins	†173	Willie Dunn	Newport GC, Newport, RI
1896	James Foulis	†152	Horace Rawlins	Shinnecock Hills GC, Southampton, NY
1897	Joe Lloyd	†162	Willie Anderson	Chicago GC, Wheaton, IL
1898	Fred Herd	328	Alex Smith	Myopia Hunt Club, Hamilton, MA
1899	Willie Smith	315	George Low	Baltimore CC, Baltimore
			Val Fitzjohn	
			W. H. Way	
1900	Harry Vardon	313	John H. Taylor	Chicago GC, Wheaton, IL
1901	*Willie Anderson (85)	331	Alex Smith (86)	Myopia Hunt Club, Hamilton, MA
1902	Laurie Auchterlonie	307	Stewart Gardner	Garden City GC, Garden City, NY
1903	*Willie Anderson (82)	307	David Brown (84)	Baltusrol GC, Springfield, NJ
1904	Willie Anderson	303	Gil Nicholls	Glen View Club, Golf, IL
1905	Willie Anderson	314	Alex Smith	Myopia Hunt Club, Hamilton, MA
1906	Alex Smith	295	Willie Smith	Onwentsia Club, Lake Forest, IL
1907	Alex Ross	302	Gil Nicholls	Philadelphia Cricket Club, Chestnut Hill, PA
1908	*Fred McLeod (77)	322	Willie Smith (83)	Myopia Hunt Club, Hamilton, MA
1909	George Sargent	290	Tom McNamara	Englewood GC, Englewood, NJ
1910	*Alex Smith (71)	298	John McDermott (75)	Philadelphia Cricket Club, Chestnut Hill, PA
			Macdonald Smith (77)	
1911	*John McDermott (80)	307	Mike Brady (82)	Chicago GC, Wheaton, IL
			George Simpson (85)	
1912	John McDermott	294	Tom McNamara	CC of Buffalo, Buffalo
1913	*Francis Ouimet (72)	304	Harry Vardon (77)	The Country Club, Brookline, MA
			Edward Ray (78)	
1914	Walter Hagen	290	Chick Evans	Midlothian CC, Blue Island, IL
1915	Jerry Travers	297	Tom McNamara	Baltusrol GC, Springfield, NJ
1916	Chick Evans	286	Jock Hutchison	Minikahda Club, Minneapolis
1917-18	No tournament			
1919	*Walter Hagen (77)	301	Mike Brady (78)	Brae Burn CC, West Newton, MA
1920	Edward Ray	295	Harry Vardon	Inverness CC, Toledo
			Jack Burke	
			Leo Diegel	
			Jock Hutchison	
1921	Jim Barnes	289	Walter Hagen	Columbia CC, Chevy Chase, MD
			Fred McLeod	
1922	Gene Sarazen	288	John L. Black	Skokie CC, Glencoe, IL
			Bobby Jones	
1923	*Bobby Jones (76)	296	Bobby Cruickshank (78)	Inwood CC, Inwood, NY
1924	Cyril Walker	297	Bobby Jones	Oakland Hills CC, Birmingham, MI
1925	*W. MacFarlane (75-72)	291	Bobby Jones (75-73)	Worcester CC, Worcester, MA
1926	Bobby Jones	293	Joe Turnesa	Scioto CC, Columbus, OH
1927	*Tommy Armour (76)	301	Harry Cooper (79)	Oakmont CC, Oakmont, PA
1928	*Johnny Farrell (143)	294	Bobby Jones (144)	Olympia Fields CC, Matteson, IL
1929	*Bobby Jones (141)	294	Al Espinosa (164)	Winged Foot GC, Mamaroneck, NY
1930	Bobby Jones	287	Macdonald Smith	Interlachen CC, Hopkins, MN
1931	*Billy Burke (149-148)	292	George Von Elm (149-149)	Inverness Club, Toledo
1932	Gene Sarazen	286	Phil Perkins	Fresh Meadows CC, Flushing, NY
			Bobby Cruickshank	
1933	Johnny Goodman	287	Ralph Guldahl	North Shore CC, Glenview, IL
1934	Olin Dutra	293	Gene Sarazen	Merion Cricket Club, Ardmore, PA
1935	Sam Parks, Jr	299	Jimmy Thompson	Oakmont CC, Oakmont, PA
1936	Tony Manero	282	Harry Cooper	Baltusrol GC (Upper Course), Springfield, NJ
1937	Ralph Guldahl	281	Sam Snead	Oakland Hills CC, Birmingham, MI
1938	Ralph Guldahl	284	Dick Metz	Cherry Hills CC, Denver, CO
1939	*Byron Nelson (68-70)	284	Craig Wood (68-73)	Philadelphia CC, Philadelphia
			Denny Shute (76)	
1940	*Lawson Little (70)	287	Gene Sarazen (73)	Canterbury GC, Cleveland
1941	Craig Wood	284	Denny Shute	Colonial Club, Fort Worth
1942-45	No tournament			
1946	*Lloyd Mangrum (72-72)	284	Vic Ghezzi (72-73)	Canterbury GC, Cleveland
			Byron Nelson (72-73)	
1947	*Lew Worsham (69)	282	Sam Snead (70)	St Louis CC, Clayton, MO
1948	Ben Hogan	276	Jimmy Demaret	Riviera CC, Los Angeles

United States Open Championship (*Cont.*)

Year	Winner	Score	Runner-Up	Site
1949	Cary Middlecoff	286	Sam Snead Clayton Heafner	Medinah CC, Medinah, IL
1950	*Ben Hogan (69)	287	Lloyd Mangrum (73) George Fazio (75)	Merion GC, Ardmore, PA
1951	Ben Hogan	287	Clayton Heafner	Oakland Hills CC, Birmingham, MI
1952	Julius Boros	281	Ed Oliver	Northwood CC, Dallas
1953	Ben Hogan	283	Sam Snead	Oakmont CC, Oakmont, PA
1954	Ed Furgol	284	Gene Littler	Baltusrol GC (Lower Course), Springfield, NJ
1955	*Jack Fleck (69)	287	Ben Hogan (72)	Olympic Club (Lake Course), San Francisco
1956	Cary Middlecoff	281	Ben Hogan Julius Boros	Oak Hill CC, Rochester, NY
1957	*Dick Mayer (72)	282	Cary Middlecoff (79)	Inverness Club, Toledo
1958	Tommy Bolt	283	Gary Player	Southern Hills CC, Tulsa
1959	Billy Casper	282	Bob Rosburg	Winged Foot GC, Mamaroneck, NY
1960	Arnold Palmer	280	Jack Nicklaus	Cherry Hills CC, Denver
1961	Gene Littler	281	Bob Goalby Doug Sanders	Oakland Hills CC, Birmingham, MI
1962	*Jack Nicklaus (71)	283	Arnold Palmer (74)	Oakmont CC, Oakmont, PA
1963	*Julius Boros (70)	293	Jacky Cupit (73) Arnold Palmer (76)	The Country Club, Brookline, MA
1964	Ken Venturi	278	Tommy Jacobs	Congressional CC, Washington, DC
1965	*Gary Player (71)	282	Kel Nagle (74)	Bellerive CC, St Louis
1966	*Billy Casper (69)	278	Arnold Palmer (73)	Olympic Club (Lake Course), San Francisco
1967	Jack Nicklaus	275	Arnold Palmer	Baltusrol GC (Lower Course), Springfield, NJ
1968	Lee Trevino	275	Jack Nicklaus	Oak Hill CC, Rochester, NY
1969	Orville Moody	281	Deane Beman Al Geiberger Bob Rosburg	Champions GC (Cypress Creek Course), Houston
1970	Tony Jacklin	281	Dave Hill	Hazeltine GC, Chaska, MN
1971	*Lee Trevino (68)	280	Jack Nicklaus (71)	Merion GC (East Course), Ardmore, PA
1972	Jack Nicklaus	290	Bruce Crampton	Pebble Beach GL, Pebble Beach, CA
1973	Johnny Miller	279	John Schlee	Oakmont CC, Oakmont, PA
1974	Hale Irwin	287	Forrest Fezler	Winged Foot GC, Mamaroneck, NY
1975	*Lou Graham (71)	287	John Mahaffey (73)	Medinah CC, Medinah, IL
1976	Jerry Pate	277	Tom Weiskopf Al Geiberger	Atlanta Athletic Club, Duluth, GA
1977	Hubert Green	278	Lou Graham	Southern Hills CC, Tulsa
1978	Andy North	285	Dave Stockton J. C. Snead	Cherry Hills CC, Denver
1979	Hale Irwin	284	Gary Player Jerry Pate	Inverness Club, Toledo
1980	Jack Nicklaus	272	Isao Aoki	Baltusrol GC (Lower Course), Springfield, NJ
1981	David Graham	273	George Burns Bill Rogers	Merion GC, Ardmore, PA
1982	Tom Watson	282	Jack Nicklaus	Pebble Beach GL, Pebble Beach, CA
1983	Larry Nelson	280	Tom Watson	Oakmont CC, Oakmont, PA
1984	*Fuzzy Zoeller (67)	276	Greg Norman (75)	Winged Foot GC, Mamaroneck, NY
1985	Andy North	279	Dave Barr T. C. Chen Denis Watson	Oakland Hills CC, Birmingham, MI
1986	Ray Floyd	279	Lanny Wadkins Chip Beck	Shinnecock Hills GC, Southampton, NY
1987	Scott Simpson	277	Tom Watson	Olympic Club (Lake Course), San Francisco
1988	*Curtis Strange (71)	278	Nick Faldo (75)	The Country Club, Brookline, MA
1989	Curtis Strange	278	Chip Beck Mark McCumber Ian Woosnam	Oak Hill CC, Rochester, NY
1990	*Hale Irwin (74) (3)	280	Mike Donald (74) (4)	Medinah CC, Medinah, IL
1991	Payne Stewart (75)	282	Scott Simpson (77)	Hazeltine GC, Chaska, MN

*Winner in playoff. Playoff scores are in parentheses. The 1990 playoff went to one hole of sudden death after an 18-hole playoff.

†Before 1898, 36 holes. From 1898 on, 72 holes.

British Open

Year	Winner	Score	Runner-Up	Site
1860†	Willie Park	174	Tom Morris, Sr	Prestwick, Scotland
1861‡	Tom Morris, Sr	163	Willie Park	Prestwick, Scotland
1862	Tom Morris, Sr	163	Willie Park	Prestwick, Scotland
1863	Willie Park	168	Tom Morris, Sr	Prestwick, Scotland
1864	Tom Morris, Sr	160	Andrew Strath	Prestwick, Scotland
1865	Andrew Strath	162	Willie Park	Prestwick, Scotland
1866	Willie Park	169	David Park	Prestwick, Scotland
1867	Tom Morris, Sr	170	Willie Park	Prestwick, Scotland
1868	Tom Morris, Jr	154	Tom Morris, Sr	Prestwick, Scotland
1869	Tom Morris, Jr	157	Tom Morris, Sr	Prestwick, Scotland
1870	Tom Morris, Jr	149	David Strath Bob Kirk	Prestwick, Scotland
1871	No tournament			
1872	Tom Morris, Jr	166	David Strath	Prestwick, Scotland
1873	Tom Kidd	179	Jamie Anderson	St Andrews, Scotland
1874	Mungo Park	159	No record	Musselburgh, Scotland
1875	Willie Park	166	Bob Martin	Prestwick, Scotland
1876	#Bob Martin	176	David Strath	St Andrews, Scotland
1877	Jamie Anderson	160	Bob Pringle	Musselburgh, Scotland
1878	Jamie Anderson	157	Robert Kirk	Prestwick, Scotland
1879	Jamie Anderson	169	Andrew Kirkaldy James Allan	St Andrews, Scotland
1880	Robert Ferguson	162	No record	Musselburgh, Scotland
1881	Robert Ferguson	170	Jamie Anderson	Prestwick, Scotland
1882	Robert Ferguson	171	Willie Fernie	St Andrews, Scotland
1883	*Willie Fernie	159	Robert Ferguson	Musselburgh, Scotland
1884	Jack Simpson	160	Douglas Rolland Willie Fernie	Prestwick, Scotland
1885	Bob Martin	171	Archie Simpson	St Andrews, Scotland
1886	David Brown	157	Willie Campbell	Musselburgh, Scotland
1887	Willie Park, Jr	161	Bob Martin	Prestwick, Scotland
1888	Jack Burns	171	Bernard Sayers David Anderson	St Andrews, Scotland
1889	*Willie Park, Jr (158)	155	Andrew Kirkaldy (163)	Musselburgh, Scotland
1890	John Ball	164	Willie Fernie	Prestwick, Scotland
1891	Hugh Kirkaldy	166	Andrew Kirkaldy Willie Fernie	St Andrews, Scotland
1892	Harold Hilton	**305	John Ball Hugh Kirkaldy	Muirfield, Scotland
1893	William Auchterlonie	322	John E. Laidlay	Prestwick, Scotland
1894	John H. Taylor	326	Douglas Rolland	Royal St George's, England
1895	John H. Taylor	322	Alexander Herd	St Andrews, Scotland
1896	*Harry Vardon (157)	316	John H. Taylor (161)	Muirfield, Scotland
1897	Harold Hilton	314	James Braid	Hoylake, England
1898	Harry Vardon	307	Willie Park, Jr	Prestwick, Scotland
1899	Harry Vardon	310	Jack White	Royal St George's, England
1900	John H. Taylor	309	Harry Vardon	St Andrews, Scotland
1901	James Braid	309	Harry Vardon	Muirfield, Scotland
1902	Alexander Herd	307	Harry Vardon	Hoylake, England
1903	Harry Vardon	300	Tom Vardon	Prestwick, Scotland
1904	Jack White	296	John H. Taylor	Royal St George's, England
1905	James Braid	318	John H. Taylor Rolland Jones	St Andrews, Scotland
1906	James Braid	300	John H. Taylor	Muirfield, Scotland
1907	Arnaud Massy	312	John H. Taylor	Hoylake, England
1908	James Braid	291	Tom Ball	Prestwick, Scotland
1909	John H. Taylor	295	James Braid Tom Ball	Deal, England
1910	James Braid	299	Alexander Herd	St Andrews, Scotland
1911	Harry Vardon	303	Arnaud Massy	Royal St George's, England
1912	Ted Ray	295	Harry Vardon	Muirfield, Scotland
1913	John H. Taylor	304	Ted Ray	Hoylake, England
1914	Harry Vardon	306	John H. Taylor	Prestwick, Scotland
1915-19	No tournament			
1920	George Duncan	303	Alexander Herd	Deal, England

British Open (*Cont.*)

Year	Winner	Score	Runner-Up	Site
1921	*Jock Hutchison (150)	296	Roger Wethered (159)	St Andrews, Scotland
1922	Walter Hagen	300	George Duncan Jim Barnes	Royal St George's, England
1923	Arthur G. Havers	295	Walter Hagen	Troon, Scotland
1924	Walter Hagen	301	Ernest Whitcombe	Hoylake, England
1925	Jim Barnes	300	Archie Compston Ted Ray	Prestwick, Scotland
1926	Bobby Jones	291	Al Watrous	Royal Lytham and St Annes GC, St Annes-on-the-Sea, England
1927	Bobby Jones	285	Aubrey Boomer	St Andrews, Scotland
1928	Walter Hagen	292	Gene Sarazen	Royal St George's, England
1929	Walter Hagen	292	Johnny Farrell	Muirfield, Scotland
1930	Bobby Jones	291	Macdonald Smith Leo Diegel	Hoylake, England
1931	Tommy Armour	296	Jose Jurado	Carnoustie, Scotland
1932	Gene Sarazen	283	Macdonald Smith	Prince's, England
1933	*Denny Shute (149)	292	Craig Wood (154)	St Andrews, Scotland
1934	Henry Cotton	283	Sidney F. Brews	Royal St George's, England
1935	Alfred Perry	283	Alfred Padgham	Muirfield, Scotland
1936	Alfred Padgham	287	James Adams	Hoylake, England
1937	Henry Cotton	290	Reginald A. Whitcombe	Carnoustie, Scotland
1938	Reginald A. Whitcombe	295	James Adams	Royal St George's, England
1939	Richard Burton	290	Johnny Bulla	St Andrews, Scotland
1940-45	No tournament			
1946	Sam Snead	290	Bobby Locke Johnny Bulla	St Andrews, Scotland
1947	Fred Daly	293	Reginald W. Horne Frank Stranahan	Hoylake, England
1948	Henry Cotton	294	Fred Daly	Muirfield, Scotland
1949	*Bobby Locke (135)	283	Harry Bradshaw (147)	Royal St George's, England
1950	Bobby Locke	279	Roberto DeVicenzo	Troon, Scotland
1951	Max Faulkner	285	Tony Cerda	Portrush, Ireland
1952	Bobby Locke	287	Peter Thomson	Royal Lytham, England
1953	Ben Hogan	282	Frank Stranahan Dai Rees Peter Thomson Tony Cerda	Carnoustie, Scotland
1954	Peter Thomson	283	Sidney S. Scott Dai Rees Bobby Locke	Royal Birkdale, England
1955	Peter Thomson	281	John Fallon	St Andrews, Scotland
1956	Peter Thomson	286	Flory Van Donck	Hoylake, England
1957	Bobby Locke	279	Peter Thomson	St Andrews, Scotland
1958	*Peter Thomson (139)	278	Dave Thomas (143)	Royal Lytham, England
1959	Gary Player	284	Fred Bullock Flory Van Donck	Muirfield, Scotland
1960	Kel Nagle	278	Arnold Palmer	St Andrews, Scotland
1961	Arnold Palmer	284	Dai Rees	Royal Birkdale, England
1962	Arnold Palmer	276	Kel Nagle	Troon, Scotland
1963	*Bob Charles (140)	277	Phil Rodgers (148)	Royal Lytham, England
1964	Tony Lema	279	Jack Nicklaus	St Andrews, Scotland
1965	Peter Thomson	285	Brian Huggett Christy O'Connor	Southport, England
1966	Jack Nicklaus	282	Doug Sanders Dave Thomas	Muirfield, Scotland
1967	Robert DeVicenzo	278	Jack Nicklaus	Hoylake, England
1968	Gary Player	289	Jack Nicklaus Bob Charles	Carnoustie, Scotland
1969	Tony Jacklin	280	Bob Charles	Royal Lytham, England
1970	*Jack Nicklaus (72)	283	Doug Sanders (73)	St Andrews, Scotland
1971	Lee Trevino	278	Lu Liang Huan	Royal Birkdale, England
1972	Lee Trevino	278	Jack Nicklaus	Muirfield, Scotland
1973	Tom Weiskopf	276	Johnny Miller	Troon, Scotland
1974	Gary Player	282	Peter Oosterhuis	Royal Lytham, England
1975	*Tom Watson (71)	279	Jack Newton (72)	Carnoustie, Scotland

British Open (*Cont.*)

Year	Winner	Score	Runner-Up	Site
1976	Johnny Miller	279	Jack Nicklaus	Royal Birkdale, England
			Seve Ballesteros	
1977	Tom Watson	268	Jack Nicklaus	Turnberry, Scotland
1978	Jack Nicklaus	281	Ben Crenshaw	St Andrews, Scotland
			Tom Kite	
			Ray Floyd	
			Simon Owen	
1979	Seve Ballesteros	283	Ben Crenshaw	Royal Lytham, England
			Jack Nicklaus	
1980	Tom Watson	271	Lee Trevino	Muirfield, Scotland
1981	Bill Rogers	276	Bernhard Langer	Royal St George's, England
1982	Tom Watson	284	Nick Price	Royal Troon, Scotland
			Peter Oosterhuis	
1983	Tom Watson	275	Andy Bean	Royal Birkdale, England
1984	Seve Ballesteros	276	Tom Watson	St Andrews, Scotland
			Bernhard Langer	
1985	Sandy Lyle	282	Payne Stewart	Royal St George's, England
1986	Greg Norman	280	Gordon Brand	Turnberry, Scotland
1987	Nick Faldo	279	Paul Azinger	Muirfield, Scotland
			Rodger Davis	
1988	Seve Ballesteros	273	Nick Price	Royal Lytham, England
1989††	*Mark Calcavecchia (4-3-3-3)	275	Wayne Grady (4-4-4-4)	Royal Troon, Scotland
			Greg Norman (3-3-4-x)	
1990	Nick Faldo	270	Payne Stewart	St Andrews, Scotland
			Mark McNulty	
1991	Ian Baker-Finch	272	Mike Harwood	Royal Birkdale, England

*Winner in playoff. Playoff scores are in parentheses.

†The first event was open only to professional golfers.

‡The second annual open was open to amateurs and pros.

#Tied, but refused playoff.

**Championship extended from 36 to 72 holes.

††Playoff cut from 18 holes to 4 holes.

PGA Championship

Year	Winner	Score	Runner-Up	Site
1916	Jim Barnes	1 up	Jock Hutchison	Siwanoy CC, Bronxville, NY
1917-18	No tournament			
1919	Jim Barnes	6 & 5	Fred McLeod	Engineers CC, Roslyn, NY
1920	Jock Hutchison	1 up	J. Douglas Edgar	Flossmoor CC, Flossmoor, IL
1921	Walter Hagen	3 & 2	Jim Barnes	Inwood CC, Far Rockaway, NY
1922	Gene Sarazen	4 & 3	Emmet French	Oakmont CC, Oakmont, PA
1923	Gene Sarazen	1 up 38 holes	Walter Hagen	Pelham CC, Pelham, NY
1924	Walter Hagen	2 up	Jim Barnes	French Lick CC, French Lick, IN
1925	Walter Hagen	6 & 5	William Mehlhorn	Olympia Fields CC, Olympia Fields, IL
1926	Walter Hagen	5 & 3	Leo Diegel	Salisbury GC, Westbury, NY
1927	Walter Hagen	1 up	Joe Turnesa	Cedar Crest CC, Dallas
1928	Leo Diegel	6 & 5	Al Espinosa	Five Farms CC, Baltimore
1929	Leo Diegel	6 & 4	Johnny Farrell	Hillcrest CC, Los Angeles
1930	Tommy Armour	1 up	Gene Sarazen	Fresh Meadow CC, Flushing, NY
1931	Tom Creavy	2 & 1	Denny Shute	Wannamoisett CC, Rumford, RI
1932	Olin Dutra	4 & 3	Frank Walsh	Keller GC, St Paul
1933	Gene Sarazen	5 & 4	Willie Goggin	Blue Mound CC, Milwaukee
1934	Paul Runyan	1 up 38 holes	Craig Wood	Park CC, Williamsville, NY
1935	Johnny Revolta	5 & 4	Tommy Armour	Twin Hills CC, Oklahoma City
1936	Denny Shute	3 & 2	Jimmy Thomson	Pinehurst CC, Pinehurst, NC
1937	Denny Shute	1 up 37 holes	Harold McSpaden	Pittsburgh FC, Aspinwall, PA
1938	Paul Runyan	8 & 7	Sam Snead	Shawnee CC, Shawnee-on-Delaware, PA
1939	Henry Picard	1 up 37 holes	Byron Nelson	Pomonok CC, Flushing, NY
1940	Byron Nelson	1 up	Sam Snead	Hershey CC, Hershey, PA

PGA Championship (*Cont.*)

Year	Winner	Score	Runner-Up	Site
1941	Vic Ghezzi	1 up 38 holes	Byron Nelson	Cherry Hills CC, Denver
1942	Sam Snead	2 & 1	Jim Turnesa	Seaview CC, Atlantic City
1943	No tournament			
1944	Bob Hamilton	1 up	Byron Nelson	Manito G & CC, Spokane, WA
1945	Byron Nelson	4 & 3	Sam Byrd	Morraine CC, Dayton
1946	Ben Hogan	6 & 4	Ed Oliver	Portland GC, Portland, OR
1947	Jim Ferrier	2 & 1	Chick Harbert	Plum Hollow CC, Detroit
1948	Ben Hogan	7 & 6	Mike Turnesa	Norwood Hills CC, St Louis
1949	Sam Snead	3 & 2	Johnny Palmer	Hermitage CC, Richmond
1950	Chandler Harper	4 & 3	Henry Williams, Jr	Scioto CC, Columbus, OH
1951	Sam Snead	7 & 6	Walter Burkemo	Oakmont CC, Oakmont, PA
1952	Jim Turnesa	1 up	Chick Harbert	Big Spring CC, Louisville
1953	Walter Burkemo	2 & 1	Felice Torza	Birmingham CC, Birmingham, MI
1954	Chick Harbert	4 & 3	Walter Burkemo	Keller GC, St Paul
1955	Doug Ford	4 & 3	Cary Middlecoff	Meadowbrook CC, Detroit
1956	Jack Burke	3 & 2	Ted Kroll	Blue Hill CC, Boston
1957	Lionel Hebert	2 & 1	Dow Finsterwald	Miami Valley CC, Dayton
1958	Dow Finsterwald	276	Billy Casper	Llanerch CC, Havertown, PA
1959	Bob Rosburg	277	Jerry Barber Doug Sanders	Minneapolis GC, St Louis Park, MN
1960	Jay Hebert	281	Jim Ferrier	Firestone CC, Akron
1961	*Jerry Barber (67)	277	Don January (68)	Olympia Fields CC, Olympia Fields, IL
1962	Gary Player	278	Bob Goalby	Aronimink GC, Newton Square, PA
1963	Jack Nicklaus	279	Dave Ragan, Jr	Dallas Athletic Club, Dallas
1964	Bobby Nichols	271	Jack Nicklaus Arnold Palmer	Columbus CC, Columbus, OH
1965	Dave Marr	280	Billy Casper Jack Nicklaus	Laurel Valley CC, Ligonier, PA
1966	Al Geiberger	280	Dudley Wysong	Firestone CC, Akron
1967	*Don January (69)	281	Don Massengale (71)	Columbine CC, Littleton, CO
1968	Julius Boros	281	Bob Charles Arnold Palmer	Pecan Valley CC, San Antonio
1969	Ray Floyd	276	Gary Player	NCR CC, Dayton
1970	Dave Stockton	279	Arnold Palmer Bob Murphy	Southern Hills CC, Tulsa
1971	Jack Nicklaus	281	Billy Casper	PGA Natl GC, Palm Beach Gardens, FL
1972	Gary Player	281	Tommy Aaron Jim Jamieson	Oakland Hills CC, Birmingham, MI
1973	Jack Nicklaus	277	Bruce Crampton	Canterbury GC, Cleveland
1974	Lee Trevino	276	Jack Nicklaus	Tanglewood GC, Winston-Salem, NC
1975	Jack Nicklaus	276	Bruce Crampton	Firestone CC, Akron
1976	Dave Stockton	281	Ray Floyd Don January	Congressional CC, Bethesda, MD
1977†	*Lanny Wadkins (4-4-4)	282	Gene Littler (4-4-5)	Pebble Beach GL, Pebble Beach, CA
1978	*John Mahaffey (4-3)	276	Jerry Pate (4-4) Tom Watson (4-5)	Oakmont CC, Oakmont, PA
1979	*David Graham (4-4-2)	272	Ben Crenshaw (4-4-4)	Oakland Hills CC, Birmingham, MI
1980	Jack Nicklaus	274	Andy Bean	Oak Hill CC, Rochester, NY
1981	Larry Nelson	273	Fuzzy Zoeller	Atlanta Athletic Club, Duluth, GA
1982	Raymond Floyd	272	Lanny Wadkins	Southern Hills CC, Tulsa
1983	Hal Sutton	274	Jack Nicklaus	Riviera CC, Pacific Palisades, CA
1984	Lee Trevino	273	Gary Player Lanny Wadkins	Shoal Creek, Birmingham, AL
1985	Hubert Green	278	Lee Trevino	Cherry Hills CC, Denver
1986	Bob Tway	276	Greg Norman	Inverness CC, Toledo
1987	*Larry Nelson (4)	287	Lanny Wadkins (5)	PGA Natl GC, Palm Beach Gardens, FL
1988	Jeff Sluman	272	Paul Azinger	Oak Tree GC, Edmond, OK
1989	Payne Stewart	276	Mike Reid	Kemper Lakes GC, Hawthorn Woods, IL
1990	Wayne Grady	282	Fred Couples	Shoal Creek, Birmingham, AL
1991	John Daly	276	Bruce Lietzke	Crooked Stick GC, Carmel, IN

*Winner in playoff. Playoff scores are in parentheses.

†Playoff changed from 18 holes to sudden death.

THE PGA TOUR
Season Money Leaders

		Earnings ($)			Earnings ($)
1934	Paul Runyan	6,767.00	1963	Arnold Palmer	128,230.00
1935	Johnny Revolta	9,543.00	1964	Jack Nicklaus	113,284.50
1936	Horton Smith	7,682.00	1965	Jack Nicklaus	140,752.14
1937	Harry Cooper	14,138.69	1966	Billy Casper	121,944.92
1938	Sam Snead	19,534.49	1967	Jack Nicklaus	188,998.08
1939	Henry Picard	10,303.00	1968	Billy Casper	205,168.67
1940	Ben Hogan	10,655.00	1969	Frank Beard	164,707.11
1941	Ben Hogan	18,358.00	1970	Lee Trevino	157,037.63
1942	Ben Hogan	13,143.00	1971	Jack Nicklaus	244,490.50
1943	No statistics compiled		1972	Jack Nicklaus	320,542.26
1944	Byron Nelson (war bonds)	37,967.69	1973	Jack Nicklaus	308,362.10
1945	Byron Nelson (war bonds)	63,335.66	1974	Johnny Miller	353,021.59
1946	Ben Hogan	42,556.16	1975	Jack Nicklaus	298,149.17
1947	Jimmy Demaret	27,936.83	1976	Jack Nicklaus	266,438.57
1948	Ben Hogan	32,112.00	1977	Tom Watson	310,653.16
1949	Sam Snead	31,593.83	1978	Tom Watson	362,428.93
1950	Sam Snead	35,758.83	1979	Tom Watson	462,636.00
1951	Lloyd Mangrum	26,088.83	1980	Tom Watson	530,808.33
1952	Julius Boros	37,032.97	1981	Tom Kite	375,698.84
1953	Lew Worsham	34,002.00	1982	Craig Stadler	446,462.00
1954	Bob Toski	65,819.81	1983	Hal Sutton	426,668.00
1955	Julius Boros	63,121.55	1984	Tom Watson	476,260.00
1956	Ted Kroll	72,835.83	1985	Curtis Strange	542,321.00
1957	Dick Mayer	65,835.00	1986	Greg Norman	653,296.00
1958	Arnold Palmer	42,607.50	1987	Curtis Strange	925,941.00
1959	Art Wall	53,167.60	1988	Curtis Strange	1,147,644.00
1960	Arnold Palmer	75,262.85	1989	Tom Kite	1,395,278.00
1961	Gary Player	64,540.45	1990	Greg Norman	1,165,477.00
1962	Arnold Palmer	81,448.33	1991	Corey Pavin	979,430.00

Note: Total money listed from 1968 through 1974. Official money listed from 1975 on.

Top Single-Season Marks

	Earnings	Year
Tom Kite	1,395,278	1989
Payne Stewart	1,201,301	1989
Greg Norman	1,165,477	1990
Curtis Strange	1,147,644	1988
Wayne Levi	1,024,647	1990
Corey Pavin	979,430	1991
Payne Stewart	976,281	1990
Paul Azinger	951,649	1989
Paul Azinger	944,731	1990
Curtis Strange	925,941	1987

Most Career Wins

	Wins
Sam Snead	81
Jack Nicklaus	70
Ben Hogan	63
Arnold Palmer	60
Byron Nelson	52
Billy Casper	51
Walter Hagen	40
Cary Middlecoff	40
Gene Sarazen	38
Lloyd Mangrum	36
Horton Smith	32
Tom Watson	32
Harry Cooper	31
Jimmy Demaret	31
Leo Diegel	30

Career Money Leaders*

		Earnings ($)			Earnings ($)
1.	Tom Kite	6,258,893	26.	Fuzzy Zoeller	2,842,944
2.	Tom Watson	5,374,232	27.	Tim Simpson	2,828,594
3.	Curtis Strange	5,292,892	28.	Peter Jacobsen	2,669,174
4.	Jack Nicklaus	5,170,465	29.	Mike Reid	2,595,390
5.	Lanny Wadkins	4,614,381	30.	Larry Mize	2,588,532
6.	Payne Stewart	4,582,988	31.	Jay Haas	2,576,308
7.	Ben Crenshaw	4,466,267	32.	Mark McCumber	2,541,795
8.	Greg Norman	4,251,270	33.	Johnny Miller	2,514,248
9.	Hale Irwin	4,066,080	34.	David Frost	2,508,968
10.	Ray Floyd	3,880,665	35.	Hubert Green	2,504,190
11.	Paul Azinger	3,687,384	36.	Scott Simpson	2,479,886
12.	Lee Trevino	3,474,916	37.	Jodie Mudd	2,409,986
13.	Bruce Lietzke	3,442,624	38.	Bob Tway	2,395,333
14.	Chip Beck	3,433,018	39.	Dan Pohl	2,328,363
15.	John Mahaffey	3,403,191	40.	Calvin Peete	2,297,385
16.	Wayne Levi	3,377,498	41.	Corey Pavin	2,293,688
17.	Fred Couples	3,330,978	42.	Joey Sindelar	2,292,585
18.	Mark O'Meara	3,325,207	43.	Tom Weiskopf	2,226,391
19.	Gil Morgan	3,309,995	44.	J. C. Snead	2,219,171
20.	Craig Stadler	3,262,895	45.	Don Pooley	2,181,005
21.	Mark Calcavecchia	3,158,742	46.	Ken Green	2,165,887
22.	Andy Bean	2,972,566	47.	Tom Purtzer	1,917,949
23.	Hal Sutton	2,931,903	48.	Nick Price	1,897,773
24.	Larry Nelson	2,896,075	49.	Arnold Palmer	1,894,960
25.	Scott Hoch	2,860,118	50.	George Archer	1,878,541

*Through 12/31/90.

Year by Year Statistical Leaders*

SCORING AVERAGE

1980	Lee Trevino	69.73
1981	Tom Kite	69.80
1982	Tom Kite	70.21
1983	Raymond Floyd	70.61
1984	Calvin Peete	70.56
1985	Don Pooley	70.36
1986	Scott Hoch	70.08
1987	David Frost	70.09
1988	Greg Norman	69.38
1989	Payne Stewart	69.485†
1990	Greg Norman	69.10

Note: Scoring average per round, with adjustments made at each round for the field's course scoring average.

DRIVING DISTANCE

		Yds
1980	Dan Pohl	274.3
1981	Dan Pohl	280.1
1982	Bill Calfee	275.3
1983	John McComish	277.4
1984	Bill Glasson	276.5
1985	Andy Bean	278.2
1986	Davis Love III	285.7
1987	John McComish	283.9
1988	Steve Thomas	284.6
1989	Ed Humenik	280.9
1990	Tom Purtzer	279.6

Note: Average computed by charting distance of two tee shots on a predetermined par-four or par-five hole (one on front nine, one on back nine).

DRIVING ACCURACY

1980	Mike Reid	.795
1981	Calvin Peete	.819
1982	Calvin Peete	.846
1983	Calvin Peete	.813
1984	Calvin Peete	.775
1985	Calvin Peete	.806
1986	Calvin Peete	.817
1987	Calvin Peete	.830
1988	Calvin Peete	.825
1989	Calvin Peete	.826
1990	Calvin Peete	.837

Note: Percentage of fairways hit on number of par-four and par-five holes played; par-three holes excluded.

*Based on minimum of 50 rounds per year.

†Had to be carried as extra decimal place to determine winner.

GREENS IN REGULATION

1980	Jack Nicklaus	.721
1981	Calvin Peete	.731
1982	Calvin Peete	.724
1983	Calvin Peete	.714
1984	Andy Bean	.721
1985	John Mahaffey	.719
1986	John Mahaffey	.720
1987	Gil Morgan	.733
1988	John Adams	.739
1989	Bruce Lietzke	.726
1990	Doug Tewell	.709

Note: Average of greens reached in regulation out of total holes played; hole is considered hit in regulation if any part of the ball rests on the putting surface in two shots less than the hole's par; a par five hit in two shots is one green in regulation.

PUTTING

1980	Jerry Pate	28.81
1981	Alan Tapie	28.70
1982	Ben Crenshaw	28.65
1983	Morris Hatalsky	27.96
1984	Gary McCord	28.57
1985	Craig Stadler	28.627†
1986	Greg Norman	1.736
1987	Ben Crenshaw	1.743
1988	Don Pooley	1.729
1989	Steve Jones	1.734
1990	Larry Rinker	1.7467†

Note: Average number of putts taken on greens reached in regulation; prior to 1986, based on average number of putts per 18 holes.

ALL-AROUND

1987	Dan Pohl	170
1988	Payne Stewart	170
1989	Paul Azinger	250
1990	Paul Azinger	162

Note: Addition of the places of standing from the other nine statistical categories; the player with the number closest to zero leads.

SAND SAVES

1980	Bob Eastwood	.654
1981	Tom Watson	.601
1982	Isao Aoki	.602
1983	Isao Aoki	.623
1984	Peter Oosterhuis	.647
1985	Tom Purtzer	.608
1986	Paul Azinger	.638
1987	Paul Azinger	.632
1988	Greg Powers	.635
1989	Mike Sullivan	.660
1990	Paul Azinger	.672

Note: Percentage of up-and-down efforts from greenside sand traps only; fairway bunkers excluded.

PAR BREAKERS

1980	Tom Watson	.213
1981	Bruce Lietzke	.225
1982	Tom Kite	.2154†
1983	Tom Watson	.211
1984	Craig Stadler	.220
1985	Craig Stadler	.218
1986	Greg Norman	.248
1987	Mark Calcavecchia	.221
1988	Ken Green	.236
1989	Greg Norman	.224
1990	Greg Norman	.219

Note: Average based on total birdies and eagles scored out of total holes played.

EAGLES

1980	Dave Eichelberger	16
1981	Bruce Lietzke	12
1982	Tom Weiskopf	10
	J. C. Snead	10
	Andy Bean	10
1983	Chip Beck	15
1984	Gary Hallberg	15
1985	Larry Rinker	14
1986	Joey Sindelar	16
1987	Phil Blackmar	20
1988	Ken Green	21
1989	Lon Hinkle	14
	Duffy Waldorf	14
1990	Paul Azinger	14

Note: Total of eagles scored.

BIRDIES

1980	Andy Bean	388
1981	Vance Heafner	388
1982	Andy Bean	392
1983	Hal Sutton	399
1984	Mark O'Meara	419
1985	Joey Sindelar	411
1986	Joey Sindelar	415
1987	Dan Forsman	409
1988	Dan Forsman	465
1989	Ted Schulz	415
1990	Mike Donald	401

Note: Total of birdies scored.

THEY SAID IT

Gary Player, on the putter he has used since 1961: "It's a marriage. If I had to choose between my wife and my putter— well, I'd miss her."

Men's Golf (Cont.)

PGA Player of the Year Award

1948 .... Ben Hogan	1963 .... Julius Boros	1977 .... Tom Watson
1949 .... Sam Snead	1964 .... Ken Venturi	1978 .... Tom Watson
1950 .... Ben Hogan	1965 .... Dave Marr	1979 .... Tom Watson
1951 .... Ben Hogan	1966 .... Billy Casper	1980 .... Tom Watson
1952 .... Julius Boros	1967 .... Jack Nicklaus	1981 .... Bill Rogers
1953 .... Ben Hogan	1968 .... Not awarded	1982 .... Tom Watson
1954 .... Ed Furgol	1969 ...... Orville Moody	1983 .... Hal Sutton
1955 .... Doug Ford	1970 ...... Billy Casper	1984 .... Tom Watson
1956 .... Jack Burke	1971 .... Lee Trevino	1985 .... Lanny Wadkins
1957 .... Dick Mayer	1972 .... Jack Nicklaus	1986 .... Bob Tway
1958 .... Dow Finsterwald	1973 .... Jack Nicklaus	1987 .... Paul Azinger
1959 .... Art Wall	1974 .... Johnny Miller	1988 .... Curtis Strange
1960 .... Arnold Palmer	1975 .... Jack Nicklaus	1989 .... Tom Kite
1961 .... Jerry Barber	1976 .... Jack Nicklaus	1990 .... Nick Faldo
1962 .... Arnold Palmer		

Vardon Trophy: Scoring Average

Year	Winner	Avg	Year	Winner	Avg
1937 .... Harry Cooper		*500	1967 .... Arnold Palmer		70.18
1938 .... Sam Snead		520	1968 .... Billy Casper		69.82
1939 .... Byron Nelson		473	1969 .... Dave Hill		70.34
1940 .... Ben Hogan		423	1970 .... Lee Trevino		70.64
1941 .... Ben Hogan		494	1971 .... Lee Trevino		70.27
1942-46 .... No award			1972 .... Lee Trevino		70.89
1947 .... Jimmy Demaret		69.90	1973 .... Bruce Crampton		70.57
1948 .... Ben Hogan		69.30	1974 .... Lee Trevino		70.53
1949 .... Sam Snead		69.37	1975 .... Bruce Crampton		70.51
1950 .... Sam Snead		69.23	1976 .... Don January		70.56
1951 .... Lloyd Mangrum		70.05	1977 .... Tom Watson		70.32
1952 .... Jack Burke		70.54	1978 .... Tom Watson		70.16
1953 .... Lloyd Mangrum		70.22	1979 .... Tom Watson		70.27
1954 .... E. J. Harrison		70.41	1980 .... Lee Trevino		69.73
1955 .... Sam Snead		69.86	1981 .... Tom Kite		69.80
1956 .... Cary Middlecoff		70.35	1982 .... Tom Kite		70.21
1957 .... Dow Finsterwald		70.30	1983 .... Raymond Floyd		70.61
1958 .... Bob Rosburg		70.11	1984 .... Calvin Peete		70.56
1959 .... Art Wall		70.35	1985 .... Don Pooley		70.36
1960 .... Billy Casper		69.95	1986 .... Scott Hoch		70.08
1961 .... Arnold Palmer		69.85	1987 .... Don Pohl		70.25
1962 .... Arnold Palmer		70.27	1988 .... Chip Beck		69.46
1963 .... Billy Casper		70.58	1989 .... Greg Norman		69.49
1964 .... Arnold Palmer		70.01	1990 .... Greg Norman		69.10
1965 .... Billy Casper		70.85	1991 .... Fred Couples		69.59
1966 .... Billy Casper		70.27			

*Point system used, 1937-41.

Note: As of 1988, based on minimum of 60 rounds per year.

The Grand Slam

In 1930 golf's Grand Slam consisted of the Open and Amateur championships of both the United States and Britain. Bobby Jones won all four tournaments that year, a feat which has never been duplicated. The modern Grand Slam—the Masters, U.S. Open, British Open, and PGA Championship—was adopted some twenty years later. Ben Hogan, Jack Nicklaus, Gary Player, and Gene Sarazen are the only players who have won all four of the modern Grand Slam events. In 1953 Hogan won three of the four Grand Slam tourneys, including the only British Open in which he ever competed. This is the closest any player in modern golf history has come to achieving the "Impregnable Quadrilateral."

All-Time PGA Tour Records*

Scoring

90 HOLES
333—(67-67-68-66-65) by Lanny Wadkins, at four courses, Palm Springs, CA, in winning the 1985 Bob Hope Classic (27 under par).

333—(66-68-64-69-66) by Craig Stadler, at four courses, Palm Springs, CA, in the 1985 Bob Hope Classic (27 under par).

333—(73-63-68-64-65) by Greg Norman, at three courses, Las Vegas, to win the 1986 Panasonic Las Vegas Invitational (27 under par).

72 HOLES
257—(60-68-64-65) by Mike Souchak, at Brackenridge Park GC, San Antonio, to win 1955 Texas Open (27 under par).

54 HOLES
Opening rounds
191—(66-64-61) by Gay Brewer, at Pensacola CC, Pensacola, FL, in winning the 1967 Pensacola Open.

Consecutive rounds
189—(63-63-63) by Chandler Harper in the last three rounds to win the 1954 Texas Open at Brackenridge Park GC, San Antonio.

36 HOLES
Opening rounds
126—(64-62) by Tommy Bolt, at Cavalier Yacht & CC, Virginia Beach, VA, in 1954 Virginia Beach Open.

126—(64-62) by Paul Azinger, at Oak Hills CC, San Antonio, in 1989 Texas Open.

Consecutive rounds
125—(63-62) by Ron Streck in the last two rounds to win the 1978 Texas Open at Oak Hills CC, San Antonio.

125—(62-63) by Blaine McCallister in the middle two rounds in winning the 1988 Hardee's Golf Classic at Oakwood CC, Coal Valley, IL.

18 HOLES
59—by Al Geiberger, at Colonial Country Club, Memphis, in second round in winning 1977 Memphis Classic.

9 HOLES
27—by Mike Souchak, at Brackenridge Park GC, San Antonio, on par-35 second nine of first round in 1955 Texas Open.

27—by Andy North at En-Joie GC, Endicott, NY, on par-34 second nine of first round in 1975 BC Open.

MOST CONSECUTIVE ROUNDS UNDER 70
19—Byron Nelson in 1945.

MOST BIRDIES IN A ROW
8—Bob Goalby at Pasadena GC, St Petersburg, FL, during fourth round in winning the 1961 St Petersburg Open.

8—Fuzzy Zoeller, at Oakwood CC, Coal Valley, IL, during first round of 1976 Quad Cities Open.

8—Dewey Arnette, Warwick Hills GC, Grand Blanc, MI, during first round of the 1987 Buick Open.

MOST BIRDIES IN A ROW TO WIN
5—Jack Nicklaus to win 1978 Jackie Gleason Inverrary Classic (last 5 holes).

Wins

MOST CONSECUTIVE YEARS WINNING AT LEAST ONE TOURNAMENT
17—Jack Nicklaus, 1962-78.
17—Arnold Palmer, 1955-71.
16—Billy Casper, 1956-71.

MOST CONSECUTIVE WINS
11—Byron Nelson, from Miami Four Ball, March 8-11, 1945, through Canadian Open, August 2-4, 1945.

MOST WINS IN A SINGLE EVENT
8—Sam Snead, Greater Greensboro Open, 1938, 1946, 1949, 1950, 1955, 1956, 1960, and 1965.

MOST CONSECUTIVE WINS IN A SINGLE EVENT
4—Walter Hagen, PGA Championships, 1924-27.

MOST WINS IN A CALENDAR YEAR
18—Byron Nelson, 1945.

MOST YEARS BETWEEN WINS
12—Leonard Thompson, 1977-89.

MOST YEARS FROM FIRST WIN TO LAST
29—Sam Snead, 1936-65.

YOUNGEST WINNERS
John McDermott, 19 years and 10 months, 1911 US Open.

OLDEST WINNER
Sam Snead, 52 years and 10 months, 1965 Greater Greensboro Open.

WIDEST WINNING MARGIN: STROKES
16—Bobby Locke, 1948 Chicago Victory National Championship.

Putting

FEWEST PUTTS, ONE ROUND
18—Andy North, at Kingsmill GC, in second round of 1990 Anheuser Busch Golf Classic.

18—Kenny Knox, at Harbour Town GL, in first round of 1989 MCI Heritage Classic.

18—Mike McGee, at Colonial CC, in first round of 1987 Federal Express St Jude Classic.

18—Sam Trahan, at Whitemarsh Valley CC, in final round of 1979 IVB Philadelphia Golf Classic.

FEWEST PUTTS, FOUR ROUNDS
93—Kenny Knox, in 1989 MCI Heritage Classic at Harbour Town GL.

*Through 12/31/90.

Old Money

Jack Nicklaus (b. 1-21-40) and Lee Trevino (b. 12-1-39) became eligible for the 1990 Senior Tour upon turning 50. Nicklaus entered four tournaments, won two of them, and earned $340,000 to quickly become the all-time Senior Tour Money Leader, with $5,510,465. That's a suspect title, though, because it combines PGA and Senior Tour earnings. Trevino entered 29 Senior tournaments, finished in the top 10 26 times, and became the first senior to win over $1 million in a season ($1,199,777). On the all-time Senior Tour list, however, he ranked second to Nicklaus with combined career earnings through 1990 of $4,674,694. As for the all-time career money leader, that's not Nicklaus, but Tom Kite, who finished 1990 with $6,258,893 in earnings on the PGA Tour alone.

THE MAJOR TOURNAMENTS
LPGA Championship

Year	Winner	Score	Runner-Up	Site
1955	†Beverly Hanson (4 and 3)	220	Louise Suggs	Orchard Ridge CC, Ft Wayne, IN
1956	*Marlene Hagge (5)	291	Patty Berg (6)	Forest Lake CC, Detroit
1957	Louise Suggs	285	Wiffi Smith	Churchill Valley CC, Pittsburgh
1958	Mickey Wright	288	Fay Crocker	Churchill Valley CC, Pittsburgh
1959	Betsy Rawls	288	Patty Berg	Sheraton Hotel CC, French Lick, IN
1960	Mickey Wright	292	Louise Suggs	Sheraton Hotel CC, French Lick, IN
1961	Mickey Wright	287	Louise Suggs	Stardust CC, Las Vegas
1962	Judy Kimball	282	Shirley Spork	Stardust CC, Las Vegas
1963	Mickey Wright	294	Mary Lena Faulk Mary Mills Louise Suggs	Stardust CC, Las Vegas
1964	Mary Mills	278	Mickey Wright	Stardust CC, Las Vegas
1965	Sandra Haynie	279	Clifford A. Creed	Stardust CC, Las Vegas
1966	Gloria Ehret	282	Mickey Wright	Stardust CC, Las Vegas
1967	Kathy Whitworth	284	Shirley Englehorn	Pleasant Valley CC, Sutton, MA
1968	*Sandra Post (68)	294	Kathy Whitworth (75)	Pleasant Valley CC, Sutton, MA
1969	Betsy Rawls	293	Susie Berning Carol Mann	Concord GC, Kiameshia Lake, NY
1970	*Shirley Englehorn (74)	285	Kathy Whitworth (78)	Pleasant Valley CC, Sutton, MA
1971	Kathy Whitworth	288	Kathy Ahern	Pleasant Valley CC, Sutton, MA
1972	Kathy Ahern	293	Jane Blalock	Pleasant Valley CC, Sutton, MA
1973	Mary Mills	288	Betty Burfeindt	Pleasant Valley CC, Sutton, MA
1974	Sandra Haynie	288	JoAnne Carner	Pleasant Valley CC, Sutton, MA
1975	Kathy Whitworth	288	Sandra Haynie	Pine Ridge GC, Baltimore
1976	Betty Burfeindt	287	Judy Rankin	Pine Ridge GC, Baltimore
1977	Chako Higuchi	279	Pat Bradley Sandra Post Judy Rankin	Bay Tree Golf Plantation, N. Myrtle Beach, SC
1978	Nancy Lopez	275	Amy Alcott	Jack Nicklaus GC, Kings Island, OH
1979	Donna Caponi	279	Jerilyn Britz	Jack Nicklaus GC, Kings Island, OH
1980	Sally Little	285	Jane Blalock	Jack Nicklaus GC, Kings Island, OH
1981	Donna Caponi	280	Jerilyn Britz Pat Meyers	Jack Nicklaus GC, Kings Island, OH
1982	Jan Stephenson	279	JoAnne Carner	Jack Nicklaus GC, Kings Island, OH
1983	Patty Sheehan	279	Sandra Haynie	Jack Nicklaus GC, Kings Island, OH
1984	Patty Sheehan	272	Beth Daniel Pat Bradley	Jack Nicklaus GC, Kings Island, OH
1985	Nancy Lopez	273	Alice Miller	Jack Nicklaus GC, Kings Island, OH
1986	Pat Bradley	277	Patty Sheehan	Jack Nicklaus GC, Kings Island, OH
1987	Jane Geddes	275	Betsy King	Jack Nicklaus GC, Kings Island, OH
1988	Sherri Turner	281	Amy Alcott	Jack Nicklaus GC, Kings Island, OH
1989	Nancy Lopez	274	Ayako Okamoto	Jack Nicklaus GC, Kings Island, OH
1990	Beth Daniel	280	Rosie Jones	Bethesda CC, Bethesda, MD
1991	Meg Mallon	274	Pat Bradley Ayako Okamoto	Bethesda CC, Bethesda, MD

*Won in playoff. Playoff scores are in parentheses. 1956 was sudden death; 1968 and 1970 were 18-hole playoffs.
†Won match play final.

U.S. Women's Open

Year	Winner	Score	Runner-Up	Site
1946	Patty Berg	5&4	Betty Jameson	Spokane CC, Spokane, WA
1947	Betty Jameson	295	Sally Sessions Polly Riley	Starmount Forest CC, Greensboro, NC
1948	Babe Zaharias	300	Betty Hicks	Atlantic City CC, Northfield, NJ
1949	Louise Suggs	291	Babe Zaharias	Prince George's G & CC, Landover, MD
1950	Babe Zaharias	291	Betsy Rawls	Rolling Hills CC, Wichita, KS
1951	Betsy Rawls	293	Louise Suggs	Druid Hills GC, Atlanta
1952	Louise Suggs	284	Marlene Bauer Betty Jameson	Bala GC, Philadelphia
1953	*Betsy Rawls (71)	302	Jackie Pung (77)	CC of Rochester, Rochester, NY

U.S. Women's Open (*Cont.*)

Year	Winner	Score	Runner-Up	Site
1954	Babe Zaharias	291	Betty Hicks	Salem CC, Peabody, MA
1955	Fay Crocker	299	Mary Lena Faulk	Wichita CC, Wichita, KS
			Louise Suggs	
1956	*Kathy Cornelius (75)	302	Barbara McIntire (82)	Northland CC, Duluth, MN
1957	Betsy Rawls	299	Patty Berg	Winged Foot GC, Mamaroneck, NY
1958	Mickey Wright	290	Louise Suggs	Forest Lake CC, Detroit
1959	Mickey Wright	287	Louise Suggs	Churchill Valley CC, Pittsburgh
1960	Betsy Rawls	292	Joyce Ziske	Worcester CC, Worcester, MA
1961	Mickey Wright	293	Betsy Rawls	Baltusrol GC (Lower Course), Springfield, NJ
1962	Murle Breer	301	Jo Ann Prentice	Dunes GC, Myrtle Beach, SC
			Ruth Jessen	
1963	Mary Mills	289	Sandra Haynie	Kenwood CC, Cincinnati
			Louise Suggs	
1964	*Mickey Wright (70)	290	Ruth Jessen (72)	San Diego CC, Chula Vista, CA
1965	Carol Mann	290	Kathy Cornelius	Atlantic City CC, Northfield, NJ
1966	Sandra Spuzich	297	Carol Mann	Hazeltine Natl GC, Chaska, MN
1967	Catherine LaCoste	294	Susie Berning	Hot Springs GC (Cascades Course), Hot Springs, VA
			Beth Stone	
1968	Susie Berning	289	Mickey Wright	Moslem Springs GC, Fleetwood, PA
1969	Donna Caponi	294	Peggy Wilson	Scenic Hills CC, Pensacola, FL
1970	Donna Caponi	287	Sandra Haynie	Muskogee CC, Muskogee, OK
			Sandra Spuzich	
1971	JoAnne Carner	288	Kathy Whitworth	Kahkwa CC, Erie, PA
1972	Susie Berning	299	Kathy Ahern	Winged Foot GC, Mamaroneck, NY
			Pam Barnett	
			Judy Rankin	
1973	Susie Berning	290	Gloria Ehret	CC of Rochester, Rochester, NY
			Shelley Hamlin	
1974	Sandra Haynie	295	Carol Mann	La Grange CC, La Grange, IL
			Beth Stone	
1975	Sandra Palmer	295	JoAnne Carner	Atlantic City CC, Northfield, NJ
			Sandra Post	
			Nancy Lopez	
1976	*JoAnne Carner (76)	292	Sandra Palmer (78)	Rolling Green CC, Springfield, PA
1977	Hollis Stacy	292	Nancy Lopez	Hazeltine Natl GC, Chaska, MN
1978	Hollis Stacy	289	JoAnne Carner	CC of Indianapolis, Indianapolis
			Sally Little	
1979	Jerilyn Britz	284	Debbie Massey	Brooklawn CC, Fairfield, CT
			Sandra Palmer	
1980	Amy Alcott	280	Hollis Stacy	Richland CC, Nashville
1981	Pat Bradley	279	Beth Daniel	La Grange CC, La Grange, IL
1982	Janet Anderson	283	Beth Daniel	Del Paso CC, Sacramento
			Sandra Haynie	
			Donna White	
			JoAnne Carner	
1983	Jan Stephenson	290	JoAnne Carner	Cedar Ridge CC, Tulsa
			Patty Sheehan	
1984	Hollis Stacy	290	Rosie Jones	Salem CC, Peabody, MA
1985	Kathy Baker	280	Judy Dickinson	Baltusrol GC (Upper Course), Springfield, NJ
1986	*Jane Geddes (71)	287	Sally Little (73)	NCR GC, Dayton
1987	*Laura Davies (71)	285	Ayako Okamoto (73)	Plainfield CC, Plainfield, NJ
			JoAnne Carner (74)	
1988	Liselotte Neumann	277	Patty Sheehan	Baltimore CC, Baltimore
1989	Betsy King	278	Nancy Lopez	Indianwood G & CC, Lake Orion, MI
1990	Betsy King	284	Patty Sheehan	Atlanta Athletic Club, Duluth, GA
1991	Meg Mallon	283	Pat Bradley	Colonial Club, Fort Worth

*Winner in playoff. 18-hole playoff scores are in parentheses.

Inflation on the Fairways	Oh, how the prize money has grown. In 1974 Johnny Miller won a remarkable eight tournaments and was the season's money leader, with earnings of $353,021.59. That total would have placed him 33rd on the 1990 money list, directly behind David Frost, who had only four top-10 finishes during the year.

Dinah Shore

Year	Winner	Score	Runner-Up
1972	Jane Blalock	213	Carol Mann, Judy Rankin
1973	Mickey Wright	284	Joyce Kazmierski
1974	*Jo Ann Prentice	289	Jane Blalock, Sandra Haynie
1975	Sandra Palmer	283	Kathy McMullen
1976	Judy Rankin	285	Betty Burfeindt
1977	Kathy Whitworth	289	JoAnne Carner, Sally Little
1978	*Sandra Post	283	Penny Pulz
1979	Sandra Post	276	Nancy Lopez
1980	Donna Caponi	275	Amy Alcott
1981	Nancy Lopez	277	Carolyn Hill
1982	Sally Little	278	Hollis Stacy, Sandra Haynie
1983	Amy Alcott	282	Beth Daniel, Kathy Whitworth
1984	*Juli Inkster	280	Pat Bradley
1985	Alice Miller	275	Jan Stephenson
1986	Pat Bradley	280	Val Skinner
1987	*Betsy King	283	Patty Sheehan
1988	Amy Alcott	274	Colleen Walker
1989	Juli Inkster	279	Tammie Green, JoAnne Carner
1990	Betsy King	283	Kathy Postlewait, Shirley Furlong
1991	Amy Alcott	273	Dottie Mochrie

*Winner in sudden-death playoff.

Note: Designated fourth major in 1983.

Played at Mission Hills CC, Rancho Mirage, CA.

du Maurier Classic

Year	Winner	Score	Runner-Up	Site
1973	*Jocelyne Bourassa	214	Sandra Haynie Judy Rankin	Montreal GC, Montreal
1974	Carole Jo Callison	208	JoAnne Carner	Candiac GC, Montreal
1975	*JoAnne Carner	214	Carol Mann	St George's CC, Toronto
1976	*Donna Caponi	212	Judy Rankin	Cedar Brae G & CC, Toronto
1977	Judy Rankin	214	Pat Meyers Sandra Palmer	Lachute G & CC, Montreal
1978	JoAnne Carner	278	Hollis Stacy	St George's CC, Toronto
1979	Amy Alcott	285	Nancy Lopez	Richelieu Valley CC, Montreal
1980	Pat Bradley	277	JoAnne Carner	St George's CC, Toronto
1981	Jan Stephenson	278	Nancy Lopez Pat Bradley	Summerlea CC, Dorion, Quebec
1982	Sandra Haynie	280	Beth Daniel	St George's CC, Toronto
1983	Hollis Stacy	277	JoAnne Carner Alice Miller	Beaconsfield GC, Montreal
1984	Juli Inkster	279	Ayako Okamoto	St George's G & CC, Toronto
1985	Pat Bradley	278	Jane Geddes	Beaconsfield CC, Montreal
1986	*Pat Bradley	276	Ayako Okamoto	Board of Trade CC, Toronto
1987	Jody Rosenthal	272	Ayako Okamoto	Islesmere GC, Laval, Quebec
1988	Sally Little	279	Laura Davies	Vancouver GC, Coquitlam, British Columbia
1989	Tammie Green	279	Pat Bradley Betsy King	Beaconsfield GC, Montreal
1990	Cathy Johnston	276	Patty Sheehan	Westmount G & CC, Kitchener, Ontario
1991	Nancy Scranton	279	Debbie Massey	Vancouver GC, Coquitlam, British Columbia

*Winner in sudden-death playoff.

Note: Designated third major in 1979.

THEY SAID IT

J. C. Snead, Senior PGA golfer, on his putting: "It's so bad I could putt off a tabletop and still leave the ball halfway down the leg."

THE LPGA TOUR

Season Money Leaders

		Earnings ($)
1950	Babe Zaharias	14,800
1951	Babe Zaharias	15,087
1952	Betsy Rawls	14,505
1953	Louise Suggs	19,816
1954	Patty Berg	16,011
1955	Patty Berg	16,492
1956	Marlene Hagge	20,235
1957	Patty Berg	16,272
1958	Beverly Hanson	12,639
1959	Betsy Rawls	26,774
1960	Louise Suggs	16,892
1961	Mickey Wright	22,236
1962	Mickey Wright	21,641
1963	Mickey Wright	31,269
1964	Mickey Wright	29,800
1965	Kathy Whitworth	28,658
1966	Kathy Whitworth	33,517
1967	Kathy Whitworth	32,937
1968	Kathy Whitworth	48,379
1969	Carol Mann	49,152
1970	Kathy Whitworth	30,235
1971	Kathy Whitworth	41,181
1972	Kathy Whitworth	65,063
1973	Kathy Whitworth	82,864
1974	JoAnne Carner	87,094
1975	Sandra Palmer	76,374
1976	Judy Rankin	150,734
1977	Judy Rankin	122,890
1978	Nancy Lopez	189,814
1979	Nancy Lopez	197,489
1980	Beth Daniel	231,000
1981	Beth Daniel	206,998
1982	JoAnne Carner	310,400
1983	JoAnne Carner	291,404
1984	Betsy King	266,771
1985	Nancy Lopez	416,472
1986	Pat Bradley	492,021
1987	Ayako Okamoto	466,034
1988	Sherri Turner	350,851
1989	Betsy King	654,132
1990	Beth Daniel	863,578

Career Money Leaders*

		Earnings ($)
1	Pat Bradley	3,346,047.03
2	Nancy Lopez	3,026,470.83
3	Betsy King	3,013,537.50
4	Beth Daniel	2,893,482.80
5	Patty Sheehan	2,830,464.01
6	Amy Alcott	2,491,855.14
7	JoAnne Carner	2,386,887.63
8	Ayako Okamoto	2,042,466.85
9	Jan Stephenson	1,832,085.00
10	Kathy Whitworth	1,719,804.01
11	Hollis Stacy	1,470,652.99
12	Donna Caponi	1,387,919.73
13	Sandra Palmer	1,291,038.86
14	Jane Blalock	1,290,943.62
15	Sally Little	1,277,178.80
16	Rosie Jones	1,263,216.97
17	Jane Geddes	1,253,138.30
18	Juli Inkster	1,234,847.23
19	Kathy Postlewait	1,202,016.27
20	Colleen Walker	1,090,294.71
21	Sandra Haynie	1,055,874.57
22	Debbie Massey	1,004,280.13
23	Chris Johnson	993,797.50
24	Sherri Turner	956,827.78
25	Judy Dickinson	955,035.92
26	Patti Rizzo	921,847.75
27	Judy Rankin	887,858.44
28	Donna White	820,104.08
29	Alice Miller	771,093.72
30	Cathy Gerring	760,881.00

*Through 12/31/90.

LPGA Player of the Year

1966	Kathy Whitworth		1979	Nancy Lopez
1967	Kathy Whitworth		1980	Beth Daniel
1968	Kathy Whitworth		1981	JoAnne Carner
1969	Kathy Whitworth		1982	JoAnne Carner
1970	Sandra Haynie		1983	Patty Sheehan
1971	Kathy Whitworth		1984	Betsy King
1972	Kathy Whitworth		1985	Nancy Lopez
1973	Kathy Whitworth		1986	Pat Bradley
1974	JoAnne Carner		1987	Ayako Okamoto
1975	Sandra Palmer		1988	Nancy Lopez
1976	Judy Rankin		1989	Betsy King
1977	Judy Rankin		1990	Beth Daniel
1978	Nancy Lopez			

Vare Trophy: Best Scoring Average

	Avg			Avg
1953 .... Patty Berg	75.00		1983 ..... JoAnne Carner	71.41
1954 .... Babe Zaharias ·	75.48		1984 ..... Patty Sheehan	71.40
1955 .... Patty Berg	74.47		1985 ..... Nancy Lopez	70.73
1956 .... Patty Berg	74.57		1986 .... Pat Bradley	71.10
1957 .... Louise Suggs	74.64		1987 ..... Betsy King	71.14
1958 .... Beverly Hanson	74.92		1988 ..... Colleen Walker	71.26
1959 .... Betsy Rawls	74.03		1989 .... Beth Daniel	70.38
1960 .... Mickey Wright	73.25		1990 ..... Beth Daniel	70.54
1961 .... Mickey Wright	73.55			
1962 .... Mickey Wright	73.67			
1963 .... Mickey Wright	72.81			
1964 .... Mickey Wright	72.46			
1965 .... Kathy Whitworth	72.61			

Most Career Wins*

	Wins
Kathy Whitworth	88
Mickey Wright	82
Patty Berg	57
Betsy Rawls	55
Louise Suggs	50
Nancy Lopez	43
JoAnne Carner	42
Sandra Haynie	42
Carol Mann	38
Babe Zaharias	31
Jane Blalock	29
Amy Alcott	28
Pat Bradley	26
Judy Rankin	26
Marlene Hagge	25
Beth Daniel	25
Patty Sheehan	25

*Through 12/31/90.

(Vare Trophy continued)

	Avg
1966 .... Kathy Whitworth	72.60
1967 .... Kathy Whitworth	72.74
1968 .... Carol Mann	72.04
1969 .... Kathy Whitworth	72.38
1970 .... Kathy Whitworth	72.26
1971 .... Kathy Whitworth	72.88
1972 .... Kathy Whitworth	72.38
1973 .... Judy Rankin	73.08
1974 .... JoAnne Carner	72.87
1975 .... JoAnne Carner	72.40
1976 .... Judy Rankin	72.25
1977 .... Judy Rankin	72.16
1978 .... Nancy Lopez	71.76
1979 .... Nancy Lopez	71.20
1980 .... Amy Alcott	71.51
1981 .... JoAnne Carner	71.75
1982 .... JoAnne Carner	71.49

All-Time LPGA Tour Records*

Scoring

72 HOLES
268—(66-67-69-66) by Nancy Lopez to win at the Willow Creek GC, High Point, NC, in the 1985 Henredon Classic (20 under par).

54 HOLES
198—(65-69-64) by Jan Stephenson to win at the Bent Tree CC, Dallas, in the 1981 Mary Kay Classic (18 under par).

36 HOLES
129—(64-65) by Judy Dickinson at Pasadena Yacht & CC, St Petersburg, in the 1985 S&H Golf Classic (15 under par).

18 HOLES
62—by Mickey Wright at Hogan Park GC, Midland, TX, in the first round in winning the 1964 Tall City Open (9 under par).

62—by Vicki Fergon at Almaden G & CC, San Jose, CA, in the second round of the 1984 San Jose Classic (11 under par).

9 HOLES
28—by Mary Beth Zimmerman at Rail GC, 1984 Rail Charity Golf Classic, Springfield, IL (par 36). Zimmerman shot 64.

28—by Pat Bradley at Green Gables CC, Denver, 1984 Columbia Savings Classic (par 35). Bradley shot 65.

28—by Muffin Spencer-Devlin at Knollwood CC, Elmsford, NY, in winning the 1985 MasterCard International Pro-Am (par 35). Spencer-Devlin shot 64.

MOST CONSECUTIVE ROUNDS UNDER 70
9—Beth Daniel, in 1990.

MOST BIRDIES IN A ROW
8—Mary Beth Zimmerman at Rail GC in Springfield, IL, in the second round of the 1984 Rail Charity Classic. She shot 64, 8 under par.

Wins

MOST CONSECUTIVE WINS IN SCHEDULED EVENTS
4—Mickey Wright, in 1962.
4—Mickey Wright, in 1963.
4—Kathy Whitworth, in 1969.

MOST CONSECUTIVE WINS IN ENTERED TOURNAMENTS
5—Nancy Lopez, in 1987.

MOST WINS IN A CALENDAR YEAR
13—Mickey Wright, in 1963.

WIDEST WINNING MARGIN, STROKES
14—Louise Suggs, 1949 US Women's Open.
14—Cindy Mackey, 1986 MasterCard International Pro-Am.

*Through 12/31/90.

U.S. Senior Open

Year	Winner	Score	Runner-Up	Site
1980	Roberto DeVicenzo	285	William C. Campbell	Winged Foot GC, Mamaroneck, NY
1981	*Arnold Palmer (70)	289	Bob Stone (74) Billy Casper (77)	Oakland Hills CC, Birmingham, MI
1982	Miller Barber	282	Gene Littler Dan Sikes, Jr	Portland GC, Portland, OR
1983	*Billy Casper (75) (3)	288	Rod Funseth (75) (4)	Hazeltine GC, Chaska, MN
1984	Miller Barber	286	Arnold Palmer	Oak Hill CC, Rochester, NY
1985	Miller Barber	285	Roberto DeVicenzo	Edgewood Tahoe GC, Stateline, NV
1986	Dale Douglass	279	Gary Player	Scioto CC, Columbus, OH
1987	Gary Player	270	Doug Sanders	Brooklawn CC, Fairfield, CT
1988	*Gary Player (68)	288	Bob Charles (70)	Medinah CC, Medinah, IL
1989	Orville Moody	279	Frank Beard	Laurel Valley GC, Ligonier, PA
1990	Lee Trevino	275	Jack Nicklaus	Ridgewood CC, Paramus, NJ
1991	Jack Nicklaus (65)	282	Chi Chi Rodriguez (69)	Oakland Hills CC, Birmingham, MI

*Winner in playoff. Playoff scores are in parentheses. The 1983 playoff went to one hole of sudden death after an 18-hole playoff.

SENIOR TOUR

Season Money Leaders

		Earnings ($)
1980	Don January	44,100
1981	Miller Barber	83,136
1982	Miller Barber	106,890
1983	Don January	237,571
1984	Don January	328,597
1985	Peter Thomson	386,724
1986	Bruce Crampton	454,299
1987	Chi Chi Rodriguez	509,145
1988	Bob Charles	533,929
1989	Bob Charles	725,887
1990	Lee Trevino	1,190,518

Most Career Wins*

	Wins
Miller Barber	24
Don January	22
Bruce Crampton	17
Chi Chi Rodriguez	16
Gary Player	15
Bob Charles	15
Peter Thomson	11
Arnold Palmer	10
Billy Casper	9
Orville Moody	9

* Through 12/31/90.

Career Money Leaders*

		Earnings ($)			Earnings ($)
1.	Bob Charles	2,494,732	16.	Walter Zembriski	1,256,660
2.	Miller Barber	2,488,787	17.	Lee Elder	1,227,268
3.	Chi Chi Rodriguez	2,235,159	18.	Lee Trevino	1,199,777
4.	Bruce Crampton	2,147,530	19.	Arnold Palmer	1,179,763
5.	Orville Moody	2,136,180	20.	Larry Mowry	1,115,624
6.	Gary Player	2,111,928	21.	Jim Ferree	1,107,833
7.	Don January	1,813,545	22.	Gay Brewer	1,080,281
8	Dale Douglass	1,768,120	23.	Peter Thomson	1,061,118
9.	Harold Henning	1,758,416	24.	Jim Dent	1,030,905
10.	Gene Littler	1,540,366	25.	Don Bies	980,595
11.	Al Geiberger	1,514,190	26.	Butch Baird	874,887
12.	Dave Hill	1,490,370	27.	Bobby Nichols	848,551
13.	Charles Coody	1,421,131	28.	George Archer	847,753
14.	Billy Casper	1,363,694	29.	Ben Smith	777,373
15.	Mike Hill	1,307,782	30.	Rives McBee	738,816

*Through 12/31/90.

THEY SAID IT

Peter Jacobsen, professional golfer, on what separates a pro from an amateur: "When a pro hits it left to right, it's called a fade. When an amateur hits it left to right, it's called a slice."

MAJOR MEN'S AMATEUR CHAMPIONSHIPS

U.S. Amateur

Year	Winner	Year	Winner	Year	Winner
1895	Charles B. Macdonald	1927	Bobby Jones	1961	Jack Nicklaus
1896	H. J. Whigham	1928	Bobby Jones	1962	Labron E. Harris, Jr
1897	H. J. Whigham	1929	Harrison R. Johnston	1963	Deane Beman
1898	Findlay S. Douglas	1930	Bobby Jones	1964	William C. Campbell
1899	H. M. Harriman	1931	Francis Ouimet	1965	Robert J. Murphy, Jr
1900	Walter Travis	1932	C. Ross Somerville	1966	Gary Cowan
1901	Walter Travis	1933	George T. Dunlap, Jr	1967	Robert B. Dickson
1902	Louis N. James	1934	Lawson Little	1968	Bruce Fleisher
1903	Walter Travis	1935	Lawson Little	1969	Steven N. Melnyk
1904	H. Chandler Egan	1936	John W. Fischer	1970	Lanny Wadkins
1905	H. Chandler Egan	1937	John Goodman	1971	Gary Cowan
1906	Eben M. Byers	1938	William P. Turnesa	1972	Marvin Giles, III
1907	Jerry Travers	1939	Marvin H. Ward	1973	Craig Stadler
1908	Jerry Travers	1940	Richard D. Chapman	1974	Jerry Pate
1909	Robert A. Gardner	1941	Marvin H. Ward	1975	Fred Ridley
1910	William C. Fownes, Jr	1942-45	No tournament	1976	Bill Sander
1911	Harold Hilton	1946	Ted Bishop	1977	John Fought
1912	Jerry Travers	1947	Skee Riegel	1978	John Cook
1913	Jerry Travers	1948	William P. Turnesa	1979	Mark O'Meara
1914	Francis Ouimet	1949	Charles R. Coe	1980	Hal Sutton
1915	Robert A. Gardner	1950	Sam Urzetta	1981	Nathaniel Crosby
1916	Chick Evans	1951	Billy Maxwell	1982	Jay Sigel
1917-18	No tournament	1952	Jack Westland	1983	Jay Sigel
1919	S. Davidson Herron	1953	Gene Littler	1984	Scott Verplank
1920	Chick Evans	1954	Arnold Palmer	1985	Sam Randolph
1921	Jesse P. Guilford	1955	E. Harvie Ward, Jr	1986	Buddy Alexander
1922	Jess W. Sweetser	1956	E. Harvie Ward, Jr	1987	Bill Mayfair
1923	Max R. Marston	1957	Hillman Robbins, Jr	1988	Eric Meeks
1924	Bobby Jones	1958	Charles R. Coe	1989	Chris Patton
1925	Bobby Jones	1959	Jack Nicklaus	1990	Phil Mickelson
1926	George Von Elm	1960	Deane Beman	1991	Mitch Voges

Note: All stroke play from 1965 to 1972.

U.S. Junior Amateur

Year	Winner	Year	Winner	Year	Winner
1948	Dean Lind	1963	Gregg McHatton	1978	Don Hurter
1949	Gay Brewer	1964	Johnny Miller	1979	Jack Larkin
1950	Mason Rudolph	1965	James Masserio	1980	Eric Johnson
1951	Tommy Jacobs	1966	Gary Sanders	1981	Scott Erickson
1952	Don Bisplinghoff	1967	John Crooks	1982	Rich Marik
1953	Rex Baxter	1968	Eddie Pearce	1983	Tim Straub
1954	Foster Bradley	1969	Aly Trompas	1984	Doug Martin
1955	William Dunn	1970	Gary Koch	1985	Charles Rymer
1956	Harlan Stevenson	1971	Mike Brannan	1986	Brian Montgomery
1957	Larry Beck	1972	Bob Byman	1987	Brett Quigley
1958	Buddy Baker	1973	Jack Renner	1988	Jason Widener
1959	Larry Lee	1974	David Nevatt	1989	David Duval
1960	Bill Tindall	1975	Brett Mullin	1990	Mathew Todd
1961	Charles McDowell	1976	Madden Hatcher, III	1991	Tiger Woods
1962	Jim Wiechers	1977	Willie Wood, Jr		

Event is for amateur golfers younger than 18 years of age.

Mid-Amateur Championship

Year	Winner	Year	Winner	Year	Winner
1981	Jim Holtgrieve	1985	Jay Sigel	1989	James Taylor
1982	William Hoffer	1986	Bill Loeffler	1990	Jim Stuart
1983	Jay Sigel	1987	Jay Sigel	1991	Jim Stuart
1984	Mike Podolak	1988	David Eger		

Event is for amateur golfers at least 25 years of age.

U.S. Senior Amateur

1955 ....J. Wood Platt	1967 ....Ray Palmer	1979 ....William C. Campbell
1956 ....Frederick J. Wright	1968 ....Curtis Person, Sr	1980 ....William C. Campbell
1957 ....J. Clark Espie	1969 ....Curtis Person, Sr	1981 ....Ed Updegraff
1958 ....Thomas C. Robbins	1970 ....Gene Andrews	1982 ....Alton Duhon
1959 ....J. Clark Espie	1971 ....Tom Draper	1983 ....William Hyndman, III
1960 ....Michael Cestone	1972 ....Lewis W. Oehmig	1984 ....Bob Rawlins
1961 ....Dexter H. Daniels	1973 ....William Hyndman, III	1985 ....Lewis W. Oehmig
1962 ....Merrill L. Carlsmith	1974 ....Dale Morey	1986 ....Bo Williams
1963 ....Merrill L. Carlsmith	1975 ....William F. Colm	1987 ....John Richardson
1964 ....William D. Higgins	1976 ....Lewis W. Oehmig	1988 ....Clarence Moore
1965 ....Robert B. Kiersky	1977 ....Dale Morey	1989 ....Bo Williams
1966 ....Dexter H. Daniels	1978 ....K. K. Compton	1990 ....Jackie Cummings
		1991 ....Bill Bosshard

Event is for golfers at least 55 years of age.

MAJOR WOMEN'S AMATEUR CHAMPIONSHIPS

U.S. Women's Amateur

1895 ....Mrs. Charles S. Brown	1927 ....Miriam Burns Horn	1961 ....Anne Quast Sander
1896 ....Beatrix Hoyt	1928 ....Glenna Collett	1962 ....JoAnne Gunderson
1897 ....Beatrix Hoyt	1929 ....Glenna Collett	1963 ....Anne Quast Sander
1898 ....Beatrix Hoyt	1930 ....Glenna Collett	1964 ....Barbara McIntire
1899 ....Ruth Underhill	1931 ....Helen Hicks	1965 ....Jean Ashley
1900 ....Frances C. Griscom	1932 ....Virginia Van Wie	1966 ....JoAnne Carner
1901 ....Genevieve Hecker	1933 ....Virginia Van Wie	1967 ....Mary Lou Dill
1902 ....Genevieve Hecker	1934 ....Virginia Van Wie	1968 ....JoAnne Carner
1903 ....Bessie Anthony	1935 ....Glenna Collett Vare	1969 ....Catherine Lacoste
1904 ....Georgianna M. Bishop	1936 ....Pamela Barton	1970 ....Martha Wilkinson
1905 ....Pauline Mackay	1937 ....Estelle Lawson Page	1971 ....Laura Baugh
1906 ....Harriot S. Curtis	1938 ....Patty Berg	1972 ....Mary Budke
1907 ....Margaret Curtis	1939 ....Betty Jameson	1973 ....Carol Semple
1908 ....Katherine C. Harley	1940 ....Betty Jameson	1974 ....Cynthia Hill
1909 ....Dorothy I. Campbell	1941 ....Elizabeth Hicks Newell	1975 ....Beth Daniel
1910 ....Dorothy I. Campbell	1942-45 ... No tournament	1976 ....Donna Horton
1911 ....Margaret Curtis	1946 ....Babe Zaharias	1977 ....Beth Daniel
1912 ....Margaret Curtis	1947 ....Louise Suggs	1978 ....Cathy Sherk
1913 ....Gladys Ravenscroft	1948 ....Grace S. Lenczyk	1979 ....Carolyn Hill
1914 ....Katherine Jackson	1949 ....Dorothy Porter	1980 ....Juli Inkster
1915 ....Florence Vanderbeck	1950 ....Beverly Hanson	1981 ....Juli Inkster
1916 ....Alexa Stirling	1951 ....Dorothy Kirby	1982 ....Juli Inkster
1917-18 ... No tournament	1952 ....Jacqueline Pung	1983 ....Joanne Pacillo
1919 ....Alexa Stirling	1953 ....Mary Lena Faulk	1984 ....Deb Richard
1920 ....Alexa Stirling	1954 ....Barbara Romack	1985 ....Michiko Hattori
1921 ....Marion Hollins	1955 ....Patricia A. Lesser	1986 ....Kay Cockerill
1922 ....Glenna Collett	1956 ....Marlene Stewart	1987 ....Kay Cockerill
1923 ....Edith Cummings	1957 ....JoAnne Gunderson	1988 ....Pearl Sinn
1924 ....Dorothy Campbell Hurd	1958 ....Anne Quast Sander	1989 ....Vicki Goetze
1925 ....Glenna Collett	1959 ....Barbara McIntire	1990 ....Pat Hurst
1926 ....Helen Stetson	1960 ....JoAnne Gunderson	1991 ....Amy Fruhwirth

Girls' Junior Championship

1949 ....Marlene Bauer	1964 ....Peggy Conley	1978 ....Lori Castillo
1950 ....Patricia Lesser	1965 ....Gail Sykes	1979 ....Penny Hammel
1951 ....Arlene Brooks	1966 ....Claudia Mayhew	1980 ....Laurie Rinker
1952 ....Mickey Wright	1967 ....Elizabeth Story	1981 ....Kay Cornelius
1953 ....Millie Meyerson	1968 ....Peggy Harmon	1982 ....Heather Farr
1954 ....Margaret Smith	1969 ....Hollis Stacy	1983 ....Kim Saiki
1955 ....Carole Jo Kabler	1970 ....Hollis Stacy	1984 ....Cathy Mockett
1956 ....JoAnne Gunderson	1971 ....Hollis Stacy	1985 ....Dana Lofland
1957 ....Judy Eller	1972 ....Nancy Lopez	1986 ....Pat Hurst
1958 ....Judy Eller	1973 ....Amy Alcott	1987 ....Michelle McGann
1959 ....Judy Rand	1974 ....Nancy Lopez	1988 ....Jamille Jose
1960 ....Carol Sorenson	1975 ....Dayna Benson	1989 ....Brandie Burton
1961 ....Mary Lowell	1976 ....Pilar Dorado	1990 ....Sandrine Mendiburu
1962 ....Mary Lou Daniel	1977 ....Althea Tome	1991 ....Emilee Klein
1963 ....Janis Ferraris		

U.S. Senior Women's Amateur

1962 ....Maureen Orcutt	1972 ....Carolyn Cudone	1982...........Edean Ihlanfeldt
1963 ....Sis Choate	1973 ....Gwen Hibbs	1983...........Dorothy Porter
1964 ....Loma Smith	1974 ....Justine Cushing	1984...........Constance Guthrie
1965 ....Loma Smith	1975 ....Alberta Bower	1985...........Marlene Streit
1966 ....Maureen Orcutt	1976 ....Cecile H. Maclaurin	1986...........Connie Guthrie
1967 ....Marge Mason	1977 ....Dorothy Porter	1987...........Anne Sander
1968 ....Carolyn Cudone	1978 ....Alice Dye	1988...........Lois Hodge
1969 ....Carolyn Cudone	1979 ....Alice Dye	1989...........Anne Sander
1970 ....Carolyn Cudone	1980 ....Dorothy Porter	1990...........Anne Sander
1971 ....Carolyn Cudone	1981 ....Dorothy Porter	1991...........Phyllis Preuss

Women's Mid-Amateur Championship

1987 .... Cindy Scholefield
1988 .... Martha Lang
1989 .... Robin Weiss
1990 .... Carol Semple Thompson
1991 .... Sarah LeBrun Ingram

International Golf

Ryder Cup Matches

Year	Results	Site
1927	United States 9½, Great Britain 2½	Worcester CC, Worcester, MA
1929	Great Britain 7, United States 5	Moortown GC, Leeds, England
1931	United States 9, Great Britain 3	Scioto CC, Columbus, OH
1933	Great Britain 6½, United States 5½	Southport and Ainsdale Courses, Southport, England
1935	United States 9, Great Britain 3	Ridgewood CC, Ridgewood, NJ
1937	United States 8, Great Britain 4	Southport and Ainsdale Courses, Southport, England
1939-1945	No tournament	
1947	United States 11, Great Britain 1	Portland GC, Portland, OR
1949	United States 7, Great Britain 5	Ganton GC, Scarborough, England
1951	United States 9½, Great Britain 2½	Pinehurst CC, Pinehurst, NC
1953	United States 6½, Great Britain 5½	Wentworth Club, Surrey, England
1955	United States 8, Great Britain 4	Thunderbird Ranch & CC, Palm Springs, CA
1957	Great Britain 7½, United States 4½	Lindrick GC, Yorkshire, England
1959	United States 8½, Great Britain 3½	Eldorado CC, Palm Desert, CA
1961	United States 14½, Great Britain 9½	Royal Lytham & St Anne's GC, St Anne's-on-the-Sea, England
1963	United States 23, Great Britain 9	East Lake CC, Atlanta
1965	United States 19½, Great Britain 12½	Royal Birkdale GC, Southport, England
1967	United States 23½, Great Britain 8½	Champions GC, Houston
1969	United States 16, Great Britain 16	Royal Birkdale GC, Southport, England
1971	United States 18½, Great Britain 13½	Old Warson CC, St Louis
1973	United States 19, Great Britain 13	Hon Co of Edinburgh Golfers, Muirfield, Scotland
1975	United States 21, Great Britain 11	Laurel Valley GC, Ligonier, PA
1977	United States 12½, Great Britain 7½	Royal Lytham & St Anne's GC, St Anne's-on-the-Sea, England
1979	United States 17, Europe 11	Greenbrier, White Sulphur Springs, WV
1981	United States 18½, Europe 9½	Walton Heath GC, Surrey, England
1983	United States 14½, Europe 13½	PGA National GC, Palm Beach Gardens, FL
1985	Europe 16½, United States 11½	Belfry GC, Sutton Coldfield, England
1987	Europe 15, United States 13	Muirfield GC, Dublin, OH
1989	Europe 14, United States 14	Belfry GC, Sutton Coldfield, England
1991	United States 14½, Europe 13½	Ocean Course, Kiawah Island, SC

Team matches held every odd year between US professionals and those of Great Britain/Europe (since 1979, prior to which was US vs GB). Team members selected on basis of finishes in PGA and European Tour events.

Walker Cup Matches

Year	Results
1922	United States 8, Great Britain 4
1923	United States 6, Great Britain 5
1924	United States 9, Great Britain 3
1926	United States 6, Great Britain 5
1928	United States 11, Great Britain 1
1930	United States 10, Great Britain 2
1932	United States 8, Great Britain 1
1934	United States 9, Great Britain 2
1936	United States 9, Great Britain 0
1938	Great Britain 7, United States 4
1940-46	No tournament
1947	United States 8, Great Britain 4
1949	United States 10, Great Britain 2
1951	United States 6, Great Britain 3
1953	United States 9, Great Britain 3
1955	United States 10, Great Britain 2
1957	United States 8, Great Britain 3

Year	Results
1959	United States 9, Great Britain 3
1961	United States 11, Great Britain 1
1963	United States 12, Great Britain 8
1965	Great Britain 11, United States 11
1967	United States 13, Great Britain 7
1969	United States 10, Great Britain 8
1971	Great Britain 13, United States 11
1973	United States 14, Great Britain 10
1975	United States 15½, Great Britain 8½
1977	United States 16, Great Britain 8
1979	United States 15½, Great Britain 8½
1981	United States 15, Great Britain 9
1983	United States 13½, Great Britain 10½
1985	United States 13, Great Britain 11
1987	United States 16½, Great Britain 7½
1989	Great Britain 12½, United States 11½
1991	United States 14, Great Britain 10

Men's amateur team competition every other year between United States and Great Britain. US team members selected by USGA.

Curtis Cup Matches

Year	Results
1932	United States 5½, British Isles 3½
1934	United States 6½, British Isles 2½
1936	United States 4½, British Isles 4½
1938	United States 5½, British Isles 3½
1940-46	No tournament
1948	United States 6½, British Isles 2½
1950	United States 7½, British Isles 1½
1952	British Isles 5, United States 4
1954	United States 6, British Isles 3
1956	British Isles 5, United States 4
1958	British Isles 4½, United States 4½
1960	United States 6½, British Isles 2½
1962	United States 8, British Isles 1
1964	United States 10½, British Isles 7½

Year	Results
1966	United States 13, British Isles 5
1968	United States 10½, British Isles 7½
1970	United States 11½, British Isles 6½
1972	United States 10, British Isles 8
1974	United States 13, British Isles 5
1976	United States 11½, British Isles 6½
1978	United States 12, British Isles 6
1980	United States 13, British Isles 5
1982	United States 14½, British Isles 3½
1984	United States 9½, British Isles 8½
1986	British Isles 13, United States 5
1988	British Isles 11, United States 7
1990	United States 14, British Isles 4

Women's amateur team competition every other year between the United States and Great Britain. US team members selected by USGA.

So Who's Counting?

Ever wonder how many dimples there are on a golf ball? Before we tell you, let's go through a little dimpleology. By the 1890s golfers had discovered that a ball flew up to 60% longer and a lot truer if it were nicked here and there. Manufacturers started turning out balls with tiny raised bumps in concentric circles. Dimples arrived in 1908 when it became apparent that they were better than bumps aerodynamically.

The size, number, and pattern of dimples all have a lot to do with a ball's carrying distance and trajectory. The deeper the dimple, the lower the ball will go; the shallower, the higher. There's no magic number of dimples a ball should have, because dimple coverage (how much of the ball is dimpled) is more important than dimple count.

So how many dimples are there? Until 1984 most golf balls had 324 or 336 dimples. Because greater dimple coverage increases carrying distance, Titleist introduced a ball in 1984 with 384 dimples. Titleist's newest product, the HVC, has 440 dimples of 11 different sizes.

Boxing

South Africa: Is the Olympic Exile Over?

APRIL 29, 1991
$2.95

Sports Illustrated

SLUGFEST

Evander Holyfield Retains His Heavyweight Title Against a Surprisingly Spry George Foreman

WILL HART

But Seriously, Folks

At 42, George Foreman gave champion Evander Holyfield
a surprisingly tough fight | by RICHARD HOFFER

GEORGE FOREMAN UNLEASHED HIMSELF upon us like a circus bear, kind of fun to watch but still pretty far removed from the wild kingdom. At first, he seemed 100% entertainment value, all mischief and monologues. He was huge and bald, yes, but there was no longer the sense of danger he carried about him when he was that fierce heavyweight champion in the 1970s. He was now some 250 pounds of merriment. He was, in a word, a joke.

But with nothing else doing in the heavyweight division in 1991, the public decided to go for laughs for once and they allowed Big George into the big tent. His four-year comeback had been a comedy caravan, some stiffs scattered about along the way, but mostly one long lounge act. It was all patter about eating and aging, and his timing with a gag was considered much better than with a jab. There was nothing he had done, really, to suggest that he was a credible opponent for the champion, Evander Holyfield, who was undefeated and physically spectacular. But George, fat and 42 and so filled with self-mockery that he often argued his rightful place in boxing history would be at the buffet, earned the fight on his sheer likability, something the division has not thought to offer in quite some time.

You know the old saying: There's a sucker born every minute. An estimated 10 million of them huddled in front of the pay-

JOHN BIEVER

Holyfield (left) had Foreman in trouble in several rounds, but could not put him away.

per-view broadcast last April, contributing to purses of $20 million for Holyfield and $12.5 million for Foreman, the part-time preacher. Most of these fans were of the variety that not even P. T. Barnum could have hoped for. These were people who had already been suckered by the Buster Douglas farce, a disgraceful affair that involved another hopeless wide-body. Holyfield had knocked out the 247-pound, one-fight champion in only three rounds the previous November. And the incredibly sculpted Holyfield had stepped up his conditioning with all sorts of sophisticated training methods. Foreman, meanwhile, was being put through his paces by old Archie Moore, who promised to impart "mental gymnastics, escapology and Mongoosiana." You may not be able to fool everybody all the time, but you can fool fight fans whenever you want.

And so who was fooled? Foreman stung Holyfield in the second, fifth, and seventh rounds and, though he was outpointed in the end, seemed just one punch away from recapturing his old title in all the other rounds. It was a magnificent competition, with the hearts and chins of both fighters tested well. Holyfield, who took Foreman more seriously than anyone else in attendance, be-

moaned the effort that was required of him. "He made me do things I didn't want to do, punch when I didn't want to punch," said the champion. The fight was no sham, and Holyfield was lucky not to have anticipated one.

Boxing was lucky to have this spectacle because, elsewhere, there was disappointment all around. Douglas, who seemed to have enlivened the heavyweight division when he clobbered the invincible Mike Tyson the year before, stunned the boxing world again when he apparently failed to train at all for his fight with Holyfield. Having weighed 220 when he beat Tyson, he evidently celebrated by eating all the food Foreman was claiming to consume. It was his grandmother's pinto beans and chicken necks, he explained. Also a $98 room service order delivered to his sauna only days before the Holyfield fight. This while Holyfield was slimming down to 208 with the help of six-time Mr. Olympia, Lee Haney.

At least Douglas could afford to pay for whatever he ordered, since he had escaped the clutches of promoter Don King and was able to hike the bidding for his services to $23.5 million. Steve Wynn, the owner of the Mirage Hotel and Casino, the new player in high-dollar promotion, promised Douglas $30 million more if he could advance past Holyfield to a rematch with Tyson. In the end Wynn got better bang for his buck from the prefight fireworks. Clocked at five minutes, the pyrotechnics lasted only a little bit less than Douglas and only cost $25,000.

Douglas not only went down quickly, falling in the third round when Holyfield countered a missed uppercut with a right cross to the jaw, but went down as if determined to stay down. He seemed to begin to rise at the count of four, then sagged back to the canvas. Referee Mills Lane seemed to voice

boxing's disappointment when he said, "I don't know if he could have got up, but he sure never tried." Douglas, who had risen to such heights the year before, would henceforth be remembered on his back. "I don't know how much James ever liked boxing," said trainer John Russell, summing up yet another enigma to come boxing's way.

The one heavyweight with an undisputed appetite for fighting was kept away from the championship table, straining relationships with his promoter and his fans. Mike Tyson spent the year in a pair of meaningless tune-ups—easy knockouts over Henry Tillman and Alex Stewart—and a pair of far more troublesome matches with Razor Ruddock. The latter bouts were not particularly distinguished. The first one in March was interest-

The Finale of A Class Act

SUGAR RAY LEONARD understood that to be a popular world figure in boxing, the most popular of the 1980s, he would have to cloak the sport's brutality in a kind of formal wear. Certainly, for all the violence he committed upon his opponents, he was the most graceful fighter of his time. And indeed, he was as elegant outside the ring as within, handsome and well-spoken at the HBO mike and elsewhere. And well-dressed? For a boxer, he spent an awful lot of time in a tuxedo.

But Leonard's sense of showmanship briefly departed him in 1991 when he allowed himself to fight Terry Norris for the WBC junior middleweight championship, his Madison Square Garden debut. This was against all good and very public advice. He was 34, had not fought in more than a year and stood to gain neither increased respect nor a great deal of money by defeating Norris, a fighter of no particular mystique or marquee value.

The comeback was foolish by any measure but Leonard's. "I have to know that I've taken my talent as far as it can go," he explained. "I want to be the guy who says, 'Leonard, it's time to quit.'"

For all the time he was logging in a cummerbund, Leonard still preferred to think of himself as an athlete, not an ambassador. Yet Norris, a 23-year-old Leonard disciple, proved the master wrong, knocking him down in the second and seventh rounds, and generally working his handsome face over to win a 12-round decision. It was not pretty. Leonard was left with torn lips, a nearly closed left eye and ugly bumps above his cheeks. Given that, the retirement he would announce immediately afterward was inevitable. Surprisingly, it was much more graceful than his fight.

The fighter who had taken other knocks during the year—during divorce proceedings his wife accused him of physical abuse and cocaine use—got right back on his feet that night, praising his opponent and expressing relief that his career was over. "It took this kind of fight to

ing more for the premature stoppage by referee Richard Steele, who halted the bout with 38 seconds left in the seventh round. It was a brutal fight to that point and Tyson was certainly winning it. But what should have been remembered for Tyson's reborn fury was clouded by controversy. Ruddock was undamaged during a Tyson attack against the ropes when Steele, for no apparent reason, stepped between the fighters, setting off a post-fight melee involving several simultaneous skirmishes among the handlers of both camps. It also set off calls for a rematch.

Tyson seemed agreeable, indeed sympathetic. "I feel sorry for the guys who want to fight me, the killer of many men," he said, recovering his old bravado if nothing else.

Later his comments were harder to unravel. Tyson's legion of amateur psychologists listened to his ravings at his press conferences—he promised to make Ruddock his girlfriend—and read accounts of his feuding with King (there were reported incidents of physical confrontations between the fighter and promoter) and wondered who he was angriest with. Right up to the fight, there were signs of Tyson's growing impatience with King, stories that he had bolted camp, that he was going to replace Richie Giachetti, King's hand-picked lead trainer, with Carlos (Panama) Lewis, who had recently spent time in prison for removing the padding from the gloves of one of his fighters. There were stories that Tyson was seeking the counsel of former promoter Harold

prove to me that it is no longer my time," he said. "I am not the fighter of the '90s."

That last fight aside, he will be remembered as one of the great ones of all time. Toward the end he fought intermittently, as his ego or the public required, beating people like Donny Lalonde or a much-faded Roberto Duran. But the '80s, during his peak, were punctuated by some of boxing's biggest events, all of them Leonard fights. His *no mas* rematch with Duran in 1981 remains a talked-about spectacle. And his fights with contemporaries Marvelous Marvin Hagler and Thomas Hearns—his recent one with Hearns ending in a draw—stole all the attention away from the heavyweight division.

Boxing will not forget Leonard, who finally retired with a 36-2-1 record and earnings of more than $100 million, unsullied and apparently unhurt by a dangerous game. But perhaps Leonard, who had retired three times before, can forget boxing. "Finally I'll feel comfortable doing something else," he said.

Leonard was king of his sport in 1981 when he was named SI's Sportsman of the Year.

JOHN IACONO

A flabby Douglas saw his reign come to a close in the third round of his bout with Holyfield.

Smith, who spent five years in prison for embezzlement during the '80s. There were stories that Tyson couldn't wait one more day to reclaim the titles that Holyfield now held.

But first he had to wait through 12 rounds of Ruddock, who took the champion the distance in their summertime rematch. Tyson broke Ruddock's jaw, perhaps as early as the fourth round, knocked him down twice, and disfigured him but still could not put him away. Critics worried anew that Tyson had forsaken the skills and tools that once made him, indeed, the killer of many men. Against Ruddock he resorted to the puncher's fight, abandoning his jab and rarely following up with combinations. Every once in a while he just loaded up and fired. As for defense, Tyson refused to bob and weave and was happier demonstrating the firmness of his chin. "Michael," said Jay Bright, one of Tyson's exasperated corner men, "no fighter has ever had greater determination. But if you would just move your head more, you wouldn't have to be so determined."

It wasn't until July that King finally delivered Holyfield to Tyson, but only after the usual shenanigans at the negotiating table. King, who lost control of the heavyweight division when Tyson lost his titles, tried to assert some leverage in his dealings with Holyfield's people, promoter Dan Duva and manager Shelly Finkel, by announcing an offer to fight Foreman. This was interesting, as Foreman had just consigned Tyson to that group of has-beens. "Tyson has become average," he said. But Big George was to be an innocent pawn in this intrigue, abused by both sides. The Holyfield camp countered by saying they had the contract with Foreman. King's bluff called, he quickly accepted Duva's original offer of $15 million for Tyson, plus 40% of the profits above $48 million—rich enough but not the split he wanted. Holyfield was to get $30 million.

No sooner had the ink dried on the contracts than Tyson found himself facing a far more serious battle. In late July, the former champion was accused of rape by a contestant in the Miss Black America competition in Indianapolis. Seven weeks later, he was indicted. All parties insisted that the bout would be held as scheduled on Nov. 8, but the indictment cast a pall over the most eagerly awaited fight in years.

In the meantime, these vast sums of money

Tyson (left) KO'd Stewart in Round 1, but
was far less impressive against other oppenents.

JOHN IACONO

produced fevers in other heavyweights and would-be heavyweights as well. Larry Holmes, long retired, started a halfhearted comeback with a one-round knockout of somebody named Tim Anderson, then got into a postfight brawl with Trevor Berbick. And former football star Mark Gastineau began preparations for a championship onslaught with a fight against somebody who was later reported to be a professional wrestler.

At all levels the succession of young talent appeared stagnant. Among the young heavyweights, only Riddick Bowe remained impressive, although he should have had an easier time with Tyrell Biggs than he did.

At middleweight, the man who would be Sugar Ray Leonard, Michael Nunn, suffered a shocking loss to James Toney. And in his own backyard, no less. Nunn, who had some of Leonard's ability but none of his fire, had invited Toney to fight him in Davenport, Iowa, a treat for Nunn's hometown fans. But Toney knocked the previously undefeated IBF champion out in the 11th round. "I got lazy," said Nunn.

Leonard, who finally ended his wonderful career when Terry Norris decisioned him, had a much better excuse. He got old. Getting older, too, was Thomas Hearns, Leonard's old foil. Hearns turned 32 in 1990 but seemed to have aged even more than Leonard and the rest of that gang from the '80s. He had slowed considerably and, as he moved up in weight from welterweight, to

Toney (right) turned out to be an imperfect guest, KO'ing Nunn in the IBF champ's hometown.

win titles in the super welterweight, middleweight, super middleweight, and light heavyweight divisions, he had lost his punch as well. The Hitman hadn't knocked out a world-class opponent since 1987. In fact, Hearns was probably one loss away from becoming one of those stepping-stone fighters, a faded name who, in defeat, lends credibility to some up-and-comer.

That was until he met WBA light heavyweight champion Virgil Hill last June. Hearns unleashed the same jab that threatened Leonard in their famous 1981 fight and destroyed Hill, winning his sixth championship. The 2-to-1 underdog pocketed $4.5 million for that, just like the old days when he and Leonard and Marvelous Marvin Hagler and Roberto Duran exchanged paydays, and began entertaining visions of winning title No. 7, perhaps in a cruiserweight match with the WBA 190-pound champion, Bobby Czyz.

Was this Big George's influence? Giving hope to those who go up in weight and age? Perhaps. Certainly Foreman's welcome congeniality could be seen washing over the sport at every division. Later in the summer, Hearns and Hill got together for a kinder and gentler rematch. They spent a weekend fishing together in North Dakota.

Current Champions

Division	Weight Limit	WBC Champion	WBA Champion	IBF Champion
Heavyweight	None	Evander Holyfield	Evander Holyfield	Evander Holyfield
Cruiserweight	190	Anaclet Wamba	Bobby Czyz	James Warring
Light heavyweight	175	Jeff Harding	Thomas Hearns	Prince Charles Williams
Super middleweight	168	Mauro Galvano	Victor Cordova	Darrin Van Horn
Middleweight	160	Julian Jackson	Mike McCallum	James Toney
Junior middleweight	154	Terry Norris	Gilbert Dele	Gianfranco Rosi
Welterweight	147	Simon Brown	Meldrick Taylor	Vacant
Junior welterweight	140	Julio Cesar Chavez	Edwin Rosario	Vacant
Lightweight	135	Pernell Whitaker	Pernell Whitaker	Pernell Whitaker
Junior lightweight	130	Azumah Nelson	Joey Gamache	Brian Mitchell
Featherweight	126	Marcos Villasana	Yong Kyun Park	Manuel Medina
Junior featherweight	122	Daniel Zaragoza	Luis Mendoza	Welcome Ncita
Bantamweight	118	Joichiro Tatsuyoshi	Luisito Espinosa	Orlando Canizales
Junior bantamweight	115	Sung-Kil Moon	Khaosai Galaxy	Robert Quiroga
Flyweight	112	Muangchai Kittikasem	Yong Kang Kim	Dave McAuley
Junior flyweight	108	Humberto Gonzales	Myung Woo Yuh	Michael Carbajal
Strawweight	105	Ricardo Lopez	Hi Yong Choi	Phalan Lukmingkwan

Note: WBC = World Boxing Council   WBA = World Boxing Association   IBF = International Boxing Federation

Championship and Major Fights of 1990 and 1991*

Abbreviations: WBC=World Boxing Council   WBA= World Boxing Association   IBF=International Boxing Federation   KO=knockout   TKO=technical knockout   Dec=decision   Split=split decision   Disq=disqualification

Heavyweight

Date	Winner	Loser	Result	Title	Site
Mar 18	Mike Tyson	Razor Ruddock	TKO 7		Las Vegas
Apr 19	Evander Holyfield	George Foreman	Dec 12	WBC, WBA, IBF	Atlantic City
June 28	Mike Tyson	Razor Ruddock	Dec 12		Las Vegas
Aug 9	Riddick Bowe	Bruce Seldon	KO 1		Atlantic City

Cruiserweight

Date	Winner	Loser	Result	Title	Site
Nov 22	Robert Daniels	Taoufik Belbouli	Draw 12	WBA	Madrid
Dec 8	Massimiliano Duran	Anaclet Wamba	Disq 12	WBC	Ferrara, Italy
Mar 8	Bobby Czyz	Robert Daniels	Split 12	WBA	Atlantic City
July 20	Anaclet Wamba	Massimiliano Duran	TKO 11	WBC	Palermo, Italy
Aug 10	Bobby Czyz	Bash Ali	Dec 12	WBA	Atlantic City
Sep 7	James Warring	James Pritchard	KO 1	IBF	Salemi, Italy

Note: Jeff Lampkin forfeited IBF title in 1991.

Light Heavyweight

Date	Winner	Loser	Result	Title	Site
Jan 6	Virgil Hill	Mike Peak	Dec 12	WBA	Las Vegas
Jan 19	Dennis Andries	Guy Waters	Dec 12	WBC	Adelaide
Apr 20	Prince Charles Williams	James Kinchen	KO 2	IBF	Atlantic City
June 3	Thomas Hearns	Virgil Hill	Dec 12	WBA	Las Vegas
July 3	Prince Charles Williams	Vincent Boulware	KO 3	IBF	San Remo, Italy
Sep 11	Jeff Harding	Dennis Andries	Split 12	WBC	London

Super Middleweight

Date	Winner	Loser	Result	Title	Site
Nov 23	Christopher Tiozzio	Danny Morgan	TKO 2	WBA	Cergy-Pontoise, France
Dec 15	Lindell Holmes	Thulani Malinga	Dec 12	IBF	Marino, Italy
Dec 15	Mauro Galvano	Dario Matteoni	Dec 12	WBC	Monte Carlo
Apr 5	Victor Cordova	Christopher Tiozzio	TKO 9	WBA	Marseille, France
May 18	Darrin Van Horn	Lindell Holmes	KO 11	IBF	Verbania, Italy
July 27	Mauro Galvano	Ron Essett	Dec 12	WBC	Capo d'Orlando, Italy
Aug 17	Darrin Van Horn	Rick Jarvis	KO 3	IBF	Irvine, CA

* November 1, 1990, through September 19, 1991.

Middleweight

Date	Winner	Loser	Result	Title	Site
Nov 24	Julian Jackson	Herol Graham	KO 4	WBC	Benalmadena, Spain
Mar 29	Mike McCallum	Sumbu Kalambay	Dec 12	WBA	Monte Carlo
May 10	James Toney	Michael Nunn	KO 11	IBF	Davenport, IA
June 29	James Toney	Reggie Johnson	Dec 12	IBF	Las Vegas
Aug 29	Mike McCallum	Carlos Cruz	Dec 10	WBA	Santa Cruz

Junior Middleweight (Super Welterweight)

Date	Winner	Loser	Result	Title	Site
Feb 9	Terry Norris	Ray Leonard	Dec 12	WBC	New York
Feb 23	Gilbert Dele	Carlos Elliot	KO 7	WBA	Point a Pitre, Guadaloupe
Mar 16	Gianfranco Rosi	Ron Amundsen	Dec 12	IBF	St Vincent, Italy
May 4	Gilbert Dele	Jun Sok Hwang	Dec 12	WBA	Paris
June 1	Terry Norris	Donald Curry	KO 8	WBC	Palm Springs, CA
July 13	Gianfranco Rosi	Glenn Wolfe	Dec 12	IBF	Avezzano, Italy
Aug 17	Terry Norris	Brett Lally	KO 1	WBC	San Diego

Welterweight

Date	Winner	Loser	Result	Title	Site
Jan 19	Meldrick Taylor	Aaron Davis	Dec 12	WBA	Atlantic City
Mar 18	Simon Brown	Maurice Blocker	TKO 10	WBC, IBF*	Las Vegas
June 1	Meldrick Taylor	Luis Garcia	Split 12	WBA	Palm Springs, CA

*Brown forfeited IBF title in 1991.

Junior Welterweight

Date	Winner	Loser	Result	Title	Site
Dec 1	Loreto Garza	Vinny Pazienz	Disq 11	WBA	Sacramento
Dec 8	Julio Cesar Chavez	Ahn Kyung-Duk	TKO 3	WBC, IBF	Atlantic City
Mar 18	Julio Cesar Chavez	John Duplessis	TKO 4	WBC, IBF*	Las Vegas
June 14	Edwin Rosario	Loreto Garza	KO 3	WBA	Sacramento

*Chavez forfeited IBF title in 1991.

Lightweight

Date	Winner	Loser	Result	Title	Site
Feb 23	Pernell Whitaker	Anthony Jones	Dec 12	WBA, WBC, IBF	Las Vegas
July 27	Pernell Whitaker	Poli Diaz	Dec 12	WBA, WBC, IBF	Norfolk, VA

Junior Lightweight (Super Featherweight)

Date	Winner	Loser	Result	Title	Site
June 28	Azumah Nelson	Jeff Fenech	Draw 12	WBC	Las Vegas
June 28	Joey Gamache	Jerry Ngobeni	TKO 10	WBA	Lewiston, ME
July 12	Tony Lopez	Lupe Gutierrez	TKO 6	IBF	Stateline, NV
Sep 13	Brian Mitchell	Tony Lopez	Dec 12	IBF	Sacramento

Note: Tony Lopez and Brian Mitchell fought to a 12-round draw in Sacramento on March 15. Lopez retained the IBF title, and Mitchell retained the WBA title, which he later forfeited.

Featherweight

Date	Winner	Loser	Result	Title	Site
Mar 30	Yong Kyun Park	Antonio Esparragoza	Dec 12	WBA	Kwangju, South Korea
Apr 11	Marcos Villasana	Rafael Zuniga	KO 6	WBC	Mexico City
June 3	Troy Dorsey	Alfred Rangel	KO 1	IBF	Las Vegas
June 15	Yong Kyun Park	Masuaki Takeda	KO 6	WBA	Taegu, South Korea
Aug 10	Manuel Medina	Troy Dorsey	Dec 12	IBF	Inglewood, CA
Aug 15	Marcos Villasana	Ricardo Cepeda	Dec 12	WBC	Marbella, Spain

Junior Featherweight (Super Bantamweight)

Date	Winner	Loser	Result	Title	Site
Nov 5	Pedro Decima	Paul Banke	TKO 4	WBC	Inglewood, CA
Jan 20	Luis Mendoza	Noree Jockygym	KO 8	WBA	Bangkok
Feb 3	Kiyoshi Hatanaka	Pedro Decima	TKO 8	WBC	Nagoya, Japan
Feb 27	Welcome Ncita	Sugar Baby Rojas	Dec 12	IBF	San Antonio
Apr 22	Luis Mendoza	Carlos Uribe	Dec 12	WBA	Cartagena
May 30	Luis Mendoza	Joao Cardosa	KO 7	WBA	Madrid
June 14	Daniel Zaragoza	Kiyoshi Hatanaka	Dec 12	WBC	Nagoya, Japan
June 15	Welcome Ncita	Hurley Snead	Dec 12	IBF	San Antonio

Bantamweight

Date	Winner	Loser	Result	Title	Site
Nov 29	Luisito Espinosa	Thanomsak Sithbaobey	Dec 12	WBA	Bangkok
Dec 17	Raul Perez	Candelario Carmona	KO 8	WBC	Tijuana
Feb 25	Greg Richardson	Raul Perez	Dec 12	WBC	Inglewood, CA
Apr 5	Orlando Canizales	Billy Hardy	KO 8	IBF	Laredo, TX
May 20	Greg Richardson	Victor Rabanales	Split 12	WBC	Inglewood, CA
Sep 19	Joichiro Tatsuyoshi	Greg Richardson	TKO 10	WBC	Osaka, Japan

Junior Bantamweight (Super Flyweight)

Date	Winner	Loser	Result	Title	Site
Dec 9	Khaosai Galaxy	Ernesto Ford	TKO 6	WBA	Bangkok
Jan 26	Robert Quiroga	Vincenzo Belcastro	Dec 12	IBF	Capo d'Orlando, Italy
Apr 6	Khaosai Galaxy	Jae Suk Park	KO 5	WBA	Bangkok
June 15	Robert Quiroga	Akeem Anifowoshe	Dec 12	IBF	San Antonio
July 20	Sung-Kil Moon	Ernesto Ford	KO 5	WBC	Seoul
July 20	Khaosai Galaxy	David Grimm	TKO 5	WBA	Bangkok

Flyweight

Date	Winner	Loser	Result	Title	Site
Nov 24	Sot Chitalada	Chang Jung-Koo	Dec 12	WBC	Seoul
Dec 6	Leopard Tamakura	Jesus Rojas	Draw 12	WBA	Aomori, Japan
Feb 15	Muangchai Kittikasem	Sot Chitalada	TKO 6	WBC	Ayuthaya, Thailand
Mar 14	Elvis Álvarez	Leopard Tamakuma	Dec 12	WBA	Tokyo
May 11	Dave McAuley	Pedro Feliciano	Dec 12	IBF	Belfast
May 18	Muangchai Kittikasem	Jung Koo Chang	KO 12	WBC	Seoul
June 1	Yong Kang Kim	Elvis Alvarez	Dec 12	WBA	Seoul
Sep 7	Dave McAuley	Jake Matlala	KO 10	IBF	Belfast

Junior Flyweight (Light Flyweight)

Date	Winner	Loser	Result	Title	Site
Nov 10	Yuh Myung Woo	Leo Gamez	Dec 12	WBA	Pohang, South Korea
Dec 8	Michael Carbajal	Leon Salazar	KO 4	IBF	Scottsdale, AZ
Dec 19	Humberto Gonzales	Rolando Pascua	KO 6	WBC	Inglewood, CA
Feb 17	Michael Carbajal	Macario Santos	KO 2	IBF	Las Vegas
Mar 17	Michael Carbajal	Javier Varguez	Dec 12	IBF	Las Vegas
Apr 28	Myung Woo Yuh	Kajkong Danphoothai	KO 10	WBA	Masan, South Korea
May 10	Michael Carbajal	Hector Luis Patri	Dec 12	IBF	Davenport, IA
June 3	Humberto Gonzales	Melchor Cob Castro	Dec 12	WBC	Las Vegas

Strawweight (Mini-Flyweight)

Date	Winner	Loser	Result	Title	Site
Nov 3	Kim Bong-Jim	Silveri Barcenas	Dec 12	WBA	Bangkok
Dec 20	Phalan Lukmingkwan	Domingo Lucas	Draw 12	IBF	Bangkok
Feb 2	Hi Yong Choi	Kim Bong-Jim	Dec 12	WBA	Pusan, South Korea
May 19	Ricardo Lopez	Kimio Hirano	KO 8	WBC	Shizuoka, Japan
June 15	Hi Yong Choi	Sugar Ray Mike	Dec 12	WBA	Shizuoka, Japan
July 2	Phalan Lukmingkwan	Abdi Ponan	Dec 12	IBF	Bangkok

Sugar Ray Leonard's Professional Career in the Ring

Date	Opponent	Result	Title	Site
1977.......Feb 5	Luis Vega	Dec 6		Baltimore
1977.......May 14	Willie Rodriguez	Dec 6		Baltimore
1977.......June 10	Vinnie DeBarros	TKO 3		Hartford
1977.......Sep 24	Frank Santore	KO 5		Baltimore
1977.......Nov 5	Augustin Estrada	KO 5		Las Vegas
1977.......Dec 17	Hector Diaz	KO 2		Washington, DC
1978.......Feb 4	Rocky Ramon	Dec 8		Baltimore
1978.......Mar 1	Art McKnight	TKO 7		Dayton, OH
1978.......Mar 19	Javier Muniz	KO 1		New Haven
1978.......Apr 13	Bobby Haymon	TKO 3		Landover, MD
1978.......May 13	Randy Milton	TKO 8		Utica
1978.......June 3	Rafael Rodriquez	Dec 10		Baltimore
1978.......July 18	Dick Eckland	Dec 10		Boston
1978.......Sep 9	Floyd Mayweather	TKO 10		Providence
1978.......Oct 6	Randy Shields	Dec 10		Baltimore
1978.......Nov 3	Bernardo Prada	Dec 10		Portland, ME
1978.......Dec 9	Armando Muniz	TKO 6		Springfield, MA
1979.......Jan 11	Johnny Gant	TKO 8		Landover, MD
1979.......Feb 11	Fernand Marcotte	TKO 8		Miami Beach
1979.......Mar 24	Daniel Gonzales	KO 1		Tucson
1979.......Apr 21	Adolfo Viruet	Dec 10		Las Vegas
1979.......May 20	Marcos Geraldo	Dec 10		New Orleans
1979.......June 24	Tony Chiaverini	TKO 4		Las Vegas
1979.......Aug 12	Pete Ranzany	TKO 4	NABF Welterweight	Las Vegas
1979.......Sep 28	Andy Price	KO 1	NABF Welterweight	Las Vegas
1979.......Nov 30	Wilfred Benitez	TKO 15	WBC Welterweight	Las Vegas
1980.......Mar 31	Dave (Boy) Green	KO 4	WBC Welterweight	Landover, MD
1980.......June 20	Roberto Duran	LDec 15		Montreal
1980.......Nov 25	Roberto Duran	TKO 8	WBC Welterweight	New Orleans
1981.......Mar 28	Larry Bonds	TKO 10	WBC Welterweight	Syracuse
1981.......June 25	Ayub Kalule	KO 9	WBA Jr Middleweight	Houston
1981.......Sep 26	Thomas Hearns	TKO 14	Welterweight*	Las Vegas
1982.......Feb 15	Bruce Finch	TKO 3	Welterweight*	Reno
1984.......May 11	Kevin Howard	TKO 9		Worcester
1987.......Apr 6	Marvin Hagler	Dec 12	WBC Middleweight	Las Vegas
1988.......Nov 7	Don Lalonde	TKO 9	WBC Super Middleweight	Las Vegas
1989.......June 12	Thomas Hearns	Draw 12	WBC Super Middleweight	Las Vegas
1989.......Dec 7	Roberto Duran	Dec 12	WBC Super Middleweight	Las Vegas
1991.......Feb 9	Terry Norris	LDec 12		New York

*Undisputed world title.

Note: NABF = North American Boxing Federation   WBA = World Boxing Association   WBC = World Boxing Council
An "L" before the result = a loss.

World Champions

Sanctioning bodies include the National Boxing Association (NBA), the New York State Athletic Commission (NY), the World Boxing Association (WBA), the World Boxing Council (WBC), and the International Boxing Federation (IBF).

Heavyweights
(Weight: Unlimited)

Champion	Reign
John L. Sullivan	1885-92
James J. Corbett	1892-97
Bob Fitzsimmons	1897-99
James J. Jeffries	1899-1905†
Marvin Hart	1905-06
Tommy Burns	1906-08
Jack Johnson	1908-15
Jess Willard	1915-19
Jack Dempsey	1919-26
Gene Tunney	1926-28
Max Schmeling	1930-32
Jack Sharkey	1932-33
Primo Carnera	1933-34
Max Baer	1934-35
James J. Braddock	1935-37
Joe Louis	1937-49†
Ezzard Charles	1949-51
Jersey Joe Walcott	1951-52

*Champion not generally recognized.
†Champion retired or relinquished title.

Champion	Reign
Rocky Marciano	1952-56†
Floyd Patterson	1956-59
Ingemar Johansson	1959-60
Floyd Patterson	1960-62
Sonny Liston	1962-64
Muhammad Ali (Cassius Clay)	1964-70
Ernie Terrell* WBA	1965-67
Joe Frazier* NY	1968-70
Jimmy Ellis* WBA	1968-70
Joe Frazier	1970-73
George Foreman	1973-74
Muhammad Ali	1974-78
Leon Spinks	1978
Ken Norton* WBC	1978
Larry Holmes* WBC	1978-80
Muhammad Ali	1978-79†
John Tate* WBA	1979-80

Champion	Reign
Mike Weaver* WBA	1980-82
Larry Holmes	1980-85
Michael Dokes* WBA	1982-83
Gerrie Coetzee* WBA	1983-84
Tim Witherspoon* WBC	1984
Pinklon Thomas* WBC	1984-86
Greg Page* WBA	1984-85
Michael Spinks	1985-87
Tim Witherspoon* WBA	1986
Trevor Berbick* WBC	1986
Mike Tyson* WBC	1986-87
James Bonecrusher Smith* WBA	1986-87
Tony Tucker* IBF	1987
Mike Tyson	1987-90
Buster Douglas	1990
Evander Holyfield	1990-

Cruiserweights
(Weight Limit: 190 pounds)

Champion	Reign
Marvin Camel* WBC	1980
Carlos De Leon* WBC	1980-82
Ossie Ocasio* WBA	1982-84
S.T. Gordon* WBC	1982-83
Carlos De Leon* WBC	1983-85
Marvin Camel* IBF	1983-84
Lee Roy Murphy* IBF	1984-86
Piet Crous* WBA	1984-85
Alfonso Ratliff* WBC	1985
Dwight Braxton* WBA	1985-86

*Champion not generally recognized.
†Champion retired or relinquished title.
Note: Division called Junior Heavyweights by the WBA.

Champion	Reign
Bernard Benton* WBC	1985-86
Carlos De Leon* WBC	1986-88
Evander Holyfield* WBA	1986-88
Ricky Parkey* IBF	1986-87
Evander Holyfield* WBA/IBF	1987-88
Evander Holyfield WBA/IBF/WBC	1988†

Champion	Reign
Toufik Belbouli* WBA	1989
Robert Daniels* WBA	1989-91
Carlos De Leon* WBC	1989-90
Glenn McCrory* IBF	1989-90
Jeff Lampkin* IBF	1990-
Massimiliano Duran* WBC	1990-91
Bobby Czyz* WBA	1991-
Anaclet Wamba* WBC	1991-

Light Heavyweights
(Weight Limit: 175 pounds)

Champion	Reign
Jack Root	1903
George Gardner	1903
Bob Fitzsimmons	1903-05
Philadelphia Jack O'Brien	1905-12†
Jack Dillon	1914-16
Battling Levinsky	1916-20
Georges Carpentier	1920-22
Battling Siki	1922-23
Mike McTigue	1923-25
Paul Berlenbach	1925-26
Jack Delaney	1926-27†
Jimmy Slattery* NBA	1927

Champion	Reign
Tommy Loughran	1927-29
Maxie Rosenbloom	1930-34
George Nichols* NBA	1932
Bob Godwin* NBA	1933
Bob Olin	1934-35
John Henry Lewis	1935-38
Melio Bettina	1939
Billy Conn	1939-40†
Anton Christoforidis	1941
Gus Lesnevich	1941-48
Freddie Mills	1948-50
Joey Maxim	1950-52
Archie Moore	1952-62†

Champion	Reign
Harold Johnson* NBA	1961
Harold Johnson	1962-63
Willie Pastrano	1963-65
Jose Torres	1965-66
Dick Tiger	1966-68
Bob Foster	1968-74†
Vicente Rondon* WBA	1971-72
John Conteh* WBC	1974-77
Victor Galindez* WBA	1974-78
Miguel A. Cuello* WBC	1977-78
Mate Parlov* WBC	1978
Mike Rossman* WBA	1978-79
Marvin Johnson* WBC	1978-79

Light Heavyweights (*Cont.*)

Champion	Reign
Matthew Saad Muhammad* WBC	1979-81
Marvin Johnson* WBA	1979-80
Eddie Mustapha Muhammad* WBA	1980-81
Michael Spinks* WBA	1981-83
Dwight Muhammad Qawi* WBC	1981-83
Michael Spinks	1983-85†

Champion	Reign
J. B. Williamson* WBC	1985-86
Slobodan Kacar* IBF	1985-86
Marvin Johnson* WBA	1986-87
Dennis Andries* WBC	1986-87
Bobby Czyz* IBF	1986-87
Leslie Stewart* WBA	1987
Virgil Hill* WBA	1987-
Prince Charles Williams* IBF	1987-

Champion	Reign
Thomas Hearns* WBC	1987†
Donny Lalonde* WBC	1987-88
Sugar Ray Leonard* WBC	1988
Dennis Andries* WBC	1989
Jeff Harding* WBC	1989-90
Dennis Andries* WBC	1990-91
Thomas Hearns* WBA	1991-
Jeff Harding* WBC	1991

*Champion not generally recognized.
†Champion retired or relinquished title.

Super Middleweights
(Weight Limit: 168 pounds)

Champion	Reign
Murray Sutherland* IBF	1984
Chong-Pal Park* IBF	1984-87
Chong-Pal Park* WBA	1987-88
Graciano Rocchigiani* IBF	1988-89

Champion	Reign
Fulgencio Obelmejias* WBA	1988-89
Sugar Ray Leonard* WBC	1988-90†
In-Chul Baek* WBA	1989-90

Champion	Reign
Lindell Holmes* IBF	1990-91
Christophe Tiozzo* WBA	1990-91
Mauro Galvano* WBC	1990-
Victor Cordova* WBA	1991-
Darrin Van Horn* IBF	1991-

*Champion not generally recognized.
†Champion retired or relinquished title.

Middleweights
(Weight Limit: 160 pounds)

Champion	Reign
Jack Dempsey	1884-91
Bob Fitzsimmons	1891-97
Kid McCoy	1897-98
Tommy Ryan	1898-1907
Stanley Ketchel	1908
Billy Papke	1908
Stanley Ketchel	1908-10
Frank Klaus	1913
George Chip	1913-14
Al McCoy	1914-17
Mike O'Dowd	1917-20
Johnny Wilson	1920-23
Harry Greb	1923-26
Tiger Flowers	1926
Mickey Walker	1926-31†
Gorilla Jones	1931-32
Marcel Thil	1932-37
Fred Apostoli	1937-39
Al Hostak* NBA	1938
Solly Krieger* NBA	1938-39
Al Hostak* NBA	1939-40
Ceferino Garcia	1939-40
Ken Overlin	1940-41

Champion	Reign
Tony Zale* NBA	1940-41
Billy Soose	1941
Tony Zale	1941-47
Rocky Graziano	1947-48
Tony Zale	1948
Marcel Cerdan	1948-49
Jake La Motta	1949-51
Sugar Ray Robinson	1951
Randy Turpin	1951
Sugar Ray Robinson	1951-52
Bobo Olson	1953-55
Sugar Ray Robinson	1955-57
Gene Fullmer	1957
Sugar Ray Robinson	1957
Carmen Basilio	1957-58
Sugar Ray Robinson	1958-60
Gene Fullmer* NBA	1959-62
Paul Pender	1960-61
Terry Downes	1961-62
Paul Pender	1962-63
Dick Tiger* WBA	1962-63
Dick Tiger	1963
Joey Giardello	1963-65

Champion	Reign
Dick Tiger	1965-66
Emile Griffith	1966-67
Nino Benvenuti	1967
Emile Griffith	1967-68
Nino Benvenuti	1968-70
Carlos Monzon	1970-77†
Rodrigo Valdez* WBC	1974-76
Rodrigo Valdez	1977-78
Hugo Corro	1978-79
Vito Antuofermo	1979-80
Alan Minter	1980
Marvin Hagler	1980-87
Sugar Ray Leonard	1987
Frank Tate* IBF	1987-88
Sumbu Kalambay* WBA	1987-89
Thomas Hearns* WBC	1987-88
Iran Barkley* WBC	1988-89
Michael Nunn* IBF	1988-91
Roberto Duran* WBC	1989-90
Mike McCallum* WBA	1989-
Julian Jackson* WBC	1990-
James Toney* IBF	1991-

*Champion not generally recognized.
†Champion retired or relinquished title.

THEY SAID IT

Wali Muhammad, cruiserweight, asked if he bit James Salerno during their Feb. 4, 1991 fight: "No, I'm a vegetarian."

Junior Middleweights
(Weight Limit: 154 pounds)

Champion	Reign
Emile Griffith (EBU)	1962-63
Dennis Moyer	1962-63
Ralph Dupas	1963
Sandro Mazzinghi	1963-65
Nino Benvenuti	1965-66
Ki-Soo Kim	1966-68
Sandro Mazzinghi	1968
Freddie Little	1969-70
Carmelo Bossi	1970-71
Koichi Wajima	1971-74
Oscar Albarado	1974-75
Koichi Wajima	1975
Miguel de Oliveira* WBC	1975-76
Jae-Do Yuh	1975-76
Elisha Obed* WBC	1975-76
Koichi Wajima	1976

Champion	Reign
Jose Duran	1976
Eckhard Dagge* WBC	1976-77
Miguel Angel Castellini	1976-77
Eddie Gazo	1977-78
Rocky Mattioli* WBC	1977-79
Masashi Kudo	1978-79
Maurice Hope* WBC	1979-81
Ayub Kalule	1979-81
Wilfred Benitez* WBC	1981-82
Sugar Ray Leonard	1981-82
Tadashi Mihara* WBA	1981-82
Davey Moore* WBA	1982-83
Thomas Hearns* WBC	1982-84
Roberto Duran* WBA	1983-84
Mark Medal* IBF	1984
Thomas Hearns	1984-86
Mike McCallum* WBA	1984-87

Champion	Reign
Carlos Santos* IBF	1984-86
Buster Drayton* IBF	1986-87
Duane Thomas* WBC	1986-87
Matthew Hilton* IBF	1987-88
Lupe Aquino* WBC	1987
Gianfranco Rosi* WBC	1987-88
Julian Jackson* WBA	1987-90
Donald Curry* WBC	1988-89
Robert Hines* IBF	1988-89
Darrin Van Horn* IBF	1989
Rene Jacquot* WBC	1989
John Mugabi* WBC	1989-90
Gianfranco Rosi* IBF	1989-
Terry Norris* WBC	1990-
Gilbert Dele* WBA	1991-

*Champion not generally recognized.
Note: Division called Super Welterweight by the WBC.

Welterweights
(Weight Limit: 147 pounds)

Champion	Reign
Paddy Duffy	1888-90
Mysterious Billy Smith	1892-94
Tommy Ryan	1894-98
Mysterious Billy Smith	1898-1900
Rube Ferns	1900
Matty Matthews	1900-01
Rube Ferns	1901
Joe Walcott	1901-04
The Dixie Kid	1904-05
Honey Mellody	1906-07
Twin Sullivan	1907-08
Jimmy Gardner	1908
Jimmy Clabby	1910-11
Waldemar Holberg	1914
Tom McCormick	1914
Matt Wells	1914-15
Mike Glover	1915
Jack Britton	1915
Ted "Kid" Lewis	1915-16
Jack Britton	1916-17
Ted "Kid" Lewis	1917-19
Jack Britton	1919-22
Mickey Walker	1922-26
Pete Latzo	1926-27
Joe Dundee	1927-29
Jackie Fields	1929-30
Young Jack Thompson	1930
Tommy Freeman	1930-31
Young Jack Thompson	1931

Champion	Reign
Lou Brouillard	1931-32
Jackie Fields	1932-33
Young Corbett III	1933
Jimmy McLarnin	1933-34
Barney Ross	1934
Jimmy McLarnin	1934-35
Barney Ross	1935-38
Henry Armstrong	1938-40
Fritzie Zivic	1940-41
Red Cochrane	1941-46
Marty Servo	1946
Sugar Ray Robinson	1946-51†
Johnny Bratton	1951
Kid Gavilan	1951-54
Johnny Saxton	1954-55
Tony DeMarco	1955
Carmen Basilio	1955-56
Johnny Saxton	1956
Carmen Basilio	1956-57
Virgil Akins	1958
Don Jordan	1958-60
Kid Paret	1960-61
Emile Griffith	1961
Kid Paret	1961-62
Emile Griffith	1962-63
Luis Rodriguez	1963
Emile Griffith	1963-66
Curtis Cokes	1966-69
Jose Napoles	1969-70
Billy Backus	1970-71

Champion	Reign
Jose Napoles	1971-75
Hedgemon Lewis* NY	1972-73
Angel Espada* WBA	1975-76
John H. Stracey	1975-76
Carlos Palomino	1976-79
Pipino Cuevas* WBA	1976-80
Wilfredo Benitez	1979
Sugar Ray Leonard	1979-80
Roberto Duran	1980
Thomas Hearns* WBA	1980-81
Sugar Ray Leonard	1980-82
Donald Curry* WBA	1983-85
Milton McCrory* WBC	1983-85
Donald Curry	1985-86
Lloyd Honeyghan	1986-87
Jorge Vaca WBC	1987-88
Lloyd Honeyghan WBC	1988-89
Mark Breland* WBA	1987
Marlon Starling* WBA	1987-88
Tomas Molinares* WBA	1988-89
Simon Brown* IBF	1988-
Mark Breland* WBA	1989-90
Marlon Starling* WBC	1989-90
Aaron Davis* WBA	1990-91
Maurice Blocker* WBC	1990-91
Meldrick Taylor* WBA	1991-
Simon Brown* WBC, IBF	1991-

*Champion not generally recognized.
†Champion retired or relinquished title.

Well, He Did Get KO'd	A Massachusetts newspaper, *The Fitchburg-Leominster Sentinel & Enterprise,* ran this correction in the fall of 1990: "Due to a typing error, Gov. [Michael] Dukakis was incorrectly identified in the third paragraph as Mike Tyson."

Junior Welterweights
(Weight Limit: 140 pounds)

Champion	Reign
Pinkey Mitchell	1922-25
Red Herring	1925
Mushy Callahan	1926-30
Jack (Kid) Berg	1930-31
Tony Canzoneri	1931-32
Johnny Jadick	1932-33
Sammy Fuller*	1932-33
Battling Shaw	1933
Tony Canzoneri	1933
Barney Ross	1933-35
Tippy Larkin	1946
Carlos Ortiz	1959-60
Duilio Loi	1960-62
Eddie Perkins	1962
Duilio Loi	1962-63
Roberto Cruz* WBA	1963
Eddie Perkins	1963-65
Carlos Hernandez	1965-66
Sandro Lopopolo	1966-67
Paul Fujii	1967-68
Nicolino Loche	1968-72
Pedro Adigue* WBC	1968-70
Bruno Arcari* WBC	1970-74

Champion	Reign
Alfonso Frazer	1972
Antonio Cervantes	1972-76
Perico Fernandez* WBC	1974-75
Saensak Muangsurin* WBC	1975-76
Wilfred Benitez	1976-79
Miguel Velasquez* WBC	1976
Saensak Muangsurin* WBC	1976-78
Antonio Cervantes* WBA	1977-80
Sang-Hyun Kim* WBC	1978-80
Saoul Mamby* WBC	1980-82
Aaron Pryor* WBA	1980-83
Leroy Haley* WBC	1982-83
Aaron Pryor* IBF	1983-85
Bruce Curry* WBC	1983-84
Johnny Bumphus WBA	1984
Bill Costello* WBC	1984-
Gene Hatcher* WBA	1984-85

Champion	Reign
Ubaldo Sacco* WBA	1985-86
Lonnie Smith* WBC	1985-86
Patrizio Oliva* WBA	1986-87
Gary Hinton* IBF	1986
Rene Arredondo* WBC	1986
Tsuyoshi Hamada* WBC	1986-87
Joe Louis Manley* IBF	1986-87
Terry Marsh* IBF	1987
Juan Martin Coggi* WBA	1987-90
Rene Arredondo* WBC	1987
Roger Mayweather* WBC	1987-89
James McGirt* IBF	1988
Meldrick Taylor* IBF	1988-90
Julio Cesar Chavez* WBC	1989-
Julio Cesar Chavez* WBC/IBF	1990-
Loreto Garza* WBA	1990-91
Juan Coggs* WBA	1991
Edwin Rosario* WBA	1991-

*Champion not generally recognized.
Note: Division called Super Lightweight by the WBC.

Lightweights
(Weight Limit: 135 pounds)

Champion	Reign
Jack McAuliffe	1886-94
Kid Lavigne	1896-99
Frank Erne	1899-1902
Joe Gans	1902-04
Jimmy Britt	1904-05
Battling Nelson	1905-06
Joe Gans	1906-08
Battling Nelson	1908-10
Ad Wolgast	1910-12
Willie Ritchie	1912-14
Freddie Welsh	1915-17
Benny Leonard	1917-25†
Jimmy Goodrich	1925
Rocky Kansas	1925-26
Sammy Mandell	1926-30
Al Singer	1930
Tony Canzoneri	1930-33
Barney Ross	1933-35†
Tony Canzoneri	1935-36
Lou Ambers	1936-38
Henry Armstrong	1938-39
Lou Ambers	1939-40
Sammy Angott* NBA	1940-41
Lew Jenkins	1940-41
Sammy Angott	1941-42†
Beau Jack* NY	1942-43
Bob Montgomery* NY	1943
Sammy Angott* NBA	1943-44
Beau Jack* NY	1943-44

Champion	Reign
Bob Montgomery* NY	1944-47
Juan Zurita* NBA	1944-45
Ike Williams	1947-51
James Carter	1951-52
Lauro Salas	1952
James Carter	1952-54
Paddy DeMarco	1954
James Carter	1954-55
Wallace Smith	1955-56
Joe Brown	1956-62
Carlos Ortiz	1962-65
Ismael Laguna	1965
Carlos Ortiz	1965-68
Carlos Teo Cruz	1968-69
Mando Ramos	1969-70
Ismael Laguna	1970
Ken Buchanan	1970-72
Roberto Duran	1972-79†
Chango Carmona* WBC	1972
Rodolfo Gonzalez* WBC	1972-74
Ishimatsu Suzuki* WBC	1974-76
Estaban DeJesus* WBC	1976-78
Jim Watt* WBC	1979-81
Ernesto Espana* WBA	1979-80
Hilmer Kenty* WBA	1980-81
Sean O'Grady* WBA	1981

Champion	Reign
Claude Noel* WBA	1981
Alexis Arguello* WBC	1981-82
Arturo Frias* WBA	1981-82
Ray Mancini* WBA	1982-84
Alexis Arguello	1982-83
Edwin Rosario* WBC	1983-84
Choo Choo Brown* IBF	1984
Livingstone Bramble* WBA	1984-86
Jose Luis Ramirez* WBC	1984-85
Harry Arroyo* IBF	1984-85
Jimmy Paul* IBF	1985-86
Hector Camacho* WBC	1985-86
Greg Haugen* IBF	1986-87
Edwin Rosario* WBA	1986-87
Julio Cesar Chavez* WBA	1987-88
Jose Luis Ramirez* WBC	1987-88
Julio Cesar Chavez	1988-89
Vinny Pazienza* IBF	1987-88
Greg Haugen* IBF	1988-89
Pernell Whitaker* WBC, IBF	1989-90
Edwin Rosario* WBA	1989-90
Juan Nazario* WBA	1990
Pernell Whitaker WBA, WBC, IBF	1990-

*Champion not generally recognized.
†Champion retired or relinquished title.

Junior Lightweights
(Weight Limit: 130 pounds)

Champion	Reign	Champion	Reign	Champion	Reign
Johnny Dundee	1921-23	Ben Villaflor	1972-73	Roger Mayweather	1983-84
Jack Bernstein	1923	Kuniaki Shibata	1973	Hector Camacho* WBC	1983-84
Johnny Dundee	1923-24	Ben Villaflor	1973-76	Rocky Lockridge	1984-85
Steve (Kid) Sullivan	1924-25	Kuniaki Shibata* WBC	1974-75	Hwan-Kil Yuh* IBF	1984-85
Mike Ballerino	1925	Alfredo Escalera* WBC	1975-78	Julio Cesar Chavez*	
Tod Morgan	1925-29	Samuel Serrano	1976-80	WBC	1984-87
Benny Bass	1929-31	Alexis Arguello* WBC	1978-80	Lester Ellis* IBF	1985-
Kid Chocolate	1931-33	Yasutsune Uehara	1980-81	Wilfredo Gomez	1985-86
Frankie Klick	1933-34	Rafael (Bazooka)		Barry Michael* IBF	1985-87
Sandy Saddler	1949-50	Limon* WBC	1980-81	Alfredo Layne* WBA	1986
Harold Gomes	1959-60	Cornelius Boza-		Brian Mitchell* WBA	1986-91
Gabriel (Flash) Elorde	1960-67	Edwards* WBC	1981	Rocky Lockridge* IBF	1987-88
Yoshiaki Numata	1967	Samuel Serrano	1981-83	Azumah Nelson* WBC	1988-
Hiroshi Kobayashi	1967-71	Rolando Navarrete*		Tony Lopez* IBF	1988-89
Rene Barrientos* WBC	1969-70	WBC	1981-82	Juan Molina* IBF	1989-90
Yoshiaki Numata* WBC	1970-71	Rafael (Bazooka)		Tony Lopez* IBF	1990-91
Alfredo Marcano	1971-72	Limon* WBC	1982	Joey Gamache, WBA	1991-
Richardo Arredondo*		Bobby Chacon* WBC	1982-83	Brian Mitchell* IBF	1991-
WBC	1971-74				

*Champion not generally recognized.

Note: Division called Super Featherweight by the WBC.

Featherweights
(Weight Limit: 126 pounds)

Champion	Reign	Champion	Reign	Champion	Reign
Torpedo Billy Murphy	1890	Leo Rodak* NBA	1938-39	Ernesto Marcel* WBA	1972-74
Young Griffo	1890-92	Joey Archibald	1939-40	Jose Legra WBC	1972-73
George Dixon	1892-97	Petey Scalzo* NBA	1940-41	Eder Jofre WBC	1973-74
Solly Smith	1897-98	Harry Jeffra	1940-41	Ruben Olivares* WBA	1974
Dave Sullivan	1898	Joey Archibald	1941	Bobby Chacon* WBC	1974-75
George Dixon	1898-1900	Richie Lamos* NBA	1941	Alexis Arguello WBA	1974-76
Terry McGovern	1900-01	Chalky Wright	1941-42	Ruben Olivares* WBC	1975
Young Corbett II	1901-04	Jackie Wilson* NBA	1941-43	Poison Kotey* WBC	1975-76
Jimmy Britt	1904	Willie Pep	1942-48	Danny Lopez WBC	1976-80
Brooklyn Tommy		Jackie Callura* NBA	1943	Rafael Ortega* WBA	1977
Sullivan	1904-05	Phil Terranova* NBA	1943-44	Cecilio Lastra* WBA	1977-78
Abe Attell	1906-12	Sal Bartolo* NBA	1944-46	Eusebio Pedroza* WBA	1978-85
Johnny Kilbane	1912-23	Sandy Saddler	1948-49	Salvador Sanchez	
Eugene Criqui	1923	Willie Pep	1949-50	WBC	1980-82
Johnny Dundee	1923-24	Sandy Saddler	1950-57†	Juan LaPorte* WBC	1982-84
"Kid" Kaplan	1925-26	Kid Bassey	1957-59	Wilfredo Gomez* WBC	1984
Benny Bass	1927-28	Davey Moore	1959-63	Min-Keun Oh* IBF	1984-85
Tony Canzoneri	1928	Sugar Ramos	1963-64	Azumah Nelson* WBC	1984-88
Andre Routis	1928-29	Vicente Saldivar	1964-67†	Barry McGuigan* WBA	1985-86
Battling Battalino	1929-32	Paul Rojas* WBA	1968	Ki Young Chung* IBF	1985-86
Tommy Paul* NBA	1932-33	Jose Legra* WBC	1968-69	Steve Cruz* WBA	1986-87
Kid Chocolate* NY	1932-33	Shozo Saijyo* WBA	1968-71	Antonio Rivera* IBF	1986-88
Freddie Miller* NBA	1933-36	Johnny Famechon*		Antonio Esparragoza*	
Mike Beloise* NY	1936-37	WBC	1969-70	WBA	1987-
Petey Sarron* NBA	1936-37	Vicente Saldivar WBC	1970	Calvin Grove* IBF	1988
Maurice Holtzer	1937-38	Kuniaki Shibata WBC	1970-72	Jorge Paez* IBF	1988-91
Henry Armstrong	1937-38	Antonio Gomez* WBA	1971-72	Jeff Fenech* WBC	1988-90†
Joey Archibald* NY	1938-39	Clemente Sanchez		Marcos Villasana* WBC	1990
		WBC	1972	Troy Dorsey* IBF	1991-

*Champion not generally recognized.

†Champion retired or relinquished title.

THEY SAID IT

Chris Dundee, fight promoter: "I'd love to be a procrastinator, but I never seem to get around to it." (1973)

Junior Featherweights
(Weight Limit: 122 pounds)

Champion	Reign
Jack (Kid) Wolfe*	1922-23
Carl Duane*	1923-24
Rigoberto Riasco* WBC	1976
Royal Kobayashi* WBC	1976
Dong-Kyun Yum* WBC	1976-77
Wilfredo Gomez* WBC	1977-83
Soo-Hwan Hong* WBC	1977-78
Ricardo Cardona* WBA	1978-80
Leo Randolph* WBA	1980
Sergio Palma* WBA	1980-82
Leonardo Cruz* WBA	1982-84
Jaime Garza* WBC	1983
Bobby Berna* IBF	1983-84
Loris Stecca* WBA	1984

*Champion not generally recognized.

Champion	Reign
Seung-Il Suh* IBF	1984-85
Victor Callejas* WBA	1984-86
Juan (Kid) Meza* WBC	1984-85
Ji-Won Kim* IBF	1985-86
Lupe Pintor* WBC	1985-86
Samart Payakaroon* WBC	1986-87
Seung-Hoon Lee* IBF	1987-88
Louie Espinoza* WBA	1987
Jeff Fenech* WBC	1987
Julio Gervacio* WBA	1987-88
Daniel Zaragoza* WBC	1988-90
Jose Sanabria* IBF	1988-89

Note: Division called Super Bantamweight by the WBC.

Champion	Reign
Bernardo Pinango* WBA	1988
Juan Jose Estrada* WBA	1988-89
Fabrice Benichou* IBF	1989-90
Jesus Salud* WBA	1989-90
Welcome Ncita* IBF	1990-
Paul Banke* WBC	1990
Luis Mendoza* WBA	1990-
Pedro Decima* WBC	1990-91
Kiyoshi Hatanaka* WBC	1991
Daniel Zaragoza* WBC	1991-

Bantamweights
(Weight Limit: 118 pounds)

Champion	Reign
Spider Kelly	1887
Hughey Boyle	1887-88
Spider Kelly	1889
Chappie Moran	1889-90
George Dixon	1890-91
Pedlar Palmer*	1895-99
Terry McGovern	1899-1900
Harry Harris	1901-2
Harry Forbes	1902-3
Frankie Neil	1903-4
Joe Bowker	1904-5
Jimmy Walsh	1905-6
Owen Moran	1907-8
Monte Attell*	1909-10
Frankie Conley	1910-11
Johnny Coulon	1911-14
Kid Williams	1914-17
Kewpie Ertle*	1915
Pete Herman	1917-20
Joe Lynch	1920-21
Pete Herman	1921
Johnny Buff	1921-22
Joe Lynch	1922-24
Abe Goldstein	1924
Cannonball Martin	1924-25
Phil Rosenberg	1925-27
Bud Taylor NBA	1927-28
Bushy Graham* NY	1928-29

*Champion not generally recognized.

Champion	Reign
Panama Al Brown	1929-35
Sixto Escobar* WBA	1934-35
Baltazar Sangchilli	1935-36
Lou Salica* NBA	1935
Sixto Escobar* NBA	1935-36
Tony Marino	1936
Sixto Escobar	1936-37
Harry Jeffra	1937-38†
Sixto Escobar	1938-39
Georgie Pace NBA	1939-40
Lou Salica	1940-42
Manuel Ortiz	1942-47
Harold Dade	1947
Manuel Ortiz	1947-50
Vic Toweel	1950-52
Jimmy Carruthers	1952-54†
Robert Cohen	1954-56
Paul Macias* NBA	1955-57
Mario D'Agata	1956-57
Alphonse Halimi	1957-59
Joe Becerra	1959-60†
Eder Jofre	1961-65
Fighting Harada	1965-68
Lionel Rose	1968-69
Ruben Olivares	1969-70
Chucho Castillo	1970-71
Ruben Olivares	1971-72
Rafael Herrera	1972
Enrique Pinder	1972-73

†Champion retired or relinquished title.

Champion	Reign
Romeo Anaya	1973
Rafael Herrera* WBC	1973-74
Soo-Hwan Hong	1974-75
Rodolfo Martinez* WBC	1974-76
Alfonso Zamora	1975-77
Carlos Zarate* WBC	1976-79
Jorge Lujan	1977-80
Lupe Pintor* WBC	1979-83
Julian Solis	1980
Jeff Chandler	1980-84
Albert Davila* WBC	1983-85
Richard Sandoval	1984-86
Satoshi Shingaki* IBF	1984-85
Jeff Fenech* IBF	1985
Daniel Zaragoza* WBC	1985
Miguel Lora* WBC	1985-88
Gaby Canizales	1986
Bernardo Pinango* WBA	1986-87
Wilfredo Vasquez* WBA	1987-88
Kevin Seabrooks* IBF	1987-88
Kaokor Galaxy* WBA	1988
Moon Sung-Kil* WBA	1988-89
Kaokor Galaxy* WBA	1989
Raul Perez* WBC	1988-91
Orlando Canizales* IBF	1988-
Luisito Espinosa* WBA	1989-
Greg Richardson* WBC	1990-91
Joichiro Tatsuyoshi, WBC	1991-

Junior Bantamweights
(Weight Limit: 115 pounds)

Champion	Reign
Rafael Orono* WBC	1980-81
Chul-Ho Kim* WBC	1981-82
Gustavo Ballas* WBA	1981
Rafael Pedroza* WBA	1981-82
Jiro Watanabe* WBA	1982-84
Rafael Orono* WBC	1982-83
Payao Poontarat* WBC	1983-84
Joo-Do Chun* IBF	1983-85

*Champion not generally recognized.

Champion	Reign
Jiro Watanabe	1984-86
Kaosai Galaxy* WBA	1984-
Ellyas Pical* IBF	1985-86
Cesar Polanco* IBF	1986
Gilberto Roman* WBC	1986-87
Ellyas Pical* IBF	1986
Santos Laciar* WBC	1987
Tae-Il Chang* IBF	1987

Note: Division called Super Flyweight by the WBC.

Champion	Reign
Sugar Rojas* WBC	1987-88
Ellyas Pical* IBF	1987-89
Giberto Roman* WBC	1988-89
Juan Polo Perez* IBF	1989-90
Nana Konadu* WBC	1989-90
Sung-Kil Moon* WBC	1990-
Robert Quiroga* IBF	1990-

Flyweights
(Weight Limit: 112 pounds)

Champion	Reign
Sid Smith	1913
Bill Ladbury	1913-14
Percy Jones	1914
Joe Symonds	1914-16
Jimmy Wilde	1916-23
Pancho Villa	1923-25
Fidel LaBarba	1925-27†
Frenchy Belanger NBA	1927-28
Corporal Izzy Schwartz NY	1927-29
Frankie Genaro NBA	1928-29
Spider Pladner NBA	1929
Frankie Genaro NBA	1929-31
Midget Wolgast* NY	1930-35
Young Perez NBA	1931-32
Jackie Brown NBA	1932-35
Benny Lynch	1935-38
Small Montana* NY	1935-37
Peter Kane	1938-43
Little Dado* NY	1938-40
Jackie Paterson	1943-48
Rinty Monaghan	1948-50
Terry Allen	1950
Dado Marino	1950-52
Yoshio Shirai	1953-54
Pascual Perez	1954-60
Pone Kingpetch	1960-62
Hiroyuki Ebihara	1963-64
Pone Kingpetch	1964-65
Salvatore Burrini	1965-66
Horacio Accavallo* WBA	1966-68
Walter McGowan	1966

Champion	Reign
Chartchai Chionoi	1966-69
Efren Torres	1969-70
Hiroyuki Ebihara* WBA	1969
Bernabe Villacampo* WBA	1969-70
Chartchai Chionoi	1970
Berkrerk Chartvanchai* WBA	1970
Masao Ohba* WBA	1970-73
Erbito Salavarria	1970-73
Betulio Gonzalez* WBA	1972
Venice Borksor* WBC	1972-73
Venice Borkorsor	1973
Chartchai Chionoi* WBA	1973-74
Betulio Gonzalez* WBA	1973-74
Shoji Oguma* WBC	1974-75
Susumu Hanagata* WBA	1974-75
Miguel Canto* WBC	1975-79
Erbito Salavarria* WBA	1975-76
Alfonso Lopez* WBA	1976
Gustavo Espadas* WBA	1976-78
Betulio Gonzalez* WBA	1978-79
Chan-Hee Park* WBC	1979-80
Luis Ibarra* WBA	1979-80
Tae-Shik Kim* WBA	1980
Shoji Oguma* WBC	1980-81
Peter Mathebula* WBA	1980-81
Santos Laciar* WBA	1981
Antonio Avelar* WBC	1981-82
Luis Ibarra* WBA	1981

Champion	Reign
Juan Herrera* WBA	1981-82
Prudencio Cardona* WBC	1982
Santos Laciar* WBA	1982-85
Freddie Castillo* WBC	1982
Eleoncio Mercedes* WBC	1982-83
Charlie Magri* WBC	1983
Frank Cedeno* WBC	1983-84
Soon-Chun Kwon* IBF	1983-85
Koji Kobayashi* WBC	1984
Gabriel Bernal* WBC	1984
Sot Chitalada* WBC	1984-88
Hilario Zapate* WBA	1985-87
Chong-Kwan Chung* IBF	1985-86
Bi-Won Chung* IBF	1986
Hi-Sup Shin* IBF	1986-87
Dodie Penalosa* IBF	1987
Fidel Bassa* WBA	1987-89
Choi-Chang Ho* IBF	1987-88
Rolando Bohol* IBF	1988
Yong-Kang Kim* WBC	1988-89
Duke McKenzie* IBF	1988-89
Sot Chitalada* WBC	1989-91
Dave McAuley* IBF	1989-
Jesus Rojas* WBA	1989-90
Yul-Woo Lee* WBA	1990
Leopard Tamakuma* WBA	1990-91
Muangchai Kittikasem* WBC	1991-
Yong Kang Kim* WBA	1991-

*Champion not generally recognized.
†Champion retired or relinquished title.

Junior Flyweights
(Weight Limit: 108 pounds)

Champion	Reign
Franco Udella* WBC	1975
Jaime Rios* WBA	1975-76
Luis Estaba* WBC	1975-78
Juan Guzman* WBA	1976
Yoko Gushiken* WBA	1976-81
Freddy Castillo* WBC	1978
Netrnoi Vorasingh* WBC	1978
Sung-Jun Kim* WBC	1978-80
Shigeo Nakajima* WBC	1980
Hilario Zapata* WBC	1980-82
Pedro Flores* WBA	1981
Hwan-Jin Kim* WBA	1981

Champion	Reign
Katsuo Tokashiki* WBA	1981-83
Amado Urzua* WBC	1982
Tadashi Tomori* WBC	1982
Hilario Zapata* WBC	1982-83
Jung-Koo Chang* WBC	1983-88
Lupe Madera* WBA	1983-84
Dodie Penalosa* IBF	1983-86
Francisco Quiroz* WBA	1984-85
Joey Olivo* WBA	1985
Myung-Woo Yuh* WBA	1985-
Jum-Hwan Choi* IBF	1986-88
Tacy Macalos* IBF	1988-89

Champion	Reign
German Torres* WBC	1988-89
Yul-Woo Lee* WBC	1989
Muangchai Kittikasem* IBF	1989-90
Humberto Gonzalez* WBC	1989-90
Michael Carbajal* IBF	1990-
Rolando Pascua* WBC	1990
Melchor Cob Castro* WBC	1991
Humberto Gonzalez* WBC	1991-

*Champion not generally recognized.
Note: Division called Light Flyweight by the WBC.

THEY SAID IT

Jake La Motta, commenting on Sugar Ray Robinson, the best man for his sixth wedding: "He was the best man in our fights, too." (1986)

All-Time Career Leaders

Most Total Bouts

Name	Years Active	Bouts
Len Wickwar	1928-47	463
Jack Britton	1905-30	350
Johnny Dundee	1910-32	333
Billy Bird	1920-48	318
George Marsden	1928-46	311
Maxie Rosenbloom	1923-39	299
Harry Greb	1913-26	298
Young Stribling	1921-33	286
Battling Levinsky	1910-29	282
Ted "Kid" Lewis	1909-29	279

Note: Based on records in *The Ring Record Book and Boxing Encyclopedia.*

Most Knockouts

Name	Years Active	KOs
Archie Moore	1936-63	130
Young Stribling	1921-33	126
Billy Bird	1920-48	125
George Odwell	1930-45	114
Sugar Ray Robinson	1940-65	110
Sandy Saddler	1944-56	103
Sam Langford	1902-26	102
Henry Armstrong	1931-45	100
Jimmy Wilde	1911-23	98
Len Wickwar	1928-47	93

Note: Based on records in *The Ring Record Book and Boxing Encyclopedia.*

World Heavyweight Championship Fights

Date	Winner	Wgt	Loser	Wgt	Result	Site
Sep 7, 1892	James J. Corbett*	178	John L. Sullivan	212	KO 21	New Orleans
Jan 25, 1894	James J. Corbett	184	Charley Mitchell	158	KO 3	Jacksonville, FL
Mar 17, 1897	Bob Fitzsimmons*	167	James J. Corbett	183	KO 14	Carson City, NV
June 9, 1899	James J. Jeffries*	206	Bob Fitzsimmons	167	KO 11	Coney Island, NY
Nov 3, 1899	James J. Jeffries	215	Tom Sharkey	183	Ref 25	Coney Island, NY
Apr 6, 1900	James J. Jeffries	n/a	Jack Finnegan	n/a	KO 1	Detroit
May 11, 1900	James J. Jeffries	218	James J. Corbett	188	KO 23	Coney Island, NY
Nov 15, 1901	James J. Jeffries	211	Gus Ruhlin	194	TKO 6	San Francisco
July 25, 1902	James J. Jeffries	219	Bob Fitzsimmons	172	KO 8	San Francisco
Aug 14, 1903	James J. Jeffries	220	James J. Corbett	190	KO 10	San Francisco
Aug 25, 1904	James J. Jeffries	219	Jack Munroe	186	TKO 2	San Francisco
July 3, 1905	Marvin Hart*	190	Jack Root	171	KO 12	Reno
Feb 23, 1906	Tommy Burns*	180	Marvin Hart	188	Ref 20	Los Angeles
Oct 2, 1906	Tommy Burns	n/a	Jim Flynn	n/a	KO 15	Los Angeles
Nov 28, 1906	Tommy Burns	172	Philadelphia Jack O'Brien	163½	Draw 20	Los Angeles
May 8, 1907	Tommy Burns	180	Philadelphia Jack O'Brien	167	Ref 20	Los Angeles
Jul 4, 1907	Tommy Burns	181	Bill Squires	180	KO 1	Colma, CA
Dec 2, 1907	Tommy Burns	177	Gunner Moir	204	KO 10	London
Feb 10, 1908	Tommy Burns	n/a	Jack Palmer	n/a	KO 4	London
Mar 17, 1908	Tommy Burns	n/a	Jem Roche	n/a	KO 1	Dublin
Apr 18, 1908	Tommy Burns	n/a	Jewey Smith	n/a	KO 5	Paris
June 13, 1908	Tommy Burns	184	Bill Squires	183	KO 8	Paris
Aug 24, 1908	Tommy Burns	181	Bill Squires	184	KO 13	Sydney
Sep 2, 1908	Tommy Burns	183	Bill Lang	187	KO 6	Melbourne
Dec 26, 1908	Jack Johnson*	192	Tommy Burns	168	TKO 14	Sydney
Mar 10, 1909	Jack Johnson	n/a	Victor McLaglen	n/a	ND 6	Vancouver
May 19, 1909	Jack Johnson	205	Philadelphia Jack O'Brien	161	ND 6	Philadelphia
June 30, 1909	Jack Johnson	207	Tony Ross	214	ND 6	Pittsburgh
Sep 9, 1909	Jack Johnson	209	Al Kaufman	191	ND 10	San Francisco
Oct 16, 1909	Jack Johnson	205½	Stanley Ketchel	170¼	KO 12	Colma, CA
July 4, 1910	Jack Johnson	208	James J. Jeffries	227	KO 15	Reno
July 4, 1912	Jack Johnson	195½	Jim Flynn	175	TKO 9	Las Vegas
Dec 19, 1913	Jack Johnson	n/a	Jim Johnson	n/a	Draw 10	Paris
June 27, 1914	Jack Johnson	221	Frank Moran	203	Ref 20	Paris
Apr 5, 1915	Jess Willard*	230	Jack Johnson	205½	KO 26	Havana
Mar 25, 1916	Jess Willard	225	Frank Moran	203	ND 10	New York
July 4, 1919	Jack Dempsey*	187	Jess Willard	245	TKO 4	Toledo, OH
Sep 6, 1920	Jack Dempsey	185	Billy Miske	187	KO 3	Benton Harbor, MI
Dec 14, 1920	Jack Dempsey	188¼	Bill Brennan	197	KO 12	New York
July 2, 1921	Jack Dempsey	188	Georges Carpentier	172	KO 4	Jersey City
July 4, 1923	Jack Dempsey	188	Tommy Givvons	175½	Ref 15	Shelby, MT
Sep 14, 1923	Jack Dempsey	192½	Luis Firpo	216½	KO 2	New York
Sep 23, 1926	Gene Tunney*	189½	Jack Dempsey	190	UD 10	Philadelphia
Sep 22, 1927	Gene Tunney	189½	Jack Dempsey	192½	UD 10	Chicago

World Heavyweight Championship Fights (*Cont.*)

Date	Winner	Wgt	Loser	Wgt	Result	Site
July 26, 1928	Gene Tunney	192	Tom Heeney	203½	TKO 11	New York
June 12, 1930	Max Schmeling*	188	Jack Sharkey	197	Foul 4	New York
July 3, 1931	Max Schmeling	189	Young Stribling	186½	TKO 15	Cleveland
June 21, 1932	Jack Sharkey*	205	Max Schmeling	188	Split 15	Long Island City
June 29, 1933	Primo Carnera*	260½	Jack Sharkey	201	KO 6	Long Island City
Oct 22, 1933	Primo Carnera	259½	Paulino Uzcudun	229¼	UD 15	Rome
Mar 1, 1934	Primo Carnera	270	Tommy Loughran	184	UD 15	Miami
June 14, 1934	Max Baer*	209½	Primo Carnera	263¼	TKO 11	Long Island City
June 13, 1935	James J. Braddock*	193¾	Max Baer	209½	UD 15	Long Island City
June 22, 1937	Joe Louis	197¼	James J. Braddock	197	KO 8	Chicago
Aug 30, 1937	Joe Louis	197	Tommy Farr	204¼	UD 15	New York
Feb 23, 1938	Joe Louis	200	Nathan Mann	193½	KO 3	New York
Apr 1, 1938	Joe Louis	202½	Harry Thomas	196	KO 5	Chicago
June 22, 1938	Joe Louis	198¼	Max Schmeling	193	KO 1	New York
Jan 25, 1939	Joe Louis	200¼	John Henry Lewis	180¾	KO 1	New York
Apr 17, 1939	Joe Louis	201¼	Jack Roper	204¾	KO 1	Los Angeles
June 28, 1939	Joe Louis	200¾	Tony Galento	233¾	TKO 4	New York
Sep 20, 1939	Joe Louis	200	Bob Pastor	183	KO 11	Detroit
Feb 9, 1940	Joe Louis	203	Arturo Godoy	202	Split 15	New York
Mar 29, 1940	Joe Louis	201½	Johnny Paychek	187½	KO 2	New York
June 20, 1940	Joe Louis	199	Arturo Godoy	201¼	TKO 8	New York
Dec 16, 1940	Joe Louis	202¼	Al McCoy	180¾	TKO 6	Boston
Jan 31, 1941	Joe Louis	202½	Red Burman	188	KO 5	New York
Feb 17, 1941	Joe Louis	203½	Gus Dorazio	193½	KO 2	Philadelphia
Mar 21, 1941	Joe Louis	202	Abe Simon	254½	TKO 13	Detroit
Apr 8, 1941	Joe Louis	203½	Tony Musto	199½	TKO 9	St Louis
May 23, 1941	Joe Louis	201½	Buddy Baer	237½	Disq 7	Washington, DC
June 18, 1941	Joe Louis	199½	Billy Conn	174	KO 13	New York
Sep 29, 1941	Joe Louis	202¼	Lou Nova	202½	TKO 6	New York
Jan 9, 1942	Joe Louis	206¾	Buddy Baer	250	KO 1	New York
Mar 27, 1942	Joe Louis	207½	Abe Simon	255½	KO 6	New York
June 9, 1946	Joe Louis	207	Billy Conn	187	KO 8	New York
Sep 18, 1946	Joe Louis	211	Tami Mauriello	198½	KO 1	New York
Dec 5, 1947	Joe Louis	211½	Jersey Joe Walcott	194½	Split 15	New York
June 25, 1948	Joe Louis	213½	Jersey Joe Walcott	194¾	KO 11	New York
June 22, 1949	Ezzard Charles*	181¾	Jersey Joe Walcott	195½	UD 15	Chicago
Aug 10, 1949	Ezzard Charles	180	Gus Lesnevich	182	TKO 8	New York
Oct 14, 1949	Ezzard Charles	182	Pat Valentino	188½	KO 8	San Francisco
Aug 15, 1950	Ezzard Charles	183¼	Freddie Beshore	184½	TKO 14	Buffalo
Sep 27, 1950	Ezzard Charles	184½	Joe Louis	218	UD 15	New York
Dec 5, 1950	Ezzard Charles	185	Nick Barone	178½	KO 11	Cincinnati
Jan 12, 1951	Ezzard Charles	185	Lee Oma	193	TKO 10	New York
Mar 7, 1951	Ezzard Charles	186	Jersey Joe Walcott	193	UD 15	Detroit
May 30, 1951	Ezzard Charles	182	Joey Maxim	181½	UD 15	Chicago
July 18, 1951	Jersey Joe Walcott*	194	Ezzard Charles	182	KO 7	Pittsburgh
June 5, 1952	Jersey Joe Walcott	196	Ezzard Charles	191½	UD 15	Philadelphia
Sep 23, 1952	Rocky Marciano*	184	Jersey Joe Walcott	196	KO 13	PHiladelphia
May 15, 1953	Rocky Marciano	184½	Jersey Joe Walcott	197¾	KO 1	Chicago
Sep 24, 1953	Rocky Marciano	185	Roland LaStarza	184¾	TKO 11	New York
June 17, 1954	Rocky Marciano	187½	Ezzard Charles	185½	UD 15	New York
Sep 17, 1954	Rocky Marciano	187	Ezzard Charles	192½	KO 8	New York
May 16, 1955	Rocky Marciano	189	Don Cockell	205	TKO 9	San Francisco
Sep 21, 1955	Rocky Marciano	188¼	Archie Moore	188	KO 9	New York
Nov 30, 1956	Floyd Patterson*	182¼	Archie Moore	187¾	KO 5	Chicago
July 29, 1957	Floyd Patterson	184	Tommy Jackson	192½	TKO 10	New York
Aug 22, 1957	Floyd Patterson	187¼	Pete Rademacher	202	KO 6	Seattle
Aug 18, 1958	Floyd Patterson	184½	Roy Harris	194	TKO 13	Los Angeles
May 1, 1959	Floyd Patterson	182½	Brian London	206	KO 11	Indianapolis
June 26, 1959	Ingemar Johansson*	196	Floyd Patterson	182	TKO 3	New York
June 20, 1960	Floyd Patterson*	190	Ingemar Johansson	194¾	KO 5	New York
Mar 13, 1961	Floyd Patterson	194¾	Ingemar Johansson	206½	KO 6	Miami Beach
Dec 4, 1961	Floyd Patterson	188½	Tom McNeeley	197	KO 4	Toronto
Sep 25, 1962	Sonny Liston*	214	Floyd Patterson	189	KO 1	Chicago
July 22, 1963	Sonny Liston	215	Floyd Patterson	194½	KO 1	Las Vegas
Feb 25, 1964	Cassius Clay	210½	Sonny Liston	218	TKO 7	Miami Beach
Mar 5, 1965	Ernie Terrell WBA*	199	Eddie Machen	192	UD 15	Chicago
May 25, 1965	Muhammad Ali	206	Sonny Liston	215¼	KO 1	Lewiston, ME

World Heavyweight Championship Fights (*Cont.*)

Date	Winner	Wgt	Loser	Wgt	Result	Site
Nov 1, 1965	Ernie Terrell WBA*	206	George Chuvalo	209	UD 15	Toronto
Nov 22, 1965	Muhammad Ali	210	Floyd Patterson	196¾	TKO 12	Las Vegas
Mar 29, 1966	Muhammad Ali	214½	George Chuvalo	216	UD 15	Toronto
May 21, 1966	Muhammad Ali	201½	Henry Cooper	188	TKO 6	London
June 28, 1966	Ernie Terrell WBA*	209½	Doug Jones	187½	UD 15	Houston
Aug 6, 1966	Muhammad Ali	209½	Brian London	201½	KO 3	London
Sep 10, 1966	Muhammad Ali	203½	Karl Mildenberger	194¼	TKO 12	Frankfurt
Nov 14, 1966	Muhammad Ali	212¾	Cleveland Williams	210½	TKO 3	Houston
Feb 6, 1967	Muhammad Ali	212¼	Ernie Terrell WBA	212½	UD 15	Houston
Mar 22, 1967	Muhammad Ali	211½	Zora Folley	202½	KO 7	New York
Mar 4, 1968	Joe Frazier*	204½	Buster Mathis	243½	TKO 11	New York
Apr 27, 1968	Jimmy Ellis*	197	Jerry Quarry	195	Maj 15	Oakland
June 24, 1968	Joe Frazier NY*	203½	Manuel Ramos	208	TKO 2	New York
Aug 14, 1968	Jimmy Ellis WBA*	198	Floyd Patterson	188	Ref 15	Stockholm
Dec 10, 1968	Joe Frazier NY*	203	Oscar Bonavena	207	UD 15	Philadelphia
Apr 22, 1969	Joe Frazier NY*	204½	Dave Zyglewicz	190½	KO 1	Houston
June 23, 1969	Joe Frazier NY*	203½	Jerry Quarry	198½	TKO 8	New York
Feb 16, 1970	Joe Frazier NY*	205	Jimmy Ellis WBA	201	TKO 5	New York
Nov 18, 1970	Joe Frazier*	209	Bob Foster	188	KO 2	Detroit
Mar 8, 1971	Joe Frazier*	205½	Muhammad Ali	215	UD 15	New York
Jan 15, 1972	Joe Frazier	215½	Terry Daniels	195	TKO 4	New Orleans
May 26, 1972	Joe Frazier	217½	Ron Stander	218	TKO 5	Omaha
Jan 22, 1973	George Foreman*	217½	Joe Frazier	214	TKO 2	Kingston, Jamaica
Sep 1, 1973	George Foreman	219½	Jose "King" Roman	196½	KO 1	Tokyo
Mar 26, 1974	George Foreman	224¼	Ken Norton	212¼	TKO 2	Caracas
Oct 30, 1974	Muhammad Ali*	216½	George Foreman	220	KO 8	Kinshasa, Zaire
Mar 24, 1975	Muhammad Ali	223½	Chuck Wepner	225	TKO 15	Cleveland
May 16, 1975	Muhammad Ali	224½	Ron Lyle	219	TKO 11	Las Vegas
July 1, 1975	Muhammad Ali	224½	Joe Bugner	230	UD 15	Kuala Lumpur, Malaysia
Oct 1, 1975	Muhammad Ali	224½	Joe Frazier	215	TKO 15	Manila
Feb 20, 1976	Muhammad Ali	226	Jean Pierre Coopman	206	KO 5	San Juan
Apr 30, 1976	Muhammad Ali	230	Jimmy Young	209	UD 15	Landover, MD
May 24, 1976	Muhammad Ali	230	Richard Dunn	206½	TKO 5	Munich
Sep 28, 1976	Muhammad Ali	221	Ken Norton	217½	UD 15	New York
May 16, 1977	Muhammad Ali	221¼	Alfredo Evangelista	209¼	UD 15	Landover, MD
Sep 29, 1977	Muhammad Ali	225	Earnie Shavers	211¼	UD 15	New York
Feb 15, 1978	Leon Spinks*	197¼	Muhammad Ali	224¼	Split 15	Las Vegas
June 9, 1978	Larry Holmes*	209	Ken Norton WBC	220	Split 15	Las Vegas
Sep 15, 1978	Muhammad Ali*	221	Leon Spinks	201	UD 15	New Orleans
Nov 10, 1978	Larry Holmes WBC*	214	Alfredo Evangelista	208¼	KO 7	Las Vegas
Mar 23, 1979	Larry Holmes WBC*	214	Osvaldo Ocasio	207	TKO 7	Las Vegas
June 22, 1979	Larry Holmes WBC*	215	Mike Weaver	202	TKO 12	New York
Sep 28, 1979	Larry Holmes WBC*	210	Earnie Shavers	211	TKO 11	Las Vegas
Oct 20, 1979	John Tate*	240	Gerrie Coetzee	222	UD 15	Pretoria
Feb 3, 1980	Larry Holmes WBC*	213½	Lorenzo Zanon	215	TKO 6	Las Vegas
Mar 31, 1980	Mike Weaver*	232	John Tate WBA	232	KO 15	Knoxville
Mar 31, 1980	Larry Holmes WBC*	211	Leroy Jones	254½	TKO 8	Las Vegas
July 7, 1980	Larry Holmes WBC*	214¼	Scott LeDoux	226	TKO 7	Minneapolis
Oct 2, 1980	Larry Holmes WBC*	211¼	Muhammad Ali	217½	TKO 11	Las Vegas
Oct 25, 1980	Mike Weaver WBA*	210	Gerrie Coetzee	226½	KO 13	Sun City, Boph'swana
Apr 11, 1981	Larry Holmes	215	Trevor Berbick	215½	UD 15	Las Vegas
June 12, 1981	Larry Holmes	212¼	Leon Spinks	200¼	TKO 3	Detroit
Oct 3, 1981	Mike Weaver WBA*	215	Quick Tillis	209	UD 15	Rosemont, IL
Nov 6, 1981	Larry Holmes	213¼	Renaldo Snipes	215¾	TKO 11	Pittsburgh
June 11, 1982	Larry Holmes	212½	Gerry Cooney	225½	TKO 13	Las Vegas
Nov 26, 1982	Larry Holmes	217½	Tex Cobb	234¼	UD 15	Houston
Dec 10, 1982	Michael Dokes*	216	Mike Weaver WBA	209¾	TKO 1	Las Vegas
Mar 27, 1983	Larry Holmes	221	Lucien Rodriguez	209	UD 12	Scranton
May 20, 1983	Michael Dokes WBA*	223	Mike Weaver	218½	Draw 15	Las Vegas
May 20, 1983	Larry Holmes	213	Tim Witherspoon	219½	Split 12	Las Vegas
Sep 10, 1983	Larry Holmes	223	Scott Frank	211¼	TKO 5	Atlantic City
Sep 23, 1983	Gerrie Coetzee*	215	Michael Dokes WBA	217	KO 10	Richfield, OH
Nov 25, 1983	Larry Holmes	219	Marvis Frazier	200	TKO 1	Las Vegas
Mar 9, 1984	Tim Witherspoon	220¼	Greg Page	239½	Maj 12	Las Vegas
Aug 31, 1984	Pinklon Thomas*	216	Tim Witherspoon WBC	217	Maj 12	Las Vegas

World Heavyweight Championship Fights (*Cont.*)

Date	Winner	Wgt	Loser	Wgt	Result	Site
Nov 9, 1984	Larry Holmes IBF	221½	James Bonecrusher Smith	227	TKO 12	Las Vegas
Dec 1, 1984	Greg Page*	236½	Gerrie Coetzee WBA	218	KO 8	Sun City, Boph'swana
Mar 15, 1985	Larry Holmes	223½	David Bey	233¼	TKO 10	Las Vegas
Apr 29, 1985	Tony Tubbs*	229	Greg Page WBA	239½	UD 15	Buffalo
May 20, 1985	Larry Holmes	224¼	Carl Williams	215	UD 15	Las Vegas
June 15, 1985	Pinklon Thomas*	220¼	Mike Weaver	211¼	KO 8	Las Vegas
Sep 21, 1985	Michael Spinks*	200	Larry Holmes IBF	221½	UD 15	Las Vegas
Jan 17, 1986	Tim Witherspoon	227	Tony Tubbs WBA	229	Maj 15	Atlanta
Mar 22, 1986	Trevor Berbick*	218½	Pinklon Thomas WBC	222¾	UD 15	Las Vegas
Apr 19, 1986	Michael Spinks	205	Larry Holmes	223	Split 15	Las Vegas
July 19, 1986	Tim Witherspoon*	234¾	Frank Bruno	228	TKO 11	Wembley, England
Sep 6, 1986	Michael Spinks	201	Steffen Tangstad	214¾	TKO 4	Las Vegas
Nov 22, 1986	Mike Tyson*	221¼	Trevor Berbick WBC	218½	TKO 2	Las Vegas
Dec 12, 1986	James Bonecrusher Smith*	228½	Tim Witherspoon WBA	233½	TKO 1	New York
Mar 7, 1987	Mike Tyson WBC*	219	James Bonecrusher Smith WBA	233	UD 12	Las Vegas
May 30, 1987	Mike Tyson*	218¾	Pinklon Thomas	217¾	TKO 6	Las Vegas
May 30, 1987	Tony Tucker	222¼	Buster Douglas	227¼	TKO 10	Las Vegas
June 15, 1987	Michael Spinks	208¾	Gerry Cooney	238	TKO 5	Atlantic City
Aug 1, 1987	Mike Tyson*	221	Tony Tucker IBF	221	UD 12	Las Vegas
Oct 16, 1987	Mike Tyson*	216	Tyrell Biggs	228¾	TKO 7	Atlantic City
Jan 22, 1988	Mike Tyson*	215¾	Larry Holmes	225¾	TKO 4	Atlantic City
Mar 20, 1988	Mike Tyson*	216¼	Tony Tubbs	238¼	KO 2	Tokyo
June 27, 1988	Mike Tyson*	218¼	Michael Spinks	212¼	KO 1	Atlantic City
Feb 25, 1989	Mike Tyson	218	Frank Bruno	228	TKO 5	Las Vegas
July 21, 1989	Mike Tyson	219¼	Carl Williams	218	TKO 1	Atlantic City
Feb 10, 1990	Buster Douglas*	231½	Mike Tyson	220½	KO 10	Tokyo
Oct 25, 1990	Evander Holyfield	208	Buster Douglas	246	KO 3	Las Vegas
Apr 19, 1991	Evander Holyfield	212	George Foreman	257	UD 12	Atlantic City

*Champion not generally recognized.

KO=knockout; TKO=technical knockout; UD=unanimous decision; Split=split decision; Ref=referee's decision; Disq=disqualification; ND=no decision.

George Foreman's Professional Career in the Ring

George Foreman's professional boxing career spans four decades during which he has won 69 of 72 fights, 65 by knockout. He gained the undisputed heavyweight title in 1973 and fought to regain it more than 18 years later. Here is a look at his remarkable record:

Date	Opponent	Result	Site
June 23, 1969	Don Waldheim	KO 3	New York City
July 1	Fred Askew	KO 1	Houston
July 14	Sylvester Dullaire	KO 1	Washington D.C.
Aug 18	Chuck Wepner	KO 3	New York City
Sep 18	John Carroll	KO 1	Seattle
Sep 23	Cookie Wallace	KO 2	Houston
Oct 7	Vernon Clay	KO 2	Houston
Oct 31	Roberto Davila	DEC 8	New York City
Nov 5	Leo Paterson	KO 4	Scranton, PA
Nov 18	Max Martinez	KO 2	Houston
Dec 6	Bob Hazleton	KO 1	Las Vegas
Dec 16	Levi Forte	DEC 10	Miami Beach
Dec 18	Gary Wiler	KO 1	Seattle
Jan 6, 1970	Charlie Polite	KO 4	Houston
Jan 26	Jack O'Halloran	KO 5	New York City
Feb 16	Gregorio Peralta	DEC 10	New York City
Mar 31	Rufus Brassell	KO 1	Houston
Apr 17	James J. Woody	KO 3	New York City
Apr 29	Aaron Easting	KO 4	Cleveland
May 16	George Johnson	TKO 7	Los Angeles

George Foreman's Professional Career in the Ring (*Cont.*)

Date	Opponent	Result	Site
(*1970 Cont.*)			
July 20	Roger Russell	KO 1	Philadelphia
Aug 4	George Chuvalo	KO 3	New York City
Nov 3	Lou Bailey	KO 3	Oklahoma City
Nov 18	Boone Kirkman	KO 2	New York City
Dec 19	Mel Turnbow	TKO 1	Seattle
Feb 8, 1971	Charlie Boston	KO 1	St. Paul
Apr 3	Stamford Harris	KO 2	Lake Geneva
May 10	Gregorio Peralta	TKO 10	Oakland, CA
Sep 14	Vic Scott	KO 1	El Paso, TX
Sep 21	Leroy Caldwell	KO 3	Beaumont
Oct 7	Ollie Wilson	KO 2	San Antonio
Oct 29	Luis Faustino Pires	TKO 4	New York City
Feb 29, 1972	Murphy Goodwin	KO 2	Austin
Mar 7	Clarence Boone	KO 2	Beaumont
Apr 10	Ted Gullick	KO 2	Los Angeles
May 11	Miguel Angel Paez	KO 2	Oakland
Oct 10	Terry Sorrels	KO 2	Salt Lake City
Jan 22, 1973	Joe Frazier	TKO 2 (World Heavyweight)	Kingston
Sep 1	Jose (King) Roman	KO 1 (World Heavyweight)	Tokyo
Mar 26, 1974	Ken Norton	TKO 2 (World Heavyweight)	Tokyo
Oct 30	Muhammad Ali	LKO 8 (World Heavyweight)	Kinshasha, Zaire
Apr 26, 1975	Charlie Polite	EXH 3	Toronto
Apr 26	Boone Kirkman	EXH 3	Toronto
Apr 26	Terry Daniels	EXH 2	Toronto
Apr 26	Jerry Judge	EXH 2	Toronto
Apr 26	Alonzo Johnson	EXH 2	Toronto
Nov 26	Jody Ballard	EXH 2	Kiamesha Lake
Dec 17	Eddie Brooks	EXH 4	San Francisco
Jan 24, 1976	Ron Lyle	KO 4	Las Vegas
June 15	Joe Frazier	KO 5	Uniondale, NY
Aug 14	Scott LeDoux	KO 3	Utica, NY
Oct 15	John Denis	TKO 4	Hollywood, FLA
Jan 22, 1977	Pedro Agosta	KO 4	Pensacola, FLA
Mar 17	Jimmy Young	LDEC 12	San Juan, PR
Mar 9, 1987	Steve Zouski	KO 4	Sacramento
July 9	Charles Hostetter	KO 3	Oakland
Sep 15	Bobby Crabtree	TKO 6	Springfield, IL
Nov 21	Tim Anderson	TKO 4	Orlando
Dec 18	Richard Sekorski	TKO 3	Las Vegas
Jan 23, 1988	Tom Trimm	KO 1	Orlando
Feb 5	Guido Trane	TKO 5	Las Vegas
Mar 19	Dwight Qawi	TKO 7	Las Vegas
May 21	Frank Williams	KO 3	Anchorage
June 26	Carlos Hernandez	TKO 4	Atlantic City
Aug 25	Ladislao Mijangos	TKO 2	Ft. Myers, FL
Sep 10	Bobby Hitzelburg	KO 1	Auburn Hills, MI
Oct 27	Tony Fulilangi	TKO 2	Marshall, TX
Dec 28	David Jaco	KO 1	Bakersfield, CA
Jan 26, 1989	Mark Young	TKO 7	Rochester, NY
Feb 16	Manuel De Almeida	TKO 3	Orlando
Apr 30	J.B. Williamson	TKO 5	Galveston, TX
June 1	Bert Cooper	TKO 2	Phoenix
July 20	Everett Martin	DEC 10	Tuscon
Jan 15, 1990	Gerry Cooney	TKO 2	Atlantic City
Apr 17	Mike Jameson	KO 4	Las Vegas
June 16	Adilson Rodrigues	KO 2	Las Vegas
July 31	Ken Lakusta	KO 3	Alberta, ED
Sep 25	Terry Anderson	KO 1	London
Apr 19, 1991	Evander Holyfield	LDEC 12	Atlantic City

Note: KO = knockout. TKO = technical knockout. DEC = decision. EXH = exhibition. An "L" before the result = a loss.

Michael was magical as the Bulls soared to their first NBA title over Earvin Johnson (32) and the Lakers.

The war in the Persian Gulf overshadowed sporting events in the early part of the year.

Bills like James Lofton took a Giant pounding from Everson Walls and other New York defenders in the Super Bowl.

Georgia Tech routed Nebraska in the Citrus Bowl and let pollsters know where they thought their team should be ranked.

No. 1 UNLV got past Seton Hall (right) but stumbled over Duke in the Final Four. No. 1 for much of the year, Virginia (below) fell to Tennessee in the women's NCAA title game.

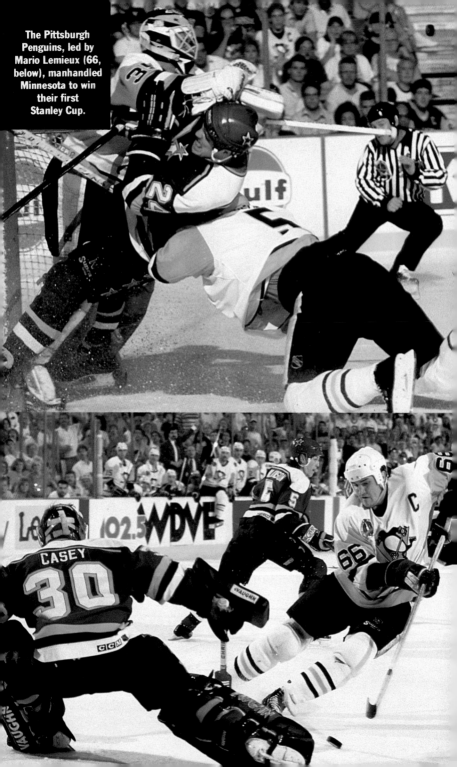

The Pittsburgh Penguins, led by Mario Lemieux (66, below), manhandled Minnesota to win their first Stanley Cup.

Jordan was the NBA's MVP but the league's championship trophy was the award he really coveted.

Payne Stewart
punched out Scott
Simpson in an 18-
hole U.S. Open
playoff at Hazeltine

The White Sox
moved across the
street, while the
National League
announced it was
moving into Miami

Oakland's Rickey Henderson tied (right), then broke, Lou Brock's all-time stolen base record. Early in the National League season Pittsburgh and L.A. (below) seemed on a collision course.

A focused Mike Tyson gave Razor Ruddock a mouthful in their June rematch in Las Vegas.

Darrell Waltrip's car rolled over Joe Ruttman's in a spectacular July 4 crash at Daytona. Neither driver was seriously injured.

Strike the Gold
struck from the
outside (pink silks
at the top of the
stretch to win the
Kentucky Derby.

Carl Lewis
ran 100 meters in
a world-record
9.86 seconds at
the World Track
and Field
Championships.

A final look? With his son as comfor[t] the Raiders' Bo Jackson limped of[f] with his two-spor[t] athletic future in limbo.

Horse Racing

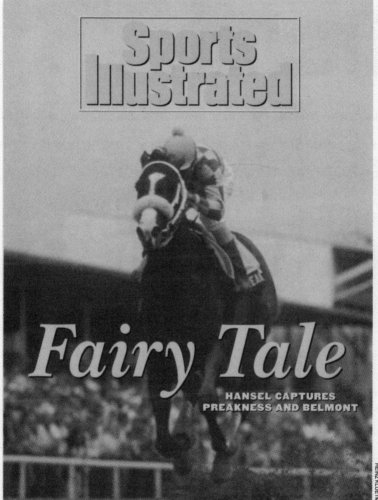

Sports Illustrated

Fairy Tale

HANSEL CAPTURES
PREAKNESS AND BELMONT

HEINZ KLUETMEIER

Triumph and Tragedy

The horse racing industry launched an exciting new series of races, but the Shoe was paralyzed and Calumet Farm went bankrupt | by WILLIAM F. REED

FOR YEARS PEOPLE IN THOROUGHBRED RACing have been trying to figure out how to lengthen the careers of the sport's star performers. Far too often, just as the public is beginning to get excited about a horse, he is whisked off to a breeding farm. It's no coincidence that some of the most beloved horses—Kelso, Forego, and John Henry, to name a few—all were geldings who were able to enjoy long careers because they had no value at stud.

So maybe, more than anything else, 1991 deserves to be remembered as the year the horse racing industry finally came up with an exciting concept that should encourage owners to keep their best horses in training well beyond their 3-year-old year. The American Championship Racing Series consisted of 10 races at nine major tracks from coast-to-coast. It offered $6.75 million in total purses and a $1.5 million bonus to

be split among the four horses amassing the most points (10 points for a win, seven for a second, and so forth).

The series got off to a rousing start when Jolie's Halo won the Donn Handicap at Florida's Gulfstream Park on Feb. 9, and it gained momentum as the year went on. The brainchild of Barry Weisbord of Matchmaker International and Tim Capps of Pimlico race course, the ACRS turned out to be the most positive concept to hit racing since the advent of the Breeders' Cup program in 1984.

Sadly, much of the racing news in 1991 wasn't cheerful. Tracks continued to grope for ways to boost sagging attendance. And the controversy over medication continued, with no uniform rules regarding the uses of Lasix and Butazolidin. Most vexing of all, racing continued to compete against itself by embracing the brave new world of high-tech TV gambling, which takes fans away from the tracks and pulls them into off-site wagering facilities.

One of the saddest stories of the year involved legendary jockey Bill Shoemaker, who was paralyzed in a car accident on April 8. The fact that the accident happened less than a month before the Kentucky Derby, his favorite race, made it especially disheartening.

Nobody in any sport has ever been as good for as long as the Shoe was. His road to glory began in 1949 and didn't end until his tearful farewell on Feb. 3, 1990, at Santa Anita Park. Along the way he had 40,350 mounts, 8,833 victories and 1,009 stakes wins, all world records.

Since he was proudest of his Kentucky Derby wins (Swaps in 1955, Tomy Lee in '59, Lucky Debonair in '65, and Ferdinand in '86), it was ironic that when the accident occurred, he was on his way to The Derby, an Arcadia, Calif., restaurant. Police reported that Shoemaker's blood-alcohol level was over the legal limit, although ex-jockey and fellow trainer Don Pierce says that the Shoe had "only a couple of beers" after their afternoon golf match.

After being transferred to a hospital in Denver, Shoemaker's condition improved to the point where he was able to resume training horses via telephone and a closed-circuit TV system that had been installed in his hospital room.

Even the Kentucky Derby win by Strike the Gold had its gloomy side. The colt was bred by Calumet Farm of Lexington, Ky. This was the home of two Triple Crown winners (Whirlaway in 1941 and Citation in 1948) and a record eight Kentucky Derby winners.

Strike the Gold was a son of Alydar, who emerged in the 1980s as one of the world's best stallions, siring such classic winners as Alysheba, Easy Goer, Turkoman, and Criminal Type. Tragically, Alydar was destroyed on Nov. 15, 1990, after breaking a leg in a freak stall accident. On that same day, Strike the Gold broke his maiden for trainer Nick Zito.

The extent of Calumet's financial problems didn't begin to become apparent until

JERRY COOKE

The Shoe's final Derby triumph was his '86 win aboard Ferdinand.

Calumet president J.T. Lundy resigned on April 3. Lundy had taken over the reins at Calumet in 1982, shortly after the death of Lucille Parker Wright Markey, who built Calumet with her first husband, Warren Wright, Sr., and sustained it after Wright's death in 1950 with her second husband, Admiral Gene Markey. By the terms of her first husband's will, the farm was inherited by Bertha Wright, widow of their adopted son Warren Wright, Jr., and their four grandchildren. The heirs picked Lundy, who is married to one of the granddaughters, to serve as president.

When Lundy took over, Calumet was debt free and profitable. But by mid-summer of 1991, it was revealed that the farm was more than $70 million in debt and besieged by creditors who had filed more than $27 million in lawsuits. Lundy's friends say he was a victim of bad luck, the sluggish economy, the death of Alydar, and poor judgment in the stallions he selected. Nevertheless, new president John T. Ward had to bring in a team of bankers, lawyers, and accountants to figure out what, if anything, could be done to keep the farm from declaring bankruptcy and being auctioned off.

Against this woeful backdrop, Strike the Gold won the April 13 Blue Grass Stakes at Keeneland, upsetting Fly So Free, the 2-year-old champion colt. But many experts disregarded the Gold as a potential Derby winner because of the Dosage Index, a complex system by which contenders are evaluated according to pedigree. No horse with a Dosage higher than 4.00 had won the Derby since 1929; Strike the Gold's Dosage was a whop-

U Can't Touch This

ON SATURDAY, JULY 6, rap megastar M.C. Hammer put on a show at New York's Belmont Park that was unlike any performance his fans had ever seen. As the splendid 3-year-old filly Lite Light pounded down the stretch in the 1¼-mile Coaching Club American Oaks, Hammer jumped onto the railing in front of his box and jerked off his aquamarine leather jacket. Bare-chested, he twirled it in triumph as Lite Light drew off to a seven-length victory over Meadow Star, who had gone into the race unbeaten against fillies. "I can't remember a more exciting moment," Hammer said. "It was one of supreme bliss—ecstasy!"

Hammer, whose real name is Stanley Burrell, grew up in Oakland and as a youngster spent a couple of summers as the visiting batboy at Oakland Athletics' baseball games. The players in the clubhouse nicknamed Burrell "Little Hammer" because of his resemblance to Hank Aaron. He later added the M.C. for master of ceremonies when he began his rap career.

He quickly became so popular, and so wealthy, that he was able to bankroll his family's quest to become thoroughbred owners. The Burrells named their stable Oaktown, after their home city. One of their first purchases was Lite Light, a 3-year-old daughter of Majestic Light out of the In Reality mare Printing Press.

After Lite Light set a stakes record in winning the Kentucky Oaks at Churchill Downs on May 3, Hammer and the other Oaktown owners—his father, Lewis E. Burrell Sr., and brothers Louis K. and Christopher—thought seriously about running her against colts in the June 8 Belmont Stakes. Instead they opted for the June 9 Mother Goose Stakes and a meeting with Meadow Star, who had run her record against fillies to 10 for 10 by winning the Acorn Stakes.

Before the Mother Goose, Hammer met Carl Icahn, chairman of the board of TWA and the owner of Meadow Star. Icahn told Hammer he was glad to see him in racing but advised him never to buy a horse farm or an airline. The two men also made a $35,000 side bet on the Mother Goose. By post time Hammer and his entourage had bet so much money that the odds on Lite Light had dropped from 4–5 to 1–2 to 1–5.

The race was one of the best seen in New York in years. The two fillies hooked up in the turn for home and battled head-to-head down the long stretch. The stewards needed seven minutes to study the photo of the finish before declaring Meadow Star the winner.

Lite Light's effort was so strenuous that after the race it was discovered that she had bled slightly from the nostrils. Trainer Jerry Hollendorfer shipped her back to California, and she wasn't expected to test Meadow Star again until the Nov. 2 Breeders' Cup Distaff. But Hammer and the other Oaktown owners decided to have Lite Light flown back to New York

ping 9.00. "Voodoo, witchcraft," said Zito.

On an overcast afternoon at Churchill Downs, Strike the Gold came from near the back of the pack, circled the field turning for home and held on for a 1¾ length victory over Best Pal, the leading contender from California.

The biggest disappointment of the Derby was Hansel, who went off as a 5–2 favorite but finished only 10th. Trainer Frank Brothers admitted he was baffled. "I'd like to be able to give you a reason why he ran so bad," Brothers said, "but I just can't." Instead of shipping Hansel to Baltimore for the Preak-

for the Coaching Club American Oaks. The wisdom of the decision was questioned by the public and the press, but Hammer remained unruffled and confident. Before the race he found Icahn and said, "Let's make it a real bet today—my $200,000 against your $150,000." Icahn agreed.

This time the theme for Lite Light's performance could well have been Hammer's hit song "U Can't Touch This." Jockey Corey Nakatani kept her three or four lengths off the early pace, tucked along the rail. In the turn for home Lite Light and Meadow Star surged past the tiring Car Gal. But instead of hooking up in another duel, Meadow Star failed to respond when Lite Light took off. The final margin was a widening seven lengths in a stakes-record time of 2:00⅖ for the mile and a quarter.

Hammer donated the $150,000 to his charity of choice, the Help the Children Foundation in Oakland. Icahn had donated his earlier winnings from Hammer to his charity of choice, the Children's Rescue Fund, which has received all monies Meadow Star has earned since Oct. 18. In the winner's circle, cheered by thousands of fans, Hammer showed the same exuberance that characterizes his performances. "Wherever Hammer goes, other people follow," said Hollendorfer. "I'm not used to it, but I hope I can get used to it."

A triumphant Hammer led his winning filly into the winner's circle at Belmont Park.

ness, Brothers sent him home to Chicago and tried to figure out what had caused the poor showing. A replay revealed nothing. Neither did a scoping of Hansel's breathing passage and a blood test. What to do? Be conservative and go to the Jersey Derby or the Ohio Derby? Or take a shot at the Preakness and risk humiliation?

On the Tuesday before the Preakness, after blowing out Hansel in Chicago, Brothers called owner Joe L. Allbritton and put the choice to him. Allbritton in turn called Frank Shipp, manager of his farm in Upperville, Va. Shipp reminded him that Snow Chief had won the 1986 Preakness after finishing 11th as the Derby favorite. That did it. All-britton called Brothers back and told him to put Hansel on a van to Baltimore.

In the Preakness, Hansel set just off the early pace set by Corporate Report and Olympio. Then jockey Jerry Bailey eased him up to second, moving with Best Pal after Olympio began to fade at the six-furlong mark. Turning for home, Hansel literally pulled Bailey to the lead and they drew off for a seven-length victory in the good time of 1:54 for the 1 3/16 miles.

The once glorious Calumet Farm was driven into bankruptcy.

As for Strike the Gold, he never fired because Chris Antley allowed long-shot Honor Grades to keep him pinned on the rail at the back of the pack in the early going. On the turn for home, when Hansel started to accelerate, Strike the Gold was back in sixth place, a position he maintained to the wire. Zito was disappointed, but he vowed that Strike the Gold would redeem himself in the Belmont.

The 1 1/2-mile Belmont unfolded pretty much as the Preakness had, with Hansel stalking the early pace and surging into the lead in the turn for home. But this time here came Strike the Gold, who had been as much as 20 lengths back. Circling the field in the turn and flying on the outside in the stretch, Strike the Gold kept eating into the tiring Hansel's lead. "Had it been a mile and a half and two jumps, we would have won," Antley said. Strike the Gold came up only a head short in a race that stamped both horses as the best of their class.

THOROUGHBRED RACING

The Triple Crown

117th Kentucky Derby

May 4, 1991. Grade I, 3-year-olds; 8th race, Churchill Downs, Louisville. All 126 lbs. Distance: 1¼ miles. Stakes purse: $905,800; Winner: $655,800; Second: $145,000; Third: $70,000; Fourth: $35,000. Track: Fast. Off: 5:36 p.m. Winner: Strike the Gold (Ch C by Alydar-Majestic Gold, by Hatchet Man); Times: 0:23⅕, 0:46 ⅖, 1:11⅕, 1:37⅖; 2:03. Won: Driving. Breeder: Calumet Farm (KY).

Horse	Finish-PP	Margin	Jockey/Owner
Strike the Gold	1-5	1¾	Chris Antley/B. Giles Brophy, William J. Condren, Joseph M. Cornacchia
Best Pal	2-15	1¾	Gary Stevens/Golden Eagle Farm
Mane Minister	3-10	Head	Alex Solis/Trudy McCaffery, John Toffan
Green Alligator	4-8	¾	Corey Nakatani/Anderson Fowler
Fly So Free	5-1	1¾	Jose Santos/Thomas Valando
Quintana	6-16	½	Angel Cordero Jr/Gary M. Garber
Paulrus	7-11	Head	Shane Sellers/Hermitage Farm
Sea Cadet	8-4	2	Chris McCarron/V.H.W. Stable, Inc.
Corporate Report	9-12	2	Pat Day/Overbrook Farm, D. Wayne Lukas
Hansel*	10-6	Head	Jerry Bailey/Lazy Lane Farm
Happy Jazz Band	11-14	½	Cash Asmussen/Straus-Medina Ranch
Lost Mountain	12-9	8½	Herbert McCauley/Loblolly Stable
Another Review	13-13	Neck	Art Madrid Jr/Buckland Farm
Alydavid	14-2	1½	Corey Black/David's Farm
Wilder Than Ever	15-3	16	Joe Deegan/Raymond H. Cottrell Sr
Forty Something	16-7	—	Andrea Seefeldt/Sam F. Morrell

116th Preakness Stakes

May 18, 1991. Grade I, 3-year-olds; 10th race, Pimlico Race Course, Baltimore. All 126 lbs. Distance: 1³⁄₁₆ miles. Stakes purse: $665,800; Winner: $432,770; Second: $133,160; Third: $66,580; Fourth: $33,200. Track: Fast. Off: 5:32 p.m. Winner: Hansel (Bc, by Woodman-Count on Bonnie, by Dancing Count); Times: 0:23⅕, 0:46⅕, 1:10⅕, 1:35, 1:54. Won: Driving. Breeder: Marvin Little Jr.

Horse	Finish-PP	Margin	Jockey/Owner
Hansel	1-4	7	Jerry Bailey/Lazy Lane Farm
Corporate Report	2-1	2¾	Pat Day/Overbrook Farm, D. Wayne Lukas
Mane Minister	3-2	½	Alex Solis/Trudy McCaffery, John Toffan
Olympio	4-7	¾	Eddie Delahoussaye/V.H.W. Stable, Inc.
Best Pal	5-5	½	Gary Stevens/Golden Eagle Farm
Strike the Gold*	6-3	1½	Chris Antley/B. Giles Brophy, William J. Condren, Joseph M. Cornacchia
Whadjathink	7-8	1¼	Jorge Velasquez/Richard L. Duchossois
Honor Grades	8-6	—	Chris McCarron/Summa Stable, Wayne Gretzky, Magic Johnson

123rd Belmont Stakes

June 8, 1991. Grade I, 3-year-olds; 8th race, Belmont Park, Elmont, NY. All 126 lbs. Distance: 1½ miles. Stakes purse: $696,800; Winner: $418,080; Second: $153,296; Third: $83,616; Fourth: $41,808. Track: Fast. Off: 5:32 p.m. Winner: Hansel (Bc, by Woodman-Count on Bonnie, by Dancing Count); Times: 0:23, 0:46⅗, 1:11⅗, 1:36⅗, 2:02, 2:28. Won: Driving. Breeder: Marvin Little Jr.

Horse	Finish-PP	Margin	Jockey/Owner
Hansel	1-5	Head	Jerry Bailey/Lazy Lane Farm
Strike the Gold*	2-11	3	Chris Antley/B. Giles Brophy, William J. Condren, Joseph M. Cornacchia
Mane Minister	3-3	2½	Alex Solis/Trudy McCaffery, John Toffan
Corporate Report	4-4	2¼	Pat Day/Overbrook Farm, D. Wayne Lukas
Scan	5-2	10¾	Chris McCarron/William Haggin Perry
Quintana	6-7	3½	Angel Cordero Jr/Gary M. Garber
Lost Mountain	7-4	¾	Craig Perret/Loblolly Stable
Smooth Performance	8-10	22½	Michael Kinane/Moyglare Stud
Subordinated Debt	9-9	¾	Julie Krone/Leslie R. Grimm
Green Alligator	10-8	—	Corey Nakatani/Anderson Fowler
Another Review	11-1	—	Richard Migliore/Buckland Farm

*The favorite.

The American Championship Racing Series

Final points and standings in the inaugural 10-race American Championship Racing Series. The 10 races are the Donn Handicap, the Santa Anita Handicap, the Oaklawn Handicap, the Pimlico Special, the Nassau County Handicap, the Hollywood Gold Cup, the New England Classic, the Pacific Classic, the Iselin Handicap, and the Woodward Stakes. Points were awarded on a 10-7-5-3-1 basis in each race, and a $1.5 million bonus was split among the top four point leaders.

Horse	Age	Sex	Starts	1	2	3	4	5	Pts.	Bonus ($)
Farma Way	4	C	7	2	3	1	0	1	47	750,000
Festin	5	H	7	2	2	1	2	0	45	375,000
Marquetry	4	C	3	2	0	0	0	1	21	225,000
Jolie's Halo	4	C	4	1	0	2	0	0	20	150,000
In Excess	4	C	2	1	0	0	1	0	13	
Silver Survivor	5	H	5	0	0	1	2	1	12	
Best Pal	3	G	1	1	0	0	0	0	10	
Black Tie Affair	5	H	1	1	0	0	0	0	10	
Primal	6	G	2	0	1	0	1	0	10	
Chief Honcho	4	C	2	0	0	1	1	0	8	
Gervazy	4	C	1	0	1	0	0	0	7	
Sports View	4	C	1	0	1	0	0	0	7	
Summer Squall	4	C	2	0	1	0	0	0	7	
Twilight Agenda	5	H	1	0	1	0	0	0	7	
Unbridled	4	C	3	0	0	1	0	1	6	
Itsallgreektome	4	G	2	0	0	1	0	0	5	
Pleasant Tap	4	C	1	0	0	1	0	0	5	
Secret Hello	4	C	1	0	0	1	0	0	5	
Anshan	4	C	3	0	0	0	1	0	3	
Strike the Gold	3	C	1	0	0	0	1	0	3	
Whiz Along	6	H	1	0	0	0	1	0	3	
Killer Diller	4	C	2	0	0	0	0	1	1	
Louis Cyphre	5	H	1	0	0	0	0	1	1	
Roanoke	4	C	2	0	0	0	0	1	1	
Sound of Cannons	4	C	1	0	0	0	0	1	1	
Sunny Serve	4	C	1	0	0	0	0	1	1	
Yonder	4	C	1	0	0	0	0	1	1	

C = Colt   G = Gelding   H = Horse   F = Filly   M = Mare

Major Stakes Races

Late 1990

Date	Race	Track	Distance	Winner	Jockey	Purse ($)
Oct 6	Champagne Stakes	Belmont	1 mile	Fly So Free	Jose Santos	636,000
Oct 6	Jockey Cup Gold Cup	Belmont	1¼ miles	Flying Continental	Corey Black	838,500
Oct 6	Oak Tree Invitational	Santa Anita	1½ miles	Rial	Rafael Meza	500,000
Oct 7	Arc de Triomphe	Longchamp	1½ miles	Saumarez	Gerald Mosse	1,450,950
Oct 7	Turf Classic	Belmont	1¼ miles	Cacoethes	Ray Cochrane	600,000
Oct 12	Meadowlands Cup	Meadowlands	1⅛ miles	Great Normand	Carlos Lopez	500,000
Oct 14	Rothmans International	Woodbine	1½ miles	French Glory	Pat Eddery	1,032,750
Oct 21	Budweiser International	Laurel	1¼ miles	Fly till Dawn	Laffit Pincay Jr	750,000
Oct 27	Breeder's Cup Distaff	Belmont	1⅛ miles	Bayakoa	Laffit Pincay Jr	1,000,000
Oct 27	Breeder's Cup Classic	Belmont	1¼ miles	Unbridled	Pat Day	3,000,000
Oct 27	Breeder's Cup Turf	Belmont	1½ miles	In the Wings	Gary Stevens	2,000,000
Oct 27	Breeder's Cup Juvenile	Belmont	1¹⁄₁₆ miles	Fly So Free	Jose Santos	1,000,000
Oct 27	Breeder's Cup Juvenile Fillies	Belmont	1¹⁄₁₆ miles	Meadow Star	Jose Santos	1,000,000
Oct 27	Breeder's Cup Mile	Belmont	1 mile	Royal Academy	Lester Piggot	1,000,000
Oct 27	Breeder's Cup Sprint	Belmont	6 furlongs	Safely Kept	Craig Perret	1,000,000
Nov 3	NYRA Mile Handicap	Aqueduct	1 mile	Quiet American	Chris McCarron	638,000
Nov 25	Hollywood Starlet Stakes	Hollywood Park	1 mile	Cuddles	Gary Stevens	500,000
Dec 9	Hollywod Futurity	Hollywood Park	1 mile	Best Pal	Jose Santos	1,000,000
Dec 16	Hollywood Turf Cup	Hollywood Park	1½ miles	Itsallgreektome	Corey Nakatani	500,000

1991 (Through September 22)

Date	Race	Track	Distance	Winner	Jockey	Purse ($)
Feb 9	Donn Handicap	Gulfstream Park	1⅛ miles	Jolie's Halo	Robin Platts	500,000
Feb 10	Charles H. Strub Stakes	Santa Anita	1¼ miles	Defensive Play	Jose Santos	500,000
Feb 23	Fountain of Youth Stakes	Gulfstream Park	1¹⁄₁₆ miles	Fly So Free	Jose Santos	122,895
Mar 9	Santa Anita Handicap	Santa Anita	1¼ miles	Farma Way	Gary Stevens	1,000,000
Mar 16	Florida Derby	Gulfstream	1⅛ miles	Fly So Free	Jose Santos	500,000
Mar 30	Jim Beam Stakes	Turfway	1⅛ miles	Hansel	Jerry Bailey	500,000
Apr 6	Santa Anita Derby	Santa Anita	1⅛ miles	Dinard	Chris McCarron	500,000
Apr 6	Gotham Stakes	Aqueduct	1 mile	Kyle's Our Man	Angel Cordero Jr	150,000
Apr 13	Blue Grass Stakes	Keeneland	1 ⅛ miles	Strike the Gold	Chris Antley	400,800
Apr 13	Oaklawn Handicap	Oaklawn Park	1⅛ miles	Festin	Eddie Dela-houssaye	500,000
Apr 20	Wood Memorial	Aqueduct	1⅛ miles	Cahill Road	Craig Perret	500,000
Apr 26	Arkansas Derby	Oakland Park	1⅛ miles	Olympio	Eddie Dela-houssaye	500,000
May 3	Kentucky Oaks	Churchill Downs	1⅛ miles	Lite Light	Corey Nakatani	318,900
May 4	Kentucky Derby	Churchill Downs	1¼ miles	Strike the Gold	Chris Antley	905,800
May 11	Pimlico Special Handicap	Pimlico	1³⁄₁₆ miles	Farma Way	Gary Stevens	750,000
May 17	Black Eyed Susan Stakes	Pimlico	1⅛ miles	Wide Country	Santos Chavez	250,000
May 18	Preakness Stakes	Pimlico	1³⁄₁₆ miles	Hansel	Jerry Bailey	665,800
May 25	Acorn Stakes	Belmont	1 mile	Meadow Star	Jerry Bailey	172,800
May 27	Hollywood Turf Handicap	Hollywood Park	1¼ miles	Exbourne	Gary Stevens	500,000
May 27	Jersey Derby	Garden State	1⅛ miles	Greek Costume	Mike Smith	300,000
May 27	Metropolitan Handicap	Belmont	1 mile	In Excess	Pat Valenzuela	500,000
June 5	English Derby	Epsom Downs	1½ miles	Generous	Alan Munroe	1,166,100
June 8	Belmont Stakes	Belmont	1½ miles	Hansel	Jerry Bailey	695,800
June 8	Nassau County Handicap	Belmont	1⅛ miles	Festin	Eddie Dela-houssaye	500,000
June 9	Mother Goose Stakes	Belmont	1⅛ miles	Meadow Star	Jerry Bailey	200,000
June 29	Hollywood Gold Cup	Hollywood Park	1¼ miles	Marquetry	David Flores	1,000,000
June 30	Irish Derby	The Currah	1½ miles	Generous	Alan Munroe	1,072,200
July 4	Suburban Handicap	Belmont	1¼ miles	In Excess	Gary Stevens	500,000
July 6	Coaching Club American Oaks	Belmont	1¼ miles	Lite Light	Corey Nakatani	250,000
July 7	Queen's Plate	Woodbine	1¼ miles	Dance Smartly	Pat Day	391,400
July 20	New England Classic	Rockingham	1⅛ miles	Marquetry	David Flores	500,000
July 27	Haskell Invitational	Monmouth	1⅛ miles	Lost Mountain	Craig Perret	500,000
July 28	Jim Dandy Stakes	Saratoga	1⅛ miles	Fly So Free	Jose Santos	179,700
Aug 3	Whitney Handicap	Saratoga	1⅛ miles	In Excess	Gary Steven	250,000
Aug 10	Alabama Stakes	Saratoga	1¼ miles	Versailles Treaty	Angel Cordera Jr	200,000
Aug 10	Pacific Classic	Del Mar	1¼ miles	Best Pal	Pat Valenzuela	1,000,000
Aug 17	Travers Stakes	Saratoga	1¼ miles	Corporate Report	Chris McCarron	1,000,000
Sep 1	Arlington Million	Arlington Int'l	1¼ miles	Tight Spot	Laffit Pincay Jr	1,000,000
Sep 1	Iselin Handicap	Monmouth Park	1⅛ miles	Black Tie Affair	Pat Day	500,000
Sep 11	Del Mar Futurity	Del Mar	1 mile	Bertrando	Alex Solis	287,500
Sep 15	Molson Export Million	Woodbine	1⅛ miles	Dance Smartly	Pat Day	1,000,000
Sep 15	Woodward	Belmont	1⅛ miles	In Excess	Gary Stevens	500,000
Sep 22	Man o' War Stakes	Belmont	1⅜ miles	Solar Splendor	Herb McCaughley	400,000
Sep 22	Super Derby XII	Louisiana Downs	1¼ miles	Free Spirit's Joy	Calvin Borel	1,000,000

1990 Statistical Leaders

Horses

Horse	Starts	1st	2nd	3rd	Purses ($)	Horse	Starts	1st	2nd	3rd	Purses ($)
Unbridled	11	4	3	2	3,718,149	Summer Squall	7	4	2	0	1,222,356
Izvestia	11	8	1	1	2,486,667	Ibn Bey	8	2	2	2	1,132,414
Criminal Type	11	7	2	0	2,270,290	Flying Continental	7	3	1	1	1,096,700
In the Wings	7	4	1	0	1,479,017	Ruhlmann	7	2	1	2	1,095,800
Bayakoa	10	7	2	0	1,234,406	With Approval	11	5	3	1	1,043,840

Jockeys

Jockey	Mounts	1st	2nd	3rd	Purses ($)	Win Pct	$ Pct*
Gary Stevens	1,504	283	245	202	13,881,198	19	49
Jose Santos	1,416	254	187	203	12,844,912	18	45
Craig Perret	732	172	143	94	11,724,403	23	56
Pat Day	1,421	364	265	222	10,424,900	26	60
Angel Cordero Jr.	1,371	263	220	202	9,777,937	19	50
Jerry Bailey	1,210	224	182	167	9,390,557	19	47
Mike Smith	1,767	250	254	230	8,990,289	14	42
Chris McCarron	963	201	145	128	8,891,469	21	49
Alex Solis	1,571	220	151	227	8,071,971	14	38
Eddie Delahoussaye	1,348	183	208	189	8,049,608	14	43

Trainers

Trainer	Starts	1st	2nd	3rd	Purses ($)	Win Pct	$ Pct*
D. Wayne Lukas	1,396	267	219	164	14,511,690	19	47
Carl Nafzger	385	56	51	64	6,114,798	15	44
Charlie Whittingham	382	58	41	52	5,688,885	15	40
Ron McAnally	498	81	54	59	5,435,327	16	39
Roger Attfield	272	67	38	30	5,053,580	25	50
Richard Mandella	430	100	61	65	3,778,362	23	53
Shug McGaughey	175	53	37	30	3,758,712	30	69
Jim Day	373	76	61	54	3,230,800	20	51
Scotty Schulhofer	351	71	46	50	3,152,810	20	48
Gary Jones	358	58	50	47	3,151,402	16	43

*Percentage in the Money (1st, 2nd, and 3rd)

Note: 1990 statistical leaders courtesy of *The American Racing Manual,* a publication of Daily Racing Form, Inc.

HARNESS RACING

Major Stakes Races

Late 1990

Date	Race	Location	Winner	Driver	Purse ($)
Oct 5	Kentucky Futurity	Red Mile	Star Mystic	Jan Johnson	180,000
Nov 2	BC Aged Horse/Gelding Pace	Pompano Park	Bays Fella	Paul Macdonell	273,458
Nov 2	BC Aged Horse/Gelding Trot	Pompano Park	No Sex Please	Ron Waples	221,458
Nov 2	BC Aged Mare Pace	Pompano Park	Caesar's Jackpot	Bill Fahy	200,000
Nov 2	BC Aged Mare Trot	Pompano Park	Peace Corps	Stig Johansson	203,458
Nov 2	BC Three-Year-Old Colt Pace	Pompano Park	Beach Towel	Ray Remmen	366,932
Nov 2	BC Three-Year-Old Colt Trot	Pompano Park	Embassy Lobell	Michel Lachance	396,932
Nov 2	BC Three-Year-Old Filly Pace	Pompano Park	Town Pro	Doug Brown	304,932
Nov 2	BC Three-Year-Old Filly Trot	Pompano Park	Me Maggie	Berndt Lindstedt	378,932
Nov 17	Governor's Cup	Garden State	Artsplace	John Campbell	655,600
Nov 30	BC 2-Yr-Old Filly Pace	Pompano Park	Miss Easy	John Campbell	514,870
Nov 30	BC 2-Yr-Old Filly Trot	Pompano Park	Jean Bi	Jan Nordin	367,402
Nov 30	BC 2-Yr-Old Colt Pace	Pompano Park	Artsplace	John Campbell	605,870
Nov 30	BC 2-Yr-Old Colt Trot	Pompano Park	Crysta's Best	Dick Richardson	355,403

1991 (Through September 21)

Date	Race	Location	Winner	Driver	Purse ($)
May 26	Elitlopp	Solvalla (Sweden)	Peace Corps	Stig Johansson	417,391
June 22	North America Cup	Greenwood Raceway	Precious Bunny	John Campbell	1,000,000
July 12	Meadowlands Pace	Meadowlands	Precious Bunny	Jack Moiseyev	1,000,000
July 13	Yonkers Trot	Yonkers Raceway	Crown's Invitation	Michel Lachance	370,392
Aug 3	Hambletonian	Meadowlands	Giant Victory	Jack Moiseyev	1,238,000
Aug 3	Peter Haughton Memorial	Meadowlands	BJ's Mac	William Gale	558,500
Aug 10	Adios	Meadows	Precious Bunny	Jack Moiseyev	428,880
Aug 16	Sweetheart Pace	Meadowlands	Summer Child	Richie Silverman	643,500
Aug 16	Woodrow Wilson Pace	Meadowlands	Sportsmaster	Ron Waples	889,000

1991 (Through September 21) (*Cont.*)

Date	Race	Location	Winner	Driver	Purse ($)
Aug 18.....	Prix D'Ete Molson	Blue Bonnets	Die Laughing	Richie Silverman	603,500
Aug 24.....	Cane Pace	Yonkers Raceway	Silky Stallone	Jack Moiseyev	523,190
Aug 31.....	World Trotting Derby	DuQuoin	Somatic	Tom Haughton	700,000
Sep 7.......	Messenger Stakes	Rosecraft	Die Laughing	Richie Silverman	475,000
Sep 19.....	Little Brown Jug	Delaware	Precious Bunny	Jack Moiseyev	575,150
Sep 21.....	Metro	Mohawk Raceway	Shipps Saint	Tim Twaddle	716,000

Major Races

The Hambletonian

Horse	Driver	PP	1/4	1/2	3/4	Stretch	Finish
Giant Victory	Jack Moiseyev	2	5	5	5	3-1	1-3/4
M.B. Felty	John Patterson Jr	1	4	4	4	1-1/2	2-3/4
Uconn Don	Michel Lachance	4	6	6	7	5-3	3-3
Somatic	William O'Donnell	7	7	7	6	4-2 3/4	4-5
Crysta's Best	Dick Richardson Jr.	5	3	3	2	2-1/2	5-6 1/4
Anders Crown	Jan Nordin	8	8	8	8	8-5 1/2	6-9 1/2
Super Pleasure	Catello Manzi	6	1	2	3	7-4 1/2	7-10 1/4
Big Brown	John Campbell	3	2	1	1	6-4 1/4	8-11 3/4
Can't Be Jimmie	Ron Pierce	10	10	10	9	9-10 1/2	9-17
Charlie Ten Hitch	Dick Williams II	9	9	9	10	10/dis	10/dis

Time: :28.1; :56.1; 1:25.2; 1:55; Fast

The Little Brown Jug

Horse	Driver	PP	1/4	1/2	3/4	Stretch	Finish
Precious Bunny	Jack Moiseyev	3	1	1	1	1-1 1/2	1-1 3/4
Nuke Skywalker	Ron Pierce	1	2	3	3	2-1 1/2	2-3/4
Three Wizzards	Bill Gale	4	5	5	6	3-3	3-1 1/4
Easy Goer	Joe Pavia Jr.	2	3	2	2	4-4 1/2	4-2 3/4
Stormin Jesse	John Campbell	5	6	6	4	6-4 3/4	5-3
Die Laughing	Richard Silverman	9	4	4	5	7-6 1/4	6-4 1/2
Complex Trooper	Ron Waples	6	8	7	8	5-4 1/2	7-4 3/4
Arcane Hanover	Norm McKnight	7	7	8	7	8-8 1/4	8-6 1/4
Nuclear Legacy	-- Scratched						

Time: :28.1; :57.2; 1:27; 155; Fast

1990 Statistical Leaders

1990 Leading Moneywinners by Age, Sex and Gait

Division	Horse	Starts	1st	2nd	3rd	Earnings ($)
2-Year-Old Pacing Colts and Geldings	Artsplace	15	11	3	0	1,189,271
2-Year-Old Trotting Colts and Geldings	Charlie Ten Hitch	8	7	0	0	366,499
2-Year-Old Pacing Fillies	Miss Easy	17	15	1	1	1,128,956
2-Year-Old Trotting Fillies	Santa Royal	11	5	3	0	427,154
3-Year-Old Pacing Colts and Geldings	Beach Towel	23	18	4	0	2,091,860
3-Year-Old Trotting Colts and Geldings	Harmonious	14	10	0	0	1,033,942
3-Year-Old Pacing Fillies	Town Pro	17	14	2	1	634,690
3-Year-Old Trotting Fillies	Working Gal	20	8	4	1	322,462
Aged Pacers	Dorunrun Bluegrass	31	17	6	2	851,755
Aged Trotters	No Sex Please	28	18	4	1	561,169

Drivers

Driver	Earnings ($)	Driver	Earnings ($)
John Campbell	11,620,878	Bill O'Donnell	4,294,221
Michel Lachance	7,165,323	Bill Fahy	4,034,219
Doug Brown	6,042,217	Ron Waples	3,683,735
Cat Manzi	5,511,211	Dave Magee	3,455,951
Herve Filion	4,309,598	Steve Condren	3,243,361

FOR THE RECORD • Year by Year

THOROUGHBRED RACING

Kentucky Derby

Run at Churchill Downs, Louisville, KY, on the first Saturday in May.

Year	Winner (Margin)	Jockey	Second	Third	Time
1875	Aristides (1)	Oliver Lewis	Volcano	Verdigris	2:37¾
1876	Vagrant (2)	Bobby Swim	Creedmoor	Harry Hill	2:38¼
1877	Baden-Baden (2)	William Walker	Leonard	King William	2:38
1878	Day Star (2)	Jimmie Carter	Himyar	Leveler	2:37¼
1879	Lord Murphy (1)	Charlie Shauer	Falsetto	Strathmore	2:37
1880	Fonso (1)	George Lewis	Kimball	Bancroft	2:37½
1881	Hindoo (4)	Jimmy McLaughin	Lelex	Alfambra	2:40
1882	Apollo (½)	Babe Hurd	Runnymede	Bengal	2:40¼
1883	Leonatus (3)	Billy Donohue	Drake Carter	Lord Raglan	2:43
1884	Buchanan (2)	Isaac Murphy	Loftin	Audrain	2:40¼
1885	Joe Cotton (Neck)	Erskine Henderson	Bersan	Ten Booker	2:37¼
1886	Ben Ali (½)	Paul Duffy	Blue Wing	Free Knight	2:36½
1887	Montrose (2)	Isaac Lewis	Jim Gore	Jacobin	2:39¼
1888	MacBeth II (1)	George Covington	Gallifet	White	2:38¼
1889	Spokane (Nose)	Thomas Kiley	Proctor Knott	Once Again	2:34½
1890	Riley (2)	Isaac Murphy	Bill Letcher	Robespierre	2:45
1891	Kingman (1)	Isaac Murphy	Balgowan	High Tariff	2:52¼
1892	Azra (Nose)	Alonzo Clayton	Huron	Phil Dwyer	2:41½
1893	Lookout (5)	Eddie Kunze	Plutus	Boundless	2:39¼
1894	Chant (2)	Frank Goodale	Pearl Song	Sigurd	2:41
1895	Halma (3)	Soup Perkins	Basso	Laureate	2:37½
1896	Ben Brush (Nose)	Willie Simms	Ben Eder	Semper Ego	2:07¼
1897	Typhoon II (Head)	Buttons Garner	Ornament	Dr. Catlett	2:12½
1898	Plaudit (Neck)	Willie Simms	Lieber Karl	Isabey	2:09
1899	Manuel (2)	Fred Taral	Corsini	Mazo	2:12
1900	Lieut. Gibson (4)	Jimmy Boland	Florizar	Thrive	2:06¼
1901	His Eminence (2)	Jimmy Winkfield	Sannazarro	Driscoll	2:07¾
1902	Alan-a-Dale (Nose)	Jimmy Winkfield	Inventor	The Rival	2:08¾
1903	Judge Himes (¾)	Hal Booker	Early	Bourbon	2:09
1904	Elwood (½)	Frankie Prior	Ed Tierney	Brancas	2:08½
1905	Agile (3)	Jack Martin	Ram's Horn	Layson	2:10¾
1906	Sir Huon (2)	Roscoe Troxler	Lady Navarre	James Reddick	2:08⅕
1907	Pink Star (2)	Andy Minder	Zal	Ovelando	2:12⅗
1908	Stone Street (1)	Arthur Pickens	Sir Cleges	Dunvegan	2:15⅕
1909	Wintergreen (4)	Vincent Powers	Miami	Dr. Barkley	2:08⅕
1910	Donau (½)	Fred Herbert	Joe Morris	Fighting Bob	2:06⅖
1911	Meridian (¾)	George Archibald	Governor Gray	Colston	2:05
1912	Worth (Neck)	Carroll H. Schilling	Duval	Flamma	2:09⅖
1913	Donerail (½)	Roscoe Goose	Ten Point	Gowell	2:04⅘
1914	Old Rosebud (8)	John McCabe	Hodge	Bronzewing	2:03⅖
1915	Regret (2)	Joe Notter	Pebbles	Sharpshooter	2:05⅖
1916	George Smith (Neck)	Johnny Loftus	Star Hawk	Franklin	2:04
1917	Omar Khayyam (2)	Charles Borel	Ticket	Midway	2:04⅗
1918	Exterminator (1)	William Knapp	Escoba	Viva America	2:10⅘
1919	Sir Barton (5)	Johnny Loftus	Billy Kelly	Under Fire	2:09⅘
1920	Paul Jones (Head)	Ted Rice	Upset	On Watch	2:09
1921	Behave Yourself (Head)	Charles Thompson	Black Servant	Prudery	2:04⅕
1922	Morvich (1½)	Albert Johnson	Bet Mosie	John Finn	2:04⅗
1923	Zev (1½)	Earl Sande	Martingale	Vigil	2:05⅖
1924	Black Gold (½)	John Mooney	Chilhowee	Beau Butler	2:05⅕
1925	Flying Ebony (1½)	Earl Sande	Captain Hal	Son of John	2:07⅗
1926	Bubbling Over (5)	Albert Johnson	Bagenbaggage	Rock Man	2:03⅗
1927	Whiskery (Head)	Linus McAtee	Osmond	Jock	2:06
1928	Reigh Count (3)	Chick Lang	Misstep	Toro	2:10⅖
1929	Clyde Van Dusen (2)	Linus McAtee	Naishapur	Panchio	2:10⅘

Year	Winner (Margin)	Jockey	Second	Third	Time
1930	Gallant Fox (2)	Earl Sande	Gallant Knight	Ned O.	2:07⅗
1931	Twenty Grand (4)	Charles Kurtsinger	Sweep All	Mate	2:01⅘
1932	Burgoo King (5)	Eugene James	Economic	Stepenfetchit	2:05⅕
1933	Brokers Tip (Nose)	Don Meade	Head Play	Charley O.	2:06⅘
1934	Cavalcade (2½)	Mack Garner	Discovery	Agrarian	2:04
1935	Omaha (1½)	Willie Saunders	Roman Soldier	Whiskolo	2:05
1936	Bold Venture (Head)	Ira Hanford	Brevity	Indian Broom	2:03⅗
1937	War Admiral (1¾)	Charles Kurtsinger	Pompoon	Reaping Reward	2:03⅕
1938	Lawrin (1)	Eddie Arcaro	Dauber	Can't Wait	2:04⅘
1939	Johnstown (8)	James Stout	Challedon	Heather Broom	2:03⅗
1940	Gallahadion (1½)	Carroll Bierman	Bimelech	Dit	2:05
1941	Whirlaway (8)	Eddie Arcaro	Staretor	Market Wise	2:01⅖
1942	Shut Out (2½)	Wayne Wright	Alsab	Valdina Orphan	2:04⅖
1943	Count Fleet (3)	John Longden	Blue Swords	Slide Rule	2:04
1944	Pensive (4½)	Conn McCreary	Broadcloth	Stir Up	2:04⅕
1945	Hoop Jr. (6)	Eddie Arcaro	Pot o' Luck	Darby Dieppe	2:07
1946	Assault (8)	Warren Mehrtens	Spy Song	Hampden	2:06⅗
1947	Jet Pilot (Head)	Eric Guerin	Phalanx	Faultless	2:06⅘
1948	Citation (3½)	Eddie Arcaro	Coaltown	My Request	2:05⅖
1949	Ponder (3)	Steve Brooks	Capot	Palestinian	2:04⅕
1950	Middleground (1¼)	William Boland	Hill Prince	Mr. Trouble	2:01⅗
1951	Count Turf (4)	Conn McCreary	Royal Mustang	Ruhe	2:02⅗
1952	Hill Gail (2)	Eddie Arcaro	Sub Fleet	Blue Man	2:01⅗
1953	Dark Star (Head)	Hank Moreno	Native Dancer	Invigorator	2:02
1954	Determine (1½)	Ray York	Hasty Road	Hasseyampa	2:03
1955	Swaps (1½)	Bill Shoemaker	Nashua	Summer Tan	2:01⅘
1956	Needles (¾)	Dave Erb	Fabius	Come On Red	2:03⅖
1957	Iron Liege (Nose)	Bill Hartack	Gallant Man	Round Table	2:02⅕
1958	Tim Tam (½)	Ismael Valenzuela	Lincoln Road	Noureddin	2:05
1959	Tomy Lee (Nose)	Bill Shoemaker	Sword Dancer	First Landing	2:02⅕
1960	Venetian Way (3½)	Bill Hartack	Bally Ache	Victoria Park	2:02⅖
1961	Carry Back (¾)	John Sellers	Crozier	Bass Clef	2:04
1962	Decidedly (2¼)	Bill Hartack	Roman Line	Ridan	2:00⅖
1963	Chateaugay (1¼)	Braulio Baeza	Never Bend	Candy Spots	2:01⅘
1964	Northern Dancer (Neck)	Bill Hartack	Hill Rise	The Scoundrel	2:00
1965	Lucky Debonair (Neck)	Bill Shoemaker	Dapper Dan	Tom Rolfe	2:01⅕
1966	Kauai King (½)	Don Brumfield	Advocator	Blue Skyer	2:02
1967	Proud Clarion (1)	Bobby Ussery	Barbs Delight	Damascus	2:00⅗
1968	Forward Pass (Disq.)	Ismael Valenzuela	Francie's Hat	T.V. Commercial	2:02⅕
1969	Majestic Prince (Neck)	Bill Hartack	Arts and Letters	Dike	2:01⅘
1970	Dust Commander (5)	Mike Manganello	My Dad George	High Echelon	2:03⅖
1971	Canonero II (3¾)	Gustavo Avila	Jim French	Bold Reason	2:03⅕
1972	Riva Ridge (3¼)	Ron Turcotte	No Le Hace	Hold Your Peace	2:01⅘
1973	Secretariat (2½)	Ron Turcotte	Sham	Our Native	1:59⅖
1974	Cannonade (2¼)	Angel Cordero Jr	Hudson County	Agitate	2:04
1975	Foolish Pleasure (1¾)	Jacinto Vasquez	Avatar	Diabolo	2:02
1976	Bold Forbes (1)	Angel Cordero Jr	Honest Pleasure	Elocutionist	2:01⅗
1977	Seattle Slew (1¾)	Jean Cruguet	Run Dusty Run	Sanhedrin	2:02⅕
1978	Affirmed (1¼)	Steve Cauthen	Alydar	Believe It	2:01⅕
1979	Spectacular Bid (2¾)	Ronald J. Franklin	General Assembly	Golden Act	2:02⅖
1980	Genuine Risk (1)	Jacinto Vasquez	Rumbo	Jaklin Klugman	2:02
1981	Pleasant Colony (¾)	Jorge Velasquez	Woodchopper	Partez	2:02
1982	Gato Del Sol (2½)	Eddie Delahoussaye	Laser Light	Reinvested	2:02⅕
1983	Sunny's Halo (2)	Eddie Delahoussaye	Desert Wine	Caveat	2:02⅕
1984	Swale (3¼)	Laffit Pincay Jr	Coax Me Chad	At the Threshold	2:02⅖
1985	Spend A Buck (5)	Angel Cordero Jr	Stephan's Odyssey	Chief's Crown	2:00⅕
1986	Ferdinand (2¼)	Bill Shoemaker	Bold Arrangement	Broad Brush	2:02⅘
1987	Alysheba (¾)	Chris McCarron	Bet Twice	Avies Copy	2:03⅖

Kentucky Derby (*Cont.*)

Year	Winner (Margin)	Jockey	Second	Third	Time
1988	Winning Colors (Neck)	Gary Stevens	Forty Niner	Risen Star	2:02 1/5
1989	Sunday Silence (2½)	Pat Valenzuela	Easy Goer	Awe Inspiring	2:05
1990	Unbridled (3½)	Craig Perret	Summer Squall	Pleasant Tap	2:02
1991	Strike the Gold (1¾)	Chris Antley	Best Pal	Mane Minister	2:03

Note: Distance: 1½ miles (1875-95), 1¼ miles (1896-present).

Preakness

Run at Pimlico Race Course, Baltimore, Md., two weeks after the Kentucky Derby.

Year	Winner (Margin)	Jockey	Second	Third	Time
1873	Survivor (10)	G. Barbee	John Boulger	Artist	2:43
1874	Culpepper (¾)	W. Donohue	King Amadeus	Scratch	2:56½
1875	Tom Ochiltree (2)	L. Hughes	Viator	Bay Final	2:43½
1876	Shirley (4)	G. Barbee	Rappahannock	Algerine	2:44¾
1877	Cloverbrook (4)	C. Holloway	Bombast	Lucifer	2:45½
1878	Duke of Magenta (6)	C. Holloway	Bayard	Albert	2:41¾
1879	Harold (3)	L. Hughes	Jericho	Rochester	2:40½
1880	Grenada (¾)	L. Hughes	Oden	Emily F.	2:40½
1881	Saunterer (½)	T. Costello	Compensation	Baltic	2:40½
1882	Vanguard (Neck)	T. Costello	Heck	Col Watson	2:44½
1883	Jacobus (4)	G. Barbee	Parnell		2:42½
1884	Knight of Ellerslie (2)	S. Fisher	Welcher		2:39½
1885	Tecumseh (2)	Jim McLaughlin	Wickham	John C.	2:49
1886	The Bard (3)	S. Fisher	Eurus	Elkwood	2:45
1887	Dunboyne (1)	W. Donohue	Mahoney	Raymond	2:39½
1888	Refund (3)	F. Littlefield	Judge Murray	Glendale	2:49
1889	Buddhist (8)	W. Anderson	Japhet		2:17½
1890*	Montague (3)	W. Martin	Philosophy	Barrister	2:36¾
1894	Assignee (3)	Fred Taral	Potentate	Ed Kearney	1:49¼
1895	Belmar (1)	Fred Taral	April Fool	Sue Kittie	1:50½
1896	Margrave (1)	H. Griffin	Hamilton II	Intermission	1:51
1897	Paul Kauvar (1½)	C. Thorpe	Elkins	On Deck	1:51¼
1898	Sly Fox (2)	C. W. Simms	The Huguenot	Nuto	1:49 3/5
1899	Half Time (1)	R. Clawson	Filigrane	Lackland	1:47
1900	Hindus (Head)	H. Spencer	Sarmation	Ten Candles	1:48 2/5
1901	The Parader (2)	F. Landry	Sadie S.	Dr. Barlow	1:47 1/5
1902	Old England (Nose)	L. Jackson	Major Daingerfield	Namtor	1:45 4/5
1903	Flocarline (½)	W. Gannon	Mackey Dwyer	Rightful	1:44 4/5
1904	Bryn Mawr (1)	E. Hildebrand	Wotan	Dolly Spanker	1:44 1/5
1905	Cairngorm (Head)	W. Davis	Kiamesha	Coy Maid	1:45 4/5
1906	Whimsical (4)	Walter Miller	Content	Larabie	1:45
1907	Don Enrique (1)	G. Mountain	Ethon	Zambesi	1:45 2/5
1908	Royal Tourist (4)	E. Dugan	Live Wire	Robert Cooper	1:46 2/5
1909	Effendi (1)	Willie Doyle	Fashion Plate	Hilltop	1:39 4/5
1910	Layminster (½)	R. Estep	Dalhousie	Sager	1:40 3/5
1911	Watervale (1)	E. Dugan	Zeus	The Nigger	1:51
1912	Colonel Holloway (5)	C. Turner	Bwana Tumbo	Tipsand	1:56 3/5
1913	Buskin (Neck)	J. Butwell	Kleburne	Barnegat	1:53 2/5
1914	Holiday (¾)	A. Schuttinger	Brave Cunarder	Defendum	1:53 4/5
1915	Rhine Maiden (1½)	Douglas Hoffman	Half Rock	Runes	1:58
1916	Damrosch (1½)	Linus McAtee	Greenwood	Achievement	1:54 4/5
1917	Kalitan (2)	E. Haynes	Al M. Dick	Kentucky Boy	1:54 2/5
1918	War Cloud (¾)	Johnny Loftus	Sunny Slope	Lanius	1:53 3/5
1918	Jack Hare, Jr (2)	C. Peak	The Porter	Kate Bright	1:53 2/5
1919	Sir Barton (4)	Johnny Loftus	Eternal	Sweep On	1:53
1920	Man o' War (1½)	Clarence Kummer	Upset	Wildair	1:51 3/5
1921	Broomspun (¾)	F. Coltiletti	Polly Ann	Jeg	1:54 1/5
1922	Pillory (Head)	L. Morris	Hea	June Grass	1:51 3/5
1923	Vigil (1¼)	B. Marinelli	General Thatcher	Rialto	1:53 3/5
1924	Nellie Morse (1½)	J. Merimee	Transmute	Mad Play	1:57 1/5
1925	Coventry (4)	Clarence Kummer	Backbone	Almadel	1:59

Year	Winner (Margin)	Jockey	Second	Third	Time
1926	Display (Head)	J. Maiben	Blondin	Mars	1:59⅘
1927	Bostonian (½)	A. Abel	Sir Harry	Whiskery	2:01⅗
1928	Victorian (Nose)	Sonny Workman	Toro	Solace	2:00⅕
1929	Dr. Freeland (1)	Louis Schaefer	Minotaur	African	2:01⅗
1930	Gallant Fox (¾)	Earl Sande	Crack Brigade	Snowflake	2:00⅗
1931	Mate (1½)	G. Ellis	Twenty Grand	Ladder	1:59
1932	Burgoo King (Head)	E. James	Tick On	Boatswain	1:59⅘
1933	Head Play (4)	Charles Kurtsinger	Ladysman	Utopian	2:02
1934	High Quest (Nose)	R. Jones	Cavalcade	Discovery	1:58⅕
1935	Omaha (6)	Willie Saunders	Firethorn	Psychic Bid	1:58⅖
1936	Bold Venture (Nose)	George Woolf	Granville	Jean Bart	1:59
1937	War Admiral (Head)	Charles Kurtsinger	Pompoon	Flying Scot	1:58⅖
1938	Dauber (7)	M. Peters	Cravat	Menow	1:59⅘
1939	Challedon (1¼)	George Seabo	Gilded Knight	Volitant	1:59⅘
1940	Bimelech (3)	F. A. Smith	Mioland	Gallahadion	1:58⅗
1941	Whirlaway (5½)	Eddie Arcaro	King Cole	Our Boots	1:58⅘
1942	Alsab (1)	B. James	Requested / Sun Again	(dead heat for second)	1:57
1943	Count Fleet (8)	Johnny Longden	Blue Swords	Vincentive	1:57⅖
1944	Pensive (¾)	Conn McCreary	Platter	Stir Up	1:59⅕
1945	Polynesian (2½)	W. D. Wright	Hoop Jr	Darby Dieppe	1:58⅘
1946	Assault (Neck)	Warren Mehrtens	Lord Boswell	Hampden	2:01⅖
1947	Faultless (1¼)	Doug Dodson	On Trust	Phalanx	1:59
1948	Citation (5½)	Eddie Arcaro	Vulcan's Forge	Bovard	2:02⅖
1949	Capot (Head)	Ted Atkinson	Palestinian	Noble Impulse	1:56
1950	Hill Prince (5)	Eddie Arcaro	Middleground	Dooley	1:59⅕
1951	Bold (7)	Eddie Arcaro	Counterpoint	Alerted	1:56⅖
1952	Blue Man (3½)	Conn McCreary	Jampol	One Count	1:57⅖
1953	Native Dancer (Neck)	Eric Guerin	Jamie K.	Royal Bay Gem	1:57⅘
1954	Hasty Road (Neck)	Johnny Adams	Correlation	Hasseyampa	1:57⅖
1955	Nashua (1)	Eddie Arcaro	Saratoga	Traffic Judge	1:54⅗
1956	Fabius (¾)	Bill Hartack	Needles	No Regrets	1:58⅖
1957	Bold Ruler (2)	Eddie Arcaro	Iron Liege	Inside Tract	1:56⅕
1958	Tim Tam (1½)	I. Valenzuela	Lincoln Road	Gone Fishin'	1:57⅕
1959	Royal Orbit (4)	William Harmatz	Sword Dancer	Dunce	1:57
1960	Bally Ache (4)	Bobby Ussery	Victoria Park	Celtic Ash	1:57⅗
1961	Carry Back (¾)	Johnny Sellers	Globemaster	Crozier	1:57⅗
1962	Greek Money (Nose)	John Rotz	Ridan	Roman Line	1:56⅕
1963	Candy Spots (3½)	Bill Shoemaker	Chateaugay	Never Bend	1:56⅕
1964	Northern Dancer (2¼)	Bill Hartack	The Scoundrel	Hill Rise	1:56⅘
1965	Tom Rolfe (Neck)	Ron Turcotte	Dapper Dan	Hail to All	1:56⅕
1966	Kauai King (1¾)	Don Brumfield	Stupendous	Amberoid	1:55⅖
1967	Damascus (2¼)	Bill Shoemaker	In Reality	Proud Clarion	1:55⅕
1968	Forward Pass (6)	I. Valenzuela	Out of the Way	Nodouble	1:56⅘
1969	Majestic Prince (Head)	Bill Hartack	Arts and Letters	Jay Ray	1:55⅗
1970	Personality (Neck)	Eddie Belmonte	My Dad George	Silent Screen	1:56⅕
1971	Canonero II (1½)	Gustavo Avila	Eastern Fleet	Jim French	1:54
1972	Bee Bee Bee (1¼)	Eldon Nelson	No Le Hace	Key to the Mint	1:55⅗
1973	Secretariat (2½)	Ron Turcotte	Sham	Our Native	1:54⅖
1974	Little Current (7)	Miguel Rivera	Neapolitan Way	Cannonade	1:54⅗
1975	Master Derby (1)	Darrel McHargue	Foolish Pleasure	Diabolo	1:56⅖
1976	Elocutionist (3)	John Lively	Play the Red	Bold Forbes	1:55
1977	Seattle Slew (1½)	Jean Cruguet	Iron Constitution	Run Dusty Run	1:54⅖
1978	Affirmed (Neck)	Steve Cauthen	Alydar	Believe It	1:54⅖
1979	Spectacular Bid (5½)	Ron Franklin	Golden Act	Screen King	1:54⅕
1980	Codex (4¾)	Angel Cordero Jr	Genuine Risk	Colonel Moran	1:54⅕
1981	Pleasant Colony (1)	Jorge Velasquez	Bold Ego	Paristo	1:54⅗
1982	Aloma's Ruler (½)	Jack Kaenel	Linkage	Cut Away	1:55⅖

Preakness (*Cont.*)

Year	Winner (Margin)	Jockey	Second	Third	Time
1983	Deputed Testamony (2¾)	Donald Miller Jr	Desert Wine	High Honors	1:55⅖
1984	Gate Dancer (1½)	Angel Cordero Jr	Play On	Fight Over	1:53⅗
1985	Tank's Prospect (Head)	Pat Day	Chief's Crown	Eternal Prince	1:53⅖
1986	Snow Chief (4)	Alex Solis	Ferdinand	Broad Brush	1:54⅘
1987	Alysheba (½)	Chris McCarron	Bet Twice	Cryptoclearance	1:55⅘
1988	Risen Star (1¼)	E. Delahoussaye	Brian's Time	Winning Colors	1:56⅕
1989	Sunday Silence (Nose)	Pat Valenzuela	Easy Goer	Rock Point	1:53⅘
1990	Summer Squall (2¼)	Pat Day	Unbridled	Mister Frisky	1:53⅗
1991	Hansel (Head)	Jerry Bailey	Corporate Report	Mane Minister	1:54

*Preakness was not run 1891–1893. In 1918, it was run in two divisions.

Note: Distance: 1½ miles (1873–88), 1¼ miles (1889), 1½ miles (1890), 11⁄16 miles (1894–1900), 1 mile and 70 yards (1901–1907), 11⁄16 miles (1908), 1 mile (1909–10), 1⅛ miles (1911–24), 1 3⁄16 miles (1925–present).

Belmont

Run at Belmont Park, Elmont, NY, three weeks after the Preakness Stakes. Held previously at two locations in the Bronx, NY: Jerome Park (1867–1889) and Morris Park (1890–1904).

Year	Winner (Margin)	Jockey	Second	Third	Time
1867	Ruthless (Head)	J. Gilpatrick	De Courcy	Rivoli	3:05
1868	General Duke (2)	R. Swim	Northumberland	Fannie Ludlow	3:02
1869	Fenian (Unknown)	C. Miller	Glenelg	Invercauld	3:04¼
1870	Kingfisher (½)	E. Brown	Foster	Midday	2:59½
1871	Harry Bassett (3)	W. Miller	Stockwood	By-the-Sea	2:56
1872	Joe Daniels (¾)	James Rowe	Meteor	Shylock	2:58¼
1873	Springbok (4)	James Rowe	Count d'Orsay	Strachino	3:01¾
1874	Saxon (Neck)	G. Barbee	Grinstead	Aaron Pennington	2:39½
1875	Calvin (2)	R. Swim	Aristides	Milner	2:40¼
1876	Algerine (Head)	W. Donahue	Fiddlestick	Barricade	2:40½
1877	Cloverbrook (1)	C. Holloway	Loiterer	Baden-Baden	2:46
1878	Duke of Magenta (2)	L. Hughes	Bramble	Sparta	2:43½
1879	Spendthrift (5)	S. Evans	Monitor	Jericho	2:42¾
1880	Grenada (½)	L. Hughes	Ferncliffe	Turenne	2:47
1881	Saunterer (Neck)	T. Costello	Eole	Baltic	2:47
1882	Forester (5)	James McLaughlin	Babcock	Wyoming	2:43
1883	George Kinney (2)	James McLaughlin	Trombone	Renegade	2:42½
1884	Panique (½)	James McLaughlin	Knight of Ellerslie	Himalaya	2:42
1885	Tyrant (3½)	Paul Duffy	St Augustine	Tecumseh	2:43
1886	Inspector B (1)	James McLaughlin	The Bard	Linden	2:41
1887	Hanover (28-32)	James McLaughlin	Oneko		2:43½
1888	Sir Dixon (12)	James McLaughlin	Prince Royal		2:40¼
1889	Eric (Head)	W. Hayward	Diable	Zephyrus	2:47
1890	Burlington (1)	S. Barnes	Devotee	Padishah	2:07¾
1891	Foxford (Neck)	E. Garrison	Montana	Laurestan	2:08¾
1892	Patron (Unknown)	W. Hayward	Shellbark		2:17
1893	Comanche (Head)(21)	Willie Simms	Dr. Rice	Rainbow	1:53¼
1894	Henry of Navarre (2-4)	Willie Simms	Prig	Assignee	1:56½
1895	Belmar (Head)	Fred Taral	Counter Tenor	Nanki Pooh	2:11½
1896	Hastings (Neck)	H. Griffin	Handspring	Hamilton II	2:24½
1897	Scottish Chieftain (1)	J. Scherrer	On Deck	Octagon	2:23¼

Belmont (*Cont.*)

Year	Winner (Margin)	Jockey	Second	Third	Time
1898	Bowling Brook (8)	P. Littlefield	Previous	Hamburg	2:32
1899	Jean Bereaud (Head)	R. R. Clawson	Half Time	Glengar	2:23
1900	Ildrim (Head)	N. Turner	Petrucio	Missionary	2:21½
1901	Commando (½)	H. Spencer	The Parader	All Green	2:21
1902	Masterman (2)	John Bullmann	Ranald	King Hanover	2:22½
1903	Africander (2)	John Bullmann	Whorler	Red Knight	2:23⅕
1904	Delhi (3½)	George Odom	Graziallo	Rapid Water	2:06⅗
1905	Tanya (½)	E. Hildebrand	Blandy	Hot Shot	2:08
1906	Burgomaster (4)	L. Lyne	The Quail	Accountant	2:20
1907	Peter Pan (1)	G. Mountain	Superman	Frank Gill	Unknown
1908	Colin (Head)	Joe Notter	Fair Play	King James	Unknown
1909	Joe Madden (8)	E. Dugan	Wise Mason	Donald MacDonald	2:21⅗
1910* ...	Sweep (6)	J. Butwell	Duke of Ormonde		2:22
1913	Prince Eugene (½)	Roscoe Troxler	Rock View	Flying Fairy	2:18
1914	Luke McLuke (8)	M. Buxton	Gainer	Charlestonian	2:20
1915	The Finn (4)	G. Byrne	Half Rock	Pebbles	2:18⅖
1916	Friar Rock (3)	E. Haynes	Spur	Churchill	2:22
1917	Hourless (10)	J. Butwell	Skeptic	Wonderful	2:17⅘
1918	Johren (2)	Frank Robinson	War Cloud	Cum Sah	2:20⅖
1919	Sir Barton (5)	Johnny Loftus	Sweep On	Natural Bridge	2:17⅖
1920	Man o' War (20)	Clarence Kummer	Donnacona		2:14⅕
1921	Grey Lag (3)	Earl Sande	Sporting Blood	Leonardo II	2:16⅘
1922	Pillory (2)	C. H. Miller	Snob II	Hea	2:18⅘
1923	Zev (1½)	Earl Sande	Chickvale	Rialto	2:19
1924	Mad Play (2)	Earl Sande	Mr. Mutt	Modest	2:18⅘
1925	American Flag (8)	Albert Johnson	Dangerous	Swope	2:16⅘
1926	Crusader (1)	Albert Johnson	Espino	Haste	2:32⅕
1927	Chance Shot (1½)	Earl Sande	Bois de Rose	Flambino	2:32⅖
1928	Vito (3)	Clarence Kummer	Genie	Diavolo	2:33⅕
1929	Blue Larkspur (¾)	Mack Garner	African	Jack High	2:32⅘
1930	Gallant Fox (3)	Earl Sande	Whichone	Questionnaire	2:31⅗
1931	Twenty Grand (10)	Charles Kurtsinger	Sun Meadow	Jamestown	2:29⅗
1932	Faireno (1½)	T. Malley	Osculator	Flag Pole	2:32⅘
1933	Hurryoff (1½)	Mack Garner	Nimbus	Union	2:32⅗
1934	Peace Chance (6)	W. D. Wright	High Quest	Good Goods	2:29⅕
1935	Omaha (1½)	Willie Saunders	Firethorn	Rosemont	2:30⅗
1936	Granville (Nose)	James Stout	Mr. Bones	Hollyrood	2:30
1937	War Admiral (3)	Charles Kurtsinger	Sceneshifter	Vamoose	2:28⅗
1938	Pasteurized (Neck)	James Stout	Dauber	Cravat	2:29⅖
1939	Johnstown (5)	James Stout	Belay	Gilded Knight	2:29⅗
1940	Bimelech (¾)	F. A. Smith	Your Chance	Andy K	2:29⅗
1941	Whirlaway (2½)	Eddie Arcaro	Robert Morris	Yankee Chance	2:31
1942	Shut Out (2)	Eddie Arcaro	Alsab	Lochinvar	2:29⅕
1943	Count Fleet (25)	Johnny Longden	Fairy Manhurst	Deseronto	2:28⅕
1944	Bounding Home (½)	G. L. Smith	Pensive	Bull Dandy	2:32⅕
1945	Pavot (5)	Eddie Arcaro	Wildlife	Jeep	2:30⅕
1946	Assault (3)	Warren Mehrtens	Natchez	Cable	2:30⅘
1947	Phalanx (5)	R. Donoso	Tide Rips	Tailspin	2:29⅖
1948	Citation (8)	Eddie Arcaro	Better Self	Escadru	2:28⅕
1949	Capot (½)	Ted Atkinson	Ponder	Palestinian	2:30⅕
1950	Middleground (1)	William Boland	Lights Up	Mr. Trouble	2:28⅗
1951	Counterpoint (4)	D. Gorman	Battlefield	Battle Morn	2:29
1952	One Count (2½)	Eddie Arcaro	Blue Man	Armageddon	2:30⅕
1953	Native Dancer (Neck)	Eric Guerin	Jamie K.	Royal Bay Gem	2:38⅗
1954	High Gun (Neck)	Eric Guerin	Fisherman	Limelight	2:30⅘
1955	Nashua (9)	Eddie Arcaro	Blazing Count	Portersville	2:29
1956	Needles (Neck)	David Erb	Career Boy	Fabius	2:29⅘
1957	Gallant Man (8)	Bill Shoemaker	Inside Tract	Bold Ruler	2:26⅗
1958	Cavan (6)	Pete Anderson	Tim Tam	Flamingo	2:30⅕
1959	Sword Dancer (¾)	Bill Shoemaker	Bagdad	Royal Orbit	2:28⅖
1960	Celtic Ash (5½)	Bill Hartack	Venetian Way	Disperse	2:29⅗
1961	Sherluck (2¼)	Braulio Baeza	Globemaster	Guadalcanal	2:29⅕

Year	Winner (Margin)	Jockey	Second	Third	Time
1962	Jaipur (Nose)	Bill Shoemaker	Admiral's Voyage	Crimson Satan	2:28⅘
1963	Chateaugay (2½)	Braulio Baeza	Candy Spots	Choker	2:30⅕
1964	Quadrangle (2)	Manuel Ycaza	Roman Brother	Northern Dancer	2:28⅖
1965	Hail to All (Neck)	John Sellers	Tom Rolfe	First Family	2:28⅖
1966	Amberold (2½)	William Boland	Buffle	Advocator	2:29⅗
1967	Damascus (2½)	Bill Shoemaker	Cool Reception	Gentleman James	2:28⅘
1968	Stage Door Johnny (1¼)	Hellodoro Gustines	Forward Pass	Call Me Prince	2:27⅕
1969	Arts and Letters (5½)	Braulio Baeza	Majestic Prince	Dike	2:28⅘
1970	High Echelon (¾)	John L. Rotz	Needles N Pins	Naskra	2:34
1971	Pass Catcher (¾)	Walter Blum	Jim French	Bold Reason	2:30⅖
1972	Riva Ridge (7)	Ron Turcotte	Ruritania	Cloudy Dawn	2:28
1973	Secretariat (31)	Ron Turcotte	Twice a Prince	My Gallant	2:24
1974	Little Current (7)	Miguel A. Rivera	Jolly Johu	Cannonade	2:29⅕
1975	Avatar (Neck)	Bill Shoemaker	Foolish Pleasure	Master Derby	2:28⅕
1976	Bold Forbes (Neck)	Angel Cordero, Jr	McKenzie Bridge	Great Contractor	2:29
1977	Seattle Slew (4)	Jean Cruguet	Run Dusty Run	Sanhedrin	2:29⅗
1978	Affirmed (Head)	Ruben Hernandez	Alydar	Darby Creek Road	2:26⅘
1979	Coastal (3¼)	Ruben Hernandez	Golden Act	Spectacular Bid	2:28⅗
1980	Temperence Hill (2)	Eddie Maple	Genuine Risk	Rockhill Native	2:29⅘
1981	Summing (Neck)	George Martens	Highland Blade	Pleasant Colony	2:29
1982	Conquistador Cielo (14½)	Laffit Pincay, Jr	Gato Del Sol	Illuminate	2:28⅕
1983	Caveat (3½)	Laffit Pincay, Jr	Slew o'Gold	Barberstown	2:27⅘
1984	Swale (4)	Laffit Pincay, Jr	Pine Circle	Morning Bob	2:27⅕
1985	Creme Fraiche (½)	Eddie Maple	Stephan's Odyssey	Chief's Crown	2:27
1986	Danzig Connection (1¼)	Chris McCarron	Johns Treasure	Ferdinand	2:29⅘
1987	Bet Twice (14)	Craig Perret	Cryptoclearance	Gulch	2:28⅕
1988	Risen Star (14¾)	Eddie Delahoussaye	Kingpost	Brian's Time	2:26⅖
1989	Easy Goer (8)	Pat Day	Sunday Silence	Le Voyageur	2:26
1990	Go and Go (8¼)	Michael Kinane	Thirty Six Red	Baron de Vaux	2:27⅕
1991	Hansel (Head)	Jerry Bailey	Strike the Gold	Mane Minister	2:28

*Race not held in 1911-1912.

Note: Distance: 1 mile 5 furlongs (1867-89), 1¼ miles (1890-1905), 1⅜ miles (1906-25), 1½ miles (1926-present).

Neighing In

Don't look now, but a 1,005-pound Dirty Diaper ran at Oklahoma City's Remington Park racetrack last spring. Not only were track officials aware of the situation, but they posted the news on 300 video monitors around the park.

The weights of Dirty Diaper and other horses are provided to fans at Remington through a program called The Right Weigh. "Handicappers throw a fit if a jockey is overweight," says track racing analyst Scott Wells, who devised the program in the fall of 1990. "Why shouldn't they care about a horse whose beer belly equals the bulk of half a jockey?"

Thirty minutes before each race, horses are led to a barn where they are walked onto a ground-level, electronic livestock scale. Within seconds, a digital readout displaying their weights is flashed on the monitors. Horseplayers can then check each weight against the program, which lists the horses' weights from previous races at Remington.

Remington is the only track in North America that releases weigh-in results to the public, but the practice has been standard in Japan and South America for years. Wells, though, claims he got the idea after betting $10 in October 1990 that Buster Douglas would beat Evander Holyfield in their heavyweight championship fight. Says Wells, "Once I saw Buster on the scale, I knew I had kissed my money goodbye."

Triple Crown Winners

Year	Horse	Jockey	Owner	Trainer
1919	Sir Barton	John Loftus	J. K. L. Ross	H. G. Bedwell
1930	Gallant Fox	Earle Sande	Belair Stud	James Fitzsimmons
1935	Omaha	William Saunders	Belair Stud	James Fitzsimmons
1937	War Admiral	Charles Kurtsinger	Samuel D. Riddle	George Conway
1941	Whirlaway	Eddie Arcaro	Calumet Farm	Ben Jones
1943	Count Fleet	John Longden	Mrs J. D. Hertz	Don Cameron
1946	Assault	Warren Mehrtens	King Ranch	Max Hirsch
1948	Citation	Eddie Arcaro	Calumet Farm	Jimmy Jones
1973	Secretariat	Ron Turcotte	Meadow Stable	Lucien Laurin
1977	Seattle Slew	Jean Cruguet	Karen L. Taylor	William H. Turner Jr
1978	Affirmed	Steve Cauthen	Harbor View Farm	Laz Barrera

Awards

Horse of the Year

Year	Horse	Owner	Trainer	Breeder
1936	Granville	Belair Stud	James Fitzsimmons	Belair Stud
1937	War Admiral	Samuel D. Riddle	George Conway	Mrs. Samuel D. Riddle
1938	Seabiscuit	Charles S. Howard	Tom Smith	Wheatley Stable
1939	Challedon	William L. Brann	Louis J. Schaefer	Branncastle Farm
1940	Challedon	William L. Brann	Louis J. Schaefer	Branncastle Farm
1941	Whirlaway	Calumet Farm	Ben Jones	Calumet Farm
1942	Whirlaway	Calumet Farm	Ben Jones	Calumet Farm
1943	Count Fleet	Mrs. John D. Hertz	Don Cameron	Mrs. John D. Hertz
1944	Twilight Tear	Calumet Farm	Ben Jones	Calumet Farm
1945	Busher	Louis B. Mayer	George Odom	Idle Hour Stock Farm
1946	Assault	King Ranch	Max Hirsch	King Ranch
1947	Armed	Calumet Farm	Jimmy Jones	Calumet Farm
1948	Citation	Calumet Farm	Jimmy Jones	Calumet Farm
1949	Capot	Greentree Stable	John M. Gaver Sr	Greentree Stable
1950	Hill Prince	C. T. Chenery	Casey Hayes	C. T. Chenery
1951	Counterpoint	C. V. Whitney	Syl Veitch	C. V. Whitney
1952	One Count	Mrs. W. M. Jeffords	O. White	W. M. Jeffords
1953	Tom Fool	Greentree Stable	John M. Gaver Sr	D. A. Headley
1954	Native Dancer	A. G. Vanderbilt	Bill Winfrey	A. G. Vanderbilt
1955	Nashua	Belair Stud	James Fitzsimmons	Belair Stud
1956	Swaps	Ellsworth-Galbreath	Mesh Tenney	R. Ellsworth
1957	Bold Ruler	Wheatley Stable	James Fitzsimmons	Wheatley Stable
1958	Round Table	Kerr Stables	Willy Molter	Claiborne Farm
1959	Sword Dancer	Brookmeade Stable	Elliott Burch	Brookmeade Stable
1960	Kelso	Bohemia Stable	C. Hanford	Mrs. R. C. duPont
1961	Kelso	Bohemia Stable	C. Hanford	Mrs. R. C. duPont
1962	Kelso	Bohemia Stable	C. Hanford	Mrs. R. C. duPont
1963	Kelso	Bohemia Stable	C. Hanford	Mrs. R. C. duPont
1964	Kelso	Bohemia Stable	C. Hanford	Mrs. R. C. duPont
1965	Roman Brother	Harbor View Stable	Burley Parke	Ocala Stud
1966	Buckpasser	Ogden Phipps	Eddie Neloy	Ogden Phipps
1967	Damascus	Mrs. E. W. Bancroft	Frank Y. Whiteley Jr	Mrs. E. W. Bancroft
1968	Dr. Fager	Tartan Stable	John A. Nerud	Tartan Farms
1969	Arts and Letters	Rokeby Stable	Elliott Burch	Paul Mellon
1970	Fort Marcy	Rokeby Stable	Elliott Burch	Paul Mellon
1971	Ack Ack	E. E. Fogelson	Charlie Whittingham	H. F. Guggenheim
1972	Secretariat	Meadow Stable	Lucien Laurin	Meadow Stud
1973	Secretariat	Meadow Stable	Lucien Laurin	Meadow Stud
1974	Forego	Lazy F Ranch	Sherrill W. Ward	Lazy F Ranch
1975	Forego	Lazy F Ranch	Sherrill W. Ward	Lazy F Ranch
1976	Forego	Lazy F Ranch	Frank Y. Whiteley Jr	Lazy F Ranch
1977	Seattle Slew	Karen L. Taylor	Billy Turner Jr	B. S. Castleman
1978	Affirmed	Harbor View Farm	Laz Barrera	Harbor View Farm
1979	Affirmed	Harbor View Farm	Laz Barrera	Harbor View Farm
1980	Spectacular Bid	Hawksworth Farm	Bud Delp	Mmes. Gilmore and Jason

Horse of the Year (*Cont.*)

Year	Horse	Owner	Trainer	Breeder
1981	John Henry	Dotsam Stable	Ron McAnally and Lefty Nickerson	Golden Chance Farm
1982	Conquistador Cielo	H. de Kwiatkowski	Woody Stephens	L. E. Iandoli
1983	All Along	Daniel Wildenstein	P. L. Biancone	Dayton
1984	John Henry	Dotsam Stable	Ron McAnally	Golden Chance Farm
1985	Spend a Buck	Hunter Farm	Cam Gambolati	Irish Hill Farm & R. W. Harper
1986	Lady's Secret	Mr. & Mrs. Eugene Klein	D. Wayne Lukas	R. H. Spreen
1987	Ferdinand	Mrs. H. B. Keck	Charlie Whittingham	H. B. Keck
1988	Alysheba	D. & P. Scharbauer	Jack Van Berg	Preston Madden
1989	Sunday Silence	Gaillard, Hancock, & Whittingham	Charlie Whittingham	Oak Cliff Thoroughbreds
1990	Criminal Type	Calumet Farm	D. Wayne Lukas	Calumet Farm

Note: From 1936 to 1970, the *Daily Racing Form* annually selected a "Horse of the Year." In 1971 the *Daily Racing Form*, with the Thoroughbred Racing Associations and the National Turf Writers Association, jointly created the Eclipse Awards.

Eclipse Award Winners

2-YEAR-OLD COLT

1971 .... Riva Ridge
1972 .... Secretariat
1973 .... Protagonist
1974 .... Foolish Pleasure
1975 .... Honest Pleasure
1976 .... Seattle Slew
1977 .... Affirmed
1978 .... Spectacular Bid
1979 .... Rockhill Native
1980 .... Lord Avie
1981 .... Deputy Minister
1982 .... Roving Boy
1983 .... Devil's Bag
1984 .... Chief's Crown
1985 .... Tasso
1986 .... Capote
1987 .... Forty Niner
1988 .... Easy Goer
1989 .... Rhythm
1990 .... Fly So Free

2-YEAR-OLD FILLY

1971 .... Numbered Account
1972 .... La Prevoyante
1973 .... Talking Picture
1974 .... Ruffian
1975 .... Dearly Precious
1976 .... Sensational
1977 .... Lakeville Miss
1978 .... Candy Eclair
      It's in the Air
1979 .... Smart Angle
1980 .... Heavenly Cause
1981 .... Before Dawn
1982 .... Landaluce
1983 .... Althea
1984 .... Outstandingly
1985 .... Family Style
1986 .... Brave Raj
1987 .... Epitome
1988 .... Open Mind
1989 .... Go for Wand
1990 .... Meadow Star

3-YEAR-OLD COLT

1971 .... Canonero II
1972 .... Key to the Mint
1973 .... Secretariat
1974 .... Little Currant
1975 .... Wajima
1976 .... Bold Forbes
1977 .... Seattle Slew
1978 .... Affirmed
1979 .... Spectacular Bid
1980 .... Temperence Hill
1981 .... Pleasant Colony
1982 .... Conquistador Cielo
1983 .... Slew o'Gold
1984 .... Swale
1985 .... Spend A Buck
1986 .... Snow Chief
1987 .... Alysheba
1988 .... Risen Star
1989 .... Sunday Silence
1990 .... Unbridled

3-YEAR-OLD FILLY

1971 .... Turkish Trousers
1972 .... Susan's Girl
1973 .... Desert Vixen
1974 .... Chris Evert
1975 .... Ruffian
1976 .... Revidere
1977 .... Our Mims
1978 .... Tempest Queen
1979 .... Davona Dale
1980 .... Genuine Risk

1981 .... Wayward Lass
1982 .... Christmas Past
1983 .... Heartlight No. One
1984 .... Life's Magic
1985 .... Mom's Command
1986 .... Tiffany Lass
1987 .... Sacahuista
1988 .... Winning Colors
1989 .... Open Mind
1990 .... Go for Wand

Sport of the King

Elvis Presley still lives, at least in the registry of The Jockey Club, where the following horses are listed: Elvis, Elvis Pelvis, Elvis Lives, Elvis' Double, Triple Elvis, Blue Suede Shoes, Jailhouse Rock, Hound Dog, Don't Be Cruel, All Shook Up, Return To Sender, Love Me Tender, In the Ghetto, Heartbreak Hotel (by Elvis), Graceland, and The King.

Eclipse Award Winners (*Cont.*)

OLDER COLT, HORSE OR GELDING

1971 .... Ack Ack (5)
1972 .... Autobiography (4)
1973 .... Riva Ridge (4)
1974 .... Forego (4)
1975 .... Forego (5)
1976 .... Forego (6)
1977 .... Forego (7)
1978 .... Seattle Slew (4)
1979 .... Affirmed (4)
1980 .... Spectacular Bid (4)
1981 .... John Henry (6)
1982 .... Lemhi Gold (4)
1983 .... Bates Motel (4)
1984 .... Slew o'Gold (4)
1985 .... Vanlandingham (4)
1986 .... Turkoman (4)
1987 .... Ferdinand (4)
1988 .... Alysheba (4)
1989 .... Blushing John (4)
1990 .... Criminal Type (5)

CHAMPION TURF HORSE

1971 ..... Run the Gantlet (3)
1972 ..... Cougar II (6)
1973 ..... Secretariat (3)
1974 ..... Dahlia (4)
1975 ..... Snow Knight (4)
1976 ..... Youth (3)
1977 ..... Johnny D (3)
1978 ..... Mac Diarmida (3)

STEEPLECHASE OR HURDLE HORSE

1971 .... Shadow Brook (7)
1972 .... Soothsayer (5)
1973 .... Athenian Idol (5)
1974 .... Gran Kan (8)
1975 .... Life's Illusion (4)
1976 .... Straight & True (6)
1977 .... Cafe Prince (7)
1978 .... Cafe Prince (8)
1979 .... Martie's Anger (4)
1980 .... Zaccio (4)
1981 .... Zaccio (5)
1982 .... Zaccio (6)
1983 .... Flatterer (4)
1984 .... Flatterer (5)
1985 .... Flatterer (6)
1986 .... Flatterer (7)
1987 .... Inlander (6)
1988 .... Jimmy Lorenzo (6)
1989 .... Highland Bud (4)
1990 .... Morley Street (7)

OLDER FILLY OR MARE

1971 .... Shuvee (5)
1972 .... Typecast (6)
1973 .... Susan's Girl (4)
1974 .... Desert Vixen (4)
1975 .... Susan's Girl (6)
1976 .... Proud Delta (4)
1977 .... Cascapedia (4)
1978 .... Late Bloomer (4)
1979 .... Waya (5)
1980 .... Glorious Song (4)
1981 .... Relaxing (5)
1982 .... Track Robbery (6)
1983 .... Ambassador of Luck (4)
1984 .... Princess Rooney (4)
1985 .... Life's Magic (4)
1986 .... Lady's Secret (4)
1987 .... North Sider (5)
1988 .... Personal Ensign (4)
1989 .... Bayakoa (5)
1990 .... Bayakoa (6)

CHAMPION MALE TURF HORSE

1979 .... Bowl Game (5)
1980 .... John Henry (5)
1981 .... John Henry (6)
1982 .... Perrault (5)
1983 .... John Henry (8)
1984 .... John Henry (9)
1985 .... Cozzene (4)
1986 .... Manila (3)
1987 .... Theatrical (5)
1988 .... Sunshine Forever (3)
1989 .... Steinlen (6)
1990 .... Itsallgreektome (3)

OUTSTANDING OWNER

1971 ... Mr. & Mrs. E. E. Fogleson
1974 ... Dan Lasater
1975 ... Dan Lasater
1976 ... Dan Lasater
1977 ... Maxwell Gluck
1978 ... Harbor View Farm
1979 ... Harbor View Farm
1980 ... Mr. & Mrs. Bertram Firestone
1981 ... Dotsam Stable
1982 ... Viola Sommer
1983 ... John Franks
1984 ... John Franks
1985 ... Mr. & Mrs. Eugene Klein
1986 ... Mr. & Mrs. Eugene Klein
1987 ... Mr. & Mrs. Eugene Klein
1988 ... Ogden Phipps
1989 ... Ogden Phipps
1990 ... Frances Genter

SPRINTER

1971 ..... Ack Ack (5)
1972 ..... Chou Croute (4)
1973 ..... Shecky Greene (3)
1974 ..... Forego (4)
1975 ..... Gallant Bob (3)
1976 ..... My Juliet (4)
1977 ..... What a Summer (4)
1978 ..... Dr. Patches (4)
        J. O. Tobin (4)
1979 ..... Star de Naskra (4)
1980 ..... Plugged Nickel (3)
1981 ..... Guilty Conscience (5)
1982 ..... Gold Beauty (3)
1983 ..... Chinook Pass (4)
1984 ..... Eillo (4)
1985 ..... Precisionist (4)
1986 ..... Smile (4)
1987 ..... Groovy (4)
1988 ..... Gulch (4)
1989 ..... Safely Kept (3)
1990 ..... Housebuster (3)

CHAMPION FEMALE TURF HORSE

1979 :... Trillion (5)
1980 .... Just a Game II (4)
1981 .... De La Rose (3)
1982 .... April Run (4)
1983 .... All Along (4)
1984 .... Royal Heroine (4)
1985 .... Pebbles (4)
1986 .... Estrapade (6)
1987 .... Miesque (3)
1988 .... Miesque (4)
1989 .... Brown Bess (7)
1990 .... Laugh and Be Merry (5)

OUTSTANDING TRAINER

1971 ... Charlie Whittingham
1972 ... Lucien Laurin
1973 ... H. Allen Jerkens
1974 ... Sherrill Ward
1975 ... Steve DiMauro
1976 ... Lazaro Barrera
1977 ... Lazaro Barrera
1978 ... Lazaro Barrera
1979 ... Lazaro Barrera
1980 ... Bud Delp
1981 ... Ron McAnally
1982 ... Charlie Whittingham
1983 ... Woody Stephens
1984 ... Jack Van Berg
1985 ... D. Wayne Lukas
1986 ... D. Wayne Lukas
1987 ... D. Wayne Lukas
1988 ... Claude R. McGaughey III
1989 ... Charlie Whittingham
1990 ... Carl Nafzger

Note: Number in parentheses is horse's age.

Awards (*Cont.*)

Eclipse Award Winners (*Cont.*)

OUTSTANDING JOCKEY

1971... Laffit Pincay Jr
1972... Braulio Baeza
1973... Laffit Pinca Jr
1974... Laffit Pincay Jr
1975... Braulio Baeza
1976... Sandy Hawley
1977... Steve Cauthen
1978... Darrel McHargue
1979... Laffit Pincay Jr
1980... Chris McCarron
1981... Bill Shoemaker
1982... Angel Cordero Jr
1983... Angel Cordero Jr
1984... Pat Day
1985... Laffit Pincay Jr
1986... Pat Day
1987... Pat Day
1988... Jose Santos
1989... Kent Desormeaux
1990... Craig Perret

OUTSTANDING APPRENTICE JOCKEY

1971 .... Gene St. Leon
1972 .... Thomas Wallis
1973 .... Steve Valdez
1974 .... Chris McCarron
1975 .... Jimmy Edwards
1976 .... George Martens
1977 .... Steve Cauthen
1978 .... Ron Franklin
1979 .... Cash Asmussen
1980 .... Frank Lovato Jr
1981 .... Richard Migliore
1982 .... Alberto Delgado
1983 .... Declan Murphy
1984 .... Wesley Ward
1985 .... Art Madrid Jr
1986 .... Allen Stacy
1987 .... Kent Desormeaux
1988 .... Steve Capanas
1989 .... Michael Luzzi
1990 .... Mark Johnston

OUTSTANDING BREEDER

1974 .... John W. Galbreath
1975 .... Fred W. Hooper
1976 .... Nelson Bunker Hunt
1977 .... Edward Plunket Taylor
1978 .... Harbor View Farm
1979 .... Claiborne Farm
1980 .... Mrs. Henry D. Paxson
1981 .... Golden Chance Farm
1982 .... Fred W. Hooper
1983 .... Edward Plunket Taylor
1984 .... Claiborne Farm
1985 .... Nelson Bunker Hunt
1986 .... Paul Mellon
1987 .... Nelson Bunker Hunt
1988 .... Ogden Phipps
1989 .... North Ridge Farm
1990 .... Calumet Farm

AWARD OF MERIT

1976 .... Jack J. Dreyfus
1977 .... Steve Cauthen
1978 .... Ogden Phipps
1979 .... Frank E. Kilroe
1980 .... John D. Schapiro
1981 .... Bill Shoemaker
1984 .... John Gaines
1985 .... Keene Daingerfield
1986 .... Herman Cohen
1987 .... J. B. Faulconer
1988 .... John Forsythe
1989 .... Michael P. Sandler

SPECIAL AWARD

1971..... Robert J. Kleberg
1974..... Charles Hatton
1976..... Bill Shoemaker
1980..... John T. Landry
Pierre E. Bellocq (Peb)
1984..... C. V. Whitney
1985..... Arlington Park
1987 .... Anheuser-Busch
1988 .... Edward J. DeBartolo Sr
1989 .... Richard Duchossois

Note: Not presented annually. For long-term and/or outstanding service to the industry.

Breeders' Cup

Location: Hollywood Park (CA) 1984, 1987; Aqueduct Racetrack (NY) 1985; Santa Anita Park (CA) 1986; Churchill Downs (KY) 1988; Gulfstream Park (FL) 1989; Belmont Park (NY) 1990.

Juveniles

Year	Winner (Margin)	Jockey	Second	Third	Time
1984	Chief's Crown (3⁄4)	Don MacBeth	Tank's Prospect	Spend a Buck	1:36 1⁄5
1985	Tasso (Nose)	Laffit Pincay Jr	Storm Cat	Scat Dancer	1:36 1⁄5
1986	Capote (1 1⁄4)	Laffit Pincay Jr	Qualify	Alysheba	1:43 4⁄5
1987	Success Express (1 3⁄4)	Jose Santos	Regal Classic	Tejano	1:35 1⁄5
1988	Is It True (1 1⁄4)	Laffit Pincay Jr	Easy Goer	Tagel	1:46 3⁄5
1989	Rhythm (2)	Craig Perret	Grand Canyon	Slavic	1:43 3⁄5
1990	Fly So Free (3)	Jose Santos	Take Me Out	Lost Mountain	1:43 2⁄5

Note: One mile (1984–85, 87); 1 1⁄16 miles (1986 and since 1988).

Juvenile Fillies

Year	Winner (Margin)	Jockey	Second	Third	Time
1984	Outstandingly*	Walter Guerra	Dusty Heart	Fine Spirit	1:37 4⁄5
1985	Twilight Ridge (1)	Jorge Velasquez	Family Style	Steal a Kiss	1:35 4⁄5
1986	Brave Raj (5 1⁄2)	Pat Valenzuela	Tappiano	Saros Brig	1:43 1⁄5
1987	Epitome (Nose)	Pat Day	Jeanne Jones	Dream Team	1:36 2⁄5
1988	Open Mind (1 3⁄4)	Angel Cordero Jr	Darby Shuffle	Lea Lucinda	1:46 3⁄5
1989	Go for Wand (2 3⁄4)	Randy Romero	Sweet Roberta	Stella Madrid	1:44 1⁄5
1990	Meadow Star (5)	Jose Santos	Private Treasure	Dance Smartly	1:44

*In 1984, winner Fran's Valentine was disqualified for interference in the stretch and placed 10th.

Note: One mile (1984–85, 87); 1 1⁄16 miles (1986 and since 1988).

Sprint

Year	Winner (Margin)	Jockey	Second	Third	Time
1984	Eillo (Nose)	Craig Perret	Commemorate	Fighting Fit	1:10⅕
1985	Precisionist (¾)	Chris McCarron	Smile	Mt. Livermore	1:08⅖
1986	Smile (1¼)	Jacinto Vasquez	Pine Tree Lane	Bedside Promise	1:08⅖
1987	Very Subtle (4)	Pat Valenzuela	Groovy	Exclusive Enough	1:08⅘
1988	Gulch (¾)	Angel Cordero Jr	Play the King	Afleet	1:10⅖
1989	Dancing Spree (Neck)	Angel Cordero Jr	Safely Kept	Dispersal	1:09
1990	Safely Kept (Neck)	Craig Perret	Dayjur	Black Tie Affair	1:09⅗

Note: Six furlongs (since 1984).

Mile

Year	Winner (Margin)	Jockey	Second	Third	Time
1984	Royal Heroine (1½)	Fernando Toro	Star Choice	Cozzene	1:32⅗
1985	Cozzene (2¼)	Walter Guerra	Al Mamoon*	Shadeed	1:35
1986	Last Tycoon (Head)	Yves St-Martin	Palace Music	Fred Astaire	1:35⅕
1987	Miesque (3½)	Freddie Head	Show Dancer	Sonic Lady	1:32⅘
1988	Miesque (4)	Freddie Head	Steinlen	Simply Majestic	1:38⅗
1989	Steinlen (¾)	Jose Santos	Sabona	Most Welcome	1:37⅕
1990	Royal Academy (Neck)	Lester Piggott	Itsallgreektome	Priolo	1:35⅕

*2nd place finisher Palace Music was disqualified for interference and placed 9th.

Distaff

Year	Winner (Margin)	Jockey	Second	Third	Time
1984	Princess Rooney (7)	Eddie Delahoussaye	Life's Magic	Adored	2:02⅖
1985	Life's Magic (6¼)	Angel Cordero Jr	Lady's Secret	Dontstop Themusic	2:02
1986	Lady's Secret (2½)	Pat Day	Fran's Valentine	Outstandingly	2:01⅕
1987	Sacahuista (2¼)	Randy Romero	Clabber Girl	Oueee Bebe	2:02⅘
1988	Personal Ensign (Nose)	Randy Romero	Winning Colors	Goodbye Halo	1:52
1989	Bayakoa (1½)	Laffit Pincay Jr	Gorgeous	Open Mind	1:47⅖
1990	Bayakoa (6¾)	Laffit Pincay Jr	Colonial Waters	Valay Maid	1:49⅕

Note: 1¼ miles (1984-87); 1⅛ miles (since 1988).

Turf

Year	Winner (Margin)	Jockey	Second	Third	Time
1984	Lashkari (Neck)	Yves St-Martin	All Along	Raami	2:25⅕
1985	Pebbles (Neck)	Pat Eddery	Strawberry Rd II	Mourjane	2:27
1986	Manila (Neck)	Jose Santos	Theatrical	Estrapade	2:25⅖
1987	Theatrical (½)	Pat Day	Trempolino	Village Star II	2:24⅖
1988	Great Communicator (½)	Ray Sibille	Sunshine Forever	Indian Skimmer	2:35⅕
1989	Prized (Head)	Eddie Delahoussaye	Sierra Roberta	Star Lift	2:28
1990	In the Wings (½)	Gary Stevens	With Approval	El Senor	2:29⅗

Note: 1½ miles.

A Game of H-O-R-S-E

This past year Magic Johnson purchased a share of the colt Honor Grades from co-owners Bruce McNall and Wayne Gretzky. Perhaps Magic should consider adding some of these horses to his stable: Slam Dunk, Knick Press, Fullcourt Press, Double Dribble, Back Court Pass, Jump Shot, Doctor J., Willis, Wilt, and Bill Russell. By the way, there is also a horse named Magic Johnson and jockeys named Larry Bird and Michael Jordan.

Classic

Year	Winner (Margin)	Jockey	Second	Third	Time
1984	Wild Again (Head)	Pat Day	Slew o'Gold*	Gate Dancer	2:03²⁄₅
1985	Proud Truth (Head)	Jorge Velasquez	Gate Dancer	Turkoman	2:00⁴⁄₅
1986	Skywalker (1¼)	Laffit Pincay Jr	Turkoman	Precisionist	2:00²⁄₅
1987	Ferdinand (Nose)	Bill Shoemaker	Alysheba	Judge Angelucci	2:01²⁄₅
1988	Alysheba (Nose)	Chris McCarron	Seeking the Gold	Waquoit	2:04⁴⁄₅
1989	Sunday Silence (½)	Chris McCarron	Easy Goer	Blushing John	2:00¹⁄₅
1990	Unbridled (1)	Pat Day	Ibn Bey	Thirty Six Red	2:02¹⁄₅

*2nd place finisher Gate Dancer was disqualified for interference and placed 3rd.

Note: 1¼ miles.

England's Triple Crown Winners

England's Triple Crown consists of the Two Thousand Guineas, held at Newmarket; the Epsom Derby, held at Epsom Downs; and the St. Leger Stakes, held at Doncaster.

Year	Horse	Owner	Year	Horse	Owner
1853	West Australian	Mr. Bowes	1900	Diamond Jubilee	Prince of Wales
1865	Gladiateur	F. DeLagrange	1903	*Rock Sand	J. Miller
1866	Lord Lyon	R. Sutton	1915	Pommern	S. Joel
1886	*Ormonde	Duke of Westminster	1917	Gay Crusader	Mr. Fairie
1891	Common	†F. Johnstone	1918	Gainsborough	Lady James Douglas
1893	Isinglass	H. McCalmont	1935	*Bahram	Aga Khan
1897	Galtee More	J. Gubbins	1970	‡Nijinsky II	C. W. Engelhard
1899	Flying Fox	Duke of Westminster			

*Imported into United States.   †Raced in name of Lord Alington in Two Thousand Guineas.   ‡Canadian-bred.

Annual Leaders

Horse—Money Won

Year	Horse	Age	Starts	1st	2nd	3rd	Winnings ($)
1919	Sir Barton	3	13	8	3	2	88,250
1920	Man o'War	3	11	11	0	0	166,140
1921	Morvich	2	11	11	0	0	115,234
1922	Pillory	3	7	4	1	1	95,654
1923	Zev	3	14	12	1	0	272,008
1924	Sarzen	3	12	8	1	1	95,640
1925	Pompey	2	10	7	2	0	121,630
1926	Crusader	3	15	9	4	0	166,033
1927	Anita Peabody	2	7	6	0	1	111,905
1928	High Strung	2	6	5	0	0	153,590
1929	Blue Larkspur	3	6	4	1	0	153,450
1930	Gallant Fox	3	10	9	1	0	308,275
1931	Gallant Flight	2	7	7	0	0	219,000
1932	Gusto	3	16	4	3	2	145,940
1933	Singing Wood	2	9	3	2	2	88,050
1934	Cavalcade	3	7	6	1	0	111,235
1935	Omaha	3	9	6	1	2	142,255
1936	Granville	3	11	7	3	0	110,295
1937	Seabiscuit	4	15	11	2	2	168,580
1938	Stagehand	3	15	8	2	3	189,710
1939	Challedon	3	15	9	2	3	184,535
1940	Bimelech	3	7	4	2	1	110,005
1941	Whirlaway	3	20	13	5	2	272,386
1942	Shut Out	3	12	8	2	0	238,872
1943	Count Fleet	3	6	6	0	0	174,055
1944	Pavot	2	8	8	0	0	179,040
1945	Busher	3	13	10	2	1	273,735
1946	Assault	3	15	8	2	3	424,195

Note: Annual leaders on pages 392-395 courtesy of *The American Racing Manual*, a publication of Daily Racing Form, Inc.

Horse—Money Won (*Cont.*)

Year	Horse	Age	Starts	1st	2nd	3rd	Winnings ($)
1947	Armed	6	17	11	4	1	376,325
1948	Citation	3	20	19	1	0	709,470
1949	Ponder	3	21	9	5	2	321,825
1950	Noor	5	12	7	4	1	346,940
1951	Counterpoint	3	15	7	2	1	250,525
1952	Crafty Admiral	4	16	9	4	1	277,225
1953	Native Dancer	3	10	9	1	0	513,425
1954	Determine	3	15	10	3	2	328,700
1955	Nashua	3	12	10	1	1	752,550
1956	Needles	3	8	4	2	0	440,850
1957	Round Table	3	22	15	1	3	600,383
1958	Round Table	4	20	14	4	0	662,780
1959	Sword Dancer	3	13	8	4	0	537,004
1960	Bally Ache	3	15	10	3	1	445,045
1961	Carry Back	3	16	9	1	3	565,349
1962	Never Bend	2	10	7	1	2	402,969
1963	Candy Spots	3	12	7	2	1	604,481
1964	Gun Bow	4	16	8	4	2	580,100
1965	Buckpasser	2	11	9	1	0	568,096
1966	Buckpasser	3	14	13	1	0	669,078
1967	Damascus	3	16	12	3	1	817,941
1968	Forward Pass	3	13	7	2	0	546,674
1969	Arts and Letters	3	14	8	5	1	555,604
1970	Personality	3	18	8	2	1	444,049
1971	Riva Ridge	2	9	7	0	0	503,263
1972	Droll Role	4	19	7	3	4	471,633
1973	Secretariat	3	12	9	2	1	860,404
1974	Chris Evert	3	8	5	1	2	551,063
1975	Foolish Pleasure	3	11	5	4	1	716,278
1976	Forego	6	8	6	1	1	401,701
1977	Seattle Slew	3	7	6	0	1	641,370
1978	Affirmed	3	11	8	2	0	901,541
1979	Spectacular Bid	3	12	10	1	1	1,279,334
1980	Temperence Hill	3	17	8	3	1	1,130,452
1981	John Henry	6	10	8	0	0	1,798,030
1982	Perrault	5	8	4	1	2	1,197,400
1983	All Along	4	7	4	1	1	2,138,963
1984	Slew o'Gold	4	6	5	1	0	2,627,944
1985	Spend A Buck	3	7	5	1	1	3,552,704
1986	Snow Chief	3	9	6	1	1	1,875,200
1987	Alysheba	3	10	3	3	1	2,511,156
1988	Alysheba	4	9	7	1	0	3,808,600
1989	Sunday Silence	3	9	7	2	0	4,578,454
1990	Unbridled	3	11	4	3	2	3,718,149

Trainer—Money Won

Year	Trainer	Wins	Winnings ($)	Year	Trainer	Wins	Winnings ($)
1908	James Rowe, Sr	50	284,335	1925	G. R. Tompkins	30	199,245
1909	Sam Hildreth	73	123,942	1926	Scott P. Harlan	21	205,681
1910	Sam Hildreth	84	148,010	1927	W. H. Bringloe	63	216,563
1911	Sam Hildreth	67	49,418	1928	John F. Schorr	65	258,425
1912	John F. Schorr	63	58,110	1929	James Rowe, Jr	25	314,881
1913	James Rowe, Sr	18	45,936	1930	Sunny Jim Fitzsimmons	47	397,355
1914	R. C. Benson	45	59,315	1931	Big Jim Healey	33	297,300
1915	James Rowe, Sr	19	75,596	1932	Sunny Jim Fitzsimmons	68	266,650
1916	Sam Hildreth	39	70,950	1933	Humming Bob Smith	53	135,720
1917	Sam Hildreth	23	61,698	1934	Humming Bob Smith	43	249,938
1918	H. Guy Bedwell	53	80,296	1935	Bud Stotler	87	303,005
1919	H. Guy Bedwell	63	208,728	1936	Sunny Jim Fitzsimmons	42	193,415
1920	L. Feustal	22	186,087	1937	Robert McGarvey	46	209,925
1921	Sam Hildreth	85	262,768	1938	Earl Sande	15	226,495
1922	Sam Hildreth	74	247,014	1939	Sunny Jim Fitzsimmons	45	266,205
1923	Sam Hildreth	75	392,124	1940	Silent Tom Smith	14	269,200
1924	Sam Hildreth	77	255,608	1941	Plain Ben Jones	70	475,318

Trainer—Money Won (*Cont.*)

Year	Trainer	Wins	Winnings ($)	Year	Trainer	Wins	Winnings ($)
1942	John M. Gaver Sr	48	406,547	1967	Eddie Neloy	72	1,776,089
1943	Plain Ben Jones	73	267,915	1968	Eddie Neloy	52	1,233,101
1944	Plain Ben Jones	60	601,660	1969	Elliott Burch	26	1,067,936
1945	Silent Tom Smith	52	510,655	1970	Charlie Whittingham	82	1,302,354
1946	Hirsch Jacobs	99	560,077	1971	Charlie Whittingham	77	1,737,115
1947	Jimmy Jones	85	1,334,805	1972	Charlie Whittingham	79	1,734,020
1948	Jimmy Jones	81	1,118,670	1973	Charlie Whittingham	85	1,865,385
1949	Jimmy Jones	76	978,587	1974	Pancho Martin	166	2,408,419
1950	Preston Burch	96	637,754	1975	Charlie Whittingham	93	2,437,244
1951	John M. Gaver Sr	42	616,392	1976	Jack Van Berg	496	2,976,196
1952	Plain Ben Jones	29	662,137	1977	Laz Barrera	127	2,715,848
1953	Harry Trotsek	54	1,028,873	1978	Laz Barrera	100	3,307,164
1954	Willie Molter	136	1,107,860	1979	Laz Barrera	98	3,608,517
1955	Sunny Jim Fitzsimmons	66	1,270,055	1980	Laz Barrera	99	2,969,151
1956	Willie Molter	142	1,227,402	1981	Charlie Whittingham	74	3,993,302
1957	Jimmy Jones	70	1,150,910	1982	Charlie Whittingham	63	4,587,457
1958	Willie Molter	69	1,116,544	1983	D. Wayne Lukas	78	4,267,261
1959	Willie Molter	71	847,290	1984	D. Wayne Lukas	131	5,835,921
1960	Hirsch Jacobs	97	748,349	1985	D. Wayne Lukas	218	11,155,188
1961	Jimmy Jones	62	759,856	1986	D. Wayne Lukas	259	12,345,180
1962	Mesh Tenney	58	1,099,474	1987	D. Wayne Lukas	343	17,502,110
1963	Mesh Tenney	40	860,703	1988	D. Wayne Lukas	318	17,842,358
1964	Bill Winfrey	61	1,350,534	1989	D. Wayne Lukas	305	16,103,998
1965	Hirsch Jacobs	91	1,331,628	1990	D. Wayne Lukas	267	14,508,871
1966	Eddie Neloy	93	2,456,250				

Jockey—Money Won

Year	Jockey	Mts	1st	2nd	3rd	Pct	Winnings ($)
1919	John Loftus	177	65	36	24	.37	252,707
1920	Clarence Kummer	353	87	79	48	.25	292,376
1921	Earl Sande	340	112	69	59	.33	263,043
1922	Albert Johnson	297	43	57	40	.14	345,054
1923	Earl Sande	430	122	89	79	.28	569,394
1924	Ivan Parke	844	205	175	121	.24	290,395
1925	Laverne Fator	315	81	54	44	.26	305,775
1926	Laverne Fator	511	143	90	86	.28	361,435
1927	Earl Sande	179	49	33	19	.27	277,877
1928	Pony McAtee	235	55	43	25	.23	301,295
1929	Mack Garner	274	57	39	33	.21	314,975
1930	Sonny Workman	571	152	88	79	.27	420,438
1931	Charles Kurtsinger	519	93	82	79	.18	392,095
1932	Sonny Workman	378	87	48	55	.23	385,070
1933	Robert Jones	471	63	57	70	.13	226,285
1934	Wayne D. Wright	919	174	154	114	.19	287,185
1935	Silvio Coucci	749	141	125	103	.19	319,760
1936	Wayne D. Wright	670	100	102	73	.15	264,000
1937	Charles Kurtsinger	765	120	94	106	.16	384,202
1938	Nick Wall	658	97	94	82	.15	385,161
1939	Basil James	904	191	165	105	.21	353,333
1940	Eddie Arcaro	783	132	143	112	.17	343,661
1941	Don Meade	1164	210	185	158	.18	398,627
1942	Eddie Arcaro	687	123	97	89	.18	481,949
1943	John Longden	871	173	140	121	.20	573,276
1944	Ted Atkinson	1539	287	231	213	.19	899,101
1945	John Longden	778	180	112	100	.23	981,977
1946	Ted Atkinson	1377	233	213	173	.17	1,036,825
1947	Douglas Dodson	646	141	100	75	.22	1,429,949
1948	Eddie Arcaro	726	188	108	98	.26	1,686,230
1949	Steve Brooks	906	209	172	110	.23	1,316,817
1950	Eddie Arcaro	888	195	153	144	.22	1,410,160
1951	Bill Shoemaker	1161	257	197	161	.22	1,329,890
1952	Eddie Arcaro	807	188	122	109	.23	1,859,591
1953	Bill Shoemaker	1683	485	302	210	.29	1,784,187

Jockey—Money Won (*Cont.*)

Year	Jockey	Mts	1st	2nd	3rd	Pct	Winnings ($)
1954	Bill Shoemaker	1251	380	221	142	.30	1,876,760
1955	Eddie Arcaro	820	158	126	108	.19	1,864,796
1956	Bill Hartack	1387	347	252	184	.25	2,343,955
1957	Bill Hartack	1238	341	208	178	.28	3,060,501
1958	Bill Shoemaker	1133	300	185	137	.26	2,961,693
1959	Bill Shoemaker	1285	347	230	159	.27	2,843,133
1960	Bill Shoemaker	1227	274	196	158	.22	2,123,961
1961	Bill Shoemaker	1256	304	186	175	.24	2,690,819
1962	Bill Shoemaker	1126	311	156	128	.28	2,916,844
1963	Bill Shoemaker	1203	271	193	137	.22	2,526,925
1964	Bill Shoemaker	1056	246	147	133	.23	2,649,553
1965	Braulio Baeza	1245	270	200	201	.22	2,582,702
1966	Braulio Baeza	1341	298	222	190	.22	2,951,022
1967	Braulio Baeza	1064	256	184	127	.24	3,088,888
1968	Braulio Baeza	1089	201	184	145	.18	2,835,108
1969	Jorge Velasquez	1442	258	230	204	.18	2,542,315
1970	Laffit Pincay Jr	1328	269	208	187	.20	2,626,526
1971	Laffit Pincay Jr	1627	380	288	214	.23	3,784,377
1972	Laffit Pincay Jr	1388	289	215	205	.21	3,225,827
1973	Laffit Pincay Jr	1444	350	254	209	.24	4,093,492
1974	Laffit Pincay Jr	1278	341	227	180	.27	4,251,060
1975	Braulio Baeza	1190	196	208	180	.16	3,674,398
1976	Angel Cordero Jr	1534	274	273	235	.18	4,709,500
1977	Steve Cauthen	2075	487	345	304	.23	6,151,750
1978	Darrel McHargue	1762	375	294	263	.21	6,188,353
1979	Laffit Pincay Jr	1708	420	302	261	.25	8,183,535
1980	Chris McCarron	1964	405	318	282	.20	7,666,100
1981	Chris McCarron	1494	326	251	207	.22	8,397,604
1982	Angel Cordero Jr	1838	397	338	227	.22	9,702,520
1983	Angel Cordero Jr	1792	362	296	237	.20	10,116,807
1984	Chris McCarron	1565	356	276	218	.23	12,038,213
1985	Laffit Pincay Jr	1409	289	246	183	.21	13,415,049
1986	Jose Santos	1636	329	237	222	.20	11,329,297
1987	Jose Santos	1639	305	268	208	.19	12,407,355
1988	Jose Santos	1867	370	287	265	.20	14,877,298
1989	Jose Santos	1459	285	238	220	.20	13,847,003
1990	Gary Stevens	1504	283	245	202	.19	13,881,198

Leading Jockeys—Career Records Through 1990

Jockey	Years Riding	Mts	1st	2nd	3rd	Win Pct	Winnings ($)
Shoemaker, W. (1990)	42	40,350	8,833	6,136	4,987	.219	123,375,524
Pincay, L. Jr	25	34,739	7,477	5,816	4,872	.215	154,659,844
Cordero, A. Jr	29	37,270	6,812	5,921	5,169	.183	154,944,152
Velasquez, J.	28	36,748	6,333	5,643	5,216	.172	113,078,159
Snyder, L.	31	33,342	6,133	4,786	3,171	.184	44,011,598
Longden, J. (1966)	40	32,413	6,032	4,914	4,273	.186	24,665,800
Hawley, S.	23	27,125	5,790	4,242	3,587	.213	72,120,057
Gall, D.	34	32,489	5,712	4,933	4,625	.176	16,120,904
Gambardella, C.	35	35,325	5,674	5,329	4,826	.161	24,597,949
McCarron, C. J.	16	24,541	5,304	4,077	3,306	.216	127,825,744
E. Fires	26	34,182	5,075	4,271	4,070	.148	54,149,113
Day, P.	18	23,779	5,006	3,943	3,281	.211	99,294,959
Vasquez, J.	31	33,604	4,787	4,301	4,078	.142	71,824,307
Arcaro E. (1961)	31	24,092	4,779	3,807	3,302	.198	30,039,543
Brumfield, D. (1989)	37	33,223	4,573	4,076	3,758	.138	48,567,861
Delahoussaye, E.	21	27,854	4,506	4,009	3,741	.162	94,768,041
Brooks, S. (1975)	34	30,330	4,451	4,219	3,658	.147	18,239,817
Blum, W. (1975)	22	28,673	4,382	3,913	3,350	.153	26,497,189
Hartack, W. (1974)	22	21,535	4,272	3,370	2,871	.198	26,466,758
Gomez, A. (1980)	34	17,028	4,081	2,947	2,405	.240	11,777,297

Jockey	Years Riding	Mts	1st	2nd	3rd	Win Pct	Winnings ($)
Dittfach, H. (1989)	33	33,905	4,000	4,092	6,113	.118	13,506,052
Maple, E.	23	29,601	3,924	3,943	3,790	.133	86,512,104
Atkinson, T. (1959)	22	23,661	3,795	3,300	2,913	.160	17,449,360
Whited, D. E.	33	27,939	3,786	3,593	3,358	.136	25,261,849
Neves, R. (1964)	21	25,334	3,772	3,547	3,352	.149	13,786,239

Note: Records include available statistics for races ridden in foreign countries. Figures in parentheses after jockey's name indicate last year in which he rode.

Leading jockeys courtesy of *The American Racing Manual*, a publication of Daily Racing Form, Inc.

National Museum of Racing Hall of Fame

HORSES

Ack Ack (1986, 1966)
Affectionately (1989, 1960)
Affirmed (1980, 1975)
All Along (1990, 1979)
Alsab (1976, 1939)
Alydar (1989, 1975)
American Eclipse (1970, 1814)
Armed (1963, 1941)
Artful (1956, 1902)
Assault (1964, 1943)
Battleship (1969, 1927)
Bed o'Roses (1976, 1947)
Beldame (1956, 1901)
Ben Brush (1955, 1893)
Bewitch (1977, 1945)
Bimelech (1990, 1937)
Black Gold (1989, 1921)
Black Helen (1991, 1932)
Blue Larkspur (1957, 1926)
Bold Ruler (1973, 1954)
Bon Nouvel (1976, 1960)
Boston (1955, 1833)
Broomstick (1956, 1901)
Buckpasser (1970, 1963)
Busher (1964, 1942)
Bushranger (1967, 1930)
Cafe Prince (1985, 1970)
Carry Back (1975, 1958)
Challedon (1977, 1936)
Chris Evert (1988, 1971)
Cicada (1967, 1959)
Citation (1959, 1945)
Coaltown (1983, 1945)
Colin (1956, 1905)
Commando (1956, 1898)
Count Fleet (1961, 1940)
Dahlia (1981, 1970)
Damascus (1974, 1964)
Dark Mirage (1974, 1965)
Davona Dale (1985, 1976)
Desert Vixen (1979, 1970)
Devil Diver (1980, 1939)
Discovery (1969, 1931)
Domino (1955, 1891)

Dr. Fager (1971, 1964)
Elkridge (1966, 1938)
Emperor of Norfolk (1988, 1885)
Equipoise (1957, 1928)
Exterminator (1957, 1915)
Fairmount (1985, 1921)
Fair Play (1956, 1905)
Fashion (1980, 1837)
Firenze (1981, 1884)
Forego (1979, 1970)
Gallant Bloom (1977, 1966)
Gallant Fox (1957, 1927)
Gallant Man (1987, 1954)
Gallorette (1962, 1942)
Gamely (1980, 1964)
Genuine Risk (1986, 1977)
Good and Plenty (1956, 1900)
Grey Lag (1957, 1918)
Hamburg (1986, 1895)
Hanover (1955, 1884)
Henry of Navarre (1985, 1891)
Hill Prince (1991, 1947)
Hindoo (1955, 1878)
Imp (1965, 1894)
Jay Trump (1971, 1957)
John Henry (1990, 1975)
Jolly Roger (1965, 1922)
Kelso (1967, 1957)
Kentucky (1983, 1861)
Kingston (1955, 1884)
L'Escargot (1977, 1963)
Lexington (1955, 1850)
Longfellow (1971, 1867)
Luke Blackburn (1956, 1877)
Majestic Prince (1988, 1966)
Man o'War (1957, 1917)
Miss Woodford (1967, 1880)
Myrtlewood (1979, 1932)
Nashua (1965, 1952)
Native Dancer (1963, 1950)
Native Diver (1978, 1959)
Neji (1966, 1950)
Northern Dancer (1976, 1961)
Oedipus (1978, 1946)

Old Rosebud (1968, 1911)
Omaha (1965, 1932)
Pan Zareta (1972, 1910)
Parole (1984, 1879)
Peter Pan (1956, 1904)
Princess Doreen (1982, 1921)
Princess Rooney (1991, 1980)
Real Delight (1987, 1949)
Regret (1957, 1912)
Reigh Count (1978, 1925)
Roamer (1981, 1911)
Roseben (1956, 1901)
Round Table (1972, 1954)
Ruffian (1976, 1972)
Ruthless (1975, 1864)
Salvator (1955, 1886)
Sarazen (1957, 1921)
Seabiscuit (1958, 1933)
Searching (1978, 1952)
Seattle Slew (1981, 1974)
Secretariat (1974, 1970)
Shuvee (1975, 1966)
Silver Spoon (1978, 1956)
Sir Archy (1955, 1805)
Sir Barton (1957, 1916)
Spectacular Bid (1982, 1976)
Stymie (1975, 1941)
Susan's Girl (1976, 1969)
Swaps (1966, 1952)
Sword Dancer (1977, 1956)
Sysonby (1956, 1902)
Ten Broeck (1982, 1872)
Tim Tam (1985, 1955)
Tom Fool (1960, 1949)
Top Flight (1966, 1929)
Tosmah (1984, 1961)
Twenty Grand (1957, 1928)
Twilight Tear (1963, 1941)
Two Lea (1982, 1946)
War Admiral (1958, 1934)
Whirlaway (1959, 1938)
Whisk Broom II (1979, 1907)
Zev (1983, 1920)

Note: Years of election and foaling in parentheses.

'Tis the Season   In a pace at New Jersey's Freehold Raceway in 1990, Chanuka finished third, a neck ahead of Thenitebeforexmas.

HARNESS RACING

Major Races

Hambletonian

Year	Horse	Driver	Year	Horse	Driver
1926	Guy McKinney	Nat Ray	1960	Blaze Hanover	Joe O'Brien
1927	Iosola's Worthy	Marvin Childs	1961	Harlan Dean	James Arthur
1928	Spenser	W. H. Leese	1962	A. C.'s Viking	Sanders Russell
1929	Walter Dear	Walter Cox	1963	Speedy Scot	Ralph Baldwin
1930	Hanover's Bertha	Tom Berry	1964	Ayres	J. Simpson, Sr
1931	Calumet Butler	R. D. McMahon	1965	Egyptian Candor	Del Cameron
1932	The Marchioness	William Caton	1966	Kerry Way	Frank Ervin
1933	Mary Reynolds	Ben White	1967	Speedy Streak	Del Cameron
1934	Lord Jim	Doc Parshall	1968	Nevele Pride	Stanley Dancer
1935	Greyhound	Sep Palin	1969	Lindy's Pride	H. Beissinger
1936	Rosalind	Ben White	1970	Timothy T.	J. Simpson, Jr
1937	Shirley Hanover	Henry Thomas	1971	Speedy Crown	H. Beissinger
1938	McLin Hanover	Henry Thomas	1972	Super Bowl	Stanley Dancer
1939	Peter Astra	Doc Parshall	1973	Flirth	Ralph Baldwin
1940	Spencer Scott	Fred Egan	1974	Christopher T.	Bill Haughton
1941	Bill Gallon	Lee Smith	1975	Bonefish	Stanley Dancer
1942	The Ambassador	Ben White	1976	Steve Lobell	Bill Haughton
1943	Volo Song	Ben White	1977	Green Speed	Bill Haughton
1944	Yankee Maid	Henry Thomas	1978	Speedy Somolli	H. Beissinger
1945	Titan Hanover	H. Pownall Sr	1979	Legend Hanover	George Sholty
1946	Chestertown	Thomas Berry	1980	Burgomeister	Bill Haughton
1947	Hoot Mon	Sep Palin	1981	Shiaway St. Pat	Ray Remmen
1948	Demon Hanover	Harrison Hoyt	1982	Speed Bowl	Tom Haughton
1949	Miss Tilly	Fred Egan	1983	Duenna	Stanley Dancer
1950	Lusty Song	Del Miller	1984	Historic Freight	Ben Webster
1951	Mainliner	Guy Crippen	1985	Prakas	Bill O'Donnell
1952	Sharp Note	Bion Shively	1986	Nuclear Kosmos	Ulf Thoresen
1953	Helicopter	Harry Harvey	1987	Mack Lobell	John Campbell
1954	Newport Dream	Del Cameron	1988	Armbro Goal	John Campbell
1955	Scott Frost	Joe O'Brien	1989	Park Avenue Joe*	Ron Waples
1956	The Intruder	Ned Bower		Probe*	Bill Fahy
1957	Hickory Smoke	J. Simpson Sr	1990	Harmonious	John Campbell
1958	Emily's Pride	Flave Nipe	1991	Giant Victory	Jack Moiseyev
1959	Diller Hanover	Frank Ervin			

*Park Avenue Joe and Probe dead-heated for win. Park Avenue Joe finished first in the summary 2-1-1 to Probe's 1-9-1 finish.

Note: Run at 1 mile since 1947.

The Little Brown Jug

Year	Winner	Driver	Year	Winner	Driver
1946	Ensign Hanover	Wayne Smart	1969	Laverne Hanover	Bill Haughton
1947	Forbes Chief	Del Cameron	1970	Most Happy Fella	Stanley Dancer
1948	Knight Dream	Frank Safford	1971	Nansemond	Herve Filion
1949	Good Time	Frank Ervin	1972	Strike Out	Keith Waples
1950	Dudley Hanover	Del Miller	1973	Melvin's Woe	Joe O'Brien
1951	Tar Heel	Del Cameron	1974	Armbro Omaha	Bill Haughton
1952	Meadow Rice	Wayne Smart	1975	Seatrain	Ben Webster
1953	Keystoner	Frank Ervin	1976	Keystone Ore	Stanley Dancer
1954	Adios Harry	Morris MacDonald	1977	Governor Skipper	John Chapman
1955	Quick Chief	Bill Haughton	1978	Happy Escort	William Popfinger
1956	Noble Adios	John Simpson Sr	1979	Hot Hitter	Herve Filion
1957	Torpid	John Simpso Sr	1980	Niatross	Clint Galbraith
1958	Shadow Wave	Joe O'Brien	1981	Fan Hanover	Glen Garnsey
1959	Adios Butler	Clint Hodgins	1982	Merger	John Campbell
1960	Bullet Hanover	John Simpson Sr	1983	Ralph Hanover	Ron Waples
1961	Henry T. Adios	Stanley Dancer	1984	Colt Fortysix	Chris Boring
1962	Lehigh Hanover	Stanley Dancer	1985	Nihilator	Bill O'Donnell
1963	Overtrick	John Patterson	1986	Barberry Spur	Bill O'Donnell
1964	Vicar Hanover	Bill Haughton	1987	Jaguar Spur	Dick Stillings
1965	Bret Hanover	Frank Ervin	1988	B. J. Scoot	Michel Lachance
1966	Romeo Hanover	George Sholty	1989	Goalie Jeff	Michel Lachance
1967	Best of All	James Hackett	1990	Beach Towel	Ray Remmen
1968	Rum Customer	Bill Haughton			

Breeders Crown

1984

Div	Winner	Driver
2PC	Dragon's Lair	Jeff Mallet
2PF	Amneris	John Campbell
3PC	Troublemaker	Bill O'Donnell
3PF	Naughty But Nice	Tommy Haughton
2TC	Workaholic	Berndt Lindstedt
2TF	Conifer	George Sholty
3TC	Baltic Speed	Jan Nordin
3TF	Fancy Crown	Bill O'Donnell

1985

Div	Winner	Driver
2PC	Robust Hanover	John Campbell
2PF	Caressable	Herve Filion
3PC	Nihilator	Bill O'Donnell
3PF	Stienam	Buddy Gilmour
2TC	Express Ride	John Campbell
2TF	JEF's Spice	Mickey McNichol
3TC	Prakas	John Campbell
3TF	Armbro Devona	Bill O'Donnell
AP	Division Street	Michel Lachance
AT	Sandy Bowl	John Campbell

1986

Div	Winner	Driver
2PC	Sunset Warrior	Bill Gale
2PF	Halcyon	Ray Remmen
3PC	Masquerade	Richard Silverman
3PF	Glow Softly	Ron Waples
2TC	Mack Lobell	John Campbell
2TF	Super Flora	Ron Waples
3TC	Sugarcane Hanover	Ron Waples
3TF	JEF's Spice	Bill O'Donnell
APM	Samshu Bluegrass	Michel Lachance
ATM	Grades Singing	Herve Filion
APH	Forrest Skipper	Lucien Fontaine
ATH	Nearly Perfect	Mickey McNichol

1987

Div	Winner	Driver
2PC	Camtastic	Bill O'Donnell
2PF	Leah Almahurst	Bill Fahy
3PC	Call For Rain	Clint Galbraith
3PF	Pacific	Tom Harmer
2TC	Defiant One	Howard Beissinger
2TF	Nan's Catch	Berndt Lindstedt
3TC	Mack Lobell	John Campbell
3TF	Armbro Fling	George Sholty
APM	Follow My Star	John Campbell
ATM	Grades Singing	Olle Goop
APH	Armbro Emerson	Walter Whelan
ATH	Sugarcane Hanover	Ron Waples

1988

Div	Winner	Driver
2PC	Kentucky Spur	Dick Stillings
2PF	Central Park West	John Campbell
3PC	Camtastic	Bill O'Donnell
3PF	Sweet Reflection	Bill O'Donnell
2TC	Valley Victory	Bill O'Donnell
2TF	Peace Corps	John Campbell
3TC	Firm Tribute	Mark O'Mara
3TF	Nalda Hanover	Mickey McNichol
APM	Anniecrombie	Dave Magee
ATM	Armbro Flori	Larry Walker
APH	Call For Rain	Clint Galbraith
ATH	Mack Lobell	John Campbell

1989

Div	Winner	Driver
2PC	Till We Meet Again	Mickey McNichol
2PF	Town Pro	Doug Brown
3PC	Goalie Jeff	Michel Lachance
3PF	Cheery Hello	John Campbell
2TC	Royal Troubador	Carl Allen
2TF	Delphi's Lobell	Ron Waples
3TC	Esquire Spur	Dick Stillings
3TF	Pace Corps	John Campbell
APM	Armbro Feather	John Kopas
ATM	Grades Singing	Olle Goop
APH	Matt's Scooter	Michel Lachance
ATH	Delray Lobell	John Campbell

1990

Div	Winner	Driver
2PC	Artsplace	John Campbell
2PF	Miss Easy	John Campbell
3PC	Beach Towel	Ray Remmen
3PF	Town Pro	Doug Brown
2TC	Crysta's Best	Dick Richardson Jr
2TF	Jean Bi	Jan Nordin
3TC	Embassy Lobell	Michel Lachance
3TF	Me Maggie	Berndt Lindstedt
APM	Caesar's Jackpot	Bill Fahy
ATM	Peace Corps	Stig Johansson
APH	Bay's Fella	Paul MacDonell
ATH	No Sex Please	Ron Waples

2 = Two-year-old
T = Trotter
C = Colt
3 = Three-year-old
P = Pacer

F = Filly
A = Aged
H = Horse
M = Mare

Spirited Wagering

Joseph Guylas was such a frequent patron of Thistledown racetrack in Cleveland that his obituary in the Akron *Beacon Journal* read: "In lieu of flowers, it is suggested that a small wager in Joe's honor be made on a nag at the track. Do not expect it to win. It celebrates Joe's ascension to the great racetrack in the sky, where he will enjoy considerably more luck."

Triple Crown Winners

Trotting

Trotting's Triple Crown consists of the Hambletonian (first run in 1926), the Kentucky Futurity (first run in 1893), and the Yonkers Trot (known as the Yonkers Futurity when it began in 1955).

Year	Horse	Owner	Breeder	Trainer/Driver
1955	Scott Frost	S.A. Camp Farms	Est of W. N. Reynolds	Joe O'Brien
1963	Speedy Scot	Castleton Farms	Castleton Farms	Ralph Baldwin
1964	Ayres	Charlotte Sheppard	Charlotte Sheppard	John Simpson Sr
1968	Nevele Pride	Nevele Acres & Lou Resnick	Mr & Mrs E. C. Quin	Stanley Dancer
1969	Lindy's Pride	Lindy Farm	Hanover Shoe Farms	Howard Beissinger
1972	Super Bowl	Rachel Dancer & Rose Hild Breeding Farm	Stoner Creek Stud	Stanley Dancer

Pacing

Pacing's Triple Crown consists of the Cane Pace (called the Cane Futurity when it began in 1955), the Little Brown Jug (first run in 1946), and the Messenger Stake (first run in 1956).

Year	Horse	Owner	Breeder	Trainer/Driver
1959	Adios Butler	Paige West & Angelo Pelillo	R. C. Carpenter	Paige West/Clint Hodgins
1965	Bret Hanover	Richard Downing	Hanover Shoe Farms	Frank Ervin
1966	Romeo Hanover	Lucky Star Stables & Morton Finder	Hanover Shoe Farms	Jerry Silverman/ William Meyer (Cane) & George Sholty (Jug & Messenger)
1968	Rum Customer	Kennilworth Farms & L. C. Mancuso	Mr. & Mrs. R. C. Larkin	Bill Haughton
1970	Most Happy Fella	Egyptian Acres Stable	Stoner Creek Stud	Stanley Dancer
1980	Niatross	Niagara Acres, C. Galbraith & Niatross Stables	Niagara Acres	Clint Galbraith
1983	Ralph Hanover	Waples Stable, Pointsetta Stable, Grant's Direct Stable & P. J. Baugh	Hanover Shoe Farms	Stew Firlotte/Ron Waples

Awards

Horse of the Year

Year	Horse	Gait	Owner
1947	Victory Song	T	Castleton Farm
1948	Rodney	T	R. H. Johnston
1949	Good Time	P	William Cane
1950	Proximity	T	Ralph and Gordon Verhurst
1951	Pronto Don	T	Hayes Fair Acres Stable
1952	Good Time	P	William Cane
1953	Hi Lo's Forbes	P	Mr. and Mrs. Earl Wagner
1954	Stenographer	T	Max Hempt
1955	Scott Frost	T	S. A. Camp Farms
1956	Scott Frost	T	S. A. Camp Farms
1957	Torpid	P	Sherwood Farm
1958	Emily's Pride	T	Walnut Hall and Castleton Farms
1959	Bye Bye Byrd	P	Mr. and Mrs. Rex Larkin
1960	Adios Butler	P	Adios Butler Syndicate
1961	Adios Butler	P	Adios Butler Syndicate
1962	Su Mac Lad	T	I. W. Berkemeyer
1963	Speedy Scot	T	Castleton Farm
1964	Bret Hanover	P	Richard Downing
1965	Bret Hanover	P	Richard Downing
1966	Bret Hanover	P	Richard Downing
1967	Nevele Pride	T	Nevele Acres
1968	Nevele Pride	T	Nevele Acres, Louis Resnick
1969	Nevele Pride	T	Nevele Acres, Louis Resnick
1970	Fresh Yankee	T	Duncan MacDonald
1971	Albatross	P	Albatross Stable

Horse of the Year (*Cont.*)

Year	Horse	Gait	Owner
1972	Albatross	P	Amicable Stable
1973	Sir Dalrae	P	A La Carte Racing Stable
1974	Delmonica Hanover	T	Delvin Miller, W. Arnold Hanger
1975	Savoir	T	Allwood Stable
1976	Keystone Ore	P	Mr. and Mrs. Stanley Dancer, Rose Hild Farms, Robert Jones
1977	Green Speed	T	Beverly Lloyds
1978	Abercrombie	P	Shirley Mitchell, L. Keith Bulen
1979	Niatross	P	Niagara Acres, Clint Galbraith
1980	Niatross	P	Niatross Syndicate, Niagara Acres, Clint Galbraith
1981	Fan Hanover	P	Dr. J. Glen Brown
1982	Cam Fella	P	Norm Clements, Norm Faulkner
1983	Cam Fella	P	JEF's Standardbred, Norm Clements, Norm Faulkner
1984	Fancy Crown	T	Fancy Crown Stable
1985	Nihilator	P	Wall Street-Nihilator Syndicate
1986	Forrest Skipper	P	Forrest L. Bartlett
1987	Mack Lobell	T	One More Time Stable and Fair Wind Farm
1988	Mack Lobell	T	John Erik Magnusson
1989	Matt's Scooter	P	Gordon and Illa Rumpel, Charles Jurasvinski
1990	Beach Towel	P	Uptown Stables

Note: Balloting is conducted by the U.S Trotting Association and U.S. Harness Writers Association.

Leading Drivers—Money Won

Year	Driver	Winnings ($)	Year	Driver	Winnings ($)
1946	Thomas Berry	121,933	1969	Del Insko	1,635,463
1947	H. C. Fitzpatrick	133,675	1970	Herve Filion	1,647,837
1948	Ralph Baldwin	153,222	1971	Herve Filion	1,915,945
1949	Clint Hodgins	184,108	1972	Herve Filion	2,473,265
1950	Del Miller	306,813	1973	Herve Filion	2,233,303
1951	John Simpson Sr	333,316	1974	Herve Filion	3,474,315
1952	Bill Haughton	311,728	1975	Carmine Abbatiello	2,275,093
1953	Bill Haughton	374,527	1976	Herve Filion	2,278,634
1954	Bill Haughton	415,577	1977	Herve Filion	2,551,058
1955	Bill Haughton	599,455	1978	Carmine Abbatiello	3,344,457
1956	Bill Haughton	572,945	1979	John Campbell	3,308,984
1957	Bill Haughton	586,950	1980	John Campbell	3,732,306
1958	Bill Haughton	816,659	1981	Bill O'Donnell	4,065,608
1959	Bill Haughton	771,435	1982	Bill O'Donnell	5,755,067
1960	Del Miller	567,282	1983	John Campbell	6,104,082
1961	Stanley Dancer	674,723	1984	Bill O'Donnell	9,059,184
1962	Stanley Dancer	760,343	1985	Bill O'Donnell	10,207,372
1963	Bill Haughton	790,086	1986	John Campbell	9,515,055
1964	Stanley Dancer	1,051,538	1987	John Campbell	10,186,495
1965	Bill Haughton	889,943	1988	John Campbell	11,148,565
1966	Stanley Dancer	1,218,403	1989	John Campbell	9,738,450
1967	Bill Haughton	1,305,773	1990	John Campbell	11,620,878
1968	Bill Haughton	1,654,463			

Sulky of Swat

On March 2, 1991, a pacer named Babe Ruth won the fourth race at Pocono Downs in Wilkes-Barre, Pa., from post position 7. The second- and third-place finishers in the race came from posts 1 and 4, respectively, which means the Big Triple combination for the race was 7–1–4. The Bambino, of course, hit 714 homers in his career.

Motor Sports

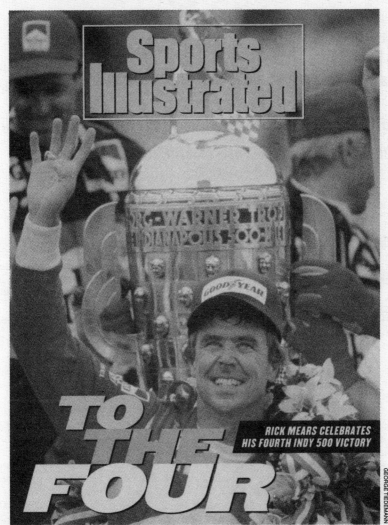

RICK MEARS CELEBRATES
HIS FOURTH INDY 500 VICTORY

Cashing in on Success

Racing is reaching new highs—with speeds of more than 220 mph and salaries of $15 million | by ED HINTON

BY AGE FOUR, MARCO ANDRETTI, SON OF Michael, grandson of Mario, had discovered the bottom line of motor racing in 1991. On Sunday afternoons, according to his mother, Sandy, Marco would head out the door toward his all-terrain vehicle and say, "O.K., Mom, let's strap on my helmet. Gotta go out and ride the four-wheeler and make some money."

In 1991, Marco's father earned a base salary estimated at $1.5 million, plus 50% of winnings that by midsummer had almost duplicated his paycheck. Still, Michael Andretti longed for the promised land of the Formula One Grand Prix tour, where his father had won the world driving championship in 1978, and where defending champion Ayrton Senna collected a base salary estimated at $15 million from McLaren International in 1991 (and was being courted with talk of a $23 million annual salary package from rival Williams Engineering for 1992).

Senna's pay, not quite $1 million per race, wasn't all that outrageous considering the cost of the machinery he controlled: $2 million for an original McLaren-Honda, counting research and development costs, and about $500,000 per copy to replace cars destroyed in crashes or worn out during practices and races.

Though other forms of racing couldn't touch Formula One for sheer dollar outlay, all is relative in motor sports. Costs at every level, in all forms, were out of sight and still accelerating upward in 1991.

It cost an estimated $10 million for team owners Carl Haas and Paul Newman to field Indy Cars for Mario and Michael Andretti over the 17-race CART season, and theirs wasn't even the biggest budget on the tour. It was only about average for a competitive Indy Car team, which in 1991 had to shell out $325,000 for each Lola car and $138,000 for each Chevy Indy V-8 engine (as well as lease a minimum of seven engines). To keep Indy 500 winner Rick Mears and teammate

Emerson Fittipaldi going, owner Roger Penske was believed to have operated on a $7 million-per-car budget. That kind of outlay pays off, as Mears won his fourth Indianapolis 500, giving Penske Racing an unprecedented seven wins in the "Greatest Spectacle in Racing."

NASCAR remained the least expensive major form of auto racing, but owner-driver Darrell Waltrip operated with a $4 million budget in 1991, double what he had raced with while driving for owner Rick Hendrick only one year earlier. Most competitive NASCAR teams were operating on $3 million and up—this in a realm where 20 years ago $100,000 a year carried a top team through a season comfortably.

NASCAR competition, compared to other racing, may have been the most inflationary of all. A NASCAR stock car still costs only about $60,000 to build, but Waltrip cites "people costs" in the upward budget spiral. Dale Earnhardt, NASCAR's defending champion and top money-earner, gets an estimated $1 million in base salary, plus 50% of winnings that can run to $3 million per season.

It has long been a saying on pit roads that "the best way to make a small fortune in racing is to start with a big one." Never has this been so true, and these days team owners

Senna began his $15 million season with a start-to-finish win at Phoenix.

rarely foot the bills themselves. Corporate sponsors have become the blood and marrow of big-time motor racing. And the economic recession in the United States caused a shakeout among racing teams in 1991.

By May, the hallowed Indianapolis 500 was barely able to fill its traditional field of 33 cars. Struggling teams, which previously had managed to find enough corporate sponsorship to run at least at Indy, had to stay home this time. Arie Luyendyk, the 1990 winner, arrived at Indy with only $500,000 in sponsorship for the entire season—and top teams figure on spending $1 million each to run Indy alone. Willy T. Ribbs, the first black driver to qualify for the Indy 500, did so largely on a personal check from comedian Bill Cosby. In August, only 21 cars started CART's Marlboro 500 at Michigan International Speedway. It was the smallest field for a 500-mile Indy Car race since the 1916 Indy 500.

At least on the surface NASCAR appeared healthy, regularly starting its standard field of 42 cars on its Super Speedways.

Corporate sponsors, hit hard by the recession, slashed budgets across the board, including those for promotion and advertising—the ones that most affect auto racing. And hanging as a further shadow over racing was the specter of federal government inquiries into the promotional involvement of tobacco and alcohol manufacturers in sporting events. RJR Nabisco, through its Winston cigarette brand, pours an estimated $15 million a year into NASCAR racing. The company is also a major sponsor of National Hot Rod Association drag racing. Philip Morris, through its Marlboro brand, is believed to spend another $15 million for Senna's McLaren Formula One team alone.

Hard-pressed brokers of sponsorships, anxious to keep up the level of their own commissions, have come up with demographic studies that have lured previously unlikely corporations into racing. When analysts found that nearly half of paying NASCAR fans are women, manufacturers of products such as coffee, laundry detergent, and TV dinners began paying for the privilege of painting their logos on the sides of cars. Discount department stores are heavily involved in Indy Cars and are believed to be headed into NASCAR in 1992.

So in spite of the economy, auto racing's rich get richer, and the champagne tastes soar from Cold Duck to Dom Perignon levels. These days, even Earnhardt's pit crewmen get paid for public appearances, travel aboard team owner Richard Childress's two

A Family Affair

THE 1991 INDIANAPOLIS 500 was so chock full of Andrettis—one family member starting in each of the first four rows of the field—that it seemed the peak of a 20-year trend toward family traditions of race driving. But people were only half-joking when they said "one day, Andrettis might fill the entire [33-car] field."

Patriarch Mario Andretti, at 51, isn't ready to retire. Elder son Michael, 29, is just hitting his prime, and younger son Jeff, 27, is feeling his way into the big time. Mario's nephew John Andretti, 28, scored his first Indy car win in 1991. Meanwhile, Adam Andretti, 12, gazes at big brother John's car and sighs, "Yeah. I want to do this." And Marco Andretti, 4, tears around the backyard in Nazareth, Pa., on the go-karts and all-terrain vehicles bought for him by dad Michael.

Down South, Adam Petty, 11, crashes go-karts with a reckless regularity, showing the instincts to become the first *fourth*-generation NASCAR driver. Lee Petty begot Richard, who begot Kyle, who begot Adam, who "had better

hurry," says Richard, if the Pettys are to beat the Andrettis to the next milestone of racing dynasties: fielding three generations in one race.

Richard Petty's old rival, Bobby Allison, hasn't raced since 1988 when he suffered a severe head injury. But Allison's son Davey has emerged as the most aggressive threat to the current supremacy of Dale Earnhardt (son of old-time dirt-tracker Ralph Earnhardt) on the Winston Cup tour.

Michael Andretti's chief rival on the CART Indy Car tour is Al Unser Jr., "Proud to be son of . . . ," he says, still in awe of a father who won the Indy 500 four times and "Uncle Bobby" who won three times at the Brickyard.

If you care to rile any of the younger-generation drivers, just insinuate that they rode into the big time solely on the strength of their surnames. "These kids didn't grow up with me mapping their careers," Mario Andretti says of his sons and nephew. "I think it was just a matter of their always being exposed to it."

Driving lineages are a matter of early environment, son Michael believes:

private planes, and stay in first-class hotels.

Hardly a star driver in the world doesn't own his own airplane—or need it. Public appearances are almost a daily affair for the top drivers, either on behalf of sponsors or for large fees from the stores or dealerships at which they appear. "It's getting to the point where you've got to be concerned about the business side as much as, if not more than, the racing side," says recently retired NASCAR driver Neil Bonnet. "Years ago I spent one day a week hustling around for sponsorship and five days a week racing. Now, you spend five days a week on sponsorship to be able to climb into a car for three or four hours on Sunday."

Despite what *Days of Thunder, Stroker Ace,* and similar movies might suggest, driver behavior on and off the track has become restrained by sponsors who demand squeaky-clean images. Formula One and NASCAR threaten drivers with time penalties, fines, and/or suspensions for the "rough driving" that once lent roguish color to auto racing. CART drivers can be fined even for horseplay with rental cars during race weekends. And, where some NASCAR drivers would once finish off their on-track disputes with fists, NASCAR will now quickly fine such unseemly behavior.

All this concern about corporate image and product exposure had, by 1991, washed much of the color out of drivers' live TV comments. Where once a driver might have

"From a very young age, I was used to speed and control of machinery." Racing drivers tend to love all sorts of motor-driven vehicles, so there usually are plenty of motorcycles, go-karts, and ATVs around for kids to play with. And if the reflexes for shooting a basketball or batting a ball are neglected, the reflexes for steering, braking, clutching, and shifting are honed from the toddler stage.

"There can be only two directions from there," says Michael Andretti. "You either get sick of it, or you want more."

The trend has been overwhelmingly toward the latter—except for A.J. Foyt's elder son, Tony, long irritated by the very sound of a racing engine, who has found happiness training thoroughbred racehorses.

The Andrettis at Indy: (from left) John, Jeff, Mario and Michael.

snarled, "That no-talent punk wrecked me because he's ox dumb, and he can just figure that next Sunday is payback time," now the standard line goes something like, "Well, the Acme Battery, Zestoid Barbecue Sauce, Golden Brown Tanning Parlor, Betta Motors Luminescent was running just great today until somebody tapped us from behind. It was just one of those unfortunate things that happen in racing. I just want to thank Acme, Zestoid, and Golden Brown once again and promise 'em we'll do a better job for 'em next week."

Some drivers concede privately that they know how silly all this sounds, but at $2 million a year from Acme, plus $500,000 each from Zestoid and Golden Brown, they memorize their lines and deliver them anytime a microphone is in sight.

And for 1991 and beyond, drivers' bowing to corporate image-consciousness will only increase in motor racing, for the costs of racing and the need for sponsorship promise only to escalate.

Indianapolis Motor Speedway began in 1991 to consider a change in its engine formula from the current turbo-charged powerplants to a projected "universal formula" of 3.5-liter, nonturbo engines such as

Close racing and corporate sponsors keep Earnhardt (3) going strong in NASCAR.

those now being used in Formula One and being introduced into prototype sports car racing. IMS president Tony George's plan is to open the Indianapolis 500 to a broader field of competitors and cars, though the change at Indy may be several years away. But along with the world-class competitors might also come Formula One-like technological costs, pushing the price of engines from the $138,000 cost for the current turbo Chevy Indy V8s to about $300,000 each for the even more sophisticated 3.5-liter engines. Such a cost probably would be absorbed by an influx of Japanese and European factory teams to Indy—in other words, deeper and wider corporate involvement.

And so little Marco Andretti, should he follow his father and grandfather into Indy Cars and Formula One, might someday look back on his "make some money" games as basic survival instincts for a motor racing world whose costs and rewards continue to come precariously close to the ragged edge of control.

FOR THE RECORD • 1990 – 1991

CART Racing

Indianapolis 500

Results of the 75th running of the Indianapolis 500 and 4th round of the 1991 CART series. Held Sunday, May 26, at the 2.5-mile Indianapolis Motor Speedway in Speedway, IN.

Distance, 500 miles; starters, 33; time of race, 2:50:00.791; average speed, 176.457 mph; margin of victory, 3.1 seconds; caution flags, 7 for 30 laps; lead changes, 18 among 6 drivers; attendance, 450,000.

Top 10 Finishers

Pos	Driver (start pos.)	Car	Qual. Speed	Laps	Status	Winnings ($)
1	Rick Mears (1)	Penske 91-Chevy	224.113	200	Running	1,219,704
2	Michael Andretti (5)	Lola 91-Chevy	220.943	200	Running	607,753
3	Arie Luyendyk (14)	Lola 91-Chevy	223.881	199	Running	317,053
4	Al Unser Jr (6)	Lola 91-Chevy	219.623	198	Running	223,916
5	John Andretti (7)	Lola 91-Chevy	219.059	197	Running	205,153
6	Gordon Johncock (33)	Lola 90-Chevy	213.812	188	Running	275,960
7	Mario Andretti (3)	Lola 91-Chevy	221.818	187	Engine	203,478
8	Stan Fox (17)	Lola 91-Buick	219.501	185	Running	201,090
9	Tony Bettenhausen (20)	Penske 90-Chevy	218.188	180	Running	170,016
10	Danny Sullivan (9)	Lola 91-Alfa	218.343	173	Engine	194,403

1991 CART Results

Date	Track/Distance	Winner (start pos.)	Car	Avg Speed	Winnings ($)
Mar 17	Gold Coast GP*	John Andretti (9)	Lola-Chevy	81.953	118,625
Apr 14	Long Beach GP*	Al Unser Jr (2)	Lola-Chevy	81.195	133,134
Apr 21	Phoenix 200	Arie Luyendyk (9)	Lola-Chevy	129.990	64,000
May 26	Indianapolis 500	Rick Mears (1)	Penske-Chevy	176.457	1,219,704
June 2	Milwaukee 200	Michael Andretti (3)	Lola-Chevy	134.557	63,476
June 16	Detroit GP*	Emerson Fittipaldi (2)	Penske-Chevy	78.824	132,700
June 23	Portland 200	Michael Andretti (4)	Lola-Chevy	115.208	79,398
July 7	Cleveland GP*	Michael Andretti (2)	Lola-Chevy	117.763	78,992
July 14	Meadowlands GP*	Bobby Rahal (4)	Lola-Chevy	95.551	80,922
July 21	Toronto	Michael Andretti (1)	Lola-Chevy	99.143	138,154
Aug 4	Michigan 500	Rick Mears (1)	Penske-Chevy	167.230	173,182
Aug 25	Denver GP	Al Unser Jr (3)	Lola-Chevy	69.576	135,700
Sep 1	Vancouver	Michael Andretti (1)	Lola-Chevy	93.888	138,920
Sep 15	Mid-Ohio 200	Michael Andretti (1)	Lola-Chevy	99.789	83,700
Sep 22	Road America 200	Michael Andretti (3)	Lola-Chevy	126.205	78,700
Oct 6	Pennsylvania 200	Arie Luyendyk (11)	Lola-Chevy	131.310	63,452
Oct 20	Laguna Seca 300K	Michael Andretti (1)	Lola-Chevy	103.604	83,700

*Temporary circuits.   Note: Distances are in miles unless followed by K (kilometers).

1991 CART Championship Standings

Driver	Starts	Wins	Pts
Michael Andretti	17	8	234
Bobby Rahal	17	1	200
Al Unser Jr	17	2	197
Rick Mears	17	2	144
Emerson Fittipaldi	17	1	140
Arie Luyendyk	17	2	134
Mario Andretti	17	0	132
John Andretti	17	1	105
Eddie Cheever	17	0	91
Scott Pruett	17	0	67

1991 CART Drivers Winnings

Driver	Winnings ($)
Rick Mears	2,213,865
Michael Andretti	1,936,234
Al Unser Jr	1,255,752
Bobby Rahal	1,211,823
Emerson Fittipaldi	1,072,473
Arie Luyendyk	1,039,464
Mario Andretti	947,217
John Andretti	809,845
Eddie Cheever	727,652
Scott Pruett	716,214

NASCAR Racing

Daytona 500

Results of the opening round of the 1991 Winston Cup series. Held Sunday, February 17, at the 2.5-mile high-banked Daytona International Speedway.

Distance, 500 miles; starters, 42; time of race, 3:22:30; average speed, 148.148 mph; margin of victory, under caution; caution flags, 9 for 36 laps; lead changes, 21 among 9 drivers; attendance, 120,000.

Top 10 Finishers

Pos	Driver (start pos.)	Car	Laps	Winnings ($)
1	Ernie Irvan (2)	Chevrolet	200	231,000
2	Sterling Marlin (12)	Ford	200	133,925
3	Joe Ruttman (14)	Oldsmobile	200	111,480
4	Rick Mast (7)	Oldsmobile	200	100,900
5	Dale Earnhardt (4)	Chevrolet	200	113,850
6	Dale Jarrett (17)	Ford	199	74,900
7	Bobby Hillin (36)	Oldsmobile	199	60,925
8	Alan Kulwicki (27)	Ford	199	52,450
9	Ricky Rudd (9)	Chevrolet	199	52,600
10	Bobby Hamilton (20)	Oldsmobile	199	43,500

Late 1990 NASCAR Results

Date	Track/Distance	Winner (start pos.)	Car	Avg Speed	Winnings ($)
Sep 30	N. Wilkesboro 400*	Mark Martin (2)	Ford	93.818	52,875
Oct 7	Charlotte 500	Davey Allison (5)	Ford	137.428	90,650
Oct 21	Rockingham 500	Alan Kulwicki (3)	Ford	126.452	53,300
Nov 4	Phoenix 500K	Dale Earnhardt (2)	Chevrolet	96.786	72,100
Nov 18	Atlanta 500	Morgan Shepherd (20)	Ford	140.911	62,250

Note: Distances are in miles unless followed by * (laps) or K (kilometers).

1991 NASCAR Results (through September 22)

Date	Track/Distance	Winner (start pos.)	Car	Avg Speed	Winnings ($)
Feb 17	Daytona 500	Ernie Irvan (2)	Chevrolet	148.148	231,000
Feb 24	Richmond 400*	Dale Earnhardt (19)	Chevrolet	105.397	67,950
Mar 3	Rockingham 500	Kyle Petty (1)	Pontiac	124.083	131,450
Mar 18	Atlanta 500	Ken Schrader (5)	Chevrolet	140.470	69,250
Apr 7	Darlington 500	Ricky Rudd (13)	Chevrolet	135.594	62,185
Apr 14	Bristol 500*	Rusty Wallace (1)	Pontiac	72.809	51,300
Apr 21	N. Wilkesboro 400*	Darrell Waltrip (13)	Chevrolet	79.604	53,800
Apr 28	Martinsville 500*	Dale Earnhardt (10)	Chevrolet	75.139	63,600
May 6	Talladega 500	Harry Gant (2)	Oldsmobile	165.620	81,950
May 26	Charlotte 600	Davey Allison (10)	Ford	138.951	137,100
June 2	Dover Downs 500	Ken Schrader (19)	Chevrolet	120.152	64,800
June 9	Sears Point 300K	Davey Allison (13)	Ford	72.970	61,950
June 16	Pocono 500	Darrell Waltrip (13)	Chevrolet	122.666	60,650
June 23	Michigan 400	Davey Allison (4)	Ford	160.912	90,650
July 6	Daytona 400	Bill Elliot (10)	Ford	159.116	75,000
July 21	Pocono 500	Rusty Wallace (10)	Pontiac	115.459	34,100
July 28	Talladega 500	Dale Earnhardt (4)	Chevrolet	147.383	88,670
Aug 11	Watkins Glen 219	Ernie Irvan (3)	Chevrolet	98.977	64,850
Aug 18	Michigan 400	Dale Jarrett (11)	Ford	142.972	74,150
Aug 24	Bristol 500	Alan Kulwicki (5)	Ford	82.028	61,400
Sep 1	Darlington 500	Harry Gant (5)	Oldsmobile	133.508	179,450
Sep 7	Richmond 400	Harry Gant (13)	Oldsmobile	101.361	63,650
Sep 15	Dover Downs 500	Harry Gant (10)	Oldsmobile	110.179	67,100
Sep 22	Martinsville 500	Harry Gant (12)	Oldsmobile	74.535	64,000

*Distance in laps.

Note: Distances are in miles unless followed by K (kilometers).

1990 Winston Cup Standings

Driver	Car	Starts	Wins	Pts
Dale Earnhardt	Chevrolet	29	9	4430
Mark Martin	Ford	29	3	4404
Geoff Bodine	Ford	29	3	4017
Bill Elliot	Ford	29	1	3999
Morgan Shepherd	Ford	29	1	3689
Rusty Wallace	Pontiac	29	2	3676
Ricky Rudd	Chevrolet	29	1	3601
Alan Kulwicki	Ford	29	1	3599
Ernie Irvan	Olds/Chevy	29	1	3593
Ken Schrader	Chevrolet	29	0	3572

1990 Winston Cup Driver Winnings

Driver	Winnings ($)
Dale Earnhardt	3,083,056
Mark Martin	1,302,958
Geoff Bodine	1,131,222
Bill Elliott	1,090,730
Rusty Wallace	954,129
Ken Schrader	769,934
Kyle Petty	746,326
Morgan Shepherd	666,915
Davey Allison	640,684
Ricky Rudd	573,650

Formula One/Grand Prix Racing

1991 Formula One Results

Date	Grand Prix	Winner	Car	Avg Speed
Mar 10	United States	Ayrton Senna	McLaren-Honda	93.018
Mar 24	Brazil	Ayrton Senna	McLaren-Honda	116.264
Apr 28	San Marino	Ayrton Senna	McLaren-Honda	120.269
May 12	Monaco	Ayrton Senna	McLaren-Honda	85.620
June 2	Canada	Nelson Piquet	Benetton-Ford	115.207
June 16	Mexico	Riccardo Patrese	Williams-Renault	122.880
July 7	France	Nigel Mansell	Williams-Renault	116.988
July 14	Britain	Nigel Mansell	Williams-Renault	131.227
July 28	Germany	Nigel Mansell	Williams-Renault	143.554
Aug 11	Hungary	Ayrton Senna	McLaren-Honda	104.301
Aug 25	Belgium	Ayrton Senna	McLaren-Honda	134.806
Sep 8	Italy	Nigel Mansell	Williams-Renault	147.109
Sep 22	Portugal	Riccardo Patrese	Williams-Renault	120.314
Sep 29	Spain	Nigel Mansell	Williams-Renault	116.561
Oct 20	Japan	Gerhard Berger	McLaren-Honda	125.702
Nov 3	Australia	Ayrton Senna	McLaren-Honda	80.262*

*Race shortened due to rain.

1991 World Championship Standings

Drivers compete in Grand Prix races for the title of World Driving Champion. Below are the official top 10 results from the 1991 season. Points are awarded for places 1-6 as follows: 10-6-4-3-2-1.

Driver, Country	Starts	Wins	Top 6	Pts
Aryton Senna, Brazil	16	7	14	96
Nigel Mansell, Great Britain	16	5	10	72
Riccardo Patrese, Italy	16	2	11	53
Gerhard Berger, Austria	16	1	9	43
Alain Prost, France	15	0	8	34
Nelson Piquet, Brazil	16	1	8	26.5
Jean Alesi, France	16	0	7	21
Stefano Modena, Italy	16	0	3	10
Andrea deCesaris, Italy	15	0	4	9
Roberto Moreno, Brazil	14	0	3	8

IMSA Racing

The 24 Hours of Daytona

Held at the Daytona International Speedway on February 2-3, 1991, the 24 Hours of Daytona annually serves as the opening round for the International Motor Sports Association sports car season.

Place	Drivers	Car	Distance
1	John Winter, Frank Jelinksi, Henri Pescarolo, Hurley Haywood, Bob Wollek	Porsche 962C	719 laps (106.633 mph)
2	Geoff Brabham, Chip Robinson, Derek Daly, Bob Earl	Nissan R90C	701 laps
3	John Hotchkis, James Adams, Chris Cord, Rob Dyson	Porsche 962C	692 laps
4	Robby Gordon, Mark Martin, Wally Dallenbach	Ford Mustang	672 laps
5	Mario Andretti, Michael Andretti, Jeff Andretti	Porsche 962C	663 laps (not running)

Late 1990 GTP Results

Date	Race	Winner (start pos.)	Car	Avg Speed	Winnings ($)
Sep 2	San Antonio GP	Juan Fangio II (11)	Toyota Eagle	163.660	30,000
Sep 30	Tampa GP	James Weaver (6)	Porsche 962C	89.538	90,500
Nov 11	San Diego GP at Del Mar	Juan Fangio II (8)	Toyota Eagle	78.836	50,000

1991 GTP Results

Date	Race	Winner (start pos.)	Car	Avg Speed	Winnings ($)
Feb 2-3	24 Hours of Daytona	Winter/Jelinski/Pescarolo/ Haywood/Wollek (7)	Porsche 962C	106.633	72,000
Mar 3	Palm Beach GP	Davy Jones (2)	Jaguar XJR10	93.122	50,500
Mar 16	12 Hours of Sebring	Geoff Brabham/Derek Daly/Gary Brabham	Nissan NPT-90	91.626	62,500
Apr 7	Miami GP	Raul Boesel	Jaguar XJR10	84.470	50,500
Apr 28	Atlanta GP at Road Atlanta	Davy Jones	Jaguar XJR16	120.932	31,500
May 5	Heartland GP	Chip Robinson	Nissan NPT-91	98.298	70,500
May 27	Lime Rock GP	Chip Robinson	Nissan NPT-91	102.340	30,500
June 2	GP of Ohio at Mid-Ohio	Davy Jones	Jaguar XJR16	107.275	30,500
June 16	GP du Mardi Gras	Wayne Taylor	Chevy Interpid	60.126	95,500
June 30	Watkins Glen	Juan Fangio II	Toyota Eagle	117.706	51,000
July 21	Monterey GP at Laguna Seca	Davy Jones	Jaguar XJR16	91.112	30,500
July 28	Portland GP	Juan Fangio II	Toyota Eagle	116.214	30,000
Aug 25	Road America GP	Davy Jones	Jaguar XJR16	122.491	30,000

1990 IMSA GTP Championship Standings

Driver	Pts
Geoff Brabham	196
Chip Robinson	175
Davy Jones	132
Juan Fangio II	115
John Nielsen	110
James Weaver	108
Prince Cobb	97
John Paul Jr	91
Derek Daly	72
Drake Olson	70

FIA World Sports Car Racing

The 24 Hours of LeMans

Held at LeMans, France, on June 22-23, 1991, the 24 Hours of LeMans is the most prestigious event in the FIA World Sports Car Championship.

Place	Drivers	Car	Distance
1	Volker Weidler, Johnny Herbert, Bertrand Gachot	Mazda 787B	362 laps (127.589 mph)
2	Davy Jones, Raul Boesel, Michel Ferte	Jaguar XJR12	360 laps
3	Teo Fabi, Bob Wollek, Kenny Acheson	Jaguar XJR12	358 laps
4	Derek Warwick, John Nielsen, Andy Wallace	Jaguar XJR12	356 laps
5	K. Wendlinger, M. Schumacher, F. Kreuzpointner	Mercedes C11	355 laps

Drag Racing

National Hot Rod Association

Race locations are the same for both Top Fuel and Funny Car drag races and are listed here with the Top Fuel events.

1991 Results

TOP FUEL

Date	Race, Site	Winner	Time	Speed
Feb 3	Winternationals, Pomona, CA	Frank Bradley	5.419	277.26
Feb 24	Arizona Nationals, Phoenix	Kenny Bernstein	5.016	287.63
Mar 3	Supernationals, Houston	Kenny Bernstein	4.957	291.54
Mar 17	Gatornationals, Gainesville, FL	Joe Amato	4.897	285.89
Apr 21	Southern Nationals, Atlanta	Kenny Bernstein	5.048	282.75
May 5	Mid-South Nationals, Memphis	Lori Johns	5.074	270.27
June 9	Springnationals, Columbus, OH	Don Prudhomme	5.084	281.86
June 23	Le Grandnational, Montreal	Kenny Bernstein	5.020	284.00
July 7	Summernationals, Englishtown, NJ	Tom McEwen	5.004	283.55
July 21	Mile-High Nationals, Denver	Joe Amato	5.052	274.64
July 28	California Nationals, Sonoma, CA	Joe Amato	4.968	277.34
Aug 4	Northwest Nationals, Seattle	Joe Amato	4.968	279.58
Aug 18	NorthStar Nationals, Brainerd, MN	Kenny Bernstein	5.051	283.37
Sep 2	US Nationals, Indianapolis	Kenny Bernstein	13.528	77.25
Sep 15	Keystone Nationals, Reading, PA	Don Prudhomme	4.954	278.20
Sep 29	Heartland Nationals, Topeka	Pat Austin	4.979	275.65
Oct 13	Texas Nationals, Dallas	Don Prudhomme	5.000	282.57
Nov 3	Winston Finals, Pomona, CA	Pat Austin	5.018	284.57

FUNNY CAR

Date	Race	Winner	Time	Speed
Feb 3	Winternationals	John Force	5.318	239.93
Feb 17	Arizona Nationals	Jim White	5.309	284.62
Mar 3	Supernationals	John Force	5.216	278.46
Mar 7	Gatornationals	Mark Oswald	5.375	258.91
Apr 21	Southern Nationals	Del Worsham	5.500	270.67
May 5	Mid-South Nationals	Mike Dunn	5.302	275.31
June 9	Springnationals	Mike Dunn	5.344	275.06
June 23	Le Grandnational	Jim White	5.595	271.90
July 7	Summernationals	Del Worsham	5.299	273.05
July 21	Mile-High Nationals	Mike Dunn	5.479	257.21
July 28	California Nationals	John Force	5.566	269.21
Aug 4	Northwest Nationals	John Force	5.360	270.83
Aug 18	NorthStar Nationals	John Force	5.409	265.40
Sep 2	US Nationals	Jim White	5.275	283.64
Sep 15	Keystone Nationals	Jim White	5.181	289.94
Sep 29	Heartland Nationals	Pat Austin	5.989	232.61
Oct 13	Texas Nationals	Al Hofmann	5.365	271.41
Nov 3	Winston Finals	Al Hofmann	5.394	271.57

1991 Standings

TOP FUEL

Driver	Wins	Pts
Joe Amato	4	14,388
Kenny Bernstein	6	13,832
Don Prudhomme	3	12,672
Frank Hawley	0	9,882
Lori Johns	1	8,986
Eddie Hill	0	8,636
Tom McEwen	1	8,248
Gene Snow	0	7,490
Dick LaHaie	0	6,980
Cory McClenathan	0	6,918

FUNNY CAR

Driver	Wins	Pts
John Force	5	15,538
Jim White	4	14,432
Mike Dunn	3	12,100
Ed McCulloch	0	11,364
Mark Oswald	2	11,172
Del Worsham	2	10,532
Al Hofmann	2	9,956
Tom Hoover	0	6,568
Richard Hartman	0	6,002
Jerry Caminito	0	5,392

CART Racing

Indianapolis 500

First held in 1911, the Indy 500—200 laps of the 2.5-mile Indianapolis Motor Speedway Track (called the Brickyard in honor of its original pavement)—has grown to become the most famous auto race in the world. Held on Memorial Day weekend, it annually draws the largest crowd of any sporting event in the world.

Year	Winner (Start Position)	Car	Avg MPH	Pole Winner	MPH
1911	Ray Harroun (28)	Marmon Wasp	74.590	Lewis Strang	Awarded pole
1912	Joe Dawson (7)	National	78.720	Gil Anderson	Drew pole
1913	Jules Goux (7)	Peugeot	75.930	Caleb Bragg	Drew pole
1914	Rene Thomas (15)	Delage	82.470	Jean Chassagne	Drew pole
1915	Ralph DePalma (2)	Mercedes	89.840	Howard Wilcox	98.90
1916	Dario Resta (4)	Peugeot	84.000	John Aitken	96.69
1917-18	No race				
1919	Howard Wilcox (2)	Peugeot	88.050	Rene Thomas	104.78
1920	Gaston Chevrolet (6)	Monroe	88.620	Ralph DePalma	99.15
1921	Tommy Milton (20)	Frontenac	89.620	Ralph DePalma	100.75
1922	Jimmy Murphy (1)	Murphy Special	94.480	Jimmy Murphy	100.50
1923	Tommy Milton (1)	H.C.S. Special	90.950	Tommy Milton	108.17
1924	L. L. Corum Joe Boyer (21)	Duesenberg Special	98.230	Jimmy Murphy	108.037
1925	Peter DePaolo (2)	Duesenberg Special	101.130	Leon Duray	113.196
1926	Frank Lockhart (20)	Miller Special	95.904	Earl Cooper	111.735
1927	George Souders (22)	Duesenberg	97.545	Frank Lockhart	120.100
1928	Louis Meyer (13)	Miller Special	99.482	Leon Duray	122.391
1929	Ray Keech (6)	Simplex Piston Ring Special	97.585	Cliff Woodbury	120.599
1930	Billy Arnold (1)	Miller Hartz Special	100.448	Billy Arnold	113.268
1931	Louis Schneider (13)	Bowes Seal-Fast Special	96.629	Russ Snowberger	112.796
1932	Fred Frame (27)	Miller Hartz Special	104.144	Lou Moore	117.363
1933	Louis Meyer (6)	Tydol Special	104.162	Bill Cummings	118.524
1934	Bill Cummings (10)	Boyle Products Special	104.863	Kelly Petillo	119.329
1935	Kelly Petillo (22)	Gilmore Speedway Special	106.240	Rex Mays	120.736
1936	Louis Meyer (28)	Ring-Free Special	109.069	Rex Mays	119.664
1937	Wilbur Shaw (2)	Shaw-Gilmore Special	113.580	Bill Cummings	123.343
1938	Floyd Roberts (1)	Burd Piston Ring Special	117.200	Floyd Roberts	125.681
1939	Wilbur Shaw (3)	Boyle Special	115.035	Jimmy Snyder	130.138
1940	Wilbur Shaw (2)	Boyle Special	114.277	Rex Mays	127.850
1941	Floyd Davis Mauri Rose (17)	Noc-Out Hose Clamp Special	115.117	Mauri Rose	128.691
1942-45	No race				
1946	George Robson (15)	Thorne Engineering Special	114.820	Cliff Bergere	126.471
1947	Mauri Rose (3)	Blue Crown Spark Plug Special	116.338	Ted Horn	126.564
1948	Mauri Rose (3)	Blue Crown Spark Plug Special	119.814	Rex Mays	130.577
1949	Bill Holland (4)	Blue Crown Spark Plug Special	121.327	Duke Nalon	132.939
1950	Johnnie Parsons (5)	Wynn's Friction Proofing	124.002	Walt Faulkner	134.343
1951	Lee Wallard (2)	Belanger Special	126.244	Duke Nalon	136.498
1952	Troy Ruttman (7)	Agajanian Special	128.922	Fred Agabashian	138.010
1953	Bill Vukovich (1)	Fuel Injection Special	128.740	Bill Vukovich	138.392
1954	Bill Vukovich (19)	Fuel Injection Special	130.840	Jack McGrath	141.033
1955	Bob Sweikert (14)	John Zink Special	128.209	Jerry Hoyt	140.045
1956	Pat Flaherty (1)	John Zink Special	128.490	Pat Flaherty	145.596
1957	Sam Hanks (13)	Belond Exhaust Special	135.601	Pat O'Connor	143.948
1958	Jim Bryan (7)	Belond AP Parts Special	133.791	Dick Rathmann	145.974
1959	Rodger Ward (6)	Leader Card 500 Roadster	135.857	Johnny Thomson	145.908
1960	Jim Rathmann (2)	Ken-Paul Special	138.767	Eddie Sachs	146.592
1961	A. J. Foyt (7)	Bowes Seal-Fast Special	139.130	Eddie Sachs	147.481
1962	Rodger Ward (2)	Leader Card 500 Roadster	140.293	Parnelli Jones	150.370
1963	Parnelli Jones (1)	Agajanian-Willard Special	143.137	Parnelli Jones	151.153
1964	A. J. Foyt (5)	Sheraton-Thompson Special	147.350	Jim Clark	158.828
1965	Jim Clark (2)	Lotus Ford	150.686	A. J. Foyt	161.233
1966	Graham Hill (15)	American Red Ball Special	144.317	Mario Andretti	165.899
1967	A. J. Foyt (4)	Sheraton-Thompson Special	151.207	Mario Andretti	168.982
1968	Bobby Unser (3)	Rislone Special	152.882	Joe Leonard	171.559
1969	Mario Andretti (2)	STP Oil Treatment Special	156.867	A. J. Foyt	170.568
1970	Al Unser (1)	Johnny Lightning 500 Special	155.749	Al Unser	170.221

Indianapolis 500 (*Cont.*)

Year	Winner (Start Position)	Car	Avg MPH	Pole Winner	MPH
1971	Al Unser (5)	Johnny Lightning Special	157.735	Peter Revson	178.696
1972	Mark Donohue (3)	Sunoco McLaren	162.962	Bobby Unser	195.940
1973	Gordon Johncock (11)	STP Double Oil Filters	159.036	Johnny Rutherford	198.413
1974	Johnny Rutherford (25)	McLaren	158.589	A. J. Foyt	191.632
1975	Bobby Unser (3)	Jorgensen Eagle	149.213	A. J. Foyt	193.976
1976	Johnny Rutherford (1)	Hy-Gain McLaren/Goodyear	148.725	Johnny Rutherford	188.957
1977	A. J. Foyt (4)	Gilmore Racing Team	161.331	Tom Sneva	198.884
1978	Al Unser (5)	FNCTC Chaparral Lola	161.361	Tom Sneva	202.156
1979	Rick Mears (1)	The Gould Charge	158.899	Rick Mears	193.736
1980	Johnny Rutherford (1)	Pennzoil Chaparral	142.862	Johnny Rutherford	192.256
1981	Bobby Unser (1)	Norton Spirit Penske PC-9B	139.084	Bobby Unser	200.546
1982	Gordon Johncock (5)	STP Oil Treatment	162.026	Rick Mears	207.004
1983	Tom Sneva (4)	Texaco Star	162.117	Teo Fabi	207.395
1984	Rick Mears (3)	Pennzoil Z-7	163.612	Tom Sneva	210.029
1985	Danny Sullivan (8)	Miller American Special	152.982	Pancho Carter	212.583
1986	Bobby Rahal (4)	Budweiser/Truesports/March	170.722	Rick Mears	216.828
1987	Al Unser (20)	Cummins Holset Turbo	162.175	Mario Andretti	215.390
1988	Rick Mears (1)	Penske-Chevrolet	144.809	Rick Mears	219.198
1989	Emerson Fittipaldi (3)	Penske-Chevrolet	167.581	Rick Mears	223.885
1990	Arie Luyendyk (3)	Domino's Pizza Chevrolet	185.981*	Emerson Fittipaldi	225.301†
1991	Rick Mears (1)	Penske-Chevrolet	176.457	Rick Mears	224.113

*Track record, winning time.

†Track record, qualifying time.

Indianapolis 500 Rookie of the Year Award

1952 ....Art Cross	1967 ....Denis Hulme	1981 ....Josele Garza
1953 ....Jimmy Daywalt	1968 ....Billy Vukovich	1982 ....Jim Hickman
1954 ....Larry Crockett	1969 ....Mark Donohue*	1983 ....Teo Fabi
1955 ....Al Herman	1970 ....Donnie Allison	1984 ....Michael Andretti
1956 ....Bob Veith	1971 ....Denny Zimmerman	.............Roberto Guerrero
1957 ....Don Edmunds	1972 ....Mike Hiss	1985 ....Arie Luyendyk
1958 ....George Amick	1973 ....Graham McRae	1986 ....Randy Lanier
1959 ....Bobby Grim	1974 ....Pancho Carter	1987 ....Fabrizio Barbazza
1960 ....Jim Hurtubise	1975 ....Bill Puterbaugh	1988 ....Billy Vukovich III
1961 ....Parnelli Jones*	1976 ....Vern Schuppan	1989 ....Bernard Jourdain
.............Bobby Marshman	1977 ....Jerry Sneva	.............Scott Pruett
1962 ....Jimmy McElreath	1978 ....Rick Mears*	1990 ....Eddie Cheever
1963 ....Jim Clark*	.............Larry Rice	1991 ....Jeff Andretti
1964 ....Johnny White	1979 ....Howdy Holmes	
1965 ....Mario Andretti*	1980 ....Tim Richmond	*Future winner of Indy 500.
1966 ....Jackie Stewart		

Indy Car Champions

From 1909 to 1955, this championship was awarded by the American Automobile Association (AAA), and from 1956 to 1979 by United States Auto Club (USAC). Since 1979, Championship Auto Racing Teams (CART) has conducted the championship.

1909 ....George Robertson	1924 ....Jimmy Murphy	1939 ....Wilbur Shaw
1910 ....Ray Harroun	1925 ....Peter DePaolo	1940 ....Rex Mays
1911 ....Ralph Mulford	1926 ....Harry Hartz	1941 ....Rex Mays
1912 ....Ralph DePalma	1927 ....Peter DePaolo	1942-45 ...No racing
1913 ....Earl Cooper	1928 ....Louis Meyer	1946 ....Ted Horn
1914 ....Ralph DePalma	1929 ....Louis Meyer	1947 ....Ted Horn
1915 ....Earl Cooper	1930 ....Billy Arnold	1948 ....Ted Horn
1916 ....Dario Resta	1931 ....Louis Schneider	1949 ....Johnnie Parsons
1917 ....Earl Cooper	1932 ....Bob Carey	1950 ....Henry Banks
1918 ....Ralph Mulford	1933 ....Louis Meyer	1951 ....Tony Bettenhausen
1919 ....Howard Wilcox	1934 ....Bill Cummings	1952 ....Chuck Stevenson
1920 ....Tommy Milton	1935 ....Kelly Petillo	1953 ....Sam Hanks
1921 ....Tommy Milton	1936 ....Mauri Rose	1954 ....Jimmy Bryan
1922 ....Jimmy Murphy	1937 ....Wilbur Shaw	1955 ....Bob Sweikert
1923 ....Eddie Hearne	1938 ....Floyd Roberts	1956 ....Jimmy Bryan

Indy Car Champions (*Cont.*)

1957 ....Jimmy Bryan	1969 ....Mario Andretti	1980 ....Johnny Rutherford
1958 ....Tony Bettenhausen	1970 ....Al Unser	1981 ....Rick Mears
1959 ....Rodger Ward	1971 ....Joe Leonard	1982 ....Rick Mears
1960 ....A. J. Foyt	1972 ....Joe Leonard	1983 ....Al Unser
1961 ....A. J. Foyt	1973 ....Roger McCluskey	1984 ....Mario Andretti
1962 ....Rodger Ward	1974 ....Bobby Unser	1985 ....Al Unser
1963 ....A. J. Foyt	1975 ....A. J. Foyt	1986 ....Bobby Rahal
1964 ....A. J. Foyt	1976 ....Gordon Johncock	1987 ....Bobby Rahal
1965 ....Mario Andretti	1977 ....Tom Sneva	1988 ....Danny Sullivan
1966 ....Mario Andretti	1978 ....Tom Sneva	1989 ....Emerson Fittipaldi
1967 ....A. J. Foyt	1979 ....A. J. Foyt	1990 ....Al Unser Jr
1968 ....Bobby Unser	1979 ....Rick Mears	

All-Time Indy Car Leaders

WINS		WINNINGS ($)		POLE POSITIONS	
A. J. Foyt*	67	Rick Mears*	10,070,993	Mario Andretti*	64
Mario Andretti*	51	Mario Andretti*	8,533,166	A. J. Foyt*	53
Al Unser*	39	Bobby Rahal*	8,274,993	Bobby Unser	49
Bobby Unser	35	Al Unser Jr*	7,670,549	Rick Mears*	39
Rick Mears*	29	Emerson Fittipaldi*	7,190,878	Al Unser*	27
Johnny Rutherford*	27	Michael Andretti*	6,978,194	Johnny Rutherford*	23
Rodger Ward	26	Danny Sullivan*	6,536,058	Gordon Johncock*	20
Gordon Johncock*	25	Al Unser*	6,129,901	Danny Sullivan*	19
Ralph DePalma	24	A. J. Foyt*	5,130,504	Rex Mays	19
Tommy Milton	23	Arie Luyendyk*	4,671,900	Michael Andretti*	16
Tony Bettenhausen	21	Tom Sneva*	4,253,215	Don Branson	15
Earl Cooper	21	Johnny Rutherford*	4,209,232	Tom Sneva*	14
Bobby Rahal*	20	Gordon Johncock*	3,285,411	Bobby Rahal*	14
Jimmy Murphy	19	Roberto Guerrero*	3,268,906	Tony Bettenhausen	14
Jimmy Bryan	19	Kevin Cogan*	2,996,253	Parnelli Jones	12
Michael Andretti*	18	Pancho Carter*	2,698,733	Emerson Fittipaldi*	11
Ralph Mulford	17	Bobby Unser	2,674,516	Danny Ongais	11
Al Unser Jr*	16	Raul Boesel*	2,609,858	Rodger Ward	11
Danny Sullivan*	15	Geoff Brabham*	2,393,123	Johnny Thomson	10
Tom Sneva*	13	Teo Fabi*	2,322,804	Dan Gurney	10

*Active driver.

Note: Indy Car Leaders through August 4, 1991.

NASCAR Racing

Stock Car Racing's Major Events

Winston offers a $1 million bonus to any driver to win 3 of NASCAR's top 4 events in the same season. These races are the richest (Daytona 500), the fastest (Winston 500 at Talladega), the longest (Coca-Cola 600 at Charlotte) and the oldest (Heinz Southern 500 at Darlington). These events form the backbone of NASCAR racing. Only 3 drivers, LeeRoy Yarbrough (1969), David Pearson (1976) and Bill Elliott (1985), have scored the 3-track hat trick.

Daytona 500

Year	Winner	Car	Avg MPH	Pole Winner	MPH
1959 ....Lee Petty		Oldsmobile	135.520	Cotton Owens	143.198
1960 ....Junior Johnson		Chevrolet	124.740	Fireball Roberts	151.556
1961 ....Marvin Panch		Pontiac	149.601	Fireball Roberts	155.709
1962 ....Fireball Roberts		Pontiac	152.529	Fireball Roberts	156.995
1963 ....Tiny Lund		Ford	151.566	Johnny Rutherford	165.183
1964 ....Richard Petty		Plymouth	154.345	Paul Goldsmith	174.910
1965 ....Fred Lorenzen		Ford	141.539	Darel Dieringer	171.151
1966 ....Richard Petty		Plymouth	160.627	Richard Petty	175.165
1967 ....Mario Andretti		Ford	149.926	Curtis Turner	180.831
1968 ....Cale Yarborough		Mercury	143.251	Cale Yarborough	189.222
1969 ....LeeRoy Yarbrough		Ford	157.950	David Pearson	190.029

Daytona 500 (*Cont.*)

Year	Winner	Car	Avg MPH	Pole Winner	MPH
1970	Pete Hamilton	Plymouth	149.601	Cale Yarborough	194.015
1971	Richard Petty	Plymouth	144.462	A. J. Foyt	182.744
1972	A. J. Foyt	Mercury	161.550	Bobby Isaac	186.632
1973	Richard Petty	Dodge	157.205	Buddy Baker	185.662
1974	Richard Petty	Dodge	140.894	David Pearson	185.017
1975	Benny Parsons	Chevrolet	153.649	Donnie Allison	185.827
1976	David Pearson	Mercury	152.181	A. J. Foyt	185.943
1977	Cale Yarborough	Chevrolet	153.218	Donnie Allison	188.048
1978	Bobby Allison	Ford	159.730	Cale Yarborough	187.536
1979	Richard Petty	Oldsmobile	143.977	Buddy Baker	196.049
1980	Buddy Baker	Oldsmobile	177.602*	A. J. Foyt	195.020
1981	Richard Petty	Buick	169.651	Bobby Allison	194.624
1982	Bobby Allison	Buick	153.991	Benny Parsons	196.317
1983	Cale Yarborough	Pontiac	155.979	Ricky Rudd	198.864
1984	Cale Yarborough	Chevrolet	150.994	Cale Yarborough	201.848
1985	Bill Elliott	Ford	172.265	Bill Elliott	205.114
1986	Geoff Bodine	Chevrolet	148.124	Bill Elliott	205.039
1987	Bill Elliott	Ford	176.263	Bill Elliott	210.364†
1988	Bobby Allison	Buick	137.531	Ken Schrader	193.823
1989	Darrell Waltrip	Chevrolet	148.466	Ken Schrader	196.996
1990	Derrike Cope	Chevrolet	165.761	Ken Schrader	196.515
1991	Earnie Irvan	Chevrolet	148.148	Davey Allison	195.955

*Track record, winning time. †Track record, qualifying time.

Note: The Daytona 500, held annually in February, now opens the NASCAR season with 200 laps around the high-banked Daytona, FL, superspeedway.

World 600

1960	Joe Lee Johnson
1961	David Pearson
1962	Nelson Stacy
1963	Fred Lorenzen
1964	Jim Paschal
1965	Fred Lorenzen
1966	Marvin Panch
1967	Jim Paschal
1968	Buddy Baker
1969	LeeRoy Yarbrough
1970	Donnie Allison
1971	Bobby Allison
1972	Buddy Baker
1973	Buddy Baker
1974	David Pearson
1975	Richard Petty
1976	David Pearson
1977	Richard Petty
1978	Darrell Waltrip
1979	Darrell Waltrip
1980	Benny Parsons
1981	Bobby Allison
1982	Neil Bonnett
1983	Neil Bonnett
1984	Bobby Allison
1985	Darrell Waltrip
1986	Dale Earnhardt
1987	Kyle Petty
1988	Darrell Waltrip
1989	Darrell Waltrip
1990	Rusty Wallace

Note: Held at the 1.5-mile Charlotte, NC, Motor Speedway on Memorial Day weekend.

Talladega 500

1970	Pete Hamilton
1971	Donnie Allison
1972	David Pearson
1973	David Pearson
1974	David Pearson
1975	Buddy Baker
1976	Buddy Baker
1977	Darrell Waltrip
1978	Cale Yarborough
1979	Bobby Allison
1980	Buddy Baker
1981	Bobby Allison
1982	Darrell Waltrip
1983	Richard Petty
1984	Cale Yarborough
1985	Bill Elliott
1986	Bobby Allison
1987	Davey Allison
1988	Phil Parsons
1989	Davey Allison
1990	Dale Earnhardt

Note: Held at the 2.66-mile high-banked Talladega, AL, Superspeedway on the last weekend in July.

Southern 500

1950	Johnny Mantz
1951	Herb Thomas
1952	Fonty Flock
1953	Buck Baker
1954	Herb Thomas
1955	Herb Thomas
1956	Curtis Turner
1957	Speedy Thompson
1958	Fireball Roberts
1959	Jim Reed
1960	Buck Baker
1961	Nelson Stacy
1962	Larry Frank
1963	Fireball Roberts
1964	Buck Baker
1965	Ned Jarrett
1966	Darel Dieringer
1967	Richard Petty
1968	Cale Yarborough
1969	LeeRoy Yarbrough
1970	Buddy Baker
1971	Bobby Allison
1972	Bobby Allison
1973	Cale Yarborough
1974	Cale Yarborough
1975	Bobby Allison
1976	David Pearson
1977	David Pearson
1978	Cale Yarborough
1979	David Pearson
1980	Terry Labonte
1981	Neil Bonnett
1982	Cale Yarborough
1983	Bobby Allison
1984	Harry Gant
1985	Bill Elliott
1986	Tim Richmond
1987	Dale Earnhardt
1988	Bill Elliott
1989	Dale Earnhardt
1990	Dale Earnhardt

Note: Held at the 1.366-mile Darlington, SC, International Raceway on Labor Day weekend.

Winston Cup NASCAR Champions

Year	Driver	Car	Wins	Poles	Winnings ($)
1949	Red Byron	Oldsmobile	2	0	5,800
1950	Bill Rexford	Oldsmobile	1	0	6,175
1951	Herb Thomas	Hudson	7	4	18,200
1952	Tim Flock	Hudson	8	4	20,210
1953	Herb Thomas	Hudson	11	10	27,300
1954	Lee Petty	Dodge	7	3	26,706
1955	Tim Flock	Chrysler	18	19	33,750
1956	Buck Baker	Chrysler	14	12	29,790
1957	Buck Baker	Chevy	10	5	24,712
1958	Lee Petty	Olds	7	4	20,600
1959	Lee Petty	Plymouth	10	2	45,570
1960	Rex White	Chevy	6	3	45,260
1961	Ned Jarrett	Chevy	1	4	27,285
1962	Joe Weatherly	Pontiac	9	6	56,110
1963	Joe Weatherly	Mercury	3	6	58,110
1964	Richard Petty	Plymouth	9	8	98,810
1965	Ned Jarrett	Ford	13	9	77,966
1966	David Pearson	Dodge	14	7	59,205
1967	Richard Petty	Plymouth	27	18	130,275
1968	David Pearson	Ford	16	12	118,824
1969	David Pearson	Ford	11	14	183,700
1970	Bobby Isaac	Dodge	11	13	121,470
1971	Richard Petty	Plymouth	21	9	309,225
1972	Richard Petty	Plymouth	8	3	227,015
1973	Benny Parsons	Chevy	1	0	114,345
1974	Richard Petty	Dodge	10	7	299,175
1975	Richard Petty	Dodge	13	3	378,865
1976	Cale Yarborough	Chevy	9	2	387,173
1977	Cale Yarborough	Chevy	9	3	477,499
1978	Cale Yarborough	Oldsmobile	10	8	530,751
1979	Richard Petty	Chevy	5	1	531,292
1980	Dale Earnhardt	Chevy	5	0	588,926
1981	Darrell Waltrip	Buick	12	11	693,342
1982	Darrell Waltrip	Buick	12	7	873,118
1983	Bobby Allison	Buick	6	0	828,355
1984	Terry Labonte	Chevy	2	2	713,010
1985	Darrell Waltrip	Chevy	3	4	1,318,735
1986	Dale Earnhardt	Chevy	5	1	1,783,880
1987	Dale Earnhardt	Chevy	11	1	2,099,243
1988	Bill Elliott	Ford	6	6	1,574,639
1989	Rusty Wallace	Pontiac	6	4	2,247,950
1990	Dale Earnhardt	Chevy	9	4	3,083,056

All-Time NASCAR Leaders

WINS

Richard Petty*	200
David Pearson	105
Bobby Allison	84
Cale Yarborough	83
Darrell Waltrip*	81
Lee Petty	54
Dale Earnhardt*	51
Junior Johnson	50
Ned Jarrett	50
Herb Thomas	48
Buck Baker	46
Tim Flock	40
Bobby Isaac	37
Fireball Roberts	34
Bill Elliott*	34
Rex White	28

WINNINGS ($)

Dale Earnhardt*	13,683,320
Darrell Waltrip*	10,927,710
Bill Elliott*	10,739,570
Richard Petty*	7,334,033
Bobby Allison	7,102,233
Rusty Wallace*	6,682,569
Terry Labonte*	6,491,308
Ricky Rudd*	5,532,770
Geoff Bodine*	5,321,011
Harry Gant*	5,196,638
Cale Yarborough	5,003,716
Benny Parsons	3,926,539
Ken Schrader*	3,854,989
Neil Bonnett	3,847,146
Buddy Baker*	3,582,221
Mark Martin*	3,359,738

POLE POSITIONS

Richard Petty*	127
David Pearson	113
Cale Yarborough	70
Bobby Allison	57
Darrell Waltrip*	57
Bobby Isaac	51
Junior Johnson	47
Buck Baker	44
Buddy Baker*	40
Bill Elliott*	39
Herb Thomas	38
Tim Flock	37
Fireball Roberts	37
Ned Jarrett	36
Rex White	36
Fred Lorenzen	33

*Active drivers.

Note: NASCAR leaders as of August 18, 1991.

Formula One/Grand Prix Racing

World Driving Champions

Year	Winner	Car	Year	Winner	Car
1950	Guiseppe Farina, Italy	Alfa Romeo	1969	Jackie Stewart, Scotland	Matra-Ford
1951	Juan-Manuel Fangio, Argentina	Alfa Romeo	1970	Jochen Rindt, Austria*	Lotus-Ford
1952	Alberto Ascari, Italy	Ferrari	1971	Jackie Stewart, Scotland	Tyrell-Ford
1953	Alberto Ascari, Italy	Ferrari	1972	Emerson Fittipaldi, Brazil	Lotus-Ford
1954	Juan-Manuel Fangio, Argentina	Maserati/ Mercedes	1973	Jackie Stewart, Scotland	Tyrell-Ford
1955	Juan-Manuel Fangio, Argentina	Mercedes	1974	Emerson Fittipaldi, Brazil	McLaren-Ford
1956	Juan-Manuel Fangio, Argentina	Ferrari	1975	Niki Lauda, Austria	Ferrari
1957	Juan-Manuel Fangio, Argentina	Maserati	1976	James Hunt, England	McLaren-Ford
1958	Mike Hawthorne, England	Ferrari	1977	Niki Lauda, Austria	Ferrari
1959	Jack Brabham, Australia	Cooper-Climax	1978	Mario Andretti, United States	Lotus-Ford
1960	Jack Brabham, Australia	Cooper-Climax	1979	Jody Scheckter, South Africa	Ferrari
1961	Phil Hill, United States	Ferrari	1980	Alan Jones, Australia	Williams-Ford
1962	Graham Hill, England	BRM	1981	Nelson Piquet, Brazil	Brabham-Ford
1963	Jim Clark, Scotland	Lotus-Climax	1982	Keke Rosberg, Finland	Williams-Ford
1964	John Surtees, England	Ferrari	1983	Nelson Piquet, Brazil	Brabham-BMW
1965	Jim Clark, Scotland	Lotus-Climax	1984	Niki Lauda, Austria	McLaren-Porsche
1966	Jack Brabham, Australia	Brabham-Climax	1985	Alain Prost, France	McLaren-Porsche
1967	Denis Hulme, New Zealand	Brabham-Repco	1986	Alain Prost, France	McLaren-Porsche
1968	Graham Hill, England	Lotus-Ford	1987	Nelson Piquet, Brazil	Williams-Honda
			1988	Ayrton Senna, Brazil	McLaren-Honda
			1989	Alain Prost, France	McLaren-Honda
			1990	Ayrton Senna, Brazil	McLaren-Honda

*The championship was awarded after Rindt was killed in practice for the Italian Grand Prix.

All-Time Grand Prix Winners

Driver	Wins
Alain Prost, France*	44
Ayrton Senna, Brazil*	31
Jackie Stewart, Scotland	27
Jim Clark, Scotland	25
Niki Lauda, Austria	25
Juan-Manuel Fangio, Argentina	24
Nelson Piquet, Brazil*	20
Nigel Mansell, England*	17
Stirling Moss, England	16
Jack Brabham, Australia	14
Graham Hill, England	14
Emerson Fittipaldi, Brazil*	14

*Active driver.

Note: Through August 11, 1991.

All-Time Grand Prix Pole Winners

Driver	Poles
Ayrton Senna, Brazil*	59
Jim Clark, Scotland	33
Juan-Manuel Fangio, Argentina	28
Alain Prost, France*	25
Niki Lauda, Austria	24
Nelson Piquet, Brazil*	24
Mario Andretti, United States*	18
Jackie Stewart, Scotland	17
Stirling Moss, England	16
Alberto Ascari, Italy	14
Ronnie Peterson, Sweden	14
James Hunt, England	14

*Active driver.

IMSA Racing

The 24 Hours of Daytona

Year	Winner	Car	Avg Speed	Distance
1962	Dan Gurney	Lotus 19-Class SP11	104.101 mph	3 hrs (312.42 mi)
1963	Pedro Rodriguez	Ferrari-Class 12	102.074 mph	3 hrs (308.61 mi)
1964	Pedro Rodriguez/Phil Hill	Ferrari 250 LM	98.230 mph	2,000 km
1965	Ken Miles/Lloyd Ruby	Ford	99.944 mph	2,000 km
1966	Ken Miles/Lloyd Ruby	Ford Mark II	108.020 mph	24 hrs (2,570.63 mi)
1967	Lorenzo Bandini/Chris Amon	Ferrari 330 P4	105.688 mph	24 hrs (2,537.46 mi)
1968	Vic Elford/Jochen Neerpasch	Porsche 907	106.697 mph	24 hrs (2,565.69 mi)
1969	Mark Donohue/Chuck Parsons	Chevy Lola	99.268 mph	24 hrs (2,383.75 mi)
1970	Pedro Rodriguez/Leo Kinnunen	Porsche 917	114.866 mph	24 hrs (2,758.44 mi)

The 24 Hours of Daytona (*Cont.*)

Year	Winner	Car	Avg Speed	Distance
1971	Pedro Rodriguez/Jackie Oliver	Porsche 917K	109.203 mph	24 hrs (2,621.28 mi)
1972*	Mario Andretti/Jacky Ickx	Ferrari 312/P	122.573 mph	6 hrs (738.24 mi)
1973	Peter Gregg/Hurley Haywood	Porsche Carrera	106.225 mph	24 hrs (2,552.7 mi)
1974	(No race)			
1975	Peter Gregg/Hurley Haywood	Porsche Carrera	108.531 mph	24 hrs (2,606.04 mi)
1976†	Peter Gregg/Brian Redman/ John Fitzpatrick	BMW CSL	104.040 mph	24 hrs (2,092.8 mi)
1977	John Graves/Hurley Haywood/ Dave Helmick	Porsche Carrera	108.801 mph	24 hrs (2,615 mi)
1978	Rolf Stommelen/ Antoine Hezemans/Peter Gregg	Porsche Turbo	108.743 mph	24 hrs (2,611.2 mi)
1979	Ted Field/Danny Ongais/ Hurley Haywood	Porsche Turbo	109.249 mph	24 hrs (2,626.56 mi)
1980	Volkert Meri/Rolf Stommelen/ Reinhold Joest	Porsche Turbo	114.303 mph	24 hrs
1981	Bob Garretson/Bobby Rahal/ Brian Redman	Porsche Turbo	113.153 mph	24 hrs
1982	John Paul, Jr/John Paul, Sr/ Rolf Stommelen	Porsche Turbo	114.794 mph	24 hrs
1983	Preston Henn/Bob Wollek/ Claude Ballot-Lena/A. J. Foyt	Porsche Turbo	98.781 mph	24 hrs
1984	Sarel van der Merwe/ Graham Duxbury/Tony Martin	Porsche March	103.119 mph	24 hrs (2,476.8 mi)
1985	A. J. Foyt/Bob Wollek/ Al Unser, Sr/Thierry Boutsen	Porsche 962	104.162 mph	24 hrs (2,502.68 mi)
1986	Al Holbert/Derek Bell/ Al Unser, Jr	Porsche 962	105.484 mph	24 hrs (2,534.72 mi)
1987	Chip Robinson/Derek Bell/ Al Holbert/Al Unser, Jr	Porsche 962	111.599 mph	24 hrs (2,680.68 mi)
1988	Martin Brundle/ John Nielsen/ Raul Boesel	Jaguar XJR-9	107.943 mph	24 hrs (2,591.68 mi)
1989	John Andretti/Derek Bell/ Bob Wollek	Porsche 962	92.009 mph	24 hrs (2,210.76 mi)
1990	Davy Jones/Jan Lammers/ Andy Wallace	Jaguar XJR-12	112.857 mph	24 hrs (2,709.16 mi)
1991	Hurley Haywood/John Winter/ Frank Jelinski/Henri Pescarolo/ Bob Wollek	Porsche 962C	106.633 mph	24 hrs (2,559.64 mi)

*Race shortened due to fuel crisis.

†Course lengthened from 3.81 miles to 3.84 miles.

FIA World Sports Car Racing

The 24 Hours of Le Mans

Year	Winning Drivers	Car
1923	André Lagache/René Léonard	Chenard & Walker
1924	John Duff/Francis Clement	Bentley 3-litre
1925	Gérard de Courcelles/André Rossignol	La Lorraine
1926	Robert Bloch/André Rossignol	La Lorraine
1927	J. Dudley Benjafield/Sammy Davis	Bentley 3-litre
1928	Woolf Barnato/Bernard Rubin	Bentley 4½
1929	Woolf Barnato/Sir Henry Birkin	Bentley Speed Six
1930	Woolf Barnato/Glen Kidston	Bentley Speed Six
1931	Earl Howe/Sir Henry Birkin	Alfa Romeo 8C-2300 sc
1932	Raymond Sommer/Luigi Chinetti	Alfa Romeo 8C-2300 sc
1933	Raymond Sommer/Tazio Nuvolari	Alfa Romeo 8C-2300 sc
1934	Luigi Chinetti/Philippe Etancelin	Alfa Romeo 8C-2300 sc
1935	John Hindmarsh/Louis Fontés	Lagonda M45R
1936	Race cancelled	
1937	Jean-Pierre Wimille/Robert Benoist	Bugatti 57G sc
1938	Eugene Chaboud/Jean Tremoulet	Delahaye 135M
1939	Jean-Pierre Wimille/Pierre Veyron	Bugatti 57G sc

The 24 Hours of Le Mans (*Cont.*)

Year	Winning Drivers	Car
1940-48	Races cancelled	
1949	Luigi Chinetti/Lord Selsdon	Ferrari 166MM
1950	Louis Rosier/Jean-Louis Rosier	Talbot-Lago
1951	Peter Walker/Peter Whitehead	Jaguar C
1952	Hermann Lang/Fritz Reiss	Mercedes-Benz 300 SL
1953	Tony Rolt/Duncan Hamilton	Jaguar C
1954	Froilan Gonzales/Maurice Trintignant	Ferrari 375
1955	Mike Hawthorn/Ivor Bueb	Jaguar D
1956	Ron Flockhart/Ninian Sanderson	Jaguar D
1957	Ron Flockhart/Ivor Buab	Jaguar D
1958	Olivier Gendebien/Phil Hill	Ferrari 250 TR58
1959	Carroll Shelby/Roy Salvadori	Aston Martin DBR1
1960	Olivier Gendebien/Paul Frère	Ferrari 250 TR59/60
1961	Olivier Gendebien/Phil Hill	Ferrari 250 TR61
1962	Olivier Gendebien/Phil Hill	Ferrari 250P
1963	Lodovico Scarfiotti/Lorenzo Bandini	Ferrari 250P
1964	Jean Guichel/Nino Vaccarella	Ferrari 275P
1965	Jochen Rindt/Masten Gregory	Ferrari 250LM
1966	Chris Amon/Bruce McLaren	Ford Mk2
1967	Dan Gurney/A. J. Foyt	Ford Mk4
1968	Pedro Rodriguez/Lucien Bianchi	Ford GT40
1969	Jacky Ickx/Jackie Oliver	Ford GT40
1970	Hans Herrmann/Richard Attwood	Porsche 917
1971	Helmut Marko/Gijs van Lennep	Porsche 917
1972	Henri Pescarolo/Graham Hill	Matra-Simca MS670
1973	Henri Pescarolo/Gérard Larrousse	Matra-Simca MS670B
1974	Henri Pescarolo/Gérard Larrousse	Matra-Simca MS670B
1975	Jacky Ickx/Derek Bell	Mirage-Ford MB
1976	Jacky Ickx/Gijs van Lennep	Porsche 936
1977	Jacky Ickx/Jurgen Barth/Hurley Haywood	Porsche 936
1978	Jean-Pierre Jaussaud/Didier Pironi	Renault-Alpine A442
1979	Klaus Ludwig/Bill Whttington/Don Whittington	Porsche 935
1980	Jean-Pierre Jaussaud/Jean Rondeau	Rondeau-Ford M379B
1981	Jacky Ickx/Derek Bell	Porsche 936-81
1982	Jacky Ickx/Derek Bell	Porsche 956
1983	Vern Schuppan/Hurley Haywood/Al Holbert	Porsche 956-83
1984	Klaus Ludwig/Henri Pescarolo	Porsche 956B
1985	Klaus Ludwig/Paolo Barilla/John Winter	Porsche 956B
1986	Derek Bell/Hans-Joachim Stuck/Al Holbert	Porsche 962C
1987	Derek Bell/Hans-Joachim Stuck/Al Holbert	Porsche 962C
1988	Jan Lammers/Johnny Dumfries/Andy Wallace	Jaguar XJR9LM
1989	Jochen Mass/Manuel Reuter/Stanley Dickens	Sauber-Mercedes C9-88
1990	John Nielsen/Price Cobb/Martin Brundle	TWR Jaguar XJR-12
1991	Volker Weidler/Johnny Herbert/Bertrand Gachof	Mazda 787B

Drag Racing: Milestone Performances

Top Fuel

ELAPSED TIME

9.00	Jack Chrisman	Feb 18, 1961	Pomona, CA
8.97	Jack Chrisman	May 20, 1961	Empona, VA
7.96	Bobby Vodnick	May 16, 1964	Bayview, MD
6.97	Don Johnson	May 7, 1967	Carlsbad, CA
5.97	Mike Snively	Nov 17, 1972	Ontario, CA
5.78	Don Garlits	Nov 18, 1973	Ontario, CA
5.698	Gary Beck	Oct 10, 1975	Ontario, CA
5.636	Don Garlits	Oct 10, 1975	Ontario, CA
5.573	Gary Beck	Oct 18, 1981	Irvine, CA
5.484	Gary Beck	Sep 6, 1982	Clermont, IN
5.391	Gary Beck	Oct 1, 1983	Fremont, CA
5.280	Darrell Gwynn	Sep 25, 1986	Ennis, TX
5.176	Darrell Gwynn	April 4, 1987	Ennis, TX

Top Fuel (*Cont.*)

ELAPSED TIME (*Cont.*)

5.090 .... Joe Amato	Oct 1, 1987	Ennis, TX
4.990 .... Eddie Hill	April 9, 1988	Ennis, TX
4.936 .... Eddie Hill	Oct 9, 1988	Baytown, TX
4.919 .... Gary Ormsby	Oct 7, 1989	Ennis, TX
4.881 .... Gary Ormsby	Sep 29, 1990	Topeka, KS

SPEED

180.36 .... Connie Kalitta	Sep 3, 1962	Clermont, IN
190.26 .... Don Garlits	Sep 21, 1963	East Haddam, CT
201.34 .... Don Garlits	Aug 1, 1964	Great Meadows, NJ
226.12 .... John Edmunds	May 7, 1967	Carlsbad, CA
232.55 .... Larry Hendrickson	July 11, 1970	Vancouver, WA
243.24 .... Don Garlits	March 18, 1973	Gainesville, FL
250.69 .... Don Garlits	Oct 11, 1975	Ontario, CA
260.11 .... Joe Amato	March 18, 1984	Gainesville, FL
272.56 .... Don Garlits	March 23, 1986	Gainesville, FL
282.13 .... Joe Amato	Sep 5, 1987	Clermont, IN
291.54 .... Connie Kalitta	Feb 11, 1989	Pomona, CA
294.88 .... Michael Brotherton	Oct 7, 1989	Ennis, TX
294.88 .... Gary Ormsby	Oct 8, 1989	Ennis, TX
296.05 .... Gary Ormsby	Sep 29, 1990	Topeka, KS

Funny Car

ELAPSED TIME

6.92 .... Leroy Goldstein	Sep 3, 1970	Clermont, IN
5.987 .... Don Prudhomme	Oct 12, 1975	Ontario, CA
5.868 .... Raymond Beadle	July 16, 1981	Englishtown, NJ
5.799 .... Tom Anderson	Sep 3, 1982	Clermont, IN
5.637 .... Don Prudhomme	Sep 4, 1982	Clermont, IN
5.588 .... Rick Johnson	Feb 3, 1985	Pomona, CA
5.425 .... Kenny Bernstein	Sep 26, 1986	Ennis, TX
5.397 .... Kenny Bernstein	April 5, 1987	Ennis, TX
5.255 .... Ed McCulloch	April 17, 1988	Ennis, TX
5.193 .... Don Prudhomme	March 2, 1989	Baytown, TX
5.132 .... Ed McCulloch	Oct 7, 1989	Ennis, TX

SPEED

200.44 .... Gene Snow	August, 1968	Houston, TX
250.00 .... Don Prudhomme	May 23, 1982	Erwinville, LA
260.11 .... Kenny Bernstein	March 18, 1984	Gainesville, FL
271.41 .... Kenny Bernstein	Aug 30, 1986	Clermont, IN
280.72 .... Mike Dunn	Oct 2, 1987	Ennis, TX
283.28 .... Mark Oswald	Oct 29, 1989	Pomona, CA
284.18 .... Mark Oswald	Oct 11, 1990	Ennis, TX

Pro Stock

ELAPSED TIME

7.778 .... Lee Shepherd	March 12, 1982	Gainesville, FL
7.655 .... Lee Shepherd	Oct 1, 1982	Fremont, CA
7.557 .... Bob Glidden	Feb 2, 1985	Pomona, CA
7.497 .... Bob Glidden	Sep 13, 1985	Maple Grove, PA
7.377 .... Bob Glidden	Aug 28, 1986	Clermont, IN
7.294 .... Frank Sanchez	Oct 7, 1988	Baytown, TX
7.256 .... Bob Glidden	March 11, 1989	Baytown, TX
7.184 .... Darrell Alderman	Oct 12, 1990	Ennis, TX

SPEED

181.08 .... Warren Johnson	Oct 1, 1982	Fremont, CA
190.07 .... Warren Johnson	Aug 29, 1986	Clermont, IN
191.32 .... Bob Glidden	Sep 4, 1987	Clermont, IN
192.18 .... Warren Johnson	Oct 13, 1990	Ennis, TX

Bowling

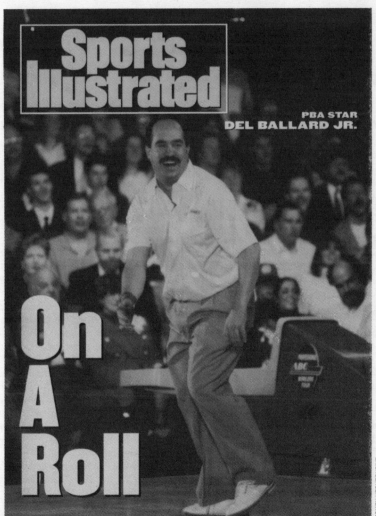

Sports Illustrated

PBA STAR
DEL BALLARD JR.

On A Roll

ERICA BERGER-NEWSDAY

Out of the Gutter

After an embarrassing start, Del Ballard Jr. enjoyed his best year ever on the PBA Tour | by STEVE WULF

DEL BALLARD JR. WENT ON A ROLL IN 1991, and it all started with a gutter ball. In the televised finals of the Professional Bowlers Association's Fair Lanes Open in Randallstown, Md., on March 2, Ballard needed two strikes and a seven in the 10th frame to beat Pete Weber. Ballard got the two strikes, but instead of safely guiding the ball down the middle for a seven, he tried to make his normal, gutter-hugging hook, and he slipped. The ball went into the channel, and the $30,000 first prize went to Weber. "I feel so bad for Del," said Weber, "it's hard to enjoy this win for the moment."

The gutter ball might have been considered one of sports' great chokes, but Ballard had the good sense—not to mention the good humor—to go along with the considerable ribbing he received. At a pro-am event the very next week, Ballard rolled his first ball into the gutter on purpose. The crowd gave him a standing ovation.

Redemption came soon enough. At the Long Island Open, in Sayville, N.Y., two weeks after the gutter ball, Ballard defeated Danny Wiseman in the semifinal and Jim Johnson Jr. in the final to collect the $20,000 winner's check. In fact, in the semifinal, Ballard faced a similar situation to the one he had against Weber. He needed a strike and an eight on his last two rolls, and after he got the strike, he threw one of his patented hooks for another strike and a 250–247 win. "I prayed I would get in a spot like that on TV again," said Ballard, a 10-year tour veteran from Richardson, Texas. "I'm thankful it came so soon, The title's the thing, but just rolling a big ball like that should erase all bad memories for me and hush the folks who had been kidding me."

Ballard went on to enjoy the best year of his career. He and Bob Benoit teamed up to win the PBA Doubles Classic in Beaumont, Texas, on June 1, and the next week he won the Kessler Open at Earl Anthony's Dublin Bowl, in Dublin, Calif. "The gutter ball has helped me in staying focused and restraining my emotions until the match is completed," said Ballard.

Joining Ballard as three-time winners in 1991 (prior to the PBA's four-event Fall Tour) were Weber, David Ozio, and John Mazza. The first jewel of the PBA's Triple Crown, the PBA Nationals in Toledo on March 30, was won by Mike Miller. Weber won the second big event of the year, the U.S. Open, on April 13 in Indianapolis, and Ozio captured the last of the big three, the Firestone Tournament of Champions in Fairlawn, Ohio, on April 27. Ozio had to overcome not only the other bowlers in that tournament but also a 40-minute delay in the television finals because of a bomb threat. ABC commentators Chris Schenkel and Nelson Burton Jr. spent part of that time discussing for viewers what the delay would do to the size of the bowlers' thumbs.

The PBA's Player of the Year in both 1989 and 1990, Amleto Monacelli of Venezuela, won the Quaker State Open and the True Value Open, but with only four events remaining as of press time, it appeared as if he might miss out on a third consecutive title. The other big news on the PBA Tour in 1991 was the conversion of two nearly impossible 7–10 splits on national television. Mazza was the first to do it, at the Bud Light Classic on Feb. 16, and fellow southpaw Jess Stayrook was the second, at the July 13 Tucson Open. In the 30 years of PBA telecasts, there had only been one previous 7–10 conversion—by Mark Roth in 1980.

On the Ladies Pro Bowlers Tour, Nikki Gianulias was the only three-time winner prior to the Fall Tour, with victories in the Okeechobee (Fla.) Classic, the Garland (Texas) Centennial Open and the Hammer Western Open (Tempe, Ariz.). The LPBT has its own Triple Crown—Triple Tiara?— and the first of the jewels, the WIBC Queens (Cedar Rapids, Iowa), was won by Dede Davidson. The second title, the BPAA U.S. Open (Fountain Valley, Calif.), went to Anne Marie Duggan, and the third of the big

three, the Sam's Town Invitational in Las Vegas, was to be contested in late November. The single best performance of the year was turned in by Leanne Barrette, who came thisclose to a perfect game in the Lady Ebonite Classic in Columbia, Tenn.; Barrette rolled 10 straight strikes in the championship match, only to have a 3-9-10 split pop up in the 10th frame. She finished with a 286.

Last, but not least, the LPBT made history in 1991 by becoming the first women's professional sports league to come up with its own trading cards. Now kids can say, "I'll give you a Vesma Grinfelds for an Aleta Sill."

Pete Weber—shown here with his Hall of Fame father, Dick, in 1985—counted the U.S. Open among his 1991 wins.

LANE STEWART

FOR THE RECORD • 1990 – 1991

The Majors

Firestone Tournament of Champions

CHAMPIONSHIP ROUND

Bowler	Total	Earnings ($)
David Ozio	476 (2 games)	50,000
Amleto Monacelli	203 (1 game)	28,000
Mike Miller	457 (2 games)	20,000
Chris Warren	466 (2 games)	15,000
Scott Devers	224 (1 game)	10,000

Playoff Results: Warren def. Devers, 248-224; Miller def. Warren, 230-218; Ozio def. Miller, 240-227; Ozio def. Monacelli, 236-203.

Held at Riviera Lanes, Fairlawn, Ohio, April 23-27, 1991

1990 Sam's Town Invitational

CHAMPIONSHIP ROUND

Bowler	Total	Earnings ($)
Wendy Macpherson	901 (4 games)	20,000
Jeanne Maiden	202 (1 game)	10,000
Debbie Bennett	228 (1 game)	7,500
Michelle Mullen	179 (1 game)	5,000
Donna Adamek	219 (1 game)	3,500

Playoff Results: Macpherson def. Adamek, 237-219; Macpherson def. Mullen, 220-179; Macpherson def. Bennett, 241-228; Macpherson def. Madden, 203-202.

Held at Sam's Town, Las Vegas, NV, Nov. 10-17, 1990

PBA Tour Results

1990 Fall Tour

Date	Event	Winner
Oct 11-14	Oronamin C Japan Cup	Chris Warren
Oct 29-Nov 3	Chevy Truck Classic	Roger Bowker
Nov 5-10	Toyota Classic	Pete Weber
Nov 10-17	Brunswick Memorial World Open	Jimmy Johnson
Nov 19-24	American Bowling Congress Fall Classic	Parker Bohn III
Nov 26-Dec 1	Budweiser Touring Players Championship	Duane Fisher
Dec 7-10	Cambridge Mixed Doubles	Tish Johnson/ Amleto Monacelli

1991 Winter Tour

Date	Event	Winner
Jan 8-12	AC-Delco Classic	David Ozio
Jan 13-19	Showboat Invitational	David Ozio
Jan 22-26	ARC Pinole Open	Brian Voss
Jan 29-Feb 2	Quaker State Open	Amleto Monacelli
Feb 5-9	Florida Open	John Mazza
Feb 11-16	Bud Light Classic	Bob Benoit
Feb 19-23	Flagship City Open	Jess Stayrook
Feb 25-Mar 2	Fair Lanes Open	Pete Weber
Mar 4-9	Johnny Petraglia Open	Pete Weber
Mar 11-16	Leisure's Long Island Open	Del Ballard Jr
Mar 18-23	Bud Light Open	Norm Duke
Mar 24-30	PBA Natl Championship	Mike Miller
Apr 1-6	True Value Open	Amleto Monacelli
Apr 7-13	BPAA US Open	Pete Weber
Apr 16-20	Tums Classic	Billy Young
Apr 23-27	Firestone Tournament of Champions	David Ozio

1991 Spring/Summer Tour

Date	Event	Winner
May 7-11	Fresno Open	John Mazza
May 14-18	Kessler Classic	Bryan Goebel
May 21-25	Celebrity Denver Open	John Mazza
May 28-	Beaumont PBA	Del Ballard Jr
June 1	Doubles Classic	Bob Benoit
June 11-15	Kessler Open	Del Ballard Jr
June 18-22	Seattle Open	Danny Wiseman
June 25-29	Oregon Open	Tony Westlake
July 2-6	El Paso Open	Ray Edwards
July 9-13	Tucson Open	Norm Duke
July 16-20	Wichita Open	Chris Warren
July 22-27	Columbia 300 Open	Brian Voss
July 28-Aug 3	Hotels Intl Summer Classic	Steve Jaros
Aug 4-8	La Mode Classic	Tony Westlake
Aug 11-15	PBA Senior/Touring Pro Doubles Championship	Rick Steelsmith, Teata Semiz

1990 Senior Fall Tour

Date	Event	Winner
Oct 18-25	Treasure Coast Senior Open	Jimmy Certain

1991 Senior Tour

Date	Event	Winner
Mar 10-14	AMF-HPL Senior Open	Darrel Curtis
Mar 17-21	Hammer Senior Open	Paul Busch
Mar 24-28	Cal Bowl Senior Open	Gene Stus
June 2-8	Showboat Senior Invitational	John Handegard
June 16-20	Flint Senior Open	Richard Beattie
June 22-27	Hammond Senior Open	Mickey Spiezio
July 6-11	St Clair Senior Open	Adam Toney
July 13-18	AMF Cobra Senior Classic	John Handegard

LPBT Tour Results

1990 Fall Tour

Date	Event	Winner
Sep 16-20	AMF Cobra Classic	Tish Johnson
Sep 23-27	Columbia 300 Delaware Open	Tish Johnson
Sep 30-Oct 4	Hammer Eastern Open	Tish Johnson
Oct 7-11	Brunswick Open	Leanne Barrette
Oct 14-18	Hammer Midwest Open	Lorrie Nichols
Oct 21-25	Lady Ebonite Classic	Nikki Gianulias
Oct 28-Nov 1	Hammer Western Open	Leanne Barrette
Nov 4-8	Los Angeles Open	Nikki Gianulias
Nov 10-17	Sam's Town Invitational	Wendy Macpherson
Dec 7-10	Cambridge Mixed Doubles	Tish Johnson/ Amleto Monacelli

1991 Winter Tour

Date	Event	Winner
Feb 2-6	Okeechobee Classic	Nikki Gianulias
Feb 10-14	Central Florida Classic	Tish Johnson
Feb 17-21	Athens Open	Sandra Jo Shiery
Feb 24-28	New Orleans Classic	Aleta Sill
Mar 2-6	Garland Centennial Open	Nikki Gianulias

1991 Spring Tour

Date	Event	Winner
Apr 7-11	Robby's Open	Donna Adamek
Apr 14-18	Lady Ebonite Classic	Leanne Barrette
Apr 21-25	Lady Fair Lanes Open	Dana Miller-Mackie
Apr 28-May 2	Ashland Blue Ribbon Classic	Rene Fleming
May 5-9	Hoffman/Schaumburg Open	Karen Ellingsworth
May 12-16	WIBC Queens	Dede Davidson
May 19-23	Hammer Western Open	Nikki Gianulias
May 30	BPAA US Open	Anne Marie Duggan

1991 Summer Tour

Date	Event	Winner
Aug 17	Gold Rush Mixed Doubles Shootout	Sherrie Dodge, Adam Apo
Aug 18-22	LPBT National Doubles	Carolyn Dorin, Lisa Wagner

1990 Tour Leaders

PBA

MONEY LEADERS

Name	Titles	Tournaments	Earnings ($)
Amleto Monacelli	3	29	204,775
Chris Warren	3	34	197,475
Parker Bohn III	3	35	172,575
Ron Palombi Jr	2	33	147,820
Brian Voss	1	30	143,370

Note: Includes ABC Masters.

AVERAGE

Name	Games	Pinfall	Average
Amleto Monacelli	1,024	223,394	218.158
Walter Ray Williams Jr	970	210,331	216.836
Norm Duke	797	172,344	216.241
Parker Bohn III	1,009	217,800	215.857
Michael Edwards	1,016	219,071	215.621

Seniors

MONEY LEADERS

Name	Titles	Tournaments	Earnings ($)
Earl Anthony	3	8	41,130
John Hricsina	1	8	30,750
Jimmy Certain	1	8	30,070
Dave Soutar	1	7	28,360
John Handegard	2	8	24,700

AVERAGE

Name	Games	Pinfall	Average
Jimmy Certain	272	58,900	216.544
Richard Beattie	110	23,802	216.382
Dave Soutar	248	53,467	215.593
John Hricsina	280	60,300	215.357
John Handegard	285	61,092	214.358

LPBT

MONEY LEADERS

Name	Titles	Tournaments	Earnings ($)
Tish Johnson	4	21	94,420
Leanne Barrette	3	21	91,390
Lisa Wagner	2	21	58,055
Dana Miller-Mackie	2	18	57,805
Nikki Gianulias	2	21	57,087.50

AVERAGE

Name	Games	Pinfall	Average
Leanne Barrette	822	173,878	211.53
Nikki Gianulias	771	161,486	209.45
Robin Romeo	862	180,364	209.24
Lisa Wagner	818	170,848	208.86
Wendy Macpherson	737	153,260	207.95

FOR THE RECORD • Year by Year

Men's Majors

BPAA United States Open

1942 ....John Crimmins	1959 ....Billy Welu	1976 ....Paul Moser
1943 ....Connie Schwoegler	1960 ....Harry Smith	1977 ....Johnny Petraglia
1944 ....Ned Day	1961 ....Bill Tucker	1978 ....Nelson Burton Jr
1945 ....Buddy Bomar	1962 ....Dick Weber	1979 ....Joe Berardi
1946 ....Joe Wilman	1963 ....Dick Weber	1980 ....Steve Martin
1947 ....Andy Varipapa	1964 ....Bob Strampe	1981 ....Marshall Holman
1948 ....Andy Varipapa	1965 ....Dick Weber	1982 ....Dave Husted
1949 ....Connie Schwoegler	1966 ....Dick Weber	1983 ....Gary Dickinson
1950 ....Junie McMahon	1967 ....Les Schissler	1984 ....Mark Roth
1951 ....Dick Hoover	1968 ....Jim Stefanich	1985 ....Marshall Holman
1952 ....Junie McMahon	1969 ....Billy Hardwick	1986 ....Steve Cook
1953 ....Don Carter	1970 ....Bobby Cooper	1987 ....Del Ballard Jr
1954 ....Don Carter	1971 ....Mike Limongello	1988 ....Pete Weber
1955 ....Steve Nagy	1972 ....Don Johnson	1989 ....Mike Aulby
1956 ....Bill Lillard	1973 ....Mike McGrath	1990 ....Ron Palombi Jr
1957 ....Don Carter	1974 ....Larry Laub	1991 ....Pete Weber
1958 ....Don Carter	1975 ....Steve Neff	

PBA National Championship

1960 ....Don Carter	1971 ....Mike Limongello	1982 ....Earl Anthony
1961 ....Dave Soutar	1972 ....Johnny Guenther	1983 ....Earl Anthony
1962 ....Carmen Salvino	1973 ....Earl Anthony	1984 ....Bob Chamberlain
1963 ....Billy Hardwick	1974 ....Earl Anthony	1985 ....Mike Aulby
1964 ....Bob Strampe	1975 ....Earl Anthony	1986 ....Tom Crites
1965 ....Dave Davis	1976 ....Paul Colwell	1987 ....Randy Pedersen
1966 ....Wayne Zahn	1977 ....Tommy Hudson	1988 ....Brian Voss
1967 ....Dave Davis	1978 ....Warren Nelson	1989 ....Pete Weber
1968 ....Wayne Zahn	1979 ....Mike Aulby	1990 ....Jim Pencak
1969 ....Mike McGrath	1980 ....Johnny Petraglia	1991 ....Mike Miller
1970 ....Mike McGrath	1981 ....Earl Anthony	

Firestone Tournament of Champions

1965 ....Billy Hardwick	1974 ....Earl Anthony	1983 ....Joe Berardi
1966 ....Wayne Zahn	1975 ....Dave Davis	1984 ....Mike Durbin
1967 ....Jim Stefanich	1976 ....Marshall Holman	1985 ....Mark Williams
1968 ....Dave Davis	1977 ....Mike Berlin	1986 ....Marshall Holman
1969 ....Jim Godman	1978 ....Earl Anthony	1987 ....Pete Weber
1970 ....Don Johnson	1979 ....George Pappas	1988 ....Mark Williams
1971 ....Johnny Petraglia	1980 ....Wayne Webb	1989 ....Del Ballard Jr
1972 ....Mike Durbin	1981 ....Steve Cook	1990 ....Dave Ferraro
1973 ....Jim Godman	1982 ....Mike Durbin	1991 ....David Ozio

ABC Masters Tournament

1951 ....Lee Jouglard	1965 ....Billy Welu	1979 ....Doug Myers
1952 ....Willard Taylor	1966 ....Bob Strampe	1980 ....Neil Burton
1953 ....Rudy Habetler	1967 ....Lou Scalia	1981 ....Randy Lightfoot
1954 ....Eugene Elkins	1968 ....Pete Tountas	1982 ....Joe Berardi
1955 ....Buzz Fazio	1969 ....Jim Chestney	1983 ....Mike Lastowski
1956 ....Dick Hoover	1970 ....Don Glover	1984 ....Earl Anthony
1957 ....Dick Hoover	1971 ....Jim Godman	1985 ....Steve Wunderlich
1958 ....Tom Hennessy	1972 ....Bill Beach	1986 ....Mark Fahy
1959 ....Ray Bluth	1973 ....Dave Soutar	1987 ....Rick Steelsmith
1960 ....Billy Golembiewski	1974 ....Paul Colwell	1988 ....Del Ballard Jr
1961 ....Don Carter	1975 ....Eddie Ressler	1989 ....Mike Aulby
1962 ....Billy Golembiewski	1976 ....Nelson Burton Jr	1990 ....Chris Warren
1963 ....Harry Smith	1977 ....Earl Anthony	1991 ....Doug Kert
1964 ....Billy Welu	1978 ....Frank Ellenburg	

Women's Majors

BPAA United States Open

1949	Marion Ladewig
1950	Marion Ladewig
1951	Marion Ladewig
1952	Marion Ladewig
1953	Not held
1954	Marion Ladewig
1955	Sylvia Martin
1956	Marion Ladewig
1957	Not held
1958	Merle Matthews
1959	Marion Ladewig
1960	Sylvia Martin
1961	Phyllis Notaro
1962	Shirley Garms
1963	Marion Ladewig

1964	LaVerne Carter
1965	Ann Slattery
1966	Joy Abel
1967	Gloria Simon
1968	Dotty Fothergill
1969	Dotty Fothergill
1970	Mary Baker
1971	Paula Carter
1972	Lorrie Koch (Nichols)
1973	Millie Martorella
1974	Pat Costello
1975	Paula Carter
1976	Patty Costello
1977	Betty Morris

1978	Donna Adamek
1979	Diana Silva
1980	Pat Costello
1981	Donna Adamek
1982	Shinobu Saitoh
1983	Dana Miller
1984	Karen Ellingsworth
1985	Pat Mercatani
1986	Wendy Macpherson
1987	Carol Norman
1988	Lisa Wagner
1989	Robin Romeo
1990	Dana Miller-Mackie
1991	Anne Marie Dugan

WIBC Queens

1961	Janet Harman
1962	Dorothy Wilkinson
1963	Irene Monterosso
1964	D. D. Jacobson
1965	Betty Kuczynski
1966	Judy Lee
1967	Millie Martorella
1968	Phyllis Massey
1969	Ann Feigel
1970	Millie Martorella
1971	Millie Martorella

1972	Dotty Fothergill
1973	Dotty Fothergill
1974	Judy Soutar
1975	Cindy Powell
1976	Pam Buckner
1977	Dana Stewart
1978	Loa Boxberger
1979	Donna Adamek
1980	Donna Adamek
1981	Katsuko Sugimoto
1982	Katsuko Sugimoto

1983	Aleta Sill
1984	Kazue Inahashi
1985	Aleta Sill
1986	Cora Fiebig
1987	Cathy Alameida
1988	Wendy Macpherson
1989	Carol Gianotti
1990	Patty Ann
1991	Dede Davidson

Sam's Town Invitational

1981	Cindy Coburn
1984	Aleta Sill
1985	Patty Costello

1986	Aleta Sill
1987	Debbie Bennett
1988	Donna Adamek

1989	Tish Johnson
1990	Wendy Macpherson

PWBA Championships

1960	Marion Ladewig
1961	Shirley Garms
1962	Stephanie Balogh
1963	Janet Harman
1964	Betty Kuczynski
1965	Helen Duval
1966	Joy Abel

1967	Betty Mivalez
1968	Dotty Fothergill
1969	Dotty Fothergill
1970	Bobbe North
1971	Patty Costello
1972	Patty Costello
1973	Betty Morris

1974	Pat Costello
1975	Pam Buckner
1976	Patty Costello
1977	Vesma Grinfelds
1978	Toni Gillard
1979	Cindy Coburn
1980	Donna Adamek

Men's Awards

BWAA Bowler of the Year

1942	Johnny Crimmins
1943	Ned Day
1944	Ned Day
1945	Buddy Bomar
1946	Joe Wilman
1947	Buddy Bomar
1948	Andy Varipapa
1949	Connie Schwoegler
1950	Junie McMahon
1951	Lee Jouglard
1952	Steve Nagy
1953	Don Carter
1954	Don Carter

1955	Steve Nagy
1956	Bill Lillard
1957	Don Carter
1958	Don Carter
1959	Ed Lubanski
1960	Don Carter
1961	Dick Weber
1962	Don Carter
1963	Dick Weber, Billy Hardwick (PBA)*
1964	Billy Hardwick, Bob Strampe (PBA)*
1965	Dick Weber

1966	Wayne Zahn
1967	Dave Davis
1968	Jim Stefanich
1969	Billy Hardwick
1970	Nelson Burton Jr
1971	Don Johnson
1972	Don Johnson
1973	Don McCune
1974	Earl Anthony
1975	Earl Anthony
1976	Earl Anthony
1977	Mark Roth
1978	Mark Roth

BWAA Bowler of the Year (*Cont.*)

1979 .... Mark Roth	1984 .... Mark Roth	1988 .... Brian Voss
1980 .... Wayne Webb	1985 .... Mike Aulby	1989 .... Mike Aulby, Amleto
1981 .... Earl Anthony	1986 .... Walter Ray	Monacelli (PBA)*
1982 .... Earl Anthony	Williams Jr	1990 .... Amleto Monacelli
1983 .... Earl Anthony	1987 .... Marshall Holman	

*The PBA began selecting a player of the year in 1963. Its selection has been the same as the BWAA's in all but three years.

Women's Awards

BWAA Bowler of the Year

1948 .... Val Mikiel	1964 .... LaVerne Carter	1979 .... Donna Adamek
1949 .... Val Mikiel	1965 .... Betty Kuczynski	1980 .... Donna Adamek
1950 .... Marion Ladewig	1966 .... Joy Abel	1981 .... Donna Adamek
1951 .... Marion Ladewig	1967 .... Millie Martorella	1982 .... Nikki Gianulias
1952 .... Marion Ladewig	1968 .... Dotty Fothergill	1983 .... Lisa Wagner
1953 .... Marion Ladewig	1969 .... Dotty Fothergill	1984 .... Aleta Sill
1954 .... Marion Ladewig	1970 .... Mary Baker	1985 .... Aleta Sill, Patty
1955 .... Marion Ladewig	1971 .... Paula Sperber Carter	Costello (LPBT)*
1956 .... Sylvia Martin	1972 .... Patty Costello	1986 .... Lisa Wagner, Jeanne
1957 .... Anita Cantaline	1973 .... Judy Soutar	Madden (LPBT)*
1958 .... Marion Ladewig	1974 .... Betty Morris	1987 .... Betty Morris
1959 .... Marion Ladewig	1975 .... Judy Soutar	1988 .... Lisa Wagner
1960 .... Sylvia Martin	1976 .... Patty Costello	1989 .... Robin Romeo
1961 .... Shirley Garms	1977 .... Betty Morris	1990 .... Tish Johnson, Leanne
1962 .... Shirley Garms	1978 .... Donna Adamek	Barrette (LPBT)*
1963 .... Marion Ladewig		

*The LPBT began selecting a player of the year in 1983. Its selection has been the same as the BWAA's in all but three years.

Career Leaders

Earnings

MEN		WOMEN	
Marshall Holman	$1,543,571	Lisa Wagner	$455,364
Mark Roth	$1,398,551	Aleta Sill	$427,201
Earl Anthony	$1,354,581	Donna Adamek	$397,694
Pete Weber	$1,306,137	Lorrie Nichols	$383,416
Mike Aulby	$1,191,045	Nikki Gianulias	$380,177

Note: Does not include PBA Senior Tour earnings.

Titles

MEN		WOMEN	
Earl Anthony	41	Lisa Wagner	26
Mark Roth	33	Patty Costello	25
Don Johnson	26	Donna Adamek	18
Dick Weber	26	Betty Morris	17
Marshall Holman	21	Aleta Sill	17

Soccer

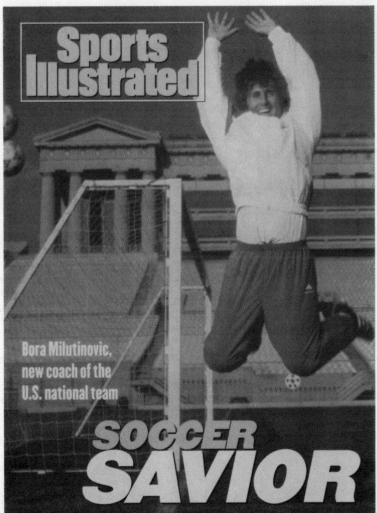

Sports Illustrated

Bora Milutinovic, new coach of the U.S. national team

SOCCER SAVIOR

GWENDOLEN CATES

Never a Dull Moment

In a year that was supposed to be quiet, soccer found its way into the headlines | by DOUGLAS S. LOONEY

I T SEEMED LIKELY THAT 1991 WOULD BE A QUIET year in soccer. After all, it followed the worldwide hoopla over the 1990 World Cup competition in Italy (which was won by West Germany) and the next World Cup wouldn't be held until 1994. Wrong. For soccer, which stirs the most unbridled passions of any sport—everywhere, of course, except in the U.S.—seems unable to slip away from the public focus, lie down in the shade and rest awhile, then rise to excite and enthrall anew. Soccer simply knows no life off the front burner.

Just 19 days into the year, the world's best and flashiest player, Argentina's Diego Maradona, abruptly announced he would retire by year's end. He was largely responsible for Argentina's 1986 World Cup win and was, arguably, the world's No. 1 sports hero. Maradona said that everybody everywhere was against him and he mused darkly, "I can't continue this way." But as happens depressingly often, this wasn't Maradona talking, it was drugs. In March, he tested positive for cocaine and was suspended for 15 months by several soccer governing bodies. The next month, he was caught in a police raid in Buenos Aires and arrested for drug possession. It was another downward spiral for another brilliant athlete. Estimates are that he stands to lose $20 million in salary and endorsements over the next two years.

Things were not placid in the U.S. either. Under coach Bob Gansler, the U.S. in 1990 qualified for the World Cup tournament (only 24 teams take part) for the first time in 40 years. As expected, the U.S. failed to win any of its three first-round games and was thus eliminated. So, naturally, talk immediately turned to firing the coach. In February, after a humiliating 1–0 loss to Bermuda—the sixth straight game in which the U.S. failed to score—Gansler resigned under pressure. His record in two years was 14–17–5. Initially, the United States Soccer Federation tried to entice former West German coach Franz Beckenbauer to sign on, but he instead became a technical adviser to a French team. So the USSF turned to Bora Milutinovic, 47, a Yugoslav who had coached Mexico to the quarterfinals in the '86 World Cup and Costa Rica in '90 to the second round. His deal pays him about $200,000 a year through 1994. In appraising the team, he said the best things about the Americans "are discipline and tactics." Notice he didn't mention talent.

The first game for the U.S. under Milutinovic was auspicious. Not only did the U.S. beat Uruguay 1–0 on May 5 in Denver, but there were 35,772 fans in Mile High Stadium. Two weeks later, though, the U.S. lost at Stanford to Argentina 1–0 in a game that wasn't that close. Is USSF president Alan Rothenberg really talking about winning the World Cup in 1994?

Meanwhile, 27 cities, from New Haven, Conn., to Corvallis, Ore., have bid for parts of the '94 World Cup (opening ceremonies and five rounds) that the U.S. will host. The USSF said it expected to select 8 to 12 of them by year's end. While the event figures to spur American interest in soccer, it was unsettling to the USSF that New York sub-

Maradona, here playing in the '86 World Cup, found troubles off the field in '91.

mitted an unenthusiastic bid and that the U.S. TV networks seemed inclined to keep the hoods on their cameras.

Women's soccer is having its first-ever world championship late in 1991, in China, and the U.S. national coach, Anson Dorrance, says of his team's chances, "We've got a shot. We're good." In part, Dorrance says that's because not only does he have outstanding players, including forwards Michelle Akers-Stahl, April Heinrichs, and Carin Jennings, but also because "there are no traditions in women's world soccer, so we haven't fallen behind yet."

Sadly, soccer also continued to get world attention for the wrong reasons. Just 13 days into the year in Oarkney, South Africa, 80 miles southwest of Johannesburg, two black teams from Soweto, the Orlando Pirates and the Kaizer Chiefs, were playing. The Chiefs scored a disputed goal which was upheld by the referee. A riot ensued in which 40 spectators were killed and another 50 injured. That the outbreak was the focus of attention for only a few days rather than weeks and months demonstrates how inured the world has become to this kind of mindless and senseless and hooliganistic behavior at soccer matches. It is unexcusable. Unfortunately, it will probably happen again.

FOR THE RECORD • 1990 – 1991

International Competition

North American Gold Cup

The first national level competition between the nations of CONCACAF (Confederation of North, Central America and Carribean Football) since 1986.

Semifinals (July 5): Honduras 2, Costa Rica 0
US 2, Mexico 0
Bronze Medal Game (July 7): Mexico 2, Costa Rica 0
Final (July 7, 1991 at Los Angeles Coliseum, Los Angeles, CA, Att: 39,873): **United States 0, Honduras 0** (4-3 in penalty kicks).

Pan Am Games

Competition between under-23 teams representing the nations of North and South America.

Final (August 13, 1991 at Havana, Cuba): **United States 2, Mexico 1 (extra time).** Ref: N. Seifert (Att: 6,000).
Goals: Mexico, Mariscal 16; US, Reyna 33; US, Moore 95.
US: Friedel, Imler, Rast, Kapper, Harty, Burns, Allnutt, Onalfo (Lagos 73), Reyna (Moore 46), Snow, Washington.
Mexico: Bernal, Cadena, Mariscal (R. Romero 97), C. Romero, Hernandez, Rangel, L. Castenada, Rameries, J. Cansteneda, Noriega, Mascereno (D. Casteneda 76).

Under-17 World Championships

The United States advanced into the quarterfinals of the Under-17 World Championships in Italy with consecutive victories over Italy, Argentina and China. In the quarters, the US was eliminated by Qatar, 5-4 on penalty kicks.

Semifinals:
August 28, 1991 at Viareggio, Italy.
Qatar 0, Ghana 0 (Ghana wins 4-2 on penalty kicks).
August 28, 1991 at Massa, Italy.
Spain 1, Argentina 0
Final (August 30, 1991 at Florence, Italy):
Ghana 1, Spain 0

Under-20 World Championships

Semifinals:
June 26, 1991 at Lisbon, Portugal:
Portugal 1, Australia 0
June 26, 1991 at Guimaraes, Portugal:
Brazil 3, USSR 0
Final (June 30, 1991 at Lisbon, Portugal):
Portugal 0, Brazil 0 (Portugal wins 3-2 on penalty kicks).

South American Championship (Copa America)

July 6-21, Chile (round robin format)

FINAL STANDINGS

Country	W	L	T	Pts
Argentina	2	0	1	5
Brazil	2	1	0	4
Chile	0	1	2	2
Colombia	0	2	1	1

U.S. Men's National Team
Results in 1991 Full International Matches

Feb 1 at Miami: US 0, Switzerland 1
Feb 21 at Hamilton, Bermuda: US 1, Bermuda 0
Mar 12 at Los Angeles: US 2, Mexico "B" 2
Mar 16 at Los Angeles: US 2, Canada 0
Apr 5 at Pusan, South Korea: US 2, South Korea 1
Apr 7 at Pohang, South Korea: US 2, South Korea 0
May 5 at Denver: US 1, Uruguay 0
May 19 at Palo Alto: US 0, Argentina 1
June 1 at Boston: US 1, Ireland 1
June 29 at Pasadena: US 2, Trinidad 1
July 1 at Pasadena: US 3, Guatemala 0
July 3 at Los Angeles: US 3, Costa Rica 2
July 5 at Los Angeles: US 2, Mexico 0
July 7 at Los Angeles: US 0, Honduras 0 (US wins 4-3 on penalty kicks)
Aug 17 at Moscow: US 1, USSR 2
Sep 4 at Istanbul, Turkey: US 1, Turkey 1
Sep 14 at High Point, N.C.: US 1, Jamaica 0

U.S. Women's National Team

Qualifying results for the first FIFA world championship for women's football, to be held Nov. 16-30, 1991, in China.

Date	Opponent	Site	Result	US Goals
4-18-91	Mexico	Port-au-Prince, Haiti	12-0 W	Hamm, Akers-Stahl (2), Heinrichs (2), Foudy, Chastain (5), Jennings
4-20-91	Martinique	Port-au-Prince, Haiti	12-0 W	Hamm (2), Heinrichs (3), Foudy, Akers-Stahl (2), Gebauer, Biefeld (2), Chastain
4-22-91	Trin. & Tobago	Port-au-Prince, Haiti	10-0 W	Hamm (2), Jennings (2), Gebauer (2), Akers-Stahl (2), Chastain, Bates
4-25-91	Haiti	Port-au-Prince, Haiti	10-0 W	Lilly, Akers-Stahl (2), Jennings (2), Bates (2), Heinrichs (2), Biefeld
4-28-91	Canada	Port-au-Prince, Haiti	5-0 W	Akers-Stahl (3), Lilly, Heinrichs

Team Members: Michelle Akers-Stahl, Amy Allman, Tracey Bates, Debbie Belkin, Joy Biefeld, Brandi Chastain, Amanda Cromwell, Julie Foudy, Wendy Gebauer, Mia Hamm, April Heinrichs, Lori Henry, Shannon Higgins, Carin Jennings, Kristine Lilly, Kim Maslin, Megan McCarthy, Carla Werden.

Club Competition

1990 Toyota Cup Final
(Competition between winners of European Champion Clubs' Cup and Libertadores Cup)

Dec 9, 1990 in Tokyo: A.C. Milan vs. Olimpia 3-0
Ref: Wright (Brazil) Att: 62,228
A.C. Milan—Pazzagli, Tassotti, Baresi, Costacurta, Maldini (Galli 22), Carbone, Donadoni (Guerreri 82), Rijkaard, Van Basten, Gullit, Stropa.
Olimpia—Almeida, Fernandez, Caceres, Guasch, Ramirez (Chamac 48), Suarez, Hoyn (Cubilla 68), Balbuena, Monzon

European Champion Clubs' Cup

League champions of the countries belonging to UEFA (Union of European Football Associations).

Semifinals (2-game/total goals series):
Olympique Marseille 3, Moscow Spartak 1
Olympique Marseille 2, Moscow Spartak 1 (Marseille wins 5-2).
Red Star 2, Bayern Munich 1
Red Star 2, Bayern Munich 2 (Red Star wins 4-3).
Final (1 game):
Red Star 0, Olympique Marseille 0 (Red Star wins on penalty kicks, 5-4).

European Cup Winners' Cup

Cup winners of countries belonging to UEFA.

Semifinals (2-game/total goals series):
Barcelona 3, Juventus 1.
Juventus 1, Barcelona 0 (Barcelona wins 3-2).
Manchester United 3, Legia Warsaw 1.
Manchester United 1, Legia Warsaw 1 (Manchester United wins 4-2).
Final (1 game):
Manchester United 2, Barcelona 1.

UEFA Cup

Competition between teams other than league champions and cup winners from UEFA.

Semifinals (2-game/total goals series):
Inter Milan 0, Sporting 0.
Inter Milan 2, Sporting 0 (Inter Milan wins 2-0).
Roma 0, Brondby 0.
Roma 2, Brondby 1 (Roma wins 2-1).
Final (2-game/total goals series):
Inter Milan 2, A.S. Roma 0.
A.S. Roma 1, Inter Milan 0 (Inter Milan wins 2-1).

Libertadores Cup

Competition between champion clubs and runners up of 10 South American National Associations.

Semifinals (2-game/total goals series):
Boca Juniors 1, Colo Colo 0.
Colo Colo 3, Boca Juniors 1 (Colo Colo wins 3-2).
Atletico Nacional 0, Olimpia 0.
Olimpia 1, Atletico Nacional 0 (Olimpia wins 1-0).

Finals (two-game/total goals series):
Olimpia 0, Colo Colo 0.
Colo Colo 3, Olimpia 0 (Colo Colo wins 3-0).

National Club Champions—Europe

Country	League Champion	League Scoring Leader, Club	Cup Winner
Austria	Austria Vienna	Danek, Tirol	Stockerau
Belgium	Anderlecht	Vandenbergh, La Gantoise	FC Malines
Czechoslovakia	AC Sparta	Kukleta, AC Sparta	Banikostrava
Denmark*	Brondby	Christensen, Brondby	
England	Arsenal	Smith, Arsenal	Tottenham Hotspur
France	Olympique Marseille	Papin, Marseille	A.S. Monaco
Finland*	Kuusysi Lahti	Czakon, HJK Helsinki	FC Ilves Tampere
Greece	Panathinaikos	Saravakos, Panathinaikos	Panathinaikos
Holland	P.S.V. Eindhoven	Romario, PSV; Bergkamp, Ajax	Feyenoord
Hungary	Budapest Honved	Gregor, Budapest Honved	Ferencvaros
Iceland*	Fram	Magnusson, Hafnafjordur	Valur
Ireland	Dundalk	Hanrahan, Dundalk	Galway United
Italy	Sampdoria	Vialli, Sampdoria	AC Roma
Malta	Hamrun	Zarb, Valletta	Sliema
Norway*	Rosenborg	Dahlum, Start	Czakon
Poland	Zableble	Dziubinski, Wisla	GKS Katowice
Portugal	Benfica	Rui Aguas, Benfoca	Porto
Romania	Uni Craiova	Hanganu, Corvinul	Uni Craiova
Scotland	Rangers	Gilhaus, Aberdeen	Motherwell
Spain	FC de Barcelona	Butragueno, Real Madrid	Atletico de Madrid
Sweden*	I.F.K. Gothenburg	Eskelinen, I.F.K. Gothenburg	Oester Vaxjo
Switzerland	Grasshopper	Zuffi, Sion Young Boys	Sion Young Boys
Turkey	Besiktas	Colak, Galatasaray	Galatasaray
USSR*	Dynamo Kiev	Protasov, Dynamo Kiev	Dynamo Kiev
W. Germany	Kaiserslautern	Wohlfarth, Bayern Munich	Werder Bremen
Yugoslavia	Red Star Belgrade	Pancev, Red Star	Hajduk

*1990 Champion. 1991 Champion decided in late fall.

National Club Champions—South America

Country	Champion	Player of the Year, Club
Argentina	Newell's Old Boys	Da Silva, River Plate
Bolivia	Oriente	Saldias, O. Petrolero
Brazil	Corinthians	Neto, Corinthians
Chile	Colo Colo	Pizarro, Colo Colo
Colombia	America Cali	Higuita, America Cali
Ecuador	LDU Quito	Capurro, Emelec
Paraguay	Cerro Porteno	Monzon, Olimpia
Peru	Universitario	Yanes, Universitario
Uruguay*	Bella Vista	Revelez, Bella Vista
Venezuela	Maritimo	Miranda, Caracas

*1990 Champion. 1991 Champion decided in late fall.

Major Soccer League

Final Standings

EASTERN DIVISION

Team	W	L	Pct	GB	GF	GA
Cleveland	29	23	.558	—	322	280
Kansas City	26	26	.500	3.0	263	283
Baltimore	21	31	.404	8.0	298	315
Wichita	21	31	.404	8.0	257	308

WESTERN DIVISION

Team	W	L	Pct	GB	GF	GA
San Diego	34	18	.654	—	302	250
St Louis	32	20	.615	2.0	320	288
Tacoma	25	27	.481	9.0	254	259
Dallas	20	32	.385	14.0	257	294

Playoff Results

WESTERN DIVISION SEMIFINALS

Date	Results	Attendance
Apr 9	Tacoma 2 at St Louis 9	5,832
Apr 11	St Louis 3 at Tacoma 4 (OT)	2,760
Apr 13	Tacoma 2 at St Louis 9	7,084
	(St Louis wins series, 2-1.)	

EASTERN DIVISION SEMIFINALS

Date	Results	Attendance
Apr 12	Wichita 0 at Kansas City 6	6,144
Apr 14	Kansas City 9 at Wichita 8	4,737
	(Kansas City wins series, 2-0.)	

WESTERN DIVISION FINALS

Date	Results	Attendance
Apr 18	St Louis 6 at San Diego 9	5,157
Apr 20	St Louis 4 at San Diego 5 (OT)	8,534
Apr 21	San Diego 4 at St Louis 5	5,751
Apr 25	San Diego 11 at St Louis 4	4,633
Apr 27	San Diego 7 at St Louis 4	6,032
	(San Diego wins series, 4-1.)	

EASTERN DIVISION FINALS

Date	Results	Attendance
Apr 18	Kansas City 2 at Cleveland 7	5,357
Apr 20	Kansas City 5 at Cleveland 7	10,021
Apr 24	Cleveland 6 at Kansas City 7(OT)	4,639
Apr 26	Cleveland 5 at Kansas City 4	9,451
Apr 28	Cleveland 4 at Kansas City 5(OT)	3,889
May 1	Kansas City 8 at Cleveland 6	7,239
May 4	Kansas City 6 at Cleveland 7	12,718
	(Cleveland wins series, 4-3.)	

CHAMPIONSHIP SERIES

Date	Results	Attendance
May 10	Cleveland 4 at San Diego 8	7,785
May 12	Cleveland 4 at San Diego 3	6,996
May 17	San Diego 6 at Cleveland 5	14,571
May 19	San Diego 5 at Cleveland 7	10,831
May 21	San Diego 6 at Cleveland 1	12,102
May 23	Cleveland 6 at San Diego 8	12,073
	(San Diego wins series, 4-2, and seventh Major Soccer League Championship.)	

Only the Men Can't Play This Game

While U.S. men struggle in international soccer, at other levels the United States had a good deal of success in 1991. The Under-23 team won the gold medal at the Pan Am Games. The Under-17 team defeated Italy, Argentina and China at the World Championships before bowing out to Quatar in the quarterfinals. And the women's national team has qualified to compete in the first-ever women's world championships in China from Nov. 16–30.

Statistical Leaders

SCORING

Rank	Player	Team	Games	Goals	Assists	Points
1	Tatu	Dall	51	78	66	144
2	Zoran Karic	Clev	47	73	48	121
	Preki	StL	52	68	53	121
4	Jan Goossens	KC	41	53	58	111
5	Hector Marinaro	Clev	45	63	44	107

GOALS

Player	Team	Games	Goals
1	Tatu	Dall	51	78
2	Zoran Karic	Clev	47	73
3	Preki	StL	52	68
4	Thompson Usiyan	StL	51	64
5	Hector Marinaro	Clev	45	63

ASSISTS

Player	Team	Games	Assists
1	Tatu	Dall	51	66
2	Jan Goossens	KC	41	58
3	Brian Quinn	SD	45	55
4	Preki	StL	52	53
5	Zoran Karic	Clev	47	48

GOALKEEPING LEADERS (Minimum 1560 minutes)

Player	Team	GP	Min	Shts	Svs	GA	GAA	W	L
1	Victor Nogueira	SD	47	2828:00	1175	569	206	4.37	31	16
2	Cris Vaccaro	Tac	16	2635:13	1178	470	208	4.65	22	22
3	Zoltan Toth	StL	36	2099:20	1126	519	176	5.03	25	10
4	P. J. Johns	Clev	38	2127:54	1128	531	180	5.08	25	10
5	Kris Peat	Wich	37	2070:49	913	435	186	5.39	14	21

American Professional Soccer League

AMERICAN CONFERENCE FINAL STANDINGS

	W	L	GF	GA	Pts	Home	Road
Ft. Lauderdale Strikers	15	6	43	23	117	10-1	5-5
Albany Capitals	10	11	27	32	92	8-3	2-8
Tampa Bay Rowdies	8	13	26	27	69	6-5	2-8
Penn-Jersey Spirit	6	15	27	52	61	4-7	2-8
Miami Freedom	6	15	20	53	52	5-6	1-9

WESTERN CONFERENCE FINAL STANDINGS

	W	L	GF	GA	Pts	Home	Road
Maryland Bays	19	2	55	23	158	11-0	8-2
S.F. Bay Blackhawks	17	4	37	17	126	10-1	7-3
Colorado Foxes	13	8	37	28	111	8-3	5-5

Point System: 6 pts. for each victory in regulation or overtime; 4 pts. for a penalty-kick tiebreaker win, 2 pts. for a penalty-kick tiebreaker loss; 1 pt. for each goal scored in regulation up to maximum of 3 (regardless of whether team wins or loses).

Playoff Results: Four teams—Maryland, Albany, Ft. Lauderdale, and San Francisco Bay—qualified for the playoffs. San Francisco Bay defeated Albany in the finals for the APSL championship.

SCORING LEADERS

Jean Harbor, Maryland	45*
Kevin Sloan, Maryland	32
Ezekiel "Zico" Doe, Colorado	26
Derek Sanderson, Ft. Lauderdale	23
Brian Haynes, Maryland	23

GOALS LEADERS

Jean Harbor, Maryland	17†
Kevin Sloan, Maryland	14
Ezekiel "Zico" Doe, Colorado	12
Derek Sanderson, Ft. Lauderdale	10
Brian Haynes, Maryland	9

ASSISTS LEADERS

Jean Harbor, Maryland	11
Andrew McKay, Ft. Lauderdale	8
Bruce Murray, Maryland	7
David Byrne, Tampa Bay	7
Chad Ashton, Colorado	7

GOALS-AGAINST-AVERAGE LEADERS

Mark Dougherty, San Francisco Bay	0.81
Scoop Stanisic, Albany	1.02
Arnie Mausser, Ft. Lauderdale	1.02
Steve Powers, Maryland	1.04
Tony Meola, Ft. Lauderdale	1.06

*APSL Record. †Ties APSL Record.

The World Cup

Results

Year	Champion	Score	Runner-Up	Winning Coach
1930	Uruguay	4-2	Argentina	Alberto Supicci
1934	Italy	2-1	Czechoslovakia	Vittorio Pozzo
1938	Italy	4-2	Hungary	Vittorio Pozzo
1950	Uruguay	2-1	Brazil	Juan Lopez
1954	West Germany	3-2	Hungary	Sepp Herberger
1958	Brazil	5-2	Sweden	Vicente Feola
1962	Brazil	3-1	Czechoslovakia	Aymore Moreira
1966	England	4-2	West Germany	Alf Ramsey
1970	Brazil	4-1	Italy	Mario Zagalo
1974	West Germany	2-1	Netherlands	Helmut Schoen
1978	Argentina	3-1	Netherlands	Cesar Menotti
1982	Italy	3-1	West Germany	Enzo Bearzot
1986	Argentina	3-2	West Germany	Carlos Bilardo
1990	West Germany	1-0	Argentina	Franz Beckenbauer

All-time World Cup Participation

Of the 55 nations which have taken part in the World Cup, only Brazil has competed in each of the 13 tournaments held to date. West Germany has played in 12 World Cups, including the 1934 and 1938 editions when the team represented an undivided Germany.

	Matches	Wins	Ties	Losses	Goals For	Goals Against		Matches	Wins	Ties	Losses	Goals For	Goals Against
Brazil	66	44	11	11	148	65	USA	10	3	0	7	14	29
*West Germany	68	39	15	14	145	90	Bulgaria	16	0	6	10	11	35
Italy	54	31	12	11	89	54	Wales	5	1	3	1	4	4
Argentina	48	24	9	15	82	59	Algeria	6	2	1	3	6	10
England	41	18	12	11	55	38	Morocco	7	1	3	3	5	8
Uruguay	37	15	8	14	61	52	Republic of Ireland	5	0	4	1	2	3
USSR	31	15	6	10	53	34	Costa Rica	4	2	0	2	4	6
France	34	15	5	14	71	56	Colombia	7	1	2	4	9	15
Yugoslavia	33	15	5	13	55	42	Tunisia	3	1	1	1	3	2
Hungary	32	15	3	14	87	57	North Korea	4	1	1	2	5	9
Spain	32	13	7	12	43	38	Cuba	3	1	1	1	5	12
Poland	25	13	5	7	39	29	Turkey	3	1	0	2	10	11
Sweden	31	11	6	14	51	52	Honduras	3	0	2	1	2	3
Czechoslovakia	30	11	5	14	44	45	Israel	3	1	0	2	1	3
Austria	26	12	2	12	40	43	Egypt	4	0	2	2	3	6
Holland	20	8	6	6	35	23	Kuwait	3	0	1	2	2	6
Belgium	25	7	4	14	33	49	Australia	3	0	1	2	0	5
Mexico	29	6	6	17	27	64	Iran	3	0	1	2	2	8
Chile	21	7	3	11	26	32	South Korea	8	0	1	7	5	29
Scotland	20	4	6	10	23	35	Norway	1	0	0	1	1	2
Portugal	9	6	0	3	19	12	Dutch East Indies	1	0	0	1	0	6
Switzerland	18	5	2	11	28	44	Iraq	3	0	0	3	1	4
Northern Ireland	13	3	5	5	13	23	Canada	3	0	0	3	0	5
Peru	15	4	3	8	19	31	United Arab Emirates	3	0	0	3	2	11
Paraguay	11	3	4	4	16	25	New Zealand	3	0	0	3	2	12
Rumania	12	3	3	6	16	20	Haiti	3	0	0	3	2	14
Cameroon	8	3	3	2	8	10	Zaire	3	0	0	3	0	14
Denmark	4	3	0	1	10	6	Bolivia	3	0	0	3	0	16
East Germany	6	2	2	2	5	5	El Salvador	6	0	0	6	1	22

*Includes Germany 1930-38.

Note: Matches decided by penalty kicks are shown as drawn games.

The Yanks Are Coming!

John Harkes of Kearny, N.J., is the first American-born soccer player ever to play in an English League Cup championship. A member of the U.S. national team, he plays for Sheffield Wednesday which won the British second division title on April 21, 1991, at London's Wembley Stadium.

All-Time Leaders

GOALS

Player, Nation	Tournaments	Goals Scored
Gerd Mueller, West Germany	1970, 1974	14
Just Fontaine, France	1958	13
Pele, Brazil	1958, 1962, 1966, 1970	12
Sandor Kocsis, Hungary	1954	11
Teofilo Cubillas, Peru	1970, 1978	10
Gregorz Lato, Poland	1974, 1978, 1982	10
Helmut Rahn, West Germany	1954, 1958	10
Gary Lineker, England	1986, 1990	10
Ademir, Brazil	1950	9
Eusebio, Portugal	1966	9
Jairzinho, Brazil	1970, 1974	9
Paolo Rossi, Italy	1982, 1986	9
Karl-Heinz Rummenigge, W. Germany	1978, 1982, 1986	9
Uwe Seeler, West Germany	1958, 1962, 1966, 1970	9
Vava, Brazil	1958, 1962	9

LEADING SCORER, CUP BY CUP

Year	Player/Nation	Goals	Year	Player/Nation	Goals
1930	Guillermo Stabile, Argentina	8	1962	Leonel Sánchez, Chile	4
1934	Oldrich Nejedly, Czechoslovakia	5		Vava, Brazil	
1938	Leonidas da Silva, Brazil	8	1966	Eusebio Ferreira, Portugal	9
1950	Ademir de Menezes, Brazil	9	1970	Gerd Mueller, West Germany	10
1954	Sandor Kocsis, Hungary	11	1974	Gregorz Lato, Poland	7
1958	Just Fontaine, France	13	1978	Mario Kempes, Argentina	6
1962	Florian Albert, Hungary	4	1982	Paolo Rossi, Italy	6
	Valentin Ivanov, USSR		1986	Gary Lineker, England	6
	Garrincha, Brazil		1990	Salvatore Schillaci, Italy	6
	Drazan Jerkovic, Yugoslavia				

Most Goals, Individual, One Game

Goals	Player, Nation	Score	Date
4	Leonidas, Brazil	Brazil-Poland, 6-5	6-5-38
4	Ernest Willimowski, Poland	Brazil-Poland, 6-5	6-5-38
4	Gustav Wetterström, Sweden	Sweden-Cuba, 8-0	6-12-38
4	Juan Alberto Schiaffino, Uruguay	Uruguay-Bolivia, 8-0	7-2-50
4	Ademir, Brazil	Brazil-Sweden, 7-1	7-9-50
4	Sandor Kocsis, Hungary	Hungary-West Germany, 8-3	6-20-54
4	Just Fontaine, France	France-West Germany, 6-3	6-28-58
4	Eusebio, Portugal	Portugal-No. Korea, 5-3	7-23-66
4	Emilio Butragueño, Spain	Spain-Denmark, 5-1	6-18-86

Note: 30 players have scored 31 World Cup hat tricks. Gerd Mueller of West Germany is the only man to have two World Cup hat tricks, both in 1970. The last hat tricks were 6-23-90, Tomas Skuhravy (Czech) vs. Costa Rica and Michel (Spain) vs. So. Korea, 6-17-90.

Attendance and Goalscoring Year by Year

Year	Site	No. of Games	Goals	Goals/Game	Attendance	Avg Att
1930	Uruguay	18	70	3.89	434,500	24,139
1934	Italy	17	70	4.12	395,000	23,235
1938	France	18	84	4.67	483,000	26,833
1950	Brazil	22	88	4.00	1,337,000	60,773
1954	Switzerland	26	140	5.38	943,000	36,269
1958	Sweden	35	126	3.60	868,000	24,800
1962	Chile	32	89	2.78	776,000	24,250
1966	England	32	89	2.78	1,614,677	50,459
1970	Mexico	32	95	2.97	1,673,975	52,312
1974	West Germany	38	97	2.55	1,774,022	46,685
1978	Argentina	38	102	2.68	1,610,215	42,374
1982	Spain	52	146	2.80	1,856,277	35,698
1986	Mexico	52	132	2.54	2,441,731	46,956
1990	Italy	52	115	2.21	2,514,443	48,354
	Totals	412	1328	3.22		

The United States in the World Cup

URUGUAY 1930: FINAL COMPETITION

Date	Opponent	Result	Scoring
7-13-30	Belgium	3-0 W	US—McGhee 2, Patenaude
7-17-30	Paraguay	3-0 W	US—Patenaude 2, Florie
7-26-30	Argentina	1-6 L	ARG—Monti 2, Scopelli 2, Stabile 2 US—Brown.

BRAZIL 1950: FINAL COMPETITION

Date	Opponent	Result	Scoring
6-25-50	Spain	1-3 L	US—Pariani SPN—Igoa, Basora, Zarra
6-29-50	England	1-0 W	US—Gaetjens.
7-2-50	Chile	2-5 L	US—Wallace, Maca CHL—Robledo, Cremaschi 3, Prieto

ITALY 1934: FINAL COMPETITION

Date	Opponent	Result	Scoring
5-27-34	Italy	1-7 L	US—Donelli ITA—Schiavio 3, Orsi 2, Meazza, Ferrari

ITALY 1990: FINAL COMPETITION

Date	Opponent	Result	Scoring
6-10-90	Czechoslovakia	1-5 L	US—Caligiuri Czech—Skuhravy 2, Hasek, Bilek, Luhovy
6-14-90	Italy	0-1 L	Italy—Giannini
6-19-90	Austria	1-2 L	US—Murray Austria—Rodax, Ogris

International Competition

Under-20 World Championship

Year	Host	Champion	Runner-Up
1977	Tunisia	USSR	Mexico
1979	Japan	Argentina	USSR
1981	Australia	W. Germany	Qatar
1983	Mexico	Brazil	Argentina
1985	USSR	Brazil	Spain
1987	Chile	Yugoslavia	W. Germany
1989	Saudi Arabia	Portugal	Nigeria
1991	Portugal	Portugal	Brazil

Under-17 World Championship

1985	Nigeria
1987	USSR
1989	Saudi Arabia
1991	Ghana

Pan American Games

1951	Argentina
1955	Argentina
1959	Argentina
1963	Brazil
1967	Mexico
1971	Argentina
1975	Brazil-Mexico (tie)
1979	Brazil
1983	Uruguay
1987	Brazil
1991	United States

European Championship

Official name: the European Football Championship. Held every four years since 1960.

Year	Champion	Score	Runner-up	Year	Champion	Score	Runner-up
1960	USSR	2-1	Yugoslavia	1976	Czechoslovakia*	2-2	West Germany
1964	Spain	2-1	USSR	1980	West Germany	2-1	Belgium
1968	Italy	2-0	Yugoslavia	1984	France	2-0	Spain
1972	West Germany	3-0	USSR	1988	Holland	2-0	USSR

*Won on penalty kicks.

South American Championship (Copa America)

Year	Champion	Host	Year	Champion	Host
1916	Uruguay	Argentina	1929	Argentina	Argentina
1917	Uruguay	Uruguay	1935	Uruguay	Peru
1919	Brazil	Brazil	1937	Argentina	Argentina
1920	Uruguay	Chile	1939	Peru	Peru
1921	Argentina	Argentina	1941	Argentina	Chile
1922	Brazil	Brazil	1942	Uruguay	Uruguay
1923	Uruguay	Uruguay	1945	Argentina	Chile
1924	Uruguay	Uruguay	1946	Argentina	Argentina
1925	Argentina	Argentina	1947	Argentina	Ecuador
1926	Uruguay	Chile	1949	Brazil	Brazil
1927	Argentina	Peru	1953	Paraguay	Peru

South American Championship (Copa America) (*Cont.*)

Year	Champion	Host	Year	Champion	Host
1955	Argentina	Chile	1975	Peru	—
1956	Uruguay	Uruguay	1979	Paraguay	—
1957	Argentina	Peru	1983	Uruguay	—
1958	Argentina	Argentina	1987	Uruguay	Argentina
1959	Uruguay	Ecuador	1989	Brazil	Brazil
1963	Bolivia	Bolivia	1990	Brazil	Argentina
1967	Uruguay	Uruguay	1991	Argentina	Chile

Awards

European Footballer of the Year

Year	Player	Team	Year	Player	Team
1956	Stanley Matthews	Blackpool	1975	Oleg Blokhin	Dynamo Kiev
1957	Alfredo Di Stefano	Real Madrid	1976	Franz Beckenbauer	Bayern Munich
1958	Raymond Kopa	Real Madrid	1977	Allan Simonsen	Borussia
1959	Alfredo Di Stefano	Real Madrid			Moenchengladbach
1960	Luis Suarez	Barcelona	1978	Kevin Keegan	SV Hamburg
1961	Omar Sivori	Juventus	1979	Kevin Keegan	SV Hamburg
1962	Josef Masopust	Dukla Prague	1980	Karl-Heinz Rummenigge	Bayern Munich
1963	Lev Yashin	Moscow Dynamo	1981	Karl-Heinz Rummenigge	Bayern Munich
1964	Denis Law	Manchester United			
1965	Eusebio	Benfica	1982	Paolo Rossi	Juventus
1966	Bobby Charlton	Manchester United	1983	Michel Platini	Juventus
1967	Florian Albert	Ferencvaros	1984	Michel Platini	Juventus
1968	George Best	Manchester United	1985	Michel Platini	Juventus
1969	Gianni Rivera	AC Milan	1986	Igor Belanov	Dynamo Kiev
1970	Gerd Mueller	Bayern Munich	1987	Ruud Gullit	AC Milan
1971	Johan Cruyff	Ajax	1988	Marco Van Basten	AC Milan
1972	Franz Beckenbauer	Bayern Munich	1989	Marco Van Basten	AC Milan
1973	Johan Cruyff	Barcelona	1990	Lothar Matthaeus	Inter Milan
1974	Johan Cruyff	Barcelona			

South American Player of the Year

Year	Player	Team	Year	Player	Team
1971	Tostao	Cruzeiro	1981	Zico	Flamengo
1972	Teofilo Cubillas	Alianza Lima	1982	Zico	Flamengo
1973	Pele	Santos	1983	Socrates	Corinthians
1974	Elias Figueroa	Internacional	1984	Enzo Francescoli	River Plate
1975	Elias Figueroa	Internacional	1985	Julio Cesar Romero	Fluminense
1976	Elias Figueroa	Internacional	1986	Antonio Alzamendi	River Plate
1977	Zico	Flamengo	1987	Carlos Valderrama	Deportivo Cali
1978	Mario Kempes	Valencia	1988	Ruben Paz	Racing Buenos Aires
1979	Diego Maradona	Argentinos Juniors	1989	Bebeto	Vasco da Gama
1980	Diego Maradona	Boca Juniors	1990	Raul Amarilla	Olimpia

African Footballer of the Year

Year	Player	National Team	Year	Player	National Team
1970	Salif Keita	Mali	1981	Lakhdar Belloumi	Algeria
1971	Ibrahim Sunday	Ghana	1982	Thomas Nkono	Cameroon
1972	Chérif Souleyman	Guinea	1983	Mahmoud Al-Khatib	Egypt
1973	Tshimimu Bwanga	Zaire	1984	Théophile Abega	Cameroon
1974	Paul Moukila	Congo	1985	Mohamed Timoumi	Morocco
1975	Ahmed Faras	Morocco	1986	Badou Zaki	Morocco
1976	Roger Milla	Cameroon	1987	Rabah Madjer	Algeria
1977	Dhiab Tarak	Tunisia	1988	Kalusha Bwalya	Zambia
1978	Abdul Razak	Ghana	1989	George Weah	Liberia
1979	Thomas Nkono	Cameroon	1990	Roger Milla	Cameroon
1980	Jean Manga Onguene	Cameroon			

Selected by *France Football*.

Club Competition

Toyota Cup

Competition between winners of European Champion Clubs' Cup and Libertadores Cup.

1960 ...Real Madrid, Spain	1971 ...Nacional, Uruguay	1981 ... Flamengo, Brazil
1961 ...Penarol, Uruguay	1972 ...Ajax, Holland	1982 ... Penarol, Uruguay
1962 ...Santos, Brazil	1973 ...Independiente, Argentina	1983 ... Gremio, Brazil
1963 ...Santos, Brazil	1974 ...Atletico de Madrid, Spain	1984 ... Independiente, Argentina
1964 ...Inter, Italy	1975 ...No tournament	1985 ... Juventus, Italy
1965 ...Inter, Italy	1976 ...Bayern Munich	1986 ... River Plate, Argentina
1966 ...Penarol, Uruguay	1977 ...Boca Juniors, Argentina	1987 ... Porto, Portugal
1967 ...Racing Club, Argentina	1978 ...No tournament	1988 ... Nacional, Uruguay
1968 ...Estudiantes, Argentina	1979 ...Olimpia, Paraguay	1989 ... Milan, Italy
1969 ...Milan, Italy	1980 ...Nacional, Uruguay	1990 ... Milan, Italy
1970 ...Feyenoord, Netherlands		

Note: Until 1968 a best-of-three-games format decided the winner. After that a two-game/total-goal format was used until Toyota became the sponsor in 1980, moved the game to Tokyo, and switched the format to a one game championship. The European Cup runner-up substituted for the winner in 1971, 1973, 1974, and 1979.

European Champion Clubs' Cup

1956 ...Real Madrid, Spain	1971 ...Ajax Amsterdam, Netherlands	1980 ... Nottingham Forest, England
1957 ...Real Madrid, Spain	1972 ...Ajax Amsterdam, Netherlands	1981 ... Liverpool, England
1958 ...Real Madrid, Spain	1973 ...Ajax Amsterdam, Netherlands	1982 ... Aston Villa, England
1959 ...Real Madrid, Spain		1983 ... SV Hamburg, West Germany
1960 ...Real Madrid, Spain	1974 ...Bayern Munich, West Germany	1984 ... Liverpool, England
1961 ...Benfica, Portugal	1975 ...Bayern Munich, West Germany	1985 ... Juventus, Italy
1962 ...Benfica, Portugal	1976 ...Bayern Munich, West Germany	1986 ... Steaua Bucharest, Romania
1963 ...A.C. Milan, Italy		
1964 ...Inter-Milan, Italy	1977 ...Liverpool, England	1987 ... Porto, Portugal
1965 ...Inter-Milan, Italy	1978 ...Liverpool, England	1988 ... P.S.V. Eindhoven, Netherlands
1966 ...Real Madrid, Spain	1979 ...Nottingham Forest, England	
1967 ...Celtic, Scotland		1989 ... A.C. Milan, Italy
1968 ...Manchester United, England		1990 ... A.C. Milan, Italy
1969 ...A.C. Milan, Italy		1991 ... Red Star, Belgrade
1970 ...Feyenoord, Netherlands		

On four occasions the European Cup winner has refused to play in the Intercontinental Cup (now Toyota Cup) and has been replaced by the runner-up: Panathinaikos (Greece) in 1971, Juventus (Italy) in 1973, Atletico Madrid (Spain) in 1974, and Malmo (Sweden) in 1979.

Libertadores Cup

Competition between champion clubs and runners-up of 10 South American National Associations.

1960 ...Penarol, Uruguay	1972 ...Independiente, Argentina	1983 ... Gremio, Brazil
1961 ...Penarol, Uruguay	1973 ...Independiente, Argentina	1984 ... Independiente, Argentina
1962 ...Santos, Brazil	1974 ...Independiente, Argentina	1985 ... Argentinos Juniors, Argentina
1963 ...Santos, Brazil	1975 ...Independiente, Argentina	
1964 ...Independiente, Argentina	1976 ...Cruzeiro, Brazil	1986 ... River Plate, Argentina
1965 ...Independiente, Argentina	1977 ...Boca Juniors, Argentina	1987 ... Penarol, Uruguay
1966 ...Penarol, Uruguay	1978 ...Boca Juniors, Argentina	1988 ... Nacional, Uruguay
1967 ...Racing Club, Argentina	1979 ...Olimpia, Paraguay	1989 ... Atletico Nacional, Colombia
1968 ...Estudiantes, Argentina	1980 ...Nacional, Uruguay	
1969 ...Estudiantes, Argentina	1981 ...Flamengo, Brazil	1990 ... Olimpia, Paraguay
1970 ...Estudiantes, Argentina	1982 ...Penarol, Uruguay	1991 ... Colo Colo, Chile
1971 ...Nacional, Uruguay		

UEFA Cup

Competition between teams other than league champions and cup winners from the Union of European Football Associations.

1958 ...Barcelona, Spain	1966 ... Barcelona, Spain	1972 ...Tottenham Hotspur, England
1959 ...No tournament	1967 ... Dynamo Zagreb, Yugoslavia	
1960 ...Barcelona, Spain		1973 ...Liverpool, England
1961 ...AS Roma, Italy	1968 ... Leeds United, England	1974 ...Feyenoord, Netherlands
1962 ...Valencia, Spain	1969 ... Newcastle United, England	1975 ...Borussia Moenchengladbach, West Germany
1963 ...Valencia, Spain		
1964 ...Real Zaragoza, Spain	1970 ... Arsenal, England	
1965 ...Ferencvaros, Hungary	1971 ... Leeds United, England	1976 ...Liverpool, England

UEFA Cup (*Cont.*)

1977 ...Juventus, Italy	1981 ...Ipswich Town, England	1988... Bayer Leverkusen, West Germany
1978 ...P.S.V. Eindhoven, Netherlands	1982 ...I.F.K. Gothenburg, Sweden	1989... Naples, Italy
1979 ...Borussia Moenchengladbach, West Germany	1983 ...Anderlecht, Belgium	1990... Juventus, Italy
1980 ...Eintracht Frankfurt, West Germany	1984 ...Tottenham Hotspur, England	1991... Inter-Milan, Italy
	1985 ...Real Madrid, Spain	
	1986 ...Real Madrid, Spain	
	1987 ...I.F.K. Gothenburg, Sweden	

European Cup Winners' Cup

Competition between cup winners of countries belonging to UEFA.

1961 ...A.C. Fiorentina, Italy	1970 ...Manchester City, England	1981... Dynamo Tbilisi, USSR
1962 ...Atletico Madrid, Spain	1971 ...Chelsea, England	1982... Barcelona, Spain
1963 ...Tottenham Hotspur, England	1972 ...Glasgow Rangers, Scotland	1983... Aberdeen, Scotland
1964 ...Sporting Lisbon, Portugal	1973 ...A.C. Milan, Italy	1984... Juventus, Italy
1965 ...West Ham United, England	1974 ...Magdeburg, East Germany	1985... Everton, England
1966 ...Borussia Dortmund, West Germany	1975 ...Dynamo Kiev, USSR	1986... Dynamo Kiev, USSR
1967 ...Bayern Munich, West Germany	1976 ...Anderlecht, Belgium	1987... Ajax Amsterdam, Netherlands
1968 ...A.C. Milan, Italy	1977 ...S.V. Hamburg, West Germany	1988... Mechelen, Belgium
1969 ...Slovan Bratislava, Czechoslovakia	1978 ...Anderlecht, Belgium	1989... Barcelona, Spain
	1979 ...Barcelona, Spain	1990... Sampdoria, Italy
	1980 ...Valencia, Spain	1991... Manchester United, England

Major Soccer League

Results

Called the Major Indoor Soccer League from 1979-90.

Year	Champion	Series	Runner-Up	Year	Champion	Series	Runner-Up
1979	NY Arrows	2-0	Philadelphia	1986	San Diego	4-3	Minnesota
1980	NY Arrows	7-4	Houston	1987	Dallas	4-3	Tacoma
1981	NY Arrows	6-5	St Louis	1988	San Diego	4-0	Cleveland
1982	NY Arrows	3-2	St Louis	1989	San Diego	4-3	Baltimore
1983	San Diego	3-2	Baltimore	1990	San Diego	4-2	Baltimore
1984	Baltimore	4-1	St Louis	1991	San Diego	4-2	Cleveland
1985	San Diego	4-1	Baltimore				

Championship format: 1979, best-of-three-games series; 1980-81, one-game championship; 1982-83, best-of-five-games series; 1984 to present, best-of-seven-games series.

Statistical Leaders

	SCORING			ASSISTS	
Year	Player/Team	Points	Year	Player/Team	Assists
1978-79	Fred Grgurev, Phil	74	1978-79	Fred Grgurev, Phil	28
1979-80	Steve Zungul, NY	136	1979-80	Steve Zungul, NY	46
1980-81	Steve Zungul, NY	152	1980-81	Jorgen Kristensen, Wich	52
1981-82	Steve Zungul, NY	163	1981-82	Steve Zungul, NY	60
1982-83	Steve Zungul, NY	122	1982-83	Stan Stamenkovic, Mem	65
1983-84	Stan Stamenkovic, Balt	97	1983-84	Stan Stamenkovic, Balt	63
1984-85	Steve Zungul, SD	136	1984-85	Steve Zungul, SD	68
1985-86	Steve Zungul, Tac	115	1985-86	Steve Zungul, Tac	60
1986-87	Tatu, Dall	111	1986-87	Kai Haaskivi, Clev	55
1987-88	Erik Rasmussen, Wich	112	1987-88	Preki, Tac	58
1988-89	Preki, Tac	104	1988-89	Preki, Tac	53
1989-90	Tatu, Dall	113	1989-90	Jan Goossens, KC	55
1990-91	Tatu, Dall	144	1990-91	Tatu, Dall	66

Major Soccer League (*Cont.*)

Statistical Leaders (*Cont.*)

GOALS			TOP GOALKEEPERS		
Year	Player/Team	Goals	Year	Player/Team	Goals Agst Avg
1978-79	Fred Grgurev, Phil	46	1978-79	Paul Hammond, Hous	4.16
1979-80	Steve Zungul, NY	90	1979-80	Sepp Gantenhammer, Hous	4.42
1980-81	Steve Zungul, NY	108	1980-81	Enzo DiPede, Chi	4.06
1981-82	Steve Zungul, NY/GB	103	1981-82	Slobo Liijevski, StL	3.85*
1982-83	Steve Zungul, NY/GB	75	1982-83	Zoltan Toth, NY	4.01
1983-84	Mark Liveric, NY	58	1983-84	Slobo Liijevski, StL	3.67
1984-85	Steve Zungul, SD	68	1984-85	Scott Manning, Balt	3.89
1985-86	Erik Rasmussen, Wich	67	1985-86	Keith Van Eron, Balt	3.66
1986-87	Tatu, Dall	73	1986-87	Tino Lettieri, Minn	3.38
1987-88	Hector Marinaro, Minn	58	1987-88	Zoltan Toth, SD	2.94
1988-89	Preki, Tac	51	1988-89	Victor Nogueira, SD	2.86
1989-90	Tatu, Dall	64	1989-90	Joe Papaleo, Dall	3.34
1990-91	Tatu, Dall	78	1990-91	Victor Nogueira, SD	4.37

North American Soccer League

Formed in 1968 by the merger of the National Professional Soccer League and the USA League, both of which had begun operations a year earlier. The NPSL's lone champion was the Oakland Clippers. The USA, which brought entire teams in from Europe, was won in 1967 by the LA Wolves, who were the English League's Wolverhampton Wanderers.

Year	Champion	Score	Runner-Up	Year	Champion	Score	Runner-Up
1968	Atlanta	0-0,3-0	San Diego	1977	NY	2-1	Seattle
1969	Kansas City	No game	Atlanta	1978	NY	3-1	Tampa Bay
1970	Rochester	3-0,1-3	Washington	1979	Vancouver	2-1	Tampa Bay
1971	Dallas	1-2, 4-1, 2-0	Atlanta	1980	NY	3-0	Ft Lauderdale
1972	NY	2-1	St Louis	1981	Chicago	1-0*	NY
1973	Philadelphia	2-0	Dallas	1982	NY	1-0	Seattle
1974	Los Angeles	4-3*	Miami	1983	Tulsa	2-0	Toronto
1975	Tampa Bay	2-0	Portland	1984	Chicago	2-1, 3-2	Toronto
1976	Toronto	3-0	Minnesota				

*Shootout.

Championship Format: 1968 & 1970: Two games/total goals. 1971 & 1984: Best-of-three game series. 1972-1983: One game championship. Title in 1969 went to the regular season champion.

Statistical Leaders

SCORING

Year	Player/Team	Pts	Year	Player/Team	Pts
1968	John Kowalik, Chi	69	1977	Steven David, LA	58
1969	Kaiser Motaung, Atl	36	1978	Giorgio Chinaglia, NY	79
1970	Kirk Apostolidis, Dall	35	1979	Oscar Fabbiani, Tampa Bay	58
1971	Carlos Metidieri, Roch	46	1980	Giorgio Chinaglia, NY	77
1972	Randy Horton, NY	22	1981	Giorgio Chinaglia, NY	74
1973	Kyle Rote, Dall	30	1982	Giorgio Chinaglia, NY	55
1974	Paul Child, San Jose	36	1983	Roberto Cabanas, NY	66
1975	Steven David, Miami	52	1984	Slavisa Zungul, Golden Bay	50
1976	Giorgio Chinaglia, NY	49			

Canada's Answer to Bo

Center Peter Zezel of hockey's Toronto Maple Leafs became Canada's answer to two-sport athletes Bo Jackson and Deion Sanders, when he made his professional soccer debut with the North York Rockets of the Canadian Soccer League on August 7, 1991.

NCAA Sports

Sports Illustrated

CRISIS IN THE NCAA

EXECUTIVE DIRECTOR DICK SCHULTZ

LANE STEWART

Stalking the NCAA

With Congress threatening to take action, the NCAA tried to clean its house | by ROBERT SULLIVAN

NINETEEN NINETY-ONE BEGAN BUOY-antly for the NCAA with a convention that passed several high-minded initiatives. But as the year progressed it became clear that college sports faced persistent problems that couldn't be solved by putting in a few new rules.

The NCAA's continuing inability to stem the flow of scandal was its most frustrating problem, which led to plenty of advice on what to do about wrongdoing. Congress began a series of hearings that would, according to Rep. Cardiss Collins (D-Ill.), who presided, "look into all aspects of college sports—the NCAA, grades, money, everything." The NCAA, which began the year on cloud nine, finished under a different cloud.

Last January in Nashville, the NCAA, led by reformist college presidents, voted to reduce the size of coaching staffs, reduce the number of scholarships by 10% in all sports, reduce the length of seasons, limit practice-time demands on athletes to 20 hours a week and place some limits on recruiting. "The convention was the great success of the year," says NCAA executive director Dick Schultz in retrospect. "It dealt with getting sports closer to their proper perspective at a university."

The reformist roll continued last spring when the Southern Association of Colleges and Schools, an 800-member group in an 11-state region from Virginia to Texas, said it would take steps to require oversight of athletics by its schools' presidents. Under the SACS plan, the chancellors would be responsible for their athletic departments' fiscal, recruiting and eligibility operations. If a school were found in serious violation of NCAA rules, it would lose its academic accreditation within SACS, thereby jeopardizing the federal aid the school receives.

By early summer Congress had begun its series of attention-grabbing hearings into "the mess of college sports," as Rep. Collins called it. Collins, chair of the House Sub-

*Brown, the LSU basketball coach, continued his longtime opposition to NCAA policies during the Washington hearings in June.*

AP PHOTO

committee on Commerce, Consumer Protection and Competitiveness, had been asked to call the hearings by two members of her subcommittee, Ed Towns (D-N.Y.) and Tom McMillen (D-Md.).

Federal lawmakers—including McMillen, a former college and professional basketball player, and Towns—became interested in college sports a few years ago when it became apparent that the NCAA was struggling to clean its increasingly dirty house. Two years ago, these fed-up legislators pushed through a bill to force colleges to report their athletes' graduation rates, thereby creating an "embarrassment factor" at schools whose academic programs were lagging. Emboldened by that success, Towns introduced The Coaches and Athletes Bill of Rights, which would require the NCAA to observe due process in all its

investigations. "Look," says Schultz, "we're in favor of due process. We started taping conversations last spring, for instance. We're still studying our enforcement procedures, and I would only hope [Congress] allows us to implement whatever recommendations come out of that."

Why, in its struggle to control college sports, does the NCAA fear the intervention of government?

Power and money.

"Our members are afraid we'll lose control of the game," says Jeffrey H. Orleans, executive director of the Ivy League. "Our guys think once Congress gets used to intervening, it'll intervene tooth and nail. It'll get into freshman eligibility, tax issues and academics. The fear among our big boys is that the feds will get into revenue-sharing and base it upon something silly, like academic performance." The NCAA has received a billion-dollar windfall from its most recent basketball TV contract, and the Oklahomas are worried that the Harvards might get a proportionate share if Congress calls the shots.

A question for the other side: Why is Congress, which had a front-page war to occupy it in '91, wasting its time on the sports section?

Says Schultz: "The reason I really think they're doing this, I can't be quoted on."

Orleans can: "These guys are politicians. They've got a juicy, populist issue." That was evident in the first hearings last June. Basketball coaches Dale Brown of LSU and Jerry Tarkanian of UNLV turned Capitol Hill into a media circus. Tarkanian, who was finally brought down last year by one too many scandals (see sidebar), reviled his longtime foes within the NCAA and pleaded with Congress to insinuate itself into college sports. "I had the thought as I watched him," says John C. Weistart, Duke law professor and co-author of *The Law of Sports,* "that here was the fox begging for better security around the henhouse."

Brown, for his part, actually had a few nice things to say about the NCAA. But then he pulled his film-at-11 stunt. He waved the NCAA manual around and said it should be burned. "I once phoned the NCAA and thought I'd gotten the Kremlin!" he went on. "If we don't get things fixed now, this will last as long as the Ottoman Empire!" Switching metaphorical tracks, he whined that coaches were "whipping boys . . . forced to the back of the bus."

Hold on right there, said Collins, who is black and represents a poor district in Chicago. "There's been some partying going on at the back of your bus!"

It was great stuff, wonderful theater. And despite its superficiality, it advanced this dead serious idea of congressional intervention.

"I expect more intervention, and I think it's the central problem for the NCAA right now," says Weistart. "Intervention will come because the NCAA can no longer say

'You can depend on us to reform ourselves.' They tinker at their conventions, but still the bad news and the cheating keep coming. I think the college presidents are enacting even better rules. But until they change the big-money nature of the thing—the profit-motive aspects of football and basketball—these rules will just mean more scandals, and that will lead to intervention.

"You want to know what a bold move would be? Reserve 15 spots in the NCAA basketball tournament for teams that are *not* colleges. Have 15 spots for club teams and AAU teams. Then kids who don't want to go to college—who don't belong in college—wouldn't *have* to go to college and might still be able to go to the pros when they matured.

The Shark Strikes Back

IN 1991 THE NCAA's epic thriller starring UNLV basketball coach Jerry Tarkanian finally ended. But not, of course, without a dramatic final act, in which The Shark, badly wounded by yet another scandal, went down thrashing.

Eighteen years ago Tarkanian became the basketball coach at UNLV. Shortly thereafter the NCAA alleged recruiting violations. Tarkanian then started what would be an 11-year court battle, charging that the association's investigative methods didn't afford due process. In 1988 the Supreme Court found for the NCAA. The NCAA went back to work on the UNLV case, trying to decide a penalty that fit the crime of long ago.

But in 1990, Tark's Runnin' Rebels, led by juniors Larry Johnson and Stacey Augmon, put an in-your-face move on the NCAA by winning the national championship. The association returned the slam several months later, accusing UNLV of 29 *new* rules violations, most of them concerning the recruitment of Lloyd Daniels, a legend on the New York City playgrounds.

The NCAA also announced a one-year probation for UNLV for the 1970s' abuses, but, after an appeal, said it would be deferred for 12 months so the Rebels could defend their title in Indianapolis in 1991. Some observers praised this decision as Solomonic: No sense visiting the sins of the great-great-great-grandfathers upon the current generation. Skeptics wondered if the NCAA would have acted the same way if the team in question were, say, McNeese State—which wouldn't add much box-office luster to its March madness.

As the 1991 season ended, Johnson and Augmon got the jitters and UNLV lost in the Final Four to eventual champion Duke. Tarkanian, rather defiantly, said that he would not follow his stellar seniors to the NBA, but would return to UNLV. Ah, but in late spring, the *Las Vegas Review-Journal* printed a 1989 photo showing three former UNLV players in a hot tub with a convicted sports fixer named Richard Perry. The players—Anderson Hunt, Moses Scurry and David Butler—had

"But the NCAA would never do such a thing. The colleges like the money too much. Since the beast is unwilling to kill itself, federal involvement will follow."

Weistart is certainly right about the unending stream of scandal: Nineteen ninety-one saw no abatement in rules-breaking and bad faith among athletes, coaches and other college officials. Consider this unsavory sampling taken from one week's—one *week's*—news in June:

- North Carolina Central was sued by six athletes who said they were cheated out of their scholarships.
- Federal investigators found that a number of Miami athletes had paid for falsified federal grant-in-aid applications to obtain money that was earmarked for poor students. Tony Russell, who sold the documents and admitted it, was an employee of the athletic department; he said he was trying to support a cocaine habit.
- *USA Today* reported that 20 universities—including N.C. State, Alabama, Colorado, Maryland, LSU, Clemson and Arizona—had graduated one or none of the minority male athletes recruited during a five-year period in the '80s.
- Texas A&M conceded 10 NCAA rules violations in *its* basketball program.
- SI reported an upsurge of criminal activity among college athletes. "I've had more incidents in the past year than I had in 10 or 12 years at other schools," said USC football coach Larry Smith, who since the year began had seen two Trojans charged

been on the national championship team. Perry had been convicted in connection with the Boston College point-shaving scheme of the early 1980s and had been convicted of fixing harness races in the 1970s in New York.

Twelve days after the damning snapshot was published, Tarkanian announced that he would step down following the 1991–92 season. "It was the hot tub thing," Tark said of his reason for finally stepping down.

The Shark's farewell chomp at the NCAA was issued before he embarked on his last UNLV hoops campaign. In testimony at the college-sports hearings on Capitol Hill, he told the lawmakers that people needed protection from the prying eyes of the NCAA. "A reign of terror," is what he called the association's rule of college sports. "The NCAA can pick on anybody and destroy their careers."

Even as Tarkanian testified, staffers at UNLV were boxing a 300-page argument and 10,000 pages of supporting transcripts for delivery to the NCAA in response to its most recent allegations.

It was too late.

Exit The Shark

Tarkanian finally gave in to his critics, announcing that he will retire at the end of the 1992 basketball season.

Football teams like Penn State, which is moving to the Big Ten, won't be playing old rivals such as Pitt.

with felonies and one—quarterback Todd Marinovich—charged with drug possession.

- The *Boulder Daily Camera* reported that Colorado football coach Bill McCartney had been paid a $75,833 bonus, in addition to his $130,000 salary, for winning the national title. The bonus clause in his contract had been approved by the university's former president.

"It's terrible—a clause like that," says Rep. Collins. "How can a coach who can get $75,000 extra be expected to urge his kids to study? Baloney! We're going to do something about that kind of baloney."

The NCAA only hopes it can placate the legislators. Toward that end, the 44-member NCAA Presidents Commission will push at the '92 convention in New Orleans for better institutional control of coaches' compensation and for tougher freshman-eligibility standards. Currently, a grade point average of 2.0 in 11 high school core courses is needed to play, and the chancellors want to up that to a 2.5 GPA in 13 courses. "The priorities for legislation will be academic standards," said NCAA president Judy

Sweet. "There is pretty strong general support for strengthening academic standards."

But the NCAA's jock element shows no great desire to reform. Last year there was continued lobbying for a football playoff, which could make a long season longer. And all year the colleges with the largest sports programs dickered like Vegas cardsharks over the realignment of their conferences. Arkansas, for example, will move in the fall of '92 from the Southwest Conference—it had been a member for 76 years—to the Southeastern. Penn State, which has always played football as an independent, will scrap most of its traditional rivalries and join the Big Ten Conference in 1993. "Conference realignment isn't bad for reasons of competitiveness," says Schultz. "But if it's done to make money in major sports, and the small sports can't afford the time or money to travel that far—well, then it's a bad idea."

So the NCAA perseveres, for now, with continuing friction between its money-making heart and its scholar-athlete conscience. At the convention in January in Anaheim, the 800-member association will tinker yet again with the rules. But time grows shorter with each new scandal, and if the tinkering of '92 doesn't produce more emphatic progress than did the tinkering of '88, '89, '90, and '91, then the NCAA will soon get some unsolicited advice that it cannot refuse.

NCAA Team Champions

Fall 1990

Cross Country

MEN

Division I:	Arkansas
Division II:	Edinboro (PA)
Division III:	WI-Oshkosh

WOMEN

Division I:	Villanova
Division II:	Cal Poly-San Luis Obispo
Division III:	Cortland St

Field Hockey

WOMEN

Division I:	Old Dominion
Division III:	Trenton St

Football

MEN

Division I-A:	Colorado
Division I-AA:	Georgia Southern
Division II:	N Dakota St
Division III:	Allegheny

Soccer

MEN

Division I:	UCLA
Division II:	Southern Connecticut St
Division III:	Glassboro St Col

WOMEN

Division I:	N Carolina
Division II:	Sonoma St
Division III:	Ithaca

Volleyball

WOMEN

Division I:	UCLA
Division II:	W Texas St
Division III:	California-San Diego

Water Polo

MEN

Champion:	California

Winter 1990–1991

Basketball

MEN

Division I:	Duke
Division II:	N Alabama
Division III:	WI-Platteville

WOMEN

Division I:	Tennessee
Division II:	N Dakota St
Division III:	St Thomas (MN)

Fencing

Champion:	Penn St

Gymnastics

MEN

Champion:	Oklahoma

WOMEN

Champion:	Alabama

Ice Hockey

MEN

Division I:	Northern Michigan
Division III:	WI-Stevens Point

Rifle

Champion:	W Virginia

Skiing

Champion:	Colorado

Swimming and Diving

MEN

Division I:	Texas
Division II:	Cal St-Bakersfield
Division III:	Kenyon

WOMEN

Division I:	Texas
Division II:	Oakland (MI)
Division III:	Kenyon

Indoor Track

MEN

Division I:	Arkansas
Division II:	St Augustine's (NC)
Division III:	WI-La Crosse

WOMEN

Division I:	Louisiana St
Division II:	Abilene Christian
Division III:	Cortland St

Wrestling

MEN

Division I:	Iowa
Division II:	NE-Omaha
Division III:	Augsburg

Spring 1991

Baseball

MEN

Division I:	Louisiana St
Division II:	Jacksonville St
Division III:	Southern Maine

Golf

MEN

Division I:	Arizona St
Division II:	Florida Southern
Division III:	Methodist (NC)

WOMEN

Champion:	UCLA

Lacrosse

MEN

Division I:	N Carolina
Division II:	Hobart

WOMEN

National Collegiate:	Virginia
Division III:	Trenton St

Softball

WOMEN

Division I:	Arizona
Division II:	Augustana (SD)
Division III:	Central Col (IA)

Tennis

MEN

Division I:	Southern Cal
Division II:	Rollins (FL)
Division III:	Kalamazoo

WOMEN

Division I:	Stanford
Division II:	Cal Poly-Pomona
Division III:	Mary Washington (VA)

Spring 1991 (*Cont.*)

Outdoor Track

MEN

Division I: Tennessee
Division II: St Augustine's (NC)
Division III: WI-La Crosse

WOMEN

Division I: Louisiana St
Division II: Cal Poly-San Luis Obispo
Division III: WI-Oshkosh

Volleyball

MEN

Champion: Cal St-Long Beach

NCAA Division I Individual Champions

Fall 1990

Cross Country

Men: Jonah Koech, Iowa St
Women: Sonia O'Sullivan, Villanova

Winter 1990–1991

Fencing

MEN

Sabre ....Vitali Nazlimov, Penn St
Foil......................Ben Atkins, Columbia
Épée ....Marc Oshima, Columbia

WOMEN

Foil......................Heidi Piper, Notre Dame

Gymnastics

MEN

All-around ....John Roethlisberger, Minnesota
Vault ....Adam Carton, Penn St
Parallel bars ....Scott Keswick, UCLA
Horizontal bar ....Luis Lopez, New Mexico
Floor exercise...........Brad Hayashi, UCLA
Pommel horse ....Mark Sohn, Penn St
Rings ....Adam Carton, Penn St

WOMEN

All-around ....Hope Spivey, Georgia
Balance beam ....Melissa Marlowe, Utah
Uneven bars ....Kelly Macy, Georgia
Floor exercise...........Hope Spivey, Georgia
Vault ....Anna Basaldua, Arizona

Rifle

Smallbore ....Soma Dutta, TX-El Paso
Air rifle ....Ann Pfiffner, W Virginia

Skiing

MEN

Slalom .... Einar Boehmer, Vermont
Giant slalom .... Toni Standteiner, Colorado
Freestyle cross country ... Bjon Svensson, Colorado
Diagonal cross country .... Stig Mattsson, AK-Anchorage

WOMEN

Slalom .... Heather Flood, Middlebury
Giant slalom .... Keri Schlopy, Vermont
Freestyle cross country .... Laura Wilson, Vermont
Diagonal cross country ..... Laura Wilson, Vermont

Swimming

MEN

50-yard freestyle .... Shaun Jordan, Texas
100-yard freestyle .... Shaun Jordan, Texas
200-yard freestyle .... Artur Wojdat, Iowa
500-yard freestyle .... Artur Wojdat, Iowa
1650-yard freestyle .... Artur Wojdat, Iowa
100-yard backstroke ..... Jeff Rouse, Stanford
200-yard backstroke ..... Martin Zubero, Florida
100-yard breaststroke ... Andrea Cecchi, UCLA
200-yard breaststroke ... Mike Barrowman, Michigan
100-yard butterfly .... Anthony Nesty, Florida
200-yard butterfly .... Melvin Stewart, Tennessee
200-yard individual medley .... Martin Zubero, Florida
400-yard individual medley .... David Wharton, Southern Cal
1-meter diving .... Dean Panaro, Miami (FL)
3-meter diving .... Jason Rhodes, Texas

WOMEN

50-yard freestyle .... Leigh Ann Fetter, Texas
100-yard freestyle .... Leigh Ann Fetter, Texas
200-yard freestyle .... Nicole Haislett, Florida
500-yard freestyle .... Janet Evans, Stanford
1650-yard freestyle .... Janet Evans, Stanford
100-yard backstroke ..... Jodi Wilson, Texas
200-yard backstroke ..... Beth Barr, Texas
100-yard breaststroke ... Lori Heisick, Stanford
200-yard breaststroke ... Dorsey Tierney, Texas
100-yard butterfly .... Cris Ahmann-Leighton, Arizona
200-yard butterfly .... Summer Sanders, Stanford
200-yard individual medley .... Summer Sanders, Stanford
400-yard individual medley .... Summer Sanders, Stanford
1-meter diving .... Krista Wilson, Southern Meth
3-meter diving .... Julie Farrell-Ovenhouse, Michigan St

Winter 1990–1991 (*Cont.*)
Indoor Track

MEN		WOMEN	
55-meter dash	Augustine Olabia, Washington St	55-meter dash	Carlette Guidry, Texas
55-meter hurdles	Tony Li, Washington St	55-meter hurdles	Mary Cobb, Louisiana St
200-meter dash	Frank Fredericks, Brigham Young	200-meter dash	Carlette Guidry, Texas
400-meter dash	Gabriel Luke, Rice	400-meter dash	Maicel Malone, Arizona St
800-meter run	George Kirsh, Mississippi	800-meter run	Edith Nakiyingi, Iowa St
Mile run	Robert Kennedy, Indiana	Mile run	Jennifer Lanctot, Boston U
3000-meter run	Reuben Reina, Arkansas	3000-meter run	Patty Weigand, Tennessee
5000-meter run	Jonah Koech, Iowa St	5000-meter run	Sonia O'Sullivan, Villanova
High jump	Tony Barton, George Mason	High jump	Tanya Hughes, Arizona
Long jump	Alan Turner, Indiana	Long jump	Diane Guthrie, Florida
Triple jump	Eugene Greene, Boise St	Triple jump	Leah Kirklin, Florida
Shot put	Eric Bergreen, UCLA	Shot put	Tracie Millett, UCLA
Pole vault	Istvan Bagyula, George Mason		
35-pound weight throw	Christophe Epalle, Southern Meth		

Wrestling

118 lb	Jeff Prescott, Penn St	150 lb	Matt Demaray, Wisconsin
126 lb	Jason Kelber, Nebraska	158 lb	Pat Smith, Oklahoma St
134 lb	Tom Brands, Iowa	167 lb	Mark Reiland, Iowa
142 lb	Scott Collins, W Virginia	177 lb	Marty Morgan, Minnesota

Spring 1991
Golf

Men: Warren Schutte, NV-Las Vegas
Women: Annika Sorenstam, Arizona

Tennis

MEN	WOMEN
Singles..... Jared Palmer, Stanford	Singles .....Sandra Birch, Stanford
Doubles ... Matt Lucena and Bent Pedersen, California	Doubles ....Jillian Alexander and Nicole Arendt, Florida

Outdoor Track

MEN		WOMEN	
100-meter dash	Frank Fredericks, Brigham Young	100-meter dash	Carlette Guidry, Texas
200-meter dash	Frank Fredericks, Brigham Young	200-meter dash	Carlette Guidry, Texas
400-meter dash	Gabriel Luke, Rice	400-meter dash	Ximena Restropo, Nebraska
800-meter run	George Kersh, Mississippi	800-meter run	Nekita Beasley, Florida
1,500-meter run	Samuel Kibiri, Washington St	1,500-meter run	Darcy Oreola, Cal St-Northridge
3,000-meter steeplechase	Mark Croghan, Ohio St	3,000-meter run	Sonia O'Sullivan, Villanova
5,000-meter run	Shannon Butler, Montana St	5,000-meter run	Laurie Gomez, N Carolina St
10,000-meter run	Terry Thornton, Louisiana St	10,000-meter run	Jamie Park, Arkansas
110-meter hurdles	Greg Williams, Texas A&M	100-meter hurdles	Dawn Bowles, Louisiana St
400-meter hurdles	Samuel Matete, Auburn	400-meter hurdles	Janeene Vickers, UCLA
High jump	Darrin Plab, Southern Illinois	High jump	Tanya Hughes, Arizona
Pole vault	Istvan Bagyula, George Mason	Long jump	Diane Guthrie, George Mason
Long jump	George Ogbeide, Washington St	Triple jump	Donna Crumety, St Joseph's (PA)
Triple jump	Brian Wellman, Arkansas	Shot put	Eileen Vanisi, Texas
Shot put	Simon Williams, Louisiana St	Discus throw	Anna Mosdell, Brigham Young
Discus throw	Kamy Kashmiri, Nevada	Javelin throw	Paula Berry, Oregon
Hammer throw	Christophe Epalle, Southern Meth	Heptathlon	Sharon Jaklofsky, Louisiana St
Javelin throw	Patrik Boden, Texas		
Decathlon	Aric Long, Tennessee		

CHAMPIONSHIP RESULTS

Baseball

Men

DIVISION I

Year	Champion	Coach	Score	Runner-Up	Most Outstanding Player
1947	California*	Clint Evans	8-7	Yale	No award
1948	Southern Cal	Sam Barry	9-2	Yale	No award
1949	Texas*	Bibb Falk	10-3	Wake Forest	Charles Teague, Wake Forest, 2B
1950	Texas	Bibb Falk	3-0	Washington St	Ray VanCleef, Rutgers, CF
1951	Oklahoma*	Jack Baer	3-2	Tennnessee	Sidney Hatfield, Tennessee, P-1B
1952	Holy Cross	Jack Barry	8-4	Missouri	James O'Neill, Holy Cross, P
1953	Michigan	Ray Fisher	7-5	Texas	J. L. Smith, Texas, P
1954	Missouri	John "Hi" Simmons	4-1	Rollins	Tom Yewcic, Michigan St, C
1955	Wake Forest	Taylor Sanford	7-6	Western Michigan	Tom Borland, Oklahoma St, P
1956	MInnesota	Dick Siebert	12-1	Arizona	Jerry Thomas, Minnesota, P
1957	California*	George Wolfman	1-0	Penn St	Cal Emery, Penn St, P-1B
1958	Southern Cal	Rod Dedeaux	8-7†	Missouri	Bill Thom, Southern Cal, P
1959	Oklahoma St	Toby Greene	5-3	Arizona	Jim Dobson, Oklahoma St, 3B
1960	Minnesota	Dick Siebert	2-1‡	Southern Cal	John Erickson, Minnesota, 2B
1961	Southern Cal*	Rod Dedeaux	1-0	Oklahoma St	Littleton Fowler, Oklahoma St, P
1962	Michigan	Don Lund	5-4	Santa Clara	Bob Garibaldi, Santa Clara, P
1963	Southern Cal	Rod Dedeaux	5-2	Arizona	Bud Hollowell, Southern Cal, C
1964	Minnesota	Dick Siebert	5-1	Missouri	Joe Ferris, Maine, P
1965	Arizona St	Bobby Winkles	2-1#	Ohio St	Sal Bando, Arizona St, 3B
1966	Ohio St	Marty Karow	8-2	Oklahoma St	Steve Arlin, Ohio St, P
1967	Arizona St	Bobby Winkles	11-2	Houston	Ron Davini, Arizona St, C
1968	Southern Cal*	Rod Dedeaux	4-3	Southern Illinois	Bill Seinsoth, Southern Cal, 1B
1969	Arizona St	Bobby Winkles	10-1	Tulsa	John Dolinsek, Arizona St, LF
1970	Southern Cal	Rod Dedeaux	2-1	Florida St	Gene Ammann, Florida St, P
1971	Southern Cal	Rod Dedeaux	7-2	Southern Illinois	Jerry Tabb, Tulsa, 1B
1972	Southern Cal	Rod Dedeaux	1-0	Arizona St	Russ McQueen, Southern Cal, P
1973	Southern Cal*	Rod Dedeaux	4-3	Arizona St	Dave Winfield, Minnesota, P-OF
1974	Southern Cal	Rod Dedeaux	7-3	Miami (FL)	George Milke, Southern Cal, P
1975	Texas	Cliff Gustafson	5-1	S Carolina	Mickey Reichenbach, Texas, 1B
1976	Arizona	Jerry Kindall	7-1	Eastern Michigan	Steve Powers, Arizona, P-DH
1977	Arizona St	Jim Brock	2-1	S Carolina	Bob Horner, Arizona St, 3B
1978	Southern Cal*	Rod Dedeaux	10-3	Arizona St	Rod Boxberger, Southern Cal, P
1979	Cal St-Fullerton	Augie Garrido	2-1	Arkansas	Tony Hudson, Cal St-Fullerton, P
1980	Arizona	Jerry Kindall	5-3	Hawaii	Terry Francona, Arizona, LF
1981	Arizona St	Jim Brock	7-4	Oklahoma St	Stan Holmes, Arizona St, LF
1982	Miami (FL)*	Ron Fraser	9-3	Wichita St	Dan Smith, Miami (FL), P
1983	Texas*	Cliff Gustafson	4-3	Alabama	Calvin Schiraldi, Texas, P
1984	Cal St-Fullerton	Augie Garrido	3-1	Texas	John Fishel, Cal St-Fullerton, LF
1985	Miami (FL)	Ron Fraser	10-6	Texas	Greg Ellena, Miami (FL), DH
1986	Arizona	Jerry Kindall	10-2	Florida St	Mike Senne, Arizona, LF
1987	Stanford	Mark Marquess	9-5	Oklahoma St	Paul Carey, Stanford, RF
1988	Stanford	Mark Marquess	9-4	Arizona St	Lee Plemel, Stanford, P
1989	Wichita St	Gene Stephenson	5-3	Texas	Greg Brummett, Wichita St, P
1990	Georgia	Steve Webber	2-1	Oklahoma St	Mike Rebhan, Georgia, P
1991	Louisiana St	Skip Bertman	6-3	Wichita St	Gary Hymel, Louisiana St, C

*Undefeated teams in College World Series play. †12 innings. ‡10 innings. #15 innings.

DIVISION II

Year	Champion	Year	Champion	Year	Champion	Year	Champion
1968	Chapman*	1974	UC-Irvine	1980	Cal Poly-Pomona*	1986	Troy St
1969	Illinois St*	1975	Florida Southern	1981	Florida Southern*	1987	Troy St*
1970	Cal St-Northridge	1976	Cal Poly-Pomona	1982	UC-Riverside*	1988	Florida Southern*
1971	Florida Southern	1977	UC-Riverside	1983	Cal Poly-Pomona*	1989	Cal Poly-SLO
1972	Florida Southern	1978	Florida Southern	1984	Cal St-Northridge	1990	Jacksonville St
1973	UC-Irvine*	1979	Valdosta St	1985	Florida Southern*	1991	Jacksonville St

*Undefeated teams.

Men (*Cont.*)

DIVISION III

Year	Champion	Year	Champion	Year	Champion
1976	Cal St-Stanislaus	1982	Eastern Connecticut St	1987	Montclair St
1977	Cal St-Stanislaus	1983	Marietta	1988	Ithaca
1978	Glassboro St	1984	Ramapo	1989	NC Wesleyan
1979	Glassboro St	1985	WI-Oshkosh	1990	Eastern Connecticut St
1980	Ithaca	1986	Marietta	1991	Southern Maine
1981	Marietta				

Cross Country

Men

DIVISION I

Year	Champion	Coach	Pts	Runner-Up	Pts	Individual Champion	Time
1938	Indiana	Earle Hayes	51	Notre Dame	61	Greg Rice, Notre Dame	20:12.9
1939	Michigan St	Lauren Brown	54	Wisconsin	57	Walter Mehl, Wisconsin	20:30.9
1940	Indiana	Earle Hayes	65	Eastern Michigan	68	Gilbert Dodds, Ashland	20:30.2
1941	Rhode Island	Fred Tootell	83	Penn St	110	Fred Wilt, Indiana	20:30.1
1942	Indiana	Earle Hayes	57			Oliver Hunter, Notre Dame	20:18.0
	Penn St	Charles Werner	57				
1943	No meet						
1944	Drake	Bill Easton	25	Notre Dame	64	Fred Feiler, Drake	21:04.2
1945	Drake	Bill Easton	50	Notre Dame	65	Fred Feiler, Drake	21:14.2
1946	Drake	Bill Easton	42	NYU	98	Quentin Brelsford, Ohio Wesleyan	20:22.9
1947	Penn St	Charles Werner	60	Syracuse	72	Jack Milne, North Carolina	20:41.1
1948	Michigan St	Karl Schlademan	41	Wisconsin	69	Robert Black, Rhode Island	19:52.3
1949	Michigan St	Karl Schlademan	59	Syracuse	81	Robert Black, Rhode Island	20:25.7
1950	Penn St	Charles Werner	53	Michigan St	55	Herb Semper Jr, Kansas	20:31.7
1951	Syracuse	Robert Grieve	80	Kansas	118	Herb Semper Jr, Kansas	20:09.5
1952	Michigan St	Karl Schlademan	65	Indiana	68	Charles Capozzoli, Georgetown	19:36.7
1953	Kansas	Bill Easton	70	Indiana	82	Wes Santee, Kansas	19:43.5
1954	Oklahoma St	Ralph Higgins	61	Syracuse	118	Allen Frame, Kansas	19:54.2
1955	Michigan St	Karl Schlademan	46	Kansas	68	Charles Jones, Iowa	19:57.4
1956	Michigan St	Karl Schlademan	28	Kansas	88	Walter McNew, Texas	19:55.7
1957	Notre Dame	Alex Wilson	121	Michigan St	127	Max Truex, Southern Cal	19:12.3
1958	Michigan St	Francis Dittrich	79	Western Michigan	104	Crawford Kennedy, Michigan St	20:07.1
1959	Michigan St	Francis Dittrich	44	Houston	120	Al Lawrence, Houston	20:35.7
1960	Houston	John Morriss	54	Michigan St	80	Al Lawrence, Houston	19:28.2
1961	Oregon St	Sam Bell	68	San Jose St	82	Dale Story, Oregon St	19:46.6
1962	San Jose St	Dean Miller	58	Villanova	69	Tom O'Hara, Loyola (IL)	19:20.3
1963	San Jose St	Dean Miller	53	Oregon	68	Victor Zwolak, Villanova	19:35.0
1964	Western Michigan	George Dales	86	Oregon	116	Elmore Banton, Ohio	20:07.5
1965	Western Michigan	George Dales	81	Northwestern	114	John Lawson, Kansas	29:24.0
1966	Villanova	James Elliott	79	Kansas St	155	Gerry Lindgren, Washington St	29:01.4
1967	Villanova	James Elliott	91	Air Force	96	Gerry Lindgren, Washington St	30:45.6
1968	Villanova	James Elliott	78	Stanford	100	Michael Ryan, Air Force	29:16.8
1969	UTEP	Wayne Vandenburg	74	Villanova	88	Gerry Lindgren, Washington St	28:59.2
1970	Villanova	James Elliott	85	Oregon	86	Steve Prefontaine, Oregon	28:00.2
1971	Oregon	Bill Dellinger	83	Washington St	122	Steve Prefontaine, Oregon	29:14.0
1972	Tennessee	Stan Huntsman	134	E Tennessee St	148	Neil Cusack, E Tennessee St	28:23.0
1973	Oregon	Bill Dellinger	89	UTEP	157	Steve Prefontaine, Oregon	28:14.0

Men (*Cont.*)

Year	Champion	Coach	Pts	Runner-Up	Pts	Individual Champion	Time
1974	Oregon	Bill Dellinger	77	Western Kentucky	110	Nick Rose, Western Kentucky	29:22.0
1975	UTEP	Ted Banks	88	Washington St	92	Craig Virgin, Illinois	28:23.3
1976	UTEP	Ted Banks	62	Oregon	117	Henry Rono, Washington St	28:06.6
1977	Oregon	Bill Dellinger	100	UTEP	105	Henry Rono, Washington St	28:33.5
1978	UTEP	Ted Banks	56	Oregon	72	Alberto Salazar, Oregon	29:29.7
1979	UTEP	Ted Banks	86	Oregon	93	Henry Rono, Washington St	28:19.6
1980	UTEP	Ted Banks	58	Arkansas	152	Suleiman Nyambui, UTEP	29:04.0
1981	UTEP	Ted Banks	17	Providence	109	Mathews Motshwarateu, UTEP	28:45.6
1982	Wisconsin	Dan McClimon	59	Providence	138	Mark Scrutton, Colorado	30:12.6
1983	Vacated			Wisconsin	164	Zakarie Barie, UTEP	29:20.0
1984	Arkansas	John McDonnell	101	Arizona	111	Ed Eyestone, Brigham Young	29:28.8
1985	Wisconsin	Martin Smith	67	Arkansas	104	Timothy Hacker, Wisconsin	29:17.88
1986	Arkansas	John McDonnell	69	Dartmouth	141	Aaron Ramirez, Arizona	30:27.53
1987	Arkansas	John McDonnell	87	Dartmouth	119	Joe Falcon, Arkansas	29:14.97
1988	Wisconsin	Martin Smith	105	Northern Arizona	160	Robert Kennedy, Indiana	29:20.0
1989	Iowa St	Bill Bergan	54	Oregon	72	John Nuttall, Iowa St	29:30.55
1990	Arkansas	John McDonnell	68	Iowa St	96	Jonah Koech, Iowa St	29:05.0

DIVISION II

Year	Champion	Year	Champion	Year	Champion
1958	Northern Illinois	1970	Eastern Michigan	1981	Millersville
1959	S Dakota St	1971	Cal St-Fullerton	1982	Eastern Washington
1960	Central St (OH)	1972	N Dakota St	1983	Cal Poly-Pomona
1961	Southern Illinois	1973	S Dakota St	1984	SE Missouri St
1962	Central St (OH)	1974	SW Missouri St	1985	S Dakota St
1963	Emporia St	1975	UC-Irvine	1986	Edinboro
1964	Kentucky St	1976	UC-Irvine	1987	Edinboro
1965	San Diego St	1977	Eastern Illinois	1988	Edinboro Mankato St
1966	San Diego St	1978	Cal Poly-SLO	1989	S Dakota St
1967	San Diego St	1979	Cal Poly-SLO	1990	Edinboro
1968	Eastern Illinois	1980	Humboldt St		
1969	Eastern Illinois				

DIVISION III

Year	Champion	Year	Champion
1973	Ashland	1982	North Central
1974	Mount Union	1983	Brandeis
1975	North Central	1984	St Thomas (MN)
1976	North Central	1985	Luther
1977	Occidental	1986	St Thomas (MN)
1978	North Central	1987	North Central
1979	North Central	1988	WI-Oshkosh
1980	Carleton	1989	WI-Oshkosh
1981	North Central	1990	WI-Oshkosh

At Long Last, Victory

The University of Utah won this year's Western Athletic Conference softball championship, but it needed to play runner-up Creighton University for 12 hours before it could claim the crown. In the final match-up of the double elimination tournament, which began at 6 p.m. on May 11, the Lady Jays beat the Utes 1–0 in a 31-inning game to give both schools one loss. The deciding game started shortly thereafter—at 12:45 a.m. on May 12—and Utah was crowned champ after it scored a run on a throwing error at 6:08 a.m. to clinch a 4–3, 25-inning victory. Afterward, Creighton pitcher Kelly Brookhart, who worked 51 1/3 innings for the Blue Jays, said, "I need ice."

Women

DIVISION I

Year	Champion	Coach	Pts	Runner-Up	Pts	Individual Champion	Time
1981	Virginia	John Vasvary	36	Oregon	83	Betty Springs, N Carolina St	16:19.0
1982	Virginia	Martin Smith	48	Stanford	91	Lesley Welch, Virginia	16:39.7
1983	Oregon	Tom Heinonen	95	Stanford	98	Betty Springs, N Carolina St	16:30.7
1984	Wisconsin	Peter Tegen	63	Stanford	89	Cathy Branta, Wisconsin	16:15.6
1985	Wisconsin	Peter Tegen	58	Iowa St	98	Suzie Tuffey, N Carolina St	16:22.53
1986	Texas	Terry Crawford	62	Wisconsin	64	Angela Chalmers, Northern Arizona	16:55.49
1987	Oregon	Tom Heinonen	97	N Carolina St	99	Kimberly Betz, Indiana	16:10.85
1988	Kentucky	Don Weber	75	Oregon	128	Michelle Dekkers, Indiana	16:30.0
1989	Villanova	Marty Stern	99	Kentucky	168	Vicki Huber, Villanova	15:59.86
1990	Villanova	Marty Stern	82	Providence	172	Sonia O'Sullivan, Villanova	16:06.0

DIVISION II

Year	Champion
1981	S Dakota St
1982	Cal Poly-SLO
1983	Cal Poly-SLO
1984	Cal Poly-SLO
1985	Cal Poly-SLO
1986	Cal Poly-SLO
1987	Cal Poly-SLO
1988	Cal Poly-SLO
1989	Cal Poly-SLO
1990	Cal Poly-SLO

DIVISION III

Year	Champion
1981	Central (IA)
1982	St Thomas (MN)
1983	WI-La Crosse
1984	St Thomas (MN)
1985	Franklin & Marshall
1986	St Thomas (MN)
1987	St Thomas (MN)
	WI-Oshkosh
1988	WI-Oshkosh
1989	Cortland St
1990	Cortland St

Fencing

Men

TEAM CHAMPIONS

Year	Champion	Coach	Pts	Runner-Up	Pts
1941	Northwestern	Henry Zettleman	28½	Illinois	27
1942	Ohio St	Frank Riebel	34	St John's (NY)	33½
1943-1946	No tournament				
1947	NYU	Martinez Castello	72	Chicago	50½
1948	CCNY	James Montague	30	Navy	28
1949	Army	Servando Velarde	63		
	Rutgers	Donald Cetrulo	63		
1950	Navy	Joseph Fiems	67½	NYU	66½
				Rutgers	66½
1951	Columbia	Servando Velarde	69	Pennsylvania	64
1952	Columbia	Servando Velarde	71	NYU	69
1953	Pennsylvania	Lajos Csiszar	94	Navy	86
1954	Columbia	Irving DeKoff	61		
	NYU	Hugo Castello	61		
1955	Columbia	Irving DeKoff	62	Cornell	57
1956	Illinois	Maxwell Garret	90	Columbia	88
1957	NYU	Hugo Castello	65	Columbia	64
1958	Illinois	Maxwell Garret	47	Columbia	43
1959	Navy	Andre Deladrier	72	NYU	65
1960	NYU	Hugo Castello	65	Navy	57
1961	NYU	Hugo Castello	79	Princeton	68
1962	Navy	Andre Deladrier	76	NYU	74
1963	Columbia	Irving DeKoff	55	Navy	50
1964	Princeton	Stan Sieja	81	NYU	79
1965	Columbia	Irving DeKoff	76	NYU	74
1966	NYU	Hugo Castello	5-0	Army	5-2
1967	NYU	Hugo Castello	72	Pennsylvania	64
1968	Columbia	Louis Bankuti	92	NYU	87
1969	Pennsylvania	Lajos Csiszar	54	Harvard	43

TEAM CHAMPIONS (*Cont.*)

Year	Champion	Coach	Pts	Runner-Up	Pts
1970	NYU	Hugo Castello	71	Columbia	63
1971	NYU	Hugo Castello	68		
	Columbia	Louis Bankuti	68		
1972	Detroit	Richard Perry	73	NYU	70
1973	NYU	Hugo Castello	76	Pennsylvania	71
1974	NYU	Hugo Castello	92	Wayne St (MI)	87
1975	Wayne St (MI)	Istvan Danosi	89	Cornell	83
1976	NYU	Herbert Cohen	79	Wayne St (MI)	77
1977	Notre Dame	Michael DeCicco	114*	NYU	114
1978	Notre Dame	Michael DeCicco	121	Pennsylvania	110
1979	Wayne St (MI)	Istvan Danosi	119	Notre Dame	108
1980	Wayne St (MI)	Istvan Danosi	111	Pennsylvania	106
				MIT	106
1981	Pennsylvania	Dave Micahnik	113	Wayne St (MI)	111
1982	Wayne St (MI)	Istvan Danosi	85	Clemson	77
1983	Wayne St (MI)	Aladar Kogler	86	Notre Dame	80
1984	Wayne St (MI)	Gil Pezza	69	Penn St	50
1985	Wayne St (MI)	Gil Pezza	141	Notre Dame	140
1986	Notre Dame	Michael DeCicco	151	Columbia	141
1987	Columbia	George Kolombatovich	86	Pennsylvania	78
1988	Columbia	George Kolombatovich Aladar Kogler	90	Notre Dame	83
1989	Columbia	George Kolombatovich Aladar Kogler	88	Penn St	85
1990	Penn St	Emmanuil Kaidanov	36	Columbia-Barnard	35
1991	Penn St	Emmanuil Kaidanov	4700	Columbia/Columbia-Barnard	4200

*Tie broken by a fence-off.
Note: Beginning in 1990, men's and women's combined teams competed for the national championship.

INDIVIDUAL CHAMPIONS

	Foil	Sabre	Épée
1941	Edward McNamara, Northwestern	William Meyer, Dartmouth	G. H. Boland, Illinois
1942	Byron Kreiger, Wayne St (MI)	Andre Deladrier, St John's (NY)	Ben Burtt, Ohio St
1947	Abraham Balk, NYU	Oscar Parsons, Temple	Abraham Balk, NYU
1948	Albert Axelrod, CCNY	James Day, Navy	William Bryan, Navy
1949	Ralph Tedeschi, Rutgers	Alex Treves, Rutgers	Richard C. Bowman, Army
1950	Robert Nielsen, Columbia	Alex Treves, Rutgers	Thomas Stuart, Navy
1951	Robert Nielsen, Columbia	Chamberless Johnston, Princeton	Daniel Chafetz, Columbia
1952	Harold Goldsmith, CCNY	Frank Zimolzak, Navy	James Wallner, NYU
1953	Ed Nober, Brooklyn	Robert Parmacek, Pennsylvania	Jack Tori, Pennsylvania
1954	Robert Goldman, Pennsylvania	Steve Sobel, Columbia	Henry Kolowrat, Princeton
1955	Herman Velasco, Illinois	Barry Pariser, Columbia	Donald Tadrawski, Notre Dame
1956	Ralph DeMarco, Columbia	Gerald Kaufman, Columbia	Kinmont Hoitsma, Princeton
1957	Bruce Davis, Wayne St (MI)	Bernie Balaban, NYU	James Margolis, Columbia
1958	Bruce Davis, Wayne St (MI)	Art Schankin, Illinois	Roland Wommack, Navy
1959	Joe Paletta, Navy	Al Morales, Navy	Roland Wommack, Navy
1960	Gene Glazer, NYU	Mike Desaro, NYU	Gil Eisner, NYU
1961	Herbert Cohen, NYU	Israel Colon, NYU	Jerry Halpern, NYU
1962	Herbert Cohen, NYU	Barton Nisonson, Columbia	Thane Hawkins, Navy
1963	Jay Lustig, Columbia	Bela Szentivanyi, Wayne St (MI)	Larry Crum, Navy
1964	Bill Hicks, Princeton	Craig Bell, Illinois	Paul Pesthy, Rutgers
1965	Joe Nalven, Columbia	Howard Goodman, NYU	Paul Pesthy, Rutgers
1966	Al Davis, NYU	Paul Apostol, NYU	Bernhardt Hermann, Iowa
1967	Mike Gaylor, NYU	Todd Makler, Pennsylvania	George Masin, NYU
1968	Gerard Esponda, San Francisco	Todd Makler, Pennsylvania	Don Sieja, Cornell
1969	Anthony Kestler, Columbia	Norman Braslow, Pennsylvania	James Wetzler, Pennsylvania
1970	Walter Krause, NYU	Bruce Soriano, Columbia	John Nadas, Case Reserve
1971	Tyrone Simmons, Detroit	Bruce Soriano, Columbia	George Szunyogh, NYU

INDIVIDUAL CHAMPIONS (*Cont.*)

	Foil	Sabre	Épée
1972	Tyrone Simmons, Detroit	Bruce Soriano, Columbia	Ernesto Fernandez, Pennsylvania
1973	Brooke Makler, Pennsylvania	Peter Westbrock, NYU	Risto Hurme, NYU
1974	Greg Benko, Wayne St (MI)	Steve Danosi, Wayne St (MI)	Risto Hurme, NYU
1975	Greg Benko, Wayne St (MI)	Yuri Rabinovich, Wayne St (MI)	Risto Hurme, NYU
1976	Greg Benko, Wayne St (MI)	Brian Smith, Columbia	Randy Eggleton, Pennsylvania
1977	Pat Gerard, Notre Dame	Mike Sullivan, Notre Dame	Hans Wieselgren, NYU
1978	Ernest Simon, Wayne St (MI)	Mike Sullivan, Notre Dame	Bjorne Vaggo, Notre Dame
1979	Andrew Bonk, Notre Dame	Yuri Rabinovich, Wayne St (MI)	Carlos Songini, Cleveland St
1980	Ernest Simon, Wayne St (MI)	Paul Friedberg, Pennsylvania	Gil Pezza, Wayne St (MI)
1981	Ernest Simon, Wayne St (MI)	Paul Friedberg, Pennsylvania	Gil Pezza, Wayne St (MI)
1982	Alexander Flom, George Mason	Neil Hick, Wayne St (MI)	Peter Schifrin, San Jose St
1983	Demetrios Valsamis, NYU	John Friedberg, North Carolina	Ola Harstrom, Notre Dame
1984	Charles Higgs-Coulthard, Notre Dame	Michael Lofton, NYU	Ettore Bianchi, Wayne St (MI)
1985	Stephan Chauvel, Wayne St (MI)	Michael Lofton, NYU	Ettore Bianchi, Wayne St (MI)
1986	Adam Feldman, Penn St	Michael Lofton, NYU	Chris O'Loughlin, Pennsylvania
1987	William Mindel, Columbia	Michael Lofton, NYU	James O'Neill, Harvard
1988	Marc Kent, Columbia	Robert Cottingham, Columbia	Jon Normile, Columbia
1989	Edward Mufel, Penn St	Peter Cox, Penn St	Jon Normile, Columbia
1990	Nick Bravin, Stanford	David Mandell, Columbia	Jubba Beshin, Notre Dame
1991	Ben Atkins, Columbia	Vitali Nazlimov, Penn St	Marc Oshima, Columbia

Women

Year	Champion	Coach	Rec	Runner-Up	Rec
1982	Wayne St (MI)	Istvan Danosi	7-0	San Jose St	6-1
1983	Penn St	Beth Alphin	5-0	Wayne St (MI)	3-2
1984	Yale	Henry Harutunian	3-0	Penn St	2-1
1985	Yale	Henry Harutunian	3-0	Pennsylvania	2-1
1986	Pennsylvania	David Micahnik	3-0	Notre Dame	2-1
1987	Notre Dame	Yves Auriol	3-0	Temple	2-1
1988	Wayne St (MI)	Gil Pezza	3-0	Notre Dame	2-1
1989	Wayne St (MI)	Gil Pezza	3-0	Columbia-Barnard	2-1

Note: Beginning in 1990, men's and women's combined teams competed for the national championship.

Field Hockey

Women

DIVISION I

Year	Champion	Coach	Score	Runner-Up
1981	Connecticut	Diane Wright	4-1	Massachusetts
1982	Old Dominion	Beth Anders	3-2	Connecticut
1983	Old Dominion	Beth Anders	3-1 (3 OT)	Connecticut
1984	Old Dominion	Beth Anders	5-1	Iowa
1985	Connecticut	Diane Wright	3-2	Old Dominion
1986	Iowa	Judith Davidson	2-1 (2 OT)	New Hampshire
1987	Maryland	Sue Tyler	2-1 (OT)	N Carolina
1988	Old Dominion	Beth Anders	2-1	Iowa
1989	N Carolina	Karen Shelton	2-1 (3 OT)*	Old Dominion
1990	Old Dominion	Beth Anders	5-0	N Carolina

*Penalty strokes.

DIVISION II (Discontinued)

Year	Champion	Coach	Score	Runner-Up
1981	Pfeiffer	Ellen Briggs	5-3	Bentley
1982	Lock Haven	Sharon Taylor	4-1	Bloomsburg
1983	Bloomsburg	Jan Hutchinson	1-0	Lock Haven

Field Hockey (*Cont.*)

DIVISION III

Year	Champion	Year	Champion
1981	Trenton St	1986	Salisbury St
1982	Ithaca	1987	Bloomsburg
1983	Trenton St	1988	Trenton St
1984	Bloomsburg	1989	Lock Haven
1985	Trenton St	1990	Trenton St

Golf

Men

DIVISION I

Results, 1897-1938

Year	Champion	Site	Individual Champion
1897	Yale	Ardsley Casino	Louis Bayard Jr, Princeton
1898	Harvard (spring)		John Reid Jr, Yale
1898	Yale (fall)		James Curtis, Harvard
1899	Harvard		Percy Pyne, Princeton
1900	No tournament		
1901	Harvard	Atlantic City	H. Lindsley, Harvard
1902	Yale (spring)	Garden City	Charles Hitchcock Jr, Yale
1902	Harvard (fall)	Morris County	Chandler Egan, Harvard
1903	Harvard	Garden City	F. O. Reinhart, Princeton
1904	Harvard	Myopia	A. L. White, Harvard
1905	Yale	Garden City	Robert Abbott, Yale
1906	Yale	Garden City	W. E. Clow Jr, Yale
1907	Yale	Nassau	Ellis Knowles, Yale
1908	Yale	Brae Burn	H. H. Wilder, Harvard
1909	Yale	Apawamis	Albert Seckel, Princeton
1910	Yale	Essex County	Robert Hunter, Yale
1911	Yale	Baltusrol	George Stanley, Yale
1912	Yale	Ekwanok	F. C. Davison, Harvard
1913	Yale	Huntingdon Valley	Nathaniel Wheeler, Yale
1914	Princeton	Garden City	Edward Allis, Harvard
1915	Yale	Greenwich	Francis Blossom, Yale
1916	Princeton	Oakmont	J. W. Hubbell, Harvard
1917-18	No tournament		
1919	Princeton	Merion	A. L. Walker Jr, Columbia
1920	Princeton	Nassau	Jess Sweetster, Yale
1921	Dartmouth	Greenwich	Simpson Dean, Princeton
1922	Princeton	Garden City	Pollack Boyd, Dartmouth
1923	Princeton	Siwanoy	Dexter Cummings, Yale
1924	Yale	Greenwich	Dexter Cummings, Yale
1925	Yale	Montclair	Fred Lamprecht, Tulane
1926	Yale	Merion	Fred Lamprecht, Tulane
1927	Princeton	Garden City	Watts Gunn, Georgia Tech
1928	Princeton	Apawamis	Maurice McCarthy, Georgetown
1929	Princeton	Hollywood	Tom Aycock, Yale
1930	Princeton	Oakmont	G. T. Dunlap Jr, Princeton
1931	Yale	Olympia Fields	G. T. Dunlap Jr, Princeton
1932	Yale	Hot Springs	J. W.Fischer, Michigan
1933	Yale	Buffalo	Walter Emery, Oklahoma
1934	Michigan	Cleveland	Charles Yates, Georgia Tech
1935	Michigan	Congressional	Ed White, Texas
1936	Yale	North Shore	Charles Kocsis, Michigan
1937	Princeton	Oakmont	Fred Haas Jr, Louisiana St
1938	Stanford	Louisville	John Burke, Georgetown

Men (Cont.)
Results, 1939-1991

Year	Champion	Coach	Score	Runner-Up	Score	Host or Site	Individual Champion
1939	Stanford	Eddie Twiggs	612	Northwestern	614	Wakonda	Vincent D'Antoni, Tulane
				Princeton	614		
1940	Princeton	Walter Bourne	601			Ekwanok	Dixon Brooke, Virginia
	Louisiana St	Mike Donahue	601				
1941	Stanford	Eddie Twiggs	580	Louisiana St	599	Ohio St	Earl Stewart, Louisiana St
1942	Louisiana St	Mike Donahue	590			Notre Dame	Frank Tatum Jr
	Stanford	Eddie Twiggs	590				
1943	Yale	William Neale Jr	614	Michigan	618	Olympia Fields	Wallace Ulrich, Carleton
1944	Notre Dame	George Holderith	311	Minnesota	312	Inverness	Louis Lick, Minnesota
1945	Ohio St	Robert Kepler	602	Northwestern	621	Ohio St	John Lorms, Ohio St
1946	Stanford	Eddie Twiggs	619	Michigan	624	Princeton	George Hamer, Georgia
1947	Louisiana St	T. P. Heard	606	Duke	614	Michigan	Dave Barclay, Michigan
1948	San Jose St	Wilbur Hubbard	579	Louisiana St	588	Stanford	Bob Harris, San Jose St
1949	N Texas	Fred Cobb	590	Purdue	600	Iowa St	Harvie Ward, N Carolina
				Texas	600		
1950	N Texas	Fred Cobb	573	Purdue	577	New Mexico	Fred Wampler, Purdue
1951	N Texas	Fred Cobb	588	Ohio St	589	Ohio St	Tom Nieporte, Ohio St
1952	N Texas	Fred Cobb	587	Michigan	593	Purdue	Jim Vickers, Oklahoma
1953	Stanford	Charles Finger	578	N Carolina	580	Broadmoor	Earl Moeller, Oklahoma St
1954	Southern Meth	Graham Ross	572	N Texas	573	Houston, Rice	Hillman Robbins, Memphis St
1955	Louisiana St	Mike Barbato	574	N Texas	583	Tennessee	Joe Campbell, Purdue
1956	Houston	Dave Williams	601	N Texas	602	Ohio St	Rick Jones, Ohio St
				Purdue	602		
1957	Houston	Dave Williams	602	Stanford	603	Broadmoor	Rex Baxter Jr, Houston
1958	Houston	Dave Williams	570	Oklahoma St	582	Williams	Phil Rodgers, Houston
1959	Houston	Dave Williams	561	Purdue	571	Oregon	Dick Crawford, Houston
1960	Houston	Dave Williams	603	Purdue	607	Broadmoor	Dick Crawford, Houston
				Oklahoma St	607		
1961	Purdue	Sam Voinoff	584	Arizona St	595	Lafayette	Jack Nicklaus, Ohio St
1962	Houston	Dave Williams	588	Oklahoma St	598	Duke	Kermit Zarley, Houston
1963	Oklahoma St	Labron Harris	581	Houston	582	Wichita St	R. H. Sikes, Arkansas
1964	Houston	Dave Williams	580	Oklahoma St	587	Broadmoor	Terry Small, San Jose St
1965	Houston	Dave Williams	577	Cal St-LA	587	Tennessee	Marty Fleckman, Houston
1966	Houston	Dave Williams	582	San Jose St	586	Stanford	Bob Murphy, Florida
1967	Houston	Dave Williams	585	Florida	588	Shawnee, PA	Hale Irwin, Colorado
1968	Florida	Buster Bishop	1154	Houston	1156	New Mexico St	Grier Jones, Oklahoma St
1969	Houston	Dave Williams	1223	Wake Forest	1232	Broadmoor	Bob Clark, Cal St-LA
1970	Houston	Dave Williams	1172	Wake Forest	1182	Ohio St	John Mahaffey, Houston

Men *(Cont.)*
Results, 1939-1991 *(Cont.)*

Year	Champion	Coach	Score	Runner-Up	Score	Host or Site	Individual Champion
1971	Texas	George Hannon	1144	Houston	1151	Arizona	Ben Crenshaw, Texas
1972	Texas	George Hannon	1146	Houston	1159	Cape Coral	Ben Crenshaw, Texas Tom Kite, Texas
1973	Florida	Buster Bishop	1149	Oklahoma St	1159	Oklahoma St	Ben Crenshaw, Texas
1974	Wake Forest	Jess Haddock	1158	Florida	1160	San Diego St	Curtis Strange, Wake Forest
1975	Wake Forest	Jess Haddock	1156	Oklahoma St	1189	Ohio St	Jay Haas, Wake Forest
1976	Oklahoma St	Mike Holder	1166	Brigham Young	1173	New Mexico	Scott Simpson, Southern Cal
1977	Houston	Dave Williams	1197	Oklahoma St	1205	Colgate	Scott Simpson, Southern Cal
1978	Oklahoma St	Mike Holder	1140	Georgia	1157	Oregon	David Edwards, Oklahoma St
1979	Ohio St	James Brown	1189	Oklahoma St	1191	Wake Forest	Gary Hallberg, Wake Forest
1980	Oklahoma St	Mike Holder	1173	Brigham Young	1177	Ohio St	Jay Don Blake, Utah St
1981	Brigham Young	Karl Tucker	1161	Oral Roberts	1163	Stanford	Ron Commans, Southern Cal
1982	Houston	Dave Williams	1141	Oklahoma St	1151	Pinehurst	Billy Ray Brown, Houston
1983	Oklahoma St	Mike Holder	1161	Texas	1168	Fresno St	Jim Carter, Arizona St
1984	Houston	Dave Williams	1145	Oklahoma St	1146	Houston	John Inman, N Carolina
1985	Houston	Dave Williams	1172	Oklahoma St	1175	Florida	Clark Burroughs, Ohio St
1986	Wake Forest	Jess Haddock	1156	Oklahoma St	1160	Wake Forest	Scott Verplank, Oklahoma St
1987	Oklahoma St	Mike Holder	1160	Wake Forest	1176	Ohio St	Brian Watts, Oklahoma St
1988	UCLA	Eddie Merrins	1176	UTEP Oklahoma Oklahoma St	1179 1179 1179	Southern Cal	E. J. Pfister, Oklahoma St
1989	Oklahoma	Gregg Grost	1139	Texas	1158	Oklahoma Oklahoma St	Phil Mickelson, Arizona St
1990	Arizona St	Steve Loy	1155	Florida	1157	Florida	Phil Mickelson, Arizona St
1991	Oklahoma St	Mike Holder	1161	N Carolina	1168	San Jose St	Warren Schutte, Nevada-Las Vegas

Notes: Match play, 1897-1964; par-70 tournaments held in 1969, 1973 and 1989; par-71 tournaments held in 1968, 1981 and 1988; all other championships par-72 tournaments. Scores are based on 4 rounds instead of 2 after 1967.

The Student-Athlete

According to a 1990 report in the *Chronicle of Higher Education,* a weekly journal that reports on the nation's colleges, a survey conducted between the years 1984 and 1989 showed that athletes graduate from college within five years of entrance at a higher rate than the student body as a whole, 56% to 48%. Participants in golf, tennis, and baseball helped boost the athletes' percentage. Football players, on the other hand, graduated at a 47% rate. And for basketball players the term student-athlete is an oxymoron. Fewer than 39% of hoopsters received a degree within five years. Interestingly, two of the schools tied for the best and worst basketball graduation rates met in March's Final Four when Duke (100%) upset Nevada-Las Vegas (0%).

Men (*Cont.*)

DIVISION II

Year	Champion
1963	SW Missouri St
1964	Southern Illinois
1965	Middle Tennessee St
1966	Cal St-Chico
1967	Lamar
1968	Lamar
1969	Cal St-Northridge
1970	Rollins
1971	New Orleans
1972	New Orleans
1973	Cal St-Northridge
1974	Cal St-Northridge
1975	UC-Irvine
1976	Troy St
1977	Troy St
1978	Columbus
1979	UC-Davis
1980	Columbus
1981	Florida Southern
1982	Florida Southern
1983	SW Texas St
1984	Troy St
1985	Florida Southern
1986	Florida Southern
1987	Tampa
1988	Tampa
1989	Columbus
1990	Florida Southern
1991	Florida Southern

DIVISION III

Year	Champion
1975	Wooster
1976	Cal St-Stanislaus
1977	Cal St-Stanislaus
1978	Cal St-Stanislaus
1979	Cal St-Stanislaus
1980	Cal St-Stanislaus
1981	Cal St-Stanislaus
1982	Ramapo
1983	Allegheny
1984	Cal St-Stanislaus
1985	Cal St-Stanislaus
1986	Cal St-Stanislaus
1987	Cal St-Stanislaus
1988	Cal St-Stanislaus
1989	Cal St-Stanislaus
1990	Methodist
1991	Methodist

Note: All championships par-72 except for 1986 and 1988, which were par-71; fourth round of 1975 championships canceled as a result of bad weather, first round of 1988 championships canceled as a result of rain.

Women

Year	Champion	Coach	Score	Runner-Up	Score	Individual Champion
1982	Tulsa	Dale McNamara	1191	Texas Christian	1227	Kathy Baker, Tulsa
1983	Texas Christian	Fred Warren	1193	Tulsa	1196	Penny Hammel, Miami (FL)
1984	Miami (FL)	Lela Cannon	1214	Arizona St	1221	Cindy Schreyer, Georgia
1985	Florida	Mimi Ryan	1218	Tulsa	1233	Danielle Ammaccapane, Arizona St
1986	Florida	Mimi Ryan	1180	Miami (FL)	1188	Page Dunlap, Florida
1987	San Jose St	Mark Gale	1187	Furman	1188	Caroline Keggi, New Mexico
1988	Tulsa	Dale McNamara	1175	Georgia	1182	Melissa McNamara, Tulsa
				Arizona	1182	
1989	San Jose St	Mark Gale	1208	Tulsa	1209	Pat Hurst, San Jose St
1990	Arizona St	Linda Vollstedt	1206	UCLA	1222	Susan Slaughter, Arizona
1991	UCLA*	Jackie Steinmann	1197	San Jose St	1197	Annika Sorenstam, Arizona

*Won sudden death playoff. Note: Par-74 tournaments held in 1983 and 1988; par-72 tournament held in 1990; all other championships par-73 tournaments.

Gymnastics

Men

Year	Champion	Coach	Pts	Runner-Up	Pts
1938	Chicago	Dan Hoffer	22	Illinois	18
1939	Illinois	Hartley Price	21	Army	17
1940	Illinois	Hartley Price	20	Navy	17
1941	Illinois	Hartley Price	68.5	Minnesota	52.5
1942	Illinois	Hartley Price	39	Penn St	30
1943-47	No tournament				
1948	Penn St	Gene Wettstone	55	Temple	34.5
1949	Temple	Max Younger	28	Minnesota	18

Men (*Cont.*)

Year	Champion	Coach	Pts	Runner-Up	Pts
1950	Illinois	Charley Pond	26	Temple	25
1951	Florida St	Hartley Price	26	Illinois	23.5
				Southern Cal	23.5
1952	Florida St	Hartley Price	89.5	Southern Cal	75
1953	Penn St	Gene Wettstone	91.5	Illinois	68
1954	Penn St	Gene Wettstone	137	Illinois	68
1955	Illinois	Charley Pond	82	Penn St	69
1956	Illinois	Charley Pond	123.5	Penn St	67.5
1957	Penn St	Gene Wettstone	88.5	Illinois	80
1958	Michigan St	George Szypula	79		
	Illinois	Charley Pond	79		
1959	Penn St	Gene Wettstone	152	Illinois	87.5
1960	Penn St	Gene Wettstone	112.5	Southern Cal	65.5
1961	Penn St	Gene Wettstone	88.5	Southern Illinois	80.5
1962	Southern Cal	Jack Beckner	95.5	Southern Illinois	75
1963	Michigan	Newton Loken	129	Southern Illinois	73
1964	Southern Illinois	Bill Meade	84.5	Southern Cal	69.5
1965	Penn St	Gene Wettstone	68.5	Washington	51.5
1966	Southern Illinois	Bill Meade	187.200	California	185.100
1967	Southern Illinois	Bill Meade	189.550	Michigan	187.400
1968	California	Hal Frey	188.250	Southern Illinois	188.150
1969	Iowa	Mike Jacobson	161.175	Penn St	160.450
	Michigan*	Newton Loken		Colorado St	
1970	Michigan	Newton Loken	164.150	Iowa St	164.050
				New Mexico St	
1971	Iowa St	Ed Gagnier	319.075	Southern Illinois	316.650
1972	Southern Illinois	Bill Meade	315.925	Iowa St	312.325
1973	Iowa St	Ed Gagnier	325.150	Penn St	323.025
1974	Iowa St	Ed Gagnier	326.100	Arizona St	322.050
1975	California	Hal Frey	437.325	Louisiana St	433.700
1976	Penn St	Gene Wettstone	432.075	Louisiana St	425.125
1977	Indiana St	Roger Counsil	434.475		
	Oklahoma	Paul Ziert	434.475		
1978	Oklahoma	Paul Ziert	439.350	Arizona St	437.075
1979	Nebraska	Francis Allen	448.275	Oklahoma	446.625
1980	Nebraska	Francis Allen	563.300	Iowa St	557.650
1981	Nebraska	Francis Allen	284.600	Oklahoma	281.950
1982	Nebraska	Francis Allen	285.500	UCLA	281.050
1983	Nebraska	Francis Allen	287.800	UCLA	283.900
1984	UCLA	Art Shurlock	287.300	Penn St	281.250
1985	Ohio St	Michael Willson	285.350	Nebraska	284.550
1986	Arizona St	Don Robinson	283.900	Nebraska	283.600
1987	UCLA	Art Shurlock	285.300	Nebraska	284.750
1988	Nebraska	Francis Allen	288.150	Illinois	287.150
1989	Illinois	Yoshi Hayasaki	283.400	Nebraska	282.300
1990	Nebraska	Francis Allen	287.400	Minnesota	287.300
1991	Oklahoma	Greg Buwick	288.025	Penn St	285.500

*Trampoline.

DIVISION II (Discontinued)

Year	Champion	Coach	Pts	Runner-Up	Pts
1968	Cal St-Northridge	Bill Vincent	179.400	Springfield	178.050
1969	Cal St-Northridge	Bill Vincent	151.800	Southern Connecticut St	145.075
1970	Northwestern Louisiana	Armando Vega	160.250	Southern Connecticut St	159.300
1971	Cal St-Fullerton	Dick Wolfe	158.150	Springfield	156.987
1972	Cal St-Fullerton	Dick Wolfe	160.550	Southern Connecticut St	153.050
1973	Southern Connecticut St	Abe Grossfeld	160.750	Cal St-Northridge	158.700
1974	Cal St-Fullerton	Dick Wolfe	309.800	Southern Connecticut St	309.400
1975	Southern Connecticut St	Abe Grossfeld	411.650	IL-Chicago	398.800
1976	Southern Connecticut St	Abe Grossfeld	419.200	IL-Chicago	388.850
1977	Springfield	Frank Wolcott	395.950	Cal St-Northridge	381.250
1978	IL-Chicago	Clarence Johnson	406.850	Cal St-Northridge	400.400
		Arnold Gentile			

Gymnastics (*Cont.*)

Men (*Cont.*)

DIVISION II (Discontinued)

Year	Champion	Coach	Pts	Runner-Up	Pts
1979	IL-Chicago	Clarence Johnson	418.550	WI-Oshkosh	385.650
1980	WI-Oshkosh	Ken Allen	260.550	Cal St-Chico	256.050
1981	WI-Oshkosh	Ken Allen	209.500	Springfield	201.550
1982	WI-Oshkosh	Ken Allen	216.050	East Stroudsburg	211.200
1983	East Stroudsburg	Bruno Klaus	258.650	WI-Oshkosh	257.850
1984	East Stroudsburg	Bruno Klaus	270.800	Cortland St	246.350

Women
Team Champions

Year	Champion	Coach	Pts	Runner-Up	Pts
1982	Utah	Greg Marsden	148.60	Cal St-Fullerton	144.10
1983	Utah	Greg Marsden	184.65	Arizona St	183.30
1984	Utah	Greg Marsden	186.05	UCLA	185.55
1985	Utah	Greg Marsden	188.35	Arizona St	186.60
1986	Utah	Greg Marsden	186.95	Arizona St	186.70
1987	Georgia	Suzanne Yoculan	187.90	Utah	187.55
1988	Alabama	Sarah Patterson	190.05	Utah	189.50
1989	Georgia	Suzanne Yoculan	192.65	UCLA	192.60
1990	Utah	Greg Marsden	194.900	Alabama	194.575
1991	Alabama	Sarah Patterson	195.125	Utah	194.375

Individual Champions

ALL-AROUND

1982 .... Sue Stednitz, Utah
1983 .... Megan McCunniff (Marsden), Utah
1984 .... Megan Marsden, Utah
1985 .... Penney Hauschild, Alabama
1986 .... Penney Hauschild, Alabama
                       Jackie Brummer, Arizona St
1987 .... Kelly Garrison-Steves, Oklahoma
1988 .... Kelly Garrison-Steves, Oklahoma
1989 .... Corrinne Wright, Georgia
1990 .... Dee Dee Foster, Alabama
1991 .... Hope Spivey, Georgia

VAULT

1982 .... Elaine Alfano, Utah
1983 .... Elaine Alfano, Utah
1984 .... Megan Marsden, Utah
1985 .... Elaine Alfano, Utah
1986 .... Kim Neal, Arizona St
                       Pam Loree, Penn St
1987 .... Yumi Mordre, Washington
1988 .... Jill Andrews, UCLA
1989 .... Kim Hamilton, UCLA
1990 .... Michele Bryant, Nebraska
1991 .... Anna Basaldva, Arizona

BALANCE BEAM

1982 .... Sue Stednitz, Utah
1983 .... Julie Goewey, Cal St-Fullerton
1984 .... Heidi Anderson, Oregon St
1985 .... Lisa Zeis, Arizona St
1986 .... Jackie Brummer, Arizona St
1987 .... Yumi Mordre, Washington
1988 .... Kelly Garrison-Steves, Oklahoma
1989 .... Jill Andrews, UCLA
                       Joy Selig, Oregon St
1990 .... Joy Selig, Oregon St
1991 .... Melissa Marlowe, Utah

FLOOR EXERCISE

1982 .... Mary Ayotte-Law, Oregon St
1983 .... Kim Neal, Arizona St
1984 .... Maria Anz, Florida
1985 .... Lisa Mitzel, Utah
1986 .... Lisa Zeis, Arizona St
                       Penney Hauschild, Alabama
1987 .... Kim Hamilton, UCLA
1988 .... Kim Hamilton, UCLA
1989 .... Corrinne Wright, Georgia
                       Kim Hamilton, UCLA
1990 .... Joy Selig, Oregon St
1991 .... Hope Spivey, Georgia

UNEVEN BARS

1982 .... Lisa Shirk, Pittsburgh
1983 .... Jeri Cameron, Arizona St
1984 .... Jackie Brummer, Arizona St
1985 .... Penney Hauschild, Alabama
1986 .... Lucy Wener, Georgia
1987 .... Lucy Wener, Georgia
1988 .... Kelly Garrison-Steves, Oklahoma
1989 .... Lucy Wener, Georgia
1990 .... Marie Roethlisberger, Minnesota
1991 .... Kelly Macy, Georgia

Women (*Cont.*)

DIVISION II (Discontinued)

Year	Champion	Coach	Pts	Runner-Up	Pts
1982	Cal St-Northridge	Donna Stuart	138.10	Jacksonville St	134.05
1983	Denver	Dan Garcia	174.80	Cal St-Northridge	174.35
1984	Jacksonville St	Robert Dillard	173.40	SE Missouri St	171.45
1985	Jacksonville St	Robert Dillard	176.85	SE Missouri St	173.95
1986	Seattle Pacific	Laurel Tindall	175.80	Jacksonville St	175.15

Ice Hockey

DIVISION I

Year	Champion	Coach	Score	Runner-Up	Most Outstanding Player
1948	Michigan	Vic Heyliger	8-4	Dartmouth	Joe Riley, Dartmouth, F
1949	Boston Col	John Kelley	4-3	Dartmouth	Dick Desmond, Dartmouth, G
1950	Colorado Col	Cheddy Thompson	13-4	Boston U	Ralph Bevins, Boston U, G
1951	Michigan	Vic Heyliger	7-1	Brown	Ed Whiston, Brown, G
1952	Michigan	Vic Heyliger	4-1	Colorado Col	Kenneth Kinsley, Colorado Col, G
1953	Michigan	Vic Heyliger	7-3	Minnesota	John Matchefts, Michigan, F
1954	Rensselaer	Ned Harkness	5-4 (OT)	Minnesota	Abbie Moore, Rensselaer, F
1955	Michigan	Vic Heyliger	5-3	Colorado Col	Philip Hilton, Colorado Col, Def
1956	Michigan	Vic Heyliger	7-5	Michigan Tech	Lorne Howes, Michigan, G
1957	Colorado Col	Thomas Bedecki	13-6	Michigan	Bob McCusker, Colorado Col, F
1958	Denver	Murray Armstrong	6-2	N Dakota	Murray Massier, Denver, F
1959	N Dakota	Bob May	4-3 (OT)	Michigan St	Reg Morelli, N Dakota, F
1960	Denver	Murray Armstrong	5-3	Michigan Tech	Bob Marquis, Boston U, F
1961	Denver	Murray Armstrong	12-2	St Lawrence	Barry Urbanski, Boston U, G
1962	Michigan Tech	John MacInnes	7-1	Clarkson	Louis Angotti, Michigan Tech, F
1963	N Dakota	Barney Thorndycraft	6-5	Denver	Al McLean, N Dakota, F
1964	Michigan	Allen Renfrew	6-3	Denver	Bob Gray, Michigan, G
1965	Michigan Tech	John MacInnes	8-2	Boston Col	Gary Milroy, Michigan Tech, F
1966	Michigan St	Amo Bessone	6-1	Clarkson	Gaye Cooley, Michigan St, G
1967	Cornell	Ned Harkness	4-1	Boston U	Walt Stanowski, Cornell, Def
1968	Denver	Murray Armstrong	4-0	N Dakota	Gerry Powers, Denver, G
1969	Denver	Murray Armstrong	4-3	Cornell	Keith Magnuson, Denver, Def
1970	Cornell	Ned Harkness	6-4	Clarkson	Daniel Lodboa, Cornell, Def
1971	Boston U	Jack Kelley	4-2	Minnesota	Dan Brady, Boston U, G
1972	Boston U	Jack Kelley	4-0	Cornell	Tim Regan, Boston U, G
1973	Wisconsin	Bob Johnson	4-2	Vacated	Dean Talafous, Wisconsin, F
1974	Minnesota	Herb Brooks	4-2	Michigan Tech	Brad Shelstad, Minnesota, G
1975	Michigan Tech	John MacInnes	6-1	Minnesota	Jim Warden, Michigan Tech, G
1976	Minnesota	Herb Brooks	6-4	Michigan Tech	Tom Vanelli, Minnesota, F
1977	Wisconsin	Bob Johnson	6-5 (OT)	Michigan	Julian Baretta, Wisconsin, G
1978	Boston U	Jack Parker	5-3	Boston Col	Jack O'Callahan, Boston U, Def
1979	Minnesota	Herb Brooks	4-3	N Dakota	Steve Janaszak, Minnesota, G
1980	N Dakota	John Gasparini	5-2	Northern Michigan	Doug Smail, N Dakota, F
1981	Wisconsin	Bob Johnson	6-3	Minnesota	Marc Behrend, Wisconsin, G
1982	N Dakota	John Gasparini	5-2	Wisconsin	Phil Sykes, N Dakota, F
1983	Wisconsin	Jeff Sauer	6-2	Harvard	Marc Behrend, Wisconsin, G
1984	Bowling Green	Jerry York	5-4 (OT)	MN-Duluth	Gary Kruzich, Bowling Green, G
1985	Rensselaer	Mike Addesa	2-1	Providence	Chris Terreri, Providence, G
1986	Michigan St	Ron Mason	6-5	Harvard	Mike Donnelly, Michigan St, F
1987	N Dakota	John Gasparini	5-3	Michigan St	Tony Hrkac, N Dakota, F
1988	Lake Superior St	Frank Anzalone	4-3 (OT)	St Lawrence	Bruce Hoffort, Lake Superior St, G
1989	Harvard	Bill Cleary	4-3 (OT)	Minnesota	Ted Donato, Harvard, F
1990	Wisconsin	Jeff Sauer	7-3	Colgate	Chris Tancill, Wisconsin, F
1991	Northern Michigan	Rick Comley	8-7 (3OT)	Boston U	Scott Beattie, Northern Michigan, F

Ice Hockey (*Cont.*)

Year	Champion	Coach	Score	Runner-Up
1978 ... Merrimack		Thom Lawler	12-2	Lake Forest
1979 ... Lowell		Bill Riley Jr	6-4	Mankato St
1980 ... Mankato St		Don Brose	5-2	Elmira
1981 ... Lowell		Bill Riley Jr	5-4	Plattsburgh St
1982 ... Lowell		Bill Riley Jr	6-1	Plattsburgh St
1983 ... Rochester Inst		Brian Mason	4-2	Bemidji St
1984 ... Bemidji St		Bob Peters	14-4*	Merrimack

*Two-game, total-goal series.

DIVISION III

Year	Champion
1984	Babson
1985	Rochester Inst
1986	Bemidji St
1987	Vacated
1988	WI-River Falls
1989	WI-Stevens Point
1990	WI-Stevens Point
1991	WI-Stevens Point

Lacrosse

Men

DIVISION I

Year	Champion	Coach	Score	Runner-Up
1971	Cornell	Richie Moran	12-6	Maryland
1972	Virginia	Glenn Thiel	13-12	Johns Hopkins
1973	Maryland	Bud Beardmore	10-9 (2 OT)	Johns Hopkins
1974	Johns Hopkins	Bob Scott	17-12	Maryland
1975	Maryland	Bud Beardmore	20-13	Navy
1976	Cornell	Richie Moran	16-13 (OT)	Maryland
1977	Cornell	Richie Moran	16-8	Johns Hopkins
1978	Johns Hopkins	Henry Ciccarone	13-8	Cornell
1979	Johns Hopkins	Henry Ciccarone	15-9	Maryland
1980	Johns Hopkins	Henry Ciccarone	9-8 (2 OT)	Virginia
1981	N Carolina	Willie Scroggs	14-13	Johns Hopkins
1982	N Carolina	Willie Scroggs	7-5	Johns Hopkins
1983	Syracuse	Roy Simmons Jr	17-16	Johns Hopkins
1984	Johns Hopkins	Don Zimmerman	13-10	Syracuse
1985	Johns Hopkins	Don Zimmerman	11-4	Syracuse
1986	N Carolina	Willie Scroggs	10-9 (OT)	Virginia
1987	Johns Hopkins	Don Zimmerman	11-10	Cornell
1988	Syracuse	Roy Simmons Jr	13-8	Cornell
1989	Syracuse	Roy Simmons Jr	13-12	Johns Hopkins
1990	Syracuse	Roy Simmons Jr	21-9	Loyola (MD)
1991	N Carolina	Dave Klarmann	18-13	Towson St

DIVISION II (Discontinued)

Year	Champion	Coach	Score	Runner-Up
1974	Towson St	Carl Runk	18-17 (OT)	Hobart
1975	Cortland St	Chuck Winters	12-11	Hobart
1976	Hobart	Jerry Schmidt	18-9	Adelphi
1977	Hobart	Jerry Schmidt	23-13	Washington (MD)
1978	Roanoke	Paul Griffin	14-13	Hobart
1979	Adelphi	Paul Doherty	17-12	MD-Baltimore County
1980	MD-Baltimore County	Dick Watts	23-14	Adelphi
1981	Adelphi	Paul Doherty	17-14	Loyola (MD)

Lacrosse (*Cont.*)

Men (*Cont.*)

DIVISION III

Year	Champion	Coach	Score	Runner-Up
1980	Hobart	Dave Urick	11-8	Cortland St
1981	Hobart	Dave Urick	10-8	Cortland St
1982	Hobart	Dave Urick	9-8 (OT)	Washington (MD)
1983	Hobart	Dave Urick	13-9	Roanoke
1984	Hobart	Dave Urick	12-5	Washington (MD)
1985	Hobart	Dave Urick	15-8	Washington (MD)
1986	Hobart	Dave Urick	13-10	Washington (MD)
1987	Hobart	Dave Urick	9-5	Ohio Wesleyan
1988	Hobart	Dave Urick	18-9	Ohio Wesleyan
1989	Hobart	Dave Urick	11-8	Ohio Wesleyan
1990	Hobart	B. J. O'Hara	18-6	Washington (MD)
1991	Hobart	B. J. O'Hara	12-11	Salisbury St

Women

DIVISION I

Year	Champion	Coach	Score	Runner-Up
1982	Massachusetts	Pamela Hixon	9-6	Trenton St
1983	Delaware	Janet Smith	10-7	Temple
1984	Temple	Tina Sloan Green	6-4	Maryland
1985	New Hampshire	Marisa Didio	6-5	Maryland
1986	Maryland	Sue Tyler	11-10	Penn St
1987	Penn St	Susan Scheetz	7-6	Temple
1988	Temple	Tina Sloan Green	15-7	Penn St
1989	Penn St	Susan Scheetz	7-6	Harvard
1990	Harvard	Carole Kleinfelder	8-7	Maryland
1991	Virginia	Jane Miller	8-6	Maryland

DIVISION III

Year	Champion	Year	Champion
1985	Trenton St	1989	Ursinus
1986	Ursinus	1990	Ursinus
1987	Trenton St	1991	Trenton St
1988	Trenton St		

Rifle

Men's and Women's Combined

Year	Champion	Coach	Score	Runner-Up	Score	Individual Champion Air Rifle	Smallbore
1980	Tennessee Tech	James Newkirk	6201	W Virginia	6150	Rod Fitz-Randolph, Tennessee Tech	Rod Fitz-Randolph, Tennessee Tech
1981	Tennessee Tech	James Newkirk	6139	W Virginia	6136	John Rost, W Virginia	Kurt Fitz-Randolph, Tennessee Tech
1982	Tennessee Tech	James Newkirk	6138	W Virginia	6136	John Rost, W Virginia	Kurt Fitz-Randolph, Tennessee Tech
1983	W Virginia	Edward Etzel	6166	Tennessee Tech	6148	Ray Slonena, Tennessee Tech	David Johnson, W Virginia
1984	W Virginia	Edward Etzel	6206	East Tennessee St	6142	Pat Spurgin, Murray St	Bob Broughton, W Virginia
1985	Murray St	Elvis Green	6150	W Virginia	6149	Christian Heller, W Virginia	Pat Spurgin, Murray St
1986	W Virginia	Edward Etzel	6229	Murray St	6163	Marianne Wallace, Murray St	Mike Anti, W Virginia
1987	Murray St	Elvis Green	6205	W Virginia	6203	Rob Harbison, TN-Martin	Web Wright, W Virginia
1988	W Virginia	Greg Perrine	6192	Murray St	6183	Deena Wigger, Murray St	Web Wright, W Virginia

Rifle (*Cont.*)

Men's and Women's Combined (*Cont.*)

					Individual Champion	
Year	Champion	Coach	Score	Runner-Up	Score	Air Rifle	Smallbore
1989 ...	W Virginia	Edward Etzel	6234	S Florida	6180	Michelle Scarborough, S Florida	Deb Sinclair, AK-Fairbanks
1990 ...	W Virginia	Marsha Beasley	6205	Navy	6101	Gary Hardy, W Virginia	Michelle Scarborough, S Florida
1991 ...	W Virginia	Marsha Beasley	6171	Alaska-Fairbanks	6110	Ann Pfiffner, W Virginia	Soma Dutta, UTEP

Skiing

Men's and Women's Combined

Year	Champion	Coach	Pts	Runner-Up	Pts	Host or Site
1954	Denver	Willy Schaeffler	384.0	Seattle	349.6	NV-Reno
1955	Denver	Willy Schaeffler	567.05	Dartmouth	558.935	Norwich
1956	Denver	Willy Schaeffler	582.01	Dartmouth	541.77	Winter Park
1957	Denver	Willy Schaeffler	577.95	Colorado	545.29	Ogden Snow Basin
1958	Dartmouth	Al Merrill	561.2	Denver	550.6	Dartmouth
1959	Colorado	Bob Beattie	549.4	Denver	543.6	Winter Park
1960	Colorado	Bob Beattie	571.4	Denver	568.6	Bridger Bowl
1961	Denver	Willy Schaeffler	376.19	Middlebury	366.94	Middlebury
1962	Denver	Willy Schaeffler	390.08	Colorado	374.30	Squaw Valley
1963	Denver	Willy Schaeffler	384.6	Colorado	381.6	Solitude
1964	Denver	Willy Schaeffler	370.2	Dartmouth	368.8	Franconia Notch
1965	Denver	Willy Schaeffler	380.5	Utah	378.,4	Crystal Mountain
1966	Denver	Willy Schaeffler	381.02	Western Colorado	365.92	Crested Butte
1967	Denver	Willy Schaeffler	376.7	Wyoming	375.9	Sugarloaf Mountain
1968	Wyoming	John Cress	383.9	Denver	376.2	Mount Werner
1969	Denver	Willy Schaeffler	388.6	Dartmouth	372.0	Mount Werner
1970	Denver	Willy Schaeffler	386.6	Dartmouth	378.8	Cannon Mountain
1971	Denver	Peder Pytte	394.7	Colorado	373.1	Terry Peak
1972	Colorado	Bill Marolt	385.3	Denver	380.1	Winter Park
1973	Colorado	Bill Marolt	381.89	Wyoming	377.83	Middlebury
1974	Colorado	Bill Marolt	176	Wyoming	162	Jackson Hole
1975	Colorado	Bill Marolt	183	Vermont	115	Fort Lewis
1976	Colorado	Bill Marolt	112			Bates
	Dartmouth	Jim Page	112			
1977	Colorado	Bill Marolt	179	Wyoming	154.5	Winter Park
1978	Colorado	Bill Marolt	152.5	Wyoming	121.5	Cannon Mountain
1979	Colorado	Tim Hinderman	153	Utah	130	Steamboat Springs
1980	Vermont	Chip LaCasse	171	Utah	151	Lake Placid and Stowe
1981	Utah	Pat Miller	183	Vermont	172	Park City
1982	Colorado	Tim Hinderman	461	Vermont	436.5	Lake Placid
1983	Utah	Pat Miller	696	Vermont	650	Bozeman
1984	Utah	Pat Miller	750.5	Vermont	684	New Hampshire
1985	Wyoming	Tim Ameel	764	Utah	744	Bozeman
1986	Utah	Pat Miller	612	Vermont	602	Vermont
1987	Utah	Pat Miller	710	Vermont	627	Anchorage
1988	Utah	Pat Miller	651	Vermont	614	Middlebury
1989	Vermont	Chip LaCasse	672	Utah	668	Jackson Hole
1990	Vermont	Chip LaCasse	671	Utah	571	Vermont
1991	Colorado	Richard Rokos	713	Vermont	682	Park City

THEY SAID IT

Elden Campbell, Los Angeles Lakers forward, when asked if he had earned his degree from Clemson: "No, but they gave me one, anyway."

Soccer

Men

DIVISION I

Year	Champion	Coach	Score	Runner-Up
1959	St Louis	Bob Guelker	5-2	Bridgeport
1960	St Louis	Bob Guelker	3-2	Maryland
1961	West Chester	Mel Lorback	2-0	St Louis
1962	St Louis	Bob Guelker	4-3	Maryland
1963	St Louis	Bob Guelker	3-0	Navy
1964	Navy	F. H. Warner	1-0	Michigan St
1965	St Louis	Bob Guelker	1-0	Michigan St
1966	San Francisco	Steve Negoesco	5-2	LIU-Brooklyn
1967	Michigan St St Louis	Gene Kenney Harry Keough	0-0	Game called due to inclement weather
1968	Maryland Michigan St	Doyle Royal Gene Kenney	2-2 (2 OT)	
1969	St Louis	Harry Keough	4-0	San Francisco
1970	St Louis	Harry Keough	1-0	UCLA
1971	Vacated		3-2	St Louis
1972	St Louis	Harry Keough	4-2	UCLA
1973	St Louis	Harry Keough	2-1 (OT)	UCLA
1974	Howard	Lincoln Phillips	2-1 (4 OT)	St Louis
1975	San Francisco	Steve Negoesco	4-0	SIU-Edwardsville
1976	San Francisco	Steve Negoesco	1-0	Indiana
1977	Hartwick	Jim Lennox	2-1	San Francisco
1978	Vacated		2-0	Indiana
1979	SIU-Edwardsville	Bob Guelker	3-2	Clemson
1980	San Francisco	Steve Negoesco	4-3 (OT)	Indiana
1981	Connecticut	Joe Morrone	2-1 (OT)	Alabama A&M
1982	Indiana	Jerry Yeagley	2-1 (8 OT)	Duke
1983	Indiana	Jerry Yeagley	1-0 (2 OT)	Columbia
1984	Clemson	I. M. Ibrahim	2-1	Indiana
1985	UCLA	Sigi Schmid	1-0 (8 OT)	American
1986	Duke	John Rennie	1-0	Akron
1987	Clemson	I. M. Ibrahim	2-0	San Diego St
1988	Indiana	Jerry Yeagley	1-0	Howard
1989	Santa Clara Virginia	Steve Sampson Bruce Arena	1-1 (2 OT)	
1990	UCLA	Sigi Schmid	1-0 (OT)	Rutgers

DIVISION II

Year	Champion
1972	SIU-Edwardsville
1973	MO-St Louis
1974	Adelphi
1975	Baltimore
1976	Loyola (MD)
1977	Alabama A&M
1978	Seattle Pacific
1979	Alabama A&M
1980	Lock Haven
1981	Tampa
1982	Florida Intl
1983	Seattle Pacific
1984	Florida Intl
1985	Seattle Pacific
1986	Seattle Pacific
1987	Southern Connecticut St
1988	Florida Tech
1989	New Hampshire Col
1990	Southern Connecticut St

DIVISION III

Year	Champion
1974	Brockport St
1975	Babson
1976	Brandeis
1977	Lock Haven
1978	Lock Haven
1979	Babson
1980	Babson
1981	Glassboro St
1982	NC-Greensboro
1983	NC-Greensboro
1984	Wheaton (IL)
1985	NC-Greensboro
1986	NC-Greensboro
1987	NC-Greensboro
1988	UC-San Diego
1989	Elizabethtown
1990	Glassboro St

Women

DIVISION I

Year	Champion	Coach	Score	Runner-Up
1982	N Carolina	Anson Dorrance	2-0	Central Florida
1983	N Carolina	Anson Dorrance	4-0	George Mason
1984	N Carolina	Anson Dorrance	2-0	Connecticut
1985	George Mason	Hank Leung	2-0	N Carolina
1986	N Carolina	Anson Dorrance	2-0	Colorado Col
1987	N Carolina	Anson Dorrance	1-0	Massachusetts
1988	N Carolina	Anson Dorrance	4-1	N Carolina St
1989	N Carolina	Anson Dorrance	2-0	Colorado Col
1990	N Carolina	Anson Dorrance	6-0	Connecticut

DIVISION II

Year	Champion
1988	Cal St-Hayward
1989	Barry
1990	Sonoma St

DIVISION III

Year	Champion
1986	Rochester
1987	Rochester
1988	William Smith
1989	UC-San Diego
1990	Ithaca

Softball

Women

DIVISION I

Year	Champion	Coach	Score	Runner-Up
1982	UCLA*	Sharron Backus	2-0†	Fresno St
1983	Texas A&M	Bob Brock	2-0‡	Cal St-Fullerton
1984	UCLA	Sharron Backus	1-0#	Texas A&M
1985	UCLA	Sharron Backus	2-1**	Nebraska
1986	Cal St-Fullerton*	Judi Garman	3-0	Texas A&M
1987	Texas A&M	Bob Brock	4-1	UCLA
1988	UCLA	Sharron Backus	3-0	Fresno St
1989	UCLA*	Sharron Backus	1-0	Fresno St
1990	UCLA	Sharron Backus	2-0	Fresno St
1991	Arizona	Mike Candrea	5-1	UCLA

*Undefeated teams in final series.   †8 innings.   ‡12 innings.   #13 innings.   **9 innings.

DIVISION II

Year	Champion
1982	Sam Houston St
1983	Cal St-Northridge
1984	Cal St-Northridge
1985	Cal St-Northridge
1986	SF Austin St
1987	Cal St-Northridge
1988	Cal St-Bakersfield
1989	Cal St-Bakersfield
1990	Cal St-Bakersfield
1991	Augustana (SO)

DIVISION III

Year	Champion
1982	Eastern Connecticut St*
1983	Trenton St
1984	Buena Vista*
1985	Eastern Connecticut St
1986	Eastern Connecticut St
1987	Trenton St*
1988	Central (IA)
1989	Trenton St*
1990	Eastern Connecticut St
1991	Central (IA)

*Undefeated teams in final series.

Yanked

With the addition this year of James Madison (Harrisonburg, Va.) and William and Mary (Williamsburg, Va.), the nine-member Yankee Conference now has four schools—Richmond and Delaware are the others—from below the Mason-Dixon line.

Men

DIVISION I

Year	Champion	Coach	Pts	Runner-Up	Pts
1937	Michigan	Matt Mann	75	Ohio St	39
1938	Michigan	Matt Mann	46	Ohio St	45
1939	Michigan	Matt Mann	65	Ohio St	58
1940	Michigan	Matt Mann	45	Yale	42
1941	Michigan	Matt Mann	61	Yale	58
1942	Yale	Robert J. H. Kiphuth	71	Michigan	39
1943	Ohio St	Mike Peppe	81	Michigan	47
1944	Yale	Robert J. H. Kiphuth	39	Michigan	38
1945	Ohio St	Mike Peppe	56	Michigan	48
1946	Ohio St	Mike Peppe	61	Michigan	37
1947	Ohio St	MIke Peppe	66	Michigan	39
1948	Michigan	Matt Mann	44	Ohio St	41
1949	Ohio St	Mike Peppe	49	Iowa	35
1950	Ohio St	Mike Peppe	64	Yale	43
1951	Yale	Robert J. H. Kiphuth	81	Michigan St	60
1952	Ohio St	Mike Peppe	94	Yale	81
1953	Yale	Robert J. H. Kiphuth	96½	Ohio St	73½
1954	Ohio St	Mike Peppe	94	Michigan	67
1955	Ohio St	Mike Peppe	90	Yale	51
				Michigan	51
1956	Ohio St	Mike Peppe	68	Yale	54
1957	Michigan	Gus Stager	69	Yale	61
1958	Michigan	Gus Stager	72	Yale	63
1959	Michigan	Gus Stager	137½	Ohio St	44
1960	Southern Cal	Peter Daland	87	Michigan	73
1961	Michigan	Gus Stager	85	Southern Cal	62
1962	Ohio St	Mike Peppe	92	Southern Cal	46
1963	Southern Cal	Peter Daland	81	Yale	77
1964	Southern Cal	Peter Daland	96	Indiana	91
1965	Southern Cal	Peter Daland	285	Indiana	278½
1966	Southern Cal	Peter Daland	302	Indiana	286
1967	Stanford	Jim Gaughran	275	Southern Cal	260
1968	Indiana	James Counsilman	346	Yale	253
1969	Indiana	James Counsilman	427	Southern Cal	306
1970	Indiana	James Counsilman	332	Southern Cal	235
1971	Indiana	James Counsilman	351	Southern Cal	260
1972	Indiana	James Counsilman	390	Southern Cal	371
1973	Indiana	James Counsilman	358	Tennessee	294
1974	Southern Cal	Peter Daland	339	Indiana	338
1975	Southern Cal	Peter Daland	344	Indiana	274
1976	Southern Cal	Peter Daland	398	Tennessee	237
1977	Southern Cal	Peter Daland	385	Alabama	204
1978	Tennessee	Ray Bussard	307	Auburn	185
1979	California	Nort Thornton	287	Southern Cal	227
1980	California	Nort Thornton	234	Texas	220
1981	Texas	Eddie Reese	259	UCLA	189
1982	UCLA	Ron Ballatore	219	Texas	210
1983	Florida	Randy Reese	238	Southern Meth	227
1984	Florida	Randy Reese	287½	Texas	277
1985	Stanford	Skip Kenney	403½	Florida	302
1986	Stanford	Skip Kenney	404	California	335
1987	Stanford	Skip Kenney	374	Southern Cal	296
1988	Texas	Eddie Reese	424	Southern Cal	369½
1989	Texas	Eddie Reese	475	Stanford	396
1990	Texas	Eddie Reese	506	Southern Cal	423
1991	Texas	Eddie Reese	476	Stanford	420

Men (*Cont.*)

	DIVISION II			DIVISION III	
Year		**Champion**	**Year**		**Champion**
1964		Bucknell	1975		Cal St-Chico
1965		San Diego St	1976		St Lawrence
1966		San Diego St	1977		Johns Hopkins
1967		UC-Santa Barbara	1978		Johns Hopkins
1968		Long Beach St	1979		Johns Hopkins
1969		UC-Irvine	1980		Kenyon
1970		UC-Irvine	1981		Kenyon
1971		UC-Irvine	1982		Kenyon
1972		Eastern Michigan	1983		Kenyon
1973		Cal St-Chico	1984		Kenyon
1974		Cal St-Chico	1985		Kenyon
1975		Cal St-Northridge	1986		Kenyon
1976		Cal St-Chico	1987		Kenyon
1977		Cal St-Northridge	1988		Kenyon
1978		Cal St-Northridge	1989		Kenyon
1979		Cal St-Northridge	1990		Kenyon
1980		Oakland	1991		Kenyon
1981		Cal St-Northridge			
1982		Cal St-Northridge			
1983		Cal St-Northridge			
1984		Cal St-Northridge			
1985		Cal St-Northridge			
1986		Cal St-Bakersfield			
1987		Cal St-Bakersfield			
1988		Cal St-Bakersfield			
1989		Cal St-Bakersfield			
1990		Cal St-Bakersfield			
1991		Cal St-Bakersfield			

Women

DIVISION I

Year	Champion	Coach	Pts	Runner-Up	Pts
1982	Florida	Randy Reese	505	Stanford	383
1983	Stanford	George Haines	418½	Florida	389½
1984	Texas	Richard Quick	392	Stanford	324
1985	Texas	Richard Quick	643	Florida	400
1986	Texas	Richard Quick	633	Florida	586
1987	Texas	Richard Quick	648½	Stanford	631½
1988	Texas	Richard Quick	661	Florida	542½
1989	Stanford	Richard Quick	610½	Texas	547
1990	Texas	Mark Schubert	632	Stanford	622½
1991	Texas	Mark Schubert	746	Stanford	653

	DIVISION II			DIVISION III	
Year		**Champion**	**Year**		**Champion**
1982		Cal St-Northridge	1982		Williams
1983		Clarion	1983		Williams
1984		Clarion	1984		Kenyon
1985		S Florida	1985		Kenyon
1986		Clarion	1986		Kenyon
1987		Cal St-Northridge	1987		Kenyon
1988		Cal St-Northridge	1988		Kenyon
1989		Cal St-Northridge	1989		Kenyon
1990		Oakland (MI)	1990		Kenyon
1991		Oakland (MI)	1991		Kenyon

Tennis

Men

DIVISION I

Year	Champion	Coach	Pts	Runner-Up	Pts	Individual Champion
1946	Southern Cal	William Moyle	9	William & Mary	6	Robert Falkenburg, Southern Cal
1947	William & Mary	Sharvey G. Umbeck	10	Rice	4	Gardner Larned, William & Mary
1948	William & Mary	Sharvey G. Umbeck	6	San Francisco	5	Harry Likas, San Francisco
1949	San Francisco	Norman Brooks	7	Rollins	4	Jack Tuero, Tulane
				Tulane	4	
				Washington	4	
1950	UCLA	William Ackerman	11	California	5	Herbert Flam, UCLA
				Southern Cal	5	
1951	Southern Cal	Louis Wheeler	9	Cincinnati	7	Tony Trabert, Cincinnati
1952	UCLA	J. D. Morgan	11	California	5	Hugh Stewart, Southern Cal
				Southern Cal	5	
1953	UCLA	J. D. Morgan	11	California	6	Hamilton Richardson, Tulane
1954	UCLA	J. D. Morgan	15	Southern Cal	10	Hamilton Richardson, Tulane
1955	Southern Cal	George Toley	12	Texas	7	Jose Aguero, Tulane
1956	UCLA	J. D. Morgan	15	Southern Cal	14	Alejandro Olmedo, Southern Cal
1957	Michigan	William Murphy	10	Tulane	9	Barry MacKay, Michigan
1958	Southern Cal	George Toley	13	Stanford	9	Alejandro Olmedo, Southern Cal
1959	Notre Dame	Thomas Fallon	8			Whitney Reed, San Jose St
	Tulane	Emmet Pare	8			
1960	UCLA	J. D. Morgan	18	Southern Cal	8	Larry Nagler, UCLA
1961	UCLA	J. D. Morgan	17	Southern Cal	16	Allen Fox, UCLA
1962	Southern Cal	George Toley	22	UCLA	12	Rafael Osuna, Southern Cal
1963	Southern Cal	George Toley	27	UCLA	19	Dennis Ralston, Southern Cal
1964	Southern Cal	George Toley	26	UCLA	25	Dennis Ralston, Southern Cal
1965	UCLA	J. D. Morgan	31	Miami (FL)	13	Arthur Ashe, UCLA
1966	Southern Cal	George Toley	27	UCLA	23	Charles Pasarell, UCLA
1967	Southern Cal	George Toley	28	UCLA	23	Bob Lutz, Southern Cal
1968	Southern Cal	George Toley	31	Rice	23	Stan Smith, Southern Cal
1969	Southern Cal	George Toley	35	UCLA	23	Joaquin Loyo-Mayo, Southern Cal
1970	UCLA	Glenn Bassett	26	Trinity (TX)	22	Jeff Borowiak, UCLA
				Rice	22	
1971	UCLA	Glenn Bassett	35	Trinity (TX)	27	Jimmy Connors, UCLA
1972	Trinity (TX)	Clarence Mabry	36	Stanford	30	Dick Stockton, Trinity (TX)
1973	Stanford	Dick Gould	33	Southern Cal	28	Alex Mayer, Stanford
1974	Stanford	Dick Gould	30	Southern Cal	25	John Whitlinger, Stanford
1975	UCLA	Glenn Bassett	27	Miami (FL)	20	Bill Martin, UCLA
1976	Southern Cal	George Toley	21			Bill Scanlon, Trinity (TX)
	UCLA	Glenn Bassett	21			
1977	Stanford	Dick Gould		Trinity (TX)		Matt Mitchell, Stanford
1978	Stanford	Dick Gould		UCLA		John McEnroe, Stanford
1979	UCLA	Glenn Bassett		Trinity (TX)		Kevin Curren, Texas
1980	Stanford	Dick Gould		California		Robert Van't Hof, Southern Cal
1981	Stanford	Dick Gould		UCLA		Tim Mayotte, Stanford
1982	UCLA	Glenn Bassett		Pepperdine		Mike Leach, Michigan
1983	Stanford	Dick Gould		Southern Meth		Greg Holmes, Utah
1984	UCLA	Glenn Bassett		Stanford		Mikael Pernfors, Georgia
1985	Georgia	Dan Magill		UCLA		Mikael Pernfors, Georgia
1986	Stanford	Dick Gould		Pepperdine		Dan Goldie, Stanford
1987	Georgia	Dan Magill		UCLA		Andrew Burrow, Miami (FL)
1988	Stanford	Dick Gould		Louisiana St		Robby Weiss, Pepperdine
1989	Stanford	Dick Gould		Georgia		Donni Leaycraft, Louisiana St
1990	Stanford	Dick Gould		Tennessee		Steve Bryan, Texas
1991	Southern Cal	Dick Leach		Georgia		Jared Palmer, Stanford

Note: Prior to 1977, individual wins counted in the team's total points. In 1977, a dual-match single-elimination team championship was initiated, eliminating the point system.

No Hits But No Runs

The longest no-hitter in NCAA tournament history belongs to Ron Darling, who threw 11 hitless innings against St. John's while he was at Yale. Unfortunately, the Bulldogs couldn't score and Darling lost the game 1–0 in 12 innings. The pitcher who threw the shutout for St. John's was Darling's future New York Mets teammate, Frank Viola.

Men (*Cont.*)

INDIVIDUAL CHAMPIONS 1883-1945

1883	Joesph Clark, Harvard (spring)
1883	Howard Taylor, Harvard (fall)
1884	W. P. Knapp, Yale
1885	W. P. Knapp, Yale
1886	G. M. Brinley, Trinity (CT)
1887	P. S. Sears, Harvard
1888	P. S. Sears, Harvard
1889	R. P. Huntington, Jr, Yale
1890	Fred Hovey, Harvard
1891	Fred Hovey, Harvard
1892	William Larned, Cornell
1893	Malcolm Chace, Brown
1894	Malcolm Chace, Yale
1895	Malcolm Chace, Yale
1896	Malcolm Whitman, Harvard
1897	S. G. Thompson, Princeton
1898	Leo Ware, Harvard
1899	Dwight Davis, Harvard
1900	Raymond Little, Princeton
1901	Fred Alexander, Princeton
1902	William Clothier, Harvard
1903	E. B. Dewhurst, Pennsylvania
1904	Robert LeRoy, Columbia
1905	E. B. Dewhurst, Pennsylvania
1906	Robert LeRoy, Columbia
1907	G. Peabody Gardner, Jr, Harvard
1908	Nat Niles, Harvard
1909	Wallace Johnson, Pennsylvania
1910	R. A. Holden, Jr, Yale
1911	E. H. Whitney, Harvard
1912	George Church, Princeton
1913	Richard Williams II, Harvard
1914	George Church, Princeton
1915	Richard Williams II, Harvard
1916	G. Colket Caner, Harvard
1917-18	No tournament
1919	Charles Garland, Yale
1920	Lascelles Banks, Yale
1921	Philip Neer, Stanford
1922	Lucien Williams, Yale
1923	Carl Fischer, Philadelphia Osteo
1924	Wallace Scott, Washington
1925	Edward Chandler, California
1926	Edward Chandler, California
1927	Wilmer Allison, Texas
1928	Julius Seligson, Lehigh
1929	Berkeley Bell, Texas
1930	Clifford Sutter, Tulane
1931	Keith Gledhill, Stanford
1932	Clifford Sutter, Tulane
1933	Jack Tidball, UCLA
1934	Gene Mako, Southern Cal
1935	Wilbur Hess, Rice
1936	Ernest Sutter, Tulane
1937	Ernest Sutter, Tulane
1938	Frank Guernsey, Rice
1939	Frank Guernsey, Rice
1940	Donald McNeil, Kenyon
1941	Joseph Hunt, Navy
1942	Frederick Schroeder, Jr, Stanford
1943	Pancho Segura, Miami (FL)
1944	Pancho Segura, Miami (FL)
1945	Pancho Segura, Miami (FL)

DIVISION II

Year	Champion	Year	Champion
1963	Cal St-LA	1976	Hampton
1964	Cal St-LA	1977	UC-Irvine
	Southern Illinois	1978	SIU-Edwardsville
1965	Cal St-LA	1979	SIU-Edwardsville
1966	Rollins	1980	SIU-Edwardsville
1967	Long Beach St	1981	SIU-Edwardsville
1968	Fresno St	1982	SIU-Edwardsville
1969	Cal St-Northridge	1983	SIU-Edwardsville
1970	UC-Irvine	1984	SIU-Edwardsville
1971	UC-Irvine	1985	Chapman
1972	UC-Irvine	1986	Cal Poly-SLO
	Rollins	1987	Chapman
1973	UC-Irvine	1988	Chapman
1974	San Diego	1989	Hampton
1975	UC-Irvine	1990	Cal Poly-SLO
	San Diego	1991	Rollins

DIVISION III

Year	Champion	Year	Champion
1976	Kalamazoo	1984	Redlands
1977	Swarthmore	1985	Swarthmore
1978	Kalamazoo	1986	Kalamazoo
1979	Redlands	1987	Kalamazoo
1980	Gustavus Adolphus	1988	Washington & Lee
1981	Claremont-M-S	1989	UC-Santa Cruz
	Swarthmore	1990	Swarthmore
1982	Gustavus Adolphus	1991	Kalamazoo
1983	Redlands		

Women

DIVISION I

Year	Champion	Coach	Runner-Up	Individual Champion
1982	Stanford	Frank Brennan	UCLA	Alycia Moulton, Stanford
1983	Southern Cal	Dave Borelli	Trinity (TX)	Beth Herr, Southern Cal
1984	Stanford	Frank Brennan	Southern Cal	Lisa Spain, Georgia
1985	Southern Cal	Dave Borelli	Miami (FL)	Linda Gates, Stanford
1986	Stanford	Frank Brennan	Southern Cal	Patty Fendick, Stanford
1987	Stanford	Frank Brennan	Georgia	Patty Fendick, Stanford
1988	Stanford	Frank Brennan	Florida	Shaun Stafford, Florida
1989	Stanford	Frank Brennan	UCLA	Sandra Birch, Stanford
1990	Stanford	Frank Brennan	Florida	Debbie Graham, Stanford
1991	Stanford	Frank Brennan	UCLA	Sandra Birch, Stanford

DIVISION II

Year	Champion
1982	Cal St-Northridge
1983	TN-Chattanooga
1984	TN-Chattanooga
1985	TN-Chattanooga
1986	SIU-Edwardsville
1987	SIU-Edwardsville
1988	SIU-Edwardsville
1989	SIU-Edwardsville
1990	UC-Davis
1991	Cal Poly-Pomona

DIVISION III

Year	Champion
1982	Occidental
1983	Principia
1984	Davidson
1985	UC-San Diego
1986	Trenton St
1987	UC-San Diego
1988	Mary Washington
1989	UC-San Diego
1990	Gustavus Adolphus
1991	Mary Washington

Indoor Track and Field

Men

DIVISION I

Year	Champion	Coach	Pts	Runner-Up	Pts
1965	Missouri	Tom Botts	14	Oklahoma St	12
1966	Kansas	Bob Timmons	14	Southern Cal	13
1967	Southern Cal	Vern Wolfe	26	Oklahoma	17
1968	Villanova	Jim Elliott	35	Southern Cal	25
1969	Kansas	Bob Timmons	41½	Villanova	33
1970	Kansas	Bob Timmons	27½	Villanova	26
1971	Villanova	Jim Elliott	22	UTEP	19¼
1972	Southern Cal	Vern Wolfe	19	Bowling Green	18
				Michigan St	18
1973	Manhattan	Fred Dwyer	18	Kansas	12
				Kent	12
				UTEP	12
1974	UTEP	Ted Banks	19	Colorado	18
1975	UTEP	Ted Banks	36	Kansas	17½
1976	UTEP	Ted Banks	23	Villanova	15
1977	Washington St	John Chaplin	25½	UTEP	25
1978	UTEP	Ted Banks	44	Auburn	38
1979	Villanova	Jim Elliott	52	UTEP	51
1980	UTEP	Ted Banks	76	Villanova	42
1981	UTEP	Ted Banks	76	Southern Meth	51
1982	UTEP	John Wedel	67	Arkansas	30
1983	Southern Meth	Ted McLaughlin	43	Villanova	32
1984	Arkansas	John McDonnell	38	Washington St	28
1985	Arkansas	John McDonnell	70	Tennessee	29
1986	Arkansas	John McDonnell	49	Villanova	22
1987	Arkansas	John McDonnell	39	Southern Meth	31
1988	Arkansas	John McDonnell	34	Illinois	29
1989	Arkansas	John McDonnell	34	Florida	31
1990	Arkansas	John McDonnell	44	Texas A&M	36
1991	Arkansas	John McDonnell	34	Georgetown	27

Men (*Cont.*)

DIVISION II

Year	Champion
1985	SE Missouri St
1987	St Augustine's
1988	Abilene Christian
	St Augustine's
1989	St Augustine's
1990	St Augustine's
1991	St Augustine's

DIVISION III

Year	Champion
1985	St Thomas (MN)
1986	Frostburg St
1987	WI-La Crosse
1988	WI-La Crosse
1989	North Central
1990	Lincoln (PA)
1991	WI-La Crosse

Women

DIVISION I

Year	Champion	Coach	Pts	Runner-Up	Pts
1983	Nebraska	Gary Pepin	47	Tennessee	44
1984	Nebraska	Gary Pepin	59	Tennessee	48
1985	Florida St	Gary Winckler	34	Texas	32
1986	Texas	Terry Crawford	31	Southern Cal	26
1987	Louisiana St	Loren Seagrave	49	Tennessee	30
1988	Texas	Terry Crawford	71	Villanova	52
1989	Louisiana St	Pat Henry	61	Villanova	34
1990	Texas	Terry Crawford	50	Wisconsin	26
1991	Louisiana St	Pat Henry	48	Texas	39

DIVISION II

Year	Champion
1985	St Augustine's
1987	St Augustine's
1988	Abilene Christian
1989	Abilene Christian
1990	Abilene Christian
1991	Abilene Christian

DIVISION III

Year	Champion
1985	MA-Boston
1986	MA-Boston
1987	MA-Boston
1988	Christopher Newport
1989	Christopher Newport
1990	Christopher Newport
1991	Cortland St

Outdoor Track and Field

Men

DIVISION I

Year	Champion	Coach	Pts	Runner-Up	Pts
1921	Illinois	Harry Gill	20†	Notre Dame	16†
1922	California	Walter Christie	28†	Penn St	19†
1923	Michigan	Stephen Farrell	29†	Mississippi St	16
1924	No meet				
1925	Stanford*	R. L. Templeton	31†		
1926	Southern Cal*	Dean Cromwell	27†		
1927	Illinois*	Harry Gill	35†		
1928	Stanford	R. L. Templeton	72	Ohio St	31
1929	Ohio St	Frank Castleman	50	Washington	42
1930	Southern Cal	Dean Cromwell	55†	Washington	40
1931	Southern Cal	Dean Cromwell	77†	Ohio St	31†
1932	Indiana	Billy Hayes	56	Ohio St	49†
1933	Louisiana St	Bernie Moore	58	Southern Cal	54
1934	Stanford	R. L. Templeton	63	Southern Cal	54†
1935	Southern Cal	Dean Cromwell	74†	Ohio St	40†
1936	Southern Cal	Dean Cromwell	103†	Ohio St	73
1937	Southern Cal	Dean Cromwell	62	Stanford	50
1938	Southern Cal	Dean Cromwell	67†	Stanford	38
1939	Southern Cal	Dean Cromwell	86	Stanford	44†
1940	Southern Cal	Dean Cromwell	47	Stanford	28†
1941	Southern Cal	Dean Cromwell	81†	Indiana	50

Men (*Cont.*)

DIVISION I (*Cont.*)

Year	Champion	Coach	Pts	Runner-Up	Pts
1942	Southern Cal	Dean Cromwell	85†	Ohio St	44†
1943	Southern Cal	Dean Cromwell	46	California	39
1944	Illinois	Leo Johnson	79	Notre Dame	43
1945	Navy	E. J. Thomson	62	Illinois	48†
1946	Illinois	Leo Johnson	78	Southern Cal	42†
1947	Illinois	Leo Johnson	59†	Southern Cal	34†
1948	Minnesota	James Kelly	46	Southern Cal	41†
1949	Southern Cal	Jess Hill	55†	UCLA	31
1950	Southern Cal	Jess Hill	49†	Stanford	28
1951	Southern Cal	Jess Mortenson	56	Cornell	40
1952	Southern Cal	Jess Mortenson	66†	San Jose St	24†
1953	Southern Cal	Jess Mortenson	80	Illinois	41
1954	Southern Cal	Jess Mortenson	66†	Illinois	31†
1955	Southern Cal	Jess Mortenson	42	UCLA	34
1956	UCLA	Elvin Drake	55†	Kansas	51
1957	Villanova	James Elliott	47	California	32
1958	Southern Cal	Jess Mortenson	48†	Kansas	40†
1959	Kansas	Bill Easton	73	San Jose St	48
1960	Kansas	Bill Easton	50	Southern Cal	37
1961	Southern Cal	Jess Mortenson	65	Oregon	47
1962	Oregon	William Bowerman	85	Villanova	40†
1963	Southern Cal	Vern Wolfe	61	Stanford	42
1964	Oregon	William Bowerman	70	San Jose St	40
1965	Oregon	William Bowerman	32		
	Southern Cal	Vern Wolfe	32		
1966	UCLA	Jim Bush	81	Brigham Young	33
1967	Southern Cal	Vern Wolfe	86	Oregon	40
1968	Southern Cal	Vern Wolfe	58	Washington St	57
1969	San Jose St	Bud Winter	48	Kansas	45
1970	Brigham Young	Clarence Robison	35		
	Kansas	Bob Timmons	35		
	Oregon	William Bowerman	35		
1971	UCLA	Jim Bush	52	Southern Cal	41
1972	UCLA	Jim Bush	82	Southern Cal	49
1973	UCLA	Jim Bush	56	Oregon	31
1974	Tennessee	Stan Huntsman	60	UCLA	56
1975	UTEP	Ted Banks	55	UCLA	42
1976	Southern Cal	Vern Wolfe	64	UTEP	44
1977	Arizona St	Senon Castillo	64	UTEP	50
1978	UCLA	Jim Bush	50		
	UTEP	Ted Banks	50		
1979	UTEP	Ted Banks	64	Villanova	48
1980	UTEP	Ted Banks	69	UCLA	46
1981	UTEP	Ted Banks	70	Southern Meth	57
1982	UTEP	John Wedel	105	Tennessee	94
1983	Southern Meth	Ted McLaughlin	104	Tennessee	102
1984	Oregon	Bill Dellinger	113	Washington St	94½
1985	Arkansas	John McDonnell	61	Washington St	46
1986	Southern Meth	Ted McLaughlin	53	Washington St	52
1987	UCLA	Bob Larsen	81	Texas	28
1988	UCLA	Bob Larsen	82	Texas	41
1989	Louisiana St	Pat Henry	53	Texas A&M	51
1990	Louisiana St	Pat Henry	44	Arkansas	36
1991	Tennessee	Doug Brown	51	Washington St	42

*Unofficial championship.   †Fraction of a point.

Men (*Cont.*)

DIVISION II

Year	Champion
1963	MD-Eastern Shore
1964	Fresno St
1965	San Diego St
1966	San Diego St
1967	Long Beach St
1968	Cal Poly-SLO
1969	Cal Poly-SLO
1970	Cal Poly-SLO
1971	Kentucky St
1972	Eastern Michigan
1973	Norfolk St
1974	Eastern Illinois
	Norfolk St
1975	Cal St-Northridge
1976	UC-Irvine
1977	Cal St-Hayward
1978	Cal St-LA
1979	Cal Poly-SLO
1980	Cal Poly-SLO
1981	Cal Poly-SLO
1982	Abilene Christian
1983	Abilene Christian
1984	Abilene Christian
1985	Abilene Christian
1986	Abilene Christian
1987	Abilene Christian
1988	Abilene Christian
1989	St Augustine's
1990	St Augustine's
1991	St Augustine's

DIVISION III

Year	Champion
1974	Ashland
1975	Southern-New Orleans
1976	Southern-New Orleans
1977	Southern-New Orleans
1978	Occidental
1979	Slippery Rock
1980	Glassboro St
1981	Glassboro St
1982	Glassboro St
1983	Glassboro St
1984	Glassboro St
1985	Lincoln (PA)
1986	Frostburg St
1987	Frostburg St
1988	WI-La Crosse
1989	North Central
1990	Lincoln (PA)
1991	WI-La Crosse

Women

DIVISION I

Year	Champion	Coach	Pts	Runner-Up	Pts
1982	UCLA	Scott Chisam	153	Tennessee	126
1983	UCLA	Scott Chisam	116½	Florida St	108
1984	Florida St	Gary Winckler	145	Tennessee	124
1985	Oregon	Tom Heinonen	52	Florida St	46
				Louisiana St	46
1986	Texas	Terry Crawford	65	Alabama	55
1987	Louisiana St	Loren Seagrave	62	Alabama	53
1988	Louisiana St	Loren Seagrave	61	UCLA	58
1989	Louisiana St	Pat Henry	86	UCLA	47
1990	Louisiana St	Pat Henry	53	UCLA	46
1991	Louisiana St	Pat Henry	78	Texas	67

DIVISION II

Year	Champion
1982	Cal Poly-SLO
1983	Cal Poly-SLO
1984	Cal Poly-SLO
1985	Abilene Christian
1986	Abilene Christian
1987	Abilene Christian
1988	Abilene Christian
1989	Cal Poly-SLO
1990	Cal Poly-SLO
1991	Cal Poly-SLO

DIVISION III

Year	Champion
1982	Central (IA)
1983	WI-La Crosse
1984	WI-La Crosse
1985	Cortland St
1986	MA-Boston
1987	Christopher Newport
1988	Christopher Newport
1989	Christopher Newport
1990	WI-Oshkosh
1991	WI-Oshkosh

Volleyball

Men

Year	Champion	Coach	Score	Runner-Up	Most Outstanding Player
1970	UCLA	Al Scates	3-0	Long Beach St	Dane Holtzman, UCLA
1971	UCLA	Al Scates	3-0	UC-Santa Barbara	Kirk Kilgore, UCLA
					Tim Bonynge, UC-Santa Barbara
1972	UCLA	Al Scates	3-2	San Diego St	Dick Irvin, UCLA
1973	San Diego St	Jack Henn	3-1	Long Beach St	Duncan McFarland, San Diego St
1974	UCLA	Al Scates	3-2	UC-Santa Barbara	Bob Leonard, UCLA
1975	UCLA	Al Scates	3-1	UC-Santa Barbara	John Bekins, UCLA
1976	UCLA	Al Scates	3-0	Pepperdine	Joe Mika, UCLA
1977	Southern Cal	Ernie Hix	3-1	Ohio St	Celso Kalache, Southern Cal
1978	Pepperdine	Marv Dunphy	3-2	UCLA	Mike Blanchard, Pepperdine
1979	UCLA	Al Scates	3-1	Southern Cal	Singin Smith, UCLA
1980	Southern Cal	Ernie Hix	3-1	UCLA	Dusty Dvorak, Southern Cal
1981	UCLA	Al Scates	3-2	Southern Cal	Karch Kiraly, UCLA
1982	UCLA	Al Scates	3-0	Penn St	Karch Kiraly, UCLA
1983	UCLA	Al Scates	3-0	Pepperdine	Ricci Luyties, UCLA
1984	UCLA	Al Scates	3-1	Pepperdine	Ricci Luyties, UCLA
1985	Pepperdine	Marv Dunphy	3-1	Southern Cal	Bob Ctvrtlik, Pepperdine
1986	Pepperdine	Rod Wilde	3-2	Southern Cal	Steve Friedman, Pepperdine
1987	UCLA	Al Scates	3-0	Southern Cal	Ozzie Volstad, UCLA
1988	Southern Cal	Bob Yoder	3-2	UC-Santa Barbara	Jen-Kai Liu, Southern Cal
1989	UCLA	Al Scates	3-1	Stanford	Matt Sonnichsen, UCLA
1990	Southern Cal	Jim McLaughlin	3-1	Long Beach St	Bryan Ivie, Southern Cal
1991	Long Beach St	Ray Ratelle	3-1	Southern Cal	Brent Hilliard, Long Beach St

Women

DIVISION I

Year	Champion	Coach	Score	Runner-Up
1981	Southern Cal	Chuck Erbe	3-2	UCLA
1982	Hawaii	Dave Shoji	3-2	Southern Cal
1983	Hawaii	Dave Shoji	3-0	UCLA
1984	UCLA	Andy Banachowski	3-2	Stanford
1985	Pacific	John Dunning	3-1	Stanford
1986	Pacific	John Dunning	3-0	Nebraska
1987	Hawaii	Dave Shoji	3-1	Stanford
1988	Texas	Mick Haley	3-0	Hawaii
1989	Long Beach St	Brian Gimmillaro	3-0	Nebraska
1990	UCLA	Andy Banachowski	3-0	Pacific

DIVISION II

Year	Champion
1981	Cal St-Sacramento
1982	UC-Riverside
1983	Cal St-Northridge
1984	Portland St
1985	Portland St
1986	UC-Riverside
1987	Cal St-Northridge
1988	Portland St
1989	Cal St-Bakersfield
1990	West Texas St

DIVISION III

Year	Champion
1981	UC-San Diego
1982	La Verne
1983	Elmhurst
1984	UC-San Diego
1985	Elmhurst
1986	UC-San Diego
1987	UC-San Diego
1988	UC-San Diego
1989	Washington (MO)
1990	UC-San Diego

Water Polo

Men

Year	Champion	Coach	Score	Runner-Up
1969	UCLA	Bob Horn	5-2	California
1970	UC-Irvine	Ed Newland	7-6 (3 OT)	UCLA
1971	UCLA	Bob Horn	5-3	San Jose St
1972	UCLA	Bob Horn	10-5	UC-Irvine

Men (*Cont.*)

Year	Champion	Coach	Score	Runner-Up
1973	California	Pete Cutino	8-4	UC-Irvine
1974	California	Pete Cutino	7-6	UC-Irvine
1975	California	Pete Cutino	9-8	UC-Irvine
1976	Stanford	Art Lambert	13-12	UCLA
1977	California	Pete Cutino	8-6	UC-Irvine
1978	Stanford	Dante Dettamanti	7-6 (3 OT)	California
1979	UC-Santa Barbara	Pete Snyder	11-3	UCLA
1980	Stanford	Dante Dettamanti	8-6	California
1981	Stanford	Dante Dettamanti	17-6	Long Beach St
1982	UC-Irvine	Ed Newland	7-4	Stanford
1983	California	Pete Cutino	10-7	Southern Cal
1984	California	Pete Cutino	9-8	Stanford
1985	Stanford	Dante Dettamanti	12-11 (2 OT)	UC-Irvine
1986	Stanford	Dante Dettamanti	9-6	California
1987	California	Pete Cutino	9-8 (OT)	Southern Cal
1988	California	Pete Cutino	14-11	UCLA
1989	UC-Irvine	Ed Newland	9-8	California
1990	California	Steve Heaston	8-7	Stanford

Wrestling

DIVISION I

Year	Champion	Coach	Pts	Runner-Up	Pts	Most Outstanding Wrestler
1928	Oklahoma St*	E. C. Gallagher				
1929	Oklahoma St	E. C. Gallagher	26	Michigan	18	
1930	Oklahoma St*	E. C. Gallagher	27	Illinois	14	
1931	Oklahoma St*	E. C. Gallagher		Michigan		
1932	Indiana*	W. H. Thom		Oklahoma St		Edwin Belshaw, Indiana
1933	Oklahoma St*	E. C. Gallagher				Allan Kelley, Oklahoma St
	Iowa St*	Hugo Otopalik				Pat Johnson, Harvard
1934	Oklahoma St	E. C. Gallagher	29	Indiana	19	Ben Bishop, Lehigh
1935	Oklahoma St	E. C. Gallagher	36	Oklahoma	18	Ross Flood, Oklahoma St
1936	Oklahoma	Paul Keen	14	Central St (OK)	10	Wayne Martin, Oklahoma
				Oklahoma St	10	
1937	Oklahoma St	E. C. Gallagher	31	Oklahoma	13	Stanley Henson, Oklahoma St
1938	Oklahoma St	E. C. Gallagher	19	Illinois	15	Joe McDaniels, Oklahoma St
1939	Oklahoma St	E. C. Gallagher	33	Lehigh	12	Dale Hanson, Minnesota
1940	Oklahoma St	E. C. Gallagher	24	Indiana	14	Don Nichols, Michigan
1941	Oklahoma St	Art Griffith	37	Michigan St	26	Al Whitehurst, Oklahoma St
1942	Oklahoma St	Art Griffith	31	Michigan St	26	David Arndt, Oklahoma St
1943-45	No tournament					
1946	Oklahoma St	Art Griffith	25	Northern Iowa	24	Gerald Leeman, Northern Iowa
1947	Cornell	Paul Scott	32	Northern Iowa	19	William Koll, Northern Iowa
1948	Oklahoma St	Art Griffith	33	Michigan St	28	William Koll, Northern Iowa
1949	Oklahoma St	Art Griffith	32	Northern Iowa	27	Charles Hetrick, Oklahoma St
1950	Northern Iowa	David McCuskey	30	Purdue	16	Anthony Gizoni, Waynesburg
1951	Oklahoma	Port Robertson	24	Oklahoma St	23	Walter Romanowski, Cornell
1952	Oklahoma	Port Robertson	22	Northern Iowa	21	Tommy Evans, Oklahoma
1953	Penn St	Charles Speidel	21	Oklahoma	15	Frank Bettucci, Cornell
1954	Oklahoma St	Art Griffith	32	Pittsburgh	17	Tommy Evans, Oklahoma
1955	Oklahoma St	Art Griffith	40	Penn St	31	Edward Eichelberger, Lehigh
1956	Oklahoma St	Art Griffith	65	Oklahoma	62	Dan Hodge, Oklahoma
1957	Oklahoma	Port Robertson	73	Pittsburgh	66	Dan Hodge, Oklahoma
1958	Oklahoma St	Myron Roderick	77	Iowa St	62	Dick Delgado, Oklahoma
1959	Oklahoma St	Myron Roderick	73	Iowa St	51	Ron Gray, Iowa St
1960	Oklahoma	Thomas Evans	59	Iowa St	40	Dave Auble, Cornell
1961	Oklahoma St	Myron Roderick	82	Oklahoma	63	E. Gray Simons, Lock Haven
1962	Oklahoma St	Myron Roderick	82	Oklahoma	45	E. Gray Simons, Lock Haven
1963	Oklahoma	Thomas Evans	48	Iowa St	45	Mickey Martin, Oklahoma
1964	Oklahoma St	Myron Roderick	87	Oklahoma	58	Dean Lahr, Colorado
1965	Iowa St	Harold Nichols	87	Oklahoma St	86	Yojiro Uetake, Oklahoma St

DIVISION I (*Cont.*)

Year	Champion	Coach	Pts	Runner-Up	Pts	Most Outstanding Wrestler
1966	Oklahoma St	Myron Roderick	79	Iowa St	70	Yojiro Uetake, Oklahoma St
1967	Michigan St	Grady Peninger	74	Michigan	63	Rich Sanders, Portland St
1968	Oklahoma St	Myron Roderick	81	Iowa St	78	Dwayne Keller, Oklahoma St
1969	Iowa St	Harold Nichols	104	Oklahoma	69	Dan Gable, Iowa St
1970	Iowa St	Harold Nichols	99	Michigan St	84	Larry Owings, Washington
1971	Oklahoma St	Tommy Chesbro	94	Iowa St	66	Darrell Keller, Oklahoma St
1972	Iowa St	Harold Nichols	103	Michigan St	72½	Wade Schalles, Clarion
1973	Iowa St	Harold Nichols	85	Oregon St	72½	Greg Strobel, Oregon St
1974	Oklahoma	Stan Abel	69½	Michigan	67	Floyd Hitchcock, Bloomsburg
1975	Iowa	Gary Kurdelmeier	102	Oklahoma	77	Mike Frick, Lehigh
1976	Iowa	Gary Kurdelmeier	123½	Iowa St	85¾	Chuch Yagla, Iowa
1977	Iowa St	Harold Nichols	95½	Oklahoma St	88¾	Nick Gallo, Hofstra
1978	Iowa	Dan Gable	94½	Iowa St	94	Mark Churella, Michigan
1979	Iowa	Dan Gable	122½	Iowa St	88	Bruce Kinseth, Iowa
1980	Iowa	Dan Gable	110¾	Oklahoma St	87	Howard Harris, Oregon St
1981	Iowa	Dan Gable	129¾	Oklahoma	100¼	Gene Mills, Syracuse
1982	Iowa	Dan Gable	131¾	Iowa St	111	Mark Schultz, Oklahoma
1983	Iowa	Dan Gable	155	Oklahoma St	102	Mike Sheets, Oklahoma St
1984	Iowa	Dan Gable	123¾	Oklahoma St	98	Jim Zalesky, Iowa
1985	Iowa	Dan Gable	145¼	Oklahoma	98½	Barry Davis, Iowa
1986	Iowa	Dan Gable	158	Oklahoma	84¼	Marty Kistler, Iowa
1987	Iowa St	Jim Gibbons	133	Iowa	108	John Smith, Oklahoma St
1988	Arizona St	Bobby Douglas	93	Iowa	85½	Scott Turner, N Carolina St
1989	Oklahoma St	Joe Seay	91¼	Arizona St	70½	Tim Krieger, Iowa St
1990	Oklahoma St	Joe Seay	117¾	Arizona St	104¾	Chris Barnes, Oklahoma St
1991	Iowa	Dan Gable	157	Oklahoma St	108¾	Jeff Prescott, Penn St

*Unofficial champions.

DIVISION II

Year	Champion
1963	Western St (CO)
1964	Western St (CO)
1965	Mankato St
1966	Cal Poly-SLO
1967	Portland St
1968	Cal Poly-SLO
1969	Cal Poly-SLO
1970	Cal Poly-SLO
1971	Cal Poly-SLO
1972	Cal Poly-SLO
1973	Cal Poly-SLO
1974	Cal Poly-SLO
1975	Northern Iowa
1976	Cal St-Bakersfield
1977	Northern Iowa
1978	Northern Iowa
1979	Cal St-Bakersfield
1980	Cal St-Bakersfield
1981	Cal St-Bakersfield
1982	Cal St-Bakersfield
1983	Cal St-Bakersfield
1984	SIU-Edwardsville
1985	SIU-Edwardsville
1986	SIU-Edwardsville
1987	Cal St-Bakersfield
1988	N Dakota St
1989	Portland St
1990	Portland St
1991	Nebraska-Omaha

DIVISION III

Year	Champion
1974	Wilkes
1975	John Carroll
1976	Montclair St
1977	Brockport St
1978	Buffalo
1979	Trenton St
1980	Brockport St
1981	Trenton St
1982	Brockport St
1983	Brockport St
1984	Trenton St
1985	Trenton St
1986	Montclair St
1987	Trenton St
1988	St Lawrence
1989	Ithaca
1990	Ithaca
1991	Augsburg

INDIVIDUAL CHAMPIONSHIP
RECORDS

Swimming and Diving

Men

Event	Time	Record Holder	Date
50-yard freestyle	19.15	Matt Biondi, California	4-2-87
100-yard freestyle	41.80	Matt Biondi, California	4-4-87
200-yard freestyle	1:33.03	Matt Biondi, California	4-3-87
500-yard freestyle	4:12.24	Artur Wojdat, Iowa	3-30-89
1650-yard freestyle	14:37.87	Jeff Kostoff, Stanford	4-5-86
100-yard backstroke	46.99	Jeff Rouse, Stanford	3-30-91
200-yard backstroke	1:42.88	Martin Zubero, Florida	3-30-91
100-yard breaststroke	52.48	Steve Lundquist, Southern Meth	3-25-83
200-yard breaststroke	1:53.77	Mike Barrowman, Michigan	3-24-90
100-yard butterfly	46.26	Pablo Morales, Stanford	4-4-86
200-yard butterfly	1:41.78	Melvin Stewart, Tennessee	3-30-91
200-yard individual medley	1:44.01	Martin Zubera, Florida	3-30-91
400-yard individual medley	3:42.23	David Wharton, Southern Cal	4-8-88

Women

Event	Time	Record Holder	Date
50-yard freestyle	21.92	Leigh Ann Fetter, Texas	3-16-90
100-yard freestyle	48.26	Dara Torres, Florida	3-19-88
200-yard freestyle	1:44.78	Mitzi Kremer, Clemson	3-17-89
500-yard freestyle	4:34.39	Janet Evans, Stanford	3-15-90
1650-yard freestyle	15:39.14	Janet Evans, Stanford	3-17-90
100-yard backstroke	53.98	Betsy Mitchell, Texas	3-20-87
200-yard backstroke	1:55.16	Betsy Mitchell, Texas	3-21-87
100-yard breaststroke	1:00.51	Tracy McFarlane, Texas	3-18-88
200-yard breaststroke	2:11.54	Dorsey Tierney, Texas	3-23-91
100-yard butterfly	52.36	Cris Ahmann-Leighton, Arizona	3-23-91
200-yard butterfly	1:54.17	Summer Sanders, Stanford	3-23-91
200-yard individual medley	1:57.02	Summer Sanders, Stanford	3-23-91
400-yard individual medley	4:05.19	Summer Sanders, Stanford	3-23-91

Indoor Track and Field

Men

Event	Mark	Record Holder	Date
55-meter dash	6.00	Lee McRae, Pittsburgh	3-14-86
55-meter hurdles	7.08	Roger Kingdom, Pittsburgh	3-10-84
200-meter dash	20.59	Michael Johnson, Baylor	3-10-89
400-meter dash	45.79	Gabriel Luke, Rice	3-10-90
500-meter run	59.82	Roddie Haley, Arkansas	3-15-86
800-meter run	1:46.19	George Kersh, Mississippi	3-9-91
1000-meter run	2:18.74	Freddie Williams, Abilene Christian	3-15-86
1500-meter run	3:43.48	Paul Donovan, Arkansas	3-9-85
3000-meter run	7:50.00	Reuben Reina, Arkansas	3-9-91
5000-meter run	13:37.94	Jonah Koech, Iowa St	3-9-90
High jump	7 ft 9¼ in	Hollis Conway, Southwestern Louisiana	3-11-89
Pole vault	18 ft 6½ in	Dean Starkey, Illinois	3-11-89
		Istvan Bagyula, George Mason	3-10-90
Long jump	27 ft 10 in	Carl Lewis, Houston	3-13-81
Triple jump	56 ft 9½ in	Keith Connor, Southern Meth	3-13-81
Shot put	69 ft 8½ in	Michael Carter, Southern Meth	3-13-81
		Soren Tallhem, Brigham Young	3-9-85
35-pound weight throw	76 ft 5½ in	Robert Weir, Southern Meth	3-11-83

Women

Event	Mark	Record Holder	Date
55-meter dash	6.56	Gwen Torrence, Georgia	3-14-87
55-meter hurdles	7.44	Lynda Tolbert, Arizona St	3-9-90
200-meter dash	22.96	Dawn Sowell, Louisiana St	3-10-89
400-meter dash	51.05	Maicel Malone, Arizona St	3-9-91
500-meter run	1:08.89	Linetta Wilson, Nebraska	3-14-87
800-meter run	2:02.77	Meredith Rainey, Harvard	3-10-90
1000-meter run	2:41.08	Trena Hull, NV-Las Vegas	3-14-87
1500-meter run	4:17.85	Tina Krebs, Clemson	3-9-85
3000-meter run	8:54.98	Stephanie Herbst, Wisconsin	3-15-86
5000-meter run	15:48.17	Valerie McGovern, Kentucky	3-9-90
High jump	6 ft 3¼ in	Lisa Bernhagen, Stanford	3-14-87
Long jump	21 ft 10¼ in	Angela Thacker, Nebraska	3-10-84
Triple jump	45 ft 9 in	Sheila Hudson, California	3-10-90
Shot put	57 ft 11¾ in	Regina Cavanaugh, Rice	3-14-86

Outdoor Track and Field

Men

Event	Mark	Record Holder	Date
100-meter dash	10.03	Stanley Floyd, Houston	6-5-82
		Joe DeLoach, Houston	6-4-88
200-meter dash	19.87	Lorenzo Daniel, Mississippi St	6-3-88
400-meter dash	44.12	Butch Reynolds, Ohio St	6-6-87
800-meter run	1:44.70	Mark Everett, Florida	6-1-90
1500-meter run	3:35.30	Sydney Maree, Villanova	6-6-81
3000-meter steeplechase	8:12.39	Henry Rono, Washington St	6-1-78
5000-meter run	13:20.63	Sydney Maree, Villanova	6-2-79
10000-meter run	28:01.30	Suleiman Nyambui, UTEP	6-1-79
110-meter high hurdles	13.22	Greg Foster, UCLA	6-2-78
400-meter intermediate hurdles	47.85	Kevin Young, UCLA	6-3-88
High jump	7 ft 9¾ in	Hollis Conway, Southwestern Louisiana	6-3-89
Pole vault	19 ft ¼ in	Istvan Bagyula, George Mason	3-31-91
Long jump	27 ft 5½ in	Leroy Burrell, Houston	6-2-89
Triple jump	57 ft 7¾ in	Keith Connor, Southern Meth	6-5-82
Shot put	71 ft 11 in	John Brenner, UCLA	6-2-84
Discus throw	218 ft 5 in	Kamy Keshmiri, Nevada	3-31-91
Hammer throw	257 ft 0 in	Ken Flax, Oregon	6-6-86
Javelin throw	295 ft 2 in	Einar Vilhjalmsson, Texas	6-2-83
Decathlon	8279 pts	Tito Steiner, Brigham Young	6-2/3-81

Women

Event	Mark	Record Holder	Date
100-meter dash	10.78	Dawn Sowell, Louisiana St	6-3-89
200-meter dash	22.04	Dawn Sowell, Louisiana St	6-2-89
400-meter dash	50.18	Pauline Davis, Alabama	6-3-89
800-meter run	1:59.11	Suzy Favor, Wisconsin	6-1-90
1500-meter run	4:08.26	Suzy Favor, Wisconsin	6-2-90
3000-meter run	8:47.35	Vicki Huber, Villanova	6-3-88
5000-meter run	15:38.47	Annette Hand, Oregon	6-4-88
10000-meter run	32:28.57	Sylvia Mosqueda, Cal St-LA	6-1-88
100-meter hurdles	12.70	Tananjalyn Stanley, Louisiana St	6-3-89
400-meter hurdles	54.64	Latanya Sheffield, San Diego St	5-31-85
High jump	6 ft 4¼ in	Katrena Johnson, Arizona	6-1-85
Long jump	22 ft 9¼ in	Sheila Echols, Louisiana St	6-5-87
Triple jump	46 ft ¾ in	Sheila Hudson, California	6-2-90
Shot put	57 ft 6½ in	Regina Cavanaugh, Rice	6-4-86
Discus throw	209 ft 10 in	Leslie Deniz, Arizona St	6-4-83
Javelin throw	206 ft 9 in	Karin Smith, Cal Poly-SLO	6-4-82
Heptathlon	6365 pts	Jackie Joyner, UCLA	5-30/31-83

Olympics

Lords of the Rings

The Games are so commercial that even NBA richies are welcome | by WILLIAM OSCAR JOHNSON

NOTHING IN THE WORLD OF SPORT OVER the past 10 years has undergone a transformation as radical as the one that has altered the face of the Olympic Games. And we may have seen only the beginning of change in that venerable institution, which celebrates its 100th anniversary in 1996.

In 1992 there will be two Olympics, Winter and Summer (the winter version of the Games joined the summer version on the sports calendar in 1924), but never again thereafter will there be two in the same year. After the '92 doubleheader—to be held, respectively, in Albertville, France, from Feb. 8 to Feb. 23 and Barcelona from July 25 to Aug. 9—the Games will take place in alternating biennial order. The next Winter Games will be in '94 in Lillehammer, Norway; the Summer Games of '96 in Atlanta; the Winter Games of '98 in Nagano, Japan; the Summer Games of 2000 in a city yet to be named, and so on. What this does is to make each Olympics more a center of attention in its own year, which in turn—or so the International Olympic Committee (IOC) devoutly hopes—will make each Games more valuable to commercial sponsors and commercial television, and thus produce more money for the Olympic movement.

Of course, one of the new truisms of the Games is that money is the root of all Olympian endeavor. After spending the better part of a century endlessly and hypocritically demanding that all Olympic competitors take an oath swearing that they were "amateurs," the Olympic movement finally got realistic in the 1980s and dropped its barriers against professional athletes. In the 1988 Summer Games in Seoul, tennis became an official sport again for the first time since 1924 and some of the richest athletes on earth went for the gold—including West Germany's Steffi Graf and Czechoslovakia's Miloslav Mecir (they won it) and Chris Evert of the U.S. (she lost it). In the '92 Games in Barcelona next summer, players from the National Basketball Association will be allowed to compete for the first time, meaning that the U.S. team could include such millionaire hoopsters as the Chicago Bulls' Michael Jordan and the Los Angeles Lakers' Magic Johnson.

But not every Olympic sport will enjoy a full roster of professionals competing in '92. The AIBA, boxing's international federation, does not allow any boxer to participate who has fought for money—which certainly eliminates the Evander Holyfields and George Foremans of the world. Baseball, which in Barcelona will be an official medal sport for the first time, doesn't allow pros, which may be just as well since the U.S. major league season coincides with the Olympics. As for ice hockey in Albertville, pros are eligible, but, again, since the NHL season parallels the dates of the Games, marquee players probably won't be going for the gold.

The man most responsible for the ongoing Olympic revolution is IOC president Juan Antonio Samaranch, 71, a native of Barcelona who served as Spain's ambassador to the Soviet Union in the 1970s. Samaranch was elected head of the IOC in 1980, replacing Lord Killanin of Ireland who had been a relatively ineffective leader for eight years following the imperious and backward-looking 20-year regime of the American curmudgeon, Avery Brundage.

When Samaranch started his term as IOC president, the Olympic movement was in a state so sorry as to seem unimaginable today. The 1972 Games in Munich had seen the murder of 11 Israelis by terrorists. The 1976 Olympics in Montreal had experienced a boycott by African nations and wound up $1 billion in debt. The 1980 Summer Games in Moscow were a sad, depleted affair when 65 nations, including the U.S., boycotted because of the Soviet invasion of Afghanistan. Fear of political and financial disasters was so rampant that when Los Angeles obtained the right to host the 1984 Games, it was the only city to bid. And then the L.A. Olympics became the target of a retaliatory boycott by the Soviet Union and its satellite countries.

The Olympic movement seemed tarnished and out of sync with reality. Then the L.A. effort suddenly took off with a high-wire act that not only produced a vibrant and largely trouble-free Olympics, but delivered a $215 million profit to boot. The secret of it all was the utter commercialization of the Olympics, masterminded by the marketing wizard, Peter Ueberroth. IOC traditionalists looked on in shock at first, but soon enough they stole the idea lock, stock and cash register and began their own strenuous campaign to fill each and every one of the five Olympic rings with dollar signs.

Of course, it worked. The IOC now has a stable of 12 international sponsors, including Coca-Cola, Visa and Kodak, who pay hefty fees to display official Olympic logos on their products. The organizing committees for each Olympics also enlist an impressive array of sponsors. Billboard advertising at venues and the display of product logos on athletes' bodies are still prohibited—but perhaps only for a while

Samaranch speaks to modern realities by treating the Olympics as big business.

RICHARD MACKSON

longer. More and more in these years of rapid change, Samaranch's IOC has chosen the expedience of hard cash over sentiments of the heart. Never was this more true than in September 1990 when the IOC convened in Tokyo to select the city to host the Summer Games of '96.

The '96 Games will commemorate the 100th anniversary of the first modern Olympics, which were held from April 6 to April 15, 1896, in Athens. Due to the mountains of Olympic corporate money available in these plummy post–L.A. days, the number of cities campaigning for bids has multiplied. For the 1996 Games, the list included: Toronto, Manchester, Belgrade, Melbourne, Atlanta and—the sentimental sweetheart and early favorite—Athens. Greece's minister of culture, Tzannis Tzannetakis, bluntly stated his case in Tokyo: "The Olympics thrive on tradition. Giving the Games to any other city than Athens would be to surrender to commercialism."

After an intense, expensive three-year campaign by the contending cities, the IOC voted to cold-shoulder the birthplace of the Olympics and gave the Games of '96 instead to Atlanta, a great convention city, one that is likely to put on an Olympics fueled, in the modern manner, by big bucks—including record-smashing TV rights that could go over $1 billion.

In fact, Atlanta was a far superior candidate to Athens in many ways. It is a sleek,

The Legacy of a Fallen Hero

WHEN THE CANADIAN SPRINTER Ben Johnson failed his drug test at the 1988 Summer Olympics in Seoul, he triggered a global ripple effect.

Three days after defeating his American archrival, Carl Lewis, in the 100-meter race in a fastest-ever time of 9.79 seconds, Johnson was stripped of both gold medal and world record when a urine test showed evidence in his system of the anabolic steroid stanozolol. He was not the only medal winner disqualified for using banned substances in Seoul: Two gold medal–winning weightlifters from Bulgaria, a silver medalist in the same sport from Hungary and a bronze judoist from Great Britain were also kicked out. Nevertheless, in all, only 10 Olympians of the 9,000-plus athletes competing were disqualified for using illicit drugs—barely one tenth of one percent. Was that an accurate representation of drug use among world-class athletes?

Not by miles and miles. A few months after the '88 Games, *The New York Times* published a series on steroid use in sports and estimated that at least half of all competitors in Seoul had used performance-enhancing drugs of some kind. After the Games, it was rumored that there had been an IOC-supported cover-up in Seoul to keep reports of positive tests at a minimum. This was fiercely denied by IOC president Juan Antonio Samaranch, and Dr. Park Jong Sei, who ran the Olympic drug-testing lab in Seoul, said, "I was very much aware of those rumors, but I don't think there was any hanky-panky going on." Johnson ultimately admitted to drug use and wound up with a two-year suspension from international track meets. The suspension ended in September 1990, and he began racing again this year, though with slower times and much less success than he had enjoyed before.

Johnson's disgrace gave birth to stepped-up efforts to eliminate the use of performance-enhancing drugs. Among other things, this has meant more rigorous testing of athletes—not only tests conducted immediately after competitions but also, in some countries, random tests

well-organized city with numerous beautiful settings for venues and plenty of available financing. By contrast, Athens offered the specter of choking air pollution, an unstable government and a shaky telecommunications system, to say nothing of a fear of terrorism in that part of the world that the Olympic organizers said they would counter by deploying 60,000 security people—four times the number of athletes.

Atlanta will be the fifth North American city to host an Olympics in 20 years. The others were Montreal (Summer) 1976, Lake Placid (Winter) 1980, Los Angeles (Summer) 1984 and Calgary (Winter) 1988. Dependable facilities, easy financing and the fact that a North American location allows coverage of many major events to be aired live during the super-profitable prime-time hours on U.S. TV have made it very tempting for the IOC to keep voting American and Canadian. Indeed, before the IOC convened in Birmingham, England, in June 1991 to pick a city to host the 1998 Winter Games, the odds-on favorite was Salt Lake City for all of the above reasons, plus its gorgeous nearby ski mountains and its impressive array of Olympic venues already in place. But, no, the IOC could not bring itself to go to North America yet again, and by a narrow vote of 46–42, it shifted to the Far East and settled on Nagano, Japan, a lovely temple town 100 miles northwest of Tokyo. Loaded with yen, the Nagano organizers pledged

during routine training periods. In 1989, The Athletics Congress (TAC), the U.S. governing body for track and field, instituted out-of-competition testing, which proved only partially effective because of a lack of qualified testers. Of 686 athletes designated for testing in 1990, no fewer than 376, or 55%, were excused because they lived farther than 75 miles from an official tester. TAC said it was addressing the problem by hiring more testers.

Nevertheless, two of the biggest track and field stars from the U.S., Randy Barnes and Butch Reynolds, world record-holders in the shotput and the 400-meter run, respectively, were suspended for two years in November 1990 by the world track governing body, the International Amateur Athletic Federation (IAAF), after they tested positive for steroids at meets the previous summer. Both claimed innocence, but barring successful appeals, both figure to be ineligible for Barcelona.

After blazing to victory and a world record in Seoul, Johnson stumbled in the drug test.

Until now, the primary tool for IOC enforcement of the drug ban has been urine tests, which are considered less effective than blood or saliva tests. The IOC's medical commission reported this year that blood tests might be the best way to detect the presence of certain drugs. The IOC has asked the commission to evaluate the legal and ethical issues involved.

Whatever kind of tests are used at the Games of '92, the sad fate of the fallen hero, Ben Johnson, offered an unmistakable lesson to Olympic sportsmen everywhere: Using drugs may enhance performance, but it is a risky proposition.

East Germans like Kristin Otto, who won six golds in '88, now compete under a new flag.

to spend lavishly on Olympic construction.

Samaranch was not at all unhappy about the IOC's switch to Asia. He fervently believes that the Games should have a global reach. He likes to emphasize the fact that each of the five Olympic rings is meant to symbolize a continent and that two of those continents—South America and Africa—have yet to host the Games. As things stand, the burdens of Third World poverty, crippling international debt and volatile, often violent, politics will probably prevent South America from putting on an Olympics in the foreseeable future. The same, sad to say, is true of most African nations—save possibly one. That is South Africa. Until this past year, South Africa had been a pariah to most of the world, cut off by most civilized nations from international trade as well as international sports competition as punishment for its cruel policies of apartheid. But in 1991 the government formally erased the last of the laws that kept the races rigidly segregated, and the sanctions against participating in both commerce and sport with

South Africa were eased. South Africa thus can expect to compete in Barcelona after being an Olympic outcast since 1960. That turnabout in itself is historic. And a few visionaries in the IOC foresee the day that an Olympics will be held in Johannesburg or Capetown.

Ostrichlike Olympic traditionalists argued vehemently for decades that politics played no part in the Olympic Games. This was absurd (witness Hitler's Nazi-showcase Olympics of 1936 as only the most obvious example), and such foolishness has pretty much died out during the pragmatic rule of Samaranch. Just in time, for in the past couple of years, world politics have gone through an extraordinary upheaval that may change the quality of competition in the Olympics more than anything in memory.

Hostility between the Soviet Union and the U.S. has ended. Eastern Europe is a collection of small, struggling independent countries instead of a Communist monolith united behind the Iron Curtain erected at the end of World War II. The Berlin Wall is gone and the Germanies are united after more than four decades apart. All of this is good for the world generally and for democracy specifically, but it remains to be seen how it may affect the Olympics.

Ever since the Soviets sent a team to the 1952 Games in Helsinki, a breathless world has watched in fascination to see which political system would prevail over the other on the sporting battlefield of the Olympics. With East-West hostility out and *perestroika* in, the Soviet sports system no longer enjoys the same immense financial and political support. And the formerly all-powerful East German sports juggernaut, which turned that nation of just 16.7 million people into the second-biggest Olympic power—after the U.S.S.R. and ahead of the U.S.—has merged with an athletically less formidable West German team. Some experts have predicted that the unified German team will be *the* Olympic power. But as a leading East German track coach, Thomas Springstein, said of the merged teams: "There are factors that will disturb athletic development. Money will be scarce. Young talents will not find support as they did in East Germany. Everything will be like it has been in West Germany—no selection system for youngsters, few full-time coaches. Perhaps we can conceal this lack of support until 1996. But after that the all-German track team will become mediocre, like the West German team is now, and I am very sad about that."

An Olympics without the built-in melodrama of the Cold War is still hard to imagine. A Winter Olympics in which there is no chance for another triumph of the American Dream, such as the one that that baby-faced U.S. hockey team pulled off in 1980 against the Soviets? A Summer Olympics without some superpatriot warning that democracy is in jeopardy because the U.S. has won fewer medals than the Soviet Union? It is impossible to guess how much the public's fascination with the Olympics will be diluted by the easing of East-West tensions.

No one will be more interested in the results than the American television networks. The first test will come in the Winter Games at Albertville in February 1992. CBS paid a shocking amount for the rights—$243 million, which was $68 million more than

Seoul opened its arms to the world's top pros, and Graf responded by winning the gold.

Atlantans rejoiced when the IOC tapped their city as the '96 summer host, shunning Athens.

NBC bid as the only other competitor and $43 million more than the IOC had asked as a minimum. Neal Pilson, president of CBS Sports, has said the network expects only a "modest profit," but even that may be too optimistic.

If American competitors do well in Albertville, CBS's ratings could climb, but early odds are against that. Women's figure skating could produce a gold, a silver, a bronze and maybe all three, and Bonnie Blair is still golden in speed skating sprints, but U.S. chances in everything else from ice hockey to alpine skiing are not bright—and neither are those of CBS. The network has plunged for another $300 million to buy the rights to the 1994 Winter Games in Lillehammer, hoping to use the short two-year lapse after Albertville to do double-header Olympic marketing by offering package deals to advertisers who buy time in both events.

This is new, but it is not as revolutionary as the idea NBC has concocted for its coverage of next summer's Games in Barcelona. The network put up $401 million for American TV rights, and plans about 160 hours of regular television coverage over the 16-day schedule of events. This is routine stuff: Where the network has departed from previous network Olympic formats is in its use of pay-per-view television. NBC will offer around-the-clock programming consisting of three different tiers of coverage at three different prices: the highest being $170 for around-the-clock broadcasts, perhaps including start-to-finish live coverage of such popular events as diving and gymnastics. The network's market researchers estimate that as many as 2.5 million homes could sign up for the coverage—meaning a windfall in the neighborhood of $250 million.

Of course, NBC is taking the optimistic view. Tom Rogers, president of the network's cable operations, says, "With the Olympics, pay-per-view will finally have a massive event to capture the imagination of the American public. This could make it a social phenomenon. This could be a win-win situation for everyone." Many experts think the $170 fee is too high. Nevertheless, whether NBC ends up in a win-win or a lose-lose situation after Barcelona, its pay-per-view experiment will be closely watched by the TV industry—and perhaps even more closely by the cool and practical businessmen of Juan Antonio Samaranch's ever-changing Olympic movement.

1988 Summer Games

TRACK AND FIELD

Men

100 METERS

1. ... Carl Lewis, United States	9.92 WR
2. ... Linford Christie, Great Britain	9.97
3. ... Calvin Smith, United States	9.99

200 METERS

1. ... Joe DeLoach, United States	19.75 OR
2. ... Carl Lewis, United States	19.79
3. ... Robson da Silva, Brazil	20.04

400 METERS

1. ... Steven Lewis, United States	43.87
2. ... Butch Reynolds, United States	43.93
3. ... Danny Everett, United States	44.09

800 METERS

1. ... Paul Ereng, Kenya	1:43.45
2. ... Joaquim Cruz, Brazil	1:43.90
3. ... Said Aouita, Morocco	1:44.06

1500 METERS

1. ... Peter Rono, Kenya	3:35.96
2. ... Peter Elliott, Great Britain	3:36.15
3. ... Jens-Peter Herold, East Germany	3:36.21

5000 METERS

1. ... John Ngugi, Kenya	13:11.70
2. ... Dieter Baumann, West Germany	13:15.52
3. ... Hansjörg Kunze, East Germany	13:15.73

10,000 METERS

1. ... Brahim Boutaib, Morocco	27:21.46 OR
2. ... Salvatore Antibo, Italy	27:23.55
3. ... Kipkemboi Kimeli, Kenya	27:25.16

MARATHON

1. ... Gelindo Bordin, Italy	2'10:32
2. ... Douglas Wakiihuri, Kenya	2'10:47
3. ... Houssein Ahmed Saleh, Djibouti	2'10:59

110-METER HURDLES

1. ... Roger Kingdom, United States	12.98 OR
2. ... Colin Jackson, Great Britain	13.28
3. ... Tonie Campbell, United States	13.38

400-METER HURDLES

1. ... Andre Phillips, United States	47.19 OR
2. ... El Hadj Dia Ba, Senegal	47.23
3. ... Edwin Moses, United States	47.56

Note: OR=Olympic record. WR=world record.
EOR=equals Olympic record.
EWR=equals world record.

3000-METER STEEPLECHASE

1. ... Julius Kariuki, Kenya	8:05.51 OR
2. ... Peter Koech, Kenya	8:06.79
3. ... Mark Rowland, Great Britain	8:07.96

4 X 100 METER RELAY

1. ... USSR: Viktor Bryzgine, Vladimir Krylov, Vladimir Mouraviev, Vitaly Savine	38.19
2. ... Great Britain	38.40
3. ... France	38.47

4 X 400 METER RELAY

1. ... United States: Danny Everett, Steven Lewis, Kevin Robinzine, Butch Reynolds	2:56.16 EWR
2. ... Jamaica	3:00.30
3. ... West Germany	3:00.56

20-KILOMETER WALK

1. ... Jozef Pribilinec, Czechoslovakia	1:19:57 OR
2. ... Ronald Weigel, East Germany	1:20:00
3. ... Maurizio Damilano, Italy	1:20:14

50-KILOMETER WALK

1. ... Vyacheslav Ivanenko, USSR	3:38:29 OR
2. ... Ronald Weigel, East Germany	3:38:56
3. ... Hartwig Gauder, East Germany	3:39:45

HIGH JUMP

1. ... Gennadiy Avdeyenko, USSR	7 ft 9¾ in OR
2. ... Hollis Conway, United States	7 ft 8¾ in
3. ... Roudolf Povarnitsyne, USSR	7 ft 8¾ in
3. ... Patrik Sjoberg, Sweden	7 ft 8¾ in

POLE VAULT

1. ... Sergei Bubka, USSR	19 ft 4¼ in OR
2. ... Radion Gataoulline, USSR	19 ft 2¼ in
3. ... Grigory Egorov, USSR	19 ft ¼ in

LONG JUMP

1. ... Carl Lewis, United States	28 ft 7½ in
2. ... Mike Powell, United States	27 ft 10¼ in
3. ... Larry Myricks, United States	27 ft 1¾ in

TRIPLE JUMP

1. ... Khristo Markov, Bulgaria	57 ft 9½ in OR
2. ... Igor Lapchine, USSR	57 ft 5¾ in
3. ... Aleksandr Kovalenko, USSR	57 ft 2 in

SHOT PUT

1. ... Ulf Timmermann, East Germany	73 ft 8¾ in OR
2. ... Randy Barnes, United States	73 ft 5½ in
3. ... Werner Günthör, Switzerland	72 ft 1¾ in

TRACK AND FIELD (*Cont.*)

DISCUS THROW

1. ... Jürgen Schult, East Germany	225 ft 9 in OR
2. ... Romas Oubartas, USSR	221 ft 5 in
3. ... Rolf Danneberg, West Germany	221 ft 1 in

HAMMER THROW

1. ... Sergei Litvinov, USSR	278 ft 2 in OR
2. ... Yuri Sedykh, USSR	274 ft 10 in
3. ... Iouri Tamm, USSR	266 ft 3 in

JAVELIN

1. .... Tapio Korjus, Finland	276 ft 6 in
2. .... Jan Zelezny, Czechoslovakia	276 ft
3. .... Seppo Raty, Finland	273 ft 2 in

DECATHLON

		Pts
1. .... Christian Schenk, East Germany		8488
2. .... Torsten Voss, East Germany		8399
3. .... Dave Steen, Canada		8328

Women

100 METERS

1. ... Florence Griffith Joyner, United States	10.54
2. ... Evelyn Ashford, United States	10.83
3. ... Heike Drechsler, East Germany	10.85

200 METERS

1. ... Florence Griffith Joyner, United States	21.34 WR
2. ... Grace Jackson, Jamaica	21.72
3. ... Heike Drechsler, East Germany	21.95

400 METERS

1. ... Olga Bryzgina, USSR	48.65 OR
2. ... Petra Mueller, East Germany	49.45
3. ... Olga Nazarova, USSR	49.90

800 METERS

1. ... Sigrun Wodars, East Germany	1:56.10
2. ... Christine Wachtel, East Germany	1:56.64
3. ... Kim Gallagher, United States	1:56.91

1500 METERS

1. ... Paula Ivan, Romania	3:53.96 OR
2. ... Lailoute Baikauskaite, USSR	4:00.24
3. ... Tatiana Samolenko, USSR	4:00.30

3000 METERS

1. ... Tatiana Samolenko, USSR	8:26.53 OR
2. ... Paula Ivan, Romania	8:27.15
3. ... Yvonne Murray, Great Britain	8:29.02

10,000 METERS

1. ... Olga Bondarenko, USSR	31:05.21 OR
2. ... Elizabeth McColgan, Great Britain	31:08.44
3. ... Elena Zhupieva, USSR	31:19.82

MARATHON

1. ... Rosa Mota, Portugal	2:25:40
2. ... Lisa Martin, Australia	2:25:53
3. ... Kathrin Doerre, East Germany	2:26:21

100-METER HURDLES

1. ... Jordanka Donkova, Bulgaria	12.38 OR
2. ... Gloria Siebert, East Germany	12.61
3. ... Claudia Zackiewicz, West Germany	12.75

400-METER HURDLES

1. .... Debra Flintoff-King, Australia	53.17 OR
2. .... Tatiana Ledovskaia, USSR	53.18
3. .... Ellen Fiedler, East Germany	53.63

4 X 100 METER RELAY

1. .... United States: Alice Brown, Sheila Echols, Florence Griffith Joyner, Evelyn Ashford	41.98
2. .... East Germany	42.09
3. .... USSR	42.75

4 X 400 METER RELAY

1. .... USSR (Tatyana Ledovskaia, Olga Nazarova, Mariya Piniguina, Olga Bryzgina)	3:15.18 WR
2. .... United States (Denean Howard, Diane Dixon, Valerie Brisco, Florence Griffith Joyner)	3:15.51
3. .... East Germany	3:18.29

HIGH JUMP

1. .... Louise Ritter, United States	6 ft 8 in OR
2. .... Stefka Kostadinova, Bulgaria	6 ft 7 in
3. .... Tamara Bykova, USSR	6 ft 6¼ in

LONG JUMP

1. .... Jackie Joyner-Kersee, United States	24 ft 3½ in OR
2. .... Heike Drechsler, East Germany	23 ft 8¼ in
3. .... Galina Tchistiakova, USSR	23 ft 4 in

SHOT PUT

1. .... Natalya Lisovskaya, USSR	72 ft 11¾ in
2. .... Kathrin Niemke, East Germany	69 ft 1½ in
3. .... Li Meisu, China	69 ft 1¼ in

DISCUS THROW

1. .... Martina Hellmann, East Germany	237 ft 2 in OR
2. .... Diana Gansky, East Germany	235 ft 10 in
3. .... Tzvetanka Hristova, Bulgaria	228 ft 10 in

Note: OR=Olympic record. WR=world record.

TRACK AND FIELD (*Cont.*)

JAVELIN

1. ... Petra Felke, East Germany — 245 ft 0 in OR
2. ... Fatima Whitbread, Great Britain — 230 ft 8 in
3. ... Beate Koch, East Germany — 220 ft 9 in

Note: OR=Olympic record. WR=world record.
EOR=equals Olympic record.
EWR=equals world record.

HEPTATHLON

		Pts
1. ... Jackie Joyner-Kersee, United States		7291 WR
2. ... Sabine John, East Germany		6897
3. ... Anke Behmer, East Germany		6858

BASKETBALL

Men

Final: USSR 76, Yugoslavia 63
United States (3rd):
Mitch Richmond, Charles E. Smith IV, Vernell Coles, Hersey Hawkins, Jeff Grayer, Charles D. Smith, Willie Anderson, Stacey Augmon, Dan Majerle, Danny Manning, J. R. Reid, David Robinson

Women

Final: United States 77, Yugoslavia 70
USSR (3rd)
United States: Teresa Edwards, Mary Ethridge, Cynthia Brown, Anne Donovan, Teresa Weatherspoon, Bridgette Gordon, Victoria Bullett, Andrea Lloyd, Katrina McClain, Jennifer Gillom, Cynthia Cooper, Suzanne McConnell

BOXING

LIGHT FLYWEIGHT (106 LB)

1. .... Ivailo Hristov, Bulgaria
2. .... Michael Carbajal, United States
3. .... Leopoldo Serantes, Philippines
3. .... Robert Isaszegi, Hungary

FLYWEIGHT (112 LB)

1. .... Kim Kwang Sun, South Korea
2. .... Andreas Tews, East Germany
3. .... Mario Gonzalez, Mexico
3. .... Timofei Skriabin, USSR

BANTAMWEIGHT (119 LB)

1. .... Kennedy McKinney, United States
2. .... Alexandar Hristov, Bulgaria
3. .... Phajol Moolsan, Thailand
3. .... Jorge Julio Rocha, Colombia

FEATHERWEIGHT (125 LB)

1. .... Giovanni Parisi, Italy
2. .... Daniel Dumitrescu, Romania
3. .... Lee Jae Hyuk, South Korea
3. .... Abdelhak Achik, Morocco

LIGHTWEIGHT (132 LB)

1. .... Andreas Zuelow, East Germany
2. .... George Cramne, Sweden
3. .... Romallis Ellis, United States
3. .... Nerguy Enkhbat, Mongolia

LIGHT WELTERWEIGHT (139 LB)

1. .... Vyacheslav Janovski, USSR
2. .... Grahame Cheney, Australia
3. .... Reiner Gies, West Germany
3. .... Lars Myrberg, Sweden

WELTERWEIGHT (147 LB)

1. .... Robert Wangila, Kenya
2. .... Laurent Boudouani, France
3. .... Jan Dydak, Poland
3. .... Kenneth Gould, United States

LIGHT MIDDLEWEIGHT (156 LB)

1. .... Park Si Hun, South Korea
2. .... Roy Jones, United States
3. .... Richard Woodhall, Great Britain
3. .... Raymond Downey, Canada

MIDDLEWEIGHT (165 LB)

1. .... Henry Maske, East Germany
2. .... Egerton Marcus, Canada
3. .... Chris Sande, Kenya
3. .... Hussain Shah Syed, Pakistan

LIGHT HEAVYWEIGHT (178 LB)

1. .... Andrew Maynard, United States
2. .... Nourmagomed Chanavazov, USSR
3. .... Damir Skaro, Yugoslavia
3. .... Henryk Petrich, Poland

HEAVYWEIGHT (201 LB)

1. .... Ray Mercer, United States
2. .... Baik Hyun Man, South Korea
3. .... Arnold Vanderlude, Netherlands
3. .... Andrzej Golota, Poland

SUPERHEAVYWEIGHT (201+ LB)

1. .... Lennox Lewis, Canada
2. .... Riddick Bowe, United States
3. .... Aleksandr Mirochnitchenko, USSR
3. .... Janusz Zarenkiewicz, Poland

GYMNASTICS

Men

ALL-AROUND

	Pts
1. ......Vladimir Artemov, USSR	119.125
2. ......Valery Lyukin, USSR	119.025
3. ......Dmitri Bilozertchev, USSR	118.975

HORIZONTAL BAR

	Pts
1. ......Vladimir Artemov, USSR	19.900
1. ......Valery Lyukin, USSR	19.900
3. ......Holger Behrendt, East Germany	19.800
3. ......Marius Gherman, Romania	19.800

PARALLEL BARS

	Pts
1. ......Vladimir Artemov, USSR	19.925
2. ......Valery Lyukin, USSR	19.900
3. ......Sven Tippelt, East Germany	19.750

VAULT

	Pts
1. ......Lou Yun, China	19.875
2. ......Sylvio Kroll, East Germany	19.862
3. ......Park Jong Hoon, South Korea	19.775

POMMEL HORSE

	Pts
1. ......Lyubomir Gueraskov, Bulgaria	19.950
1. ......Zsolt Borkai, Hungary	19.950
1. ......Dmitri Bilozertchev, USSR	19.950

RINGS

	Pts
1. ......Holger Behrendt, East Germany	19.925
1. ......Dmitri Bilozertchev, USSR	19.925
3. ......Sven Tippelt, East Germany	19.875

FLOOR EXERCISE

	Pts
1. ......Sergei Kharikov, USSR	19.925
2. ......Vladimir Artemov, USSR	19.900
3. ......Lou Yun, China	19.850
3. ......Yukio Iketani, Japan	19.850

TEAM COMBINED EXERCISES

	Pts
1. ......USSR	593.350
2. ......East Germany	588.450
3. ......Japan	585.600

Women

ALL-AROUND

	Pts
1. ......Elena Shushunova, USSR	79.662
2. ......Daniela Silivas, Romania	79.637
3. ......Svetlana Boguinskaya, USSR	79.400

VAULT

	Pts
1. ......Svetlana Boguinskaya, USSR	19.905
2. ......Gabriela Potorac, Romania	19.830
3. ......Daniela Silivas, Romania	19.818

UNEVEN BARS

	Pts
1. ......Daniela Silivas, Romania	20.000
2. ......Dagmar Kersten, East Germany	19.987
3. ......Elena Shushunova, USSR	19.962

BALANCE BEAM

	Pts
1. ......Daniela Silivas, Romania	19.924
2. ......Elena Shushunova, USSR	19.875
3. ......Gabriela Potorac, Romania	19.837
3. ......Phoebe Mills, United States	19.837

FLOOR EXERCISE

	Pts
1. ......Daniela Silivas, Romania	19.937
2. ......Svetlana Boguinskaya, USSR	19.887
3. ......Diana Doudeva, Bulgaria	19.850

TEAM COMBINED EXERCISES

	Pts
1. ......USSR	395.475
2. ......Romania	394.125
3. ......East Germany	390.875

RHYTHMIC ALL-AROUND

	Pts
1. ......Marina Lobatch, USSR	60.000
2. ......Adriana Dounavska, Bulgaria	59.950
3. ......Aleksandra Timochenko, USSR	59.875

THEY SAID IT

Ed Temple, who has coached eight women's Olympic track gold medalists during his 38 years at Tennessee State: "I'm the only man alive whose wife approves of him going around with fast women."

SWIMMING

Men

50-METER FREESTYLE

1. ... Matt Biondi, United States — 22.14 WR
2. ... Tom Jager, United States — 22.36
3. ... Gennadi Prigoda, USSR — 22.71

100-METER FREESTYLE

1. ... Matt Biondi, United States — 48.63 OR
2. ... Chris Jacobs, United States — 49.08
3. ... Stephan Caron, France — 49.62

200-METER FREESTYLE

1. ... Duncan Armstrong, Australia — 1:47.25 WR
2. ... Anders Holmertz, Sweden — 1:47.89
3. ... Matt Biondi, United States — 1:47.99

400-METER FREESTYLE

1. ... Uwe Dassler, East Germany — 3:46.95 WR
2. ... Duncan Armstrong, Australia — 3:47.15
3. ... Artur Wojdat, Poland — 3:47.34

1500-METER FREESTYLE

1. ... Vladimir Salnikov, USSR — 15:00.40
2. ... Stefan Pfeiffer, West Germany — 15:02.69
3. ... Uwe Dassler, East Germany — 15:06.15

100-METER BACKSTROKE

1. ... Daichi Suzuki, Japan — 55.05
2. ... David Berkoff, United States — 55.18
3. ... Igor Polianski, USSR — 55.20

200-METER BACKSTROKE

1. ... Igor Polianski, USSR — 1:59.37
2. ... Frank Baltrusch, East Germany — 1:59.60
3. ... Paul Kingsman, New Zealand — 2:00.48

100-METER BREASTSTROKE

1. ... Adrian Moorhouse, Great Britain — 1:02.04
2. ... Karoly Guttler, Hungary — 1:02.05
3. ... Dmitri Volkov, USSR — 1:02.20

200-METER BREASTSTROKE

1. ... Jozsef Szabo, Hungary — 2:13.52
2. ... Nick Gillingham, Great Britain — 2:14.12
3. ... Sergio Lopez, Spain — 2:15.21

100-METER BUTTERFLY

1. ... Anthony Nesty, Suriname — 53:00 OR
2. ... Matt Biondi, United States — 53:01
3. ... Andy Jameson, Great Britain — 53.30

200-METER BUTTERFLY

1. ... Michael Gross, West Germany — 1:56.94 OR
2. ... Benny Nielsen, Denmark — 1:58.24
3. ... Anthony Mosse, New Zealand — 1:58.28

200-METER INDIVIDUAL MEDLEY

1. ... Tamas Darnyi, Hungary — 2:00.17 WR
2. ... Patrick Kuehl, Great Britain — 2:01.61
3. ... Vadim Iarochtchouk, USSR — 2:02.40

400-METER INDIVIDUAL MEDLEY

1. ... Tamas Darnyi, Hungary — 4:14.75 WR
2. ... David Wharton, United States — 4:17.36
3. ... Stefano Battistelli, Italy — 4:18.01

4 X 100 METER MEDLEY RELAY

1. ... United States: David Berkoff, Richard Schroeder, Matt Biondi, Chris Jacobs — 3:36.93 WR
2. ... Canada — 3:39.28
3. ... USSR — 3:39.96

4 X 100 METER FREESTYLE RELAY

1. ... United States: Chris Jacobs, Troy Dalbey, Tom Jager, Matt Biondi — 3:16.53 WR
2. ... USSR — 3:18.33
3. ... East Germany — 3:19.82

4 X 200 METER FREESTYLE RELAY

1. ... United States: Troy Dalbey, Matt Cetlinski, Doug Gjertsen, Matt Biondi — 7:12.51 WR
2. ... East Germany — 7:13.68
3. ... West Germany — 7:14.35

Note: OR=Olympic record. WR=world record.
EOR=equals Olympic record.
EWR=equals world record.

Women

50-METER FREESTYLE

1. ... Kristin Otto, East Germany — 25.49 OR
2. ... Yang Wenyi, China — 25.64
3. ... Katrin Meissner, East Germany — 25.71
3. ... Jill Sterkel, United States — 25.71

100-METER FREESTYLE

1. ... Kristin Otto, East Germany — 54.93
2. ... Zhuang Yong, China — 55.47
3. ... Catherine Plewinski, France — 55.49

SWIMMING (*Cont.*)

Women (*Cont.*)

200-METER FREESTYLE

1. ... Heike Friedrich, East Germany	1:57.65 OR
2. ... Silvia Poll, Costa Rica	1:58.67
3. ... Manuela Stellmach, East Germany	1:59.01

400-METER FREESTLYE

1. ... Janet Evans, United States	4:03.85 WR
2. ... Heike Friedrich, East Germany	4:05.94
3. ... Anke Moehring, East Germany	4:06.62

800-METER FREESTYLE

1. ... Janet Evans, United States	8:20.20 OR
2. ... Astrid Stauss, East Germany	8:22.09
3. ... Julie McDonald, Australia	8:22.93

100-METER BACKSTROKE

1. ... Kristin Otto, East Germany	1:00.89
2. ... Krisztina Egerszegi, Hungary	1:01.56
3. ... Cornelia Sirch, East Germany	1:01.57

200-METER BACKSTROKE

1. ... Krisztina Egerszegi, Hungary	2:09.29 OR
2. ... Kathrin Zimmermann, East Germany	2:10.61
3. ... Cornelia Sirch, East Germany	2:11.45

100-METER BREASTSTROKE

1. ... Tania Dangalakova, Bulgaria	1:07.95 OR
2. ... Antoaneta Frenkeva, Bulgaria	1:08.74
3. ... Silke Hoerner, East Germany	1:08.83

200-METER BREASTSTROKE

1. ... Silke Hoerner, East Germany	2:26.71 WR
2. ... Huang Xioamin, China	2:27.49
3. ... Antoaneta Frenkeva, Bulgaria	2:28.34

Note: OR=Olympic record. WR=world record.
EOR=equals Olympic record.
EWR=equals world record.

100-METER BUTTERFLY

1. ....Kristin Otto, East Germany	59.00 OR
2. ....Birte Weigang, East Germany	59.45
3. ....Qian Hong, China	59.52

200-METER BUTTERFLY

1. ....Kathleen Nord, East Germany	2:09.51
2. ....Birte Weigang, East Germany	2:09.91
3. ....Mary T. Meagher, United States	2:10.80

200-METER INDIVIDUAL MEDLEY

1. ....Daniela Hunger, East Germany	2:12.59 OR
2. ....Elena Dendeberova, USSR	2:13.31
3. ....Noemi Ildiko Lung, Romania	2:14.85

400-METER INDIVIDUAL MEDLEY

1. ....Janet Evans, United States	4:37.76
2. ....Noemi Ildiko Lung, Romania	4:39.36
3. ....Daniela Hunger, East Germany	4:39.76

4 X 100 METER MEDLEY RELAY

1. ....East Germany: (Kristin Otto, Silke Hoerner, Birte Weigang, Katrin Meissner)	4:03.74 OR
2. ....United States (Beth Barr, Tracey McFarlane, Janel Jorgensen, Mary Wayte)	4:07.90
3. ....Canada	4:10.49

4 X 100 METER FREESTYLE RELAY

1. ....East Germany: (Kristin Otto, Katrin Meissner, Daniela Hunger, Manula Stellmach)	3:40.63 OR
2. ....Holland	3:43.39
3. ....United States (Mary Wayte, Mitzi Kremer, Laura Walker, Dana Torres)	3:44.25

DIVING

Men		**Women**	

SPRINGBOARD

	Pts		Pts
1. ......Greg Louganis, United States	730.80	1. ......Gao Min, China	580.23
2. ......Tan Liangde, China	704.88	2. ......Li Qing, China	534.33
3. ......Li Deliang, China	665.28	3. ......Kelly McCormick, United States	533.19

PLATFORM

	Pts		Pts
1. ......Greg Louganis, United States	638.61	1. ......Xu Yanmei, China	445.20
2. ......Xiong Ni, China	637.47	2. ......Michele Mitchell, United States	436.95
3. ......Jesus Mena, Mexico	594.39	3. ......Wendy Lian Williams, United States	400.44

MEDALISTS IN OTHER SPORTS

Men's Individual Archery

Jay Barrs, United States.. 338

Women's Individual Archery

Kim Soo Nyung, South Korea 344

Men's Cycling

100 KM TEAM TIME TRIAL

East Germany: Uwe Ampler, Mario
Kummer, Maik Landsmann, Jan Schur 1:57:47.7

1 KM TIME TRIAL

Aleksandr Kirichenko, USSR........................... 1:04.50

4000 METER INDIVIDUAL PURSUIT

Gintaoutas Umaras, USSR 4:32.0

4000 METER TEAM PURSUIT

USSR: Viatcheslav Ekimov,
Artouras Kasputis, Dmitri Nelubine,
Gintaoutas Umaras 4:13.31

POINTS RACE

Dan Frost, Denmark 038

ROAD RACE

Olaf Ludwig, East Germany 4:32:22

Women's Cycling

SPRINT

Erika Saloumiae, USSR

ROAD RACE

Monique Knol, Netherlands 2:00:52

Equestrian

3-DAY TEAM

West Germany: Claus Erhorn,
Matthias Baumann, Thies Kaspareit,
Ralf Ehrenbrink.. 225.95

3-DAY INDIVIDUAL

Mark Todd, New Zealand 42.60

TEAM DRESSAGE

West Germany: Reiner Klimke,
Annkathrin Linsenhoff, Monica Theodorescu,
Nicole Uphoff.. 4302

INDIVIDUAL DRESSAGE

Nicole Uphoff, West Germany......................... 1521

TEAM JUMPING

West Germany: Ludger Beerbaum,
Wolfgang Brinkmann, Dirk Hafemeister, Franke
Sloothaak 17.25

Equestrian (*Cont.*)

INDIVIDUAL JUMPING

Pierre Durand, France..1.25

Men's Fencing

FOIL

Stefano Cerioni, Italy

SABRE

Jean-Francois Lamour, France

EPEE

Arnd Schmitt, West Germany

Women's Fencing

FOIL

Anja Fichtel, West Germany

Men's Field Hockey

1. .... Great Britain
2. .... West Germany
3. .... Netherlands

Women's Field Hockey

1. .... Australia
2. .... South Korea
3. .... Netherlands

Men's Handball

1. .... USSR
2. .... South Korea
3. .... Yugoslavia

Women's Handball

1. .... South Korea
2. .... Norway
3. .... USSR

THEY SAID IT

Heather Percy, mother of Karen Percy, Canada's bronze medalist in the women's downhill, confirming her daughter's reputation as a klutz: "I will never understand how she can ski down a mountain 50 or 60 miles an hour, then come home and fall down the stairs."

MEDALISTS IN OTHER SPORTS (*Cont.*)

Judo

EXTRA-LIGHTWEIGHT
Kim Jae Yup, South Korea

HALF-LIGHTWEIGHT
Lee Kyung Keun, South Korea

LIGHTWEIGHT
Marc Alexandre, France

HALF-MIDDLEWEIGHT
Waldemar Legien, Poland

MIDDLEWEIGHT
Peter Seisenbacher, Austria

HALF-HEAVYWEIGHT
Aurelio Miguel, Brazil

HEAVYWEIGHT
Hitoshi Saito, Japan

Modern Pentathlon

TEAM
Hungary

INDIVIDUAL
Janos Martinek, Hungary

Men's Rowing

SINGLE SCULL
Thomas Lange, East Germany 6:49.86

DOUBLE SCULL
Netherlands 6:21.13

COXLESS PAIR
Great Britain 6:36.84

COXED FOUR
East Germany 6:10.74

COXED PAIR
Italy 6:58.79

QUADRUPLE SCULL
Italy 5:53.37

COXLESS FOUR
East Germany 6:03.11

EIGHT-OARS
West Germany 5:46.05

Women's Rowing

SINGLE SCULL
Jutta Behrendt, East Germany 7:47.19

DOUBLE SCULL
East Germany 7:00.48

COXLESS PAIR
Romania 7:28.13

COXED FOUR
East Germany 6:56.0

QUADRUPLE SCULL
East Germany 6:21.06

EIGHT-OARS
East Germany 6:15.17

Soccer

1. .... USSR
2. .... Brazil
3. .... West Germany

Synchronized Swimming

SOLO

	Pts
Carolyn Waldo, Canada	200.150

DUET
Michelle Cameron & Carolyn Waldo, Canada ... 197.717

THEY SAID IT

Doug Russell, who beat the then-unpopular Mark Spitz in the 100-meter butterfly at Mexico City in 1968, on Spitz's seven gold medals at Munich: "It could have happened to a nicer guy."

A Gold for All Seasons

Eddie Eagan of the United States is the only person to have won a gold medal in both the summer and winter Olympics. At the 1920 Summer Games in Antwerp, Belgium, Eagan won the gold in the light heavyweight boxing competition. Twelve years later, he competed on the gold medal-winning four-man bobsled team at Lake Placid.

MEDALISTS IN OTHER SPORTS (*Cont.*)

Men's Table Tennis

SINGLES
Yoo Nam Kyu, South Korea

DOUBLES
Chen Longcan & Wei Qingguang, China

Women's Table Tennis

SINGLES
Chen Jing, China

DOUBLES
Hyun Jung Hwa & Yang Young Ja, South Korea

Men's Tennis

SINGLES
Miloslav Mecir, Czechoslovakia

DOUBLES
Ken Flach & Robert Seguso, United States

Women's Tennis

SINGLES
Steffi Graf, West Germany

DOUBLES
Pam Shriver & Zina Garrison, United States

Men's Volleyball

1. .... United States: Troy Tanner, David Saunders, Jon Root, Bob Ctvrtlik, Bob Partie, Steve Timmons, Craig Buck, Scott Fortune, Ricci Luyties, Jeff Stork, Eric Sato, Karch Kiraly
2. .... USSR
3. .... Argentina

Women's Volleyball

1. .... USSR
2. .... Peru
3. .... China

Water Polo

1. .... Yugoslavia
2. .... United States: James Bergeson, Greg Boyer, Jeff Campbell, Jody Campbell, Peter Campbell, Chris DuPlanty, Mike Evans, Doug Kimbell, Craig Klass, Alan Mouchawar, Kevin Robertson, Terry Schroeder, Craig Wilson
3. .... USSR

Weightlifting

115 POUNDS
Sevdalin Marinov, Bulgaria.......................... 595 lb WR

123 POUNDS
Oxen Mirzoian, USSR .... 645 lb OR

132 POUNDS
Naim Suleymanoglu, Turkey .... 755 lb WR

149 POUNDS
Joachim Kunz, East Germany.................... 749 lb

165 POUNDS
Borislav Guidikov, Bulgaria .... 827 lb OR

182 POUNDS
Israil Arsamakov, USSR............................. 832 lb

198 POUNDS
Anatoly Khrapatyi, USSR .... 910 lb OR

220 POUNDS
Pavel Kouznetsov, USSR............................ 937 lb OR

243 POUNDS
Yuri Zakharevitch, USSR .... 1003 lb WR

243+ POUNDS
Alexandre Kourlovitch, USSR .... 1020 lb OR

Freestyle Wrestling

106 POUNDS	Takashi Kobayashi, Japan
115 POUNDS	Mitsuru Sato, Japan
126 POUNDS	Sergei Beloglazov, USSR
137 POUNDS	John Smith, United States
150 POUNDS	Arsen Fadzaev, USSR
163 POUNDS	Kenneth Monday, United States
181 POUNDS	Han Myung Woo, South Korea
198 POUNDS	Makharbek Khadartsev, USSR
220 POUNDS	Vasile Puscasu, Romania
286 POUNDS	David Gobedjichvili, USSR

Note: OR=Olympic Record; WR=World Record; EOR=Equals Olympic Record; EWR=Equals World Record; WB=World Best.

MEDALISTS IN OTHER SPORTS (*Cont.*)

Greco-Roman Wrestling

106 POUNDS	Vincenzo Maenza, Italy
115 POUNDS	Jon Ronningen, Norway
126 POUNDS	Andras Sike, Hungary
137 POUNDS	Kamandar Madjidov, USSR
150 POUNDS	Levon Djoulfalakian, USSR
163 POUNDS	Kim Young Nam, South Korea
181 POUNDS	Mikhail Mamiachvili, USSR
198 POUNDS	Atanas Komchev, Bulgaria
220 POUNDS	Andrzej Wronski, Poland
286 POUNDS	Aleksandr Kareline, USSR

Yachting

SOLING CLASS	East Germany
STAR CLASS	Great Britain
FLYING DUTCHMAN CLASS	Denmark
FINN CLASS	Jose Luis Doreste, Spain
TORNADO CLASS	France
DIVISION II	Bruce Kendall, New Zealand
MEN'S 470 CLASS	France
WOMEN'S 470 CLASS	United States

1988 Winter Games

BIATHLON

10 KILOMETERS

1.	Frank-Peter Roetsch, East Germany	25:08.1
2.	Valeri Medvedtsev, USSR	25:23.7
3.	Sergei Tchepikov, USSR	25:29.4

20 KILOMETERS

1.	Frank-Peter Roetsch, East Germany	56:33.33
2.	Valeri Medvedtsev, USSR	56:54.6
3.	Johann Passler, Italy	57:10.1

4 X 7.5 KILOMETER RELAY

1.	USSR	1:22:30.0
2.	West Germany	1:23:37.4
3.	Italy	1:23:51.5

BOBSLED

4-MAN BOB

1.	Switzerland	3:47.51
2.	East Germany	3:47.58
3.	USSR	3:48.26

2-MAN BOB

1.	USSR	3:53.48
2.	East Germany	3:54.19
3.	East Germany II	3:54.64

ICE HOCKEY

1.	USSR
2.	Finland
3.	Sweden

LUGE

Men's

SINGLES

1.	Jens Mueller, East Germany	3:05.548
2.	Georg Hackl, West Germany	3:05.916
3.	Iouri Khartchenko, USSR	3:06.274

PAIRS

1.	East Germany	1:31.940
2.	East Germany	1:32.039
3.	West Germany	1:32.724

Women's

SINGLES

1.	Steffi Walter, East Germany	3:03.973
2.	Ute Oberhoffner, East Germany	3:04.105
3.	Cerstin Schmidt, East Germany	3:04.181

Note: OR=Olympic Record; WR=World Record;
EOR=Equals Olympic Record; EWR=Equals World Record;
WB=World Best.

FIGURE SKATING

Men

1..... Brian Boitano, United States
2..... Brian Orser, Canada
3..... Viktor Petrenko, USSR

Women

1..... Katarina Witt, East Germany
2..... Elizabeth Manley, Canada
3..... Debi Thomas, United States

Pairs

1. ... Ekaterina Gordeeva & Sergei Grinkov, USSR
2. ... Elena Valova & Oleg Vasiliev, USSR
3. ... Jill Watson & Peter Oppegard, United States

Ice Dancing

1. ... Natalia Bestemianova & Andrei Bukin, USSR
2. ... Marina Klimova & Sergei Ponomarenko, USSR
3. ... Tracy Wilson & Robert McCall, Canada

SPEED SKATING

Men

500 METERS

1. ....Jens-Uwe Mey, East Germany	36.45 WR
2. ....Jan Ykema, Netherlands	36.76
3. ....Akira Kuroiwa, Japan	36.77

1000 METERS

1. ....Nikolai Gulyaev, USSR	1:13.03 OR
2. ....Jens-Uwe Mey, East Germany	1:13.11
3. ....Igor Zhelezovski, USSR	1:13.19

1500 METERS

1. ....Andre Hoffmann, East Germany	1:52.06 WR
2. ....Eric Flaim, United States	1:52.12
3. ....Michael Hadschieff, Austria	1:52.31

5000 METERS

1. ....Tomas Gustafson, Sweden	6:44.63 WR
2. ....Leo Visser, Netherlands	6:44.98
3. ....Gerard Kemkers, Netherlands	6:45.92

10,000 METERS

1. ....Tomas Gustafson, Sweden	13:48.20 WR
2. ....Michael Hadschieff, Austria	13:56.11
3. ....Leo Visser, Netherlands	14:00.55

Women

500 METERS

1. ....Bonnie Blair, United States	39.10 WR
2. ....Christa Rothenburger, East Germany	39.12
3. ....Karin Kania, East Germany	39.24

1000 METERS

1. ....Christa Rothenburger, East Germany	1:17.65 WR
2. ....Karin Kania, East Germany	1:17.70
3. ....Bonnie Blair, United States	1:18.31

1500 METERS

1. ....Yvonne van Gennip, Netherlands	2:00.68 OR
2. ....Karin Kania, East Germany	2:00.82
3. ....Andrea Ehrig, East Germany	2:01.49

3000 METERS

1. ....Yvonne van Gennip, Netherlands	4:11.94 WR
2. ....Andrea Ehrig, East Germany	4:12.09
3. ....Gabi Zange, East Germany	4:16.92

5000 METERS

1. ....Yvonne van Gennip, Netherlands	7:14.13 WR
2. ....Andrea Ehrig, East Germany	7:17.12
3. ....Gabi Zange, East Germany	7:21.61

ALPINE SKIING

Men

DOWNHILL

1. ....Pirmin Zurbriggen, Switzerland	1:59.63
2. ....Peter Mueller, Switzerland	2:00.14
3. ....Franck Piccard, France	2:01.24

SUPER GIANT SLALOM

1. ....Franck Piccard, France	1:39.66
2. ....Helmut Mayer, Austria	1:40.96
3. ....Lars-Börje Eriksson, Sweden	1:41.08

GIANT SLALOM

1. ....Alberto Tomba, Italy	2:06.37
2. ....Hubert Strolz, Austria	2:07.41
3. ....Pirmin Zurbriggen, Switzerland	2:08.39

SLALOM

1. ....Alberto Tomba, Italy	1:39.47
2. ....Frank Woerndl, West Germany	1:39.53
3. ....Paul Frommelt, Liechtenstein	1:39.84

Women

DOWNHILL

1. ....Marina Kiehl, West Germany	1:25.86
2. ....Brigitte Oertli, Switzerland	1:26.61
3. ....Karen Percy, Canada	1:26.62

SUPER GIANT SLALOM

1. ....Sigrid Wolf, Austria	1:19.03
2. ....Michela Figini, Switzerland	1:20.03
3. ....Karen Percy, Canada	1:20.29

GIANT SLALOM

1. ....Vreni Schneider, Switzerland	2:06.49
2. ....C. Kinshofer-Güthlein, West Germany	2:07.42
3. ....Maria Walliser, Switzerland	2:07.72

SLALOM

1. ....Vreni Schneider, Switzerland	1:36.69
2. ....Mateja Svet, Yugoslavia	1:38.37
3. ....C. Kinshofer-Güthlein, West Germany	1:38.40

ALPINE SKIING (*Cont.*)

Men (*Cont.*)

COMBINED

	Pts
1. ....Hubert Strolz, Austria	36.55
2. ....Bernhard Gstrein, Austria	43.45
3. ....Paul Accola, Switzerland	48.24

Women (*Cont.*)

COMBINED

	Pts
1. ....Anita Wachter, Austria	29.25
2. ....Brigitte Oertli, Switzerland	29.48
3. ....Maria Walliser, Switzerland	51.28

NORDIC SKIING

Men

15 KILOMETERS

1. ....Mikhail Deviatiarov, USSR	41:18.9
2. ....Pal Mikkelsplass, Norway	41:33.4
3. ....Vladimir Smirnov, USSR	41:48.5

30 KILOMETERS

1. ....Aleksei Prokourorov, USSR	1:24:26.3
2. ....Vladimir Smirnov, USSR	1:24:35.1
3. ....Vogard Ulvang, Norway	1:25:11.6

50 KILOMETERS

1. ....Gunde Svan, Sweden	2:04:30.9
2. ....Maurilio De Zolt, Italy	2:05:36.4
3. ....Andy Gruenenfelder, Switzerland	2:06:01.9

4 X 10 KILOMETER RELAY

1. .... Sweden	1:43:58.6
2. .... USSR	1:44:11.3
3. .... Czechoslovakia	1:45:22.7

COMBINED CROSS-COUNTRY & JUMPING

1. .... Hippolyt Kempf, Switzerland
2. .... Klaus Sulzenbacher, Austria
3. .... Allar Levandi, USSR

TEAM SKI JUMPING

	Pts
1. .... Finland	634.4
2. .... Yugoslavia	625.5
3. .... Norway	596.1

SKI JUMPING (90 METERS)

	Pts
1. ... Matti Nykänen, Finland	224.0
2. ... Erik Johnsen, Norway	207.9
3. ... Matjaz Debelak, Yugoslavia	207.7

TEAM COMBINED

1. .... West Germany
2. .... Switzerland
3. .... Austria

SKI JUMPING (70 METERS)

	Pts
1. ....Matti Nykänen, Finland	229.1
2. ....Pavel Ploc, Czechoslovakia	212.1
3. ....Jiri Malec, Czechoslovakia	211.8

Women

5 KILOMETERS

1. ....Marjo Matikainen, Finland	15:04.0
2. ....Tamara Tikhonova, USSR	15:05.3
3. ....Vida Ventsane, USSR	15:11.1

10 KILOMETERS

1. ....Vida Ventsane, USSR	30:08.3
2. ....Raisa Smetanina, USSR	30:17.0
3. ....Marjo Matikainen, Finland	30:20.5

4 X 5 KILOMETERS

1. ....Tamara Tikhonova, USSR	55:53.6
2. ....Anfissa Reztsova, USSR	56:12.8
3. ....Raisa Smetanina, USSR	57:22.1

4 X 5 KILOMETER RELAY

1. .... USSR	59:51.1
2. .... Norway	1:01:33.0
3. .... Finland	1:01:53.8

Bahamas: Solid Gold

When gold medal totals are adjusted for population, the Bahamas in 1964 is the biggest winner in Summer Olympic history. Its single gold in yachting's Star class represented a country of only 108,000 people. By comparison, the U.S.'s 83 gold medals in the '84 Games, skipped by the USSR and most of its Eastern bloc comrades, represent a meager 1-for-3 million ratio.

THEY SAID IT

Center David Robinson, when asked what was missing from the U.S. basketball team's disappointing bronze medal performance at the 1988 Summer Games: "We didn't have enough points."

Olympic Games Locations and Dates

Summer

	Year	Site	Dates	Men	Women	Nations	Most Medals	US Medals
I	1896	Athens, Greece	Apr 6-15	311	0	13	Greece (10-19-18 — 47)	11-6-2 — 19 (2nd)
II	1900	Paris, France	May 20-Oct 28	1319	11	22	France (29-41-32 — 102)	20-14-19 — 53 (2nd)
III	1904	St Louis, United States	July 1-Nov 23	681	6	12	United States (80-86-72 — 238)	
—	1906	Athens, Greece	Apr 22-May 2	877	7	20	France (15-9-16 — 40)	12-6-5 — 23 (4th)
IV	1908	London, Great Britain	Apr 27-Oct 31	1999	36	23	Britain (56-50-39 — 145)	23-12-12 — 47 (2nd)
V	1912	Stockholm, Sweden	May 5-July 22	2490	57	28	Sweden (24-24-17 — 65)	23-19-19 — 61 (2nd)
VI	1916	Berlin, Germany	Cancelled because of war					
VII	1920	Antwerp, Belgium	Apr 20-Sep 12	2543	64	29	United States (41-27-28 — 96)	
VIII	1924	Paris, France	May 4-July 27	2956	136	44	United States (45-27-27 — 99)	
IX	1928	Amsterdam, Netherlands	May 17-Aug 12	2724	290	46	United States (22-18-16 — 56)	
X	1932	Los Angeles, United States	July 30-Aug 14	1281	127	37	United States (41-32-31 — 104)	
XI	1936	Berlin, Germany	Aug 1-16	3738	328	49	Germany (33-26-30 — 89)	24-20-12 — 56 (2nd)
XII	1940	Tokyo, Japan	Cancelled because of war					
XIII	1944	London, Great Britain	Cancelled because of war					
XIV	1948	London, Great Britain	July 29-Aug 14	3714	385	59	United States (38-27-19 — 84)	
XV	1952	Helsinki, Finland	July 19-Aug 3	4407	518	69	United States (40-19-17 — 76)	
XVI	1956	Melbourne, Australia*	Nov 22-Dec 8	2958	384	67	USSR (37-29-32 — 98)	32-25-17 — 74 (2nd)
XVII	1960	Rome, Italy	Aug 25-Sep 11	4738	610	83	USSR (43-29-31 — 103)	34-21-16 — 71 (2nd)
XVIII	1964	Tokyo, Japan	Oct 10-24	4457	683	93	United States (36-26-28 — 90)	
XIX	1968	Mexico City, Mexico	Oct 12-27	4750	781	112	United States (45-28-34 — 107)	
XX	1972	Munich, West Germany	Aug 26-Sep 10	5848	1299	122	USSR (50-27-22 — 99)	33-31-30 — 94 (2nd)
XXI	1976	Montreal, Canada	July 17-Aug 1	4834	1251	92†	USSR (49-41-35 — 125)	34-35-25 — 94 (3rd)
XXII	1980	Moscow, USSR	July 19-Aug 3	4265	1088	81‡	USSR (80-69-46 — 195)	Did not compete
XXIII	1984	Los Angeles, United States	July 28-Aug 12	5458	1620	141#	United States (83-61-30 — 174)	
XXIV	1988	Seoul, South Korea	Sep 17-Oct 2	7105	2476	160	USSR (55-31-46 — 132)	36-31-27 — 94 (3rd)
XXV	1992	Barcelona, Spain	July 25-Aug 9					

*The equestrian events were held in Stockholm, Sweden, June 10-17, 1956.

†This figure includes Cameroon, Egypt, Morocco, and Tunisia, countries that boycotted the 1976 Olympics after some of their athletes had already competed.

‡The US was among 65 countries that refused to participate in the 1980 Summer Games in Moscow.

#The USSR, East Germany, and 14 other countries skipped the Summer Games in Los Angeles.

Winter

	Year	Site	Dates	Competitors Men	Women	Nations	Most Medals	US Medals
I	1924	Chamonix, France	Jan 25-Feb 4	281	13	16	Norway (4-7-6 — 17)	1-2-1 — 4 (3rd)
II	1928	St Moritz, Switzerland	Feb 11-19	468	27	25	Norway (6-4-5 — 15)	2-2-2 — 6 (2nd)
III	1932	Lake Placid, United States	Feb 4-15	274	32	17	United States (6-4-2 — 12)	
IV	1936	Garmisch-Partenkirchen, Germany	Feb 6-16	675	80	28	Norway (7-5-3 — 15)	1-0-3 — 4 (T-5th)
—	1940	Garmisch-Partenkirchen, Germany	Cancelled because of war					
—	1944	Cortina d'Ampezzo, Italy	Cancelled because of war					
V	1948	St Moritz, Switzerland	Jan 30-Feb 8	636	77	28	Norway (4-3-3 — 10) Sweden (4-3-3 — 10) Switzerland (3-4-3 — 10)	3-4-2 — 9 (4th)
VI	1952	Oslo, Norway	Feb 14-25	623	109	30	Norway (7-3-6 — 16)	4-6-1 — 11 (2nd)
VII	1956	Cortina d'Ampezzo, Italy	Jan 26-Feb 5	686	132	32	USSR (7-3-6 — 16)	2-3-2 — 7 (T-4th)
VIII	1960	Squaw Valley, United States	Feb 18-28	521	144	30	USSR (7-5-9 — 21)	3-4-3 — 10 (2nd)
IX	1964	Innsbruck, Austria	Jan 29-Feb 9	986	200	36	USSR (11-8-6 — 25)	1-2-3 — 6 (7th)
X	1968	Grenoble, France	Feb 6-18	1081	212	37	Norway (6-6-2 — 14)	1-5-1 — 7 (T-7th)
XI	1972	Sapporo, Japan	Feb 3-13	1015	217	35	USSR (8-5-3 — 16)	3-2-3 — 8 (6th)
XII	1976	Innsbruck, Austria	Feb 4-15	900	228	37	USSR (13-6-8 — 27)	3-3-4 — 10 (T-3rd)
XIII	1980	Lake Placid, United States	Feb 14-23	833	234	37	USSR (10-6-6 — 22)	6-4-2 — 12 (3rd)
XIV	1984	Sarajevo, Yugoslavia	Feb 7-19	1002	276	49	USSR (6-10-9 — 25)	4-4-0 — 8 (T-5th)
XV	1988	Calgary, Canada	Feb 13-28	1128	317	57	USSR (11-9-9 — 29)	2-1-3 — 6 (T-8th)
XVI	1992	Albertville, France	Feb 8-23					

Summer Games Champions

TRACK AND FIELD

Men

100 METERS

1896 .... Thomas Burke, United States	12.0	
1900 .... Frank Jarvis, United States	11.0	
1904 .... Archie Hahn, United States	11.0	
1906 .... Archie Hahn, United States	11.2	
1908 .... Reginald Walker, South Africa	10.8 OR	
1912 .... Ralph Craig, United States	10.8	
1920 .... Charles Paddock, United States	10.8	
1924 .... Harold Abrahams, Great Britain	10.6 OR	
1928 .... Percy Williams, Canada	10.8	
1932 .... Eddie Tolan, United States	10.3 OR	
1936 .... Jesse Owens, United States	10.3	
1948 .... Harrison Dillard, United States	10.3	
1952 .... Lindy Remigino, United States	10.4	
1956 .... Bobby Morrow, United States	10.5	
1960 .... Armin Hary, West Germany	10.2 OR	
1964 .... Bob Hayes, United States	10.0 EWR	
1968 .... Jim Hines, United States	9.95 WR	
1972 .... Valery Borzov, USSR	10.14	
1976 .... Hasely Crawford, Trinidad	10.06	
1980 .... Allan Wells, Great Britain	10.25	
1984 .... Carl Lewis, United States	9.99	
1988 .... Carl Lewis, United States*	9.92 WR	

*Ben Johnson, Canada, disqualified.

TRACK AND FIELD (*Cont.*)

Men

200 METERS

1900	John Walter Tewksbury, United States	22.2
1904	Archie Hahn, United States	21.6 OR
1906	Not held	
1908	Robert Kerr, Canada	22.6
1912	Ralph Craig, United States	21.7
1920	Allen Woodring, United States	22.0
1924	Jackson Scholz, United States	21.6
1928	Percy Williams, Canada	21.8
1932	Eddie Tolan, United States	21.2 OR
1936	Jesse Owens, United States	20.7 OR
1948	Mel Patton, United States	21.1
1952	Andrew Stanfield, United States	20.7
1956	Bobby Morrow, United States	20.6 OR
1960	Livio Berruti, Italy	20.5 EWR
1964	Henry Carr, United States	20.3 OR
1968	Tommie Smith, United States	19.83 WR
1972	Valery Borzov, USSR	20.00
1976	Donald Quarrie, Jamaica	20.23
1980	Pietro Mennea, Italy	20.19
1984	Carl Lewis, United States	19.80 OR
1988	Joe DeLoach, United States	19.75 OR

400 METERS

1896	Thomas Burke, United States	54.2
1900	Maxey Long, United States	49.4 OR
1904	Harry Hillman, United States	49.2 OR
1906	Paul Pilgrim, United States	53.2
1908	Wyndham Halswelle, Great Britain	50.0
1912	Charles Reidpath, United States	48.2 OR
1920	Bevil Rudd, South Africa	49.6
1924	Eric Liddell, Great Britain	47.6 OR
1928	Ray Barbuti, United States	47.8
1932	William Carr, United States	46.2 WR
1936	Archie Williams, United States	46.5
1948	Arthur Wint, Jamaica	46.2
1952	George Rhoden, Jamaica	45.9
1956	Charles Jenkins, United States	46.7
1960	Otis Davis, United States	44.9 WR
1964	Michael Larrabee, United States	45.1
1968	Lee Evans, United States	43.86 WR
1972	Vincent Matthews, United States	44.66
1976	Alberto Juantorena, Cuba	44.26
1980	Viktor Markin, USSR	44.60
1984	Alonzo Babers, United States	44.27
1988	Steven Lewis, United States	43.87

800 METERS

1896	Edwin Flack, Australia	2:11
1900	Alfred Tysoe, Great Britain	2:01.2
1904	James Lightbody, United States	1:56 OR
1906	Paul Pilgrim, United States	2:01.5
1908	Mel Sheppard, United States	1:52.8 WR
1912	James Meredith, United States	1:51.9 WR
1920	Albert Hill, Great Britain	1:53.4
1924	Douglas Lowe, Great Britain	1:52.4
1928	Douglas Lowe, Great Britain	1:51.8 OR
1932	Thomas Hampson, Great Britain	1:49.8 WR

800 METERS (*Cont.*)

1936	John Woodruff, United States	1:52.9
1948	Mal Whitfield, United States	1:49.2 OR
1952	Mal Whitfield, United States	1:49.2 EOR
1956	Thomas Courtney, United States	1:47.7 OR
1960	Peter Snell, New Zealand	1:46.3 OR
1964	Peter Snell, New Zealand	1:45.1 OR
1968	Ralph Doubell, Australia	1:44.3 EWR
1972	Dave Wottle, United States	1:45.9
1976	Alberto Juantorena, Cuba	1:43.50 WR
1980	Steve Ovett, Great Britain	1:45.40
1984	Joaquim Cruz, Brazil	1:43.00 OR
1988	Paul Ereng, Kenya	1:43.45

1500 METERS

1896	Edwin Flack, Australia	4:33.2
1900	Charles Bennett, Great Britain	4:06.2 WR
1904	James Lightbody, United States	4:05.4 WR
1906	James Lightbody, United States	4:12.0
1908	Mel Sheppard, United States	4:03.4 OR
1912	Arnold Jackson, Great Britain	3:56.8 OR
1920	Albert Hill, Great Britain	4:01.8
1924	Paavo Nurmi, Finland	3:53.6 OR
1928	Harry Larva, Finland	3:53.2 OR
1932	Luigi Beccali, Italy	3:51.2 OR
1936	Jack Lovelock, New Zealand	3:47.8 WR
1948	Henri Eriksson, Sweden	3:49.8
1952	Josef Barthel, Luxemburg	3:45.1 OR
1956	Ron Delany, Ireland	3:41.2 OR
1960	Herb Elliott, Australia	3:35.6 WR
1964	Peter Snell, New Zealand	3:38.1
1968	Kipchoge Keino, Kenya	3:34.9 OR
1972	Pekkha Vasala, Finland	3:36.3
1976	John Walker, New Zealand	3:39.17
1980	Sebastian Coe, Great Britain	3:38.4
1984	Sebastian Coe, Great Britain	3:32.53 OR
1988	Peter Rono, Kenya	3:35.96

5000 METERS

1912	Hannes Kolehmainen, Finland	14:36.6 WR
1920	Joseph Guillemot, France	14:55.6
1924	Paavo Nurmi, Finland	14:31.2 OR
1928	Villie Ritola, Finland	14:38
1932	Lauri Lehtinen, Finland	14:30 OR
1936	Gunnar Höckert, Finland	14:22.2 OR
1948	Gaston Reiff, Belgium	14:17.6 OR
1952	Emil Zatopek, Czechoslovakia	14:06.6 OR
1956	Vladimir Kuts, USSR	13:39.6 OR
1960	Murray Halberg, New Zealand	13:43.4
1964	Bob Schul, United States	13:48.8
1968	Mohamed Gammoudi, Tunisia	14:05.0
1972	Lasse Viren, Finland	13:26.4 OR
1976	Lasse Viren, Finland	13:24.76
1980	Miruts Yifter, Ethiopia	13:21.0
1984	Said Aouita, Morocco	13:05.59 OR
1988	John Ngugi, Kenya	13:11.70

Note: OR=Olympic Record; WR=World Record; EOR=Equals Olympic Record; EWR=Equals World Record; WB=World Best.

TRACK AND FIELD (*Cont.*)
Men

10,000 METERS

1912	Hannes Kolehmainen, Finland	31:20.8
1920	Paavo Nurmi, Finland	31:45.8
1924	Villie Ritola, Finland	30:23.2 WR
1928	Paavo Nurmi, Finland	30:18.8 OR
1932	Janusz Kusocinski, Poland	30:11.4 OR
1936	Ilmari Salminen, Finland	30:15.4
1948	Emil Zatopek, Czechoslovakia	29:59.6 OR
1952	Emil Zatopek, Czechoslovakia	29:17.0 OR
1956	Vladimir Kuts, USSR	28:45.6 OR
1960	Pyotr Bolotnikov, USSR	28:32.2 OR
1964	Billy Mills, United States	28:24.4 OR
1968	Naftali Temu, Kenya	29:27.4
1972	Lasse Viren, Finland	27:38.4 WR
1976	Lasse Viren, Finland	27:40.38
1980	Miruts Yifter, Ethiopia	27:42.7
1984	Alberto Cova, Italy	27:47.54
1988	Brahim Boutaib, Morocco	27:21.46 OR

MARATHON

1896	Spiridon Louis, Greece	2:58:50
1900	Michel Theato, France	2:59:45
1904	Thomas Hicks, United States	3:28:53
1906	William Sherring, Canada	2:51:23.6
1908	John Hayes, United States	2:55:18.4 OR
1912	Kenneth McArthur, South Africa	2:36:54.8
1920	Hannes Kolehmainen, Finland	2:32:35.8 WB
1924	Albin Stenroos, Finland	2:41:22.6
1928	Boughera El Ouafi, France	2:32:57
1932	Juan Zabala, Argentina	2:31:36 OR
1936	Kijung Son, Japan (Korea)	2:29:19.2 OR
1948	Delfo Cabrera, Argentina	2:34:51.6
1952	Emil Zatopek, Czechoslovakia	2:23:03.2 OR
1956	Alain Mimoun, France	2:25
1960	Abebe Bikila, Ethiopia	2:15:16.2 WB
1964	Abebe Bikila, Ethiopia	2:12:11.2 WB
1968	Mamo Wolde, Ethiopia	2:20:26.4
1972	Frank Shorter, United States	2:12:19.8
1976	Waldemar Cierpinski, East Germany	2:09:55 OR
1980	Waldemar Cierpinski, East Germany	2:11:03.0
1984	Carlos Lopes, Portugal	2:09:21.0 OR
1988	Gelindo Bordin, Italy	2:10:32

Note: Marathon distances: 1896, 1904—40,000 meters; 1900—40,260 meters; 1906—41,860 meters; 1912—40,200 meters; 1920—42,750 meters; 1908 and since 1924—42,195 meters (26 miles, 385 yards).

110-METER HURDLES

1896	Thomas Curtis, United States	17.6
1900	Alvin Kraenzlein, United States	15.4 OR
1904	Frederick Schule, United States	16.0
1906	Robert Leavitt, United States	16.2
1908	Forrest Smithson, United States	15.0 WR
1912	Frederick Kelly, United States	15.1
1920	Earl Thomson, Canada	14.8 WR
1924	Daniel Kinsey, United States	15
1928	Sydney Atkinson, South Africa	14.8
1932	George Saling, United States	14.6
1936	Forrest Towns, United States	14.2
1948	William Porter, United States	13.9 OR
1952	Harrison Dillard, United States	13.7 OR
1956	Lee Calhoun, United States	13.5 OR
1960	Lee Calhoun, United States	13.8
1964	Hayes Jones, United States	13.6
1968	Willie Davenport, United States	13.3 OR
1972	Rod Milburn, United States	13.24 EWR
1976	Guy Drut, France	13.30
1980	Thomas Munkelt, East Germany	13.39
1984	Roger Kingdom, United States	13.20 OR
1988	Roger Kingdom, United States	12.98 OR

400-METER HURDLES

1900	John Walter Tewksbury, United States	57.6
1904	Harry Hillman, United States	53.0
1906	Not held	
1908	Charles Bacon, United States	55.0 WR
1912	Not held	
1920	Frank Loomis, United States	54.0 WR
1924	F. Morgan Taylor, United States	52.6
1928	David Burghley, Great Britain	53.4 OR
1932	Robert Tisdall, Ireland	51.7
1936	Glenn Hardin, United States	52.4
1948	Roy Cochran, United States	51.1 OR
1952	Charles Moore, United States	50.8 OR
1956	Glenn Davis, United States	50.1 EOR
1960	Glenn Davis, United States	49.3 EOR
1964	Rex Cawley, United States	49.6
1968	Dave Hemery, Great Britain	48.12 WR
1972	John Akii-Bua, Uganda	47.82 WR
1976	Edwin Moses, United States	47.64 WR
1980	Volker Beck, East Germany	48.70
1984	Edwin Moses, United States	47.75
1988	Andre Phillips, United States	47.19 OR

Summer Cool

Before the first winter games were held in Chamonix, France, in 1924, figure skating was an event at the 1908 and 1920 *Summer* Games. The first Olympic ice hockey game was played at the 1920 Summer Games in Antwerp, Belgium.

TRACK AND FIELD (*Cont.*)

Men

3000-METER STEEPLECHASE

1920	Percy Hodge, Great Britain	10:00.4 OR
1924	Villie Ritola, Finland	9:33.6 OR
1928	Toivo Loukola, Finland	9:21.8 WR
1932	Volmari Iso-Hollo, Finland*	10:33.4
1936	Volmari Iso-Hollo, Finland	9:03.8 WR
1948	Thore Sjöstrand, Sweden	9:04.6
1952	Horace Ashenfelter, United States	8:45.4 WR
1956	Chris Brasher, Great Britain	8:41.2 OR
1960	Zdzislaw Krzyszkowiak, Poland	8:34.2 OR
1964	Gaston Roelants, Belgium	8:30.8 OR
1968	Amos Biwott, Kenya	8:51
1972	Kipchoge Keino, Kenya	8:23.6 OR
1976	Anders Gärderud, Sweden	8:08.2 WR
1980	Bronislaw Malinowski, Poland	8:09.7
1984	Julius Korir, Kenya	8:11.8
1988	Julius Kariuki, Kenya	8:05.51 OR

*About 3450 meters; extra lap by error.

4 X 100-METER RELAY

1912	Great Britain	42.4 OR
1920	United States	42.2 WR
1924	United States	41.0 EWR
1928	United States	41.0 EWR
1932	United States	40.0 EWR
1936	United States	39.8 WR
1948	United States	40.6
1952	United States	40.1
1956	United States	39.5 WR
1960	West Germany	39.5 EWR
1964	United States	39.0 WR
1968	United States	38.2 WR
1972	United States	38.19 EWR
1976	United States	38.33
1980	USSR	38.26
1984	United States	37.83 WR
1988	USSR	38.19

4 X 400-METER RELAY

1908	United States	3:29.4
1912	United States	3:16.6 WR
1920	Great Britain	3:22.2
1924	United States	3:16 WR
1928	United States	3:14.2 WR
1932	United States	3:08.2 WR
1936	Great Britain	3:09.0
1948	United States	3:10.4 WR
1952	Jamaica	3:03.9 WR
1956	United States	3:04.8
1960	United States	3:02.2 WR
1964	United States	3:00.7 WR
1968	United States	2:56.16 WR
1972	Kenya	2:59.8
1976	United States	2:58.65
1980	USSR	3:01.1
1984	United States	2:57.91
1988	United States	2:56.16 EWR

Note: OR=Olympic Record; WR=World Record;

EOR=Equals Olympic Record; EWR=Equals World Record;
WB=World Best.

20-KILOMETER WALK

1956	Leonid Spirin, USSR	1:31:27.4
1960	Vladimir Golubnichiy, USSR	1:33:07.2
1964	Kenneth Mathews, Great Britain	1:29:34.0 OR
1968	Vladimir Golubnichiy, USSR	1:33:58.4
1972	Peter Frenkel, East Germany	1:26:42.4 OR
1976	Daniel Bautista, Mexico	1:24:40.6 OR
1980	Maurizio Damilano, Italy	1:23:35.5 OR
1984	Ernesto Canto, Mexico	1:23:13.0 OR
1988	Jozef Pribilinec, Czechoslovakia	1:19:57.0 OR

50-KILOMETER WALK

1932	Thomas Green, Great Britain	4:50:10
1936	Harold Whitlock, Great Britain	4:30:41.4 OR
1948	John Ljunggren, Sweden	4:41:52
1952	Giuseppe Dordoni, Italy	4:28:07.8 OR
1956	Norman Read, New Zealand	4:30:42.8
1960	Donald Thompson, Great Britain	4:25:30 OR
1964	Abdon Parnich, Italy	4:11:12.4 OR
1968	Christoph Höhne, East Germany	4:20:13.6
1972	Bernd Kannenberg, West Germany	3:56:11.6 OR
1980	Hartwig Gauder, East Germany	3:49:24.0 OR
1984	Raul Gonzalez, Mexico	3:47:26.0 OR
1988	Viacheslav Ivanenko, USSR	3:38:29.0 OR

HIGH JUMP

1896	Ellery Clark, United States	5 ft 11¼ in
1900	Irving Baxter, United States	6 ft 2¾ in OR
1904	Samuel Jones, United States	5 ft 11 in
1906	Cornelius Leahy, Great Britain/Ireland	5 ft 10 in
1908	Harry Porter, United States	6 ft 3 in OR
1912	Alma Richards, United States	6 ft 4 in OR
1920	Richmond Landon, United States	6 ft 4 in OR
1924	Harold Osborn, United States	6 ft 6 in OR
1928	Robert W. King, United States	6 ft 4½ in
1932	Duncan McNaughton, Canada	6 ft 5½ in
1936	Cornelius Johnson, United States	6 ft 8 in OR
1948	John L. Winter, Australia	6 ft 6 in
1952	Walter Davis, United States	6 ft 8½ in OR
1956	Charles Dumas, United States	6 ft 11½ in OR
1960	Robert Shavlakadze, USSR	7 ft 1 in OR
1964	Valery Brumel, USSR	7 ft 1¾ in OR
1968	Dick Fosbury, United States	7 ft 4¼ in OR
1972	Yuri Tarmak, USSR	7 ft 3¾ in
1976	Jacek Wszola, Poland	7 ft 4½ in OR
1980	Gerd Wessig, East Germany	7 ft 8¾ in WR
1984	Dietmar Mögenburg, West Germany	7 ft 8½ in
1988	Gennadiy Avdeyenko, USSR	7 ft 9¾ in OR

TRACK AND FIELD (*Cont.*)
Men

POLE VAULT

1896 ...	William Hoyt, United States	10 ft 10 in
1900 ...	Irving Baxter, United States	10 ft 10 in
1904 ...	Charles Dvorak, United States	11 ft 5¾ in
1906 ...	Fernand Gonder, France	11 ft 5¾ in
1908 ...	Alfred Gilbert, United States	12 ft 2 in OR
	Edward Cooke, Jr, United States	
1912 ...	Harry Babcock, United States	12 ft 11½ in OR
1920 ...	Frank Foss, United States	13 ft 5 in WR
1924 ...	Lee Barnes, United States	12 ft 11½ in
1928 ...	Sabin Carr, United States	13 ft 9¼ in OR
1932 ...	William Miller, United States	14 ft 1¾ in OR
1936 ...	Earle Meadows, United States	14 ft 3¼ in OR
1948 ...	Guinn Smith, United States	14 ft 1¼ in
1952 ...	Robert Richards, United States	14 ft 11 in OR
1956 ...	Robert Richards, United States	14 ft 11½ in OR
1960 ...	Don Bragg, United States	15 ft 5 in OR
1964 ...	Fred Hansen, United States	16 ft 8¾ in OR
1968 ...	Bob Seagren, United States	17 ft 8½ in OR
1972 ...	Wolfgang Nordwig, East Germany	18 ft ½ in OR
1976 ...	Tadeusz Slusarski, Poland	18 ft ½ in EOR
1980 ...	Wladyslaw Kozakiewicz, Poland	18 ft 11½ in WR
1984 ...	Pierre Quinon, France	18 ft 10¼ in
1988 ...	Sergei Bubka, USSR	19 ft 9¼ in OR

LONG JUMP

1896 ...	Ellery Clark, United States	20 ft 10 in
1900 ...	Alvin Kraenzlein, United States	23 ft 6¾ in OR
1904 ...	Meyer Prinstein, United States	24 ft 1 in OR
1906 ...	Meyer Prinstein, United States	23 ft 7½ in
1908 ...	Frank Irons, United States	24 ft 6½ in OR
1912 ...	Albert Gutterson, United States	24 ft 11¼ in OR
1920 ...	William Peterssen, Sweden	23 ft 5½ in
1924 ...	DeHart Hubbard, United States	24 ft 5 in
1928 ...	Edward B. Hamm, United States	25 ft 4½ in OR
1932 ...	Edward Gordon, United States	25 ft ¾ in
1936 ...	Jesse Owens, United States	26 ft 5½ in OR
1948 ...	William Steele, United States	25 ft 8 in
1952 ...	Jerome Biffle, United States	24 ft 10 in

LONG JUMP (*Cont.*)

1956 ...	Gregory Bell, United States	25 ft 8¼ in
1960 ...	Ralph Boston, United States	26 ft 7¾ in OR
1964 ...	Lynn Davies, Great Britain	26 ft 5¾ in
1968 ...	Bob Beamon, United States	29 ft 2½ in WR
1972 ...	Randy Williams, United States	27 ft ½ in
1976 ...	Arnie Robinson, United States	27 ft 4¾ in
1980 ...	Lutz Dombrowski, East Germany	28 ft ¼ in
1984 ...	Carl Lewis, United States	28 ft ¼ in
1988 ...	Carl Lewis, United States	28 ft 7½ in

TRIPLE JUMP

1896 ...	James Connolly, United States	44 ft 11¾ in
1900 ...	Meyer Prinstein, United States	47 ft 5¾ in OR
1904 ...	Meyer Prinstein, United States	47 ft 1 in
1906 ...	Peter O'Connor, Great Britain/Ireland	46 ft 2¼ in
1908 ...	Timothy Ahearne, Great Britain/Ireland	48 ft 11¼ in OR
1912 ...	Gustaf Lindblom, Sweden	48 ft 5¼ in
1920 ...	Vilho Tuulos, Finland	47 ft 7 in
1924 ...	Anthony Winter, Australia	50 ft 11¼ in WR
1928 ...	Mikio Oda, Japan	49 ft 11 in
1932 ...	Chuhei Nambu, Japan	51 ft 7 in WR
1936 ...	Naoto Tajima, Japan	52 ft 6 in WR
1948 ...	Arne Ahman, Sweden	50 ft 6¼ in
1952 ...	Adhemar da Silva, Brazil	53 ft 2¾ in WR
1956 ...	Adhemar da Silva, Brazil	53 ft 7¾ in OR
1960 ...	Jozef Schmidt, Poland	55 ft 2 in
1964 ...	Jozef Schmidt, Poland	55 ft 3½ in OR
1968 ...	Viktor Saneyev, USSR	57 ft ¾ in WR
1972 ...	Viktor Saneyev, USSR	56 ft 11¾ in
1976 ...	Viktor Saneyev, USSR	56 ft 8¾ in
1980 ...	Jaak Uudmae, USSR	56 ft 11¼ in
1984 ...	Al Joyner, United States	56 ft 7½ in
1988 ...	Khristo Markov, Bulgaria	57 ft 9½ in OR

SHOT PUT

1896 ...	Robert Garrett, United States	36 ft 9¾ in
1900 ...	Richard Sheldon, United States	46 ft 3¼ in OR
1904 ...	Ralph Rose, United States	48 ft 7 in WR
1906 ...	Martin Sheridan, United States	40 ft 5¼ in
1908 ...	Ralph Rose, United States	46 ft 7½ in
1912 ...	Pat McDonald, United States	50 ft 4 in OR
1920 ...	Ville Porhola, Finland	48 ft 7¼ in
1924 ...	Clarence Houser, United States	49 ft 2¼ in
1928 ...	John Kuck, United States	52 ft ¾ in WR
1932 ...	Leo Sexton, United States	52 ft 6 in OR
1936 ...	Hans Woellke, Germany	53 ft 1¾ in OR
1948 ...	Wilbur Thompson, United States	56 ft 2 in OR
1952 ...	Parry O'Brien, United States	57 ft ½ in OR

TRACK AND FIELD (*Cont.*)

Men

SHOT PUT (*Cont.*)

1956 ...	Parry O'Brien, United States	60 ft 11¼ in OR
1960 ...	William Nieder, United States	64 ft 6¾ in OR
1964 ...	Dallas Long, United States	66 ft 8½ in OR
1968 ...	Randy Matson, United States	67 ft 4¾ in
1972 ...	Wladyslaw Komar, Poland	69 ft 6 in OR
1976 ...	Udo Beyer, East Germany	69 ft ¾ in
1980 ...	Vladimir Kiselyov, USSR	70 ft ½ in OR
1984 ...	Alessandro Andrei, Italy	69 ft 9 in
1988 ...	Ulf Timmermann, East Germany	73 ft 8¾ in OR

DISCUS THROW

1896 ...	Robert Garrett, United States	95 ft 7½ in
1900 ...	Rudolf Bauer, Hungary	118 ft 3 in OR
1904 ...	Martin Sheridan, United States	128 ft 10½ in OR
1906 ...	Martin Sheridan, United States	136 ft
1908 ...	Martin Sheridan, United States	134 ft 2 in OR
1912 ...	Armas Taipale, Finland	148 ft 3 in OR
1920 ...	Elmer Niklander, Finland	146 ft 7 in
1924 ...	Clarence Houser, United States	151 ft 4 in OR
1928 ...	Clarence Houser, United States	155 ft 3 in OR
1932 ...	John Anderson, United States	162 ft 4 in OR
1936 ...	Ken Carpenter, United States	165 ft 7 in OR
1948 ...	Adolfo Consolini, Italy	173 ft 2 in OR
1952 ...	Sim Iness, United States	180 ft 6 in OR
1956 ...	Al Oerter, United States	184 ft 11 in OR
1960 ...	Al Oerter, United States	194 ft 2 in OR
1964 ...	Al Oerter, United States	200 ft 1 in OR
1968 ...	Al Oerter, United States	212 ft 6 in OR
1972 ...	Ludvik Daněk, Czechoslovakia	211 ft 3 in
1976 ...	Mac Wilkins, United States	221 ft 5 in OR
1980 ...	Viktor Rashchupkin, USSR	218 ft 8 in
1984 ...	Rolf Dannenberg, West Germany	218 ft 6 in
1988 ...	Jürgen Schult, East Germany	225 ft 9 in OR

HAMMER THROW

1900 ...	John Flanagan, United States	163 ft 1 in
1904 ...	John Flanagan, United States	168 ft 1 in OR
1906 ...	Not held	
1908 ...	John Flanagan, United States	170 ft 4 in OR
1912 ...	Matt McGrath, United States	179 ft 7 in OR
1920 ...	Pat Ryan, United States	173 ft 5 in
1924 ...	Fred Tootell, United States	174 ft 10 in
1928 ...	Patrick O'Callaghan, Ireland	168 ft 7 in
1932 ...	Patrick O'Callaghan, Ireland	176 ft 11 in
1936 ...	Karl Hein, Germany	185 ft 4 in OR
1948 ...	Imre Nemeth, Hungary	183 ft 11 in

HAMMER THROW (*Cont.*)

1952 ...	Jozsef Csermak, Hungary	197 ft 11 in WR
1956 ...	Harold Connolly, United States	207 ft 3 in OR
1960 ...	Vasily Rudenkov, USSR	220 ft 2 in OR
1964 ...	Romuald Klim, USSR	228 ft 10 in OR
1968 ...	Gyula Zsivotsky, Hungary	240 ft 8 in OR
1972 ...	Anatoli Bondarchuk, USSR	247 ft 8 in OR
1976 ...	Yuri Sedykh, USSR	254 ft 4 in OR
1980 ...	Yuri Sedykh, USSR	268 ft 4 in WR
1984 ...	Juha Tiainen, Finland	256 ft 2 in
1988 ...	Sergei Litvinov, USSR	278 ft 2 in OR

JAVELIN

1908 ...	Erik Lemming, Sweden	179 ft 10 in
1912 ...	Erik Lemming, Sweden	198 ft 11 in WR
1920 ...	Jonni Myyrä, Finland	215 ft 10 in OR
1924 ...	Jonni Myyrä, Finland	206 ft 6 in
1928 ...	Eric Lundkvist, Sweden	218 ft 6 in OR
1932 ...	Matti Jarvinen, Finland	238 ft 6 in OR
1936 ...	Gerhard Stöck, Germany	235 ft 8 in
1948 ...	Kai Rautavaara, Finland	228 ft 10½ in
1952 ...	Cy Young, United States	242 ft 1 in OR
1956 ...	Egil Danielson, Norway	281 ft 2¼ in WR
1960 ...	Viktor Tsibulenko, USSR	277 ft 8 in
1964 ...	Pauli Nevala, Finland	271 ft 2 in
1968 ...	Janis Lusis, USSR	295 ft 7 in OR
1972 ...	Klaus Wolfermann, West Germany	296 ft 10 in OR
1976 ...	Miklos Nemeth, Hungary	310 ft 4 in WR
1980 ...	Dainis Kuta, USSR	299 ft 23⁄8 in
1984 ...	Arto Härkönen, Finland	284 ft 8 in
1988 ...	Tapio Korjus, Finland	276 ft 6 in

DECATHLON

		Pts
1904	Thomas Kiely, Ireland	6036
1912	Jim Thorpe, United States*	8412 WR
1920	Helge Lövland, Norway	6803
1924	Harold Osborn, United States	7711 WR
1928	Paavo Yrjölä, Finland	8053.29 WR
1932	James Bausch, United States	8462 WR
1936	Glenn Morris, United States	7900 WR
1948	Robert Mathias, United States	7139
1952	Robert Mathias, United States	7887 WR
1956	Milton Campbell, United States	7937 OR
1960	Rafer Johnson, United States	8392 OR
1964	Willi Holdorf, West Germany	7887
1968	Bill Toomey, United States	8193 OR
1972	Nikolai Avilov, USSR	8454 WR
1976	Bruce Jenner, United States	8617 WR
1980	Daley Thompson, Great Britain	8495
1984	Daley Thompson, Great Britain	8798 EWR
1988	Christian Schenk, East Germany	8488

*In 1913, Thorpe was disqualified for having played professional baseball in 1910. His record was restored in 1982.

Note: OR=Olympic Record; WR=World Record; EOR=Equals Olympic Record; EWR=Equals World Record; WB=World Best.

TRACK AND FIELD (*Cont.*)
Women

100 METERS

1928	Elizabeth Robinson, United States	12.2 EWR
1932	Stella Walsh, Poland	11.9 EWR
1936	Helen Stephens, United States	11.5
1948	Francina Blankers-Koen, Netherlands	11.9
1952	Marjorie Jackson, Australia	11.5 EWR
1956	Betty Cuthbert, Australia	11.5 EWR
1960	Wilma Rudolph, United States	11.0
1964	Wyomia Tyus, United States	11.4
1968	Wyomia Tyus, United States	11.0 WR
1972	Renate Stecher, East Germany	11.07
1976	Annegret Richter, West Germany	11.08
1980	Lyudmila Kondratyeva, USSR	11.06
1984	Evelyn Ashford, United States	10.97 OR
1988	Florence Griffith Joyner, United States	10.54

200 METERS

1948	Francina Blankers-Koen, Netherlands	24.4
1952	Marjorie Jackson, Australia	23.7
1956	Betty Cuthbert, Australia	23.4 EOR
1960	Wilma Rudolph, United States	24.0
1964	Edith McGuire, United States	23.0 OR
1968	Irena Szewinska, Poland	22.5 WR
1972	Renate Stecher, East Germany	22.40 EWR
1976	Bärbel Eckert, East Germany	22.37 OR
1980	Bärbel Wöckel (Eckert), East Germany	22.03 OR
1984	Valerie Brisco-Hooks, United States	21.81 OR
1988	Florence Griffith Joyner, United States	21.34 WR

400 METERS

1964	Betty Cuthbert, Australia	52.0 OR
1968	Colette Besson, France	52.0 EOR
1972	Monika Zehrt, East Germany	51.08 OR
1976	Irena Szewinska, Poland	49.29 WR
1980	Marita Koch, East Germany	48.88 OR
1984	Valerie Brisco-Hooks, United States	48.83 OR
1988	Olga Bryzgina, USSR	48.65 OR

800 METERS

1928	Lina Radke, Germany	2:16.8 WR
1932	Not held 1932-1956	
1960	Lyudmila Shevtsova, USSR	2:04.3 EWR
1964	Ann Packer, Great Britain	2:01.1 OR
1968	Madeline Manning, United States	2:00.9 OR
1972	Hildegard Falck, West Germany	1:58.55 OR
1976	Tatyana Kazankina, USSR	1:54.94 WR
1980	Nadezhda Olizarenko, USSR	1:53.42 WR
1984	Doina Melinte, Romania	1:57.6
1988	Sigrun Wodars, East Germany	1:56.10

1500 METERS

1972	Lyudmila Bragina, USSR	4:01.4 WR
1976	Tatyana Kazankina, USSR	4:05.48
1980	Tatyana Kazankina, USSR	3:56.6 OR
1984	Gabriella Dorio, Italy	4:03.25
1988	Paula Ivan, Romania	3:53.96 OR

3000 METERS

1984	Maricica Puica, Romania	8:35.96 OR
1988	Tatyana Samolenko, USSR	8:26.53 OR

10,000 METERS

1988	Olga Boldarenko, USSR	31:05.21 OR

MARATHON

1984	Joan Benoit, United States	2:24:52
1988	Rosa Mota, Portugal	2:25:40

80-METER HURDLES

1932	Babe Didrikson, United States	11.7 WR
1936	Trebisonda Valla, Italy	11.7
1948	Francina Blankers-Koen, Netherlands	11.2 WR
1952	Shirley Strickland, Australia	10.9 WR
1956	Shirley Strickland, Australia	10.7 OR
1960	Irina Press, USSR	10.8
1964	Karin Balzer, East Germany	10.5
1968	Maureen Caird, Australia	10.3 WR

100-METER HURDLES

1972	Annelie Ehrhardt, East Germany	12.59 WR
1976	Johanna Schaller, East Germany	12.77
1980	Vera Komisova, USSR	12.56 OR
1984	Benita Fitzgerald-Brown, United States	12.84
1988	Jordanka Donkova, Bulgaria	12.38 OR

400-METER HURDLES

1984	Nawal el Moutawakel, Morocco	54.61 OR
1988	Debra Flintoff-King, Australia	53.17 OR

4 X 100-METER RELAY

1928	Canada	48.4 WR
1932	United States	46.9 WR
1936	United States	46.9
1948	Netherlands	47.5
1952	United States	45.9 WR
1956	Australia	44.5 WR
1960	United States	44.5
1964	Poland	43.6
1968	United States	42.8 WR
1972	West Germany	42.81 EWR
1976	East Germany	42.55 OR
1980	East Germany	41.60 WR
1984	United States	41.65
1988	United States	41.98

Note: OR=Olympic Record; WR=World Record; EOR=Equals Olympic Record; EWR=Equals World Record; WB=World Best.

TRACK AND FIELD (*Cont.*)
Women

4 X 400-METER RELAY

1972	East Germany	3:23 WR
1976	East Germany	3:19.23 WR
1980	USSR	3:20.02
1984	United States	3:18.29 OR
1988	USSR	3:15.18 WR

HIGH JUMP

1928	Ethel Catherwood, Canada	5 ft 2½ in
1932	Jean Shiley, United States	5 ft 5¼ in WR
1936	Ibolya Csak, Hungary	5 ft 3 in
1948	Alice Coachman, United States	5 ft 6 in OR
1952	Esther Brand, South Africa	5 ft 5¾ in
1956	Mildred L. McDaniel, United States	5 ft 9¼ in WR
1960	Iolanda Balas, Romania	6 ft ¾ in OR
1964	Iolanda Balas, Romania	6 ft 2¾ in OR
1968	Miloslava Reskova, Czechoslovakia	5 ft 11½ in
1972	Ulrike Meyfarth, West Germany	6 ft 3½ in EWR
1976	Rosemarie Ackermann, East Germany	6 ft 4 in OR
1980	Sara Simeoni, Italy	6 ft 5½ in OR
1984	Ulrike Meyfarth, West Germany	6 ft 7½ in OR
1988	Louise Ritter, United States	6 ft 8 in OR

LONG JUMP

1948	Olga Gyarmati, Hungary	18 ft 8¼ in
1952	Yvette Williams, New Zealand	20 ft 5¾ in OR
1956	Elzbieta Krzeskinska, Poland	20 ft 10 in EWR
1960	Vyera Krepkina, USSR	20 ft 10¾ in OR
1964	Mary Rand, Great Britain	22 ft 2¼ in WR
1968	Viorica Viscopoleanu, Romania	22 ft 4½ in WR
1972	Heidemarie Rosendahl, West Germany	22 ft 3 in
1976	Angela Voigt, East Germany	22 ft ¾ in
1980	Tatyana Kolpakova, USSR	23 ft 2 in OR
1984	Anisoara Stanciu, Romania	22 ft 10 in
1988	Jackie Joyner-Kersee, United States	24 ft 3½ in OR

SHOT PUT

1948	Micheline Ostermeyer, France	45 ft 1½ in
1952	Galina Zybina, USSR	50 ft 1¾ in WR
1956	Tamara Tyshkevich, USSR	54 ft 5 in OR
1960	Tamara Press, USSR	56 ft 10 in OR
1964	Tamara Press, USSR	59 ft 6¼ in OR
1968	Margitta Gummel, East Germany	64 ft 4 in WR
1972	Nadezhda Chizhova, USSR	69 ft WR
1976	Ivanka Hristova, Bulgaria	69 ft 5¼ in OR
1980	Ilona Slupianek, East Germany	73 ft 6¼ in OR
1984	Claudia Losch, West Germany	67 ft 2¼ in
1988	Natalya Lisovskaya, USSR	72 ft 11¾ in

DISCUS THROW

1928	Helena Konopacka, Poland	129 ft 11¾ in WR
1932	Lillian Copeland, United States	133 ft 2 in OR
1936	Gisela Mauermayer, Germany	156 ft 3 in OR
1948	Micheline Ostermeyer, France	137 ft 6 in
1952	Nina Romaschkova, USSR	168 ft 8 in OR
1956	Olga Fikotova, Czechoslovakia	176 ft 1 in OR
1960	Nina Ponomaryeva, USSR	180 ft 9 in OR
1964	Tamara Press, USSR	187 ft 10 in OR
1968	Lia Manoliu, Romania	191 ft 2 in OR
1972	Faina Melnik, USSR	218 ft 7 in OR
1976	Evelin Schlaak, East Germany	226 ft 4 in OR
1980	Evelin Jahl (Schlaak), East Germany	229 ft 6 in OR
1984	Ria Stalman, Netherlands	214 ft 5 in
1988	Martina Hellmann, East Germany	237 ft 2 in OR

JAVELIN THROW

1932	Babe Didrikson, United States	143 ft 4 in OR
1936	Tilly Fleischer, Germany	148 ft 3 in OR
1948	Herma Bauma, Austria	149 ft 6 in
1952	Dana Zatopkova, Czechoslovakia	165 ft 7 in
1956	Inese Jaunzeme, USSR	176 ft 8 in
1960	Elvira Ozolina, USSR	183 ft 8 in OR
1964	Mihaela Penes, Romania	198 ft 7 in
1968	Angela Nemeth, Hungary	198 ft
1972	Ruth Fuchs, East Germany	209 ft 7 in OR
1976	Ruth Fuchs, East Germany	216 ft 4 in OR
1980	Maria Colon, Cuba	224 ft 5 in OR
1984	Tessa Sanderson, Great Britain	228 ft 2 in OR
1988	Petra Felke, East Germany	245 ft OR

PENTATHLON

Year	Athlete	Pts
1964	Irina Press, USSR	5246 WR
1968	Ingrid Becker, West Germany	5098
1972	Mary Peters, Great Britain	4801 WR*
1976	Siegrun Siegl, East Germany	4745
1980	Nadezhda Tkachenko, USSR	5083 WR

*In 1971, 100-meter hurdles replaced 80-meter hurdles, necessitating a change in scoring tables.

HEPTATHLON

Year	Athlete	Pts
1984	Glynis Nunn, Australia	6390 OR
1988	Jackie Joyner-Kersee, United States	7291 WR

BASKETBALL

Men

1936

Final: United States 19, Canada 8
United States: Ralph Bishop, Joe Fortenberry, Carl Knowles, Jack Ragland, Carl Shy, William Wheatley, Francis Johnson, Samuel Balter, John Gibbons, Frank Lubin, Arthur Mollner, Donald Piper, Duane Swanson, Willard Schmidt

1948

Final: United States 65, France 21
United States: Cliff Barker, Don Barksdale, Ralph Beard, Lewis Beck, Vince Boryla, Gordon Carpenter, Alex Groza, Wallace Jones, Bob Kurland, Ray Lumpp, Robert Pitts, Jesse Renick, Bob Robinson, Ken Rollins

1952

Final: United States 36, USSR 25
United States: Charles Hoag, Bill Hougland, Melvin Dean Kelley, Bob Kenney, Clyde Lovellette, Marcus Freiberger, Victor Wayne Glasgow, Frank McCabe, Daniel Pippen, Howard Williams, Ronald Bontemps, Bob Kurland, William Lienhard, John Keller

1956

Final: United States 89, USSR 55
United States: Carl Cain, Bill Hougland, K. C. Jones, Bill Russell, James Walsh, William Evans, Burdette Haldorson, Ron Tomsic, Dick Boushka, Gilbert Ford, Bob Jeangerard, Charles Darling

1960

Final: United States 90, Brazil 63
United States: Jay Arnette, Walt Bellamy, Bob Boozer, Terry Dischinger, Jerry Lucas, Oscar Robertson, Adrian Smith, Burdette Haldorson, Darrall Imhoff, Allen Kelley, Lester Lane, Jerry West

1964

Final: United States 73, USSR 59
United States: Jim Barnes, Bill Bradley, Larry Brown, Joe Caldwell, Mel Counts, Richard Davies, Walt Hazzard, Lucius Jackson, John McCaffrey, Jeff Mullins, Jerry Shipp, George Wilson

1968

Final: United States 65, Yugoslavia 50
United States: John Clawson, Ken Spain, Jo-Jo White, Michael Barrett, Spencer Haywood, Charles Scott, William Hosket, Calvin Fowler, Michael Silliman, Glynn Saulters, James King, Donald Dee

1972

Final: USSR 51, United States 50
United States: Kenneth Davis, Doug Collins, Thomas Henderson, Mike Bantom, Bobby Jones, Dwight Jones, James Forbes, James Brewer, Tom Burleson, Tom McMillen, Kevin Joyce, Ed Ratleff

1976

Final: United States 95, Yugoslavia 74
United States: Phil Ford, Steve Sheppard, Adrian Dantley, Walter Davis, Quinn Buckner, Ernie Grunfield, Kenny Carr, Scott May, Michel Armstrong, Tom La Garde, Phil Hubbard, Mitch Kupchak

1980

Final: Yugoslavia 86, Italy 77
U.S. participated in boycott.

1984

Final: United States 96, Spain 65
United States: Steve Alford, Leon Wood, Patrick Ewing, Vern Fleming, Alvin Robertson, Michael Jordan, Joe Kleine, Jon Koncak, Wayman Tisdale, Chris Mullin, Sam Perkins, Jeff Turner

1988

Final: USSR 76, Yugoslavia 63
United States (3rd): Mitch Richmond, Charles E. Smith, IV, Vernell Coles, Hersey Hawkins, Jeff Grayer, Charles D. Smith, Willie Anderson, Stacey Augmon, Dan Majerle, Danny Manning, J. R. Reid, David Robinson

Women

1976

Gold, USSR; Silver, United States*
United States: Cindy Brogdon, Susan Rojcewicz, Ann Meyers, Lusia Harris, Nancy Dunkle, Charlotte Lewis, Nancy Lieberman, Gail Marquis, Patricia Roberts, Mary Anne O'Connor, Patricia Head, Julienne Simpson

*In 1976 the women played a round-robin tournament, with the gold medal going to the team with the best record. The USSR won with a 5-0 record, and the USA, with a 3-2 record, was given the silver by virtue of a 95-79 victory over Bulgaria, which was also 3-2.

1980

Final: USSR 104, Bulgaria 73
U.S. participated in boycott.

1984

Final: United States 85, Korea 55
United States: Teresa Edwards, Lea Henry, Lynette Woodard, Anne Donovan, Cathy Boswell, Cheryl Miller, Janice Lawrence, Cindy Noble, Kim Mulkey, Denise Curry, Pamela McGee, Carol Menken-Schaudt

1988

Final: United States 77, Yugoslavia 70
United States: Teresa Edwards, Mary Ethridge, Cynthia Brown, Anne Donovan, Teresa Weatherspoon, Bridgette Gordon, Victoria Bullett, Andrea Lloyd, Katrina McClain, Jennifer Gillom, Cynthia Cooper, Suzanne McConnell

BOXING

LIGHT FLYWEIGHT (106 LB)

1968	Francisco Rodriguez, Venezuela
1972	Gyorgy Gedo, Hungary
1976	Jorge Hernandez, Cuba
1980	Shamil Sabyrov, USSR
1984	Paul Gonzalez, United States
1988	Ivailo Hristov, Bulgaria

FLYWEIGHT (112 LB)

1904	George Finnegan, United States
1906-1912	Not held
1920	Frank Di Gennara, United States
1924	Fidel LaBarba, United States
1928	Antal Kocsis, Hungary
1932	Istvan Enekes, Hungary
1936	Willi Kaiser, Germany
1948	Pascual Perez, Argentina
1952	Nathan Brooks, United States
1956	Terence Spinks, Great Britain
1960	Gyula Torok, Hungary
1964	Fernando Atzori, Italy
1968	Ricardo Delgado, Mexico
1972	Georgi Kostadinov, Bulgaria
1976	Leo Randolph, United States
1980	Peter Lessov, Bulgaria
1984	Steve McCrory, United States
1988	Kim Kwang Sun, South Korea

BANTAMWEIGHT (119 LB)

1904	Oliver Kirk, United States
1906	Not held
1908	A. Henry Thomas, Great Britain
1912	Not held
1920	Clarence Walker, South Africa
1924	William Smith, South Africa
1928	Vittorio Tamagnini, Italy
1932	Horace Gwynne, Canada
1936	Ulderico Sergo, Italy
1948	Tibor Csik, Hungary
1952	Pentti Hamalainen, Finland
1956	Wolfgang Behrendt, East Germany
1960	Oleg Grigoryev, USSR
1964	Takao Sakurai, Japan
1968	Valery Sokolov, USSR
1972	Orlando Martinez, Cuba
1976	Yong Jo Gu, North Korea
1980	Juan Hernandez, Cuba
1984	Maurizio Stecca, Italy
1988	Kennedy McKinney, United States

FEATHERWEIGHT (125 LB)

1904	Oliver Kirk, United States
1906	Not held
1908	Richard Gunn, Great Britain
1912	Not held
1920	Paul Fritsch, France
1924	John Fields, United States
1928	Lambertus van Klaveren, Netherlands
1932	Carmelo Robledo, Argentina
1936	Oscar Casanovas, Argentina
1948	Ernesto Formenti, Italy
1952	Jan Zachara, Czechoslovakia
1956	Vladimir Safronov, USSR

FEATHERWEIGHT (*Cont.*)

1960	Francesco Musso, Italy
1964	Stanislav Stephashkin, USSR
1968	Antonio Roldan, Mexico
1972	Boris Kousnetsov, USSR
1976	Angel Herrera, Cuba
1980	Rudi Fink, East Germany
1984	Meldrick Taylor, United States
1988	Giovanni Parisi, Italy

LIGHTWEIGHT (132 LB)

1904	Harry Spanger, United States
1906	Not held
1908	Frederick Grace, Great Britain
1912	Not held
1920	Samuel Mosberg, United States
1924	Hans Nielsen, Denmark
1928	Carlo Orlandi, Italy
1932	Lawrence Stevens, South Africa
1936	Imre Harangi, Hungary
1948	Gerald Dreyer, South Africa
1952	Aureliano Bolognesi, Italy
1956	Richard McTaggart, Great Britain
1960	Kazimierz Pazdzior, Poland
1964	Jozef Grudzien, Poland
1968	Ronald Harris, United States
1972	Jan Szczepanski, Poland
1976	Howard Davis, United States
1980	Angel Herrera, Cuba
1984	Pernell Whitaker, United States
1988	Andreas Zuelow, East Germany

LIGHT WELTERWEIGHT (139 LB)

1952	Charles Adkins, United States
1956	Vladimir Yengibaryan, USSR
1960	Bohumil Nemecek, Czechoslovakia
1964	Jerzy Kulej, Poland
1968	Jerzy Kulej, Poland
1972	Ray Seales, United States
1976	Ray Leonard, United States
1980	Patrizio Oliva, Italy
1984	Jerry Page, United States
1988	Viatcheslav Janovski, USSR

WELTERWEIGHT (147 LB)

1904	Albert Young, United States
1906-1912	Not held
1920	Albert Schneider, Canada
1924	Jean Delarge, Belgium
1928	Edward Morgan, New Zealand
1932	Edward Flynn, United States
1936	Sten Suvio, Finland
1948	Julius Torma, Czechoslovakia
1952	Zygmunt Chychla, Poland
1956	Nicolae Linca, Romania
1960	Giovanni Benvenuti, Italy
1964	Marian Kasprzyk, Poland
1968	Manfred Wolke, East Germany
1972	Emilio Correa, Cuba
1976	Jochen Bachfeld, East Germany
1980	Andres Aldama, Cuba
1984	Mark Breland, United States
1988	Robert Wangila, Kenya

BOXING (*Cont.*)

LIGHT MIDDLEWEIGHT (156 LB)

1952	Laszlo Papp, Hungary
1956	Laszlo Papp, Hungary
1960	Wilbert McClure, United States
1964	Boris Lagutin, USSR
1968	Boris Lagutin, USSR
1972	Dieter Kottysch, West Germany
1976	Jerzy Rybicki, Poland
1980	Armando Martinez, Cuba
1984	Frank Tate, United States
1988	Park Si-Hun, South Korea

MIDDLEWEIGHT (165 LB)

1904	Charles Mayer, United States
1908	John Douglas, Great Britain
1912	Not held
1920	Harry Mallin, Great Britain
1924	Harry Mallin, Great Britain
1928	Piero Toscani, Italy
1932	Carmen Barth, United States
1936	Jean Despeaux, France
1948	Laszlo Papp, Hungary
1952	Floyd Patterson, United States
1956	Gennady Schatkov, USSR
1960	Edward Crook, United States
1964	Valery Popenchenko, USSR
1968	Christopher Finnegan, Great Britain
1972	Vyacheslav Lemechev, USSR
1976	Michael Spinks, United States
1980	Jose Gomez, Cuba
1984	Shin Joon Sup, South Korea
1988	Henry Maske, East Germany

LIGHT HEAVYWEIGHT (178 LB)

1920	Edward Eagan, United States
1924	Harry Mitchell, Great Britain
1928	Victor Avendano, Argentina
1932	David Carstens, South Africa
1936	Roger Michelot, France
1948	George Hunter, South Africa
1952	Norvel Lee, United States

LIGHT HEAVYWEIGHT (*Cont.*)

1956	James Boyd, United States
1960	Cassius Clay, United States
1964	Cosimo Pinto, Italy
1968	Dan Poznyak, USSR
1972	Mate Parlov, Yugoslavia
1976	Leon Spinks, United States
1980	Slobodan Kacer, Yugoslavia
1984	Anton Josipovic, Yugoslavia
1988	Andrew Maynard, United States

HEAVYWEIGHT (OVER 201 LB)

1904	Samuel Berger, United States
1906	Not held
1908	Albert Oldham, Great Britain
1912	Not held
1920	Ronald Rawson, Great Britain
1924	Otto von Porat, Norway
1928	Arturo Rodriguez Jurado, Argentina
1932	Santiago Lovell, Argentina
1936	Herbert Runge, Germany
1948	Rafael Inglesias, Argentina
1952	H. Edward Sanders, United States
1956	T. Peter Rademacher, United States
1960	Franco De Piccoli, Italy
1964	Joe Frazier, United States
1968	George Foreman, United States
1972	Teofilo Stevenson, Cuba
1976	Teofilo Stevenson, Cuba
1980	Teofilo Stevenson, Cuba

HEAVYWEIGHT (201* LB)

1984	Henry Tillman, United States
1988	Ray Mercer, United States

SUPER HEAVYWEIGHT (UNLIMITED)

1984	Tyrell Biggs, United States
1988	Lennox Lewis, Canada

*Until 1984 the heavyweight division was unlimited. With the addition of the super heavyweight division, a limit of 201 pounds was imposed.

SWIMMING

Men

50-METER FREESTYLE

1904	Zoltan Halmay, Hungary (50 yds)	28.0
1988	Matt Biondi, United States	22.14 WR

100-METER FREESTYLE

1896	Alfred Hajos, Hungary	1:22.2 OR
1904	Zoltan Halmay, Hungary (100 yds)	1:02.8
1906	Charles Daniels, United States	1:13.4
1908	Charles Daniels, United States	1:05.6 WR
1912	Duke Kahanamoku, United States	1:03.4
1920	Duke Kahanamoku, United States	1:00.4 WR
1924	John Weissmuller, United States	59.0 OR

100-METER FREESTLYE (*Cont.*)

1928	John Weissmuller, United States	58.6 OR
1932	Yasuji Miyazaki, Japan	58.2
1936	Ferenc Csik, Hungary	57.6
1948	Wally Ris, United States	57.3 OR
1952	Clarke Scholes, United States	57.4
1956	Jon Henricks, Australia	55.4 OR
1960	John Devitt, Australia	55.2 OR
1964	Don Schollander, United States	53.4 OR
1968	Mike Wenden, Australia	52.2 WR
1972	Mark Spitz, United States	51.22 WR
1976	Jim Montgomery, United States	49.99 WR
1980	Jörg Woithe, East Germany	50.40
1984	Rowdy Gaines, United States	49.80 OR
1988	Matt Biondi, United States	48.63 OR

SWIMMING (*Cont.*)
Men

200-METER FREESTYLE

1900 ... Frederick Lane, Australia	2:25.2 OR
1904 ... Charles Daniels, United States	2:44.2
1906 ... Not held 1906-1964	
1968 ... Michael Wenden, Australia	1:55.2 OR
1972 ... Mark Spitz, United States	1:52.78 WR
1976 ... Bruce Furniss, United States	1:50.29 WR
1980 ... Sergei Kopliakov, USSR	1:49.81 OR
1984 ... Michael Gross, West Germany	1:47.44 WR
1988 ... Duncan Armstrong, Australia	1:47.25 WR

400-METER FREESTYLE

1896 ... Paul Neumann, Austria (500 yds)	8:12.6
1904 ... Charles Daniels, United States (440 yds)	6:16.2
1906 ... Otto Scheff, Austria (440 yds)	6:23.8
1908 ... Henry Taylor, Great Britain	5:36.8
1912 ... George Hodgson, Canada	5:24.4
1920 ... Norman Ross, United States	5:26.8
1924 ... John Weissmuller, United States	5:04.2 OR
1928 ... Albert Zorilla, Argentina	5:01.6 OR
1932 ... Buster Crabbe, United States	4:48.4 OR
1936 ... Jack Medica, United States	4:44.5 OR
1948 ... William Smith, United States	4:41.0 OR
1952 ... Jean Boiteux, France	4:30.7 OR
1956 ... Murray Rose, Australia	4:27.3 OR
1960 ... Murray Rose, Australia	4:18.3 OR
1964 ... Don Schollander, United States	4:12.2 WR
1968 ... Mike Burton, United States	4:09.0 OR
1972 ... Brad Cooper, Australia	4:00.27 OR
1976 ... Brian Goodell, United States	3:51.93 WR
1980 ... Vladimir Salnikov, USSR	3:51.31 OR
1984 ... George DiCarlo, United States	3:51.23 OR
1988 ... Uwe Dassler, East Germany	3:46.95 WR

1500-METER FREESTYLE

1908 ... Henry Taylor, Great Britain	22:48.4 WR
1912 ... George Hodgson, Canada	22:00.0 WR
1920 ... Norman Ross, United States	22:23.2
1924 ... Andrew Charlton, Australia	20:06.6 WR
1928 ... Arne Borg, Sweden	19:51.8 OR
1932 ... Kusuo Kitamura, Japan	19:12.4 OR
1936 ... Noboru Terada, Japan	19:13.7
1948 ... James McLane, United States	19:18.5
1952 ... Ford Konno, United States	18:30.3 OR
1956 ... Murray Rose, Australia	17:58.9
1960 ... John Konrads, Australia	17:19.6 OR
1964 ... Robert Windle, Australia	17:01.7 OR
1968 ... Mike Burton, United States	16:38.9 OR
1972 ... Mike Burton, United States	15:52.58 OR
1976 ... Brian Goodell, United States	15:02.40 WR
1980 ... Vladimir Salnikov, USSR	14:58.27 WR
1984 ... Michael O'Brien, United States	15:05.20
1988 ... Vladimir Salnikov, USSR	15:00.40

Note: OR=Olympic Record; WR=World Record;
EOR=Equals Olympic Record; EWR=Equals World Record;
WB=World Best.

100-METER BACKSTROKE

1904 ... Walter Brack, Germany (100 yds)	1:16.8
1908 ... Arno Bieberstein, Germany	1:24.6 WR
1912 ... Harry Hebner, United States	1:21.2
1920 ... Warren Kealoha, United States	1:15.2
1924 ... Warren Kealoha, United States	1:13.2 OR
1928 ... George Kojac, United States	1:08.2 WR
1932 ... Masaji Kiyokawa, Japan	1:08.6
1936 ... Adolph Kiefer, United States	1:05.9 OR
1948 ... Allen Stack, United States	1:06.4
1952 ... Yoshi Oyakawa, United States	1:05.4 OR
1956 ... David Thiele, Australia	1:02.2 OR
1960 ... David Thiele, Australia	1:01.9 OR
1964 ... Not held	
1968 ... Roland Matthes, East Germany	58.7 OR
1972 ... Roland Matthes, East Germany	56.58 OR
1976 ... John Naber, United States	55.49 WR
1980 ... Bengt Baron, Sweden	56.33
1984 ... Rick Carey, United States	55.79
1988 ... Daichi Suzuki, Japan	55.05

200-METER BACKSTROKE

1900 ... Ernst Hoppenberg, Germany	2:47.0
1904 ... Not held 1904-1960	
1964 ... Jed Graef, United States	2:10.3 WR
1968 ... Roland Matthes, East Germany	2:09.6 OR
1972 ... Roland Matthes, East Germany	2:02.82 EWR
1976 ... John Naber, United States	1:59.19 WR
1980 ... Sandor Wladar, Hungary	2:01.93
1984 ... Rick Carey, United States	2:00.23
1988 ... Igor Polianski, USSR	1:59.37

100-METER BREASTSTROKE

1968 ... Don McKenzie, United States	1:07.7 OR
1972 ... Nobutaka Taguchi, Japan	1:04.94 WR
1976 ... John Hencken, United States	1:03.11 WR
1980 ... Duncan Goodhew, Great Britain	1:03.44
1984 ... Steve Lundquist, United States	1:01.65 WR
1988 ... Adrian Moorhouse, Great Britain	1:02.04

200-METER BREASTSTROKE

1908 ... Frederick Holman, Great Britain	3:09.2 WR
1912 ... Walter Bathe, Germany	3:01.8 OR
1920 ... Haken Malmroth, Sweden	3:04.4
1924 ... Robert Skelton, United States	2:56.6
1928 ... Yoshiyuki Tsuruta, Japan	2:48.8 OR
1932 ... Yoshiyuki Tsuruta, Japan	2:45.4
1936 ... Tetsuo Hamuro, Japan	2:41.5 OR
1948 ... Joseph Verdeur, United States	2:39.3 OR
1952 ... John Davies, Australia	2:34.4 OR
1956 ... Masura Furukawa, Japan	2:34.7 OR
1960 ... William Mulliken, United States	2:37.4
1964 ... Ian O'Brien, Australia	2:27.8 WR
1968 ... Felipe Munoz, Mexico	2:28.7
1972 ... John Hencken, United States	2:21.55 WR
1976 ... David Wilkie, Great Britain	2:15.11 WR
1980 ... Robertas Zhulpa, USSR	2:15.85
1984 ... Victor Davis, Canada	2:13.34 WR
1988 ... Jozsef Szabo, Hungary	2:13.52

SWIMMING (*Cont.*)

Men

100-METER BUTTERFLY

1968 ...	Doug Russell, United States	55.9 OR
1972 ...	Mark Spitz, United States	54.27 WR
1976 ...	Matt Vogel, United States	54.35
1980 ...	Pär Arvidsson, Sweden	54.92
1984 ...	Michael Gross, West Germany	53.08 WR
1988 ...	Anthony Nesty, Suriname	53.00 OR

200-METER BUTTERFLY

1956 ...	William Yorzyk, United States	2:19.3 OR
1960 ...	Michael Troy, United States	2:12.8 WR
1964 ...	Kevin Berry, Australia	2:06.6 WR
1968 ...	Carl Robie, United States	2:08.7
1972 ...	Mark Spitz, United States	2:00.70 WR
1976 ...	Mike Bruner, United States	1:59.23 WR
1980 ...	Sergei Fesenko, USSR	1:59.76
1984 ...	Jon Sieben, Australia	1:57.04 WR
1988 ...	Michael Gross, West Germany	1:56.94 OR

200-METER INDIVIDUAL MEDLEY

1968 ...	Charles Hickcox, United States	2:12.0 OR
1972 ...	Gunnar Larsson, Sweden	2:07.17 WR
1984 ...	Alex Baumann, Canada	2:01.42 WR
1988 ...	Tamas Darnyi, Hungary	2:00.17 WR

400-METER INDIVIDUAL MEDLEY

1964 ...	Richard Roth, United States	4:45.4 WR
1968 ...	Charles Hickcox, United States	4:48.4
1972 ...	Gunnar Larsson, Sweden	4:31.98 OR
1976 ...	Rod Strachan, United States	4:23.68 WR
1980 ...	Aleksandr Sidorenko, USSR	4:22.89 OR
1984 ...	Alex Baumann, Canada	4:17.41 WR
1988 ...	Tamas Darnyi, Hungary	4:14.75 WR

4 X 100-METER MEDLEY RELAY

1960 ...	United States	4:05.4 WR
1964 ...	United States	3:58.4 WR
1968 ...	United States	3:54.9 WR
1972 ...	United States	3:48.16 WR
1976 ...	United States	3:42.22 WR
1980 ...	Australia	3:45.70
1984 ...	United States	3:39.30 WR
1988 ...	United States	3:36.93 WR

4 X 400-METER FREESTYLE RELAY

1964 ...	United States	3:32.2 WR
1968 ...	United States	3:31.7 WR
1972 ...	United States	3:26.42 WR
1976-1980 ...	Not held	
1984 ...	United States	3:19.03 WR
1988 ...	United States	3:16.53 WR

4 X 200-METER FREESTYLE RELAY

1906 ...	Hungary (1000 m)	16:52.4
1908 ...	Great Britain	10:55.6
1912 ...	Australia/New Zealand	10:11.6 WR
1920 ...	United States	10:04.4 WR
1924 ...	United States	9:53.4 WR
1928 ...	United States	9:36.2 WR
1932 ...	Japan	8:58.4 WR
1936 ...	Japan	8:51.5 WR
1948 ...	United States	8:46.0 WR
1952 ...	United States	8:31.1 OR
1956 ...	Australia	8:23.6 WR
1960 ...	United States	8:10.2 WR
1964 ...	United States	7:52.1 WR
1968 ...	United States	7:52.33
1972 ...	United States	7:35.78 WR
1976 ...	United States	7:23.22 WR
1980 ...	USSR	7:23.50
1984 ...	United States	7:15.69 WR
1988 ...	United States	7:12.51 WR

Women

50-METER FREESTYLE

1988 ...	Kristin Otto, East Germany	25.49 OR

100-METER FREESTYLE

1912 ...	Fanny Durack, Australia	1:22.2
1920 ...	Ethelda Bleibtrey, United States	1:13.6 WR
1924 ...	Ethel Lackie, United States	1:12.4
1928 ...	Albina Osipowich, United States	1:11.0 OR
1932 ...	Helene Madison, United States	1:06.8 OR
1936 ...	Hendrika Mastenbroek, Netherlands	1:05.9 OR
1948 ...	Greta Andersen, Denmark	1:06.3
1952 ...	Katalin Szöke, Hungary	1:06.8
1956 ...	Dawn Fraser, Australia	1:02.0 WR
1960 ...	Dawn Fraser, Australia	1:01.2 OR
1964 ...	Dawn Fraser, Australia	59.5 OR
1968 ...	Jan Henne, United States	1:00.0
1972 ...	Sandra Neilson, United States	58.59 OR
1976 ...	Kornelia Ender, East Germany	55.65 WR

100-METER FREESTYLE (*Cont.*)

1980 ...	Barbara Krause, East Germany	54.79 WR
1984 ...	Carrie Steinseifer, United States	55.92
	Nancy Hogshead, United States	55.92
1988 ...	Kristin Otto, East Germany	54.93

200-METER FREESTYLE

1968 ...	Debbie Meyer, United States	2:10.5 OR
1972 ...	Shane Gould, Australia	2:03.56 WR
1976 ...	Kornelia Ender, East Germany	1:59.26 WR
1980 ...	Barbara Krause, East Germany	1:58.33 OR
1984 ...	Mary Wayte, United States	1:59.23
1988 ...	Heike Friedrich, East Germany	1:57.65 OR

Note: OR=Olympic Record; WR=World Record;
EOR=Equals Olympic Record; EWR=Equals World Record;
WB=World Best.

SWIMMING (*Cont.*)

Women

400-METER FREESTYLE

1924 ... Martha Norelius, United States — 6:02.2 OR
1928 ... Martha Norelius, United States — 5:42.8 WR
1932 ... Helene Madison, United States — 5:28.5 WR
1936 ... Hendrika Mastenbroek, Netherlands — 5:26.4 OR
1948 ... Ann Curtis, United States — 5:17.8 OR
1952 ... Valeria Gyenge, Hungary — 5:12.1 OR
1956 ... Lorraine Crapp, Australia — 4:54.6 OR
1960 ... Chris von Saltza, United States — 4:50.6 OR
1964 ... Virginia Duenkel, United States — 4:43.3 OR
1968 ... Debbie Meyer, United States — 4:31.8 OR
1972 ... Shane Gould, Australia — 4:19.44 WR
1976 ... Petra Thümer, East Germany — 4:09.89 WR
1980 ... Ines Diers, East Germany — 4:08.76 WR
1984 ... Tiffany Cohen, United States — 4:07.10 OR
1988 ... Janet Evans, United States — 4:03.85 WR

800-METER FREESTYLE

1968 ... Debbie Meyer, United States — 9:24.0 OR
1972 ... Keena Rothhammer, United States — 8:53.68 WR
1976 ... Petra Thümer, East Germany — 8:37.14 WR
1980 ... Michelle Ford, Australia — 8:28.90 OR
1984 ... Tiffany Cohen, United States — 8:24.95 OR
1988 ... Janet Evans, United States — 8:20.20 WR

100-METER BACKSTROKE

1924 ... Sybil Bauer, United States — 1:23.2 OR
1928 ... Marie Braun, Netherlands — 1:22.0
1932 ... Eleanor Holm, United States — 1:19.4
1936 ... Dina Senff, Netherlands — 1:18.9
1948 ... Karen Harup, Denmark — 1:14.4 OR
1952 ... Joan Harrison, South Africa — 1:14.3
1956 ... Judy Grinham, Great Britain — 1:12.9 OR
1960 ... Lynn Burke, United States — 1:09.3 OR
1964 ... Cathy Ferguson, United States — 1:07.7 WR
1968 ... Kaye Hall, United States — 1:06.2 WR
1972 ... Melissa Belote, United States — 1:05.78 OR
1976 ... Ulrike Richter, East Germany — 1:01.83 OR
1980 ... Rica Reinisch, East Germany — 1:00.86 WR
1984 ... Theresa Andrews, United States — 1:02.55
1988 ... Kristin Otto, East Germany — 1:00.89

200-METER BACKSTROKE

1968 ... Pokey Watson, United States — 2:24.8 OR
1972 ... Melissa Belote, United States — 2:19.19 WR
1976 ... Ulrike Richter, East Germany — 2:13.43 OR
1980 ... Rica Reinisch, East Germany — 2:11.77 WR
1984 ... Jolanda De Rover, Netherlands — 2:12.38
1988 ... Krisztina Egerszegi, Hungary — 2:09.29 WR

100-METER BREASTSTROKE

1968 ... Djurdjica Bjedov, Yugoslavia — 1:15.8 OR
1972 ... Catherine Carr, United States — 1:13.58 WR
1976 ... Hannelore Anke, East Germany — 1:11.16
1980 ... Ute Geweniger, East Germany — 1:10.22
1984 ... Petra Van Staveren, Netherlands — 1:09.88 OR
1988 ... Tania Dangalakova, Bulgaria — 1:07.95 OR

200-METER BREASTSTROKE

1924 ... Lucy Morton, Great Britain — 3:33.2 OR
1928 ... Hilde Schrader, Germany — 3:12.6
1932 ... Clare Dennis, Australia — 3:06.3 OR
1936 ... Hideko Maehata, Japan — 3:03.6
1948 ... Petronella Van Vliet, Netherlands — 2:57.2
1952 ... Eva Szekely, Hungary — 2:51.7 OR
1956 ... Ursula Happe, West Germany — 2:53.1 OR
1960 ... Anita Lonsbrough, Great Britain — 2:49.5 WR
1964 ... Galina Prozumenshikova, USSR — 2:46.4 OR
1968 ... Sharon Wichman, United States — 2:44.4 OR
1972 ... Beverly Whitfield, Australia — 2:41.71 OR
1976 ... Marina Koshevaia, USSR — 2:33.35 WR
1980 ... Lina Kaciusyte, USSR — 2:29.54 OR
1984 ... Anne Ottenbrite, Canada — 2:30.38
1988 ... Silke Hoerner, East Germany — 2:26.71 WR

100-METER BUTTERFLY

1956 ... Shelley Mann, United States — 1:11.0 OR
1960 ... Carolyn Schuler, United States — 1:09.5 OR
1964 ... Sharon Stouder, United States — 1:04.7 WR
1968 ... Lynn McClements, Australia — 1:05.5
1972 ... Mayumi Aoki, Japan — 1:03.34 WR
1976 ... Kornelia Ender, East Germany — 1:00.13 EWR
1980 ... Caren Metschuck, East Germany — 1:00.42
1984 ... Mary T. Meagher, United States — 59.26
1988 ... Kristin Otto, East Germany — 59.00

200-METER BUTTERFLY

1968 ... Ada Kok, Netherlands — 2:24.7 OR
1972 ... Karen Moe, United States — 2:15.57 WR
1976 ... Andrea Pollack, East Germany — 2:11.41 OR
1980 ... Ines Geissler, East Germany — 2:10.44 OR
1984 ... Mary T. Meagher, United States — 2:06.90 OR
1988 ... Kathleen Nord, East Germany — 2:09.51

200-METER INDIVIDUAL MEDLEY

1968 ... Claudia Kolb, United States — 2:24.7 OR
1972 ... Shane Gould, Australia — 2:23.07 WR
1976 ... Not held 1976-1980
1984 ... Tracy Caulkins, United States — 2:12.64 OR
1988 ... Daniela Hunger, East Germany — 2:12.59 OR

400-METER INDIVIDUAL MEDLEY

1964 ... Donna de Varona, United States — 5:18.7 OR
1968 ... Claudia Kolb, United States — 5:08.5 OR
1972 ... Gail Neall, Australia — 5:02.97 WR
1976 ... Ulrike Tauber, East Germany — 4:42.77 WR
1980 ... Petra Schneider, East Germany — 4:36.29 WR
1984 ... Tracy Caulkins, United States — 4:39.24
1988 ... Janet Evans, United States — 4:37.76

4 X 100-METER MEDLEY RELAY

1960 .... United States — 4:41.1 WR
1964 .... United States — 4:33.9 WR
1968 .... United States — 4:28.3 OR
1972 .... United States — 4:20.75 WR
1976 .... East Germany — 4:07.95 WR

SWIMMING (*Cont.*)

Women

4 X 100-METER MEDLEY RELAY (*Cont.*)

1980	East Germany	4:06.67 WR
1984	United States	4:08.34
1988	East Germany	4:03.74 OR

4 X 100-METER FREESTYLE RELAY

1912	Great Britain	5:52.8 WR
1920	United States	5:11.6 WR
1924	United States	4:58.8 WR
1928	United States	4:47.6 WR
1932	United States	4:38.0 WR
1936	Netherlands	4:36.0 OR

4 X 100-METER FREESTYLE RELAY (*Cont.*)

1948	United States	4:29.2 OR
1952	Hungary	4:24.4 WR
1956	Australia	4:17.1 WR
1960	United States	4:08.9 WR
1964	United States	4:03.8 WR
1968	United States	4:02.5 OR
1972	United States	3:55.19 WR
1976	United States	3:44.82 WR
1980	East Germany	3:42.71 WR
1984	United States	3:43.43
1988	East Germany	3:40.63 OR

DIVING

Men

SPRINGBOARD

		Pts
1908	Albert Zürner, Germany	85.5
1912	Paul Günther, Germany	79.23
1920	Louis Kuehn, United States	675.40
1924	Albert White, United States	97.46
1928	Pete DesJardins, United States	185.04
1932	Michael Galitzen, United States	161.38
1936	Richard Degener, United States	163.57
1948	Bruce Harlan, United States	163.64
1952	David Browning, United States	205.29
1956	Robert Clotworthy, United States	159.56
1960	Gary Tobian, United States	170.00
1964	Kenneth Sitzberger, United States	159.90
1968	Bernie Wrightson, United States	170.15
1972	Vladimir Vasin, USSR	594.09
1976	Phil Boggs, United States	619.05
1980	Aleksandr Portnov, USSR	905.02
1984	Greg Louganis, United States	754.41
1988	Greg Louganis, United States	730.80

PLATFORM

		Pts
1904	George Sheldon, United States	12.66
1906	Gottlob Walz, Germany	156.0
1908	Hjalmar Johansson, Sweden	83.75
1912	Erik Adlerz, Sweden	73.94
1920	Clarence Pinkston, United States	100.67
1924	Albert White, United States	97.46
1928	Pete DesJardins, United States	98.74
1932	Harold Smith, United States	124.80
1936	Marshall Wayne, United States	113.58
1948	Sammy Lee, United States	130.05
1952	Sammy Lee, United States	156.28
1956	Joaquin Capilla, Mexico	152.44
1960	Robert Webster, United States	165.56
1964	Robert Webster, United States	148.58
1968	Klaus Dibiasi, Italy	164.18
1972	Klaus Dibiasi, Italy	504.12
1976	Klaus Dibiasi, Italy	600.51
1980	Falk Hoffmann, East Germany	835.65
1984	Greg Louganis, United States	710.91
1988	Greg Louganis, United States	638.61

Women

SPRINGBOARD

		Pts
1920	Aileen Riggin, United States	539.90
1924	Elizabeth Becker, United States	474.50
1928	Helen Meany, United States	78.62
1932	Georgia Coleman, United States	87.52
1936	Marjorie Gestring, United States	89.27
1948	Victoria Draves, United States	108.74
1952	Patricia McCormick, United States	147.30
1956	Patricia McCormick, United States	142.36
1960	Ingrid Krämer, East Germany	155.81
1964	Ingrid Engel Krämer, East Germany	145.00
1968	Sue Gossick, United States	150.77
1972	Micki King, United States	450.03
1976	Jennifer Chandler, United States	506.19
1980	Irina Kalinina, USSR	725.91
1984	Sylvie Bernier, Canada	530.70
1988	Gao Min, China	580.23

PLATFORM

		Pts
1912	Greta Johansson, Sweden	39.90
1920	Stefani Fryland-Clausen, Denmark	34.60
1924	Caroline Smith, United States	33.20
1928	Elizabeth B. Pinkston, United States	31.60
1932	Dorothy Poynton, United States	40.26
1936	Dorothy Poynton Hill, United States	33.93
1948	Victoria Draves, United States	68.87
1952	Patricia McCormick, United States	79.37
1956	Patricia McCormick, United States	84.85
1960	Ingrid Krämer, East Germany	91.28
1964	Lesley Bush, United States	99.80
1968	Milena Duchkova, Czechoslovakia	109.59
1972	Ulrika Knape, Sweden	390.00
1976	Elena Vaytsekhovskaya, USSR	406.59
1980	Martina Jäschke, East Germany	596.25
1984	Zhou Jihong, China	435.51
1988	Xu Yanmei, China	445.20

Note: OR=Olympic Record; WR=World Record;
EOR=Equals Olympic Record; EWR=Equals World Record;
WB=World Best.

BOBSLED

4-MAN BOB

1924 ...	Switzerland (Eduard Scherrer)	5:45.54
1928 ...	United States (William Fiske) (5-man)	3:20.50
1932 ...	United States (William Fiske)	7:53.68
1936 ...	Switzerland (Pierre Musy)	5:19.85
1948 ...	United States (Francis Tyler)	5:20.10
1952 ...	Germany (Andreas Ostler)	5:07.84
1956 ...	Switzerland (Franz Kapus)	5:10.44
1960 ...	Not held	
1964 ...	Canada (Victor Emery)	4:14.46
1968 ...	Italy (Eugenio Monti) (2 runs)	2:17.39
1972 ...	Switzerland (Jean Wicki)	4:43.07
1976 ...	East Germany (Meinhard Nehmer)	3:40.43
1980 ...	East Germany (Meinhard Nehmer)	3:59.92
1984 ...	East Germany (Wolfgang Hoppe)	3:20.22
1988 ...	Switzerland (Ekkehard Fasser)	3:47.51

Note: Driver in parentheses.

2-MAN BOB

1932 ...	United States (Hubert Stevens)	8:14.74
1936 ...	United States (Ivan Brown)	5:29.29
1948 ...	Switzerland (Felix Endrich)	5:29.20
1952 ...	Germany (Andreas Ostler)	5:24.54
1956 ...	Italy (Lamberto Dalla Costa)	5:30.14
1960 ...	Not held	
1964 ...	Great Britain (Anthony Nash)	4:21.90
1968 ...	Italy (Eugenio Monti)	4:41.54
1972 ...	West Germany (Wolfgang Zimmerer)	4:57.07
1976 ...	East Germany (Meinhard Nehmer)	3:44.42
1980 ...	Switzerland (Erich Schärer)	4:09.36
1984 ...	East Germany (Wolfgang Hoppe)	3:25.56
1988 ...	USSR (Janis Kipours)	3:53.48

Note: Driver in parentheses.

ICE HOCKEY

1920*	Canada, United States, Czechoslovakia
1924	Canada, United States, Great Britain
1928	Canada, Sweden, Switzerland
1932	Canada, United States, Germany
1936	Great Britain, Canada, United States
1948	Canada, Czechoslovakia, Switzerland
1952	Canada, United States, Sweden
1956	USSR, United States, Canada
1960	United States, Canada, USSR
1964	USSR, Sweden, Czechoslovakia
1968	USSR, Czechoslovakia, Canada
1972	USSR, United States, Czechoslovakia
1976	USSR, Czechoslovakia, West Germany
1980	United States, USSR, Sweden
1984	USSR, Czechoslovakia, Sweden
1988	USSR, Finland, Sweden

*Competition held at summer games in Antwerp.
Note: Gold, silver, and bronze medals.

FIGURE SKATING

Men

SINGLES

1908*	Ulrich Salchow, Sweden
1920†	Gillis Grafström, Sweden
1924	Gillis Grafström, Sweden
1928	Gillis Grafström, Sweden
1932	Karl Schäfer, Austria
1936	Karl Schäfer, Austria
1948	Dick Button, United States
1952	Dick Button, United States
1956	Hayes Alan Jenkins, United States
1960	David Jenkins, United States
1964	Manfred Schnelldorfer, West Germany
1968	Wolfgang Schwarz, Austria
1972	Ondrej Nepela, Czechoslovakia
1976	John Curry, Great Britain
1980	Robin Cousins, Great Britain
1984	Scott Hamilton, United States
1988	Brian Boitano, United States

Women

SINGLES

1908*	Madge Syers, Great Britain
1920†	Magda Julin, Sweden
1924	Herma Szabo-Planck, Austria
1928	Sonja Henie, Norway
1932	Sonja Henie, Norway
1936	Sonja Henie, Norway
1948	Barbara Ann Scott, Canada
1952	Jeanette Altwegg, Great Britain
1956	Tenley Albright, United States
1960	Carol Heiss, United States
1964	Sjoukje Dijkstra, Netherlands
1968	Peggy Fleming, United States
1972	Beatrix Schuba, Austria
1976	Dorothy Hamill, United States
1980	Anett Pötzsch, East Germany
1984	Katarina Witt, East Germany
1988	Katarina Witt, East Germany

*Competition held at summer games in London.
†Competition held at summer games in Antwerp.

FIGURE SKATING (*Cont.*)

Mixed

PAIRS

1908* ....Anna Hübler & Heinrich Burger, Germany
1920† ...Ludovika & Walter Jakobsson, Finland
1924 .....Helene Engelmann & Alfred Berger, Austria
1928 .....Andree Joly & Pierre Brunet, France
1932 .....Andree Brunet (Joly) & Pierre Brunet, France
1936 .....Maxi Herber & Ernst Baier, Germany
1948 .....Micheline Lannoy & Pierre Baugniet, Belgium
1952 .....Ria Falk and Paul Falk, West Germany
1956 .....Elisabeth Schwartz & Kurt Oppelt, Austria
1960 .....Barbara Wagner & Robert Paul, Canada
1964 .....Lyudmila Beloussova & Oleg Protopopov, USSR
1968 .....Lyudmila Beloussova & Oleg Protopopov, USSR
1972 .....Irina Rodnina & Alexei Ulanov, USSR
1976 .....Irina Rodnina & Aleksandr Zaitzev, USSR
1980 .....Irina Rodnina & Aleksandr Zaitzev, USSR
1984 .....Elena Valova & Oleg Vasiliev, USSR
1988 .....Ekaterina Gordeeva & Sergei Grinkov, USSR

ICE DANCING

1976 ....Lyudmila Pakhomova & Aleksandr Gorshkov, USSR
1980 ....Natalia Linichuk & Gennadi Karponosov, USSR
1984 ....Jayne Torvill & Christopher Dean, Great Britain
1988 ....Natalia Bestemianova & Andrei Bukin, USSR

THEY SAID IT

Bob Mathias, when asked how he intended to celebrate his victory in the decathlon at the tender age of 17: "I'll start shaving, I guess."

SPEED SKATING

Men

500 METERS

1924 ... Charles Jewtraw, United States	44.0	
1928 ... Clas Thunberg, Finland	43.4 OR	
Bernt Evensen, Norway	43.4 OR	
1932 ... John Shea, United States	43.4 OR	
1936 ... Ivar Ballangrud, Norway	43.4 EOR	
1948 ... Finn Helgesen, Norway	43.1 OR	
1952 ... Kenneth Henry, United States	43.2	
1956 ... Yevgeny Grishin, USSR	40.2 EWR	
1960 ... Yevgeny Grishin, USSR	40.2 EWR	
1964 ... Terry McDermott, United States	40.1 OR	
1968 ... Erhard Keller, West Germany	40.3	
1972 ... Erhard Keller, West Germany	39.44 OR	
1976 ... Yevgeny Kulikov, USSR	39.17 OR	
1980 ... Eric Heiden, United States	38.03 OR	
1984 ... Sergei Fokichev, USSR	38.19	
1988 ... Jens-Uwe Mey, East Germany	36.45 WR	

1000 METERS

1976 ... Peter Mueller, United States — 1:19.32
1980 ... Eric Heiden, United States — 1:15.18 OR
1984 ... Gaetan Boucher, Canada — 1:15.80
1988 ... Nikolai Gulyaev, USSR — 1:13.03 OR

1500 METERS

1924 ... Clas Thunberg, Finland	2:20.8	
1928 ... Clas Thunberg, Finland	2:21.1	
1932 ... John Shea, United States	2:57.5	
1936 ... Charles Mathisen, Norway	2:19.2 OR	
1948 ... Sverre Farstad, Norway	2:17.6 OR	
1952 ... Hjalmar Andersen, Norway	2:20.4	
1956 ... Yevgeny Grishin, USSR	2:08.6 WR	
Yuri Mikhailov, USSR	2:08.6 WR	
1960 ... Roald Aas, Norway	2:10.4	
Yevgeny Grishin, USSR	2:10.4	

1500 METERS (*Cont.*)

1964 ... Ants Anston, USSR	2:10.3	
1968 ... Cornelis Verkerk, Netherlands	2:03.4 OR	
1972 ... Ard Schenk, Netherlands	2:02.96 OR	
1976 ... Jan Egil Storholt, Norway	1:59.38 OR	
1980 ... Eric Heiden, United States	1:55.44 OR	
1984 ... Gaetan Boucher, Canada	1:58.36	
1988 ... Andre Hoffmann, East Germany	1:52.06 WR	

5000 METERS

1924 ... Clas Thunberg, Finland	8:39.0	
1928 ... Ivar Ballangrud, Norway	8:50.5	
1932 ... Irving Jaffee, United States	9:40.8	
1936 ... Ivar Ballangrud, Norway	8:19.6 OR	
1948 ... Reidar Liaklev, Norway	8:29.4	
1952 ... Hjalmar Andersen, Norway	8:10.6 OR	
1956 ... Boris Shilkov, USSR	7:48.7 OR	
1960 ... Viktor Kosichkin, USSR	7:51.3	
1964 ... Knut Johannesen, Norway	7:38.4 OR	
1968 ... Fred Anton Maier, Norway	7:22.4 WR	
1972 ... Ard Schenk, Netherlands	7:23.61	
1976 ... Sten Stensen, Norway	7:24.48	
1980 ... Eric Heiden, United States	7:02.29 OR	
1984 ... Sven Tomas Gustafson, Sweden	7:12.28	
1988 ... Tomas Gustafson, Sweden	6:44.63 WR	

SPEED SKATING (*Cont.*)

Men

10,000 METERS

1924 ... Julius Skutnabb, Finland	18:04.8	
1928 ... Not held, thawing of ice		
1932 ... Irving Jaffee, United States	19:13.6	
1936 ... Ivar Ballangrud, Norway	17:24.3 OR	
1948 ... Ake Seyffarth, Sweden	17:26.3	
1952 ... Hjalmar Andersen, Norway	16:45.8 OR	
1956 ... Sigvard Ericsson, Sweden	16:35.9 OR	
1960 ... Knut Johannesen, Norway	15:46.6 WR	

1964 ... Jonny Nilsson, Sweden	15:50.1
1968 ... Johnny Höglin, Sweden	15:23.6 OR
1972 ... Ard Schenk, Netherlands	15:01.35 OR
1976 ... Piet Kleine, Netherlands	14:50.59 OR
1980 ... Eric Heiden, United States	14:28.13 WR
1984 ... Igor Malkov, USSR	14:39.90
1988 ... Tomas Gustafson, Sweden	13:48.20 WR

Women

500 METERS

1960 ... Helga Haase, East Germany	45.9
1964 ... Lydia Skoblikova, USSR	45.0 OR
1968 ... Lyudmila Titova, USSR	46.1
1972 ... Anne Henning, United States	43.33 OR
1976 ... Sheila Young, United States	42.76 OR
1980 ... Karin Enke, East Germany	41.78 OR
1984 ... Christa Rothenburger, East Germany	41.02 OR
1988 ... Bonnie Blair, United States	39.10 WR

1500 METERS

1960 ... Lydia Skoblikova, USSR	2:25.2 WR
1964 ... Lydia Skoblikova, USSR	2:22.6 OR
1968 ... Kaija Mustonen, Finland	2:22.4 OR
1972 ... Dianne Holum, United States	2:20.85 OR
1976 ... Galina Stepanskaya, USSR	2:16.58 OR
1980 ... Anne Borckink, Netherlands	2:10.95 OR
1984 ... Karin Enke, East Germany	2:03.42 WR
1988 ... Yvonne van Gennip, Netherlands	2:00.68 OR

1000 METERS

1960 ... Klara Guseva, USSR	1:34.1
1964 ... Lydia Skoblikova, USSR	1:33.2 OR
1968 ... Carolina Geijssen, Netherlands	1:32.6 OR
1972 ... Monika Pflug, West Germany	1:31.40 OR
1976 ... Tatiana Averina, USSR	1:28.43 OR
1980 ... Natalya Petruseva, USSR	1:24.10 OR
1984 ... Karin Enke, East Germany	1:21.61 OR
1988 ... Christa Rothenburger, East Germany	1:17.65 WR

3000 METERS

1960 ... Lydia Skoblikova, USSR	5:14.3
1964 ... Lydia Skoblikova, USSR	5:14.9
1968 ... Johanna Schut, Netherlands	4:56.2 OR
1972 ... Christina Baas-Kaiser, Netherlands	4:52.14 OR
1976 ... Tatiana Averina, USSR	4:45.19 OR
1980 ... Bjorg Eva Jensen, Norway	4:32.13 OR
1984 ... Andrea Schöne, East Germany	4:24.79 OR
1988 ... Yvonne van Gennip, Netherlands	4:11.94 WR

Note: OR=Olympic Record; WR=World Record; EOR=Equals Olympic Record; EWR=Equals World Record; WB=World Best.

5000 METERS

1988 ... Yvonne van Gennip, Netherlands	7:14.13 WR

ALPINE SKIING

Men

DOWNHILL

1948 ... Henri Oreiller, France	2:55.0
1952 ... Zeno Colo, Italy	2:30.8
1956 ... Anton Sailer, Austria	2:52.2
1960 ... Jean Vuarnet, France	2:06.0
1964 ... Egon Zimmermann, Austria	2:18.16
1968 ... Jean-Claude Killy, France	1:59.85
1972 ... Bernhard Russi, Switzerland	1:51.43
1976 ... Franz Klammer, Austria	1:45.73
1980 ... Leonhard Stock, Austria	1:45.50
1984 ... Bill Johnson, United States	1:45.59
1988 ... Pirmin Zurbriggen, Switzerland	1:59.63

SUPER GIANT SLALOM

1988 ... Franck Piccard, France	1:39.66

Women

DOWNHILL

1948 ... Hedy Schlunegger, Switzerland	2:28.3
1952 ... Trude Jochum-Beiser, Austria	1:47.1
1956 ... Madeleine Berthod, Switzerland	1:40.7
1960 ... Heidi Biebl, West Germany	1:37.6
1964 ... Christl Haas, Austria	1:55.39
1968 ... Olga Pall, Austria	1:40.87
1972 ... Marie-Theres Nadig, Switzerland	1:36.68
1976 ... Rosi Mittermaier, West Germany	1:46.16
1980 ... Annemarie Moser-Pröll, Austria	1:37.52
1984 ... Michela Figini, Switzerland	1:13.36
1988 ... Marina Kiehl, West Germany	1:25.86

SUPER GIANT SLALOM

1988 ... Sigrid Wolf, Austria	1:19.03

ALPINE SKIING (*Cont.*)

<table>
<tr><td colspan="2">

Men

GIANT SLALOM

</td><td colspan="2">

Women

GIANT SLALOM

</td></tr>
</table>

Men

GIANT SLALOM

1952 ...	Stein Eriksen, Norway	2:25.0
1956 ...	Anton Sailer, Austria	3:00.1
1960 ...	Roger Staub, Switzerland	1:48.3
1964 ...	Francois Bonlieu, France	1:46.71
1968 ...	Jean-Claude Killy, France	3:29.28
1972 ...	Gustav Thöni, Italy	3:09.62
1976 ...	Heini Hemmi, Switzerland	3:26.97
1980 ...	Ingemar Stenmark, Sweden	2:40.74
1984 ...	Max Julen, Switzerland	2:41.18
1988 ...	Alberto Tomba, Italy	2:06.37

SLALOM

1948 ...	Edi Reinalter, Switzerland	2:10.3
1952 ...	Othmar Schneider, Austria	2:00.0
1956 ...	Anton Sailer, Austria	3:14.7
1960 ...	Ernst Hinterseer, Austria	2:08.9
1964 ...	Josef Stiegler, Austria	2:11.13
1968 ...	Jean-Claude Killy, France	1:39.73
1972 ...	Francisco Fernandez Ochoa, Spain	1:49.27
1976 ...	Piero Gros, Italy	2:03.29
1980 ...	Ingemar Stenmark, Sweden	1:44.26
1984 ...	Phil Mahre, United States	1:39.41
1988 ...	Alberto Tomba, Italy	1:39.47

COMBINED

		Pts
1936 ...	Franz Pfnür, Germany	99.25
1948 ...	Henri Oreiller, France	3.27
1988 ...	Hubert Strolz, Austria	36.55

Women

GIANT SLALOM

1952 ...	Andrea Mead Lawrence, United States	2:06.8
1956 ...	Ossi Reichert, West Germany	1:56.5
1960 ...	Yvonne Rüegg, Switzerland	1:39.9
1964 ...	Marielle Goitschel, France	1:52.24
1968 ...	Nancy Greene, Canada	1:51.97
1972 ...	Marie-Theres Nadig, Switzerland	1:29.90
1976 ...	Kathy Kreiner, Canada	1:29.13
1980 ...	Hanni Wenzel, Liechtenstein (2 runs)	2:41.66
1984 ...	Debbie Armstrong, United States	2:20.98
1988 ...	Vreni Schneider, Switzerland	2:06.49

SLALOM

1948 ...	Gretchen Fraser, United States	1:57.2
1952 ...	Andrea Mead Lawrence, United States	2:10.6
1956 ...	Renee Colliard, Switzerland	1:52.3
1960 ...	Anne Heggtveigt, Canada	1:49.6
1964 ...	Christine Goitschel, France	1:29.86
1968 ...	Marielle Goitschel, France	1:25.86
1972 ...	Barbara Cochran, United States	1:31.24
1976 ...	Rosi Mittermaier, West Germany	1:30.54
1980 ...	Hanni Wenzel, Liechtenstein	1:25.09
1984 ...	Paoletta Magoni, Italy	1:36.47
1988 ...	Vreni Schneider, Switzerland	1:36.69

COMBINED

		Pts
1988 ...	Anita Wachter, Austria	29.25

Track and Field

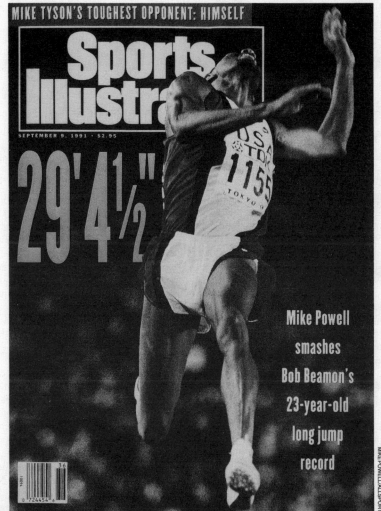

MIKE TYSON'S TOUGHEST OPPONENT: HIMSELF

Sports Illustrated

SEPTEMBER 9, 1991 · $2.95

29'4½"

USA
TDK
1155
TOKYO

Mike Powell
smashes
Bob Beamon's
23-year-old
long jump
record

The Great Leap Forward

Mike Powell set an astounding record in the long jump at the World Championships | by MERRELL NODEN

O BRAVE NEW WORLD INDEED! TRACK AND field seemed to brim with fresh possibilities after the summer of 1991. The 20-foot barrier fell in the pole vault; Leroy Burrell and Carl Lewis, training partners and Santa Monica Track Club teammates, swapped the title of world's fastest human; and the oldest record in the books, Bob Beamon's 29'2½" in the long jump, finally fell, not to Lewis, as almost everyone expected it would, but to Mike Powell, the silver medalist at the 1988 Seoul Olympics, who had never beaten Lewis before. The third outdoor World Track and Field Championships, held in Tokyo from Aug. 24 to Sept. 1, were a stirring prelude to the Olympic Games in Barcelona.

The indoor season belonged to pole vaulter Sergei Bubka, the 27-year-old Ukrainian who seems now to have been the world's best vaulter forever. Between Feb. 9 and Aug. 5, Bubka set eight world records in the vault, four indoors and four outdoors. That brought his career total to 28. Only distance runner Paavo Nurmi had more world bests—

29. At the end of the summer, Bubka's marks stood at 20'1" indoors and 20'0" outdoors. He won the world indoor title and in Tokyo defended his world outdoor title with a last-attempt clearance of 19'6¼".

Lewis was also putting together a good season. On June 14, at the TAC Championships in New York City, he ran 9.93 in the 100, finishing second to Burrell's world record of 9.90. In the long jump, he ran his win streak to 65 meets with a leap of 28'4¼", edging Powell by half an inch.

It had long been assumed that if anyone was going to break Beamon's mark, it would be Lewis. This summer he claimed to be in the best shape of his life and, though he turned 30 on July 1, he looked it. Lewis's chances seemed even better when, on Aug. 25 in Tokyo, he beat the fastest 100 field ever, clocking 9.86 to edge his U.S. teammates Burrell (9.88) and Dennis Mitchell (9.91). That set the stage for the long jump final on Aug. 30.

On his third jump on a humid, windy night, Lewis leaped a wind-aided 28'11¾", farther than he had ever jumped. After a foul

by Powell, Lewis sailed 29′2¾″, beyond Beamon's 1968 record but again wind-assisted. On his fifth jump, Powell hit the board perfectly and landed close to the nine-meter mark. The wind turned out to be legal and the mark came up as 8.95 meters: 29′4½″. Lewis came back with jumps of 29′1¼″ and 29′. As Lewis himself later pointed out, his was the greatest series of jumps in history. But only one jump counts and Powell, a 27-year-old from Alta Loma, Calif., was the winner. Lewis would come back two days later to anchor a U.S. team of Andre Cason, Burrell, and Mitchell in obliterating the world record in the 4 x 100-meter relay with a time of 37.50. Lewis must surely be regarded now as the greatest track and field athlete in history, with 13 golds in Olympic and World Championship competition.

The long sprints again belonged to Michael Johnson of Waco, Texas, who paced the world in the 200 and 400 this year with bests of 19.88 and 44.17 through the summer. In Tokyo, Johnson ran 20.01 into a strong head wind, beating the field by .33, the largest winning margin in a major 200 since 1936, when Jesse Owens won the 200 at the Berlin Olympics. Another easy winner

Lewis beat Burrell, far right, with his 9.86 clocking for the 100 meters in Tokyo.

in Tokyo was decathlete Dan O'Brien, who decimated the field with a score of 8,812. Barring injury, he should easily be history's first 9,000-point scorer.

Curiously, for the third straight year, not a single world record was set by a woman in an Olympic event. Before 1989, that had happened just once (in 1966) since the International Amateur Athletic Federation began keeping world marks in 1921. It may be evidence that the random drug testing programs are having their intended deterrent effect.

In Tokyo, Katrin Krabbe was a double dash victor, winning with comparative ease in 10.99 and 22.09. Jackie Joyner-Kersee won the long jump (24′¼″) and seemed well on her way to at least a win and maybe a world record in the heptathlon when she pulled a hamstring in the 200 and had to withdraw. With South Africa eligible for the '92 Olympics, watch out for Zola Budd Pieterse and her countrywoman Elana Meyer, who ran the fastest since the Seoul Olympics in both the 3,000 (8:32.00) and 5,000 (14:49.35).

World Track and Field Championships

Tokyo, August 24-September 1
Men

TRACK EVENTS

Event	Winner	Time
100 meters	Carl Lewis, US	9.86*
200 meters	Michael Johnson, US	20.01
400 meters	Antonio Pettigrew, US	44.57
800 meters	Billy Konchellah, Kenya	1:43.99
1,500 meters	Noureddine Morceli, Algeria	3:32.84
Steeplechase	Moses Kiptanui, Kenya	8:12.59
5,000 meters	Yobes Ondieki, Kenya	13:14.45
10,000 meters	Moses Tanui, Kenya	27:38.74
Marathon	Hiromi Taniguchi, Japan	2:14:57
110-meter hurdles	Greg Foster, US	13.06
400-meter hurdles	Samuel Matete, Zambia	47.64
20-kilometer walk	Maurizio Damilano, Italy	1:19:37
50-kilometer walk	Aleksandr Potashov, USSR	3:53:09
4x100-meter relay	United States (Andre Cason, Leroy Burrell, Dennis Mitchell, Carl Lewis)	37.50*
4x400-meter relay	Great Britain (Roger Black, Derek Redmond, John Regis, Kriss Akabusi)	2:57.53

*World record.

FIELD EVENTS

Event	Winner	Mark
High jump	Charles Austin, US	7 ft 9¾ in
Pole vault	Sergei Bubka, USSR	19 ft 6¼ in
Long jump	Mike Powell, US	29 ft 4½ in*
Triple jump	Kenny Harrison, US	58 ft 4 in
Shot put	Werner Gunthor, Switzerland	71 ft 1¼ in
Discus	Lars Riedel, Germany	217 ft 2 in
Hammer	Yuriy Sedykh, USSR	268 ft
Javelin	Kimmo Kinnunen, Finland	297 ft 11 in

DECATHLON

Event	Winner	Mark
Decathlon	Dan O'Brien, US	8812 pts

THEY SAID IT

Billy Olsen, 32-year-old pole vaulter: "I'm between the twilight and the no-light of my career."

Women

TRACK EVENTS

Event	Winner	Time
100 meters	Katrin Krabbe, Germany	10.99
200 meters	Katrin Krabbe, Germany	22.09
400 meters	Marie-Josee Perec, France	49.13
800 meters	Lilia Nurutdinova, USSR	1:57.50
1,500 meters	Hassiba Boulmerka, Algeria	4:02.21
3,000 meters	Tatyana Dorovskikh, USSR	8:35.82
10,000 meters	Liz McColgan, Great Britain	31:14.31
Marathon	Wanda Panfil, Poland	2:29:53
100-meter hurdles	Lyudmila Narozhilenko, USSR	12.59
400-meter hurdles	Tatyana Ledovskaya, USSR	53.11
10-kilometer walk	Alina Ivanova, USSR	42:57
4x100-meter relay	Jamaica (Dahlia Duhaney, Juliet Cuthbert, Beverley McDonald, Merlene Ottey)	41.94
4x400-meter relay	USSR (Tatyana Ledovskaya, Lyudmila Dzhigalova, Olga Nazarova, Olga Bryzgina)	3:18.43

*World record.

FIELD EVENTS

Event	Winner	Mark
High jump	Heike Henkel, Germany	6 ft 8¾ in
Long jump	Jackie Joyner-Kersee, US	24 ft ¼ in
Shot put	Zhihong Huang, China	68 ft 4¼ in
Discus	Tsvetanka Khristova, Bulgaria	233 ft
Javelin	Demei Xu, China	225 ft 8 in

HEPTATHLON

Event	Winner	Mark
Heptathlon	Sabine Braun, Germany	6672 pts

IAAF World Cross-Country Championships

Antwerp, Belgium, March 24, 1991

MEN (11,764 meters; 7.30 miles)

1.	Khalid Skah, Morocco	33:53
2.	Moses Tanui, Kenya	33:54
3.	Simon Karori, Kenya	33:54

WOMEN (6,425 meters; 3.99 miles)

1.	Lynn Jennings, US	20:24
2.	Derartu Tula, Ethiopia	20:27
3.	Liz McColgan, Scotland	20:28

MEN'S TEAM

		Pts
1.	Kenya	38
2.	Ethiopia	104
3.	Spain	198

WOMEN'S TEAM

		Pts
1.	Kenya	36
2.	Ethiopia	36
3.	USSR	48

Major Marathons

New York City, November 4, 1990

MEN

1.	Douglas Wakiihuri, Kenya	2:12:39
2.	Salvador Garcia, Mexico	2:13:19
3.	Steve Brace, Great Britain	2:13:32

WOMEN

1.	Wanda Panfil, Poland	2:30:45
2.	Kim Jones, US	2:30:50
3.	Katrin Dörre, Germany	2:33:21

Fukuoka, Japan, December 2, 1990

MEN

1.	Belayneh Densimo, Ethiopia	2:11:35
2.	Tsutomu Hiroyama, Japan	2:11:37
3.	Mike O'Reilly, Ireland	2:14:01

Osaka, Japan, January 27, 1991

WOMEN

1.	Katrin Dörre, Germany	2:27:43
2.	Yuko Arimori, Japan	2:28:01
3.	Chen Qingmei, China	2:29:44

Tokyo, February 10, 1991

MEN

1.	Abebe Mekonnen, Ethiopia	2:10:26
2.	Toru Kozasu, Japan	2:10:26
3.	Maurilio Castillo, Mexico	2:10:47

Boston, April 15, 1991

MEN

1.	Ibrahim Hussein, Kenya	2:11:06
2.	Abebe Mekonnen, Ethiopia	2:11:22
3.	Andy Ronan, Ireland	2:11:27

WOMEN

1.	Wanda Panfil, Poland	2:24:18
2.	Kim Jones, US	2:26:40
3.	Uta Pippig, Germany	2:26:52

London (IAAF World Cup), April 21, 1991

MEN

1.	Yakov Tolstikov, USSR	2:09:17
2.	Manuel Matius, Portugal	2:10:21
3.	Jan Huruk, Poland	2:10:21

WOMEN

1.	Rosa Mota, Portugal	2:26:14
2.	Francie Larrieu-Smith, US	2:27:35
3.	Valentina Yegorova, USSR	2:28:18

MEN'S TEAM

1.	Great Britain	6:34:59
2.	Portugal	6:35:55
3.	Poland	6:36:12

WOMEN'S TEAM

1.	USSR	7:30:21
2.	Italy	7:36:37
3.	France	7:38:51

Rotterdam, April 21, 1991

MEN

1.	Rob de Castella, Australia	2:09:42
2.	Dionicio Ceron, Mexico	2:10:02
3.	Tesfaye Dadi, Ethiopia	2:10:08

THEY SAID IT

Ron Laird, U.S. racewalker, after he went off course in the Pan American Games' 20,000-meter walk: "I knew something was wrong when I came to a locked gate."
(1967)

TRACK AND FIELD

World Records

As of September 23, 1991. World outdoor records are recognized by the International Amateur Athletics Federation (IAAF).

MEN'S TRACK EVENTS

Event	Mark	Record Holder	Date	Site
100 meters	9.86	Carl Lewis, United States	8-25-91	Tokyo
200 meters	19.72	Pietro Mennea, Italy	9-12-79	Mexico City
400 meters	43.29	Butch Reynolds, United States	8-17-88	Zurich
800 meters	1:41.73	Sebastian Coe, Great Britain	6-10-81	Florence
1,000 meters	2:12.18	Sebastian Coe, Great Britain	7-11-81	Oslo
1,500 meters	3:29.46	Said Aouita, Morocco	8-23-85	Berlin
Mile	3:46.32	Steve Cram, Great Britain	7-27-85	Oslo
2,000 meters	4:50.81	Said Aouita, Morocco	7-16-87	Paris
3,000 meters	7:29.45	Said Aouita, Morocco	8-20-89	Cologne
Steeplechase	8:05.35	Peter Koech, Kenya	7-3-89	Stockholm
5,000 meters	12:58.39	Said Aouita, Morocco	7-22-87	Rome
10,000 meters	27:08.23	Arturo Barrios, Mexico	8-18-89	Berlin
20,000 meters	56:55.6	Arturo Barrios, Mexico	3-30-91	La Flèche, France
Hour	21,101 meters	Arturo Barrios, Mexico	3-30-91	La Flèche, France
25,000 meters	1:13:55.8	Toshihiko Seko, Japan	3-22-81	Christchurch, New Zealand
30,000 meters	1:29:18.8	Toshihiko Seko, Japan	3-22-81	Christchurch, New Zealand
Marathon	2:06:50	Belayneh Densimo, Ethiopia	4-17-88	Rotterdam
110-meter hurdles	12.92	Roger Kingdom, United States	8-16-89	Zurich
400-meter hurdles	47.02	Edwin Moses, United States	8-31-83	Koblenz, Germany
20 kilometer walk	1:18:40.0	Ernesto Canto, Mexico	5-5-84	Bergen, Norway
30 kilometer walk	2:03:56.5	Thierry Toutain, France	3-24-91	Héricourt, France
50 kilometer walk	3:41:38.4	Raúl Gonzáles, Mexico	5-25-79	Bergen, Norway
4x100-meter relay	37.50	United States (Andre Cason, Leroy Burrell, Dennis Mitchell, Carl Lewis)	9-1-91	Tokyo
4x200-meter relay	1:19.38	United States (Danny Everett, Leroy Burrell, Floyd Heard, Carl Lewis)	8-23-89	Koblenz, Germany
4x400-meter relay	2:56.16	United States (Vince Matthews, Ron Freeman, Larry James, Lee Evans)	10-20-68	Mexico City
		United States (Danny Everett, Steve Lewis, Kevin Robinzine, Butch Reynolds)	10-1-88	Seoul
4x800-meter relay	7:03.89	Great Britain (Peter Elliott, Garry Cook, Steve Cram, Sebastian Coe)	8-30-82	London
4x1500-meter relay	14:38.8	West Germany (Thomas Wessinghage, Harald Hudak, Michael Lederer, Karl Fleschen)	8-17-77	Cologne

MEN'S FIELD EVENTS

Event	Mark	Record Holder	Date	Site
High jump	8 ft 0 in	Javier Sotomayor, Cuba	7-29-89	San Juan
Pole vault	20 ft 0 in	Sergei Bubka, USSR	8-5-91	Malmö, Sweden
Long jump	29 ft 4½ in	Mike Powell, United States	8-30-91	Tokyo
Triple jump	58 ft 11½ in	Willie Banks, United States	6-16-85	Indianapolis
Shot put	75 ft 10¼ in	Randy Barnes, United States	5-20-90	Westwood, CA
Discus throw	243 ft 0 in	Jurgen Schult, East Germany	6-6-86	Neubrandenburg, Germany
Hammer throw	284 ft 7 in	Yuri Syedikh, USSR	8-30-86	Stuttgart
Javelin throw	318 ft 1 in	Seppo Räty, Finland	6-2-91	Punkalaidun, Finland

DECATHLON

Event	Mark	Record Holder	Date	Site
Decathlon	8847 pts	Daley Thompson, Great Britain	8-8-9-84	Los Angeles

Note: The decathlon consists of 10 events—the 100 meters, long jump, shot put, high jump and 400 meters on the first day; the 110-meter hurdles, discus, pole vault, javelin and 1500 meters on the second.

World Records (Cont.)

WOMEN'S TRACK EVENTS

Event	Mark	Record Holder	Date	Site
100 meters	10.49	Florence Griffith Joyner, United States	7-16-88	Indianapolis
200 meters	21.34	Florence Griffith Joyner, United States	9-29-88	Seoul
400 meters	47.60	Marita Koch, East Germany	10-6-85	Canberra
800 meters	1:53.28	Jarmila Kratochvilova, Czechoslovakia	7-26-83	Munich
1,500 meters	3:52.47	Tatyana Kazankina, USSR	8-13-80	Zurich
Mile	4:15.61	Paula Ivan, Romania	7-10-89	Nice
2,000 meters	5:28.69	Maricica Puica, Romania	7-11-86	London
3,000 meters	8:22.62	Tatyana Kazankina, USSR	8-26-84	Leningrad
5,000 meters	14:37.33	Ingrid Kristiansen, Norway	8-5-86	Stockholm
10,000 meters	30:13.74	Ingrid Kristiansen, Norway	7-5-86	Oslo
25,000 meters	1:29:29.2	Karolina Szabó, Hungary	4-22-88	Budapest
30,000 meters	1:49:05.6	Karolina Szabó, Hungary	4-22-88	Budapest
Marathon	2:21:06	Ingrid Kristiansen, Norway	4-21-85	London
100-meter hurdles	12.21	Yordanka Donkova, Bulgaria	8-20-88	Stara Zagora, Bulgaria
400-meter hurdles	52.94	Marina Stepanova, USSR	9-17-86	Tashkent, USSR
5-kilometer walk	20:07.52	Beate Anders, East Germany	6-23-90	Rostock, Germany
10-kilometer walk	41:56.23	Nadezhda Ryashkina, USSR	7-24-90	Seattle
4x100-meter relay	41.37	East Germany (Silke Gladisch, Sabine Reiger, Ingrid Auerswald, Marlies Göhr)	10-6-85	Canberra
4x200-meter relay	1:28.15	East Germany (Marlies Göhr, Romy Müller, Bärbel Wöckel, Marita Koch)	8-9-80	Jena, East Germany
4x400-meter relay	3:15.17	USSR (Tatyana Ledovskaya, Olga Nazarova, Maria Pinigina, Olga Bryzgina)	10-1-88	Seoul
4x800-meter relay	7:50.17	USSR (Nadezhda Olizarenko, Lyubov Gurina, Lyudmila Borisova, Irina Podyalovskaya)	8-5-84	Moscow

WOMEN'S FIELD EVENTS

Event	Mark	Record Holder	Date	Site
High jump	6 ft 10¼ in	Stefka Kostadinova, Bulgaria	8-30-87	Rome
Long jump	24 ft 8¼ in	Galina Chistyakova, USSR	6-11-88	Leningrad
Shot put	74 ft 3 in	Natalya Lisovskaya, USSR	6-7-87	Moscow
Discus throw	252 ft 0 in	Gabriele Reinsch, East Germany	7-9-88	Neubrandenburg, Germany
Javelin throw	262 ft 5 in	Petra Felke, East Germany	9-9-88	Berlin

HEPTATHLON

Event	Mark	Record Holder	Date	Site
Heptathlon	7291 pts	Jackie Joyner-Kersee, United States	9-23-24-88	Seoul

Note: The heptathlon consists of 7 events—the 100-meter hurdles, high jump, shot put and 200 meters on the first day; the long jump, javelin and 800 meters on the second.

20 Feet for America

Soviet pole vaulter Sergei Bubka already held the world indoor record of 19' 11 1/4" (as well as the outdoor record of 19' 10 1/2") when he arrived in San Sebastian, Spain for an indoor meet last March 15. In fact Bubka, twice world champion and twice Olympic gold medalist, had set 12 indoor and nine outdoor world records in his career. In 1985 he had become the first vaulter ever to clear the landmark height of six meters (19' 8 1/4"). Bubka knew, however, that for the non-metric minded fans of the U.S. a more significant barrier still loomed. In San Sebastian he broke it, clearing 6.10 meters—20 feet—on his first attempt at that height. "Twenty feet will mean more to Americans than to Europeans," said a happy Bubka after the meet. "This record is a gift to the United States."

American Records

As of September 23, 1991. American outdoor records are recognized by The Athletics Congress (TAC). WR=world record.

MEN'S TRACK EVENTS

Event	Mark	Record Holder	Date	Site
100 meters	9.86 WR	Carl Lewis	8-25-91	Tokyo
200 meters	19.75	Carl Lewis	6-19-83	Indianapolis
		Joe DeLoach	9-28-88	Seoul
400 meters	43.29 WR	Butch Reynolds	8-17-88	Zurich
800 meters	1:42.60	Johnny Gray	8-28-85	Koblenz, Germany
1,000 meters	2:13.9	Rick Wohlhuter	7-30-74	Oslo
1,500 meters	3:29.77	Sydney Maree	8-25-85	Cologne
Mile	3:47.69	Steve Scott	7-7-82	Oslo
2,000 meters	4:52.44	Jim Spivey	9-15-87	Lausanne
3,000 meters	7:35.84	Doug Padilla	7-9-83	Oslo
Steeplechase	8:09.17	Henry Marsh	8-28-85	Koblenz, Germany
5,000 meters	13:01.15	Sydney Maree	7-27-85	Oslo
10,000 meters	27:20.56	Mark Nenow	9-5-86	Brussels
20,000 meters	58:25.0	Bill Rodgers	8-9-77	Boston
Hour	20,547 meters	Bill Rodgers	8-9-77	Boston
25,000 meters	1:14:11.8	Bill Rodgers	2-21-79	Saratoga, CA
30,000 meters	1:31:49	Bill Rodgers	2-21-79	Saratoga, CA
Marathon	2:10:04	Pat Petersen	4-23-89	London
110-meter hurdles	12.92 WR	Roger Kingdom	8-16-89	Zurich
400-meter hurdles	47.02 WR	Edwin Moses	8-31-83	Koblenz, Germany
20-kilometer walk	1:24:50	Tim Lewis	5-7-88	Seattle
30-kilometer walk	2:23:14.0	Goetz Klopfer	11-15-70	Seattle
50-kilometer walk	4:04:23.8	Herm Nelson	10-29-89	Seattle
4x100-meter relay	37.50 WR	National Team (Andre Cason, Leroy Burrell, Dennis Mitchell, Carl Lewis)	9-1-91	Tokyo
4x200-meter relay	1:19.38 WR	Santa Monica Track Club (Danny Everett, Leroy Burrell, Floyd Heard, Carl Lewis)	8-23-89	Koblenz, Germany
4x400-meter relay	2:56.16 WR	Olympic Team (Vince Matthews, Ron Freeman, Larry James, Lee Evans)	10-20-68	Mexico City
		Olympic Team (Danny Everett, Steve Lewis, Kevin Robinzine, Butch Reynolds)	10-1-88	Seoul
4x800-meter relay	7:06.5	Santa Monica Track Club (James Robinson, David Mack, Earl Jones, Johnny Gray)	4-26-86	Walnut, CA
4x1500-meter relay	14:46.3	National Team (Dan Aldredge, Andy Clifford, Todd Harbour, Tom Duits)	6-24-79	Bourges, France

MEN'S FIELD EVENTS

Event	Mark	Record Holder	Date	Site
High jump	7 ft 10½ in	Charles Austin	8-15-91	Zurich
Pole vault	19 ft 6½ in	Joe Dial	6-18-87	Norman, OK
Long jump	29 ft 4½ in WR	Mike Powell	8-30-91	Tokyo
Triple jump	58 ft 11½ in WR	Willie Banks	6-16-85	Indianapolis
Shot put	75 ft 10¼ in WR	Randy Barnes	5-20-90	Westwood, CA
Discus throw	237 ft 4 in	Ben Plucknett	7-7-81	Stockholm
Hammer throw	268 ft 8 in	Jud Logan	4-22-88	University Park, PA
Javelin throw	280 ft 1 in	Tom Petranoff	7-7-86	Helsinki

DECATHLON

Event	Mark	Record Holder	Date	Site
Decathlon	8812 pts	Dan O'Brien	8–29-30–91	Tokyo

WOMEN'S TRACK EVENTS

Event	Mark	Record Holder	Date	Site
100 meters	10.49 WR	Florence Griffith Joyner	7-16-88	Indianapolis
200 meters	21.34 WR	Florence Griffith Joyner	9-29-88	Seoul
400 meters	48.83	Valerie Brisco-Hooks	8-6-84	Los Angeles
800 meters	1:56.90	Mary Decker Slaney	8-16-85	Bern
1,500 meters	3:57.12	Mary Decker Slaney	7-26-83	Stockholm
Mile	4:16.71	Mary Decker Slaney	8-21-85	Zurich
2,000 meters	5:32.7	Mary Decker Slaney	8-3-84	Eugene, OR
3,000 meters	8:25.83	Mary Decker Slaney	9-7-85	Rome
5,000 meters	15:00.00	PattiSue Plumer	7-3-89	Stockholm
10,000 meters	31:28.92	Francie Larrieu Smith	4-4-91	Austin, TX
Marathon	2:21:21	Joan Samuelson	10-20-85	Chicago
100-meter hurdles	12.48	Gail Devers-Roberts	9-10-91	Berlin
400-meter hurdles	53.37	Sandra Farmer-Patrick	7-22-89	New York City
5-kilometer walk	22:36.8	Teresa Vaill	4-28-90	Philadelphia
10-kilometer walk	45:28.4	Debbi Lawrence	7-19-91	Westwood, CA
4x100-meter relay	41.55	National Team (Alice Brown, Diane Williams, Florence Griffith, Pam Marshall)	8-21-87	Berlin
4x200-meter relay	1:32.57	Louisiana State (Tananjalyn Stanley, Sylvia Brydson, Esther Jones, Dawn Sowell)	4-28-89	Des Moines
4x400-meter relay	3:15.51	Olympic Team (Denean Howard, Diane Dixon, Valerie Brisco, Florence Griffith Joyner)	10-1-88	Seoul
4x800-meter relay	8:17.09	Athletics West (Sue Addison, Lee Arbogast, Mary Decker, Chris Mullen)	4-24-83	Walnut, CA

WOMEN'S FIELD EVENTS

Event	Mark	Record Holder	Date	Site
High jump	6 ft 8 in	Louise Ritter	7-8-88	Austin
		Louise Ritter	9-30-88	Seoul
Long jump	24 ft 5½ in	Jackie Joyner-Kersee	8-13-87	Indianapolis
Triple jump	46 ft ¾ in	Sheila Hudson	6-2-90	Durham, NC
Shot put	66 ft 2½ in	Ramona Pagel	6-25-88	San Diego
Discus throw	216 ft 10 in	Carol Cady	5-31-86	San Jose
Javelin throw	227 ft 5 in	Kate Schmidt	9-10-77	Fürth, West Germany

HEPTATHLON

Event	Mark	Record Holder	Date	Site
Heptathlon	7291 pts WR	Jackie Joyner-Kersee	9-23-24–88	Seoul

Racing with the Moon

Inspired, perhaps, by the ancient Greeks, who competed at the Olympics in the nude, 45 men and women from 10 university track teams shed their clothes at 2:30 a.m. on March 31 and took off running. Jerry Falwell's worst nightmare? A complete breakdown in traditional values? No, just the second annual Nude Relays, an unsanctioned track meet following the Florida Relays in Gainesville.

A few athletes initiated the instant tradition last year, sneaking onto pitch-dark Percy Beard Track and running relays naked after the postmeet party. The legend was passed along the college track grapevine, so the second run-as-you-are party generated a lot of interest. Too much, in fact.

The revelers trying to watch from the stands made enough noise to wake up the neighbors, who called the campus police. After the first heat, the police turned on the lights, and the runners scattered. The Villanova team had won a chaotic 400-meter relay, so the Wildcats were declared the winners. "This wasn't just a bunch of drunks," said Phil Wharton, a former Florida runner and the self-described Nude Relays coordinator. "We were getting down to the essence of the sport, without all the commercialization. No baton, no shoes, just the bare essence."

Upon uncovering the Nude Relays, University of Florida officials kept their shirts on. No one was arrested. University president John Lombardi confessed, "If I had known about it, I would have watched."

Will there be a third annual Nude Relays? Florida track coach John Webb recognizes the public relations value. "We could break a world record and not get this kind of publicity," lamented Webb. "But this will be the last one at Florida."

Said Wharton, "The venue might change, but the event will continue."

Historically, the Olympics have served as the outdoor world championships for track and field. In 1983 the International Amateur Athletic Federation (IAAF) instituted a separate World Championship meet, to be held every 4 years between the Olympics. The first was held in Helsinki in 1983, the second in Rome in 1987, the third in Tokyo in 1991.

HELSINKI 1983

Men

TRACK EVENTS

Event	Winner	Time
100 meters	Carl Lewis, United States	10.07
200 meters	Calvin Smith, United States	20.14
400 meters	Bert Cameron, Jamaica	45.05
800 meters	Willi Wulbeck, West Germany	1:43.65
1,500 meters	Steve Cram, Great Britain	3:41.59
Steeplechase	Patriz Ilg, West Germany	8:15.06
5,000 meters	Eamonn Coghlan, Ireland	13:28.53
10,000 meters	Alberto Cova, Italy	28:01.04
Marathon	Rob de Castella, Australia	2:10:03
110-meter hurdles	Greg Foster, United States	13.42
400-meter hurdles	Edwin Moses, United States	47.50

WALKING

Event	Winner	Time
20 kilometers	Ernesto Canto, Mexico	1:20:49
50 kilometers	Ronald Weigel, East Germany	3:43:08

DECATHLON

Event	Winner	Pts
Decathlon	Daley Thompson, Great Britain	8666

RELAYS

Event	Winner	Time
4x100 meters	United States (Emmit King, Willie Gault, Calvin Smith, Carl Lewis)	37.86
4x400 meters	USSR (Sergei Lovachev, Alecksandr Troschilo, Nikolay Chernyetski, Viktor Markin)	3:00.79

FIELD EVENTS

Event	Winner	Mark
High jump	Gennadi Avdeyenko, USSR	7 ft 7¼ in
Pole vault	Sergei Bubka, USSR	18 ft 8¼ in
Long jump	Carl Lewis, United States	28 ft 3¾ in
Triple jump	Zdzislaw Hoffmann, Poland	57 ft 2 in
Shot put	Edward Sarul, Poland	70 ft 2¼ in
Discus throw	Imrich Bugar, Czechoslovakia	222 ft 2 in
Hammer throw	Sergei Litvinov, USSR	271 ft 3 in
Javelin throw	Detlef Michel, East Germany	293 ft 7 in

Women

TRACK EVENTS

Event	Winner	Time
100 meters	Marlies Göhr, East Germany	10.97
200 meters	Marita Koch, East Germany	22.13
400 meters	Jarmila Kratochvilova, Czechoslovakia	47.99
800 meters	Jarmila Kratochvilova, Czechoslovakia	1:54.68
1,500 meters	Mary Decker Slaney, United States	4:00.90
3,000 meters	Mary Decker Slaney, United States	8:34.62
Marathon	Grete Waitz, Norway	2:28:09
100-meter hurdles	Bettine Jahn, East Germany	12.35
400-meter hurdles	Yekaterina Fesenko, USSR	54.14

RELAYS

Event	Winner	Time
4x100 meters	East Germany (Silke Gladisch, Marita Koch, Averswald, Marlies Göhr)	41.76
4x400 meters	East Germany (Kerstin Walther, Sabine Busch, Marita Koch, Dagmar Rubsam)	3:19.73

Women (*Cont.*)

FIELD EVENTS

Event	Winner	Mark
High jump	Tamara Bykova, USSR	6 ft 7 in
Long jump	Heike Daute, East Germany	23 ft 10¼ in
Shot put	Helena Fibingerova, Czechoslovakia	69 ft ¾ in
Discus throw	Martina Opitz, East Germany	226 ft 2 in
Javelin throw	Tiina Lillak, Finland	232 ft 4 in

HEPTATHLON

Event	Winner	Pts
Heptathlon	Ramona Neubert, East Germany	6714

ROME 1987

Men

TRACK EVENTS

Event	Winner	Time
100 meters	Ben Johnson, Canada	9.83
200 meters	Calvin Smith, United States	20.16
400 meters	Thomas Schönlebe, East Germany	44.33
800 meters	Billy Konchellah, Kenya	1:43.06
1,500 meters	Abdi Bile, Somalia	3:36.80
Steeplechase	Francesco Panetta, Italy	8:08.57
5,000 meters	Said Aouita, Morocco	13:26.44
10,000 meters	Paul Kipkoech, Kenya	27:38.63
Marathon	Douglas Wakiihuri, Kenya	2:11:48
110-meter hurdles	Greg Foster, United States	13.21
400-meter hurdles	Edwin Moses, United States	47.46

WALKING

Event	Winner	Time
20 kilometers	Maurizio Damilano, Italy	1:20:45
50 kilometers	Hartwig Gauder, East Germany	3:40:53

DECATHLON

Event	Winner	Pts
Decathlon	Torsten Voss, East Germany	8680

RELAYS

Event	Winner	Time
4x100	United States (Lee McRae, Lee McNeil, Harvey Glance, Carl Lewis)	37.90
4x400	United States (Danny Everett, Rod Haley, Antonio McKay, Butch Reynolds)	2:57.29

FIELD EVENTS

Event	Winner	Mark
High jump	Patrik Sjoberg, Sweden	7 ft 9¾ in
Pole vault	Sergei Bubka, USSR	19 ft 2¼ in
Long jump	Carl Lewis, United States	28 ft 5¼ in
Triple jump	Khristo Markov, Bulgaria	58 ft 9½ in
Shot put	Werner Gunthor, Switzerland	72 ft 11¼ in
Discus throw	Juergen Schult, East Germany	225 ft 6 in
Hammer throw	Sergei Litvinov, USSR	272 ft 6 in
Javelin throw	Seppo Räty, Finland	274 ft 1 in

Women

TRACK EVENTS

Event	Winner	Time
100 meters	Silke Gladisch, East Germany	10.90
200 meters	Silke Gladisch, East Germany	21.74
400 meters	Olga Bryzgina, USSR	49.38
800 meters	Sigrun Wodars, East Germany	1:55.26
1,500 meters	Tatyana Samolenko, USSR	3:58.56
3,000 meters	Tatyana Samolenko, USSR	8:38.73
10,000 meters	Ingrid Kristiansen, Norway	31:05.85
Marathon	Rosa Mota, Portugal	2:25:17
100-meter hurdles	Ginka Zagorcheva, Bulgaria	12.34
400-meter hurdles	Sabine Busch, East Germany	53.62

Women (*Cont.*)

WALKING

Event	Winner	Time
10 kilometers	Irina Strakhova, USSR	44:12

RELAYS

Event	Winner	Time
4x100 meters	United States (Alice Brown, Diane Williams, Florence Griffith, Pam Marshall)	41.58
4x400 meters	East Germany (Dagmar Neubauer, Kirsten Emmelmann, Petra Müller, Sabine Busch)	3:18.63

FIELD EVENTS

Event	Winner	Mark
High jump	Stefka Kostadinova, Bulgaria	6 ft 10¼ in
Long jump	Jackie Joyner-Kersee, United States	24 ft 1¾ in
Shot put	Natalya Lisovskaya, USSR	69 ft 8¼ in
Discus throw	Martina Hellmann, East Germany	235 ft 0 in
Javelin throw	Fatima Whitbread, Great Britain	251 ft 5 in

HEPTATHLON

Event	Winner	Pts
Heptathlon	Jackie Joyner-Kersee, United States	7128

Track & Field News Athlete of the Year

Each year (since 1959 for men and since 1974 for women) Track & Field News has chosen the outstanding athlete in the sport.

Men

Year	Athlete	Event
1959	Martin Lauer, West Germany	110-meter hurdles/Decathlon
1960	Rafer Johnson, United States	Decathlon
1961	Ralph Boston, United States	Long jump
1962	Peter Snell, New Zealand	800/1500 meters
1963	C. K. Yang, Taiwan	Decathlon/Pole vault
1964	Peter Snell, New Zealand	800/1500 meters
1965	Ron Clarke, Australia	5,000/10,000 meters
1966	Jim Ryun, United States	800/1500 meters
1967	Jim Ryun, United States	1500 meters
1968	Bob Beamon, United States	Long jump
1969	Bill Toomey, United States	Decathlon
1970	Randy Matson, United States	Shot put
1971	Rod Milburn, United States	110-meter hurdles
1972	Lasse Viren, Finland	5,000/10,000 meters
1973	Ben Jipcho, Kenya	1500/5000 meters/Steeplechase
1974	Rick Wohlhuter, United States	800/1500 meters
1975	John Walker, New Zealand	800/1500 meters
1976	Alberto Juantorena, Cuba	400/800 meters
1977	Alberto Juantorena, Cuba	400/800 meters
1978	Henry Rono, Kenya	5,000/10,000 meters/Steeplechase
1979	Sebastian Coe, Great Britain	800/1500 meters
1980	Edwin Moses, United States	400-meter hurdles
1981	Sebastian Coe, Great Britain	800/1500 meters
1982	Carl Lewis, United States	100/200 meters/Long jump
1983	Carl Lewis, United States	100/200 meters/Long jump
1984	Carl Lewis, United States	100/200 meters/Long jump
1985	Said Aouita, Morocco	1500/5000 meters
1986	Yuri Syedikh, USSR	Hammer throw
1987	Ben Johnson, Canada	100 meters
1988	Sergei Bubka, USSR	Pole vault
1989	Roger Kingdom, United States	110-meter hurdles
1990	Michael Johnson, United States	200/400 meters

Track & Field News Athlete of the Year (*Cont.*)

Women

Year	Athlete	Event
1974	Irena Szewinska, Poland	100/200/400 meters
1975	Faina Melnik, USSR	Shot put/Discus
1976	Tatyana Kazankina, USSR	800/1500 meters
1977	Rosemarie Ackermann, East Germany	High jump
1978	Marita Koch, East Germany	100/200/400 meters
1979	Marita Koch, East Germany	100/200/400 meters
1980	Ilona Briesenick, East Germany	Shot put
1981	Evelyn Ashford, United States	100/200 meters
1982	Marita Koch, East Germany	100/200/400 meters
1983	Jarmila Kratochvilova, Czechoslovakia	200/400/800 meters
1984	Evelyn Ashford, United States	100 meters
1985	Marita Koch, East Germany	100/200/400 meters
1986	Jackie Joyner-Kersee, United States	Long jump/Heptathlon
1987	Jackie Joyner-Kersee, United States	100-meter hurdles/Long jump/Heptathlon
1988	Florence Griffith Joyner, United States	100/200 meters
1989	Ana Quirot, Cuba	400/800 meters
1990	Merlene Ottey, Jamaica	100/200 meters

MARATHON

World Record Progression

Men

Record Holder	Time	Date	Site
John Hayes, United States	2:55:18.4	7-24-08	Shepherd's Bush, London
Robert Fowler, United States	2:52:45.4	1-1-09	Yonkers, NY
James Clark, United States	2:46:52.6	2-12-09	New York City
Albert Raines, United States	2:46:04.6	5-8-09	New York City
Frederick Barrett, Great Britain	2:42:31	5-26-09	Shepherd's Bush, London
Harry Green, Great Britain	2:38:16.2	5-12-13	Shepherd's Bush, London
Alexis Ahlgren, Sweden	2:36:06.6	5-31-13	Shepherd's Bush, London
Johannes Kolehmainen, Finland	2:32:35.8	8-22-20	Antwerp, Belgium
Albert Michelsen, United States	2:29:01.8	10-12-25	Port Chester, NY
Fusashige Suzuki, Japan	2:27:49	3-31-35	Tokyo
Yasuo Ikenaka, Japan	2:26:44	4-3-35	Tokyo
Kitei Son, Japan	2:26:42	11-3-35	Tokyo
Yun Bok Suh, Korea	2:25:39	4-19-47	Boston
James Peters, Great Britain	2:20:42.2	6-14-52	Chiswick, England
James Peters, Great Britain	2:18:40.2	6-13-53	Chiswick, England
James Peters, Great Britain	2:18:34.8	10-4-53	Turku, Finland
James Peters, Great Britain	2:17:39.4	6-26-54	Chiswick, England
Sergei Popov, USSR	2:15:17	8-24-58	Stockholm
Abebe Bikila, Ethiopia	2:15:16.2	9-10-60	Rome
Toru Terasawa, Japan	2:15:15.8	2-17-63	Beppu, Japan
Leonard Edelen, United States	2:14:28	6-15-63	Chiswick, England
Basil Heatley, Great Britain	2:13:55	6-13-64	Chiswick, England
Abebe Bikila, Ethiopia	2:12:11.2	6-21-64	Tokyo
Morio Shigematsu, Japan	2:12:00	6-12-65	Chiswick, England
Derek Clayton, Australia	2:09:36.4	12-3-67	Fukuoka, Japan
Derek Clayton, Australia	2:08:33.6	5-30-69	Antwerp, Belgium
Rob de Castella, Australia	2:08:18	12-6-81	Fukuoka, Japan
Steve Jones, Great Britain	2:08:05	10-21-84	Chicago
Carlos Lopes, Portugal	2:07:12	4-20-85	Rotterdam, Netherlands
Belayneh Densimo, Ethiopia	2:06:50	4-17-88	Rotterdam, Netherlands

An Unprecedented Double	In 1990, America's Michael Johnson, *Track & Field News* Athlete of the Year, became the first man ever to be ranked No. 1 in the world for both the 200 and the 400 meters.

Women

Record Holder	Time	Date	Site
Dale Greig, Great Britain	3:27:45	5-23-64	Ryde, England
Mildred Simpson, New Zealand	3:19:33	7-21-64	Auckland, New Zealand
Maureen Wilton, Canada	3:15:22	5-6-67	Toronto
Anni Pede-Erdkamp, West Germany	3:07:26	9-16-67	Waldniel, West Germany
Caroline Walker, United States	3:02:53	2-28-70	Seaside, OR
Elizabeth Bonner, United States	3:01:42	5-9-71	Philadelphia
Adrienne Beames, Australia	2:46:30	8-31-71	Werribee, Australia
Chantal Langlace, France	2:46:24	10-27-74	Neuf Brisach, France
Jacqueline Hansen, United States	2:43:54.5	12-1-74	Culver City, CA
Liane Winter, West Germany	2:42:24	4-21-75	Boston
Christa Vahlensieck, West Germany	2:40:15.8	5-3-75	Dülmen, West Germany
Jacqueline Hansen, United States	2:38:19	10-12-75	Eugene, OR
Chantal Langlace, France	2:35:15.4	5-1-77	Oyarzun, France
Christa Vahlensieck, West Germany	2:34:47.5	9-10-77	West Berlin, West Germany
Grete Waitz, Norway	2:32:29.9	10-22-78	New York City
Grete Waitz, Norway	2:27:32.6	10-21-79	New York City
Grete Waitz, Norway	2:25:41.3	10-26-80	New York City
Grete Waitz, Norway	2:25:29	4-17-83	London
Joan Benoit Samuelson, United States	2:22:43	4-18-83	Boston
Ingrid Kristiansen, Norway	2:21:06	4-21-85	London

Boston Marathon

The Boston Marathon began in 1897 as a local Patriot's Day event. Run every year but 1918 since, it has grown into one of the world's premier marathons.

Men

Year	Winner	Time	Year	Winner	Time
1897	John J. McDermott, United States	2:55:10	1931	James "Hinky" Henigan, United States	2:46:45
1898	Ronald J. McDonald, United States	2:42:00	1932	Paul de Bruyn, Germany	2:33:36
1899	Lawrence J. Brignolia, United States	2:54:38	1933	Leslie Pawson, United States	2:31:01
1900	James J. Caffrey, Canada	2:39:44	1934	Dave Komonen, Canada	2:32:53
1901	James J. Caffrey, Canada	2:29:23	1935	John A. Kelley, United States	2:32:07
1902	Sammy Mellor, United States	2:43:12	1936	Ellison M. "Tarzan" Brown, United States	2:33:40
1903	John C. Lorden, United States	2:41:29	1937	Walter Young, Canada	2:33:20
1904	Michael Spring, United States	2:38:04	1938	Leslie Pawson, United States	2:35:34
1905	Fred Lorz, United States	2:38:25	1939	Ellison M. "Tarzan" Brown, United States	2:28:51
1906	Timothy Ford, United States	2:45:45	1940	Gerard Cote, Canada	2:28:28
1907	Tom Longboat, Canada	2:24:24	1941	Leslie Pawson, United States	2:30:38
1908	Thomas Morrissey, United States	2:25:43	1942	Bernard Joseph Smith, United States	2:26:51
1909	Henri Renaud, United States	2:53:36	1943	Gerard Cote, Canada	2:28:25
1910	Fred Cameron, United States	2:28:52	1944	Gerard Cote, Canada	2:31:50
1911	Clarence H. DeMar, United States	2:21:39	1945	John A. Kelley, United States	2:30:40
1912	Mike Ryan, United States	2:21:18	1946	Stylianos Kyriakides, Greece	2:29:27
1913	Fritz Carlson, United States	2:25:14	1947	Yun Bok Suh, Korea	2:25:39
1914	James Duffy, Canada	2:25:01	1948	Gerard Cote, Canada	2:31:02
1915	Edouard Fabre, Canada	2:31:41	1949	Karl Gosta Leandersson, Sweden	2:31:50
1916	Arthur Roth, United States	2:27:16	1950	Kee Yong Ham, Korea	2:32:39
1917	Bill Kennedy, United States	2:28:37	1951	Shigeki Tanaka, Japan	2:27:45
1918	No race		1952	Doroteo Flores, Guatemala	2:31:53
1919	Carl Linder, United States	2:29:13	1953	Keizo Yamada, Japan	2:18:51
1920	Peter Trivoulidas, Greece	2:29:31	1954	Veikko Karvonen, Finland	2:20:39
1921	Frank Zuna, United States	2:18:57	1955	Hideo Hamamura, Japan	2:18:22
1922	Clarence H. DeMar, United States	2:18:10	1956	Antti Viskari, Finland	2:14:14
1923	Clarence H. DeMar, United States	2:23:37	1957	John J. Kelley, United States	2:20:05
1924	Clarence H. DeMar, United States	2:29:40	1958	Franjo Mihalic, Yugoslavia	2:25:54
1925	Chuck Mellor, United States	2:33:00	1959	Eino Oksanen, Finland	2:22:42
1926	John C. Miles, Canada	2:25:40	1960	Paavo Kotila, Finland	2:20:54
1927	Clarence H. DeMar, United States	2:40:22	1961	Eino Oksanen, Finland	2:23:39
1928	Clarence H. DeMar, United States	2:37:07	1962	Eino Oksanen, Finland	2:23:48
1929	John C. Miles, Canada	2:33:08	1963	Aurele Vandendriessche, Belgium	2:18:58
1930	Clarence H. DeMar, United States	2:34:48	1964	Aurele Vandendriessche, Belgium	2:19:59

Men (*Cont.*)

Year	Winner	Time	Year	Winner	Time
1965	Morio Shigematsu, Japan	2:16:33	1979	Bill Rodgers, United States	2:09:27
1966	Kenji Kimihara, Japan	2:17:11	1980	Bill Rodgers, United States	2:12:11
1967	David McKenzie, New Zealand	2:15:45	1981	Toshihiko Seko, Japan	2:09:26
1968	Amby Burfoot, United States	2:22:17	1982	Alberto Salazar, United States	2:08:52
1969	Yoshiaki Unetani, Japan	2:13:49	1983	Gregory A. Meyer, United States	2:09:00
1970	Ron Hill, England	2:10:30	1984	Geoff Smith, England	2:10:34
1971	Alvaro Mejia, Colombia	2:18:45	1985	Geoff Smith, England	2:14:05
1972	Olavi Suomalainen, Finland	2:15:39	1986	Rob de Castella, Australia	2:07:51
1973	Jon Anderson, United States	2:16:03	1987	Toshihiko Seko, Japan	2:11:50
1974	Neil Cusack, Ireland	2:13:39	1988	Ibrahim Hussein, Kenya	2:08:43
1975	Bill Rodgers, United States	2:09:55	1989	Abebe Mekonnen, Ethiopia	2:09:06
1976	Jack Fultz, United States	2:20:19	1990	Gelindo Bordin, Italy	2:08:19
1977	Jerome Drayton, Canada	2:14:46	1991	Ibrahim Hussein, Kenya	2:11:06
1978	Bill Rodgers, United States	2:10:13			

Women

Year	Winner	Time	Year	Winner	Time
1966	Roberta Gibb, United States	3:21:40*	1979	Joan Benoit, United States	2:35:15
1967	Roberta Gibb, United States	3:27:17*	1980	Jacqueline Gareau, Canada	2:34:28
1968	Roberta Gibb, United States	3:30:00*	1981	Allison Roe, New Zealand	2:26:46
1969	Sara Mae Berman, United States	3:22:46*	1982	Charlotte Teske, West Germany	2:29:33
1970	Sara Mae Berman, United States	3:05:07*	1983	Joan Benoit, United States	2:22:43
1971	Sara Mae Berman, United States	3:08:30*	1984	Lorraine Moller, New Zealand	2:29:28
1972	Nina Kuscsik, United States	3:10:36	1985	Lisa Larsen Weidenbach, United States	2:34:06
1973	Jacqueline A. Hansen, United States	3:05:59	1986	Ingrid Kristiansen, Norway	2:24:55
1974	Miki Gorman, United States	2:47:11	1987	Rosa Mota, Portugal	2:25:21
1975	Liane Winter, West Germany	2:42:24	1988	Rosa Mota, Portugal	2:24:30
1976	Kim Merritt, United States	2:47:10	1989	Ingrid Kristiansen, Norway	2:24:33
1977	Miki Gorman, United States	2:48:33	1990	Rosa Mota, Portugal	2:25:24
1978	Gayle Barron, United States	2:44:52	1991	Wanda Panfil, Poland	2:24:18

*Unofficial.

Note: Over the years the Boston course has varied in length. The distances have been 24 miles, 1232 yards (1897-1923); 26 miles, 209 yards (1924-1926); 26 miles 385 yards (1927-1952); and 25 miles, 958 yards (1953-1956). Since 1957, the course has been certified to be the standard marathon distance of 26 miles, 385 yards.

New York City Marathon

From 1970 through 1975 the New York City Marathon was a small local race run in the city's Central Park. In 1976 it was moved to the streets of New York's 5 boroughs. It has since become one of the biggest and most prestigious marathons in the world.

Men

Year	Winner	Time	Year	Winner	Time
1970	Gary Muhrcke, United States	2:31:38	1981	Alberto Salazar, United States	2:08:13
1971	Norman Higgins, United States	2:22:54	1982	Alberto Salazar, United States	2:09:29
1972	Sheldon Karlin, United States	2:27:52	1983	Rod Dixon, New Zealand	2:08:59
1973	Tom Fleming, United States	2:21:54	1984	Orlando Pizzolato, Italy	2:14:53
1974	Norbert Sander, United States	2:26:30	1985	Orlando Pizzolato, Italy	2:11:34
1975	Tom Fleming, United States	2:19:27	1986	Gianni Poli, Italy	2:11:06
1976	Bill Rodgers, United States	2:10:10	1987	Ibrahim Hussein, Kenya	2:11:01
1977	Bill Rodgers, United States	2:11:28	1988	Steve Jones, Great Britain	2:08:20
1978	Bill Rodgers, United States	2:12:12	1989	Juma Ikangaa, Tanzania	2:08:01
1979	Bill Rodgers, United States	2:11:42	1990	Douglas Wakiihuri, Kenya	2:12:39
1980	Alberto Salazar, United States	2:09:41			

Women

Year	Winner	Time	Year	Winner	Time
1970	No finisher		1981	Allison Roe, New Zealand	2:25:29
1971	Beth Bonner, United States	2:55:22	1982	Grete Waitz, Norway	2:27:14
1972	Nina Kuscsik, United States	3:08:41	1983	Grete Waitz, Norway	2:27:00
1973	Nina Kuscsik, United States	2:57:07	1984	Grete Waitz, Norway	2:29:30
1974	Katherine Switzer, United States	3:07:29	1985	Grete Waitz, Norway	2:28:34
1975	Kim Merritt, United States	2:46:14	1986	Grete Waitz, Norway	2:28:06
1976	Miki Gorman, United States	2:39:11	1987	Priscilla Welch, Great Britain	2:30:17
1977	Miki Gorman, United States	2:43:10	1988	Grete Waitz, Norway	2:28:07
1978	Grete Waitz, Norway	2:32:30	1989	Ingrid Kristiansen, Norway	2:25:30
1979	Grete Waitz, Norway	2:27:33	1990	Wanda Panfil, Poland	2:30:45
1980	Grete Waitz, Norway	2:25:41			

WORLD CROSS-COUNTRY CHAMPIONSHIPS

Conducted by the International Amateur Athletic Federation (IAAF), this meet annually brings together the best runners in the world at every distance from the mile to the marathon to compete in the same cross-country race.

Men

Year	Winner	Winning Team	Year	Winner	Winning Team
1973	Pekka Paivarinta, Finland	Belgium	1983	Bekele Debele, Ethiopia	Ethiopia
1974	Eric DeBeck, Belgium	Belgium	1984	Carlos Lopes, Portugal	Ethiopia
1975	Ian Stewart, Scotland	New Zealand	1985	Carlos Lopes, Portugal	Ethiopia
1976	Carlos Lopes, Portugal	England	1986	John Ngugi, Kenya	Kenya
1977	Leon Schots, Belgium	Belgium	1987	John Ngugi, Kenya	Kenya
1978	John Treacy, Ireland	France	1988	John Ngugi, Kenya	Kenya
1979	John Treacy, Ireland	England	1989	John Ngugi, Kenya	Kenya
1980	Craig Virgin, United States	England	1990	Khalid Skah, Morocco	Kenya
1981	Craig Virgin, United States	Ethiopia	1991	Khalid Skah, Morocco	Kenya
1982	Mohammed Kedir, Ethiopia	Ethiopia			

Women

Year	Winner	Winning Team	Year	Winner	Winning Team
1973	Paola Cacchi, Italy	England	1983	Grete Waitz, Norway	United States
1974	Paola Cacchi, Italy	England	1984	Maricica Puica, Romania	United States
1975	Julie Brown, United States	United States	1985	Zola Budd, England	United States
1976	Carmen Valero, Spain	USSR	1986	Zola Budd, England	England
1977	Carmen Valero, Spain	USSR	1987	Annette Sergent, France	United States
1978	Grete Waitz, Norway	Romania	1988	Ingrid Kristiansen, Norway	USSR
1979	Grete Waitz, Norway	United States	1989	Annette Sergent, France	USSR
1980	Grete Waitz, Norway	USSR	1990	Lynn Jennings, United States	USSR
1981	Grete Waitz, Norway	USSR	1991	Lynn Jennings, United States	Kenya
1982	Maricica Puica, Romania	USSR			

THEY SAID IT

Steve Smith, world-class pole vaulter, noting that he has been vaulting half his life and yet fears heights: "If you put me up 18 feet on a ladder and asked me to jump into a foam rubber pit, I wouldn't do it."
(1973)

Swimming

Sports Illustrated

Making Waves

World Record Holder Janet Evans of the U.S.

More Room at the Top

In the new world order, the U.S. women made gains, while Hungary emerged as a power | by MERRELL NODEN

N 1991 THE WORLD OF SWIMMING SEEMED TO reflect the upheavals taking place in the world around it. The year was more intriguing for who did *not* swim well than for who did. With the fall of the Berlin Wall in 1989 and the subsequent unification of the two Germanys, swimming fans wondered what would become of the formidable East German women, who had dominated the sport since the 1973 World Championships.

The answer, when it came in January at the World Swimming Championships in Perth, Australia, was a shock. The German women did not win a single gold medal in an individual event. Indeed, the only German individual to win in Perth was freestyler Joerg Hoffmann, who won both the 400 (3:48.04) and the 1,500 (14:50.36). The latter time smashed the oldest and perhaps most revered of all men's swimming records, Vladimir Salnikov's 14:54.76, which had stood for eight years. In August, at the European Championships in Athens, the

German women won only two gold medals—Simone Osygus in the 50-meter freestyle and Daniela Hunger in the 200-meter individual medley—the same number as the Norwegians and the Danes.

Benefiting most from the new order were the U.S. women. Janet Evans (400 and 800 freestyle), Summer Sanders (200 butterfly), and Nicole Haislett (100 freestyle) all won world titles in Perth. Haislett's time was an American record (55.17) that lasted until August, when Angel (Meyers) Martino swam a 55.14 in the prelims of the Pan Pacific Swimming Championships in Edmonton. For Martino, that time—the fastest in the world for the year—and her victory over world champion Haislett in the final were especially gratifying. The Pan Pacific meet was her first international competition after having served a 16-month suspension for testing positive for the steroid nandrolone at the 1988 U.S. Olympic Trials in Austin, Texas.

For Evans, 1991 was a time of transition.

She began her sophomore year at Stanford, but was unhappy with coach Richard Quick's training schedules and his decision to overhaul her breaststroke technique. Evans was also concerned about the new NCAA limitations on workout times, so she took a leave from Stanford and moved to Austin, where she could train for the Barcelona Olympics under University of Texas coach Mark Schubert.

Though Matt Biondi won the 100-meter freestyle at Perth and Edmonton, he had to share the year's world-best time of 49.18 with Alexander Popov of the improving Soviet team. In Perth the top American men were breaststroker Mike Barrowman and butterflyer Melvin Stewart. Stewart caught Germany's Michael Gross off the final turn of the 200-meter butterfly to win in 1:55.69, more than half a second under Gross's 1985 world record. Barrowman, using the new "wave-action" breaststroke technique developed by his Hungarian coach Jozsef Nagy, broke his own world record for the 200 breaststroke, swimming a 2:11.23. Barrowman lowered the mark again at the U.S. Nationals in Fort Lauderdale, where he swam a 2:10.60.

Hungary also emerged as a world power, setting five world records, two by Tamas Darnyi, the Olympic champion in both individual medleys and arguably the finest all-around swimmer in history. Darnyi took his specialty to unheard-of levels, setting world records in both the 200 (1:59.36) and 400

With his 1:59.36, Darnyi became the first swimmer to go under two minutes for the 200 IM.

(4:12.36) IMs. No one had previously broken two minutes in the 200.

In the 100-meter breaststroke at the world championships, Hungary's Norbert Rozsa set a world record (1:01.45) that was later tied by Soviet Vasily Ivanov in Moscow. Rozsa regained sole possession of the record at the European Championships, swimming a 1:01.29. His countrywoman Krisztina Egerszegi won world titles in the 100 and 200 backstrokes, and at the Europeans added world records in both, with a 1:00.31 in the 100 and a 2:06.62 in the 200.

FINA, swimming's governing body, made two significant changes in the rules for the backstroke. One permits backstrokers to turn without first touching the wall with their hand. The other requires them to break the surface of the water with their heads within 15 meters of the starting blocks. Previously, the rule said that backstrokers' feet could not surface past the 10-meter mark. Both changes allowed backstrokers to go faster. At the U.S. Nationals in Fort Lauderdale, Martin Zubero of Spain set a world record in the 200 backstroke with a time of 1:57.30, while at Edmonton, Jeff Rouse led off the U.S.'s 400 medley relay team with a 53.93, swimming's first sub-54 for the 100 backstroke.

1991 Major Competitions

Men

	WORLD CHAMPIONSHIPS Perth, Australia, Jan 7-13	PAN AMERICAN GAMES Havana, Aug 12-18	PAN PACIFIC CHAMPIONSHIPS Edmonton, Alberta, Aug 22-25
50 free	Tom Jager, US, 22.16*	Todd Pace, US, 22.60	Tom Jager, US, 22.21
100 free	Matt Biondi, US, 49.18	Gustavo Borges, Bra, 49.48*	Matt Biondi, US, 49.72
200 free	Giorgio Lamberti, Italy,1:47.27*	Eric Diehl, US, 1:49.67*	Ian Brown, Aus, 1:49:48
400 free	Joerg Hoffman, Ger, 3:48.04*	Sean Killion, US, 3:50.38*	Kieren Perkins, Aus, 3:50.08*
800 free	Not held	Not held	Kieren Perkins, Aus, 7:50.68*
1500 free	Joerg Hoffman, Ger, 14:50.36†	Alex Kostich, US, 15:21.36	Kieren Perkins, Aus, 14:59.79‡
100 back	Jeff Rouse, US, 55.23*	Andrew Gill, US, 55.79	Jeff Rouse, US, 54.67
200 back	Martin Zubero, Spain, 1:59.52	Rogerio Romero, Bra, 2:01.07	Jeff Rouse, US, 2:00.85
100 breast	Norbert Rozsa, Hun, 1:01.45†	Hans Dersh, US, 1:02.57	Mike Barrowman, US, 1:02.02*
200 breast	Mike Barrowman, US, 2:11.23†	Mario Gonzales, Cuba, 2:15.50*	Mike Barrowman, US, 2:11.96*
100 fly	Anthony Nesty, Sur, 53.29*	Anthony Nesty, Sur, 53.45*	Matt Biondi, US, 54.24
200 fly	Melvin Stewart, US, 1:55.69†	Mark Dean, US, 2:00.11	Melvin Stewart, US, 1:57.92*
200 IM	Tamas Darnyi, Hun, 1:59.36†	Ronald Karnaugh, US, 2:00.92*	Gary Anderson, Can, 2:02.93
400 IM	Tamas Darnyi, Hun, 4:12.36†	Alex Kostich, US, 4:23.96	Eric Namesnik, US, 4:18.40
400 m relay	United States, 3:39.66*	United States, 3:42.84	United States#, 3:37.15*
400 f relay	United States, 3:17.15*	Brazil, 3:23.28	United States, 3:19.22
800 f relay	Germany, 7:13.50*	United States, 7:23.39	United States, 7:19.77
1-m spgbd	Edwin Jongejans, Hol	Mark Lenzi, US	Wang Yijie, China**
3-m spgbd	Kent Ferguson, US	Kent Ferguson, US	Mark Lenzi, US**
Platform	Sun Shuwei, China	Rioger Ramirez, Cuba	Sun Shuwei, China**

*Meet record. †World record. ‡800 meter split set a world record at 7:47.85. #Jeff Rouse set a world 100-meter backstroke record of 53.93 on 1st leg of relay.
**Event not held at Pan Pacific Championships. Result is from FINA World Diving Cup, May 1-5, in Winnipeg, Manitoba.

Women

50 free	Zhuang Yong, China, 25.47	Kristen Topham, Can, 26.01*	Jenny Thompson, US, 25.77
100 free	Nicole Haislett, US, 55.17†	Ashley Tappin, US, 56.51	Angel Martino, US, 55.34‡
200 free	Hayley Lewis, Aus, 2:00.48	Lisa Jacob, US, 2:02.06	Nicole Haislett, US, 2:00.31
400 free	Janet Evans, US, 4:08.63	Jane Skillman, US, 4:13.69	Janet Evans, US, 4:10.45
800 free	Janet Evans, US, 8:24.05*	Jane Skillman, US, 8:43.26	Janet Evans, US, 8:28.69
100 back	Krisztina Egerszegi, Hun, 1:01.78	Sylvia Poll, CosRic, 1:03.15	Janie Wagstaff, US, 1:01.00†
200 back	Krisztina Egerszegi, Hun, 2:09.15*	Diana Trimble, US, 2:15.80	Anna Simcic, NZ, 2:10.79*
100 breast	Linley Frame, Aus, 1:08.81	Dorsey Tierney, US, 1:10.30*	Linley Frame, Aus, 1:09.98
200 breast	Elena Vulkova, USSR, 2:29.53	Dorsey Tierney, US, 2:28.69*	Kristine Quance, US, 2:27.55*
100 fly	Qian Hong, China, 59.68	Kristen Topham, Can, 1:01.19	Susan O'Neill, Aus, 59.93
200 fly	Summer Sanders, US, 2:09.24	Susan Gottlieb, US, 2:12.35	Summer Sanders, US, 2:09.84
200 IM	Lin Li, China, 2:13.40	Lisa Summers, US, 2:16.86	Summer Sanders, US, 2:14.04*
400 IM	Lin Li, China, 4:41.45	Amy Shaw, US, 4:50.39	Summer Sanders, US, 4:41.46
400 m relay	United States, 4:06.51	United States, 4:12.51*	United States, 4:05.98
400 f relay	United States, 3:43.26†	United States, 3:48.88	United States, 3:43.67
800 f relay	Germany, 8:02.56	United States, 8:11.47*	United States, 8:03.70
1-m spgbd	Gao Min, China	A. Jill Schlabach, US	Yu Xiaoling, China#
3-m spgbd	Gao Min, China	Karen LaFace, US	Brita Baldus, Germany#
Platform	Fu Mingxia, China	Eileen Richetelli, US	Elena Mirochina, USSR#

*Meet record. †National record. ‡American record (55.14) in prelims.
#Event not held at Pan Pacific Championships. Result is from FINA World Diving Cup, May 1-5, in Winnipeg, Manitoba.

Barrowman Takes Bathe

Mike Barrowman, the world record holder in the 200-meter breaststroke, decided in October of 1991 to chase an ancient mark, the 6:29.6 that Walter Bathe of Germany swam in winning the 400-meter breaststroke at the 1912 Olympics. That event was discontinued not long thereafter because several swimmers almost drowned while swimming it. We are happy to report that Barrowman not only destroyed Bathe's mark with his 4:47.99, he also lived to tell about it.

World and American Records Through August 25, 1991

MEN

Freestyle

Event	Time	Record Holder	Site	Date
50 meters	21.81	Tom Jager (W,A)	Nashville	3-24-90
100 meters	48.42	Matt Biondi (W,A)	Austin	8-10-88
200 meters	1:46.69	Giorgio Lamberti, Italy (W)	Bonn	8-15-89
	1:47.72	Matt Biondi (A)	Austin	8-8-88
400 meters	3:46.95	Uwe Dassler, East Germany (W)	Seoul	9-23-88
	3:48.06	Matt Cetlinski (A)	Austin	8-11-88
800 meters	7:47.85*	Kieren Perkins, Australia (W)	Edmonton, Alberta	8-25-91
	7:52.45	Sean Killion (A)	Clovis, CA	7-27-87
1500 meters	14:50.36	Joerg Hoffman, Germany (W)	Perth, Australia	1-13-91
	15:01.51	George DiCarlo (A)	Indianapolis	6-30-84

*Set during 1500-m freestyle.

Backstroke

Event	Time	Record Holder	Site	Date
100 meters	53.93*	Jeff Rouse (W,A)	Edmonton, Alberta	8-25-91
200 meters	1:57.30	Martin Zubero, Spain (W)	Fort Lauderdale, FL	8-13-91
	1:58.86	Rick Carey (A)	Indianapolis	6-27-84

*Set on first leg of relay.

Breaststroke

Event	Time	Record Holder	Site	Date
100 meters	1:01.29	Norbert Rosza, Hungary (W)	Athens, Greece	8-20-91
	1:01.65	Steve Lundquist (A)	Los Angeles	7-29-84
200 meters	2:10.60	Mike Barrowman (W,A)	Fort Lauderdale, FL	8-13-91

Butterfly

Event	Time	Record Holder	Site	Date
100 meters	52.84	Pablo Morales (W,A)	Orlando, FL	6-23-86
200 meters	1:55.69	Melvin Stewart (W,A)	Perth, Australia	1-12-91

Individual Medley

Event	Time	Record Holder	Site	Date
200 meters	1:59.36	Tamas Darnyi, Hungary (W)	Perth, Australia	1-13-91
	2:00.11	Dave Wharton (A)	Tokyo	8-20-89
400 meters	4:12.36	Tamas Darnyi, Hungary (W)	Perth, Australia	1-8-91
	4:15.21	Eric Namesnik (A)	Perth, Australia	1-8-91

Relays

Event	Time	Record Holder	Site	Date
400-meter medley	3:36.93	United States (David Berkoff, Rich Schroeder, Matt Biondi, Chris Jacobs) (W,A)	Seoul	9-25-88
400-meter freestyle	3:16.53	United States (Chris Jacobs, Troy Dalbey, Tom Jager, Matt Biondi) (W,A)	Seoul	9-23-88
800-meter freestyle	7:12.51	United States (Troy Dalbey, Matt Cetlinski, Doug Gjertsen, Matt Biondi) (W,A)	Seoul	9-21-88

The Birth of the Butterfly

In the early 1930s some U.S. breaststrokers discovered that, without breaking any existing rules, they could increase their speed by bringing their arms back above the water upon recovery. Breaststroke traditionalists were greatly relieved when this technique, known as the butterfly, was officially recognized as a separate Olympic stroke in 1952.

WOMEN

Freestyle

Event	Time	Record Holder	Site	Date
50 meters	24.98	Yang Wenyi, China (W)	Shanghai	4-11-88
	25.50	Leigh Ann Fetter (A)	Austin	8-13-88
		Leigh Ann Fetter (A)	Perth, Australia	1-13-91
100 meters	54.73*	Kristin Otto, East Germany (W)	Madrid	8-19-86
	55.14	Angel Martino (A)	Edmonton, Alberta	8-23-91
200 meters	1:57.55	Heike Friedrich, East Germany (W)	Berlin	6-18-86
	1:58.23	Cynthia Woodhead (A)	Tokyo	9-3-79
400 meters	4:03.85	Janet Evans (W,A)	Seoul	9-22-88
800 meters	8:16.22	Janet Evans (W,A)	Tokyo	8-20-89
1500 meters	15:52.10	Janet Evans (W,A)	Orlando, FL	3-26-88

*Set on first leg of relay.

Backstroke

Event	Time	Record Holder	Site	Date
100 meters	1:00.31	Krisztina Egerszegi, Hungary (W)	Athens, Greece	8-22-91
	1:01.00	Janie Wagstaff (A)	Edmonton, Alberta	8-22-91
200 meters	2:06.62	Krisztina Egerszegi, Hungary (W)	Athens, Greece	8-25-91
	2:08.60	Betsy Mitchell (A)	Orlando, FL	6-27-86

Breaststroke

Event	Time	Record Holder	Site	Date
100 meters	1:07.91	Silke Hoerner, East Germany (W)	Strasbourg, France	8-21-87
	1:08.91	Tracey McFarlane (A)	Austin	8-11-88
200 meters	2:26.71	Silke Hoerner, East Germany (W)	Seoul	9-21-88
	2:27.08	Anita Nall (A)	Seattle	4-4-91

Butterfly

Event	Time	Record Holder	Site	Date
100 meters	57.93	Mary T. Meagher (W,A)	Brown Deer, WI	8-16-81
200 meters	2:05.96	Mary T. Meagher (W,A)	Brown Deer, WI	8-13-81

Individual Medley

Event	Time	Record Holder	Site	Date
200 meters	2:11.73	Uta Geweniger, East Germany (W)	Berlin	7-4-81
	2:12.64	Tracy Caulkins (A)	Los Angeles	8-3-84
400 meters	4:36.10	Petra Schneider, East Germany (W)	Guayaquil, Ecuador	8-1-82
	4:37.75	Janet Evans (A)	Seoul	9-19-88

Relays

Event	Time	Record Holder	Site	Date
400-meter medley	4:03.69	East Germany (Ina Kleber, Sylvia Gerasch, Ines Geissler, Birgit Meineke) (W)	Moscow	8-24-84
	4:05.98	United States (Janie Wagstaff, Kelli King, Crissy Ahmann-Leighton, Nicole Haislett) (A)	Edmonton, Alberta	8-25-91
400-meter freestyle	3:40.57	East Germany (Kristin Otto, Manuela Stellmach, Sabina Schulze, Heike Friedrich) (W)	Madrid	8-19-86
	3:43.26	United States (Nicole Haislett, Julie Cooper, Whitney Hedgepeth, Jenny Thompson) (A)	Perth, Australia	1-9-91
800-meter freestyle	7:55.47	East Germany (Manuela Stellmach, Astrid Strauss, Anke Mohring, Heike Friedrich) (W)	Strasbourg, France	8-18-87
	8:02.12	United States (Betsy Mitchell, Mary T. Meagher, Kim Brown, Mary Wayte) (A)	Madrid	8-22-86

Championship venues: Belgrade, Yugoslavia, Sep 4-9, 1973; Cali, Colombia, July 18-27, 1975; West Berlin, Aug 20-28, 1978; Guayaquil, Equador, Aug 1-7, 1982; Madrid, Aug 17-22, 1986; Perth, Australia, Jan 7-13, 1991.

MEN

50-meter Freestyle

1986	Tom Jager, United States	22.49‡
1991	Tom Jager, United States	22.16‡

100-meter Freestyle

1973	Jim Montgomery, United States	51.70
1975	Andy Coan, United States	51.25
1978	David McCagg, United States	50.24
1982	Jorg Woithe, East Germany	50.18
1986	Matt Biondi, United States	48.94
1991	Matt Biondi, United States	49.18

200-meter Freestyle

1973	Jim Montgomery, United States	1:53.02
1975	Tim Shaw, United States	1:52.04‡
1978	Billy Forrester, United States	1:51.02‡
1982	Michael Gross, West Germany	1:49.84
1986	Michael Gross, West Germany	1:47.92
1991	Giorgio Lamberti, Italy	1:47.27‡

400-meter Freestyle

1973	Rick DeMont, United States	3:58.18‡
1975	Tim Shaw, United States	3:54.88‡
1978	Vladimir Salnikov, USSR	3:51.94‡
1982	Vladimir Salnikov, USSR	3:51.30‡
1986	Rainer Henkel, West Germany	3:50.05
1991	Joerg Hoffman, Germany	3:48.04‡

1500-meter Freestyle

1973	Stephen Holland, Australia	15:31.85
1975	Tim Shaw, United States	15:28.92‡
1978	Vladimir Salnikov, USSR	15:03.99‡
1982	Vladimir Salnikov, USSR	15:01.77‡
1986	Rainer Henkel, West Germany	15:05.31
1991	Joerg Hoffman, Germany	14:50.36*

100-meter Backstroke

1973	Roland Matthes, East Germany	57.47
1975	Roland Matthes, East Germany	58.15
1978	Bob Jackson, United States	56.36‡
1982	Dirk Richter, East Germany	55.95
1986	Igor Polianski, USSR	55.58‡
1991	Jeff Rouse, United States	55.23‡

200-meter Backstroke

1973	Roland Matthes, East Germany	2:01.87†
1975	Zoltan Varraszto, Hungary	2:05.05
1978	Jesse Vassallo, United States	2:02.16
1982	Rick Carey, United States	2:00.82‡
1986	Igor Polianski, USSR	1:58.78‡
1991	Martin Zubero, Spain	1:59.52

100-meter Breaststroke

1973	John Hencken, United States	1:04.02†
1975	David Wilkie, Great Britain	1:04.26‡
1978	Walter Kusch, West Germany	1:03.56‡
1982	Steve Lundquist, United States	1:02.75‡
1986	Victor Davis, Canada	1:02.71
1991	Norbert Rozsa, Hungary	1:01.45*

200-meter Breaststroke

1973	David Wilkie, Great Britain	2:19.28†
1975	David Wilkie, Great Britain	2:18.23‡
1978	Nick Nevid, United States	2:18.37
1982	Victor Davis, Canada	2:14.77*
1986	Jozsef Szabo, Hungary	2:14.27‡
1991	Mike Barrowman, United States	2:11.23*

100-meter Butterfly

1973	Bruce Robertson, Canada	55.69
1975	Greg Jagenburg, United States	55.63
1978	Joe Bottom, United States	54.30
1982	Matt Gribble, United States	53.88‡
1986	Pablo Morales, United States	53.54‡
1991	Anthony Nesty, Suriname	53.29‡

200-meter Butterfly

1973	Robin Backhaus, United States	2:03.32
1975	Bill Forrester, United States	2:01.95‡
1978	Mike Bruner, United States	1:59.38‡
1982	Michael Gross, East Germany	1:58.85‡
1986	Michael Gross, East Germany	1:56.53‡
1991	Melvin Stewart, United States	1:55.69*

200-meter Individual Medley

1973	Gunnar Larsson, Sweden	2:08.36
1975	Andras Hargitay, Hungary	2:07.72
1978	Graham Smith, Canada	2:03.65*
1982	Alexander Sidorenko, USSR	2:03.30‡
1986	Tamas Darnyi, Hungary	2:01.57‡
1991	Tamas Darnyi, Hungary	1:59.36*

400-meter Individual Medley

1973	Andras Hargitay, Hungary	4:31.11
1975	Andras Hargitay, Hungary	4:32.57
1978	Jesse Vassallo, United States	4:20.05*
1982	Ricardo Prado, Brazil	4:19.78*
1986	Tamas Darnyi, Hungary	4:18.98†‡
1991	Tamas Darnyi, Hungary	4:12.36*

* World record.
†National record.
‡World championship record.

400-meter Medley Relay

1973	United States (Mike Stamm, John Hencken, Joe Bottom, Jim Montgomery)	3:49.49
1975	United States (John Murphy, Rick Colella, Greg Jagenburg, Andy Coan)	3:49.00
1978	United States (Robert Jackson, Nick Nevid, Joe Bottom, David McCagg)	3:44.63
1982	United States (Rick Carey, Steve Lundquist, Matt Gribble, Rowdy Gaines)	3:40.84*
1986	United States (Dan Veatch, David Lundberg, Pablo Morales, Matt Biondi)	3:41.25
1991	United States (Jeff Rouse, Eric Wunderlich, Mark Henderson, Matt Biondi)	3:39.66‡

400-meter Freestyle Relay

1973	United States (Mel Nash, Joe Bottom, Jim Montgomery, John Murphy)	3:27.18
1975	United States (Bruce Furniss, Jim Montgomery, Andy Coan, John Murphy)	3:24.85
1978	United States (Jack Babashoff, Rowdy Gaines, Jim Montgomery, David McCagg)	3:19.74
1982	United States (Chris Cavanaugh, Robin Leamy, David McCagg, Rowdy Gaines)	3:19.26*
1986	United States (Tom Jager, Mike Heath, Paul Wallace, Matt Biondi)	3:19.89
1991	United States (Tom Jager, Brent Lang, Doug Gjertsen, Matt Biondi)	3:17.15‡

800-meter Freestyle Relay

1973	United States (Kurt Krumpholz, Robin Backhaus, Rick Klatt, Jim Montgomery)	7:33.22*
1975	West Germany (Klaus Steinbach, Werner Lampe, Hans Joachim Geisler, Peter Nocke)	7:39.44
1978	United States (Bruce Furniss, Billy Forrester, Bobby Hackett, Rowdy Gaines)	7:20.82
1982	United States (Rich Saeger, Jeff Float, Kyle Miller, Rowdy Gaines)	7:21.09
1986	East Germany (Lars Hinneburg, Thomas Flemming, Dirk Richter, Sven Lodziewski)	7:15.91†‡
1991	Germany (Peter Sitt, Steffan Zesner, Stefan Pfeiffer, Michael Gross)	7:13.50‡

WOMEN

50-meter Freestyle

1986	Tamara Costache, Romania	25.28*
1991	Zhuang Yong, China	25.47

100-meter Freestyle

1973	Kornelia Ender, East Germany	57.54†
1975	Kornelia Ender, East Germany	56.50†
1978	Barbara Krause, East Germany	55.68‡
1982	Birgit Meineke, East Germany	55.79
1986	Kristin Otto, East Germany	55.05‡
1991	Nicole Haislett, United States	55.17†

200-meter Freestyle

1973	Keena Rothhammer, United States	2:04.99
1975	Shirley Babashoff, United States	2:02.50
1978	Cynthia Woodhead, United States	1:58.53*
1982	Annemarie Verstappen, Netherlands	1:59.53†
1986	Heike Friedrich, East Germany	1:58.26‡
1991	Hayley Lewis, Australia	2:00.48

400-meter Freestyle

1973	Heather Greenwood, United States	4:20.28
1975	Shirley Babashoff, United States	4:22.70
1978	Tracey Wickham, Australia	4:06.28*
1982	Carmela Schmidt, East Germany	4:08.98
1986	Heike Friedrich, East Germany	4:07.45
1991	Janet Evans, United States	4:08.63

800-meter Freestyle

1973	Novella Calligaris, Italy	8:52.97
1975	Jenny Turrall, Australia	8:44.75‡
1978	Tracey Wickham, Australia	8:24.94‡
1982	Kim Linehan, United States	8:27.48
1986	Astrid Strauss, East Germany	8:28.24
1991	Janet Evans, United States	8:24.05‡

* World record.
†National record.
‡World championship record.

THEY SAID IT

U.S. Diver Mark Lenzi, speaking enviously of the 1991 World Championships' women's platform champion, 12-year-old Fu Mingxia of China, who stands 4'9" and weighs 77 pounds: "It's kind of like dropping a broom handle off a 10-meter platform. She could land flat on her back and still rip the entry."

100-meter Backstroke

1973	Ulrike Richter, East Germany	1:05.42†
1975	Ulrike Richter, East Germany	1:03.30‡
1978	Linda Jezek, United States	1:02.55†‡
1982	Kristin Otto, East Germany	1:01.30‡
1986	Betsy Mitchell, United States	1:01.74
1991	Krisztina Egerszegi, Hungary	1:01.78

200-meter Backstroke

1973	Melissa Belote, United States	2:20.52
1975	Birgit Treiber, East Germany	2:15.46*
1978	Linda Jezek, United States	2:11.93*
1982	Cornelia Sirch, East Germany	2:09.91*
1986	Cornelia Sirch, East Germany	2:11.37
1991	Krisztina Egerszegi, Hungary	2:09.15‡

100-meter Breaststroke

1973	Renate Vogel, East Germany	1:13.74
1975	Hannalore Anke, East Germany	1:12.72
1978	Julia Bogdanova, USSR	1:10.31*
1982	Ute Geweniger, East Germany	1:09.14‡
1986	Sylvia Gerasch, East Germany	1:08.11*
1991	Linley Frame, Australia	1:08.81

200-meter Breaststroke

1973	Renate Vogel, East Germany	2:40.01
1975	Hannalore Anke, East Germany	2:37.25‡
1978	Lina Kachushite, USSR	2:31.42*
1982	Svetlana Varganova, USSR	2:28.82‡
1986	Silke Hoerner, East Germany	2:27.40*
1991	Elena Volkova, USSR	2:29.53

100-meter Butterfly

1973	Kornelia Ender, East Germany	1:02.53
1975	Kornelia Ender, East Germany	1:01.24*
1978	Joan Pennington, United States	1:00.20†‡
1982	Mary T. Meagher, United States	59.41‡
1986	Kornelia Gressler, East Germany	59.51
1991	Qian Hong, China	59.68

200-meter Butterfly

1973	Rosemarie Kother, East Germany	2:13.76†
1975	Rosemarie Kother, East Germany	2:15.92
1978	Tracy Caulkins, United States	2:09.87*
1982	Ines Geissler, East Germany	2:08.66‡
1986	Mary T. Meagher, United States	2:08.41‡
1991	Summer Sanders, United States	2:09.24

200-meter Individual Medley

1973	Andrea Huebner, East Germany	2:20.51
1975	Kathy Heddy, United States	2:19.80
1978	Tracy Caulkins, United States	2:14.07*
1982	Petra Schneider, East Germany	2:11.79
1986	Kristin Otto, East Germany	2:15.56
1991	Lin Li, China	2:13.40

* World record.
†National record.
‡World championship record.

400-meter Individual Medley

1973	Gudrun Wegner, East Germany	4:57.71†
1975	Ulrike Tauber, East Germany	4:52.76‡
1978	Tracy Caulkins, United States	4:40.83*
1982	Petra Schneider, East Germany	4:36.10*
1986	Kathleen Nord, East Germany	4:43.75
1991	Lin Li, China	4:41.45

400-meter Medley Relay

1973	East Germany (Ulrike Richter, Renate Vogel, Rosemarie Kother, Kornelia Ender)	4:16.84
1975	East Germany (Ulrike Richter, Hannelore Anke, Rosemarie Kother, Kornelia Ender)	4:14.74
1978	United States (Linda Jezek, Tracy Caulkins, Joan Pennington, Cynthia Woodhead)	4:08.21†‡
1982	East Germany (Kristin Otto, Ute Gewinger, Ines Geissler, Birgit Meineke)	4:05.8*
1986	East Germany (Kathrin Zimmermann, Sylvia Gerasch, Kornelia Gressler, Kristin Otto)	4:04.82
1991	United States (Janie Wagstaff, Tracey McFarlane, Crissy Ahmann-Leighton, Nicole Haislett)	4:06.51†

400-meter Freestyle Relay

1973	East Germany (Kornelia Ender, Andrea Eife, Andrea Huebner, Sylvia Eichner)	3:52.45†
1975	East Germany (Kornelia Ender, Barbara Krause, Claudia Hempel, Ute Bruckner)	3:49.37
1978	United States (Tracy Caulkins, Stephanie Elkins, Joan Pennington, Cynthia Woodhead)	3:43.43*
1982	East Germany (Birgit Meineke, Susanne Link, Kristin Otto, Caren Metschuk)	3:43.97
1986	East Germany (Kristin Otto, Manuela Stellmach, Sabine Schulze, Heike Friedrich)	3:40.57*
1991	United States (Nicole Haislett, Julie Cooper, Whitney Hedgepeth, Jenny Thompson)	3:43.26†

800-meter Freestyle Relay

1986	East Germany (Manuela Stellmach, Astrid Strauss, Nadja Bergknecht, Heike Friedrich)	7:59.33*
1991	Germany (Kerstin Kielgass, Manuela Stellmach, Dagmar Hase, Stephanie Ortwig)	8:02.56

MEN

1-meter Springboard

	Pts
1991 ...... Edwin Jongejans, Holland	588.51

3-meter Springboard

	Pts
1973 ...... Phil Boggs, United States	618.57
1975 ...... Phil Boggs, United States	597.12
1978 ...... Phil Boggs, United States	913.95
1982 ...... Greg Louganis, United States	752.67
1986 ...... Greg Louganis, United States	750.06
1991 ...... Kent Ferguson, United States	650.25

Platform

	Pts
1973 ...... Klaus Dibiasi, Italy	559.53
1975 ...... Klaus Dibiasi, Italy	547.98
1978 ...... Greg Louganis, United States	844.11
1982 ...... Greg Louganis, United States	634.26
1986 ...... Greg Louganis, United States	668.58
1991 ...... Sun Shuwei, China	626.79

WOMEN

1-meter Springboard

	Pts
1991 ...... Gao Min, China	478.26

3-meter Springboard

	Pts
1973 ...... Christa Koehler, East Germany	442.17
1975 ...... Irina Kalinina, USSR	489.81
1978 ...... Irina Kalinina, USSR	691.43
1982 ...... Megan Neyer, United States	501.03
1986 ...... Gao Min, China	582.90
1991 ...... Gao Min, China	539.01

Platform

	Pts
1973 ...... Ulrike Knape, Sweden	406.77
1975 ...... Janet Ely, United States	403.89
1978 ...... Irina Kalinina, USSR	412.71
1982 ...... Wendy Wyland, United States	438.79
1986 ...... Chen Lin, China	449.67
1991 ...... Fu Mingxia, China	426.51

Less Is More

In swimming it has been theorized that for speed in the water the best swimsuit might well be no swimsuit at all. As a result the major issue in the design of women's competitive swimwear has long been functionality versus propriety. In 1973 the East Germans struck a telling blow for functionality. Having won not a single gold medal at the '72 Olympics, they showed up for the 1973 World Aquatic Championships in Belgrade, Yugoslavia, in skin-tight, semi-see-through spandex. That's going too far, said the rest of the swimming world. Whereupon the East German women won 10 of a possible 14 gold medals. The rest of the swimming world switched to spandex.

Skiing

Sports Illustrated

WHITE HEAT

Luxembourg's Marc Girardelli Is Tops in the World

ellesse

Saalbach Hinterglemm

4

HEINZ KLUETMEIER

Downhill All the Way

Personal tragedies and a war in the desert overshadowed the ski season | by WILLIAM OSCAR JOHNSON

THIS WORLD CUP SKI RACING SEASON HAD bad news written all over it. For the U.S. team the bad news began early and went on and on. Though Americans had had mediocre results in recent years, it was considered likely that the women's team would be the strongest in a long time. Tamara McKinney, 27, was simply the best U.S. woman ever, with 18 career World Cup victories and a gold medal in the combined event at the 1989 World Championships in Vail; Kristi Terzian, 23, had scored points in 17 separate World Cup events in the 1989–90 season, an American women's record for one-year consistency; and Diann Roffe, 23, winner of the gold medal in the giant slalom at the 1985 World Championships, was coming on strong again.

Unfortunately, the glow went off the season even before it started. Terzian wrecked her knee so badly during October training that she was out for the year. In November, McKinney announced that she would retire because of a bad knee injury from the previous season. And in December Roffe fell during downhill training, tore a ligament in her left knee and she, too, was benched for the year.

The U.S. men's team, in general, was much weaker than the women's, but the downhillers began to look impressive in December, leading nicely up to the 1991 World Championships, to be held in the Austrian villages of Saalbach and Hinterglemm in January. Then, in a period of six days, three of the U.S.'s top four men downhillers suffered championship-ruining injuries—"just as we were beginning to think we were pretty damned good," said A. J. Kitt, 22, a downhiller who survived the whole year though he never finished better than fourth.

The World Championships, scheduled to

Tomba was a Bomba at the World Championships, but finished second in the overall World Cup standings.

HEINZ KLUETMEIER

begin Jan. 22, were hit by bad news, too. A pall lay over the event for two reasons: (1) Three days before the championships were to start, a promising Austrian rookie, Gernot Reinstadler, 20, took a 50-mph fall during a downhill qualifying race on the Lauberhorn in Wengen, Switzerland, and died after six hours of surgery. It was the first World Cup racing death since 1970. And (2) there was the Gulf War, which had begun on Jan. 16 with allied air attacks against Iraq. That led to fear that Iraqi president Saddam Hussein would retaliate with terrorist assaults against citizens of the U.S. and its allies. The U.S. Ski Team immediately flew home from Europe, and organizers of the World Championships canceled the opening ceremonies. ABC Sports, in turn, canceled its coverage of the event.

After that, things got a little better. The Americans returned to the Worlds, though two days late, and some of skiing's heroes and heroines began to perform at their peak. Marc Girardelli, 27, of Luxembourg, who is arguably the best racer today—now that Switzerland's Pirmin Zurbriggen has retired—won the gold medal in the men's slalom. Rudolf Nierlich, 24, a pleasant, handsome Austrian who was virtually unknown when he won gold medals in the slalom and giant slalom at the '89 Worlds in Vail, won the GS at Saalbach-Hinterglemm, bringing great joy to the home-country crowds.

The Austrian of whom most was expected was Petra Kronberger, 21, an apple-cheeked bank clerk from the village of Pfarrwerfen. In the World Cup season up to the championships, she had blown out the field, winning eight of the 16 races she had entered

and becoming the first woman ever to win a race in each of the five Alpine skiing disciplines. Before the Worlds, Kronberger's fans talked eagerly of a five-gold-medal performance. She started with a bang, winning the women's downhill easily, but in her next event, the Super G, the season's bad news syndrome nailed Kronberger too. Thirty yards from the finish, she caught a ski edge and hurtled across the finish. Doctors found a ligament in her right knee slightly torn. Though Kronberger skied no more at the championships, she returned to the regular-season circuit and won the overall World Cup title as well as the slalom crown for the year.

Alberto Tomba, 24, the Italian glamour boy, playboy and sometime slalom specialist, was a Bomba at the World Championships. But he pulled himself together to win the giant slalom World Cup title and finished second in the overall World Cup standings, a mere 20 points behind Girardelli, who joined Italy's Gustavo Thöni and Zurbriggen as the only men to win the Cup four times. Girardelli also won the World Cup slalom and combined titles. For the Americans, some good tidings finally came at the end of the season in Waterville Valley, N.H., where Julie Parisien, 19, became the first U.S. skier to win a World Cup race since McKinney accomplished the feat in 1987.

With the season over late in March, ski fans breathed a little easier in the belief that the Year of Bad News had ended. Unfortunately, it hadn't. On May 18, Nierlich, who was a national hero in Austria, was driving on a rain-drenched road near his home in St. Wolfgang when his car smashed into a restaurant. He died on the way to a hospital.

Taking a Powder   The Massachusetts high school cross-country ski championships were held last Feb. 13—in Vermont. For the second time in three years the event had to be moved from the Bay State to the Green Mountain State because of lack of snow.

FOR THE RECORD • 1990 – 1991

World Cup Season Race Results

Men

Date	Event	Site	Winner
8-8-90	Slalom	Mount Hutt, New Zealand	Peter Roth, Germany
8-9-90	Giant slalom	Mount Hutt, New Zealand	Fredrik Nyberg, Sweden
12-2-90	Super G	Valloire, France	Franck Piccard, France
12-8-90	Downhill	Val d'Isère, France	Leonhard Stock, Austria
12-11-90	Slalom	Sestriere, Italy	Alberto Tomba, Italy
12-14-90	Downhill	Val Gardena, Italy	Franz Heinzer, Switzerland
12-15-90	Downhill	Val Gardena, Italy	Atle Skaardal, Norway
12-16-90	Giant slalom	Alta Badia, Italy	Alberto Tomba, Italy
12-18-90	Slalom	Madona di Campiglio, Italy	Ole Christian Furuseth, Norway
12-21-90	Giant slalom	Kranjska Gora, Yugoslavia	Alberto Tomba, Italy
12-22-90	Slalom	Kranjska Gora, Yugoslavia	Ole Christian Furuseth, Norway
1-5-91	Downhill	Garmisch-Partenkirchen, Germany	Daniel Mahrer, Switzerland
1-6-91	Super G	Garmisch-Partenkirchen, Germany	Günther Mader, Austria
1-12-91	Downhill	Kitzbühel, Austria	Franz Heinzer, Switzerland
1-13-91	Slalom	Kitzbühel, Austria	Marc Girardelli, Luxembourg
1-12,1-13-91	Combined	Kitzbühel, Austria	Marc Girardelli, Luxembourg
1-15-91	Giant slalom	Adelboden, Switzerland	Marc Girardelli, Luxembourg
2-26-91	Slalom	Oppdal, Norway	Rudolf Nierlich, Austria
3-1-91	Giant slalom	Lillehammer, Norway	Alberto Tomba, Italy
3-2-91	Slalom	Lillehammer, Norway	Michael Tritscher, Austria
3-8-91	Downhill	Aspen, CO	Franz Heinzer, Switzerland
3-9-91	Giant slalom	Aspen, CO	Alberto Tomba, Italy
3-10-91	Slalom	Aspen, CO	Rudolf Nierlich, Austria
3-15-91	Downhill	Lake Louise, Alberta	Atle Skaardal, Norway
3-16-91	Downhill	Lake Louise, Alberta	Franz Heinzer, Switzerland
3-17-91	Super G	Lake Louise, Alberta	Marcus Wasmeier, Germany
3-21-91	Giant slalom	Waterville Valley, NH	Alberto Tomba, Italy
3-23-91	Slalom	Waterville Valley, NH	Tomas Fogdoe, Sweden

Women

Date	Event	Site	Winner
12-1-90	Giant slalom	Valzoldana, Italy	Petra Kronberger, Austria
12-2-90	Slalom	Valzoldana, Italy	Petra Kronberger, Austria
12-8-90	Downhill	Altenmarkt, Austria	Katrin Knopf, Germany
12-9-90	Super G	Altenmarkt, Austria	Petra Kronberger, Austria
12-16-90	Super G	Hasliberg, Switzerland	Chantal Bournissen, Switzerland
12-21-90	Downhill	Morzine, France	Petra Kronberger, Austria
12-22-90	Slalom	Morzine, France	Blanca Fernandez-Ochoa, Spain
12-21,12-22-90	Combined	Morzine, France	Ingrid Stockl, Austria
1-6-91	Downhill	Bad-Kleinkirchheim, Austria	Katrin Gutensohn, Germany
1-7-91	Slalom	Bad-Kleinkirchheim, Austria	Pernilla Wiberg, Sweden
1-6,1-7-91	Combined	Bad-Kleinkirchheim, Austria	Petra Kronberger, Austria
1-11-91	Giant slalom	Kranjska Gora, Yugoslavia	Vreni Schneider, Switzerland
1-12-91	Slalom	Kranjska Gora, Yugoslavia	Natasa Bokal, Yugoslavia
1-13-91	Slalom	Kranjska Gora, Yugoslavia	Petra Kronberger, Austria
1-18-91	Downhill	Meribel, France	Petra Kronberger, Austria
1-19-91	Super G	Meribel, France	Petra Kronberger, Austria
2-8-91	Downhill	Garmisch-Partenkirchen, Germany	Chantal Bournissen, Switzerland
2-9-91	Super G	Garmisch-Partenkirchen, Germany	Carole Merle, France
2-10-91	Giant slalom	Zweisel, Germany	Anita Wachter, Austria
2-23-91	Downhill	Furano, Japan	Anja Haas, Austria
2-24-91	Super G	Furano, Japan	Carole Merle, France
3-9-91	Downhill	Lake Louise, Alberta	Sabine Ginther, Austria
3-10-91	Giant slalom	Lake Louise, Alberta	Pernilla Wiberg, Sweden
3-11-91	Slalom	Lake Louise, Alberta	Vreni Schneider, Switzerland
3-15-91	Downhill	Vail, CO	Sabine Ginther, Austria
3-16-91	Downhill	Vail, CO	Chantal Bournissen, Switzerland
3-17-91	Super G	Vail, CO	Vreni Schneider, Switzerland
3-20-91	Slalom	Waterville Valley, NH	Pernilla Wiberg, Sweden
3-22-91	Giant slalom	Waterville Valley, NH	Julie Perisien, United States

FOR THE RECORD • Year by Year

Event Descriptions

Downhill: A speed event entailing a single run on a course with a minimum vertical drop of 500 meters (800 for Men's World Cup) and very few control gates.
Slalom: A technical event in which times for runs on 2 courses are totaled to determine the winner. Skiers must make many quick, short turns through a combination of gates (55-75 gates for men, 40-60 for women) over a short course (140-220-meter vertical drop for men, 120-180 for women).

Giant Slalom: A faster technical event with fewer, more broadly spaced gates than in the slalom. Times for runs on 2 courses with vertical drops of 250-400 meters (250-300 for women) are combined to determine the winner.
Super G: A speed event that is a cross between the downhill and the giant slalom.
Combined: An event in which scores from designated slalom and downhill races are combined to determine finish order.

FIS World Championships

Sites

1931	Mürren, Switzerland
1932	Cortina d'Ampezzo, Italy
1933	Innsbruck, Austria
1934	St Moritz, Switzerland
1935	Mürren, Switzerland
1936	Innsbruck, Austria
1937	Chamonix, France
1938	Engelberg, Switzerland
1939	Zakopane, Poland

Men

DOWNHILL

1931	Walter Prager, Switzerland
1932	Gustav Lantschner, Austria
1933	Walter Prager, Switzerland
1934	David Zogg, Switzerland
1935	Franz Zingerle, Austria
1936	Rudolf Rominger, Switzerland
1937	Émile Allais, France
1938	James Couttet, France
1939	Hans Lantschner, Germany

SLALOM

1931	David Zogg, Switzerland
1932	Friedrich Dauber, Germany
1933	Anton Seelos, Austria
1934	Franz Pfnür, Germany
1935	Anton Seelos, Austria
1936	Rudi Matt, Austria
1937	Émile Allais, France
1938	Rudolf Rominger, Switzerland
1939	Rudolf Rominger, Switzerland

Women

DOWNHILL

1931	Esme Mackinnon, Great Britain
1932	Paola Wiesinger, Italy
1933	Inge Wersin-Lantschner, Austria
1934	Anni Rüegg, Switzerland
1935	Christel Cranz, Germany
1936	Evie Pinching, Great Britain
1937	Christel Cranz, Germany
1938	Lisa Resch, Germany
1939	Christel Cranz, Germany

SLALOM

1931	Esme Mackinnon, Great Britain
1932	Rösli Streiff, Switzerland
1933	Inge Wersin-Lantschner, Austria
1934	Christel Cranz, Germany
1935	Anni Rüegg, Switzerland
1936	Gerda Paumgarten, Austria
1937	Christel Cranz, Germany
1938	Christel Cranz, Germany
1939	Christel Cranz, Germany

A Fitting Farewell

The greatest career in World Cup history came to a close when Ingemar Stenmark retired following the 1989 season. In 16 years Stenmark won a record 86 World Cup races, the last in a giant slalom at Aspen in February of '89. After the Aspen win the stoic Swede, who had won three overall World Cup titles and eight world championship and Olympic medals, said, "I wished for that last victory with all my heart. I didn't want to retire a beaten man, and now I can go without regrets."

FIS World Alpine Ski Championships

Sites

1950 ....Aspen, Colorado	1978 ....Garmisch-Partenkirchen, West Germany
1954 ....Are, Sweden	1982 ....Schladming, Austria
1958 ....Badgastein, Austria	1985 ....Bormio, Italy
1962 ....Chamonix, France	1987 ....Crans-Montana, Switzerland
1966 ....Portillo, Chile	1989 ....Vail, Colorado
1970 ....Val Gardena, Italy	1991 ....Saalbach-Hinterglemm, Austria
1974 ....St Moritz, Switzerland	

Men

DOWNHILL

1950 ....Zeno Colo, Italy	1978 ....Josef Walcher, Austria
1954 ....Christian Pravda, Austria	1982 ....Harti Weirather, Austria
1958 ....Toni Sailer, Austria	1985 ....Pirmin Zurbriggen, Switzerland
1962 ....Karl Schranz, Austria	1987 ....Peter Müller, Switzerland
1966 ....Jean-Claude Killy, France	1989 ....Hansjörg Tauscher, West Germany
1970 ....Bernard Russi, Switzerland	1991 ....Franz Heinzer, Switzerland
1974 ....David Zwilling, Austria	

SLALOM

1950 ....Georges Schneider, Switzerland	1978 ....Ingemar Stenmark, Sweden
1954 ....Stein Eriksen, Norway	1982 ....Ingemar Stenmark, Sweden
1958 ....Josl Rieder, Austria	1985 ....Jonas Nilsson, Sweden
1962 ....Charles Bozon, France	1987 ....Frank Wörndl, West Germany
1966 ....Carlo Senoner, Italy	1989 ....Rudolf Nierlich, Austria
1970 ....Jean-Noël Augert, France	1991 ....Marc Girardelli, Luxembourg
1974 ....Gustavo Thöni, Italy	

GIANT SLALOM

1950 ....Zeno Colo, Italy	1978 ....Ingemar Stenmark, Sweden
1954 ....Stein Eriksen, Norway	1982 ....Steve Mahre, United States
1958 ....Toni Sailer, Austria	1985 ....Markus Wasmaier, West Germany
1962 ....Egon Zimmermann, Austria	1987 ....Pirmin Zurbriggen, Switzerland
1966 ....Guy Périllat, France	1989 ....Rudolf Nierlich, Austria
1970 ....Karl Schranz, Austria	1991 ....Rudolf Nierlich, Austria
1974 ....Gustavo Thöni, Italy	

COMBINED

1982 ....Michel Vion, France	1989 ....Marc Girardelli, Luxembourg
1985 ....Pirmin Zurbriggen, Switzerland	1991 ....Stefan Eberharter, Austria
1987 ....Marc Girardelli, Luxembourg	

SUPER G

1987 ....Pirmin Zurbriggen, Switzerland	1991 ....Stefan Eberharter, Austria
1989 ....Martin Hangl, Switzerland	

Women

DOWNHILL

1950 ....Trude Beiser-Jochum, Austria	1978 ....Annemarie Moser-Pröll, Austria
1954 ....Ida Schopfer, Switzerland	1982 ....Gerry Sorensen, Canada
1958 ....Lucile Wheeler, Canada	1985 ....Michela Figini, Switzerland
1962 ....Christl Haas, Austria	1987 ....Maria Walliser, Switzerland
1966 ....Erika Schinegger, Austria	1989 ....Maria Walliser, Switzerland
1970 ....Anneroesli Zryd, Switzerland	1991 ....Petra Kronberger, Austria
1974 ....Annemarie Moser-Pröll, Austria	

SLALOM

1950 ....Dagmar Rom, Austria	1978 ....Lea Sölkner, Austria
1954 ....Trude Klecker, Austria	1982 ....Erika Hess, Switzerland
1958 ....Inger Bjornbakken, Norway	1985 ....Perrine Pelen, France
1962 ....Marianne Jahn, Austria	1987 ....Erika Hess, Switzerland
1966 ....Annie Famose, France	1989 ....Mateja Svet, Yugoslavia
1970 ....Ingrid Lafforgue, France	1991 ....Vreni Schneider, Switzerland
1974 ....Hanni Wenzel, Liechtenstein	

Women (*Cont.*)

GIANT SLALOM

1950 ....Dagmar Rom, Austria	1978 ....Maria Epple, West Germany
1954 ....Lucienne Schmith-Couttet, France	1982 ....Erika Hess, Switzerland
1958 ....Lucile Wheeler, Canada	1985 ....Diann Roffe, United States
1962 ....Marianne Jahn, Austria	1987 ....Vreni Schneider, Switzerland
1966 ....Marielle Goitschel, France	1989 ....Vreni Schneider, Switzerland
1970 ....Betsy Clifford, Canada	1991 ....Pernilla Wiberg, Sweden
1974 ....Fabienne Serrat, France	

COMBINED

1982 ....Erika Hess, Switzerland	1989 ....Tamara McKinney, United States
1985 ....Erika Hess, Switzerland	1991 ....Chantal Bournissen, Switzerland
1987 ....Erika Hess, Switzerland	

SUPER G

1987 ....Maria Walliser, Switzerland	1991 ....Ulrike Maier, Austria
1989 ....Ulrike Maier, Austria	

World Cup Season Title Holders

Men

OVERALL

1967 ....Jean-Claude Killy, France	1980 ....Andreas Wenzel, Liechtenstein
1968 ....Jean-Claude Killy, France	1981 ....Phil Mahre, United States
1969 ....Karl Schranz, Austria	1982 ....Phil Mahre, United States
1970 ....Karl Schranz, Austria	1983 ....Phil Mahre, United States
1971 ....Gustavo Thöni, Italy	1984 ....Pirmin Zurbriggen, Switzerland
1972 ....Gustavo Thöni, Italy	1985 ....Marc Girardelli, Luxembourg
1973 ....Gustavo Thöni, Italy	1986 ....Marc Girardelli, Luxembourg
1974 ....Piero Gros, Italy	1987 ....Pirmin Zurbriggen, Switzerland
1975 ....Gustavo Thöni, Italy	1988 ....Pirmin Zurbriggen, Switzerland
1976 ....Ingemar Stenmark, Sweden	1989 ....Marc Girardelli, Luxembourg
1977 ....Ingemar Stenmark, Sweden	1990 ....Pirmin Zurbriggen, Switzerland
1978 ....Ingemar Stenmark, Sweden	1991 ....Marc Girardelli, Luxembourg
1979 ....Peter Lüscher, Switzerland	

DOWNHILL

1967 ....Jean-Claude Killy, France	1980 ....Peter Müller, Switzerland
1968 ....Gerhard Nenning, Austria	1981 ....Harti Weirather, Austria
1969 ....Karl Schranz, Austria	1982 ....Steve Podborski, Canada
1970 ....Karl Schranz, Austria	Peter Müller, Switzerland
Karl Cordin, Austria	1983 ....Franz Klammer, Austria
1971 ....Bernhard Russi, Switzerland	1984 ....Urs Raber, Switzerland
1972 ....Bernhard Russi, Switzerland	1985 ....Helmut Höflehner, Austria
1973 ....Roland Collumbin, Switzerland	1986 ....Peter Wirnsberger, Austria
1974 ....Roland Collumbin, Switzerland	1987 ....Pirmin Zurbriggen, Switzerland
1975 ....Franz Klammer, Austria	1988 ....Pirmin Zurbriggen, Switzerland
1976 ....Franz Klammer, Austria	1989 ....Marc Girardelli, Luxembourg
1977 ....Franz Klammer, Austria	1990 ....Helmut Höflehner, Austria
1978 ....Franz Klammer, Austria	1991 ....Franz Heinzer, Switzerland
1979 ....Peter Müller, Switzerland	

Girardelli Makes His Marc

Through 1988 Marc Girardelli, the oft-injured Austrian native who skies for Luxembourg, had won several slalom, giant slalom, and overall titles in 10 years on the World Cup circuit, but never a downhill race. In '89, however, he won the downhill season title, as well as the combined and overall crowns. His eight victories included at least one in each discipline, a feat previously achieved only by Jean-Claude Killy, and Killy did it when there was no super G.

Men (*Cont.*)

SLALOM

1967	Jean-Claude Killy, France	1979	Ingemar Stenmark, Sweden
1968	Domeng Giovanoli, Switzerland	1980	Ingemar Stenmark, Sweden
1969	Jean-Noël Augert, France	1981	Ingemar Stenmark, Sweden
1970	Patrick Russel, France	1982	Phil Mahre, United States
	Alain Penz, France	1983	Ingemar Stenmark, Sweden
1971	Jean-Noël Augert, France	1984	Marc Girardelli, Luxembourg
1972	Jean-Noël Augert, France	1985	Marc Girardelli, Luxembourg
1973	Gustavo Thöni, Italy	1986	Rok Petrovic, Yugoslavia
1974	Gustavo Thöni, Italy	1987	Bojan Krizaj, Yugoslavia
1975	Ingemar Stenmark, Sweden	1988	Alberto Tomba, Italy
1976	Ingemar Stenmark, Sweden	1989	Armin Bittner, West Germany
1977	Ingemar Stenmark, Sweden	1990	Armin Bittner, West Germany
1978	Ingemar Stenmark, Sweden	1991	Marc Girardelli, Luxembourg

GIANT SLALOM

1967	Jean-Claude Killy, France	1981	Ingemar Stenmark, Sweden
1968	Jean-Claude Killy, France	1982	Phil Mahre, United States
1969	Karl Schranz, Austria	1983	Phil Mahre, United States
1970	Gustavo Thöni, Italy	1984	Ingemar Stenmark, Sweden
1971	Patrick Russel, France		Pirmin Zurbriggen, Switzerland
1972	Gustavo Thöni, Italy	1985	Marc Girardelli, Luxembourg
1973	Hans Hinterseer, Austria	1986	Joël Gaspoz, Switzerland
1974	Piero Gros, Italy	1987	Joël Gaspoz, Switzerland
1975	Ingemar Stenmark, Sweden		Pirmin Zurbriggen, Switzerland
1976	Ingemar Stenmark, Sweden	1988	Alberto Tomba, Italy
1977	Heini Hemmi, Switzerland	1989	Pirmin Zurbriggen, Switzerland
	Ingemar Stenmark, Sweden	1990	Ole Kristian Furuseth, Norway
1978	Ingemar Stenmark, Sweden		Günther Mader, Austria
1979	Ingemar Stenmark, Sweden	1991	Alberto Tomba, Italy
1980	Ingemar Stenmark, Sweden		

SUPER G

1986	Markus Wasmeier, West Germany	1989	Pirmin Zurbriggen, Switzerland
1987	Pirmin Zurbriggen, Switzerland	1990	Pirmin Zurbriggen, Switzerland
1988	Pirmin Zurbriggen, Switzerland	1991	Franz Heinzer, Switzerland

COMBINED

1979	Andreas Wenzel, Liechtenstein	1986	Markus Wasmaier, West Germany
1980	Andreas Wenzel, Liechtenstein	1987	Pirmin Zurbriggen, Switzerland
1981	Phil Mahre, United States	1988	Hubert Strolz, Austria
1982	Phil Mahre, United States	1989	Marc Girardelli, Luxembourg
1983	Phil Mahre, United States	1990	Pirmin Zurbriggen, Switzerland
1984	Andreas Wenzel, Liechtenstein	1991	Marc Girardelli, Luxembourg
1985	Andreas Wenzel, Liechtenstein		

Women

OVERALL

1967	Nancy Greene, Canada	1980	Hanni Wenzel, Liechtenstein
1968	Nancy Greene, Canada	1981	Marie-Thérèse Nadig, Switzerland
1969	Gertrud Gabl, Austria	1982	Erika Hess, Switzerland
1970	Michèle Jacot, France	1983	Tamara McKinney, United States
1971	Annemarie Pröll, Austria	1984	Erika Hess, Switzerland
1972	Annemarie Pröll, Austria	1985	Michela Figini, Switzerland
1973	Annemarie Pröll, Austria	1986	Maria Walliser, Switzerland
1974	Annemarie Moser-Pröll, Austria	1987	Maria Walliser, Switzerland
1975	Annemarie Moser-Pröll, Austria	1988	Michela Figini, Switzerland
1976	Rosi Mitermaier, West Germany	1989	Vreni Schneider, Switzerland
1977	Lise-Marie Morerod, Switzerland	1990	Petra Kronberger, Austria
1978	Hanni Wenzel, Liechtenstein	1991	Petra Kronberger, Austria
1979	Annemarie Moser-Pröll, Austria		

Women (*Cont.*)

DOWNHILL

1967 .... Marielle Goitschel, France	1979 .... Annemarie Moser-Pröll, Austria
1968 .... Isabelle Mir, France	1980 .... Marie-Thérèse Nadig, Switzerland
Olga Pall, Austria	1981 .... Marie-Thérèse Nadig, Switzerland
1969 .... Wiltrud Drexel, Austria	1982 .... Marie-Cecile Gros-Gaudenier, France
1970 .... Isabelle Mir, France	1983 .... Doris De Agostini, Switzerland
1971 .... Annemarie Pröll, Austria	1984 .... Maria Walliser, Switzerland
1972 .... Annemarie Pröll, Austria	1985 .... Michela Figini, Switzerland
1973 .... Annemarie Pröll, Austria	1986 .... Maria Walliser, Switzerland
1974 .... Annemarie Moser-Pröll, Austria	1987 .... Michela Figini, Switzerland
1975 .... Annemarie Moser-Pröll, Austria	1988 .... Michela Figini, Switzerland
1976 .... Brigitte Totschnig, Austria	1989 .... Michela Figini, Switzerland
1977 .... Brigitte Totschnig-Habersatter, Austria	1990 .... Katrin Gutensohn-Knopf, Germany
1978 .... Annemarie Moser-Pröll, Austria	1991 .... Chantal Bournissen, Switzerland

SLALOM

1967 ....Marielle Goitschel, France	1980 ....Perrine Pelen, France
1968 ....Marielle Goitschel, France	1981 ....Erika Hess, Switzerland
1969 ....Gertrud Gabl, Austria	1982 ....Erika Hess, Switzerland
1970 ....Ingrid Lafforgue, France	1983 ....Erika Hess, Switzerland
1971 ....Britt Lafforgue, France	1984 ....Tamara McKinney, United States
1972 ....Britt Lafforgue, France	1985 ....Erika Hess, Switzerland
1973 ....Patricia Emonet, France	1986 ....Roswitha Steiner, Austria
1974 ....Christa Zechmeister, West Germany	Erika Hess, Switzerland
1975 ....Lise-Marie Morerod, Switzerland	1987 ....Corrine Schmidhauser, Switzerland
1976 ....Rosi Mittermaier, West Germany	1988 ....Roswitha Steiner, Austria
1977 ....Lise-Marie Morerod, Switzerland	1989 ....Vreni Schneider, Switzerland
1978 ....Hanni Wenzel, Liechtenstein	1990 ....Vreni Schneider, Switzerland
1979 ....Regina Sackl, Austria	1991 ....Petra Kronberger, Austria

GIANT SLALOM

1967 ....Nancy Greene, Canada	1980 ....Hanni Wenzel, Liechtenstein
1968 ....Nancy Greene, Canada	1981 ....Marie-Thérèse Nadig, Switzerland
1969 ....Marilyn Cochran, United States	1982 ....Irene Epple, West Germany
1970 ....Michèle Jacot, France	1983 ....Tamara McKinney, United States
Françoise Macchi, France	1984 ....Erika Hess, Switzerland
1971 ....Annemarie Pröll, Austria	1985 ....Maria Keihl, West Germany
1972 ....Annemarie Pröll, Austria	Michela Figini, Switzerland
1973 ....Monika Kaserer, Austria	1986 ....Vreni Schneider, Switzerland
1974 ....Hanni Wenzel, Liechtenstein	1987 ....Vreni Schneider, Switzerland
1975 ....Annemarie Moser-Pröll, Austria	Maria Walliser, Switzerland
1976 ....Lise-Marie Morerod, France	1988 ....Mateja Svet, Yugoslavia
1977 ....Lise-Marie Morerod, France	1989 ....Vreni Schneider, Switzerland
1978 ....Lise-Marie Morerod, France	1990 ....Anita Wachter, Austria
1979 ....Christa Kinshofer, West Germany	1991 ....Vreni Schneider, Switzerland

SUPER G

1986 ....Maria Kiehl, West Germany	1989 ....Carole Merle, France
1987 ....Maria Walliser, Switzerland	1990 ....Carole Merle, France
1988 ....Michela Figini, Switzerland	1991 ....Carole Merle, France

COMBINED

1979 ....Annemarie Moser-Pröll, Austria	1985 ....Brigitte Oertli, Switzerland
Hanni Wenzel, Liechtenstein	1986 ....Maria Walliser, Switzerland
1980 ....Hanni Wenzel, Liechtenstein	1987 ....Brigitte Oertli, Switzerland
1981 ....Marie-Thérèse Nadig, Switzerland	1988 ....Brigitte Oertli, Switzerland
1982 ....Irene Epple, West Germany	1989 ....Brigitte Oertli, Switzerland
1983 ....Hanni Wenzel, Liechtenstein	1990 ....Anita Wachter, Austria
1984 ....Erika Hess, Switzerland	1991 ....Sabine Ginther, Austria

Figure Skating

Sports Illustrated

Ice Queen

Kristi Yamaguchi
of the U.S.
Wins the World Title

HEINZ KLUETMEIER

Three for the Show

Kristi Yamaguchi led a U.S. sweep at the world figure skating championships | by E. M. SWIFT

T WAS THE YEAR OF THE AMERICAN WOMEN. At the World Championships in Munich, historic in that they were the first ever competed without the compulsory figures, Kristi Yamaguchi, the stylish 19-year-old from Fremont, Calif., won her first world title. U.S. champion Tonya Harding, 20, a newcomer to the world team, took silver, and elegant Nancy Kerrigan, a 21-year-old from Stoneham, Mass., completed the U.S. sweep by capturing the bronze. It was the first time three women from one nation had gone 1-2-3, a feat made all the more astonishing by the absence of defending world and three-time national champion Jill Trenary, who was recovering from surgery on her right ankle. Informed of the ladies' coup moments after completion of the competition, Trenary sighed, "It means next year's Nationals are going to be like the Olympics."

Indeed, in 1991 the favorites for the Winter Games in Albertville, France, stepped to the fore. In men's figure skating Kurt Browning of Canada won his third straight world title by edging the Soviet Union's Viktor Petrenko for the second year in a row. Petrenko, a heartthrob who is called "the Baryshnikov of skating" by his admirers, got three first-place votes from the judges to Browning's six. But in the end it was Browning's three triple-triple combinations in the free skating program, where Petrenko had none, that tipped the balance. Two-time U.S. champion Todd Eldredge, who's only 19, finished a strong third.

For the seventh year in a row, and the 24th time in 27 years, the Soviet Union proved strongest in pairs, despite the retirement from amateur competition of Olympic and four-time world champions Ekaterina Gordeeva and Sergei Grinkov. In their place stepped Natalia Miskutienok and Artur Dmitriev, who completed the most breathtaking performance of the year in Munich during their free skating routine to Franz Liszt's "Dream of Love." Miskutienok, who is as flexible as Gumby, seemed to drift weightlessly toward the rafters until her partner, employing his little finger, kept returning her to the ice. The Canadian pair of Isabelle Brasseur and Lloyd Eisler took second, while Natasha Kuchiki and Todd Sand of the U.S., who had skated together just 18 months, won the bronze, the first American medal in the pairs since 1987.

The ice dance competition, meanwhile, continued to test the limits of the sport. Torn costumes, inscrutable themes and lasciviously entwined bodies were the dominant flavors of 1991. The gold medal duo from France, Isabelle and Paul Duchesnay, actually issued a press release explaining their program, which was entitled *Missing II*. It's a sequel to *Missing,* the previous year's silver medal hit about repression in a South American dictatorship, and in *Missing II* the dictatorship is over! This was apparently swell news to the audience at Munich's Olympiahalle, because the Duchesnays received their first standing ovation merely for showing up in tattered garments and looking tortured. The judges, who ever since the 1988 Olympics in Calgary have been booed for failing to put the Duchesnays in first, succumbed to popular sentiment and gave this brother-sister pair its first world title. One had the feeling they would have won for skating *Jack and Jill Went up the Hill.* Care to guess who'll waltz to ice dancing gold in Albertville in '92?

As for the American women, they have always been both deep and strong in the international echelon of figure skating. But they had never so utterly dominated the event as they did in 1991. The only two challengers who had a chance to prevent a sweep were European champion Surya Bonaly of France and Midori Ito of Japan. Bonaly, just 17, came within a quarter turn of becoming the first woman to land a quadruple revolution jump. The problem was that within seconds of touching down, Bonaly stubbed her toepick into the ice while applauding herself and belly-flopped like a mattress. See ya, Surya. Meanwhile, Ito, the world champion in 1989, was undone by a frightening fall in her original program when she mistimed her combina-

tion jump and launched herself kamikaze-style over a 12-inch wooden barrier and into a television camera. Ito finished fourth, enabling Kerrigan, appearing at her first worlds, to take third.

The battle for gold then came down to Harding and Yamaguchi. Harding, a pepperpot from Portland, Ore., jumps nearly as explosively as Ito. In February, while winning the U.S. Nationals, she became the first American woman to land a triple Axel in competition. Yamaguchi floats over the ice like a baton in a whimsical hand and her programs always seem to end too soon. Each skater offered a different style, but on that day in March it was the five-foot, 90-pound Yamaguchi who was flawless, landing six triples and earning, from the Italian judge, the first 6.0 of her career for artistic impression. Yamaguchi had proved that, despite the abolition of the compulsory figures, the era of the stylish skater—as opposed to the athletic jumper—had not yet passed. Nor, certainly, had the era of the American women.

The brother-sister team of the Duchesnays finally found gold with a routine they called *Missing II*.

FOR THE RECORD • 1990 – 1991

World Champions

Munich, Germany, March 11–17

Women

1. ....Kristi Yamaguchi, United States
2. ....Tonya Harding, United States
3. ....Nancy Kerrigan, United States

Men

1. ....Kurt Browning, Canada
2. ....Viktor Petrenko, USSR
3. ....Todd Eldredge, United States

Pairs

1. .... Natalia Mishkutienok and Artur Dmitriev, USSR
2. .... Isabelle Brasseur and Lloyd Eisler, Canada
3. .... Natasha Kuchiki and Todd Sand, United States

Dance

1. .... Isabelle Duchesnay and Paul Duchesnay, France
2. .... Marina Klimova and Sergei Ponomarenko, USSR
3. .... Maia Usova and Alexander Zhulin, USSR

Champions of the United States

Minneapolis, Minnesota, February 10–17

Women

1. .... Tonya Harding, Carousel FSC
2. .... Kristi Yamaguchi, St Moritz ISC
3. .... Nancy Kerrigan, Colonial FSC

Men

1. .... Todd Eldredge, Los Angeles FSC
2. .... Christopher Bowman, Los Angeles FSC
3. .... Paul Wylie, SC of Boston

Pairs

1. ....Natasha Kuchiki and Todd Sand,
   Los Angeles FSC
2. ....Calla Urbanski and Rocky Marval,
   U of Delaware FSC, SC of New York
3. ....Jenni Meno and Scott Wendland,
   Winterhurst FSC, All Year FSC

Dance

1. ....Elizabeth Punsalan and Jerod Swallow,
   Broadmoor SC
2. ....April Sargent and Russ Witherby,
   U of Delaware FSC
3. ....Jeanne Miley and Michael Verlich,
   Los Angeles FSC

World Figure Skating Championships Medals Table

Country	Gold	Silver	Bronze	Total
United States	1	1	3	5
USSR	1	2	1	4
Canada	1	1	0	2
France	1	0	0	1

Special Achievements

Men successfully landing a quadruple jump in competition:
   Kurt Browning, Canada, 1988 World Championship.
   Aleksei Urmanov, USSR, 1991 European Championship.
   Elvis Stojko, Canada, 1991 World Championship.

Women successfully landing a triple Axel in competition:
   Midori Ito, Japan, 1988 free-skating competition at Aichi, Japan.
   Tonya Harding, United States, 1991 U.S. Figure Skating Championship.

Shut Out

Brian Boitano, the men's 1988 Olympic figure skating champion, got the equivalent of straight 0.0 scores from the International Skating Union (ISU), his sport's governing body. The ISU voted to allow figure skaters to skate professionally from now on without losing their Olympic eligibility, but opted not to restore the eligibility of current pros. "People are calling this the Brian Boitano rule," says Boitano. "I was really the only [pro] who had expressed any interest in coming back to compete."

FOR THE RECORD • Year by Year

World Champions

Women

1906	Madge Sayers-Cave, Great Britain
1907	Madge Sayers-Cave, Great Britain
1908	Lily Kronberger, Hungary
1909	Lily Kronberger, Hungary
1910	Lily Kronberger, Hungary
1911	Lily Kronberger, Hungary
1912	Opika von Meray Horvath, Hungary
1913	Opika von Meray Horvath, Hungary
1914	Opika von Meray Horvath, Hungary
1915-21	No competition
1922	Herma Plank-Szabo, Austria
1923	Herma Plank-Szabo, Austria
1924	Herma Plank-Szabo, Austria
1925	Herma Jaross-Szabo, Austria
1926	Herma Jaross-Szabo, Austria
1927	Sonja Henie, Norway
1928	Sonja Henie, Norway
1929	Sonja Henie, Norway
1930	Sonja Henie, Norway
1931	Sonja Henie, Norway
1932	Sonja Henie, Norway
1933	Sonja Henie, Norway
1934	Sonja Henie, Norway
1935	Sonja Henie, Norway
1936	Sonja Henie, Norway
1937	Cecilia Colledge, Great Britain
1938	Megan Taylor, Great Britain
1939	Megan Taylor, Great Britain
1940-46	No competition
1947	Barbara Ann Scott, Canada
1948	Barbara Ann Scott, Canada
1949	Alena Vrzanova, Czechoslovakia
1950	Aja Vrzanova, Czechoslovakia
1951	Jeannette Altwegg, Great Britain
1952	Jacqueline duBief, France
1953	Tenley Albright, United States
1954	Gundi Busch, West Germany
1955	Tenley Albright, United States
1956	Carol Heiss, United States
1957	Carol Heiss, United States
1958	Carol Heiss, United States
1959	Carol Heiss, United States
1960	Carol Heiss, United States
1961	No competition
1962	Sjoukje Dijkstra, Netherlands
1963	Sjoukje Dijkstra, Netherlands
1964	Sjoukje Dijkstra, Netherlands
1965	Petra Burka, Canada
1966	Peggy Flemming, United States
1967	Peggy Flemming, United States
1968	Peggy Flemming, United States
1969	Gabriele Seyfert, East Germany
1970	Gabriele Seyfert, East Germany
1971	Beatrix Schuba, Austria
1972	Beatrix Schuba, Austria
1973	Karen Magnussen, Canada
1974	Christine Errath, East Germany
1975	Dianne DeLeeuw, Netherlands
1976	Dorothy Hamill, United States
1977	Linda Fratianne, United States
1978	Annett Poetzsch, East Germany
1979	Linda Fratianne, United States
1980	Annett Poetzsch, East Germany
1981	Denise Biellmann, Switzerland
1982	Elaine Zayak, United States
1983	Rosalynn Sumners, United States
1984	Katarina Witt, East Germany
1985	Katarina Witt, East Germany
1986	Debi Thomas, United States
1987	Katarina Witt, East Germany
1988	Katarina Witt, East Germany
1989	Midori Ito, Japan
1990	Jill Trenary, United States
1991	Kristi Yamaguchi, United States

Men

1896	Gilbert Fuchs, Germany
1897	Gustav Hugel, Austria
1898	Henning Grenander, Sweden
1899	Gustav Hugel, Austria
1900	Gustav Hugel, Austria
1901	Ulrich Salchow, Sweden
1902	Ulrich Salchow, Sweden
1903	Ulrich Salchow, Sweden
1904	Ulrich Salchow, Sweden
1905	Ulrich Salchow, Sweden
1906	Gilbert Fuchs, Germany
1907	Ulrich Salchow, Sweden
1908	Ulrich Salchow, Sweden
1909	Ulrich Salchow, Sweden
1910	Ulrich Salchow, Sweden
1911	Ulrich Salchow, Sweden
1912	Fritz Kachler, Austria
1913	Fritz Kachler, Austria
1914	Gosta Sandhal, Sweden
1915-21	No competition
1922	Gillis Grafstrom, Sweden
1923	Fritz Kachler, Austria
1924	Gillis Grafstrom, Sweden
1925	Willy Bockl, Austria
1926	Willy Bockl, Austria
1927	Willy Bockl, Austria
1928	Willy Bockl, Austria
1929	Gillis Grafstrom, Sweden
1930	Karl Schafer, Austria
1931	Karl Schafer, Austria
1932	Karl Schafer, Austria
1933	Karl Schafer, Austria
1934	Karl Schafer, Austria
1935	Karl Schafer, Austria
1936	Karl Schafer, Austria
1937	Felix Kaspar, Austria
1938	Felix Kaspar, Austria
1939	Graham Sharp, Great Britain
1940-46	No competition
1947	Hans Gerschwiler, Switzerland
1948	Dick Button, United States
1949	Dick Button, United States
1950	Dick Button, United States
1951	Dick Button, United States
1952	Dick Button, United States
1953	Hayes Alan Jenkins, United States

Men (*Cont.*)

1954 .... Hayes Alan Jenkins, United States	1973 .... Andrej Nepela, Czechoslovakia
1955 .... Hayes Alan Jenkins, United States	1974 .... Jan Hoffmann, East Germany
1956 .... Hayes Alan Jenkins, United States	1975 .... Sergei Volkov, USSR
1957 .... David W. Jenkins, United States	1976 .... John Curry, Great Britain
1958 .... David W. Jenkins, United States	1977 .... Vladimir Kovalev, USSR
1959 .... David W. Jenkins, United States	1978 .... Charles Tickner, United States
1960 .... Alan Giletti, France	1979 .... Vladimir Kovalev, USSR
1961 .... No competition	1980 .... Jan Hoffmann, East Germany
1962 .... Donald Jackson, Canada	1981 .... Scott Hamilton, United States
1963 .... Donald McPherson, Canada	1982 .... Scott Hamilton, United States
1964 .... Manfred Schneldorfer, West Germany	1983 .... Scott Hamilton, United States
1965 .... Alain Calmat, France	1984 .... Scott Hamilton, United States
1966 .... Emmerich Danzer, Austria	1985 .... Aleksander Fadeev, USSR
1967 .... Emmerich Danzer, Austria	1986 .... Brian Boitano, United States
1968 .... Emmerich Danzer, Austria	1987 .... Brian Orser, Canada
1969 .... Tim Wood, United States	1988 .... Brian Boitano, United States
1970 .... Tim Wood, United States	1989 .... Kurt Browning, Canada
1971 .... Andrej Nepela, Czechoslovakia	1990 .... Kurt Browning, Canada
1972 .... Andrej Nepela, Czechoslovakia	1991 .... Kurt Browning, Canada

Pairs

1908 .... Anna Hubler, Heinrich Burger, Germany	1939 .... Maxi Herber, Ernst Bajer, Germany
1909 .... Phyllis Johnson, James H. Johnson, Great Britain	1940-46 .... No competition
1910 .... Anna Hubler, Heinrich Burger, Germany	1947 .... Micheline Lannoy, Pierre Baugniet, Belgium
1911 .... Ludowika Eilers, Walter Jakobsson, Germany/Finland	1948 .... Micheline Lannoy, Pierre Baugniet, Belgium
1912 .... Phyllis Johnson, James H. Johnson, Great Britain	1949 .... Andrea Kekessy, Ede Kiraly, Hungary
1913 .... Helene Engelmann, Karl Majstrik, Austria	1950 .... Karol Kennedy, Peter Kennedy, United States
1914 .... Ludowika Jakobsson-Eilers, Walter Jakobsson-Eilers, Finland	1951 .... Ria Baran, Paul Falk, West Germany
1915-21 .... No competition	1952 .... Ria Baran Falk, Paul Falk, West Germany
1922 .... Helene Engelmann, Alfred Berger, Austria	1953 .... Jennifer Nicks, John Nicks, Great Britain
1923 .... Ludowika Jakobsson-Eilers, Walter Jakobsson-Eilers, Finland	1954 .... Frances Dafoe, Norris Bowden, Canada
1924 .... Helene Engelmann, Alfred Berger, Austria	1955 .... Frances Dafoe, Norris Bowden, Canada
1925 .... Herma Jaross-Szabo, Ludwig Wrede, Austria	1956 .... Sissy Schwarz, Kurt Oppelt, Austria
1926 .... Andree Joly, Pierre Brunet, France	1957 .... Barbara Wagner, Robert Paul, Canada
1927 .... Herma Jaross-Szabo, Ludwig Wrede, Austria	1958 .... Barbara Wagner, Robert Paul, Canada
1928 .... Andree Joly, Pierre Brunet, France	1959 .... Barbara Wagner, Robert Paul, Canada
1929 .... Lilly Scholz, Otto Kaiser, Austria	1960 .... Barbara Wagner, Robert Paul, Canada
1930 .... Andree Brunet-Joly, Pierre Brunet-Joly, France	1961 .... No competition
1931 .... Emilie Rotter, Laszlo Szollas, Hungary	1962 .... Maria Jelinek, Otto Jelinek, Canada
1932 .... Andree Brunet-Joly, Pierre Brunet-Joly, France	1963 .... Marika Kilius, Hans-Jurgen Baumler, West Germany
1933 .... Emilie Rotter, Laszlo Szollas, Hungary	1964 .... Marika Kilius, Hans-Jurgen Baumler, West Germany
1934 .... Emilie Rotter, Laszlo Szollas, Hungary	1965 .... Ljudmila Protopopov, Oleg Protopopov, USSR
1935 .... Emilie Rotter, Laszlo Szollas, Hungary	1966 .... Ljudmila Protopopov, Oleg Protopopov, USSR
1936 .... Maxi Herber, Ernst Bajer, Germany	1967 .... Ljudmila Protopopov, Oleg Protopopov, USSR
1937 .... Maxi Herber, Ernst Bajer, Germany	1968 .... Ljudmila Protopopov, Oleg Protopopov, USSR
1938 .... Maxi Herber, Ernst Bajer, Germany	1969 .... Irina Rodnina, Alexsei Ulanov, USSR

Pairs (*Cont.*)

1970	Irina Rodnina, Alexsei Ulanov, USSR
1971	Irina Rodnina, Sergei Ulanov, USSR
1972	Irina Rodnina, Sergei Ulanov, USSR
1973	Irina Rodnina, Aleksandr Zaitsev, USSR
1974	Irina Rodnina, Aleksandr Zaitsev, USSR
1975	Irina Rodnina, Aleksandr Zaitsev, USSR
1976	Irina Rodnina, Aleksandr Zaitsev, USSR
1977	Irina Rodnina, Aleksandr Zaitsev, USSR
1978	Irina Rodnina, Aleksandr Zaitsev, USSR
1979	Tai Babilonia, Randy Gardner, United States
1980	Maria Cherkasova, Sergei Shakhrai, USSR
1981	Irina Vorobieva, Igor Lisovsky, USSR
1982	Sabine Baess, Tassilio Thierbach, East Germany
1983	Elena Valova, Oleg Vasiliev, USSR
1984	Barbara Underhill, Paul Martini, Canada
1985	Elena Valova, Oleg Vasiliev, USSR
1986	Yekaterina Gordeeva, Sergei Grinkov, USSR
1987	Yekaterina Gordeeva, Sergei Grinkov, USSR
1988	Elena Valova, Oleg Vasiliev, USSR
1989	Yekaterina Gordeeva, Sergei Grinkov, USSR
1990	Yekaterina Gordeeva, Sergei Grinkov, USSR
1991	Natalia Mishkutienok, Artur Dmitriev, USSR

Dance

1950	Lois Waring, Michael McGean, United States
1951	Jean Westwood, Lawrence Demmy, Great Britain
1952	Jean Westwood, Lawrence Demmy, Great Britain
1953	Jean Westwood, Lawrence Demmy, Great Britain
1954	Jean Westwood, Lawrence Demmy, Great Britain
1955	Jean Westwood, Lawrence Demmy, Great Britain
1956	Pamela Wieght, Paul Thomas, Great Britain
1957	June Markham, Courtney Jones, Great Britain
1958	June Markham, Courtney Jones, Great Britain
1959	Doreen D. Denny, Courtney Jones, Great Britain
1960	Doreen D. Denny, Courtney Jones, Great Britain
1961	No competition
1962	Eva Romanova, Pavel Roman, Czechoslovakia
1963	Eva Romanova, Pavel Roman, Czechoslovakia
1964	Eva Romanova, Pavel Roman, Czechoslovakia
1965	Eva Romanova, Pavel Roman, Czechoslovakia
1966	Diane Towler, Bernard Ford, Great Britain
1967	Diane Towler, Bernard Ford, Great Britain
1968	Diane Towler, Bernard Ford, Great Britain
1969	Diane Towler, Bernard Ford, Great Britain
1970	Ljudmila Pakhomova, Aleksandr Gorshkov, USSR
1971	Ljudmila Pakhomova, Aleksandr Gorshkov, USSR
1972	Ljudmila Pakhomova, Aleksandr Gorshkov, USSR
1973	Ljudmila Pakhomova, Aleksandr Gorshkov, USSR
1974	Ljudmila Pakhomova, Aleksandr Gorshkov, USSR
1975	Irina Moiseeva, Andreij Minenkov, USSR
1976	Ljudmila Pakhomova, Aleksandr Gorshkov, USSR
1977	Irina Moiseeva, Andreij Minenkov, USSR
1978	Natalia Linichuk, Gennadi Karponosov, USSR
1979	Natalia Linichuk, Gennadi Karponosov, USSR
1980	Krisztina Regoeczy, Andras Sallai, Hungary
1981	Jayne Torvill, Christopher Dean, Great Britain
1982	Jayne Torvill, Christopher Dean, Great Britain
1983	Jayne Torvill, Christopher Dean, Great Britain
1984	Jayne Torvill, Christopher Dean, Great Britain
1985	Natalia Bestemianova, Andrei Bukin, USSR
1986	Natalia Bestemianova, Andrei Bukin, USSR
1987	Natalia Bestemianova, Andrei Bukin, USSR
1988	Natalia Bestemianova, Andrei Bukin, USSR
1989	Marina Klimova, Sergei Ponomarenko, USSR
1990	Marina Klimova, Sergei Ponomarenko, USSR
1991	Isabelle Duchesnay, Paul Duchesnay, France

Champions of the United States

The championships held in 1914, 1918, 1920 and 1921 under the auspices of the International Skating Union of America were open to Canadians, although they were considered to be United States championships. Beginning in 1922, the championships have been held under the auspices of the United States Figure Skating Association.

Women

1914 ....Theresa Weld, SC of Boston	1954 ....Tenley E. Albright, SC of Boston
1915-17 ......No competition	1955 ....Tenley E. Albright, SC of Boston
1918 ....Rosemary S. Beresford, New York SC	1956 ....Tenley E. Albright, SC of Boston
1919 ....No competition	1957 ....Carol E. Heiss, SC of New York
1920 ....Theresa Weld, SC of Boston	1958 ....Carol E. Heiss, SC of New York
1921 ....Theresa Weld Blanchard, SC of Boston	1959 ....Carol E. Heiss, SC of New York
1922 ....Theresa Weld Blanchard, SC of Boston	1960 ....Carol E. Heiss, SC of New York
1923 ....Theresa Weld Blanchard, SC of Boston	1961 ....Laurence R. Owen, SC of Boston
1924 ....Theresa Weld Blanchard, SC of Boston	1962 ....Barbara Roles Pursley,
1925 ....Beatrix Loughran, New York SC	.............................Arctic Blades FSC
1926 ....Beatrix Loughran, New York SC	1963 ....Lorraine G. Hanlon, SC of Boston
1927 ....Beatrix Loughran, New York SC	1964 ....Peggy Fleming, Arctic Blades FSC
1928 ....Maribel Y. Vinson, SC of Boston	1965 ....Peggy Fleming, Arctic Blades FSC
1929 ....Maribel Y. Vinson, SC of Boston	1966 ....Peggy Fleming, City of Colorado Springs
1930 ....Maribel Y. Vinson, SC of Boston	1967 ....Peggy Fleming, Broadmoor SC
1931 ....Maribel Y. Vinson, SC of Boston	1968 ....Peggy Fleming, Broadmoor SC
1932 ....Maribel Y. Vinson, SC of Boston	1969 ....Janet Lynn, Wagon Wheel FSC
1933 ....Maribel Y. Vinson, SC of Boston	1970 ....Janet Lynn, Wagon Wheel FSC
1934 ....Suzanne Davis, SC of Boston	1971 ....Janet Lynn, Wagon Wheel FSC
1935 ....Maribel Y. Vinson, SC of Boston	1972 ....Janet Lynn, Wagon Wheel FSC
1936 ....Maribel Y. Vinson, SC of Boston	1973 ....Janet Lynn, Wagon Wheel FSC
1937 ....Maribel Y. Vinson, SC of Boston	1974 ....Dorothy Hamill, SC of New York
1938 ....Joan Tozzer, SC of Boston	1975 ....Dorothy Hamill, SC of New York
1939 ....Joan Tozzer, SC of Boston	1976 ....Dorothy Hamill, SC of New York
1940 ....Joan Tozzer, SC of Boston	1977 ....Linda Fratianne, Los Angeles FSC
1941 ....Jane Vaughn, Philadelphia SC & HS	1978 ....Linda Fratianne, Los Angeles FSC
1942 ....Jane Vaughn Sullivan,	1979 ....Linda Fratianne, Los Angeles FSC
.............................Philadelphia SC & HS	1980 ....Linda Fratianne, Los Angeles FSC
1943 ....Gretchen Van Zandt Merrill, SC of Boston	1981 ....Elaine Zayak, SC of New York
1944 ....Gretchen Van Zandt Merrill, SC of Boston	1982 ....Rosalynn Sumners, Seattle SC
1945 ....Gretchen Van Zandt Merrill, SC of Boston	1983 ....Rosalynn Sumners, Seattle SC
1946 ....Gretchen Van Zandt Merrill, SC of Boston	1984 ....Rosalynn Sumners, Seattle SC
1947 ....Gretchen Van Zandt Merrill, SC of Boston	1985 ....Tiffany Chin, San Diego FSC
1948 ....Gretchen Van Zandt Merrill, SC of Boston	1986 ....Debi Thomas, Los Angeles FSC
1949 ....Yvonne Claire Sherman, SC of New York	1987 ....Jill Trenary, Broadmoor SC
1950 ....Yvonne Claire Sherman, SC of New York	1988 ....Debi Thomas, Los Angeles FSC
1951 ....Sonya Klopfer, Junior SC of New York	1989 ....Jill Trenary, Broadmoor SC
1952 ....Tenley E. Albright, SC of Boston	1990 ....Jill Trenary, Broadmoor SC
1953 ....Tenley E. Albright, SC of Boston	1991 ....Tonya Harding, Carousel FSC

Men

1914 ....Norman M. Scott, WC of Montreal	1934 ....Roger F. Turner, SC of Boston
1915-17 ......No competition	1935 ....Robin H. Lee, SC, New York
1918 ....Nathaniel W. Niles, SC of Boston	1936 ....Robin H. Lee, SC, New York
1919 ....No competition	1937 ....Robin H. Lee, SC, New York
1920 ....Sherwin C. Badger, SC of Boston	1938 ....Robin H. Lee, Chicago FSC
1921 ....Sherwin C. Badger, SC of Boston	1939 ....Robin H. Lee, St Paul FSC
1922 ....Sherwin C. Badger, SC of Boston	1940 ....Eugene Turner, Los Angeles FSC
1923 ....Sherwin C. Badger, SC of Boston	1941 ....Eugene Turner, Los Angeles FSC
1924 ....Sherwin C. Badger, SC of Boston	1942 ....Robert Specht, Chicago FSC
1925 ....Nathaniel W. Niles, SC of Boston	1943 ....Arthur R. Vaughn, Jr,
1926 ....Chris I. Christenson, Twin City FSC	.............................Philadelphia SC & HS
1927 ....Nathaniel W. Niles, SC of Boston	1944-45 ......No competition
1928 ....Roger F. Turner, SC of Boston	1946 ....Dick Button, Philadelphia SC & HS
1929 ....Roger F. Turner, SC of Boston	1947 ....Dick Button, Philadelphia SC & HS
1930 ....Roger F. Turner, SC of Boston	1948 ....Dick Button, Philadelphia SC & HS
1931 ....Roger F. Turner, SC of Boston	1949 ....Dick Button, Philadelphia SC & HS
1932 ....Roger F. Turner, SC of Boston	1950 ....Dick Button, SC of Boston
1933 ....Roger F. Turner, SC of Boston	1951 ....Dick Button, SC of Boston

Men (*Cont.*)

1952 ....Dick Button, SC of Boston	1972 ....Kenneth Shelley, Arctic Blades FSC
1953 ....Hayes Alan Jenkins, Cleveland SC	1973 ....Gordon McKellen, Jr, SC of Lake Placid
1954 ....Hayes Alan Jenkins, Broadmoor SC	1974 ....Gordon McKellen, Jr, SC of Lake Placid
1955 ....Hayes Alan Jenkins, Broadmoor SC	1975 ....Gordon McKellen, Jr, SC of Lake Placid
1956 ....Hayes Alan Jenkins, Broadmoor SC	1976 ....Terry Kubicka, Arctic Blades FSC
1957 ....David Jenkins, Broadmoor SC	1977 ....Charles Tickner, Denver FSC
1958 ....David Jenkins, Broadmoor SC	1978 ....Charles Tickner, Denver FSC
1959 ....David Jenkins, Broadmoor SC	1979 ....Charles Tickner, Denver FSC
1960 ....David Jenkins, Broadmoor SC	1980 ....Charles Tickner, Denver FSC
1961 ....Bradley R. Lord, SC of Boston	1981 ....Scott Hamilton, Philadelphia SC & HS
1962 ....Monty Hoyt, Broadmoor SC	1982 ....Scott Hamilton, Philadelphia SC & HS
1963 ....Thomas Litz, Hershey FSC	1983 ....Scott Hamilton, Philadelphia SC & HS
1964 ....Scott Ethan Allen, SC of New York	1984 ....Scott Hamilton, Philadelphia SC & HS
1965 ....Gary C. Visconti, Detroit SC	1985 ....Brian Boitano, Peninsula FSC
1966 ....Scott Ethan Allen, SC of New York	1986 ....Brian Boitano, Peninsula FSC
1967 ....Gary C. Visconti, Detroit SC	1987 ....Brian Boitano, Peninsula FSC
1968 ....Tim Wood, Detroit SC	1988 ....Brian Boitano, Peninsula FSC
1969 ....Tim Wood, Detroit SC	1989 ....Christopher Bowman, Los Angeles FSC
1970 ....Tim Wood, City of Colorado Springs	1990 ....Todd Eldredge, Los Angeles FSC
1971 ....John Misha Petkevich, Great Falls FSC	1991 ....Todd Eldredge, Los Angeles FSC

Pairs

1914 .... Jeanne Chevalier, Norman M. Scott	1956 .... Carole Ann Ormaca, Robin Greiner
1915-17... No competition	1957 .... Nancy Rouillard Ludington,
1918 .... Theresa Weld, Nathaniel W. Niles	Ronald Ludington
1919 .... No competition	1958 .... Nancy Rouillard Ludington,
1920 .... Theresa Weld, Nathaniel W. Niles	Ronald Ludington
1921 .... Theresa Weld Blanchard, Nathaniel W. Niles	1959 .... Nancy Rouillard Ludington,
1922 .... Theresa Weld Blanchard, Nathaniel W. Niles	Ronald Ludington
1923 .... Theresa Weld Blanchard, Nathaniel W. Niles	1960 .... Nancy Rouillard Ludington,
1924 .... Theresa Weld Blanchard, Nathaniel W. Niles	Ronald Ludington
1925 .... Theresa Weld Blanchard, Nathaniel W. Niles	1961 .... Maribel Y. Owen, Dudley S. Richards
1926 .... Theresa Weld Blanchard, Nathaniel W. Niles	1962 .... Dorothyann Nelson, Pieter Kollen
1927 .... Theresa Weld Blanchard, Nathaniel W. Niles	1963 .... Judianne Fotheringill, Jerry J. Fotheringill
1928 .... Maribel Y. Vinson, Thornton L. Coolidge	1964 .... Judianne Fotheringill, Jerry J. Fotheringill
1929 .... Maribel Y. Vinson, Thornton L. Coolidge	1965 .... Vivian Joseph, Ronald Joseph
1930 .... Beatrix Loughran, Sherwin C. Badger	1966 .... Cynthia Kauffman, Ronald Kauffman
1931 .... Beatrix Loughran, Sherwin C. Badger	1967 .... Cynthia Kauffman, Ronald Kauffman
1932 .... Beatrix Loughran, Sherwin C. Badger	1968 .... Cynthia Kauffman, Ronald Kauffman
1933 .... Maribel Y. Vinson, George E. B. Hill	1969 .... Cynthia Kauffman, Ronald Kauffman
1934 .... Grace E. Madden, James L. Madden	1970 .... Jo Jo Starbuck, Kenneth Shelley
1935 .... Maribel Y. Vinson, George E. B. Hill	1971 .... Jo Jo Starbuck, Kenneth Shelley
1936 .... Maribel Y. Vinson, George E. B. Hill	1972 .... Jo Jo Starbuck, Kenneth Shelley
1937 .... Maribel Y. Vinson, George E. B. Hill	1973 .... Melissa Militano, Mark Militano
1938 .... Joan Tozzer, M. Bernard Fox	1974 .... Melissa Militano, Johnny Johns
1939 .... Joan Tozzer, M. Bernard Fox	1975 .... Melissa Militano, Johnny Johns
1940 .... Joan Tozzer, M. Bernard Fox	1976 .... Tai Babilonia, Randy Gardner
1941 .... Donna Atwood, Eugene Turner	1977 .... Tai Babilonia, Randy Gardner
1942 .... Doris Schubach, Walter Noffke	1978 .... Tai Babilonia, Randy Gardner
1943 .... Doris Schubach, Walter Noffke	1979 .... Tai Babilonia, Randy Gardner
1944 .... Doris Schubach, Walter Noffke	1980 .... Tai Babilonia, Randy Gardner
1945 .... Donna Jeanne Pospisil, Jean-Pierre Brunet	1981 .... Caitlin Carruthers, Peter Carruthers
1946 .... Donna Jeanne Pospisil, Jean-Pierre Brunet	1982 .... Caitlin Carruthers, Peter Carruthers
1947 .... Yvonne Claire Sherman, Robert J. Swenning	1983 .... Caitlin Carruthers, Peter Carruthers
1948 .... Karol Kennedy, Peter Kennedy	1984 .... Caitlin Carruthers, Peter Carruthers
1949 .... Karol Kennedy, Peter Kennedy	1985 .... Jill Watson, Peter Oppegard
1950 .... Karol Kennedy, Peter Kennedy	1986 .... Gillian Wachsman, Todd Waggoner
1951 .... Karol Kennedy, Peter Kennedy	1987 .... Jill Watson, Peter Oppegard
1952 .... Karol Kennedy, Peter Kennedy	1988 .... Jill Watson, Peter Oppegard
1953 .... Carole Ann Ormaca, Robin Greiner	1989 .... Kristi Yamaguchi, Rudi Galindo
1954 .... Carole Ann Ormaca, Robin Greiner	1990 .... Kristi Yamaguchi, Rudi Galindo
1955 .... Carole Ann Ormaca, Robin Greiner	1991 .... Natasha Kuchiki, Todd Sand

Dance

1914	Waltz	1935	Waltz
	Theresa Weld, Nathaniel W. Niles		Nettie C. Prantel, Roy Hunt
1915-19...	No competition	1936	Marjorie Parker, Joseph K. Savage
1920	Waltz	1937	Nettie C. Prantel, Harold Hartshorne
	Theresa Weld, Nathaniel W. Niles	1938	Nettie C. Prantel, Harold Hartshorne
	Fourteenstep	1939	Sandy Macdonald, Harold Hartshorne
	Gertrude Cheever Porter, Irving Brokaw	1940	Sandy Macdonald, Harold Hartshorne
1921	Waltz and Fourteenstep	1941	Sandy Macdonald, Harold Hartshorne
	Theresa Weld Blanchard,	1942	Edith B. Whetstone, Alfred N. Richards, Jr
	Nathaniel W. Niles	1943	Marcella May, James Lochead, Jr
1922	Waltz	1944	Marcella May, James Lochead, Jr
	Beatrix Loughran, Edward M. Howland	1945	Kathe Mehl Williams, Robert J. Swenning
	Fourteenstep	1946	Anne Davies, Carleton C. Hoffner, Jr
	Theresa Weld Blanchard,	1947	Lois Waring, Walter H. Bainbridge, Jr
	Nathaniel W. Niles	1948	Lois Waring, Walter H. Bainbridge, Jr
1923	Waltz	1949	Lois Waring, Walter H. Bainbridge, Jr
	Mr. & Mrs. Henry W. Howe	1950	Lois Waring, Michael McGean
	Fourteenstep	1951	Carmel Bodel, Edward L. Bodel
	Sydney Goode, James B. Greene	1952	Lois Waring, Michael McGean
1924	Waltz	1953	Carol Ann Peters, Daniel C. Ryan
	Rosaline Dunn, Frederick Gabel	1954	Carmel Bodel, Edward L. Bodel
	Fourteenstep	1955	Carmel Bodel, Edward L. Bodel
	Sydney Goode, James B. Greene	1956	Joan Zamboni, Roland Junso
1925	Waltz and Fourteenstep	1957	Sharon McKenzie, Bert Wright
	Virginia Slattery, Ferrier T. Martin	1958	Andree Anderson, Donald Jacoby
1926	Waltz	1959	Andree Anderson Jacoby, Donald Jacoby
	Rosaline Dunn, Joseph K. Savage	1960	Margie Ackles, Charles W. Phillips, Jr
	Fourteenstep	1961	Diane C. Sherbloom, Larry Pierce
	Sydney Goode, James B. Greene	1962	Yvonne N. Littlefield, Peter F. Betts
1927	Waltz and Fourteenstep	1963	Sally Schantz, Stanley Urban
	Rosaline Dunn, Joseph K. Savage	1964	Darlene Streich, Charles D. Fetter, Jr
1928	Waltz	1965	Kristin Fortune, Dennis Sveum
	Rosaline Dunn, Joseph K. Savage	1966	Kristin Fortune, Dennis Sveum
	Fourteenstep	1967	Lorna Dyer, John Carrell
	Ada Bauman Kelly, George T. Braakman	1968	Judy Schwomeyer, James Sladky
1929	Waltz and Original Dance combined	1969	Judy Schwomeyer, James Sladky
	Edith C. Secord, Joseph K. Savage	1970	Judy Schwomeyer, James Sladky
1930	Waltz	1971	Judy Schwomeyer, James Sladky
	Edith C. Secord, Joseph K. Savage	1972	Judy Schwomeyer, James Sladky
	Original	1973	Mary Karen Campbell, Johnny Johns
	Clara Rotch Frothingham, George E. B. Hill	1974	Colleen O'Connor, Jim Millns
1931	Waltz	1975	Colleen O'Connor, Jim Millns
	Edith C. Secord, Ferrier T. Martin	1976	Colleen O'Connor, Jim Millns
	Original	1977	Judy Genovesi, Kent Weigle
	Theresa Weld Blanchard,	1978	Stacey Smith, John Summers
	Nathaniel W. Niles	1979	Stacey Smith, John Summers
1932	Waltz	1980	Stacey Smith, John Summers
	Edith C. Secord, Joseph K. Savage	1981	Judy Blumberg, Michael Seibert
	Original	1982	Judy Blumberg, Michael Seibert
	Clara Rotch Frothingham, George E. B. Hill	1983	Judy Blumberg, Michael Seibert
1933	Waltz	1984	Judy Blumberg, Michael Seibert
	Ilse Twaroschk, Frederick F. Fleishmann	1985	Judy Blumberg, Michael Seibert
	Original	1986	Renee Roca, Donald Adair
	Suzanne Davis, Frederick Goodridge	1987	Suzanne Semanick, Scott Gregory
1934	Waltz	1988	Suzanne Semanick, Scott Gregory
	Nettie C. Prantel, Roy Hunt	1989	Susan Wynne, Joseph Druar
	Original	1990	Susan Wynne, Joseph Druar
	Suzanne Davis, Frederick Goodridge	1991	Elizabeth Punsalan, Jerod Swallow

Miscellaneous Sports

Sports Illustrated

Miguel Induráin
Of Spain Wins the
Tour de France

TOUR DE FORCE

GOUVERNEUR/GAMMA

Archery

National Men's Champions

1879 .... Will H. Thompson	1915 ...... Dr. Robert Elmer	1957 .... Joe Fries
1880 .... L. L. Pedinghaus	1916 ...... Dr. Robert Elmer	1958 .... Robert Bitner
1881 .... F. H. Walworth	1919 ...... Dr. Robert Elmer	1959 .... Wilbert Vetrovsky
1882 .... D. H. Nash	1920 ...... Dr. Robert Elmer	1960 .... Robert Kadlec
1883 .... Col. Robert Williams	1921 ...... James Jiles	1961 .... Clayton Sherman
1884 .... Col. Robert Williams	1922 ...... Dr. Robert Elmer	1962 .... Charles Sandlin
1885 .... Col. Robert Williams	1923 ...... Bill Palmer	1963 .... Dave Keaggy, Jr.
1886 .... W. A. Clark	1924 ...... James Jiles	1964 .... Dave Keaggy, Jr.
1887 .... W. A. Clark	1925 ...... Dr. Paul Crouch	1965 .... George Slinzer
1888 .... Lewis Maxson	1926 ...... Stanley Spencer	1966 .... Hardy Ward
1889 .... Lewis Maxson	1927 ...... Dr. Paul Crouch	1967 .... Ray Rogers
1890 .... Lewis Maxson	1928 ...... Bill Palmer	1968 .... Hardy Ward
1891 .... Lewis Maxson	1929 ...... Dr. E. K. Roberts	1969 .... Ray Rogers
1892 .... Lewis Maxson	1930 ...... Russ Hoogerhyde	1970 .... Joe Thornton
1893 .... Lewis Maxson	1931 ...... Russ Hoogerhyde	1971 .... John Williams
1894 .... Lewis Maxson	1932 ...... Russ Hoogerhyde	1972 .... Kevin Erlandson
1895 .... W. B. Robinson	1933 ...... Ralph Miller	1973 .... Darrell Pace
1896 .... Lewis Maxson	1934 ...... Russ Hoogerhyde	1974 .... Darrell Pace
1897 .... W. A. Clark	1935 ...... Gilman Keasey	1975 .... Darrell Pace
1898 .... Lewis Maxson	1936 ...... Gilman Keasey	1976 .... Darrell Pace
1899 .... M. C. Howell	1937 ...... Russ Hoogerhyde	1977 .... Rick McKinney
1900 .... A. R. Clark	1938 ...... Pat Chambers	1978 .... Darrell Pace
1901 .... Will H. Thompson	1939 ...... Pat Chambers	1979 .... Rick McKinney
1902 .... Will H. Thompson	1940 ...... Russ Hoogerhyde	1980 .... Rick McKinney
1903 .... Will H. Thompson	1941 ...... Larry Hughes	1981 .... Rick McKinney
1904 .... George Bryant	1946 ...... Wayne Thompson	1982 .... Rick McKinney
1905 .... George Bryant	1947 ...... Jack Wilson	1983 .... Rick McKinney
1906 .... Henry Richardson	1948 ...... Larry Hughes	1984 .... Darrell Pace
1907 .... Henry Richardson	1949 ...... Russ Reynolds	1985 .... Rick McKinney
1908 .... Will H. Thompson	1950 ...... Stan Overby	1986 .... Rick McKinney
1909 .... Geroge Bryant	1951 ...... Russ Reynolds	1987 .... Rick McKinney
1910 .... Henry Richardson	1952 ...... Robert Larson	1988 .... Jay Barrs
1911 .... Dr. Robert Elmer	1953 ...... Bill Glackin	1989 .... Ed Eliason
1912 .... George Bryant	1954 ...... Robert Rhode	1990 .... Ed Eliason
1913 .... George Bryant	1955 ...... Joe Fries	1991 .... Ed Eliason
1914 .... Dr. Robert Elmer	1956 ...... Joe Fries	

National Women's Champions

1879 .... Mrs. S. Brown	1904 ...... Mrs. M. C. Howell	1931 .... Doroth Cummings
1880 .... Mrs. T. Davies	1905 ...... Mrs. M. C. Howell	1932 .... Ilda Hanchette
1881 .... Mrs. Gibbes	1906 ...... Mrs. E. C. Cook	1933 .... Madelaine Taylor
1882 .... Mrs. A. H. Gibbes	1907 ...... Mrs. M. C. Howell	1934 .... Desales Mudd
1883 .... Mrs. M. C. Howell	1908 ...... Harriet Case	1935 .... Ruth Hodgert
1884 .... Mrs. H. Hall	1909 ...... Harriet Case	1936 .... Gladys Hammer
1885 .... Mrs. M. C. Howell	1910 ...... J. V. Sullivan	1937 .... Gladys Hammer
1886 .... Mrs. M. C. Howell	1911 ...... Mrs. J. S. Taylor	1938 .... Jean Tenney
1887 .... Mrs. A. M. Phillips	1912 ...... Mrs. Witwer Tayler	1939 .... Belvia Carter
1888 .... Mrs. A. M. Phillips	1913 ...... Mrs. P. Fletcher	1940 .... Ann Weber
1889 .... Mrs. A. M. Phillips	1914 ...... Mrs. B. P. Gray	1941 .... Ree Dillinger
1890 .... Mrs. M. C. Howell	1915 ...... Cynthia Wesson	1946 .... Ann Weber
1891 .... Mrs. M. C. Howell	1916 ...... Cynthia Wesson	1947 .... Ann Weber
1892 .... Mrs. M. C. Howell	1919 ...... Dorothy Smith	1948 .... Jean Lee
1893 .... Mrs. M. C. Howell	1920 ...... Cynthia Wesson	1949 .... Jean Lee
1894 .... Mrs. Albert Kern	1921 ...... Mrs. L. C. Smith	1950 .... Jean Lee
1895 .... Mrs. M. C. Howell	1922 ...... Dorothy Smith	1951 .... Jean Lee
1896 .... Mrs. M. C. Howell	1923 ...... Norma Pierce	1952 .... Ann Weber
1897 .... Mrs. J. S. Baker	1924 ...... Dorothy Smith	1953 .... Ann Weber
1898 .... Mrs. M. C. Howell	1925 ...... Dorothy Smith	1954 .... Luarette Young
1899 .... Mrs. M. C. Howell	1926 ...... Dorothy Smith	1955 .... Ann Clark
1900 .... Mrs. M. C. Howell	1927 ...... Mrs. R. Johnson	1956 .... Carole Meinhart
1901 .... Mrs. C. E. Woodruff	1928 ...... Beatrice Hodgson	1957 .... Carole Meinhart
1902 .... Mrs. M. C. Howell	1929 ...... Audrey Grubbs	1958 .... Carole Meinhart
1903 .... Mrs. M. C. Howell	1930 ...... Audrey Grubbs	1959 .... Carole Meinhart

National Women's Champions (*Cont.*)

1960 .... Ann Clark	1971 ...... Doreen Wilber	1982 ....Luann Ryon
1961 .... Victoria Cook	1972 ...... Ruth Rowe	1983 ....Nancy Myrick
1962 .... Nancy Vonderheide	1973 ...... Doreen Wilber	1984 ....Ruth Rowe
1963 .... Nancy Vonderheide	1974 ...... Doreen Wilber	1985 ....Terri Pesho
1964 .... Victoria Cook	1975 .... Irene Lorensen	1986 ....Debra Ochs
1965 .... Nancy Pfeiffer	1976 ...... Luann Ryon	1987 ....Terry Quinn
1966 .... Helen Thornton	1977 ...... Luann Ryon	1988 ....Debra Ochs
1967 .... Ardelle Mills	1978 ...... Luann Ryon	1989 ....Debra Ochs
1968 .... Victoria Cook	1979 ...... Lynette Johnson	1990 ....Denise Parker
1969 ..... Doreen Wilber	1980 ...... Judi Adams	1991 ....Denise Archer
1970 .... Nancy Myrick	1981 ...... Debra Metzger	

Chess

World Champions

1866-94 ....Wilhelm Steinitz, Austria	1958-59 ....Mikhail Botvinnik, USSR
1894-1921 ....Emanuel Lasker, Germany	1960-61 ....Mikhail Tal, USSR
1921-27 ....Jose Capablanca, Cuba	1961-63 ....Mikhail Botvinnik, USSR
1927-35 ....Alexander Alekhine, France	1963-69 ....Tigran Petrosian, USSR
1935-37 ....Max Euwe, Holland	1969-72 ....Boris Spassky, USSR
1937-46 ....Alexander Alekhine, France	1972-75 ....Bobby Fischer, United States*
1948-57 ....Mikhail Botvinnik, USSR	1975-85 ....Anatoly Karpov, USSR
1957-58 ....Vassily Smyslov, USSR	1985- ....Garry Kasparov, USSR

*Defaulted championship.

United States Champions

1857-71 ....Paul Morphy	1969-72 ....Samuel Reshevsky
1871-76 ....George Mackenzie	1972-73 ....Robert Byrne
1876-80 ....James Mason	1973-74 ....Lubomir Kavalek
1880-89 ....George Mackenzie	John Grefe
1889-90 ....Samuel Lipschutz	1974-77 ....Walter Browne
1890 ....Jackson Showalter	1978-80 ....Lubomir Kavalek
1890-91 ....Max Judd	1980-81 ....Larry Evans
1891-92 ....Jackson Showalter	Larry Christiansen
1892-94 ....Samuel Lipschutz	Walter Browne
1894 ....Jackson Showalter	1981-83 ....Walter Browne
1894-95 ....Albert Hodges	Yasser Seirawan
1895-97 ....Jackson Showalter	1983 ....Roman Dzindzichashvili
1897-1906 ....Harry Pillsbury	Larry Christiansen
1906-09 ....Vacant	Walter Browne
1909-36 ....Frank Marshall	1984-85 ....Lev Alburt
1936-44 ....Samuel Reshevsky	1986 ....Yasser Seirawan
1944-46 ....Arnold Denker	1987 ....Joel Benjamin
1946-48 ....Samuel Reshevsky	Nick DeFirmian
1948-51 ....Herman Steiner	1988 ....Michael Wilder
1951-54 ....Larry Evans	1989 ....Roman Dzindzichashvili
1954-57 ....Arthur Bisguier	Stuart Rachels
1957-61 ....Bobby Fischer	Yasser Seirawan
1961-62 ....Larry Evans	1990 ....Lev Alburt
1962-68 ....Bobby Fischer	1991 ....Gata Kamski
1968-69 ....Larry Evans	

Curling

World Champions

Year	Country, Skip	Year	Country, Skip
1972 ....Canada, Crest Melesnuk		1977 ....Sweden, Ragnar Kamp
1973 ....Sweden, Kjell Oscarius		1978 ....United States, Bob Nichols
1974 ....United States, Bud Somerville		1979 ....Norway, Kristian Soerum
1975 ....Switzerland, Otto Danieli		1980 ....Canada, Rich Folk
1976 ....United States, Bruce Roberts		1981 ....Switzerland, Jurg Tanner

Curling (Cont.)

World Champions (Cont.)

Year	Country, Skip	Year	Country, Skip
1982	Canada, Al Hackner	1987	Canada, Russ Howard
1983	Canada, Ed Werenich	1988	Norway, Eigil Ramsfjell
1984	Norway, Eigil Ramsfjell	1989	Canada, Pat Ryan
1985	Canada, Al Hackner	1990	Canada, Ed Werenich
1986	Canada, Ed Luckowich	1991	Scotland, David Smith

U.S. Men's Champions

Year	Site	Winning Club	Skip
1957	Chicago, IL	Hibbing, MN	Harold Lauber
1958	Milwaukee, WI	Detroit, MI	Douglas Fisk
1959	Green Bay, WI	Hibbing, MN	Fran Kleffman
1960	Chicago, IL	Grafton, ND	Orvil Gilleshammer
1961	Grand Forks, ND	Seattle, WA	Frank Crealock
1962	Detroit, MI	Hibbing, MN	Fran Kleffman
1963	Duluth, MN	Detroit, MI	Mike Slyziuk
1964	Utica, NY	Duluth, MN	Robert Magle, Jr.
1965	Seattle, WA	Superior, WI	Bud Somerville
1966	Hibbing, MN	Fargo, ND	Joe Zbacnik
1967	Winchester, MA	Seattle, WA	Bruce Roberts
1968	Madison, WI	Superior, WI	Bud Somerville
1969	Grand Forks, ND	Superior, WI	Bud Somerville
1970	Ardsley, NY	Grafton, ND	Art Tallackson
1971	Duluth, MN	Edmore, ND	Dale Dalziel
1972	Wilmette, IL	Grafton, ND	Robert Labonte
1973	Colorado Springs, CO	Winchester, MA	Charles Reeves
1974	Schenectady, NY	Superior, WI	Bud Somerville
1975	Detroit, MI	Seattle, WA	Ed Risling
1976	Wausau, WI	Hibbing, MN	Bruce Roberts
1977	Northbrook, IL	Hibbing, MN	Bruce Roberts
1978	Utica, NY	Superior, WI	Bob Nichols
1979	Superior, WI	Bemidji, MN	Scott Baird
1980	Bemidji, MN	Hibbing, MN	Paul Pustovar
1981	Fairbanks, AK	Superior, WI	Bob Nichols
1982	Brookline, MA	Madison, WI	Steve Brown
1983	Colorado Springs, CO	Colorado Springs, CO	Don Cooper
1984	Hibbing, MN	Hibbing, MN	Bruce Roberts
1985	Mequon, WI	Wilmette, IL	Tim Wright
1986	Seattle, WA	Madison, WI	Steve Brown
1987	Lake Placid, NY	Seattle, WA	Jim Vukich
1988	St. Paul, MN	Seattle, WA	Doug Jones
1989	Detroit, MI	Seattle, WA	Jim Vukich
1990	Superior, WI	Seattle, WA	Doug Jones
1991	Utica, NY	Madison, WI	Steve Brown

U.S. Women's Champions

Year	Site	Winning Club	Skip
1977	Wilmette, IL	Hastings, NY	Margaret Smith
1978	Duluth, MN	Wausau, WI	Sandy Robarge
1979	Winchester, MA	Seattle, WA	Nancy Langley
1980	Seattle, WA	Seattle, WA	Sharon Kozal
1981	Kettle Moraine, WI	Seattle, WA	Nancy Langley
1982	Bowling Green, OH	Oak Park, IL	Ruth Schwenker
1983	Grafton, ND	Seattle, WA	Nancy Langley
1984	Wauwatosa, WI	Duluth, MN	Amy Hatten
1985	Hershey, PA	Fairbanks, AK	Bev Birklid
1986	Chicago, IL	St. Paul, MN	Gerri Tilden
1987	St. Paul, MN	Seattle, WA	Sharon Good
1988	Darien, CT	Seattle, WA	Nancy Langley
1989	Detroit, MI	Rolla, ND	Jan Lagasse
1990	Superior, WI	Denver, CO	Bev Behnka
1991	Utica, NY	Houston, TX	Maymar Gemmell

Cycling

Tour de France Winners

Year	Winner	Time
1903	Maurice Garin, France	94 hrs, 33 min
1904	Henri Cornet, France	96 hrs, 5 min, 56 sec
1905	Louis Trousselier, France	110 hrs, 26 min, 58 sec
1906	Rene Pottier, France	Not available
1907	Lucien Petit-Breton, France	158 hrs, 54 min, 5 sec
1908	Lucien Petit-Breton, France	Not available
1909	Francois Faber, Luxembourg	157 hrs, 1 min, 22 sec
1910	Octave Lapize, France	162 hrs, 41 min, 30 sec
1911	Gustave Garrigou, France	195 hrs, 37 min
1912	Odile Defraye, Belgium	190 hrs, 30 min, 28 sec
1913	Philippe Thys, Belgium	197 hrs, 54 min
1914	Philippe Thys, Belgium	200 hrs, 28 min, 48 sec
1915-18	No race	
1919	Firmin Lambot, Belgium	231 hrs, 7 min, 15 sec
1920	Philippe Thys, Belgium	228 hrs, 36 min, 13 sec
1921	Leon Scieur, Belgium	221 hrs, 50 min, 26 sec
1922	Firmin Lambot, Belgium	222 hrs, 8 min, 6 sec
1923	Henri Pelissier, France	222 hrs, 15 min, 30 sec
1924	Ottavio Bottechia, Italy	226 hrs, 18 min, 21 sec
1925	Ottavio Bottechia, Italy	219 hrs, 10 min, 18 sec
1926	Lucien Buysse, Belgium	238 hrs, 44 min, 25 sec
1927	Nicolas Frantz, Luxembourg	198 hrs, 16 min, 42 sec
1928	Nicolas Frantz, Luxembourg	192 hrs, 48 min, 58 sec
1929	Maurice Dewaele, Belgium	186 hrs, 39 min, 16 sec
1930	Andre Leducq, France	172 hrs, 12 min, 16 sec
1931	Antonin Magne, France	177 hrs, 10 min, 3 sec
1932	Andre Leducq, France	154 hrs, 12 min, 49 sec
1933	Georges Speicher, France	147 hrs, 51 min, 37 sec
1934	Antonin Magne, France	147 hrs, 13 min, 58 sec
1935	Romain Maes, Belgium	141 hrs, 32 min
1936	Sylvere Maes, Belgium	142 hrs, 47 min, 32 sec
1937	Roger Lapebie, France	138 hrs, 58 min, 31 sec
1938	Gino Bartali, Italy	148 hrs, 29 min, 12 sec
1939	Sylvere Maes, Belgium	132 hrs, 3 min, 17 sec
1940-46	No race	
1947	Jean Robic, France	148 hrs, 11 min, 25 sec
1948	Gino Bartali, Italy	147 hrs, 10 min, 36 sec
1949	Fausto Coppi, Italy	149 hrs, 40 min, 49 sec
1950	Ferdi Kubler, Switzerland	145 hrs, 36 min, 56 sec
1951	Hugo Koblet, Switzerland	142 hrs, 20 min, 14 sec
1952	Fausto Coppi, Italy	151 hrs, 57 min, 20 sec
1953	Louison Bobet, France	129 hrs, 23 min, 25 sec
1954	Louison Bobet, France	140 hrs, 6 min, 5 sec
1955	Louison Bobet, France	130 hrs, 29 min, 26 sec
1956	Roger Walkowiak, France	124 hrs, 1 min, 16 sec
1957	Jacques Anquetil, France	129 hrs, 46 min, 11 sec
1958	Charly Gaul, Luxembourg	116 hrs, 59 min, 5 sec
1959	Federico Bahamontes, Spain	123 hrs, 46 min, 45 sec
1960	Gastone Nencini, Italy	112 hrs, 8 min, 42 sec
1961	Jacques Anquetil, France	122 hrs, 1 min, 33 sec
1962	Jacques Anquetil, France	114 hrs, 31 min, 54 sec
1963	Jacques Anquetil, France	113 hrs, 30 min, 5 sec
1964	Jacques Anquetil, France	127 hrs, 9 min, 44 sec
1965	Felice Gimondi, Italy	116 hrs, 42 min, 6 sec
1966	Lucien Aimar, France	117 hrs, 34 min, 21 sec
1967	Roger Pingeon, France	136 hrs, 53 min, 50 sec
1968	Jan Janssen, Netherlands	133 hrs, 49 min, 32 sec
1969	Eddy Merckx, Belgium	116 hrs, 16 min, 2 sec
1970	Eddy Merckx, Belgium	119 hrs, 31 min, 49 sec
1971	Eddy Merckx, Belgium	96 hrs, 45 min, 14 sec
1972	Eddy Merckx, Belgium	108 hrs, 17 min, 18 sec
1973	Luis Ocana, Spain	122 hrs, 25 min, 34 sec
1974	Eddy Merckx, Belgium	116 hrs, 16 min, 58 sec
1975	Bernard Thevenet, France	114 hrs, 35 min, 31 sec
1976	Lucien Van Impe, Belgium	116 hrs, 22 min, 23 sec

Cycling (*Cont.*)

Tour de France Winners (*Cont.*)

Year	Winner	Time
1977	Bernard Thevenet, France	115 hrs, 38 min, 30 sec
1978	Bernard Hinault, France	108 hrs, 18 min
1979	Bernard Hinault, France	103 hrs, 6 min, 50 sec
1980	Joop Zoetemelk, Netherlands	109 hrs, 19 min, 14 sec
1981	Bernard Hinault, France	96 hrs, 19 min, 38 sec
1982	Bernard Hinault, France	92 hrs, 8 min, 46 sec
1983	Laurent Fignon, France	105 hrs, 7 min, 52 sec
1984	Laurent Fignon, France	112 hrs, 3 min, 40 sec
1985	Bernard Hinault, France	113 hrs, 24 min, 23 sec
1986	Greg LeMond, United States	110 hrs, 35 min, 19 sec
1987	Stephen Roche, Ireland	115 hrs, 27 min, 42 sec
1988	Pedro Delgado, Spain	84 hrs, 27 min, 53 sec
1989	Greg LeMond, United States	87 hrs, 38 min, 35 sec
1990	Greg LeMond, United States	90 hrs, 43 min, 20 sec
1991	Miguel Induráin, Spain	101 hrs, 1 min, 20 sec

Sled Dog Racing

Iditarod

Year	Winner	Time	Year	Winner	Time
1973	Dick Wilmarth	20 days, 00:49:41	1983	Dick Mackey	12 days, 14:10:44
1974	Carl Huntington	20 days, 15:02:07	1984	Dean Osmar	12 days, 15:07:33
1975	Emmitt Peters	14 days, 14:43:45	1985	Libby Riddles	18 days, 00:20:17
1976	Gerald Riley	18 days, 22:58:17	1986	Susan Butcher	11 days, 15:06:00
1977	Rick Swenson	16 days, 16:27:13	1987	Susan Butcher	11 days, 02:05:13
1978	Dick Mackey	14 days, 18:52:24	1988	Susan Butcher	11 days, 11:41:40
1979	Rick Swenson	15 days, 10:37:47	1989	Joe Runyan	11 days, 05:24:34
1980	Joe May	14 days, 07:11:51	1990	Susan Butcher	11 days, 01:53:23
1981	Rick Swenson	12 days, 08:45:02	1991	Rick Swenson	12 days, 16:34:39
1982	Rick Swenson	16 days, 04:40:10			

Fishing

Saltwater Fishing Records

Species	Weight	Where Caught	Date	Angler
Albacore	88 lb 2 oz	Port Mogan, Canary Islands	Nov 19, 1977	Siegfried Dickemann
Amberjack, greater	155 lb 10 oz	Challenger Bank, Bermuda	June 24, 1981	Joseph Dawson
Amberjack, Pacific	104 lb	Baja California, Mexico	July 4, 1984	Richard Cresswell
Barracuda, great	83 lb	Lagos, Nigeria	Jan 13, 1952	K. J. W. Hackett
Barracuda, Mexican	21 lb	Phantom Isle, Costa Rica	Mar 27, 1987	E. Greg Kent
Barracuda, slender	17 lb 4 oz	Sitra Channel, Bahrain	Nov 21, 1985	Roger Cranswick
Bass, barred sand	13 lb 3 oz	Huntington Beach, CA	Aug 29, 1988	Robert Halaj
Bass, black sea	9 lb 8 oz	Virginia Beach, VA	Jan 9, 1987	Joe Mizelle, Jr
Bass, European	20 lb 11 oz	Stes Maries de la Mer, France	May 6, 1986	Jean Baptiste Bayle
Bass, giant sea	563 lb 8 oz	Anacapa Island, CA	Aug 20, 1968	James D. McAdam, Jr
Bass, striped	78 lb 8 oz	Atlantic City, NJ	Sep 21, 1982	Albert McReynolds
Bluefish	31 lb 12 oz	Hatteras Inlet, NC	Jan 30, 1972	James M. Hussey
Bonefish	19 lb	Zululand, South Africa	May 26, 1962	Brian W. Batchelor
Bonito, Atlantic	18 lb 14 oz	Fayal Island, Azores	July 8, 1953	D. G. Higgs
Bonito, Pacific	23 lb 8 oz	Victoria, Mahe Seychelles	Feb 19, 1975	Anne Cochain
Cabezon	23 lb	Juan De Fuca Strait, WA	Aug 4, 1990	Wesley Hunter
Cobia	135 lb 9 oz	Shark Bay, Australia	July 9, 1985	Peter W. Goulding
Cod, Atlantic	98 lb 12 oz	Isle of Shoals, NH	June 8, 1969	Alphonse Bielevich
Cod, Pacific	30 lb	Andrew Bay, AK	June 7, 1984	Donald Vaughn
Conger	104 lb 8 oz	Brixham, England	June 5, 1988	Philip John Greenway
Dolphin	87 lb	Papagallo Gulf, Costa Rica	Sep 25, 1976	Manual Salazar
Drum, black	113 lb 1 oz	Lewes, DE	Sep 15, 1975	Gerald Townsend
Drum, red	94 lb 2 oz	Avon, NC	Nov 7, 1984	David Deuel
Eel, African mottled	36 lb 1 oz	Durban, South Africa	June 10, 1984	Ferdie van Nooten
Eel, American	7 lb 8 oz	Mashpee, MA	May 8, 1990	Paul Pietavino

Saltwater Fishing Records (*Cont.*)

Species	Weight	Where Caught	Date	Angler
Flounder, southern	20 lb 9 oz	Nassau Sound, FL	Dec 23, 1983	Larenza Mungin
Flounder, summer	22 lb 7 oz	Montauk, NY	Sep 15, 1975	Charles Nappi
Grouper, Warsaw	436 lb 12 oz	Destin, FL	Dec 22, 1985	Steve Haeusler
Halibut, Atlantic	255 lb 4 oz	Gloucester, MA	July 28, 1989	Sonny Manley
Halibut, California	53 lb 4 oz	Santa Rosa Island, CA	July 7, 1988	Russell Harmon
Halibut, Pacific	356 lb	Juneau, AK	June 30, 1982	Vern S. Foster
Jack, crevalle	54 lb 7 oz	Port Michel, Gabon	Jan 15, 1982	Thomas Gibson, Jr
Jack, horse-eye	24 lb 8 oz	Miami, FL	Dec 20, 1982	Tilo Schnau
Jack, Pacific crevalie	24 lb	Baja California, Mexico	Apr 30, 1987	Sharon Swanson
Jewfish	680 lb	Femandina Beach, FL	May 20, 1961	Lynn Joyner
Kawakawa	29 lb	NSW, Australia	Dec 17, 1986	Ronald Nakamura
Lingcod	64 lb	Elfin Cove, AK	Aug 2, 1988	David Bauer
Mackerel, cero	17 lb 2 oz	Islamorada, FL	Apr 5, 1986	G. Michael Mills
Mackerel, king	90 lb	Key West, FL	Feb 16, 1976	Norton Thomton
Mackerel, Spanish	13 lb	Ocracoke Inlet, NC	Nov 4, 1987	Robert Cranton
Marlin, Atlantic blue	1282 lb	St Thomas, Virgin Islands	Aug 6, 1977	Larry Martin
Marlin, black	1560 lb	Cabo Blanco, Peru	Aug 4, 1953	A. C. Glassell, Jr
Marlin, Pacific blue	1376 lb	Kaaiwa Point, HI	May 31, 1982	J. W. deBeaubien
Marlin, striped	494 lb	Tutukaka, New Zealand	Jan 16, 1986	Bill Boniface
Marlin, white	181 lb 14 oz	Vitoria, Brazil	Dec 8, 1979	Evandro Luiz Caser
Permit	51 lb 8 oz	Lake Worth, FL	Apr 28, 1978	William M. Kenney
Pollock	46 lb 7 oz	Brielle, NJ	May 26, 1975	John Tomes Holton
Pompano, African	50 lb 8 oz	Daytona Beach, FL	Apr 21, 1990	Tom Sargent
Roosterfish	114 lb	La Paz, Mexico	June 1, 1960	Abe Sackheim
Runner, blue	8 lb 4 oz	Bimini, Bahamas	Sep 9, 1990	Brent Rowland
Runner, rainbow	33 lb 10 oz	Clarion Island, Mexico	Mar 14, 1976	Ralph A. Mikkelsen
Sailfish, Atlantic	128 lb 1 oz	Luanda, Angola	Mar 27, 1974	Harm Steyn
Sailfish, Pacific	221 lb	Santa Cruz Island, Ecuador	Feb 12, 1947	C. W. Stewart
Seabass, white	83 lb 12 oz	San Felipe, Mexico	Mar 31, 1953	L. C. Baumgardner
Seatrout, spotted	16 lb	Mason's Beach, VA	May 28, 1977	William Katko
Shark, blue	437 lb	Catherine Bay, NSW, Australia	Oct 2, 1976	Peter Hyde
Shark, Greenland	1708 lb 9 oz	Trondheim, Norway	Oct 18, 1987	Terje Nordtvedt
Shark, hammerhead	991 lb	Sarasota, FL	May 30, 1982	Allen Ogle
Shark, man-eater or white	2664 lb	Ceduna, Australia	Apr 21, 1959	Alfred Dean
Shark, mako	1115 lb	Black River, Mauritius	Nov 16, 1988	Patrick Guillanton
Shark, porbeagle	465 lb	Cornwall, England	July 23, 1976	Jorge Potier
Shark, thresher	802 lb	Tutukaka, New Zealand	Feb 8, 1981	Dianne North
Shark, tiger	1780 lb	Cherry Grove, SC	June 14, 1964	Walter Maxwell
Skipjack, black	20 lb 5 oz	Baja California, Mexico	Oct 14, 1983	Roger Torriero
Snapper, cubera	121 lb 8 oz	Cameron, LA	July 5, 1982	Mike Hebert
Snook	53 lb 10 oz	Costa Rica	Oct 18, 1978	Gilbert Ponzi
Spearfish	90 lb 13 oz	Madeira Island, Portugal	June 2, 1980	Joseph Larkin
Swordfish	1182 lb	Iquique, Chile	May 7, 1953	L. Marron
Tanguigue	99 lb	Natal, South Africa	Mar 14, 1982	Michael J. Wilkinson
Tarpon	283 lb	Lake Maracaibo, Venezuela	Mar 19, 1956	M. Salazar
Tautog	24 lb	Wachapreagee, VA	Aug 25, 1987	Gregory Bell
Tope	72 lb 12 oz	Parengarenga Harbor, New Zealand	Dec 19, 1986	Melanie Feldman
Trevally, bigeye	15 lb	Isla Coiba, Panama	Jan 18, 1984	Sally Timms
Trevally, giant	137 lb 9 oz	McKenzie State Park, HI	July 13, 1983	Roy Gushiken
Tuna, Atlantic bigeye	375 lb 8 oz	Ocean City, MD	Aug 26, 1977	Cecil Browne
Tuna, blackfin	42 lb	Bermuda	June 2, 1978	Alan J. Card
Tuna, bluefin	1496 lb	Aulds Cove, Nova Scotia	Oct 26, 1979	Ken Fraser
Tuna, longtail	79 lb 2 oz	Montague Island, NSW, Australia	Apr 12, 1982	Tim Simpson
Tuna, Pacific bigeye	435 lb	Cabo Blanco, Peru	Apr 17, 1957	Russel Lee
Tuna, skipjack	41 lb 14 oz	Mauritius	Nov 12, 1985	Edmund Heinzen
Tuna, southern bluefin	348 lb 5 oz	Whakatane, New Zealand	Jan 16, 1981	Rex Wood
Tuna, yellowfin	388 lb 12 oz	San Benedicto Is, Mexico	Apr 1, 1977	Curt Wiesenhutter
Tunny, little	35 lb 2 oz	Cape de Garde, Algeria	Dec 14, 1988	Jean Yves Chatard
Wahoo	155 lb 8 oz	San Salvador, Bahamas	Apr 3, 1990	William Bourne
Weakfish	19 lb 2 oz	Jones Beach Inlet, NY	Oct 11, 1984	Dennis Rooney
Yellowtail, California	78 lb	Alijos Rocks, Mexico	June 27, 1987	Richard Cresswell
Yellowtail, southern	114 lb 10 oz	Tauranga, New Zealand	Feb 5, 1984	Mike Godfrey

Freshwater Fishing Records

Species	Weight	Where Caught	Date	Angler
Barramundi	59 lb 12 oz	Port Stuart, Australia	Apr 7, 1983	Andrew Davern
Bass, largemouth	22 lb 4 oz	Montgomery Lake, GA	June 2, 1932	George W. Perry
Bass, peacock	26 lb 8 oz	Matevini River, Colombia	Jan 26, 1982	Rod Neubert
Bass, redeye	8 lb 3 oz	Flint River, GA	Oct 23, 1977	David A. Hubbard
Bass, rock	3 lb	York River, Ontario	Aug 1, 1974	Peter Gulgin
Bass, smallmouth	11 lb 15 oz	Dale Hollow Lake, KY	July 9, 1955	David L. Hayes
Bass, Suwannee	3 lb 14 oz	Suwannee River, FL	Mar 2, 1985	Ronnie Everett
Bass, white	6 lb 13 oz	Orange, VA	July 31, 1989	Ronald Sprouse
Bass, whiterock	24 lb 3 oz	Leesville Lake, VA	May 12, 1989	David Lambert
Bass, yellow	2 lb 4 oz	Lake Monroe, IN	Mar 27, 1977	Donald L. Stalker
Bluegill	4 lb 12 oz	Ketona Lake, AL	Apr 9, 1950	T. S. Hudson
Bowfin	21 lb 8 oz	Florence, SC	Jan 29, 1980	Robert Harmon
Buffalo, bigmouth	70 lb 5 oz	Bastrop, LA	Apr 21, 1980	Delbert Sisk
Buffalo, black	55 lb 8 oz	Cherokee Lake, TN	May 3, 1984	Edward McLain
Buffalo, smallmouth	68 lb 8 oz	Lake Hamilton, AR	May 16, 1984	Jerry Dolezal
Bullhead, brown	5 lb 8 oz	Veal Pond, GA	May 22, 1975	Jimmy Andrews
Bullhead, yellow	4 lb 4 oz	Mormon Lake, AZ	May 11, 1984	Emily Williams
Burbot	18 lb 4 oz	Pickford, MI	Jan 31, 1980	Thomas Courtemanche
Carp	75 lb 11 oz	Lac de St Cassien, France	May 21, 1987	Leo van der Gugten
Catfish, blue	97 lb	Missouri River, SD	Sep 16, 1959	E. B. Elliott
Catfish, channel	58 lb	Santee-Cooper Reservoir, SC	July 7, 1964	W. B. Whaley
Catfish, flathead	98 lb	Lewisville, TX	June 2, 1986	William Stephens
Catfish, white	17 lb 7 oz	Success Lake, Tulare, CA	Nov 15, 1981	Chuck Idell
Char, Arctic	32 lb 9 oz	Tree River, Canada	July 30, 1981	Jeffrey Ward
Crappie, white	5 lb 3 oz	Enid Dam, MS	July 31, 1957	Fred L. Bright
Dolly Varden	12 lb	Noatak River, AK	July 10, 1987	Kenneth Alt
Dorado	51 lb 5 oz	Corrientes, Argentina	Sep 27, 1984	Armando Giudice
Drum, freshwater	54 lb 8 oz	Nickajack Lake, TN	Apr 20, 1972	Benny E. Hull
Gar, alligator	279 lb	Rio Grande River, TX	Dec 2, 1951	Bill Valverde
Gar, Florida	21 lb 3 oz	Boca Raton, FL	June 3, 1981	Jeff Sabol
Gar, longnose	50 lb 5 oz	Trinity River, TX	July 30, 1954	Townsend Miller
Gar, shortnose	5 lb	Sally Jones Lake, OK	Apr 26, 1985	Buddy Croslin
Gar, spotted	8 lb 12 oz	Tennessee River, AL	Aug 26, 1987	Winston Baker
Grayling, Arctic	5 lb 15 oz	Katseyedie River, Northwest Territories	Aug 16, 1967	Jeanne P. Branson
Inconnu	53 lb	Pah River, AK	Aug 20, 1986	Lawrence Hudnall
Kokanee	9 lb 6 oz	Okanagan Lake, Vernon, BC	June 18, 1988	Norm Kuhn
Muskellunge	69 lb 15 oz	St Lawrence River, NY	Sep 22, 1957	Arthur Lawton
Muskellunge, tiger	51 lb 3 oz	Lac Vieux-Desert, WI, MI	July 16, 1919	John Knobla
Perch, Nile	154 lb 5 oz	Nkumba Bay, Uganda	June 3, 1990	Frederick Dale
Perch, white	4 lb 12 oz	Messalonskee Lake, ME	June 4, 1949	Mrs Earl Small
Perch, yellow	4 lb 3 oz	Bordentown, NJ	May 1865	C. C. Abbot
Pickerel, chain	9 lb 6 oz	Homerville, GA	Feb 17, 1961	Baxley McQuaig, Jr
Pike, northern	55 lb 1 oz	Lake of Grefeern, West Germany	Oct 16, 1986	Lothar Louis
Redhorse, shorthead	9 lb 3 oz	Salmon River, Pulaski, NY	May 11, 1985	Jason Wilson
Redhorse, silver	11 lb 7 oz	Plum Creek, WI	May 29, 1985	Neal Long
Salmon, Atlantic	79 lb 2 oz	Tana River, Norway	1928	Henrik Henriksen
Salmon, chinook	97 lb 4 oz	Kenai River, AK	May 17, 1985	Les Anderson
Salmon, chum	32 lb	Behm Canal, AK	June 7, 1985	Fredrick Thynes
Salmon, coho	33 lb 4 oz	Pulaski, NY	Sept 27, 1989	Jerry Lifton
Salmon, pink	12 lb 9 oz	Morse, Kenai rivers, AK	Aug 17, 1974	Steven A. Lee
Salmon, sockeye	15 lb 3 oz	Kenai River, AK	Aug 9, 1987	Stan Roach
Sauger	8 lb 12 oz	Lake Sakakawea, ND	Oct 6, 1971	Mike Fischer
Shad, American	11 lb 4 oz	Connecticut River, MA	May 19, 1986	Bob Thibodo
Sturgeon, white	468 lb	Benicia, CA	July 9, 1983	Joey Pallotta III
Sunfish, green	2 lb 2 oz	Stockton Lake, MO	June 18, 1971	Paul M. Dilley
Sunfish, redbreast	1 lb 12 oz	Suwannee River, FL	May 29, 1984	Alvin Buchanan
Sunfish, redear	4 lb 13 oz	Marianna, FL	Mar 13, 1986	Joey Floyd
Tigerfish	97 lb	Zaire River, Kinshasa, Zaire	July 9, 1988	Raymond Houtmans
Tilapia	6 lb 6 oz	Clewiston, FL	June 24, 1989	Joseph Tucker
Trout, Apache	2 lb 10 oz	White Mt Apache Res, AZ	June 27, 1989	Mike Shannon
Trout, brook	14 lb 8 oz	Nipigon River, Ontario	July 1916	W. J. Cook
Trout, brown	35 lb 15 oz	Nahuel Huapi, Argentina	Dec 16, 1952	Eugenio Cavaglia
Trout, bull	32 lb	Lake Pend Oreille, ID	Oct 27, 1949	N. L. Higgins

Freshwater Fishing Records (*Cont.*)

Species	Weight	Where Caught	Date	Angler
Trout, cutthroat	41 lb	Pyramid Lake, NV	Dec 1925	J. Skimmerhorn
Trout, golden	11 lb	Cook's Lake, WY	Aug 5, 1948	Charles S. Reed
Trout, lake	65 lb	Great Bear Lake, Northwest Territories	Aug 8, 1970	Larry Daunis
Trout, rainbow	42 lb 2 oz	Bell Island, AK	June 22, 1970	David Robert White
Trout, tiger	20 lb 13 oz	Lake Michigan, WI	Aug 12, 1978	Pete Friedland
Walleye	25 lb	Old Hickory Lake, TN	Aug 1, 1960	Mabry Harper
Warmouth	2 lb 7 oz	Yellow River, Holt, FL	Oct 19, 1985	Tony D. Dempsey
Whitefish, lake	14 lb 6 oz	Meaford, Ontario	May 21, 1984	Dennis Laycock
Whitefish, mountain	5 lb 6 oz	Rioh River, Saskatchewan, Canada	June 15, 1988	John Bell
Whitefish, river	11 lb 2 oz	Nymoua, Sweden	Dec 9, 1984	Jorgen Larsson
Whitefish, round	6 lb	Putahow River, Manitoba	June 14, 1984	Allen Ristori
Zander	22 lb 2 oz	Trosa, Sweden	June 12, 1986	Harry Lee Tennison

Gymnastics

National Champions

Year	Men's Overall	Women's Overall	Rhythmic
1980	Peter Vidmar	Julianne McNamara	Sue Soffe
1981	Jim Hartung	Tracee Talavera	Sue Soffe
1982	Peter Vidmar	Tracee Talavera	Lydia Bree
1983	Mitch Gaylord	Dianne Durham	Michelle Berube
1984	Mitch Gaylord	Mary Lou Retton	Valerie Zimring
1985	Brian Babcock	Sabrina Mar	Marina Kunyavsky
1986	Tim Daggett	Jennifer Sey	Marina Kunyavsky
1987	Scott Johnson	Kristie Phillips	Marina Kunyavsky
1988	Dan Hayden	Phoebe Mills	Diane Simpson
1989	Tim Ryan	Brandy Johnson	Alexandra Feldman
1990	John Roethlisberger	Kim Zmeskal	Tracey Lepore
1991	Chris Waller	Kim Zmeskal	Jenifer Lovell

Lacrosse

United States Club Lacrosse Association Champions

1960	Mt Washington Club	1976	Mt Washington Club
1961	Baltimore Lacrosse Club	1977	Mt Washington Club
1962	Mt Washington Club	1978	Long Island Athletic Club
1963	University Club	1979	Maryland Lacrosse Club
1964	Mt Washington Club	1980	Long Island Athletic Club
1965	Mt Washington Club	1981	Long Island Athletic Club
1966	Mt Washington Club	1982	Maryland Lacrosse Club
1967	Mt Washington Club	1983	Maryland Lacrosse Club
1968	Long Island Athletic Club	1984	Maryland Lacrosse Club
1969	Long Island Athletic Club	1985	Long Island-Hofstra Lacrosse Club
1970	Long Island Athletic Club	1986	Long Island-Hofstra Lacrosse Club
1971	Long Island Athletic Club	1987	Long Island-Hofstra Lacrosse Club
1972	Carling	1988	Maryland Lacrosse Club
1973	Long Island Athletic Club	1989	Long Island-Hofstra Lacrosse Club
1974	Long Island Athletic Club	1990	Mt Washington Club
1975	Mt Washington Club	1991	Mt Washington Club

THEY SAID IT

Milton Berle, at a roast of Howard Cosell:
"Why are we honoring this man? Have we
run out of human beings?" (1984)

Motor Boat Racing

American Power Boat Association Gold Cup Champions

Year	Boat	Driver	Avg MPH
1904..........	Standard (June)	Carl Riotte	23.160
1904..........	Vingt-et-Un II (Sep)	W. Sharpe Kilmer	24.900
1905..........	Chip I	J. Wainwright	15.000
1906..........	Chip II	J. Wainwright	25.000
1907..........	Chip II	J. Wainwright	23.903
1908..........	Dixie II	E. J. Schroeder	29.938
1909..........	Dixie II	E. J. Schroeder	29.590
1910..........	Dixie III	F. K. Burnham	32.473
1911..........	MIT II	J. H. Hayden	37.000
1912..........	P.D.Q. II	A. G. Miles	39.462
1913..........	Ankle Deep	Cas Mankowski	42.779
1914..........	Baby Speed Demon II	Jim Blackton & Bob Edgren	48.458
1915..........	Miss Detroit	Johnny Milot & Jack Beebe	37.656
1916..........	Miss Minneapolis	Bernard Smith	48.860
1917..........	Miss Detroit II	Gar Wood	54.410
1918..........	Miss Detroit II	Gar Wood	51.619
1919..........	Miss Detroit III	Gar Wood	42.748
1920..........	Miss America I	Gar Wood	62.022
1921..........	Miss America I	Gar Wood	52.825
1922..........	Packard Chriscraft	J. G. Vincent	40.253
1923..........	Packard Chriscraft	Caleb Bragg	43.867
1924..........	Baby Bootlegger	Caleb Bragg	45.302
1925..........	Baby Bootlegger	Caleb Bragg	47.240
1926..........	Greenwich Folly	George Townsend	47.984
1927..........	Greenwich Folly	George Townsend	47.662
1928..........	No race		
1929..........	Imp	Richard Hoyt	48.662
1930..........	Hotsy Totsy	Vic Kliesrath	52.673
1931..........	Hotsy Totsy	Vic Kliesrath	53.602
1932..........	Delphine IV	Bill Horn	57.775
1933..........	El Lagarto	George Reis	56.260
1934..........	El Lagarto	George Reis	55.000
1935..........	El Lagarto	George Reis	55.056
1936..........	Impshi	Kaye Don	45.735
1937..........	Notre Dame	Clell Perry	63.675
1938..........	Alagi	Theo Rossi	64.340
1939..........	My Sin	Z. G. Simmons, Jr	66.133
1940..........	Hotsy Totsy III	Sidney Allen	48.295
1941..........	My Sin	Z. G. Simmons, Jr	52.509
1942-45......	No race		
1946..........	Tempo VI	Guy Lombardo	68.132
1947..........	Miss Peps V	Danny Foster	57.000
1948..........	Miss Great Lakes	Danny Foster	46.845
1949..........	My Sweetie	Bill Cantrell	73.612
1950..........	Slo-Mo-Shun IV	Ted Jones	78.216
1951..........	Slo-Mo-Shun V	Lou Fageol	90.871
1952..........	Slo-Mo-Shun IV	Stan Dollar	79.923
1953..........	Slo-Mo-Shun IV	Joe Taggart & Lou Fageol	99.108
1954..........	Slo-Mo-Shun IV	Joe Taggart & Lou Fageol	92.613
1955..........	Gale V	Lee Schoenith	99.552
1956..........	Miss Thriftaway	Bill Muncey	96.552
1957..........	Miss Thriftaway	Bill Muncey	101.787
1958..........	Hawaii Kai III	Jack Regas	103.000
1959..........	Maverick	Bill Stead	104.481
1960..........	No race		
1961..........	Miss Century 21	Bill Muncey	99.678
1962..........	Miss Century 21	Bill Muncey	100.710
1963..........	Miss Bardahl	Ron Musson	105.124
1964..........	Miss Bardahl	Ron Musson	103.433
1965..........	Miss Bardahl	Ron Musson	103.132
1966..........	Tahoe Miss	Mira Slovak	93.019
1967..........	Miss Bardahl	Bill Shumacher	101.484
1968..........	Miss Bardahl	Bill Shumacher	108.173
1969..........	Miss Budweiser	Bill Sterett	98.504

Motor Boat Racing (*Cont.*)

American Power Boat Association Gold Cup Champions (*Cont.*)

Year	Boat	Driver	Avg MPH
1970	Miss Budweiser	Dean Chenoweth	99.562
1971	Miss Madison	Jim McCormick	98.043
1972	Atlas Van Lines	Bill Muncey	104.277
1973	Miss Budweiser	Dean Chenoweth	99.043
1974	Pay 'n Pak	George Henley	104.428
1975	Pay 'n Pak	George Henley	108.921
1976	Miss U.S.	Tom D'Eath	100.412
1977	Atlas Van Lines	Bill Muncey	111.822
1978	Atlas Van Lines	Bill Muncey	111.412
1979	Atlas Van Lines	Bill Muncey	100.765
1980	Miss Budweiser	Dean Chenoweth	106.932
1981	Miss Budweiser	Dean Chenoweth	116.932
1982	Atlas Van Lines	Chip Hanauer	120.050
1983	Atlas Van Lines	Chip Hanauer	118.507
1984	Atlas Van Lines	Chip Hanauer	130.175
1985	Miller American	Chip Hanauer	120.643
1986	Miller American	Chip Hanauer	116.523
1987	Miller American	Chip Hanauer	127.620
1988	Miss Circus Circus	Chip Hanauer & Jim Prevost	123.756
1989	Miss Budweiser	Tom D'Eath	131.209
1990	Miss Budweiser	Tom D'Eath	143.176
1991	Winston Eagle	Mark Tate	137.771

Polo

United States Open Polo Champions

1904	Wanderers	
1905-09	Not played for	
1910	Ranelagh	
1911	Not played for	
1912	Cooperstown	
1913	Cooperstown	
1914	Meadow Brook Magpies	
1915	Not played for	
1916	Meadow Brook	
1917-18	Not played for	
1919	Meadow Brook	
1920	Meadow Brook	
1921	Great Neck	
1922	Argentine	
1923	Meadow Brook	
1924	Midwick	
1925	Orange County	
1926	Hurricanes	
1927	Sands Point	
1928	Meadow Brook	
1929	Hurricanes	
1930	Hurricanes	
1931	Santa Paula	
1932	Templeton	
1933	Aurora	
1934	Templeton	
1935	Greentree	
1936	Greentree	
1937	Old Westbury	
1938	Old Westbury	
1939	Bostwick Field	
1940	Aknusti	
1941	Gulf Stream	
1942-45	Not played for	
1946	Mexico	
1947	Old Westbury	
1948	Hurricanes	
1949	Hurricanes	
1950	Bostwick	
1951	Milwaukee	
1952	Beverly Hills	
1953	Meadow Brook	
1954	C.C.C.—Meadow Brook	
1955	C.C.C.	
1956	Brandywine	
1957	Detroit	
1958	Dallas	
1959	Circle F	
1960	Oak Brook C.C.C.	
1961	Milwaukee	
1962	Santa Barbara	
1963	Tulsa	
1964	Concar Oak Brook	
1965	Oak Brook—Santa Barbara	
1966	Tulsa	
1967	Bunntyco—Oak Brook	
1968	Midland	
1969	Tulsa Greenhill	
1970	Tulsa Greenhill	
1971	Oak Brook	
1972	Milwaukee	
1973	Oak Brook	
1974	Milwaukee	
1975	Milwaukee	
1976	Willow Bend	
1977	Retama	
1978	Abercrombie & Kent	
1979	Retama	
1980	Southern Hills	
1981	Rolex A & K	
1982	Retama	
1983	Ft. Lauderdale	
1984	Retama	
1985	Carter Ranch	
1986	Retama II	
1987	Aloha	
1988	Les Diables Bleus	
1989	Les Diables Bleus	
1990	Les Diables Bleus	
1991	Grant's Farm Manor	

Top-Ranked Players

The United States Polo Association ranks its registered players from minus 2 to plus 10 goals, with 10 Goal players being the game's best. At present, the USPA recognizes five 10-Goal and eight 9-Goal players:

10-GOAL

Benjamin Araya (Palm Beach)
Carlos Gracida (San Antonio)
Guillermo Gracida Jr (Palm Beach)
Gonzalo Heguy (Myopia)
Ernesto Trotz (Palm Beach)

9-GOAL

Mariano Aguerre (Greenwich)
Michael Azzaro (San Antonio)
Hector J. Crotto (Palm Beach)
Horacio Heguy Jr (Palm Beach)
Christian La Prida (Palm Beach)
Juan Merlos (Palm Beach)
Owen R. Rinehart (Palm Beach)
Martin Zubia (Palm Beach)

Rodeo

All-Around Champions

1929 ...... Earl Thode	1951 ...... Casey Tibbs	1972 ...... Phil Lyne
1930 ...... Clay Carr	1952 ...... Harry Tompkins	1973 ...... Larry Mahan
1931 ...... John Schneider	1953 ...... Bill Linderman	1974 ...... Tom Ferguson
1932 ...... Donald Nesbit	1954 ...... Buck Rutherford	1975 ...... Tom Ferguson
1933 ...... Clay Carr	1955 ...... Casey Tibbs	1976 ...... Tom Ferguson
1934 ...... Leonard Ward	1956 ...... Jim Shoulders	1977 ...... Tom Ferguson
1935 ...... Everett Bowman	1957 ...... Jim Shoulders	1978 ...... Tom Ferguson
1936 ...... John Bowman	1958 ...... Jim Shoulders	1979 ...... Tom Ferguson
1937 ...... Everett Bowman	1959 ...... Jim Shoulders	1980 ...... Paul Tierney
1938 ...... Burel Mulkey	1960 ...... Harry Tompkins	1981 ...... Jimmie Cooper
1939 ...... Paul Carney	1961 ...... Benny Reynolds	1982 ...... Chris Lybbert
1940 ...... Fritz Truan	1962 ...... Tom Nesmith	1983 ...... Roy Cooper
1941 ...... Homer Pettigrew	1963 ...... Dean Oliver	1984 ...... Dee Picket
1942 ...... Gerald Roberts	1964 ...... Dean Oliver	1985 ...... Lewis Feild
1943 ...... Louis Brooks	1965 ...... Dean Oliver	1986 ...... Lewis Feild
1944 ...... Louis Brooks	1966 ...... Larry Mahan	1987 ...... Lewis Feild
1945-46 ...... No championship	1967 ...... Larry Mahan	1988 ...... Dave Appleton
1947 ...... Todd Whatley	1968 ...... Larry Mahan	1989 ...... Ty Murray
1948 ...... Gerald Roberts	1969 ...... Larry Mahan	1990 ...... Ty Murray
1949 ...... Jim Shoulders	1970 ...... Larry Mahan	
1950 ...... Bill Linderman	1971 ...... Phil Lyne	

Rowing

National Collegiate Rowing Champions

MEN		WOMEN	
1982 ...... Yale		1979 ...... Yale	
1983 ...... Harvard		1980 ...... California	
1984 ...... Washington		1981 ...... Washington	
1985 ...... Harvard		1982 ...... Washington	
1986 ...... Wisconsin		1983 ...... Washington	
1987 ...... Harvard		1984 ...... Washington	
1988 ...... Harvard		1985 ...... Washington	
1989 ...... Harvard		1986 ...... Wisconsin	
1990 ...... Wisconsin		1987 ...... Washington	
1991 ...... Pennsylvania		1988 ...... Washington	
		1989 ...... Cornell	
		1990 ...... Princeton	
		1991 ...... Boston University	

Sailing

America's Cup Champions

SCHOONERS AND J-CLASS BOATS

Year	Winner	Skipper	Series	Loser	Skipper
1851	America	Richard Brown			
1870	Magic	Andrew Comstock	1-0	Cambria, Great Britain	J. Tannock
1871	Columbia (2-1)	Nelson Comstock	4-1	Livonia, Great Britain	J. R. Woods
	Sappho (2-0)	Sam Greenwood			
1876	Madeleine	Josephus Williams	2-0	Countess of Dufferin, Canada	J. E. Ellsworth
1881	Mischief	Nathanael Clock	2-0	Atalanta, Canada	Alexander Cuthbert
1885	Puritan	Aubrey Crocker	2-0	Genesta, Great Britain	John Carter
1886	Mayflower	Martin Stone	2-0	Galatea, Great Britain	Dan Bradford
1887	Volunteer	Henry Haff	2-0	Thistle, Great Britain	John Barr
1893	Vigilant	William Hansen	3-0	Valkyrie II, Great Britain	William Granfield
1895	Defender	Henry Haff	3-0	Valkyrie III, Great Britain	William Granfield
1899	Columbia	Charles Barr	3-0	Shamrock I, Great Britain	Archie Hogarth
1901	Columbia	Charles Barr	3-0	Shamrock II, Great Britain	E. A. Sycamore
1903	Reliance	Charles Barr	3-0	Shamrock III, Great Britain	Bob Wringe
1920	Resolute	Charles F. Adams	3-2	Shamrock IV, Great Britain	William Burton
1930	Enterprise	Harold Vanderbilt	4-0	Shamrock V, Great Britain	Ned Heard
1934	Rainbow	Harold Vanderbilt	4-2	Endeavour, Great Britain	T. O. M. Sopwith
1937	Ranger	Harold Vanderbilt	4-0	Endeavour II, Great Britain	T. O. M. Sopwith

12-METER BOATS

Year	Winner	Skipper	Series	Loser	Skipper
1958	Columbia	Briggs Cunningham	4-0	Sceptre, Great Britain	Graham Mann
1962	Weatherly	Bus Mosbacher	4-1	Gretel, Australia	Jock Sturrock
1964	Constellation	Bob Bavier & Eric Ridder	4-0	Sovereign, Australia	Peter Scott
1967	Intrepid	Bus Mosbacher	4-0	Dame Pattie, Australia	Jock Sturrock
1970	Intrepid	Bill Ficker	4-1	Gretel II, Australia	Jim Hardy
1974	Courageous	Ted Hood	4-0	Southern Cross, Australia	John Cuneo
1977	Courageous	Ted Turner	4-0	Australia	Noel Robins
1980	Freedom	Dennis Conner	4-1	Australia	Jim Hardy
1983	Australia II	John Bertrand	4-3	Liberty, United States	Dennis Conner
1987	Stars & Stripes	Dennis Conner	4-0	Kookaburra III, Australia	Iain Murray

60-FOOT CATAMARAN VS 133-FOOT MONOHULL

Year	Winner	Skipper	Series	Loser	Skipper
1988	Stars & Stripes	Dennis Conner	2-0	New Zealand	David Barnes

Note: Winning entry was from the United States every year but 1983, when an Australian vessel won.

Softball

Men

MAJOR FAST PITCH

1933	J. L. Gill Boosters, Chicago	1950	Clearwater (FL) Bombers
1934	Ke-Nash-A, Kenosha, WI	1951	Dow Chemical, Midland, MI
1935	Crimson Coaches, Toledo, OH	1952	Briggs Beautyware, Detroit
1936	Kodak Park, Rochester, NY	1953	Briggs Beautyware, Detroit
1937	Briggs Body Team, Detroit	1954	Clearwater (FL) Bombers
1938	The Pohlers, Cincinnati	1955	Raybestos Cardinals, Stratford, CT
1939	Carr's Boosters, Covington, KY	1956	Clearwater (FL) Bombers
1940	Kodak Park, Rochester, NY	1957	Clearwater (FL) Bombers
1941	Bendix Brakes, South Bend, IN	1958	Raybestos Cardinals, Stratford, CT
1942	Deep Rock Oilers, Tulsa	1959	Sealmasters, Aurora, IL
1943	Hammer Air Field, Fresno	1960	Clearwater (FL) Bombers
1944	Hammer Air Field, Fresno	1961	Sealmasters, Aurora, IL
1945	Zollner Pistons, Fort Wayne, IN	1962	Clearwater (FL) Bombers
1946	Zollner Pistons, Fort Wayne, IN	1963	Clearwater (FL) Bombers
1947	Zollner Pistons, Fort Wayne, IN	1964	Burch Tool, Detroit
1948	Briggs Beautyware, Detroit	1965	Sealmasters, Aurora, IL
1949	Tip Top Tailors, Toronto	1966	Clearwater (FL) Bombers

Men (*Cont.*)

MAJOR FAST PITCH (*Cont.*)

1967 ....Sealmasters, Aurora, IL	1980 ....Peterbilt Western, Seattle
1968 ....Clearwater (FL) Bombers	1981 ....Archer Daniels Midland, Decatur, IL
1969 ....Raybestos Cardinals, Stratford, CT	1982 ....Peterbilt Western, Seattle
1970 ....Raybestos Cardinals, Stratford, CT	1983 ....Franklin Cardinals, Stratford, CT
1971 ....Welty Way, Cedar Rapids, IA	1984 ....California Kings, Merced, CA
1972 ....Raybestos Cardinals, Stratford, CT	1985 ....Pay'n Pak, Seattle
1973 ....Clearwater (FL) Bombers	1986 ....Pay'n Pak, Seattle
1974 ....Gianella Bros, Santa Rosa, CA	1987 ....Pay'n Pak, Seattle
1975 ....Rising Sun Hotel, Reading, PA	1988 ....TransAire, Elkhart, IN
1976 ....Raybestos Cardinals, Stratford, CT	1989 ....Penn Corp, Sioux City, IA
1977 ....Billard Barbell, Reading, PA	1990 ....Penn Corp, Sioux City, IA
1978 ....Billard Barbell, Reading, PA	1991 ....Guanella Brothers, Rohnert Park, CA
1979 ....McArdle Pontiac/Cadillac, Midland, MI	

SUPER SLOW PITCH

1981 ....Howard's/Western Steer, Denver, NC	1987 ....Steele's Sports, Grafton, OH
1982 ....Jerry's Catering, Miami	1988 ....Starpath, Monticello, KY
1983 ....Howard's/Western Steer, Denver, NC	1989 ....Ritch's Salvage, Harrisburg, NC
1984 ....Howard's/Western Steer, Denver, NC	1990 ....Steele's Silver Bullets, Grafton, OH
1985 ....Steele's Sports, Grafton, OH	1991 ....Sunbelt/Worth, Centerville, GA
1986 ....Steele's Sports, Grafton, OH	

MAJOR SLOW PITCH

1953 ....Shields Construction, Newport, KY	1973 ....Howard's Furniture, Denver, NC
1954 ....Waldneck's Tavern, Cincinnati	1974 ....Howard's Furniture, Denver, NC
1955 ....Lang Pet Shop, Covington, KY	1975 ....Pyramid Cafe, Lakewood, OH
1956 ....Gatliff Auto Sales, Newport, KY	1976 ....Warren Motors, Jacksonville, FL
1957 ....Gatliff Auto Sales, Newport, KY	1977 ....Nelson Painting, Oklahoma City
1958 ....East Side Sports, Detroit	1978 ....Campbell Carpets, Concord, CA
1959 ....Yorkshire Restaurant, Newport, KY	1979 ....Nelco Mfg Co, Oklahoma City
1960 ....Hamilton Tailoring, Cincinnati	1980 ....Campbell Carpets, Concord, CA
1961 ....Hamilton Tailoring, Cincinnati	1981 ....Elite Coating, Gordon, CA
1962 ....Skip Hogan A.C., Pittsburgh	1982 ....Triangle Sports, Minneapolis
1963 ....Gatliff Auto Sales, Newport, KY	1983 ....No. 1 Electric & Heating, Gastonia, NC
1964 ....Skip Hogan A.C., Pittsburgh	1984 ....Lilly Air Systems, Chicago
1965 ....Skip Hogan A.C., Pittsburgh	1985 ....Blanton's, Fayetteville, NC
1966 ....Michael's Lounge, Detroit	1986 ....Non-Ferrous Metals, Cleveland
1967 ....Jim's Sport Shop, Pittsburgh	1987 ....Starpath, Monticello, KY
1968 ....County Sports, Levittown, NY	1988 ....Bell Corp/FAF, Tampa, FL
1969 ....Copper Hearth, Milwaukee	1989 ....Ritch's Salvage, Harrisburg, NC
1970 ....Little Caesar's, Southgate, MI	1990 ....New Construction, Shelbyville, IN
1971 ....Pile Drivers, Virginia Beach, VA	1991 ....Riverside Paving, Louisville, KY
1972 ....Jiffy Club, Louisville, KY	

Women

MAJOR FAST PITCH

1933 ....Great Northerns, Chicago	1949 ....Arizona Ramblers, Phoenix
1934 ....Hart Motors, Chicago	1950 ....Orange (CA) Lionettes
1935 ....Bloomer Girls, Cleveland	1951 ....Orange (CA) Lionettes
1936 ....Nat'l Screw & Mfg, Cleveland	1952 ....Orange (CA) Lionettes
1937 ....Nat'l Screw & Mfg, Cleveland	1953 ....Betsy Ross Rockets, Fresno
1938 ....J. J. Krieg's, Alameda, CA	1954 ....Leach Motor Rockets, Fresno
1939 ....J. J. Krieg's, Alameda, CA	1955 ....Orange (CA) Lionettes
1940 ....Arizona Ramblers, Phoenix	1956 ....Orange (CA) Lionettes
1941 ....Higgins Midgets, Tulsa	1957 ....Hacienda Rockets, Fresno
1942 ....Jax Maids, New Orleans	1958 ....Raybestos Brakettes, Stratford, CT
1943 ....Jax Maids, New Orleans	1959 ....Raybestos Brakettes, Stratford, CT
1944 ....Lind & Pomeroy, Portland, OR	1960 ....Raybestos Brakettes, Stratford, CT
1945 ....Jax Maids, New Orleans	1961 ....Gold Sox, Whittier, CA
1946 ....Jax Maids, New Orleans	1962 ....Orange (CA) Lionettes
1947 ....Jax Maids, New Orleans	1963 ....Raybestos Brakettes, Stratford, CT
1948 ....Arizona Ramblers, Phoenix	1964 ....Erv Lind Florists, Portland, OR

Women (*Cont.*)

MAJOR FAST PITCH (*Cont.*)

1965 .... Orange (CA) Lionettes	1979 .... Sun City (AZ) Saints
1966 .... Raybestos Brakettes, Stratford, CT	1980 .... Raybestos Brakettes, Stratford, CT
1967 .... Raybestos Brakettes, Stratford, CT	1981 .... Orlando (FL) Rebels
1968 .... Raybestos Brakettes, Stratford, CT	1982 .... Raybestos Brakettes, Stratford, CT
1969 .... Orange (CA) Lionettes	1983 .... Raybestos Brakettes, Stratford, CT
1970 .... Orange (CA) Lionettes	1984 .... Los Angeles Diamonds
1971 .... Raybestos Brakettes, Stratford, CT	1985 .... Hi-Ho Brakettes, Stratford, CT
1972 .... Raybestos Brakettes, Stratford, CT	1986 .... Southern California Invasion,
1973 .... Raybestos Brakettes, Stratford, CT	Los Angeles
1974 .... Raybestos Brakettes, Stratford, CT	1987 .... Orange County Majestics, Anaheim, CA
1975 .... Raybestos Brakettes, Stratford, CT	1988 .... Hi-Ho Brakettes, Stratford, CT
1976 .... Raybestos Brakettes, Stratford, CT	1989 .... Whittier (CA) Raiders
1977 .... Raybestos Brakettes, Stratford, CT	1990 .... Raybestos Brakettes, Stratford, CT
1978 .... Raybestos Brakettes, Stratford, CT	1991 .... Raybestos Brakettes, Stratford, CT

MAJOR SLOW PITCH

1959 .... Pearl Laundry, Richmond, VA	1976 .... Sorrento's Pizza, Cincinnati
1960 .... Carolina Rockets, High Pt, NC	1977 .... Fox Valley Lassies, St Charles, IL
1961 .... Dairy Cottage, Covington, KY	1978 .... Bob Hoffman's Dots, Miami
1962 .... Dana Gardens, Cincinnati	1979 .... Bob Hoffman's Dots, Miami
1963 .... Dana Gardens, Cincinnati	1980 .... Howard's Rubi-Otts, Graham, NC
1964 .... Dana Gardens, Cincinnati	1981 .... Tifton (GA) Tomboys
1965 .... Art's Acres, Omaha	1982 .... Richmond (VA) Stompers
1966 .... Dana Gardens, Cincinnati	1983 .... Spooks, Anoka, MN
1967 .... Ridge Maintenance, Cleveland	1984 .... Spooks, Anoka, MN
1968 .... Escue Pontiac, Cincinnati	1985 .... Key Ford Mustangs, Pensacola, FL
1969 .... Converse Dots, Hialeah, FL	1986 .... Sur-Way Tomboys, Tifton, GA
1970 .... Rutenschruder Floral, Cincinnati	1987 .... Key Ford Mustangs, Pensacola, FL
1971 .... Gators, Ft Lauderdale, FL	1988 .... Spooks, Anoka, MN
1972 .... Riverside Ford, Cincinnati	1989 .... Canaan's Illusions, Houston
1973 .... Sweeney Chevrolet, Cincinnati	1990 .... Spooks, Anoka, MN
1974 .... Marks Brothers Dots, Miami	1991 .... Kannan's Illusions, San Antonio, TX
1975 .... Marks Brothers Dots, Miami	

Squash

National Men's Champions

Year	Champion, Hometown	Year	Champion, Hometown
1907 .... John A. Miskey, Philadelphia		1932 .... Beckman H. Pool, New York	
1908 .... John A. Miskey, Philadelphia		1933 .... Beckman H. Pool, New York	
1909 .... William L. Freeland, Philadelphia		1934 .... Neil J. Sullivan II, Philadelphia	
1910 .... John A. Miskey, Philadelphia		1935 .... Donald Strachan, Philadelphia	
1911 .... Francis S. White, Philadelphia		1936 .... Germain G. Glidden, New York	
1912 .... Constantine Hutchins, Boston		1937 .... Germain G. Glidden, New York	
1913 .... Morton L. Newhall, Philadelphia		1938 .... Germain G. Glidden, New York	
1914 .... Constantine Hutchins, Boston		1939 .... Donald Strachan, Philadelphia	
1915 .... Stanley W. Pearson, Philadelphia		1940 .... A. Willing Patterson, Philadelphia	
1916 .... Stanley W. Pearson, Philadelphia		1941 .... Charles M. P. Britton, Philadelphia	
1917 .... Stanley W. Pearson, Philadelphia		1942 .... Charles M. P. Britton, Philadelphia	
1918-19 .... No tournament		1943-45 .... No tournament	
1920 .... Charles C. Peabody, Boston		1946 .... Charles M. P. Britton, Philadelphia	
1921 .... Stanley W. Pearson, Philadelphia		1947 .... Charles M. P. Britton, Philadelphia	
1922 .... Stanley W. Pearson, Philadelphia		1948 .... Stanley W. Pearson Jr., Philadelphia	
1923 .... Stanley W. Pearson, Philadelphia		1949 .... H. Hunter Lott Jr., Philadelphia	
1924 .... Gerald Roberts, England		1950 .... Edward J. Hahn, Detroit	
1925 .... W. Palmer Dixon, New York		1951 .... Edward J. Hahn, Detroit	
1926 .... W. Palmer Dixon, New York		1952 .... Harry B. Conlon, Buffalo	
1927 .... Myles Baker, Boston		1953 .... Ernest Howard, Toronto	
1928 .... Herbert N. Rawlins Jr., New York		1954 .... G. Diehl Mateer Jr., Philadelphia	
1929 .... J. Lawrence Pool New York		1955 .... Henri R. Salaun, Hartford, CT	
1930 .... Herbert N. Rawlins Jr., New York		1956 .... G. Diehl Mateer Jr., Philadelphia	
1931 .... J. Lawrence Pool, New York		1957 .... Henri R. Salaun, Boston	

National Men's Champions (*Cont.*)

Year	Champion, Hometown	Year	Champion, Hometown
1958	Henri R. Salaun, Boston	1975	Victor Niederhoffer, New York
1959	Benjamin H. Heckscher, Philadelphia	1976	Peter Briggs, New York
1960	G. Diehl Mateer Jr., Philadelphia	1977	Thomas E. Page, Philadelphia
1961	Henri R. Salaun, Hartford, CT	1978	Michael Desaulniers, Montreal
1962	Samuel P. Howe III, Philadelphia	1979	Mario Sanchez, Mexico
1963	Benjamin H. Heckscher, Philadelphia	1980	Michael Desaulniers, Montreal
1964	Ralph E. Howe, New York	1981	Mark Alger, Tacoma, WA
1965	Stephen T. Vehslage, New York	1982	John Nimick, Narberth, PA
1966	Victor Niederhoffer, Chicago	1983	Kenton Jernigan, Newport, RI
1967	Samuel P. Howe III, Philadelphia	1984	Kenton Jernigan, Newport, RI
1968	Colin Adair, Montreal	1985	Kenton Jernigan, Newport, RI
1969	Anil Nayar, Boston	1986	Hugh LaBossier, Seattle
1970	Anil Nayar, Boston	1987	Frank J. Stanley IV, Princeton, NJ
1971	Colin Adair, Montreal	1988	Scott Dulmage, Toronto
1972	Victor Niederhoffer, New York	1989	Rodolfo Rodriquez, Mexico
1973	Victor Niederhoffer, New York	1990	Hector Barragan, Mexico
1974	Victor Niederhoffer, New York	1991	Hector Barragan, Mexico

National Women's Champions

Year	Champion, Hometown	Year	Champion, Hometown
1928	Eleanora Sears, Boston	1962	Margaret Varner, Wilmington, DE
1929	Margaret Howe, Boston	1963	Margaret Varner, Wilmington, DE
1930	Hazel Wightman, Boston	1964	Ann Wetzel, Philadelphia
1931	Ruth Banks, Philadelphia	1965	Joyce Davenport, Philadelphia
1932	Margaret Howe, Boston	1966	Betty Meade, Philadelphia
1933	Susan Noel, England	1967	Betty Meade, Philadelphia
1934	Margaret Howe, Boston	1968	Betty Meade, Philadelphia
1935	Margot Lumb, England	1969	Joyce Davenport, Philadelphia
1936	Anne Page, Philadelphia	1970	Nina Moyer, Princeton, NJ
1937	Anne Page, Philadelphia	1971	Carol Thesieres, Philadelphia
1938	Cecile Bowes, Philadelphia	1972	Nina Moyer, Princeton, NJ
1939	Anne Page, Philadelphia	1973	Gretchen Spruance, Wilmington, DE
1940	Cecile Bowes, Philadelphia	1974	Gretchen Spruance, Wilmington, DE
1941	Cecile Bowes, Philadelphia	1975	Ginny Akabane, Rochester, NY
1942-46	No tournament	1976	Gretchen Spruance, Wilmington, DE
1947	Anne Page Homer, Philadelphia	1977	Gretchen Spruance, Wilmington, DE
1948	Cecile Bowes, Philadelphia	1978	Gretchen Spruance, Wilmington, DE
1949	Janet Morgan, England	1979	Heather McKay, Toronto
1950	Betty Howe, New Haven, CT	1980	Barbara Maltby, Philadelphia
1951	Jane Austin, Philadelphia	1981	Barbara Maltby, Philadelphia
1952	Margaret Howe, Boston	1982	Alicia McConnell, New York
1953	Margaret Howe, Boston	1983	Alicia McConnell, New York
1954	Lois Dilks, Philadelphia	1984	Alicia McConnell, New York
1955	Janet Morgan, England	1985	Alicia McConnell, New York
1956	Betty Howe Constable, Princeton, NJ	1986	Alicia McConnell, Bala Cynwyd, PA
1957	Betty Howe Constable, Princeton, NJ	1987	Alicia McConnell, New York
1958	Betty Howe Constable, Princeton, NJ	1988	Alicia McConnell, New York
1959	Betty Howe Constable, Princeton, NJ	1989	Demer Holleran, Hanover, NH
1960	Margaret Varner, Wilmington, DE	1990	Demer Holleran, Hanover, NH
1961	Margaret Varner, Wilmington, DE	1991	Demer Holleran, Hanover, NH

Triathlon

Ironman Championship

MEN

Date	Winner	Time	Site
1978	Gordon Haller	11:46	Waikiki Beach
1979	Tom Warren	11:15:56	Waikiki Beach
1980	Dave Scott	9:24:33	Ala Moana Park
1981	John Howard	9:38:29	Kailua-Kona
1982	Scott Tinley	9:19:41	Kailua-Kona

Ironman Championship (*Cont.*)

Date	Winner	Time	Site
1982	Dave Scott	9:08:23	Kailua-Kona
1983	Dave Scott	9:05:57	Kailua-Kona
1984	Dave Scott	8:54:20	Kailua-Kona
1985	Scott Tinley	8:50:54	Kailua-Kona
1986	Dave Scott	8:28:37	Kailua-Kona
1987	Dave Scott	8:34:13	Kailua-Kona
1988	Scott Molina	8:31:00	Kailua-Kona
1989	Mark Allen	8:09:15	Kailua-Kona
1990	Mark Allen	8:28:17	Kailua-Kona

WOMEN

Date	Winner	Time	Site
1978	No finishers		
1979	Lyn Lemaire	12:55	Waikiki Beach
1980	Robin Beck	11:21:24	Ala Moana Park
1981	Linda Sweeney	12:00:32	Kailua-Kona
1982	Kathleen McCartney	11:09:40	Kailua-Kona
1982	Julie Leach	10:54:08	Kailua-Kona
1983	Sylviane Puntous	10:43:36	Kailua-Kona
1984	Sylviane Puntous	10:25:13	Kailua-Kona
1985	Joanne Ernst	10:25:22	Kailua-Kona
1986	Paula Newby-Fraser	9:49:14	Kailua-Kona
1987	Erin Baker	9:35:25	Kailua-Kona
1988	Paula Newby-Fraser	9:01:01	Kailua-Kona
1989	Paula Newby-Fraser	9:00:56	Kailua-Kona
1990	Erin Baker	9:13:42	Kailua-Kona

Note: The Ironman Championship was contested twice in 1982.

Volleyball

U.S. Men's Open Champions—Gold Division

1928	Germantown, PA YMCA	1961	Hollywood, CA YMCA
1929	Hyde Park YMCA, IL	1962	Hollywood, CA YMCA
1930	Hyde Park YMCA, IL	1963	Hollywood, CA YMCA
1931	San Antonio, TX YMCA	1964	Hollywood, CA YMCA Stars
1932	San Antonio, TX YMCA	1965	Westside JCC, CA
1933	Houston, TX YMCA	1966	Sand & Sea Club, CA
1934	Houston, TX YMCA	1967	Fresno, CA VBC
1935	Houston, TX YMCA	1968	Westside JCC, L.A., CA
1936	Houston, TX YMCA	1969	Los Angeles, CA YMCA
1937	Duncan YMCA, IL	1970	Chart House, San Diego
1938	Houston, TX YMCA	1971	Santa Monica, CA YMCA
1939	Houston, TX YMCA	1972	Chart House, San Diego
1940	Los Angeles AC, CA	1973	Chuck's Steak, L.A., CA
1941	North Ave. YMCA, IL	1974	Un of CA Santa Barbara
1942	North Ave. YMCA, IL	1975	Chart House, San Diego
1943-44	No Championships	1976	Maliabu, L.A., CA
1945	North Ave. YMCA, IL	1977	Chuck's, Santa Barbara
1946	Pasadena, CA YMCA	1978	Chuck's, Los Angeles
1947	North Ave. YMCA, IL	1979	Nautilus, Long Beach
1948	Hollywood, CA YMCA	1980	Olympic Club, San Francisco
1949	Downtown YMCA, CA	1981	Nautilus, Long Beach
1950	Long Beach, CA YMCA	1982	Chuck's, Los Angeles
1951	Hollywood, CA YMCA	1983	Nautilus Pacifica, CA
1952	Hollywood, CA YMCA	1984	Nautilus Pacifica, CA
1953	Hollywood, CA YMCA	1985	Molten/SSI Torrance, CA
1954	Stockton, CA YMCA	1986	Molten, Torrance, CA
1955	Stockton, CA YMCA	1987	Molten, Torrance, CA
1956	Hollywood, CA YMCA Stars	1988	Molten, Torrance, CA
1957	Hollywood, CA YMCA Stars	1989	Not held
1958	Hollywood, CA YMCA Stars	1990	Nike, Carson, CA
1959	Hollywood, CA YMCA Stars	1991	Offshore, Woodland Hills, CA
1960	Westside JCC, CA		

Volleyball (*Cont.*)

U.S. Women's Open Champions—Gold Division

1949 ....Eagles, Houston TX	1971 ....Renegades, Los Angeles, CA
1950 ....Voit #1, Santa Monica, CA	1972 ....E Pluribus Unum, Houston
1951 ....Eagles, Houston, TX	1973 ....E Pluribus Unum, Houston
1952 ....Voit #1, Santa Monica, CA	1974 ....Renegades, Los Angeles, CA
1953 ....Voit #1, Los Angeles, CA	1975 ....Adidas, Norwalk, CA
1954 ....Houstonettes, Houston, TX	1976 ....Pasadena, TX
1955 ....Mariners, Santa Monica, CA	1977 ....Spoilers, Hermosa, CA
1956 ....Mariners, Santa Monica, CA	1978 ....Nick's, Los Angeles, CA
1957 ....Mariners, Santa Monica, CA	1979 ....Mavericks, Los Angeles, CA
1958 ....Mariners, Santa Monica, CA	1980 ....NAVA, Fountain Valley, CA
1959 ....Mariners, Santa Monica, CA	1981 ....Utah State, Logan, UT
1960 ....Mariners, Santa Monica, CA	1982 ....Monarchs, Hilo, HI
1961 ....Breakers, Long Beach, CA	1983 ....Syntex, Stockton, CA
1962 ....Shamrocks, Long Beach, CA	1984 ....Chrysler, Palo Alto, CA
1963 ....Shamrocks, Long Beach, CA	1985 ....Merrill Lynch, Arizona
1964 ....Shamrocks, Long Beach, CA	1986 ....Merrill Lynch, Arizona
1965 ....Shamrocks, Long Beach, CA	1987 ....Chrysler, Pleasanton, CA
1966 ....Renegades, Los Angeles, CA	1988 ....Chrysler, Hayward, CA
1967 ....Shamrocks, Long Beach, CA	1989 ....Plymouth, Hayward, CA
1968 ....Shamrocks, Long Beach, CA	1990 ....Plymouth, Hayward, CA
1969 ....Shamrocks, Long Beach, CA	1991 ....Fitness, Champaign, IL
1970 ....Shamrocks, Long Beach, CA	

Wrestling

United States National Champions

FREESTYLE		1983	GRECO-ROMAN	
105.5	Rich Salamone		105.5	T. J. Jones
114.5	Joe Gonzales		114.5	Mark Fuller
125.5	Joe Corso		125.5	Rob Hermann
136.5	Rich Dellagatta*		136.5	Dan Mello
149.5	Bill Hugent		149.5	Jim Martinez
163	Lee Kemp		163	James Andre
180.5	Chris Campbell		180.5	Steve Goss
198	Pete Bush		198	Steve Fraser*
220	Greg Gibson		220	Dennis Koslowski
Hvy	Bruce Baumgartner		Hvy	No champion
Team	Sunkist Kids		Team	Minnesota Wrestling Club

1984

105.5	Rich Salamone		105.5	T. J. Jones
114.5	Charlie Heard		114.5	Mark Fuller
125.5	Joe Corso		125.5	Frank Famiano
136.5	Rick Dellagatta		136.5	Dan Mello
149.5	Andre Metzger		149.5	Jim Martinez*
163	Dave Schultz*		163	John Matthews
180.5	Mark Schultz		180.5	Tom Press
198	Steve Fraser		198	Mike Houck
220	Harold Smith		220	No champion
Hvy	Bruce Baumgartner		Hvy	No champion
Team	Sunkist Kids		Team	Adirondack Three-Style, WA

1985

105.5	Tim Vanni		105.5	T. J. Jones
114.5	Jim Martin		114.5	Mark Fuller
125.5	Charlie Heard		125.5	Eric Seward*
136.5	Darryl Burley		136.5	Buddy Lee
149.5	Bill Nugent*		149.5	Jim Martinez
163	Kenny Monday		163	David Butler
180.5	Mike Sheets		180.5	Chris Catallo
198	Mark Schultz		198	Mike Houck
220	Greg Gibson		220	Greg Gibson
286	Bruce Baumgartner		286	Dennis Koslowski
Team	Sunkist Kids		Team	U.S. Marine Corps

United States National Champions (*Cont.*)

FREESTYLE		GRECO-ROMAN	

1986

	FREESTYLE		GRECO-ROMAN
105.5	Rich Salamone	105.5	Eric Wetzel
114.5	Joe Gonzales	114.5	Shawn Sheldon
125.5	Kevin Darkus	125.5	Anthony Amado
136.5	John Smith	136.5	Frank Famiano
149.5	Andre Metzger*	149.5	Jim Martinez
163	Dave Schultz	163	David Butler*
180.5	Mark Schultz	180.5	Darryl Gholar
198	Jim Scherr	198	Derrick Waldroup
220	Dan Severn	220	Dennis Koslowski
286	Bruce Baumgartner	286	Duane Koslowski
Team	Sunkist Kids (Div. I)	Team	U.S. Marine Corps (Div. I)
	Hawkeye Wrestling Club (Div. II)		U.S. Navy (Div. II)

1987

	FREESTYLE		GRECO-ROMAN
105.5	Takashi Irie	105.5	Eric Wetzel
114.5	Mitsuru Sato	114.5	Shawn Sheldon
125.5	Barry Davis	125.5	Eric Seward
136.5	Takumi Adachi	136.5	Frank Famiano
149.5	Andre Metzger	149.5	Jim Martinez
163	Dave Schultz*	163	David Butler
180.5	Mark Schultz	180.5	Chris Catallo
198	Jim Scherr	198	Derrick Waldroup*
220	Bill Scherr	220	Dennis Koslowski
286	Bruce Baumgartner	286	Duane Koslowski
Team	Sunkist Kids (Div. I)	Team	U.S. Marine Corp (Div. I)
	Team Foxcatcher (Div. II)		U.S. Army (Div. II)

1988

	FREESTYLE		GRECO-ROMAN
105.5	Tim Vanni	105.5	T. J. Jones
114.5	Joe Gonzales	114.5	Shawn Sheldon
125.5	Kevin Darkus	125.5	Gogi Parseghian*
136.5	John Smith*	136.5	Dalen Wasmund
149.5	Nate Carr	149.5	Craig Pollard
163	Kenny Monday	163	Tony Thomas
180.5	Dave Schultz	180.5	Darryl Gholar
198	Melvin Douglas III	198	Mike Carolan
220	Bill Scherr	220	Dennis Koslowski
286	Bruce Baumgartner	286	Duane Koslowski
Team	Sunkist Kids (Div. I)	Team	U.S. Marine Corps (Div. I)
	Team Foxcatcher (Div. II)		Sunkist Kids (Div. II)

1989

	FREESTYLE		GRECO-ROMAN
105.5	Tim Vanni	105.5	Lew Dorrance
114.5	Zeke Jones	114.5	Mark Fuller
125.5	Brad Penrith	125.5	Gogi Parseghian
136.5	John Smith	136.5	Isaac Anderson
149.5	Nate Carr	149.5	Andy Seras*
163	Rob Koll	163	David Butler
180.5	Rico Chiapparelli	180.5	John Morgan
198	Jim Scherr*	198	Michial Foy
220	Bill Scherr	220	Steve Lawson
286	Bruce Baumgartner	286	Craig Pittman
Team	Sunkist Kids (Div. I)	Team	U.S. Marine Corps (Div. I)
	Team Foxcatcher (Div. II)		Jets USA (Div. II)

United States National Champions (*Cont.*)

FREESTYLE		GRECO-ROMAN	
1990			
105.5	Rob Eiter	105.5	Lew Dorrance
114.5	Zeke Jones	114.5	Sam Henson
125.5	Joe Melchiore	125.5	Mark Pustelnik
136.5	John Smith	136.5	Isaac Anderson
149.5	Nate Carr	149.5	Andy Seras
163	Rob Koll	163	David Butler
180.5	Royce Alger	180.5	Derrick Waldroup
198	Chris Campbell*	198	Randy Coutre*
220	Bill Scherr	220	Chris Tironi
286	Bruce Baumgartner	286	Matt Ghaffari
Team	Sunkist Kids (Div. I)	Team	Jets USA (Div. I)
	Team Foxcatcher (Div. II)		California Jets (Div. II)
1991			
105.5	Tim Vanni	105.5	Eric Wetzel
114.5	Zeke Jones	114.5	Shawn Sheldon
125.5	Brad Penrith	125.5	Frank Famiano
136.5	John Smith*	136.5	Buddy Lee
149.5	Townsend Saunders	149.5	Andy Seras
163	Kenny Monday	163	Gordy Morgan
180.5	Kevin Jackson	180.5	John Morgan*
198	Chris Campbell	198	Michial Foy
220	Mark Coleman	220	Dennis Koslowski
286	Bruce Baumgartner	286	Craig Pittman
Team	Sunkist Kids (Div. I)	Team	Jets USA (Div. I)
	Jets USA (Div. II)		Sunkist Kids (Div. II)

*Outstanding wrestler

Making a List

Why anyone would want to smell like a thoroughbred, or like Mike Ditka for that matter, is beyond our comprehension. But in the last few years, sports fragrances have become quite popular. Here are 10 such scents, some of which did not experience the sweet smell of success.

Muhammad Ali Cologne: *"Elegant and daring,"* according to its advertisers, this 1989 cologne had a scent of labdanum and vanilla. Float like a butterfly, smell like Ali.

adidas: *No, this is not the aroma of an old sneaker. Rather, it blends Singaporean patchouli, Indian tagette and Antillean ylang-ylang.*

Bjorn Borg: *Like its namesake, this citrusy scent was retired. It, too, is unlikely to make a comeback.*

Harley-Davidson: *When a biker wants to feel like a real man, he dabs his patchouli-and-sage concoction on his secret places. Come on, Snake, pamper yourself. You deserve it.*

Bully: *The Philadelphia Flyers unveiled their signature scent in 1989 with the slogan, "Splash on Bully and head out for the evening with icy abandon."*

Gabriela Sabatini: *A big hit in Europe. Like Gaby, it's "independent but not overbearing, lively and feminine."*

Hai Karate: *According to its '70s TV ads, this, the granddaddy of all sports scents, made beautiful women lose control over nebbishes who wore it.*

Iron Mike: *By getting his cologne on the market first, Bears coach Iron Mike Ditka beat Iron Mike Tyson to the punch. "Woodsy and fresh with tobacco and cinnamon."*

Thoroughbred for Women: *Roses merge with white jasmine and violet to make this an appealing perfume to satisfy even the most finicky filly.*

Wimbledon for Gentlemen: *The purple and green of the All England Club are represented by lavender and rosemary. With this scent, every game ends in love.*

The Sports Market

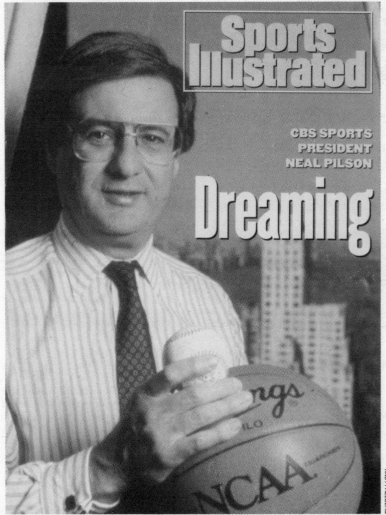

Sports Illustrated

CBS SPORTS
PRESIDENT
NEAL PILSON

Dreaming

A Spending Spree

Skyrocketing salaries and broken dreams highlighted a busy year in sports | by JOHN STEINBREDER

THINGS MAY HAVE BEEN A LITTLE SLOW ON Wall Street last year, but for those who like games of high finance and multi-million dollar winners and losers, the world of sports had plenty to offer. A baseball player signed a contract that will pay him more than $5 million a year. Businessmen bought and sold $100 million franchises like kids trading marbles. Countries committed godlike sums for the rights to hold the Olympic Games. Even the collectibles market went a little crazy, and a baseball card sold for a record $410,000.

Nowhere were the stakes higher, the dollar amounts larger and the mood swings more dramatic than at CBS. The broadcast network had spent $3.5 billion for the television rights to a slew of major sports properties—including an astonishing four-year, $1.06 billion contract for major league baseball—and its lineup for 1990 featured the Super Bowl, the NCAA basketball tournament, the NBA playoffs, the NFL regular season, and the baseball playoffs and World Series. CBS Sports president Neal Pilson called it his dream season, and he hoped it would lift the network out of the ratings cellar.

But Pilson's dream season turned into a nightmare. The advertising market softened, and corporate billings plummeted. As the losses mounted, it became clear that CBS had greatly overpaid for some sports. The network lost $100 million on baseball alone, and when the 1990 World Series was over, it asked the team owners for a partial refund. Not surprisingly, the request was denied. In January, CBS reported total losses of $156 million for the fourth quarter of 1990. It was the largest quarterly deficit in the company's history.

Considering all that went on in baseball, it's no wonder the owners didn't want to give CBS a refund. They needed every penny for themselves. Salaries soared about 60% in the off-season. Boston ace Roger Clemens became baseball's first $5 million

man when he signed a four-year deal that guarantees him $21.5 million. Pittsburgh Pirate starter Doug Drabek, the National League's 1990 Cy Young winner, set a salary arbitration record when he was awarded a one-year, $3.35 million contract. Even journeymen players were lavished with rich, multiyear deals. Lefthander Bud Black was only a career .500 pitcher, yet he finessed a four-year, $10 million contract from the San Francisco Giants.

And every team had to cough up cash when the collusion case was settled last winter. The owners agreed to pay the players $280 million, about $11 million per club, for conspiring to hold down free-agent salaries from 1986–1990.

But last year wasn't a total loss for the lords of baseball. Miami and Denver were awarded expansion franchises, to begin play in 1993, and the two new teams will each pay $95 million to join the National League. For the first time ever, both leagues will share the expansion fees, with the American League receiving 22% (about $3 million a team) and the National League getting the rest.

The NBA doesn't have baseball's financial problems, largely because it is the only

With the NFLPA out of the picture, McNeil filed an antitrust suit against the league.

professional sports league that has a salary cap. Its players have never been richer, and on average they earned $900,000 last year, more than double what they made five years ago. But that's not a sign of concern. Under the salary cap system, it simply means the league is thriving and all but a couple of teams are profitable.

Commissioner David Stern runs the NBA with a firm hand, and he is rightfully credited with leading the league into an era of unprecedented prosperity. But his grip might have been loosened by a court decision last January. At issue is the number of games that can be carried by the superstations. Previously the NBA had allowed them to show a maximum of 25 contests a season. In April of 1990 the NBA voted to lower that figure to 20 for 1990–91, and it was said to be considering decreasing the number in five-game increments each year until the superstations had no more games in '94–95. The Chicago Bulls and superstation WGN sued the league, and they nailed down a first-round victory when U.S. District Court Judge Hubert Will ruled that the reduction from 25 to

20 games constituted "a significant restraint of trade." The decision itself might be significant because if Judge Will's ruling stands, then any kind of control the league tries to exercise might easily be considered illegal. An NBA appeal is pending.

The NFL also spent a fair amount of time in court last year, mostly in battle with the Players Association. Two years ago the union moved to stop functioning as the players' collective bargaining agent in an effort to strip the NFL of its antitrust exemption. Without that exemption, the league would have to liberalize its restrictive free-agency system. It was a risky move, and the union was roundly criticized for quitting negotiations and decertifying. But there are signs that its strategy may actually be working. U.S. District Court Judge David Doty ruled in Minneapolis last June that since the union no longer exists for collective bargaining purposes, then neither does the NFL's antitrust exemption. That allowed an antitrust suit by New York Jets running back Freeman McNeil and seven other players to move forward to a February trial date. A

The Squeeze Is On

ALTHOUGH MAJOR LEAGUE BASEBALL has never been richer, it is under tremendous financial pressure. Commissioner Fay Vincent says that 10 of baseball's 26 teams lost money in 1990, and as many as half the ball clubs will run deficits in 1991. While baseball is still profitable on the whole, total earnings are dropping and the top eight teams make most of the money. So wide is the gulf between the haves and the have-nots that the payroll for the Oakland A's, for example, is greater than the total *revenues* of the Seattle Mariners. Many fans worry that the game's competitive balance is being threatened as a result, and some are even concerned that a couple of teams may go out of business.

There is reason to be concerned. What happens after the billion-dollar CBS contract expires in 1993? It's unlikely that any of the television networks will put up loads of cash the next time around, especially considering CBS's losses. How will the owners cover the big salaries they have agreed to pay their stars? And if they make an attempt to cut back on their wild spending, will the Players Association cry collusion again?

Like a hitter down two strikes in the count, baseball must adjust. It will probably have to institute a salary cap for its players, a sensible system that ties pay to revenues. The NBA has used a cap for the past eight years, and it has enriched both the players and the owners. Revenue sharing is another issue. As it stands now, teams equally divide money from the national television contracts and keep whatever they make from local broadcasters for themselves. That leads to huge revenue disparities. The Yankees, for example, get more than $40 million from their local broadcast contracts while the Pittsburgh Pirates get a little more than $3 million. Baseball has to bridge some of that gap in the next few years by getting teams to share at least a portion of their local broadcast money.

Ball clubs also have to find new streams of revenue. Many of them will move to own and operate their own stadiums (like the Toronto Blue Jays do with SkyDome) because teams can make a lot more money when they control the concessions, parking, and advertising. In addition, the owners will probably cut back on the subsidies they give their minor league affiliates. And they will look much

couple of weeks later in Washington, D.C., U.S. District Court Judge Royce Lambeth made a similar decision in a suit filed on behalf of the NFL developmental squad players, saying that the league lost its antitrust exemption when the last collective bargaining agreement expired in 1987. The NFL is appealing both rulings.

There was at least one bright spot for the NFL: The league's new international subsidiary, the World League of American Football, made a successful debut.

It was a year of growth for the National Hockey League. The expansion San Jose Sharks played their first regular-season game in October, and the league agreed to let in two new teams for the 1992–93 season, the Ottawa Senators and the Tampa Bay Lightning. The price per franchise was $50 million. Hall-of-Famer Phil Esposito heads the Tampa ownership group, and he will also serve as president and general manager. His original backers bowed out at the last minute, and Espo had to go to Japan to find new investors. No word yet on whether the Lightning will be serving sushi in the new,

harder at pay-per-view. It's a politically sensitive issue, to be sure, but the economic potential is so vast that the owners will do nearly anything to make it work. It probably won't be too much longer before the playoffs and World Series become pay-per-view events.

The players and owners generally don't agree on many things, but they both seem to acknowledge that baseball is facing a difficult time. They demonstrated their mutual concern last year by forming a committee to study the game's economic condition.

It shouldn't take the committee long to figure out that baseball has to make a number of changes if it wants to thrive into the next century. It will be a different game, but it can also be a stronger one.

More teams will need stadiums like SkyDome if they are to remain financially competitive.

MANNY MILLAN

Sampras won the '90 U.S. Open, but he hit a $2 million jackpot in the Grand Slam Cup.

17,000-seat arena now being built in Tampa.

The NHL had its share of legal problems, and last spring seven former players, including Hall of Famers Bobby Hull and Gordie Howe, filed suit against the league and other parties, accusing them of improperly allocating more than $25 million from their pension fund. The players contend that surplus money was wrongly channeled from the old-timers' pension fund to another retirement plan benefiting current players. The NHL denies the charges.

Money flowed like Gatorade when a dozen of the top men's tennis players gathered in Munich last December for the Grand Slam Cup, the richest tournament in the history of the game. Pete Sampras earned $2 million for beating Brad Gilbert in the finals.

Gilbert won $1 million as runner-up, and David Wheaton pulled in $450,000 for advancing to the semis, only $32,000 less than he had made in his two years on the pro tour. Even the alternates cashed in: Thierry Champion and Karel Novacek got $50,000 apiece just for being there in case they were needed to fill in for an injured player.

The city of Atlanta won a surprising victory when the International Olympic Committee awarded it the right to host the 1996 Summer Games. Atlanta spent some $7 million on its bid and successfully turned back a strong sentimental challenge by Athens to become the site for the 100th anniversary of the modern Games. The delegates from Atlanta propose to spend about $1.2 billion to hold the Games and expect to generate about $1.4 billion in revenues from television ($549 million), tickets ($337 million), commercial sponsorship ($331 million), and other promotions.

Salt Lake City made a strong bid for the 1998 Winter Games, but lost out to Nagano, Japan, on the fifth ballot, 46 votes to 42. Nagano is about 110 miles northwest from Tokyo, and it will be the first Asian city to host the Winter Games since 1972, when they were held in Sapporo, Japan.

The great realignment of college athletic conferences continued, and nothing symbolized that better than Penn State officially joining the Big Ten. Spurred by television money and exposure, universities all over the U.S. moved from conference to conference, creating new rivalries and new business opportunities in the process.

And finally, there was hockey star Wayne Gretzky and owner-collector Bruce McNall. Somewhere between the racehorses they bought together and the Canadian football team they co-own with actor John Candy, Gretzky and McNall got into baseball cards. At a May auction at Sotheby's in New York City, the two men spent $500,000 on a full set of 1910 cards. The gem of that lot was a Honus Wagner, and it alone went for $410,000, more than any other card in history.

The dollar amounts were huge, but it was just that kind of year.

SPORTS POLL '91, commissioned by Sports Illustrated and carried out by Lieberman Research, Inc., is a follow-up to SPORTS POLL '86—a nationwide survey conducted five years ago.

The current poll, like the earlier one, is one of the most wide-ranging investigations ever done on Americans' attitudes toward sports and their involvement with the sports world.

SPORTS POLL '91 is based on mail questionnaires completed by a nationwide sample of 2,320 adult Americans, 18 years old and over.

How interested are you in sports?

	1986	1991
Fans	**71%**	**73%**
Very interested	29	30
Fairly interested	42	43
Nonfans	**29**	**27**
Not too interested	23	21
Not interested at all	6	6

In which sports are you interested?

	1986	1991	Change
Pro football	60%	60%	0%
Baseball	59	52	−7
College football	42	40	−2
Fishing	43	37	−6
Pro basketball	32	34	+2
College basketball	30	32	+2
Professional boxing	31	30	−1
Bowling	35	29	−6
Auto racing	31	27	−4
Hunting	26	24	−2
Ice skating	25	24	−1
Snow skiing	25	23	−2
Golf	23	22	−1
Pool/billiards	26	22	−4
Tennis	22	22	0
Boating (except sailing)	20	19	−1
Volleyball	19	19	0
Ice hockey	18	17	−1
Track and field	22	16	−6
Horce racing	20	16	−4
Water skiing	18	15	−3
Pro wrestling	22	14	−8
Horseback riding	17	14	−3
Snorkeling/scuba diving	10	12	+2
Soccer	11	9	−2
Sailing	9	7	−2
Squash/racquetball	8	6	−2
Handball	5	3	−2

Which sports did you pay to attend in the past 12 months?

	1986	1991	Change
Baseball	30%	27%	−3%
Pro football	16	16	0
College football	15	16	+1
College basketball	8	11	+3
Auto racing	9	9	0
Pro basketball	7	9	+2
Horse racing	7	7	0
Ice hockey	6	6	0
Pro wrestling	7	5	−2
Golf	4	5	+1
Pro boxing	4	4	0
Soccer	3	2	−1
Tennis	3	2	−1
Track and field meet	3	2	−1

How often did you participate in sports or fitness activities in the past 12 months?

	1986	1991
Participated	73%	73%
Did not participate	27	27
Average number of times participated—among those who participated	53.2	73.7

In which sports and fitness activities did you participate in the past 12 months? Five-Year Trend

	1986	1991	Change
Swimming	48%	45%	−3%
Bicycling	37	34	−3
Fishing	35	33	−2
Using exercise machines	30	33	+3
Bowling	23	26	+3
Calisthenics/aerobics	30	24	−6
Baseball/softball	28	24	−4
Pool/billiards	22	24	+2
Jogging	30	23	−7
Hiking/backpacking	23	22	−1
Boating (except sailing)	20	21	+1
Weightlifting	21	19	−2
Basketball	15	19	+4
Volleyball	16	18	+2
Hunting	18	17	−1
Golf	14	16	+2
Football	13	12	−1
Tennis	11	11	0
Water skiing	10	9	−1
Snow skiing	9	9	0

1991—By Sex

	Men	Women
Swimming	48%	43%
Fishing	41	24
Bicycling	35	33
Using exercise machines	34	33
Baseball/softball	33	17
Pool/billiards	31	17
Weightlifting	29	10
Bowling	27	26
Jogging	27	20
Basketball	27	11
Hunting	27	8
Hiking/backpacking	24	19
Boating (except sailing)	24	18
Golf	24	8
Football	19	5
Volleyball	18	18
Calisthenics/aerobics	16	32
Tennis	11	11
Water skiing	11	8
Snow skiing	11	7

Major League Baseball
Address: 350 Park Avenue
              New York, NY 10022
Telephone: (212) 339-7800
Commissioner: Francis T. Vincent Jr.
Deputy Commissioner: Stephen D. Greenberg
Director of Public Relations: Richard Levin

Major League Baseball Players Association
Address: 805 Third Avenue
              New York, NY 10022
Telephone: (212) 826-0808
Executive Director: Donald Fehr
Director of Marketing: Allyne Price

American League

American League Office
Address: 350 Park Avenue
              New York, NY 10022
Telephone: (212) 339-7600
President: Bobby Brown
Director of Public Relations: Phyllis Merhige

Baltimore Orioles
Address: Memorial Stadium
              Baltimore, MD 21218
Telephone: (301) 243-9800
Stadium (Capacity): Memorial Stadium (54,017)*
Chairman: Eli Jacobs
General Manager: Roland Hemond
Manager: Johnny Oates
Director of Public Relations: Rick Vaughn

* Orioles to move to new ballpark, capacity
(47,000) in 1992.

Boston Red Sox
Address: Fenway Park
              Boston, MA 02215
Telephone: (617) 267-9440
Stadium (Capacity): Fenway Park (34,182)
Majority Owner and Chairman of the Board: Jean
  Yawkey
General Manager: Lou Gorman
Manager: Butch Hobson
Vice President, Public Relations: Dick Bresciani

California Angels
Address: Anaheim Stadium
              Anaheim, CA 92803
Telephone: (714) 937-7200 or (213) 625-1123
Stadium (Capacity): Anaheim Stadium (64,573)
Chairman of the Board: Gene Autry
Senior Vice President: Whitey Herzog
General Manager: Dan O'Brien
Manager: Buck Rodgers
Director of Media Relations: Tim Mead

Chicago White Sox
Address: Comiskey Park
              Chicago, IL 60616
Telephone: (312) 924-1000
Stadium (Capacity): Comiskey Park (44,702)
Chairman: Jerry Reinsdorf
General Manager: Ron Schueler
Manager: TBA
Director of Publc Relations: Doug Abel

Cleveland Indians
Address: Cleveland Stadium
              Cleveland, OH 44114
Telephone: (216) 861-1200
Stadium (Capacity): Cleveland Stadium (74,483)
Chairman of the Board and Chief Executive Officer:
  Richard Jacobs
President and Chief Operating Officer: Rick Bay
Manager: Mike Hargrove
Vice President, Public Relations: Bob DiBiasio

Detroit Tigers
Address: Tiger Stadium
              Detroit, MI 48216
Telephone: (313) 962-4000
Stadium (Capacity): Tiger Stadium (52,416)
Owner: Tom Monaghan
President and Chief Operating Officer: Bo
  Schembechler
Manager: Sparky Anderson
Vice President, Media and Public Relations: Dan
  Ewald

Kansas City Royals
Address: P.O. Box 419969
              Kansas City, MO 64141
Telephone: (816) 921-2200
Stadium (Capacity): Royals Stadium (40,625)
Owner and Chairman of the Board: Ewing Kauffman
General Manager: Herk Robinson
Manager: Hal McRae
Vice President, Public Relations: Dean Vogelaar

Milwaukee Brewers
Address: Milwaukee County Stadium
              Milwaukee, WI 53214
Telephone: (414) 933-4114
Stadium (Capacity): Milwaukee County Stadium
  (53,192)
President and Chief Executive Officer: Bud Selig
General Manager: Harry Dalton
Manager: Phil Garner
Director of Publicity: Tom Skibosh

Minnesota Twins
Address: Hubert H. Humphrey Metrodome
              Minneapolis, MN 55415
Telephone: (612) 375-1366
Stadium (Capacity): Hubert H. Humphrey Metrodome
  (55,883)
Owner: Carl Pohlad
General Manager: Andy MacPhail
Manager: Tom Kelly
Director of Media Relations: Rob Antony

New York Yankees
Address: Yankee Stadium
              Bronx, NY 10451
Telephone: (212) 293-4300
Stadium (Capacity): Yankee Stadium (57,545)
Managing General Partner: Robert Nederlander
General Manager: Gene Michael
Manager: Buck Showalter
Director of Media Relations and Publicity: Jeff Idelson

American League (*Cont.*)

Oakland Athletics
Address:　Oakland-Alameda County Coliseum
　　　　　Oakland, CA 94621
Telephone: (415) 638-4900
Stadium (Capacity): Oakland-Alameda County Coliseum (48,219)
Owner/Managing General Partner: Walter Haas
General Manager: Sandy Alderson
Manager: Tony LaRussa
Director of Baseball Information: Jay Alves

Seattle Mariners
Address:　P.O. Box 4100
　　　　　Seattle, WA 98104
Telephone: (206) 628-3555
Stadium (Capacity): The Kingdome (58,150)
Chairman: Jeff Smulyan
General Manager: Woody Woodward
Manager: Bill Plummer
Director of Public Relations: Dave Aust

Texas Rangers
Address:　P.O. Box 90111
　　　　　Arlington, TX 76004
Telephone: (817) 273-5222
Stadium (Capacity): Arlington Stadium (43,508)
General Partners: George W. Bush, Rusty Rose
General Manager: Tom Grieve
Manager: Bobby Valentine
Vice President, Public Relations: John Blake

Toronto Blue Jays
Address:　SkyDome
　　　　　300 Bremner Boulevard
　　　　　Suite 3200
　　　　　Toronto
　　　　　Ontario, Canada M5V 3B3
Telephone: (416) 341-1000
Stadium (Capacity): SkyDome (50,516)
Chairman: William Ferguson
General Manager: Pat Gillick
Manager: Cito Gaston
Director of Public Relations: Howard Starkman

National League

National League Office
Address:　350 Park Avenue
　　　　　New York, NY 10022
Telephone: (212) 339-7700
President: Bill White
Director of Public Relations: Katy Feeney

Atlanta Braves
Address:　P.O. Box 4064
　　　　　Atlanta, GA 30302
Telephone: (404) 522-7630
Stadium (Capacity): Atlanta-Fulton County Stadium (52,007)
Owner: Ted Turner
General Manager: John Schuerholz
Manager: Bobby Cox
Director of Public Relations: Jim Schultz

Chicago Cubs
Address:　Wrigley Field
　　　　　Chicago, IL 60613
Telephone: (312) 404-2827
Stadium (Capacity): Wrigley Field (38,710)
President: Don Grenesko
General Manager: Jim Frey
Manager: TBA
Director of Media Relations: Sharon Panozzo

Cincinnati Reds
Address:　Riverfront Stadium
　　　　　Cincinnati, OH 45202
Telephone: (513) 421-4510
Stadium (Capacity): Riverfront Stadium (52,392)
General Partner: Marge Schott
General Manager: Bob Quinn
Manager: Lou Piniella
Publicity Director: Jon Braude

Houston Astros
Address:　P.O. Box 288
　　　　　Houston, TX 77001
Telephone: (713) 799-9500
Stadium (Capacity): Astrodome (54,816)
Chairman: John McMullen
General Manager: Bill Wood
Manager: Art Howe
Director of Public Relations: Rob Matwick

Los Angeles Dodgers
Address:　Dodger Stadium
　　　　　Los Angeles, CA 90012
Telephone: (213) 224-1500
Stadium (Capacity): Dodger Stadium (56,000)
President: Peter O'Malley
General Manager: Fred Claire
Manager: Tom Lasorda
Director of Publicity: Jay Lucas

Montreal Expos
Address:　P.O. Box 500
　　　　　Station M
　　　　　Montreal
　　　　　Quebec, Canada H1V 3P2
Telephone: (514) 253-3434
Stadium (Capacity): Olympic Stadium (60,011)
President: Claude Brochu
General Manager: Dan Duquette
Manager: Tom Runnells
Director, Media Relations: Rich Griffin

New York Mets
Address:　Shea Stadium
　　　　　Flushing, NY 11368
Telephone: (718) 507-6387
Stadium (Capacity): Shea Stadium (55,601)
Chairman: Nelson Doubleday
Chief Operating Officer and Senior Executive Vice President: Frank Cashen
Executive Vice President and General Manager: Al Harazin
Manager: Jeff Torborg
Director of Public Relations: Jay Horwitz

Philadelphia Phillies
Address:　P.O. Box 7575
　　　　　Philadelphia, PA 19101
Telephone: (215) 463-6000
Stadium (Capacity): Veterans Stadium (62,382)
President: Bill Giles
General Manager: Lee Thomas
Manager: Jim Fregosi
Vice President, Public Relations: Larry Shenk

National League (*Cont.*)

Pittsburgh Pirates
Address: P.O. Box 7000
           Pittsburgh, PA 15212
Telephone: (412) 323-5000
Stadium (Capacity): Three Rivers Stadium (58,729)
Chairman: Doug Danforth
General Manager: Larry Doughty
Manager: Jim Leyland
Director of Media Relations: Jim Lachimia

St. Louis Cardinals
Address: Busch Stadium
           St. Louis, MO 63102
Telephone: (314) 421-3060
Stadium (Capacity): Busch Stadium (54,224)
Chairman of the Board: August Busch III
General Manager: Dal Maxvill
Manager: Joe Torre
Director of Public Relations: Jeff Wehling

San Diego Padres
Address: P.O. Box 2000
           San Diego, CA 92112
Telephone: (619) 283-7294
Stadium (Capacity): San Diego Jack Murphy Stadium
(59,022)
Chairman: Tom Werner
General Manager: Joe McIllvaine
Manager: Greg Riddoch
Director of Media Relations: Jim Ferguson

San Francisco Giants
Address: Candlestick Park
           San Francisco, CA 94124
Telephone: (415) 468-3700
Stadium (Capacity): Candlestick Park (58,000)
Chairman: Bob Lurie
General Manager: Al Rosen
Manager: Roger Craig
Vice President, Public Relations: Duffy Jennings
Director of Media Relations: Matt Fischer

Expansion Clubs (Begin play in 1993)

Colorado Rockies
Address: 1700 Lincoln Street, Suite 3710
           Denver, CO 80203
Telephone: (303) 866-0428
Stadium (Capacity): Mile High Stadium (76,000)
President: Steve Ehrhart
Senior Vice President and General Manager: Bob
  Gebhard
Manager: TBA
Publicity Director: TBA

Florida Marlins
Address: 100 N.E. 3rd Avenue
           Fort Lauderdale, FL 33301
Telephone: (305) 779-7070
Stadium (Capacity): Joe Robbie Stadium (55,000)
Owner: Wayne Huizenga
President: Carl Barger
Vice President and General Manager: David
  Dombrowski
Manager: TBA
Publicity Director: TBA

Pro Football Directory

National Football League
Address: 410 Park Avenue
           New York, New York 10022
Telephone: (212) 758-1500
Commissioner: Paul Tagliabue
Director of Communications: Greg Aiello

National Football League Players Association
Address: 2021 L Street, N.W.
           Washington, D.C. 20036
Telephone: (202) 463-2200
Executive Director: Gene Upshaw
Director, Public Relations: Frank Woschitz

National Conference

Atlanta Falcons
Address: I-85 and Suwanee Road
           Suwanee, GA 30175
Telephone: (404) 945-1111
Stadium (Capacity): Atlanta Fulton County Stadium
(59,643)
Chairman of the Board: Rankin M. Smith Sr.
General Manager: Ken Herock
Coach: Jerry Glanville
Publicity Director: Charlie Taylor

Chicago Bears
Address: 250 N. Washington Road
           Lake Forest, IL 60045
Telephone: (708) 295-6600
Stadium (Capacity): Soldier Field (66,946)
President: Michael McCaskey
General Manager: Bill Tobin
Coach: Mike Ditka
Director of Public Relations: Bryan Harlan

Dallas Cowboys
Address: One Cowboys Parkway
           Irving, TX 75063
Telephone: (214) 556-9900
Stadium (Capacity): Texas Stadium (65,024)
Owner, President, and General Manager: Jerry Jones
Coach: Jimmy Johnson
Public Relations Director: Rich Dalrymple

Detroit Lions
Address: 1200 Featherstone Road
           Box 4200
           Pontiac, MI 48342
Telephone: (313) 335-4131
Stadium (Capacity): Pontiac Silverdome (80,500)
President and Owner: William Clay Ford
General Manager: Chuck Schmidt
Coach: Wayne Fontes
Public Relations Director: Bill Keenist

National Conference (*Cont.*)

Green Bay Packers
Address: 1265 Lombardi Avenue
              Green Bay, WI 54307
Telephone: (414) 496-5700
Stadium (Capacity): Lambeau Field (59,543), Milwaukee County Stadium (56,051)
President: Bob Harlan
General Manager: Tom Braatz
Coach: Lindy Infante
Public Relations Director: Lee Remmel

Los Angeles Rams
Address: 2327 W. Lincoln Avenue
              Anaheim, CA 92801
Telephone: (714) 535-7267
Stadium (Capacity): Anaheim Stadium (69,008)
President: Georgia Frontiere
General Manager: John Shaw
Coach: John Robinson
Director of Public Relations: John Oswald

Minnesota Vikings
Address: 9520 Viking Drive
              Eden Prairie, MN 55344
Telephone: (612) 828-6500
Stadium (Capacity): Metrodome (63,000)
President: Roger L. Hendrick
General Manager: Jeff Diamond
Coach: Jerry Burns
Public Relations Director: Merrill Swanson

New Orleans Saints
Address: 1500 Poydras Street
              New Orleans, LA 70112
Telephone: (504) 733-0255
Stadium (Capacity): Louisiana Superdome (69,065)
Owner: Tom Benson
President and General Manager: Jim Finks
Coach: Jim Mora
Director of Media Relations: Rusty Kasmiersky

New York Giants
Address: Giants Stadium
              East Rutherford, NJ 07073
Telephone: (201) 935-8111
Stadium (Capacity): Giants Stadium (77,311)
President: Wellington T. Mara
General Manager: George Young
Coach: Ray Handley
Director of Media Services: Ed Croke

Philadelphia Eagles
Address: Veterans Stadium
              Broad Street and Pattison Avenue
              Philadelphia, PA 19148
Telephone: (215) 463-2500
Stadium (Capacity): Veterans Stadium (65,356)
Owner: Norman Braman
General Manager: Harry Gamble
Coach: Rich Kotite
Director of Public Relations: Ron Howard

Phoenix Cardinals
Address: P.O. Box 888
              Phoenix, AZ 85001
Telephone: (602) 379-0101
Stadium (Capacity): Sun Devil Stadium (72,608)
President: Bill Bidwill
General Manager: Larry Wilson
Coach: Joe Bugel
Director of Public Relations: Paul Jensen

San Francisco 49ers
Address: 4949 Centennial Boulevard
              Santa Clara, CA 95054
Telephone: (408) 562-4949
Stadium (Capacity): Candlestick Park (66,455)
Owner: Edward J. DeBartolo Jr.
General Manager: John McVay
Coach: George Seifert
Public Relations Director: Jerry Walker

Tampa Bay Buccaneers
Address: One Buccaneer Place
              Tampa, FL 33607
Telephone: (813) 870-2700
Stadium (Capacity): Tampa Stadium (74,315)
Owner: Hugh F. Culverhouse
General Manager: Phil Krueger
Coach: Richard Williamson
Director of Public Relations: Rick Odioso

Washington Redskins
Address: Redskin Park Drive
              Ashburn, VA 22011
Telephone: (703) 478-8900
Stadium (Capacity): RFK Memorial Stadium (55,683)
Owner: Jack Kent Cooke
General Manager: Charley Casserly
Coach: Joe Gibbs
Vice President of Communications: Charlie Dayton

American Conference

Buffalo Bills
Address: One Bills Drive
              Orchard Park, NY 14127
Telephone: (716) 648-1800
Stadium (Capacity): Rich Stadium (80,290)
President: Ralph C. Wilson Jr.
General Manager: Bill Polian
Coach: Marv Levy
Manager of Media Relations: Scott Berchtold

Cincinnati Bengals
Address: 200 Riverfront Stadium
              Cincinnati, OH 45202
Telephone: (513) 621-3550
Stadium (Capacity): Riverfront Stadium (60,389)
President: John Sawyer
General Manager: Mike Brown
Coach: Sam Wyche
Director of Public Relations: Allan Heim

Sports Poll '91— Continued

In response to the question "How often did you pay to attend sports events in the past 12 months?", 52% of respondents said never. The 48% who paid broke down as follows: 14% attended 10 or more times, 10% went five-to-nine times, and 24% went one-to-four times.

American Conference (*Cont.*)

Cleveland Browns

Address: Cleveland Stadium
           Cleveland, OH 44114
Telephone: (216) 696-5555
Stadium (Capacity): Cleveland Stadium (80,098)
President: Art Modell
General Manager: Ernie Accorsi
Coach: Bill Belichick
Director of Public Relations: Kevin Byrne

Denver Broncos

Address: 13665 Broncos Parkway
           Englewood, CO 80112
Telephone: (303) 649-9000
Stadium (Capacity): Mile High Stadium (76,273)
President: Pat Bowlen
General Manager: John Beake
Coach: Dan Reeves
Director of Media Relations: Jim Saccomano

Houston Oilers

Address: 6910 Fannin
           Houston, TX 77030
Telephone: (713) 797-9111
Stadium (Capacity): Astrodome (60,502)
President: K. S. "Bud" Adams Jr.
General Manager: Mike Holovak
Coach: Jack Pardee
Director of Media Relations: Chip Namias

Indianapolis Colts

Address: P.O. Box 535000
           Indianapolis, IN 45253
Telephone: (317) 297-2658
Stadium (Capacity): Hoosier Dome (60,129)
Owner: Robert Irsay
General Manager: Jim Irsay
Coach: Rick Venturi
Public Relations Director: Craig Kelley

Kansas City Chiefs

Address: One Arrowhead Drive
           Kansas City, MO 64129
Telephone: (816) 924-9300
Stadium (Capacity): Arrowhead Stadium (78,067)
Founder: Lamar Hunt
President and General Manager: Carl Peterson
Coach: Marty Schottenheimer
Public Relations Director: Bob Moore

Los Angeles Raiders

Address: 332 Center Street
           El Segundo, CA 90245
Telephone: (213) 322-3451
Stadium (Capacity): Los Angeles Memorial Coliseum
  (92,488)
Managing General Partner: Al Davis
Coach: Art Shell
Executive Assistant: Al LoCasale

Miami Dolphins

Address: Joe Robbie Stadium
           2269 N.W. 199 Street
           Miami, FL 33056
Telephone: (305) 620-5000
Stadium (Capacity): Joe Robbie Stadium (73,000)
President: Timothy J. Robbie
General Manager: Eddie J. Jones
Coach: Don Shula
Director of Publicity: Harvey Greene

New England Patriots

Address: Foxboro Stadium
           Route 1
           Foxboro, MA 02035
Telephone: (508) 543-8200
Stadium (Capacity): Foxboro Stadium (60,794)
Owner: Victor K. Kiam II
General Manager: Sam Jankovich
Coach: Dick MacPherson
Director of Media Relations: Pat Hanlon

New York Jets

Address: 1000 Fulton Avenue
           Hempstead, NY 11550
Telephone: (516) 538-6600
Stadium (Capacity): Giants Stadium (76,891)
Chairman of the Board: Leon Hess
General Manager: Dick Steinberg
Coach: Bruce Coslet
Director of Public Relations: Frank Ramos

Pittsburgh Steelers

Address: Three Rivers Stadium
           300 Stadium Circle
           Pittsburgh, PA 15212
Telephone: (412) 323-1200
Stadium (Capacity): Three Rivers Stadium (59,492)
President: Dan Rooney
Coach: Chuck Noll
Public Relations Director: Dan Edwards

San Diego Chargers

Address: San Diego Jack Murphy Stadium
           P.O. Box 609609
           San Diego, CA 92160
Telephone: (619) 280-2111
Stadium (Capacity): San Diego Jack Murphy Stadium
  (60,835)
President: Alex G. Spanos
General Manager: Bobby Beathard
Coach: Dan Henning
Director of Public Relations: Bill Johnston

Seattle Seahawks

Address: 11220 N.E. 53rd Street
           Kirkland, WA 98033
Telephone: (206) 827-9777
Stadium (Capacity): The Kingdome (64,984)
Owner: Ken Behring
President and General Manager: Tom Flores
Coach: Chuck Knox
Director of Public Relations: Gary Wright

Sports Poll '91— Continued

"How often did you pay to attend sports events in the past 12 months?" The average for the 48% who said they had paid was 8.4 times. That amounted to an average of 4.4 paid attendances for every respondent.

Other Leagues

Canadian Football League
Address: 110 Eglinton Avenue West, 5th floor
             Toronto, Ontario M4R 1A3
Telephone: (416) 322-9650
Commissioner: Donald Crump
Communications Director: Norm Miller

World League of American Football
Address: 540 Madison Avenue
             New York, NY 10022
Telephone: (212) 838-9400
Chief Operating Officer: Joe Bailey
Vice President of Communications: Bob Rose

Pro Basketball Directory

National Basketball Association
Address: 645 Fifth Avenue
             New York, NY 10022
Telephone: (212) 826-7000
Commissioner: David Stern
Deputy Commissioner: Russell Granik
Vice President, Public Relations: Brian McIntyre

National Basketball Association Players Association
Address: 1775 Broadway
             Suite 2401
             New York, NY 10019
Telephone: (212) 333-7510
Executive Director: Charles Crantham
Publicity Director: Lori Mandracchia

Atlanta Hawks
Address: One CNN Center, South Tower
             Suite 405
             Atlanta, GA 30303
Telephone: (404) 827-3800
Arena (Capacity): The Omni (16,371)
Owner: Ted Turner
President: Stan Kasten
General Manager: Pete Babcock
Coach: Bob Weiss
Director of Public Relations: Arthur Triche

Boston Celtics
Address: 151 Merrimac Street
             Boston, MA 02114
Telephone: (617) 523-6050
Arena (Capacity): Boston Garden (14,890)
Owner and Chairman of the Board: Don F. Gaston
President: Arnold "Red" Auerbach
Senior Executive Vice President: David Gavitt
General Manager: Jan Volk
Coach: Chris Ford
Director of Public Relations: R. Jeffrey Twiss

Charlotte Hornets
Address: Hive Drive
             Charlotte, NC 28217
Telephone: (704) 357-0252
Arena (Capacity): Charlotte Coliseum (23,901)
Owner: George Shinn
Executive Vice President: Tony Renaud
Coach: Allan Bristow
Director of Media Relations: Harold Kaufman

Chicago Bulls
Address: 980 N. Michigan Avenue
             Suite 1600
             Chicago, IL 60611
Telephone: (312) 943-5800
Arena (Capacity): Chicago Stadium (17,339)
Chairman: Jerry Reinsdorf
General Manager: Jerry Krause
Coach: Phil Jackson
Director of Media Services: Tim Hallam

Cleveland Cavaliers
Address: The Coliseum, 2923 Streetsboro Road
             Richfield, OH 44286
Telephone: (216) 659-9100
Arena (Capacity): The Coliseum (20,273)
Cochairmen of the Board: George Gund III and
     Gordon Gund
Vice President and General Manager: Wayne Embry
Coach: Lenny Wilkens
Director of Public Relations: Bob Price

Dallas Mavericks
Address: Reunion Arena
             777 Sports Street
             Dallas, TX 75207
Telephone: (214) 748-1808
Arena (Capacity): Reunion Arena (17,007)
Owner and President: Donald Carter
General Manager: Norm Sonju
Coach: Richie Adubato
Director of Public Relations: Kevin Sullivan

Denver Nuggets
Address: McNichols Sports Arena
             1635 Clay Street
             Denver, CO 80204
Telephone: (303) 893-6700
Arena (Capacity): McNichols Sports Arena (17,022)
Owners: Peter Bynoe and Robert Wussler
General Manager: Bernie Bickerstaff
Coach: Paul Westhead
Media Relations Director: Jay Clark

Detroit Pistons
Address: The Palace of Auburn Hills
             Two Championship Drive
             Auburn Hills, MI 48326
Telephone: (313) 377-0100
Arena (Capacity): The Palace of Auburn Hills (21,454)
Owner: William M. Davidson
General Manager: Jack McCloskey
Coach: Chuck Daly
Director of Public Relations: Matt Dobek

Golden State Warriors
Address: Oakland Coliseum Arena
          Oakland, CA 94621
Telephone: (415) 638-6300
Arena (Capacity): Oakland Coliseum Arena (15,025)
Chairman: James F. Fitzgerald
Coach and General Manager: Don Nelson
Media Relations Director: Julie Marvel

Houston Rockets
Address: The Summit
          Ten Greenway Plaza
          Houston, TX 77046
Telephone: (713) 627-0600
Arena (Capacity): The Summit (16,279)
Owner: Charlie Thomas
General Manager: Steve Patterson
Coach: Don Chaney
Director of Media Information: Jay Goldberg

Indiana Pacers
Address: 300 E. Market Street
          Indianapolis, IN 46204
Telephone: (317) 263-2100
Arena (Capacity): Market Square Arena (16,912)
Owners: Melvin Simon and Herbert Simon
General Manager: Donnie Walsh
Coach: Bob Hill
Media Relations Director: Dale Ratermann

Los Angeles Clippers
Address: L.A. Memorial Sports Arena
          3939 S. Figueroa Street
          Los Angeles, CA 90037
Telephone: (213) 748-8000
Arena (Capacity): L.A. Memorial Sports Arena
    (15,645)
Owner: Donald T. Sterling
General Manager: Elgin Baylor
Coach: Mike Schuler
Director of Public Relations: Mike Williams

Los Angeles Lakers
Address: Great Western Forum
          3900 West Manchester Boulevard
          Inglewood, CA 90306
Telephone: (213) 419-3100
Arena (Capacity): The Great Western Forum (17,505)
Owner: Dr. Jerry Buss
General Manager: Jerry West
Coach: Mike Dunleavy
Director of Public Relations: John Black

Miami Heat
Address: The Miami Arena
          Miami, FL 33136-4102
Telephone: (305) 577-4328
Arena (Capacity): Miami Arena (15,008)
Managing Partner: Lewis Schaffel
Director of Player Personnel: Stu Inman
Coach: Kevin Loughery
Director of Public Relations: Mark Pray

Milwaukee Bucks
Address: The Bradley Center
          1001 N. Fourth Street
          Milwaukee, WI 53203-1312
Telephone: (414) 227-0500
Arena (Capacity): The Bradley Center (18,633)
Owner: Herb Kohl
Vice President of Basketball Operations and Coach:
  Del Harris
Public Relations Director: Bill King II

Minnesota Timberwolves
Address: 600 First Avenue North
          Minneapolis, MN 55403
Telephone: (612) 337-3865
Arena (Capacity): Timberwolves Arena (18,500)
Owners: Harvey Ratner and Marv Wolfenson
General Manager and Director of Player Personnel:
  Billy McKinney
Coach: Jimmy Rodgers
Director of Media Relations: Bill Robertson

New Jersey Nets
Address: Meadowlands Arena
          East Rutherford, NJ 07073
Telephone: (201) 935-8888
Arena (Capacity): Meadowlands Arena (20,049)
Owner: Robert Casciola
General Manager: Willis Reed
Coach: Bill Fitch
Director of Public Relations: John Mertz

New York Knickerbockers
Address: Madison Square Garden
          Four Pennsylvania Plaza
          New York, NY 10001
Telephone: (212) 465-6000
Arena (Capacity): Madison Square Garden (18,212)
Owner: Paramount Communications, Inc.
President: David Checketts
General Manager: Ernie Grunfeld
Coach: Pat Riley
Vice President, Public Relations: John Cirillo

Orlando Magic
Address: One Magic Place
          Orlando Arena
          Orlando, FL 32801
Telephone: (407) 649-3200
Arena (Capacity): Orlando Arena (15,077)
Owner: Rich DeVos
General Manager: Pat Williams
Coach: Matt Guokas
Director of Publicity/Media Relations: Alex Martins

Philadelphia 76ers
Address: Veterans Stadium
          P.O. Box 25040
          Broad Street and Pattison Avenue
          Philadelphia, PA 19147
Telephone: (215) 339-7600
Arena (Capacity): The Spectrum (18,168)
Owner and President: Harold Katz
General Manager: Gene Shue
Coach: Jim Lynam
Public Relations Director: Zack Hill

Phoenix Suns
Address: 2910 N. Central Avenue
Phoenix, AZ 85012
Telephone: (602) 266-5753
Arena (Capacity): Arizona Veterans Memorial Coliseum (14,487)
Owner: Jerry Colangelo
Coach and Director of Player Personnel: Cotton Fitzsimmons
Media Relations Director: Barry Ringel

Portland Trail Blazers
Address: 700 N.E. Multnomah Street
Suite 600
Portland, OR 97232
Telephone: (503) 234-9291
Arena (Capacity): Memorial Coliseum (12,880)
Chairman of the Board: Paul Allen
General Manager: Morris "Bucky" Buckwalter
Coach: Rick Adelman
Director of Media Services: John Lashway

Sacramento Kings
Address: One Sports Parkway
Sacramento, CA 95834
Telephone: (916) 928-0000
Arena (Capacity): ARCO Arena (17,014)
Owners: Joseph Benevenuti, Gregg Lukenbill, Frank Lukenbill, Bob A. Cook and Stephen H. Cippa
General Manager: Jerry Reynolds
Coach: Dick Motta
Director of Public Relations: Julie Fie

San Antonio Spurs
Address: 600 E. Market
Suite 102
San Antonio, TX 78205
Telephone: (512) 554-7787
Arena (Capacity): HemisFair Arena (15,861)
Owner and Chairman: Red McCombs
President: Gary Woods
Coach: Larry Brown
Director of Public Relations: Wayne Witt

Seattle Supersonics
Address: 190 Queen Anne Avenue North
Suite 200
Seattle, WA 98109
Telephone: (206) 281-5800
Arena (Capacity): The Coliseum (14,250)
Owner: Barry Ackerley
President: Bob Whitsitt
Coach: K. C. Jones
Director of Public/Media Relations: Jim Rupp

Utah Jazz
Address: Five Triad Center
Suite 500
Salt Lake City, UT 84180
Telephone: (801) 575-7800
Arena (Capacity): Salt Palace (12,444)
Owner: Larry H. Miller
General Manager: R. Tim Howells
Coach: Jerry Sloan
Director of Media Services/Special Events: Kim Turner

Washington Bullets
Address: One Harry S. Truman Drive
Landover, MD 20785
Telephone: (301) 773-2255
Arena (Capacity): Capital Centre (18,756)
Owner: Abe Pollin
General Manager: John Nash
Coach: Wes Unseld
Director of Public Relations and Communications: Rick Moreland

Other League

Continental Basketball Association
Address: 425 South Cherry Street, Suite 230
Denver, CO 80222
Telephone: (303) 331-0404
Commissioner: Terdema L. Ussery
Director of Media Relations: Greg Anderson

Hockey Directory

National Hockey League
Address: 650 Fifth Avenue
33rd floor
New York, NY 10019
Telephone: (212) 398-1100
President: John Ziegler
Executive Vice President: Brian O'Neill
Vice President, Marketing and Public Relations: Steve Ryan

National Hockey League Players Association
Address: Maitland House
37 Maitland Street
Toronto, Ontario
Canada M4Y 1C8
Telephone: (416) 924-7800
Executive Director: Alan Eagleson

Boston Bruins
Address: Boston Garden
150 Causeway Street
Boston, MA 02114
Telephone: (617) 227-3206
Arena (Capacity): Boston Garden (14,448)
Owner and Governor: Jeremey M. Jacobs
Alternative Governor, President and General Manager: Harry Sinden
Coach: Rick Bowness
Director of Media Relations: Heidi Holland

Buffalo Sabres
Address: Memorial Auditorium
Buffalo, NY 14202
Telephone: (716) 856-7300
Arena (Capacity): Memorial Auditorium (16,433)
Chairman of the Board and President: Seymour H. Knox III
General Manager: Gerry Meehan
Coach: Rick Dudley
Director of Media Relations: John Gurtler

Calgary Flames
Address: Olympic Saddledome
           P.O. Box 1540, Station M
           Calgary, Alberta T2P 3B9
Telephone: (403) 261-0475
Arena (Capacity): Olympic Saddledome (20,130)
Owners: Harley N. Hotchkiss, Norman L. Kwong, Sonia
  Scurfield, Byron J. Seaman, and Daryl K. Seaman
President and Governor: William Hay
Coach and General Manager: Doug Risebrough
Director of Public Relations: Rick Skaggs

Chicago Blackhawks
Address: 1800 W. Madison Street
           Chicago, IL 60612
Telephone: (312) 733-5300
Arena (Capacity): Chicago Stadium (17,317)
President: William W. Wirtz
Coach and General Manager: Mike Keenan
Public Relations Director: Jim DeMaria

Detroit Red Wings
Address: Joe Louis Sports Arena
           600 Civic Center Drive
           Detroit, MI 48226
Telephone: (313) 567-7333
Arena (Capacity): Joe Louis Sports Arena (19,275)
Owner and President: Michael Illitch
Coach and General Manager: Bryan Murray
Director of Public Relations: Bill Jamieson

Edmonton Oilers
Address: Northlands Coliseum
           Edmonton, Alberta T5B 4M9
Telephone: (403) 474-8561
Ticket Information Number: (403) 471-2171
Arena (Capacity): Northlands Coliseum (17,313;
  standing: 190)
Owner and Governor: Peter Pocklington
General Manager: Glen Sather
Coach: Ted Green
Director of Public Relations: Bill Tuele

Hartford Whalers
Address: 242 Trumbull Street, 8th floor
           Hartford, CT 06103
Telephone: (203) 728-3366
Arena (Capacity): Hartford Civic Center Coliseum
  (15,635)
Managing General Partner and Governor: Richard
  Gordon
General Partner and Alternate Governor: Ben J. Sisti
General Manager: Ed Johnston
Coach: Jim Roberts
Director of Public Relations: John H. Forslund

Los Angeles Kings
Address: The Great Western Forum
           3900 West Manchester Boulevard
           P.O. Box 17013
           Inglewood, CA 90308
Telephone: (213) 419-3160
Arena (Capacity): The Great Western Forum (16,005)
Governor and President: Bruce McNall
General Manager: Rogatien Vachon
Coach: Tom Webster
Media Relations: Susan Carpenter

Minnesota North Stars
Address: Metropolitan Sports Center
           7901 Cedar Avenue South
           Bloomington, MN 55425
Telephone: (612) 853-9333
Arena (Capacity): Metropolitan Sports Center (15,093)
Owner: Norman N. Green
General Manager: Bob Clarke
Coach: Bob Gainey
Director of Public Relations: Joan Preston

Montreal Canadiens
Address: Montreal Forum
           2313 St. Catherine Street West
           Montreal, Quebec H3H 1N2
Telephone: (514) 932-2582
Arena (Capacity): Montreal Forum (16,197)
Chairman of the Board, President and Governor:
  Ronald Corey
General Manager: Serge A. Savard
Coach: Pat Burns
Director of Public Relations: Claude Mouton

New Jersey Devils
Address: Byrne Meadowlands Arena
           P.O. Box 504
           East Rutherford, NJ 07073
Telephone: (201) 935-6050
Arena (Capacity): Byrne Meadowlands Arena (19,040)
Chairman: John J. McMullen
President and General Manager: Lou Lamoriello
Coach: Tom McVie
Publicity Director: Dave Freed

New York Islanders
Address: Nassau Veterans' Memorial Coliseum
           Uniondale, NY 11553
Telephone: (516) 794-4100
Arena (Capacity): Nassau Veterans' Memorial Coli-
  seum (16,297)
Owner: John O. Pickett Jr.
General Manager: Bill Torrey
Coach: Al Arbour
Publicity Director: Greg Bouris

New York Rangers
Address: Madison Square Garden
           4 Pennsylvania Plaza
           New York, NY 10001
Telephone: (212) 465-6000
Arena (Capacity): Madison Square Garden (17,520)
Owner: Paramount Communications, Inc.
Vice President and General Manager: Neil Smith
Coach: Roger Neilson
Director of Communications: Barry Watkins

Philadelphia Flyers
Address: The Spectrum
           Pattison Place
           Philadelphia, PA 19148
Telephone: (215) 465-4500
Arena (Capacity): The Spectrum (17,423)
Majority Owners: Ed Snider and family
Limited Partners: Sylvan and Fran Tobin
General Manager: Russ Farwell
Coach: Paul Holmgren
Director of Public Relations: Rodger Gottlieb

Pittsburgh Penguins

Address: Civic Arena
                Pittsburgh, PA 15219
Telephone: (412) 642-1800
Arena (Capacity): Civic Arena (16,164)
Chairman of the Board: Edward J. DeBartolo Sr.
General Manager: Craig Patrick
Coach: Bob Johnson
Acting Coach: Scotty Bowman
Director of Press Relations: Cindy Himes

Quebec Nordiques

Address: Colisee de Quebec
                2205 Ave du Colisee
                Quebec City, Quebec G1L 4W7
Telephone: (418) 529-8441
Arena (Capacity): Colisee de Quebec
President and Governor: Marcel Aubut
General Manager: Pierre Page
Coach: Dave Chambers
Vice President, Marketing and Communications:
   Jean-D. Legault

St. Louis Blues

Address: St. Louis Arena
                5700 Oakland Avenue
                St. Louis, MO 63110
Telephone: (314) 781-1397
Arena (Capacity): St. Louis Arena (17,188)
Owner: Kiel Partnership
General Manager: Ron Caron
Coach: Brian Sutter
Vice President and Director of Marketing and Public
   Relations: Susie Mathieu

San Jose Sharks

Address: 10 Almaden Boulevard, Suite 600
                San Jose, CA 95113
Telephone: (408) 287-4275
Arena (Capacity): Cow Palace (10,800)
Owner: George and Gordon Gund
General Manager: Jack Ferreira
Coach: George Kingston
Publicity Director: Tim Bryant

Toronto Maple Leafs

Address: Maple Leaf Gardens
                60 Carlton Street
                Toronto, Ontario M5B 1L1
Telephone: (416) 977-1641
Arena (Capacity): Maple Leaf Gardens (16,182;
   standing: 200)
Board of Directors: Thor Eaton, Donald P. Giffin, Edward Lawrence, Edward McDowell, Edward Rogers, Douglas H. Roxborough, and Steve Stavro
General Manager: Cliff Fletcher
Coach: Tom Watt
Director of Business Operations and Communications: Bob Stellick

Vancouver Canucks

Address: Pacific Coliseum
                100 North Renfrew Street
                Vancouver, B.C. V5K 3N7
Telephone: (604) 254-5141
Arena (Capacity): Pacific Coliseum (16,123)
Board of Directors: (Northwest Sports Enterprises Ltd.) J. Lawrence Dampier, Arthur R. Griffiths, Frank A. Griffiths, F. W. Griffiths, Coleman E. Hall, Senator E. M. Lawson, W. L. McEwen, David S. Owen, Senator Ray Perrault, J. Raymond Peters, Peter Paul Saunders, Andrew E. Saxton, Peter W. Webster, Sydney W. Welsh, D. A. Williams, D. Alexander Farac (Sec.)
Coach, President, and General Manager: Pat Quinn
Director of Public and Media Relations: Steve Tambellini

Washington Capitals

Address: Capital Centre
                Landover, MD 20785
Telephone: (301) 386-7000
Arena (Capacity): Capital Centre (18,130)
Board of Directors: Abe Pollin, David P. Binderman, Stewart L. Binderman, James E. Cafritz, A. James Clark, Albert Cohen, J. Martin Irving, James T. Lewis, R. Robert Linowes, Arthur K. Mason, Dr. Jack Meshel, David M. Osnos, Richard M. Patrick
General Manager: Dave Poile
Coach: Terry Murray
Director of Public Relations: Lou Corletto

Winnipeg Jets

Address: Winnipeg Arena
                15–1430 Maroons Road
                Winnipeg, Manitoba R3G 0L5
Telephone: (204) 783-5387
Arena (Capacity): Winnipeg Arena (15,393)
Board of Directors: Barry L. Shenkarow, Jerry Kruk, Bob Chapman, Marvin Shenkarow, Don Binda, Steve Bannatyne, Harvey Secter, Bill Davis
General Manager: Mike Smith
Coach: John Paddock
Director of Communications: Mike O'Hearn

Sports Poll '91—Continued

Baseball fans vs. pro football fans: 60% of respondents called themselves pro football fans compared to 52% who claimed to be baseball fans. Men preferred pro football over baseball 72% to 60%; women preferred it 48% to 45%.

College Sports Directory

NATIONAL COLLEGIATE ATHLETIC ASSOCIATION (NCAA)

Address: 6201 College Boulevard
                Overland Park, KS 66211
Telephone: (913) 339-1906
Executive Director: Richard D. Schultz
Assistant Executive Director, Communications:
   Dave Cawood

ATLANTIC COAST CONFERENCE

Address: P.O. Drawer ACC
                Greensboro, NC 27419
Telephone: (919) 854-8787
Commissioner: Eugene F. Corrigan
Publicity Director: Thomas Mickle

Clemson University
Address: Clemson, SC 29633
Nickname: Tigers
Telephone: (803) 656-2101
Football Stadium (Capacity): Clemson Memorial
  Stadium (79,854)
Basketball Arena (Capacity): Littlejohn Coliseum
  (11,020)
President: Max Lennon
Athletic Director: Bobby Robinson
Football Coach: Ken Hatfield
Basketball Coach: Cliff Ellis
Sports Information Director: Tim Bourret

Duke University
Address: Durham, NC 27706
Nickname: Blue Devils
Telephone: (919) 684-8111
Football Stadium (Capacity): Wallace Wade Stadium
  (33,941)
Basketball Arena (Capacity): Cameron Indoor
  Stadium (8,564)
President: Dr. H. Keith H. Brodie
Athletic Director: Tom Butters
Football Coach: Barry Wilson
Basketball Coach: Mike Krzyzewski
Sports Information Director: Mike Cragg

Florida State University
Address: Tallahassee, FL 32304
Nickname: Seminoles
Telephone: (904) 644-1403
Football Stadium (Capacity): Doak S. Campbell
  Stadium (60,519)
Basketball Arena (Capacity): Leon County Civic
  Center (12,500)
President: Dr. Dale W. Lick
Athletic Director: Bob Goin
Football Coach: Bobby Bowden
Basketball Coach: Pat Kennedy
Sports Information Director: Wayne Hogan

Note: Played 1991 football season as independent; all other
1991–92 sports in the ACC.

Georgia Tech
Address: 150 Bobby Dodd Way
           Atlanta, GA 30332
Nickname: Yellow Jackets
Telephone: (404) 894-2000
Football Stadium (Capacity): Bobby Dodd Stadium
  (46,000)
Basketball Arena (Capacity): Alexander Memorial
  Coliseum (10,000)
President: Dr. John P. Crecine
Athletic Director: Dr. Homer Rice
Football Coach: Bobby Ross
Basketball Coach: Bobby Cremins
Sports Information Director: Mike Finn

University of Maryland
Address: P.O. Box 295
           College Park, MD 20740
Nickname: Terrapins
Telephone: (301) 314-3131
Football Stadium (Capacity): Byrd Stadium (45,000)
Basketball Arena (Capacity): Cole Fieldhouse
  (14,500)
President: Dr. Donald N. Langerberg
Athletic Director: Andy Geiger
Football Coach: Joe Krivak
Basketball Coach: Gary Williams
Sports Information Director: Herb Hartnett

University of North Carolina
Address: P.O. Box 2126
           Chapel Hill, NC 27514
Nickname: Tar Heels
Telephone: (919) 962-2211
Football Stadium (Capacity): Kenan Memorial
  Stadium (52,000)
Basketball Arena (Capacity): Dean E. Smith Activities
  Center (21,572)
Chancellor: Paul Hardin
Athletic Director: John Swofford
Football Coach: Mack Brown
Basketball Coach: Dean Smith
Sports Information Director: Rick Brewer

North Carolina State University
Address: P.O. Box 8501
           Raleigh, NC 27695
Nickname: Wolfpack
Telephone: (919) 737-2101
Football Stadium (Capacity): Carter-Finley Stadium
  (47,000)
Basketball Arena (Capacity): Reynolds Coliseum
  (12,400)
Chancellor: Dr. Larry K. Monteith
Athletic Director: Todd Turner
Football Coach: Dick Sheridan
Basketball Coach: Les Robinson
Sports Information Director: Mark Bockelman

University of Virginia
Address: P.O. Box 3785
           Charlottesville, VA 22903
Nickname: Cavaliers
Telephone: (804) 982-5151
Football Stadium (Capacity): Scott Stadium (42,000)
Basketball Arena (Capacity): University Hall (8,864)
President: John Casteen III
Athletic Director: Jim Copeland
Football Coach: George Welsh
Basketball Coach: Jeff Jones
Sports Information Director: Rich Murray

Wake Forest University
Address: P.O. Box 7265
           Winston-Salem, NC 27109
Nickname: Demon Deacons
Telephone: (919) 759-5000
Football Stadium (Capacity): Groves Stadium
  (31,500)
Basketball Arena (Capacity): Lawrence Joel
  Coliseum (14,407)
President: Dr. Thomas K. Hearn Jr.
Athletic Director: Dr. Gene Hooks
Football Coach: Bill Dooley
Basketball Coach: Dave Odom
Sports Information Director: John Justus

BIG EAST CONFERENCE
Address: 56 Exchange Terrace
           Providence, RI 02903
Telephone: (401) 272-9108
Commissioner: Michael A. Tranghese
Publicity Director: John Paquette

Boston College
Address: Chestnut Hill, MA 02167
Nickname: Eagles
Telephone: (617) 552-2628
Football Stadium (Capacity): Alumni Stadium (32,000)
Basketball Arena (Capacity): Silvio O. Conte Forum
   (8,604)
President: J. Donald Monan, S.J.
Athletic Director: Chet Gladchuk
Football Coach: Tom Coughlin
Basketball Coach: Jim O'Brien
Sports Information Director: Reid Oslin

University of Connecticut
Address: 2111 Hillside Road
           Storrs, CT 06269
Nickname: Huskies
Telephone: (203) 486-2041
Football Stadium (Capacity): Memorial Stadium
   (16,200)
Basketball Arena (Capacity): Gampel Pavilion (8,241)
President: Dr. Harry J. Hartley
Athletic Director: Lew Perkins
Football Coach: Tom Jackson
Basketball Coach: Jim Calhoun
Sports Information Director: Tim Tolokan

Note: Division I-AA football

Georgetown University
Address: McDonough Gymnasium
           Washington, DC 20057
Nickname: Hoyas
Telephone: (202) 687-2435
Football Stadium (Capacity): Kehoe Field (4,000)
Basketball Arena (Capacity): Capital Centre (19,035)
President: Rev. Leo J. O'Donovan, S.J.
Athletic Director: Francis X. Rienzo
Football Coach: Scott Glacken
Basketball Coach: John Thompson
Sports Information Director: Bill Shapland

Note: Division III football

University of Miami
Address: One Hurricane Drive
           Coral Gables, FL 33146
Nickname: Hurricanes
Telephone: (305) 284-3244
Football Stadium (Capacity): Orange Bowl (75,500)
Basketball Arena (Capacity): Miami Arena (15,008)
President: Edward Foote
Athletic Director: Dave Maggard
Football Coach: Dennis Erickson
Basketball Coach: Leonard Hamilton
Sports Information Director: Linda Venzon

University of Pittsburgh
Address: Dept. of Athletics, P.O. Box 7436
           Pittsburgh, PA 15213
Nickname: Panthers
Telephone: (412) 648-8240
Football Stadium (Capacity): Pitt Stadium (56,500)
Basketball Arena (Capacity): Fitzgerald Field House
   (6,798), Pittsburgh Civic Arena (16,798)
President: J. Dennis O'Connor
Athletic Director: Oval Jaynes
Football Coach: Paul Hackett
Basketball Coach: Paul Evans
Sports Information Director: Ron Wahl

Providence College
Address: River Avenue
           Providence, RI 02918
Nickname: Friars
Telephone: (401) 865-2265
Basketball Arena (Capacity): Providence Civic Center
   (13,203)
President: Rev. John Cunningham, O.P.
Athletic Director: John Marinatto
Basketball Coach: Rick Barnes
Sports Information Director: Gregg Burke

Note: No football program

Rutgers University
Address: New Brunswick, NJ 08091
Nickname: Scarlet Knights
Telephone: (908) 932-4200
Football Stadium (Capacity): Rutgers Stadium
   (25,000), Giants Stadium (76,000)
Basketball Arena (Capacity): Louis Brown Athletic
   Center (8,000)
President: Dr. Francis L. Lawrence
Athletic Director: Frederick Gruninger
Football Coach: Doug Graber
Basketball Coach: Bob Wenzel
Sports Information Director: Bob Smith

Note: Plays football in Big East, basketball in Atlantic 10
Conference.

St. John's University
Address: Jamaica, NY 11439
Nickname: Redmen
Telephone: (718) 990-6367
Football Stadium (Capacity): Redmen Field (3,000)
Basketball Arena (Capacity): Alumni Hall (6,008),
   Madison Square Garden (18,100)
President: Very Rev. Donald Harrington
Athletic Director: John W. Kaiser
Football Coach: Bob Rica
Basketball Coach: Lou Carnesecca
Sports Information Director: Frank Racaniello

Note: Division III football

Seton Hall University
Address: 400 South Orange Avenue
           South Orange, NJ 07079
Nickname: Pirates
Telephone: (201) 761-9497
Basketball Arena (Capacity): Walsh Gym (3,200),
   The Meadowlands (19,761)
Chancellor: Rev. Thomas R. Peterson
Athletic Director: Larry Keating
Basketball Coach: P. J. Carlesimo
Sports Information Director: John Wooding

Note: No football program.

Syracuse University
Address: Manley Field House
           Syracuse, NY 13244
Nickname: Orangemen
Telephone: (315) 443-2384
Football Stadium (Capacity): Carrier Dome (50,000)
Basketball Arena (Capacity): Carrier Dome (32,683)
Chancellor: Dr. Kenneth Shaw
Athletic Director: Jake Crouthamel
Football Coach: Paul Pasqualoni
Basketball Coach: Jim Boeheim
Sports Information Director: Larry Kimball

Temple University
Address: McGonigle Hall
             Philadelphia, PA 19122
Nickname: Owls
Telephone: (215) 787-7000
Football Stadium (Capacity): Veterans Stadium
  (66,592)
Basketball Arena (Capacity): McGonigle Hall (3,900)
President: Peter Liacouras
Athletic Director: Charles Theokas
Football Coach: Jerry Berndt
Basketball Coach: John Chaney
Sports Information Director: Al Shrier

Note: Plays football in Big East, basketball in Atlantic 10 Conference.

Villanova University
Address: Lancaster Avenue
             Villanova, PA 19085
Nickname: Wildcats
Telephone: (215) 645-4110
Football Stadium (Capacity): Villanova Stadium
  (13,400)
Basketball Arena (Capacity): duPont Pavilion (6,500),
  The Spectrum (18,497)
President: Rev. Edmund Dobbin, O.S.A.
Athletic Director: Dr. Ted Aceto
Football Coach: Andy Talley
Basketball Coach: Rollie Massimino
Sports Information Director: Jim DeLorenzo

Note: Division I-AA football

Virginia Tech
Address: Jamerson Athletic Center
             Blacksburg, VA 24060
Nickname: Hokies
Telephone: (703) 231-6726
Football Stadium (Capacity): Lane Stadium (51,000)
Basketball Arena (Capacity): Cassell Coliseum
  (10,000)
President: Dr. James McComas
Athletic Director: Dave Braine
Football Coach: Frank Beamer
Basketball Coach: Bill Foster
Sports Information Director: Dave Smith

Note: Plays football in Big East, basketball in Metro Conference.

West Virginia University
Address: P.O. Box 877
             Morgantown, WV 26507
Nickname: Mountaineers
Telephone: (304) 293-2821
Football Stadium (Capacity): Mountaineer Field
  (63,500)
Basketball Arena (Capacity): WVU Coliseum (14,000)
President: Neil Bucklew
Athletic Director: Ed Pastilong
Football Coach: Don Nehlen
Basketball Coach: Gale Catlett
Sports Information Director: Shelley Poe

Note: Plays football in Big East, basketball in Atlantic 10 Conference.

BIG EIGHT CONFERENCE
Address: 104 West Ninth Street
             Kansas City, MO 64105
Telephone: (816) 471-5088
Commissioner: Carl C. James
Publicity Director: Jeff Bolling

University of Colorado
Address: Campus Box 368
             Boulder, CO 80309
Nickname: Buffaloes
Telephone: (303) 492-0111
Football Stadium (Capacity): Folsom Field (51,941)
Basketball Arena (Capacity): Coors Event Center
  (11,199)
President: William H. Baughn
Athletic Director: Bill Marolt
Football Coach: Bill McCartney
Basketball Coach: Joe Harrington
Sports Information Director: David Plati

Iowa State University
Address: Oslen Building
             Ames, IA 50011
Nickname: Cyclones
Telephone: (515) 294-3662
Football Stadium (Capacity): Cyclone Stadium-Trice
  Field (50,000)
Basketball Arena (Capacity): Hilton Coliseum (14,020)
President: Milton Glick
Athletic Director: Max Urick
Football Coach: Jim Walden
Basketball Coach: Johnny Orr
Sports Information Director: Dave Starr

University of Kansas
Address: Allen Field House
             Lawrence, KS 66045
Nickname: Jayhawks
Telephone: (913) 864-2700
Football Stadium (Capacity): Memorial Stadium
  (50,250)
Basketball Arena (Capacity): Allen Field House
  (15,800)
Chancellor: Dr. Gene Budig
Athletic Director: Dr. Bob Fredrick
Football Coach: Glen Mason
Basketball Coach: Roy Williams
Sports Information Director: Doug Vance

Kansas State University
Address: Manhattan, KS 66506
Nickname: Wildcats
Telephone: (913) 532-6011
Football Stadium (Capacity): KSU Stadium (42,000)
Basketball Arena (Capacity): Bramlage Coliseum
  (13,500)
President: Dr. J. Wefald
Athletic Director: Milt Richards
Football Coach: Bill Snyder
Basketball Coach: Dana Altman
Sports Information Director: Kenny Mossman

University of Missouri
Address: P.O. Box 677
             Columbia, MO 65205
Nickname: Tigers
Telephone: (314) 882-2121
Football Stadium (Capacity): Faurot Field (62,000)
Basketball Arena (Capacity): Hearnes Center (13,143)
Chancellor: Haskell Monroe
Athletic Director: Dick Tamburo
Football Coach: Bob Stull
Basketball Coach: Norm Stewart
Sports Information Director: Bob Brendel

University of Nebraska
Address: 116 South Stadium
            Lincoln, NE 68588
Nickname: Cornhuskers
Telephone: (402) 472-7211
Football Stadium (Capacity): Memorial Stadium
   (73,650)
Basketball Arena (Capacity): Bob Devaney Sports
   Center (14,302)
Chancellor: Dr. Martin Massengale
Athletic Director: Bob Devaney
Football Coach: Tom Osborne
Basketball Coach: Danny Nee
Sports Information Director: Don Bryant

University of Oklahoma
Address: 180 W. Brooks
            Norman, OK 73019
Nickname: Sooners
Telephone: (405) 325-0311
Football Stadium (Capacity): Owen Field (74,993)
Basketball Arena (Capacity): Lloyd Noble Center
   (10,861)
President: Richard Van Horn
Athletic Director: Donnie Duncan
Football Coach: Gary Gibbs
Basketball Coach: Billy Tubbs
Sports Information Director: Mike Treps

Oklahoma State University
Address: 202 Gallagher-Iba Arena
            Stillwater, OK 74078
Nickname: Cowboys
Telephone: (405) 744-5749
Football Stadium (Capacity): Lewis Field (50,440)
Basketball Arena (Capacity): Gallagher-Iba Arena
   (6,381)
President: Dr. John R. Campbell
Athletic Director: Jim Garner
Football Coach: Pat Jones
Basketball Coach: Eddie Sutton
Sports Information Director: Steve Buzzard

BIG TEN CONFERENCE
Address: 1500 West Higgins Road
            Park Ridge, IL 60068
Telephone: (708) 696-1010
Commissioner: James E. Delany
Publicity Director: Mark Rudner

University of Illinois
Address: 115 Assembly Hall
            1800 S. First Street
            Champaign, IL 61820
Nickname: Fighting Illini
Telephone: (217) 333-1000
Football Stadium (Capacity): Memorial Stadium
   (69,200)
Basketball Arena (Capacity): Assembly Hall (16,153)
Chancellor: Morton Weir
Athletic Director: John Mackovic
Football Coach: John Mackovic
Basketball Coach: Lou Henson
Sports Information Director: Mike Pearson

Indiana University
Address: 17th Street and Fee Lane/Assembly Hall
            Bloomington, IN 47405
Nickname: Hoosiers
Telephone: (812) 855-4848
Football Stadium (Capacity): Memorial Stadium
   (52,354)
Basketball Arena (Capacity): Assembly Hall (17,311)
President: Thomas Ehrlich
Athletic Director: Clarence Doninger
Football Coach: Bill Mallory
Basketball Coach: Bob Knight
Sports Information Director: Kit Klingelhoffer

University of Iowa
Address: 205 Carver-Hawkeye Arena
            Iowa City, IA 52242
Nickname: Hawkeyes
Telephone: (319) 335-3500
Football Stadium (Capacity): Kinnick Stadium
   (70,311)
Basketball Arena (Capacity): Carver-Hawkeye Arena
   (15,500)
President: Hunter Rawlings III
Athletic Director: Robert Bowlsby
Football Coach: Hayden Fry
Basketball Coach: Tom Davis
Sports Information Director: George Wine

University of Michigan
Address: 1000 S. State Street
            Ann Arbor, MI 48109
Nickname: Wolverines
Telephone: (313) 764-1817
Football Stadium (Capacity): Michigan Stadium
   (101,701)
Basketball Arena (Capacity): Crisler Arena (13,609)
President: James Duderstadt
Athletic Director: Jack Weidenbach
Football Coach: Gary Moeller
Basketball Coach: Steve Fisher
Sports Information Director: Bruce Madej

Michigan State University
Address: East Lansing, MI 48824
Nickname: Spartans
Telephone: (517) 355-1855
Football Stadium (Capacity): Spartan Stadium
   (76,000)
Basketball Arena (Capacity): Jack Breslin Student
   Center (15,100)
President: Dr. John DiBiaggio
Athletic Director: George Perles
Football Coach: George Perles
Basketball Coach: Jud Heathcote
Sports Information Director: Ken Hoffman

University of Minnesota
Address: 516 15th Avenue S.E.
            Minneapolis, MN 55455
Nickname: Golden Gophers
Telephone: (612) 625-5000
Football Stadium (Capacity): Hubert H. Humphrey
   Metrodome (63,699)
Basketball Arena (Capacity): Williams Arena (16,991)
President: Nils Hasselmo
Acting Athletic Director: Dan Meinert
Football Coach: John Gutekunst
Basketball Coach: Clem Haskins
Sports Information Director: Bob Peterson

Northwestern University
Address: 1501 Central Street
             Evanston, IL 60208
Nickname: Wildcats
Telephone: (708) 491-2300
Football Stadium (Capacity): Dyche Stadium (49,256)
Basketball Arena (Capacity): Welsh-Ryan Arena
  (8,117)
President: Arnold Weber
Athletic Director: Bruce Corrie
Football Coach: Francis Peay
Basketball Coach: Bill Foster
Sports Information Director: Tim Clodjeaux

Ohio State University
Address: 410 Woody Hayes Drive
             Columbus, OH 43210
Nickname: Buckeyes
Telephone: (614) 292-6446
Football Stadium (Capacity): Ohio Stadium (86,071)
Basketball Arena (Capacity): St. John Arena (13,276)
President: E. Gordon Gee
Athletic Director: Jim Jones
Football Coach: John Cooper
Basketball Coach: Randy Ayers
Sports Information Director: Steve Snapp

Penn State University
Address: Recreation Building
             University Park, PA 16802
Nickname: Nittany Lions
Telephone: (814) 865-4700
Football Stadium (Capacity): Beaver Stadium (93,000)
Basketball Arena (Capacity): Recreation Building
  (6,846)
President: Joab Thomas
Athletic Director: Jim Tarman
Football Coach: Joe Paterno
Basketball Coach: Bruce Parkhill
Sports Information Director: Budd Thalman

Note: Plays 1992 football season as independent.

Purdue University
Address: Mackey Arena
             West Lafayette, IN 47907
Nickname: Boilermakers
Telephone: (317) 494-4600
Football Stadium (Capacity): Ross-Ade Stadium
  (67,861)
Basketball Arena (Capacity): Mackey Arena (14,123)
President: Dr. Steven C. Beering
Athletic Director: George S. King Jr.
Football Coach: Jim Colletto
Basketball Coach: Gene Keady
Sports Information Director: Mark Adams

University of Wisconsin
Address: 1440 Monroe Street
             Madison, WI 53711
Nickname: Badgers
Telephone: (608) 262-1234
Football Stadium (Capacity): Camp Randall Stadium
  (77,745)
Basketball Arena (Capacity): UW Fieldhouse (11,895)
Chancellor: Donna Shalala
Athletic Director: Pat Richter
Football Coach: Barry Alvarez
Basketball Coach: Steve Yoder
Sports Information Director: Steve Malchow

PACIFIC-10 CONFERENCE
Address: 800 S. Broadway, Suite 400
             Walnut Creek, CA 94596
Telephone: (415) 932-4411
Commissioner: Thomas C. Hansen
Publicity Director: Jim Muldoon

University of Arizona
Address: McKale Center
             Tucson, AZ 85721
Nickname: Wildcats
Telephone: (602) 621-2211
Football Stadium (Capacity): Arizona Stadium
  (56,197)
Basketball Arena (Capacity): McKale Center (13,477)
President: Henry Koffler
Athletic Director: Dr. Cedric Dempsey
Football Coach: Dick Tomey
Basketball Coach: Lute Olson
Sports Information Director: Butch Henry

Arizona State University
Address: Tempe, AZ 85287
Nickname: Sun Devils
Telephone: (602) 965-9011
Football Stadium (Capacity): Sun Devil Stadium
  (74,865)
Basketball Arena (Capacity): University Activity
  Center (14,287)
President: Lattie Coor
Athletic Director: Charles Harris
Football Coach: Larry Marmie
Basketball Coach: Bill Frieder
Sports Information Director: Mark Brand

University of California
Address: Berkeley, CA 94720
Nickname: Golden Bears
Telephone: (415) 642-5363
Football Stadium (Capacity): Memorial Stadium
  (76,700)
Basketball Arena (Capacity): Harmon Gym (6,600)
Chancellor: Chang-Lin Tien
Athletic Director: Robert L. Bockrath
Football Coach: Bruce Snyder
Basketball Coach: Lou Campanelli
Sports Information Director: Kevin Reneau

University of California at Los Angeles
Address: 405 Hilgard Avenue
             Los Angeles, CA 90024
Nickname: Bruins
Telephone: (213) 825-8699
Football Stadium (Capacity): Rose Bowl (102,083)
Basketball Arena (Capacity): Pauley Pavilion (12,543)
Chancellor: Dr. Charles Young
Athletic Director: Peter T. Dalis
Football Coach: Terry Donahue
Basketball Coach: Jim Harrick
Sports Information Director: Marc Dellins

University of Oregon
Address: McArthur Court
           Eugene, OR 97403
Nickname: Ducks
Telephone: (503) 346-4481
Football Stadium (Capacity): Autzen Stadium (41,698)
Basketball Arena (Capacity): McArthur Court (10,063)
President: Myles Brand
Athletic Director: Bill Byrne
Football Coach: Rich Brooks
Basketball Coach: Don Monson
Sports Information Director: Steve Hellyer

Oregon State University
Address: Gill Coliseum
           Corvallis, OR 97331
Nickname: Beavers
Telephone: (503) 737-0123
Football Stadium (Capacity): Parker Stadium (35,000)
Basketball Arena (Capacity): Gill Coliseum (10,400)
President: Dr. John V. Bryne
Athletic Director: Dutch Baughman
Football Coach: Jerry Pettibone
Basketball Coach: Jim Anderson
Sports Information Director: Hal Cowan

University of Southern California
Address: Los Angeles, CA 90089
Nickname: Trojans
Telephone: (213) 740-2311
Football Stadium (Capacity): Los Angeles Memorial
   Coliseum (92,516)
Basketball Arena (Capacity): Los Angeles Memorial
   Sports Arena (15,509)
President: Dr. Steven Sample
Athletic Director: Mike McGee
Football Coach: Larry Smith
Basketball Coach: George Raveling
Sports Information Director: Tim Tessalone

Stanford University
Address: Stanford, CA 94305
Nickname: Cardinal
Telephone: (415) 723-2300
Football Stadium (Capacity): Stanford Stadium
   (86,019)
Basketball Arena (Capacity): Maples Pavilion (7,500)
President: Dr. Donald Kennedy
Athletic Director: Dr. Ted Leland
Football Coach: Dennis Green
Basketball Coach: Mike Montgomery
Sports Information Director: Gary Migdol

University of Washington
Address: 202 Graves
           Seattle, WA 98195
Nickname: Huskies
Telephone: (206) 543-2100
Football Stadium (Capacity): Husky Stadium (72,500)
Basketball Arena (Capacity): Hec Edmundson
   Pavilion (8,000)
President: Dr. William P. Gerberding
Athletic Director: Barbara Hedges
Football Coach: Don James
Basketball Coach: Lynn Nance
Sports Information Director: Dave Senko

Washington State University
Address: 107 Bohler Gym
           Pullman, WA 99164
Nickname: Cougars
Telephone: (509) 335-0311
Football Stadium (Capacity): Martin Stadium (40,000)
Basketball Arena (Capacity): Friel Court (12,058)
President: Samuel Smith
Athletic Director: Jim Livengood
Football Coach: Mike Price
Basketball Coach: Kelvin Sampson
Sports Information Director: Rod Commons

SOUTHEASTERN CONFERENCE
Address: 200 Civic Center Boulevard
           Birmingham, AL 35203
Telephone: (205) 458-3000
Commissioner: Roy Kramer
Publicity Director: Mark Whitworth

University of Alabama
Address: P.O. Box 870391
           Paul Bryant Drive
           Tuscaloosa, AL 35487
Nickname: Crimson Tide
Telephone: (205) 348-3600
Football Stadium (Capacity): Bryant-Denny Stadium
   (70,123)
Basketball Arena (Capacity): Coleman Coliseum
   (15,043)
President: Dr. Roger Sayers
Athletic Director: Cecil "Hootie" Ingram
Football Coach: Gene Stallings
Basketball Coach: Wimp Sanderson
Sports Information Director: Larry White

University of Arkansas
Address: Broyles Athletic Complex
           Fayetteville, AR 72702
Nickname: Razorbacks
Telephone: (501) 575-2751
Football Stadium (Capacity): Razorback Stadium
   (52,968)
Basketball Arena (Capacity): Barnhill Arena (9,000)
Chancellor: Dr. Dan Ferritor
Athletic Director: Frank Broyles
Football Coach: Jack Crowe
Basketball Coach: Nolan Richardson
Sports Information Director: Rick Schaeffer
Note: Played 1991 football season in SWC; all other 1991–92
sports in SEC.

Auburn University
Address: P.O. Box 351
           Auburn, AL 36831-0351
Nickname: Tigers
Telephone: (205) 844-9800
Football Stadium (Capacity): Jordan Hare Stadium
   (85,214)
Basketball Arena (Capacity): Joel H. Eaves Memorial
   Coliseum (13,500)
President: Dr. James E. Martin
Athletic Director: Pat Dye
Football Coach: Pat Dye
Basketball Coach: Tommy Joe Eagles
Sports Information Director: David Housel

University of Florida
Address: P.O. Box 14485
Gainesville, FL 32604
Nickname: Gators
Telephone: (904) 375-4683
Football Stadium (Capacity): Ben Hill Griffin Stadium (83,000)
Basketball Arena (Capacity): Stephen O'Connell Center (12,000)
President: Dr. John Lombardi
Athletic Director: Bill Arnsparger
Football Coach: Steve Spurrier
Basketball Coach: Lon Kruger
Sports Information Director: John Humenik

University of Georgia
Address: P.O. Box 1472
Athens, GA 30613
Nickname: Bulldogs
Telephone: (404) 542-1621
Football Stadium (Capacity): Sanford Stadium (85,434)
Basketball Arena (Capacity): The Coliseum (10,512)
President: Dr. Charles Knapp
Athletic Director: Vince Dooley
Football Coach: Ray Goff
Basketball Coach: Hugh Durham
Sports Information Director: Claude Felton

University of Kentucky
Address: Memorial Coliseum
Lexington, KY 40506
Nickname: Wildcats
Telephone: (606) 257-3838
Football Stadium (Capacity): Commonwealth Stadium (57,800)
Basketball Arena (Capacity): Rupp Arena (23,000)
President: Dr. Charles Wellington Jr.
Athletic Director: C. M. Newton
Football Coach: Bill Curry
Basketball Coach: Rick Pitino
Sports Information Director: Chris Cameron

Louisiana State University
Address: Baton Rouge, LA 70894
Nickname: Fighting Tigers
Telephone: (504) 388-8226
Football Stadium (Capacity): Tiger Stadium (80,140)
Basketball Arena (Capacity): Pete Maravich Assembly Center (14,236)
Chancellor: Dr. Bud Davis
Athletic Director: Joe Dean
Football Coach: Curley Hallman
Basketball Coach: Dale Brown
Sports Information Director: Herb Vincent

University of Mississippi
Address: P.O. Box 217
University, MS 38677
Nickname: Rebels
Telephone: (601) 232-7522
Football Stadium (Capacity): Vaught-Hemingway Stadium (42,577)
Basketball Arena (Capacity): C. M. "Tad" Smith Coliseum (9,000)
President: Dr. R. Gerald Turner
Athletic Director: Warner Alford
Football Coach: Billy Brewer
Basketball Coach: Ed Murphy
Sports Information Director: Langston Rogers

Mississippi State University
Address: P.O. Drawer 5308
Mississippi St., MS 39762
Nickname: Bulldogs
Telephone: (601) 325-2703
Football Stadium (Capacity): Scott Field (41,200)
Basketball Arena (Capacity): Humphrey Coliseum (10,000)
President: Dr. Donald Zacharias
Athletic Director: Larry Templeton
Football Coach: Jackie Sherrill
Basketball Coach: Richard Williams
Sports Information Director: Joe Dier

University of South Carolina
Address: Rex Enright Athletic Center
Rosewood Drive
Columbia, SC 29208
Nickname: Gamecocks
Telephone: (803) 777-5204
Football Stadium (Capacity): Williams-Brice Stadium (72,400)
Basketball Arena (Capacity): Carolina Coliseum (12,401)
President: Dr. John Palms
Athletic Director: King Dixon
Football Coach: Sparky Woods
Basketball Coach: Steve Newton
Sports Information Director: Kerry Tharp

Note: Played 1991 football season as independent; all other 1991–92 sports in the SEC.

University of Tennessee
Address: P.O. Box 15016
Knoxville, TN 37901
Nickname: Volunteers
Telephone: (615) 974-1212
Football Stadium (Capacity): Neyland Stadium (91,110)
Basketball Arena (Capacity): Thompson Boling Assembly Center (24,535)
President: Dr. Joseph E. Johnson
Athletic Director: Doug Dickey
Football Coach: Johnny Majors
Basketball Coach: Wade Houston
Sports Information Director: Bud Ford

Vanderbilt University
Address: P.O. Box 120158
Nashville, TN 37212
Nickname: Commodores
Telephone: (615) 322-4121
Football Stadium (Capacity): Vanderbilt Stadium (41,000)
Basketball Arena (Capacity): Memorial Gym (15,378)
Chancellor: Joe B. Wyatt
Athletic Director: Paul Hoolahan
Football Coach: Gerry DiNardo
Basketball Coach: Eddie Folger
Sports Information Director: Lew Harris

SOUTHWEST ATHLETIC CONFERENCE
Address: P.O. Box 569420
Dallas, TX 75356
Telephone: (214) 634-7353
Commissioner: Fred Jacoby
Publicity Director: Bo Carter

Baylor University
Address: 3031 Dutton
Waco, TX 76711
Nickname: Bears
Telephone: (817) 755-1234
Football Stadium (Capacity): Floyd Casey Stadium (48,500)
Basketball Arena (Capacity): Ferrell Center (10,080)
President: Dr. Herbert H. Reynolds
Athletic Director: Bill Menefee
Football Coach: Grant Teaff
Basketball Coach: Gene Iba
Sports Information Director: Maxie Parrish

University of Houston
Address: 3855 Holman
Houston, TX 77204-5121
Nickname: Cougars
Telephone: (713) 749-2180
Football Stadium (Capacity): Astrodome (60,000)
Basketball Arena (Capacity): Hofheinz Pavilion (10,060)
President: Dr. Marguerite Ross Barnett
Athletic Director: Rudy Davalos
Football Coach: John Jenkins
Basketball Coach: Pat Foster
Sports Information Director: Ted Nance

Rice University
Address: P.O. Box 1892
Houston, TX 77251
Nickname: Owls
Telephone: (713) 527-4034
Football Stadium (Capacity): Rice Stadium (70,000)
Basketball Arena (Capacity): Autry Court (5,000)
President: Dr. George Rupp
Athletic Director: Bobby May
Football Coach: Fred Goldsmith
Basketball Coach: Scott Thompson
Sports Information Director: Bill Cousins

Southern Methodist University
Address: SMU Box 216
Dallas, TX 75275
Nickname: Mustangs
Telephone: (214) 692-2883
Football Stadium (Capacity): Ownby Stadium (23,783)
Basketball Arena (Capacity): Moody Coliseum (9,007)
President: A. Kenneth Pye
Athletic Director: Forrest Gregg
Football Coach: Tom Rossley
Basketball Coach: John Shumate
Sports Information Director: Ed Wisneski

University of Texas
Address: P.O. Box 7399
Austin, TX 78713
Nickname: Longhorns
Telephone: (512) 471-7437
Football Stadium (Capacity): Memorial Stadium (77,809)
Basketball Arena (Capacity): Irwin Special Events Center (16,201)
President: Dr. William Cunningham
Athletic Director: DeLoss Dodds
Football Coach: David McWilliams
Basketball Coach: Tom Penders
Sports Information Director: Bill Little

Texas A&M University
Address: Joe Routt Boulevard
College Station, TX 77843-1228
Nickname: Aggies
Telephone: (409) 845-3218
Football Stadium (Capacity): Kyle Field (72,387)
Basketball Arena (Capacity): G. Rollie White Coliseum (7,500)
President: Dr. William H. Mobley
Athletic Director: John David Crow
Football Coach: R. C. Slocum
Basketball Coach: Tony Barone
Sports Information Director: Alan Cannon

Texas Christian University
Address: P.O. Box 32924
Fort Worth, TX 76129
Nickname: Horned Frogs
Telephone: (817) 921-7969
Football Stadium (Capacity): Amon G. Carter Stadium (46,000)
Basketball Arena (Capacity): Daniel-Meyer Coliseum (7,166)
Chancellor: Dr. William E. Tucker
Athletic Director: Frank Windegger
Football Coach: Jim Wacker
Basketball Coach: Moe Iba
Sports Information Director: Glen Stone

Texas Tech University
Address: P.O. Box 43021
Lubbock, TX 79409
Nickname: Red Raiders
Telephone: (806) 742-2770
Football Stadium (Capacity): Jones Stadium (50,500)
Basketball Arena (Capacity): Lubbock Municipal Coliseum (8,196)
President: Dr. Robert Lawless
Athletic Director: T. Jones
Football Coach: Spike Dykes
Basketball Coach: James Dickey
Sports Information Director: Joe Hornaday

WESTERN ATHLETIC CONFERENCE
Address: 14 West Dry Creek Circle
Littleton, CO 80120
Telephone: (303) 795-1962
Commissioner: Dr. Joe Kearney
Publicity Director: Jeff Hurd

Air Force
Address: Colorado Springs, CO 80840-5461
Nickname: Falcons
Telephone: (719) 472-4008
Football Stadium (Capacity): Falcon Stadium (52,153)
Basketball Arena (Capacity): Cadet Field House (6,007)
President: Lt. Gen. Bradley C. Hosmer
Athletic Director: Kenneth L. Schweitzer
Football Coach: Fisher DeBerry
Basketball Coach: Reggie Minton
Sports Information Director: David Kellogg

Brigham Young University

Address: Smith Field House
Provo, UT 84602
Nickname: Cougars
Telephone: (801) 378-2096
Football Stadium (Capacity): Cougar Stadium (65,000)
Basketball Arena (Capacity): Marriott Center (23,000)
President: Rex Lee
Athletic Director: Glen Tuckett
Football Coach: LaVell Edwards
Basketball Coach: Roger Reid
Sports Information Director: Ralph Zobell

Colorado State University

Address: Moby Arena
Fort Collins, CO 80523
Nickname: Rams
Telephone: (303) 491-5300
Football Stadium (Capacity): Hughes Stadium (30,000)
Basketball Arena (Capacity): Moby Arena (9,001)
President: Dr. Albert C. Yates
Athletic Director: Chuck Bell
Football Coach: Earle Bruce
Basketball Coach: Stew Morrill
Sports Information Director: Gary Ozello

University of Hawaii

Address: 1337 Lower Campus Road
Honolulu, HI 96822-2370
Nickname: Rainbow Warriors
Telephone: (808) 956-8111
Football Stadium (Capacity): Aloha Stadium (50,000)
Basketball Arena (Capacity): Neal Blaisedell Center Arena (7,575)
President: Dr. Albert Simone
Athletic Director: Stan Sheriff
Football Coach: Bob Wagner
Basketball Coach: Riley Wallace
Sports Information Director: Ed Inouye

University of New Mexico

Address: 14 University S.E.
Albuquerque, NM 87131
Nickname: Lobos
Telephone: (505) 277-6375
Football Stadium (Capacity): University Stadium (30,646)
Basketball Arena (Capacity): University Arena—The Pit (18,100)
President: Dr. Richard Peck
Athletic Director: Dr. Gary Ness
Football Coach: Mike Sheppard
Basketball Coach: Dave Bliss
Sports Information Director: Greg Remington

San Diego State University

Address: San Diego, CA 92182
Nickname: Aztecs
Telephone: (619) 594-5163
Football Stadium (Capacity): San Diego Jack Murphy Stadium (60,409)
Basketball Arena (Capacity): San Diego Sports Arena (13,741)
President: Dr. Thomas B. Day
Athletic Director: Dr. Fred Miller
Football Coach: Al Luginbill
Basketball Coach: Jim Brandenburg
Sports Information Director: John Rosenthal

University of Texas at El Paso

Address: 500 West University Avenue
El Paso, TX 79968
Nickname: Miners
Telephone: (915) 747-5347
Football Stadium (Capacity): Sun Bowl (52,000)
Basketball Arena (Capacity): Special Events Center (12,222)
President: Dr. Diana Natalicio
Athletic Director: Dr. Brad Hovious
Football Coach: David Lee
Basketball Coach: Don Haskins
Sports Information Director: Eddie Mullens

University of Utah

Address: Huntsman Center
Salt Lake City, UT 84112
Nickname: Utes
Telephone: (801) 581-8171
Football Stadium (Capacity): Rice Stadium (35,000)
Basketball Arena (Capacity): Huntsman Center (15,000)
President: Dr. Arthur K. Smith
Athletic Director: Dr. Chris Hill
Football Coach: Ron McBride
Basketball Coach: Rick Majerus
Sports Information Director: Liz Abel

University of Wyoming

Address: P.O. Box 3414
Laramie, WY 82071-3414
Nickname: Cowboys
Telephone: (307) 766-2292
Football Stadium (Capacity): War Memorial Stadium (33,500)
Basketball Arena (Capacity): Arena-Auditorium (15,028)
President: Terry Roark
Athletic Director: Paul Roach
Football Coach: Joe Tiller
Basketball Coach: Benny Dees
Sports Information Director: Kevin McKinney

Independents

Army

Address: West Point, NY 10996
Nickname: Black Knights
Telephone: (914) 938-3303
Football Stadium (Capacity): Michie Stadium (40,157)
Basketball Arena (Capacity): Cristl Arena (5,043)
President: Lt. Gen. David Palmer
Athletic Director: Col. Al Vanderbush
Football Coach: Bob Sutton
Basketball Coach: Tom Miller
Sports Information Director: Bob Kinney

Note: Plays football as independent, basketball in Metro Atlantic Athletic Conference.

University of Louisville

Address: Louisville, KY 40292
Nickname: Cardinals
Telephone: (502) 588-6581
Football Stadium (Capacity): Cardinal Stadium (35,500)
Basketball Arena (Capacity): Freedom Hall (18,865)
President: Dr. Donald Swain
Athletic Director: William Olsen
Football Coach: Howard Schnellenberger
Basketball Coach: Denny Crum
Sports Information Director: Kenny Klein

Note: Plays football as independent, basketball in Metro Conference.

Navy
Address: Annapolis, MD 21402
Nickname: Midshipmen
Telephone: (301) 268-6226
Football Stadium (Capacity): Navy-Marine Corps Memorial Stadium (30,000)
Basketball Arena (Capacity): Alumni Hall (5,710)
Superintendent: Rear Adm. Thomas C. Lynch, USN
Athletic Director: Jack Lengyel
Football Coach: George Chaump
Basketball Coach: Pete Herrmann
Sports Information Director: Thomas Bates

Note: Plays football as independent, basketball in Colonial Athletic Association.

University of Notre Dame
Address: Notre Dame, IN 46556
Nickname: Fighting Irish
Telephone: (219) 239-5000
Football Stadium (Capacity): Notre Dame Stadium (59,075)
Basketball Arena (Capacity): Joyce Athletic and Convocation Center (11,418)
President: Rev. Edward A. Malloy
Athletic Director: Richard Rosenthal
Football Coach: Lou Holtz
Basketball Coach: John MacLeod
Sports Information Director: John Heisler

University of Southern Mississippi
Address: Southern Station
            Hattiesburg, MS 39406
Nickname: Golden Eagles
Telephone: (601) 266-5017
Football Stadium (Capacity): M. M. Roberts Stadium (33,000)
Basketball Arena (Capacity): Green Coliseum (8,532)
President: Dr. Aubrey K. Lucas
Athletic Director: Bill McLellan
Football Coach: Jeff Bower
Basketball Coach: M. K. Turk
Sports Information Director: Regiel Napier

Note: Plays football as independent, basketball in Metro Conference.

Tulane University
Address: New Orleans, LA 70118
Nickname: Green Wave
Telephone: (504) 865-5501
Football Stadium (Capacity): Louisiana Superdome (69,065)
Basketball Arena (Capacity): Fogelman Arena (3,500)
President: Dr. Eamon Kelly
Athletic Director: Dr. Kevin White
Football Coach: Greg Davis
Basketball Coach: Perry Clark
Sports Information Director: Lenny Vanglider

Note: Plays football as independent, basketball in Metro Conference.

Olympic Sports Directory

United States Olympic Committee
Address: Olympic House
            1750 East Boulder Street
            Colorado Springs, CO 80909
Telephone: (719) 632-5551
Executive Director: Dr. Harvey Schiller
Public Information and Media Relations
    Director: Mike Moran
    Associate Director: Bob Condron
    Assistant Director: Jeff Cravens
    Senior Coordinator: Gayle Plant
Telephone: (719) 578-4529

U.S. Olympic Training Center
Address: 1776 East Boulder Street
            Colorado Springs, CO 80909
Telephone: (719) 578-4500
Director: Charles Davis

U.S. Olympic Training Center
Address: 421 Old Military Road
            Lake Placid, NY 12946
Telephone: (518) 523-1570
Director: Gloria Chadwick

International Olympic Committee
Address: Chateau de Vidy
            CH-1007 Lausanne
            Switzerland
Telephone: (41.21) 25 3271/3272
President: Juan Antonio Samaranch
Director General: Francois Carrard
Public Relations Officer: Michele Verdier

Albertville Olympic Organizing Committee (COJO)
Address: 11, rue Pargoux
            73200 Albertville, France
Telephone: (33) 7945-1992
Copresidents: M. Michel Barnier and Jean-Claude Killy
Director General: Jean Corrand
Director of Information: M. Cone Croce-Spinelli
(XVIth Olympic Winter Games; February 8–23, 1992)

Barcelona Olympic Organizing Committee (COOB)
Address: COOB '92, S.A.
            Edificio Hellos
            C/Mejia Lequerica, S/N
            08028 Barcelona, Spain
Telephone: (34.3) 411-1992
Maternitat Complex
Travessera de les Corts, 191
08029 Barcelona, Spain
Telephone: (34.3) 490-1992
President and Chairman: M. Pasqual Maragall
Chief Executive Officer: Josep Miquel Abad
(Games of the XXVth Olympiad; July 25– August 9, 1992)

Lillehammer Olympic Organizing Committee
Address: Storgatan 95
            P.O. Box 106
            N-2601 Lillehammer, Norway
Telephone: (47.62) 57455
President: Gerhard Heiberg
Director of Planning: Osmund Uelaud
Director of Communication: Aage Enghaug
(XVIIth Olympic Winter Games; February 12–27, 1994)

Atlanta Olympic Organizing Committee
Address: Suite 3450, One Atlantic Center
         1201 West Peachtree Street
         Atlanta, GA 30309
Telephone: (404) 874-1996
Chairman: Hon. Andrew Young
President: William Porter Payne
Executive Director: Doug Gatlin
(Games of the XXVIth Olympiad; Tentative Dates:
  July 20–August 4, 1996)

U.S. Olympic Organizations

Archery
National Archery Association (NAA)
Address: 1750 East Boulder Street
         Colorado Springs, CO 80909
Telephone: (719) 578-4576
President: Harold Kremer
Executive Director: Christine McCartney

Athletics (Track & Field)
The Athletics Congress (TAC)
Address: P.O. Box 120
         Indianapolis, IN 46206
Telephone: (317) 261-0500
President: Frank Greenberg
Executive Director: Ollan Cassell
Press Information Director: Pete Cava

Badminton
U.S. Badminton Association (USBA)
Address: 920 O Street
         Lincoln, NE 68508
Telephone: (402) 438-2473
President: Martin French
Executive Director: Len Williams

Baseball
U.S. Baseball Federation (USBF)
Address: 2160 Greenwood Avenue
         Trenton, NJ 08609
Telephone: (609) 586-2381
President: Mark Marquess
Executive Director: Richard Case
Communications Director: Bob Bensch

Basketball
USA Basketball
Address: 1750 East Boulder Street
         Colorado Springs, CO 80909
Telephone: (719) 632-7687
President: Dave Gavitt
Executive Director: Bill Wall
Assistant Executive Director for Public Relations:
  Craig Miller

Biathlon
U.S. Biathlon Association (USBA)
Address: P.O. Box 5515
         Essex Junction, VT 05453
Telephone: (802) 655-4524
President: Howard Buxton
Executive Director: Jed Williamson
Marketing and Public Relations: Ted Fay

Bobsled
U.S. Bobsled and Skeleton Federation
Address: P.O. Box 828
         Lake Placid, NY 12946
Telephone: (518) 523-1842
President: William Napier

Bowling
U.S. Tenpin Bowling Federation
Address: 5301 South 76th Street
         Greendale, WI 53129
Telephone: (414) 421-9008
President: Joyce Dietch
Executive Director: Gerald Koenig
Public Relations Coordinator: Maureen Boyle

Boxing
USA Amateur Boxing Federation (USA/ABF)
Address: 1750 East Boulder Street
         Colorado Springs, CO 80909
Telephone: (719) 578-4506
President: Billy Dove
Executive Director: Jim Fox
Director of Communications: Jay Miller

Canoe/Kayak
U.S. Canoe and Kayak Team
Address: Pan American Plaza, Suite 470
         201 South Capitol Avenue
         Indianapolis, IN 46225
Telephone: (317) 237-5690
Chairman: Steve Parsons
Executive Director: Chuck Wielgus
Communications Director: Craig Bohnert

Cycling
U.S. Cycling Federation (USCF)
Address: 1750 East Boulder Street
         Colorado Springs, CO 80909
Telephone: (719) 578-4581
President: Richard DeGarmo
Executive Director: Jerry Lace
Media and Public Relations Director: Steve Penny

Diving
United States Diving, Inc. (USD)
Address: Pan American Plaza, Suite 430
         201 South Capitol Avenue
         Indianapolis, IN 46225
Telephone: (317) 237-5252
President: Micki King Hogue
Executive Director: Todd Smith
Director of Communications: Dave Shalkowski

Equestrian
U.S. Equestrian Team (USET)
Address: Gladstone, NJ 07934
Telephone: (201) 234-1251
President: Finn Casperson
Executive Director: Bob Standish
Director of Public Relations: Marty Bauman

Fencing

U.S. Fencing Association (USFA)
Address: 1750 East Boulder Street
            Colorado Springs, CO 80909
Telephone: (719) 578-4511
President: Michel Mamlouk
Executive Director: Carla-Mae Richards
Media Relations Director: Colleen Walker

Field Hockey

Field Hockey Association of America (FHAA) (Men)

U.S. Field Hockey Association (USFHA) (Women)
Address: 1750 East Boulder Street
            Colorado Springs, CO 80909
Telephone: (719) 578-4587 (FHAA)
Telephone: (719) 578-4567 (USFHA)
President: Allan Woods (FHAA)
Executive Director: Edwin R. Cliatt (FHAA)
Project Administrator: Ann M. Cuka (FHAA)
President: Dr. Judith Davidson (USFHA)
Executive Director: Carolyn Moody (USFHA)
Director of Public Relations: Noreen Landis-Tyson
    (USFHA)

Figure Skating

U.S. Figure Skating Association (USFSA)
Address: 20 First Street
            Colorado Springs, CO 80906
Telephone: (719) 635-5200
President: Franklin S. Nelson
Executive Director: Ian Anderson
Public Relations and Media Manager: Kristin Matta

Gymnastics

U.S. Gymnastics Federation (USGF)
Address: Pan American Plaza, Suite 300
            201 South Capitol Avenue
            Indianapolis, IN 46225
Telephone: (317) 237-5050
President: Mike Donahue
Executive Director: Mike Jacki
Media and Public Relations Coordinator: Patti Auer

Ice Hockey

USA Hockey
Address: 2997 Broadmoor Valley Road
            Colorado Springs, CO 80906
Telephone: (719) 576-4990
President: Walter Bush
Executive Director: Baaron Pittenger
Public Relations Coordinator: Tom Douglis

Judo

United States Judo, Inc. (USJ)
Address: P.O. Box 10013
            El Paso, TX 79991
Telephone: (915) 565-8754
President and Media Contact: Frank Fullerton

Luge

U.S. Luge Association (USLA)
Address: P.O. Box 651
            Lake Placid, NY 12946
Telephone: (518) 523-2071
President: Dwight Bell
Executive Director: Ron Rossi
Public Relations and Media Coordinator: Christina
    Compeau

Modern Pentathlon

U.S. Modern Pentathlon Association (USMPA)
Address: P.O. Box 8178
            San Antonio, TX 78208
Telephone: (512) 246-3000
President: Guy Troy
Executive Director: William Hanson

Racquetball

American Amateur Racquetball Association (AARA)
Address: 815 North Weber
            Colorado Springs, CO 80903
Telephone: (719) 635-5396
President: Keith Calkins
Executive Director: Luke St. Onge
Public Relations Director: Linda Mojer

Roller Skating

U.S. Amateur Confederation of Roller Skating (USAC/RS)
Address: 4730 South Street
            P.O. Box 6579
            Lincoln, NE 68506
Telephone: (402) 483-7551
President: Charles Wahlig
Executive Director: George H. Pickard
Sports Information Director: Dwain Hebda

Rowing

U.S. Rowing Association (USRA)
Address: Pan American Plaza, Suite 400
            201 South Capitol Avenue
            Indianapolis, IN 46225
Telephone: (317) 237-5656
President: Peter Zandbergen
Executive Director: Paula Oyer
Director of Communications: Maureen Merhoff

Shooting

National Rifle Association (NRA)
Address: 1600 Rhode Island Avenue, N.W.
            Washington, DC 20036
Telephone: (202) 828-6000
President: Richard Riley
Executive Director, General Operations: Gary Anderson
U.S. Shooting Team Director: Lones Wigger
1750 East Boulder Street
Colorado Springs, CO 80909
Telephone: (719) 578-4559

Skiing

U.S. Skiing
Address: P.O. Box 100
             Park City, UT 84060
Telephone: (801) 649-9090
Chairman: Thomas Weisel
President and CEO: Howard Peterson
President, U.S. Ski Association: Serge Lussi
President, U.S. Ski Educational Foundation: Vinton
   Sommerville
Director of Communications: Tom Kelly
News Bureau Coordinator: Ron Goch
Press Officer: Jolene Aubel

Soccer

U.S. Soccer Federation (USSF)
Address: 1750 East Boulder Street
             Colorado Springs, CO 80909
Telephone: (719) 578-4678
President: Alan Rothenberg
Executive Director: Hank Steinbrecher
Director of Marketing: Kevin Payne
Director of Public Relations: John Polis

Softball

Amateur Softball Association (ASA)
Address: 2801 N.E. 50th Street
             Oklahoma City, OK 73111
Telephone: (405) 424-5266
President: O. W. Bill Smith
Executive Director: Don Porter
Director of Communications: Bill Plummer

Speedskating

**U.S. International Speedskating
Association (USISA)**
Address: c/o U.S. Ski Association
             P.O. Box 100
             Park City, UT 84060
Telephone: (801) 649-0903/0920
President: Bill Cushman
Program Director: Katie Class
Director of Public Relations and Publicity: Sean
   Callahan
Public Relations Telephone: (414) 475-7465/5489

Swimming

U.S. Swimming, Inc. (USS)
Address: 1750 East Boulder Street
             Colorado Springs, CO 80909
Telephone: (719) 578-4578
President: Bill Maxson
Executive Director: Ray Essick
Director of Information Services: Jeff Dimond

Synchronized Swimming

U.S. Synchronized Swimming, Inc. (USSS)
Address: Pan American Plaza, Suite 510
             201 South Capitol Avenue
             Indianapolis, IN 46225
Telephone: (317) 237-5700
President: Barbara McNamee
Executive Director: Betty Watanabe
Membership and Communications: Laura LaMarca

Table Tennis

U.S. Table Tennis Association (USTTA)
Address: 1750 East Boulder Street
             Colorado Springs, CO 80909
Telephone: (719) 578-4583
President: Dan Seemiller
Office Manager: Linda Gleeson

Taekwondo

U.S. Taekwondo Union (USTU)
Address: 1750 East Boulder Street
             Colorado Springs, CO 80909
Telephone: (719) 578-4632
President: Kyongwon Ahn
Secretary General: Sang Lee

Team Handball

U.S. Team Handball Federation (USTHF)
Address: 1750 East Boulder Street
             Colorado Springs, CO 80909
Telephone: (719) 578-4582
President: Dr. Peter Buehning
Executive Director: Michael D. Cavanaugh
Media Contact: Evelyn Anderson

Tennis

U.S. Tennis Association
Address: 1212 Avenue of the Americas, 12th floor
             New York, NY 10036
Telephone: (212) 302-3322
President: David Markin
Executive Director: M. Marshall Happer III
Director of Communications: Ed Fabricius

Volleyball

U.S. Volleyball Association (USVBA)
Address: 3595 East Fountain Boulevard, Suite I-2
             Colorado Springs, CO 80909-1740
Telephone: (719) 637-8300
President: William Baird
Executive Director: Cliff McPeak
Media Relations and Publications: Rich Wanninger
Media Relations Telephone: (619) 692-4162

Water Polo

United States Water Polo (USWP)
Address: Pan American Plaza, Suite 520
             201 South Capitol Avenue
             Indianapolis, IN 46225
Telephone: (317) 237-5599
President: Richard Foster
Executive Director: John Duir
Director of Media and Public Relations: Eileen Sexton

Weightlifting

U.S. Weightlifting Federation (USWF)
Address: 1750 East Boulder Street
             Colorado Springs, CO 80909
Telephone: (719) 578-4508
President: Jim Schmitz
Executive Director: George Greenway
Communications Director: Mary Ann Rinehart

Wrestling

USA Wrestling
Address: 225 South Academy Boulevard
            Colorado Springs, CO 80910
Telephone: (719) 597-8333
President: Terry McCann
Executive Director: Jim Scherr
Director of Communications: Gary Abbott

Yachting

U.S. Yacht Racing Union (USYRU)
Address: P.O. Box 209
            Newport, RI 02840
Telephone: (401) 849-5200
President: William Martin
Executive Director: John B. Bonds
Acting Communications Director: Deirdre Wilde
Olympic Yachting Director: Jonathan R. Harley

Affiliated Sports Organizations

Amateur Athletic Union (AAU)
Address: 3400 West 86th Street
            P.O. Box 68207
            Indianapolis, IN 46268
Telephone: (317) 872-2900
President: Gussie Crawford
Executive Director: Stan Hooley

Curling

U.S. Curling Association (USCA)
Address: 1100 Center Point Drive
            Box 971
            Stevens Point, WI 54481
Telephone: (715) 344-1199
President: Thomas L. Satrom
Executive Director: David Garber

Gymnastics

United States Sports Acrobatics Federation
Address: 3595 East Fountain Boulevard, Suite J-1
            Colorado Springs, CO 80910
Telephone: (719) 596-5222
President: Thomas Blalock
Executive Director: Dr. Jed Friend
Marketing Director: Tracey Jo Mancini

Karate

USA Karate Federation
Address: 1300 Kenmore Boulevard
            Akron, OH 44314
Telephone: (216) 753-3114
President: George Anderson

Orienteering

U.S. Orienteering Federation
Address: P.O. Box 1444
            Forest Park, GA 30051
Telephone: (404) 363-2110
President: Larry Pedersen
Executive Director: Robin Shannonhouse
Media and Publicity Contact: John Nash
Publicity telephone: (914) 941-0896

Squash

U.S. Squash Racquets Association
Address: 23 Cynwyd Road
            P.O. Box 1216
            Bala Cynwyd, PA 19004
Telephone: (215) 667-4006
President: George A. Haggarty
Executive Director: Darwin Kingsley III

Trampoline and Tumbling

American Trampoline and Tumbling Association
Address: 1610 East Cardwell
            Brownfield, TX 79316
Telephone: (806) 637-8670
President: Connie Mara
Executive Director: Ann Sims
Public Relations Director: Kathy Wells

Triathlon

Triathlon Federation USA
Address: 3595 East Fountain Boulevard, Suite F-1
            Colorado Springs, CO 80910
Telephone: (719) 597-9090
President: Michael Gilmore
Executive Director: Mark Sisson
Deputy Director and Media Contact: Gary Scott

Underwater Swimming

Underwater Society of America
Address: 849 West Orange Avenue
            No. 1002
            South San Francisco, CA 94080
Telephone: (415) 583-8492
President: George Rose

Water Skiing

American Water Ski Association
Address: 799 Overlook Drive, S.E.
            Winter Haven, FL 33884
Telephone: (813) 324-4341
President: Tony Baggiano
Executive Director: Duke Cullimore
Public Relations Manager: Don Cullimore

Miscellaneous Sports Directory

Major Soccer League
Address: 7101 College Boulevard, Suite 320
            Overland Park, KS 66210
Telephone: (913) 339-6475
Commissioner: Earl Foreman
Director of Communications: John Griffin

Ladies Professional Golf Association
Address: 2570 Volusia Avenue, Suite B
            Daytona Beach, FL 32114
Telephone: (904) 254-8800
Commissioner: William Blue
Director of Communications: Holly Geogheghan

Professional Golfers Association

Address: Sawgrass, 112 TPC Boulevard
Ponte Vedra, FL 32082
Telephone: (904) 285-3700
Commissioner: Deane Beman
Director of Public Relations: Sid Wilson

United States Golf Association

Address: P.O. Box 708, Golf House
Far Hills, NJ 07931-0708
Telephone: (908) 234-2300
President: Grant Spaeth

Association of Tennis Professionals Tour

Address: 200 Tournament Players Road
Ponte Vedra Beach, FL 32082
Telephone: (904) 285-8000
Chief Executive Officer: Hamilton Jordan
Director of Communications: Jay Beck

Women's Tennis Association

Address: 133 First Street N.E.
St. Petersburg, FL 33701
Telephone: (813) 895-5000
Executive Director: Gerard Smith
President: Chris Evert
Director of Public Relations: Ana Leaird

United States Tennis Association

Address: 1212 Avenue of the Americas
New York, NY 10036
Telephone: (212) 302-3322
President: Robert Cookson
Executive Director: Marshall Happer
Director of Communications: Ed Fabricus

National Association for Stock Car Auto Racing

Address: P.O. Box 2875, 1801 Volusia Avenue
Daytona Beach, FL 32114-1243
Telephone: (904) 253-0611
President: Bill France Jr.
Manager of Public Relations: Bill Seaborn

Championship Auto Racing Teams

Address: 390 Enterprise Court
Bloomfield Hills, MI 48013
Telephone: (313) 334-8500
Executive Vice President: John Capels
Director of Communications: Mel Poole

National Hot Rod Association

Address: 2035 Financial Way
Glendora, CA 91740-4602
Telephone: (818) 914-4761
President: Dallas Gardner
Director of Communications: Rick Lalor

International Motor Sports Association

Address: 3502 Henderson Boulevard
Tampa, FL 33609
Telephone: (813) 877-4672
President: Mark Raffauf
Media Director: Lynn Myfelt

Professional Rodeo Cowboys Association

Address: 101 Pro Rodeo Drive
Colorado Springs, CO 80919
Telephone: (719) 593-8840
Commissioner: Lewis Cryer
Director of Media Relations: Steve Fleming

Thoroughbred Racing Associations of America

Address: 420 Fair Hill Drive, Suite 1
Elkton, MD 21921
Telephone: (301) 392-9200
President: Thomas Meeker
Director of Service Bureau: Rich Schulhoff

Thoroughbred Racing Communications, Inc.

Address: 40 East 52nd Street
New York, NY 10022
Telephone: (212) 371-5910
Executive Director: Tom Merritt
Director of Media Relations and Development:
Bob Curran

Breeders' Cup Limited

Address: 2525 Harrodsburg Road
Lexington, KY 40504-3359
Telephone: (606) 223-5444
President: James Bassett
Media Relations Director: James Gluckson

The Jockeys' Guild, Inc.

Address: 250 West Main Street
Lexington, KY 40507
Telephone: (606) 259-3211
President: Jerry Bailey
National Manager: John Giovanni

United States Trotting Association

Address: 750 Michigan Avenue
Columbus, OH 43215
Telephone: (614) 224-2291
President: Corwin Nixon
Publicity Department: John Pawlak

Professional Bowlers Association

Address: 1720 Merriman Road, P.O. Box 5118
Akron, OH 44334-0118
Telephone: (216) 836-5568
Commissioner: Joe Antenora
Public Relations Director: Kevin Shippy

Ladies Pro Bowlers Tour

Address: 7171 Cherryvale Boulevard
Rockford, IL 61112
Telephone: (815) 332-5756
Executive Director: Fran Wolf
Media Director: Jeff Allen

Women's International Bowling Congress

Address: 5301 South 76th Street
Greendale, WI 53129-1191
Telephone: (414) 421-9000
President: Gladys Banker
Public Relations Manager: Jerry Topczewski

American Bowling Congress

Address: 5301 South 76th Street
Greendale, WI 53129-1191
Telephone: (414) 421-6400
President: Max Skelton
Communications Executive: Steve James

Association of Volleyball Professionals

Address: 100 Corporate Pointe, #195
Culver City, CA 90230
Telephone: (213) 337-4842
President: Jon Stevenson
Public Relations: Debbie Rubio

Awards

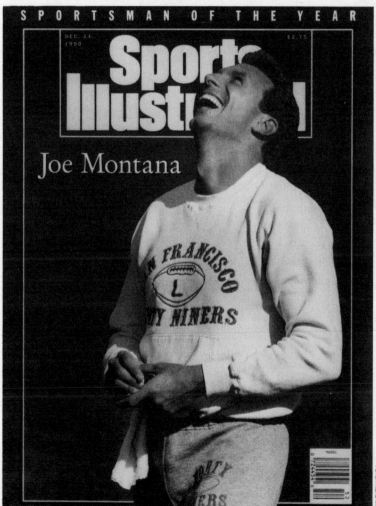

SPORTSMAN OF THE YEAR

DEC. 24, 1990

$2.75

Sports Illustrated

Joe Montana

SAN FRANCISCO FORTY NINERS

PETER READ MILLER

Athlete Awards

Sports Illustrated Sportsman of the Year

1954	Roger Bannister, Track
1955	Johnny Podres, Baseball
1956	Bobby Morrow, Track
1957	Stan Musial, Baseball
1958	Rafer Johnson, Track
1959	Ingemar Johansson, Boxing
1960	Arnold Palmer, Golf
1961	Jerry Lucas, Basketball
1962	Terry Baker, Football
1963	Pete Rozelle, Pro Football
1964	Ken Venturi, Golf
1965	Sandy Koufax, Baseball
1966	Jim Ryun, Track
1967	Carl Yastrzemski, Baseball
1968	Bill Russell, Pro Basketball
1969	Tom Seaver, Baseball
1970	Bobby Orr, Hockey
1971	Lee Trevino, Golf
1972	Billie Jean King, Tennis
	John Wooden, Basketball
1973	Jackie Stewart, Auto Racing
1974	Muhammad Ali, Boxing
1975	Pete Rose, Baseball
1976	Chris Evert, Tennis
1977	Steve Cauthen, Horse Racing
1978	Jack Nicklaus, Golf
1979	Terry Bradshaw, Pro Football
	Willie Stargell, Baseball
1980	US Olympic Hockey Team
1981	Sugar Ray Leonard, Boxing
1982	Wayne Gretzky, Hockey
1983	Mary Decker, Track
1984	Mary Lou Retton, Gymnastics
	Edwin Moses, Track
1985	Kareem Abdul-Jabbar, Pro Basketball
1986	Joe Paterno, Football
1987	Athletes Who Care
	Bob Bourne, Hockey
	Kip Keino, Track
	Judi Brown King, Track
	Dale Murphy, Baseball
	Chip Rives, Football
	Patty Sheehan, Golf
	Rory Sparrow, Pro Basketball
	Reggie Williams, Pro Football
1988	Orel Hershiser, Baseball
1989	Greg LeMond, Cycling
1990	Joe Montana, Pro Football

Associated Press Athletes of the Year

	MEN	WOMEN
1931	Pepper Martin, Baseball	Helene Madison, Swimming
1932	Gene Sarazen, Golf	Babe Didrikson, Track
1933	Carl Hubbell, Baseball	Helen Jacobs, Tennis
1934	Dizzy Dean, Baseball	Virginia Van Wie, Golf
1935	Joe Louis, Boxing	Helen Wills Moody, Tennis
1936	Jesse Owens, Track & Field	Helen Stephens, Track
1937	Don Budge, Tennis	Katherine Rawls, Swimming
1938	Don Budge, Tennis	Patty Berg, Golf
1939	Nile Kinnick, Football	Alice Marble, Tennis
1940	Tom Harmon, Football	Alice Marble, Tennis
1941	Joe DiMaggio, Baseball	Betty Hicks Newell, Golf
1942	Frank Sinkwich, Football	Gloria Callen, Swimming
1943	Gunder Haegg, Track	Patty Berg, Golf
1944	Byron Nelson, Golf	Ann Curtis, Swimming
1945	Bryon Nelson, Golf	Babe Didrikson Zaharias, Golf
1946	Glenn Davis, Football	Babe Didrikson Zaharias, Golf
1947	Johnny Lujack, Football	Babe Didrikson Zaharias, Golf
1948	Lou Boudreau, Baseball	Fanny Blankers-Koen, Track
1949	Leon Hart, Football	Marlene Bauer, Golf
1950	Jim Konstanty, Baseball	Babe Didrikson Zaharias, Golf
1951	Dick Kazmaier, Football	Maureen Connolly, Tennis
1952	Bob Mathias, Track	Maureen Connolly, Tennis
1953	Ben Hogan, Golf	Maureen Connolly, Tennis
1954	Willie Mays, Baseball	Babe Didrikson Zaharias, Golf
1955	Hopalong Cassidy, Football	Patty Berg, Golf
1956	Mickey Mantle, Baseball	Pat McCormick, Diving
1957	Ted Williams, Baseball	Althea Gibson, Tennis
1958	Herb Elliot, Track	Althea Gibson, Tennis
1959	Ingemar Johansson, Boxing	Maria Bueno, Tennis
1960	Rafer Johnson, Track	Wilma Rudolph, Track
1961	Roger Maris, Baseball	Wilma Rudolph, Track
1962	Maury Wills, Baseball	Dawn Fraser, Swimming

Associated Press Athletes of the Year (*Cont.*)

	MEN	WOMEN
1963	Sandy Koufax, Baseball	Mickey Wright, Golf
1964	Don Schollander, Swimming	Mickey Wright, Golf
1965	Sandy Koufax, Baseball	Kathy Whitworth, Golf
1966	Frank Robinson, Baseball	Kathy Whitworth, Golf
1967	Carl Yastrzemski, Baseball	Billie Jean King, Tennis
1968	Denny McLain, Baseball	Peggy Fleming, Skating
1969	Tom Seaver, Baseball	Debbie Meyer, Swimming
1970	George Blanda, Pro Football	Chi Cheng, Track
1971	Lee Trevino, Golf	Evonne Goolagong, Tennis
1972	Mark Spitz, Swimming	Olga Korbut, Gymnastics
1973	O. J. Simpson, Pro Football	Billie Jean King, Tennis
1974	Muhammad Ali, Boxing	Chris Evert, Tennis
1975	Fred Lynn, Baseball	Chris Evert, Tennis
1976	Bruce Jenner, Track	Nadia Comaneci, Gymnastics
1977	Steve Cauthen, Horse Racing	Chris Evert, Tennis
1978	Ron Guidry, Baseball	Nancy Lopez, Golf
1979	Willie Stargell, Baseball	Tracy Austin, Tennis
1980	US Olympic Hockey Team	Chris Evert Lloyd, Tennis
1981	John McEnroe, Tennis	Tracy Austin, Tennis
1982	Wayne Gretzky, Hockey	Mary Decker, Track
1983	Carl Lewis, Track	Martina Navratilova, Tennis
1984	Carl Lewis, Track	Mary Lou Retton, Gymnastics
1985	Dwight Gooden, Baseball	Nancy Lopez, Golf
1986	Larry Bird, Pro Basketball	Martina Navratilova, Tennis
1987	Ben Johnson, Track	Jackie Joyner-Kersee, Track
1988	Orel Hershiser, Baseball	Florence Griffith Joyner, Track
1989	Joe Montana, Pro Football	Steffi Graf, Tennis
1990	Joe Montana, Pro Football	Beth Daniel, Golf

James E. Sullivan Award

Presented annually by the Amateur Athletic Union to the athlete who "by his or her performance, example and influence as an amateur, has done the most during the year to advance the cause of sportsmanship."

1930	Bobby Jones, Golf	1961	Wilma Rudolph, Track
1931	Barney Berlinger, Track	1962	Jim Beatty, Track
1932	Jim Bausch, Track	1963	John Pennel, Track
1933	Glenn Cunningham, Track	1964	Don Schollander, Swimming
1934	Bill Bonthron, Track	1965	Bill Bradley, Basketball
1935	Lawson Little, Golf	1966	Jim Ryun, Track
1936	Glenn Morris, Track	1967	Randy Matson, Track
1937	Don Budge, Tennis	1968	Debbie Meyer, Swimming
1938	Don Lash, Track	1969	Bill Toomey, Track
1939	Joe Burk, Rowing	1970	John Kinsella, Swimming
1940	Greg Rice, Track	1971	Mark Spitz, Swimming
1941	Leslie MacMitchell, Track	1972	Frank Shorter, Track
1942	Cornelius Warmerdam, Track	1973	Bill Walton, Basketball
1943	Gilbert Dodds, Track	1974	Rich Wohlhuter, Track
1944	Ann Curtis, Swimming	1975	Tim Shaw, Swimming
1945	Doc Blanchard, Football	1976	Bruce Jenner, Track
1946	Arnold Tucker, Football	1977	John Naber, Swimming
1947	John B. Kelly, Jr, Rowing	1978	Tracy Caulkins, Swimming
1948	Bob Mathias, Track	1979	Kurt Thomas, Gymnastics
1949	Dick Button, Skating	1980	Eric Heiden, Speed Skating
1950	Fred Wilt, Track	1981	Carl Lewis, Track
1951	Bob Richards, Track	1982	Mary Decker, Track
1952	Horace Ashenfelter, Track	1983	Edwin Moses, Track
1953	Sammy Lee, Diving	1984	Greg Louganis, Diving
1954	Mal Whitfield, Track	1985	Joan B. Samuelson, Track
1955	Harrison Dillard, Track	1986	Jackie Joyner-Kersee, Track
1956	Pat McCormick, Diving	1987	Jim Abbott, Baseball
1957	Bobby Morrow, Track	1988	Florence Griffith Joyner, Track
1958	Glenn Davis, Track	1989	Janet Evans, Swimming
1959	Parry O'Brien, Track	1990	John Smith, Wrestling
1960	Rafer Johnson, Track		

The Sporting News Man of the Year

1968 ....Denny McLain, Baseball	1980 ....George Brett, Baseball
1969 ....Tom Seaver, Baseball	1981 ....Wayne Gretzky, Hockey
1970 ....John Wooden, Basketball	1982 ....Whitey Herzog, Baseball
1971 ....Lee Trevino, Golf	1983 ....Bowie Kuhn, Baseball
1972 ....Charles O. Finley, Baseball	1984 ....Peter Ueberroth, LA Olympics
1973 ....O. J. Simpson, Pro Football	1985 ....Pete Rose, Baseball
1974 ....Lou Brock, Baseball	1986 ....Larry Bird, Pro Basketball
1975 ....Archie Griffin, Football	1987 ....No award
1976 ....Larry O'Brien, Pro Basketball	1988 ....Jackie Joyner-Kersee, Track
1977 ....Steve Cauthen, Horse Racing	1989 ....Joe Montana, Pro Football
1978 ....Ron Guidry, Baseball	1990 ....Nolan Ryan, Baseball
1979 ....Willie Stargell, Baseball	

United Press International Sportsman and Sportswoman of the Year

MEN	WOMEN
1974 ....Muhammad Ali, Boxing	Irena Szewinska, Track and Field
1975 ....Joao Oliveira, Track and Field	Nadia Comaneci, Gymnastics
1976 ....Alberto Juantorena, Track and Field	Nadia Comaneci, Gymnastics
1977 ....Alberto Juantorena, Track and Field	Rosie Ackermann, Track and Field
1978 ....Henry Rono, Track and Field	Tracy Caulkins, Swimming
1979 ....Sebastian Coe, Track and Field	Marita Koch, Track and Field
1980 ....Eric Heiden, Speed Skating	Hanni Wenzel, Alpine Skiing
1981 ....Sebastian Coe, Track and Field	Chris Evert Lloyd, Tennis
1982 ....Daley Thompson, Track and Field	Marita Koch, Track and Field
1983 ....Carl Lewis, Track and Field	Jarmila Kratochvilova, Track and Field
1984 ....Carl Lewis, Track and Field	Martina Navratilova, Tennis
1985 ....Steve Cram, Track and Field	Mary Decker Slaney, Track and Field
1986 ....Diego Maradona, Soccer	Heike Drechsler, Track and Field
1987 ....Ben Johnson, Track and Field	Steffi Graf, Tennis
1988 ....Matt Biondi, Swimming	Florence Griffith Joyner, Track and Field
1989 ....Boris Becker, Tennis	Steffi Graf, Tennis
1990 ....Stefan Edberg, Tennis	Merlene Ottey, Track and Field

Dial Award

Presented annually by the Dial Corporation to the male and female national high school athlete/scholar of the year.

MEN	WOMEN
1979 ....Herschel Walker, Football	No award
1980 ....Bill Fralic, Football	Carol Lewis, Track
1981 ....Kevin Willhite, Football	Cheryl Miller, Basketball
1982 ....Mike Smith, Basketball	Elaine Zayak, Skating
1983 ....Chris Spielman, Football	Melanie Buddemeyer, Swimming
1984 ....Hart Lee Dykes, Football	Nora Lewis, Basketball
1985 ....Jeff George, Football	Gea Johnson, Track
1986 ....Scott Schaffner, Football	Mya Johnson, Track
1987 ....Todd Marinovich, Football	Kristi Overton, Water Skiing
1988 ....Carlton Gray, Football	Courtney Cox, Basketball
1989 ....Robert Smith, Football	Lisa Leslie, Basketball
1990 ....Derrick Brooks, Football	Vicki Goetze, Golf

Profiles

APRIL 15, 1991 · $2.95

Sports Illustrated

BASEBALL
ISSUE 1991

Miracle
Man

Ageless
Nolan Ryan
Launches His
25th Season

RONALD C. MODRA

Henry Aaron (b. 2-5-34): Baseball OF. "Hammerin' Hank." All-time leader in HR (755) and RBI (2,297); third in hits (3,771). 1957 MVP. Led league in HR and RBI 4 times each, runs scored 3 times, hits and batting average 2 times. No. 44, he 44 homers 4 times. Had 40+ HR 8 times; 100+ RBI 11 times; .300+ average 14 times. 24-time All-Star. Career span 1954–76; jersey number retired by Atlanta and Milwaukee.

Kareem Abdul-Jabbar (b. 4-16-47): Born Lew Alcindor. Basketball C. All-time leader points scored (38,387), field goals attempted (28,307), field goals made (15,837), blocked shots (3,189), games played (1,560), and years played (20); third all-time rebounds (17,440). Won 6 MVP awards (1971–72, 1974, 1976–77, 1980). Career scoring average was 24.6, rebounding average 11.2. Led league in blocks 4 times, scoring 2 times, rebounding and field goal percentage 1 time each. Averaged 30+ points 4 times, 20+ points 13 other times. 10-time All-Star, All-Defensive team 5 times. 1970 Rookie of the Year. Played on 6 championship teams; was playoff MVP in 1971, 1985. Career span 1969–88 with Milwaukee, Los Angeles. Also played on 3 NCAA championship teams with UCLA; tournament MVP 1967–69; Player of the Year 2 times.

Affirmed (b. 2-21-75): Thoroughbred race horse. Triple Crown winner in 1978 with jockey Steve Cauthen aboard. Trained by Laz Barrera.

Tenley Albright (b. 7-18-35): Figure skater. Gold medalist at 1956 Olympics, silver medalist at 1952 Olympics. World champion 2 times (1953, 1955) and U.S. champion 5 consecutive years (1952–56).

Grover Cleveland Alexander (b. 2-26-1887, d. 11-4-50): Baseball RHP. Third all-time most wins (373), second most shutouts (90). Won 30+ games 3 times, 20+ games 6 other times. Set rookie record with 28 wins in 1911. Career span 1911–30 with Philadelphia (NL), Chicago (NL), St Louis (NL).

Vasili Alexeyev (b. 1942): Soviet weightlifter. Gold medalist at 2 consecutive Olympics, 1972, 1976. World champion 8 times.

Muhammad Ali (b. 1-17-42): Born Cassius Clay. Boxer. Heavyweight champion 3 times (1964–67, 1974–78, 1978–79). Stripped of title in 1967 because he refused to serve in the Vietnam War. Career record 56–5 with 37 KOs. Defended title 19 times. Also light heavyweight gold medalist at 1960 Olympics.

Phog Allen (b. 11-18-1885, d. 9-16-74): College basketball coach. Fourth all-time most wins (746); .739 career winning percentage. Won 1952 NCAA championship. Most of career, 1920–56, with Kansas.

Bobby Allison (b. 12-3-37): Auto racer. Third all-time in NASCAR victories (84). Won Daytona 500 3 times (1978, 1982, 1988). Also NASCAR champion in 1983.

Naty Alvarado (b. 7-25-55): Mexican handball player. "El Gato (The Cat)". Won a record 11 U.S. pro four-wall handball titles starting in 1977.

Sparky Anderson (b. 2-22-34): Baseball manager. Only manager to win World Series in both leagues (Detroit, 1984, Cincinnati, 1975–76); only manager to win 100 games in both leagues. Postseason record of 34–21 (.619) is best ever. .557 career winning percentage since 1970.

Willie Anderson (b. 1880, d. 1910): Scottish golfer. Won U.S. Open 4 times (1901 and an unmatched three straight, 1903–05). Also won 4 Western Opens between 1902 and 1909.

Mario Andretti (b. 2-28-40): Auto racer. The only driver in history to win Daytona 500 (1967), Indy 500 (1969): and Formula 1 world championship (1978). Second all-time in CART victories (51 as of 10/1/91). Also 12 career Formula 1 victories. USAC/CART champion 4 times (consecutively 1965–66, 1969, 1984). Named Indy 500 Rookie of the Year in 1965.

Earl Anthony (b. 4-27-38): Bowler. Won PBA National Championship 6 times, more than any other bowler (consecutively 1973–75, 1981–83) and Tournament of Champions 2 times (1974, 1978). First bowler to top $1 million in career earnings. Bowler of the Year 6 times (consecutively 1974–76, 1981–83). Has won 45 career PBA titles since 1970.

Said Aouita (b. 11-2-60): Track and field. Moroccan holds world record in 1,500 meters (3:29.46 set in 1985), 2,000 meters (4:50.81 set in 1987), 3,000 meters (7:29.45 set in 1989): and 5,000 meters (12:58.39 set in 1987).

Al Arbour (b. 11-1-32): Hockey D-coach. Entering 1991-92 season, all-time leader in playoff wins (114—tied with Scotty Bowman), third in regular season wins (671). Led NY Islanders to 4 consecutive Stanley Cup championships (1980–83). Also played on 3 Stanley Cup champions: Detroit, Chicago and Toronto, from 1953 to 1971.

Eddie Arcaro (b. 2-19-16): Horse racing jockey. The only jockey to win the Triple Crown 2 times (aboard Whirlaway in 1941, Citation in 1948). Rode Preakness Stakes winner (1941, 1948, consecutively 1950–51, 1955, 1957) and Belmont Stakes winner (consecutively 1941–42, 1945, 1948, 1952, 1955) 6 times each and Kentucky Derby winner 5 times (1938, 1941, 1945, 1948, 1952). 4,779 career wins.

Henry Armstrong (b. 12-12-12): Boxer. Champion in 3 different weight classes: featherweight (1937—relinquished 1938), welterweight (1938–40) and lightweight (1938–39). Career record 145–20–9 with 98 KOs (27 consecutively, 1937–38) from 1931 to 1945.

Arthur Ashe (b. 7-10-43): Tennis player. First black man to win U.S. Open (1968, as an amateur), Australian Open (1970) and Wimbledon singles titles (1975). 33 career tournament victories. Member of Davis Cup team 1963–78; captain 1980–85.

Red Auerbach (b. 9-20-17): Basketball coach-executive. All-time leader in wins (938). Coached Boston from 1946 to 1966, winning 9 championships, 8 consecutively. Had .662 career winning percentage, with 50+ wins 8 consecutive seasons. Also won 7 championships as general manager.

Hobey Baker (b. 1-15-1892, d. 12-21-18): Sportsman. Member of both college football and hockey Halls of Fame. College hockey and football star with Princeton, 1911–14. Fighter pilot in World War I, died in plane crash. College hockey Player of the Year award named in his honor.

Ernie Banks (b. 1-31-31): Baseball SS-1B. "Mr. Cub." Won 2 consecutive MVP awards, in 1958–59. 512 career HR. League leader in HR, RBI 2 times each; 40+ HR 5 times; 100+ RBI 8 times. Most HR by a shortstop with 47 in 1958. Career span 1953–71 with Chicago.

Roger Bannister (b. 3-23-29): Track and field. British runner broke the 4-minute mile barrier, running 3:59.4 on May 6, 1954.

Red Barber (b. 2-17-08): Sportscaster. TV-radio baseball announcer was the voice of Cincinnati, Brooklyn and NY Yankees. His expressions, such as "sitting in the catbird seat," "pea patch" and "rhubarb" captivated audiences from 1934 to 1966.

Charles Barkley (b. 2-20-63): Basketball F. Four-time first-team All-Star. All-Star MVP, 1991. All-Rookie team, 1985. Led NBA in rebounding, 1987. Has averaged 20+ points in six of seven seasons with Philadelphia. Selected, 1992 Olympic team.

Rick Barry (b. 3-28-44): Basketball F. Only player in history to win scoring titles in NBA (San Francisco, 1967) and ABA (Oakland, 1969). All-time highest free throw percentage (.900). Career scoring average 23.2. Led league in free throw percentage 6 times, steals and scoring 1 time each. Averaged 30+ points 2 times, 20+ points 6 other times. 5-time All-Star. 1975 playoff MVP with Golden State. 1966 Rookie of the Year. Career span 1967–79.

Sammy Baugh (b. 3-17-14): Football QB-P. Set records by leading league in passing 6 times and punting 4 times. Also holds record for highest career punting average (45.1) and highest season average (51.0 in 1940). Career span 1937–52 with Washington. Also All-America with Texas Christian 3 consecutive seasons.

Elgin Baylor (b. 9-16-34): Basketball F. Third all-time highest scoring average (27.4), ninth all-time most points scored (23,149). Averaged 30+ points 3 consecutive seasons, 20+ points 8 other times. 10-time All-Star. 1962 Rookie of the Year. Played in 8 finals without winning championship. Career span 1958–71 with Los Angeles. Also 1958 MVP in NCAA tournament with Seattle.

Bob Beamon (b. 8-29-46): Track and field. Gold medalist in long jump at 1968 Olympics with world record jump of 29′2½″ that stood until 1991.

Franz Beckenbauer (b. 1945): West German soccer player. Captain of 1974 World Cup champions and coach of 1990 champions. Also played for NY Cosmos from 1977 to 1980.

Boris Becker (b. 11-22-67): German tennis player. The youngest male player to win a Wimbledon singles title at age 17 in 1985. Has won 3 Wimbledon titles (consecutively 1985–86, 1989), 1 U.S. Open (1989) and 1 Australian Open title (1991). Led West Germany to 2 consecutive Davis Cup victories (1988–89).

Chuck Bednarik (b. 5-1-25): Football C-LB. Last of the great two-way players, was named All-Pro at both center and linebacker. Missed only 3 games in 14 seasons with Philadelphia from 1949–62. Also All-America 2 times at Pennsylvania.

Clair Bee (b. 3-2-1896, d. 5-20-83): Basketball coach. Originated 1-3-1 defense, helped develop three-second rule, 24-second clock. Won 82.7 percent of games as coach for Rider College and Long Island University. Coach Baltimore Bullets, 1952–54. Author, 23-volume Chip Hilton series for children, 21 nonfiction sports books.

Jean Beliveau (b. 8-31-31): Hockey C. Won MVP award 2 times (1956, 1964), playoff MVP in 1965. Led league in assists 3 times, goals 2 times and points 1 time. 507 career goals, 712 assists. All-Star 6 times. Played on 10 Stanley Cup champions with Montreal from 1950 to 1971.

Bert Bell (b. 2-25-1895, d. 10-11-59): Football executive. Second NFL commissioner (1946–59). Also owner of Philadelphia (1933–40) and Pittsburgh (1941–46). Proposed the first college draft in 1936.

Lyudmila Belousova/Oleg Protopov (no dates of birth available): Soviet figure skaters. Won Olympic gold medal in pairs competition in 1964 and 1968. Won four consecutive World and European championships (1965–68) and eight consecutive Soviet titles (1961–68).

Deane Beman (b. 4-22-38): Commissioner of the PGA Tour since 1974. Won British Amateur title in 1959 and U.S. Amateur titles in 1960 and 1963.

Johnny Bench (b. 12-7-47): Baseball C. MVP in 1970, 1972; World Series MVP in 1976; Rookie of the Year in 1968. 389 career HR. League leader in HR 2 times, RBI 3 times. Career span 1967–83 with Cincinnati.

Patty Berg (b. 2-13-18): Golfer. All-time women's leader in major championships (16), third all-time in career wins (57). Won Titleholders Championship (1937–39, 1948, 1953–54, 1957) and Western Open (1941, 1943, 1948, 1951, 1955, 1957–58) 7 times each, the most of any golfer. Also won U.S. Women's Amateur (1938) and U.S. Women's Open (1946).

Yogi Berra (b. 5-12-25): Baseball C. Played on 10 World Series winners. All-time Series leader in games, at bats, hits and doubles. MVP in 1951 and consecutively 1954–55. 358 career HR. Career span 1946–65. Also managed pennant-winning Yankees (1964) and NY Mets (1973).

Jay Berwanger (b. 3-19-14): College football RB. Won the first Heisman Trophy and named All-America with Chicago in 1935.

George Best (b. 5-22-46): Irish soccer player. Led Manchester United to European Cup title in 1968. Named England's and Europe's Player of the Year in 1968. Played in North American Soccer League for Los Angeles (1976–78), Fort Lauderdale (1978–79) and San Jose (1980–81). Suspended from San Jose in 1982 for failure to report to two matches. Frequent troubles with alcohol and gambling overshadowed career.

Abebe Bikila (b. 8-7-32, d. 10-25-73): Track and field. Ethiopian barefoot runner won consecutive gold medals in the marathon at Olympics in 1960 and 1964.

Dmitri Bilozerchev (b. 12-22-66): Soviet gymnast. Won 3 gold medals at 1988 Olympics. Made comeback after shattering his left leg into 44 pieces in 1985. Two-time world champion (1983, 1987). At 16, became youngest to win all-around world championship title in 1983.

Matt Biondi (b. 10-8-65): Swimmer. Winner of 5 gold medals, 1 silver medal and 1 bronze medal at 1988 Olympics. Holds world record in 100-meter freestyle (48.42 set in 1988).

Larry Bird (b. 12-7-56): Basketball F. Won 3 consecutive MVP awards (1984–86) and 2 playoff MVP awards (1984, 1986). Also Rookie of the Year (1980) and All-Star 9 consecutive seasons. Has led league in free throw percentage 4 times. Averaged 20+ points 10 times. Career span since 1979 with Boston. Also named Player of the Year in 1979 with Indiana State.

Bonnie Blair (b. 3-18-64): Speed skater. Won gold medal in 500 meters and bronze medal in 1,000 meters at 1988 Olympics. Also 1989 World Sprint champion.

Toe Blake (b. 8-21-12): Hockey LW and coach. Second all-time highest winning percentage (.640): and fifth in wins (582). Led Montreal to 8 Stanley Cup championships from 1955 to 1968 (consecutively 1956–60, 1965–66, 1968). Also MVP and scoring leader in 1939. Played on 2 Stanley Cup champions with Montreal from 1932 to 1948.

Doc Blanchard (b. 12-11-24): College football FB. "Mr. Inside." Teamed with Glenn Davis to lead Army to 3 consecutive undefeated seasons (1944–46) and 2 consecutive national championships (1944–45). Won Heisman Trophy and Sullivan Award in 1945. Also All-America 3 times.

George Blanda (b. 9-17-27): Football QB-K. All-time leader in seasons played (26), games played (340), points scored (2,002) and points after touchdown (943); second in field goals (335). Also passed for 26,920 career yards and 236 touchdowns. Tied record with 7 touchdown passes on Nov. 19, 1961. Player of the Year 2 times (1961, 1970). Retired at age 48, the oldest to ever play. Career span 1949–75 with Chicago, Houston, Oakland.

Fanny Blankers-Koen (b. 4-26-18): Track and field. Dutch athlete won four gold medals at 1948 Olympics, in 100-meters; 200 meters; 80-meter hurdles; and 400-meter relay. Versatile, she also set world records in high jump (5′7¼″ in 1943), long jump (20′6″ in 1943) and pentathlon (4,692 points in 1951).

Wade Boggs (b. 6-15-58): Baseball 3B. Fifth all-time highest batting average (.344) and 5 batting titles (1983, consecutively 1985–88); has had .350+ average 5 times, 200+ hits 7 times. Career span since 1982 with Boston.

Nick Bolletieri (b. 7-31-31): Tennis coach. Since 1976, has run Nick Bolletieri Tennis Academy in Bradenton, Fla. Former residents of the academy include Andre Agassi, Monica Seles and Jim Courier.

Bjorn Borg (b. 6-6-56): Swedish tennis player. Second all-time men's leader in Grand Slam singles titles (11—tied with Rod Laver). Set modern record by winning 5 consecutive Wimbledon titles (1976–80). Won 6 French Open titles (consecutively 1974–75, 1978–81). Reached U.S. Open final 4 times, but title eluded him. 65 career tournament victories. Led Sweden to Davis Cup win in 1975.

Ralph Boston (b. 5-9-39): Track and field. Long jumper won medals at 3 consecutive Olympics; gold in 1960, silver in 1964, bronze in 1968.

Scotty Bowman (b. 9-18-33): Hockey coach. Entered 1991–92 season with Pittsburgh as all-time leader in regular season wins (739) and in regular season winning percentage (.661). Also all-time leader in playoff wins (114—tied with Al Arbour). Led Montreal to 5 Stanley Cups, and has also coached St Louis and Buffalo. Won Jack Adams Award, Coach of the Year, 1976–77.

Bill Bradley (b. 7-28-43): Basketball F. Played on 2 NBA championship teams with New York from 1967 to 1977. Player of the Year and NCAA tournament MVP in 1965 with Princeton; All-America 3 times; Sullivan Award winner in 1965. Rhodes scholar. U.S. Senator (D-NJ) since 1979.

Terry Bradshaw (b. 9-2-48): Football QB. Played on 4 Super Bowl champions (consecutively 1974–75, 1978–79); named Super Bowl MVP 2 consecutive seasons (1978–79). 212 career touchdown passes; 27,989 yards passing. Player of the Year in 1978. Career span 1970–83 with Pittsburgh.

George Brett (b. 5-15-53): Baseball 3B-1B. MVP in 1980 with .390 batting average; 3 batting titles, in 1976, 1980, 1990; and .300+ average 11 times. Led league in hits and triples 3 times. Career span since 1973 with Kansas City.

Bret Hanover (b. 5-19-62): Horse. Son of Adios. Won 62 of 68 harness races and earned $922,616. Undefeated as two-year-old. From total of 1,694 foals, he sired winners of $61 million and 511 horses which have recorded sub-2:00 performances.

Lou Brock (b. 6-18-39): Baseball OF. Second all-time most stolen bases (938); second most season steals (118). Led league in steals 8 times, with 50+ steals 12 consecutive seasons. All-time World Series leader in steals (14—tied with Eddie Collins); second in Series batting average (.391). 3,023 career hits. Career span 1961–79 with St Louis.

Jim Brown (b. 2-17-36): Football FB. All-time leader in touchdowns (126): and third in yards rushing (12,312). Led league in rushing a record 8 times. His 5.22-yards per carry average is also the best ever. Player of the Year 4 times (consecutively 1957–58, 1963, 1965) and Rookie of the Year in 1957. Rushed for 1,000+ yards in 7 seasons, 200+ yards in 4 games, 100+ yards in 54 other games. Career span 1957–65 with Cleveland; never missed a game. Also All-America with Syracuse.

Paul Brown (b. 9-7-08, d. 8-5-91): Football coach. Led Cleveland to 10 consecutive championship games. Won 4 consecutive AAFC titles (1946–49) and 3 NFL titles (1950, consecutively 1954–55). Coached Cleveland from 1946 to 1962; became first coach of Cincinnati, 1968–75, and then general manager. Career coaching record 222–113–9. Also won national championship with Ohio State in 1942.

Avery Brundage (b. 9-28-1887, d. 5-5-75): Amateur sports executive. President of International Olympic Committee 1952–72. Served as president of U.S. Olympic Committee 1929–53. Also president of Amateur Athletic Union 1928–35. Member of 1912 U.S. Olympic track and field team.

Paul "Bear" Bryant (b. 9-11-13, d. 1-26-83): College football coach. All-time Division I-A leader in wins (323). Won 6 national championships (1961, consecutively 1964–65, 1973, consecutively 1978–79) with Alabama. Career record 323–85–17, including 4 undefeated seasons. Also won 15 bowl games. Career span 1945–82 with Maryland, Kentucky, Texas A&M, Alabama.

Sergei Bubka (b. 12-4-63): Track and field. Soviet pole vaulter was gold medalist at 1988 Olympics. World champion 3 times (1983, 1987, 1991). First man to break the 20-foot barrier, holds world indoor record of 20′1″ and world outdoor record of 20′¼″, both set in 1991.

Don Budge (b. 6-13-15): Tennis player. First player to achieve the Grand Slam, in 1938. Won 2 consecutive Wimbledon and U.S. singles titles (1937–38), 1 French and 1 Australian title (1938).

Dick Butkus (b. 12-9-42): Football LB. Recovered 25 opponents' fumbles, second most in history. Selected for Pro Bowl 8 times. Career span 1965–73 with Chicago. Also All-America 2 times with Illinois. Award recognizing the outstanding college linebacker named in his honor.

Dick Button (b. 7-18-29): Figure skater. Gold medalist at 2 consecutive Olympics in 1948, 1952. World champion 5 consecutive years (1948–52) and U.S. champion 7 consecutive years (1946–52). Sullivan Award winner in 1949.

Walter Byers (b. 3-13-22): Amateur sports executive. First executive director of NCAA, served from 1952 to 1987.

Frank Calder (b. 11-17-1877, d. 2-4-43): Hockey executive. First commissioner of NHL, served from 1917 to 1943. Rookie of the Year award named in his honor.

Walter Camp (b. 4-7-1859, d. 3-14-25): Football pioneer. Played for Yale in its first football game vs. Harvard on Nov. 17, 1876. Proposed rules such as 11 men per side, scrimmage line, center snap, yards and downs. Founded the All-America selections in 1889.

Roy Campanella (b. 11-19-21): Baseball C. Career span 1948–57, ended when paralyzed in car crash. MVP in 1951, 1953, 1955. Played on 5 pennant winners; 1955 World Series winner with Brooklyn Dodgers.

Earl Campbell (b. 3-29-55): Football RB. Ninth all-time yards rushing (9,407); third all-time season yards rushing (1,934 in 1980) and touchdowns rushing (19 in 1979). Led league in rushing 3 consecutive seasons. Rushed for 1,000+ yards in 5 seasons, 100+ yards in 40 games, 200+ yards in 4 other games. Scored 74 career touchdowns. Player of the Year 2 consecutive seasons (1978–79). Rookie of the Year in 1978. Career span 1978–85 with Houston, New Orleans. Won Heisman Trophy with Texas in 1977.

John Campbell (b. 4-8-55): Canadian harness racing driver. All-time leading money winner closing in on $100 million in earnings. Leading money winner 1986–90. Has more than 5,500 career wins.

Billy Cannon (b. 2-8-37): Football RB. Led Louisiana State to national championship in 1958 and won Heisman Trophy in 1959. Signed contract in both NFL (Los Angeles) and AFL (Houston). Houston won lawsuit for his services. Played in 6 AFL championship games with Houston, Oakland, Kansas City. Career span 1960–70. Served three-year jail term for 1983 conviction on counterfeiting charges.

Harry Caray (b. 3-1-17): Sportscaster. TV-radio baseball announcer since 1945 with St Louis (NL), Oakland, Chicago (AL) and Chicago (NL). Achieved celebrity status on Cubs' superstation WGN by singing "Take Me Out to the Ballgame" with Wrigley Field fans.

Rod Carew (b. 10-1-45): Baseball 2B-1B. Won 7 batting titles (1969, consecutively 1972–75, 1977–78). Had .328 career average, 3,053 career hits, and .300+ average 15 times. 1977 MVP; 1967 Rookie of the Year. Career span 1967–85; jersey number (29) retired by Minnesota and California.

Steve Carlton (b. 12-22-44): Baseball LHP. Second all-time most strikeouts (4,136). 4 Cy Young awards (1972, 1977, 1980, 1982). 329 career wins; won 20+ games 6 times. League leader in wins 4 times, innings pitched and strikeouts 5 times each. Struck out 19 batters in 1 game in 1969. Career span 1965–88 with St. Louis, Philadelphia and four other teams in last two years.

Don Carter (b. 7-29-26): Bowler. Won All-Star Tournament 4 times (1952, 1954, 1956, 1958) and PBA National Championship in 1960. Voted Bowler of the Year 6 times (consecutively 1953–54, 1957–58, 1960, 1962).

Alexander Cartwright (b. 4-17-1820, d. 7-12-1892): Baseball pioneer. Organized the first baseball game on June 19, 1846, and set the basic rules of bases 90 feet apart, 9 men per side, 3 strikes per out and 3 outs per inning. In that first game his New York Knickerbockers lost to the New York Nine 23–1 at Elysian Fields in Hoboken, NJ.

Tracy Caulkins (b. 1-11-63): Swimmer. Won 3 gold medals at 1984 Olympics. Won 48 U.S. national titles, more than any other swimmer, from 1978 to 1984. Also won Sullivan Award in 1978.

Bill Chadwick (b. 10-10-15): Hockey referee. Spent 16 years as a referee despite vision in only one eye. Developed hand signals to signify penalties. Also former television announcer for the New York Rangers.

Wilt Chamberlain (b. 8-21-36): Basketball C. All-time leader in rebounds (23,924) and rebounding average (22.9). All-time season leader in points scored (4,029 in 1962), scoring average (50.4 in 1962), rebounding average (27.2 in 1961) and field goal percentage (.727 in 1973). All-time single-game most points scored (100 in 1962) and most rebounds (55 in 1960). Second all-time most points scored (31,419) and most field goals made (12,681). 4 MVP awards (1960, consecutively 1966–68); playoff MVP in 1972 and 1960 Rookie of the Year. 7-time All-Star. 30.1 career scoring average. Led league in rebounding 11 times, field goal percentage 9 times, scoring 7 consecutive seasons, assists 1 time. Averaged 50+ points and 40+ points 1 time each; 30+ points and 20+ points 5 other times each. Career span 1959–72 with Philadelphia, Los Angeles. Also named College Player of the Year in 1957 at Kansas.

Colin Chapman (b. 1928, d. 12-16-83): Auto racing engineer. Founded Lotus race and street cars, designing the first Lotus racer in 1948. Introduced the monocoque design for Formula One cars in 1962 and ground effects in 1978. Four of his drivers, including Mario Andretti, won Formula One world championships.

Julio Cesar Chavez (b. 7-12-62): Boxer. As of October 1991, the current super lightweight and junior welterweight champion has a career record of 75–0. Also won titles as super featherweight (1984–87) and lightweight (1987–89).

Citation (b. 4-11-45, d. 8-8-70): Thoroughbred race horse. Triple Crown winner in 1948 with jockey Eddie Arcaro aboard. Trained by Ben A. Jones.

King Clancy (b. 2-25-03, d. 11-6-86): Hockey D. Four-time All-Star. Coach, Montreal Maroons, Toronto. Referee. Trophy named in his honor, recognizing leadership qualities and contribution to community.

Jim Clark (b. 3-4-36, d. 4-7-68): Scottish auto racer. Third all-time in Formula 1 victories (25—tied with Niki Lauda). Formula 1 champion 2 times (1963, 1965). Won Indy 500 1 time (1965). Named Indy 500 Rookie of the Year in 1963. Killed during competition in 1968 at age 32.

Bobby Clarke (b. 8-13-49): Hockey C. Won MVP award 3 times (1973, consecutively 1975–76). 358 career goals, 852 assists. Led league in assists 2 consecutive seasons and scored 100+ points 3 times. Played on 2 consecutive Stanley Cup champions (1974–75) with Philadelphia. Career span 1969 to 1984. Also general manager with Philadelphia from 1984 to 1990 and Minnesota since 1991.

Roger Clemens (b. 8-4-62): Baseball RHP. Fourth all-time best winning percentage (.687). Record 20 strikeouts in 1 game. Won 2 consecutive Cy Young Awards in 1986, 1987. Also 1986 MVP. League leader in ERA 3 times, wins and strikeouts 2 times each. Career span since 1984 with Boston.

Roberto Clemente (b. 8-18-34, d. 12-31-72): Baseball OF. Killed in plane crash while still an active player. Had 3,000 career hits and .317 career average. 4 batting titles; .300+ average 13 times. 1966 MVP; 1971 World Series MVP. 12 consecutive Gold Gloves; led league in assists 5 times. Career span 1955–72 with Pittsburgh.

Ty Cobb (b. 12-18-1886, d. 7-17-61): Baseball OF. All-time leader in batting average (.367) and runs scored (2,245); second most hits (4,191); third most stolen bases (892). 1911 MVP and 1909 Triple Crown winner. 12 batting titles. Had .400+ average 3 times, .350+ average 13 other times; 200+ hits 9 times. Led league in hits 7 times, steals 6 times and runs scored 5 times. Career span 1905–28 with Detroit.

Mickey Cochrane (b. 4-6-03, d. 6-28-62): Baseball C. All-time highest career batting average among catchers (.320). MVP in 1928, 1934. Had .300+ average 8 times. Career span 1925–37 with Philadelphia, Detroit.

Sebastian Coe (b. 9-29-56): Track and field. British runner was gold medalist in 1,500 meters and silver medalist in 800 meters at 2 consecutive Olympics in 1980, 1984. World record holder in 800 meters (1:41.73 set in 1981) and 1,000 meters (2:12.18 set in 1981).

Eddie Collins (b. 5-2-1887, d. 3-25-51): Baseball 2B. All-time leader among 2nd basemen in games, chances and assists; led league in fielding 9 times. 3,311 career hits; .333 career average; .330+ average 12 times. Fourth all-time most stolen bases (743); all-time most World Series steals (14—tied with Lou Brock); all-time leader in single-game steals (6, twice). 1914 MVP. Career span 1906–30 with Philadelphia, Chicago.

Nadia Comaneci (b. 11-12-61): Romanian gymnast. First ever to score a perfect 10 at Olympics (on uneven parallel bars in 1976). Won 3 gold, 2 silver and 1 bronze medal at 1976 Olympics. Also won 2 gold and 2 silver medals at 1980 Olympics.

Dennis Conner (b. 9-16-42): Sailing. Captain of America's Cup winner 2 times (1980, 1987).

Maureen Connolly (b. 9-17-34, d. 6-21-69): Tennis player. "Little Mo" first woman to achieve the Grand Slam, in 1953. Won the U.S. singles title in 1951 at age 16. Thereafter lost only 4 matches before retiring in 1954 because of a broken leg caused by a riding accident. Was never beaten in singles at Wim-

bledon, winning 3 consecutive titles (1952–54). Won 3 consecutive U.S. singles titles (1951–53) and 2 consecutive French titles (1953–54). Also won 1 Australian title (1953).

Jimmy Connors (b. 9-2-52): Tennis player. All-time men's leader in tournament victories (109). Held men's #1 ranking a record 159 consecutive weeks, July 29, 1974 through Aug. 16, 1977. Won 5 U.S. Open singles titles on 3 different surfaces (grass 1974, clay 1976, hard 1978, consecutively 1982–83). Won 2 Wimbledon singles titles (1974, 1982) farther apart than anyone since Bill Tilden. Also won 1974 Australian Open title. Reached Grand Slam final 7 other times.

Howard Cosell (b. 3-25-20): Sportscaster. Lawyer turned TV-radio sports commentator in 1953. Best known for his work on "Monday Night Football." His nasal voice and "tell it like it is" approach made him a controversial figure.

James "Doc" Counsilman (b. 12-28-20): Swimming coach. Coached Indiana from 1957 to 1990. Won 6 consecutive NCAA championships (1968–73). Career record 287–36–1. Coached U.S. men's team at Olympics in 1964, 1976. Also oldest person to swim English Channel (58 in 1979).

Count Fleet (b. 3-24-40, d. 12-3-73): Thoroughbred race horse. Triple Crown winner in 1943 with jockey Johnny Longden aboard. Trained by Don Cameron.

Margaret Smith Court (b. 7-16-42): Australian tennis player. All-time leader in Grand Slam singles titles (26) and total Grand Slam titles (66). Achieved Grand Slam in 1970 and mixed doubles Grand Slam in 1963 with Ken Fletcher. Won 11 Australian singles titles (consecutively 1960–66, 1969–71, 1973), 5 French titles (1962, 1964, consecutively 1969–70, 1973), 5 U.S. titles (1962, 1965, consecutively 1969–70, 1973) and 3 Wimbledon titles (1963, 1965, 1970). Also won 19 Grand Slam doubles titles and 19 mixed doubles titles.

Bob Cousy (b. 8-9-28): Basketball G. Fifth all-time most assists (6,955), second all-time most assists in a game (28 in 1958). League leader in assists 8 consecutive seasons. Averaged 18+ points and named to All-Star team 10 consecutive seasons. 1957 MVP. Played on 6 championship teams with Boston from 1950 to 1969. Also played on NCAA championship team in 1947 with Holy Cross.

Chuck Daly (b. 7-20-30): Basketball coach. Won 2 consecutive championships with Detroit (1989–90). Won 50+ games 4 consecutive seasons. Coach of 1992 Olympic team. Career span as pro coach 1983–present.

Stanley Dancer (b. 7-25-27): Harness racing driver. Only driver to win the Trotting Triple Crown 2 times (Nevele Pride in 1968, Super Bowl in 1972). Also won Pacing Triple Crown driving Most Happy Fella in 1970. Won The Hambletonian 4 times (1968, 1972, 1975, 1983). Driver of the Year in 1968.

Tamas Darnyi (b. 6-3-67): Hungarian swimmer. Gold medalist in 200-meter and 400-meter individual medleys at 1988 Olympics. Also won both events at World Championships in 1986 and 1991. Set world record in these events at 1991 Championships (1:59.36—the only person to break the 2-minute barrier, and 4:12.36).

Al Davis (b. 7-4-29): Football executive. Owner and general manager of Oakland-LA Raiders since 1963.

Built winningest franchise in sports history (289–143–11—a .673 winning percentage entering the 1991 season). Team has won 3 Super Bowl championships (1976, 1980, 1983). Also served as AFL commissioner in 1966, helped negotiate AFL–NFL merger.

Ernie Davis (b. 12-14-39, d. 5-18-63): Football RB. Won Heisman Trophy in 1961, the first black man to win the award. All-America 3 times at Syracuse. First selection in 1962 NFL draft, but became ill with leukemia and never played professionally.

Glenn Davis (b. 12-26-24): College football HB. "Mr. Outside." Teamed with Doc Blanchard to lead Army to 3 consecutive undefeated seasons (1944–46) and 2 consecutive national championships (1944–45). Won Heisman Trophy in 1946. Also named All-America 3 times.

John Davis (b. 1-12-21, d. 7-13-84): Weightlifter. Gold medalist at 2 consecutive Olympics in 1948, 1952. World champion 6 times.

Pete Dawkins (b. 3-8-38): Football RB. Starred at Army 1956–58. Won Heisman Trophy 1958. Was first captain of cadets, class president, top 5 percent of class academically, and football team captain; first man to do all four at West Point. Did not play pro football. Attended Oxford on Rhodes scholarship, won two Bronze Stars in Vietnam, rose to brigadier general before leaving Army to become investment banker. Made unsuccessful run for Senate from New Jersey in 1988.

Dizzy Dean (b. 1-16-11, d. 7-17-74): Baseball RHP. 1934 MVP with 30 wins. League leader in strikeouts, complete games 4 times each. 150 career wins. Arm trouble shortened career after 134 wins by age 26. Career span 1930–47 with St Louis.

Pierre de Coubertin (b. 1-1-1863, d. 9-2-37): Frenchman called the father of the Modern Olympics. President of International Olympic Committee from 1896 to 1925.

Jack Dempsey (b. 6-24-1895, d. 5-31-83): Boxer. Heavyweight champion (1919–26), lost title to Gene Tunney and rematch in the famous "long count" bout in 1927. Career record 62–6–10 with 49 KOs from 1914 to 1928.

Klaus Dibiasi (b. 10-6-47): Italian diver. Gold medalist in platform at 3 consecutive Olympics (1968, 1972, 1976) and silver medalist at 1964 Olympics.

Eric Dickerson (b. 9-2-60): Football RB. All-time season leader in yards rushing (2,105 in 1984), fifth all-time most career yards rushing (11,903 entering 1991 season). Rushed for 1,000+ yards a record 7 consecutive seasons; 100+ yards in 61 games, including a record 12 times in 1984. Led league in rushing 4 times. Rookie of the Year in 1983. Career span since 1983 with Los Angeles, Indianapolis.

Harrison Dillard (b. 7-8-23): Track and field. Only man to win Olympic gold medal in sprint (100 meters in 1948) and hurdles (110 meters in 1952). Sullivan Award winner in 1955.

Joe DiMaggio (b. 11-25-14): Baseball OF. Voted baseball's greatest living player. Record 56-game hitting streak in 1941. MVP in 1939, 1941, 1947. Had .325 career batting average; .300+ average 11 times; 100+ RBI 9 times. League leader in batting average, HR, and RBI 2 times each. Played on 10 World Series winners with NY Yankees. Career span 1936–51.

Tony Dorsett (b. 4-7-54): Football RB. Second all-time in yards rushing (12,739), third in attempts

(2,936). Rushed for 1,000+ yards in 8 seasons. Set record for longest run from scrimmage with 99-yard touchdown run on January 3, 1983. Scored 91 career touchdowns. Named Rookie of the Year in 1977. Career span 1977–88 with Dallas, Denver. Also won Heisman Trophy in 1976, leading Pittsburgh to national championship. All-time NCAA leader in yards rushing and only man to break 6,000-yard barrier (6,082).

Abner Doubleday (b. 6-26-1819, d. 1-26-1893): Civil War hero incorrectly credited as the inventor of baseball in Cooperstown, New York, in 1839. More recent research calls Alexander Cartwright the true father of the game.

Ken Dryden (b. 8-8-47): Hockey G. Goaltender of the Year 5 times (1973, consecutively 1976–79). Playoff MVP as a rookie in 1971, maintained rookie status and named Rookie of the Year in 1972. Led league in goals against average 5 times, wins and shutouts 4 times each. Career record 258–57–74, including 46 shutouts. Career 2.24 goals against average is the modern record. Second all-time in playoff wins (80). Tied record of 4 playoff shutouts in 1977. Played on 6 Stanley Cup champions with Montreal from 1970 to 1979.

Roberto Duran (b. 6-16-51): Panamanian boxer. Champion in 3 different weight classes: lightweight (1972–79), welterweight (1980, lost rematch to Sugar Ray Leonard in famous "no mas" bout) and junior middleweight (1983–84). Current career record 86–9 with 60 KOs since 1967.

Leo Durocher (b. 7-27-05, d. 10-7-91): Baseball manager. "Leo the Lip." Said "Nice guys finish last." Managed 3 pennant winners and 1954 World Series winner. Won 2,008 games in 24 years. Led Brooklyn 1939–48; New York 1948–55; Chicago 1966–72; and Houston 1972–73.

Eddie Eagan (b. 4-26-1898, d. 6-14-67): Only American athlete to win gold medal at Summer and Winter Olympic Games (boxing 1920, bobsled 1932).

Alan Eagleson (b. 4-24-33): Hockey labor leader. Founder of NHL Players' Association and its executive director since 1967.

Dale Earnhardt (b. 4-29-52): Auto racer. NASCAR champion 4 times (1980, 1986–87, 1990). Currently 50 career victories.

Stefan Edberg (b. 1-19-66): Swedish tennis player. Has won 2 Wimbledon singles titles (1988, 1990), 2 Australian Open titles (1985, 1987) and 1 U.S. Open title (1991). Led Sweden to 3 Davis Cup victories (consecutively 1984–85, 1987).

Gertrude Ederle (b. 10-23-06): Swimmer. First woman to swim the English Channel, in 1926. Swam 21 miles from France to England in 14:39. Also won 3 medals at the 1924 Olympics.

Herb Elliott (b. 2-25-38): Track and field. Australian runner was gold medalist in 1960 Olympic 1,500 meters in world record 3:35.6. Also set world mile record of 3:54.5 in 1958. Undefeated at 1500 meters/mile in international competition. Retired at 21.

Roy Emerson (b. 11-3-36): Australian tennis player. All-time men's leader in Grand Slam singles titles (12). Won 6 Australian titles, 5 consecutively (1961, 1963–67), 2 consecutive Wimbledon titles (1964–65), 2 U.S. titles (1961, 1964): and 2 French titles (1963, 1967). Also won 13 Grand Slam doubles titles.

Kornelia Ender (b. 10-25-58): East German swimmer. Won 4 gold medals at 1976 Olympics and 3 silver medals at 1972 Olympics.

Julius Erving (b. 2-22-50): "Dr. J." Basketball F. Third all-time most points scored for combined ABA and NBA career (30,026). 24.2 scoring average. Averaged 20+ points 14 consecutive seasons. 4 MVP awards, consecutively 1974–76, 1981; playoff MVP 1974, 1976. All-Star 9 times. Led league in scoring 3 times. Played on 3 championship teams, with New York (ABA) and Philadelphia (NBA). Career span 1971 to 1986.

Phil Esposito (b. 2-20-42): Hockey C. "Espo." First to break the 100-point barrier (126 in 1969). Fourth all-time in points (1,590) and goals (717), fifth in assists (873). Led league in goals 6 consecutive seasons, points 5 times and assists 3 times. Won MVP award 2 times (1969, 1974). Scored 30+ goals 13 consecutive seasons and 100+ points 6 times. All-Star 6 times. Career span 1963–81 with Chicago, Boston, NY Rangers. Also general manager of NY Rangers from 1986 to 1989. Brother Tony was Goaltender of the Year 3 times.

Janet Evans (b. 8-28-71): Swimmer. Won 3 gold medals at 1988 Olympics. Holds world record in 400-meter freestyle (4:03.85 set in 1988), 800-meter freestyle (8:16.22 set in 1989) and 1,500-meter freestyle (15:52.10 set in 1988). Sullivan Award winner in 1989.

Lee Evans (b. 2-25-47): Track and field. Gold medalist in 400 meters at 1968 Olympics with world record time of 43.86 that stood until 1988.

Chris Evert (b. 12-21-54): Also Chris Evert Lloyd. Tennis player. All-time leader in tournament victories (157). Third all-time in women's Grand Slam singles titles (18—tied with Martina Navratilova). Won at least 1 Grand Slam singles title every year from 1974 to 1986. Won 7 French Open titles (1974–75, 1979–1980, 1983, 1985–86), 6 U.S. Open titles (1975–77, 1978, 1980, 1982), 3 Wimbledon titles (1974, 1976, 1981) and 2 Australian Open titles (1982, 1984). Reached Grand Slam finals 16 other times. Reached semifinals at 52 of her last 56 Grand Slam tournaments.

Patrick Ewing (b. 8-5-62): Basketball C. 1986 Rookie of the Year with New York. Played on 3 NCAA final teams with Georgetown (1982, 1984–85); tournament MVP in 1984. All-America 3 times.

Nick Faldo (b. 7-18-57): British golfer. Winner of the Masters 2 consecutive years (1989–90) and British Open 2 times (1987, 1990).

Juan Manuel Fangio (b. 6-24-11): Argentinian auto racer. Fourth all-time in Formula 1 victories (24, but in just 51 starts). Formula 1 champion 5 times, the most of any driver (1951, consecutively 1954–57). Retired in 1958.

Bob Feller (b. 11-3-18): Baseball RHP. League leader in wins 6 times, strikeouts 7 times, innings pitched 5 times. Pitched 3 no-hitters and 12 one-hitters. 266 career wins; 2,581 career strikeouts. Won 20+ games 6 times. Served 4 years in military during career. Career span 1936–41, 1945–56 with Cleveland.

Tom Ferguson (b. 12-20-50): Rodeo. First to top $1 million in career earnings. All-Around champion 6 consecutive years (1974–79).

Enzo Ferrari (b. 2-8-1898, d. 8-14-88): Auto racing engineer. Team owner since 1929, he built first

Ferrari race car in Italy in 1947 and continued to preside over Ferrari race and street cars until his death. In 61 years of competition, Ferrari's cars have won over 5,000 races.

Mark Fidrych (b. 8-14-54): Baseball RHP. "The Bird." Rookie of the Year in 1976 with Detroit. Had 19–9 record with league-best 2.39 ERA and 24 complete games. Habit of talking to the ball on the mound made him a cult hero. Arm injuries curtailed career.

Cecil Fielder (b. 9-21-63): Baseball 1B. The last man to hit 50+ HR (51 in 1990). Has led the major leagues in HR and RBI 2 consecutive seasons (1990–91) after spending 1989 season in Japanese league. Career span since 1985 with Toronto, Detroit.

Herve Filion (b. 2-1-40): Harness racing driver. All-time leader in career wins (more than 13,000). Driver of the Year 10 times, more than any other driver (consecutively 1969–74, 1978, 1981, 1989).

Rollie Fingers (b. 8-25-46): Baseball RHP. All-time leader in saves (341); third in relief wins (107); fourth in appearances (944). 1981 Cy Young and MVP winner; 1974 World Series MVP. All-time Series leader in saves (6). Career span 1968–85 with Oakland, San Diego, Milwaukee.

Bobby Fischer (b. 3-9-43): Chess. World champion from 1972 to 1975, the only American to hold title. Never played competitive chess during his reign. Forfeited title to Anatoly Karpov by refusing to play him.

Carlton Fisk (b. 12-26-47): Baseball C. Ended 1991 season as all-time HR leader among catchers (348) and second in games caught (2,147). 372 career HR, including a record 68 after age 40. Rookie of the Year in 1972 and All-Star 11 times. Hit dramatic 12th-inning HR to win Game 6 of 1975 World Series. Career span since 1969 with Boston, Chicago (AL).

Emerson Fittipaldi (b. 12-12-46): Brazilian auto racer. Won Indy 500 and CART championship in 1989. Currently 13 career CART victories and 14 career Formula 1 victories. Formula 1 champion 2 times (1972, 1974).

James Fitzsimmons (b. 7-23-1874, d. 3-11-66): Horse racing trainer. "Sunny Jim." Trained Triple Crown winner 2 times (Gallant Fox in 1930, Omaha in 1935). Trained Belmont Stakes winner 6 times (1930, 1932, consecutively 1935–36, 1939, 1955), Preakness Stakes winner 4 times (1930, 1935, 1955, 1957) and Kentucky Derby winner 3 times (1930, 1935, 1939).

Peggy Fleming (b. 7-27-48): Figure skater. Gold medalist at 1968 Olympics. World champion 3 consecutive years (1966–68) and U.S. champion 5 consecutive years (1964–68).

Curt Flood (b. 1-18-38): Baseball OF. Won 7 consecutive Gold Gloves from 1963 to 1969. Career batting average of .293. Refused to be traded after 1969 season, challenging baseball's reserve clause. Supreme Court rejected his plea, but baseball was eventually forced to adopt free agency system. Career span 1956–69 with St. Louis.

Whitey Ford (b. 10-21-26): Baseball LHP. All-time World Series leader in wins, losses, games started, innings pitched, hits allowed, walks and strikeouts. 236 career wins, 2.75 ERA. Third all-time best career winning percentage (.690). Led league in wins and winning percentage 3 times each; ERA, shutouts, innings pitched 2 times each. 1961 Cy Young winner and World Series MVP. Career span 1950, 1953–67 with New York Yankees.

George Foreman (b. 1-22-48): Boxer. Heavyweight champion (1973–74). Retired in 1977, but returned to the ring in 1987. Lost 12–round decision to champion Evander Holyfield in 1991. Current career record 69–3 with 65 KOs since 1969. Also heavyweight gold medalist at 1968 Olympics.

Dick Fosbury (b. 3-6-47): Track and field. Gold medalist in high jump at 1968 Olympics. Back-to-the-bar style of high jumping, called the "Fosbury Flop."

Jimmie Foxx (b. 10-22-07, d. 7-21-67): Baseball 1B. Won 3 MVP awards, consecutively 1932–33, 1938. Fourth all-time highest slugging average (.609), with 534 career HR; hit 30+ HR 12 consecutive seasons, 100+ RBI 13 consecutive seasons. Won Triple Crown in 1933. Led league in HR 4 times, batting average 2 times. Career span 1925–45 with Philadelphia, Boston.

A. J. Foyt (b. 1-16-35): Auto racer. All-time leader in Indy Car victories (67). Won Indy 500 4 times (1961, 1964, 1967, 1977), Daytona 500 1 time (1972), 24 Hours of Daytona 2 times (1983, 1985) and 24 Hours of LeMans 1 time (1967). USAC champion 7 times, more than any other driver (consecutively 1960–61, 1963–64, 1967, 1975, 1979).

William H. G. France (b. 9-26-09): Auto racing executive. Founder of NASCAR and president from 1948 to 1972, succeeded by his son Bill Jr. Builder of Daytona and Talladega speedways.

Dawn Fraser (b. 9-4-37): Australian swimmer. Only swimmer to win gold medal in same event at 3 consecutive Olympics (100-meter freestyle in 1956, 1960, 1964). First woman to break the 1-minute barrier at 100 meters (59.9 in 1962).

Joe Frazier (b. 1-12-44): Boxer. "Smokin' Joe." Heavyweight champion (1970–73). Best known for his 3 epic bouts with Muhammad Ali. Career record 32–4–1 with 27 KOs from 1965 to 1976. Also heavyweight gold medalist at 1964 Olympics.

Dan Gable (b. 10-25-48): Wrestler. Gold medalist in 149–pound division at 1972 Olympics. Also NCAA champion 2 times (in 1968 at 130 pounds, in 1969 at 137 pounds). Career record 118–1. Coached Iowa to NCAA championship 9 consecutive years (1978–86).

Clarence Gaines (b. 5-21-23): College basketball coach. "Bighouse." Entering 1991–92 season with 816 career wins in 44 seasons at Division II Winston-Salem State since 1947.

John Galbreath (b. 8-10-1897, d. 7-20-88): Horse racing owner. Owner of Darby Dan Farms from 1935 until his death and of baseball's Pittsburgh Pirates from 1946 to 1985. Only man to breed and own winners of both the Kentucky Derby (Chateaugay in 1963 and Proud Clarion in 1967) and the Epsom Derby (Roberto in 1972).

Gallant Fox (b. 3-23-27, d. 11-13-54): Thoroughbred race horse. Triple Crown winner in 1930 with jockey Earle Sande aboard. Trained by James Fitzsimmons. The only Triple Crown winner to sire another Triple Crown winner (Omaha in 1935).

Don Garlits (b. 1-14-32): Auto racer. "Big Daddy." Has won 35 National Hot Rod Association top fuel events. Fourth on all-time NHRA national event win list. Won 3 NHRA top fuel points titles (1975, 1985–86). First top fuel driver to surpass 190 mph (1963),

200 mph (1964), 240 mph (1973), 250 mph (1975) and 270 mph (1986). Credited with developing rear engine dragster.

Lou Gehrig (b. 6-19-03, d. 6-2-41): Baseball 1B. "The Iron Horse." All-time leader in consecutive games played (2,130) and grand slam HR (23), third in RBI (1,990) and slugging average (.632). MVP in 1927, 1936; won Triple Crown in 1934. .340 career average; 493 career HR. 100+ RBI 13 consecutive seasons. Led league in RBI 5 times and HR 3 times. Played on 7 World Series winners with New York Yankees. Died of disease since named for him. Career span 1923–39.

Althea Gibson (b. 8-25-27): Tennis player. Won 2 consecutive Wimbledon and U.S. singles titles (1957–58), the first black player to win these tournaments. Also won 1 French title (1956).

Bob Gibson (b. 11-9-35): Baseball RHP. 1968 Cy Young and MVP award winner, with all-time National League best in ERA (1.12); and second most shutouts (13). Also 1970 Cy Young award winner. Record holder for most strikeouts in a World Series game (17); Series MVP in 1964, 1967. Won 20+ games 5 times. 251 career wins; 3,117 strikeouts. Pitched no-hitter in 1971. Career span 1959–75 with St. Louis.

Josh Gibson (b. 12-21-11, d. 1-20-47): Baseball C in Negro leagues. "The Black Babe Ruth." Couldn't play in major leagues because of color. Credited with 950 HR (75 in 1931, 69 in 1934) and .350 batting average. Had .400+ average 2 times. Career span 1930–46 with Homestead Grays, Pittsburgh Crawfords.

Kirk Gibson (b. 5-28-57): Baseball OF. Played on 2 World Series champions (Detroit in 1984 and Los Angeles in 1988). Hit dramatic pinch-hit HR in 9th inning to win Game 1 of 1988 series. MVP in 1988. Career span since 1979, currently with Kansas City. Also starred in baseball and football with Michigan State.

Sid Gillman (b. 10-26-11): Football coach. Developed wide-open, pass-oriented style of offense, introduced techniques for situational player substitutions and the study of game films. Won one division title with Los Angeles Rams and five division titles and one AFL championship (1963) with Los Angeles/San Diego Chargers. Career span 1955–59 Los Angeles Rams; 1960 Los Angeles Chargers; 1961–69 San Diego; 1973–74 Houston. Lifetime record 124–101–7. Also general manager in San Diego and Houston.

Pancho Gonzales (b. 5-9-28): Tennis player. Won 2 consecutive U.S. singles titles (1948–49). In 1969, at age 41, beat Charlie Pasarell 22–24, 1–6, 16–14, 6–3, 11–9 in longest Wimbledon match ever (5:12).

Shane Gould (b. 11-23-56): Australian swimmer. Won 3 gold medals, 1 silver and 1 bronze medal at 1972 Olympics. Set 11 world records over 23-month period beginning in 1971. Held world record in 5 freestyle distances ranging from 100 meters to 1,500 meters in late 1971 and 1972. Retired at age 16.

Steffi Graf (b. 6-14-69): German tennis player. Achieved the Grand Slam in 1988. Has won 3 Australian Open singles titles (1988–90), 3 Wimbledon titles (1988–89, 1991), 2 French Open titles (1987–88) and 2 U.S. Open titles (1988–89). Held the #1 ranking a record 186 weeks; Aug. 17, 1987 through March 10, 1991. Also, gold medalist at 1988 Olympics.

Otto Graham (b. 12-6-21): Football QB. Led Cleveland to 10 championship games in his 10-year career. Played on 4 consecutive AAFC champions (1946–49) and 3 NFL champions (1950, consecutively 1954–55). Combined league totals: 23,584 yards passing, 174 touchdown passes. Player of the Year 2 times (1953, 1955). Led league in passing 6 times. Career span 1946–55.

Red Grange (b. 6-13-03, d. 1-28-91): Football HB. "The Galloping Ghost." All-America 3 consecutive seasons with Illinois (1923–25), scoring 31 touchdowns in 20–game collegiate career. Signed by George Halas of Chicago in 1925, attracted sellout crowds across the country. Established the first AFL with manager C. C. Pyle in 1926, but league folded after 1 year. Career span 1925–34 with Chicago, New York.

Rocky Graziano (b. 6-7-22, d. 5-22-90): Boxer. Middleweight champion from 1947 to 1948. Career record 67–13. Endured 3 brutal title fights against Tony Zale, with Zale winning by KO in 1946 and 1948, and Graziano winning by KO in 1947.

Hank Greenberg (b. 1-1-11, d. 9-4-86): Baseball 1B. 331 career HR (58 in 1938). MVP in 1935, 1940. League leader in HR and RBI 4 times each. Fifth all-time highest slugging average (.605). 100+ RBI 7 times. Career span 1933–41, 1945–47 with Detroit, Pittsburgh.

Joe Greene (b. 9–24–46): Football DT. "Mean Joe." Anchored Pittsburgh's famed "Steel Curtain" defense. Selected for Pro Bowl 10 times. Played on 4 Super Bowl champions (consecutively 1974–75, 1978–79). Career span 1969 to 1981.

Wayne Gretzky (b. 1-26-61): Hockey C. "The Great One." Most dominant player in history, has set 57 records. All-time scoring leader in points (2,142) and assists (1,424), third in goals (718) through 1990–91 season. All-time season scoring leader in points (215 in 1986), goals (92 in 1982) and assists (163 in 1986). Has won MVP award 9 times, more than any other player (consecutively 1980–87, 1989). Led league in assists 11 times, scoring 9 times, goals 4 times. Scored 200+ points 4 times, 100+ points 8 other times; 70+ goals 4 consecutive seasons, 50+ goals 5 other times; 100+ assists 11 consecutive seasons. Also all-time playoff scoring leader in points (299), goals (93) and assists (206). Playoff MVP 2 times (1985, 1988). All-Star 7 times. Played on 5 Stanley Cup champions with Edmonton from 1978 to 1988. Traded to Los Angeles on Aug. 9, 1988.

Archie Griffin (b. 8-21-54): College football RB. Only player to win the Heisman Trophy 2 times (consecutively 1974–75), with Ohio State. Fourth all-time NCAA most yards rushing (5,177), his 6.13 yards per carry is the collegiate record. Professional career span 1976–83 with Cincinnati; totaled 2,808 yards rushing and 192 receptions.

Lefty Grove (b. 3-6-00, d. 5-22-75): Baseball LHP. 300 career wins and fourth all-time highest winning percentage (.680). League leader in ERA 9 times, strikeouts 7 consecutive seasons. Won 20+ games 8 times. 1931 MVP. Career span 1925–41 with Philadelphia, Boston.

Tony Gwynn (b. 5-9-60): Baseball OF. 4 batting titles (1984, consecutively 1987–89). League leader in hits 4 times, with .300+ average 8 times, 200+ hits 4 times. .327 career average. Career span since 1982 with San Diego.

Walter Hagen (b. 12-21-1892, d. 10-5-69): Golfer. Third all-time leader in major championships (11). Won PGA Championship 5 times (1921, consecu-

tively 1924–27), British Open 4 times (1922, 1924, consecutively 1928–29) and U.S. Open 2 times (1914, 1919). Won 40 career tournaments.

Marvin Hagler (b. 5-23-54): Boxer. "Marvelous." Middleweight champion (1980–87). Career record 62–3–2 with 52 KOs from 1973 to 1987. Defended title 13 times.

George Halas (b. 2-2-1895, d. 10-31-83): Football owner and coach. "Papa Bear." All-time leader in seasons coaching (40) and wins (325). Career record 325–151–31 intermittently from 1920 to 1967. Remained as owner until his death. Chicago won a record 7 NFL championships during his tenure.

Arthur B. "Bull" Hancock (b. 1-24-10, d. 9-14-72): Horse racing owner. Owner of Claiborne Farm and arguably the greatest breeder in history. For 15 straight years, from 1955 to 1969, a Claiborne stallion led the sire list. Foaled at Claiborne Farm were 4 Horses of the Year (Kelso, Round Table, Bold Ruler and Nashua).

Tom Harmon (b. 9-28-19, d. 3-17-90): Football RB. Won Heisman Trophy in 1940 with Michigan, the only Wolverine to win award. Triple-threat back led nation in scoring and named All-America 2 consecutive seasons (1939–40). Awarded Silver Star and Purple Heart in World War II. Played in NFL with Los Angeles (1946–47).

Franco Harris (b. 3-7-50): Football RB. Fourth all-time most rushing yards (12,120): and rushing touchdowns (91). Rushed for 1,000+ yards in 8 seasons, 100+ yards in 47 games. Scored 100 career touchdowns. Selected for Pro Bowl 9 times. Rookie of the Year in 1972. Played on 4 Super Bowl champions (consecutively 1974–75, 1978–79) with Pittsburgh. Super Bowl MVP in 1974. Holds Super Bowl record for most rushing yards (354) and most rushing touchdowns (4). Made the "Immaculate Reception" to win 1972 playoff game against Oakland. Career span 1972–83 with Pittsburgh.

Leon Hart (b. 11-2-28): Football DE. Won Heisman Trophy in 1949, the last lineman to win the award. Played on 3 national champions with Notre Dame (consecutively 1946–47, 1949) and the Irish were undefeated during his 4 years (36–0–2). Also played on 3 NFL champions with Detroit. Career span 1950–57.

Bill Hartack (b. 12-9-32): Horse racing jockey. Rode Kentucky Derby winner 5 times (1957, 1960, 1962, 1964, 1969), Preakness Stakes winner 3 times (1956, 1964, 1969) and Belmont Stakes winner 1 time (1960).

Doug Harvey (b. 12-19-24, d. 12-26-90): Hockey D. Defensive Player of the Year 7 times (consecutively 1954–57, 1959–61). Led league in assists in 1954. All-Star 10 times. Played on 6 Stanley Cup champions with Montreal from 1947 to 1968.

Billy Haughton (b. 11-2-23, d. 7-15-86): Harness racing driver. Won the Pacing Triple Crown driving Rum Customer in 1968. Won The Hambletonian 4 times (1974, consecutively 1976–77, 1980).

Woody Hayes (b. 2-14-13, d. 3-12-87): College football coach. Fourth all-time in wins (238). Won national championship 3 times (1954, 1957, 1968) and Rose Bowl 4 times. Career record 238–72–10, including 4 undefeated seasons, with Ohio State from 1951 to 1978. Forced to resign after striking an opposing player during 1978 Gator Bowl.

Marques Haynes (b. 10-3-26): Basketball G. Known as "The World's Greatest Dribbler." Since 1946 has barnstormed more than 4 million miles throughout 97 countries for the Harlem Globetrotters, Harlem Magicians, Meadowlark Lemon's Bucketeers, Harlem Wizards.

Thomas Hearns (b. 10-18-58): Boxer. "Hit Man." Champion in 5 different weight classes: junior middleweight, light heavyweight, middleweight, super middleweight, and light heavyweight. As of 6-18-91 career record 50–3–1 with 40 KOs.

Eric Heiden (b. 6-14-58): Speed skater. Won 5 gold medals at 1980 Olympics. World champion 3 consecutive years (1977–79). Also won Sullivan Award in 1980.

Carol Heiss (b. 1-20-40): Figure skater. Gold medalist at 1960 Olympics, silver medalist at 1956 Olympics. World champion 5 consecutive years (1956–60) and U.S. champion 4 consecutive years (1957–60). Married 1956 gold medalist Hayes Jenkins.

Rickey Henderson (b. 12-25-57): Baseball OF. All-time career stolen base leader (994); all-time season stolen base record holder (130) in 1982. Led league in steals 11 times. Scored 100+ runs 10 times. 1990 MVP. All-time most HR leading off game (50). Career span since 1979 with Oakland, New York.

Sonja Henie (b. 4-8-12, d. 10-12-69): Norwegian figure skater. Gold medalist at 3 consecutive Olympics (1928, 1932, 1936). World champion 10 consecutive years (1927–36).

Orel Hershiser (b. 9-16-58): Baseball RHP. All-time leader most consecutive scoreless innings pitched (59 in 1988). Cy Young Award winner in 1988 and World Series MVP. Career span since 1983 with Los Angeles.

Foster Hewitt (b. 11-21-02, d. 4-22-85): Hockey sportscaster. In 1923, aired one of hockey's first radio broadcasts. Became the voice of hockey in Canada on radio and later television. Famous for the phrase, "He shoots ... he scores!"

Tommy Hitchcock (b. 2-11-00, d. 4-19-44): Polo. 10-goal rating 18 times in his 19-year career from 1922 to 1940. Killed in plane crash in World War II.

Lew Hoad (b. 11-23-34): Australian tennis player. Won 2 consecutive Wimbledon singles titles (1956–57). Also won French title and Australian title in 1956, but failed to achieve the Grand Slam when defeated at Forest Hills by countryman Ken Rosewall.

Ben Hogan (b. 8-13-12): Golfer. Third all-time in career wins (63). Won U.S. Open 4 times (1948, consecutively 1950–51, 1953), the Masters (1951, 1953) and PGA Championship (1946, 1948) 2 times each and British Open once (1953). PGA Player of the Year 4 times (1948, consecutively 1950–51, 1953).

Marshall Holman (b. 9-29-54): Bowler. Won 21 PBA titles between 1975 and 1988. Had leading average in 1987 (213.54) and was named PBA Bowler of the Year.

Nat Holman (b. 10-18-1896): College basketball coach. Only coach in history to win NCAA and NIT championships in same season in 1950 with CCNY. 423 career wins, a .689 winning percentage.

Larry Holmes (b. 11-3-49): Boxer. Heavyweight champion (1978–85). Career record 48–3 with 34 KOs from 1973 to 1988. Defended title 21 times. Began comeback in 1991.

Evander Holyfield (b. 10-19-62): Boxer. Undefeated heavyweight champion since Oct. 25, 1990 when he beat James "Buster" Douglas in Las Vegas. Career record as of 11-1-91 26–0 with 21 KOs.

Harry Hopman (b. 8-12-06, d. 12-27-85): Australian tennis coach. As nonplaying captain, led Australia to 15 Davis Cup titles between 1950 and 1969. Mentor to Lew Hoad, Ken Rosewall, Rod Laver and John Newcombe.

Willie Hoppe (b. 10-11-1887, d. 2-1-59): Billiards. Won 51 world championship matches from 1904 to 1952.

Rogers Hornsby (b. 4-27-1896, d. 1-5-63): Baseball 2B. Second all-time highest career batting average (.358) and 7 batting titles, including .424 average in 1924. 200+ hits 7 times; .400+ average 3 times and .300+ average 12 other times. Led league in slugging average 9 times. Triple Crown winner in 1922, 1925; MVP award winner in 1925, 1929. Career span 1915–37 with St Louis (NL), New York (NL), Boston, Chicago (NL).

Paul Hornung (b. 12-23-35): Football RB-K. Led league in scoring 3 consecutive seasons, including a record 176 points in 1960 (15 touchdowns, 15 field goals, 41 extra points). Player of the Year in 1961. Career span 1957–66 with Green Bay. Suspended for 1963 season by Pete Rozelle for gambling. Also won Heisman Trophy in 1956 with Notre Dame.

Gordie Howe (b. 3-31-28): Hockey RW. All-time leader in goals (801), years played (26) and games (1,767). Second all-time scoring leader in points (1,850) and assists (1,049). Won MVP award 6 times (consecutively 1952–53, 1957–58, 1960, 1963). Led league in scoring 6 times, goals 5 times and assists 3 times. Scored 40+ goals 5 times, 30+ goals 13 other times, 100+ points 3 times. All-Star 12 times. Played on 4 Stanley Cup champions with Detroit from 1946 to 1971. Teamed with sons Mark and Marty in the WHA with Houston and New England from 1973 to 1979, in NHL with Hartford in 1980.

Carl Hubbell (b. 6-22-03, d. 11-21-88): Baseball LHP. 253 career wins. MVP in 1933, 1936. League leader in wins and ERA 3 times each. Won 24 consecutive games from 1936 to 1937. Struck out Ruth, Gehrig, Foxx, Simmons and Cronin consecutively in 1934 All-Star game. Pitched no-hitter in 1929. Career span 1928–43 with New York.

Bobby Hull (b. 1-3-39): Hockey LW. "The Golden Jet." Fifth all-time in goals scored (610). Led league in goals 7 times and points 3 times. Scored 50+ goals 5 times, 30+ goals 8 other times. Won MVP award 2 consecutive seasons (1965–66). Son Brett won MVP award in 1991, the only father and son to be so honored. All-Star 10 times. Career span 1957–72 with Chicago, 1973–80 with Winnipeg of WHA.

Jim "Catfish" Hunter (b. 4-8-46): Baseball RHP. 1974 Cy Young award winner. Won 20+ games 5 consecutive seasons. Led league in wins and winning percentage 2 times each, ERA 1 time. 250+ innings pitched 8 times. Pitched perfect game in 1968. Member of 5 World Series champions for Oakland and New York Yankees. Career span 1965–79.

Don Hutson (b. 1-31-13): Football WR. Second all-time in touchdown receptions (99). Led league in pass receptions 8 times, receiving yards 7 times and scoring 5 consecutive seasons. Caught at least 1 pass in 95 consecutive games. Player of the Year 2 consecutive seasons (1941–42). Career span 1935–45 with Green Bay.

Jackie Ickx (b. 1-1-45): Belgian auto racer. Won the 24 Hours of LeMans a record six times (1969, consecutively 1975–77, 1981–82) before retiring in 1985.

Punch Imlach (b. 3-15-18, d. 12-1-87): Hockey coach. Seventh all-time in wins (467). With Toronto from 1958 to 1969. Won 4 Stanley Cup championships (consecutively 1962–64, 1967).

Bo Jackson (b. 11-30-62): Baseball OF and Football RB. Only person in history to be named to baseball All-Star game and football Pro Bowl game. 1985 Heisman Trophy winner at Auburn. First pick in 1986 NFL draft by Tampa Bay, but opted to play baseball at Kansas City. 1989 All-Star game MVP. Signed with football's LA Raiders in 1988. Sustained football injury in 1990, released from baseball contract by KC, signed by Chicago and returned from injury in early September 1991. Career span since 1986.

Joe Jackson (b. 7-16-1889, d. 12-5-51): Baseball OF. "Shoeless Joe." Third all-time highest career batting average (.356), with .300+ average 11 times. 1 of the "8 men out" banned from baseball for throwing 1919 World Series. Career span 1908–20 with Cleveland, Chicago.

Reggie Jackson (b. 5-18-46): Baseball OF. "Mr. October." All-time leader in World Series slugging average (.755). 1977 Series MVP, hit 3 HR in final game on 3 consecutive pitches. 563 career HR total is sixth best all-time. Led league in HR 4 times. 1973 MVP. All-time strikeout leader (2,597). In a 12-year period played on 10 first-place teams, 5 World Series winners. Career span 1967–87 with Oakland, New York, California.

Bruce Jenner (b. 10-28-49): Track and Field. Gold medalist in decathlon at 1976 Olympics. Sullivan Award winner in 1976.

John Henry (b. 1975): Thoroughbred race horse. Sold as yearling for $1,100, the gelding was Horse of the Year in 1981 and in 1984 and retired with then-record $6,597,947 in winnings.

Ben Johnson (b. 12-30-61): Track and field. Canadian sprinter set world record in 100 meters (9.83 in 1987). Won event at 1988 Olympics in 9.79, but gold medal revoked for failing drug test. Both world records revoked for steroids usage.

Earvin "Magic" Johnson (b. 8-14-59): Basketball G. Entering the 1991–92 season all-time leader in assists (9,921); all-time playoff leader in assists (2,320) and steals (358). MVP award 3 times (1987, consecutively 1989–90) and playoff MVP 1980, 1982, 1987. Played on 5 championship teams with Los Angeles since 1979. All-Star 8 consecutive seasons. League leader in assists 4 times, steals 2 times, free throw percentage 1 time. Also won NCAA championship and named tournament MVP in 1979 with Michigan State.

Jack Johnson (b. 3-31-1878, d. 6-10-46): Boxer. First black heavyweight champion (1908–15). Career record 78–8–12 with 45 KOs from 1897 to 1928.

Walter Johnson (b. 11-6-1887, d. 12-10-46): Baseball RHP. "Big Train." All-time leader in shutouts (110), second in wins (416), third in losses (279) and innings pitched (5,923). His 2.17 career ERA and 3,508 career strikeouts are seventh best all-time. MVP in 1913, 1924. Won 20+ games 12 times.

League leader in strikeouts 12 times, ERA 5 times, wins 6 times. Pitched no-hitter in 1920. Career span 1907–27 with Washington.

Ben A. Jones (b. 12-31-1882, d. 6-13-61): Horse racing trainer. Trained Triple Crown winner 2 times (Whirlaway in 1941, Citation in 1948). Trained Kentucky Derby winner 6 times, more than any other trainer (1938, 1941, 1944, consecutively 1948–49, 1952), Preakness Stakes winner 2 times (1941, 1944) and Belmont Stakes winner 1 time (1941).

Bobby Jones (b. 3-17-02, d. 12-18-71): Golfer. Achieved golf's only recognized Grand Slam in 1930. Second all-time in major championships (13). Won U.S. Amateur 5 times, more than any golfer (consecutively 1924–25, 1927–28, 1930), U.S. Open 4 times (1923, 1926, consecutively 1929–30), British Open 3 times (consecutively 1926–27, 1930) and British Amateur (1930). Also designed Augusta National course, site of the Masters, and founded the tournament. Winner of Sullivan Award in 1930.

Robert Trent Jones (b. 6-20-06): English-born golf course architect designed or remodelled over 400 courses, including Baltusrol, Hazeltine, Oak Hill and Winged Foot. In the mid-60s five straight U.S. Opens were played on courses designed or remodelled by Jones.

Michael Jordan (b. 2-17-63): Basketball G. "Air." Entering 1991–92 season, all-time highest regular season scoring average (32.8) and most points scored in a playoff game (63 in 1986). Has led league in scoring 5 consecutive seasons, steals 2 times. MVP in 1988, 1991; playoff MVP in 1991; Rookie of the Year in 1985. All-Star team 4 consecutive seasons, All-Defensive team 3 consecutive seasons. Career span since 1984 with Chicago. Also College Player of the Year in 1984. Played on NCAA championship team with North Carolina in 1982. Member of gold medal-winning 1984 Olympic team. Selected, 1992 Olympic team.

Florence Griffith Joyner (b. 12-21-59): Track and field. Won 3 gold medals (100 meters, 200 meters, 4x100-meter relay) at 1988 Olympics; silver medalist at 1984 Olympics. Women's world record holder in 100 meters (10.49 set in 1988) and 200 meters (21.34 set at 1988 Olympics). Sullivan Award winner in 1988.

Jackie Joyner-Kersee (b. 3-3-62): Track and field. Gold medalist in heptathlon and long jump at 1988 Olympics. Heptathlon world record holder (7,291 points set at 1988 Olympics). Also won silver medal in heptathlon at 1984 Olympics. Sullivan Award winner in 1986.

Alberto Juantorena (b. 3-12-51): Track and field. Cuban gold medalist in 400 meters and 800 meters at 1976 Olympics.

Duke Kahanamoku (b. 8-24-1890, d. 1-22-68): Swimmer. Won a total of 5 medals (3 gold and 2 silver) at 3 Olympics in 1912, 1920, 1924. Introduced the crawl stroke to America. Surfing pioneer and water polo player. Later sheriff of Honolulu.

Al Kaline (b. 12-19-34): Baseball OF. 3,007 career hits and 399 career HR. Youngest player to win batting title with .340 average as a 20-year-old in 1955. Had .300+ average 9 times. Played in 18 All-Star games. Career span 1953–74 with Detroit.

Anatoly Karpov (b. 5-23-61): Soviet chess player. First world champion to receive title by default, in

1975, when Bobby Fischer chose not to defend his crown. Champion until 1985 when beaten by Gary Kasparov.

Gary Kasparov (b. 4-13-63): Born Harry Weinstein. Soviet chess player. World champion since 1985.

Kip Keino (b. 1-17-40): Track and field. Kenyan was gold medalist in 1,500 meters at 1968 Olympics and in steeplechase at 1972 Olympics.

Kelso (b. 1957, d. 1983): Thoroughbred race horse. Gelding was Horse of the Year 5 straight years (1960–64). Finished in the money in 53 of 63 races. Career earnings $1,977,896.

Harmon Killebrew (b. 6-29-36): Baseball 3B-1B. 573 career HR total is fifth most all-time. 100+ RBI 9 times, 40+ HR 8 times. League leader in HR 6 times and RBI 4 times. 1969 MVP. 100+ walks and strikeouts 7 times each. Career span 1954–75 with Washington, Minnesota.

Jean Claude Killy (b. 8-30-43): French skier. Won 3 gold medals at 1968 Olympics. World Cup overall champion 2 consecutive years (1967–68).

Ralph Kiner (b. 10-27-22): Baseball OF. Second to Babe Ruth in all-time HR frequency (7.1 HR every 100 at bats). 369 career HR. Led league in HR 7 consecutive seasons, with 50+ HR 2 times; 100+ RBI and runs scored in same season 6 times; 100+ walks 6 times. Career span 1946–55 with Pittsburgh.

Billie Jean King (b. 11-22-43): Tennis player. Won a record 20 Wimbledon titles, including 6 singles titles (consecutively 1966–68, 1972–73, 1975). Won 4 U.S. singles titles (1967, consecutively 1971–72, 1974), and singles titles at Australian Open (1968) and French Open (1972). Won 27 Grand Slam doubles titles—total of 39 Grand Slam titles is third all-time. Helped found the women's pro tour in 1970, serving as president of the Women's Tennis Association 2 times. Helped form Team Tennis. Also won the "Battle of the Sexes" match against Bobby Riggs in straight sets on Sept. 20, 1973, at the Houston Astrodome.

Nile Kinnick (b. 7-9-18, d. 6-2-43): College football RB. Won the Heisman Trophy in 1939 with Iowa. Premier runner, passer and punter was killed in plane crash during routine Navy training flight. Stadium in Iowa City named in his honor.

Franz Klammer (b. 12-3-54): Austrian alpine skier. Greatest downhiller ever. Gold medalist at 1976 Olympics. Also won four World Cup downhill titles (1975–78).

Bob Knight (b. 10-25-40): College basketball coach. Won 3 NCAA championships with Indiana in 1976, 1981, 1987. Coached U.S. Olympic team to gold medal in 1984. 532 career wins and .729 career winning percentage entering 1991–92 season. Career span since 1966.

Olga Korbut (b. 5-16-55): Soviet gymnast. First ever to complete backward somersault on balance beam. Won 3 gold medals at 1972 Olympics.

Sandy Koufax (b. 12-30-35): Baseball LHP. Cy Young Award winner 3 times (1963, consecutively 1965–66); and MVP in 1963; World Series MVP in 1963, 1965. Pitched 1 perfect game, 3 no-hitters. League leader in ERA 5 consecutive seasons, strikeouts 4 times. Won 25+ games 3 times. Career record 165–87, with 2.76 ERA. Career span 1955–66 with Brooklyn/Los Angeles.

Jack Kramer (b. 8-1-21): Tennis player. Won 2 consecutive U.S. singles titles (1946–47) and 1 Wimbledon title (1947). Also won 6 Grand Slam doubles titles. Served as executive director of Association of Tennis Professionals from 1972 to 1975.

Ingrid Kristiansen (b. 3-21-56): Track and field. Norwegian runner is only person—male or female—to hold world records in 5,000 meters (14:37.33 set in 1986), 10,000 meters (30:13.74 set in 1986) and marathon (2:21.06 set in 1985). Also won Boston Marathon 2 times (1986, 1989).

Rene Lacoste (b. 7-2-05): French tennis player. "The Crocodile." One of France's "Four Musketeers" of the 1920s. Won 3 French singles titles (1925, 1927, 1929), 2 consecutive U.S. titles (1926–27) and 2 Wimbledon titles (1925, 1928). Also designed casual shirt with embroidered crocodile that bears his name.

Marion Ladewig (b. 10-30-14): Bowler. Won All-Star Tournament 8 times (consecutively 1949–52, 1954, 1956, 1959, 1963) and WPBA National Championship once (1960). Also voted Bowler of the Year 9 times, more than any other bowler (consecutively 1950–54, 1957–59, 1963).

Guy Lafleur (b. 9-20-51): Hockey RW. Won MVP award 2 consecutive seasons (1977–78), playoff MVP in 1977. Scored 50+ goals and 100+ points 6 consecutive seasons. Led league in points scored 3 consecutive seasons, goals and assists 1 time each. 560 career goals, 793 assists. Played on 5 Stanley Cup champions with Montreal from 1971 to 1985.

Jack Lambert (b. 7-8-52): Football LB. Anchored Pittsburgh's famed "Steel Curtain" defense. Selected for Pro Bowl 9 times. Played on 4 Super Bowl champions (consecutively 1974–75, 1978–79) with Pittsburgh from 1974 to 1984.

Kenesaw Mountain Landis (b. 11-20-1866, d. 11-25-44): Baseball's first and most powerful commissioner from 1920 to 1944. By banning the 8 Black Sox he restored public confidence in the integrity of baseball.

Tom Landry (b. 9-11-24): Football coach. Third all-time in wins (271). The first coach in Dallas history, from 1960 to 1988. Led team to 13 division titles, 7 championship games and 5 Super Bowls. Won 2 Super Bowl championships (1971, 1977). Career record 271–180–6.

Dick "Night Train" Lane (b. 4-16-28): Football DB. Third all-time in interceptions (68) and second in interception yardage (1,207). Set record with 14 interceptions as a rookie in 1952. Career span 1952–65 with Los Angeles, Chicago Cardinals, Detroit.

Joe Lapchick (b. 4-12-00, d. 8-10-70): Basketball C-coach. One of the first big men in basketball, member of New York's Original Celtics. Coached St. John's (1936–47, 1956–65) winning four NIT Tournaments. Coached New York Knicks, 1947–56.

Steve Largent (b. 9-28-54): Football WR. All-time leader in pass receptions (819), consecutive games with reception (177), touchdown receptions (100), seasons with 50+ receptions (10), receiving yards (13,089) and seasons with 1,000+ yards receiving (8). Career span 1976–89 with Seattle.

Don Larsen (b. 8-7-29): Baseball RHP. Pitched only perfect game in World Series history for the NY

Yankees on Oct. 8, 1956, beating the Dodgers 2–0; named World Series MVP. Career span 1953–67 for many teams.

Tommy Lasorda (b. 9-22-27): Baseball manager. Has spent nearly his entire minor and major league career in Dodgers organization as a pitcher, coach and manager. Has managed Dodgers since 1977, winning 4 pennants and 2 World Series championships (1981, 1988).

Rod Laver (b. 8-9-38): Australian tennis player. "Rocket." Only player to achieve the Grand Slam twice (as an amateur in 1962 and as a pro in 1969). Second all-time in men's Grand Slam singles titles (11—tied with Bjorn Borg). Won 4 Wimbledon titles (consecutively 1961–62, 1968–69), 3 Australian titles (1960, 1962, 1969), 2 U.S. titles (1962, 69) and 2 French titles (1962, 1969). Also won 8 Grand Slam doubles titles. First player to earn $1 million in prize money. 47 career tournament victories. Member of undefeated Australian Davis Cup team from 1959 to 1962.

Andrea Mead Lawrence (b. 4-19-32): Skier. Gold medalist in slalom and giant slalom at 1952 Olympics.

Sammy Lee (b. 8-1-20): Diver. Gold medalist at 2 consecutive Olympics (highboard in 1948, 1952); bronze medalist in springboard at 1948 Olympics. Won the 1953 Sullivan Award. Also 1960 U.S. Olympic diving coach.

Mario Lemieux (b. 10-5-65): Hockey C. Won MVP award in 1988, playoff MVP in 1991. Led league in most points and goals scored 2 consecutive seasons, assists 1 season. Scored 40+ goals and 100+ points 6 consecutive seasons, including 85 goals and 199 points in 1989. Rookie of the Year in 1985. Tied playoff game record for points (8) and goals (5) on April 25, 1989. Career span since 1984 with Pittsburgh.

Greg LeMond (b. 6-26-61): Cyclist. Only American to win Tour de France; won event 3 times (1986, consecutively 1989–90). Recovered from hunting accident to win in 1989.

Ivan Lendl (b. 3-7-60): Tennis player. Second all-time men's most career tournament victories (90). Won 3 consecutive U.S. Open singles titles (1985–87) and 3 French Open titles (1984, consecutively 1985–86). Also won 2 consecutive Australian Open titles (1989–90). Reached Grand Slam final 9 other times. All-time leader in prize money, with more than $16 million.

Suzanne Lenglen (b. 5-24-1899, d. 7-4-38): French tennis player. Lost only 1 match from 1919 to her retirement in 1926. Won 6 Wimbledon singles and doubles titles (consecutively 1919–23, 1925). Won 6 French singles and doubles titles (consecutively 1920–23, 1925–26).

Sugar Ray Leonard (b. 5-17-56): Boxer. Champion in 5 different weight classes: welterweight, junior middleweight, middleweight, light heavyweight and super middleweight. Career record 36–2–1 with 25 KOs from 1977 to 1991. Also light welterweight gold medalist at 1976 Olympics.

Carl Lewis (b. 7-1-61): Track and field. Set world record for 100 meters (9.86) on 8-25-91 at World Championships in Tokyo. Duplicated Jesse Owens's feat by winning 4 gold medals at 1984 Olympics (100 and 200 meters, 4x100-meter relay and long jump). Also

won 2 gold medals (100 meters, long jump) and 1 silver (200 meters) at 1988 Olympics. Sullivan Award winner in 1981.

Nancy Lieberman (b. 7-1-58): Basketball G. Three-time All-America at Old Dominion. Player of the Year (1979, 1980). Olympian, 1976, and selected for 1980 team, but quit because of Moscow boycott. Promoter of women's basketball, played in WPBL, WABA. First woman to play basketball in a men's professional league (USBL) in 1986.

Sonny Liston (b. 5-8-32, d. 12-30-70): Boxer. Heavyweight champion from 1962 to 1964. Lost title to Cassius Clay (Muhammad Ali) in 1964 and then lost rematch in 1965 when KOd in first round.

Vince Lombardi (b. 6-11-13, d. 9-3-70): Football coach. All-time highest winning percentage (.736). Career record 106–36–6. Won 3 NFL championships and 2 consecutive Super Bowl titles with Green Bay from 1959 to 1967. Coached Washington in 1969. Super Bowl trophy named in his honor.

Johnny Longden (b. 2-14-07): Horse racing jockey. Rode Triple Crown winner Count Fleet in 1943. Fifth all-time most wins (6,032).

Nancy Lopez (b. 1-6-57): Golfer. LPGA Player of the Year 4 times (consecutively 1978–79, 1985, 1988). Winner of LPGA Championship 3 times (1978, 1985, 1989). Youngest member of the LPGA Hall of Fame.

Greg Louganis (b. 1-29-60): Diver. Gold medalist in platform and springboard at 2 consecutive Olympics in 1984, 1988. World champion 5 times (platform in 1978, 1982, 1986; springboard in 1982, 1986). Also Sullivan Award winner in 1984.

Joe Louis (b. 5-13-14, d. 4-12-81): Boxer. "The Brown Bomber." Longest title reign of any heavyweight champion (11 years, 9 months) from June 1937 through March 1949. Career record 63–3 with 49 KOs from 1934 to 1951. Defended title 25 times.

Sid Luckman (b. 11–21–16): Football QB. Played on 4 NFL champions (consecutively 1940–41, 1943, 1946) with Chicago. Player of the Year in 1943. Tied record with 7 touchdown passes on Nov. 14, 1943. All-Pro 6 times. 137 career touchdown passes. Career span 1939–50. Also All-America with Columbia.

Jon Lugbill (b. 5-27-61): White water canoe racer. Won 5 world singles titles from 1979 to 1989.

Hank Luisetti (b. 6-16-16): Basketball F. The first player to use the one-handed shot. All-America at Stanford 3 consecutive years from 1936–38.

D. Wayne Lukas (b. 9-2-35): Horse racing trainer. Former college basketball coach and quarter horse trainer takes mass production approach with stables at most major tracks around country. Trained two Horses of the Year, Lady's Secret in 1986 and Criminal Type in 1990. Won 1988 Kentucky Derby with a filly, Winning Colors.

Connie Mack (b. 2-22-1862, d. 2-8-56): Born Cornelius McGillicuddy. Baseball manager. Managed Philadelphia for 50 years (1901–50) until age 87. All-time leader in games (7,755), wins (3,731) and losses (3,948). Won 9 pennants and 5 World Series (1910–11, 1913, 1929–30).

Larry Mahan (b. 11-21-43): Rodeo. All-Around champion 6 times (consecutively 1966–70, 1973).

Phil Mahre (b. 5-10-57): Skier. Gold medalist in slalom at 1984 Olympics (twin brother Steve won silver medal). World Cup champion 3 consecutive years (1981–83).

Joe Malone (b. 2-28-1890, d. 5-15-69): Hockey F. "Phantom Joe." Led the NHL in its first season, 1917–18, with 44 goals in 20 games with Montreal. Led league in scoring 2 times (1918, 1920). Holds NHL record with most goals scored, single game (7) in 1920.

Karl Malone (b. 7-24-63): Basketball F. "The Mailman." Three-time first-team All-Star. All-Star MVP, 1989. All-Rookie team, 1986. Scored 20+ points in five of six seasons with Utah. Selected, 1992 Olympic team.

Moses Malone (b. 3-23-55): Basketball C. Entering 1991–92 season all-time leader free throws made (7,999), fifth in rebounds (15,150) and seventh in points scored (25,737). 3 MVP awards in 1979, consecutively 1982–83; playoff MVP in 1983. 4-time All-Star. Led league in rebounding 6 times, 5 consecutively. Career span since 1976 with Houston, Philadelphia, Washington, Atlanta, Milwaukee.

Man o' War (b. 1917, d. 1947): Thoroughbred race horse. Won 20 of 21 races from 1919 to 1920. Only loss was in 1919 in Sanford Stakes to Upset. Passed up Derby but won both Preakness and Belmont. Winner of $249,465. Sire of War Admiral, 1937 Triple Crown winner.

Mickey Mantle (b. 10-20-31): Baseball OF. Won 3 MVP awards, consecutively 1956–57 and 1962; won Triple Crown in 1956. 536 career HR. Led league in runs scored 6 times, HR and slugging average 4 times. 50+ HR 2 times, 30+ HR 7 other times. Led league in walks and strikeouts 5 times each. Greatest switch hitter in history. Played in 20 All-Star games. All-time World Series leader in HR (18), RBI (40) and runs scored (42). No. 7 was a member of 7 World Series winners with NY Yankees. Career span 1951–68.

Diego Maradona (b. 10-30-60): Argentinian soccer player. Led Argentina to 1986 World Cup victory and to 1990 World Cup finals. Led Naples to Italian League titles (1987, 1990), Italian Cup (1987) and to European Champion Clubs' Cup title (1989). Throughout 1980s often acknowledged as best player in the world. Tested positive for cocaine and suspended by FIFA and Italian Soccer Federation for 15 months in March 1991.

Pete Maravich (b. 6-22-47, d. 1-5-88): Basketball G. "Pistol Pete." All-time NCAA leader in points scored (3,667), scoring average (44.2) and games scoring 50+ points (28, including then Division I record 69 points in 1970). All-time season leader in points scored (1,381) and scoring average (44.5) in 1970. College Player of the Year in 1970. NCAA scoring leader and All-America 3 consecutive seasons from 1968 to 1970 with Louisiana State. Also led NBA in scoring in 1977. Averaged 20+ points 8 times. All-Star 2 times. Career span 1970–79 with Atlanta, New Orleans/Utah, Boston.

Rocky Marciano (b. 9-1-23, d. 8-31-69): Boxer. Heavyweight champion (1952–56). Career record 49-0 with 43 KOs from 1947 to 1956. Retired as undefeated champion.

Juan Marichal (b. 10-24-37): Baseball RHP. 243 career wins, 2.89 career ERA. Won 20+ games 6 times; 250+ innings pitched 8 times; 200+ strikeouts 6 times. Pitched no-hitter in 1963. Career span 1960–75 with San Francisco.

Dan Marino (b. 9-15-61): Football QB. Set all-time season record for yards passing (5,084) and touchdown passes (48) in 1984. Prior to 1991 season had passed for 4,000+ yards 3 other seasons and 400+ yards a record 10 games. Player of the Year in 1984. Career totals: 31,416 yards passing, 241 touchdown passes. Career span since 1983 with Miami.

Roger Maris (b. 9-10-34, d. 12-14-85): Baseball OF. Broke Babe Ruth's all-time season HR record with 61 in 1961. Won consecutive MVP awards and led league in RBI 1960–61. Career span 1957–68 with Kansas City, New York (AL), St Louis.

Billy Martin (b. 5-16-28, d. 12-25-89): Baseball 2B-manager. Volatile manager was hired and fired by Minnesota, Detroit, Texas, New York Yankees (5 times!) and Oakland from 1969 to 1988. Won World Series with Yankees as manager in 1977 and as player 4 times.

Eddie Mathews (b. 10-13-31): Baseball 3B. 512 career HR and 30+ HR 9 consecutive seasons. League leader in HR 2 times, walks 4 times. Career span 1952–68 with Milwaukee.

Christy Mathewson (b. 8-12-1880, d. 10-7-25): Baseball RHP. Third all-time most wins (373) and shutouts (80); fifth all-time best ERA (2.13). Led league in wins 5 times; won 30+ games 4 times and 20+ games 9 other times. Led league in ERA and strikeouts 5 times each. 300+ innings pitched 11 times. Pitched 2 no-hitters. Pitched 3 shutouts in 1905 World Series. Career span 1900–16 with New York.

Bob Mathias (b. 11-17-30): Track and field. At age 17, youngest to win gold medal in decathlon at 1948 Olympics. First decathlete to win gold medal at consecutive Olympics (1948, 1952). Also won Sullivan Award in 1948.

Ollie Matson (b. 5-1-30): Football RB. Versatile runner totalled 12,844 combined yards rushing, receiving and kick returning. His 9 touchdowns on punt and kickoff returns is an NFL record. Scored 73 career touchdowns, including a 105-yard kickoff return on Oct. 14, 1956, the second longest ever. Career span 1952–66 with Chicago Cardinals, Los Angeles, Detroit, Philadelphia. Also won bronze medal in 400-meters at 1952 Olympics.

Roland Matthes (b. 11-17-50): German swimmer. Gold medalist in 100-meter and 200-meter backstroke at 2 consecutive Olympics (1968, 1972). Set 16 world records from 1967 to 1973.

Willie Mays (b. 5-6-31): Baseball OF. "Say Hey Kid." MVP in 1954, 1965; Rookie of the Year in 1951. Third all-time most HR (660), with 50+ HR 2 times, 30+ HR 9 other times. Led league in HR 4 times. 100+ RBI 10 times; 100+ runs scored 12 consecutive seasons. 3,283 career hits. Led league in stolen bases 4 consecutive seasons. 30 HR and 30 steals in same season 2 times and first man in history to hit 300+ HR and steal 300+ bases. Won 11 consecutive Gold Gloves; set record for career putouts by an outfielder and league record for total chances. His catch in the 1954 World Series off the bat of Vic Wertz called the greatest ever. Career span 1951–73 with New York and San Francisco Giants, New York Mets.

Bill Mazeroski (b. 9-5-36): Baseball 2B. Hit dramatic 9th-inning home run in Game 7 to win 1960 World Series, the only Series to end on a home run.

Also a great fielder, won Gold Glove 8 times. Led league in assists 9 times, double plays 8 times and putouts 5 times.

Joe McCarthy (b. 4-21-1887, d. 1-3-78): Baseball manager. All-time highest winning percentage among managers for regular season (.615) and World Series (.698). First manager to win pennants in both leagues (Chicago (NL), 1929, New York (AL), 1932). From 1926 to 1950 his teams won 7 World Series and 9 pennants.

Mark McCormack (b. 11-6-30): Sports marketing agent. Founded International Management Group in 1962. Also author of best-selling business advice books.

Pat McCormick (b. 5-12-30): Diver. Gold medalist in platform and springboard at 2 consecutive Olympics (1952, 1956). Also won Sullivan Award in 1956.

John McEnroe (b. 2-26-59): Tennis player. Has won 4 U.S. Open singles titles (consecutively 1979–81, 1984) and 3 Wimbledon titles (1981, consecutively 1983–84). Also won 8 Grand Slam doubles titles. Third all-time men's most career tournament victories (76), second most doubles titles (74). Led U.S. to 4 Davis Cup victories (1978–79, 1981–82).

John McGraw (b. 4-7-1873, d. 2-25-34): Baseball manager. Second all-time most games (4,801) and wins (2,784). Guided New York Giants to 3 World Series titles and 10 pennants from 1902 to 1932.

Denny McLain (b. 3-29-44): Baseball RHP. Last pitcher to win 30+ games in a season (Detroit, 1968); won 20+ games 2 other times. Won 2 consecutive Cy Young Awards (1968–69). Led league in innings pitched 2 times. Served 2½-year jail term for 1985 conviction of extortion, racketeering and drug possession. Career span 1963–72.

Mary T. Meagher (b. 10-27-64): Swimmer. "Madame Butterfly." Won 3 gold medals at 1984 Olympics (100-meter butterfly, 200-meter butterfly and 400-medley relay). World record holder in 100-meter butterfly (57.93 set in 1981) and 200-meter butterfly (2:05.96 set in 1981).

Rick Mears (b. 12-3-51): Auto racer. Has won Indy 500 4 times (1979, 1984, 1988, 1991). Fifth all-time in CART victories (28 as of 8-13-91) and CART champion 3 times (1979, consecutively 1981–82). Named Indy 500 Rookie of the Year in 1978.

George Mikan (b. 6-18-24): Basketball C. Averaged 20+ points and named to All-Star team 6 consecutive seasons. Led league in scoring 3 times, rebounding 1 time. Played on 5 championship teams in 6 years (1949–54) with Minneapolis. Also played on 1945 NIT championship team with DePaul. All-America 3 times. Served as ABA Commissioner from 1968 to 1969.

Stan Mikita (b. 5-20-40): Hockey C. Won MVP award 2 consecutive seasons (1967–68). Fifth all-time in assists (1,467). Led league in assists 4 consecutive seasons and points 4 times. 541 career goals. All-Star 6 times. Career span 1958–80 with Chicago.

Del Miller (b. 7-5-13): Harness racing driver. Has raced in 8 decades since 1929, the longest career of any athlete. Won The Hambletonian in 1950. As of 8-13-91 has won 2,435 career races.

Marvin Miller (b. 4-14-17): Labor negotiator. Union chief of Major League Baseball Players Association from 1966 to 1984. Led strikes in 1972 and 1981. Negotiated 5 labor contracts with owners that increased minimum salary and pension fund, allowed for agents and arbitration, and brought about the end of the reserve clause and the beginning of free agency.

Joe Montana (b. 6-11-56): Football QB. Entering 1991 season all-time highest-rated passer (93.4), third in completions (2,914), fourth in passing yards (34,998) and sixth in touchdown passes (242). Has won 4 Super Bowl championships (1981, 1984, consecutively 1988–89) with San Francisco since 1979. Named Super Bowl MVP 3 times (1981, 1984, 1989). Player of the Year in 1989. Also led Notre Dame to national championship in 1977.

Carlos Monzon (b. 8-7-42): Argentinian boxer. Longest title reign of any middleweight champion (6 years, 9 months) from Nov. 1970 through Aug. 1977. Career record 89–3–9 with 61 KOs from 1963 to 1977. Won 82 consecutive bouts from 1964 to 1977. Defended title 14 times. Retired as champion.

Helen Wills Moody (b. 10-6-05): Tennis player. Second all-time most women's Grand Slam singles titles (19). Her 8 Wimbledon titles are second most all-time (consecutively 1927–30, 1932–33, 1935, 1938). Won 7 U.S. titles (consecutively 1923–25, 1927–29, 1931) and 4 French titles (consecutively 1928–30, 1932). Also won 12 Grand Slam doubles titles.

Archie Moore (b. 12-13-16): Boxer. Longest title reign of any light heavyweight champion (9 years, 1 month) from Dec. 1952 through Feb. 1962. Career record 199–26–8 with an all-time record 145 KOs from 1935 to 1965. Retired at age 52.

Joe Morgan (b. 9-19-43): Baseball 2B. Won 2 consecutive MVP awards in 1975–76. Third all-time most walks (1,865), seventh most stolen bases (689). Led league in walks 4 times. 100+ walks and runs scored 8 times each; 40+ stolen bases 9 times. Won 5 Gold Gloves. Second all-time most games played by 2nd baseman (2,527). Career span 1963–84 with Houston, Cincinnati.

Willie Mosconi (b. 6-27-13): Pocket billiards player. Won world title a record 15 straight times between 1941 and 1957. Once pocketed 526 balls without a miss.

Edwin Moses (b. 8-31-55): Track and field. Gold medalist in 400-meter hurdles at 2 Olympics, in 1976, 1984 (U.S. boycotted 1980 Games); bronze medalist at 1988 Olympics. World record holder in 400-meter hurdles (47.02 set in 1983). Also won 122 consecutive races from 1977 to 1987. Won Sullivan Award in 1983.

Marion Motley (b. 6-5-20): Football FB. All-time AAFC leader in yards rushing (3,024). Also led NFL in rushing 1 time. Combined league totals: 4,712 yards rushing, 39 touchdowns. Played on 4 consecutive AAFC champions (1946–49), 1 NFL champion (1950) with Cleveland from 1946 to 1953.

Shirley Muldowney (b. 6-19-40): Drag racer. First woman to win the Top Fuel championship, which she won 3 times (1977, 1980, 1982).

Isaac Murphy (b. 4-16-1861, d. 2-12-1896): Horse racing jockey. Top jockey of his era, Murphy, who was black, won 3 Kentucky Derbys (aboard Buchanan in 1884, Riley in 1890 and Kingman in 1891).

Jim Murray (b. 12-29-19): Sportswriter. Won Pulitzer Prize in 1990. Named Sportswriter of the Year 14 times. Columnist for *Los Angeles Times* since 1961.

Ty Murray (b. 10-11-69): Rodeo cowboy. All-Around world champion, 1989, 1990. Set single-season earnings record, 1990 ($213,771). Rookie of the Year, 1988. At 20 in 1989, became youngest man ever to win national all-around title.

Stan Musial (b. 11-21-20): Baseball OF-1B. "Stan the Man." Had .331 career batting average and 475 career HR. MVP award winner 1943, 1946, 1948. Fourth all-time in hits (3,630) and third in doubles (725). Won 7 batting titles. Led league in hits 6 times, slugging average 5 times, doubles 8 times. Had .300+ batting average 17 times, 200+ hits 6 times, 100+ RBI 10 times, and 100+ runs scored 11 times. 24-time All-Star. Career span 1941–63 with St. Louis.

John Naber (b. 1-20-56): Swimmer. Won 4 gold medals and 1 silver medal at 1976 Olympics. Sullivan Award winner in 1977.

Bronko Nagurski (b. 11-3-08, d. 1-7-90): Football FB. Punishing runner played on 3 NFL champions (consecutively 1932–33, 1943) with Bears. Rushed for 2,778 career yards, 1930–37 and 1943 with Chicago. Also All-America with Minnesota.

James Naismith (b. 11-6-1861, d. 11-28-39): Invented basketball in 1891 while an instructor at YMCA Training School in Springfield, Mass. Refined the game while a professor at Kansas from 1898 to 1937. Hall of Fame is named in his honor.

Joe Namath (b. 5-31-43): Football QB. "Broadway Joe." Super Bowl MVP in 1968 after he guaranteed victory for AFL. 173 career touchdown passes. Led league in yards passing 3 times, including 4,007 yards in 1967. Player of the Year in 1968, Rookie of the Year in 1965. Career span 1965–77 with NY Jets, LA Rams.

Martina Navratilova (b. 10-18-56): Tennis player. Third all-time most women's Grand Slam singles titles (18—tied with Chris Evert). Won a record 9 Wimbledon titles, including 6 consecutively (1978–79, 1982–87, 1990). Won 4 U.S. Open titles (consecutively 1983–84, 1986–87), 3 Australian Open titles (1981, 1983, 1985) and 2 French Open titles (1982, 1984). Reached Grand Slam final 12 other times. Also won 36 Grand Slam doubles titles. Her total of 54 Grand Slam titles is second all-time to Margaret Court's. Completed a non-calendar year Grand Slam in 1984–85. Set mark for longest winning streak with 74 matches in 1984. Also won the doubles Grand Slam in 1984 with Pam Shriver. Won 109 consecutive matches with Shriver from 1983 to 1985.

Byron Nelson (b. 2-14-12): Golfer. Won the Masters (1937, 1942) and PGA Championship (1940, 1945) 2 times each and U.S. Open once (1939). Won 52 career tournaments, including 11 consecutively in 1945.

Ernie Nevers (b. 6-11-03, d. 5-3-76): Football FB. Set all-time pro single game record for points scored (40) and touchdowns (6) on Nov. 28, 1929. Career span 1926–31 with Duluth, Chicago. Also a pitcher with St. Louis, surrendered 2 of Babe Ruth's 60 HR in 1927. All-America at Stanford, earned 11 letters in 4 sports.

John Newcombe (b. 5-23-44): Australian tennis player. Won 3 Wimbledon singles titles (1967, consecutively 1970–71), 2 U.S. titles (1967, 1973) and 2 Australian Open titles (1973, 1975). Also won 17 Grand Slam doubles titles.

Jack Nicklaus (b. 1-21-40): Golfer. "The Golden Bear." All-time leader in major championships (20).

Second all-time in career wins (70). Winner of the Masters 6 times, more than any golfer (1963, consecutively 1965–66, 1972, 1975, 1986—at age 46, the oldest player to win event), PGA Championship 5 times (1963, 1971, 1973, 1975, 1980), U.S. Open 4 times (1962, 1967, 1972, 1980), British Open 3 times (1966, 1970, 1978) and U.S. Amateur 2 times (1959, 1961). PGA Player of the Year 5 times (1967, consecutively 1972–73, 1975–76). Also NCAA champion with Ohio State in 1961.

James D. Norris (b. 11-6-06, d. 2-25-66): Hockey executive. Owner of Detroit from 1933 to 1943 and Chicago from 1946 to 1966. Teams won 4 Stanley Cup championships (consecutively 1936–37, 1943, 1961). Defensive Player of the Year award named in his honor. Also a boxing promoter, operated International Boxing Club from 1949 to 1958.

Paavo Nurmi (b. 6-13-1897, d. 10-2-73): Track and field. Finnish middle- and long-distance runner won a total of 9 gold medals at 3 Olympics in 1920, 1924, 1928

Matti Nykänen (b. 7-17-63): Finnish ski jumper. Three-time Olympic gold medalist. Won 90-meter jump (1984, 1988) and 70-meter jump (1988). World champion on 90-meter jump in 1982. Won four World Cups (1983, 1985, 1986, 1988).

Parry O'Brien (b. 1-28-32): Track and field. Shot putter who revolutionized the event with his "glide" technique and won Olympic gold medals in 1952 and 1956, silver in 1960. Set 10 world records from 1953 to 1959, topped by a put of 63′4″ in 1959. Sullivan Award winner in 1959.

Al Oerter (b. 8-19-36): Track and field. Gold medalist in discus at 4 consecutive Olympics (1956, 1960, 1964, 1968), setting Olympic record each time. First to break the 200-foot barrier, throwing 200′5″ in 1962.

Sadaharu Oh (b. 5-20-40): Baseball 1B in Japanese league. 868 career HR in 22 seasons for the Tokyo Giants. Led league in HR 15 times, RBI 13 times, batting 5 times and runs 13 consecutive seasons. Awarded MVP 9 times; won 2 consecutive Triple Crowns and 9 Gold Gloves.

Bobby Orr (b. 3-20-48): Hockey D. Defensive Player of the Year more than any other player, 8 consecutive seasons (1968–75). Won MVP award 3 consecutive seasons (1970–72), playoff MVP 2 times (1970, 1972). Also Rookie of the Year in 1967. Led league in assists 5 times and scoring 2 times. Career span 1966–77 with Boston.

Mel Ott (b. 3-2-09, d. 11-21-58): Baseball OF. 511 career HR, 1,861 RBI, .304 batting average. League leader in HR and walks 6 times each. 100+ RBI 9 times and 100+ walks 10 times. Career span 1926–47 with New York.

Kristin Otto (b. 1966): East German swimmer. Won 6 gold medals at 1988 Olympics. World record holder in 100-meter freestyle (54.73 set in 1986).

Jesse Owens (b. 9-12-13, d. 3-31-80): Track and field. Gold medalist in 4 events (100 meters and 200 meters; 4x100-meter relay and long jump) at 1936 Olympics.

Satchel Paige (b. 7-7-06, d. 6-8-82): Baseball RHP. All-time greatest black pitcher, didn't pitch in major leagues until 1948 at age 42 with Cleveland. Oldest pitcher in major league history at age 59 with Kansas City in 1965. Pitched in the Negro leagues from 1926 to 1950 with Birmingham Black Barons, Pittsburgh Crawfords and Kansas City Monarchs. Estimated career record is 2,000 wins, 250 shutouts, 30,000 strikeouts, 45 no-hitters. Said "Don't look back. Something may be gaining on you."

Arnold Palmer (b. 9-10-29): Golfer. Fourth all-time in career wins (60). Won the Masters 4 times (1958, 1960, 1962, 1964), British Open 2 consecutive years (1961–62) and U.S. Open (1960) and U.S. Amateur (1954) once each. PGA Player of the Year 2 times (1960, 1962). The first golfer to surpass $1 million in career earnings. Also won Seniors Championship 2 times (1980, 1984) and U.S. Senior Open once (1981). 10 career seniors titles as of 8-13-91.

Jim Palmer (b. 10-15-45): Baseball RHP. 268 career wins, 2.86 ERA. Won 3 Cy Young Awards (1973, consecutively 1975–76). Won 20+ games 8 times. Led league in wins 3 times, innings pitched 4 times, ERA 2 times. Never allowed a grand slam HR. Pitched on 6 World Series teams with Baltimore, including shutout at 20 years old in 1966. Pitched no-hitter in 1969. Jockey underwear pitchman. Career span 1965–84.

Bernie Parent (b. 4-3-45): Hockey G. All-time leader for wins in a season (47 in 1974). Goaltender of the Year, playoff MVP, league leader in wins, goals against average and shutouts 2 consecutive seasons (1974–75). Career record 270–197–121, including 55 shutouts. Career 2.55 goals against average. Tied record of 4 playoff shutouts in 1975. Played on 2 consecutive Stanley Cup champions (1974–75). Career span 1965 to 1979 with Philadelphia. Also the first NHL player to sign with the WHA in 1972, with Philadelphia.

Joe Paterno (b. 12-21-26): College football coach. Going into 1991 season sixth all-time in wins in Division I-A (229—the most of any active coach at that level). Has won 2 national championships (1982, 1986) with Penn State since 1966. Career record 229–60–3, including 4 undefeated seasons. Has also won 13 bowl games.

Lester Patrick (b. 12-30-1883, d. 6-1-60): Hockey coach. Led NY Rangers to only Stanley Cup championships (1928, 1933, 1940). Originated the NHL's farm system and developed playoff format.

Floyd Patterson (b. 1-4-35): Boxer. Heavyweight champion 2 times (1956–59, 1960–62). First heavyweight to regain title, in rematch with Ingemar Johansson. Career record 55–8–1 with 40 KOs from 1952 to 1972. Also middleweight gold medalist at 1952 Olympics.

Walter Payton (b. 7-25-54): Football RB. All-time leader in yards rushing (16,726), rushing attempts (3,838), games gaining 100+ yards rushing (77), seasons gaining 1,000+ yards rushing (10) and rushing touchdowns (110). His 125 total touchdowns rank second. Rushed for a record 275 yards on Nov. 20, 1977. Selected for Pro Bowl 9 times. Player of the Year 2 times (1977, 1985). Led league in rushing 5 consecutive seasons. Career span 1975–87 with Chicago.

Pele (b. 10-23-40): Born Edson Arantes do Nascimento. Brazilian soccer player. Soccer's great ambassador. Played on 3 World Cup winners with Brazil (1958, 1962, 1970). Helped promote soccer in U.S. by playing with NY Cosmos from 1975 to 1977. Scored 1,281 goals in 22 years.

Willie Pep (b. 9-19-22): Boxer. Featherweight champion 2 times (1942–48, 1949–50). Lost title to Sandy Saddler, won it back in rematch, then lost it to Saddler again. Career record 230–11–1 with 65 KOs from 1940 to 1966. Won 73 consecutive bouts from 1940 to 1943. Defended title 9 times.

Fred Perry (b. 5-18-09): British tennis player. Won 3 consecutive Wimbledon singles titles (1934–36), the last British man to win the tournament. Also won 3 U.S. titles (consecutively 1933–34, 1936), 1 French title (1935) and 1 Australian title (1934).

Gaylord Perry (b. 9-15-38): Baseball RHP. Only pitcher to win Cy Young Award in both leagues (Cleveland 1972, San Diego 1978). 314 career wins, 3,534 strikeouts. 20+ wins 5 times; 200+ strikeouts 8 times; 250+ innings pitched 12 times. Pitched no-hitter in 1968. Admittedly threw a spitter. Career span 1962–83 with San Francisco, Cleveland, San Diego.

Bob Pettit (b. 12-12-32): Basketball F. First player in history to break 20,000-point barrier (20,880 career points scored). Fifth all-time highest scoring average (26.4), seventh most free throws made (6,182) and tenth most rebounds (12,849 for 16.2 average). MVP in 1956, 1959; Rookie of the Year in 1955. All-Star 10 consecutive seasons. Led league in scoring 2 times, rebounding 1 time. Career span 1954–64 with St Louis.

Richard Petty (b. 7-2-37): Auto racer. All-time leader in NASCAR victories (currently 200). Daytona 500 winner (1964, 1966, 1971, consecutively 1973–74, 1979, 1981) and NASCAR champion (1964, 1967, consecutively 1971–72, 1974–75, 1979) 7 times each, the most of any driver. First stock car racer to reach $1 million in earnings. Son of Lee Petty, 3-time NASCAR champion (1954, consecutively 1958–59).

Jacques Plante (b. 1-17-29, d. 2-27-86): Hockey G. First goalie to wear a mask. Second all-time in wins (434) and second lowest modern goals against average (2.38). Goaltender of the Year 7 times, more than any other goalie (consecutively 1955–59, 1961, 1968). Won MVP award in 1961. Led league in goals against average 8 times, wins 6 times and shutouts 4 times. Was on 5 Stanley Cup champions with Montreal from 1952 to 1962 and played for 4 other teams until retirement in 1972.

Gary Player (b. 11-1-36): South African golfer. Won the Masters (1961, 1974, 1978) and British Open (1959, 1968, 1974) 3 times each, PGA Championship 2 times (1962, 1972) and U.S. Open (1965). Also won Seniors Championship 3 times (1986, 1988, 1990) and U.S. Senior Open 2 consecutive years (1987–88).

Sam Pollock (b. 12-15-25): Hockey executive. As general manager of Montreal from 1964 to 1978 won 9 Stanley Cup championships (1965–66, 1968–69, 1971, 1973, 1976–78).

Mike Powell (b. 11-10-63): Track and field. Long jumper broke Bob Beamon's 23-year-old world record at 1991 World Championships in Tokyo with a jump of 29 ′4½″.

Annemarie Moser-Pröll (b. 3-27-53): Austrian skier. Gold medalist in downhill at 1980 Olympics. World Cup overall champion 6 times, more than any other skier (consecutively 1971–75, 1979).

Alain Prost (b. 2-24-55): French auto racer. All-time leader in Formula 1 victories (44 as of 8-13-91). Formula 1 champion 3 times (consecutively 1985–86, 1989).

Mary Lou Retton (b. 1-24-68): Gymnast. Won 1 gold, 1 silver and 2 bronze medals at 1984 Olympics.

Grantland Rice (b. 11-1-1880, d. 7-13-54): Sportswriter. Legendary figure during sport's Golden Age of the 1920s. Wrote "When the Last Great Scorer comes / To mark against your name, / He'll write not 'won' or 'lost' / But how you played the game." Also named the 1924–25 Notre Dame backfield the "Four Horsemen."

Jerry Rice (b. 10-13-62): Football WR. All-time leader in consecutive games with touchdown reception (13 in 1988). Player of the Year in 1987 and led league in scoring (138 points on 23 touchdowns). Super Bowl MVP in 1989 with record 215 receiving yards on 11 catches. Also set Super Bowl record with 3 touchdown receptions in 1990. Career span since 1985.

Henri Richard (b. 2-29-36): Hockey C. "The Pocket Rocket." Played on 11 Stanley Cup champions with Montreal. Four-time All-Star. Career span from 1955 to 1975.

Maurice Richard (b. 8-4-21): Hockey RW. "The Rocket." First player ever to score 50 goals in a season, in 1945. Led league in goals 5 times. 544 career goals. Won MVP award in 1947. All-Star 8 times. Tied playoff game record for most goals (5 on March 23, 1944). Played on 8 Stanley Cup champions with Montreal from 1942 to 1959.

Bob Richards (b. 2-2-26): Track and field. The only pole vaulter to win gold medal at 2 consecutive Olympics (1952, 1956). Also won Sullivan Award in 1951.

Branch Rickey (b. 12-20-1881, d. 12-9-65): Baseball executive. Integrated major league baseball in 1947 by signing Jackie Robinson to contract with Brooklyn Dodgers. Conceived minor league farm system in 1919 at St Louis; instituted batting cage and sliding pit.

Pat Riley (b. 3-20-45): Basketball coach. Going into 1991–92 season all-time highest winning percentage (.725) and most playoff wins (102). Coached Los Angeles to 4 championships, 2 consecutively, from 1981 to 1989. 60+ wins 5 times (4 times consecutively), 50+ wins 4 other times. Currently coaching New York Knicks.

Cal Ripken Jr (b. 8-24-60): Baseball SS. Ended 1991 season with second longest consecutive game streak (1,573 since May 29, 1982). Set record for consecutive errorless games by a shortstop (95 in 1990). MVP in 1983 and Rookie of the Year in 1982. Has hit 20+ HRs in 10 consecutive seasons and started in 8 consecutive All-Star games.

Glenn "Fireball" Roberts (b. 1-20-31, d. 7-2-64): Auto racer. Won 34 NASCAR races. Died as a result of fiery accident in World 600 at Charlotte Motor Speedway in May 1964. At time of his death had won more major races than any other driver in NASCAR history.

Oscar Robertson (b. 11-24-38): Basketball G. "The Big O." Second all-time most assists (9,887) and free throws made (7,694), fourth most points scored (26,710), sixth most field goals made (9,508) and eighth highest scoring average (25.7). MVP in 1964, All-Star 9 consecutive seasons and 1961 Rookie of

the Year. Led league in assists 6 times, free throw percentage 2 times. Averaged 30+ points 6 times in 7 seasons, 20+ points 4 other times. Only player in history to average a season triple-double (1961). Career span 1960–72 with Cincinnati, Milwaukee. Also College Player of the Year, All-America and NCAA scoring leader 3 consecutive seasons from 1958 to 1960 with Cincinnati. Third all-time NCAA highest scoring average (33.8); sixth most points scored (2,973).

Brooks Robinson (b. 5-18-37): Baseball 3B. All-time leader in assists, putouts, double plays and fielding average among 3rd baseman. Won 16 consecutive Gold Gloves. Led league in fielding average a record 11 times. MVP in 1964—led league in RBIs—and MVP in 1970 World Series. Career span 1955–77 with Baltimore.

Eddie Robinson (b. 2-13-19): College football coach. Going into 1991 season has had all-time college record 366 career wins at Division I-AA Grambling State since 1941.

Frank Robinson (b. 8-31-35): Baseball OF-manager. Only player to win MVP awards in both leagues (Cincinnati, 1961, Baltimore, 1966). Won Triple Crown and World Series MVP in 1966. Rookie of the Year in 1956. Fourth all-time most HR (586). 30+ HR 11 times; 100+ RBI 6 times; 100+ runs scored 8 times (led league 3 times). Had .300+ batting average 9 times. Became first black manager in major leagues, with Cleveland in 1975. Career span as player 1956–76. Career span as manager 1975–77 with Cleveland; 1981–84 with San Francisco; 1988–91 with Baltimore.

Jackie Robinson (b. 1-13-19, d. 10-24-72): Baseball 2B. Broke the color barrier as first black player in major leagues in 1947 with Brooklyn Dodgers. 1947 Rookie of the Year; 1949 MVP with .342 batting average to lead league. Had .311 career batting average. Led league in stolen bases 2 times; stole home 19 times. Played on 6 pennant winners in 10 years with Brooklyn.

Sugar Ray Robinson (b. 5-3-21, d. 4-12-89): Born Walker Smith, Jr. Boxer. Called best pound-for-pound boxer in history. Welterweight champion (1946–51) and middleweight champion 5 times. Career record 174–19–6 with 109 KOs from 1940 to 1965. Won 91 consecutive bouts from 1943 to 1951. 15 of his 19 losses came after age 35. Retired at age 45.

Knute Rockne (b. 3-4-1888, d. 3-31-31): College football coach. Won national championship 3 times (1924, consecutively 1929–30). All-time highest winning percentage (.881). Career record 105–12–5, including 5 undefeated seasons, with Notre Dame from 1918 to 1930.

Bill Rodgers (b. 12-23-47): Track and field. Won the Boston and New York City marathons 4 times each between 1975 and 1980.

Murray Rose (b. 1-6-39) Australian swimmer. Won 3 gold medals (including 400- and 1500-meter free-style) at 1956 Olympics. Also won 1 gold, 1 silver and 1 bronze medal at 1960 Olympics.

Pete Rose (b. 4-14-41): Baseball OF-IF. "Charlie Hustle." All-time leader in hits (4,256), games played (3,562) and at bats (14,053); second in doubles (746); fourth in runs scored (2,165). Had .303 career average and won 3 batting titles. Averaged .300+ 15 times, 200+ hits and 100+ runs scored each 10 times. Led league in hits 7 times, runs scored 4 times, doubles 5 times. 1963 Rookie of the Year;

1973 MVP; 1975 World Series MVP. Had 44-game hitting streak in 1978. Played in 17 All-Star games, starting at 5 different positions. Career span 1963–86 with Cincinnati, Philadelphia. Manager of Cincinnati from 1984 to 1989. Banned from baseball for life by Commissioner Bart Giamatti in 1989 for betting activities. Served 5-month jail term for tax evasion in 1990. Ineligible for Hall of Fame.

Ken Rosewall (b. 11-2-34): Australian tennis player. Won Grand Slam singles titles at ages 18 and 35. Won 4 Australian titles (1953, 1955, consecutively 1971–72), 2 French titles (1953, 1968) and 2 U.S. titles (1956, 1970). Reached 4 Wimbledon finals, but title eluded him.

Art Ross (b. 1-13-1886, d. 8-5-64): Hockey D-coach. Improved design of puck and goal net. Manager-coach of Boston, 1924–45, won Stanley Cup, 1938–39. The Art Ross Trophy is awarded to the NHL scoring champion.

Donald Ross (b. 1873, d. 4-26-48): Scottish-born golf course architect. Trained at St. Andrews under Old Tom Morris. Designed over 500 courses, including Pinehurst No. 2 course and Oakland Hills.

Pete Rozelle (b. 3-1-26): Football executive. Fourth NFL commissioner, served from 1960 to 1989. During his term, league expanded from 12 to 28 teams. Created Super Bowl in 1966 and negotiated merger with AFL. Devised plan for revenue sharing of lucrative TV monies among owners. Presided during players' strikes of 1982, 1987.

Wilma Rudolph (b. 6-23-40): Track and field. Gold medalist in 3 events (100-, 200- and 4x100-meter relay) at 1960 Olympics. Also won Sullivan Award in 1961.

Adolph Rupp (b. 9-2-01, d. 12-10-77): College basketball coach. All-time NCAA leader in wins (875) and third highest winning percentage (.822). Won 4 NCAA championships: consecutively 1948–49, 1951, 1958. Career span 1930–72 with Kentucky.

Amos Rusie (b. 5-3-1871, d. 12-6-42): Baseball RHP. Fastball was so intimidating that in 1893 the pitching mound was moved back 5 ′6 ″ to its present distance of 60 ′6 ″. Led league in strikeouts and walks 5 times each. Career record 246-174, 3.07 ERA with New York (NL) from 1889–1901.

Bill Russell (b. 2-12-34): Basketball C. Won MVP award 5 times (1958, consecutively 1961–63, 1965). Played on 11 championship teams, 8 consecutively, with Boston (1957, 1959–66, 1968–69). Player-coach 1968–69 (league's first black coach). Second all-time most rebounds (21,620) and second highest rebounding average (22.5); second most rebounds in a game (51 in 1960). Led league in rebounding 4 times. Also played on 2 consecutive NCAA championship teams with San Francisco in 1955–56; tournament MVP in 1955. Member of gold medal-winning 1956 Olympic team.

Babe Ruth (b. 2-6-1895, d. 8-16-48): Given name George Herman Ruth. Baseball P-OF. Most dominant player in history. All-time leader in slugging average (.690), HR frequency (8.5 HR every 100 at bats) and walks (2,056); second all-time most HR (714), RBI (2,211) and runs scored (2,174). Holds season record for most walks (170 in 1923) and highest slugging average (.847 in 1920). 1923 MVP. League leader in slugging average 13 times, HR 12 times, walks 11 times, runs scored 8 times and RBI 6 times. 1 batting title. Had .342 career batting average and 2,873 hits.

60 HR in 1927, 50+ HR 3 other times and 40+ HR 7 other times; 100+ RBI and 100+ walks 13 times each; 100+ runs scored 12 times. Second all-time most World Series HR (15), including his "called shot" in 1932. Began career as a pitcher for Boston Red Sox: 94 career wins and 2.28 ERA. Won 20+ games 2 times; ERA leader in 1916. Played on 10 pennant winners, 7 World Series winners (3 with Boston, 4 with New York). Sold to Yankees in 1920 (Boston hasn't won World Series since). Career span 1914–35.

Nolan Ryan (b. 1-31-47): Baseball RHP. Pitched record 7th no hitter on May 1, 1991. All-time leader in 1-hitters (12), strikeouts (5,511), walks (2,686). League leader in strikeouts 11 times, walks 8 times, shutouts 3 times, ERA 2 times. 300+ strikeouts 6 times, including season record of 383 in 1973. 314 career wins. Career span since 1966 with New York (NL), California, Houston, Texas.

Jim Ryun (b. 4-29-47): Track and field. Youngest ever to run under four minutes for the mile (3:59.0 at 17 years, 37 days). Set two world records in mile (3:51.3 in 1966 and 3:51.1 in 1967) and one in 1,500 (3:33.1 in 1967). Plagued by bad luck at Olympics; won silver medal in 1968 1,500 meters despite mononucleosis; was bumped and fell in 1972. Won Sullivan Award in 1967.

Toni Sailer (b. 11-17-35): Austrian skier. Won gold medals in 1956 Olympics in slalom, giant slalom and downhill, the first skier to accomplish the feat.

Juan Antonio Samaranch (b. 7-17-20): Amateur sports executive. Spaniard has been president of International Olympic Committee since 1980.

Joan Benoit Samuelson (b. 5-16-57): Track and field. Gold medalist in first ever women's Olympic marathon (1984). Won Boston Marathon 2 times (1979, 1983). Sullivan Award winner in 1985.

Barry Sanders (b. 7-16-68): Football RB. All-time NCAA season leader in yards rushing (2,628 in 1988). Won Heisman Trophy in 1988 at Oklahoma State. Entered NFL in 1989 with Detroit and named Rookie of the Year. Gained 1,000+ yards rushing and named to Pro Bowl each of his first 2 seasons. Led league in rushing in 1990.

Gene Sarazen (b. 2-27-02): Golfer. Won PGA Championship 3 times (consecutively 1922–23, 1933), U.S. Open 2 times (1922, 1932), British Open once (1932) and the Masters once (1935). His win at the Masters included golf's most famous shot, a double eagle on the 15th hole of the final round to tie Craig Wood (Sarazen then won the playoff). Won 38 career tournaments. Also won Seniors Championship 2 times (1954, 1958). Pioneered the sand wedge in 1930.

Glen Sather (b. 9-2-43): Hockey coach and general manager. As coach, third all-time highest winning percentage (.634) and sixth in wins (535). Led Edmonton to 4 Stanley Cup championships (consecutively 1984–85, 1987–88) from 1979 to 1989. Relinquished coaching duties in 1989. Also played for 6 teams from 1966 to 1976.

Terry Sawchuk (b. 12-28-29): Hockey G. All-time leader in wins (435) and shutouts (103). Career 2.52 goals against average. Goaltender of the Year 4 times (consecutively 1951–52, 1954, 1964). Led league in wins and shutouts 3 times and goals against average 2 times. Rookie of the Year in 1950.

Tied record of 4 playoff shutouts in 1952. Played on 4 Stanley Cup champions with Detroit and Toronto from 1949 to 1969.

Gale Sayers (b. 5-30-43): Football RB. All-time leader in kickoff return average (30.6). Scored 56 career touchdowns, including a rookie record 22 in 1965. Led league in rushing and gained 1,000+ yards rushing 2 times. Averaged 5 yards per carry, third best in history. Rookie of the Year in 1965. Tied record with 6 rushing touchdowns on Dec. 12, 1965. Career span 1965–71 with Chicago cut short due to knee injury. Also All-America 2 times with Kansas.

Mike Schmidt (b. 9-27-49): Baseball 3B. Won 3 MVP awards (consecutively 1980–81, 1986). 548 career HR. Led league in HR 8 times, slugging average 5 times and RBI, walks and strikeouts 4 times each. 40+ HR 3 times, 30+ HR 10 other times; 100+ RBI 9 times, 100+ runs scored 7 times, 100+ strikeouts 12 times and third all-time most strikeouts (1,883). 100+ walks 7 times. Won 10 Gold Gloves. Career span 1972–89 with Philadelphia.

Don Schollander (b. 4-30-46): Swimmer. Won 4 gold medals (including 100- and 400-meter freestyle) at 1964 Olympics; won 1 gold and 1 silver medal at 1968 Olympics. Also won Sullivan Award in 1964.

Dick Schultz (b. 9-5-29): Amateur sports executive. Second executive director of the NCAA, has served since 1987. Also served as athletic director at Cornell (1976–81) and Virginia (1981–87).

Tom Seaver (b. 11-17-44): Baseball RHP. "Tom Terrific." 311 career wins, 2.86 ERA. Cy Young Award winner 3 times (1969, 1973, 1975) and Rookie of the Year 1967. Third all-time most strikeouts (3,640). Led league in strikeouts 5 times, winning percentage 4 times and wins and ERA 3 times each. Won 20+ games 5 times; 200+ strikeouts 10 times. Struck out 19 batters in 1 game in 1970, including the final 10 in succession. Pitched no-hitter in 1978. Career span 1967–86 with New York (NL), Cincinnati, Chicago (AL), Boston.

Secretariat (b. 3-30-70, d. 10-4-89): Thoroughbred race horse. Triple Crown winner in 1973 with jockey Ron Turcotte aboard. Trained by Lucien Laurin.

Monica Seles (b. 12-2-73): Tennis player. Has won 2 consecutive French Open singles titles (1990–91), 1 Australian Open title (1991) and 1 U.S. Open title (1991).

Wilbur Shaw (b. 10-31-02, d. 10-30-54): Auto racer. Won Indy 500 3 times in 4 years (1937, consecutively 1939–40). AAA champion 2 times (1937, 1939). Also pioneered the use of the crash helmet after suffering skull fracture in 1923 crash.

Fred Shero (b. 10-23-25, d. 11-24-90): Hockey coach. Fourth all-time highest winning percentage (.612, regular season). Led Philadelphia to 2 Stanley Cup championships (1974–75). Also coached NY Rangers. Played defense for NY Rangers, 1947–50.

Bill Shoemaker (b. 8-19-31): Horse racing jockey. All-time leader in wins (8,833). Rode Belmont Stakes winner 5 times (1957, 1959, 1962, 1967, 1975), Kentucky Derby winner 4 times (1955, 1959, 1965, 1986—at age 54, the oldest jockey to win Derby) and Preakness Stakes winner 2 times (1963, 1967). Also won Eclipse Award in 1981.

Eddie Shore (b. 11-25-02, d. 3-16-85): Hockey D. Won MVP award 4 times (1933, consecutively 1935–36, 1938). All-Star 7 times. Played on 2 Stanley Cup champions with Boston from 1926 to 1940.

Frank Shorter (b. 10-31-47): Track and field. Gold medalist in marathon at 1972 Olympics, the first American to win the event since 1908. Olympic silver medalist in 1976 marathon. Sullivan Award winner in 1972.

Jim Shoulders (b. 5-13-28): Rodeo. All-time leader in career titles (16). All-Around champion 5 times (1949, consecutively 1956–59).

Don Shula (b. 1-4-30): Football coach. Second all-time in wins (got 300th on 9-22-91, the most of any active coach). Won 2 consecutive Super Bowl championships (1972–73) with Miami, including NFL's only undefeated season in 1972. Also reached Super Bowl 4 other times. Career span since 1963 with Baltimore and Miami.

O. J. Simpson (b. 7-9-47): Given name Orenthal James. Football RB. Seventh all-time in yards rushing (11,236). Gained 1,000+ yards rushing 5 consecutive seasons, including then-record 2,003 yards in 1973. Player of the Year 3 times (consecutively 1972–73, 1975). Led league in rushing 4 times. Gained 200+ yards rushing in a game a record 6 times, including 273 yards on Nov. 25, 1976. Scored 61 career touchdowns, including 23 in 1975. Also won Heisman Trophy with USC in 1968.

George Sisler (b. 3-24-1893, d. 3-26-73): Baseball 1B. All-time most hits in a season (257 in 1920). League leader in hits 2 times, with 200+ hits 6 times. Won 2 batting titles, including .420 average in 1922; averaged .400+ 2 times and .300+ 11 other times. Had 2,812 career hits and .340 average. Career span 1915–30 with St Louis.

Mary Decker Slaney (b. 8-4-58): Track and field. American record holder in 5 events ranging from 800 to 3,000 meters. Won 1,500 and 3,000 meters at World Championships in 1983. Lost chance for medal at 1984 Olympics when she tripped and fell after contact with Zola Budd. Won Sullivan Award in 1982.

Dean Smith (b. 2-28-31): College basketball coach. Entered 1991–92 season sixth all-time in wins (717), the most among active coaches; fifth all-time highest winning percentage (.774). All-time most NCAA tournament appearances (21), reached Final Four 8 times. Won NCAA championship in 1982. Coached 1976 Olympic team to gold medal. Career span since 1962 with North Carolina.

Ozzie Smith (b. 12-26-54): Baseball SS. "The Wizard of Oz." May be the best defensive shortstop in history. Holds all-time record for most assists in a season among shortstops (621 in 1980). 10 consecutive starts in All-Star game. Entered 1991 with 11 consecutive Gold Gloves. Career span since 1978 with San Diego, St Louis.

Red Smith (b. 9-25-05, d. 1-15-82): Sportswriter. Won Pulitzer Prize in 1976. After Grantland Rice, the most widely syndicated sports columnist. His literate essays appeared in the *NY Herald Tribune* from 1945 to 1971 and the *NY Times* from 1971 to 1982.

Tommy Smith (b. 6-5-44): Track and field. Sprinter won 1968 Olympic 200 meters in world record of 19.83, then was expelled from Olympic Village, along with bronze medalist John Carlos, for raising black-gloved fist and bowing head during playing of national anthem to protest racism in U.S.

Conn Smythe (b. 2-1-1895, d. 11-18-80): Hockey executive. As general manager with Toronto from 1929 to 1961 won 7 Stanley Cup championships (1932, 1942, 1945, consecutively 1947–49, 1951). Award for playoff MVP named in his honor.

Sam Snead (b. 5-27-12): Golfer. All-time leader in career wins (81). Won the Masters (1949, 1952, 1954) and PGA Championship (1942, 1949, 1951) 3 times each and British Open (1946). Runner-up at U.S. Open 4 times, but title eluded him. PGA Player of the Year in 1949. Won Seniors Championship 6 times, more than any golfer (1964–65, 1967, 1970, 1972–73).

Peter Snell (b. 12-17-38): Track and field. New Zealand runner was gold medalist in 800 meters at 2 consecutive Olympics in 1960, 1964. Also gold medalist in 1,500 meters at 1964 Olympics.

Duke Snider (b. 9-19-26): Baseball OF. Career .295 average, 407 HR and 1,333 RBIs. Hit 40+ HR 5 consecutive seasons and 100+ RBIs 6 times. Also led league in runs scored 3 consecutive seasons. Played on 6 pennant winners with the Brooklyn Dodgers. World Series total of 11 HR and 26 RBIs are NL best. Career span from 1947–64.

Javier Sotomayor (b. 10-13-67): Track and field. Cuban high jumper broke the 8-foot barrier with world record jump of 8′0″ in 1989.

Warren Spahn (b. 4-23-21): Baseball LHP. All-time leader in games won for a lefthander (363): 20+ wins 13 times. League leader in wins 8 times (5 seasons consecutively), complete games 9 times (7 seasons consecutively), strikeouts 4 consecutive seasons, innings pitched 4 times and ERA 3 times. 1957 Cy Young award. 63 career shutouts. Pitched 2 no-hitters after age 39. Career span 1942–65, all but last year with Boston (NL), Milwaukee.

Tris Speaker (b. 4-4-1888, d. 12-8-58): Baseball OF. All-time leader in doubles (792), fifth in hits (3,515) and seventh in batting average (.344). 1 batting title (.386 in 1916), but .375+ average 6 times and .300+ average 12 other times. League leader in doubles 8 times, hits 2 times and HR and RBI 1 time each. 200+ hits 4 times, 40+ doubles 10 times and 100+ runs scored 7 times. MVP in 1912. All-time leader among outfielders in assists and double plays, second in putouts and total chances. Career span 1907–28 with Boston, Cleveland.

Mark Spitz (b. 2-10-50): Swimmer. Won a record 7 gold medals (2 in freestyle, 2 in butterfly, 3 in relays) at 1972 Olympics, setting world record in each event. Also won 2 gold medals and 1 silver and 1 bronze medal at 1968 Olympics. Sullivan Award winner in 1971.

Amos Alonzo Stagg (b. 8-16-1862, d. 3-17-65): College football coach. Second all-time in wins (314). Won national championship with Chicago in 1905. Coach of the Year with Pacific in 1943 at age 81. Career record 314–199–35, including 5 undefeated seasons, from 1892 to 1946. Only person elected to both college football and basketball Halls of Fame. Played in the first basketball game in 1892.

Bart Starr (b. 1-9-34): Football QB. Played on 3 NFL champions (consecutively 1961–62, 1965) and first two Super Bowl champions (1966–67) with Green Bay. Also named MVP of first two Super Bowls. Player of the Year in 1966. Led league in passing 3 times. Also coached Green Bay to 53–77–3 record from 1975 to 1983.

Roger Staubach (b. 2-5-42): Football QB. Won Heisman Trophy with Navy as a junior in 1963. Served 4-year military obligation before turning pro. Led Dallas to 6 NFC Championships, 4 Super Bowls and 2 Super Bowl titles (1971, 1977). Player of the Year and Super Bowl MVP in 1971. Also led league in passing 4 times. Career span 1969–79.

Casey Stengel (b. 7-30-1890, d. 9-29-75): Baseball manager. "The Ol' Perfesser." Managed New York Yankees to 10 pennants and 7 World Series titles (5 consecutively) in 12 years from 1949 to 1960. All-time leader in World Series games (63) and wins (37), second in winning percentage (.587) and losses (26). Platoon system was his trademark strategy, Stengelese his trademark language ("You could look it up"). Managed New York Mets from 1962 to 1965. Jersey number (37) retired by Yankees and Mets.

Ingemar Stenmark (b. 3-18-56): Swedish skier. Gold medalist in slalom and giant slalom at 1980 Olympics. World Cup overall champion 3 consecutive years (1976–78).

Woody Stephens (b. 9-1-13): Horse racing trainer. Trained 2 Kentucky Derby winners (Cannonade, who won the 100th Derby in 1974 and Swale in 1984) and an incredible 5 straight Belmont winners from 1982–86, starting with 1982 Horse of the Year Conquistador Cielo.

David Stern (b. 9-22-42): Fourth NBA commissioner. Served since 1984. Average worth of a franchise has tripled from $20 million to $65 million. Owners rewarded him with 5-year, $27.5 million contract extension in 1990.

Jackie Stewart (b. 6-11-39): Scottish auto racer. Second all-time in Formula 1 victories (27); Formula 1 champion 3 times (1969, 1971, 1973). Also Indy 500 Rookie of the Year in 1966. Retired in 1973.

John L. Sullivan (b. 10-15-1858, d. 2-2-18): Boxer. Last bare knuckle champion. Heavyweight title holder (1882–92), lost to Jim Corbett. Career record 38–1–3 with 33 KOs from 1878 to 1892.

Paul Tagliabue (b. 11-24-40): Football executive. Fifth NFL commissioner, has served since 1989.

Anatoli Tarasov (b. 1918): Hockey coach. Orchestrated Soviet Union's emergence as a hockey power. Won 9 consecutive world amateur championships (1963–71) and 3 Olympic gold medals in 1964, 1968, 1972.

Fran Tarkenton (b. 2-3-40): Football QB. All-time leader in touchdown passes (342), yards passing (47,003), pass attempts (6,467) and pass completions (3,686). Player of the Year in 1975. Career span 1961–78 with Minnesota, NY Giants.

Lawrence Taylor (b. 2-4-59): Football LB. Revolutionized the linebacker position. Entered 1991 season as the all-time leader in sacks (115). Also named to Pro Bowl a record 10 consecutive seasons. Player of the Year in 1986. Has played on 2 Super Bowl champions with New York Giants (1986, 1990). Career span since 1981.

Daley Thompson (b. 7-30-58): Track and field. British decathlete was gold medalist at 2 consecutive Olympics in 1980, 1984. Set world record with 8,847 points at 1984 Olympics.

Bobby Thomson (b. 10-25-23): Baseball OF. Hit dramatic 9th-inning playoff home run to win NL pennant for New York Giants on Oct. 3, 1951. The Giants came from 13½ games behind the Brooklyn Dodgers on Aug. 11 to win the pennant on Thomson's 3-run homer off Ralph Branca in the final game of the 3-game playoff.

Jim Thorpe (b. 5-28-1888, d. 3-28-53): Sportsman. Gold medalist in decathlon and pentathlon at 1912 Olympics. Played pro baseball with New York (NL) and Cincinnati from 1913 to 1919, and pro football with several teams from 1919 to 1926. Also All-America 2 times with Carlisle.

Bill Tilden (b. 2-10-1893, d. 6-5-53): Tennis player. "Big Bill." Won 7 U.S. singles titles, 6 consecutively (1920–25, 1929) and 3 Wimbledon titles (consecutively 1920–21, 1930). Also won 6 Grand Slam doubles titles. Led U.S. to 7 consecutive Davis Cup victories (1920–26).

Ted Tinling (b. 6-23-10, d. 5-23-90): British tennis couturier. The premier source on women's tennis from Suzanne Lenglen to Steffi Graf. Also designed tennis clothes, most notably the frilled lace panties worn by Gorgeous Gussy Moran at Wimbledon in 1949.

Jayne Torvil/Christopher Dean (b. 10-7-57/ b. 7-27-58): British figure skaters. Won 4 consecutive ice dancing world championships (1981–84) and Olympic ice dancing gold medal (1984). Won world professional championships in 1985.

Vladislav Tretiak (b. 4-25-52): Hockey G. Led Soviet Union to 3 gold medals at Olympics in 1972, 1976, 1984. Played on 13 world amateur champions from 1970 to 1984.

Lee Trevino (b. 12-1-39): Golfer. Won U.S. Open (1968, 1971), British Open (consecutively 1971–72) and PGA Championship (1974, 1984) 2 times each. PGA Player of the Year in 1971. Also won U.S. Senior Open in 1990. First Senior $1 million season.

Emlen Tunnell (b. 3-29-25, d. 7-23-75): Football S. All-time leader in interception yardage (1,282) and second in interceptions (79). All-Pro 9 times. Career span 1948–61 with New York Giants and Green Bay.

Gene Tunney (b. 5-25-1897, d. 11-7-78): Boxer. Heavyweight champion (1926–28). Defeated Jack Dempsey 2 times, including famous "long count" bout. Career record 65–2–1 with 43 KOs from 1915 to 1928. Retired as champion.

Ted Turner (b. 11-19-38): Sportsman. Skipper who successfully defended the America's Cup in 1977. Also owner of the Atlanta Braves since 1976 and Hawks since 1977. Founded the Goodwill Games in 1986.

Mike Tyson (b. 6-30-66): Boxer. Youngest heavyweight champion at 19 years old in 1986. Held title until knocked out by James "Buster" Douglas in Tokyo on Feb. 10, 1990. Career record as of 10-1-91 40–1 with 36 KOs since 1985.

Johnny Unitas (b. 5-7-33): Football QB. All-time leader for consecutive games throwing touchdown pass (47, 1956–60), second all-time touchdown passes (290), third all-time yards passing (40,239). Led league in touchdown passes a record 4 consecutive seasons. Player of the Year 3 times (1959, 1964, 1967). Career span 1956–72 with Baltimore, San Diego.

Al Unser Sr (b. 5-29-39): Auto racer. Won Indy 500 4 times (consecutively 1970–71, 1978, 1987). Third all-time in CART victories (39). USAC/CART champion 3 times (1970, 1983, 1985). Brother of Bobby.

Bobby Unser (b. 2-20-34): Auto racer. Won Indy 500 3 times (1968, 1975, 1981). Fourth all-time in CART victories (35). USAC champion 2 times (1968, 1974). Brother of Al, Sr.

Harold S. Vanderbilt (b. 7-6-1884, d. 7-4-70): Sailer. Owner and skipper who successfully defended the America's Cup 3 consecutive times (1930, 1934, 1937).

Glenna Collett Vare (b. 6-20-03, d. 2-2-89): Golfer. Won U.S. Women's Amateur 6 times, more than any golfer (1922, 1925, consecutively 1928–30, 1935).

Bill Veeck (b. 2-9-14, d. 1-2-86): Baseball owner. From 1946 to 1980, owned ballclubs in Cleveland, St Louis (AL), Chicago (AL). In 1948, Cleveland became baseball's first team to draw 2 million in attendance. That year Veeck integrated AL by signing Larry Doby and then Satchel Paige. A brilliant promoter, Veeck sent midget Eddie Gaedel up to bat for St Louis in 1951. Brought exploding scoreboard to stadiums and put players' names on uniforms.

Lasse Viren (b. 7-22-49): Track and field. Finnish runner was gold medalist in 5,000 and 10,000 meters at 2 consecutive Olympics (1972, 1976).

Honus Wagner (b. 2-24-1874, d. 12-6-55): Baseball SS. Had .327 career batting average, 3,415 hits and 8 batting titles. Averaged .300+ 15 consecutive seasons. Led league in RBI 4 times, with 100+ RBI 9 times. Third all-time in triples (252) and league leader in doubles 8 times. Sixth all-time in stolen bases (722) and league leader 5 times. Career span 1897–1917 with Pittsburgh.

Grete Waitz (b. 10-1-53): Track and field. Norwegian runner has won New York City Marathon a record 9 times (consecutively 1978–80, 1982–86, 1988).

Jersey Joe Walcott (b. 10-31-14): Boxer. Heavyweight champion from 1951 to 1952. Won title at age 37 on fifth attempt before surrendering it to Rocky Marciano. Later became sheriff of Camden, NJ.

Doak Walker (b. 1-1-27): Football HB. Led league in scoring 2 times, his first and final seasons. All-Pro 5 times. Played on 2 consecutive NFL champions (1952–53) with Detroit. Career span 1950 to 1955. Also won Heisman Trophy as a junior in 1948. All-America 3 consecutive seasons with SMU.

Herschel Walker (b. 3-3-62): Football RB. Won Heisman Trophy in 1982 with Georgia. Turned pro by entering USFL with New Jersey. Gained 7,000+ rushing yards and scored 61 touchdowns in 3 seasons before league folded. Entered NFL in 1986 with Dallas and led league in rushing yards (1,606 in 1987). Currently with Minnesota.

Bill Walton (b. 11-5-52): Basketball C. MVP in 1978, playoff MVP in 1977. Led league in rebounding and blocks in 1977. Career span 1974–86 with Portland, San Diego, Boston. Also College Player of the Year 3 consecutive seasons (1972–74). Played on 2 consecutive NCAA championship teams (1972–73) with UCLA; tournament MVP twice (1972–73). Sullivan Award winner in 1973.

Glenn "Pop" Warner (b. 4-5-1871, d. 9-7-54): College football coach. Third all-time in wins (313). Won 3 national championships with Pittsburgh (1916, 1918) and Stanford (1926). Career record 313–106–32 with 6 teams from 1896 to 1938.

Tom Watson (b. 9-4-49): Golfer. Winner of British Open 5 times (1975, 1977, 1980, consecutively 1982–83), the Masters 2 times (1977, 1981) and U.S. Open once (1982). PGA Player of the Year 6 times, more than any golfer (consecutively 1977–80, 1982, 1984).

Dick Weber (b. 12-23-29): Bowler. Won All-Star Tournament 4 times (consecutively 1962–63, 1965–66). Voted Bowler of the Year 3 times (1961, 1963, 1965). Won 31 career PBA titles.

Johnny Weissmuller (b. 6-2-04, d. 1-21-84): Swimmer. Won 3 gold medals (including 100- and 400-meter freestyle) at 1924 Olympics and 2 gold medals at 1928 Olympics. Also played Tarzan in the movies.

Jerry West (b. 5-28-38): Basketball G. 10 time All-Star; All-Defensive Team 4 times; 1969 playoff MVP. Set season record for most free throws made (840 in 1966). Led league in assists and scoring 1 time each. Career span 1960–72 with Los Angeles. Currently general manager. Also NCAA tournament MVP in 1959. All-America 2 times with West Virginia. Played on 1960 gold medal-winning Olympic team.

Whirlaway (b. 4-2-38, d. 4-6-53): Thoroughbred race horse. Triple Crown winner in 1941 with jockey Eddie Arcaro aboard. Trained by Ben A. Jones.

Byron "Whizzer" White (b. 6-8-17): Football RB. Led NFL in rushing 2 times (Pittsburgh in 1938, Detroit in 1940). Led NCAA in scoring and rushing with Colorado in 1937; named All-America. Supreme Court justice since 1962.

Hoyt Wilhelm (b. 7-26-23): Baseball RHP. Only relief pitcher in Hall of Fame. Threw knuckleball until age 48. All-time pitching leader in games (1,070) and relief wins (124). Career record: 143–122, 2.52 ERA, 227 saves. Hit home run in his first at bat (never hit another) and pitched no-hitter in 1958. Career span with 9 teams from 1952–72.

Bud Wilkinson (b. 4-23-15): Football coach. All-time NCAA leader in consecutive wins (47, 1953–57). Won 3 national championships (1950, consecutively 1955–56) with Oklahoma, where he coached from 1947 to 1963. Won Orange Bowl 4 times and Sugar Bowl 2 times. Career record 145–29–4, including 4 undefeated seasons. Also coached with St Louis of NFL in 1978–79.

Ted Williams (b. 8-30-18): Baseball OF. "The Splendid Splinter." Last player to hit .400 (.406 in 1941). MVP in 1946, 1949 and Triple Crown winner in 1942, 1947. Sixth all-time highest batting average (.344), second most walks (2,019) and second highest slugging average (.634). Tenth most HR (521) and RBI (1,839). League leader in batting average and runs scored 6 times each, RBI and HR 4 times each, walks 8 times and doubles 2 times. Had .300+ average 15 consecutive seasons; 100+ RBI and runs scored 9 times each; 30+ HR 8 times; and 100+ walks 11 times. Lost nearly 5 seasons to military service. Career span 1939–42 and 1946–60 with Boston.

Major W. C. Wingfield (b. 19-16-1833, d. 4-18-12): British tennis pioneer. Credited with inventing the game of tennis, which he called "Sphairistike" or "sticky" and patented in February 1874.

Colonel Matt Winn (b. 6-30-1861, d. 10-6-49): As general manager of Churchill Downs from 1904 until his death, promoted the Kentucky Derby into the premier race in the country.

Katarina Witt (b. 12-3-65): East German figure skater. Gold medalist at 2 consecutive Olympics in 1984, 1988. Also world champion 4 times (consecutively 1984–85, 1987–88).

John Wooden (b. 10-14-10): College basketball coach. Only member of basketball Hall of Fame as coach and player. Coached UCLA to 10 NCAA championships in 12 years (consecutively 1964–65, 1967–73, 1975). All-time winning streak 88 games (1971–74). 664 career wins and fourth all-time highest winning percentage (.804). Career span 1949–75 with UCLA. Also 1932 College Player of the Year at Purdue.

Mickey Wright (b. 2-14-35): Golfer. Second all-time in career wins (82) and major championships (13—tied with Louise Suggs). Won U.S. Open 4 times (consecutively 1958–59, 1961, 1964), LPGA Championship 4 times, more than any golfer (1958, consecutively 1960–61, 1963), Western Open 3 times (consecutively 1962–63, 1966) and Titleholders Championship twice (1961–62).

Cale Yarborough (b. 3-27-40): Auto racer. Won Daytona 500 4 times (1968, 1977, consecutively 1983–84). Fourth all-time in NASCAR victories (83). Also NASCAR champion 3 consecutive years (1976–78).

Carl Yastrzemski (b. 8-22-39): Baseball OF. "Yaz." 3,419 career hits, 452 HR. 1967 MVP and Triple Crown winner. 3 batting titles, including .301 in 1968, the lowest ever to win. Second all-time in games played (3,308) and fourth in walks (1,845). Led league in slugging average, runs scored and doubles 3 times each, hits and walks 2 times each. Holds league record for most times intentionally walked (190) and seasons leading in outfield assists (6). Career span 1961–83 with Boston.

Cy Young (b. 3-29-1867, d. 11-4-55): Baseball RHP. All-time leader in wins (511), losses (315), innings pitched (7,356) and complete games (750); fourth in shutouts (76). Had 2.63 career ERA. Led league in shutouts 7 times; wins 4 times; complete games 3 times; and ERA, innings pitched and strikeouts 2 times each. 30+ wins 5 times, 20+ wins 10 other times; 400+ innings pitched 5 times, 300+ innings pitched 11 other times. Pitched 3 no-hitters, including a perfect game in 1904. Pitching award named in his honor. Career span 1890–1911 with Cleveland, Boston.

Babe Didrikson Zaharias (b. 6-26-14, d. 9-27-56): Sportswoman. The greatest female athlete. Gold medalist in 80-meter hurdles and javelin throw at 1932 Olympics; also won silver medal in high jump (her gold medal jump was disallowed for using the then-illegal western roll). Became a golfer in 1935 and won 12 major titles, including U.S. Open 3 times (1948, 1950, 1954—a year after cancer surgery). Also helped found the LPGA in 1949.

Emil Zatopek (b. 9-19-22): Track and field. Czechoslovakian runner became only athlete to win gold medal in 5,000 and 10,000 meters and marathon, at 1952 Olympics. Also gold medalist in 10,000 meters at 1948 Olympics.

Obituaries

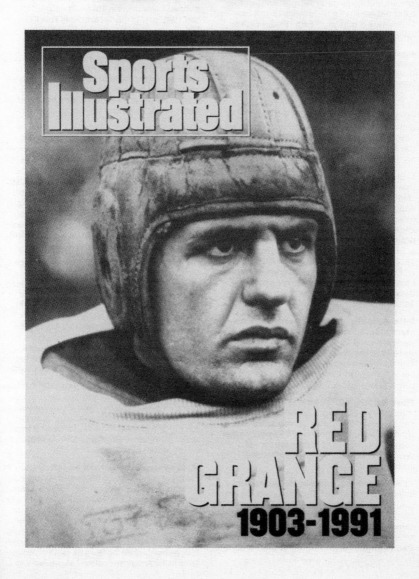

Sports Illustrated

RED GRANGE
1903-1991

George Allen, 72, football coach. Allen guided the Los Angeles Rams to a 49–19–4 record from 1966 to 1970, and the Washington Redskins to a 67–30–1 mark from 1971 to 1977. His 1972 "Over the Hill Gang" reached the first Super Bowl in Redskins history. Allen earlier coached at Whittier and Morningside colleges, and he came out of retirement in 1990 to coach Long Beach State to a 6–5 season. In Palos Verdes Estates, CA, of a coronary spasm, December 31, 1990.

Alydar, 15, thoroughbred race horse. The runner-up to Affirmed in all three Triple Crown races in 1978—losing the Kentucky Derby by 1¼ lengths, the Preakness Stakes by a neck and the Belmont Stakes by a head—Alydar went on to sire more than 40 stakes winners. Among his progeny are Alysheba, winner of the Kentucky Derby and the Preakness in 1987, and Easy Goer, the 1989 Belmont champion. In Lexington, KY, by lethal injection after he broke his right rear leg in a fall, November 15, 1990.

Luke Appling, 83, baseball player. A two-time American League batting champion, with a .388 average in 1936 and a .328 mark in 1943. Appling played his entire 20-year major league career as an infielder for the Chicago White Sox. Known as Old Aches and Pains because of his penchant for complaining about his health, he had a .310 lifetime batting average when he retired in 1950. He served as a minor league hitting instructor for the Atlanta Braves for many years, retiring from that post only two days before his death. In Cumming, GA, during emergency surgery for an aortic aneurysm, January 3.

Pete Axthelm, 47, writer and TV commentator. A former sports columnist for *Newsweek* and writer for *Sports Illustrated*, Axthelm was best known for his book on basketball, *The City Game*, and for his work on TV as a handicapper of horse races and pro football games. In Pittsburgh, of liver failure, February 2.

Mary Bacon, 43, jockey. One of the first female jockeys, Bacon rode her first winner in 1969 and her last in 1990, when her career was cut short by cancer. She rode in 3,526 races, winning 286 and earning $997,117 in purses. In Fort Worth, of a gunshot wound, apparently self-inflicted, June 8.

Laz Barrera, 66, thoroughbred trainer. A four-time winner of the Eclipse Award as the top U.S. trainer, Barrera won the Triple Crown in 1978 with Affirmed. He said the proudest moment of his career occurred two years earlier, on his birthday, when Bold Forbes upset heavily favored Honest Pleasure in the Kentucky Derby and two of his

other horses won the Illinois Derby and the Carter Handicap. Born in Cuba, Barrera came to the U.S. in 1948. In Downey, CA, of heart failure, April 25.

Oscar Barrera, 63, thoroughbred trainer. The most successful trainer in New York State during the 1980s, Barrera, younger brother of Laz, saddled 148 winners in 1984—98 each in 1983 and 1985, and 112 in 1986. In New York City, of heart failure, April 4.

Gene Barth, 61, football referee. Barth, an oil company executive, moonlighted as an NFL referee for 20 years before ill health curtailed his career at the end of the 1990 season. Considered one of the league's best, he worked Super Bowl XVIII and was an alternate referee for three other Super Bowls. In St. Charles, MO, of cancer, October 11.

James "Cool Papa" Bell, 87, baseball player. Considered the fastest man in the Negro leagues, Bell played from 1919, when he was 16, until 1946. A lefthanded-hitting centerfielder, he starred for the Homestead Grays, St. Louis Stars, Chicago American Giants, Pittsburgh Crawfords and Kansas City Monarchs, but he was barred from playing major league baseball because of the color barrier. At one time he was the highest-paid player in the Negro leagues, at $90 a month. In St. Louis, after a brief illness, March 8.

Floyd "Bill" Bevens, 75, baseball player. Pitching for the New York Yankees in Game 4 of the 1947 World Series against the Brooklyn Dodgers, Bevens did not allow a hit for the first 8⅔ innings. However, he had walked 10 batters, including two in the ninth, and when pinch-hitter Cookie Lavagetto lined a two-run double off the wall, he lost his no-hitter and the game to the Dodgers, 3–2. Bevens never won another major league game, finishing with a 40–36 career record. In Salem, OR, of natural causes, October 26.

P. J. Boatwright, Jr., 63, golf administrator. As the U.S. Golf Association's executive director for rules and competition, Boatwright was considered the world's leading authority on the rules of golf. He also served as joint secretary of the World Amateur Golf Council. In Morristown, NJ, of cancer, April 5.

Paul Brown, 82, football coach. Founder of the Cleveland Browns in 1946 and the Cincinnati Bengals in 1968, Brown led the Cleveland team, which was named after him, to all four championships in the short-lived All-America Football Conference (1946–49) and, after the Browns joined the established league, three NFL crowns during the 1950s. Fired by Cleveland after the 1962 season, he established the Bengals as an expansion team in the American Football League two years before the AFL-NFL merger, coaching the team through 1975 and later serving as vice president and general manager. A member of the Pro Football Hall of Fame, Brown had a coaching record of 213–104–9. He is credited with being the first coach to use game films to grade players' performances and the first to call plays from the sideline. In Cincinnati, of complications from pneumonia, August 5.

Milt Bruhn, 78, football coach. The last coach to take Wisconsin to the Rose Bowl, Bruhn had a record from 1955 to 1966 of 52–45–6. The Badgers won Big Ten titles in 1959 and 1962, leading to Rose Bowl appearances in 1960 and 1963. They lost the 1960 game in a rout; against USC in 1963 they came back from a 42–14 deficit in the fourth quarter before losing 42–37. In Madison, WI, of a heart attack, May 14.

Pierre Brunet, 89, figure skater. Winner of 10 French national singles championships during the 1920s and 1930s, Brunet, along with his wife, Andrée Joly, also won four world pairs championships and gold medals in the 1928 and 1932 Winter Olympics. He came to the U.S. in 1940 to coach, eventually settling in Michigan. His most famous protégée, Carol Heiss, won five world titles and a gold medal in the 1960 Winter Olympics. In Boyne City, MI, of complications from Parkinson's disease, July 27.

Smokey Burgess, 64, baseball player. A catcher who batted .295 overall during 17 seasons with the Philadelphia Phillies, Cincinnati Reds, Pittsburgh Pirates and Chicago White Sox, Burgess became celebrated late in his career for his pinch-hitting prowess. When the five-time All-Star retired in 1967, he had 145 pinch hits, more than anyone else in history. The record stood until 1979. In Asheville, NC, of natural causes, September 15.

Fred "Cappy" Capossela, 88, horse racing announcer. A race caller at New York thoroughbred tracks from 1934 to 1971, Capossela was credited with popularizing the phrase, "Aaaand they're off!" which he uttered in a signature nasal twang. One of the last things he said on his deathbed was, "It is now post time." In Upland, CA, following two strokes, April 3.

A. B. "Happy" Chandler, 92, baseball commissioner. The former Kentucky governor and U.S. Senator became baseball's second commissioner in 1945, succeeding Kenesaw Mountain Landis. His decision to allow the Dodgers to promote Jackie Robinson to the majors in 1947 resulted in the breaking of the sport's color barrier. Dismissed by the owners in 1951, Chandler later served a second term as Kentucky's governor and ran unsuccessfully for president as a favorite-son candidate, receiving 36½ votes at the 1956 Democratic convention. He became the grand old man

of Kentucky politics, and he rarely missed a University of Kentucky football or basketball game. In Versailles, KY, in his sleep, June 15.

Walker Cooper, 76, baseball player. A six-time All-Star, Cooper formed a battery with his brother, Mort, for the St. Louis Cardinals in the early 1940s. He spent most of 18 seasons in the majors, catching 1,223 games and batting .285 lifetime. Cooper said he knew it was time to retire in 1957, when he was 42 and his daughter married one of his Cardinal teammates. In Scottsdale, AZ, of respiratory disease, April 11.

Jack Crawford, 83, tennis player. A four-time Australian singles champion, Crawford narrowly missed completing the Grand Slam in 1933, when he won titles at Wimbledon, the French and the Australian national tournaments, then lost to Fred Perry in the U.S. finals. In Sydney, of a brain tumor, September 10.

Roy Cullenbine, 77, baseball player. In 10 major league seasons with six teams, including five years with his hometown Detroit Tigers, Cullenbine hit 110 home runs. He batted .335 with the Tigers in 1946. An outfielder, Cullenbine had a .276 career batting average. In Mount Clemens, MI, of heart failure, May 28.

Joseph Dey, 83, golf administrator. Often referred to as Mr. Golf, Dey served as executive director of the U.S. Golf Association from 1934 to 1969, and from 1969 to 1974 he was the first commissioner of the Tournament Players Division of the Professional Golf Association, now known as the PGA Tour. Dey had a yearning to be a minister and once said, "The ministry can be practiced in many ways: a writer molding words into a message, a painter transferring his heart to a canvas, a musician composing a beautiful hymn, or a golf official trying to protect the standards of the game." In Locust Valley, NY, of cancer, March 3.

Bo Diaz, 37, baseball player. A two-time All-Star catcher, with the Cleveland Indians in 1981 and the Cincinnati Reds in 1987, Diaz batted .255 for four teams during a 13-year major league career that ended in 1989 after two seasons troubled by injuries. He also played for the Boston Red Sox and the Philadelphia Phillies. For the Phillies, he hit .288 with 18 homers and 85 RBIs in 1982, and he batted .333 in the 1983 World Series, which the Baltimore Orioles won in five games. In Caracas, Venezuela, of injuries sustained when he was crushed by a satellite dish antenna he was attempting to install on the roof of his home, November 24, 1990.

Leo Durocher, 86, baseball manager and player. The abrasive, aggressive Durocher managed the 1941 Brooklyn Dodgers and the '51 and '54 New York Giants into the World Series; the '54 Giants won it. In 24 seasons with the Dodgers, Giants, Chicago Cubs and Houston Astros, his teams won 2,008 games, sixth on the all-time list, and his winning percentage was .540. As an infielder for the New York Yankees, Cincinnati Reds, St. Louis Cardinals and Brooklyn Dodgers, he batted .247 in 17 seasons and played on teams that won three pennants and two World Series. In 1947, he was barred from managing the Dodgers for the season by commissioner A. B. "Happy" Chandler for associating with shady characters. He was reinstated the following year but never made the Hall of Fame, possibly because of the suspension. Durocher's legacy may be a phrase he coined: "Nice guys finish last." In Palm Springs, CA, of natural causes, October 7.

Frank Ervin, 87, harness racer. Ervin won 1,213 races and more than $4.3 million in prize money during a 59-year career. The first driver to crack the two-minute barrier on a half-mile track, in 1951, he eventually had 108 sub-two minute times. He guided Bret Hanover to consecutive harness Horse of the Year titles in 1965 and '66, won the Hambletonian in 1959 with Diller Hanover and in 1966 with Kerry Way, and was inducted into harness racing's Hall of Fame of the Trotter in 1968. In Orlando, FL, following a seizure, September 30.

Walter "Hoot" Evers, 69, baseball player and administrator. Evers played 12 years in the major leagues, including two All-Star seasons for the Detroit Tigers—1948, when he hit .314 with 10 homers and 103 RBIs, and 1950, when he hit .323 with 21 homers and 103 RBIs. Traded to the Boston Red Sox in 1952, he also played for the New York Giants, the Baltimore Orioles and the Cleveland Indians before retiring in 1956 with a .278 career batting average. In 1970, after 14 years with the Indians' front office, he returned to the Tigers as director of player development, and since 1978, he had been a special-assignment scout for the team. In Houston, following a heart attack, January 25.

Ray Felix, 60, basketball player. The NBA Rookie of the Year in 1953 and 1954, the 6′11″ center averaged 17.6 points and 13.3 rebounds a game for the Baltimore Bullets. Traded to the New York Knicks in 1954, Felix became a consistent performer and played all 72 games for five straight seasons. He spent two years with the Lakers, in Minneapolis and Los Angeles, before retiring in 1962 with career averages of 10.6 points and 8.9 rebounds per game. In New York City, of heart failure, July 28.

John Fetzer, 89, baseball owner. After making his fortune operating the Michigan radio network he founded in the early 1930s, Fetzer headed a group of investors that bought the Detroit Tigers for $5.5 million in 1956. He remained in control of the club until 1983, when Domino's Pizza chief Tom Monaghan purchased it for $53 million. Under Fetzer's hands-off stewardship, the

Tigers won the 1968 World Series and the American League East title in 1972. In Detroit, of an undisclosed cause, February 21.

Ralph Floyd, 65, administrator. During Floyd's tenure as athletic director at Indiana University, from December 1978 until his death, Hoosier teams won two-thirds of all their games or matches, including 41 Big Ten championships and five NCAA titles, two in basketball. In Indianapolis, of cancer, December 15, 1990.

Bob Goldham, 69, hockey player. A defenseman, Goldham played on four Stanley Cup winners (Toronto in 1942, Detroit in '52, '54, and '55). After retiring in 1956, Goldham was an analyst on the *Hockey Night in Canada* television broadcasts of NHL games. In Toronto, following a stroke, September 6.

Charles Goren, 90, bridge champion. Inventor of the most widely used bidding system in bridge, Goren achieved a celebrity status unequaled by the game's other world champions. His playing partners included President Eisenhower, Nelson Rockefeller and Humphrey Bogart. A *Sports Illustrated* contributing editor for 17 years, he also had a television series, wrote a syndicated newspaper column and produced 40 books on the game. In Encino, CA, of heart failure, April 3.

Harold "Red" Grange, 87, football player. The "Galloping Ghost" starred as a running back, first at Illinois, where he was an All-America from 1923 to 1925, and then for seven seasons with the Chicago Bears. Grange captured the imagination of pro football fans and became an ambassador for the fledgling sport. The Bears went on a barnstorming tour after his signing, playing 19 games in 17 cities in 66 days and drawing NFL-record crowds of 73,000 in New York and 75,000 in Los Angeles. Wrote Damon Runyon: "He is three or four men rolled into one. He is Jack Dempsey, Babe Ruth, Al Jolson, Paavo Nurmi and Man o' War." In Lake Wales, FL, of complications from pneumonia, January 28.

Helen Meany Gravis, 86, diver. The gold medalist in the springboard event at the 1928 Summer Olympics in Amsterdam, Gravis was a U.S. champion at age 15 in 1920, when she participated in her first of three consecutive Olympics. She was inducted into the Swimming Hall of Fame in 1971. In Greenwich, CT, of pancreatic cancer, July 21.

Howard Head, 76, inventor. He revolutionized tennis with his Prince oversized racket and skiing with his Head aluminum skis. In 1946 Head, a failure as a movie scriptwriter, began redesigning athletic products to improve his own performance. Head's daughter, Nancy Everly, once said of her father, "If he gets annoyed with something, he changes it." In Baltimore, of complications after quadruple-bypass surgery, March 3.

Howard Hobson, 87, basketball coach. In 1939, Hobson coached Oregon to the first NCAA championship. That year, Oregon went 29–5 and defeated Ohio State for the title. Hobson, who had a 212–124 record in 11 years at Oregon and later went 121–118 in nine seasons at Yale, produced a doctoral thesis on basketball in 1944 that proposed, among other things, a three-point field goal and a shot clock. He was named to the Basketball Hall of Fame in 1965. In Portland, OR, of heart failure, June 9.

Abel Kiviat, 99, distance runner. In 1912 Kiviat broke the world record in the 1,500 meters three times in 13 days; Kiviat's Olympic qualifying time, 3:55.8, remained a world record for six years. At that year's Summer Games in Stockholm, though, he was beaten down the stretch by Britain's Arnold Strode Jackson and finished second for a silver medal in the event. A member of the National Track and Field Hall of Fame and the International Jewish Sports Hall of Fame, Kiviat was the oldest living U.S. Olympian. In Lakehurst, NJ, of cancer, August 24.

Bob Kullen, 41, hockey coach. Kullen was an All-America defenseman at Bowdoin College in 1971 and a member of the silver-medal-winning 1972 U.S. Olympic hockey team. A year after he became head coach at the University of New Hampshire in 1986, he underwent a heart transplant. After returning to his duties in 1988–89, Kullen was named New England Division I coach of the year. His triumphant comeback lasted only one more season before poor health forced him to step down. In Durham, NH, of heart failure, November 3, 1990.

Herbie Lewis, 85, hockey player. A left-winger, Lewis captained the Detroit Red Wing teams that won Stanley Cups in 1936 and 1937. A tenacious defender, he was considered the fastest skater in the NHL during most of his 11-year career. In 1935, his salary was $8,000, making him the league's highest-paid player. He was inducted into the Hockey Hall of Fame in 1989. In Indianapolis, of heart failure, January 20.

Dale Long, 64, baseball player. The 1956 season was the peak of Long's major league career, which spanned 11 years with six teams. That year as a first baseman with the Pittsburgh Pirates, he became the first player to hit a home run in eight consecutive games; for the season he batted .263, with 27 homers and 91 RBIs, and started for the National League in the All-Star game. In Palm Coast, FL, of cancer, January 27.

Steve Lowe, 35, volleyball coach. In five years as the University of Wisconsin women's volleyball coach, Lowe directed the Badgers to a

108–64 record, including a Big Ten championship and NCAA tournament appearance, both in 1990. In Madison, WI, of cancer, August 22.

J. D. McDuffie, 52, race car driver. A longtime competitor on the NASCAR circuit, McDuffie, who disdained sponsorships, was of an increasingly rare type—the independent stock car driver. His best year was 1971, when he finished 9th in the Winston Cup standings; in 1990, his last full year, he finished 40th. In Watkins Glen, NY, of injuries suffered in a crash during the Budweiser at the Glen NASCAR race, August 11.

Bill McPeak, 64, football player and coach. A three-time All-Pro defensive end with the Pittsburgh Steelers (1949–57), McPeak coached the Washington Redskins to a 21–46–3 record from 1961 to 1965. He later was an assistant coach with the Detroit Lions and Miami Dolphins, and from 1979 until his death he was director of professional scouting for the New England Patriots. In Foxboro, MA, of heart failure, May 7.

Hank Majeski, 74, baseball player. During his 13-season major league career, Majeski, a third baseman with a .279 career batting average, played for the Boston Braves, New York Yankees, Philadelphia Athletics, Chicago White Sox, Cleveland Indians and Baltimore Orioles. In New York City, of cancer, August 9.

Alice Marble, 77, tennis champion. The top female player in the U.S. from 1936 to 1940, Marble was the first woman to play serve-and-volley, winning U.S. singles titles in 1936, 1938, 1939 and 1940, and Wimbledon in 1939. She led a colorful life, spying for U.S. Army Intelligence during World War II, later designing sportswear and giving lessons to movie stars like Marlene Dietrich, Charlie Chaplin and Carole Lombard, and campaigning for the integration of women's tennis. In Palm Springs, CA, of an undisclosed cause, December 13, 1990.

E. E. "Rip" Miller, 90, football player and coach. Miller was the last surviving member of the Seven Mules, the linemen who blocked for the Four Horsemen at Notre Dame from 1922 to 1924. The Fighting Irish, coached by Knute Rockne, went 27–2–1 during those years, winning the national championship in '24. Miller, a tackle, was elected to the College Football Hall of Fame in 1966. In Annapolis, MD, of natural causes, October 1.

John Mullen, 66, baseball executive. An administrator for the Braves in Boston, Milwaukee and Atlanta, Mullen was responsible for signing future home-run king Henry Aaron in 1952. From 1966 to 1979, he was with the Houston Astros; then he rejoined the Braves as general manager, a job he held until 1985, when he was reassigned as vice president and assistant general manager. In Palm Beach Gardens, FL, of a heart attack, April 3.

Roy Lee "Chucky" Mullins, 21, football player. A defensive back for the University of Mississippi in 1989, Mullins, who was black, shattered four vertebrae in his neck while making a tackle in a game against Vanderbilt. Paralyzed by the injury, he received an outpouring of sympathy and support from Mississippians of both races and became a symbol of the potential for racial harmony in the state. In Memphis, of complications from a blood clot in his lungs, May 6.

***The National*, 1, daily sports newspaper.** The first U.S. all-sports daily, *The National* was launched on Jan. 31, 1990, amid high expectations. Frank Deford was editor-in-chief, and the paper spent lavishly to hire top talent, including columnists Mike Lupica, Dave Kindred and Scott Ostler. But advertising and single-copy sales (less than 200,000 at the end) lagged far below the break-even point, and when the owner, Mexican media mogul Emilio Azcarraga, pulled the plug, the paper had lost a cool $100 million. In New York City, of a financial hemorrhage, June 13.

Rudolf Nierlich, 25, skier. A three-time world champion, once in the slalom and twice in the giant slalom, Nierlich won eight World Cup races in his career. He began skiing at age three and won the 1984 junior world championship in the giant slalom. Near St. Wolfgang, Austria, in an automobile accident, May 18.

Northern Dancer, 29, thoroughbred race horse. Winner of the Kentucky Derby and the Preakness in 1964, Northern Dancer became one of racing's top stud horses, siring 143 stakes winners, including Nijinsky II, the 1970 European Horse of the Year. In Chesapeake City, MD, by lethal injection after he was stricken with colic, November 16, 1990.

Lou Nova, 76, boxer. In 1938, Nova was the No. 1-ranked heavyweight contender, behind champion Joe Louis and ahead of Max Baer. He lost a fight to Tony Galento, and didn't get to face Louis until 1941; Louis won in six rounds. In Las Vegas, of cancer, September 29.

Gary Ormsby, 49, drag racer. The 1989 National Hot Rod Association Top Fuel champion, Ormsby spent 20 years on the professional circuit. In July 1990 he challenged the U.S. Navy to race an A-6 Intruder attack jet against his car; the plane won. Two months later, in September 1990, he set an NHRA record with a run of 4.881 seconds at 296.05 mph. In Roseville, CA, of cancer, August 28.

Gernot Reinstadler, 20, skier. A rookie on the World Cup circuit, the native of Austria was fatally injured in a 50-mph spill near the end of a downhill qualifying race. His death was the first

associated with World Cup competition since 1970. In Wengen, Switzerland, of internal injuries, January 19.

Johnny Revolta, 79, golfer. Revolta rose to prominence in 1935, at age 23, when he won the PGA Championship. He won 19 events on the professional tour between 1932 and 1952, after which he became the full-time head pro at the Evanston Golf Club, in Skokie, IL. He moved to California in 1966 and took a teaching position at the Mission Hills Country Club in Rancho Mirage. He was elected to the PGA Hall of Fame in 1963. In Palm Springs, CA, of natural causes, March 3.

Greg Rice, 75, distance runner. Winner of the 1940 Sullivan Award as the top amateur athlete in the U.S., Rice won 65 consecutive races before finishing second in his final race, in 1943. He set world indoor records in the two-mile (8:51 in 1943) and three-mile (13:46 in 1942) runs. The Athletics Congress recently named him the finest men's indoor distance runner of all time. In River Edge, NJ, of a stroke, May 19.

Bill Riordan, 71, tennis promoter. The promoter of the U.S. national men's indoor championships in Salisbury, MD, from 1963 to 1976, Riordan was better known as Jimmy Connors's first manager. His unconventional style was controversial; in 1975, he booked Connors into a series of made-for-TV, "winner take all" matches with stars like Rod Laver, John Newcombe and Ilie Nastase—events that actually included guaranteed payments to Connors and his opponents. In Naples, FL, of heart failure, January 20.

Pete Runnells, 63, baseball player. Runnells won two American League batting titles: in 1960, when he hit .320, and in 1962, when he hit .326, both for the Boston Red Sox. He also played for the Washington Senators from 1951 to 1957 before spending five seasons with the Red Sox. He finished his career with the Houston Colt .45s in 1964 and had a lifetime batting average of .291. In Pasadena, TX, following a stroke, May 20.

Schottzie, 9, Cincinnati Reds mascot. Schottzie became the Reds' mascot after her owner, Marge Schott, took over as the club's general partner in 1984. A St. Bernard, Schottzie was involved in a number of Reds promotions, often appeared on the field before games wearing a Reds cap, and for a while even had her own air-conditioned office at Riverfront Stadium. In Cincinnati, by lethal injection after developing incurable bone cancer, August 7.

Marchmont "Marchie" Schwartz, 82, football player and coach. A two-time All-America running back at Notre Dame, Schwartz starred on the undefeated 1930 national championship team coached by Knute Rockne and set a school record when he rushed for 960 yards in 1931. In 1942, he became head coach at Stanford, a position he kept during a three-year suspension of the football program during World War II. He then coached for five more seasons before he resigned in 1950 to go into business. Schwartz's record as a coach was 28–28–4. He was named to the College Football Hall of Fame in 1974. In Walnut Creek, CA, of heart failure, April 18.

Wendell Scott, 69, race car driver. The first black to compete in Grand National auto racing, Scott drove in more than 500 races, finished in the top five 20 times and won once. On other circuits, he won 128 races during a 24-year career that began in 1949. In 1977, the film *Greased Lightning*, starring Richard Pryor as Scott, brought him belated celebrity. In Danville, VA, of cancer, December 23, 1990.

William Shea, 84, lawyer. After the Brooklyn Dodgers and New York Giants moved to the West Coast in the fall of 1957, New York City mayor Robert Wagner asked the politically influential Shea to head the effort to secure another National League baseball team for the city. Less than five years later the New York Mets were born. In 1964 the Mets' new ballpark was named Shea Stadium in his honor. In New York, of natural causes, October 3.

Fred Shero, 65, hockey coach. The creative, talented Shero coached the Philadelphia Flyers from 1971 to 1978 and the New York Rangers from 1978 to 1980, guiding the brawling Flyers to Stanley Cups in 1974 and 1975. He popularized the diagramming of plays and designed innovative drills that helped his players learn to skate in complex patterns to confuse opponents. His career record was 390–225–119, and his .612 winning percentage is fourth-best among NHL coaches. In Camden, NJ, of cancer, November 24, 1990.

Chris Short, 53, baseball player. Short, a lefthander, won 135 games for the Philadelphia Phillies in 14 seasons, placing him fourth on the club's all-time list. His 1,585 strikeouts rank third. He won 17 or more games four times in a five-year period beginning in 1964. Including one season with the Milwaukee Brewers before his retirement in 1973, his lifetime record was 135–132. In Wilmington, DE, of complications from a ruptured brain aneurysm that had left him in a coma since 1988, August 1.

Shelby Strother, 44, columnist. Winner of more than 100 awards as a sportswriter for the *Detroit News*, *The Denver Post*, the *St. Petersburg Times* and *Florida Today*, Strother had been a columnist for the Detroit paper since 1985. His distinctive prose often dealt with out-of-the-way places and characters, and he was considered one of the profession's best storytellers. In Detroit, of liver cancer, March 3.

N. B. "Bim" Stults, 83, swimming coach. Stults built the swimming program he founded at Florida State into one of the strongest in the South. In his 25 years as coach, FSU teams were 185–43 in dual meets and had six undefeated seasons. The FSU aquatic center is named after Stults, who retired in 1973. In Tallahassee, following a brief illness, April 7.

Cedric Tallis, 76, baseball executive. As general manager of the Kansas City Royals from 1968, a year before the team played a game, until 1975, Tallis helped assemble baseball's most successful expansion franchise. He later served as general manager of the New York Yankees and as director of Tampa's unsuccessful effort to secure an expansion team. His career in baseball began in Thomasville, GA, in 1948 and included jobs in six minor league cities before he broke into the majors in 1961 as business manager of the Los Angeles Angels. In Tampa, of a heart attack, May 7.

Russ Thomas, 66, football executive. As general manager of the NFL's Detroit Lions from 1967 until he retired in 1989, Thomas built a reputation as a tough but fair negotiator. He spent 42 years with the Lions, as offensive tackle, scout, broadcaster, assistant coach, financial officer, personnel director and general manager. In Detroit, in his sleep of an undetermined cause, March 19.

Earl Torgeson, 66, baseball player. Nicknamed the "Earl of Snohomish," after his hometown of Snohomish, WA, the first baseman batted .265 with 149 home runs during a major league career that lasted from 1947 to 1961. In 1950, Torgeson's best season, he batted .290 with 23 homers and 87 RBIs for the Boston Braves and led the National League with 120 runs scored. He also played for the Philadelphia Phillies, the Detroit Tigers, the Chicago White Sox and the New York Yankees before returning to Snohomish, where he later served as a county commissioner. In Everett, WA, of leukemia, November 8, 1990.

Forrest "Spec" Towns, 77, hurdler. Gold medalist in the 110-meter hurdles at the 1936 Olympics in Berlin, a few weeks later Towns became the first man to break 14 seconds for the event when he ran 13.7 in Oslo. He later became track coach at his alma mater, Georgia, which had offered him a scholarship after a neighbor spotted him in his backyard, barefoot and in overalls, jumping over a broomstick. In Athens, GA, of heart failure, April 9.

Max Truex, 55, distance runner. The 5' 5" dynamo, whose training meal often consisted of a quart of ice cream, won the 1957 NCAA cross-country title while at USC and set U.S. distance records in several events. At the 1960 Olympics in Rome, Truex became the first American to break 29 minutes in the 10,000 meters when he ran a 28:50.2, finishing sixth. Olympic teammate Jim Beatty once referred to Truex as "a gutsy little runner who pounded at you all the way around the track." In Milton, MA, after an extended illness, March 24.

Frank Umont, 73, baseball umpire. In 20 years as an American League umpire, the bespectacled Umont worked four World Series, four All-Star Games and a league championship series before retiring in 1973. In Fort Lauderdale, of heart failure, June 20.

James Van Alen, 88, tennis revolutionary. Van Alen invented the VASSS, best-of-nine-point tiebreaker, which he introduced in 1958 and relentlessly promoted. After it was adopted at the 1970 U.S. Open, it evolved into the current tiebreaker, in which the first player to reach seven and have a two-point margin wins the set. In 1954, he founded the International Tennis Hall of Fame in Newport, RI, and later served as the institution's president. In Newport, of injuries suffered in a fall at his home, July 3.

Bill Vukovich, III, 27, race car driver. Rookie of the Year at the 1988 Indianapolis 500 when he finished 14th, he was a third-generation driver—his father, Bill, Jr., raced Indy Cars for 12 years, and his grandfather, Bill, Sr., was killed in a crash while he was leading the Indy 500 in 1955. In Bakersfield, CA, after a sprint-type car he was driving crashed into a wall at Mesa Marin Speedway during a practice lap, November 25, 1990.

Bucky Walters, 82, baseball player. A three-time 20-game winner for the Cincinnati Reds, Walters also pitched for the Boston Braves, the Boston Red Sox and the Philadelphia Phillies during a 19-year major league career. The righthander, a six-time All-Star, finished with a lifetime record of 198–160. In 1939, he went 27–11 with a 2.29 ERA for the Reds and was named the National League's MVP. The following year, also for the Reds, he won 22 games during the regular season and two more to help Cincinnati take the World Series. In Abington, PA, of an undisclosed cause, April 20.

Fred Washington, 23, football player. A rookie defensive tackle out of Texas Christian University, Washington was the Chicago Bears' 2nd pick in the 1990 NFL draft, the 32nd player selected overall. In Lake Forest, IL, of injuries suffered in an automobile accident, December 21, 1990.

Arthur Watson, 61, television executive. As president of NBC Sports from 1979 to 1989 and as executive vice president of the network after that, Watson spearheaded NBC's deals to broadcast the 1980, 1988 and 1992 Summer Olympics. After NBC lost the rights to major league baseball to CBS in 1990, he successfully pursued the NBA, which previously had been televised by CBS. He also helped create horse racing's splashy Breeders' Cup series of races. In Ridgewood, NJ, of an undisclosed cause, June 27.

Alan Wiggins, 32, baseball player. A switch-hitting second baseman for the San Diego Padres from 1981 to 1985 and the Baltimore Orioles from 1985 to 1987, Wiggins helped San Diego win the 1984 National League pennant, stealing 70 bases and scoring 106 runs. He was suspended from baseball for 30 days in 1982, after an arrest for cocaine possession, and indefinitely in 1987, for failing a drug test. In Los Angeles, reportedly of AIDS-related complications, January 6.

Travis Williams, 45, football player. In 1967, his rookie season with the Green Bay Packers, Williams set an NFL record by returning four kickoffs for touchdowns. He played four seasons with the Packers. A knee injury ended his career in 1972, and he later struggled with alcohol abuse and homelessness. In Martinez, CA, of heart failure, February 17.

Lee Wulff, 86, sports fisherman. A master with the rod and reel, Wulff popularized dry-fly fishing for salmon and the use of small fly rods. He pioneered sportfishing for giant bluefin tuna in the North Atlantic, twice establishing world records. He also wrote eight books and produced award-winning films on fishing and hunting. In Hancock, NY, when the light plane he was piloting crashed into a hillside after he apparently suffered a heart attack, April 28.

Jim Wynne, 60, powerboat designer and racer. Wynne developed and perfected the special hulls and the inboard-outboard, stern-drive engines that revolutionized high-speed offshore motorboat racing. He and a companion became the first to cross the Atlantic Ocean in a boat with an outboard motor, an 11-day trip from Copenhagen to New York City in 1958. In 1964 and 1966, he won powerboat racing's open class world championship. In Miami, after an extended illness, December 21, 1990.

Joe Yancey, 80, track coach. Elected to the Track and Field Hall of Fame in 1986, Yancey coached the five-member Jamaican track team to two gold and three silver medals in the 1952 Olympic Games in Helsinki, where the Jamaicans set a world record of 3:03.9 in the 4x400-meter relay. He founded the New York Pioneers track and field club, and he coached Olympic teams from the Bahamas, Trinidad and British Guiana. In Teaneck, NJ, of heart failure, February 22.